THE
CAMBRIDGE
MEDIEVAL HISTORY

VOLUME VIII

THE
CAMBRIDGE
MEDIEVAL HISTORY

PLANNED BY THE LATE

J. B. BURY, M.A., F.B.A.

EDITED BY

C. W. PREVITÉ-ORTON, Litt.D., F.B.A.
Z. N. BROOKE, Litt.D.

VOLUME VIII

THE CLOSE OF THE MIDDLE AGES

CAMBRIDGE
AT THE UNIVERSITY PRESS
1969

PUBLISHED BY
THE SYNDICS OF THE CAMBRIDGE UNIVERSITY PRESS

Bentley House, 200 Euston Road, London, N.W.1
American Branch: 32 East 57th Street, New York, NY 10022

First Edition 1936
Reprinted 1959
1964
1969

First printed in Great Britain at the University Press, Cambridge
Reprinted in Great Britain by Photolithography by
Unwin Brothers Limited
Woking and London

PREFACE.

WITH the appearance of Volume VIII, the *Cambridge Medieval History*, the first volume of which was published in 1911, has at last reached its conclusion. Apart from the major calamity of the War, which necessitated a pause of four years and numerous changes of contributors, the *History* has experienced a number of vicissitudes in the course of its compilation. It has suffered the loss not only of its architect, Professor Bury, but also, by death or resignation, of the three editors who were originally entrusted with the task of executing his scheme, and of two others who were subsequently appointed. In the construction of the later volumes there has been less disturbance, for the present editors have been jointly concerned in the production of the last five volumes; and their partnership, which began when most of the chapters of Volume IV were already in print, has lasted for fourteen years. It is not without a sigh of relief that they sign their initials for the last time; but besides the satisfaction that the task has been accomplished, there is also a feeling of pride in reviewing the distinguished body of historians who have been associated with them in their work. Along with scholars from England, Wales, Scotland, and Ireland, the *Cambridge Medieval History* can number among its contributors scholars from Austria, Belgium, Czechoslovakia, France, Germany, Holland, Hungary, Italy, Norway, Russia, Spain, Switzerland, Yugoslavia, and the United States of America. There are certain objections, often voiced, to co-operative histories; but there can be little doubt of the gain to historical knowledge when so many scholars from so many countries contribute their learning and their matured experience to a joint undertaking of this kind. The editors would like to take this opportunity of expressing in a public manner, what they have already expressed privately, their sincere thanks to each and all of the contributors who have co-operated in the writing of the *Cambridge Medieval History*.

Of those who contributed chapters to Volume VIII, we regret to say that no fewer than five have died before the publication of the volume— Mr Edward Armstrong, whose death we already had occasion to deplore when Volume VII was published; Professor W. T. Waugh and Dr G. H. Orpen, who rendered us valuable assistance in that volume as well as in this; Professor Paul Fournier, for forty years eminent as the historian of canon law, who had before that made his name as the historian of the kingdom of Arles, the subject of his chapter in this volume; and, most recently, Professor Henri Pirenne, the great historian of Belgium, an honorary doctor of the University of Cambridge, who has given us what must now be his final summary of the medieval history of his country. The last four, at any rate, had seen their chapters in print and given us their corrections, so that their work is in the form that they themselves desired; and we had the expert assistance of Miss C. M. Ady in correcting the proofs of Mr Armstrong's chapter.

The Maps on this occasion have been prepared by Dr Previté-Orton, but we have to thank Professor Bruce-Boswell for the map of East Central Europe in the fifteenth century, and Mr McFarlane for the map of England in the fifteenth century as well as the Oxford University Press for permission for him to make use of the map in the Oxford Historical Atlas. The Index has been compiled by Mr F. Donal Ward, and we are indebted to him for important corrections which he has brought to our notice. Finally, Mr C. C. Scott has once more undertaken the editing of the Bibliographies. His association with the *History* is as long as our own, and it would be impossible for us to exaggerate what we owe to his knowledge, his thoroughness, and his patient care in the most difficult and tedious of all editorial work.

C. W. P.-O.
Z. N. B.

January, 1936.

CORRIGENDA.

Vol. I.

p. 697. *For* 481 The *Henoticon* of Zeno. Schism in the Church. *read* 482, etc. *and transfer after next entry.*

Vol. II.

p. 357, l. 21. *For* Mūsā *read* Abū Mūsā.

p. 648, l. 16. *For* was afterwards called trinoda necessitas *read* has been called *trimoda necessitas.*

p. 706 at bottom *Add* Note. In this chapter Popes Stephen II and Stephen III are called Stephen III and Stephen IV in accordance with the modern official numbering.

Index.

p. 822, col. 2. *Insert entry* Abū Mūsā al-Ash'arī, 357.

p. 865, col. 1. *Delete entry* Mūsā al-Ash'arī.

Vol. III.

p. 111, ll. 18–17 from bottom. *For* Adela, daughter of Henry I of England *read* Adela, sister of Henry I of France.

Index.

p. 682, col. 1. *Under* Mesco I *for* 322 *read* 222.

Vol. IV.

p. 148, par. 4, l. 1. *For* 986 *read* 976.

p. 148, par. 4, l. 2. *For* thirty *read* forty.

p. 149, par. 2, l. 6. *For* campaigning in *read* at war with.

p. 209, l. 4 from bottom. *For* a revolt in *read* the war with.

p. 240, l. 8 from bottom. *For* 981 *read* 986.

p. 240, l. 5 from bottom. *For* Fifteen *read* Ten.

p. 531, l. 13. *For* Smilec *read* Smilets.

Vol. V.

p. 186, last line. *For* 1133 *read* 1132.

pp. 616–17. *For* when Louis VII's sister Constance was married to the Dauphin of Viennois, *read* when Louis VII's nephew Alberic of Toulouse was married to the heiress of Viennois.

p. 662, l. 10 from bottom. *For* in the Jura *read* east of the Jura.

p. 767, l. 19 from bottom. *For* Peckham *read* Pecham.

p. 855 *under* Aimé of Monte Cassino. *Add* Also ed. Bartholomaeis, V. de. (Fonti.) Rome. 1935.

p. 858. *Add entries* Jamison, E. M. The administration of the county of Molise in the twelfth and thirteenth centuries. EHR. xliv, xlv. 1929, 30.

—— I conti di Molise e Marsia nei secoli xii e xiii. *In* Atti del Convegno Storico Abruzzese-Molisano, 1931. Casalbordino. 1932.

p. 860. *Under* II. Sources. A. *Add*

Anonymus Ticinensis. Liber de laudibus civitatis Ticinensis. Ed. Maiocchi, R. and Quintavalle, F. RR.II.SS. New edn. xi. Pt. 1. [Opicino de Canestris.]

Instituta regalia regum Longobardorum (Honorancie civitatis Papie). Ed. Hofmeister, A. MGH. Script. xxx. Pt. 2. 1933.

Johannes de Viterbo. Liber de regimine civitatum. Ed. Gaudenzi, A. *in* Bibliotheca Iuridica Medii Aevi. iii. Bologna. 1901.

p. 860. *Under* II. Sources. A. (*cont.*)

Oculus pastoralis. Ed. Muratori, L. A. *in* Antiquitates Italiae. IV.

—— *Under* Landulfus Junior. *Add Also* ed. Castiglioni, C. RR.II.SS. New edn. Vol. V. Pt. 3.

—— *Under* Marago. *For* Ed. Bonaini, F. ASI. Vol. VI, 2. 1845 *read* Ed. Gentile, M. L. RR.II.SS. New edn. Vol. VI. Pt. 2.

—— *Under* Rangerius. *Add Also* ed. Schmeidler, B. etc. MGH. Script. XXX. Pt. 2. 1933.

p. 861. *Under* Codice diplomatico Barese. *For* VIII *read* XI.

p. 871. *Under* III. Modern Works. *Add*

La Monte, J. L. Feudal Monarchy in the Latin Kingdom of Jerusalem, 1100 to 1291. Cambridge, Mass. 1932.

Grousset, R. Histoire des Croisades et du Royaume Franc de Jerusalem. 3 vols. Paris. 1934 ff.

p. 876. *Under* Marago. *For* Ed. Bonaini, F. ASI. Vol. VI, 2. 1845 *read* Ed. Gentile, M. L. RR.II.SS. New edn. Vol. VI. Pt. 2.

p. 876. *Under* Otto Morena. *For* Ed. Jaffé, P. MGH. Script. XVIII *read* Ed. Güterbock, F. MGH. Script. rer. Germ. VII. 1930.

p. 830. *For* Güterbock, E. *read* Güterbock, F.

INDEX.

p. 948, col. 2. *Insert entry* Alberic of Toulouse, Dauphin of Viennois, 616 sq.

p. 960, col. 1. *Under entry* Constance, sister of Louis VII *delete* ; 616.

p. 974, col. 2. *Under entry* Hugh of Crécy. *For* Louis IV *read* Louis VI.

VOL. VI.

pp. xxix and xl, title of Chap. XII. *Read* Spain, 1031–1248.

p. 15, l. 17. *For* whomsoever *read* whosoever.

p. 134, 2nd par., l. 4. *For* 1201 *read* 1202.

p. 168, note 1. *For* 2 *read* 11.

p. 193, l. 5 from bottom. *For* 1276 *read* 1275.

p. 201, ll. 19 and 15 from bottom. *For* Campofranco *read* Canfranc.

p. 290, l. 5. *For* Ida *read* Matilda.

p. 359, l. 13 from bottom. *For* Luxembourg *read* Luxemburg.

p. 393, Chap. XII, title. *Read* Spain, 1031–1248.

p. 393, l. 1. *For* 1034 *read* 1031.

p. 393, l. 6. *For* 1034 *read* 1031.

p. 394, l. 1. *For* Three *read* Six.

p. 585, par. 2, l. 10 from bottom. *For* Consequently in 1352 a bull was *read* Already in 1360 a bull had been.

p. 600, note 1. *For* Vol. VII *read* Vol. VIII, Chap. XXIII.

p. 749, l. 5. *For* confessions *read* confessors.

p. 877. *For entry* Ptolomaeus Lucensis. Annales, etc. *read* Ptolomaeus (Tholomeus) Lucensis. Annales. Ed. Schmeidler, B. with Gesta Florentinorum and Gesta Lucanorum. MGH. Script. rer. Germ. VIII. 1930.

p. 912, Chap. XII, title. *Read* Spain, 1031–1248.

p. 981. *Read* 1031 Fall of Caliphate of Cordova.

p. 985. *Read* 1285 Death of Peter III of Aragon.

INDEX.

p. 995, col. 2. *For* Campofranco *read* Canfranc.

p. 1014, col. 1. *Delete entry* Ida.

p. 1022, col. 1. *Insert entry* Matilda of Boulogne, 290.

p. 1034, col. 2, *under* Rodrigo Diaz, l. 3. *For* IV *read* VI.

Vol. VII.

p. 7, l. 4 from bottom. *For* 1301 Corrado Doria *read* 1300 Roger Loria.

p. 14, par. 2, l. 6. *For* 1 November *read* 7 November.

p. 22, par. 2, l. 12. *For* cards *read* chess.

p. 30, l. 3. *For* This was granted *read* This was finally granted.

p. 30, l. 4. *For* 15 June 1310 *read* early in 1313.

p. 41, l. 18. *For* death *read* fall.

p. 60, l. 19 from bottom. *For* nephew *read* great-nephew.

p. 83, ll. 4 and 9. *For* Woeringen *read* Worringen.

p. 350, par. 2, l. 6. *For* lightly *read* slowly.

p. 382, l. 1. *For* 24 November *read* 23 November.

p. 408, l. 14. *For* pointed out to the clergy that their promise *read* pointed out that the clergy's promise.

p. 408, l. 15. *For* they decided that *read* they decided in Convocation (January 1297) that.

p. 408, l. 22. *For* 1296 *read* 1297.

p. 408, l. 31. *For* The following year, however, opposition arose *read* In the meantime, however, opposition had arisen.

p. 409, l. 4 from bottom. *For* 10 October *read* 12 October.

p. 571, l. 11 from bottom. *For* 1285 *read* 1284.

p. 591, l. 19 from bottom. *For* his brother *read* his brother Ferdinand.

p. 819 *under* Savio, F. *For* Pt. II. Milan. 1932 *read* Pt. II. 2 vols. Bergamo. 1929, 32.

p. 829 *under* C. Tuscany. *Insert* Cronache Senesi. Ed. Lisini, A. and Jacometti, F. RR.II.SS. New edn. Vol. xv. Pt. 6.

pp. 883, 892. *Under* Records illustrating Parliamentary History *insert* Rotuli Parliamentorum Anglie hactenus inediti, 1279–1373. Ed. Richardson, H. G. and Sayles, G. (Roy. Hist. Soc., Camden 3rd ser. LI). London. 1935.

p. 931 *under* B. Modern Works. *Insert* Soldevila, F. Història de Catalunya. Vol. I. Barcelona. 1934.

p. 966 *under* Vergerio, P. P. *Insert* Epistolario. Ed. Smith, L. (Fonti.) Rome. 1934.

p. 980. *For* 1376–80 Wenceslas, King of the Romans *read* 1376–1400 Wenceslas, King of the Romans.

Index.

p. 1006, col. 1. *Delete entry* Doria, Corrado, 7.

p. 1072, col. 2. *For* Woeringen *read* Worringen.

Vol. VIII.

p. 16, l. 9. *For* from that of Nicaea to that of *read* and the general Councils of the Lateran, Lyons, and.

p. 95, l. 12 from bottom. *For* Magdalene *read* Madeleine.

TABLE OF CONTENTS

CHAPTER I.

THE COUNCILS OF CONSTANCE AND BASLE.

By the late W. T. Waugh, M.A., F.R.S.C., sometime Kingsford
Professor of History in McGill University, Montreal.

CHAPTER II.
JOHN HUS.

By Dr KAMIL KROFTA, Professor of Bohemian History in the University of Prague, Minister of Foreign Affairs in Czechoslovakia.

CHAPTER III.
BOHEMIA IN THE FIFTEENTH CENTURY.
By Dr KAMIL KROFTA.

CHAPTER IV.

THE EMPIRE IN THE FIFTEENTH CENTURY.

By R. G. D. Laffan, M.A., Fellow and Tutor of Queens' College, Cambridge.

CHAPTER V.

THE PAPACY AND NAPLES IN THE FIFTEENTH CENTURY.

By the late EDWARD ARMSTRONG, M.A., F.B.A., sometime
Fellow of the Queen's College, Oxford.

CHAPTER VI.

FLORENCE AND NORTH ITALY, 1414—1492.

By Cecilia Mary Ady, M.A., Fellow of St Hugh's College, Oxford.

CHAPTER VII.

FRANCE: THE REIGN OF CHARLES VII AND THE END OF THE HUNDRED YEARS' WAR.

By Joseph Calmette, Membre de l'Institut, Professor of History in the Faculty of Letters in the University of Toulouse, Director of the *Annales du Midi*.

CHAPTER VIII.

FRANCE: LOUIS XI.

By Charles Petit-Dutaillis, Dʳ-ès-Lettres, Membre de l'Institut, Director of the National Office of French Universities and Schools.

CHAPTER IX.

THE KINGDOM OF BURGUNDY OR ARLES FROM THE ELEVENTH TO THE FIFTEENTH CENTURY.

By the late PAUL FOURNIER, Membre de l'Institut, sometime Professor in the Faculty of Law of the University of Paris.

CHAPTER X.

THE LOW COUNTRIES.

By the late HENRI PIRENNE, F.B.A., Membre de l'Institut, Secretary of the Royal Belgian Commission of History, sometime Professor of Medieval and Belgian History in the University of Ghent.

CHAPTER XI.

ENGLAND: THE LANCASTRIAN KINGS, 1399–1461.

By K. B. McFarlane, M.A., Fellow and Tutor of Magdalen College, Oxford.

CHAPTER XII.

ENGLAND: THE YORKIST KINGS, 1461–1485.

By C. H. WILLIAMS, M.A., Professor of History at King's College
in the University of London.

CHAPTER XIII.

IRELAND, 1315–*c.* 1485.

By the late GODDARD H. ORPEN, Litt.D., Trinity College, Dublin.

CHAPTER XIV.

SCOTLAND, 1328–1488.

By C. SANFORD TERRY, Litt.D., Hon. Mus.D., Honorary Fellow of Clare College, Cambridge, Emeritus Professor of History in the University of Aberdeen.

CHAPTER XV.

SPAIN, 1412–1516.

By Dr RAFAEL ALTAMIRA, Judge in the permanent Court of International Justice at the Hague; formerly Professor of Jurisprudence in the University of Oviedo.

CHAPTER XVI.

PORTUGAL IN THE MIDDLE AGES.

By EDGAR PRESTAGE, D.Litt., Professor of Portuguese language,
literature, and history in the University of London.

CHAPTER XVII.

THE SCANDINAVIAN KINGDOMS DURING THE FOURTEENTH
AND FIFTEENTH CENTURIES.

By Dr HALVDAN KOHT, F.B.A., Minister of Foreign Affairs in Norway,
Professor of History in the University of Oslo.

CHAPTER XVIII.

POLAND AND LITHUANIA IN THE FOURTEENTH AND FIFTEENTH CENTURIES.

By ALEXANDER BRUCE-BOSWELL, M.A., Bowes Professor of Russian history, language, and literature in the University of Liverpool.

CHAPTER XIX.

HUNGARY, 1301–1490.

By Bálint Hóman, Royal Hungarian Minister for Worship
and Public Education.

CHAPTER XX.

POLITICAL THEORY IN THE LATER MIDDLE AGES.

By Harold J. Laski, M.A., Professor of Political Science in the
University of London.

CHAPTER XXI.

THE ART OF WAR IN THE FIFTEENTH CENTURY.

By Sir Charles Oman, K.B.E., M.A., Hon. D.C.L., F.B.A., F.S.A., Chichele Professor of Modern History in the University of Oxford.

CHAPTER XXII.

MAGIC, WITCHCRAFT, ASTROLOGY, AND ALCHEMY.

By Lynn Thorndike, Ph.D., Professor of History at Columbia University.

CHAPTER XXIII.

EDUCATION IN THE FOURTEENTH AND FIFTEENTH CENTURIES.

By G. R. POTTER, M.A., Ph.D., St John's College, Professor of Modern History in the University of Sheffield.

CHAPTER XXIV.

PAINTING, SCULPTURE, AND THE ARTS.

By W. G. CONSTABLE, M.A., F.S.A., Fellow of St John's College and Slade Professor of Fine Art in the University of Cambridge, Director of the Courtauld Institute of Art, London University.

CHAPTER XXV.

THE RENAISSANCE IN EUROPE.

By ARTHUR A. TILLEY, M.A., Fellow of King's College, Cambridge.

EPILOGUE.

LIST OF BIBLIOGRAPHIES

LIST OF MAPS.

VOLUME VIII.

CHAPTER I

THE COUNCILS OF CONSTANCE AND BASLE

THAT the Council of Constance met was due in the first place to a wide-spread desire that it should meet. Without such a desire no summons, however authoritative and peremptory, would have given rise to such an assembly. But public opinion on the matter might have remained in-effective for years had it not been for the initiative of the King of the Romans. One need not look too closely into Sigismund's motives. No doubt he expected that much political advantage might be gained by an adroit manipulation of a Council's proceedings. No doubt he thought of the prestige which would be his if a Council, summoned at his instance and sitting under his protection, were to end the Schism and accomplish a serious reform of ecclesiastical abuses. No doubt, too, he was concerned for the good estate of the Christian Church. Judge him as we may, he wanted a Council, and when, early in the summer of 1413, it became evident that the abortive Council of Rome[1] would never re-assemble, he seized the opportunity to secure the meeting of a new one on German soil.

Much inferior to Sigismund in influence, yet not to be passed over as promoters of the Council, were the Italian potentátes, Carlo Malatesta of Rimini and Ladislas, King of Naples. Malatesta, a great pillar of the cause of Gregory XII, had been an advocate of the cession of all three Popes, but, convinced that the plan was impracticable, he became an ad-vocate of the Council. As for Ladislas, no one would suspect him of a concern for the good of Christendom or even the unity of the Church, but his services to the conciliar party, though unintentional, were never-theless great. The reconciliation effected in 1412 between him and Pope John XXIII did not last long. In the early summer of 1413 he invaded the Papal States, and on 7 June his troops entered Rome, whence Pope and Curia departed in confused flight. John took refuge first in Florence, then in Bologna. Even there he felt unsafe, and in his alarm and de-spondency he turned to Sigismund, who was in North Italy pursuing his designs against Milan. The price of Sigismund's support, he well knew, was the summons of a General Council; but he counted on holding it in a place where his influence would be strong enough to render it harmless. Unfortunately for himself, he allowed too wide a discretion to the envoys who on his behalf met Sigismund at Como in October 1413. They seem to have been carried away by the vigour and address of the king, who knew exactly what he wanted; and in John's name they agreed that the Council should meet at the imperial city of Constance on 1 November 1414.

[1] 1412–13; see Valois, *La France et le Grand Schisme de l'Occident*, IV, pp. 199 sqq.

Before the Pope had heard of the agreement, Sigismund published it and addressed invitations to John XXIII's two rivals and all Christian princes and prelates. Within the next weeks Sigismund and John met more than once on outwardly amicable terms; but the king refused to modify the arrangement, and on 9 December the Pope issued bulls convoking the Council according to its conditions. He also tried to placate the king by giving him a large and much-needed sum of money.

For some time, however, the king's zeal for the Council remained far more evident than the Pope's. It was again Ladislas who overcame John's obduracy. In March 1414 he once more occupied Rome, whence he advanced northward. John XXIII began to make active preparations for his journey to Germany, to take steps to raise the necessary funds, and to urge the French and English to participate in the Council. The Pope's vigour, however, slackened when Florence made with Ladislas a treaty which halted his march, and ceased altogether when on 6 August he died. Rome soon went back to papal allegiance, and John, there is no doubt, would have liked to return thither. But the death of the King of Naples had come just too late. All over western Europe preparations for the Council were afoot, and the reform party was eager for action. The cardinals recognised that for John to go back on his word would mean ruin for him and perhaps for them. They held him to his undertakings, and on 1 October he reluctantly set out from Bologna to fulfil them. On his journey he met Frederick of Habsburg, Count of Tyrol, and appointed him captain-general of the papal troops at a salary of 6000 florins[1], while Frederick promised to protect the Pope while he was in Constance, or if he decided to leave it. John made his solemn entry into the city, on 28 October, with the feeling that he was walking into a trap.

It must not be forgotten that there were three rival Popes, and that many people, including Sigismund, were disposed to treat them all alike. At first Gregory XII refused to countenance a gathering summoned by a usurper of the Holy See, though he protested that he would have recognised one convoked by representatives of all three Popes, or even by Sigismund alone. Soon, however, he had to weaken. His chief supporter in Germany, Lewis Count Palatine of the Rhine, wished to take part, and eventually, probably under pressure from Malatesta, Gregory decided to send two envoys.

Benedict XIII, every one knew, would recognise the Council only in the last extremity. Envoys from Sigismund and France went to Spain in the summer of 1414, and at Morella, near the border of Catalonia and Valencia, took part in a series of conferences with the Pope, numerous clergy of his obedience, members of the royal family of Aragon, and envoys from Castile. But they could gain nothing more than an undertaking by Benedict to meet Sigismund next spring at Villefranche, near Nice, where the question of union might be discussed.

[1] Hardt, ii, pt. ix. 146.

On 5 November 1414 Pope John XXIII officially opened the Council of Constance. On 16 November the first formal General Session was held in the cathedral. John Hus had arrived on the 3rd, but Sigismund did not appear till Christmas Eve. Most of the other members of the Council displayed true medieval unpunctuality, and very little business could be done before the end of the year. Among those present, however, there was much informal discussion, which helped to clear the way for the treatment of hard questions later on.

The Council of Constance proved to be larger in size and longer in duration than any ecclesiastical assembly that had hitherto met. It was as if the medieval Church, powerless to avert decay and disruption, had been granted a last opportunity of displaying in a living pageant the extent of its dominion and the catholicity of its interests. Every country in Europe was concerned in the Council's proceedings. Every problem of the time, religious or political, attracted its notice or affected its fortunes. The failure of the Council to achieve many parts of its task must not spoil our appreciation of the marvel that such a gathering should have assembled, deliberated for three years and a half, and separated without losing its dignity or self-respect. When at its largest, the Council included three patriarchs, twenty-nine cardinals, thirty-three archbishops, one hundred and fifty bishops, more than a hundred abbots, about fifty provosts and deans, and some three hundred other doctors. While these figures were based on a careful computation, it is wise to be sceptical of contemporary estimates of the total number of strangers in the city, the most modest of which is forty thousand. It cannot, however, be doubted that the concourse was huge, several times greater than the normal population, at most six thousand. For the assemblage was more than a deliberative and legislative Council of the Church. The business of the Curia must be carried on, and its comparative accessibility attracted to it from northern Europe crowds of benefice-hunters and privilege-seekers. Sigismund had announced, too, that he would transact imperial business at Constance, and thus drew thither many who did not even pretend an interest in ecclesiastical affairs. Many of those present, clerical and lay, treated the Council as an occasion for unwonted self-indulgence; and their demands were met by hosts of craftsmen, pedlars, minstrels, and prostitutes. All things considered, it is astonishing that there was so little open disorder in the place, that after the first winter there was no serious apprehension of a dearth of food, and that it was possible to arrange with the civic authorities a tariff of maximum prices for food and lodging, which was not only enforced but seems to have given general satisfaction[1]. There was evidently high organising ability among both the officials of the Council and the magistrates of the city.

The case of John Hus was the only business on which real progress

---

[1] For most valuable information about prices for board and lodging, see Richental, pp. 38 sqq.

was made before the end of the year. He was arrested on 28 November, and on 4 December a commission was appointed to deal with him. The career, trial, and fate of Hus are treated elsewhere in this volume[1], and need be touched upon here only in so far as they affected other issues before the Council. It should be remembered, in fact, that while the proceedings against Hus were of supreme interest to the Bohemians and of deep concern to many Germans, and while to Protestant historians of later times they seemed more momentous than any other episodes of the Council, they were hardly of the first importance to the majority of those present. There was at Constance no desire to alter the Faith, and in general estimation Hus was a reckless agitator who must undergo condign punishment, if it were proved that he obstinately denied Catholic doctrine. A criminal case like this, even though the accused might be a man of unusual ability and influence, seemed trivial compared with the problems raised by the Schism and the need of reform[2].

When the Council began, nine members out of ten were thinking mainly of the restoration of union. The failure of the Council of Pisa had caused widespread fear lest the schism in the West might prove as incurable as that of the Greeks. Desperate remedies were being discussed, and the character and conduct of John XXIII had impaired the loyalty of many of his supporters. Unfortunately for the Pope, the Italians, who were mostly faithful to him, tried to use their temporary majority in the Council to secure him from future attack. They urged that the decrees of Pisa should be confirmed, that measures should be taken for the meeting of a General Council every twenty-five years, and that, having transacted this business, the Council might be dissolved. This hardy suggestion brought into the field the Conciliar Party, headed by Cardinals d'Ailly and Fillastre, who gained the sympathy of Sigismund soon after his arrival. It was urged by them in speech and writing that those who advocated a premature dissolution were under suspicion of heresy, that the Council was superior to the Pope, especially in matters of faith, that the three rival Popes should resign, and that, if John refused, the Council might depose him. During December and January such views met with great and growing approval. John's apprehension was increased by the Council's resolve to receive the envoys of Benedict and of Gregory. Those of the former, indeed, simply reiterated their master's willingness to confer with Sigismund; but an excellent impression was made by Gregory's representatives, who said that he would resign if his rivals would, and that his supporters consented to deliberate with the Council

[1] See *infra*, Chap. ii.

[2] On 1 January 1415, Sigismund spoke of "factum Johannis Hus et alia minora," which must not be allowed to delay the reform of the Church and the Empire (Cerretanus, in Finke, *Acta*, ii, 203). The copious journal of Cardinal Fillastre contains only three short references to Hus prior to his death, though he inserts the full text of his sentence (*ibid.*, pp. 17, 40, 48). Cerretanus does not allude to Hus' death in the part of his journal which covers July 1415.

on reform, union, and other business, though they did not pledge themselves to accept its decrees.

The numbers of the Council were now rapidly increasing. The French were at last able to influence the course of affairs, and late in January there arrived the English deputation. The question of procedure had to be solved. Hitherto there had been but one formal session of the whole Council. In the transaction of such business as had been accomplished a rough division into "nations" seems to have been followed, but the Council was not bound to this arrangement. The papal party, hoping to turn the situation to their advantage, proposed that voting should be by heads and that only bishops and abbots might vote, a suggestion which would have given an assured predominance to the Italians. D'Ailly and Fillastre, while advocating a much wider franchise, agreed that heads should be counted; but the Germans and the English demanded that each "nation" should constitute a voting unit, the French acceded to their views, and the Italians perforce gave way. The scheme was apparently adopted without any formal decree, and each "nation" seems to have decided who might share and vote in its deliberations. As a rule, it seems, they admitted all prelates and university graduates in theology and law, together with such representatives of secular authorities as were in holy orders. When all four "nations"—Italian, French, German, and English[1]—had made up their minds on an issue, it was laid before the whole Council, and the decision reached was confirmed[2]. This manner of doing business was unfavourable to the cause of John XXIII and also, as the event shewed, to the plans of the reform party.

Defeated on the question of procedure, John began to waver. After an offer to resign on conditions which the Council could not possibly accept, he went so far as to declare, on 2 March, that he would abdicate if in the Council's opinion such action would give union to the Church. Unluckily for him, however, the embassy of the King of France arrived at this juncture, and their expressions of devotion deluded him into believing that they would prove unfaltering supporters. At the same time the Council was sharply divided in opinion as to the powers which should be bestowed on the mission which was to negotiate with Benedict XIII. John thought that it would take little to plunge the Council into chaos.

---

[1] In the German "nation" were included all from northern or eastern Europe, in the English "nation" all from the British Isles.

[2] Fillastre in Finke, II, 19; Cerretanus, *ibid.*, 210 sq. Cf. *ibid.* 742, 747. There was a general committee, consisting of four members from each "nation," with three cardinals, to prepare the work of the nations and to lay their conclusions before the whole Council (*ibid.* 743). A "General Session" was a very solemn and formal affair, at which perpetual decrees were enacted (see, *e.g.*, Finke, II, 746). Other meetings of the whole Council were known as "General Congregations." They were much more frequent. They could pass resolutions which were not meant to be of permanent or universal validity. As a rule matters were not brought before the whole Council until all the "nations" were in agreement upon them, though in cases of urgency a majority vote was deemed sufficient (*ibid.* II, 65, 746).

On 20 March he assured Sigismund that he would rather die than desert
it, and that night he left Constance disguised as a groom, making his way
to Schaffhausen, where, according to plan, he was joined by Frederick
of Habsburg.

In messages to the Council John used fair words, pretending that he
had left for reasons of health; but it was soon known that in letters to
the King and princes of France he was denouncing the Council bitterly.
A few days later, indeed, he cast off pretence by fleeing to Laufenburg
and retracting all the promises made by him at Constance. He had
grievously miscalculated, for the effect of his escape was to make the
Council almost unanimous against him. The cardinals tried in vain to
moderate its implacability. Whatever may be thought of the principles
on which it based its doings, there is no denying that it acted with great
dignity and effectiveness. With the enthusiastic concurrence of the French,
German, and English "nations," a series of vital decrees was passed, culminating in those of the Fifth General Session, held on 6 April. The
Council of Constance, it was resolved, held its power immediately of
Christ, and everyone, even the Pope, must obey it in matters concerning
the Faith, the extinction of schism, and the reform of the Church in head
and members. Whosoever should refuse to conform to the decrees of this
or any other General Council rendered himself liable to punishment. It
was also decreed that the Pope was bound to abdicate if and when, in the
opinion of the Council, it was in the interest of the Church that he should
do so. John XXIII was summoned to return, and threatened, in the
event of refusal, with proceedings as a promoter of schism and heresy[1].

Meanwhile Sigismund had been taking military measures against
Frederick of Habsburg. They caused John, now deserted by most of his
cardinals, to flee to Freiburg-im-Breisgau, whence he made frantic efforts
to cross the Rhine in the hope of gaining protection from the Duke of
Burgundy. Frederick, however, lost heart, and constrained the Pope to
meet a deputation from the Council at Freiburg, where on 28 April, in
terms prescribed by the Council, he appointed plenipotentiaries to resign
on his behalf, stipulating nevertheless that he was to retain the title of
cardinal, receive the office of papal vicar, and exercise papal authority
throughout Italy[2]. Again he had misconstrued the situation. Frederick
had already surrendered, and the Council had agreed to take judicial
action against the Pope, who on 2 May was summoned to answer charges
of heresy, simony, misuse of the Church's goods, and moral turpitude.
Three days later, Frederick publicly and ceremoniously humiliated himself before Sigismund, to whom he handed over all his lands, promising
to have John brought back to Constance.

[1] For what was said and done at Constance concerning the flight of John XXIII,
see in particular Hardt, II, pts. ix–xiv.

[2] On the exciting and amusing goings and comings of the Pope and the Council's
ambassadors, see the spirited account of Fillastre in Finke, II, 29.

On 13 May a commission of thirteen was appointed to collect evidence on the charges against the Pope. A long list of accusations was hurriedly made, and even before it was complete the questioning of witnesses began. This initial inquiry was "summary," its purpose being to establish a *prima facie* case against John's official conduct and private life. Next day the Council felt warranted in decreeing his suspension from office[1].

Feeling against the shifty and obstinate Pope arose yet higher when on 15 May there was read a bull of Gregory XII, in which he declared himself ready to abdicate and to recognise the Council, provided that John XXIII did not attend. Next day there began the detailed investigation of John's case[2]. Some seventy articles, unsystematically arranged and hastily drafted, were laid to his charge. The Pope, it was alleged, had been a naughty boy. His subsequent advancement was due wholly to corruption. He was guilty—many particulars are given—of simony and fraud of every kind both before and after his election to the Holy See. He had betrayed Rome to Ladislas. His attempts to frustrate the Council had been caused by a desire to prolong the Schism. He was guilty of fornication, adultery, incest, and sodomy, had poisoned Pope Alexander V and his physician, and had denied the immortality of the soul. When medieval man threw mud, he did so generously, and standing by themselves the accusations would not carry much weight. But (though the witnesses were not subject to cross-examination) the report of the evidence gives on the whole a favourable impression of the sincerity and fairness of those who bore testimony. We have altogether reports of the evidence of thirty-nine, of whom six were cardinals and seven bishops—personages of weight and responsibility—while many were officials of the Curia, who ran some risk in telling tales of their master. Some of those examined were obviously reluctant to testify at all. Most of the witnesses state, with reference to each count on which they were questioned, whether they are speaking from personal knowledge or repeating hearsay. Only in one or two cases is there any indication of personal hostility to the Pope. The inquiry was careful and thorough, and took in all more than eight days.

Meanwhile, Frederick of Hohenzollern, at the head of a deputation from the Council, had arrested John XXIII and imprisoned him at Radolfzell. The Pope was lachrymose and submissive, and on hearing of his suspension declared that he bowed to the Council's judgment. But

---

[1] Mansi, xxvii, 652 sqq.

[2] Until some thirty years ago historians knew only the number and rank of the witnesses by whom the charges were declared to have been substantiated. Valois then discovered (*La France et le Grand Schisme*, iv, 309) a summary of the evidence on each charge, with the names of the witnesses who testified. This record has lately been printed in full by Finke (*Acta*, iii, 157 sqq.) Still more recently, however, Finke found a much fuller report of the depositions of the individual witnesses (*ibid.*, iv, 758 sqq.), and thanks to this we now have a far more thorough understanding of the process against John XXIII than was previously possible.

the Council was unrelenting. At its eleventh General Session, on 25 May, the Cardinal of Viviers (Ostia) presiding and fifteen other cardinals and the King of the Romans being present, a report of the commission of inquiry was read, and fifty-four of the accusations were recited and declared to have been proved[1]. Now that we know something of the evidence on which this judgment was based, no candid historian can apply even the thinnest coat of whitewash to John XXIII. Yet one cannot but feel a little sorry for him. He was a bad man. But his misdoings were notorious when he was elected, and he had grown no worse since. He had a just grievance against the cardinals who failed him in his adversity. Both d'Ailly and Fillastre had accepted the cardinal's hat at his hands.

On hearing the result of the inquisition, John merely repeated that he submitted himself wholly to the Council. On 29 May, at the twelfth General Session, the Council formally declared that his flight had been prejudicial to the peace and union of the Church, that he was a notorious simoniac, that he had wasted ecclesiastical property, and that by his abominable life he had scandalised the Church of God and proved himself incorrigible[2]. His deposition was solemnly pronounced, and was ratified by him two days later.

John was taken to Gottlieben castle, where he was kept under the surveillance of the Elector Palatine. He was soon removed to Heidelberg. In 1416, on the discovery of a plot for his escape, he was transferred to Mannheim. There he stayed until the close of the Council.

During the month following the Pope's deposition, John Hus was perhaps the main centre of interest at Constance. But on 15 June there arrived Carlo Malatesta, accredited to Sigismund and empowered to resign the Papacy on behalf of Gregory XII. He behaved with scrupulous correctness, negotiating amicably with the four "nations" but refraining from any recognition of the validity of the Council. All went well; and at the fourteenth General Session, on 4 July, Malatesta and Cardinal Dominici of Ragusa, one of Gregory's representatives, summoned as a General Council the assembly gathered at Constance at the bidding of Sigismund. Dominici joined the other cardinals, and it was decreed that the election of a new Pope should be made only with the assent of the Council, who should decide how, when, and where it should be conducted, that no one should leave before the new Pope was chosen, that Gregory's decrees were

---

[1] More than twelve articles were altogether passed over, out of consideration, it was asserted, for the Pope's "honour." As some of them were not particularly scandalous, it has been contended that the real reason was that these articles—which included charges of murdering Alexander V, sexual immorality, and the utterance of heresy—had not been substantiated. The documents recently printed by Finke, however, shew that in the summary of the evidence only three are noted as not proven, and that for several of them the evidence was just as strong as for some of those that were publicly treated as established. It is, in short, impossible to say for certain why the omission was made.

[2] Mansi, xxvii, 715 sqq.

to be held valid, and that he and his cardinals were to form part of the Sacred College. Malatesta then announced Gregory's resignation[1]. The Council named him legate of Ancona, and he lived quietly till his death in 1417. The selfish stubbornness which he had long shewn was somewhat compensated by the dignity and graciousness with which he finally accepted the inevitable.

Two days after the abdication of Gregory, Hus was burned, and the teaching ascribed to Jean Petit on what was miscalled "tyrannicide" was condemned in general terms. The most pressing business was now the elimination of Benedict XIII. Accordingly, on 18 July, Sigismund, with twelve delegates from the Council, set out for Nice.

So far, from its own standpoint, the Council had not done badly. Substantial progress towards ending the Schism had been made. The execution of Hus, it was believed, was a deadly blow at heresy. And the Council's work had been done, considering its nature, with singularly little controversy. It was confident and zealous.

As the event shewed, it had really reached the height of its prosperity and success. Sigismund was away for eighteen months. He had asked that nothing of the first consequence should be decided in his absence, and his wishes could not be ignored. Even had he returned quickly, however, the Council's activities would have been narrowly restricted, for it could do little towards union or reform until the countries in Benedict's obedience sent representatives to the Council. And that they were slow to do.

Though the Council attempted to prepare the ground for effective re-forming measures, the truth is that for many months it hardly had enough proper work to do. In the circumstances, it is not to be greatly blamed for allowing itself to be diverted to business with which it was not fitted to deal. For instance, in its distrust of the cardinals, the Council tried to take the place and perform the functions of the Papacy. It was a task unsuited to a great deliberative body; and the minds of many of the Council's members were diverted from their lawful concerns. It was still more unfortunate that the Council should have entertained highly controversial questions with which it really had no concern; the passions thus generated impaired the unity which at best was maintained with difficulty.

The Council's task was rendered harder by changes in the political situation of western Europe during Sigismund's absence. In August 1415 Henry V landed in Normandy. Relations between Armagnacs and Bur-gundians soon began to deteriorate again after a temporary improvement. From the spring of 1416 Sigismund was in Armagnac eyes an unfriendly neutral, who soon became a bitter and dangerous enemy. All the fight-ing, hatred, and malice among the potentates of Europe had their repercussions at Constance; and only if enthusiasm for its true work had been kept at white heat could the Council have escaped injury from them.

[1] Mansi, xxvii, 731 sqq.

Most of the Council's troubles were due to Benedict XIII. In the negotiations with him—conducted not at Nice but at Perpignan—Sigismund shewed no lack of tact or address. But the old man had not bated a jot of his claims or hopes. He still had with him Castile, Aragon, Navarre, the counties of Foix and Armagnac, and Scotland; and he believed that he stood a chance of recovering Naples, nay France itself, and even of winning the Papal States. Now that his rivals were removed, he hoped to bring about the unanimous election of himself. All his old tricks were used with his habitual adroitness. But Sigismund was determined to secure his unconditional surrender, and he won over most of Benedict's supporters at Perpignan[1]. The Pope was finally urged to resign by the King of Aragon himself. He refused. On 6 November Sigismund broke off the negotiations and withdrew to Narbonne. Next day Benedict retired to the impregnable castle of Peñiscola, in the province of Valencia.

Nevertheless, the King of Aragon and the envoys of others of Benedict's supporters soon resumed discussions with Sigismund, and on 13 December the Capitulation of Narbonne was sworn to by the delegates of Castile, Aragon, Navarre, and Foix, and approved by Sigismund, the Council's delegation, and a representative of the King of France. The Council was to summon the kings, princes, and prelates obeying Benedict, and these in their turn were to summon the assembly gathered in Constance to a General Council in that town. If Benedict would not abdicate, the Council might depose him. No new Pope should be chosen until the Council had been joined by Benedict's supporters and he had been formally deposed.

Benedict remaining obdurate, Ferdinand of Aragon withdrew obedience from him on 6 January 1416. But some of the Aragonese clergy opposed the king's policy, and his death in the spring caused yet more delay in its execution. Castile's obedience was officially renounced on 15 January, but the Archbishops of Toledo and Seville used their formidable influence to prevent the Capitulation of Narbonne from taking further effect. It was not until July that Navarre and until August that Foix abandoned Benedict. By the Count of Armagnac and the Regent of Scotland the Capitulation was ignored.

The Council welcomed the agreement, ratified it on 4 February 1416, and issued its invitation to the followers of Benedict. It was not, however, until 5 September 1416 that the embassy of the King of Aragon reached Constance. On 15 October a Spanish "nation," composed of Aragonese and Portuguese, was added to the four others; on 5 November a commission was appointed to investigate the culpability of Benedict, and its report led the Council, on 28 November, to cite him as a promoter of schism and under suspicion of heresy. Next month the representatives of the Count of Foix and the King of Navarre joined the Council; but the Castilians had not yet appeared when Sigismund returned.

[1] Mansi, xxvii, 812 sqq. Much new material about the negotiations at Perpignan and Narbonne was published by Finke in Vol. iii of the *Acta Concilii Constanciensis*.

Meanwhile, the one important matter on which the Council had been able to take vigorous and united action was the suppression of heresy. For this the most zealous reformers and the most radical advocates of conciliar sovereignty were even more eager than the conservatives, since they were anxious to shew that their views did not diminish their concern for the Faith. Their victim was Jerome of Prague, whose character and career are described elsewhere[1]. Though in September 1415 he presented a written retractation of false doctrine, which was accepted by the commission in charge of his case, he was not released, and in February 1416 a new commission was set up to collect evidence against him. He soon perceived that he was marked down for destruction, and his last speeches were masterpieces of defiant eloquence. He met his end, on 30 May, with a debonair courage which impressed beholders even more than the pious resignation of Hus.

The Council's other doings had not only been singularly futile but stirred up much bad blood among its members. A great deal of breath and ink had been wasted over Jean Petit. The whole affair was part of the internecine struggle between Armagnacs and Burgundians. In 1414 an ecclesiastical Council at Paris had condemned Petit's "justification" of the murder of the Duke of Orleans, and John the Fearless had appealed to the Pope. The case was still pending when the General Council opened; and the Armagnacs prepared to agitate for the condemnation of Petit by the Council itself. At the last moment, however, both the royal government and Duke John, being for the moment in outward harmony, forbade their respective representatives to raise the issue at Constance. The truce was broken, it seems, by Gerson, who on this issue had lost all sense of proportion. Sigismund supported him, and the Council, compelled to consider the question, passed on 6 July a decree denouncing "tyrannicide" in general terms, but mentioning no names. Neither side was satisfied, and the struggle continued as fiercely as ever. On 15 January 1416, a judicial commission appointed by John XXIII to consider the appeal from the Duke of Burgundy annulled the sentence of the Paris Council, on the ground that it had acted *ultra vires*. Acting now under express orders from Charles VI, Gerson and his associates nevertheless continued to clamour, in both speech and writing, for an express condemnation of Petit's doctrines by the Council. Duke John's agents resisted stubbornly and adroitly; no agreement could be reached; indeed, few in the Council wanted an official pronouncement. In the summer of 1416 the Council became weary of the topic, and for some time little was heard of it; and small success attended Gerson when he tried to revive it early in 1417. His lack of moderation had irremediably injured his prestige at Constance, a fact of great moment[2].

[1] See *infra*, Chap. II.
[2] The Petit controversy may be studied in the documents collected in Mansi, xxviii, 731 sqq. and Finke, *Acta*, iv, 237 sqq.

Another matter which took up much time and did much harm was the case of William of Diest, Bishop-elect of Strasbourg, who had administered the goods of the see for eighteen years without taking holy orders. Accused of wasting the goods of his church and of intending to sell some of them in order to promote a marriage for himself, he had been imprisoned by the chapter of the cathedral and the magistrates of the city. The scandal was laid before the Council near the end of 1415, and a commission was appointed to investigate the affair. When its decision was rejected by the Strasbourgers, the Council wavered and set up another commission. Urged to decisive action by Sigismund, it proved unable to achieve anything without his forcible intervention; and a further commission was sitting on the question when he returned to Constance. The Council cut no better figure in its attempt to settle a long-standing quarrel between the Bishop of Trent and Pope John's old protector, Frederick of Habsburg, who, heedless of experience, defied it.

These ephemeral disputes must be noticed if one is to understand how the Council occupied its time during Sigismund's absence. Its failure to deal with them promptly and trenchantly weakened its self-confidence and prestige. One must be careful, however, not to judge it unfairly. All the while it was trying to prepare for the subsequent achievement of a genuine reform. Very soon after Sigismund left, a commission[1] of thirty-five—eight from each "nation," with three cardinals—was appointed to draw up a programme. It began work immediately, and remained in being for two years. Each proposal formally considered by it was subjected to an elaborate procedure, which necessitated the extensive use of sub-committees. It had also to undergo discussion by each "nation" before it could be submitted to the whole Council. We have no report from this commission, and indeed it is not certain that it ever presented one. It soon became clear that its task was most difficult; while few denied the need of some kind of reform, everyone's mind was fixed on the sins and shortcomings of all classes but his own. The most vital problems were the Papacy's pecuniary exactions and its encroachments on the rights of electors and patrons. The Italians were mostly hostile to any drastic measures on these matters. The English, all delegates of the secular authority, took their orders from the king, and knew very well that the Crown was able and willing to limit the Papacy's dealings with England. The German "nation" was perhaps more earnestly in favour of a thorough reform than any other. Among the French there were indeed many zealous reformers, but on the most important questions there was much difference of opinion, the universities, especially Paris, being ready to accord to the Papacy the fullest control over ecclesiastical appointments, since it was believed to be more favourable than ordinary patrons to university graduates[2].

[1] On the work of the various reform commissions, see Finke, *Acta*, II, 549 sqq.
[2] For differences of opinion in the French "nation," see Mansi, xxviii, 161 sqq.

To complicate the work of reform, there had been a revival of controversy respecting the relative authority of a General Council and the Papacy. After the victory of the Conciliar Party in the spring of 1415, the dispute had slumbered, but in October 1416 Leonard Statius, general of the Dominicans, raised his voice for papal supremacy, and initiated a sharp debate which was still lively when Sigismund returned[1]. The papalists were the more formidable since the cardinals—even those who had taken the lead against John XXIII—were openly or covertly with them. The upholders of conciliar authority were largely to blame for this. For some time after Pope John's deposition the Sacred College had been treated with bare civility. It was not represented on the delegation which accompanied Sigismund to Perpignan. Business was sometimes submitted to the Council for its final approval before many of the cardinals had heard anything about it. Their position improved, however, after Charles VI, in June 1416, appointed d'Ailly and Fillastre his proctors at Constance, and, as in the Council's early days, the cardinals now sometimes voted as a body at General Sessions or Congregations. There soon grew up a kind of entente between the Sacred College and the French "nation." D'Ailly, unstable but clever, flung himself into his new rôle with ardour. From now to the end of the Council his motives seem to have been chiefly political, and his main purpose was to thwart the Germans and the English. He was much aided by the arrival of the envoys from Aragon. They at once began to bargain as to the terms on which they were to join the Council, and were particularly concerned lest the English should have precedence of them in voting and signing documents. D'Ailly had already been criticising the procedure and organisation of the Council, and challenging the right of the English, so few in number, to constitute a separate "nation"; and encouraged by the attitude of the Aragonese, he worked himself into a passionate anglophobia which caused disorder in the Council's sessions and threatened to lead to armed conflict in the streets. Nor did the arrival of Sigismund, on 27 January 1417, tend to allay the passions excited by this particular dispute. He was now in alliance with Henry V, and at Constance he ostentatiously manifested his friendliness towards the English. Thus to the French he was merely an enemy, and his well-meant efforts to promote the Council's work were regarded by them with suspicion. Indeed, d'Ailly, some of the other cardinals, and the envoys of Charles VI wanted to wreck the Council. The French believed, no doubt with some truth, that Sigismund expected to derive much political advantage out of its further proceedings and to secure the election of a Pope who would be at his beck and call. The attack[2] on the English "nation" continued; but the Englishmen themselves, supported by Sigismund, the Germans, and the

[1] For examples of the arguments employed, see Finke, *Acta*, II, 705 sqq.

[2] For the nature of this attack, see Mansi, XXVII, 1022 sqq. The arguments are most instructive to anyone who wishes to understand what was meant by a "nation" in the fifteenth century. The English reply is dated 31 March 1417 (*ibid.* 1050 sqq.).

Burgundians of the French "nation," were able to hold their own. No change was made. To avoid disputes as to precedence it was decreed that when all the "nations" were in favour of a proposal, the president at the General Session should say *placet* for all. It was also decided that the consent of the cardinals must be secured for every conciliar act[1].

The dispute about the English "nation" fell into the background owing to the emergence of another question, which seemed to offer an equally good opportunity for annoying Sigismund. When should a new Pope be chosen? When the Council has finished its work, answered the reform party; but the papalists, backed by the cardinals and many of the French, urged that the election should take place at the earliest possible moment. The matter became urgent when on 29 March the envoys of Castile made their tardy appearance. Following their instructions, they at once asked, among other things, how the papal election was to be conducted. They refused to join the Council until they had clear answers to their questions, and announced that they would resist any proposal to exclude the cardinals from a share in the election. Indeed, they and most of the Italians would have had it conducted in the usual way. To this, however, no other "nation" would agree; while Sigismund, the Germans, the English, and some Italians did not want the question to be discussed at all until a reform of the Church had been carried out. But the Castilians stood firm, and were in a strong position, since they might frustrate the completion of union. There followed some weeks of great excitement and obscure intrigue. Towards the end of May d'Ailly produced a treatise, known from its opening words as *Ad laudem*, which was offered by the cardinals as their answer to the Castilian inquiry about the papal election. It suggested that the new Pope should be elected by the cardinals and an equal number of other members of the Council. To be successful, a candidate must have two-thirds of the votes of each section. The Castilians approved the scheme, soon to be followed by the greater part of the French and the Italians. The Aragonese said that they would concur if the Castilians would unite with the Council. This they did on 18 June[2].

In the next weeks, nevertheless, the Council almost broke up. The cardinals, Italians, French, and Spaniards virtually went on strike, declaring that Sigismund was planning violence against them and demanding from him a new guarantee of security. But Sigismund's enemies were nearly as suspicious of one another as of him; and in July an agreement was patched up between him and the cardinals. Sigismund gave new undertakings about freedom of speech, while the cardinals declared that they were ready to reform the Papacy and the Curia before making arrangements for a papal election.

After this the proceedings against Benedict XIII were pressed forward, and on 26 July he was solemnly deposed as a heretic and an incorrigible promoter of schism[3].

---

[1] Finke, ii, 91.   [2] Mansi, xxvii, 1127.   [3] Mansi, xxvii, 1140 sqq.

To deal with reform, it was considered well to appoint a new commission. Each "nation" contributed five delegates, the four old "nations" each choosing two of those who had represented them on the previous commission. The new body took up the work of its predecessor; it also inherited its difficulties. The old differences at once reappeared; and it was soon seen that the Spaniards cared nothing at all about reform and the Germans had lost some of their zeal for it. Meanwhile the papal party, heedless of the pledge given by the cardinals to Sigismund, were again agitating for an early election, arguing that a commission to decide its mode might work simultaneously with that on reform. Sigismund, the Germans, and the English resisted, and once more there was almost an open breach between the king and the cardinals.

Early in September there occurred the death of Robert Hallam, Bishop of Salisbury, a confidential adviser of Sigismund, a strong advocate of reform, and the man to whose skilful leadership the English at Constance owed their remarkable influence over the Council. Immediately afterwards the English suddenly consented to appoint representatives on a commission to consider arrangements for the papal election. They were apparently obeying instructions from Henry V which happened to reach Constance at this moment; but they would probably have acted less precipitately had Hallam been alive. Another stormy time ensued, though it is hard to see why tempers rose so high at this particular moment. Only the vigour of Sigismund's measures prevented a general disruption of the Council; tactless and overbearing as he often was, he had a sincere and rare concern for ecclesiastical union and reform, and he little deserved the charge of heresy which was shouted at him in a debate or the insult offered him by the cardinals when they appeared in their red hats in token of their readiness to endure the martyrdom which they were in no danger of incurring.

Though the papal party was gaining ground, there was every likelihood of a long struggle. The situation, however, was unexpectedly changed by the arrival of Henry Beaufort, Bishop of Winchester, uncle of the English king, who was ostensibly breaking his journey on pilgrimage to Jerusalem. There is little doubt that Henry V had instructed him to work for the speedy election of a Pope who would be favourable to the English and Sigismund. Beaufort evidently had much weight with Sigismund, for through his mediation it was quickly agreed that the election should be held as soon as possible, that such reforms as were generally acceptable should forthwith be embodied in decrees, and that the new Pope, with the aid of the Council or a special commission, should reform the Papacy and Curia on the basis of proposals already laid before the commission on reform.

In consequence several decrees were passed at the thirty-ninth session, held on 9 October 1417. In the first and most important, the decree *Frequens*[1],

---

[1] Mansi, xxvii, 1159 sqq.

it was laid down that General Councils were to be held periodically, the first five years after the termination of the Council of Constance, the second seven years after the end of the first, and the third and following at intervals of ten years. Another decree enacted that if a new schism should occur, a General Council should assemble within a year. On election, it was decided, every Pope should solemnly profess his acceptance of the Catholic Faith, according to the traditions of the Apostles, General Councils, and Fathers, and especially of the eight oecumenical Councils from that of Nicaea to that of Vienne. Bishops were not to be translated, except with the consent of a majority of the cardinals and after having an opportunity of stating objections. The Pope was to renounce the procurations which properly belonged to bishops and other prelates, nor was he to seize their *spolia* on their decease. These decrees were assuredly not trivial, but they were a poor harvest considering all the labour that had been expended on reform.

A committee was now chosen to determine the mode of electing the Pope. Despite furious disputes among its members, it agreed on a scheme which was approved by the Council on 30 October. All the cardinals were to take part in the election, and also six representatives of each "nation." To be elected a candidate must have two-thirds of the cardinals' votes, and, in addition, four votes from each of the "nations." It was furthermore decreed that before the dissolution of the Council the new Pope, with the Council's assistance, should reform the Church on eighteen points, the most notable being the number and character of the cardinals, annates and kindred impositions, the collation of benefices, appeals to the Curia, the fees charged there, the grounds and method of correcting or deposing Popes, simony, indulgences, and the levy of papal tenths[1].

On 8 November the electors entered the conclave. On the first vote Cardinal Oddone Colonna had the support of all the English, four of the Italians, and eight cardinals; and he alone had some support from each nation. Further voting gave him the needful majorities on 11 November, the French being the last to adhere to him. The new Pope, who took the name of Martin V, had been made cardinal by Innocent VII, but had joined the conciliar party and figured at the Council of Pisa. He had studied law, but was of no renown as a scholar. At Constance he had successfully run with the hare and hunted with the hounds. Men believed him to be amiable and somewhat colourless. His election, however, caused wild rejoicing. Many of those at Constance considered their work to be over. Fillastre's diary, for instance, betrays its compiler's lack of interest in the business of the next months.

It was thought that Martin V would be willing to consent to effective measures of reform. It is true that on 12 November he laid down for the conduct of the papal chancery rules which not only renewed but increased

[1] Mansi, xxvii, 1163 sqq.

the claims of his predecessor respecting provisions and reservations[1]. But these regulations were not published for more than three months, and a new reform commission, consisting of six from each "nation" and six cardinals, was confidently appointed to treat with the Pope concerning the eighteen points enumerated in the decree of 30 October. As before, however, it was almost impossible to reach agreement on anything that mattered. So hard was it to make progress that shortly before Christmas the commission suspended business for a month.

It was probably at the request of the Pope that the several "nations" now drew up statements of their views on the eighteen points. The memoranda presented by the French and by the Germans are still extant[2]. On 20 January 1418 Martin laid before the "nations" a number of projected decrees on matters calling for reform, while declaring that in regard to the punishment or deposition of Popes the majority of the "nations" were opposed to enacting anything new. But on few of the Pope's proposals was there any approach to agreement. Martin pressed for unanimous decisions; even if he did not really want them, it was safe for him to do so, for the diversity of opinions was beyond remedy. On the whole matter of reform, indeed, a spirit of hopelessness came over the Council, and soon led to negotiations between individual "nations" and the Pope for the arrangement of national concordats.

There was still, however, one subject on which the Council was harmonious—the Hussite heresy. On 22 February Martin, with the consent of the Council, published the bull *Inter cunctas*, which was designed to facilitate the suppression of Hus' followers. Numerous statements from the works of Wyclif and Hus were denounced as heretical, and there was appended a *questionnaire* to which those under suspicion of heresy were to answer on oath. They would be asked, for instance, whether every General Council, including that of Constance, represented the Church universal, whether the decrees of this Council touching the Faith and the salvation of souls were to be held by all believers, and whether its proceedings against Wyclif, Hus, and Jerome were lawful and just. These questions must be answered in the affirmative, and their inclusion was later held by many to constitute a recognition by Martin of the doctrine of conciliar sovereignty, though the papal party contended that this had nothing to do with faith or salvation.

At the moment, however, few were in a mood for controversy. A deputation from the Orthodox Church, which alleged as its purpose the restoration of union between East and West, was politely received and answered; but the long speeches must have been infuriating to those who heard them. The Pope evaded a renewed demand for a definite decision in the case of Petit and the kindred process against the Pomeranian friar, Falken-

[1] For the text see Mansi, xxviii, 499. No reasonable person should have expected reforms from a Pope whose first concern was to uphold the claims which this document sets forth.

[2] Finke, *Acta*, ii, 673 sqq.; Hardt, i, 999.

berg. On 21 March, at the forty-third General Session, seven reforming decrees were approved[1]. They represented the greatest common measure of the views of the "nations" on reform, and were mainly based on clauses in the Pope's proposals of 20 January. They concerned exemption from canonical obligations, the union and incorporation of churches, the revenues of vacant benefices, simony, dispensations, papal tenths, and the life and honour of the clergy. Though the Pope renounced his claim to the income of vacant benefices and accepted restrictions on his right to levy tenths, most of the new decrees did little but enjoin the observance of the existing law. It was a miserable climax to all the eager advocacy of reform with which Constance had resounded for over three years. Nevertheless, the Council accepted Martin's declaration that by these decrees, together with the concordats then under consideration, the object of the decree of the previous 30 October had been attained.

On 15 April the concordats with the Germans and the Latin "nations" were registered, the two having a strong resemblance. The number of cardinals was to be limited. Reservations and provisions were restricted, concessions being made to both ordinary patrons and the universities, but much discretion in these matters was still left to the Pope. Annates were to be lightened, the encroachments of the papal Curia in the judicial sphere to be checked. But the contents matter little. Each concordat was to be in force for only five years; in France the Armagnac party would not recognise the one that affected it, and in the other countries concerned they were nowhere effectually executed[2].

The English concordat—not finally concluded till July—had no time limit, but this fact is of no consequence. It promised that the number of cardinals should be reduced, and that new ones should be chosen with the approval of the Sacred College and from all parts of Christendom. There were timid clauses about indulgences, dispensations, and the appropriation of churches. Pontifical insignia were not to be permitted to lesser prelates, and Englishmen were to be appointed to some of the offices of the Curia. Such were the "reforms" with which the once vigorous English "nation" professed itself content[3]. After a little while the concordat fell into total oblivion.

The close of the Council witnessed a revival of animosity which was of ill omen for the future. Martin V decided that the next council should be held after five years at Pavia. Four of the "nations" assented; but the French, objecting to the place, absented themselves from the session at which the announcement was made. The formalities which marked the dissolution of the Council at its forty-fifth session, on 22 April 1418, were interrupted by the advocates of the Poles and the Lithuanians, who tried at the last moment to secure the condemnation of Falkenberg, asserting that the Council had approved of such action. The Pope took occasion

[1] Mansi, xxvii, 1174 sqq.   [2] The text of the concordats is in Mansi, xxvii, 1178 sqq.
[3] Mansi, xxvii, 1194 sqq.

to declare that he approved and ratified all that the Council had done "in materiis fidei conciliariter," words of pregnant ambiguity[1]. The Poles, dissatisfied, appealed to a future Council. Thus the Council of Constance ended with its relations to the Papacy unsettled.

Once the Council was over, Martin V bent his energies to recovering for the Papacy the temporal power and spiritual authority which had been so seriously impaired by recent events. His efforts to restore papal rule in the States of the Church belong rather to the political history of Italy than to the subject of this chapter. It must be remembered, nevertheless, that he was extraordinarily successful. At the close of the Council, the Papal States were partly in a condition of anarchy and partly under the control of *condottieri*, Rome itself being held by Sforza Attendolo, the general of Queen Joanna of Naples. Martin cautiously moved southward to Florence, which gave him asylum for eighteen months. During that time he played with great skill on the jealousy and treachery which marked the relations of the *condottieri* of central Italy, and on the dissensions within the Neapolitan kingdom. The upshot was that, having recovered a considerable part of the Papal States, he was able in September 1420 to enter the sorely dilapidated city of Rome.

For the next few years Naples was in confusion, and in 1423 Louis III of Anjou, whose claims to the Neapolitan throne Martin had countenanced, was adopted as heir by the childless queen. For some time the Papacy had nothing to fear from that quarter. In the next year the untimely deaths of the famous generals Sforza and Braccio gave Martin the chance of recovering the whole of the Papal States. A modern Protestant writer has declared that "it is the great merit of Martin V that he won back from confusion and restored to obedience and order, the disorganised States of the Church."[2]

Nevertheless, these achievements, as a Catholic historian has more recently remarked, "viennent beaucoup après l'obligation à conduire l'Église de Christ à sa perfection."[3] And for this supreme task Martin was in a most favourable position. He had little to fear from rivals. The erstwhile supporters of Gregory XII and John XXIII had submitted, and the latter, ransomed by Martin himself, had accepted the new Pope in 1419, been recognised as cardinal, and died a few months later. Benedict XIII had indeed remained obdurate in his stronghold of Peñiscola. But, except for the King of Aragon, the Count of Armagnac, and a few scattered individuals, all his followers had abandoned him by the end of 1418; and though after Benedict's death in 1422 or 1423 a successor, called Clement VIII, retained the support of Aragon and Armagnac till his abdication in 1429, he never constituted a serious danger to Martin.

Notwithstanding his opportunities, Martin was not merely lukewarm but actually hostile towards such a reform as alone could have saved the Church from lasting disruption. Attempts to palliate his conduct break

---

[1] *Ibid.* 1199.   [2] Creighton, *History of the Papacy* (ed. 1905), ii, 153.
[3] H. Leclercq, in Hefele, *Histoire des Conciles* (trans. from German), vii, ii, p. 669.

down: both at Constance and later he shewed plainly that he would make only those changes which he felt unable to avoid. It is, of course, true that to remedy certain crying evils he would have had to surrender claims which the Papacy had long enforced. That, however, he must have known when at Constance he promised to further the work of reform. And there is no doubt that by his attitude he imperilled the very office which he was striving to uphold, and that he was in great measure responsible for the troubles of his successor during the Council of Basle. His judgment was probably affected by the fact that zealous reformers were also, as a rule, upholders of conciliar supremacy. That this was so arose from the widespread suspicion, amply justified by events, that it was only through a General Council that any substantial reform could be accomplished. It is likely, however, that if Martin had put himself at the head of the reformers, they would soon have forgotten their theories about Councils, just as the nationalists in nineteenth-century Germany, when Bismarck made himself their leader, soon forgot their liberalism. But to Martin a desire for reform and a belief in the sovereignty of General Councils were inseparable. And the latter doctrine, rightly or wrongly, he was resolved to defeat.

In his attitude towards Councils it behoved Martin to be wary. After all it was a General Council that had put him where he was. And even if he argued that he had been elected by a sufficient majority of the Sacred College, he was still faced by the disquieting precedent of John XXIII's fate at the hands of his own followers. Martin, indeed, had early proof of the need for judicious dissimulation. Whether before the Council closed he had recognised its supremacy has been much debated. Probably he meant the Council to think he had, while the ambiguous wording of his utterances on the matter left the way open for a subsequent denial. But he was alarmed by the appeal of the Poles to a future Council, and while still at Constance, on 10 May 1418, he caused to be read in consistory, Sigismund being present, a bull in which he declared it unlawful to appeal from judgments or pronouncements of the Pope, the supreme judge, even in matters of faith. The outcry raised was prompt and great. Some began to talk of heresy, for which few denied that a Pope might be deposed; and Gerson wrote a treatise pointing out that, if Martin's assertion were accepted, the Councils of Pisa and Constance had met in vain, and either Benedict XIII or John XXIII was the true Pope. Martin bowed before the storm; the bull was never otherwise published or placed officially on record; and he never again raised the issue in express terms.

The Pope did not dare to defy the decree *Frequens* or go back on his announcement that the next General Council would be held in 1423. But he regretted the choice of Pavia as the meeting-place because of the enmity between himself and the Duke of Milan; and when, on 22 February 1423, he appointed four legates to preside over the Council, he empowered them to transfer it to another city if circumstances demanded. The reform of the clergy, the restoration of unity with the Greeks, the pacification of Europe, the defence of ecclesiastical liberties, and the extirpation of heresy—such, it was officially declared, were the objects of the Council.

The Council was formally opened at Pavia on 23 April, but very few save local clergy were present. It was not long before the transference of the Council elsewhere was mooted, the Pope's wishes being aided by an outbreak of epidemic disease. The "fathers" could not agree, and the decision was remitted to the legates, who, having their instructions, forthwith decreed a move to Siena. At this point there were present only four of the German "nation" and only six of the French; the English, strange to say, were more numerous, but the only Italians, apart from local ecclesiastics, were the papal legates, and there were no Spaniards at all.

Even had the Pope been friendly to the Council, it could hardly have been successful. It came too soon after the wearisome and expensive Council of Constance. The keenest of reformers had not yet recovered their vigour. There was no serious schism to heal, no fresh heresy to condemn. The nations most likely to be interested—France, Germany, England—were preoccupied by vital political concerns. But it was Martin's fault that the Council failed as miserably as it did.

The first formal session at Siena was held on 21 July 1423. The second did not take place till 8 November. The length of the interval was caused partly by the Pope's promise—probably insincere—that he would attend personally, and partly by the difficulty of arranging guarantees of safety which satisfied the members of the Council, who were a little suspicious of the civic authorities and much afraid of the Pope. At the second session there were present two cardinals and twenty-five mitred prelates. The agenda had been discussed beforehand with Martin V, who had already approved the four decrees that were passed. Heresy was denounced, the decrees of Constance against Wyclif and Hus were confirmed, and all the faithful were exhorted and stimulated to aid in the suppression of their disciples. Benedict XIII and his followers were once more condemned. Union with the Greeks having been found impracticable at the moment, the Council, it was announced, would proceed to the work of reform.

The work of reform was soon faced by obstacles. There was at Siena a party which supported the Pope's view of his relations with the Council. In view of the impossibility of reaching agreement under such conditions, it was decided that each "nation" should draw up its own reform programme, so that it might be ascertained how much all had in common. The French were ready first. Their programme was for the most part no more drastic than what the more earnest reformers had put forward at Constance. Perhaps their most startling proposals were that the Pope should choose cardinals from lists submitted to him by the various "nations," and that he should levy no taxes whatever save on the laity of the States of the Church. The "liberties" of the Church of France were demanded, and it was hinted that the measures advocated represented only the beginning of what ought to be done. The legates were much alarmed, and thenceforth it was their chief aim to dissolve the Council. Soon after the beginning of 1424 their intention was known and admitted. The two parties in the Council threatened, and indeed tried, to have recourse to force.

The reform party made a poor fight. The legates soon impaired the unity of the French "nation," partly by intrigue, partly by introducing a number of French officials of the Curia, some of whom, it was alleged, were not qualified to attend. The other "nations" seemed to despair; members of the Council began to go away. The reformers gained some encouragement by the arrival in February of the delegation of the University of Paris and of the Archbishop of Rouen, who had been sent by the Duke of Bedford, and whom the French promptly elected president of their "nation." The archbishop, however, played a part very like that of Beaufort at Constance. He was really in favour of an accommodation with the Pope; and it was doubtless due in great measure to his influence that a few days later delegates of the four "nations" designated Basle as the seat of the next Council. It was idle to declare that the Council of Siena was unaffected by this announcement. In vain did the Sienese authorities bar their gates to prevent members of the Council from leaving, in vain did a rump of the French "nation" elect a new president and continue the discussion of reform after the departure of the Archbishop of Rouen. On 7 March the papal legates fled, and when on Florentine territory caused to be affixed to the doors of Siena cathedral a proclamation dissolving the Council. The Abbot of Paisley, who had been conspicuous among the reformers, drew up an angry protest and appeal; but he could get only one member to sign and two members to witness it. The rest of those who had remained at Siena acquiesced in the dissolution. Martin blamed the Sienese for the Council's failure, and it was only grudgingly that he later restored them to his favour. He had attained his end, and had shewn a real gift for low intrigue.

When he dissolved the Council, the Pope set up a committee of three cardinals to investigate and amend the abuses in the Curia and the Church[1]. Their labours bore fruit in a constitution published on 13 April 1425. Cardinals were to do their duty and behave themselves. New rules for the conduct of the officials of the Curia were to be formulated. The clergy in general were to do what they were supposed to do. Various familiar abuses were once again denounced. Provincial councils were to be held at least once every three years. By not one jot was the Pope's power limited. Ostensible concessions to patrons of benefices really made the Pope's control of them greater than it had been since the Council of Constance. The bull would thus have achieved nothing wonderful if any attempt had been made to enforce it[2]. Naturally the reform party was

---

[1] Raynaldus, ix (xxviii), 2 sq. It is fair to recognise that he had appointed a similar committee at some uncertain date before the Council, but it had led to nothing. See *Conc. Basil.* i, 163 sqq.

[2] It is printed by Döllinger, *Beiträge*, ii, 335 sqq., and summarised at some length in Hefele-Leclercq, vii, i, 645 sqq.

unimpressed; indeed, after the Council of Siena it recognised Martin as an enemy.

The Pope's respite from Councils was not so complete as he wished. There was no chance of the Council of Basle being forgotten. Everyone who wanted for his own ends to put a little pressure on the Pope urged the speedy summons of that assembly. Sigismund did so in 1424, the Duke of Bedford in 1425, perhaps Charles VII in the following year. So in 1429 did the University of Paris, which still had a real concern for ecclesiastical reform and the doctrine of conciliar sovereignty. During the year 1430 there were widespread rumours that the Pope meant to evade summoning the Council, which, according to the decree *Frequens*, ought to meet early in 1431. Pleas and protests poured in, the University of Paris being particularly insistent. Still the Pope gave no sign that he meant to fulfil his obligations. Then, on 8 November 1430, a manifesto was placarded at a number of conspicuous spots in Rome. It announced that, as no one seemed concerned to assist in the suppression of the Hussites (then at the height of their power), two Christian princes wished to submit certain propositions. These asserted that Christian princes were bound to defend the Catholic faith, that, since the ancient heresies had been worsted by means of Councils, it was absolutely necessary to hold one next March because of the Hussites, that if the Pope did not open the Council at the time named those who had assembled to attend it ought to withdraw their obedience from him, and that if he and the cardinals did not promote the Council or appear at it, the Council might depose them. The identity of the two princes is not certain; Frederick of Hohenzollern, Elector of Brandenburg, was probably one. The document made no small stir, and encouraged the conciliar party in Rome to increase its efforts. As before the Council of Constance, some of the cardinals dissuaded the Pope from evading his duty, notwithstanding that he "held the very name of Council in horror." On 1 February 1431 he named as president of the Council, with the same powers as those enjoyed by the presidents at Pavia and Siena, Julian Cesarini, Cardinal-deacon of Sant' Angelo, a man thirty-two years old, of noble birth, and held in respect for his chastity (which seemed to contemporaries singular in a cardinal), the elegance and profundity of his learning, the moderation of his judgment, and the charm of his manner. He was already on his way to Germany as papal legate, to direct a crusade against the Hussites. Before Cesarini heard of his new appointment, Martin V, on 20 February, died of apoplexy.

On 3 March the cardinals elected Gabriel Condulmer, commonly called the Cardinal of Siena. He was a Venetian, forty-seven years old, a nephew of Gregory XII, to whom he owed his red hat. Under Martin V he had acquitted himself successfully as governor of Romagna and the Marches. He was not a great scholar; but his private life was respectable, he was believed to be keen on reform, and he had been in favour of the summoning of the Council. His principal defect was said to be obstinacy. It is to be noticed that on entering the conclave the cardinals had agreed that whoever became Pope should reform the Holy See and the Curia with the advice of the Sacred College, that he should accept their recommendations as to the time and place of the Council, and that the reform undertaken by that assembly should concern both clergy and laity but not the Pope or his court.

The new Pope, who took the name of Eugenius IV, confirmed Cesarini's authority with respect to the Crusade, and asked him for information as to the prospects of the Council. For this Cesarini shewed no concern. According to the decree *Frequens* the Council should have begun by the end of February, but during March only one stranger, the Abbot of Vézelay, appeared at Basle to attend it. The first delegates of the University of Paris arrived early in April. Then no one came for a long time. On 30 May, nevertheless, Eugenius authorised Cesarini to preside if a sufficient number of prelates attended. Cesarini nominated two deputy-presidents, who officially opened the Council on 23 July 1431[1]. The attendance was ludicrously small, and Martin V would have jumped at the chance of ending the life of so feeble an infant. But Eugenius, in bad health and engaged in civil war with the Colonna, could not apply his mind to the situation in Basle, and in any case would hardly have shewn his hand so soon. And then the Council was saved by the Bohemian heretics.

On 14 August, near Taus (Domažlice), the crusading army, under Frederick of Brandenburg and Cesarini, heard the Hussites coming and fled. On 9 September Cesarini appeared at Basle, convinced that only through a General Council could the Bohemian heresy be stemmed. At his instance letters were sent to all parts urging the clergy to gather in haste. Eugenius was besought to appear in person. On 15 October the Council wrote to the Bohemian leaders inviting them to send to Basle a delegation which should discuss with the Fathers the restoration of unity, the most lavish promises respecting safe-conducts and freedom of speech being given. As advocates of reasonableness and tolerance the sanctity and learning of Hus and Jerome were much inferior to the wagons and hand-guns of Žižka and Procop.

There followed a confusing series of events. Most of the messengers who passed between Basle and Rome seem to have been unwarrantably slow; it often happened, therefore, that by the time a communication from one to the other received its reply, the situation had entirely changed. The first formal session of the Council was held on 14 December[2]. Business transacted in less solemn gatherings was confirmed; the decree *Frequens* was renewed; the objects of the Council were declared to be the extirpation of heresy, the re-establishment of peace in Europe, and the reform of the Church. Enthusiasm was now running high at Basle, and one may well understand the dismay aroused by a rumour that the Bishop of Parenzo, papal treasurer, who arrived just before Christmas, had brought a bull dissolving the Council. It was

[1] Mansi, xxix, 1.   [2] Mansi, xxix, 3 sqq.; *Conc. Basil.* ii, 18.

true, though the bishop, taken aback by the size and zeal of the Council, denied it, and left it to a member of his suite to publish the obnoxious instrument after his own flight from the city. It caused immense indignation, soon intensified by the arrival of a second bull of similar effect, dated 18 December[1], and dictated largely by the Pope's anger and alarm at the Council's invitation to the Hussites. The effect of the two documents was that the Council was declared dissolved, that all prelates were enjoined to assemble at Bologna in eighteen months to hold an extra Council, that the next Council under the decree *Frequens* was summoned to Avignon in ten years' time, and that the war against the Czechs was to be carried on.

The Pope had altogether misapprehended the situation. The Council refused to dissolve. It expostulated by letters and envoys, justifying its resistance by the decrees of Constance and hinting that it might withdraw obedience from the Pope. It passed decrees denying the authority of anyone to dissolve or transfer it. Though Cesarini, at the Pope's command, resigned the presidency, he remained at Basle, defended the Council's policy towards the Hussites, and warned Eugenius of the perils to which he was exposing the Holy See. The King of the Romans had already taken the Council under his patronage, and had appointed William, Duke of Bavaria, as its protector.

Issue was now fairly joined, and there followed a bewildering struggle which continued till the end of 1433. Few would deny that the honours of this conflict lay with the Council. It is not merely that it won; but it shewed a dignity and steadfastness which contrast most favourably with the vacillation and trickery of the Pope. The Hussites were still the Council's greatest asset. Western Europe believed that only the Council could tame them, and so the Council must go on. But in the Council itself the ruling motive was a desire for reform. It was generally assumed at Basle that no reform could be secured through a Pope. So conciliar supremacy must be upheld, in order that the Pope might legally be overridden. The Council had no wish to go to extremes; but the maladroit hostility of Eugenius stirred men's tempers, and some advanced views were expressed. While, however, there was an almost unanimous refusal to accept the absolute monarchy claimed by the Pope, there was no agreement on what should be put in its place. To some, while the Pope's faith and conduct were subject to scrutiny by a General Council, which might reprimand, punish, or even depose him in the interest of the Church Universal, he was nevertheless head of the Church by divine right, and, unless in conflict with those of a General Council, his decrees and ordinances were universally binding. To others, on the contrary, he was no more than the *caput ministeriale* of the Church, his function being merely to execute its decrees, his own being only administrative ordinances. Some, indeed, thought that such a constitutional monarch,

[1] Mansi, xxix, 564 sqq., cf. xxx, 75 sq.

for all his lack of independent authority, had been instituted by God; but many held that the Papacy was a human invention and that the Church might entrust its executive power to a Council or Committee. There were in fact not a few who would have ascribed very great authority to the Cardinals. To no small number, furthermore, sovereignty lay with the bishops, whose powers came to them direct from God; the Church, to use modern terminology, was regarded as a federation or bishoprics, federal authority being vested in the Papacy, which, however, might exercise only such functions as had been expressly allotted to it. In the eyes of others, who were strongly represented at Basle, sovereignty belonged to the whole body of clergy. General Councils, through which this sovereignty was exercised, must therefore be constituted on a democratic basis. It is plain that, in face of these theories, some of which were mutually incompatible, the Papacy, with its clear, definite principles and claims, was in a very advantageous position.

During 1432 the Council grew stronger. Its numbers increased steadily though slowly. In April there were over eighty members, including thirty or forty mitred prelates. The King of the Romans promised to stand by them to the death. Charles VII of France, after long hesitation, accepted the advice of a council of the clergy of his obedience, and in July gave French ecclesiastics leave to attend. About the same time the English government reached a similar decision. Castile and Burgundy were also favourable. Meanwhile, negotiations with the Hussites were progressing, and in May, by the convention of Eger, they agreed, on terms which testify to the terror they had inspired, to send representatives to discuss with the Council the possibility of reconciliation.

All this while the Council was increasing its pressure on the Pope. In April it renewed the decrees of the fifth session of Constance, and called upon Eugenius to revoke his bulls of dissolution, and either to appear at Basle, or, if in bad health, to send a representative. At the same time, the cardinals, several of whom were notoriously out of sympathy with the Pope's policy, were peremptorily cited to join the Council within three months. In May Cesarini again attached himself to the Council and accepted the doctrine of conciliar supremacy. A little later the Council declared that, if the Papacy fell vacant while it was in being, the new Pope must be elected wherever it was sitting, denied the Pope's right to create cardinals as long as he absented himself, and named a Vicar of the papal territory of the Venaissin in opposition to the nephew of Eugenius.

In the early summer the Pope shewed the first sign of being impressed by the Council's firmness. While refusing any concession on matters of principle, he offered to allow the Council to remain at Basle until the Bohemian problem was solved and then to choose any place it liked in the Papal States as the scene of a new Council, which should not be dissolved until it had extinguished heresy, given peace to Europe, and reformed the Church. But the Council refused to be diverted from the principle at issue, and in its reply asserted in the bluntest language the superiority of a General Council to a Pope, who, even if he might be styled head of the Church, was only *caput ministeriale*. It also hinted that the case of Cardinal Capranica and all its implications would be investigated[1].

Meanwhile, out of twenty-one cardinals fifteen had either appeared at Basle, named proxies, or offered satisfactory excuses. In September Cesarini agreed to resume the presidency. There followed a lull in the conflict, but in December the Council decreed that, if Eugenius did not withdraw the bull of dissolution within sixty days and adhere to the Council without reserve, it would take such measures as the Holy Ghost should inspire[2].

Before the stern summons of the Council many members of the Curia were beginning to waver. Eugenius himself had already offered to submit to arbitration the question whether the Council should be moved to Italy or to another place in Germany. The latest conciliar decree, backed as it was by an urgent embassy from the German Electors, forced the Pope to admit defeat. On 14 February 1433 he issued a bull authorising the holding of a General Council at Basle. He tried to save his face by alleging that many of his previous objections to Basle had been removed by the march of events, and by announcing that he would send legates to preside. He furthermore wrote letters to the princes, universities, and ecclesiastical authorities of Catholic Europe, calling on them to attend the Council or send representatives.

When the bull became known at Basle it altogether failed to conciliate the Council. What was the Pope's view of what the Council had already done? On this no light had been shed. Consequently, at its eleventh session, held on 27 April 1433, the Council ignored the change in the Pope's attitude. It was decreed that, if he failed to attend the Council or send representatives within four months, he would be liable to suspension; if a further two months passed without his submission, the Council might depose him. The Council safeguarded itself by enacting that it might not dissolve itself without the consent of two-thirds of each of the deputations into which it was divided.

To preside over the Council, the Pope named six cardinals, one of whom was Cesarini. He refused to act; the Council rejected the others until the

---

[1] In 1426 Capranica had been created a cardinal by Martin V, who had kept his act secret until shortly before his death. In consequence Capranica had not completed all the customary formalities when Martin died. Nevertheless, he claimed the right to attend the conclave, but for political reasons a majority of the Sacred College decided to exclude him. Now, of those cardinals who had advocated his admission, the majority had not at first voted for Eugenius, and if Capranica's claim was just, there was thus some doubt of the validity of the election. With great folly, Eugenius behaved very harshly towards Capranica, who, a ruined man, went to Basle and laid his case before the Council.

[2] Mansi, xxix, 43 sq.

Pope should acknowledge that the Council had been from the beginning
a true Council, should adhere to it unconditionally, and should withdraw
the bull of dissolution. The Pope's envoys grievously mishandled their
case, and when, abandoning conciliatory talk, they openly advocated papal
supremacy, they were easily worsted in argument by Cesarini. The Council
was eager for action against Eugenius, and in July a resolution in favour
of delay was defeated by 363 votes to 23[1].

The Council, as these figures indicate, had been growing fast. In the
spring of this year seven cardinals, five archbishops, and forty-three bishops
were present[2]. The embassies of temporal potentates continued to arrive.
Those of England and Burgundy appeared in March; the French delegation, present in part since the previous November, was complete in May.
In size and representative character the Council remained inferior to that
of Constance, but it could now claim without absurdity that it spoke with
the voice of the Church Universal.

Most of the lay rulers represented at Basle, while not in sympathy
with the Pope's theories, dreaded a new schism and wished the Council
to move slowly while they tried to arrange an amicable settlement. But
the majority of the Fathers were disinclined to listen, and the urgent
remonstrances of Sigismund only secured, on 13 July, a sixty days' extension of the term within which Eugenius must comply with the Council's
demands[3]. The Council's confidence in itself may be measured by the
fact that the German Electors, England, and Burgundy were all sympathetic
towards Sigismund's efforts.

At the moment, as it happened, relations were particularly intimate
between Eugenius and Sigismund, whom the Pope had crowned Emperor
on 31 May 1433. Believing him to have been won over to the papal
cause, Eugenius was encouraged to greater boldness than he had shewn
for some time. On 1 July he forbade the Council to attempt anything
beyond its three tasks of suppressing heresy, restoring peace, and reforming the Church. On 29 July, in the bull *Inscrutabilis*, he annulled everything
it had done outside its proper field, including all its acts against himself,
the Holy See, and the Curia. This he followed three days later by the
bull *Dudum sacrum*[4]. There he recognised that the Council had been
valid from the first, though in terms which implied that he was granting
a favour, not acknowledging a fact; he also withdrew the bull of dissolution and declared his adherence to the Council. The bull *Dudum sacrum*
was prepared in two texts, one of which contained certain provisos—not
shewn to Sigismund—the most notable being that the presidents named
by the Pope should be accepted by the Council and that everything done
against the Papacy and its supporters should be annulled. If the Council
would accept the Pope's terms, he would revoke everything he had done
against its members.

[1] *Monumenta conciliorum*, ii, 393.   [2] Lazarus, *Das Basler Konzil*, App. ii.
[3] Mansi, xxix, 61.   [4] *Ibid.* 574 sq.

Very soon afterwards Eugenius heard of the Council's refusal to suspend for more than a few weeks its proceedings against him. Without waiting to ascertain the effect of the bull *Dudum sacrum*, he denounced the Council's behaviour in a circular letter to a number of kings and princes, and on 11 September the bull *In arcano* annulled the decrees passed by the Council on 13 July and declared that anyone accepting benefices taken away from his supporters would be for ever incapacitated for holding any. A further bull, *Deus novit*, dated 13 September, was quite uncompromising. It contains an outspoken statement of the Pope's case, declares that the conduct of the members of the Council approximates to heresy, expressly refuses approval to many of their acts, and denies that the Council has had a continuous existence since its beginning. The Pope agrees that the assembly in Basle may henceforth be called a General Council, on condition that it withdraws all its decrees against himself and admits his presidents. All conciliar decrees must be confirmed by the Pope, for he has authority over all Councils, save in matters which concern the Faith or the peace of the whole Church. The assertion that a General Council is above the Pope is heretical. If the Council will not change its policy, it is the duty of Christian princes to resist it.

This document has occasioned much controversy. According to the Council it was known far and wide; and it seems certain that it was published and discussed at places so remote from Rome as Vannes and Angers. The Pope, however, denied its authenticity, and modern historians have usually regarded it as a mere draft, which, whether through accident or through malice, was circulated without his knowledge. The truth of the matter will probably never be ascertained; but we have seen Martin V trying the effect of a bull unfavourable to conciliar authority and dropping it when it provoked strong opposition, and Eugenius IV had played strange tricks with the bulls dissolving the Council of Basle and quite lately had drawn up two versions of *Dudum sacrum*. It may well be that the bull was a *ballon d'essai*, which Eugenius repudiated when he found that few people liked it[1].

During the autumn of 1433 the Council's truculence was so far mitigated by political pressure that its anti-papal proceedings were suspended. The position of Eugenius, however, grew worse. The bull *Deus novit* made a bad impression on all sides. Sigismund, France, Burgundy, even his own Venice, urged him to accept the demands of the Council. What perhaps influenced him still more, the *condottieri* Sforza and Fortebraccio, probably at the instance of the Duke of Milan, entered the Papal States and occupied a great part of them. At all events, on 15 December 1433 Eugenius accepted one of the formulas proposed to him by the Council and issued

[1] Valois, *Pape et Concile*, i, 253 sqq., has shewn that the bull was drawn up by Antonio de Roselli, then a consistorial advocate, but his inference that it had never received the approval of the Pope is not borne out by the wording of the document on which he relies. Cf. Haller, in H.Z., cx, 350 sq.

a second bull *Dudum sacrum.* In this he recognises that the Council has been canonical since its opening, that its dissolution was invalid, and that it should continue in order to deal with its oft-mentioned three tasks. He declares that he will loyally promote the Council, and revokes the bulls *Inscrutabilis, In arcano,* and *Deus novit* (though, he protests, the last was published without his knowledge), together with everything he had done to the Council's prejudice.

On 5 February 1434, at the sixteenth General Session, the Council accepted the Pope's bull and declared that he had given full satisfaction. It is true that there soon followed a little dispute over the terms on which the presidents named by the Pope were to be admitted. On 24 April, however, they agreed to a form of oath acceptable to the Council, whereby they undertook to observe and defend its decrees[1]. After this there ensued some fifteen months in which the relations of the Pope and the Council were outwardly amicable.

The Council was at the height of its prestige and power. Its conflict with the Papacy, however, had not aroused popular enthusiasm, and its hold on public esteem was due mainly to its dealings with the Hussites. Most of the negotiations, it is true, were conducted on Bohemian or Moravian soil, and are best treated as part of the history of Bohemia. But what arrested the attention of Europe was the appearance at Basle in January 1433 of fifteen Bohemian envoys, including Jan Rokycana, the leading preacher of the Hussites, Peter Payne, an English disciple of Wyclif, their most formidable dialectician, and the great Prokop himself, who had caused the mood of sweet reasonableness which the Council, with obvious difficulty, maintained. Not only did the Fathers condescend to debate with condemned heretics, but, in deference to Hussite prejudices, harlots were banished from the Basle streets and members of the Council were ordered to keep sober and abstain from dancing and gambling. In accordance with the prearranged programme, the debates turned almost entirely on the famous Four Articles of Prague, in which the Hussites demanded communion under both kinds, freedom of preaching, the reduction of the clergy to apostolic poverty, and the punishment of public sins. Thanks largely to the suavity and tact of Cesarini, the heretics were allowed to state their views fully and treated with a politeness which rarely lapsed and sometimes verged on cordiality. As controversialists their leading speakers were well equipped. Their weakness was that the delegation contained representatives of every shade of Hussite opinion. Nevertheless, though the Council tried to play upon the divisions among the envoys, they were skilful enough to maintain a united front against the common enemy. Convinced, after some weeks, that their hopes of winning the Council to their views were vain, they declared that they had not been authorised to join it or make any compromise, and that, if negotiations

---

[1] For the Pope's surrender and the Council's acceptance of it, see Mansi, xxix, 78 sqq.

were to go farther, the Council must send a mission to Bohemia to confer with the Diet.

When in April 1433 the Hussites left Basle, a deputation from the Council consequently went with them. Its real task was to spy out the land. Its debates with the Diet led to no agreement, but on their return to Basle the envoys could report with truth that the Hussites were utterly disunited and that the grant of the cup to the laity in the Eucharist would win over the Utraquist or Calixtin party, which was supported by most of the Bohemian nobles. The Council resolved to make this concession, but to keep its decision secret until there had been further discussion on the other matters raised by the Articles of Prague. A second mission, which reached Prague in the autumn of 1433, found the Hussites even more at variance than before and their army in a state of mutiny. The party for reconciliation was stronger; the Council's envoys displayed great skill and address; and in November, notwithstanding the opposition of a powerful minority, the Diet accepted an agreement, commonly known as *The Compacts* of Prague, whereby Bohemia and Moravia were to make peace with all men, and any in those lands who had been wont to communicate under both kinds might continue to do so, merely verbal concessions being made on other points of the Four Articles. Almost immediately, however, there arose disputes as to the interpretation of this treaty, and nothing was really settled when, in February 1434, the Council's delegation got back to Basle. There were indeed some sharp passages between the Council and a Bohemian envoy, and there might even now have been a total breach but for the solicitous intervention of Sigismund.

Reaction, however, was spreading apace in Bohemia. The Catholics and the Utraquists arrayed themselves in arms against the Orphans and the Taborites. On 30 May 1434 Prokop was defeated and killed at Lipany. The commander of the victorious army had been an officer of Žižka, and he had under him many of the soldiery who had made the Hussite name terrible throughout Europe. But men estimated rightly that with the overthrow of Prokop the aggressive force of the Hussite cause had departed. The reconciliation of Bohemia to the Church seemed to require only a little face-saving talk. And, in the eyes of Europe, it was the Council that was chiefly to be thanked for this happy result.

Commanding widespread respect, the Council apparently stood a good chance of succeeding in its task of reform. It now had about five hundred members. It had nothing to fear from external hostility. Despite complaints of the high cost of food and lodging, it is evident that men of modest means managed to stay in Basle fairly comfortably for years. Nevertheless, the Council laboured under certain grave disadvantages. Though almost unanimous in resisting Eugenius, it was, as we have seen, irreconcilably divided in opinion as to the Pope's rightful position. It was, moreover, rent by national animosities. This fact needs emphasis,

having often been overlooked by historians, since at Basle the division
into "nations" was not formally adopted for the transaction of business.
Instead, the members were grouped into four committees or "deputations,"
which dealt respectively with the suppression of heresy, the pacification
of Europe, the reform of the Church, and what was called "common and
necessary business." The clergy of each grade were as far as possible distributed equally among the deputations, and so were the representatives
of each "nation." When one deputation had finished with a topic, its report
was communicated to the others, and if two were in favour of a proposal,
it was laid before a General Congregation[1]. Before it could be promulgated
as a conciliar decree, however, a resolution had to be passed at a General
Session, a very magnificent and solemn ceremony, to which the public
were admitted, but in which only formalities were transacted[2]. Nevertheless, while these arrangements seem to have worked fairly well, "nations"
formed themselves unofficially very soon after the beginning of the Council
and came to have a great influence on its proceedings. They debated
severally, appointed committees, and sometimes conferred with one
another. It was not to be expected that members of the Council, when
sitting in a General Congregation or a deputation, would ignore what
they had been doing and saying in their "nations," and the existence of
these was soon recognised when appointments had to be made to the
deputations and to certain conciliar offices. The Italian, French, German,
and Spanish "nations" received semi-official countenance, but the English
failed to establish their claim to form a separate group. Each "nation"
had its president and a number of officials. At first the most influential
"nations" were the Italian and the German (which included Scandinavians,
Poles, and Hungarians); but after the conclusion of the Treaty of Arras
in 1435, the French, previously divided, became very formidable, having
in their ranks most of the distinguished men attending the Council. The
Spaniards, on the other hand, were never very numerous, and it was only
after 1436 that their "nation" had any influence. The doings of each
of these bodies were swayed largely by political considerations or by the
particular interests of the regions whence their members came. They gave
instructions to their representatives on the delegations, and sometimes,
it seems, voted as solid blocks in General Congregations. It is probable,
indeed, that national and political rivalries had as much weight at Basle
as formerly at Constance[3].

It has often been asserted that the efficiency and prestige of the Council
were seriously damaged by the character of many of its members. In its
early days, when its numbers were small and its fate was uncertain, almost

[1] The Council's main rules for the conduct of business are printed in Mansi, xxix,
377 sq., and in *Mon. Conc.* ii, 260 sqq.

[2] On the Council's procedure, Lazarus (pp. 111 sqq.) may be consulted, though he
does not always interpret his authorities correctly.

[3] On this whole subject, see Lazarus, pp. 157 sqq. For illustrations of the effect of
national animosities, see *e.g. Conc. Basil.* v, 100 *et passim*.

any would-be member seems to have been admitted[1]. Later, rules concerning qualifications for membership were repeatedly made, and after 1435 the composition of the Council was theoretically little if at all more democratic than that of the Council of Constance[2]. But the Committee charged with the application of the rules seems to have paid small regard to them[3], and though references to cooks and grooms as figuring among the Fathers may have been rhetorical flights, there is no doubt that the Council comprised many who were clergy in no more than title, and some who were not even that.

In the heyday of its triumph over Papacy and heresy, this body's judgment failed it. Some members of the Council were moved by personal hatred of Eugenius. It tickled the vanity of the less responsible to feel that they were lording it over the Church and humiliating the Pope. And Eugenius, it must be admitted, was constantly giving ground for suspicion that his surrender had been insincere. Whatever its motives, the Council behaved as though the papal office were in suspension. As early as 1432 it had set up a whole judicial apparatus to take the place of the papal court[4]. It attempted to divert to itself money which had been raised by papal collectors, and claimed the right of levying taxes on the clergy of the whole Church. At the same time, it meddled in all sorts of matters, ecclesiastical and political, for which machinery already existed or which did not concern it at all. Such conduct was trebly foolish. It wasted time which the Council should have bestowed on its proper tasks; it alienated public opinion, which had no wish to see the Pope superseded by the Council and disliked its interfering fussiness; and it stiffened the hostility of Eugenius, who came to the conclusion that conciliation only encouraged radicalism.

Many modern writers have maintained that the Council's folly was due to its democratic organisation. It is true that the inferior clergy greatly outnumbered the prelates[5], that voting was by heads, and that the humblest members of a deputation might sway the course of its debates. But, while an assembly of prelates would doubtless have behaved very differently, there is no reason to believe that it would have acted more wisely. For that matter, the most extravagant views found spokesmen at Basle in bishops and even cardinals. The truth is that the Fathers, with a few striking exceptions, were not of high moral or intellectual calibre. They could endure adversity but not success. One may well doubt whether there was in the Church at that time enough devotion to principle to render possible the successful achievement of any of the tasks which the Council of Basle was striving to accomplish.

[1] *Mon. Conc.* II, 190. Cf. Mansi, XXIX, 1230. The question is discussed at some length, though not very convincingly, in Lazarus, 28 sqq.

[2] *Mon. Conc.* II, 579 sq.; *Conc. Basil.* III, 461.

[3] *Mon. Conc.* II, 650 sq.   [4] *Conc. Basil.* I, 58.

[5] There were never more than 105 mitred prelates at any meeting. That number was reached at the 17th General Session, on 26 April 1434 (*Mon. Conc.* II, 649).

Nevertheless, from 1434 to 1436 things seemed to be going fairly well for the Council. The negotiations with the Bohemians dragged on unexpectedly, for even the mildest Hussites struggled to secure recognition of communion in both kinds as the normal practice in Bohemia and Moravia and to obtain guarantees for the future autonomy of the Church in those lands. Eventually, the Compacts of Prague were signed at Iglau (Jihlava) on 5 July 1436, and the Bohemians reconciled with the Church— a hollow formality and due in any case to Sigismund rather than to the Council. The Council's envoys, however, had been conspicuous at the various conferences which led to this result, and most people supposed that their part had been decisive.

The Council also concerned itself with the work of reform. Though so drafted as almost to invite evasion, a decree of July 1433, doing away with the general papal reservation of electoral benefices, dignities, and offices, had testified to the widespread determination to curtail the Pope's absolutism[1]. But it was temptingly easy to reform the absent and the few. Thus, in November 1433 there had been passed a decree prescribing the regular and frequent holding of provincial and diocesan synods and defining their procedure and functions, its purpose being to subject metropolitans and bishops to a control like that to which the Pope was to be subjected by General Councils. In the summer of 1434 there was issued a reaffirmation of the decree of the Council of Vienne enjoining on all universities the appointment of professors of oriental languages. Such measures were naturally criticised as inadequate, nor could much be said in favour of four decrees of January 1435, against clerical concubinage, the abuse of excommunication and the interdict, and unreasonable appeals in ecclesiastical causes—the topics touched upon being either of minor consequence or adequately covered by existing legislation. At length, however, at its twenty-first General Session, in June 1435, the Council, along with ten decrees of no particular account, issued one which was equivalent to a revolution. No payment, it laid down, was to be demanded at any stage of an appointment to an ecclesiastical benefice or office, or for ordination, or for the sealing of bulls, or under the name of annates, first-fruits, or any similar designation. Officials of the papal or other chanceries were to receive appropriate salaries, with which they must be content. If the Pope resisted this decree, he would be dealt with by the Council[2].

The application of this measure would, of course, have turned upside down the government of the Catholic Church as it had been constituted since the days of Hildebrand. The Papacy, in the sense attached to the

---

[1] Mansi, xxix, 62 sqq. Cf. Zwölfen, *Die Reform der Kirchenverfassung an dem Konzil zu Basel* (*Basler Zeitschrift für Gesch. u. Altertumskunde*, xxviii, 162 sqq. The charge that the Council, when it came to the point, was lukewarm on reform must be dismissed in view of Zwölfen's arguments, which are mainly based on evidence in *Concilium Basiliense* (cf. *op. cit.* xxix, 40 sqq.).

[2] Mansi, xxix, 104.

term for more than three centuries, would have ceased to exist. It is true that when communicating the decree to Eugenius the Council declared its readiness to give to him and the others adversely affected adequate compensation, and that Cesarini, who was the principal author of the measure, urged insistently that this should be the next subject to be taken up. Nevertheless, the Pope's legates at Basle were warranted in protesting against the decree.

Eugenius himself took the blow with apparent coolness, and his envoys, while instructed to maintain the Pope's supremacy and his right to annates, were told to hint that, if arrangements for compensation were immediately made and if one or two points of detail could be amicably settled, the Pope would confirm the decree. Cesarini, however, upheld the action of the Council when it refused to bargain. It had already ordered that all sums of money due to the Pope should be sent to Basle. Eugenius for a while adopted a non-committal attitude. Really, however, he was much more confident than he had been for some time. Forced by the populace to flee ignominiously from Rome, he had been an exile in Florence since June 1434, but the political situation in Italy had lately become much more favourable to him[1]. His agents at Basle, moreover, reported that many distinguished members of the Council thought that the majority had been going too far. What gave him most hope, however, was his position in relation to the Greeks.

The question of union with the Greeks had been brought to the fore by Eugenius. The Eastern Emperor and the leading prelates of the Greek Church were particularly anxious at the moment for the healing of the Schism, since only if this were achieved could they hope for substantial help from the West against the Turks. The accessibility of Italy to the Greeks had been one of the arguments whereby Eugenius sought to justify the summons of a Council to Bologna. The Council of Basle was therefore compelled to interest itself in the matter, and it was naturally anxious that the conference between Catholics and Orthodox should be held at Basle itself. For some three years both Council and Pope had been trying to convince the Greeks that no practical results could come from dealings with the other. The Greeks refused to go to Basle, and insisted that the Pope should be present in person at the conference. On the other hand, the Council succeeded in defeating a project, to which the Pope was willing to agree, for holding a Council at Constantinople. After much tortuous negotiation, it was settled between the Council and the Greeks, in the autumn of 1435, that the conference should be held in some town on the coast, that the Council of Basle should bear the expenses of the Greeks, and that the Pope must be present in person. The situation was developing very agreeably for Eugenius.

The Council was the more determined to shew the Greeks that the

---

[1] On this see Wittram, *Die französische Politik auf dem Basler Konzil*, pp. 67 sqq.

Pope was really of small consequence; and, in view of its financial commitments, it was well for it to make good its claim to control the pecuniary resources of the Catholic Church. It had already complained, on good grounds, that the Pope had ignored some of the reforming decrees which it had passed, and that he had countenanced vexatious and frivolous proceedings in the Curia against members of the Council. To the scandal of many of its erstwhile supporters, it had discussed the issue of an indulgence to raise funds for the expenses of the Greeks. The more hot-headed of its members now led a new offensive against the Pope. In January 1436 he was called upon to withdraw everything he had done against the Council and to confirm all its decrees. He was held up to obloquy in a circular which the Council addressed to all Christian princes, praising its own conduct[1]. In March more reforms were decreed. New rules about the Pope's conduct, personal and official, were laid down. Every new Pope was to swear that he would maintain the Faith as proclaimed by General Councils, notably those of Constance and Basle, and that he would continue to hold such gatherings. There were fresh and minute regulations about the qualifications and behaviour of cardinals. Certain previous decrees very obnoxious to the Papacy were confirmed or strengthened[2]. In April, at a thinly attended session, the Council voted the grant of a plenary indulgence to all who should contribute towards the Council of union with the Greeks[3]. To the Pope's overtures on annates and the Greek question, uncompromising and aggressive answers were returned.

Meanwhile Eugenius had continued to treat the Council politely, gaining time and conceding nothing. In the summer of 1436, however, he evidently thought that he need no longer dissemble. In a memorandum to the princes of Catholic Europe he reviewed the proceedings of the Council in a hostile spirit, accusing it of a factious temper, of interfering in matters beyond its competence, of sterility even within its usurped sphere, and of a desire to destroy the authority of the Pope and to make the government of the Church a democracy.

The renewal of open strife between Council and Pope alarmed the Greeks, who had no wish to unite with a disunited Church. They were also perturbed by the policy of the Council respecting the place of meeting. Although they had bargained for a town on the coast and their Emperor had declared that he would not go to Basle, the Council most foolishly resolved, on 5 December 1436, that the conference should take place either there, at Avignon, or somewhere in Savoy[4]. Cesarini refused to put the motion, and a strong minority shared his views.

A Greek envoy insisted that the meeting must take place in one of the places already approved. Though Avignon was not one of these, the Council continued to favour it, even when it had acquiesced in the rejec-

[1] Mansi, xxx, 1044 sqq.   [2] *Ibid.* xxix, 110 sqq.   [3] *Ibid.* 128 sqq.
[4] This decision was due mainly to the French, who, there is reason to believe, hoped to get the Papacy back to Avignon (*Conc. Basil.* v, 177 sqq. *passim*).

tion of Basle. Avignon delayed beyond the prescribed term in complying with the conditions which the Council sought to impose upon it as the price of the honour and profit which it was to receive[1]; but the majority of the Council refused to change their minds[2], and, under the leadership of Louis d'Aleman, known as the Cardinal of Arles, bitterly denounced Cesarini, who, with some fifty followers—mainly prelates—asserted that another place, preferably in Italy, should be chosen. It was in vain that the twenty-fifth session was postponed to avert violence, for when on 7 May 1437 it was at last held, each party tried to seize the high altar and the president's chair, swords were drawn and blows were struck. Eventually two bishops started simultaneously to read rival decrees. The minority, whose decree was the shorter[3], sang *Te Deum* when its recital was finished, the majority beginning the hymn as soon as they could and going steadily through it a few lines in the wake of their competitors. The majority decree[4] stated that the Council of Union was to be at Basle, or, if the Greeks were immovably opposed to that, at Avignon or somewhere in Savoy. The minority had chosen Florence or any other town already designated which should be agreeable to the Pope and the Greeks. Some of those belonging to it, at the instance or with the connivance of the Archbishop of Taranto, a papal legate, stole the conciliar seal to authenticate their decree[5].

After this the Council would have done well to dissolve. It was irremediably split, and both parties had lost their dignity and sense of proportion. They acted together a little longer, however, and one party still had years of futile life before it. But there is no need to linger over the details of the sequel.

Not being ready to surrender to Eugenius, the Council, with sound tactical judgment, continued its attack on him. At the twenty-sixth General Session, on 31 July 1437, he was cited to answer charges of having refused to introduce reform, raised new scandals in the Church, and caused schism by refusing to obey the decrees of the Council[6]. Cesarini refused to preside at this session. Eugenius making no response, the Council, on 1 October, pronounced him guilty of contumacy[7].

Meanwhile the Pope had issued the bull *Doctoris gentium*, dated 18 September 1437[8]. If the Council persisted in its action against the Pope, it was to be transferred to Ferrara after 30 days (allowed for the completion of business with the Bohemians). Even if it gave up its anti-papal proceedings, it must go there as soon as the Greeks reached Italy. At Ferrara the Pope would appear with a full vindication of his conduct. On

[1] *Conc. Basil.* i, 156; *Mon. Conc.* ii, 955, v, 215 sqq.
[2] The case of the majority is fully and plausibly put in its report to the Emperor Sigismund (*Conc. Basil.* i, 442 sqq.).
[3] Mansi, xxxi, 1361 sqq. [4] *Ibid.* xxix, 133 sqq.
[5] *Conc. Basil.* i, 158, v, 253; *Mon. Conc.* ii, 979, 987.
[6] Mansi, xxix, 137 sqq. [7] *Ibid.* 147 sqq.
[8] Mansi, xxxi, 1388.

CH. I.

12 October the Council defiantly answered the Pope point by point, announcing that, unless he yielded, he would be suspended at the end of four months and deposed at the end of six after the issue of his last bull[1].

At these threats, however, the Pope could laugh, for he had decisively worsted the Council in the rivalry for the confidence of the Greeks. After the breach in the Council in the spring, he had confirmed the minority decree of the twenty-fifth session and the Greeks declared that they recognised only the minority as the true Council. In August, a deputation chosen partly by Eugenius, partly by the minority at Basle, sailed from Venice, and in September arrived in Constantinople with 300 archers for the defence of the city. They were soon followed by ships from the majority at Basle[2], but the envoys on these made no impression on the Greeks, who in November embarked on the vessels sent by Eugenius. On hearing this news, Cesarini tried to induce the Council at Basle to meet the Greeks in Italy and to effect a reconciliation with the Pope. It was prudent advice, but it is not astonishing that the majority rejected it. A few days later Eugenius announced that the Council had now been transferred to Ferrara, but before this could have been known at Basle, Cesarini left the city with his supporters, to be warmly welcomed in Italy.

For the next eighteen months the attempt to unify Eastern and Western Christendom interested Europe more than what was happening at Basle. It is hard to say, nevertheless, which of the two Councils was the more futile. At Ferrara the principal motive of nearly all the Greeks was political, while the Pope was thinking mainly of enhancing the prestige of the Holy See and scoring points off his enemies at Basle. It is no injustice to say that very few of those concerned were thinking first of the welfare of Christendom.

The Emperor John Palaeologus, the Patriarch of Constantinople, and twenty-two Orthodox bishops, with a train of priests, officials, and others, numbering in all seven hundred persons, landed at Venice in February 1438. The Council of Ferrara had been opened on 5 January; the Pope was already there; and it had appropriately denounced the Fathers of Basle. Owing to discussion on points of etiquette and procedure, it was not until 9 April that the Greeks were present at a formal session.

The Emperor hoped to secure military aid from Western Europe without risking a defeat of his Church in theological discussion. The Greeks therefore deliberately wasted time, and it was only when the indifference of the princes of the West became manifest that serious debate started. Preliminary skirmishes shewed that neither side was inclined to make concessions, and the prospect of agreement seemed dark when in October the Council at last approached the crucial question—the doctrine of the

---

[1] Mansi, xxix, 151 sqq., 289 sqq.

[2] For a description of the delays to which these had been subjected on the way, see *Conc. Basil.* v, 304 sqq.

procession of the Holy Ghost. Was it ever lawful for a section of the Church to make an addition to the Creed? And if it were, did the Holy Ghost proceed from the Son as well as from the Father? The debate was leisurely and verbose, both sides showing much dialectical acumen, and comporting themselves on the whole with dignity and good temper. Soon, however, the Pope, pleading the presence of plague in Ferrara, the disturbed state of the neighbourhood, and his lack of money, persuaded the Greeks to move to Florence, where the inhabitants had promised a loan. The transference of the Council was formally decreed on 10 January 1439, but it was not for nearly two months that the debates were resumed. There was still no agreement about the procession of the Holy Ghost, but the Emperor and many of his advisers had become more accommodating, inasmuch as they did not wish to go home without accomplishing anything whatever. Ultimately in June the Greeks accepted a formula which alleged that the addition to the Creed was warranted by the Fathers and that the Holy Ghost proceeded from the Father and the Son as from one origin and cause. A few points, deemed of minor importance, were next settled without trouble; but at the last moment there was nearly a complete breach over papal supremacy. Most of the Greeks were willing to acknowledge the primacy of the See of Rome, and the Patriarch of Constantinople, who had just died, had left behind a timely paper recognising it; but all the Greeks wished their Church to retain a considerable measure of autonomy. Eugenius was for some time intransigent, but finally both sides adopted an inconclusive and indeed meaningless formula. In consequence the decree of Union was signed on 5 July by 115 Catholic prelates and all the Greek prelates at Florence save one, Mark, Archbishop of Ephesus, an honest and unbending zealot. Though the Pope wanted to discuss other subjects, the Greeks hurried home as soon as they could.

The Pope, as he had promised, sent three hundred soldiers and two galleys to aid the defence of Constantinople. But, once the terms of the Union were known, the Greeks who had signed them became the targets of a furious outburst of popular indignation. Mark of Ephesus was the hero and leader of the opposition. The Emperor, while personally upholding what had been done, did not venture on the official promulgation of the decree of Union. Bessarion of Nicaea and Isidore of Kiev identified themselves with the Western Church and accepted cardinals' hats; and the archbishopric of Kiev, and a few Russian bishoprics, recognised the decree; but otherwise the Orthodox Church scarcely noticed the work of the Council of Ferrara and Florence. To the Pope the Council brought a temporary increase of prestige, very welcome at the moment, and reinforced by the formal and fruitless "reconciliation" of the Armenians, Jacobites, Maronites, and what not during the next few years[1].

---

[1] For a fuller account of the proceedings at Ferrara and Florence, see above, vol. IV, pp. 621 sqq.

The Council of Florence did not end with the departure of the Greeks. On 4 September 1439, in the important decree *Moyses*, it denied the assertions, lately reiterated at Basle, that a General Council was superior to the Pope, and that a Pope might not dissolve, adjourn, or transfer a General Council[1]. It was kept officially alive for six more years, perhaps longer, though after the Pope's return to Rome in 1443 it was transferred to the Lateran. Its sole function was to pass decrees of union with Eastern sects, but the Pope found it convenient to say that he was in consultation with a General Council. How and when it ended is not known.

Meanwhile, the depleted Council of Basle kept up its fight with more success than might have been anticipated. On 24 January 1438 it decreed the suspension of the Pope from the exercise of his functions, spiritual and temporal[2]. The deposition of Eugenius, which, according to the Council's plans, should have followed two months later, was, however, deferred owing to the reluctance of the princes of western Europe to see a fresh schism. The Council, indeed, had lost the countenance of England and the greater part of Italy; but it still had something to gain by humouring Germany and France.

The Emperor Sigismund died in December 1437. In March 1438 the Electors chose Albert of Austria to succeed him, and declared their neutrality as between Eugenius and the Council of Basle. This attitude they officially upheld for nearly eight years. Their object was to derive from the situation whatever advantage they could for themselves and, secondly, for the German Church; and in pursuit of such a policy their conduct naturally exhibited much inconsistency. For a while they seemed to be inclining towards the Council; and in March 1439, at a Diet at Mayence, they drew up a manifesto declaring that they accepted the Basle decrees respecting the supremacy of General Councils, reservations and provisions, the freedom of ecclesiastical elections, annates, and other matters. In acting thus the Electors were copying the French. At a Council held at Bourges in the summer of 1438 there was promulgated the celebrated Pragmatic Sanction, which favoured the Council's views on ecclesiastical sovereignty and applied to the Church in France the most notable of the reforming decrees enacted at Basle.

Emboldened by the happenings in France and Germany, the Council again became very active. On 16 May 1439 the theory of conciliar supremacy, as stated at Constance, was declared to be a dogma[3]. On 17 September a like decree was passed regarding the doctrine of the Immaculate Conception[4]. In the meantime, on 23 June, Eugenius was

---

[1] Mansi, xxxi, 716.   [2] Mansi, xxix, 165 sqq.

[3] *Ibid.* 178 sq.

[4] *Ibid.* 182 sq. These two decrees were subsequently ignored by the Church. Modern admirers of the Council have commented ironically on the fact that the doctrine of the Immaculate Conception was eventually recognised as a dogma by the very Pope who bestowed the same authority on the theory of Papal Infallibility.

formally pronounced a heretic for opposing the doctrines that a General Council had authority over all Christians and that a Pope might not dissolve, prorogue, or transfer it. Two days later, in the presence of 39 prelates and about 300 other clergy, he was solemnly deposed[1].

The election of a new Pope was deferred for some months, but on 5 November 1439[2] an electoral commission, specially chosen by the Council, gave the necessary majority to Amadeus VIII, Duke of Savoy, who took the name of Felix V. Amadeus, a widower with several children, had ruled Savoy successfully for forty years, but since 1431 he had withdrawn with seven companions to Ripaille, where he led a secluded though hardly austere life. He had shewn special interest in the Council, and in its final dispute with Eugenius had been more sympathetic towards it than any other European prince. His election as Pope was not unexpected by either the Council or himself.

The sequel was disappointing to both. Between Felix and the Council, to begin with, relations were never satisfactory. Felix was not content with the position and dignity which the radicals of the Council were willing to accord him. It was not until July 1440 that preliminary difficulties were sufficiently adjusted to admit of his coronation. He had been chosen largely because he was a rich man, who would cost the Church little or nothing; but he had no intention of dissipating his private resources in the interests of the Council, and he insisted on being allotted a proper revenue for himself and the cardinals whom the Council had allowed him to appoint. The Council was forced to transgress some of its own decrees about the taxation of benefices. But even after this Felix complained that insufficient regard was shewn for his needs, while the Council criticised him for inactivity and his officers for rapacity[3]. The truth was that both Felix and the Council were disappointed at his reception in Europe. Many universities and a few German princes accepted him. So did Elizabeth of Hungary, widow of the lately deceased King Albert of the Romans. Aragon and Milan wavered deliberately. But France, Castile, England, and most of Italy recognised Eugenius as true Pope, even though they might not always be willing to support him as against the Council of Basle. It was the ambiguous attitude of Germany that really kept the Council in existence and Felix on his throne for several more years. But late in the autumn of 1442, tired of the bickering of the Council, Felix left Basle and went to live at Lausanne.

Meanwhile there were many signs that the Council was growing weary. In numbers, indeed, it remained astonishingly strong; about the time of the election of Felix it still had over 300 members[4]. But thereafter its

---

[1] Mansi, xxix, 179 sqq.
[2] *Conc. Basil.* vii, pt. ii, p. liii.
[3] Mansi, xxix, 208; cf. *Conc. Basil.* vii, pp. xlv sqq.
[4] *Mon. Conc.* iii, 528.

interest in reform evaporated and it became more and more immersed in petty business concerning individuals[1]. The attendance at meetings of committees and at General Congregations became bad[2].

On 16 May 1443 the Council of Basle held its forty-fifth General Session[3]. It was decreed that in three years' time a new General Council should be held at Lyons; until then the present Council should continue to sit at Basle, or, if Basle should become unsuitable, at Lausanne. It was the last General Session held at Basle. Henceforth, with dwindling numbers, the Council busied itself with little save petty litigation, mostly about disputed benefices.

As long, however, as the policy of Germany remained unsettled the Council had some reason for remaining in being. The intrigues which ultimately led to an agreement between the Emperor, the princes, and the Papacy belong really to German history, and demand notice here only in so far as they are indispensable to an understanding of the fate of the Council of Basle. From 1440 to 1445 relations between Germany and Eugenius changed little. For a while both the Electors and Frederick III, Albert II's successor as King of the Romans, favoured the summons of a new General Council, but as no one outside Germany shewed any enthusiasm for the plan, it was dropped. Gradually Frederick and the Electors drifted apart. The former inclined towards Eugenius, the latter towards Basle; but there was no departure from the neutrality officially upheld.

In 1445, however, political exigencies in Hungary made friendship with Eugenius particularly desirable to Frederick. Thanks largely to the unscrupulous skill of his envoy, Aeneas Sylvius (a rat from the sinking Council), a treaty between him and the Pope was concluded early in 1446. In return for recognition Eugenius allowed Frederick the right of nomination to various sees and benefices in his territories and paid him a substantial sum of money.

The Electors regarded the treaty as a breach of a recent agreement between them and Frederick. The Pope, moreover, deposed the Elector-Archbishops of Cologne and Trèves, who were conspicuous for their friendliness towards the Council. Six of the Electors consequently agreed to demand of Eugenius that he should confirm the decrees of Constance about General Councils, accept the reforms embodied in the declaration issued at Mayence in 1439, and summon a new General Council; if he refused they would adhere to the Council of Basle on easy terms. It looked like a formidable move. But the plans of the Electors were betrayed to the Pope by Frederick III, and at the Diet of Frankfort, in September 1446, the agents of the Pope and the king, Aeneas Sylvius conspicuous

---

[1] *Conc. Basil.* vi, pt. ii, 74, vii, pp. xlii sq.

[2] *Ibid.* vii, pp. xvii sq.

[3] Herre (*Conc. Basil.* vii, p. xxiii) reckons the 44th General Session, of 9 August 1442, as the last held at Basle; but see Hefele-Leclercq, vii, ii, 1098.

among them, used bribery, cajolery, and argument in a resolute effort to break up the unity of the opposition. Two Electors and many lesser princes were won over; and a modified form of the Electors' demands was presented at Rome by a deputation. The morale of the national or reform party in Germany was ruined; nearly everyone in the country was eager for some settlement, and few seemed to care about its terms.

Eugenius IV, who was at the point of death, issued a series of instruments which the Germans accepted. Their terms fell short even of the diluted demands that had been made. He gave a personal promise to convoke a General Council after more than two years. He accepted, vaguely, the decree *Frequens*, but avoided giving countenance to any other specific decree of the Council of Constance. He recognised the "eminence" of General Councils, but not their "pre-eminence," which he had been asked to acknowledge. There is, however, little purpose in enumerating the details of these so-called concessions, for they never had any practical consequences. It was characteristic that Eugenius drew up a secret protest, in which he said that sickness had prevented him from giving full attention to everything that had been laid before him, but if anything granted was contrary to the teaching of the Fathers or prejudicial to the Holy See, it was to be void. On 23 February 1447 the Holy See was relieved of him.

Against the new Pope, Nicholas V, few felt any personal animosity, such as Eugenius had excited far and wide. He at once devoted himself, with the assistance of Aeneas Sylvius, to completing the conquest of Germany. Though there were still recalcitrant elements, a very large number of princes obeyed Frederick's summons to an assembly at Aschaffenburg in July 1447, in order to sanction the proclamation of Nicholas throughout Germany as lawful Pope. Nicholas was to confirm the concessions made by Eugenius, and a Diet was to be held shortly to settle outstanding questions, unless in the meantime a special Concordat should be concluded with the papal legate.

That astute diplomatist, John Carvajal, at once began to bargain with Frederick III, and a Concordat was signed at Vienna in February 1448. Formally it was concluded between the Pope and the king only, though the consent of several Electors was claimed and a good many princes must have been consulted. This pitiable agreement was concerned solely with reservations and provisions of benefices and with ecclesiastical elections. It was to last for ever, but otherwise bore a close resemblance to the Concordat of 1418 between the German Church and Martin V, such changes as were made being on the whole in favour of the Papacy. The meagre concessions of Eugenius IV were, it is true, confirmed, "so far as they are not contrary to the present agreement"; but most of them were incompatible with it, and the promise of a new General Council was quietly ignored. The German princes and German Church acquiesced with singular meekness in this ignominious surrender; but seventy years later Germany took the lead in the rebellion which the failure of the reform movement rendered inevitable.

The outlook of the Council of Basle was now utterly dark. In the summer of 1447 Frederick III had ordered the civic authorities to expel its members; but he had to repeat his command more than once and threaten the city with the ban of the Empire before the Fathers were asked to depart. On 7 July 1448 they were escorted to Lausanne, whither, they declared, the Council was transferred. They soon held a formal session, in which they proclaimed themselves ready to do all they could to restore peace and unity to the Church. Just as things were becoming comic, however, the mediation of Charles VII of France, backed by Henry VI of England, brought them to a dignified end. Nicholas V was prepared to be conciliatory, and Felix asserted his willingness to abdicate. After amicable negotiations, Felix, on 7 April 1449, in the second General Session of the Council of Lausanne, solemnly announced his resignation[1]. On 19 April the Council elected as Pope Thomas of Sarzana, called in his obedience Nicholas V, having been assured of his belief that a General Council holds its authority immediately of Christ and that all Christians must obey it in things which concern the Faith, the extirpation of schism, and the reform of the Church in head and members[2]. On 25 April 1449, at its fifth session, having been assured of the concurrence of Nicholas, it bestowed various offices and honours upon Felix, who had been made a cardinal by his victorious rival. Then the Council voted its own dissolution[3]. Had it always considered facts and its dignity as it did in its last days, it would have achieved more and left a better name behind it. Yet, though modern historians of all beliefs have found plenty of reason for deriding it, one should not forget that in its best days it shewed a steadfastness in face of the Pope, a restraint in face of the Bohemians, and an earnestness in face of the evil prevalent throughout the Church which deserve the applause of men of all creeds. And as the instrument of the last attempt of the medieval Church to reform itself, the Council, in its folly and wisdom alike, should command at least an unprejudiced interest.

[1] For the text, see *e.g.* Mansi, xxxv, 75 sqq.
[2] *Ibid.* 77 sqq.
[3] *Ibid.* 80.

CHAPTER II

JOHN HUS

An outstanding feature of Czech history in the second half of the fourteenth century was the powerful movement for Church reform which arose in Bohemia in the reign of Charles IV and rapidly expanded while gaining in intensity. Various causes contributed to this. There was the important political and cultural position of the Czechs in the Europe of that day when the King of Bohemia was at the same time Holy Roman Emperor, and the capital of Bohemia—Prague—was the seat not only of his court but also of the first university established in Central Europe, an institution attended by many foreigners of various nationalities; there was the material and intellectual wealth of the country, which at that time was an important centre of political and cultural activity in Central Europe; there were the almost limitless wealth and power of the Church of Rome, two factors which resulted in extravagance and immorality among the priesthood; there was the undue interference, so unfortunate in its consequences, of the Papal See in the internal affairs of the Church in Bohemia—the appointment of prebendaries, the levying of all kinds of dues—and the general relaxation of morals which all this encouraged; and, finally, the zealous and extraordinarily effective activity of a few chosen spirits against the moral degeneration of the day. The Emperor Charles and his chief adviser, Ernest, the first Archbishop of Prague, had already not only themselves taken action against various evils in the Church and among the priests, but had also protected and supported two famous preachers, the Austrian Conrad Waldhauser of the Augustinian Order (*ob.* 1369) and the Moravian priest, John Milíč of Kroměříž (*ob.* 1374), in their denunciations of depravity among the burghers of Prague and the priests of the Church. The movement for moral reformation inspired by the activities of these two men continued to develop even after their death. At the close of the fourteenth century two outstanding Czech thinkers and moralists, the knight Thomas of Štítný (*ob. c.* 1401) and the learned Matthias of Janov (*ob.* 1394), who had studied at the University of Paris, worked in the spirit of Milíč. The people of Prague at this period demonstrated their fidelity to the memory of Milíč by their unswerving regard for the preachers who came forward on behalf of true morals. The popularity of these preachers led, in 1391, to the foundation of the Bethlehem Chapel at Prague, the ministers of which were charged by the founders with the duty of preaching twice on every Sunday and holy day in the Czech tongue. It was undoubtedly the intention of the founders that the sermons should be preached in the spirit of Milíč's reforming aims, and although the first preachers at the Bethlehem Chapel were already noted for their denunciation of vice and disorder, this place of divine worship did not become the actual inheritor of Milíč's aims and the executor, as it were, of his testament, until it was placed in charge of a man who raised the Bohemian reformation movement, till then of only local significance, to a place in world history. That man was John Hus.

John Hus was born about the year 1370. His birthplace was probably the village of Husinec near Prachatice in southern Bohemia, although some serious investigators consider that he was born at the village of the same name near Prague. It is certain that he was called John of Husinec after the name of his birthplace, a designation subsequently abbreviated into Hus, which became so usual that he himself used it, and it entered with him into the pages of history. Somewhere about the year 1390 Hus came as a poor student to the University of Prague. The aim of his university studies was doubtless at the outset to enable him to become a priest, a profession to which, as he later reproaches himself, he was, like many others of his contemporaries, attracted mainly by the prospects of a good living. Nor did Hus' mode of life differ from that of other students of that day. He got a livelihood by serving in the churches, nor did he shun the gay or even exuberant entertainments of his fellow students, but throughout all he preserved the uprightness of his religious feelings. In 1393 he secured the degree of Bachelor of Arts, and in 1396 became Master of Arts. Devoting himself then to theological studies he obtained the degree of Bachelor of Theology, but he never became Master or Doctor of Theology. As a Master of Arts he lectured at the university, examined candidates for the Bachelor's degree, and was a member of various university commissions. The prestige which he enjoyed at the university is evidenced by the fact that in the autumn of 1401 he was elected Dean of the Faculty of Arts.

Previous to that, in 1400 or 1401, Hus had been ordained priest. This event, it would seem, marked a great turning-point in his life. Up to this time, Hus, though certainly at all times far removed from any debauchery or immorality, had none the less, like other "masters," found pleasure in secular entertainment and pursuits. He liked fine dress, he did not despise a good table, and he was a passionate player of chess. On becoming a priest he turned away from all such secular vanities and devoted himself with fervent sincerity to the work of his spiritual calling. He took up preaching with especial zeal, and speedily won great popularity among the people of Prague. It was apparently his qualities as a preacher that resulted in 1402 in his appointment to the pulpit of Bethlehem Chapel. In his preaching at Bethlehem Chapel Hus followed in the footsteps of men who, as we have seen, endeavoured in the second half of the fourteenth century, either by their sermons or by their writings, to raise the morals of the day by inveighing against the degeneration they saw around them, and who are generally known as the precursors of Hus. Although it cannot be shewn that Hus personally knew any of these his precursors—two of them, Waldhauser and Milíč, he could not, of course, possibly have known—or that he made use of their writings, there is nevertheless not the slightest doubt that in his activities at the Bethlehem Chapel he is closely connected with them and is their true successor. Like Waldhauser and Milíč he succeeded by his preaching in dominating the hearts of his hearers, whom he led to true religion and virtuous lives, and whose affection and devotion he won for himself. Lacking the fierce pungency of Waldhauser and the mystical flights of Milíč, Hus influenced his audiences more by the simplicity, clarity, and ingenuousness of his sermons and especially by his vivid sense for the needs, the interests, and the feelings of the common people, whose favourite and truly spiritual leader he was. In his endeavours to bring about an improvement in morals and a better, sincerer religious sense, Hus did not confine himself merely to preaching, but with profound comprehension of the simple minds of the people made use of other means as well. He devoted special attention to congregational singing in the churches. Not only did he exhort his hearers to sing the old Czech hymns, of which up to that time there were but few, but he himself composed several new hymns. Whereas, however, up to then, popular hymns had been sung only outside the actual divine service—during processions or after sermons—Hus introduced at the Bethlehem Chapel the singing of hymns by the congregation as part of the service itself. The congregation were not to be mere onlookers during the services, but were to take active part in them with their hymn-singing. Thus was given the impulse to the splendid development of Czech hymnology which followed.

It was not only among the common people, however, that Hus won many faithful friends and admirers; he found them also among the leading burghers of Prague, in the ranks of the nobles, among the courtiers of King Wenceslas (Václav); and Queen Sophia herself was so attracted by him that she made him her chaplain and perhaps even her confessor. Although Hus, like his predecessors, sharply castigated the moral short-comings of the clergy in particular, he had many friends among the priesthood, and he was also greatly esteemed by his ecclesiastical superiors. The Archbishop of Prague, Zbyněk, who had been appointed to the see as a young man of no great learning but upright and well-intentioned, himself shewed Hus favour and confidence, and more than once appointed him preacher at the synods of the Prague clergy.

Like every endeavour towards reform, all this practical effort on the part of Hus directed towards an improvement of morals was a manifestation of dissatisfaction with the conditions then existing, and his protests against the undisciplined clergy and against all manner of evils in the Church involuntarily placed him in opposition to the Church. The fate of Hus' precursors also shewed plainly enough how efforts towards a betterment of morals, coupled with a severe criticism of actual conditions, could lead to views in conflict with the general doctrines of the Church and cause the zealous protesters to be suspected of heresy—a suspicion welcomed and encouraged by those who were directly affected by the attack on immorality. It is possible, too, that Hus, endeavouring to bring about a reform in ecclesiastical and religious practice, arrived, through his own studies of ancient Church writings, at doubts concerning certain articles of Church doctrine, that he found a divergence between the teaching of Christ and that of the oldest Fathers of the Church on the one hand and doctrines which the Church of his day asked its adherents to believe on the other, that he was dissatisfied with the manner in which the scholasticism of his day settled the fundamental questions of the Christian faith. Finally, Hus was perhaps acquainted with some of the ideas to be found in the writings of his Czech precursors, ideas which not infrequently diverged from those commonly held by the Church. We have no proofs of this, however. On the other hand, the records that have come down to us concerning Hus' beginnings shew that it was by a different path that he was led to the views over which he came into conflict with the Church.

From the accusations brought by his opponents against Hus in the course of the years 1409 to 1414 it appears that the first signs of heretical views were observed in him in the very first year of his priesthood, some time in the year 1401. At the time he is said to have contended in a private conversation at one of the Prague rectories that the elements in the Eucharist even after consecration contained the substance of bread, and that a priest in mortal sin could not validly consecrate the elements. Even if we do not altogether believe this assertion, since it comes from witnesses hostile to Hus, we may assume from it with tolerable certainty that Hus, soon after his ordination as priest, took part in conversation on certain points of religion in the course of which the views were also broached for which he was afterwards condemned at Constance, that already those views were not unknown to him, and that if he did not actually adhere to them, he did not at any rate reject them with due decision. As those views are obviously a reflex of the recent teaching of the English theologian, John Wyclif, it is clear that Hus was already influenced by that teaching which subsequently assumed such fateful significance for him, that he was already acquainted with it and had turned it over in his mind.

The comparatively brisk intercourse between Bohemia and England at the time when Anne, the sister of the Bohemian King Wenceslas, was Queen of England, and when many young Czechs studied at English universities, caused a knowledge of the teachings of Wyclif as well as copies of his writings soon to penetrate to Bohemia. Wyclif's philosophical works were brought to Bohemia soon after the year 1380, that is, while their author was still alive (Wyclif died in 1384), and attained no small popularity among the Czech masters at the University of Prague, who, mainly through Hus' chief teacher, the learned Stanislav of Znojmo, preferred Wyclif's philosophic realism to the nominalistic tendencies in vogue among the other nationalities represented at Prague University. Hus himself made in 1398 copies of several of Wyclif's philosophical treatises, probably in order to use them as the basis of his own university lectures, and his annotations to these copies give evidence of the powerful impression made on him by Wyclif's works. Somewhat later than Wyclif's philosophical views, but still before the close of the fourteenth century, the English reformer's theological views began to penetrate into Bohemia. Old Thomas of Štítný obviously has in mind Wyclif's teaching on consubstantiation when, in his last work written about the year 1400, he confesses that in his seventieth year he was shaken in his belief in the elements by several masters, so that he did not know whether the substance of bread remains in the elements after consecration, or not. And practically at the same time, as we have already seen, we hear of Hus taking part in conversations in which theological views obviously emanating from Wyclif were discussed. Wyclif's theological teaching, then, was not unknown in Bohemia before the young Master, Jerome of Prague, Hus' subsequent companion in his struggles as well as in his death, somewhere about the year 1401 or 1402 brought over from England, where he had been studying, the two main theological works of Wyclif, the *Dialogus* and *Trialogus*.

A knowledge of Wyclif's teachings subsequently spread with rapidity among the masters of Prague University. As early as the beginning of the year 1403, the chapter of the cathedral at Prague—then the supreme ecclesiastical authority in the country, since the archiepiscopal see was vacant—deemed it well to submit the 45 articles of Wyclif to the university for an opinion upon them. To the 24 articles condemned in 1382 by the Synod of London there were added 21 others collected from Wyclif's writings by one of the German masters of Prague University. In response to the chapter's request, the rector of the university convened a meeting of the whole university for 28 May 1403 to deliberate upon Wyclif's articles. Thus came about in Bohemia the first public controversy concerning Wyclif, a skirmish which revealed the attitude of Prague University to his teaching. That attitude was not a unanimous one. The Czech masters championed the articles of Wyclif, though not all with the same determination. Among the defenders of the articles was Hus, but two other Czech masters, Stanislav of Znojmo, mentioned above as Hus' teacher, and Hus' friend, Stephen of Páleč, were much more decisive in their championship. On a vote being taken, the view of the Czech masters was rejected; the majority of the university, composed apparently of graduates of other nationalities, declared that no one should, either in public or in private, adhere to or defend any of the 45 articles submitted.

The verdict of the university failed to check the study of Wyclif's writings or the spread of his doctrines among the masters of the Czech University. In particular, Master Stanislav of Znojmo never ceased to defend Wyclif's articles. Not long after the university meeting he wrote a treatise on the elements in which he entirely accepted Wyclif's teaching that the substance of bread remained in the elements even after consecration. On an accusation being made against him by one of the German masters at the university, he was summoned to Rome together with Stephen of Páleč who had zealously championed him against his German opponent. In the autumn of 1408 the two Czech masters set out for Rome, but at Bologna they were arrested by order of Cardinal Baldassare Cossa, who subsequently became Pope under the name of John XXIII, and Stanislav of Znojmo was ordered by the College of Cardinals, which regarded itself as the supreme ecclesiastical tribunal in place of the dethroned Pope, Gregory XII, to declare that he recanted everything in his writings which could be regarded as in conflict with Holy Scripture and the judgment of the Church, and submitted himself to the judgment of the Apostolic See and of the appropriate ecclesiastical authorities.

Previous to this, in May 1408, a meeting of the Czechs at the University of Prague, convened, doubtless, at the instance of King Wenceslas and Archbishop Zbyněk, had deliberated upon the teaching of Wyclif. The 45 articles of Wyclif were again submitted to this gathering, which was attended by a large number of masters, graduates, and students. The object of the meeting was apparently to constrain those Czech masters who, in the year 1403 at the great university assembly, had made a stand for Wyclif or had subsequently taken his part, to declare their dissent from his teaching. In this, at least to outward view, the meeting was successful. On the one hand it was unanimously resolved that mere bachelors of arts should not be allowed to read the main theological writings of Wyclif, *Dialogus, Trialogus,* and *De Corpore Christi,* and on the other hand that no Czech member of the university should assent to or defend those of Wyclif's articles which were "heretical, misleading, or causes of offence." This description was apparently added to meet the views of those Czech masters who were unwilling to subscribe to the statement that all Wyclif's articles were misleading or heretical. Among these undoubtedly was Hus who, according to his own admission, did not agree with an absolute condemnation of Wyclif's articles, being convinced that several of them, properly interpreted, were correct. It is certain that at the meeting of the Czechs he supported the two resolutions above mentioned.

From the conduct of Hus at the meeting of the Czechs at Prague University, it may be assumed that at that time he had not as yet inclined to Wyclif's teachings so far as to be able to declare himself directly and openly for them. He certainly did not accede to Wyclif's view concerning the elements, which had been the main point of contention up till then in Bohemia, nor to Wyclif's other articles of faith. He was, however, greatly attracted by the fervour of the English reformer in his attack upon the various evils in the Church, and by his determined efforts to bring about a better state of affairs. Hus' own efforts to uplift the morality of the people and the priesthood took on, thereby, a sharper tone, increased decision and definiteness. He directed those efforts directly against certain features of Church administration mercilessly attacked by Wyclif, and particularly against the evils of simony, prevalent among the priesthood of the day. This brought upon him the wrath of those priests who were able to apply his emphatic accusations to themselves. Influenced by them, Archbishop Zbyněk also began to turn away from Hus. Thus it came about that at the synod of the diocese of Prague held in June 1408, at which Hus was no longer the preacher, a resolution was passed directed against his activities, prohibiting in particular any deriding of the priesthood in the course of sermons preached to the public. At the same time it was directed that anyone possessing a copy of any book by Wyclif must hand it in by a certain date to the archbishop's officials for examination. Although it was to be suspected that the archbishop had the intention of destroying all these books, Hus and almost all the other masters handed over to the archbishop within the given time all the works of Wyclif they possessed. Only five students refused to surrender Wyclif's works and appealed to the Pope. The prohibition to criticise the faults of the priests in public was not, however, observed by Hus. Not only did he attack them in a special work but he also opposed them by action, preaching unceasingly to the masses in condemnation of unworthy priests. He did not even abandon the condemned views of Wyclif: on the contrary, after the enforced repression of Stanislav of Znojmo's enthusiasm for Wyclif, Hus began more and more to be recognised as the leader of those who championed his teaching.

The tension which all this produced between Hus and the Archbishop of Prague was made more acute by developments in the general condition of the Church. After many fruitless attempts to rid the Church of the schism which had lasted since the year 1378, the cardinals on both sides finally, in the year 1408, decided to convoke a General Council at Pisa which should make a determined effort to unite the divided Church and to remove what were universally felt to be evils in ecclesiastical administration. To bring this about more easily, the cardinals urged the Christian rulers to observe, until the Council should have arrived at its decision, strict neutrality towards the two Popes, acknowledging neither the one nor the other. King Wenceslas readily acceded to the wishes of the cardinals, but Archbishop Zbyněk, at the head of his clergy, was unwilling to abandon allegiance to the Roman Pope, Gregory XII, who up till then had been acknowledged in Bohemia. Desirous of breaking down the opposition of the archbishop, the king called upon the University of Prague for an expression of its opinion on the question of neutrality. He manifestly expected that, influenced by the leading Czech masters who had joyfully greeted the attempt of the cardinals to give unity and reform to the Church, the whole university would declare in favour of neutrality. In this, however, he was disappointed. At the meeting of the university only the Czech masters signified their agreement with the king's standpoint, while the masters of the other three "nations[1]" at the university opposed him. Although the majority was thus against neutrality, the rector did not venture to announce to the king an unwelcome result; so the university meeting dispersed without a definite resolution being passed. The Czech masters, however, did not abandon their standpoint, and Hus in particular was active in support of neutrality, winning over influential personages as well as preaching to the people and clergy in its favour. This roused Archbishop Zbyněk, the faithful supporter of the Roman Pope Gregory, to such an extent that he issued public letters in both Latin and Czech, forbidding all the masters of Prague University and Hus in particular, whom he specially named therein as a disobedient son of the Church, to exercise any of the priestly functions in the diocese of Prague, thus prohibiting them from preaching the Word of God.

The question of neutrality which caused this public and severe action by the archbishop against Hus also provoked a notable change at the university. Early in 1409 King Wenceslas summoned the leading masters of the four "nations" at the university to meet him at Kutná Hora, where he was then residing, and whither an embassy had come from the French king to discuss the repudiation of obedience to both Popes. King Wenceslas desired to obtain a final verdict from the university in favour of neutrality. Among the Czech masters was John Hus with his young friend, Jerome of Prague. The king was soon able to convince himself of the divergent attitude to neutrality adopted by the Czech masters on the one hand and those of foreign nationality on the other. It was plain that the university would decide according to the king's wishes for neutrality if the decision should lie with the Czech masters. Thus arose the idea of altering the statutes of the university in favour of the Czech masters. The king was not at first inclined to agree to this change, since he was offended with several of the Czech masters, especially Hus and Jerome, for continuing to champion Wyclif. When, however, the representatives of the three foreign "nations" at the university persisted in their opposition to a declaration of neutrality, the king resolved to take a decisive step. By the decree of Kutná Hora, promulgated on 18 January 1409, he gave the Czechs at the university three votes in all university matters, and the other three "nations" had to be content with one. The university, which up to now had been dominated by the three foreign "nations," thus passed into the control of the Czechs.

This was not only a great national victory for the Czechs, who thus secured the power in the university that had been founded in their capital, but it was also a great triumph for the Hus party, whose position in the university was considerably enhanced by it, for the decisive factor now

[1] The four "nations" were the Czechs, Saxons, Bavarians, and Poles, but the Polish "nation" was also mainly composed of Germans.

was the voice of the Czechs, most of whom belonged to the Hus party. An obvious outcome of this success was the election of Hus himself as rector of the university in the autumn of 1409. In the dispute with Archbishop Zbyněk, which became more and more aggravated, the Hus party also derived advantage from the fact that the archbishop had completely fallen out with the king on the question of neutrality. Immediately after the issue of the decree of Kutná Hora the king strictly forbade his subjects, and particularly the clergy, to render obedience to Pope Gregory XII. This prohibition was, indeed, obeyed by Hus and his friends, but not by the archbishop, the prelates, and the bulk of the clergy. Thus the Czech clergy were split into two camps—one under the leadership of Hus and protected by the king, the other following the archbishop in allegiance to Pope Gregory XII, and defying the king's injunctions to observe neutrality. The dissension between the two parties broke out publicly in Lent 1409. The archbishop, instigated doubtless by the university debates in January of that year, in the course of which Jerome of Prague had recommended a study of the works of Wyclif, launched a sentence of excommunication against Hus and several of his friends, and anathematised on that occasion not only the religious teachings of Hus but also his philosophic realism. When those excommunicated did not cease exercising their functions as priests, and in particular continued to preach, the archbishop placed Prague and its neighbourhood under interdict. Hus and his supporters, of course, took no heed of this interdict, and the king himself sternly brought to account all persons who complied with the archbishop's interdict and thus manifested their disregard of Wenceslas' injunctions in the matter of neutrality. It was not until after the General Council of Pisa, in June 1409, had deposed the two existing Popes and elected a new pontiff who took the name of Alexander V, that Archbishop Zbyněk, some three months later, abandoned the deposed Gregory XII, and, together with all the clergy of his diocese, gave in his allegiance to the conciliar Pope.

Now that the cause of the dispute between king and archbishop had disappeared, the position of the archbishop improved so greatly that he was able to take more decisive and effective steps than hitherto against Hus. Urged on by accusations brought by Hus' enemies among the Prague priesthood, he began to make difficulties for him in his preaching and other activities at the Bethlehem Chapel. He secured in 1409 from the Pope a prohibition of all preaching outside cathedral, collegiate, parish, and monastic churches, to none of which categories, of course, the Bethlehem Chapel belonged, and further an order to demand the surrender of all books of Wyclif in order that they might be "removed from the sight of the faithful." Making use of this authorisation, the archbishop decided at the June synod in 1410 that all Wyclif's books surrendered to him should be burnt; he prohibited, on pain of severe penãlties, the teaching and defence of the errors of Wyclif, and forbade all preaching in Prague outside churches of the four categories allowed in the Pope's bull; there-fore the prohibition applied in particular to the Bethlehem Chapel.

Having no intention of submitting to this prohibition, to comply with which would have meant the end of his efforts at reform, Hus, together with several other members of the University of Prague, appealed to the Pope, at that time the notorious John XXIII. The archbishop, however, despite the protest of the university and the wishes of the king himself, caused all Wyclif's works that had been surrendered to his officials to be burnt on 16 July 1410 in the courtyard of the archiepiscopal palace in a bonfire which he lighted with his own hand. During this ceremony the *Te Deum* was sung and bells tolled as if for the dead. Immediately after-wards he launched the ban of excommunication against Hus and all those who had joined him in appealing to the Pope. In the struggle that now broke out with new force between the archbishop and the Hus party, the archbishop had, it is true, the full support of the Holy See, but against him not only the people of Prague but also King Wenceslas himself stood by Hus. The king even had the estates of the archbishop and the prelates confiscated to provide compensation for those whose books had been burnt. When the archbishop therefore again placed Prague under inter-dict, the king began to persecute the clergy who, in obedience to the archbishop's orders, ceased to celebrate the Church services. Wenceslas' energetic action finally compelled the archbishop to recede, and through the king's intervention a truce was brought about between the two parties in the summer of 1411.

Soon afterwards, perhaps at the suggestion of the king, Hus sent a petition to Pope John XXIII denying the charges made against him and asking to be relieved of the duty of appearing in person before the Papal Court, since his conflict with the archbishop had been completely settled. In this letter, which shews of itself that at that time he had not ceased to recognise the Pope as the supreme head of the Church, nor had denied in principle his supreme power of decision in questions of religion, Hus also solemnly declares his attitude to several of the fundamental articles of Wyclif's doctrine. Never, he says, had he taught that the sub-stance of bread remained in the elements after consecration, nor that a priest in a state of mortal sin could not consecrate; never had he called upon secular lords to take the property of the priests, to refuse to pay tithes, or to punish them with the secular sword; nor, again, had he re-jected indulgences or in any way promulgated errors or heresy. Nor was it his fault, as was asserted by his opponents, that the German masters at the university had departed from Prague.

Although Hus thus expressly disavows the main articles of Wyclif's teachings of which he had been accused, it would nevertheless seem that even then he was already more affected by Wyclif's heresies than he admitted or perhaps was himself aware. Certainly his forbearance towards those who obviously championed Wyclif's teaching, his ostentatious talk in favour of Wyclif and continued use of his works, not only put a welcome weapon into the hands of his personal enemies but also confirmed in their opposition to him those who were against him because they were honestly afraid of Wyclif's heresies. Thus neither the truce secured through the king between the archbishop's party and the party of Hus in 1411, nor the petition sent by Hus to the Pope following the truce, nor even the death of Archbishop Zbyněk in September of the same year, brought to an end the struggles between Hus and the power of the Church. Whereas, however, up to now Archbishop Zbyněk of Prague had represented this power, his place was henceforth taken by the Holy See itself.

Though Hus, throughout the whole period of his conflict with the archbishop, had never ceased to acknowledge the supreme power of the Pope, and continued to manifest his readiness to submit to papal commands, it is nevertheless possible at this very time to observe in him and his friends a serious change in their views of the Papacy. The lamentable state of the Papacy of that day, especially after the election of John XXIII had added to the two existing Popes a third of very doubtful character, and still more a deeper penetration into the teachings of Wyclif, undermined the faith of Hus and his friends in the Pope. This was publicly manifested in the spring of 1412 when, in accordance with a bull of John XXIII, there was proclaimed at Prague a crusade against his opponent, King Ladislas of Naples, and ample indulgences were granted to all who should personally join in the crusade or contribute funds towards it. Those who proclaimed these benefits went about their mission in such a way that their action was hardly distinguishable from an actual sale of indulgences. It is not to be wondered at that this caused great indignation, especially as in Bohemia voices had already been raised in opposition to indulgences altogether. This traffic in indulgences moved Hus to open revolt against the commands of the Pope. He preached and wrote against indulgences, and at a public disputation at the university on 7 June, supported by his friends, particularly by the eloquent Jerome of Prague, he produced reasons, mainly taken from Wyclif's writings, why it was improper for the faithful to approve of the papal bull proclaiming a crusade against the King of Naples or to give money for the spilling of Christian blood. On this occasion Hus adopted the revolutionary principle that the faithful are not bound to obey papal commands so far as they are in conflict with the law of Christ.

The opposition to indulgences had in the meantime so much increased among the masses that various disturbances occurred, in the course of which the vendors of indulgences, as well as the preachers who recommended them to the people, were abused and held up to ridicule. Even the strict orders given by the king and the city councillors, to the effect that none should speak against the preachers or the papal bulls, failed to check this. One Sunday, 10 July 1412, three youths, probably workmen, were arrested for this offence in three of the principal churches of Prague and haled to the Old Town Hall. In vain Hus begged the councillors not to punish the prisoners, since he himself was the cause of the opposition to the indulgences. The very next day they had the three youths beheaded. The people, however, favouring Hus' aims, refused to be intimidated. A great procession of masters, bachelors, and students of the university, and other persons, singing hymns, accompanied the bodies of the three young men to the Bethlehem Chapel, and there buried them as martyrs.

While the excitement among the people inspired by Hus' campaign against indulgences had increased in menacing fashion, the faculty of theology at the university led by Stanislav of Znojmo and Stephen of Páleč, who had become the most determined opponents of the views and aims for which they had themselves formerly fought with such fervour, and who had completely separated from Hus, rose up against the reformer. Doctors of theology condemned in a new pronouncement not only the 45 articles of Wyclif but six further heretical articles—a judgment directed against Hus and his friends, and particularly against their denial of indulgences. This action had the result that in the king's name there was issued, on 16 July, a strict prohibition of all these articles, and all persons disobeying the prohibition were threatened with the king's displeasure and banishment from the realm. Rome, too, issued an excommunication at this time against Hus and all who should have any relations with him, and another bull ordered that Hus should be arrested and punished under the Canon Law and that the Bethlehem Chapel should be razed to the ground. When, in accordance with a bull of excommunication, service was suspended in the autumn of 1412 in all churches throughout Prague, and the priests were forbidden to baptise the children and to bury the dead, Hus, in order to remove the cause of the interdict, left Prague for the country some time in October 1412. He remained there until the summer of 1414, staying in various places in the south-west of Bohemia and visiting Prague only for short periods. During his sojourn in the country he devoted himself indefatigably to preaching and to writing works in Latin and in Czech. Of his Czech works of that period the most important are his great *Exposition of Belief, the Ten Commandments and the Lord's Prayer*, the sharply polemical *On Simony*, and his excellent *Postilla*, or exposition of the lections from Scripture on Sundays. Of his Latin works the outstanding one is *De Ecclesia*. In composing these works Hus found a model and a fruitful source of ideas in the writings of Wyclif, to whose views he was gradually succumbing more and more, though he did not accept them without considerable changes more in keeping with the general views then held in the Church.

King Wenceslas had, in the meantime, made several attempts to bring about a reconciliation between Hus' party and his opponents, but an extraordinary synod of the clergy held with this purpose at the command of the king early in 1413 only demonstrated the fact that there was an unbridgeable gulf between the views of the two parties. When a new attempt by the king to settle the differences between them by means of the findings of a special commission failed because of the unyielding attitude of Hus' opponents, who declined to recognise him and his supporters as true Christians, the king banished their leaders from the country, expelled them from the university, and deprived them of their ecclesiastical dignities and emoluments. Among them were Stanislav of Znojmo, who soon afterwards died, and Stephen of Páleč, whom Hus met again a little later at the Council of Constance. Whereas, in Bohemia, Hus' party had at the beginning of 1413 scored a great success through the intervention of the king, the opposing party's views now again secured recognition at Rome. Pope John XXIII issued a new bull condemning all the works of Wyclif, ordering them to be burnt, strictly forbidding them to be read, elucidated, used, or even their author's name to be mentioned.

In this struggle over the very foundations of ecclesiastical theory and practice a decisive change of situation was produced by the convocation of a General Council at Constance for 1 November 1414. It came about chiefly through Sigismund, the Hungarian king, who, having been elected King of the Romans in 1410, made himself the defender of the Roman Church. In addition to the renewal of Church unity and the general reform of morals, the Council called at Constance was to occupy itself with the question of faith, that is, to express its opinion on several doctrines declared to be errors or heresy. It was clear that Wyclif's teachings and the dispute waged round the person of Hus would come up for consideration. Moreover, King Sigismund, who, as heir apparent to the throne of Bohemia, his brother King Wenceslas being childless, was anxious to see Bohemia cleansed of the disgrace of heresy, conceived the idea of prompting Hus, who had hitherto refused to present himself before the Court at Rome, to attempt his justification before the Council of Constance. In the spring of 1414 he had negotiations to this end opened with Hus, promising him not only a safe-conduct to Constance and a public hearing in the presence of the Council, but also a free and safe return to his country should he not wish to submit to the judgment of the Council. Rejecting the warnings of his friends, Hus decided to accept Sigismund's invitation. He doubtless cherished the idea that he would be successful in defending himself before the Council on the charge of heresy, but he was also determined to meet death, if need be, for his convictions. Some time in August 1414 Hus informed Sigismund that he was ready to proceed to the Council under the king's safe-conduct, and he also made this intention public. After having prepared his defence and the speeches which he designed to make before the Council, and after securing various evidence concerning his activities in the past, including the fact that he had never been proved guilty of heresy, Hus set out for Constance at the beginning of October, accompanied by the three Czech nobles who had been appointed for this task by King Wenceslas (Wenceslas, Knight of

Dubá, John, Knight of Chlum, and Henry of Chlum) and several other Czechs. Travelling through Nuremberg, Hus arrived at Constance on 3 November 1414.

During the first few days of his sojourn at Constance Hus met with no humiliation. Even the ban against him and the prohibition to celebrate divine service in the place where he was staying were temporarily suspended, since they would have had unfavourable consequences for Constance itself. Hus was also allowed to attend churches and to say the services in his abode. But this changed shortly owing to the action of his opponents. These were in particular the representatives of the Czech clergy hostile to Hus, Bishop John of Litomyšl and Michael, nicknamed "de Causis," procurator of the Prague Chapter at the Papal Court, as well as Stephen of Páleč, who had come to Constance on his own account. These compatriots of Hus endeavoured to persuade the Council, by means of public declarations and formal accusations in writing, of Hus' heresy and of the danger threatening all the clergy from his activities. They brought it about that on 28 November Hus was summoned to the Pope's palace, subjected to a hearing by the cardinals, and then thrust into prison. He was imprisoned first in the house of the precentor of Constance, but at the end of a week was thrown into a dark and dirty cell in the Dominican convent on the shores of the Lake of Constance. There he soon became so ill that his life was despaired of. In vain King Sigismund endeavoured to get him released, for the king had guaranteed his personal safety by giving him a safe-conduct. Unwilling to permit any restriction of its right to pass judgment upon a heretic, the Council brusquely refused to admit itself bound by Sigismund's safe-conduct, and the king, allowing himself to be intimidated by the threat that the Council would break up if he persisted in his request, gave way and admitted the complete liberty of the Council in the trial of a heretic.

As soon as Hus had somewhat recovered, he was obliged to answer the accusations brought against him. He was, in particular, required to express himself in writing on the 45 articles of Wyclif, and the 42 articles extracted by Stephen Páleč from Hus' own work *De Ecclesia*. In his answer Hus rejected several of Wyclif's articles most decidedly, on others he expressed himself evasively, and with some he expressed agreement. Some of the articles selected by Páleč he shewed were not correctly extracted from his work, while others he acknowledged and endeavoured to prove their truth. At the same time he never ceased to demand a hearing before the whole Council. This he obtained only at the repeated request of the Czech nobles, and not until the beginning of June 1415.

Meanwhile, after the flight of Pope John XXIII from Constance, Hus had been transferred from the Dominican convent to the fortress of Gottlieben on the Rhine, in the tower of which he suffered imprisonment more than two months (April and May 1415), in fetters and inadequately supplied with food and drink, so that he was soon again afflicted with various maladies. A few days after the transfer of Hus to Gottlieben, his friend Jerome of Prague appeared in Constance. He caused letters to be nailed to the city gates, to the doors of the churches, and to the houses of the cardinals, asking King Sigismund and the Council to grant him a safe-conduct to enable him to appear before the Council and give a public answer to anyone who might desire to accuse him of any error or heresy. In a few days he received an answer in the form of a communication summoning him before the Council. Meanwhile, however, Jerome, urged by Hus' friends, had left Constance to return to Bohemia. On the way he was arrested, was brought back to Constance at the end of May, and flung into a dark cell in the municipal tower near the church and cemetery of St Paul.

By the cruel imprisonment of Hus and Jerome the Council gave very clear expression of the disfavour with which it regarded the two Czechs. The Council also proclaimed at that time with great clarity its opinion of Wyclif's works. On the proposal of a commission appointed to conduct the dispute centring round Hus and to examine the works of Wyclif, it confirmed at the beginning of May the condemnation of them launched two years previously by Pope John XXIII, and in addition expressly rejected several articles selected from among them. All this boded ill for the public hearing of Hus before the Council, to which the reformer had looked forward with so much hope. The trial was appointed to begin on 5 June. A short time previous to this Hus was brought from Gottlieben to Constance and imprisoned in the Franciscan convent, in the refectory of which the Council held its sessions. His public hearing before the Council took place in three sessions, on 5, 7, and 8 June, and was marked by many dramatic scenes. Here, too, Hus very decidedly rejected several of Wyclif's articles (notably his teaching concerning the presence of the substance of bread in the elements after consecration), denying that he had ever taught it, but he admitted his agreement with other articles. He confessed that he did not approve of the condemnation of all the well-known 45 articles of Wyclif, since he could not regard some of them as heresy or error; he agreed, too, that he had spoken with approbation of Wyclif, that he had appealed from the archbishop to the Pope against the burning of Wyclif's books, and that, when his emissaries had failed to find a hearing at the Papal Court, he had finally appealed to Christ. The trial before the Council shewed further that on the whole Hus accepted the teaching of St Augustine and Wyclif which regarded the Church as the company of all those predestined to be saved, and the majority of the consequences deduced therefrom by Wyclif against the then Church of Rome and its institutions, especially against the papal power. Refusing to recant the articles which had been falsely concocted against him, Hus expressed his readiness to recant those which he had really professed, could he be convinced by evidence from Holy Scripture that they were untrue. The Council, of course, insisted on Hus recanting all the articles completely and unreservedly. This he could not be persuaded to do, either by the arguments of various members of the Council or by the persuasion of his friends, although it was clear that, if he did not recant completely and without reserve, he would be condemned to death as a confirmed heretic.

Before the Council delivered final judgment in the case of Hus, it occupied itself with a question closely connected therewith. This was the question of communion in both kinds (bread and wine), which, either shortly before or soon after Hus' departure from Prague, had begun to find favour with his followers there. The author of this innovation, which in the subsequent development of the Czech religious movement became of such pre-eminent importance, was not Hus himself but his friend and right-hand man, Jakoubek of Stříbro (Jacobellus de Misa), who, from a study of the writings of Matthias of Janov with his reasons for frequent communion, came to the conviction that laymen had the same right as priests to communicate in both kinds. In this conclusion he found agreement and effective support in two German masters, Nicholas and Peter of Dresden, who had spent some years at Prague taking a prominent part in the Czech religious struggles of the day on the side of Hus. Although Hus apparently agreed with Jakoubek's view from the very outset, he requested his friend, previous to his own departure for Constance, to postpone the contest over this subject. Afterwards, however, when disputes upon it arose in his absence among his own followers, threatening to produce a split in their ranks, Hus gave his approval to communion in both kinds in a special work written shortly after his arrival at Constance. The Council, however, at its general meeting on 15 June forbade lay communion in both kinds, and ordered that the communion by laymen in one kind, introduced in the Church for good reasons in place of the original communion in both kinds, was to be maintained as an unalterable practice.

A few days later the Council decided that Hus' Latin and Czech works ought to be destroyed on the ground that they contained doctrinal errors. In the meantime negotiations proceeded with Hus himself touching the manner of the recantation which he was to make in accordance with the wishes of the Council, but these proved in vain. A commission was sent to him in jail and he was required to give a final answer. On 1 July Hus again declared in writing that he was unable to recant all the articles which had been brought forward against him, since several of them were based upon false witness; that as to the articles selected from his own writings he was willing to recant everything contained in them that was not true, but that he could not recant all, since he did not wish to abuse truth. And when on 5 July the Czech nobles, Wenceslas of Dubá and John of Chlum, interviewed him for the last time at King Sigismund's request in order to persuade him to recant, he repeated with tears that he could only do so if convinced by better and more powerful reasons taken from Holy Writ.

Perceiving that Hus was not to be moved to make the recantation demanded of him, the Council proceeded to. pass judgment upon him. This was delivered in solemn assembly of the Council held on 6 July in the cathedral of Constance, King Sigismund himself presiding. First of all there were condemned 260 heretical passages extracted from Wyclif's works, then there was read in Hus' presence a document describing the whole case against him with the accusations, which he was no longer permitted to answer, together with thirty passages taken from his own works, and finally sentence was delivered upon the works of Hus and upon his person. His writings were condemned to be burnt, and he himself as a manifest heretic who taught false, demoralising, and revolutionary doctrines, who had led many astray, had slandered the honour and power of the Apostolic See and the Church, and obstinately persevered in his errors, was condemned to be degraded from the priesthood and to be punished by the secular powers. The sentence was at once carried out. Hus was unfrocked in the usual ceremony and as a heretic handed over to the King of the Romans. By order of King Sigismund he was at once led away from the town to the place of execution and placed on the pyre that had been prepared. Hus, on being appealed to for the last time to save himself, refused to recant, the fire was lighted, and in a short time, chanting a hymn, he breathed his last.

Less than a year after the death of Hus a like fate overtook his friend, Jerome of Prague. Jerome, it is true, soon after the burning of Hus, was moved by the fear of death and a yearning for liberty to recant publicly before the Council the errors of Wyclif and Hus, to acknowledge the condemnation of Hus as just, and to submit himself in all things to the judgment of the Council (September 1415). Since, however, he was still kept in prison and subjected to a new examination, he demanded a public hearing before the Council, and having obtained it (May 1416) he not only championed the condemned doctrines of Wyclif and Hus, but declared that his greatest sin had been denial of that good and holy man and his teachings. By this he sealed his own fate. On 30 May 1416 he was condemned by the Council and handed over to the secular arm to be burnt at the stake. On the spot where a year previously Hus had perished, Jerome of Prague met death with courage, dignity, and pious devotion.

The terrible death which Hus had suffered for his convictions has given him the martyr's halo, won him the universal respect of the whole civilised world, and placed him in the ranks of the greatest and noblest figures of history. But the significance of his death grows when one considers for what it was he suffered. According to a view widely accepted, the real cause of Hus' death was his fight against the evils in the Church and the immorality of the priests, which brought upon him the hostility of the clergy at home and also influenced the mind of the Council against him. The condemnation of Hus would thus become the work of petty, one might almost say personal, revenge on the part of the priesthood smarting under his accusations. This view is certainly not correct. It is doubtless true that many of Hus' opponents were against him for some such mean reasons, but the actual causes of the struggle between Hus and his main opponents, especially between him and the Council, certainly lay elsewhere and much deeper.

It was above all a question of several grave differences in belief. In this connexion Hus was mainly accused of championing and proclaiming the heretical doctrine of Wyclif touching the presence of the substance of bread in the elements after consecration (*consubstantiatio*). This accusation, as we know, Hus very emphatically and with entire truth denied, yet from the Council's point of view he could not be entirely freed from guilt, in that he had not opposed this doctrine with sufficient resolution when it spread among his supporters. Another of Wyclif's doctrines which was heretical in the eyes of the Council Hus himself admitted that he accepted. This was the doctrine, derived from St Augustine, that the Church is composed of all persons predestined to salvation. Hus did not accept all the extreme consequences of Wyclif's doctrine; in particular he did not agree with the view that a priest in a state of sin is unable to minister the sacrament, thus being as it were deprived of his office; but he accepted fully the substantial part of Wyclif's doctrine. Although doctrine concerning the Church and the Papacy and other questions connected therewith had not up to that time been laid down as a definite article of faith, there was no doubt that what Hus, following Wyclif, believed and taught regarding this was in absolute conflict with the entire spirit of the universal Catholic standpoint, and could only be regarded as heresy by those who upheld the Catholic conception.

Hus' attitude also to the prevailing Church order could not secure him any mercy from the Council. In his sharpest criticism and rejection of that order Hus did not, it is true, go as far as Wyclif, who rejected practically all the rules of the Church in so far as they were not based on Scripture or were not practised by the primitive Church; but he none the less fiercely attacked many customs and rules established by centuries of development, without which the Church could not be imagined even by those who recognised the need of altering the system of administration which had developed in the course of the thirteenth and fourteenth centuries, who acknowledged the need of breaking the excessive power of the Pope over the individual branches of the Church, and of putting an end to the financial exploitation of these branches by the Papacy. Great indignation was aroused, for example, at the Council by Hus' views against ecclesiastical tithes, and his condemnation of the originators of the secular power of the Church. Hus, it is true, did not reject as decidedly as had Wyclif the right of the Church and priests to possess secular wealth, nor did he directly declare that secular lords should have the right to deprive unworthy priests of their property, but from various utterances of his own

and from the fact that several of his friends and adherents openly proclaimed such views, it may be assumed that they were not altogether
alien to him.

If some of the views actually proclaimed by Hus, or at least attributed
to him, aroused the Council against him, he was perhaps even more
damaged in its eyes by the fact that he declined to recant them even when
they had been condemned by the Council, and that he refused to submit
simply to the decision of the Council, but demanded that he should be
shewn the falsity of these opinions by the evidence of Holy Scripture. By
opposing the Council, which just at that moment had been given supreme
power of decision in all ecclesiastical questions and the right to dictate
to the faithful what they were to believe, Hus assumed for himself and
thus for every believer the right to be his own judge in matters of faith.
Although he himself placed limits to the freedom of this right of judgment, desiring that Holy Writ should be acknowledged as a law from
which there must be no departure in anything soever, his attitude, nevertheless, was in absolute conflict with that principle of one sole supreme
authority in matters of faith, upon which the Roman Church had been
erected.

If then the Council, from its own point of view, had grave cause for
condemning Hus, it cannot be doubted that exactly therein lies the historical significance of the Czech reformer. From the opinions for which
Hus was condemned by the Council there was born a great movement
rich in ideas and imposing in its outward manifestations, a movement
rightly called the Hussite movement after Hus himself, and a movement
which gives Czech and Bohemian history its characteristic feature and a
world-wide significance. The ideas underlying the movement were, it is
true, not entirely original, having for the most part been taken over from
Wyclif, but it was Hus and the movement which he enkindled in Bohemia
that first made them an important factor in the spiritual evolution of
mankind, such a factor as, without Hus and the Hussite movement, they
would certainly never have become. The very fact that, in championing
these ideas, Hus not only himself undertook an heroic struggle with the
supreme ecclesiastical powers on behalf of the liberty of the individual
conscience, but also that by his life and death he was able to impel his
nation to a grand and successful struggle for that right, contributed undoubtedly very substantially to liberating the human mind from the
heavy fetters laid upon it by the authority of the medieval Church.

Over and above this Hus rendered special services to his own nation.
His activities as a Czech author have no small significance for the history
of the Czech language and literature. Through his Czech writings Hus
put into practice new principles of Czech composition, which meant a
considerable simplification and therefore an improvement of Czech orthography. Also from the point of view of the language itself his writings
introduced an important innovation. They were not composed in the

obsolete tongue, already remote from the living language spoken by the masses, that heavy and hard style that we meet with in the works of the best Czech authors previous to Hus, but in a speech such as was actually spoken in his own environment at Prague, a speech light and supple but at the same time pure and avoiding the use of unnecessary foreign expressions. Thus Hus not only contributed substantially by his Czech writings to the formation of a Czech literary tongue, but he also, through his whole activity as an author, laid the foundations of the subsequent rich development of Czech religious literature. Religious questions had been dealt with in Bohemia before Hus in both Latin and Czech, but these older religious writings of Czech origin, not excluding the Czech works of Thomas of Štitný or the great Latin work of Matthias of Janov, never attained much circulation and could thus have but small effect. It was only with Hus that there began the systematic development of Czech religious literature (to a considerable extent composed in Latin), which for a long time was the most significant element in Czech literature generally and ranks among the most important intellectual productions of the Czech nation as a whole.

But over and above Hus' services to Czech orthography, language, and literature, his importance for his nation appears still more in his securing for it a place among those peoples who have contributed a share to the general progress of humanity, in his uplifting in no mean measure the national conscience and giving it a new content. The great struggle which Hus himself, and the Czech nation in his spirit, carried on for the reform of the Church and the triumph of the pure law of God was, in the case of the Czech Hussites, from the very outset a fight in defence of national honour and dignity against the reproach of heresy, and soon became in the eyes of the nation the fulfilment of an exalted task for which the Czech nation had been chosen by God. This pious conviction was for a long period a source of noble self-consciousness for the Czechs, giving them an impregnable strength against the hugely superior material forces of their enemies, and later representing a source of consolation for them in their sufferings. To this very day Hus is a great national hero alike for his services to Czech language and literature and for all that he did to cause his name and that of his nation to be inscribed in the annals of the world's history.

CHAPTER III

BOHEMIA IN THE FIFTEENTH CENTURY

THE splendid position which Bohemia had attained in the fourteenth century as the premier electorate of the Holy Roman Empire, as the seat of the imperial Court, and at the same time of the greatest—and for sixteen years the only—university in Central Europe, was lost in the fifteenth century. Wenceslas (Václav) IV, deposed from the imperial throne in 1400, ceased to be the head of the Empire; and Prague University, having already lost much of its original importance through the founding of other universities in the neighbouring countries, was deprived of its international character by the Decree of Kutná Hora in 1409, and became an institution serving first and foremost the interests of the inhabitants of the Bohemian State, especially those of the Czech nation. It looked as if Bohemia had thus ceased to be an important factor in the history of Europe. It was not long, however, before it again became such a factor, though for reasons very different from before. The impulse came from the great religious movement which, starting in the preceding century, first acquired at the beginning of the fifteenth such force as caused it not merely to dominate the history of the Czech nation for several decades, but also to attract the anxious attention of practically the whole of Christian Europe. It was, above all, John Hus who lent this force to the religious movement in Bohemia. This movement, rightly known as the Hussite, did not end with the death of Hus; on the contrary, his death gave the impulse to an expansion of the struggle, with the introduction of a new element, for the cause of Hus had become that of the whole nation. With a determination and a perseverance little anticipated by those who had been responsible for the condemnation of Hus, the Czechs entered upon a struggle for his cause the like of which history has never seen before or since.

Early in May 1415, two months before the death of Hus, large gatherings of Bohemian and Moravian nobles met at Prague and at Brno (Brünn), and letters of intercession for him were sent from both to King Sigismund. Under the impression that, after the flight of Pope John XXIII from Constance, Sigismund had Hus in his power, the nobles and gentry of Bohemia and Moravia asked the king to bring about his release and to give him a free hearing, for they regarded accusations against Hus as accusations against and an affront to the Czech nation and the Bohemian Crown. The Czech nobles, too, who were at Constance joined with a number of Polish nobles there in presenting to the Council a written protest against the inhuman treatment to which Hus was being subjected, at the same time emphatically refuting the calumnies spread at the Council concerning the Czech nation by the enemies and ill-wishers of the kingdom of Bohemia.

Although it could thus have been no secret that Hus had not only numerous devoted followers but also powerful supporters in Bohemia and in Moravia, the Council apparently hoped that it would be able to stifle the movement he had kindled. Immediately after the burning of Hus, it decided to call upon the clergy and all ranks of the laity in Bohemia to oppose the further spread of the condemned errors. The letters dispatched by the Council to Bohemia at the end of July, however, contained not only this demand but also a threat that the Council would punish in accordance with Canon Law all who continued to adhere to the heresy or who gave help to heretics.

Appeals and threats proved equally ineffective in the storm of indignation which the tidings of the death of Hus aroused in Bohemia. Apart from occasional acts of violence the opposition to the Council was organised in a dignified manner by the Bohemian and Moravian nobility. At a general assembly, convened on their own initiative and not, as was usual, on the king's summons, they resolved (on 2 September) to submit a joint protest to the Council at Constance. In this memorable document, to which five hundred nobles and gentry from all parts of Bohemia and Moravia attached their seals, a solemn tribute was paid to Hus, for it bore witness that he was a good and righteous Catholic who led men not into error but to Christian love and to the keeping of God's commandments. It went on to reproach the Council that in condemning Hus on the perjured evidence of the mortal foes of the kingdom of Bohemia and the margravate of Moravia, it had calumniated these countries and their inhabitants. The protest denied most emphatically the accusation of heresy brought against the two lands, and declared that the wrong done them would be brought before the Pope as soon as a universally recognised Pope should be enthroned. Finally, it declared the determination of the signatories to defend to the last drop of their blood the doctrines of Christ and those who preached them, regardless of all laws that man might pass in conflict with those doctrines. At the same time the assembled nobles and gentry formed themselves (on 5 September) into a union, the members of which bound themselves as follows: not to acknowledge the decrees of the Council; to tender obedience to a new and regularly elected Pope only in such matters as should not be contrary to the will of God and His laws; in spiritual matters to obey the country's bishops only in so far as those bishops acted in accord with the divine law; on their estates to permit every priest freely to preach the Word of God, in so far as such priest had not been convicted of error by Holy Writ, on which matter the final decision was to lie not with the bishops but with the University of Prague. Thus, the Bohemian and Moravian nobles entered upon the path of open revolt against the supreme ecclesiastical power. Some few Bohemian nobles only, by an agreement reached a few days later, declared that they persevered in full obedience to the Church.

The Council discussed the protest of the Bohemian and Moravian nobility in February 1416, and decided to summon before it all who had appended their seals to the document, to answer the charge of heresy. The summons was at once issued, but it was obvious that little faith was manifested in its efficacy, for the Council even then considered the declaration of a crusade against the Czechs in order to destroy heresy root and branch. Meanwhile its wrath descended upon the head of the one Czech heretic in their power—Master Jerome of Prague, who was burnt at the stake on 30 May 1416.

Soon after the burning of Jerome, the Council began to deal sternly with the University of Prague. In September 1415 the university had made a pronouncement in which Hus was referred to as a holy martyr and a tribute of praise was paid to Jerome. Towards the close of the year the Council issued a ban suspending indefinitely all the university's activities. The majority of the masters at the university, however, paid no heed whatsoever to the prohibition. On its side the Council caused the Archbishop of Prague, Conrad of Vechta, a man of weak character, to begin a policy of refusing to ordain adherents of the Hussite party and to demand from all priests applying for benefices an abjuration of the errors of Wyclif and of communion in both kinds. In some cases, indeed, priests who declared themselves adherents of Hus and administered communion in both kinds were deprived of their cures. On the other hand, the clergy of those churches which were under the patronage of the Utraquist nobles or of Queen Sophia were dismissed if they refused to administer the chalice and declined to renounce obedience to the Council. The recognised leader of the Hussite nobility, Čeněk of Vartenberk, took energetic measures to remedy the lack of priests who were willing to administer communion in both kinds. He compelled one of the suffragan bishops at Prague on several occasions to ordain candidates for holy orders without any regard to the conditions laid down by the Archbishop of Prague.

While this struggle between the adherents of Hus and his opponents was proceeding, it became increasingly clear that the former were beginning to shew divergences among themselves in their views on faith and order. The dispute over communion in both kinds had been decided by Hus' declaration in favour of granting the chalice, and the last doubts on this point were dissipated by the decision of Prague University, delivered in the spring of 1417, in which the use of the Cup was approved of as the unalterable command of Christ. Communion in both kinds became the strongest bond among all who adhered to the cause of Hus and his memory, and the chalice was adopted as the universal emblem of Hussitism. Other innovations introduced or recommended by the more zealous failed to meet the approval of all the supporters of the chalice, not infrequently, indeed, meeting with strong opposition. Thus, some approved of children partaking of holy communion while others were against it. The attacks, too, of some of the more radical wing on the taking of an oath, on capital punishment, on the doctrine of purgatory, on prayers and masses for the dead, the veneration of the relics and images of the saints, on some of the sacraments and rites of the Church, aroused opposition among the more conciliatory. Possibly as early as the August Synod of 1417 a formal definition of principles common to all the followers of Hus was arrived at, principles which were solemnly promulgated in 1420 as the "Four Articles of Prague."

The following were the main demands made in this document: the Word of God to be preached without let or hindrance; the sacrament to be administered in both kinds to all believers; the dominion exercised by priests and monks over large secular possessions to be abolished; all mortal sins and all evils contrary to the divine law, including the heresy of simony, deeply rooted in the Church of that day, to be duly punished. A year after the synod, at a general assembly of masters of the University of Prague and Utraquist clergy held at Prague in September 1418, an attempt was made to settle disputed points. The assembly ratified the administration of holy communion to children, but decisively rejected the principle that nothing was to be believed that was not expressly contained in Holy Writ, as well as various innovations based in the main upon that principle. Needless to say, this did not check the spread of the innovations.

The resolutions of the synod of 1417 and the general assembly of the masters and priests in 1418, though attempting to raise a barrier against extreme radical views, provided little hope of a smooth and speedy settlement of the great conflict between the Czech nation and the Church of Rome. Nor did the trend of affairs at the Council offer much prospect in this direction. There had, it is true, been finally drafted in the Council and submitted to its full assembly a rigorous measure of ecclesiastical reform directed against every form of simony and such evils as had been attacked by Wyclif, Hus, and the latter's predecessors and followers, but no jot of it had been carried into effect. The Council had merely elected a new Pope in the person of Martin V and had then, in April 1418, dispersed. Martin V ratified all the measures taken by the Council against the Czech heretics, and ordered the stern suppression of all who championed the errors of Wyclif, Hus, and Jerome. Yielding to the pressure of his brother Sigismund, King Wenceslas, till then very tolerant towards the adherents of the Hussite movement, also began to take sharper action against them. At the beginning of 1419 he ordered the expelled clergy to be restored. In July he caused all the seats on the council of the New Town at Prague to be filled by extreme opponents of the Hussite party, and the new council at once began to take punitive action. This only exacerbated the situation, and a tendency to acts of real violence shewed itself among the masses. The first great outburst of violence occurred on 30 July 1419. On that day a monk, Jan of Želivo, a preacher at one of the three churches where communion in both kinds was permitted, led a huge procession of Utraquists through the city. When the procession arrived at the New Town Hall and the councillors declined to accede to the crowd's demand for the release of some persons lately imprisoned for religious disorder, the angry crowd forced its way into the building and threw the councillors and others whom they hated from the lofty windows into the square, where they were immediately slain. A general assembly of the townsfolk was at once summoned, and four *hetmen* (captains) were appointed to administer the city for the time being. The king, shocked and alarmed as he was, made no attempt to oppose the revolutionary act. Three days after the slaughter of the councillors he confirmed the election of their successors, chosen by the townsfolk of the New Town. The emotion caused by these events, however, so affected his health that he had a stroke and died on 16 August. With his death fell the last barrier that had hitherto held back the tide of the Hussite revolution. Its waves were now able to spread freely over the entire territory of the Bohemian lands.

Of fundamental importance for the fate of the Hussite movement after the death of King Wenceslas was the question whether the legal heir to the throne, his brother Sigismund, King of the Romans and of Hungary, would be accepted as king. At first, not only the nobles—and particularly the high nobility—but also the burghers of Prague shewed readiness to accept him, though practically all parties made it a condition that the new monarch should recognise the main points of the Hussite programme, the "Four Articles of Prague." Sigismund, however, in view of his position in Christendom could not, nor did he desire to, accept such a condition, At the outset he cautiously concealed his real sentiments on the matter, but by the spring of 1420 he had plainly revealed them. During his sojourn at Breslau in Silesia, when a crusade was proclaimed against the Czech Hussites, Sigismund simultaneously issued strict orders that the Hussites should abandon "Wyclifism" and render obedience to the Church in all things. At Breslau he caused a Prague burgher who refused to renounce the Cup to be burnt at the stake. This attitude prompted the citizens of Prague and a portion of the Bohemian nobility to make a determined stand against him. Armed masses of Hussites hastened from all parts of Bohemia and Moravia to defend Prague, threatened as it was by the proposed crusade. An especially powerful military force was sent by the strongest Hussite organisation in the provinces—that which had been formed in South Bohemia in a newly founded town to which the Biblical name of Tábor had been given. At the head of the Tábor troops was their one-eyed general, Jan Žižka, who had begun to win a great reputation among the people. Towards the end of June Sigismund marched on

Prague at the head of a large crusading army (said to be close on 100,000 men). Occupying Prague Castle, Sigismund had himself crowned there as King of Bohemia, but that was his only success. In an attempt to capture the Vitkov Height just outside the city, his army was shamefully routed by Žižka (Vitkov was subsequently called Žižkov), and suffering from disease and lack of supplies it was soon compelled to retire. In the autumn of the same year (1 November) Sigismund marched with a new army against Prague, but again suffered a crushing defeat, this time under the heights of Vyšehrad.

Sigismund's two military disasters marred all attempts at a reconciliation and gave a powerful impulse to the Hussite resistance. At a general Bohemian Diet summoned in the summer of 1421 at Čáslav, the Bohemian Estates who had subscribed to the Four Articles of Prague resolved not to accept Sigismund as king, on the ground that he was a professed calumniator of the sacred truths embodied in those Articles and an enemy of the honour and life of all who spoke the Czech tongue. In place of Sigismund (who was, however, still recognised as king by the lesser provinces of the Bohemian Crown, Silesia and Lusatia, and had also numerous supporters in Bohemia and Moravia among those who had not joined the Utraquists) the Czechs began at once to seek another king. They entered into negotiations with Vladyslav (Jagiello), King of Poland, proposing that either he himself or his cousin Vitold, Great Prince of Lithuania, should accept the Bohemian crown; but the condition that the future monarch must recognise the Hussite programme proved a stumbling-block here too[1]. While refusing the Bohemian crown himself, the Polish king agreed to allow his nephew Zygmunt (Sigismund) Korybutovich, known usually as Korybut, to proceed to Bohemia. Korybut arrived in Bohemia in the spring of 1422, and was accepted by the Hussite nobility and the burghers of Prague as administrator, or regent, of the country. A year later (in the spring of 1423) he departed, but returned in the summer of 1424 as "the desired and elected king"; he was, however, acknowledged by only a section of the Hussite Czechs. His efforts to reconcile Bohemia with the Church were not only unsuccessful, but they also caused him to forfeit the confidence of the responsible elements among the Hussites. In the spring of 1427 they raised a revolt against him, took him prisoner, and finally drove him from the country.

Thus, from the death of Wenceslas IV in the year 1419 until 1436, when the country again turned to his brother Sigismund, Bohemia had no universally recognised king capable of actually exercising sovereign power. The place of a regular ruler was for some time taken by Prince Korybut. For the rest, the Czechs appointed special councils of administration which were equipped with a large measure of the prerogatives of a ruler. All these temporary governing bodies were appointed by the diets, the importance of which at that period vastly increased, while their composition and

[1] Cf. *infra*, Chap. xviii.

character underwent very substantial changes. Like the two great diets or assemblies of the Estates which took place in the closing years of the reign of Wenceslas IV they were not summoned by the king as had previously been the rule, but came together on the initiative of the Estates, which took into their own hands all right of deciding upon the fortunes of the country. In contradistinction to the diets of the pre-Hussite period in which the representatives of the royal towns had been of but little significance, the towns represented at the diets of the Hussite epoch, led partly by Prague and partly by Tábor, the new centre of radical Hussite tendencies in South Bohemia, advanced so greatly in power that more than once they proved the deciding factor. It was the Hussite movement itself that had raised Prague and Tábor to this position of importance.

Before the death of Wenceslas IV Hussitism had ceased to be merely a spiritual and moral movement. Against the opponents of truth, as it was understood by the Hussites, violence was beginning to be used. At first it was only a matter of individual and isolated outbursts of wrath without any conscious aim, but soon after the death of Wenceslas elements gained the upper hand in the Hussite movement which made an armed struggle one of the express points of its programme. This was in large measure the result of a fanatic, chiliastic tendency which manifested itself particularly at great gatherings or camp meetings, held in the mountains even after the death of King Wenceslas. This chiliasm was at first merely a belief in the early Second Coming of Christ and of a paradise of love and peace which would be established without violence. Ere long, however, when the date had passed for which the Coming of Christ had been prophesied, chiliasm took a predominantly bellicose tone. It was proclaimed that the millennial kingdom of Christ, where mankind would live in primal innocence without sin and without suffering, must be founded upon the destruction of all evil. And when the fervidly longed-for miracle by which all the godless were to be destroyed was not forthcoming, relentless warfare for their extermination began to be preached. The belligerent enthusiasm of the masses, who began to come to the gatherings in the mountains with weapons in their hands, conflicted with the doubts of the more tolerant of the Hussite clergy, whether and to what extent it was permissible for a Christian to fight with physical weapons for divine truth, and whether in particular it was permissible to fight for that truth against those duly in authority. This conflict of opinion was submitted for solution to the masters of the University of Prague, who decided that a Christian community possessed such a right only as a last resort, when the superior authority was manifestly opposed to divine truth and thus forfeited all its rights. Thus, when King Sigismund and the Pope, as the representatives of secular and spiritual authority, declared war at the beginning of 1420 upon all defenders of the divine law, the Hussites were, according to the opinion of the university masters, justified in offering resistance. Among the opponents of the Hussites, both at home and abroad, the idea of a suppression of the Czech heretics by force of arms was generally accepted, and so the war became a war in defence of divine truth—a "Holy War" as it was termed in the Hussite watchword.

In the struggle that ensued, Prague and Tábor—in many matters, as we have seen, of divergent views—were the foremost representatives and deciding factors of the Hussite movement, indeed, we may say of all Hussite Bohemia. Prague owed its position not only to the fact that it was the capital of Bohemia and the whole Bohemian State, though its population hardly exceeded 40,000, and the main fortress in the country, but also to its significance for the rise and growth of the Hussite movement, which had germinated and reached its greatest expansion there. Tábor, an insignificant country-town of recent foundation, had won a leading place alongside Prague mainly because it had become the headquarters and citadel of the radical elements among the Hussites, and because of the military talent and wide experience of Jan Žižka of Trocnov. This South Bohemian knight of no great position or wealth, who had possibly served for some years at the Court of King Wenceslas, and had certainly been in the service of various nobles, had taken active part in the numerous and not infrequently serious fights waged in those troublous days among the nobility, the towns, and the religious Orders, and had gained still further experience during a lengthy sojourn in Poland, where he had fought on behalf of the Poles against the Teutonic Knights, taking part in particular in the famous Battle of Tannenberg (1410) At the time of the outbreak of the Hussite troubles Žižka was already an elderly man—about sixty years of age—and blind of one eye, but he quickly revealed himself as a military organiser of splendid qualities. In arming his troops, artisans from the towns and peasants from the country, full of religious zeal and enthusiasm but utterly untrained for war, he made chief use of implements and equipment to which they had been accustomed. In addition to iron-tipped flails he utilised ordinary farm wagons. Barricades of these, ingeniously arranged, soon proved not only an excellent defence for Žižka's simple foot-soldiers against the heavy cavalry of their knightly opponents but also a very effective means of attack. The efficacy of these wagon barricades, whether for defence or attack, was augmented by the use of light and easily transportable cannon of the howitzer type. Žižka's troops, thus provided with a simple and gradually perfected equipment for battle, acquired their truly astonishing strength partly from the extraordinary military talent of their leader and partly from his conviction that he was an instrument chosen of God to execute the divine law.

Just as they had united in the struggle against the opponents of the Cup at home, over whom they soon won notable successes, so did Prague and Tábor join again and again at critical junctures, despite their steadily growing differences on religious matters, in defence of the country against Sigismund and his crusading armies. Here, too, their successes were remarkable. The second crusade against the Hussites, undertaken in the year 1421, ended with the same lamentable result as the one that had preceded it. The imperial forces penetrated, it is true, into Western Bohemia, and in the middle of September, after fiercely ravaging the country, laid siege to the town of Žatec (Saaz) which was held by the Hussites. At the beginning of October, when false reports arrived that the Czech army was approaching, Sigismund's forces retired in complete disorder without a blow being struck. A similar fate soon afterwards befell the expedition, headed by the king himself, which, advancing through Moravia, compelled the nobles there to abjure the Articles of Prague, and entered Eastern Bohemia. The invaders succeeded in seizing Kutná Hora (Kuttenberg) where the king had many partisans among the burghers, but within a few days he was driven out (January 1422) by Žižka, and in the precipitate flight that ensued his troops suffered heavy losses. After this defeat of Sigismund at Kutná Hora the crusades against the Hussites ceased for a number of years.

The internal struggle, of course, continued, and to the fights of the Hussites against their common enemies, the opponents of the Cup, were added their conflicts among themselves, divided as they were not only by religious differences but also by divergent views on fundamental questions of policy. In the spring of 1423 Žižka betook himself with a small force to Eastern Bohemia, there to found a party more closely identified with his views on religious questions, on which he was not in accord with the majority of the Taborites. The nucleus of Žižka's new party was the Horeb Brotherhood which had arisen in Bohemia almost simultaneously with the Tábor Brotherhood, and their religious views were nearer Žižka's own in that they avoided the extreme radicalism of the Taborites. Žižka's new "Union," which took the place of the Horeb Brotherhood, secured the adherence of Hradec (Königgrätz) and three other towns of Eastern Bohemia, as well as that of several Hussite nobles. Žižka at once supplied the new body with a new military organisation—a standing army was also established at Tábor. Straightway in 1423 Žižka and his new body, which proclaimed inexorable warfare on all who opposed the Word of God, came into armed conflict not only with the Catholic foes of Hussitism but also with the moderate Hussite party at Prague. Desirous of restoring peace and order in the land, the moderate Hussites under the leadership of Prague were prepared to make various political and religious concessions of which the inflexible Žižka would not hear; now and then, indeed, they allied themselves with the Catholic opponents of the Cup. Thus it came about that in September 1424 Žižka and his army stood before the walls of Prague with the design of compelling it to support his policy. The threatened struggle, however, was averted by the conclusion of a six months' armistice, to which immediately afterwards the Utraquists as well as the old Tábor party subscribed. The fruit of this truce was a joint expedition of the Hussite parties to Moravia, which was to be conquered from Albert of Austria. During this expedition, however, Žižka died suddenly at the castle of Přibyslav on 11 October 1424.

The party which he had lately formed did not disperse on his death. They took the name of "The Orphans" in token of the fact that they regarded the dead general as their father, and they pursued his policy of determined opposition to Sigismund whenever the other Hussite parties attempted to come to terms with him. The internal conflicts among these parties continued, and the allied forces of the Taborites and the Orphans inflicted grievous losses on those of Prague. None the less the main Hussite factions again and again came to agreements which for a time suspended their internecine warfare, and enabled them to join against their common foe. A new joint expedition was undertaken to Moravia in October 1425, and at the close of the same year the Orphans carried their arms into Silesia, which thenceforward suffered from similar inroads till the end of the war. In the following years the Hussite armies made more and more incursions to the neighbouring countries. Among their leaders the most distinguished, and a worthy heir of the military fame of Žižka, was the Tábor priest and captain Prokop Holý (Prokop the Bald), who in these years was more than once not merely the military but also the political chief of all the Hussites. He first distinguished himself in the great struggles between the allied Hussite forces and the armies of the princes of Saxony in the year 1426, struggles which culminated in a magnificent victory for the Hussites at Ústí (Aussig) over the more numerous German forces. The profound impression made by this victory confirmed German public opinion in its belief in the invincibility of the Hussites. This conviction, coupled with the chaotic political state of Germany, caused the repeated postponement of further crusades against the Hussites, and contributed largely to their lamentable failure when they were finally undertaken. Thus, for example, the crusade which was undertaken against the Hussites in the summer of 1427, after an interval of five years, and in which Cardinal Henry Beaufort took part, ended in a disorderly flight of the crusading army from Tachov before the fight with the Czechs could begin. No fresh crusade took place until the year 1431, while on the other hand Czech expeditions were continually being made into the surrounding countries, where the Hussites captured numerous strategic points and occupied them with garrisons.

These expeditions, by which the Hussite leaders, particularly Prokop the Bald, obviously desired above all to constrain their hostile neighbours to submission and to acknowledgment of the supremacy of the Word of God, aroused among the troops a keen lust for booty which soon weakened and thrust into the background the original fanatic zeal of the "Warriors of God"—all the more so as they were joined by all manner of adventurers, largely of foreign origin. Apart from the booty, however, these expeditions brought here and there no small moral gain to the Hussites. Particularly in the minor territories of the Bohemian Crown—Silesia and

Upper Lusatia—not only were truces and unions made with the invading Hussites, but also large sections of the population, especially the lower strata of the townspeople and the peasants, joined the Hussite movement. A particularly impressive inroad was that made into Germany in the winter of 1429–30, when the united forces of the Hussites (some 40,000 infantry and 3,500 cavalry) passed through Saxony, entered the territories of the Bishop of Bamberg and of Frederick of Brandenburg in Franconia, and constrained Frederick to make peace with them. Still farther than the expeditions of the Hussite armies penetrated the flaming manifestos by means of which the Hussite parties in the years 1430 and 1431 acquainted the world with their bold programme. These reached France, Spain, and England, where a theologian of the University of Cambridge wrote a polemic against one of them. It was not till a year later (1431) that a fresh crusade was undertaken against the Hussites. In August of that year a large crusading army marched to Domažlice (Taus) but, on the approach of the Hussites, fled in total disorder without a show of fight, leaving not only large numbers of prisoners but also a huge booty in the hands of the enemy. The victory of Domažlice caused the opponents of the Hussites to lose any desire to repeat a crusade against them. Even at the Council of Basle, the view, supported especially by Cardinal Julian Cesarini, who had been mainly responsible for the promotion and organisation of the latest inglorious crusade and who had taken personal part in the expedition, gained the upper hand—that it was advisable, in face of the impossibility of suppressing the Hussites by force, to secure their return to the bosom of the universal Church by conciliatory measures.

Meanwhile, readiness for a compromise with the Church had gained ground among the Hussites themselves. The exhausted state of the country and the chaos in public administration, resulting from the long years of warfare, were largely responsible for the growing spirit of conciliation. The more moderate Hussites were also impelled to compromise with the Church by the religious and social radicalism of several sections of the party and their fanatical rage not only against the opponents of the Cup but also against every relic of Christian culture dating from the pre-Hussite era, an iconoclasm that included the destruction and burning of churches, organs, statues, and other ecclesiastical ornaments. There had been divergences among the Hussites in these matters practically from the very beginning. The famous Four Articles of Prague had expressed in substance the views of Hus and his immediate followers. From various sources, however, there had penetrated into the ideas of the Hussite movement elements that were either entirely alien to Hus or of no significance in his eyes, and which led soon after his death to the division of the Hussites into parties widely at variance, and sometimes therefore very bitterly opposed to one another. Even the logical consideration of several of the principles proclaimed by Hus—notably the doctrine that the Word of God should be the supreme or indeed the only rule of life and faith—

gave rise to views and aims considerably at variance with those of Hus himself. Other divergences were a result of direct foreign influences.

Of these influences by far the most powerful was that of the "evangelical doctor," John Wyclif, from whom the Hussites, regarding him almost as a fifth evangelist, borrowed more than from any other source, including, indeed, doctrines which Hus himself had never recognised. This was in no small measure due to the activities of Wyclif's compatriot, the Oxford "master" Peter Payne, who, as a Lollard, had fled from England to escape persecution, and had taken refuge in Bohemia. From the autumn of 1414 he took prominent part in the religious disputes there, representing for the most part very radical views. The Waldensian heresy, too, had been fairly widespread in Bohemia long before Hus, especially in the south, whence came the leading apostles of the Bohemian Reformation. It was not, however, by this route that the Waldensian doctrines influenced the Hussites most strongly, but rather through the literary activity and teaching of a notable German follower of Hus—Master Nicholas of Dresden— who during the closing years of Hus' life had conducted, with other Dresden masters, a school at Prague which was in intimate touch with the leaders of the Hussite movement and played a prominent rôle in the growth of Hussitism. Together with his companions, Peter Payne among them, Nicholas took a determined stand by the side of Master Jakoubek of Stříbro when the latter began to introduce communion in both kinds, and contributed not a little to his victory. Moreover, alongside the Waldensian beliefs, and sometimes perhaps in close connexion with them, there had penetrated to Bohemia even prior to the time of Hus some of the elements of the Catharist teachings (possibly through the Catharo-Waldensian sect of the Runcarii), an echo of which we find in the more eccentric currents among the Hussites. In 1418 there also arrived in Bohemia a party of Picards who had been driven into exile from the North of France on account of their dangerous heresy. A mystical, bitterly anti-Church spiritualism was combined in this heresy with a hard rationalism which went to the length of a complete denial of the divine presence in the sacrament of the altar.

It was mainly these foreign elements—Wyclifite, Waldensian, Catharist, and Picard—that were responsible for the fact that among the Hussites, when in 1420 they submitted the Four Articles of Prague to the whole world as their common programme, there existed parties and tendencies, the views and aims of which went much farther than the Articles. In connexion with chiliasm, radical currents vastly at variance with Hussitism proper came to the surface among the adherents of the Cup. From this fanatic belief in the early coming of Christ to found His millennial kingdom in which mortals would live in a state of paradisiacal innocence, without sin and without suffering, where there would be no place for human inventions, for secular or ecclesiastical orders introduced by man, where social distinctions would be no more and where Church and State would cease to exist, there were deduced at once demands that tended to a complete revolution in the relations of both society and State, such as the abolition of the royal power, community of property, the abolition of all taxes, the possession of women in common.

Simultaneously with these fanatic and revolutionary principles, which were in places at once put into practice, there came to the forefront at Tábor, now the headquarters of radical tendencies, the extreme rationalist tenets of the Picards, who denied the presence of Christ in the consecrated elements, and declared them to be a mere symbol of Christ's sacrifice and their adoration to be idolatry. This doctrine, however, aroused indignation even in Tábor, and those who preached it were driven out. Their leader, Martinek a priest, commonly known as Lokvis, was burnt at the stake in 1421, and his former supporters, who went on to indulge in pantheist Adamitism, were the same year extirpated by Žižka, who was inexorable in this matter. In like manner the Hussites—even their radical sections —rejected the various revolutionary ideas and demands of the chiliastic fanatics, put forward at Tábor and elsewhere in the years 1419 and 1420, which, however, nowhere gained a permanent hold.

None the less, certain of these ideas penetrated into the Hussite movement, especially among the more radical elements at Tábor. In the first place, the Taborites accepted far more completely than other Hussites the teachings of Wyclif, and put the principles preached by him far more consistently into practice. Moreover, partly as a result, in all probability, of contact with the Waldensians in their close neighbourhood, and partly from a study of the writings of Master Nicholas of Dresden and Peter Payne, they adopted various Waldensian teachings. The principle laid down in the Four Articles of Prague, to the effect that the divine law, that is the Word of God, is the supreme rule of life and faith, they endeavoured to put into practice with the strictest consistency, absolutely rejecting everything in the doctrine and organisation of the Church that appeared to be in conflict with that law, or which in their view was unsupported by it. They rejected belief in purgatory, so that prayers, alms, and masses for the dead became to them superfluous. They did away with the sacraments, with the exception of baptism and communion, in respect of which, after some hesitation, they followed Wyclif in teaching that Christ, whose body was in Heaven, was present in the elements only sacrificially and spiritually, and not materially and personally. They rejected veneration of the saints, pictures, and relics, and abolished all holy days, except Sundays and fast days. In clerical organisation they endeavoured to renew the original simplicity of the apostolic Church, rejecting all orders, regulations, and rites later introduced into the Catholic Church, which the Hussites proper had never ceased to recognise. They therefore abolished Church ritual and vestments, while divine service, which among them consisted, apart from ceremonial partaking of the body and blood of Christ, merely in the singing of Czech hymns, in the offering up of prayer and the reading and explanation of Scripture in the Czech tongue, they caused to be conducted by priests in ordinary lay garb. They did not, however, stop there, but went on relentlessly to destroy altars and their ornaments, statues and pictures of the saints, organs and all the splendour of Church decoration, and they demolished monasteries, which they regarded as dens of iniquity. They did not recognise, nor did they possess, any ecclesiastical Orders other than the offices of priest, deacon, and bishop. The bishop, who had no considerable powers, being merely *primus inter pares*, could, according to the Tábor doctrine which here followed the bold ideas of Marsilio of Padua, be elected merely by the priests without regard to the traditional apostolic succession. Already in September 1420 the Taborites had elected a bishop, the choice falling upon Nicholas of Pelhřimov, subsequently known as Biskupec, who was distinguished not only as an eminent theologian but also as the author of a great historical work in defence of the Tábor party. Thus the Taborites formally broke away from the universal Church, of which the other Hussites never ceased to regard themselves as members. The serious nature of this step was further accentuated by the fact that in their religious radicalism the Taborites were by no means isolated among the Hussites. In close affinity to them was the Horeb Brotherhood, at the head of which Žižka had placed himself towards the close of his life. But even in Prague itself religious radicalism closely allied to that of the Taborites was rampant, largely the work of Jan of Želivo, the priest who had attracted attention on the occasion of the first outburst of revolt at the capital in 1419, and who from that moment had dominated the New Town quarter, where he won the allegiance of the masses by sermons and by his demagogic and political fervour. His career lasted till early in 1422, when he and several of his followers were beheaded. In time, of course, this original radicalism everywhere diminished very considerably, and even at Tábor itself there began to be manifested a readiness to settle political and religious conflicts by conciliatory means, a tendency which was supported in particular by Žižka's successor, the priest Prokop the Bald.

On the other hand, there were many who were prepared to compromise in the matter of the Articles, so as to draw nearer to the views of the Church. These, the most moderate section of the Hussites, consisting mainly of the high nobility and numbers of the Masters of the University of Prague, were ready, in the interests of reconciliation with the Church, to sacrifice not only all those points in which the Articles went farther than Hus, and not only much that had been taken over from Wyclif, recognised even by them at an earlier date as their teacher, but also various teachings of Hus himself, and to content themselves practically with merely the Cup and the abolition of certain abuses. The leading advocate of these moderates was the learned and bellicose Master of Prague University, Jan of Příbram. His determined attacks upon Wyclifite teachings in the years 1426–27 met, however, with opposition from Wyclif's compatriot, Peter Payne, who had become acclimatised among the Hussites under the name of Master English, and who later went over completely to the "Orphans." The standpoint of the group of Jan of Příbram was far from being common to all the supporters of a moderate tendency among the Hussites, at the head of which, after the death of its leader, Jakoubek of Stříbro, in 1429, stood not Příbram but Master Jan Rokycana, whose spiritual views were closely identified with those of Jakoubek and who was subsequently for many years the head of the Utraquists; yet it was none the less a significant expression of the atmosphere of conciliation which had spread among them. Despite, however, all this genuine desire for a restoration of unity with the Church, even the most moderate Hussites of the Příbram group declined to take the step which had long been in the eyes of the Church more or less an understood condition of reconciliation, that of simple submission to its decision without reserve and without compromise, and thus the acknowledgment of its unrestricted authority in matters of faith. As long as the Church insisted upon maintaining the attitude which it had adopted towards Hus at the Council of Constance, agreement between it and the Czech Hussites was impossible, however much the latter moderated their demands.

An obstacle to such agreement was, moreover, presented by the development of ecclesiastical organisation in the Utraquist party itself. The act of Conrad of Vechta, Archbishop of Prague, in going over to Hussitism had spared this party the necessity of providing themselves, as the Taborites had done, with a new bishop of their own without regard, if need be, to the principle of apostolic succession. The position and power of Archbishop Conrad were, however, afterwards substantially different from what they had been. Alongside him there were first appointed for a while four Masters of Prague University, elected at a synod of the Czech clergy in 1421, as Church Administrators with extensive powers. And when, after the fall of Korybut, a temporary conflict arose between the archbishop and the Utraquists, Master Jan Rokycana was elected by the Prague clergy as the "official" or "superior" whom all had to obey. Archbishop Conrad himself, after the Utraquist clergy in 1429 had again acknowledged allegiance to him, recognised Rokycana as his vicar *in spiritualibus*. So this Hussite Master, though formally only the archbishop's official on the old lines, continued to be the real spiritual leader and head of the Utraquist party.

The internal development of the Hussite parties which has been broadly outlined was obviously little favourable to the efforts to reconcile the Hussites with the Church undertaken immediately in 1420 from different quarters and frequently renewed. It was repeatedly seen that on the one hand the internal conditions in Bohemia were not yet ripe for a conciliatory settlement with the Church, and on the other hand that the supreme authorities in the Church were not prepared to facilitate such a settlement by concessions of any fundamental character, or indeed to negotiate about such concessions, for the Church persevered in the unequivocal demand that the Hussites must first of all render complete submission to it.

The military successes of the Hussites gradually brought about a change in this unyielding attitude. First of all the Hussites succeeded in moving, if not the Papacy itself, at any rate its devoted adherents in Bohemia and beyond the frontiers to enter into negotiations upon the questions in dispute. Prokop the Bald himself decided in the spring of 1429 to enter into direct negotiations with King Sigismund. In the course of an inroad into Austria, Prokop, accompanied by a Hussite delegation of which he was joint leader with Peter Payne, proceeded to Bratislava (Pressburg) to meet Sigismund. The negotiations centred chiefly round the method by which it would be possible to settle the Bohemian religious problem at the General Council to be convoked at Basle in 1431. The Czechs were in principle ready to send envoys to the Council, but they demanded to be heard as equals and not to be placed on trial. They declined, of course, to surrender their faith; on the contrary, they suggested that Sigismund should adopt and defend it. Under these conditions it was only natural that no agreement could be arrived at. It was not until the famous victory of the Hussites at Domažlice that Western Christendom became convinced of the need of entering into negotiations with the Czech heretics. The Council of Basle itself sent on 15 October 1431 an invitation to the Czechs to come to Basle on terms which they had previously put forward in vain, namely, to a hearing at which "The Holy Spirit itself would be in the midst as arbiter and judge."

The invitation sent by the Council of Basle, though it was a great moral success for the Czechs, was not accepted unhesitatingly by all the Hussite sections. The Taborites, who would have wished a settlement of their conflict with the Church to be entrusted rather to laymen, were dissatisfied with the proposed hearing before the Council. The Orphans, too, were at first very reserved in their attitude to the invitation. At the beginning of 1432, however, Rokycana, who since the death of Archbishop Conrad (in December 1431) had been the spiritual head of the Utraquist party, agreed with Prokop to accept the invitation to Basle. In May 1432 representatives of the Council met the Czech delegates at Cheb (Eger) in order to settle the conditions under which the Czechs were to be heard at the Council. Here the Czechs won a fresh important success. According to the terms settled with the Council's plenipotentiaries the decision in the Czech conflict with the Church was not to lie with the Council but with another, higher judge. This judge, as the Hussites had demanded, was to be in part the divine law, that is, the Scriptures, and in part the custom (that is, the practice) of Christ, His apostles, and the primitive Church, together with the Councils and the Fathers of the Church in so far as their teachings were rightly based upon Holy Scripture and the practice of the primitive Church. In all their subsequent dealings with the Council the Hussites again and again appealed to this criterion of judgment agreed upon at Cheb—or the "Cheb Judge" as it was called.

Shortly before the Council assembled, the Taborites and the Orphans, disregarding the principles of the agreement for the attendance at Basle, joined in a great military expedition to Lusatia, Silesia, and Brandenburg, in the course of which they penetrated about the middle of April to the neighbourhood of Berlin. Later still Prokop resolutely rejected the request of the Council that the Czechs should conclude a truce for the period of their negotiations with the Council. Indeed, early in 1433 when the negotiations with the Czechs at the Council were in active progress, the Orphan captain, Jan Čapek of Sany, as an ally of the Poles against the Teutonic Knights, undertook a great expedition through Lusatia and Silesia to Neumark and Prussia, in the course of which the Hussite army advanced to the Baltic Sea near the mouth of the Vistula.

In the meantime, the negotiations at Basle, where the Czech delegation had arrived on 4 January 1433, made difficult progress. Whereas the Czechs were only disposed to accept such decisions as in their opinion were in harmony with the laws of God, the Council demanded that the Czechs should render absolute submission to it. While, too, the Czechs (in particular Rokycana, Nicholas of Pelhřimov, and Peter English) resolutely championed the Four Articles of Prague, albeit in their milder formulation as drafted in 1418 by the University of Prague, the Council rejected every article, except for the fact that privately the Czechs were offered a limited recognition of the Cup.

Being unable to move the Czech envoys to concessions the Council sent a delegation to Prague to negotiate there directly with the Bohemian diet. The Basle delegates, among whom the papal auditor, Juan Palomar, was an outstanding figure by reason of his diplomatic talents, remained at Prague two months (from May to July 1433), but even there the negotiations with the Czechs produced no result. On the other hand, confidential *pourparlers* with the most moderate section of the Hussites under Přibram prepared the way for an agreement at Prague touching all the Four Articles. This agreement, with some additions, was accepted by both sides on 30 November and sealed by the delegate priests and the Utraquist masters clasping hands; some formal changes, and the decision of the "Cheb Judge," being reserved for final settlement when matters still outstanding should be discussed (general obligation of communion in both kinds, and participation of children in the Cup). By this agreement, to which the name of *The Compacts* was applied, assent was given to all the Four Articles of Prague, but in such style and with such clauses that their original meaning was almost completely obliterated. Apart from communion in both kinds, which was permitted with some reservations, the Hussites were conceded practically nothing. Further, the agreement was not ratified by the Bohemian Estates at a new diet in January 1434, but the Council insisted that it was binding, while it was acknowledged by the moderate Hussites who interpreted the Compacts in a sense much more favourable to themselves than the Council understood them. The Taborites and Orphans, however, were decisively opposed to it. Weight was given to their opposition by the military power of their armies in the field. These forces had formerly by their military successes forced both domestic and foreign opponents of Hussitism and even the Council itself to yield, thus indirectly preparing the way to conciliation, but now they had become the main obstacle to agreement. Since the summer of 1432 troops had vainly laid siege to the main bulwark of the Catholic power in West Bohemia, the town of Plzeň (Pilsen), and by their hunt for booty had caused great damage in the whole country round. Resentment at their conduct aggravated by the growing desire for agreement with the Church and the restoration of normal conditions to the country led the Hussite nobles in the spring of 1434 to conclude an alliance with the governor of Bohemia, Aleš Vřeštovský, who had recently been elected by the diet, and the troops were ordered to disband if they did not wish to be regarded as the enemies of their country. Determined to rid the land of the Taborite and Orphan troops the Hussite nobles now did not hesitate to join with the Catholic nobles. A decisive battle was fought at Lipany on 30 May 1434, in which the army of the Taborites and Orphans was defeated, and their eminent general, Prokop the Bald, perished on the field.

This defeat of the radical elements among the Hussites facilitated the subsequent negotiations of the Czechs both with Sigismund and with the Council of Basle. Those with Sigismund proceeded smoothly and rapidly. They concerned mainly the use of the Cup in communion and Church government. With regard to the Cup the Czechs were gradually compelled to surrender their demand that the Cup should be universally compulsory. They insisted, however, that the diet, jointly with the clergy, should elect the archbishop and two bishops, that the archbishop should be an adherent of communion in both kinds, and that all the clergy in the country should be subordinate to him. This demand, though it met with keen opposition from the Council envoys, who upheld the right of the chapter to elect the bishops, was readily enough conceded by Sigismund, who was convinced that this right pertained to him as king, and that he could thus pass it on to the Estates.

The agreement between the king and the Bohemian Estates was ratified by the diet in September 1435, and the election was at once made of Master Jan Rokycana as Archbishop of Prague, and of two bishops. The election, which was made by sixteen delegates—eight representing the secular Estates, and eight representing the clergy—was immediately ratified by the diet, but it was not till July 1436 that it was confirmed by

Sigismund in a royal charter in which he averred that till Rokycana's death he did not desire to have any other as archbishop, and that he would do his utmost to get the election confirmed by the Church. This confirmation was forthcoming at a notable meeting of the Czechs with Sigismund and delegates of the Council which took place at Jihlava (Iglau) in July 1436. There, some few days prior to the issue of the charter relating to the episcopal elections, seals were affixed to the Compacts as agreed upon at the close of 1433, and on 5 July a ceremonial exchange of documents followed at Jihlava in the presence of Sigismund. In addition to the charter touching the election of Rokycana, Sigismund gave the Czechs another confirming several of their demands and thus supplementing the Compacts. At the end of August Sigismund entered Prague, and a month later was present at his first Bohemian diet as the accepted King of Bohemia.

The Compacts merely closed the first period of the great struggle; they were no final solution, the disputes breaking out again with new force. The first period, however, had profoundly affected the internal organism of the Czech State and nation, and brought about far-reaching changes.

First of all, the unity of the Czech State suffered seriously from the fact that its main territory, Bohemia, had definitively rejected Sigismund as lawful heir to the throne, and was thus for the whole period without a king, while the bulk of the minor provinces of the Bohemian Crown did not follow its example. The danger that this state of affairs presented for the unity of the Czech State was aggravated by the bitter hostility shewn towards the mother country in those parts that had fallen away from her, hostility which developed on religious as well as on racial grounds. By the recognition of Sigismund as king throughout the whole territory of the Bohemian Crown which was effected simultaneously with the acceptance of the Compacts, the shattered unity of the Czech State was restored, though not completely, for the mutual hostility of the various territories was not permanently obliterated. Three years later, on the death of Sigismund's successor, a long period of interregnum and religious conflict, aggravated by racial differences, again led to a temporary drifting asunder.

The absence of a duly recognised king in Bohemia had furthermore the result of forcing the Czechs to manage their own government. The Estates, represented by their diets, thus appeared as the actual source of all State power in Bohemia. This came to an end, it is true, on the acceptance of Sigismund as king in 1435, but it left deep traces on the relations between the king and the Estates. Sigismund was obliged not only to confirm the Estates in their old liberties and rights, but also to accept various religious and political conditions which they laid down. Moreover, although afterwards the actual influence of the Estates on all decisions in public affairs was far greater than it had been in the pre-Hussite era, even this augmented authority did not satisfy their increased consciousness of power. The disputes between king and Estates which threatened to arise were checked for the time being by the death of Sigismund. They remained, however, to be fought out at a later date.

Although Hussitism was in origin and substance a moral, religious, and ecclesiastical movement, there entered into it practically at the very outset certain endeavours to alter social and economic conditions, and these became an important element of the movement. Both the higher and the lower nobility, inclining towards the religious movement inspired by Hus, longed to break down the intolerable economic predominance of the Church, to deprive the prelates and monasteries of their vast landed possessions and to get this property into their own hands. The artisans and working classes in the towns wished to overthrow the power of the wealthy patricians, to secure some influence on municipal administration, and to improve their own economic condition. The villeins on the land cherished the hope of escaping from their irksome duties and obligations. The lowest ranks of the clergy were desirous of ending the humiliating inequality of their social and economic position compared with that of the wealthy prelates, canons, and rectors of great parishes. All these aims and desires, often unconscious and ill-defined, merged not only into one another but also into the religious and nationalist aims and sentiments.

The Hussite movement, however, though arousing and giving support to these multifarious aims and desires, did not make their fulfilment a positive article of the Hussite programme. Only the demands that the priests should be deprived of undue enjoyment of great worldly possessions, and should live lives according to the Gospel and the example of Christ and His apostles, became important articles of that programme. Other far-reaching social demands were put forward only by the extreme sections of the Hussites, particularly the Taborites. At Tábor in 1420, at a time when the chiliastic heresy was prevalent, there was proclaimed not only the abolition of serfdom and of villein dues and services, but also the replacement of private property by ownership in common. Communistic principles were put into practice by the establishment of common treasuries to which the wealthier farmers on selling their produce handed over the proceeds. Very soon, however, this ceased. The serfs did not even acquire the promised exemption from the payment of interest and dues to the large landowners. The revolutionary ideas of the extreme Taborites took no hold whatsoever on the other Hussite parties, except here and there among the lower classes of the townsfolk, where they soon disappeared in the same manner as at Tábor itself. Some of these views find, it is true, an echo in the writings of the Southern Bohemian thinker, Peter Chelčický, which appeared at the beginning of the Hussite wars, and in which the author, with impressive eloquence and fervid conviction, shews the absolute incompatibility of the relation of master and serf with the pure law of God; but Chelčický's doctrine that the true Christian must never resist the supreme secular power even when it does him wrong caused his views, at that time still little known, to lose all practical effect.

The demand—an upheaval in the social and economic conditions of the time—for the abolition or at least a great reduction in the vast possessions of the Church, especially landed property, was largely brought into effect, at least in Bohemia. During the Hussite tumults, the Church there was deprived of the major part of its secular property, the wealthy monasteries were either demolished or ·impoverished, the former economic predominance of the Church over the lay classes was broken once and for all, and the prelates were deprived of all political importance. The landed estates taken from the Church enriched, it is true, in the first place a number of the houses of the higher nobility, but the gains of the lower nobility also, the knights and gentry, were not inconsiderable. Thus, not only the nobility proper but also the knights and the gentry in Bohemia made an advance in economic and political power owing to the Hussite wars, the latter perhaps a relatively greater advance than the former. It was not indeed till the Hussite wars that the knights and gentry became factors of real consequence in public life, secured representation in the highest offices of State and the law courts, and won an influential voice in the deliberations of the diet. In like manner the Hussite movement increased the importance of the towns, which likewise frequently obtained a considerable portion of the property confiscated from the Church. The leading position which the burgher class, represented especially by the burghers of Prague, secured for themselves during the Hussite wars was not indeed permanently maintained; nevertheless, even after these wars the measure of political rights still possessed by them was such that their voice could not be disregarded in public affairs. This fact had all the greater significance because in the towns themselves it was the Hussite movement that helped the more popular and nationalistic elements to victory.

While the Hussite movement thus brought on the whole more good than harm to the nobility, the knights, and the towns, the villeins on the land not only gained nothing of what the Taborite chiliasts had dreamed, but even suffered greatly in consequence of the prolonged fighting; and the injurious effect of war on the general condition of the country contributed, as became apparent later, to a considerable deterioration in their position.

Profound and significant were the effects of the Hussite movement on the development of Czech nationality and a national Czech consciousness. There culminated in it, first and foremost, the opposition of the native Czech population to the Germans who had migrated to the country during the preceding two centuries and were to a large extent in the enjoyment of a privileged position. The Hussite upheavals accelerated and completed a development tending to the gradual Czechisation of the towns in Bohemia. Many German burghers were driven from the country on account of their hostile attitude towards the Czech religious movement, and the lower classes, of Czech nationality and of Hussite sentiments, became the ruling powers in the towns. The majority of towns in Bohemia thus became wholly Czech. In Moravia, where the Hussite movement was not so strong as in Bohemia, the German element suffered less severe losses. In particular, the towns there remained in the hands of the Germans even throughout the Hussite wars.

The Hussite struggles did not, indeed, drive all the Germans out of Bohemia and Moravia, but the privileged position which they enjoyed out of proportion to their actual strength and numbers was utterly lost. In the chief territories of the Czech State, especially in Bohemia, they became an insignificant minority of practically no importance in politics. The Latin tongue, too, was displaced by the Czech language in official correspondence, in all dealings in the public offices, the courts of justice, and the diets.

The Hussite movement had a further effect on the national character. The struggle was carried on by the Czechs not merely in the effort to cleanse the Czech State and nation from the accusation of heresy but also in the conviction that, acknowledging the purity of the truth of God above all other races, they were under the obligation of assisting it to victory, of becoming champions of the divine Word and warriors of God. This naturally gave rise in their minds to the idea of some special sacred character attaching to the Czech nation, of its call to great deeds in the service of God and the divine law. The national consciousness of the Czechs thus acquired a special mystical tinge and impressive fervour, and the Czech national idea was enriched by the thought that the nation, apart from its defensive struggle against the German menace, had had a great positive task laid upon it—a fight for the pure truth of God.

The economic harm caused to the Czech territories by the Hussite wars was certainly great. These struggles not only directly destroyed much material wealth, but also in large measure paralysed all the economic life of the country and held up its trade with other countries, which had developed so satisfactorily, especially in the preceding century. Similarly, the Hussite wars put an end to the splendid progress of the plastic arts by virtue of which in the reigns of Charles IV and Wenceslas IV Bohemia had become the leading centre of art in the Europe of that day. Many works of art dating from earlier periods fell a sacrifice to the Hussite upheaval. The opposition of the radical parties among the Hussites to art, in the works of which they saw a sinful luxury, led to the demolition and burning of churches and monasteries, to the destruction of statues, pictures, and other works of art. During the Hussite era nothing, of course, was done to make good this loss by the production of new works. The Hussite period severed, almost for good and all, the tradition of a native art, so that when at a later period the plastic arts in Bohemia were awakened to new life, they no longer stood in the forefront of

European evolution, but were for long lacking in independence, and frequently a considerably belated imitation of foreign works.

In the sphere of intellectual culture, too, the Hussite wars substantially weakened, and for the most part entirely severed, the former intimate connexion with the rest of Europe. By retarding, and for some time entirely preventing, the influx of new currents of thought from the civilised West, Hussitism checked the development of the Czech nation in more than one branch of culture. On the other hand, of course, by the ideas and moral force it possessed it inspired in some directions an intellectual activity of truly astonishing power.

To the numerous Czech and Latin works which issued from the Bohemian reformation movement at its very beginnings, and whose authors included, beside Hus himself, several of his predecessors (Thomas of Štítný, Matthias of Janov) and of his followers, the time of the Hussite wars added a large number of works of similar character, written in either Czech or Latin by the spiritual leaders of the Hussite parties, such as Master Jakoubek of Stříbro, Jan of Příbram, Peter Payne, and Nicholas of Pelhřímov. All these learned masters, however, were surpassed in ability, ideas, and power of presentation by Peter Chelčický, a farmer of South Bohemia, who knew but little Latin and whose works, all written in Czech, were mostly composed during the Hussite upheavals. Inclining to the movement inspired by Hus, Chelčický was especially attracted by the radical faction at Tábor. But he severed his connexion both with the Prague masters and with the Taborites as early as 1420, when he declared in opposition to both that war of any kind was forbidden to a Christian, even in defence of the Word of God. He thus stood aside from the great struggles within the Hussite movement itself, enshrining his thoughts in works which rank among the most precious treasures of Czech literature. In these works, along with views which are well-known from the writings of Wyclif and Hus and which are common to the entire Hussite movement, we find other views substantially different from them, obviously the effect of semi-Catharist influences. Like the Cathari, Chelčický proclaimed that the taking of life in any form, and thus war, was a sin, that whoever killed a man in battle was guilty of " hideous murder "; like them he rejected all secular power, worldly offices, human laws and rights, despised worldly learning and especially the writings of the learned " doctors," fiercely attacked the powerful and the rich, and with fervid sympathy championed the simple and the poor. Although Chelčický took the individual elements of his teaching from various sources, he projected himself as it were so completely into them that he gave them an independent, personal impress. His writings, indeed, are among the few medieval literary works which can even to-day captivate our interest.

Alongside the theological writings that arose in Bohemia during the Hussite struggles there appeared also a number of by no means unimportant literary works of a different character. They consist partly of historical works, among which the so-called *Old Annals of Bohemia*, simple and vivid records made by anonymous plebeians, give a lively account of the great national revolution, and partly of numerous Czech and Latin compositions in verse of a satirical, bellicose, derisive, and not infrequently historical nature. Finally, popular hymns, which the leading Hussite parties made a large element of their divine service, reached a high level of development. The simple words of these hymns were adapted to effective tunes which have given the hymns a very prominent place in the evolution of the art of music.

The Compacts of Prague failed to bring about a complete and genuine reconciliation between the Hussites and the Church, for neither party was wholly satisfied with them. The Church saw in them only a temporary concession forced upon it by circumstances, and did not abandon the hope that in time it would be able to deprive them of all significance. The Czechs on the other hand looked upon the Compacts as merely the foundation for a final adjustment which should satisfy them with regard to the outstanding religious and Church questions. They hoped that such an adjustment would, in particular, be forthcoming in the important question of a universal obligation to accept the Cup in all the Czech territories. As early as the end of 1437, however, the Council of Basle issued a decree to the effect that communion in both kinds was not ordained by Christ, and that it was the prerogative of the Church to determine the manner in which the sacrament of the altar should be administered, in which, whatever its form, the whole body and blood of Christ were present. This was a complete denial of one of the fundamental articles of Hussitism, and a serious whittling down of the Compacts in the point that for the Czechs was the most important of all. Little wonder that the Czechs, apart from the most moderate section led by Jan of Příbram, refused to recognise the validity of this decision, so that the conflict between them and the Church in the matter of the Cup continued.

Further disappointments were inflicted upon the Utraquist Czechs by the Council and King Sigismund in matters of Church government. Not only was the election of Rokycana as Archbishop of Prague not ratified, but also the administration of the Bohemian Church, including the Utraquist section, hitherto in Rokycana's charge, was transferred for the time being to special plenipotentiary legates appointed by the Council, the first of whom was Bishop Philibert. These legates proved extremely zealous in ridding the Church of all special rites and customs introduced by the Utraquist party. They were also instrumental in restoring the ecclesiastical institutions of the party adhering to communion in one kind, especially monasteries, and they confirmed the appointments of new incumbents to churches at Prague and in the provinces in place of the old incumbents who, in the eyes of the Church, had been wrongfully instituted. In this manner Rokycana himself was deprived of the benefice of the Tyn church at Prague. He fled from Prague to Eastern Bohemia, choosing Hradec Králové as his seat and remaining there till 1448. A large proportion of the Utraquist clergy still regarded him as their head, while the others were placed under an administrator elected for this purpose in 1437 with the consent of the king and the legates. A unification of Church administration in Bohemia, desired, though for different reasons, by the Utraquists and by the party adhering to communion in one kind, was thus not attained. At the same time dissatisfaction with the Church policy of Sigismund and with his rule generally increased among the more radical adherents of the Utraquist party. Seeing the growing opposition to himself, Sigismund left Prague early in November; and he died at Znojmo (Znaim) on his way to Hungary on 9 December 1437.

The brief period of Sigismund's rule, during which Bohemia had at last possessed a generally acknowledged king, was soon exchanged for another interregnum. It is true that, in accord with Sigismund's wishes, a portion of the Bohemian Estates acknowledged the hereditary claim of his son-in-law Albert of Austria and chose him as king at the end of 1437. The majority of the Estates, however, unable to obtain from him an undertaking to fulfil various demands, especially those touching religious matters, offered the crown to Casimir, the brother of Vladyslav, King of Poland. Before the struggle for the throne could be decided, however, Albert died in October 1439 as he was returning from an unsuccessful expedition against the Turks. In the meantime the candidature of Casimir had been dropped, so that those who had supported Albert—mainly the nobles upholding communion in one kind and the moderate Utraquists—were able at the beginning of 1440 to conclude a general peace with the party of the more determined Hussites led by Hynce Ptáček of Pirkštejn. By the terms of this general peace there were constituted in the various counties (of which there were then twelve in Bohemia) companies for defence, a kind of militia, drawn from all parties without distinction. The counties elected *hetmen* and instructed them to settle in their courts the conflicts among the different classes, to maintain peace and security, and to uphold the agreed organisation in the land even by force of arms. At a time when there was no recognised royal power nor any uniform central government in the country these county militia companies became the actual organ of public administration. They won special importance, moreover, when Ptáček, the leader of the more extreme section of the Hussites, succeeded in the spring of 1440 in uniting four eastern counties into a single body of which he himself became the head. This union, which was voluntarily joined by a fifth county, that of Boleslav, where one of the two *hetmen* was the young George of Poděbrady, then only twenty years of age, became ere long not only the nucleus of the Utraquist party now in process of reorganisation, but also the centre of a new political development in Bohemia. In ecclesiastical matters its main support and counsel was found in Rokycana. Its importance increased with the failure of attempts to fill the Bohemian throne, which was vacant till 1452 when Ladislas Posthumus, son of Albert of Austria, became king.

Meanwhile the organisation formed by Ptáček, which was gradually augmented by fresh elements, had become increasingly the moving force in Bohemian history. In it was concentrated the nucleus of the Utraquist party, which had never ceased to recognise Rokycana as its leader; he had been formally acknowledged in the summer of 1441 as the head (administrator) of the Hussite clergy in the united eastern counties. Rokycana's party systematically fixed and unified the official doctrines of the Hussite ecclesiastical organisation, both as against the moderate Hussite tendency under Příbram and the more radical Taborites. While an agreement with the Příbram party was attained, a settlement with the Taborites, owing to the important differences in doctrine, was more difficult. The political and military pressure exerted by Ptáček, however, constrained even the Taborites to agree to their clergy attending a conference at Kutná Hora in July 1443 to discuss disputed Church questions, and, should they not be settled there, to allow the Bohemian diet to decide upon them according to the "Cheb Judge." As a reconciliation between the two parties was not reached at Kutná Hora, it became necessary to submit the disputed points to the diet.

Thus it came about that the diet which met at Prague in January 1444, after hearing the report of a special committee chosen to study the disputed points, gave its approval to the teaching of the Rokycana party touching the real presence in the sacrament of the altar, and other matters, such as the maintenance of the seven sacraments, purgatory, invocation of the saints, fasting, penance, the use of vestments, and the preservation of the ancient ritual. The Taborite teachings were thus decisively condemned once and for all, and the Taborites were called upon to accept the teachings of the Rokycana party, for by the decision of the diet those teachings were given the force of law incumbent upon all adherents of the Hussite movement. As all previously existing differences between the Rokycana and Příbram sections had been settled, nothing more was lacking for the attainment of complete unity among the Hussites than that the Taborites should surrender their existing independence in accordance with the ruling of the diet. Although it was clear that this could not be attained at once or without difficulty, the decisions of the diet of January 1444 were a distinct step forward towards the attainment of unity among all the adherents of the Cup, and a great success for the Ptáček party. This party soon afterwards suffered a severe blow through the premature death of their leader, but they at once found a fitting successor to him in the youthful George of Poděbrady, who had already at a congress in the preceding September been elected supreme *hetman* of the allied militia of the eastern counties, and from that time onwards became, both at home and abroad, the acknowledged leader of Hussite Bohemia.

George of Poděbrady was a scion of the house of the Lords of Kunštát, which was of Moravian origin and formerly had had considerable estates there. In the middle of the fourteenth century one branch of this family migrated to Bohemia, where the town of Poděbrady became its main seat. It was noted for its nationalist sentiments and its support of reforming tendencies. While not quite fourteen years of age George took part with his guardian in the battle of Lipany. From the age of eighteen he was in the service of Ptáček of Pirknštejn, who was his teacher and master in practical politics. At the age of twenty he was elected *hetman* of Boleslav county, and on the death of Ptáček in the year 1444 was chosen to succeed him as supreme *hetman* of the eastern counties. In continuing the work of Ptáček, George of Poděbrady found his main support in the eastern counties' Union, which henceforward began to be known as the Poděbrady Unity.

Although George had from the outset enjoyed no little esteem even among the party of communion in one kind, his political activities met with the opposition of the leading noble of that party, the powerful and wealthy Oldřich of Rožmberk (Rosenberg) who, with his supporters, placed obstacles in the way of the young Hussite statesman. They were unable, however, to frustrate his plans. George sought in particular a solution for the outstanding ecclesiastical questions, among which a foremost place was occupied by the problem of the confirmation of the election of Rokycana as Archbishop of Prague. The Papacy, however, which at this period had already secured predominance over the Council of Basle, turned an absolutely deaf ear to the Czech demands. When the papal legate, Cardinal Carvajal, who was specially sent to Bohemia in the spring of 1448, attempted, like Bishop Philibert before him, to reintroduce the old order and customs into the government of the Czech Church, he met with determined resistance from the entire Utraquist party, who unanimously demanded the confirmation of Rokycana's election as archbishop. The negotiations with the papal legate shewed that the uncompromisingly negative attitude of the Holy See towards the Czech demands in the matter of the Compacts and the confirmation of Rokycana had caused even the most moderate of the Hussites to abandon the idea of complete unity with the universal Church. Carvajal was compelled by disorders which broke out in Prague to hasten his departure from the country, and immediately afterwards not only the Estates assembled in the diet but also the entire population of Prague proclaimed their determination to stand faithfully by the Compacts. The anti-Roman reaction in the Utraquist party culminated at the beginning of September 1448, when George of Poděbrady and his Unity troops occupied Prague, which, since the year 1436, had been under the joint administration of the party of communion in one kind and the most moderate wing of the Utraquists who were in close affinity with them. As George's troops entered Prague, the priests who had been accused of breaking the Compacts fled, and the canons departed for Plzeň, which thenceforward became the seat of the administration of the party of communion in one kind. Rokycana, once more installed in his old charge of the Tyn church, was again acknowledged as the supreme head of all the Utraquist clergy.

The occupation of Prague, accompanied as it was by an internal unification of the Utraquists(apart from the Taborites)under the leadership of Rokycana, augmented George's power, which, though he formally looked for support only to the Poděbrady Unity, acquired a more general character. George began both at home and abroad to appear as the real political power in the land, though in name he had not yet become so. He was opposed, it is true, by the nobles of the party adhering to communion in one kind, who, at the beginning of 1449, met at Strakonice and formed a compact union; but George succeeded in keeping them in check. While his opponents hoped that by the accession of the young Ladislas to the throne of Bohemia they would be able to deprive George of his post in the administration of the kingdom, the German king, Frederick of Austria, the guardian of Ladislas, preferred to come to terms with George. Frederick was moved to this partly by Aeneas Sylvius, Bishop of Siena, the famous humanist who subsequently became Pope under the title of Pius II. He had acted as Frederick's representative at the Bohemian diet held at Benešov in June 1451, had made the personal acquaintance of the young Lord of Poděbrady, and saw that he was not only the best man for the post of governor but also that his political circumspection and his conciliatory outlook on religion made him competent above all others to undertake a peaceful solution of the Church problem in Bohemia. Not long after the Benešov diet, in October 1451, Frederick gave his approval to the appointment of George as governor, but with the reservation that it was "on sufferance," thus leaving himself a free hand for the future. In the spring of 1452 the Bohemian diet passed a vote making George of Poděbrady governor of the land for a term of two years.

At the end of August he betook himself with a considerable force southwards to Tábor, which declined to recognise the new order of things. He succeeded without a struggle in obtaining the surrender of Tábor, which accepted the diet's decision to make him governor of the kingdom, and undertook to submit in all disputed religious matters to the verdict of six arbiters. The diet's decision was then quickly acknowledged by George's other opponents. At the October diet at Prague the Tábor question likewise was settled in such a manner that the movement really came to an end. A majority of the Taborites accepted an arbitration judgment which was nothing but a revival of the unfavourable decision of 1444. Some few unyielding priests, among them the Tábor bishop, Nicholas of Pelhřimov, were imprisoned in George's castles, which they never left alive.

The unity of the Utraquist party, completed by the subjection of Tábor in 1453, proved no small obstacle to the efforts of the Church of Rome.

It was now no longer possible to exploit the one section of the Utraquist party which was ready for entire reconciliation with the Church against the more determined group which held steadfastly to the Compacts. A general and genuine return of the Czechs to the bosom of the Church would now have called for a public agreement between the supreme authority of the Church and the official representatives of Hussitism. Most depended, of course, on Rokycana. The archbishop was by no means, in principle, opposed to an honourable settlement with the Church of Rome, and even as the acknowledged spiritual head of the Utraquist party he never ceased to endeavour to bring about reunion with the Church. In this he was inspired not merely by a genuine desire for a restoration of Church unity but also by practical needs. Among the Utraquists Rokycana had almost the same powers as the bishops in the rest of the Church, and he exercised them jointly with a consistory composed of twenty members, priests and masters. But he was lacking in that important right of Catholic bishops, the power of ordaining priests. As long as the Utraquist party insisted upon the principle of apostolic succession Rokycana could only acquire this right with the assent of the Holy See, and as long as he was not confirmed by the Holy See and consecrated bishop with its consent the party of communion in both kinds possessed no one who was able to ordain priests. It was thus with great difficulty that the ranks of the Utraquist priesthood could be replenished. The neighbouring bishops and the Bishop of Olomouc, though placed by the Compacts under the obligation of ordaining them, denied ordination to the Hussite theological students, who were thus compelled to resort to Italy, where several bishops were more easily prevailed upon to be accommodating, though in a manner not wholly above suspicion. This was not enough, however, and the scarcity of priests among the Utraquists continued to increase, a condition of affairs which militated against the building up of a normal Church organisation and the maintenance of moral discipline among the clergy and among the lay masses. The only way out of this *impasse* was for the Hussites either to submit unconditionally to Rome or to secure a bishop and priesthood without reference to the Papal See, just as the Taborites had done already in 1420, and thus cut themselves off completely from the Church.

There is little doubt that the Czech Utraquists, aroused to indignation by the unflinching obstinacy of the Papacy in the matter of the confirmation of Rokycana as Archbishop of Prague, frequently inclined towards the second of these alternatives. An idea was cherished among them in particular that they might secure a bishop from Constantinople from the Eastern Church. In that Church the Hussites had long displayed considerable interest, having learnt, probably from Wyclif, that it had preserved intact many of the doctrines and rites of the primitive Church. In their religious disputations the Hussite theologians had more than once appealed to the example of the Eastern Church, calling it the daughter and disciple of the apostles, and the teacher of the Church of Rome, and they took particular pleasure in pointing out that it had preserved the administration of communion in both kinds. It was not till 1452, however, that the Hussites got into direct touch with the Eastern Church and opened actual negotiations. The intermediary in these negotiations was a mysterious doctor of theology, who had gone from Bohemia to Constantinople, had adopted the Orthodox faith, and went by the name of Constantine Anglicus. It is not impossible that under this name was concealed the well-known English Hussite, Peter Payne, who had left Bohemia for Constantinople some time after 1448. Certain it is that this Constantine Anglicus arrived early in 1452 in Bohemia, bringing with him a letter from the leading dignitaries of the Greek Church inviting the Czechs to join that Church and promising to provide them with clergy and bishops. The Hussite consistory accepted in principle this invitation, but when Constantine Anglicus returned to Constantinople with their reply, he found a changed situation there, unfavourable to union with the Hussite Czechs owing to the effort made by the Greek Emperor Constantine XI for union with Rome. The fall of Constantinople in May 1453 put an end once and for all to the attempt to bring about an *entente* or union between the Hussites and the Eastern Church, the success of which would in any case have been extremely problematical.

On the other hand, failure also attended the second effort, made at this time, to secure the return of the Czechs to the fold of the Church of Rome. The noisy and ostentatious tour of the bellicose Italian monk and preacher, Giovanni Capistrano, through Moravia and Bohemia in the years 1451–52 aroused a storm of resentment among the Utraquists, while it enhanced the anti-Hussite sentiments of the Czech Catholics, but it had no great effect otherwise. Failure likewise attended the diplomatic negotiations of the learned papal legate, Nicholas of Cusa, with the official delegates of the Hussite Czechs at Ratisbon and Vienna in June and November 1452.

Soon afterwards a change occurred in the question of the throne. A revolt of the Austrian Estates under Ulrich of Cilli had compelled the Emperor Frederick to hand over the youthful Ladislas to the Estates. Ulrich opened negotiations with the Czechs for the acknowledgment of Ladislas as king. George of Poděbrady offered no objection, but with the approval of the majority of the Estates demanded that Ladislas should ascend the throne not on the basis of hereditary right but on that of election by the Bohemian Estates, and that he should undertake to fulfil certain Czech demands. After lengthy negotiations Ladislas, at a personal meeting with George at Vienna in the spring of 1453, accepted these terms. He promised in particular to respect the Compacts and the additions to them signed by Sigismund, and to secure confirmation of Rokycana's appointment as archbishop from the Pope. At the same time he appointed George as governor of the kingdom for a further period of six years after the expiry of the two years for which he had originally been appointed by the Bohemian diet. In conformity with this agreement Ladislas took the oath as elected king in the presence of the Bohemian Estates on a frontier meadow at Jihlava on 19 October, and was crowned at Prague on 28 October. A minority recognised Ladislas' hereditary right, as did also all the minor provinces of the Bohemian Crown. The Moravian nobles, indeed, did not hesitate to do homage to Ladislas as their king by hereditary right even prior to his coronation in Bohemia (6 July 1453).

King Ladislas Posthumus stayed for more than a year after his coronation in Prague (until November 1454), continuing on friendly terms with George of Poděbrady. George, as governor, did not cease to direct the fortunes of the State during the king's residence at Prague and during his subsequent absence which lasted till the autumn of 1457. Supported by the legal powers of a properly recognised king, George was able to display very considerable activity. Although he devoted attention—and not without success—to a restoration and strengthening of the Czech influence in the minor provinces of the Bohemian Crown (especially in Silesia, whose ties with Bohemia had become very loose during the Hussite wars), it was to Bohemia itself that he gave most of his care. There, by energetic and systematic measures, he restored peace and order, and undid the evil effects of the Hussite upheavals on the legal, social, and economic conditions of the country.

The accession of Ladislas to the throne encouraged the party of communion in one kind to adopt a bolder attitude towards the official Hussite Church and its spiritual head, Archbishop Rokycana. In these conflicts George of Poděbrady observed an admirable moderation, and never ceased to make efforts for reconciliation with the universal Church. He was supported by Rokycana himself. When, in 1457, Calixtus III became Pope, it seemed as if this reconciliation would really be accomplished. The Pope was desirous of peace with the Czechs, and entered into direct correspondence with Rokycana, inviting him to go to Rome to discuss the matter. But before any substantial *rapprochement* could be attained, the young king died. He had arrived at the close of September 1457 in Prague, where his marriage with the French princess Magdalene was to take place; two months later (23 November) he fell a victim to the plague.

The death of Ladislas without an heir left the Bohemian throne vacant, for the hereditary claims of other members of the House of Habsburg, based on the old succession treaties made between the Czech Luxemburgs and the Austrian Habsburgs, were not recognised by the majority of the Bohemian Estates. Such claims, moreover, could hardly have been properly prosecuted in view of the family quarrels then rampant among the agnates of the house of Habsburg, to which the Emperor Frederick belonged. Serious hereditary claims were, however, advanced by William, Duke of Saxony, and by Casimir, King of Poland, as husbands of the sisters of Ladislas. A number of aspirants to the Bohemian crown with no hereditary claim whatsoever also came forward.

Of these latter the most serious was the native candidate, George of Poděbrady, who had the support not only of the Bohemian nobles of the Utraquist party but also of several influential members of the party of communion in one kind. George, who had immediately on the death of Ladislas been confirmed by the Bohemian diet in his office as governor, himself took steps towards his election, believing that it would give him an opportunity of completing the work he had begun of a general rehabilitation of his native land. The campaign for his election was conducted largely from the angle of Hussite ideas, but there was also a strong national sentiment behind it. When on 2 March 1458 the Bohemian diet, assembled in the great hall of the Old Town Hall at Prague, elected George, the Roman Catholic nobles being also among those who voted for him, the Czechs at last had a monarch who was united with them both in national consciousness and in religious beliefs—a king who was a Czech by birth and a Hussite.

The new king, who had thus mounted the Bohemian throne against so many other claimants, and who as a Hussite, even after the signing of the Compacts, could hardly expect his election to be unreservedly accepted by the leading authorities of Western Christendom, was naturally eager speedily to secure as wide a recognition as possible. He therefore took immediate steps for his coronation. Having no bishops in his own country able and willing to crown him according to the ancient ceremonial, he asked Matthias, King of Hungary, to lend him Hungarian bishops for the purpose. Matthias was under considerable obligations to George, to whose daughter Catherine he was betrothed, for George had released Matthias from prison where he had been flung by the late King Ladislas on the death of his father and elder brother, and had effectively supported his election as King of Hungary. Matthias could hardly therefore refuse the request, but an agreement with the Hungarian bishops as to the form of the coronation ceremonial proved no easy matter. The bishops demanded that the coronation oath should contain an abjuration of the Compacts, but to this George could not, of course, consent, unless he were to disavow the whole of his policy hitherto in ecclesiastical matters, which had been based primarily on the Compacts, and indeed his entire past. A way out of the dilemma was found by George and his consort taking a secret oath on the day before the coronation, to the effect that they would uphold obedience to the Papal See and in agreement with Rome lead their subjects away from all error. From a strict Catholic point of view it was possible to interpret this indefinite formula as a condemnation of the Compacts, but King George, who could not doubt their binding nature on both Bohemia and the Church and regarded them as truly Catholic, certainly did not understand his oath in that sense. And when on the day following the secret oath (7 May) he publicly pledged himself to preserve all the liberties of the land, this pledge applied also to the Compacts, which in the eyes of a majority of the Estates were the chief privilege of all. Later on (in 1461) the Bohemian Estates obtained from King George a written confirmation of the liberties of the land containing an express reference to the Compacts.

Even after the coronation ceremony George was not acknowledged king throughout the entire territory of the Bohemian State, for the unity which had been shaken by the Hussite upheavals had not yet been completely restored. In Bohemia itself there was no serious opposition to him, but in Moravia the four leading German and Catholic towns—Brno (Brünn), Olomouc (Olmütz), Jihlava (Iglau), and Znojmo (Znaim)—rose against him, and were encouraged by the more extensive and resolute opposition against George that was fomented in Silesia by the people of Breslau, the sworn enemies of the Czech Hussites and the former governor of Bohemia. It took George several months to break down the opposition of the German and Catholic elements in the territories of the Bohemian Crown, an opposition born of religious and national distaste for Czech Hussitism. By the close of 1458 the whole of Moravia had submitted to him, and in the year 1459 he received the homage of the entire population of Upper Lusatia and Silesia with the exception of Breslau, which only after the energetic intervention of the Papacy in 1460 submitted to George, with the reservation that not until the lapse of another three years should it do homage to him as "lawful and undoubted Catholic and Christian King of Bohemia."

Previous to this George had been formally recognised as King of Bohemia by the Emperor Frederick III, who, needing George's help both in Austria and in Hungary, invested him personally at Brno on 31 July 1459 with the regalia. The recognition of King George by the Papacy proved a more difficult matter. Pope Calixtus III, who expected much of him both in respect of peace with the Czechs and of the struggle against the Turks, had shewn a readiness to recognise George without making difficulties, but he died before he could do so. His successor was Cardinal Aeneas Sylvius, who as legate had become well acquainted at first hand with conditions in Hussite Bohemia, and who had then re-commended the Papacy to come to terms with George and Rokycana, but who now, as Pius II, was very reserved in granting recognition. He supported George, it is true, in his conflict with Breslau, but he did so in the belief that George would not only help the Papacy to carry out its great plans against the Turks but would also settle the dispute with the Czechs to the satisfaction of the Church. Like his predecessors, Pius II deceived himself in imagining that King George could or would abjure the Compacts in order to make complete reconciliation with the Church possible. George himself realised the danger of a conflict with the Papacy on this point. He therefore endeavoured to consolidate his international position. This was also the object of a plan put forward on the initiative of the famous German jurist and diplomat, Martin Mair, to make George King of the Romans, as a partner of the Emperor Frederick, and to enable him as the actual ruler of the Empire to carry out the urgent reforms needed in its administration. Although for this plan, which was broached in the year 1459, George succeeded in 1461 in gaining the support of several of the leading German princes, the scheme was finally frustrated by the opposition of others besides that of the Emperor himself. George's power and the esteem in which he was held in the Empire were, however, soon afterwards demonstrated when his military and diplomatic intervention compelled the quarrelling German princes to make a truce (November 1461).

It was doubtless in order to convince both the Papacy and his German allies of his determination not to suffer within his territories any heresies inconsistent with the Compacts that as early as 1461 George took decisive steps against a new religious body that had arisen—the Unity of the Brotherhood. But he did not escape conflict with the Papacy. At the beginning of 1462, and with the approval of the Estates, George finally dispatched an embassy to Rome to tender to Pope Pius II the customary pledge of obedience, and to urge a final confirmation of the Compacts. At the end of several days, during which eloquent but vain appeals had been made to the Czech envoys to abandon the Compacts and to come to terms unconditionally with the Church, the Pope, in solemn consistory, gave the Czech envoys a flat refusal. He declared that he could not accept the obedience of King George until the king had eradicated all error from his kingdom, that he forbade the common people to receive communion in both kinds, and that he revoked the Compacts. If the Pope imagined that he would succeed in getting his decision obeyed in Bohemia, he deceived himself most completely. At an assembly of all the Estates held in August at Prague, King George replied to the Pope's challenge with the firm declaration that he and his whole family would stake not only their worldly possessions but also their lives for the Cup. And when the papal envoy, Fantino della Valle, began to accuse all those who partook of communion in both kinds of heresy, and to reproach the king with violating his coronation oath, George had him thrown into prison.

At this time considerable importance attached to a bold plan which had previously been broached to the king by the French diplomat, Antoine Marini, who had been some years in his service, representing him, among other things, at the papal Court. This scheme envisaged a union of Christian States or princes, the main object of which was to be the defence of Christendom against the Turks, and the members of which were to undertake to settle all disputes among themselves by a special court of their own, a so-called "parliament." George now endeavoured to realise this scheme without regard to the Papacy. He wished the French king as the head of this union to become, as it were, the political head of the Christian world, and it was his intention that the question of the

Bohemian Church should be brought before the "parliament." That question, in view of the defensive struggle against the Turks which was the main purpose of the union, was of no small political importance. All efforts to put this plan into effect, opposed as it was in multifarious ways by the papal diplomacy, proved vain. George merely succeeded in negotiating friendly treaties with a number of rulers, particularly with Casimir of Poland, with the French king, Louis XI, and with several of the German princes. He even secured the adherence of the Emperor Frederick by military aid in October 1462, which freed him from a difficult situation in Austria into which he had been forced by his enemies.

The favourable international position of the King of Bohemia restrained, it is true, the Papacy from decided action against him, but the Pope succeeded in causing a number of his subjects to revolt by absolving them from their allegiance to the king. In 1462 he declared George's compact with the people of Breslau, made in 1460, to be invalid, and in the spring of 1463 took Breslau under his own protection. In June 1464 he even summoned King George to appear before his Court on a charge of heresy, but he himself died two months later.

Even after the death of Pius II, the Papacy secured increasing support from the king's own subjects. These were mainly the Czech nobles of the party of communion in one kind, who were dissatisfied with the government of King George not only for religious reasons but also because the monarch, unduly disregarding, as they imagined, their own voice in the country's affairs, looked for support more particularly to the lower orders, the knights and the towns. In the autumn of 1465 these nobles formed a league, that of Zelená Hora (Grünberg), with the object, they said, of defending the liberties of the country; and, influenced by conditions beyond the frontier, open hostilities broke out between the league and the king.

In the meantime the Papacy continued its hostility, and in August 1465 George was again summoned to appear before the papal Court. He defended himself by a diplomatic manoeuvre, directed at first by the well-known Martin Mair and later by the famous German jurist, politician, and humanist, Gregory of Heimburg. The aim was to call together a congress at which the Emperor and other princes should, with the object of maintaining order in their own lands, endeavour to bring about a peaceful settlement of the Czech dispute. At the same time it was designed to win over the individual princes to the Czech point of view. This plan was not, it is true, successful, but it at any rate resulted in public opinion, especially in the Empire, not allowing itself to be drawn into sharp hostility to the Bohemian king, nor did a single German prince let himself become an instrument of the Papacy for his punishment. When the Church of Rome in December 1466 declared George guilty of confirmed heresy, deprived him of his royal dignity, and freed his subjects from their oaths of allegiance, it did not yet know who would assist it in the execution of this fateful judgment. King George, of course, did not submit. In April 1467 he announced that he would appeal to the Papacy, and, should the Pope not receive the appeal, to a General Council. At the same time he dealt with the hostile League of Zelená Hora. Although the Catholic nobles of Moravia and the other lands of the Bohemian Crown had joined this league *en masse*, King George kept the upper hand over them. He would doubtless ere long have entirely crushed their resistance had they not succeeded in finding in the spring of 1468 a powerful foreign ally in the person of the Hungarian king, Matthias, whose friendly relations with King George had much cooled, particularly since the death of Matthias' first wife, George's daughter, in February 1464. Matthias allowed ambition to seduce him into becoming the agent to execute the judgment of the papal Court upon the Bohemian king[1]. In the wars against Matthias and his Bohemian allies King George suffered severe losses in the very first year in Moravia. When, however, Matthias invaded Bohemia at the beginning of 1469, hoping not only to seize the Bohemian crown but also, with the aid of the Emperor Frederick, the Roman crown, he and all his army were entrapped. From this inglorious position he was liberated on terms negotiated at a personal meeting with King George (27 February 1469). Matthias solemnly promised to bring about a reconciliation with the Pope on the basis of the Compacts, if only the Czechs would render obedience to the Apostolic See on that footing. George, on the other hand, agreed to support Matthias' candidature for the Roman crown. This compact, however, failed to produce the expected reconciliation. While he was negotiating with George, who believed in the uprightness of Matthias' efforts to bring about a reconciliation between the Czechs and the Church, Matthias exerted secret pressure upon the Zelená Hora league of nobles to cause them to offer the crown of Bohemia to himself. Thus, less than three months after the compact with George, Matthias was elected King of Bohemia by George's enemies (3 May 1469). War, of course, broke out anew, and clashes occurred without any decisive success being achieved by either side.

King George and his supporters met Matthias' efforts by diplomatic moves among the neighbouring princes. Of these the most important were their negotiations with King Casimir of Poland with a view to his son Vladislav succeeding George on the throne of Bohemia. In earlier years George had entertained the idea of preserving the succession to the throne in his own family, and had endeavoured to get the Bohemian Estates to accept or elect his elder son Victorin as king during his own lifetime. The external and internal difficulties, however, which he encountered in his great conflict with the Papacy compelled him to abandon this design. In the course of his wars with Matthias of Hungary he decided to offer the crown of Bohemia to the son of the Polish king. This offer, made by a vote of the Bohemian diet in June 1469, was conveyed by a special

---

[1] Cf. for these events *infra*, Chapter xix.

Czech embassy sent to Poland to wait upon Casimir with the request that both he and his son should endeavour to bring about a reconciliation between all the Utraquists and the Pope, and that the Crown Prince Vladislav should take the youngest daughter of King George to wife. The fulfilment of this latter request encountered great opposition, since the Polish queen and her advisers were horrified at the thought that her son should take to wife the daughter of heretic parents. The negotiations were therefore prolonged, but Casimir shewed his agreement in principle with the Czech offer by supporting the Czechs against Matthias.

The position of King George was improved also by the circumstance that opposition to Matthias arose not only in Hungary, where much resentment was felt that the monarch neglected the defence of the country against the Turks while finding time for military enterprises in the West, but also among his allies and supporters in the West, who abandoned him because of his lack of success in the long and costly struggle. In Bohemia the league of nobles supporting Matthias had been weakened by the secession of several of its members and the vacillation of its leaders. In Silesia, which had suffered not only from Czech inroads but also from the harshness of Matthias' government, a distaste for further fighting had likewise gained ground. Again, among the German neighbours of the Bohemian king there was a distinct desire for a settlement of the Bohemian question. In these circumstances Matthias himself attempted in the winter of 1470–71 to arrive at a direct understanding with George: George was to remain King of Bohemia as long as he lived and then be succeeded by Matthias who, in the meantime, was to rule over the subsidiary territories of the Bohemian Crown and, of course, to endeavour to secure the favour of the Pope for the Utraquists and a confirmation of the Compacts of Basle. As at the same time sentiment at the imperial Court as well as at Rome itself had taken a turn in favour of the Bohemian king, hopes rose high that a happy conclusion of the great struggle was at hand. But the king, who had been ailing for some years past, died suddenly on 21 March 1471 at the age of fifty-one, and his death put an end to all these hopes.

In George of Poděbrady Bohemia lost one of her greatest rulers. Since the extinction of the Přemyslid dynasty he was the first and last king of native birth, sprung from Czech soil and brought up in intimate touch with the life of the Czech nation. In learning he was not to be compared with his great predecessor, Charles IV, or with many princes, especially in Italy, of his own day. He knew no Latin, and but little German. But in natural gifts, in his talents as a ruler and in his skill as a diplomatist, he surpassed most of the crowned heads who were his contemporaries. The period during which he was at the head of his country, first as governor and afterwards as king, was for Bohemia a breathing space after the stormy years of the Hussite upheavals. His strength and energy as a ruler restored peace and order to the land, softening the passions of the political and religious parties, and suppressing the seditious intrigues of individuals and social groups. He succeeded in reviving the respect for the royal power in the minor provinces of the Bohemian Crown and thus consolidating the shattered unity of the Czech State. The serious religious struggles in the Czech lands did not, it is true, cease even under his rule, but George overcame countless difficulties arising therefrom by his resolute defence of existing legal order. The firm basis of that order he saw in the Compacts of Basle, which by ratification in the diet had become part of the law of the land, and he was therefore inflexible in their defence. He preserved a strict impartiality towards both the great religious parties recognised by the Compacts, but he mercilessly suppressed all divergences from the Compacts, whether on the part of the Taborites or the Unity of the Brotherhood. Although there was within him none of that sacred passion for the Hussite cause which had inspired the Czech warriors of God in the preceding era, he had nevertheless been reared in so Hussite an atmosphere that it proved impossible to induce him to purchase the religious unity of the Czech State and its reconciliation with the Church by any surrender of the fundamental principles of Hussitism or a denial of the great Hussite past. On the contrary, he assisted his nation to defend, in face of practically the whole world, the spiritual and moral heritage of the Hussite movement— a movement which, though it had not made the life of the nation more comfortable or easy, was certainly richer in content and more characteristic than the life of the majority of nations of that day.

In his championship of this heritage, moreover, King George served the common weal. Proceeding in the direction indicated by Hus, he made a path for the moral and intellectual liberation of humanity from the heavy fetters of medieval Church authority, he accustomed the world of his day to toleration in matters ecclesiastical, and he taught his contemporaries to distinguish between religion and politics. From this point of view, the friendly relations existing between numerous princes who were good Catholics and the heretic King of Bohemia, subject as he was to papal excommunication, have almost revolutionary significance. The same may be affirmed of the faithful devotion of many Catholic subjects to King George, whom they refused to abandon even at the direct command of the Papacy, for they desired, as one of them put it, "that spiritual and secular matters should not be confused with one another," that they should not be compelled to abandon their king under the pretext of owing obedience to the Pope "in matters touching secular government and administration." The reign of King George thus paved the way, possibly involuntarily rather than consciously, for the modern view of the relations between Church and State. Far ahead of his own day also were his efforts to bring about a union of Christian States not unlike the present-day League of Nations. The idea of this union did not originate in George's own brain, but it acquired historical significance through the fact that he took it up and placed his diplomatic talents and his international prestige at its service. In this he displayed more than ordinary intellectual and moral courage, rare political foresight, and true statesmanship. To carry this bold scheme into effect was not vouchsafed him, and in the end not all the statesmanship which had won him so many triumphs was able to save his country from fresh struggles calculated to menace once again the integrity of the Czech State.

Meanwhile internal, and especially ecclesiastical, conditions in the lands of the Bohemian Crown had undergone many changes. Even after the signing of the Compacts the Hussite Czechs failed to unite with the Church of Rome, and all subsequent efforts on the part of Rome to bring them once more within the bosom of the Church proved in vain. On the death of King George and of Archbishop Rokycana, the Hussites, the majority of the Czech nation, were as remote from the universal Church as they had been in 1436, possibly even more remote, especially as the moderate Hussite party had become practically extinct. The Taborites, who from the beginning had broken completely with Rome, had been exterminated in the year 1452, but shortly afterwards a new religious body, not less radical in its attitude towards the universal Church, began to appear—the Unity of the Brotherhood, whose spiritual father was the original thinker and philosopher, Peter Chelčický. At the very outset of its career the Unity met with sharp opposition from King George. He saw in it a serious obstacle to his Church policy, which was based on the Compacts, and he caused its adherents to be persecuted. Despite this the Unity instituted in the year 1467 its own order of priesthood without reference to the Church of Rome, and constituted itself as a wholly independent Church. It thus became the first reformed Church which consciously and expressly renounced the Catholic principle of the apostolic succession and created its own priesthood by independent election. At the outset it was a comparatively small association of simple people faithfully embodying the ideal which Chelčický had outlined in his writings, conducting themselves in his spirit strictly according to the pure Word of Christ, disdaining the world, and patiently suffering every kind of enmity. By the institution of its own order of priesthood the Brotherhood broke away not merely from the Church of Rome but also from the Utraquists, and the Brethren were suppressed as disturbers of Utraquist unity by Rokycana as well. It was not until later, however, that the Unity of the Brotherhood became an important factor not merely in the religious life but also in the political and intellectual development of the nation.

In these circumstances, even after the signing of the Compacts, it was impossible for new vital currents to mark the life of the party of communion in one kind. The ecclesiastical government of this party was in the hands of the Prague Chapter and of administrators elected by it or nominated by the Pope from the ranks of the Chapter. In the year 1448 the Chapter had fled to Plzeň, but five years later, when the young

Ladislas was accepted as future king, it returned to Prague. Having its seat on the Castle Hill, it was known as the upper consistory in contradistinction to the nether consistory, that of the Hussites, which had its seat in the town below. The upper consistory, during the closing years of the reign of King George, when the bellicose Hilarius of Litoměřice was at its head as administrator, took a very active and important part in the religious disputes in Bohemia. Hilarius, who had been brought up in a Utraquist atmosphere, had spent a considerable time in Italy, whither he had been sent by Rokycana to secure ordination and a higher university training, and there he had cast off the Hussite faith of his youth and become one of its bitterest foes.

The Hussite wars exercised, as we have already seen, a profound influence upon the relations between the royal power and the power of the Bohemian Estates. The great authority which during these wars the Estates had secured for themselves at the expense of the kingship could not indeed be maintained when the land once more possessed its properly recognised rulers, but as these rulers rapidly changed and as more than one interregnum intervened, the monarchy could not be restored to its former status. It was again a drawback to the most distinguished monarch of this period, George of Poděbrady, that as one of the native nobility he could not appeal to the prestige of his race, and that a considerable and powerful section of the Bohemian nobles, who were opposed to him on religious grounds, could ally themselves against him with strong foreign powers, in particular with the Roman Curia. In 1467 the legal relations between the king and the Estates were indeed fixed by a royal rescript on more or less the lines obtaining at the close of the pre-Hussite period, but before long open conflict between the king and the nobles adhering to communion in one kind broke out once more, culminating in 1469 in the election of Matthias of Hungary.

On the social organism of the Czech nation the Hussite wars left a deep impress, since bands of soldiers to whom warfare had become a profession were to be found throughout the country. These bands, which included not only natives of the country but also numerous soldiers of fortune who had come from abroad, never ceased to be a menace to the peaceful inhabitants. Sigismund, after his recognition as King of Bohemia, recruited Czech companies for the wars against the Turks, and his example was followed by his successor Albert. Thus there arose in Hungary, and particularly in Slovakia, where Hussite troops had already made frequent and lengthy inroads, permanent garrisons composed of Czechs which there became the main support of the Habsburg power. Soon after 1440 the famous Czech general, Jan Jiskra of Brandýs, who had been appointed the supreme *hetman* of the Habsburgs in Upper Hungary—the present-day Slovakia—founded a small realm of his own, and defended it against all comers. With a mercenary army, composed for the most part of Hussite warriors, Jiskra, who was probably himself a Catholic, occupied the major part of Slovakia, and, in alliance with him, other Czech leaders with their troops fought in Slovakia in the service of King Ladislas. Jiskra's dominion in Slovakia did not come to an end even when John Hunyadi, whom he refused to acknowledge, became Regent of Hungary. His power, however, gradually declined, and in 1462 he was persuaded by King Matthias to disband his armies. Many Czech mercenaries continued long afterwards to fight in the service of Matthias, whose famous "Black Brigade" was composed almost exclusively of Czechs from Bohemia and Moravia and of Serbs. Czech veterans, noted for their valour, were sought also by other countries, notably Germany, Poland, and Prussia. There was scarcely a war in Central or Eastern Europe in which Czechs did not take part, often on both sides, as officers and private soldiers.

In other ways, too, the Hussite wars affected the social structure of the Czech nation. The complete overthrow of the secular dominion of the clergy, the advance in the economic position not only of the higher nobility but also of the knights, gentry, and burgesses, and the increased import-ance of these latter classes in public affairs—these were long-lasting results of the wars. In the royal towns, which never ceased to be important factors in public life and, especially in the reign of King George, a powerful support for the royal power, there was a definite growth of municipal self-government. The position of the villeins and unfree peasants on the land, who had suffered severely from the Hussite wars, deteriorated still further on their conclusion. Although here and there a reduction of dues and labour services had been secured, in the great majority of cases these services were increased after the Hussite wars in multifarious ways. The Hussite wars likewise paved the way for an increased dependence of the serfs upon their masters and a further limitation of their personal freedom. They not only caused a decline in population but they turned large numbers of the peasantry away from work on the land to take up arms as a profession. In order to remedy this state of affairs, which was certainly having a disastrous effect upon the economic life of the country, measures were adopted with the object of preventing the migration of peasants from place to place, to check their flight from estates which were lying fallow, and to bind them to the soil so that they should cultivate it properly and regularly and, of course, render the appropriate dues from it to the landlords. Thus, already in the Poděbrady era the foundation was laid for a legal restriction of the personal liberty of the peasants, and this process was later continued.

From a national and racial point of view the Poděbrady era saw the triumph of the Czech element in the public life of Bohemia, when the governor, and later the king, was a man of Czech birth. The Czech language was used in all the proceedings of the diets, the departments of government, and the courts of justice, in the provincial, municipal, and district offices; and all public documents were issued in that tongue. At the same time there was a purity and strength, a conciseness and clarity about the language which it had never before attained and which it never afterwards possessed.

The great expansion of the Czech language was accompanied by an immense growth of a Czech national consciousness, which sometimes took a deeply passionate form. It was tinged with sharp opposition to the Germans, whom the Hussite Czechs regarded as dangerous enemies not merely of the Word of God but also of their native tongue. Remembering the periods previous to the Hussite wars, when the Germans in Bohemia predominated and held sway in practically all the royal towns, frequently enjoying a privileged position there, the Czechs rejected German candidates for the Bohemian crown and opposed all tendencies to increase the German element in Bohemia. At the same time there was observable among them a strong consciousness of close affinity with the neighbouring Slav nations, especially with the Poles. Despite the divergence of religious belief, the political and cultural relations between the Czechs and Poles were close. Again, King George, surrendering for his sons all hereditary rights to the Bohemian throne in favour of the royal house of Poland, was instrumental in causing the Bohemian throne to be occupied, after his own death, by one of its members.

Now, just as in the preceding period, the religious interest continued to be the most powerful element in the intellectual life of the Czech nation, an element permeating and dominating the nation, so that only slightly, and by degrees, did other elements find a place there. The direction and the nature of this interest, as determined by the religious struggles of the past, underwent but little change during this period, except for the fact that just at the close a current wholly hostile to the Hussite past was more plainly observable in contrast to the absolute predominance of Hussite sentiment heretofore. In the early years following the Hussite wars there is to be seen a continuation, and not infrequently a culmination, of the literary activity of a number of Czech Hussite writers which had its beginnings in the first epoch of the Hussite movement. The outstanding figure among these writers is Peter Chelčický, who in the early forties wrote his maturest and best known work, *The Shield of Faith*; this gives a most complete and systematic synthesis of his views and is justly esteemed as one of the most beautiful and memorable outpourings of the Czech mind and spirit. Master Jan Rokycana, for almost the whole of this period the supreme head of the Utraquist Church, left some notable works including in particular an excellent collection of Czech sermons. Besides these adherents of Hussitism there appears in Czech theological literature at the close of the Poděbrady period a firm opponent of the Hussite tradition, the bellicose defender of the doctrines of Rome, the priest Hilarius of Litoměřice (*ob.* 1468), who wrote slashing attacks in Latin and Czech on his Hussite opponents.

Humanism, early indications of which appeared in Bohemia in the reign of Charles IV, was completely suppressed by the Hussite wars but began to shew itself once more in Bohemia in the reign of King George, finding adherents especially among the nobility and the higher ranks of the clergy of the party of communion in one kind. A powerful impulse came to it from the fact that the Italian humanist, Aeneas Sylvius, was moved by the striking story of the Hussite movement to write his *Historia Bohemiae,* in which he gave a magnificent, albeit biased and classically draped, picture of the Bohemian past and especially the stirring struggle of the Czech nation against the Church of Rome. This work, which appeared in 1458 and was only at a later date translated into Czech, had, even at a time when the majority of the people were Hussite in sentiment, a strong influence upon the nation's conception of its own past. At the same time the work displayed, despite its dislike of Hussitism, a vivid sense of its historical significance, and spread a knowledge of the Czechs in the civilised world of the time.

Taken as a whole, the Czech literature of this period, rich and varied in no small measure, bears witness, like other features of Czech national culture of the day, to a growing endeavour to renew the broken links with the West, without however sacrificing the great ideals of the first Hussite epoch. The first fruits of this endeavour appear in the reign of King George, and as the effort grew subsequently more intense it achieved, at least in several departments, no mean success.

It was clear on King George's death that the choice of a successor would lie between two candidates only—Matthias of Hungary, and the Polish crown prince. Of these two, Matthias had even in the lifetime of George been chosen as king by George's opponents, and held the subsidiary territories of the Bohemian Crown already in his power. An obstacle to his universal acceptance as Bohemian king, to which even some of the former supporters of George were ready to assent, existed on the one hand in the fact that he insisted upon the validity of his previous election and declined to submit to a new one, and on the other hand in the negotiations which had begun while King George was alive for the candidature of Crown Prince Vladislav. At a diet, convoked in May 1471 at Kutná Hora, Vladislav II, then just fifteen years of age, was unanimously elected king (27 May). Although the close kinship of the Polish and Czech nations was not lost sight of, and there was even broached a scheme of a great Slavonic Jagiellonid empire to include Czechs, Poles, Lithuanians, and Russians, the main aim of the Bohemian Estates—a vain one as it turned out—was to ensure Polish aid in obtaining a satisfactory solution for the great conflict between the Czechs and the Church.

Matthias insisted on the validity of his previous election, which was finally confirmed by the Pope on the day following the election of Vladislav, so that there were now two rival Kings of Bohemia. Poland joined the struggle not only because one of the combatants was a Pole, but also because a strong Hungarian party opposed to Matthias had offered the Hungarian crown to the Jagiellonids, who were inclined to accept it. But Polish assistance failed to supply Vladislav with the reinforcements necessary for a speedy and successful settlement. In the spring of 1472 a truce for one year, which was subsequently prolonged, was concluded at Buda between the Czechs, Poles, and Hungarians.

Matthias' position was at this juncture strengthened by the fact that the Papacy was definitely on his side. The new Pope, Sixtus IV, not only renewed the recognition of Matthias as King of Bohemia, but also empowered his legate to pronounce excommunication against Casimir, Vladislav, and their adherents. This did not decide the struggle, nor did various conferences between the contending parties convoked in hope of a settlement lead at first to the desired goal.

As, at the same time, little success attended the Czecho-Polish military operations against Matthias, the belief gained ground in Bohemia that the conflict could be settled by a temporary division of the territories of the Bohemian Crown between the two rivals. Negotiations were opened at the Bohemian diet as early as 1475, but it was not until 1478 that an agreement was secured. Matthias received not only Moravia but also the whole of Silesia and the two Lusatias, so that Vladislav had to content himself with Bohemia only for the term of his life. It was agreed that, should Matthias die first, all these territories were to go to Vladislav on payment of a sum of 400,000 florins as compensation for Matthias' heirs. Should Vladislav predecease Matthias leaving no heir and Matthias or his successor be chosen King of Bohemia, the minor provinces were to be united with the Bohemian Crown without any payment. Vladislav subscribed to this arrangement without hesitation, but Matthias accepted it only after some delay and with the important addition that he should retain the title of King of Bohemia. The peace of Olomouc on 7 December 1478 divided the lands of the Bohemian Crown between two rulers, each of whom ruled over his own territories as King of Bohemia, a great menace to the unity of the Czech State and nation, although the treaty ensured the reunion of all the Bohemian lands under the rule of a single monarch.

The efficacy of these provisions was, it is true, not a little dubious. The sum which Vladislav was to pay to recover the whole on Matthias' death was so huge that it was doubtful whether it could be fully paid. Moreover, it soon became apparent that Matthias was designing to secure the succession to his vast dominions for his illegitimate son John Corvinus. The premature death of Matthias, however, who died on 6 April 1490, changed the situation at a stroke. Vladislav obtained his ambition, without paying any indemnity, by being elected at Buda on 11 July 1490 to succeed Matthias on the throne of Hungary. The Hungarian Estates, it is true, thought that the minor provinces of the Bohemian Crown should remain attached to the Hungarian Crown until payment of the indemnity, and as that was never paid, the dispute concerning it continued to the close of the rule of the Jagiellonid dynasty in Bohemia. This, however, did not seriously affect the actual unity which the tradition of their historical evolution hitherto had created among the Bohemian lands, and which, in the case of Bohemia and Moravia, was based on the common racial and religious consciousness of the great majority of their inhabitants. The year 1490 thus saw the removal of all danger of a dissolution of the Czech State.

The religious danger, however, still continued. Immediately on his election Vladislav gave an undertaking to the Bohemian Estates that he would defend Bohemia in preserving the Compacts according to the rescripts of his predecessors, and would enter into negotiations with the Pope for their confirmation, and for the appointment of an archbishop who would observe the Compacts in their original form and according to the rescripts of the kings from Sigismund to George. As he had not been recognised as King of Bohemia by the Papacy, in whose eyes Matthias was the rightful king, Vladislav could not at the outset shew hostility to the Utraquist party, though his religious convictions made him by no means well disposed to them. None the less it would seem that even in the early years of his reign the party of communion in one kind adopted a bolder front against the Hussites.

The Olomouc settlement of 1478 also gave them a further advantage. Having been acknowledged under the terms of that settlement as king by the party of communion in one kind which had previously supported Matthias, Vladislav henceforth shewed greater indulgence and favour to that party, and began to display hostility to the Utraquists. The Prague Chapter returned from its exile at Plzeň, which had lasted since 1467, and in conjunction with the monastic Orders set about turning the people from allegiance to the Cup. Still more high-handed was the conduct of some of the nobles of the party. Although, according to previous agreements, the churches throughout the country had been permanently distributed between the two parties without regard to the religious persuasions of the nobles who held the patronage, many nobles of the party of communion in one kind began to deprive the Utraquist party of churches in their patronage, drove out the Utraquist priests, and replaced them by priests of their own persuasion.

All this aroused a storm of indignation among those who stood faithfully by the Cup, and at Prague in particular the tension between the two parties increased to such a pitch that riots and affrays again occurred. The opponents of the Cup also multiplied the difficulties which the Utraquists encountered in getting their clergy ordained. In 1482, however, the Utraquists succeeded in persuading an Italian bishop, Augustine Sanctorius, to settle in Bohemia, and to perform for them the episcopal functions for which their own Hussite "administrator" was not qualified. Thus the Utraquist party was, at least for the time being, relieved of the irksome lack of priests, and of the humiliating necessity of sending

Hussite scholars to Italy, there to beg for ordination from one of the local bishops. Bishop Augustine's sojourn in Bohemia minimised the menace of a complete split between the Hussites and the Church of Rome, but it in no way encouraged their union with the Church. Since it was done without the knowledge of the papal Curia and against its wishes, it was rather a fresh manifestation of Hussite defiance of Rome. The fact, moreover, that a foreign bishop had not hesitated to come to Bohemia, to enter into the service of the Utraquist party and recognise them as of the true faith, filled the Czech adherents of the Cup with exultation and strengthened their resolve to abide inflexibly by the Cup and the Compacts, and to defend themselves not only against the party of communion in one kind but also against the king himself.

For a complete reconciliation with the Church of Rome, which it would have been necessary to purchase at the price of abandoning the Cup and the Compacts, there existed at this time scarcely any more readiness than there had been formerly in the reigns of Sigismund and George. In fact, the aggressive conduct of the party of communion in one kind had provoked increased opposition among the Hussite masses. How great the tension was, especially at Prague, between the adherents of the two parties was shewn by the great disorders which broke out in the year 1483. The result of these disorders was that all the three municipal bodies of Prague formed a league in 1483, in which they undertook to maintain the partaking of communion in both kinds by both adults and children, the singing of hymns in the Czech tongue, and other rights based on the Scriptures, and at the same time to insist that all who desired to dwell among them should be of their belief. Appealing to the rescript of King Sigismund and to earlier documents, they forbade anyone openly or secretly within the precincts of Prague to administer communion in one kind, or to preach that there was the same measure of grace and benefit in communion in one kind as in both, or to accuse those who adhered to the Cup of heresy. All the monks and priests who were opposed to communion in both kinds, as well as those inhabitants who had of recent times seceded from the Cup, or gone over to the "Picards," that is, the Brotherhood, were at once expelled from the city. Only foreign merchants, traders, and artisans were left full liberty, provided they did not calumniate those who communicated in both kinds.

The disorders of the year 1483 and this document, which was designed to be a kind of fundamental law of the Prague communities for all time, swept away at one stroke all the advantages which Catholicism had gained in the capital by royal favour since the death of King George. Prague became once more—not merely owing to the sentiments of the vast majority of its inhabitants but also in its administration—radically a Hussite city in which the Catholic element was thrust completely into the background. In vain did the king attempt to constrain the authorities at Prague to go back on their agreement. All he could accomplish was to secure a free return to Prague for the monks and priests who had been expelled, but otherwise he was compelled to acknowledge the document of 1483. In this dispute with the king Prague was effectively supported by the Utraquist nobles. Their firm stand in defence of the Cup and the Compacts finally compelled the party of communion in one kind to yield ground. This enabled the two parties to come to an agreement in the memorable Treaty of Kutná Hora, concluded early in 1485 at a diet held there. Under the terms of this treaty the two parties undertook for a period of thirty-two years to observe the Compacts and the agreements with Sigismund regarding them, as well as the recent decision of the diet concerning parish churches, which provided that each party's rites should be maintained in their respective parishes, and that all persons should be able freely to receive communion in one kind, or in both kinds, as they wished. The party of communion in one kind thus abandoned, at least for the time being, their opposition to the Compacts as well as their standpoint that no decision on these points could be made without the sanction of the Pope. It was only because the Bohemian Estates adhering to communion in one kind, constrained by the actual strength of the Utraquists, ceased to consider themselves bound by the unyielding attitude of the Papacy and acted without its assent, that the Treaty of Kutná Hora was possible. The revolution produced in Prague by the events of 1483 long checked all attempts to undermine the predominance of the Utraquists in the capital—attempts which, had they succeeded, would have dealt a grievous blow at Hussitism throughout the whole country—and now, by the Treaty of Kutná Hora, peace was maintained for three decades between the two religious parties, each of which was guaranteed its existing position. The adherents of both parties, moreover, the villeins not excepted, were secured the right to be subject only to their own Church organisation and customs. At Prague, however, the liberties of the party of communion in one kind were seriously restricted by the agreement of the three Prague communities of the year 1483, which refused burgess rights to its adherents. Nevertheless, soon after 1483, the number of burgesses adhering to the party of communion in one kind shewed an increase, and a few years later the first monks again appeared in Prague. In 1496 an agreement between the king and the Prague authorities enabled the monks to return to their monasteries on condition that they did not accuse the Utraquists of heresy or carry the host from house to house.

Thus, although the Treaty of Kutná Hora was followed by a greater measure of toleration on the part of the Utraquists towards the adherents of communion in one kind, they shewed no willingness to surrender the Compacts or any of the points in their ecclesiastical organisation or customs which were an obstacle to unity between the Czech Hussites and the universal Church. Nor were the Hussites able to avoid friction with their Italian bishop, Augustine. The stern Hussite masters found him lacking in industry as a preacher of the Word of God, and censured his somewhat lax morals, his mendacity and profanity, and the avarice which they saw in the "simony" he had introduced into the Utraquist party, the unaccustomed fees, fines, and the like which he had taken. The tension between the bishop and the Hussite consistory increased so much that the bishop left Prague and went to Kutná Hora, where he died in 1493, almost completely alienated from the consistory. Left once more without a bishop to ordain their clergy, the Utraquists attempted several times in the following years to obtain a confirmation of the Compacts from the Papacy, but never with success. The Czech Hussites remained cut off from the universal Church until such time as Bohemia, under the influence of Luther's revolt against Rome, entered upon a path that led to a complete break with the Church.

In the meantime there was a steady increase in the religious society which had split off from the Utraquist party and had also severed itself from the universal Church, the Unity of the Brotherhood. After the deaths of King George and Rokycana, the Unity continued to be persecuted by the Utraquists, who naturally wished to check the spread of a new sect within their ranks. Nevertheless, the Unity early won powerful patrons, not only among the nobles but also among the clergy and the masters of the Utraquists. The rapid growth of the Unity in Bohemia and Moravia was facilitated by a notable revolution which had taken place within the body itself. Abandoning the strict principles of its founder, which involved an absolute rejection of all secular things, the Unity accommodated itself to the requirements of actual life, and permitted its members to participate in worldly affairs by occupying all kinds of offices. This made it much easier for adherents to join it from among the wealthier and more intelligent classes of the nation, and the number of its members taken from the nobility and the ranks of the more cultured increased. Before the century closed, the leadership of the Unity, whose congregations in Bohemia alone were then estimated at between 300 and 400, had passed into the hands of these " learned " members.

The entire era of the Jagiellonid sway over the lands of the Bohemian Crown was filled not only with religious conflicts but also with a continuous struggle for power between the king and the Estates on the one hand, and among the Estates themselves on the other. The long struggle for the Bohemian crown between King Vladislav and Matthias of Hungary, and the subsequent division of the Bohemian lands until Matthias' death in 1490, were not calculated to augment the royal power, nor was the weak and undecided character of Vladislav. While the two upper Estates consolidated and increased their power as against that of the monarch, they attempted to limit the rights of the burgesses. The latter, though not represented in any of the supreme offices or courts of the land or in the king's council, yet had a third voice in the diets, and the right to participate as an Estate in public affairs. As early as 1479, however, the suggestion was made to deprive the burgesses of this right, and in 1485 King Vladislav himself declared that the burgesses as an Estate had no right to vote at the diet on matters which did not directly concern them.

Among the rights of the Estates, that of passing legislation acquired great significance in the Jagiellonid period. This right, which had never been conceded to the Estates by express enactment, was exercised in practice partly by the collaboration of the Estates in the proclamation of laws and the activities of the High Court, and partly, in a negative fashion, by the opposition shewn by the Estates to the promulgation of a written code. This opposition was based partly on the unwillingness of the Estates to be limited in their powers at the High Court by any written prescriptions. After the restoration of normal conditions in the country, however, under King Vladislav, the Estates themselves acknowledged that the rules by which the Court was accustomed to give judgment and the important decisions of the Court should be formed into a written code, as a guide for the Court. The two upper Estates urged the issue of a code, because they desired to assure and extend their own rights at the expense of the royal power and the rights of the burgesses. The compilation of the code was entrusted to commissions of the Estates successively appointed for this purpose by the diet. The work was printed and published in 1500, and after being ratified by the king under the title of the *Land Ordinance* or *Bohemian Constitution* became the first Bohemian code of universal application.

The rivalry between the two upper Estates and the burgesses shewed itself also in the economic sphere. The new prosperity of the towns, which had begun under George Poděbrady, had for a time been checked by the war with Matthias of Hungary, but it proceeded apace again when that war was over. Economic relations with other countries were rapidly renewed, and commerce and trade made a considerable advance. As early as the reign of George of Poděbrady the towns had succeeded in obtaining the prohibition of trading in the rural districts outside the markets of the towns, and of the brewing and sale of beer in the neighbourhood of the towns. This was directed mainly against the unfree peasantry but partly also against their masters, the nobles, and became a fruitful source of disputes between the towns and the two upper Estates, who devoted themselves more and more to the systematic cultivation and economic exploitation of their domains.

Economic causes likewise prompted the higher category of nobles to aim at a further limitation of the liberties of their unfree dependents. This movement culminated in the decision of King Vladislav in 1497 that villeins should for ever be unable, without special permission from their masters, to migrate to the towns or to the estate of another landlord. The decision of 1497 was entered in the land records and also incorporated in Vladislav's *Ordinance,* so that it became the law of the land. Although it introduced nothing substantially new, it is nevertheless

8

a significant expression of the steadily growing personal dependence of the villein element on their masters, which began even prior to the Hussite wars and continued after them, drawing the villeins gradually into a condition of serfdom.

Parallel with the increase in the personal dependence of the villeins on their masters there proceeded an increase in their duties. The landowners were constrained to this by the declining value of money, which greatly reduced the value of the ordinary dues paid by the villeins. To make good the losses arising from this, the landowners turned more and more to the cultivation of the land themselves. Owing to lack of labour they introduced pisciculture, and frequently caused great harm to their villeins, from whom they forcibly took land that was suitable for the location of fishponds and placed it under water. Thus were increased, in many cases at the cost of the villeins, the economic resources of the noble landlords, who augmented the returns of their estates by establishing upon them industries previously pursued only by the burgesses (the brewing and sale of beer, etc.). The political power of the upper Estates, especially that of the nobles, thus gained a firm economic foundation.

The triumph of the Czech element in the public life of the country was maintained. Soon after the conclusion of the war with Matthias it was provided, first in Moravia (1480) and subsequently in Bohemia (1495), that all entries in the public records of the realm, except the royal charters and rescripts, which could be also couched in Latin and German, must be in Czech alone. Similarly in the towns, which mostly preserved their German character, Czech was the language in which the municipal records were kept.

Intellectual life during the early years of the reign of Vladislav was marked by a gradual change from the old religious absorption to practical and secular interests. The religious disputes within the Utraquist party still gave rise in this period to a considerable number of, often lengthy, polemical works, but it was writings of another character that came most to the fore. The need for the introduction of order into constitutional and judicial conditions in the lands of the Bohemian Crown gave rise to other legal works besides Vladislav's *Ordinance*. Even prior to the close of the fifteenth century the learned master Victorin Kornel of Vyšehrad, son of a Utraquist burgher of Chrudim and a friend of the Unity of the Brotherhood, had completed his famous work on Bohemian law, a splendid example of practical experience, legal perspicacity, profound humanistic culture, and devoted affection for the author's native tongue. Humanism in Victorin Kornel finds expression in refinement of thought, polished form, and heightened cultivation of the Czech language. In others, however, it produced contempt for the native language and native ideas, as in the case of the famous Czech humanist of the Jagiellonid era, Bohuslav Hasištejnský of Lobkovicz, in whom a patriotism of an antique stamp mingled with humanistic cosmopolitanism and manifested itself largely in a sharp criticism, touched with satire, of conditions in his native country.

In the sphere of the plastic arts the slight revival that had set in during the reign of George of Poděbrady made further progress. At Prague and at Kutná Hora in particular, the last quarter of the fifteenth century saw the rise of some notable Gothic buildings. The leading figures in Czech architecture of this period were Matthias Rejsek, a Czech of Prostějov, and Benedikt Rejt (or Ried), obviously a German and probably of Austrian origin, both of whom were born about the middle of the fifteenth century. Thanks mainly to these two men Czech architecture—by its own resources and without foreign aid—once more attained a European level. Czech sculpture and painting likewise flourished considerably. Following the isolated attempts in King George's reign to enter into contact with the world of art in the rest of Europe, the reign of his successor saw a powerful influx of foreign, especially German, art into Bohemia, which was obviously endeavouring to catch up with the rest of Europe. Before the end of the fifteenth century Czech plastic art attained a really high level, so that in this department Bohemia had already made good the setback caused by the Hussite wars, even if she could not lead the developments in European art as she had done at the close of the pre-Hussite era.

The Czech nation as a whole, although in its religious life it was sharply contrasted with its neighbours, was again coming into closer contact with the intellectual and material culture around it, and was once more winning a very honourable place even in those departments from the cultivation of which it had been distracted by the purely religious interests of the Hussite era. How it was influenced by the Reformation and the accession of the Habsburg dynasty (1526) belongs to modern history.

CHAPTER IV

THE EMPIRE IN THE FIFTEENTH CENTURY

I. THE AGE OF THE SCHISM

WENCESLAS had already had experience as king and imperial vicegerent when Charles IV died on 29 November 1378. For the first time for nearly two hundred years son succeeded to father as head of the Empire without dispute. This in itself seemed an earnest of better times for Germany. And the new king, though only seventeen years of age, had enjoyed a liberal education and the companionship of his father. Wenceslas is described as learned, witty, friendly in manner, swift and shrewd in business. He continued Charles' building schemes and patronage of literature. As King of Bohemia he was for his first dozen years respected and successful[1]. But the difficulties which surrounded a monarch in Germany were too much for his powers. As he grew older he appears to have devoted himself excessively to the chase and he then began to drink so heavily as to become unbalanced and violent, till he ceased to attempt the wearisome effort to rule in Germany, while he was unable to cope with the factions of his own Bohemia, and his reign ended in manifold humiliations.

In Germany the main problems which awaited solution may be summarised as the Schism and the anarchy due to the alliances, armaments, and secret diplomacy of the leading Estates. In the ecclesiastical question Wenceslas did not attempt the rôle of impartial arbitrator, but continued his father's policy of whole-hearted support of Urban VI against the French Papacy at Avignon. At the Reichstag at Frankfort in February 1379, the king and the Rhenish Electors called upon all members of the Empire to give their adhesion to Urban. To Cardinal Pileus of Ravenna, who came to Prague with Urban's offer of the imperial coronation at Rome, Wenceslas gave assurances that he proposed to make the Italian expedition as soon as possible. The project, however, remained unfulfilled; for later in the same year the Schism entered Germany and served to increase the existing anarchy. Adolf of Nassau, the *de facto* but as yet unlegalised occupant of the see of Mayence, declared openly for Pope Clement, from whom he received the pallium. His action should have received attention at the Reichstag at Frankfort in September; but in the absence of Wenceslas nothing was done. The Electors of Cologne, Trèves, and the Palatinate, therefore, met at Ober-Wesel in January 1380, issued a manifesto against all opponents of Urban, and wrote to Wenceslas demanding that he should either govern the Empire or leave it to the Electors. Thus early in his reign did the king encounter the threat,

---

[1] See *supra*, Vol. VII, Chap. VI, pp. 174 sqq.

often repeated later, that he might be deposed. In March he came to the Rhineland, but refused to attack Adolf. On the contrary he accepted him as archbishop, and thus peacefully induced him to abandon Avignon and return to the Roman fold.

But Adolf's example of ecclesiastical desertion had been followed by Leopold of Habsburg, with whom it was Wenceslas' policy to maintain a close alliance, and by a number of Estates on the left bank of the Rhine, where French influence was strong. Mercifully for Germany Wenceslas refused to start a war of religion, though the Schism placed endless difficulties in the way of royal government. He seems to have seriously intended to proceed to the imperial coronation, and, in reply to Urban's pressing invitations, announced his departure for Rome for the spring of 1380. But, in addition to the troubles of Germany, preoccupation with eastern questions caused him again to postpone the expedition, which ultimately never took place.

When Lewis the Great of Hungary and Poland died on 11 September 1382, leaving two daughters but no son, he also left a succession dispute of the utmost importance, for which Charles IV and other princes had been waiting and preparing. Mary, the elder daughter, was affianced to Wenceslas' brother Sigismund; Hedwig (Jadviga), the younger, to Duke William of Habsburg. But neither couple was as yet married. It had been the dead king's intention that Sigismund should succeed him in both kingdoms, thus exalting the house of Luxemburg to domination over all central Europe and securing Germany's eastern frontiers. But there were those in Hungary who supported the claims of Charles of Durazzo, King of Naples, of the younger line of Anjou. The Queen-mother Elizabeth was a Slav and detested a German succession. The French royal family came forward, with the support of Avignon, claiming to succeed the Angevin kings of Hungary by providing a husband for Mary. Lastly, the Polish Estates had no intention of being governed from Hungary by a foreigner. Thus great political, racial, and ecclesiastical issues were involved in the struggles which followed Lewis' death.

The Polish question was settled first, for the Poles accepted Hedwig as their queen, and then forced her in 1386 to marry Jagiello, the heathen Grand Prince of Lithuania, who thereupon received baptism and the Christian name of Vladyslav. Sigismund succeeded in marrying Mary in 1385; but not till 1387 was he able, with Wenceslas' help, to obtain coronation as King of Hungary and the liberation of his wife, who had meanwhile been carried off by her mother. Thus Hungary was won for the house of Luxemburg, even if a powerful Slavonic Poland arose to threaten northern Germany. But Wenceslas had succeeded in winning the Danube plain for his brother only by renouncing his own imperial coronation and by giving inadequate attention to Germany, to the exasperation of the Electors.

Despite the efforts of Charles IV in the Golden Bull to stabilise the

public law of the Empire, various Estates attempted to secure for themselves the independence granted to the Electors. The towns and the lesser
rural nobility maintained a constant mutual hatred; and many princes
supported the lesser nobles in order to induce the wealthy towns to
submit to princely government and taxation. To protect themselves the
leading towns of Swabia and the Rhineland made leagues, which temporarily united and attempted to connect their unions with the powerful
northern Hansa and the Swiss communities. In opposition arose leagues
of knights and lesser princes. At successive Reichstags it was proposed to
promulgate a general Public Peace, which should render the town-leagues
unnecessary. But the towns refused to put their trust in decrees. A *modus
vivendi* was effected by Wenceslas at an assembly at Heidelberg in July
1384, when a truce was arranged between the town-leagues and the
princely alliance formed at Nuremberg in the previous year. Wenceslas
did not, as king, recognise the town-leagues, but unofficially he entered
into friendly negotiations with the towns. With them he adopted an
agreement on currency questions and for the plundering of the Jews, from
whom he and they extorted large sums in 1385.

The peace was broken in the far south. To secure themselves against
Leopold of Habsburg, four of the Swiss communities entered into an
alliance with the Swabian town-league in February 1385. They were
further encouraged by the estrangement between the houses of Luxemburg and Habsburg. For Wenceslas had been provoked by the Habsburg
opposition to his brother in Hungary and by Leopold's continued
adhesion to Avignon; and in August 1385 he relieved Leopold of his
imperial office as *Landvogt* in Upper and Lower Swabia. The encroachments of the Swiss on Habsburg territory eventually caused Leopold to
attempt, with an army of Swabian nobles, the recovery of his town of
Sempach, where he was defeated and killed in 1386[1]. The war, however,
was localised; and in the next year Wenceslas' deputies were able to
extend the settlement of Heidelberg for three more years. This truce
was but the prelude to a general conflagration in 1388–89. The occasion
was furnished by the Wittelsbachs. The Bavarian Dukes, Stephen and
Frederick, and Rupert the younger of the Palatinate, treacherously
captured and imprisoned Pilgrim, Archbishop of Salzburg, an ally of the
Swabian towns and confidential agent of Wenceslas. Although the king
supported the towns and tried to keep the peace, war broke out and
spread rapidly through Swabia and Franconia. Pitched battles were few
and went against the towns. Eberhard of Wurtemberg scattered the
army of the Swabian league at Döffingen; and Rupert, the Elector Palatine, defeated the Rhenish league near Worms. But the war dragged on,
the princes being unable to reduce any of the towns, while the latter were
impoverished by the interruption of their trade and the devastation of
their rural districts. In the spring of 1389 peace was made between the

---

[1] See *supra*, Vol. vii, Chap. vii, pp. 195 sq.

Habsburgs and the Swiss, to the advantage of the latter; and Wenceslas was able to gather the representatives of the princes and towns to a Reichstag at Eger. Here on 5 May a Public Peace for all southern Germany was accepted and promulgated. The existing law was declared in force. General leagues of towns were prohibited, as well as the reception of *pfahlbürger;* but the towns received a concession in the establishment of regional courts of arbitration, each consisting of two princely and two citizen judges with a president appointed by the king.

Thus the southern towns failed in their most serious effort to assert their ambitions against the conservative and feudal character of German public law. Their geographical separation from each other and their parochial outlook had rendered them no match for the arms and legal arguments of their knightly opponents. Further, many of them were distracted by internal strife. Unlike the powerful towns of the North, they were not dependent for their prosperity on the skill and experience in overseas trade of big capitalists. Consequently they were the scene of many struggles by the craftsmen to wrest a share in town government from the patrician families. In the fifteenth century most of the southern towns experienced a democratic evolution, which diminished their external power and political enterprise.

Germany's hope of law and order depended on the strength of the monarch; and that in turn depended on the monarch's command of the resources of his hereditary lands. It was, therefore, a disaster that in the last decade of the century Wenceslas was engaged in long and unsuccessful struggles with the Bohemian clergy and nobles. Soon the house of Luxemburg was divided, the malcontents being supported by Sigismund and by Wenceslas' cousin Jošt, Margrave of Moravia and Brandenburg. In 1394 Wenceslas was even captured and for a time imprisoned. Thus the royal power fell into abeyance in Germany, except in so far as the Rhenish Electors took it upon themselves to act as a government for the West. Wenceslas made occasional gestures of authority. To Gian Galeazzo Visconti, *de facto* ruler of Milan, he sold investiture as Duke in 1395, to the wrath of the Electors. In 1398 he held a Reichstag at Frankfort and there promulgated for the whole of Germany a Public Peace, which was without effect. From Frankfort he went to meet Charles VI of France at Rheims with a view to common action to end the Schism. The mad King of France and the drunken King of the Romans agreed to press both Popes to resign, but their joint efforts failed of any effect for the healing of the nations. Various plans for the deposition of Wenceslas at last resulted in the agreement of the Rhenish Electors and numerous princes to renounce their allegiance and to set up another king. For this purpose they summoned a meeting of Estates at Ober-Lahnstein for 11 August 1400. Neither Wenceslas nor the Electors of Brandenburg and Saxony were present; and the towns carefully abstained from taking part in the revolutionary proceedings. On 20 August the Rhenish Electors declared Wenceslas deposed, and on the next day at Rense they elected the only layman amongst them, Rupert III of the Palatinate.

Thus Germany entered on a schism in the monarchy as well as in the Church. The Electors' declaration that Wenceslas had done nothing to forward ecclesiastical unity or to restore order in Germany was justified by the events of the previous ten years. It remained to be seen if his opponent could do any better.

His contemporaries are united in praising Rupert's piety, his honourable dealing and respect for law; but his career gives no evidence of the insight, skill, and force required by the German monarch of his day. The record of his reign is one of the best intentions, but of complete failure. Unable to gain admittance to Aix-la-Chapelle, he received his crown at Cologne at Epiphany 1401, amid a small gathering of supporters. As soon as possible he set out for Italy. Wenceslas had been denounced for abandoning the Roman Pope and for resigning the imperial control of Lombardy. Rupert intended to support Boniface IX, to obtain the imperial crown, and, if possible, to chastise the upstart Visconti. On 15 September he left Augsburg to cross the Brenner with a small force collected chiefly by his relatives. But Verona and Brescia barred the approaches to the plain, and he wasted a month in a laborious détour through the Pustertal before he was able to reach Padua. Here his inadequate resources of men and money forced him to halt while he bargained with the Florentines for the financial help which they had promised, and tried to raise troops. By April he had to admit the humiliating fact of his failure, and on 2 May he was back in Munich. Nevertheless, he continued to negotiate with Boniface for recognition of his kingship. The Pope was in need of any support which he could find, and finally on 1 October 1403 he accorded Rupert the barren honour of papal recognition, though he did not fail to insist that the Electors had no right to depose the King of the Romans without papal permission.

The futility of Rupert's Italian expedition diminished his slender chances of successful rule in Germany. He summoned assemblies in 1403 and 1404 to establish a Public Peace, but his constant demands for money and his inability to gain widespread recognition in the Empire caused the southern towns once more to form a general league. On the other hand his not wholly unsuccessful efforts to assert the royal power over his neighbours embroiled him with various princes of the Rhineland. In September 1405, Strasbourg and seventeen Swabian towns united with Bernhard of Baden, Eberhard of Wurtemberg, and even John, Elector of Mayence, who had been the chief promoter of Rupert's election, to form the league of Marbach for five years. The nominal purpose of the league was the maintenance of peace and order; but the members undertook to defend each other's rights even against the king, of whose actions they thus took it upon themselves to judge. How inadequate they found Rupert's protection of the law is clearly expressed in a letter from Basle to Strasbourg:

"if princes and towns may not form leagues without the royal permission, no one will be able to enjoy the freedom which ancient custom guarantees to him." In 1407 Rupert managed to make peace with John of Mayence and Bernhard of Baden and to secure their promise that the league should not be continued beyond its original term. Even so the league outlived him, though it ceased to offer any active opposition to royal policy.

Rupert gained a few adherents. Among them was Reinald of Guelders, whose support enabled him to enjoy the ceremony of a second coronation at Aix-la-Chapelle. But his effective power hardly extended beyond the neighbourhood of the Palatinate. When the Duchess Joan of Brabant died on 1 December 1406, the Estates of the duchy fulfilled her wishes and accepted Antony of Burgundy as her heir. To Rupert's protests at this violation of imperial rights over a lapsed fief they gave no answer; while from Bohemia Wenceslas hastily recognised the young duke and gave him the hand of Elizabeth of Görlitz together with the succession to the duchy of Luxemburg on the death of its holder, his cousin Jošt of Moravia and Brandenburg.

Most of Germany was ceasing, however, to be interested in the claims of either Wenceslas or Rupert. In treaties it was being provided that the parties might recognise the king whom they preferred. Finally, the conciliar movement made Rupert's kingship more than ever an irrelevance. When the cardinals of both obediences met, in June 1408, to provide for a General Council of Christendom to heal the Schism, they were overwhelmingly supported by the public opinion of Germany. At an assembly of princes in Frankfort in January 1409, the majority declared in favour of the cardinals' project, despite Rupert's determined loyalty to the Roman Pope, Gregory XII. The cardinals then approached Wenceslas, from whom they received assurances of whole-hearted support. In vain Rupert from Heidelberg commanded the Estates of the Empire to support the true Pope and ignore the schismatic Council of Pisa. The Council enjoyed the approval of Christendom and the recognition of the great majority of German princes. Rupert was one of the negligible number of rulers whose envoys attended Gregory XII's farcical little council at Cividale.

Despite his inability to control Germany, Rupert was still the most powerful prince of the Rhineland, and he was engaged in successful war against the turbulent John of Mayence, when he died at his castle near Oppenheim on 18 May 1410. He left the memory of a noble character, but also of complete failure to restore peace and order to Germany.

II. THE EMPEROR SIGISMUND

The experiment of a king from western Germany was not repeated, and the Electors decided to revert to the house of Luxemburg with its wide possessions in the east. But who of that house was to be elected? King

Wenceslas, who had the Bohemian vote, was supported by his cousin Jošt of Moravia and Brandenburg, and by the Saxon Elector. But these three votes could not restore Wenceslas to undisputed kingship against the opposition of the Rhenish Electors. Further, the Rhenish Electors were divided on the ecclesiastical issue. The Archbishops of Mayence and Cologne stood for the conciliar Pope; while Lewis III of the Palatinate inherited Rupert's devotion to Gregory XII and was supported by the Archbishop of Trèves. The choice of the conciliar party fell upon Jošt, while their opponents turned to Wenceslas' brother Sigismund, King of Hungary, who had hitherto kept aloof from the papal question. Sigismund claimed the vote of Brandenburg himself, despite his alienation of the Mark to Jošt, and sent Frederick of Hohenzollern, Burgrave of Nuremberg, to exercise the electoral function. Thus reinforced, Sigismund's supporters acted first. The choir of Frankfort cathedral being locked by order of the Archbishop of Mayence, they met behind the high altar and elected Sigismund king on 20 September 1410. But Wenceslas had meanwhile agreed to support the candidature of Jošt, who was accordingly elected on 1 October by the votes of Bohemia, Cologne, Mayence, Saxony, and Brandenburg, as represented by Jošt himself.

Thus during the autumn there were three German kings. But Jošt died in January 1411, leaving Sigismund with no serious competitor. The condition of Italian politics ensured him the support of Pope John XXIII, who was suffering the attacks of Sigismund's enemy, Ladislas of Naples. Sigismund now came forward as a supporter of the conciliar Pope. He also made terms with Wenceslas, to whom he guaranteed the Bohemian kingdom and the status of German king with half of the royal revenues, an inexpensive generosity. The Mark of Brandenburg had returned to him on Jošt's death. It was with little difficulty that Sigismund was unanimously elected on 21 July 1411.

The election was somewhat of a leap in the dark. Sigismund's spiritual home was Hungary, at whose court he had been educated. Germany knew little of her new king except that he had proved himself a vigorous fighter in many a Balkan and Bohemian campaign and that, unlike his brother, he was likely to make himself felt in imperial affairs. Sigismund was indeed a vivid character. He had laid low many opponents in the tournament. He spoke several languages and, unlike most German princes, was a Latinist and a patron of learning. Aeneas Sylvius Piccolomini calls him "liberal and munificent above all previous princes." He was certainly a man of ideas and of action, the most radical would-be reformer amongst Emperors before Maximilian I. He was also a dignified figure, with a fine sense of the dramatic. But his weaknesses were many. His devotion to the ladies exceeded the generous allowance conceded to monarchs. He could be savagely cruel. Windecke recounts that Sigismund had 171 Bosnian notables decapitated at Doboj, and that he made a captured Venetian commander cut off the right hands of 180 of his fellow-prisoners and take back the hands to the doge's government. His dignity was apt to degenerate into vanity, his official policy to be subordinated to personal prejudice or the whims of the moment. Above all he was hampered by constant poverty, which rendered futile his grandiose projects and made him the accomplice of anyone with money to spare.

The task that confronted a German king in the fifteenth century was formidable. On all sides arose complaints that the laws were not observed, that might was right, that no supreme power ensured peace or upheld justice. The towns and the nobility were divided by a deep gulf of suspicion and dislike. All the Estates cherished the right of waging private war and often practised it for frivolous reasons. Indeed they stood to each other in much the same relation as did the European States of the nineteenth century. They could at any moment legally break off relations with each other and have recourse to self-help, unless a special Public Peace (*Landfriede*), which was the fifteenth-century equivalent of the eleventh-century Truce of God, had been accepted by the Reichstag, or the Estates of a particular region, and was in operation. The Golden Bull had removed the territories of the Electors from the royal jurisdiction and made them virtually independent. The royal surrender of the right of evoking suits from the Electors' courts had been in practice extended in favour of many princes, lords, towns, and churches. Perhaps the best illustration of Germany's lack of governance is found in the institution of the Veme. The courts of the Veme, whose special sphere was Westphalia, were survivals from old folk-moots, long since restricted in composition to a local "free count" and his assessors. These courts, which operated where ordinary justice failed, tried cases of perjury and violence, even extending their competence to heresy. The proceedings of the courts, though conducted in the open air, were secret, and death was meted out to the assessor who blabbed. But any freeman could become an assessor of the Veme, which thus had something in common with modern American secret societies with their unofficial jurisdiction. Of these courts there were some four hundred in Westphalia, and the system had spread into other districts. A man accused before the Veme was required to clear himself with the support of twenty oath-helpers, all of whom must be assessors. Consequently every community in Germany desired to number some assessors amongst its members. Augsburg at one time possessed thirty-six assessors of the Veme. The greatest princes, as Sigismund himself and Frederick of Hohenzollern, were assessors. But the predominant element was drawn from the class of free knights claiming to hold direct of the Empire. The verdicts of the Veme were pronounced in the name of the king, and the system was accepted by the kings of the house of Luxemburg as a check on the power of the greater princes. With its immense growth in the fifteenth century the Veme deteriorated. Its courts gave conflicting decisions, and there was no provision for appeal. The worst abuse of the Veme became its venality. Assessorship and the tenure of a court were sold, and the Veme enabled the poorer nobility to earn a dishonest livelihood or to prosecute private feuds. The thing became a public nuisance. A Vemic court laid its ban for nine years on all the citizens of Groningen. Frederick III himself and his chancellor found themselves cited. The Veme had outlived its usefulness. In 1468 Augsburg condemned to death burgesses who cited others before a Vemic court. With the consolidation of orderly government in the greater principalities the Veme was stamped out.

For the task of creating order out of the German chaos the kingship suffered from many disadvantages. Its elective nature permitted the Electors to impose conditions upon their nominee and made easy the way to deposition. Successive kings had bartered away royal rights and revenues in their efforts to secure the crown to their families. Shortly after his election Sigismund estimated the royal revenue at only 13,000 florins. The connexion of the kingship with the Empire had both distributed the attention of the German monarch over an impossibly wide area and introduced to a peculiar degree the disturbing element of papal authority. There was no traditional centre of royal government. Prague, the residence of the Luxemburg kings, was far removed from the Swabian and Rhenish towns which were the nerves of the Empire; and Prague was becoming increasingly Slavonic and separatist in the heat of ecclesiastical controversy. Germany had never undergone conquest by an alien race, and consequently there was no ruling caste, attached to the monarchy and foreign to the subject population, to serve as the devoted agents of royalty. Local governors, supported by the particularist traditions of the ancient German tribes, developed easily into independent rulers. The nobility, the knights, and the towns were accustomed to forming leagues for mutual protection and self-government; and this expedient, rendered necessary by the weakness of the monarchy, tended to make the monarchy's activity superfluous, somewhat as the alliances of modern States have disguised the need for an international authority. Unlike the French or Spaniards, the Germans had not been obliged to fight for their national existence. Even the Hussite wars only afflicted the Eastern marches and that for a short time, while the Magyars and Yugoslavs took the shock of the Turkish onslaught. The fifteenth century did indeed see the German frontiers pass under quasi-foreign rule. Schleswig-Holstein became permanently attached to the Danish Crown; and in the West the Burgundian power gathered many imperial fiefs under a more than half-French dynasty. In the north-east the Teutonic Order slowly sank into helplessness and ultimately held the remnant of its territory from the Polish king. But all these losses were far removed from the centres of German public opinion. Germany did not experience the unifying force of foreign invasion till the French monarchy began to look on the Rhine as its natural boundary.

Against these disadvantages the kingship could count some elements of strength. The imperial dignity was an asset in the matrimonial market, a lesson which the Luxemburg and Habsburg houses took to heart. The control of lapsed fiefs offered opportunities for buying the adherence of powerful princes. Some sort of contact could be maintained with the provinces by the attraction which the imperial chancery and diplomatic service had for the nobility. The prevailing anarchy made the less fortunate classes of society look anxiously for the self-assertion of the monarchy; while the confusion caused by the Schism cried aloud for action by the secular lord of the world.

The institution through which the king might be expected to bid for the support of the nation was the Reichstag. But the Reichstag, which was still in the process of formation, resembled neither an English Parliament nor the Estates of other monarchies. It was dominated by the Electors, who formed a virtual oligarchy with divergent interests. Theoretically all tenants-in-chief of the Empire also had the right to attend; but in practice attendance was usually confined to princes and nobles of central and southern Germany. These did not form a separate college and were too numerous and divided to develop a corporate consciousness. The large class of smaller nobles and knights was habitually unrepresented, though their leagues were sometimes specially invited to send delegates. By the opening of the fifteenth century a number of towns had acquired a prescriptive claim to representation, and during a period of crisis, such as the Hussite wars, their wealth increased their importance in the body politic. But usually their comparative insignificance in the Reichstag was such that their adhesion to its proclamations was expressed in preambles, even when their agents had shewn opposition. The towns indeed looked on their representation only as a means of opposing undesirable measures, an aim which was more effectively achieved by ignoring the Reichstag's decisions when promulgated. The towns had too nearly attained the mentality of city-states to be easily included in a national organisation.

As German king Sigismund could either attempt immediately to exalt the authority of the monarchy, or devote himself to the strengthening of his recently recovered hereditary possession, the Mark of Brandenburg. For three years he did neither. He was deeply engaged in eastern affairs, and neither appeared in Germany nor appointed a vicegerent; while in the summer of 1411 he alienated the Mark to Frederick of Hohenzollern. Frederick had abandoned the unprofitable service of King Rupert to make his fortune in that of Sigismund in Hungary. There he had prospered; and now he was placed in charge of Brandenburg, which the king was only to resume on payment of 100,000 Hungarian gulden. So successfully did Frederick cope with the unruly baronage of the Mark that three years later he was able to leave his wife in charge, while he attended the Council at Constance. In April 1415, Sigismund conferred on him and his heirs the Electorate of Brandenburg, redeemable only with 400,000 gulden; and two years later, at another Reichstag in Constance, Frederick was solemnly invested with his high dignity. It is to be noted, as an omen of much later events, that the Hohenzollern obtained Brandenburg at the expense of the Habsburgs. Charles IV's cross-remainder agreement of 1364 had provided for the union of the territories of the houses of Luxemburg and Habsburg, should either dynasty be extinguished. In pursuance of that agreement Sigismund had secured the acknowledgment of Albert IV of Austria as his heir in Hungary, and in October 1411 he betrothed his two-year-old daughter, Elizabeth, to the youthful Albert V. Since Wenceslas was unlikely to have an heir, Albert V was the prospective inheritor of the Luxemburg dominions. But the accident of Albert's youth and Sigismund's temporary attachment to Frederick robbed the Habsburgs of Brandenburg and raised up a new dynasty of the first rank.

During the year before his definitive election Sigismund had been attempting to mitigate the fate of the Teutonic Order, after its crushing defeat by the Poles at Tannenberg in July 1410. The days of the Order seemed to be numbered. But the heroic defence of Marienburg gave time for Sigismund, to whom the Order had made a handsome pecuniary gift, to attack the Poles and induce King Vladyslav to grant the unexpectedly lenient terms of the Peace of Thorn (February 1411), whereby the Order only surrendered Samogitia. Yet the Knights could not recover their strength. Weakened by internal dissension, they were hated by the gentry and towns of their own territory, from which they would admit no member to their ranks. Their recent (1402) acquisition of the Neumark was sure to bring them into conflict with active rulers of Brandenburg. Impoverished and unable to offer Sigismund more money, they yet refused to hold Prussia or Pomerellen of him. Claiming complete freedom from royal control, they could not expect royal support. The conversion of the Lithuanians to Christianity had robbed the Order of its *raison d'être* as a crusading force. Slowly it sank before the aggression of the Poles and the revolts of its own subjects; and the standard of Germanism in the north-east passed from its nerveless fingers into the grasp of the Hohenzollern.

Sigismund then turned to the South, announcing the need for recovering the lost imperial lands in Italy. With the Venetian Republic he had many scores to settle. She had acquired the Dalmatian ports and so excluded his Hungaro-Croatian kingdom from the sea; she had extended her territory westward to the Mincio and so controlled the southern exit of the Brenner; she was attempting to absorb the Patriarchate of Aquileia with its high-roads from Vienna and Hungary; she had urged the Poles to hostility against Sigismund. The Venetian war occupied his attention till the five years' armistice of April 1413 freed him to devote himself to a task congenial to his soaring imagination. As King of the

Romans he would assemble a Council of Christendom and heal the schism. The Council should also settle the ecclesiastical disputes in Sigismund's prospective kingdom of Bohemia, and provide for the general reform of the Church. To appear at the Council as the first of secular monarchs, he at last tore himself away from Italian politics, traversed Germany, and was crowned king at Aix-la-Chapelle on 8 November 1414.

The Council of Constance belongs rather to ecclesiastical than to national history. But events of importance peculiar to Germany occurred during the Council's session. When it was known that Frederick of Habsburg, Count of Tyrol, had defied the king and organised Pope John XXIII's flight from Constance, he was put to the ban of the Empire on 30 March 1415. The unfortunate prince's collapse was rapid. Some four hundred challenges poured in upon him. Frederick of Hohenzollern led an imperial force to the capture of some of the Habsburg towns in Swabia and along the upper Rhine; another force broke into Tyrol; Lewis of the Palatinate invaded Alsace. Sigismund persuaded the Swiss confederates to disregard their fifty years' peace, concluded with Frederick of Habsburg three years before, on the ground of the latter's excommunication. The Berners, Lucerners, and Zürichers each seized what they coveted of adjacent Habsburg territory and united to attack the Habsburg stronghold of Baden in Aargau. Overwhelmed by these disasters, Frederick surrendered himself to the royal mercy. Sigismund thereupon forbade further proceedings against his vassal. But his envoys could not restrain the Swiss, and the fortress of Baden went up in flames. When on 5 May Frederick was solemnly led before Sigismund to make his submission, the German magnates saw such an assertion of royal authority as had been unknown since the days of the Hohenstaufen. Frederick's life was spared, but his possessions were declared forfeit to the Empire. Sigismund's treatment of this windfall illustrates his imperialist, non-dynastic aims. He was obliged to recognise the Swiss as imperial administrators in their acquisitions, but he conferred the freedom of the Empire on the captured Rhenish and Swabian towns and declared the rest of Frederick's inheritance imperial property. Little came of all this plan. During Sigismund's absence from the Council, Frederick escaped and re-established himself in Tyrol, where he had many friends. In May 1418, with the help of the new Pope, he made his peace with Sigismund. The Swiss kept most of their winnings and Schaffhausen remained a free town; but Frederick recovered his other possessions. It was evident that the German king could not in normal times and by his own power reduce a rebellious vassal. The chief outcome of the incident was the increased independence of the Swiss. They had been accustomed to play off the Empire against their Habsburg neighbour. They had now refused to surrender their booty to the Empire. When the Empire later passed to the Habsburg house itself, any chance of asserting imperial authority over them disappeared.

Sigismund held two Reichstags at Constance, in 1415 and 1417, at which he developed his ideas of imperial reform. He aimed at the establishment of public security, the suppression of illegal tolls, and the reform of the currency. These were objects agreeable to the townsmen, to whom he looked for support of the Empire against the disintegrating influence of the princes. As practical measures he proposed that the towns should accept imperial agents to preside over their leagues, and that southern and central Germany should be organised into four districts, each under an imperial *Hauptmann* and each bound to assist the others in maintaining the public peace. These suggestions were admirable; but Sigismund, despite his popularity, was distrusted. When he asked the towns to present their petitions, they found him unwilling to attend to a mass of petty details. His mind was revolving distant matters, the Turkish menace, his promise to help Henry V of England against the French, his grievances against the Venetians whom at one time he hoped to ruin by diverting Germany's southern trade to Genoa. It was felt that Sigismund wished to plan reforms, but to leave others to pay for and execute them. The towns hesitated to commit themselves. Amongst the princes Sigismund's plans found little favour. The opposition was led by John of Nassau, Archbishop of Mayence, and Lewis of the Palatinate, who made up their old differences in view of the common danger to their particularist interests. They joined with the other two Rhenish Electors to return a united answer to Sigismund's proposals in 1417. As the Council drew to a close, the four Electors entered into a defensive alliance against the "bourgeois" king. Thereupon the towns drew back in alarm, and Sigismund's plans collapsed.

The Council's treatment of the Bohemian reformers had disastrous effects upon Sigismund's prospective kingdom. The Hussite question dominated Central European affairs for the next twenty years. Already, during the Council's sessions, disquieting news of the progress of heresy had arrived from Bohemia. Sigismund's influence had prevented the assembled fathers from anathematising Wenceslas, and moved the latter to attempt measures of repression in the summer of 1419. These provoked Hussite disturbances, which caused the unfortunate king to have an apoplectic fit and die. With the resumption of the Venetian war in 1418 Sigismund had appointed Frederick of Brandenburg to be his vicegerent in Germany, and had betaken himself to Hungary. As Wenceslas' heir he now appointed regents in Bohemia. But the autumn saw that country given over to civil war. During a temporary lull Sigismund received the homage of the Bohemian Estates at Brno (Brünn) in December, and passed on to meet a Reichstag at Breslau in March 1420.

This assembly was summoned to consider the two questions of arbitration between the Polish king and the Teutonic Order and of the measures to be taken against heresy. Sigismund was anxious to uphold the Order out of consideration for the Germanism of the Electors, and he had begun to be haunted by the fear of a Polish-Czech Pan-Slav alliance. His verdict on the first question, therefore, was favourable to the Order, and Vladyslav was bidden to restore Pomerellen and Kulmerland to the knights. The papal legate then preached a crusade against the Hussites and produced a bull condemning their heresy. It is difficult to blame Sigismund for supporting the papal decision and launching the Empire upon the long tragedy of the Hussite wars. For the reform of the Empire the support of the Church was essential; if he wished to shew himself worthy of the imperial crown he must clear himself of that unfounded suspicion of lukewarm orthodoxy which he had incurred at Constance; Prague and the moderate elements among the Czechs might go over to the Hussites, if he shewed weakness; the cause of German civilisation, which seemed an essential element in Bohemian life, was at stake.

In the invasion of Bohemia, Sigismund was joined by the German princes of the eastern marches, the Dukes of Bavaria, the Margrave of Meissen, and young Albert of Austria. Thus supported, Sigismund occupied part of Prague at the end of June. On 28 July he was crowned in St Vitus' Cathedral with the assent of the loyalist Czechs, who, however, made it a condition that the imperial army should leave the country. The Germans thereupon dispersed, spreading the rumour broadcast that a victory over the Hussites had only been prevented by Sigismund's unwillingness to push matters to extremes against his own subjects. Once more Sigismund incurred German distrust. Nor did his moderation avail him with the Bohemian rebels. Without his German troops he could make no headway, and in March 1421 he retired to Hungary, where the Venetians, the Turks, and internal disputes demanded his presence.

Sigismund's chief interest was to prevent an hostile encirclement of Hungary, which would occur if Poland made an alliance with the successful rebels in Bohemia. It was therefore a severe blow to him when his former supporter, Frederick of Brandenburg, affianced his second son, Frederick, to Hedwig, heiress of the aged Vladyslav of Poland, on 8 April 1421. Frederick's argument, that by this arrangement a German would soon be ruling in Poland and able to prevent any threat to Germanism or orthodoxy from that quarter, does not seem to have carried any weight with Sigismund, who suspected the Elector of merely desiring to strengthen his own position against the Teutonic Order and Duke Eric of Pomerania, and considered him a traitor to himself and the Empire. Thus between the two ablest German rulers there grew up a mutual relation of suspicion and antipathy which could not fail to affect adversely the unity of imperial action.

In Sigismund's absence the Rhenish Electors took the lead at a Reichstag at Wesel in May 1421, and summoned the armed forces of Germany to join them at Eger for a Bohemian campaign in August. The response was considerable and over 100,000 men, it is said, assembled for the crusade. But divided counsels and the dilatory methods of Sigismund, as well as the military efficiency of the Hussites, caused the expedition to end in a fiasco. The German host fled homewards in disorder, and the Hussites welcomed the Polish prince Zygmunt Korybut as their regent. Precisely that Czecho-Polish entente, which Sigismund had feared, had occurred.

Feeling in Germany was now rising against the absentee king. Frederick of Brandenburg, who had taken no part in the Reichstags and crusades of 1420 and 1421, joined the Rhenish Electors in January 1422, and a joint message was sent to Sigismund, telling him in effect to come to Germany or be deposed. Sigismund thereupon summoned a Reichstag to Ratisbon for July. But the Electors, not expecting him to arrive, counter-ordered it to Nuremberg, whither Sigismund was forced to betake himself. At Nuremberg two questions had to be considered: the Bohemian war and the news of a Polish attack on the Teutonic Order. On the latter point Sigismund was able to appeal to the patriotism of the Rhenish Electors against Frederick, who alone showed sympathy for Poland. It was decided to make an offer of arbitration ; but the Order made peace precipitately, restoring to Vladyslav what he had lost by Sigismund's arbitration at Breslau in 1420. As to Bohemia a twofold decision was made. A (very defective) list of the princes and towns of the Empire was drawn up, and each was assessed for contribution to a mercenary force, to be embodied for one year. Secondly, a force of nearly 50,000 men was to be raised for a short autumn campaign. The command of both forces was given by Sigismund to Frederick, an appointment no doubt intended to embroil the Elector with his Polish friends. Before returning eastwards Sigismund appointed an imperial vicar for Germany. His choice fell on Archbishop Conrad of Mayence, to the disgust of Lewis, the Elector Palatine, who considered himself entitled to the position in virtue of clause 5 of the Golden Bull.

All these decisions came to nothing. The towns which, as centres of wealth, were most heavily assessed for the mercenary force, objected to publishing their resources and short-sightedly refused to undertake obligations which might have greatly increased their constitutional importance. The expeditionary force, which started in October, was not more than a fifth of the proposed size and the Elector Frederick soon gave up the attempt to attack Bohemia. The jealousy of the other Rhenish Electors caused Conrad of Mayence to resign his post, to the greater confusion of German affairs and the satisfaction of Sigismund, who did not wish to see a too powerful lieutenant ruling in Germany.

The tension between Sigismund and Frederick was now increased by the death of the Elector Albert III, the last Ascanian Duke of Saxe-Wittenberg. Frederick, whose eldest son, John, was married to Albert's only child, hoped to secure the Saxon electorate for his family. But Sigismund, determined to prevent any further aggrandisement of the Hohenzollern, hastily made over the electorate in January 1423 to Frederick the Quarrelsome, Margrave of Meissen, from whom he had received, and hoped to receive, much assistance. Frederick of Brandenburg sustained a further blow in 1425, when King Vladyslav, at the age of seventy-six, became the father of a son and thus defeated the sure hope of a Hohenzollern succession in Poland.

Meanwhile Sigismund seemed to have abandoned Germany, with its endless discussions and quarrels, in favour of his hereditary lands. The Electors, who had made the' regent's task impossible, now proposed to assert themselves as a committee of regency. Meeting at Bingen on 17 January 1424, they formed a union for mutual defence and for united action against heresy and any reduction of imperial territory. Although Sigismund, unlike Wenceslas in 1399, was not openly defied, the Electors clearly proposed to act in his place. But the electoral unity was short-lived. The archbishops had little feeling against Sigismund, and Frederick of Saxony probably only joined the union to obtain his colleagues' recognition of his electorate. As a neighbour of Bohemia, he was naturally led to support Sigismund in the Hussite war. In July 1425, he went to Hungary and concluded an alliance with the king at Vácz, promising to support 'the succession of Albert of Austria (now married to Sigismund's daughter Elizabeth and enfeoffed with Moravia) not only in Bohemia, but also as King of the Romans. Frederick thereupon received the formal investiture of his Saxon electorate in Buda on 1 August. The union of Electors received a further and decisive blow in March 1426, when Frederick of Brandenburg made his peace with Sigismund at Vienna, abandoning the Polish policy which had so much disquieted the king. Sigismund gratified the Electors by transferring the Reichstag from Vienna to Nuremberg, and the danger of an anti-royalist government in Germany was exorcised.

During 1426–27 Sigismund was fully occupied in repelling the Turks. Albert of Austria and Frederick of Saxony carried on the struggle with the Hussites from opposite sides of Bohemia without success. Frederick of Brandenburg was active in attempts to consolidate the forces of Germany. A considerable army, raised by the Electors, advanced into Bohemia, but retired from the siege of Mies (Stříbro) on the appearance of the Taborite host. The Cardinal Henry of Winchester, who had taken part in this campaign as papal legate, also attempted to pull Germany together. At a Reichstag in Frankfort (November 1427) he pressed for a general tax to meet the expenses of a permanent force and an efficient organisation of government for war purposes. Despite the opposition of the towns, some agreement was reached. The clergy were to pay 5 per cent. on their property, a heavy burden on an estate already taxed in other ways; a count 25 gulden, a knight 5 gulden, an *edelknecht* 3; in the towns every Jew should pay a gulden and every Christian a poll-tax of at least one Bohemian groschen (the common penny) rising in the proportion of $\frac{1}{4}$ per cent. of capital to a maximum of one gulden. For purposes of collection Germany was divided into five districts with a central exchequer at Nuremberg. And a war cabinet of six representatives of the Electors and three of the towns was to meet at stated intervals under the presidency of the cardinal. But the particularism of the towns and the passive resistance of the knights, who had not been consulted, as well as of many princes, caused this effort to fail like its predecessors. By 1429 the subject had been dropped.

Sigismund was still occupied with eastern politics, not unsuccessfully. His great object was to prevent the creation of a Pan-Slav power, by setting Polish Catholicism in opposition to Bohemian Hussitism and by the erection of an independent Lithuanian kingdom. In January 1429 he secured Vladyslav's assent to the grant of a royal crown to Vitold, Grand Prince of Lithuania, a diplomatic coup not wholly defeated by Vitold's death in 1430 and the succession of Vladyslav's brother, Swidrygiello, to the grand-principality. In December 1429 he met the Archbishop of Mayence, Frederick of Brandenburg, and other princes at Bratislava (Pressburg), and poured out to them his zeal for the Hussite war, his complaints of the wretched support accorded him from Germany, and his threats to resign the German crown. The two Electors insisted on a Reichstag in Germany, but promised Sigismund their support.

In February 1430 Frederick of Brandenburg arranged a truce with the Hussites, who were ravaging Franconia and threatening Nuremberg, with a view to a discussion of their demands. This necessitated reference to the General Council which would be due in 1431, a development that accorded well with Sigismund's partiality for gathering Christendom into conference under his auspices. In August 1430 he was again in Germany, after eight years of absence, preparing the ground for the Council. But the German Estates insisted on war, to be waged by the usual medieval army summoned for a short campaign, instead of by a permanent force. Despite the usual niggardliness of the towns, a majestic host under Frederick of Brandenburg's command moved into Bohemia, only to be repulsed in disorder at Taus (Domažlice) on 14 August 1431. This defeat marked the end of the efforts of the Empire in arms. The military prestige of the princes was gone; the towns refused to part with any more money; feeling against the Church was rising; and fears were entertained lest the Hussite heresy should spread into Germany. A spirit of moderation, therefore, marked German opinion at the Council of Basle. Similar moderation by the aristocratic party in Bohemia, the death of Vladyslav of Poland in 1434, above all the victory of the Czech moderates over the Taborites at Liban (Lipany) in the same year made possible the compromise which ended the long wars. Sigismund was able to enter Prague on 23 August 1436, but only as national king of the Czechs. German influence in Bohemia was broken.

After his imperial coronation in 1433 Sigismund returned to the

discussion of imperial reform. In September 1434, he issued a programme
of sixteen articles, in which he revised his project of organising four
circles to enforce the public peace and urged the necessity of reforming
the relations of the secular and ecclesiastical powers. His proposals were
discussed at Frankfort in December, but evoked no serious support. His
attention was distracted by his recovery of Bohemia and by the widening
rift between the Papacy and the Council of Basle. One last Reichstag
he called to Eger in Bohemia, and there was much talk of the reform of
justice, of the currency, of the public peace, as well as of the ecclesiastical
question and of Burgundian aggression in Luxemburg; but any decision
was postponed and the Reichstag was dissolved (September 1437).
Messengers from the Electors urging Sigismund to impose terms on both
the Council and the Papacy, under threat of severing relations with the
recalcitrant party, found the Emperor dead. Sigismund had passed away
at Znojmo (Znaim) on 9 December 1437, after commending his faithful
son-in-law, Albert of Habsburg, to the loyalty of the Bohemian and
Hungarian nobles. His body was borne eastwards and buried in Magyar
soil at Nagy Várad (now Oradea Mare).

As German king, Sigismund had been faced with a thankless task.
His only territorial resources in the Empire had been Bohemia and
Brandenburg. The former had been lost to him by Hussitism; the latter
he had conferred on the Hohenzollern, since it was too distant for a King
of Hungary and an anti-Turk champion to control. Of the twenty years
that followed the Council of Constance he only spent two and a half in
Germany. If he constantly complained of the lack of German support,
the princes as constantly complained of his impracticability and absence.
His reign was indeed a rehearsal of subsequent Habsburg imperial policy.
Yet his rule had not been without merit. The anarchy of Germany, if
it had not diminished, had not increased. He had revived the prestige
of the Empire at Constance and Basle. He had saved Bohemia for the
Empire and averted Slav dangers. He had tried to induce the towns to
take their share in national affairs and made it certain that they would
later find a place in the Reichstag. If the numerous efforts to reform the
machinery of government were chiefly due to the pressure of the Hussite
war, it was also true that he had raised the question before the war
began. It was with sufficient justice that the author of the *Reformation
Kaiser Sigmunds*, published soon after Sigismund's death, attributed his
programme to the Emperor. The manifesto illustrates the growing
demand for social as well as political reform, owing to the growth of
German capitalism and the anomalies of ecclesiastical power. The
writer demanded the secularisation of ecclesiastical principalities and
property, and the payment of salaries to the clergy; stricter discipline of
religious houses; equality of income for men pursuing the same calling;
that no man should follow more than one vocation; the abolition of
serfdom, freedom of movement, and facilities for acquiring burgher rights;

the establishment of maximum prices for necessities of life and the prohibition of capitalist associations; that tolls should only be levied to cover the cost of maintaining bridges and roads; and that four imperial vicars should ensure the operation of the law in the four quarters of the Empire.

III. THE HABSBURGS.

Sigismund's successor was in many ways well qualified to fill the rôle of saviour of Germany. Albert of Austria had the reputation of a man of vigour who had reduced his territorial nobles to order and forced his towns to pay their taxes. He was in the prime of life, he was a thorough German, and he united in himself the claims and possessions of the houses of Luxemburg and Habsburg. After Sigismund's wayward brilliance Albert's straightforward honesty, blameless private life, indifference to popularity, perhaps even his innocence of foreign tongues, were a relief. Even a Czech chronicler says that "though a German, he was good, brave, and gentle." The circumstances of his election strengthened Albert's position. Frederick of Hohenzollern was the most considerable figure in German affairs and, though sixty-six years of age, seems to have been considered the favourite for the crown. But the Saxon and ecclesiastical votes went to the man who was marked out as the defender of the Empire's eastern frontiers, and the crown passed to the house of Habsburg, not to leave it for 300 years. On 18 March 1438, Albert II was unanimously elected. Nevertheless the Electors tried to impose conditions on the man of their choice. Albert was to reduce the power and independence of the towns, to consult the Electors in the government of the country, to reform the Veme, to select a true German as his chancellor (a reference to the Bohemian chancellor, Kaspar Schlick). They further declared their neutrality between Pope and Council for six months. But Albert was not anxious for the royal dignity and had promised his Magyars not to accept the German crown without their consent. He was able therefore to reject the Electors' conditions and then to accept the crown with his hands free.

Albert was now a threefold king; but each crown brought with it heavy obligations. He had been crowned King of Hungary at Székesfehérvár (Stuhlweissenburg) on 1 January 1438; but the Turk was soon to cross the Danube and to tax the whole resources of the Magyar realm. The Bohemian Diet had elected him their king, and on St Peter's day he was crowned in Prague. But the nationalist minority rejected him and invited Casimir, brother of Vladyslav of Poland, to dispute the succession. During August and September a Polish army was in Bohemia and its withdrawal was followed by an invasion of Silesia. In the autumn Albert advanced northwards, with support from Saxony, Bavaria, and Albert Achilles of Hohenzollern, and drove back the Poles. An armistice in January 1439 enabled him to turn to the problem of defence against the Turks.

Meanwhile, after vainly trying to induce the towns of Swabia and Franconia to state an agreed plan of reform, Albert summoned a Reichstag to Nuremberg for 13 July 1438. Schlick and the other royal agents arrived punctually to hear the proposal of the Electors, which took the familiar form of the division of Germany into four circles with a nominated prince at the head of each, and a number of provisions against disorder. The royal proposal suggested six circles, each with a governor elected by the local estates and subordinated to a royal court of appeal. In both proposals Albert's own lands were excluded from the circles. Germany was to stand in loose relation to a half-foreign king, a foretaste of the character of Habsburg rule. But Albert's scheme was disliked by the princes and did not induce the towns to abandon their attitude of sullen suspicion either in July or in October, when Schlick also asked for military assistance in Silesia. Constitutional reform was once more postponed. But ecclesiastical reform was brought up at a third Reichstag, at Mayence, in March 1439. The Electors had prolonged their ecclesiastical neutrality, with the support of Albert and a number of princes. They now proceeded to action, which took the form of the *Acceptatio* of Mayence, *i.e.* a promulgation of such portions of the Council of Basle's anti-papal legislation as suited the princely point of view, with additions and modifications. But the "acceptation" was little more than a manifesto of policy. It was never confirmed by Albert nor put into general operation. Nor was obedience formally withdrawn from either Pope or Council, when those two authorities fell apart in open schism in June 1439. In the absence of governance, German princes and even the Conciliar Fathers themselves observed or disregarded the liberties announced at Basle and Mayence as it suited them. German unity was to receive no impetus from a German national Church.

Albert summoned another Reichstag for 1 November, but before it could meet he was dead. He had spent the summer in vain endeavours to induce the Magyar nobles to co-operate against the Turks or to accept the help of a German host. The fortress of Semendria and the greater part of Serbia fell to the Muslims, and the little Hungarian army was wasted by disease in the summer heat of the marshy plains of Bácska. Albert himself was struck down by dysentery and tried to recover his health by a hasty return to his beloved Vienna. But he died on the journey on 27 October, at the early age of forty-two. In the general confusion of Central Europe he had seemed the one hope of order, defence, and reform, and "by high and low, by rich and poor, he was more lamented than any prince since Christ's birth."[1]

The long reign of Albert's successor was a period of great importance in the development of Germany. Throughout it the public opinion of princes, churchmen, and townsfolk was alive to the deplorable lack of governance in the Empire. But circumstances rendered any remedy well-

[1] Windecke.

nigh impossible. The one expression of German national life, the Reichstag, was frequently summoned to the various cities of Franconia and the Rhineland; but it was seldom attended, and never dominated, by the sovereign, while it was paralysed by the divergent interests of the leading princes. Meanwhile the distant north, from the lower Rhine to the Polish frontier, pursued its destiny without attention to any national assembly. The break-up of Albert's threefold power—Austria, Bohemia, Hungary—opened the way for the re-creation of strong non-German kingdoms in Bohemia and Hungary, whose rulers intervened powerfully in German affairs. Germany itself was a mass of warring authorities, controlled not by a system of public law but by private agreements, interpreted not by public officials but by arbitrators chosen by the parties concerned. The Church, divided by the aftermath of the Conciliar movement or surrendered by papal bargainers to the control of the greater princes, was incapable of providing a framework for national unity. The towns, by their timidity and mutual distrust, never assumed the power to which their wealth and culture might have entitled them. Meanwhile the sovereign was far removed from the national centre of gravity, never relinquishing a claim or a right, but seldom taking any action or emerging from his retreat at Graz or Wiener Neustadt. By his tenacity, by his diplomatic skill, by the mere length of his life, Frederick III did much to ensure the permanence of the Empire in the house of Habsburg. But during his reign Germany was in conflagration. The confused scrap-heap of the Middle Ages was largely consumed in the heat of conflict, and Germany emerged divided between a number of independent territorial princes, soon to be made despots by the reception of the Roman Law and the complete subjection of their territorial clergy in the age of the Reformation; though many towns continued to enjoy their independence, protected by their walls, absorbed in parochial interests, and permanently estranged from the military caste which had won political power.

Albert II had no son. His widow was with child; but, even if it turned out to be a boy, the Electors would not burden the Empire with an infant sovereign and a regency. On 2 February 1440, they elected the eldest Habsburg prince, Frederick of Styria. The towns rejoiced at the elevation of another Habsburg. But it was to the particularist princes that the election was most welcome. Frederick was but twenty-four; his only inheritance the poor and mountainous duchies of Styria, Carniola, and Carinthia, which he shared with his troublesome brother Albert VI. He was also guardian of the young Sigismund, heir of Tyrol. He would be forced to assume the rôle of defender of Germany's eastern marches against Slavs, Magyars, and Turks, and his claims to the regency of Albert's kingdoms would divert his attention from the interior of the Empire. Further, Frederick, though cultured, moral, abstemious, and intelligent, soon shewed that he was no man of action.

His first attention was given to the Luxemburg-Habsburg inheritance. Albert's will[1] provided for a council of regency, consisting of his widow Elizabeth, the eldest Habsburg prince, three Magyar, four Czech, and two Austrian councillors, with Bratislava as a convenient seat of government. The will was not executed. On 22 February Elizabeth gave birth to a son, Ladislas Posthumus, whom she placed under Frederick's guardianship and who was duly crowned King of Hungary at Székesfehérvár on 15 May. But the majority of the Magyar magnates felt the need of vigorous leadership against the Turks and offered the crown to Vladyslav II of Poland. Civil war followed, till a truce was arranged through the mediation of Cardinal Cesarini in 1443. On Vladyslav's death at Varna in 1444, the Magyar Diet acknowledged the boy Ladislas as king. The acknowledgment remained formal, however, for Frederick refused to surrender the care of one who was also heir of Bohemia and Austria. The Magyars, therefore, accepted the regency of their national hero, John Hunyadi; Frederick was excluded from Hungarian affairs; and there matters rested for the time being.

Nor was Frederick more successful in Bohemia. The Czech Diet, after conditional and fruitless offers of the crown to Albert of Bavaria and to Frederick himself, acknowledged young Ladislas in 1443. But, as Frederick refused to part with his ward, the Bohemian kingdom remained without a head and disturbed by civil strife, till in 1452 the Diet recognised the moderate Hussite leader, George of Poděbrady, as regent.

In the hereditary lands of the Habsburgs it was only with difficulty that Frederick asserted his rule. The Habsburg inheritance had suffered division. Since 1379 Austria had been the share of the Albertine or elder line, the rest falling to the Leopoldine line; and the·latter portion had been subdivided in 1411 between the Styrian and the Tyrolese branches. When Frederick of Tyrol died on 24 June 1439, leaving an heir, Sigismund, only eleven years old, Frederick saw his opportunity of restoring unity of government to the Leopoldine lands. He hastened to make terms with the Diet of Tyrol, which acknowledged him as regent for four years, on condition that he co-operated with a council of Tyrolese and did not remove Sigismund from the county. The news of King Albert's death, opening out far larger visions of power, caused Frederick to hurry off, taking Sigismund with him, contrary to his obligations, to meet the Austrian Estates of Perchtoldsdorf. From them in November he obtained recognition as regent till Albert's son (if the child should be a son) should reach the age of sixteen. In thus obtaining the regencies of Tyrol and Austria, Frederick had defeated the ambitions of his brother Albert VI, to whom he was forced to allot considerable estates and pensions. Dissatisfied with his share, Albert VI continued to be a thorn in Frederick's side for more than twenty years, till his death in 1463.

[1] This instrument was a forgery, probably the work of the Chancellor, Schlick, and Ulrich von Eizing. See O. Stowasser, *Ulrich von Eizing.*

Preoccupied with disputes with his various Diets, with the insub-ordinate Austrian nobility, with the unsuccessful attempts of Queen Elizabeth to recover her son Ladislas, with the Counts of Cilli, whom Sigismund had raised to the rank of Princes of the Empire, Frederick did not attend to the affairs of Germany till 1442. In accepting the crown he had given no undertaking to join the Electors in their ecclesiastical neutrality, which appeared to many of the lesser estates, the inferior clergy, the universities, and the towns, as no more than an expedient for extending the power of the greater princes. In 1441 Frederick neither appeared at the Reichstag nor announced any definite policy. In 1442 he made a progress to Aix-la-Chapelle to be crowned on 17 June, and returned to the Reichstag at Frankfort, at which much discussion of the ecclesiastical and secular anarchy of Germany resulted only in an ineffective edict against lawlessness. By December he was back in Tyrol.

Frederick was feeling his way carefully. Most of the Electors were moving towards an open declaration in favour of Basle and its Pope. But Frederick, advised by his Chancellor, Schlick, and his secretary, Aeneas Sylvius Piccolomini, was inclined to see both his own advantage and the best hopes of peace and order in Germany's recognition of Eugenius IV, who commanded the adhesion of the Western kingdoms. To prevent the Electors from openly supporting Basle, Frederick appeared at the Reichstag of Nuremberg in August 1444, and succeeded in post-poning any decision until he should have appealed to both Eugenius and Basle to support the convocation of an impartial general council to end the schism. Both parties rejected the suggestion; but Frederick had gained time, and in December he opened negotiations with Eugenius, who was prepared to grant him extensive rights of ecclesiastical appoint-ment and visitation in the Habsburg lands in return for his declaration of obedience to Rome. By cautious procrastination and by convincing a number of princes of the advantages to be gained from Rome, Frederick succeeded at last in October 1446 in persuading the Electors to join him in negotiations with Eugenius. The general disgust at the protracted schism and the ecclesiastical confusion was discrediting all policies of defiance of Rome. At Eugenius' death-bed in February 1447, the main lines of the Papal-German peace were laid down. The Pope recognised elections made during the German neutrality and withdrew the penalties pronounced on neutrals and supporters of Basle. It remained to make the definitive peace with the new Pope, Nicholas V. Frederick's supporters, the Party of Obedience, led by the Elector of Mayence and the Princes of Hohenzollern, met the royal agents at Aschaffenburg in July 1447, agreed to recognise Nicholas, and left to Frederick the settlement of the liberties of the German Church and of the papal revenue from Germany. Meanwhile the other Electors, perhaps to save their faces, perhaps to obtain French help for their various ambitions, made their peace with

Rome through the mediation of King Charles VII. The final concordat, however, was effected by Frederick in February 1448, at Vienna, in the name of the Electors and Princes, and marked the complete triumph of the Papacy over the conciliar movement. All the Estates of the Empire in time acceded to it, beginning with the Archbishop of Salzburg in April 1448, and ending with Strasbourg in 1476. But not all the victory went to the Pope. The greater princes sold their adhesion at a high price: the exclusion from their territories of external episcopal juris- diction, rights of presentation to benefices, a share in ecclesiastical taxation. In this rush to join in the profits of the old system the public good of the Church and the Empire was ignored. The reform of papal taxation and of abuses, all the hopes centred in the Council of Basle, demanded an idealism of which the German princes were incapable. Yet in the universities and towns lingered a devotion to the idea of ecclesiastical reform. As Aeneas Sylvius wrote, "We have a truce, but no peace." The Papacy had temporarily broken the movement for reform by taking the princes into partnership. By doing so it increased the princely authority over the German Church, an authority which, two generations later, was to turn against Rome and, by canalising the streams of a more vigorous reforming movement, to establish itself in independence of both Church and Empire.

The schism was not the only topic for discussion at the Reichstag of Nuremberg in August 1444. Besides the Turkish danger and the need of a Public Peace in Germany, Frederick raised the urgent question of the Swiss. The death of the last Count of Toggenburg (1436) had embroiled Zürich and Schwyz in a desperate struggle for the Toggenburg lands. Zürich, worsted and empty-handed, remembered her German alle- giance and concluded an alliance with the Habsburg king on 14 June 1443.

Frederick hoped to recover the Habsburg lands seized by the con- federates in 1415, while the Zürichers saw a chance of placing their city at the head of a new league of the Upper Rhine. In September Frederick came south of the Rhine, was enthusiastically welcomed at Zürich, and received the town's homage. He refused the requests of the Confederation for confirmation of its liberties, unless it were willing to return to the *status quo* of the "fifty years' peace" of 1412. The result was a con- federate attack upon Zürich in 1443. For an imperial war against the confederates Frederick could count on the enthusiastic support of the impecunious nobles of Swabia. But he needed more adequate force. Unable to secure the help of the Swabian towns, which had little sympathy for an attack on bourgeois liberties, or that of the Duke of Burgundy, to whom he had refused Luxemburg, Frederick adopted the unfortunate expedient of demanding the loan of some 6000 troops from the King of France. Charles VII was glad of an excuse to rid France of the unruly soldiery who had fought his battles against the English. In the summer of 1444 the Dauphin Louis with a horde of 40,000 Armagnacs advanced through the Sundgau towards Basle. Diverted by the desperate resistance of 1500 Swiss who attempted to bar their way at St Jakob on the Birs on 26 August, the Armagnacs poured into Alsace. It was evident that Frederick's allies, far from co-operating in war against the Confederation, intended to spoil the defenceless Rhine valley. The dauphin made peace with the Swiss in October, and seemed to treat Alsace as conquered French territory. Frederick appeared in the ignominious character of a king who had deliberately exposed his people to foreign invasion, while he himself remained preoccupied with the Swiss war. The defence of German soil was undertaken by others. The Elector Palatine, Lewis IV, co-operated with the citizens of Strasbourg in harassing the French. The news of a Burgundian agreement with the Elector Palatine and the fear of seeing his retreat cut off caused Louis to abandon his Armagnacs and retire to France in December. He had succeeded in exporting thousands of dangerous ruffians from France and depositing them in Germany. In February 1445 a treaty concluded at Trèves provided for the evacuation of Alsace; but the infuriated inhabitants cut off and massacred considerable numbers of the French troops as they retired through the Vosges.

Meanwhile, in October 1444, Frederick had retired to Austria. His experience of electoral opposition at the Reichstag and the distressing consequences of his French alliance gave him a distaste for personal appearance at the national assembly. For the next twenty-seven years he did not visit Germany west of his hereditary lands. His attempt to reassert the control of the Empire and of the Habsburgs over the Swiss came to nothing; but the dispute was continued until Sigismund of Tyrol, when allied with the confederates against Burgundy in 1474, abandoned the Habsburg claims.

As the effort for conciliar reform degenerated into ecclesiastical confusion, the internal feuds, from which Germany had enjoyed comparative peace, blazed out on all sides. The princes looked with resentment at the growing wealth and power of the towns and were seldom at a loss for causes of dispute with each other. Peculiarly German were the struggles of princely houses for the acquisition of bishoprics. The fortunes of the house of Mörs afford a striking example. The earlier half of the fifteenth century witnessed a great extension of the family's power. From 1414 till 1463 Dietrich von Mörs was Archbishop of Cologne, and therefore Duke of Westphalia and Count of Arnsberg. His elder brother Frederick was Count of Mörs, and his youngest brother John married the heiress of Mahlberg-Lahr. But it was the Church which provided most richly for the family. Dietrich secured the bishopric of Paderborn for himself in 1415; and for his brother Henry the bishopric of Münster in 1424, and in 1442, after severe fighting, also the administration of that of Osnabrück; while his remaining brother, Walram, in 1433 possessed himself of part of the disputed see of Utrecht.

As Dietrich was on good terms with Duke Gerhard of Juliers-Berg-Ravensberg, the house of Mörs seemed to dominate all north-western Germany and to threaten the existence of the only other Westphalian principality of any importance, the Duchy of Cleve, whose Duke, Adolf II, was obliged in 1430 to surrender Mark to his brother Gerhard, a protégé of Dietrich. Nevertheless, Adolf of Cleve maintained a vigorous opposition to his powerful neighbour. He forbade his clergy to pay a tenth collected by Dietrich in 1433, and tried to secure ecclesiastical independence for his duchy. Such was the position on the lower Rhine when Dietrich entered on a struggle with the Hansa town of Soest.

Soest was a territorial town with no claim to independence of the archbishop. Dietrich was not an unsympathetic overlord, and had intervened in 1432 to secure to the community a share in municipal government, hitherto monopolised by the patrician families. But the town continually encroached upon the rights of the see, until Dietrich took his case before the royal court at Graz in 1443. Soest, as an ancient Saxon town, refused to plead except on Saxon (North German) soil. Frederick III appointed a Saxon arbitrator, who gave his award in favour of Dietrich. Thereupon Soest opened negotiations with Adolf of Cleve, and together they declared war on the archbishop in June 1444, Soest transferring its allegiance to Adolf's son John. The five years of war which followed illustrate well the difficulty of securing any decision amid the fluctuating combinations of force in Germany and the practical limitations on all forms of political authority. Frederick III put Soest to the ban of the Empire and Dietrich placed it under an interdict. But Dietrich's loyalty to ecclesiastical neutrality estranged him from Frederick, as the latter drew nearer to Eugenius IV. In January 1445, the Pope, strong in Burgundian support, transferred the territories of Cleve, including Soest, to the ecclesiastical control of Rudolf, Bishop of Utrecht, who raised the interdict; while in July Eugenius quashed all sentences laid upon the territories of Cleve. The Bishop of Münster and Gerhard of Mark supported Dietrich, but the knights and towns of their territories stood for Cleve and Soest. Finally, in January 1446, Dietrich, together with his colleague of Trèves, was deposed, as a heretic and schismatic, and the two electorates were transferred respectively to Adolf of Cleve's second son, Adolf, and to Philip of Burgundy's bastard brother, John, Bishop of Cambrai. Not until he had opened negotiations with Nicholas V and was sure of formal restoration to his see, could Dietrich hope to deal with the rebellion of Soest. He then had the help of Duke William III, the Saxon Elector's brother, who had married Anne, daughter of King Albert II, and on her account laid claim to Luxemburg against Philip of Burgundy. Dietrich promised to support the claim, and William brought a fierce horde of 16,000 Czech and Saxon mercenaries across the Weser. Together they besieged Soest in July 1447. But hunger and racial animosities, as well as the resistance of the townsmen, took the spirit out of the attack. The siege was abandoned and the mercenaries marched off eastwards. After Burgundian, royal, and papal efforts at mediation had failed, the war was resumed in 1448. Young John of Cleve, anxious to end the devastation, challenged the Elector to a decisive battle. Dietrich refused; but, as a true shepherd of his flock, offered single combat. John accepted. But Germany was denied the piquant spectacle of the elderly archbishop engaged in a duel; for Dietrich withdrew, pleading his priestly character. All parties were now financially exhausted, and war died down. The final peace was made in April 1449, at a conference at Maestricht, when Cardinal Carvajal presided and pronounced an arbitral award. The territorial settlement followed the war map; and Soest thus passed to Cleve. The ecclesiastical authority of Cologne over Cleve was restored, though Dietrich's subsequent efforts to tax the clergy of Cleve were so firmly resisted by Duke John as to give rise to the saying that the Duke of Cleve was Pope in his own lands. All claims to reparation and other outstanding questions were referred to the Pope, and so in time found decent burial.

In the next year Dietrich of Cologne entered upon another wearisome struggle. His brother Henry died in June 1450, and Dietrich induced the chapter of Münster to elect his younger brother Walram on 15 July. But the house of Mörs was now opposed by that of Hoya. Albert of Hoya was Bishop of Minden; his cousin Gerhard was Archbishop of Bremen. Albert's brother John converted the chapter of Münster to the support of another brother, Eric, and persuaded the city to nominate himself as administrator of the territory on Eric's behalf. Meanwhile the chapter of Osnabrück elected Albert of Hoya, who however received no countenance from Rome. Dietrich was strong in the papal confirmation of Walram's election, and in September had gained a great accession of strength by the purchase of the succession to Juliers and Berg from Duke Gerhard. This decided John of Cleve to support the Hoya cause and to resume his struggle with Cologne. Nicholas of Cusa vainly endeavoured to mediate between the conflicting parties, and the war dragged on until the knights and burgesses of the territory of Münster, feeling that their interests were ignored by both sides, agreed in October 1452 to the compromise of Coesfeld by which both claimants to the bishopric were to be set aside. John of Hoya temporarily yielded to public opinion and withdrew from Münster. But in February 1453 he was back in the city, relying on the support of the poorer classes and carrying out a red terror at the expense of the patrician families and the more substantial craft-gilds. The aristocratic government of the city was abrogated in favour of extremely democratic institutions, which hardly veiled John's incipient despotism. Emigrant citizens laid their complaints before the Hanseatic League at Lübeck, and in October 1454 Münster was expelled from the League. Various princes joined in the struggle with little effect. In 1455 Conrad of Diepholz, to whom Walram made over his claims before his own death in October 1456, was elected Bishop of Osnabrück and received confirmation from Calixtus III. On 22 November 1456, the chapter of Münster proceeded to another election. Two canons braved the papal disfavour and voted for Eric of Hoya; the majority elected Conrad of Diepholz. Both parties appealed to Rome. Calixtus rejected both candidates and nominated John of Wittelsbach, Count of Simmern-Zweibrücken. The new bishop was not only able and conciliatory, but was also acceptable to the Duke of Cleve. Both the disappointed candidates saw their supporters losing interest in their claims, and on 23 October 1457 the feud was ended by the treaty of Kranenburg. Münster accepted the papal nominee; John and Eric of Hoya were relieved of all ecclesiastical censures and received compensation, as did John of Cleve. Under Bishop John's rule Münster once more knew peace and order, the city coming under a mixed constitution which gave half the council to the patrician families and half to the other citizens. The long struggle had weakened both Dietrich (who also lost Juliers and Berg through the unexpected paternity of Duke Gerhard) and the Counts of Hoya; the only gainers being the Papacy and the Duke of Cleve, who in 1466 further succeeded in securing the bishopric of Münster for his nephew Henry of Schwarzburg.

Meanwhile in southern Germany there were numerous cross-currents of strife. Many princes joined in the family feud of the Dukes of Bavaria-Ingolstadt and the disputes which followed the extinction of that line in 1447, when the whole inheritance passed to Henry of Bavaria-Landshut. But the chief characteristic of the south German feuds was the opposition of the princes and the towns. In the absence of any effective royal authority the many causes of dispute—rights of jurisdiction, tolls, mints, the debts and highway robbery of the princes, the towns' acceptance of *pfahlbürger*, etc.—could find no issue but in war. The princes maintained that their legal rights were constantly being infringed by the townsmen; while the latter replied with bitterness that the feudal countryside was the scene of robbery and violence and that the towns alone provided security and comfort to the non-noble. In 1441 a number of Swabian towns formed a league for mutual defence against the dangers of the trade-routes, and this was developed in 1446 into a working confederation of thirty-one towns under the leadership of Nuremberg, Augsburg, Ulm, and Esslingen. In opposition to this movement was formed a league of princes, inspired and guided chiefly by the Margrave Albert Achilles of Hohenzollern, brother of Frederick II, Elector of Brandenburg. Albert Achilles was the perfect type of conservative and feudal prince, ambitious of re-creating for himself the duchy of Franconia, an upholder of royal authority which alone could legalise such a re-creation, contemptuous of the burgher class, cunning in diplomacy, delighting in war, which he declared to be adorned by arson as is Vespers by the Magnificat. His inextensive territories of Ansbach and part of Baireuth were surrounded

by the lands of numerous petty princes and towns and were divided from
each other by the town of Nuremberg, which had extended its jurisdiction
and protection far over the countryside. Nuremberg was the chief centre
of commercial distribution in southern Germany; its urban aristocracy
the wealthiest and most powerful. Aeneas Sylvius expressed the opinion
that "the Kings of Scotland would gladly be housed as luxuriously as
the ordinary citizens of Nuremberg." The mutual hostility of the margrave and the town led to open war in June 1449, over the behaviour of
the Lord of Heideck, who had left the service of Albert Achilles for
that of Nuremberg and had then added the offence of sinking a mine in
co-operation with some townsmen and asserting his right freely to do so
as a vassal of the Empire. Towns, princes, and knights on all sides took
part in the great "town-war" that followed. Peasants took refuge behind
the walls and artillery of the towns, while their villages were destroyed.
The Nurembergers succeeded in inflicting a severe defeat on the margrave
at the fish-ponds of Pillenreut in March 1450; but the citizen army was
incapable of forcing a decision, while the princely forces could not carry
the defences of the town. As the enthusiasm for war subsided, arbitrators put
an end to various subsidiary feuds, usually to the disadvantage of the towns;
but the main feud continued, for Albert Achilles would not surrender his
conquests without compensation, and that Nuremberg refused to pay.

The appeals made by both sides to Frederick III in 1452 were
useless, for Frederick was then facing insurrection in his own Habsburg
lands and unwilling to give a decision which might lose him possible
supporters. Albert Achilles himself went to Wiener Neustadt, refused
to submit to the jurisdiction of imperial officials, and forced the helpless
Emperor to promise the formation of a princely court to decide the
dispute. On getting rid of his unwelcome visitor, Frederick did not fulfil
this undertaking, but commissioned Duke Lewis of Bavaria-Landshut to
effect a settlement. In April 1453, the treaty of Lauf, by which Albert
Achilles surrendered his conquests in return for a heavy payment of
money, put an end to the war. Nuremberg remained as strong and
independent as ever. But in one respect the "town-war" is a landmark
in German history. It had shewn the impossibility of maintaining a
defensive league of towns in view of the narrowly selfish policy of the
members, many of whom had enough to do controlling the revolutionary
aspirations of their artisans. Henceforward the towns stood on the
defensive and refused to risk the dangers of war on behalf of each other.
When Donauwörth was seized by Lewis of Bavaria-Landshut in 1458
and Mayence by its Elector in 1462, no town moved to the assistance of
the burgher cause. In the combinations, plans, and discussions for the
reform of the Empire the voice of the towns was hardly heard. The issue
might sometimes appear to be between imperial or princely control of
the central government; but, with the Empire in the hands of the preoccupied and harassed Frederick, it resolved itself rather into a confused

struggle between princes, such as the Hohenzollern, who nominally stood for the imperial idea, and others, such as the Wittelsbachs, who opposed them. Both types followed their own interests wherever they perceived them. The future lay with the feudal prince, armed, wary, and blessed with a progeny not so numerous as to cause excessive division of his inheritance.

Meanwhile Frederick III had no peace in the Habsburg lands. The cost of his early struggles had caused him to pledge his meagre revenues for many years ahead and left him without the means to enforce his will. He provided for an extension of his guardianship over young Sigismund of Tyrol for six years from 1443; but the Tyrolese broke into revolt, and Frederick was forced in 1446 to agree to an arrangement by which Sigismund received the administration of Tyrol and the Archduke Albert VI that of the Habsburg territories on the Rhine. Far from uniting his family's inheritance, as a first step towards a strong German monarchy, Frederick had embittered his brother and his nephew without rendering them powerless. In November Austria endured an invasion by Hunyadi and the Magyars, who demanded the person of their king, Ladislas. Although Frederick received no support from Austria or from Germany, he obstinately clung to his guardianship, and peace was made in 1447 by the universal arbitrator, Cardinal Carvajal, who diverted Hunyadi to the Turkish crusade. Soon Austria turned against Frederick. The Austrian Estates laid the blame for the prevalent lack of law and order upon Frederick, whom they denounced as a Styrian who would not live in Vienna. They demanded the rule of young Ladislas and an Austrian council. Their leader was Ulrich von Eizing, who proposed to be in Austria what Hunyadi was in Hungary and Poděbrady in Bohemia. On 12 December 1451, the Austrian Diet met. Eizing harangued the populace and presented to the Estates Ladislas' sister Elizabeth, dressed in rags and begging their help. An Austrian council of regency, with Eizing at its head, was proclaimed and an ultimatum was addressed to Frederick, then about to start for Italy to marry Eleanora of Portugal and to receive the imperial crown from Nicholas V. Frederick made haste to escape from such worries, taking Ladislas with him. He enjoyed six months' peace in Italy, whence he returned, a husband and an Emperor, to Wiener Neustadt in June 1452, to find that his enemies had made good use of the interval. The Austrian insurgents were now supported by Ulrich of Cilli, Ladislas' cousin and alternative guardian, by many Magyars, and by the Catholic Bohemians, who hoped to use Ladislas for the undoing of Poděbrady and his Hussite friends. In August a force of 16,000 men attacked Wiener Neustadt. Frederick's position was not desperate, for neither Poděbrady nor Hunyadi wished to see their regencies disturbed by the liberation of Ladislas; and Poděbrady, as well as a Styrian force, was preparing to advance to the Emperor's relief. But Frederick never met force with force. He preferred negotiation, and at last brought himself to surrender Ladislas. The twelve-year-old boy was entrusted to Ulrich of Cilli, who took him to Vienna. Peace was made in March 1453, Frederick receiving compensation and comforting himself meanwhile by the promulgation of Rudolf IV's Habsburg Privilege, which attributed to the members of that house the title of Archduke of Austria and virtually relieved their territories of all obligations towards the Empire—a provision which did little harm to German unity, since the kingship remained henceforth for centuries in the Habsburg house.

But Ulrich of Cilli found that his efforts to rule Austria autocratically were opposed by Eizing, the clergy, the lesser nobles, and the towns. In September he was ejected from Vienna, and a council of twelve, representing the four Estates, took over the regency. Ladislas, however, had barely reached the age of fifteen when he asserted himself, recalled Ulrich, and began to undermine the position of the regents in his two kingdoms. These designs were checked by the urgent need of opposing the great Turkish invasions which followed the fall of Constantinople. That event spread alarm throughout central Europe. St Giovanni Capistrano and other preachers raised much enthusiasm and large sums of money for the crusade. But the German princes would not move. Three Reichstags in 1454 and 1455 produced no plan of co-operation. The championship of Christendom fell upon Hungary, and was effected by Hunyadi's heroic defence of Belgrade in July 1456. After Hunyadi's death and the retreat of the Turks, Ladislas came south to Belgrade with a small force of Austrian and Magyar crusaders. Here Ulrich of Cilli was killed by Hunyadi's son Ladislas, who represented his victim as the aggressor and obtained a sworn promise from King Ladislas that he should not be held guilty of murder. In March 1457, the king nevertheless seized and executed Ladislas Hunyadi, and carried off Hunyadi's younger son, Matthias Corvinus.

Having thus alienated the Magyars, who loved the house of Hunyadi, Ladislas turned to Bohemia. He had not time to fall out with Poděbrady, for on 23 November he died suddenly at Prague. His death snapped the slender bonds which united the Habsburg threefold monarchy. In Bohemia the Habsburg claims were set aside, and the Diet elected Poděbrady king. Frederick III, whose thoughts turned rather to the Hungarian succession, abandoned Bohemia to the king of its choice, and in 1459 invested him with the electoral dignity. Strong in the submission of Moravia and Silesia and in his alliances with the Wettin and Hohenzollern princes, Poděbrady began to play an increasingly important part in the affairs of Germany and to entertain hopes of becoming King of the Romans, the Emperor's coadjutor and prospective successor. In Hungary there was civil war again. A Magyar Diet elected Matthias Corvinus, liberated by Poděbrady on Ladislas' death, as king; while an anti-Hunyadi group of magnates, in February 1459, elected Frederick III. The efforts of the inevitable Cardinal Carvajal eventually resulted in 1463 in a settlement, by which Frederick surrendered the sacred crown of St Stephen in consideration of 80,000 ducats and the retention of several fortresses, though he characteristically stipulated that he should also retain the title of King of Hungary and that, if Matthias should die sonless, the kingdom should pass to Frederick or one of his heirs male. Frederick's foresight and his confidence in the destiny of his house, illustrated by his monogram A.E.I.O.U. (*Austriae est imperare orbi universo*), were to be justified in the future. For a time the great Habsburg inheritance was broken up. Bohemia and Hungary went their several ways. But two generations later both the kingdoms were to return to the Habsburg line, when a Habsburg Emperor ruled most of Christendom and the new world across the Atlantic.

In Austria also, the death of Ladislas was followed by succession disputes. Sigismund of Tyrol, however, surrendered his claims to Albert VI in exchange for the latter's Rhenish lands; and a Czech invasion in 1458 caused Frederick and Albert to come to terms, Frederick retaining Lower and Albert Upper Austria. Under this divided rule the unfortunate country suffered more than ever from disturbance, which the Habsburg princes had not the resources to control. Unable to pay his troops Frederick allowed their commanders to coin money, and Austria was afflicted with debased currency. This inflation, accompanied by bad harvests, brought on acute misery and even starvation. Taking advantage of the Emperor's unpopularity, Albert declared war on him in June 1461. In November of the next year Frederick was being besieged in the castle of Vienna by Albert and the citizens, when his councillors sent a desperate appeal to Poděbrady. Anxious to secure the Emperor's good offices with Pius II over the ecclesiastical difficulties in Bohemia and yet not to offend Albert whose support he needed in Germany, Poděbrady responded to the call, and in December brought about a peace by which Frederick surrendered the whole of Austria to his brother for eight years at an annual rent.

Frederick owed his safety to the powerful Bohemian, to whom he committed the guardianship of his son Maximilian in the event of his own death. He rode out of Vienna amid the derision of the populace. But in December 1463 Albert died suddenly. As Sigismund of Tyrol was then deeply engaged in a struggle with the Papacy and the Swiss, to whom he lost the last Habsburg possessions south of the Lake of Constance, Frederick became undisputed lord of reunited Austria. The Habsburg fortunes now began to revive. Frederick was at peace with Hungary; while Poděbrady was occupied with the papal offensive against Hussitism, which led to his excommunication in 1466, the rebellion of Moravia and Silesia, and the Hungarian invasion of his territories in the name of the Church. Frederick's hands were at last moderately free, and he was able to give some attention to the affairs of Germany.

As the Hussite wars of the twenties had raised the question of the constitutional reform of the Empire, so in the fifties the Turkish triumphs were accompanied by a revival of that controversy. The decade 1454–64 was filled with schemes, plots, and shifting alliances between the leading princes, ending in four years of war throughout southern Germany. Owing to the absence of the Emperor the main question was whether or not the Electors could co-operate in some scheme of national government. The issues were confused by many considerations. The most ardent reformers were anxious also to resume the struggle for ecclesiastical reform against a Papacy which seemed determined to make good its financial losses in other countries at the expense of Germany. This threw the Pope on to the side of the Emperor in opposition to all reform. Again, the leading lay Elector and the head of the Wittelsbach connexion, Frederick I of the Palatinate, had his private reasons for opposition to the Emperor, whose deposition he strongly advocated. His brother, the Elector Lewis IV, had died in 1449, leaving a baby son, Philip. To avoid the weakness of a regency and with the consent of the child's mother and of the magnates (there was no assembly of Estates in the Palatinate) Frederick "arrogated" to himself the Electorate, undertaking that the child should succeed him and that he himself would never marry. For the Palatinate the arrangement was excellent; but the Emperor, who never surrendered any legal advantage against a possible opponent, obstinately refused to recognise the arrogation. This question divided the Electors, since it was impossible for the Emperor and the Elector Palatine to work in harmony, while two Electors, Brandenburg and Saxony, would not countenance the election of another king in defiance of Frederick III. Further, the efforts of the Electors encountered the opposition of the other Estates, to whom they affected to dictate. The towns were unlikely to show enthusiasm for constitutional reform when their deputies were informed by Albert Achilles at the Reichstag of Frankfort in September 1454 that they were not there to discuss but to obey, and to see that their principals provided the quota of troops required of them. Reichstag followed Reichstag; much was said, and very little done. The chief event of the assembly at Ratisbon in 1454 was the proposal to elect another king, the most likely candidate at first being Philip of Burgundy. The Rhenish Electors then united in favour of the Archduke Albert, but shewed how slight was their interest in the reform of the central government by bargaining with their candidate for an increase of their own princely powers. Albert's candidature did not survive the Emperor's emphatic refusal to countenance it. Unable to induce the Emperor to come to central Germany, the Electors, represented by Jakob of Trèves, laid before him at Wiener Neustadt in February 1455 a constitutional scheme providing for a *Reichsregiment*, or supreme council, of the Emperor and his natural councillors, the Electors; an imperial court of justice with salaried judges; and a general imperial tax, only to be levied after the scheme had begun to operate. But Frederick refused to share supreme authority, and bought out Jakob with financial advantages and the expectation of the bishopric of Metz. In September 1456, the Rhenish Electors summoned Frederick III to attend an assembly at Nuremberg on St Andrew's Day, failing which they would "take council with another." Frederick, sure of the support of Albert Achilles and of his own brother-in-law, the Saxon Elector, refused to budge. At Nuremberg the Electors declared that they would elect a king who should live within thirty miles of Frankfort—obviously the Elector Palatine. This candidature also came to nothing, in face of the opposition of the imperialist party.

The antipathy between the Wittelsbach and the Hohenzollern-Wettin connexions was becoming acute, and flared up over the sudden seizure of Donauwörth by Lewis of Bavaria-Landshut in October 1458. War did not, however, follow at once, owing to attempts at mediation during 1459 by Pius II, who was making his great effort at Mantua to organise a general European crusade, and by Poděbrady, now undisputed King of Bohemia, in favour with the Pope, and prepared to play the part of "honest broker" in German disputes. Nothing shews the non-national outlook of the German princes more clearly than the widespread agreement amongst them from 1459 to 1461 to support this Czech, who spoke German but indifferently, as a candidate for the royal crown. So confident was Poděbrady that he tried to extract money from Francesco Sforza, the usurping Duke of Milan, in return for a promise of that legal investiture which Frederick III had steadily refused. In 1460 war broke out in Franconia and on the Rhine, and went all in favour of the Wittelsbachs. In February 1461, Poděbrady gathered both sides to an assembly at Eger, and the majority agreed that he should be king. But he found the Electors' demands for ecclesiastical reform incompatible with papal support, while the Hohenzollern princes were at one with general German feeling in refusing to accept a Czech and a doubtful Catholic as their ruler. Poděbrady's candidature fell through, and in the summer war broke out again. So far as the confusion can be given shape, the war may be said to have taken two forms—first, the support given by Lewis of Bavaria-Landshut to Albert of Austria's attack on Frederick III, and Frederick's retaliation by nominating Albert Achilles and others as commanders of the imperial host against the Wittelsbachs; secondly, the sudden deposition by Pius II of Diether, Elector of Mayence, the ally of the Elector Palatine and the chief advocate of ecclesiastical reform, and the Elector Palatine's conflict with the papal nominee, Adolf of Nassau, a struggle rendered memorable by Diether's use of the printing-press when issuing an appeal to the German nation. In both theatres of war the Wittelsbachs were successful, and were able to retain their conquests in Bavaria and the Rhineland and to exorcise the phantom of Albert Achilles' projected duchy of Franconia. The treaties which restored peace in Bavaria were effected under the auspices of Poděbrady at Prague in August 1463. The war in the Rhineland, which ended in November, was marked by Archbishop Adolf's sudden seizure of Mayence on 28 October 1462, when he expelled some 800 citizens, abolished the city's liberties, and reduced it to its legal condition of obedience to his see. An accidental result of this severity was that the exiled citizens spread abroad in Germany their city's mystery of printing. A more immediately obvious outcome was the triumph of the Pope in imposing his candidate on Mayence and in defeating the movement for ecclesiastical reform.

In 1464 the discussions over imperial reform were resumed. Three main lines of provision for governance may be distinguished. Poděbrady's plan included a supreme council of the Emperor himself, the Elector Palatine, Lewis of Bavaria-Landshut, and Albert Achilles; a permanent salaried supreme court; an imperial tax; and an imperial monopoly of printing. These were the usual suggestions, except that it is noticeable that five Electors, including the three ecclesiastics, did not figure in the council, whereas two non-electoral princes were included. Poděbrady's council was based on effective power rather than on traditional claims. It assumed, however, the reconciliation of as yet unreconciled forces and it came to nothing. Lewis of Bavaria-Landshut meanwhile was engaged in the creation of a Swabian league, which should ensure the co-operation of the princes, nobility, and towns in maintaining the peace in southern Germany. This Wittelsbach project was wrecked by the opposition of Albert Achilles, who secured its condemnation by the Emperor. Thirdly, Albert Achilles attempted to establish a similar, but "loyalist" league, with the Emperor at its head and excluding the Wittelsbach princes. This scheme met with no support from the Swabian towns, who distrusted the Hohenzollern's profession of peacefulness and protested that the Wittelsbach territories commanded all their northern and eastern trade-routes.

It was clear that amongst the princes the balance of power and the mutual distrust were such that no scheme of effective imperial government could be applied to any considerable area of Germany. Frederick III accordingly fell back upon what seemed possible. He reasserted his authority in the Empire by a series of judicial pronouncements and summoned Reichstags to Nuremberg in November 1466 and July 1467, to provide military help against the Turks and the excommunicated Poděbrady, and to discuss provisions for a general peace. The only outcome of the discussions was that in August 1467 Frederick promulgated a decree of imperial peace which forbade recourse to arms for five years. The next few years were indeed peaceful for most of Germany, thanks to the general exhaustion and to the papal resumption of the anti-Hussite crusades. But Frederick III was once more surrounded by difficulties. He alternately opposed and supported Poděbrady and, after the latter's death in 1471, hovered between the rival candidates for Bohemia, Matthias Corvinus and Vladislav of Poland; while Austria was in a constant state of insurrection, even faithful Styria broke into revolt in 1469, and the

Turks appeared in Carniola. Twice he fled from this sea of troubles, in December 1468 on pilgrimage to Rome in fulfilment of a vow taken in the unhappy days of November 1462, and in June 1471 to attend an unusually full Reichstag at Ratisbon. It was his first appearance west of Austria since 1444. For four weeks the Reichstag discussed his demand for immediate help against the Turks, and eventually only agreed to a general tenth for the provision of 60,000 men in the next year. In return Frederick put forward a scheme of imperial peace for four years. In opposition to the princely proposal for princely courts enforcing the peace over large areas, he provided that a continued policy of violence should be met by the armed resistance of all Estates within thirty miles of the offence, and that the royal court should be open to all complaints of violence. Further, all claims supported by violence should *ipso facto* fall to the ground. This amounted to a serious effort to outlaw war by flexible regional arrangements and the provision of a central court. Unfortunately the old problem remained. A central court unsupported by adequate force, while it might prevent violence amongst the lesser estates, could not control the great princes. Indeed a number of princes were exempted from the court's jurisdiction, which ensured the towns' passive resistance to the whole scheme. Frederick, however, proclaimed the peace and provided the royal court with a president and six assessors, who should receive salaries derived from the fees of litigants. Under the energetic presidency of the Imperial Chancellor, Adolf of Mayence, the court operated with considerable effect; but after his death in 1475 less recourse was had to it, the assessors' zeal was somewhat damped by the uncertainty of their incomes, and by 1480 the court had ceased to function.

By that time Frederick had turned from efforts to reorganise the Empire to the true method of ensuring royal authority, the extension of the Habsburg hereditary domains. In the East the Turks were ever present, and Frederick only secured a temporary relief from Matthias Corvinus by recognising him as King of Bohemia. In central Germany Frederick was defied by the Elector Palatine and his brother Rupert, Elector of Cologne. But in the west a new situation had developed. Already in 1472 the rumour ran through Germany that Charles the Bold of Burgundy, having made his peace with France, was preparing to take a leading part in the affairs of the Empire. Charles had only one daughter, and Frederick set himself by his favourite method of dynastic arrangement to convert the great western duchy *ad maiorem Habsburgi gloriam*. His diplomatic contest with Charles was intricate in the extreme. Charles' object was the kingship of the Romans, or the creation in his favour of a Burgundian kingdom stretching from the North Sea to the Jura. Frederick's aim was the marriage of the heiress, Mary, with his own son Maximilian, if it could be secured without any surrender of imperial authority in the West. In September 1473, Frederick met Charles at Trèves, but no agreement was reached, and Charles proceeded to consolidate his position in the Rhineland, supported Archbishop Rupert against the estates of Cologne, refused imperial arbitration, and laid siege to Neuss (1474). The issues were now complicated by the general German resentment at Charles' growing power, which aroused the armed opposition of Sigismund of Tyrol (who in 1469 had pledged the Rhenish Habsburg territories to him and now wanted to recover them), of the Swiss, of René of Lorraine, and of the bishops and towns of the upper Rhine; a combination supported by French money and encouragement. Frederick was moved by the Electors of Mayence and Saxony and by Albert Achilles, now Elector of Brandenburg, to summon an imperial army to the relief of Neuss. The Estates responded with unusual liberality, and the German host forced Charles to abandon the siege and to make peace with the Emperor. Charles' subsequent attacks on the Swiss brought about what Frederick's diplomacy had failed to achieve; for with Charles' death the possibility of a Burgundian kingdom disappeared, while the marriage of Maximilian and Mary was celebrated on 19 August 1477.

The Burgundian marriage had far-reaching consequences in the history of Germany and of the world. By it and by his subsequent military prowess Maximilian brought to the house of Habsburg the free county of Burgundy (Franche Comté) and the vast wealth of the Low Countries. The most powerful of the princely houses of Germany was thus raised far above its competitors. In future the Electors could hardly refuse it the royal crown without plunging Germany into civil war. For the crown was henceforth necessary to the Habsburgs to bind together their widely-scattered possessions from the North Sea to the middle Danube. Further, the Habsburgs became the defenders of Germany on the west as well as on the east. Across the dead body of Charles the Bold broke out the age-long struggle over the frontier between France and Germany. For centuries the *illustris domus Austriae* was to be the champion of Germany on both her fronts, till in the age of nationalism its position was undermined by another princely house, less cumbered with non-German possessions and interests.

Frederick's last years saw both his deepest humiliation and his final triumph. Matthias Corvinus, now lord of Moravia, Silesia, and Lausitz (Lusatia) as a result of his anti-Hussite crusades, attacked Austria, whose disturbed condition invited his intervention. In 1485 he established his residence at Vienna and seemed almost to have recreated the threefold monarchy of King Albert II. Frederick, ejected from his hereditary lands, wandered poverty-stricken through Germany. In his extremity he abandoned his opposition to the creation of a King of the Romans and agreed to the election of his son Maximilian on 16 February 1486. The new king's first act was the proclamation of a ten years' public peace, and in the next year steps were taken to ensure support for the royal government. The two powers of southern Germany most hostile to control by the Empire were the Swiss and the Dukes of Bavaria. Albert of Bavaria-Munich defied the peace and seized the free city of Ratisbon in the summer of 1486. His cousin George of Bavaria-Landshut was a constant source of alarm to the lesser estates of Swabia. Albert crowned his offences by his seizure of, and marriage with, Cunigunda, the Emperor's daughter, in January 1487. Frederick and Maximilian in July invited the nobles, knights, prelates, and towns of Swabia to an assembly at Esslingen, whose outcome was the Swabian League, with its council, court of justice, and machinery for raising an armed force of 13,000 men. The League was for many years a leading factor in German affairs. It checked the drift of towns from the imperial to the Swiss system and gave the Habsburgs a weapon of defence against the ambitions of the Wittelsbach dukes.

During '1488 Maximilian's Burgundian lands, far from proving a source of strength, necessitated the march of the Swabian League's army to Flanders, to rescue him from the burghers of Bruges and to insist on Flemish recognition of Maximilian as regent for his son Philip. In December Maximilian returned to Germany and set about the restoration of Habsburg power. The dynasty seemed about to lose its only remaining considerable territory, Tyrol. Sigismund's mismanagement, extravagance, and many illegitimate children had provoked his subjects beyond bearing and reduced him to hopeless debt. Detesting his cousin, the Emperor, Sigismund had sought help from the Bavarian dukes, to whom he had pledged the silver mines of Schwaz and other resources and finally the succession to Tyrol as well as to his Rhenish and Swabian lands. By skilful negotiation and strong in the support of the Tyrolese estates, Maximilian induced Sigismund, on 16 March 1490, to surrender Tyrol to himself in return for a fixed income. Further success soon followed. On 6 April Matthias Corvinus died; and his dominions were afflicted with the succession dispute of the Jagiello brothers, Vladislav of Bohemia and Albert of Poland. The Austrians were delighted to be rid of the Magyar domination, and Maximilian's reconquest of his native land was but a triumphal progress. The citizens of Vienna, who had unhappy memories of his father, now gave their oath of allegiance only to Maximilian. He then crossed the Raab and for a year disputed the Hungarian crown with Vladislav; but his lack of money and his controversy with Charles VIII of France over Brittany induced him to abandon the hopeless quest. By a treaty at Bratislava on 7 November 1491, Vladislav was recognised as King of Hungary, though, failing male heirs, the crown was to pass to Maximilian.

The old Emperor had thus lived to see the restoration and union of the Habsburg lands. But his enjoyment of this sudden recovery was clouded by his own effacement behind his too successful son and by his desire for revenge on the Bavarian dukes. In 1492 the discontented nobles of Bavaria-Munich united with the Swabian League in opposition to their Duke, Albert. Frederick put Albert to the ban of the Empire and would have plunged southern Germany once more into war, had not

Maximilian pacified his father by transferring to him the allegiance of the Austrian dominions and by inducing the Bavarian dukes to restore Ratisbon to the Empire and to cancel their claims on Tyrol.

Frederick's continued life seemed to be only a handicap to his son. But it at least enabled Maximilian to gain the support of the reformers by promises of constitutional amendment, the fulfilment of which would be prevented by the old Emperor's opposition. When Frederick at last died, at Linz on 19 August 1493, Maximilian was left undisputed lord of all the Habsburg lands, but faced with the intricate problems of imperial reform as well as those of his Burgundian inheritance, of the Turkish danger, and of his grandiose plans for the restoration of imperial power in Italy.

Maximilian's accession to sole kingship opens a new chapter in German history. At this point, therefore, we may pause to consider one characteristic of Germany in the fifteenth century, territorialism. The power of the German princes originated both in their official character as local officers of the Empire and in various rights of jurisdiction and military command, which they purchased or received from the churches, nobles, or towns in their sphere of influence. Territorialism was the process of consolidation of these various rights into a single, uniform, and exclusive authority over a defined territory. The process was greatly assisted by the ecclesiastical anarchy of the age of the Councils and by the decline of the feudal military system and the substitution of mercenary forces, the taxation for which was granted by assemblies of Estates, prepared to entrust the preservation of local peace to the prince. It was completed by the reception of the Roman Law and the exclusion of papal authority in the age of the Reformation. The strength of the prince lay in the mutual hostility of the Estates. The nobles detested the townsmen and held to the prince from fear of peasant insurrections and in the hope of ecclesiastical benefices for their families. The clergy looked to the prince for protection from the exactions of Rome and from the growing popular anti-clericalism. The towns were often recalcitrant, especially where they formed part of an external league, but a prince of vigour and shrewdness could often find in civic disputes an opportunity to impose his authority. The principality became the object of loyalty, and in the interests of unity Estates often insisted on the rule of primogeniture and the indivisibility of the territory.

We may take as a type of territorial consolidation that principality which was destined ultimately to become the unifier of Germany, the Mark of Brandenburg. Frederick I, the first Elector of the Hohenzollern line, was not only Margrave of Brandenburg, but also lord of Ansbach and Baireuth in Franconia. Imperial affairs and the leadership of anti-Hussite crusades held more attraction for him than the prosaic task of creating the machinery of government in the more primitive north, especially when his estrangement from Sigismund wrecked his hope of acquiring further north-eastern fiefs. In January 1426, he made over the government of Brandenburg to his eldest son, John. Under John, whose retiring nature and sedentary preoccupations are suggested by his nickname of "the Alchemist," the Mark relapsed into disorder. Baronial brigandage recommenced and the towns, unprotected against Hussite invasions, formed leagues which defied the princely authority. The aged Elector therefore decided to redistribute his territories. By an act of 1437 he assigned the Mark to his second son, Frederick, who thus became in 1440 the Elector Frederick II. To John was given only a half of Baireuth, while the third son, Albert Achilles, received Ansbach and the other half of Baireuth. Thus the Franconian and imperialist interests of the family were entrusted to the vigorous Albert Achilles, and Frederick II was able to concentrate on his electorate.

Frederick II was the real founder of Hohenzollern power in the north. So successful was his policy from the first that his peaceful succession to his father in 1440 passed almost unnoticed. By skill and patience he wore down the insubordinate nobility, attracting them to his service and using them for the reduction of the more powerful towns. In the chief town, Berlin-Kölln, he was able to intervene as arbitrator in a dispute between the craftsmen and the patrician council in 1442. He used his opportunity to nominate a new and more popular council, tore the seals from the town's charters, and began the erection of a castle in Kölln. This suppression of civic independence made a profound impression, increased by the final destruction of the patriciate in the town-war of 1449–50. In dealing with the clergy Frederick shewed both piety and firmness. He did much to remove clerical ignorance and indiscipline. And he used his adhesion to Nicholas V to obtain two bulls in 1447, ordering the Courts Christian of the Mark not to interfere with the electoral jurisdiction, guaranteeing the electorate against the interference of any external bishop, and conferring upon the Elector the nominations to the three territorial bishoprics of Havelberg, Brandenburg, and Lebus. Further, he set up at Tangermünde a supreme court for the Mark and laid the bases of an efficient administrative and fiscal system. With his reign the medieval confusion of authorities began to disappear from Brandenburg.

But in external relations Frederick was not so successful. For some twenty years the preoccupation of his eastern neighbours left him in peace, and he was able to obtain a footing in Lausitz in 1445 by the purchase of Kottbus, Peitz, and Teupitz, and to repurchase the Neumark in 1455 from the impoverished Teutonic Order. But with George Poděbrady's consolidation of Bohemian power and Poland's final triumph in the north and her annexation of Pomerellen in 1466, Frederick found himself the lonely champion of Germanism in the north-east against the powerful Slavs whom it was his policy to keep apart. In 1464 the ducal line of Pomerania-Stettin died out. Frederick claimed that the dukedom ought by old agreement to lapse to Brandenburg. But the elder line of Pomerania-Wolgast, strong in their alliance with Casimir IV of Poland, seized the inheritance, though they agreed to recognise Frederick's suzerainty. Frederick appealed in vain to the Emperor, who resented his unwillingness to oppose Poděbrady and now recognised the Pomeranian dukes as immediate princes of the Empire. This affront was too much for Frederick, who attempted unsuccessfully to assert his claims over Pomerania by force. Discouraged by lack of military success and by ill-health, Frederick resigned Brandenburg to his brother Albert Achilles, and retired to spend the last year of his life in the more congenial surroundings of Franconia.

In Albert Achilles (1470–86) the Mark again received a ruler whose chief attention was directed elsewhere. The new margrave only spent three of the sixteen years of his rule in Brandenburg, and after 1476 confided its internal government to his son John. Nevertheless, his reign was marked by external expansion and internal consolidation. Supported by the Emperor's goodwill, he was able to impose the treaty of Prenzlau (1472) on the Pomeranian Duke Eric, who admitted the suzerainty of Brandenburg and surrendered the banks of the Oder as far north as Gartz. He also attempted to extend his dominions up the Oder by marrying his daughter Barbara to Henry XI of Glogau-Krossen, with reversion to Brandenburg in case of failure of issue. On the death of Henry in 1476, however, John of Sagan claimed the inheritance, and it cost Albert six years of wasteful war before he secured Krossen and its dependent territories. This dynastic dispute was complicated by larger issues. It was the period of the struggle between Matthias Corvinus and Vladislav of Poland for the succession to Poděbrady in Bohemia. Albert Achilles supported the Poles, as the weaker side, and played off the Slavs against the Magyars in the interests of Germanism. The crisis came in and after 1478, when the Pomeranians, the Teutonic Order, the Silesian dukes, and the Hansa towns all joined in attacking Brandenburg in alliance with the conquering Magyar king. In 1478 Albert Achilles came north, raised a force of nearly 20,000 men, and defeated each of his enemies in turn. The Mark was not only saved, but slightly extended at the expense of Pomerania; and Matthias Corvinus was checked at the summit of his power, failing to conquer Bohemia, though he retained Silesia, Moravia, and Lausitz during his lifetime.

Amid these distractions Albert Achilles had little time for questions of the domestic government of the Mark. Nevertheless, his letters to his son, in which he advised the latter laboriously to seek power in Brandenburg rather than the more congenial life of Franconia, shew the greatest interest and pride in his northern electorate. His military necessities and the heavy debts of his predecessor caused him to make large demands for taxation. The towns resisted, complaining that he only visited the Mark to extract money. Albert insisted that the Mark must be financially self-supporting and discontinued the contributions of the Franconian lands; but by careful economy he brought order into the electoral budget.

After a long struggle he gained the support of the assembly of Estates for a tonnage on herrings, tar, and beer; and his son on the whole successfully forced the towns to submit to the decision of the community. The Elector and his son could at least point out that they were encouraging commerce by their vigorous suppression of brigandage and their control of the unruly, imperfectly assimilated, nobles of the Neumark. But perhaps Albert's chief contribution to the greatness of his dynasty was his famous *Dispositio Achillea* (1473), which served as a fundamental law of succession for the house of Hohenzollern. He provided that his eldest son should receive the electoral title and the Mark with its dependencies as an indivisible unit, to be subsequently inherited by primogeniture. The Franconian territories were allotted, also as indivisible units, to two other sons. For the future all younger sons might receive only pecuniary or ecclesiastical provision. The unity guaranteed to Brandenburg made possible the vigorous growth of a State which has been primarily the creation of its dynasty.

CHAPTER V

THE PAPACY AND NAPLES, IN THE FIFTEENTH CENTURY

DURING the Conclave of 1378, which resulted in the election of Urban VI, the mob outside the Vatican had shouted—"A Roman, a Roman, or at least an Italian." In the Merchants' Hall at Constance, in November 1417, the electors chose, not only an Italian, but a Roman of the Romans, for the new Pope Martin V, Oddone Colonna, sprang from one of the two Roman families, Orsini and Colonna, foremost in the city for some centuries past. This election of a Roman was of abiding consequence to the Papacy and to Rome. Colonna's chief rival had been Pierre d'Ailly. It is hardly probable that this Frenchman would have made Rome his permanent seat. The long abandonment had, indeed, immediately resulted from the Babylonian exile, yet, for more than a century before, the Popes had rarely made Rome their home. Even now it was not universally believed that Martin would make it the seat of the Papacy. He never, however, hesitated, doubtful as the prospects of return appeared. From Geneva he passed through Milan to Mantua, whence, after four months, the Papal Court found its home in Florence from February 1418 to September 1420.

Rome during the Schism had become a No Man's Land. Ladislas of Naples had occupied it, and, had he lived, might have annexed the Patrimony to his kingdom. The Perugian *condottiere*, Braccio da Montone, had then seized the city, to be in turn ejected by Sforza in the service of Joanna II of Naples. The queen made her peace with Martin, for he recognised her title, and she withdrew her troops. For all this he could not return, since Braccio, now lord of Perugia, Assisi, Spoleto, and Todi, blocked one of the main roads from Florence, while his troopers could raid the route which led through Siena. Through Florentine mediation Martin compromised with Braccio, who received the greater part of his conquests as a Vicariate, repressing in return the republican independence of Bologna. The road to Rome now being clear, Martin made his entrance on 30 September 1420.

Since his election Martin had done little for the ecclesiastical reforms so urgently demanded at Constance. His difficulty was real, for the demands entailed shrinkage of the papal resources, while, at the present crisis, increment rather than decrease was required. He was forced to base his hopes on the restoration of the temporal power, on the creation of an Italian State which could hold its own against its neighbours. This, though a prominent characteristic of the fifteenth century, was nothing new. It was a return to the practice of Popes before the exile, notably of Nicholas III, an Orsini, and of Boniface VIII. Nor had the Avignon Popes abandoned their temporal claims; Clement V had even annexed Ferrara to his direct dominions, a success not repeated till the last years of the sixteenth century.

On a cursory survey Martin's outlook was far from hopeful. The Papacy laboured under signal drawbacks, if compared with the secular Italian States. It may be conceived as being surrounded by rings of concentric circles, each, from time to time, pressing inwards to contract its power; while the rulers of Naples and Milan had around them a subservient Council, mere agents of their wishes, the Pope was encircled by jealous cardinals, few of them of his own appointment, striving to extend their independence. If the Papacy became a State, might it not be an oligarchy rather than a monarchy? This fate it had narrowly escaped. Had the proposal for limiting the Pope's power of creation been passed at Constance, he would have lost his chief weapon of defence. Behind the cardinals lay the city of Rome. Here tradition took two forms, both hostile to the Papacy, the one republican, the other imperial, both in a measure pagan, resenting the government of priests. The welcome given to Henry VII and Lewis IV had proved the pride of Rome as imperial city, electing its Emperor in defiance of the Pope. Cola di Rienzo was but one of the republicans who had revived the ambitions of pre-imperial Rome. Even if the loyalty of the city could be assured, she was totally unfit to be the capital of a modern State; her civilisation was years behind that of Naples, Milan, Florence, or Venice. Her ancient buildings had served as quarries, and yet her churches were in ruins. The population, apart from the greater nobles, was poor and squalid. A visitor praised the ladies for their beauty and amiability, adding that they passed their lives in the kitchen and their faces shewed it. Of trade and manufacture there was none; the chief source of wealth was the cattle of the Campagna, the chief gild of the city that of the herdsmen. Ostia had long ceased to be a port of importance; trade passed upwards to the head of the Tuscan or Adriatic gulfs. All roads might lead to Rome, but all were the haunts of brigandage.

Around Rome on the Ciminian, Sabine, Hernican, and Alban hills were encamped the great feudal houses, supporting a numerous cavalry, for whose operations the rolling, grass country of the Campagna was admirably suited. These families clustered round the two most powerful, the Orsini and Colonna, the former Guelf, the latter Ghibelline, but neither disposed to yield practical obedience to a Pope. To the north from near Civita Vecchia ran the Orsini sphere of influence, tending south-eastwards past Lake Bracciano, crossing the Tiber towards the little hill towns of Alba and Tagliacozzo, almost east of Rome. Towards this same point converged the territories of the Colonna and allied houses from the sea near Nettuno, across the Alban hills to their capital Palestrina, and thence north-eastwards.

The two families were not only rival magnates but the chief urban nobles, the Orsini quartered in the Campus Martius near the Tiber and conveniently close to the Vatican, the Colonna holding a strong position on the Quirinal, seat of the ancient imperial and modern royal monarchy. For long periods the Senatorship was shared by these two families, while one or other pulled the strings of most disturbances in Rome. Nor was it conducive to peace that both were frequently represented in the cardinalate, where they naturally took opposite sides. Thus a quarrel might arise across the floor of the Consistory and spread through Rome to distant villages in the Sabine hills, or local feuds therein might infect the city and the college.

Behind the feudatories of the Campagna stood the dynasts of the Tuscan Patrimony, Umbria, Romagna, and the March. In each city-state the head of the leading house in the conquering faction had become by force or election its lord. Many of these were old Roman colonies with a wide space of territory, which lent itself to autonomy, and each was, as a rule, a diocese accustomed to regard itself as a separate entity. The dynasts varied in power from the great lords of Este, whose rule in Ferrara dated from the first half of the thirteenth century, down to the lordlings of Camerino or Todi. Most now held the title of Papal Vicar, a system due in great measure to Cardinal Albornoz, who, unable to reduce them by force, had persuaded them to secure their *de facto* power by a *de iure* title. The oath of fealty and the tribute had meant little, so that on Martin's arrival the Vicars were virtually independent. Among them a few cities, such as Ancona, preserved municipal republicanism. In two important cases, Bologna and Perugia, the dynastic process was still incomplete. Bologna wavered between republican freedom, submission to a papal legate, and the sway of a family faction. At this moment it was in revolt against the Papacy, while Perugia under Braccio da Montone was the centre of a considerable *condottiere* State.

Behind the ring of feudatories were the four Italian powers, Naples, Milan, Venice, Florence, three of them likely to be aggressive. Ladislas and even his feeble successor Joanna II had proved how vulnerable Rome was from the south, while in the near future it was exposed to direct attack by Milan from the north. The papal dominions most endangered were Romagna and the March. Neapolitan horse might easily ford the Tronto on the south; the eastern coast was open to Venetian galleys; Ancona, indeed, had offered herself to Venice, but strangely enough had been refused. Milanese mercenaries had an easy route along the Emilian Road to Bologna and beyond. Even less venturesome Florence pushed her commerce across the Apennines to the Adriatic, especially down the Val Lamone to Faenza, where the Manfredi were almost under her protectorate. The furious factions of the hot-headed in a territory where men are still "more stomachy" than elsewhere, and the quarrels of the numerous dynasts, made Romagna the nervous centre of Italy, wherein all disorders were likely to germinate. Finally, in the distant background the European powers were now accustomed to threaten the refusal of supplies, the withdrawal of allegiance, the meddlesome interference of a General Council.

A link connecting the several rings which were compressing the Papacy was found in the *condottieri*. These might be great soldiers of fortune such as the Sforza or Braccio and his successors, fighting under command of the Italian powers; they might be Papal Vicars themselves, such as the Malatesta or Montefeltri, whose courts formed the *cadres* of a standing force, capable of indefinite expansion; or again they might be Colonna or Orsini nobles, acting upon political parties in Rome itself, or upon the very college of cardinals.

To danger from one or other, or even all, of these quarters every Pope of this century was exposed. How much more might this have affected Martin, who had slight administrative foundations upon which to build, no certain pecuniary resources, no spiritual terrors wherewith to impress sceptical or self-seeking Italian rulers! Yet, perhaps, a more favourable moment for the restoration of the Papacy could scarcely have been found, if only the man chosen were capable of taking full advantage. The very cardinals had been brought to feel that their own fortunes depended upon those of the Pope. Only through him could they amass benefices, or win provincial governorships or the wealthy offices of the Court. Papal patronage, indeed, throughout the century was to count for much. That Martin was a Roman made him secure of Rome, if only he could get there. Her very occupation by Neapolitan troops or those of Braccio made her the readier to welcome any Pope who could free her from such a scourge, could scour her streets, rebuild her churches, fill her lodging-houses, and replenish her shopkeepers' tills.

Martin's position as Pope concentrated all the resources of the Colonna; they could provide him with troops and generals, and place a wide area south of Rome under his control. It is true that this very fact might cause trouble with the Orsini. But Martin and his Orsini colleagues in the cardinalate, both men of moderation, had been on unusually good terms. Without support from Italian powers the feudatories could scarcely be actively aggressive, and could be pitted against each other. The greater States were too busy to be troublesome. The unquestioned suzerainty over Naples gave the Pope an incalculable advantage in the disputed succession between Anjou-Durazzo and the second house of Anjou. Filippo Maria Visconti of Milan was laboriously recovering his father's State, which had been broken up into its original municipal units by *condottieri* or the old local families. Venice, traditionally friendly, had not yet begun to covet actual dominion in Romagna, contenting herself with commercial concessions and the precious monopoly of the saltpans of Cervia. Florence proved her active goodwill by offering Martin hospitality. She was a weak military power as compared with Milan or Naples, but her prestige at this time was relatively high, owing to her recent resistance to the

Visconti and Ladislas, and to the internal troubles of the two monarchies.
European nations were full of turmoil. The Emperor became immersed
in the Hussite wars; France was distracted by civil war, followed by the
English invasion; England herself was before long enfeebled by a weak
minority. Thus if the Powers could not help, they could not hinder; at
all events the Council of Constance had proved that the Holy See had
nothing to fear from a European Concert.

Such were the chances open to Martin, who was the very man to use
them to the full. Moderate, conciliatory, and attractive, he had nevertheless an iron will, and would brook no rivalry. Practical and thrifty, even
to avarice, he treated the Papacy as a business concern. He was too
prudent to force political openings, but utilised those which offered
themselves with consummate skill. Fortune usually favours such a man.
On his tomb he is dubbed *Temporum suorum felicitas*, the good fortune
of his times, but the times were also fortunate for Martin.

Most opportune of all circumstances was the disputed succession to
Naples, which will best be treated later from the Neapolitan side. Apart
from this, Martin's first success was due to Florentine mediation with
Braccio, which cleared the road to Rome. The *condottiere* undertook the
submission of Bologna, receiving investiture with the Vicariate of Perugia
and neighbouring cities. This was a dangerous step for the future. Braccio
was no mere local lordling in distant Romagna, but the leader of half the
soldiery of Italy, entrenched west of the Apennines, imperilling communication with Romagna and even Tuscany. From this Martin was
saved by the accident of Braccio's death, an episode in the Neapolitan
war. The Pope was now firmly lord in Umbria. Romagna was the next
objective. Here the Malatesta were threatening to become a first-rate
power, stretching across the mountains to Gubbio and Borgo San Sepolcro,
while not till 1421 was Pandolfo Malatesta evicted from Brescia and
Bergamo. As Martin had set Braccio against Bologna, so now he countered
the Malatesta by the lord of Urbino. Then death once more came to his
aid, for the heads of the lines of Rimini and Pesaro died, and disputed
succession enabled the suzerain to confine the heirs to the earlier limits
of the two houses. Bologna, indeed, once more rebelled before the reign
closed, but obedience was restored by help of Carlo Malatesta, an old
enemy of the city.

Martin's position enabled him largely to increase the Colonna territories.
His nepotism recalls that of Nicholas III, the great Orsini Pope of the
thirteenth century. Convenient kinswomen were married to the lords of
Urbino and Piombino, and to the Orsini Prince of Taranto, the greatest
noble in the Neapolitan kingdom. Martin's brother Giordano was created
Duke of Amalfi and Prince of Salerno, another, Lorenzo, became Grand
Justiciar and Duke of Alba in the Abruzzi, recently held by the Orsini.
More substantial was the increase of the family possessions, especially
Nettuno on the coast, Marino on the great south road, Rocca di Papa on

the summit of the Alban hills. Other accretions of property north of Rome caused friction with the Orsini, but hostility was allayed by the bestowal of fiefs and arrangements for profitable marriages. In Rome order was persistently enforced, while the restoration of the Vatican, the Lateran, and other buildings gave employment to the lower classes.

Homage was done to the Renaissance by the engagement of Gentile da Fabriano and Pisanello, a worthy example to Martin's successors. Even for the future there were brilliant possibilities. Giordano died without issue, but Lorenzo's son Prospero was the obvious candidate for the Papacy, while for another son there was just a prospect of the kingdom of Naples. The only cloud upon the horizon was the conciliar question. Martin had bent the Council of Siena to his will, reducing rather than increasing, as was demanded, the authority of cardinals and bishops. In spite of his reluctance, however, the disasters of the Hussite war and pressure from the European powers compelled him to summon the fateful Council of Basle. The bull was sealed on 1 February 1431; on the twentieth day of the month the fortunate Pope was dead.

Naples, of all States, needed the rule of a strong man. Joanna II, a widow of forty-five, who succeeded her brother Ladislas, had no capacity or interest except for love. Her present favourite, Pandolfello Alopo, as Grand Chamberlain, controlled the finances and patronage of the State. The striking figure from the first is, however, Sforza Attendolo, whom Alopo, fearing his manly attractions for the queen, imprisoned. Of the Roman possessions of Ladislas, Ostia and the castle of Sant' Angelo alone remained, while the road to their recovery was blocked by rebellious lords, who occupied Capua and Aquila. Sforza, released under pressure from the Council, recovered these cities. Joanna's life became a public scandal; marriage seemed the only remedy, and James, the Bourbon Count of La Marche, of French royal blood, was bold enough to wed her. He was not to be styled King, but Vicar General, Duke of Calabria, and Prince of Taranto. On his way from Manfredonia to Naples the nobles who met him proclaimed him king, and arrested Sforza. On the bridegroom's arrival at Naples in August 1415, Alopo was executed; Joanna was placed in close confinement; places of trust were monopolised by Frenchmen. Popular sympathy was aroused by the queen's humiliation. In November 1416 a rising headed by Ottino Caracciolo resulted in the queen's release, her consort's surrender, and the expulsion of the French.

Sforza, set free, was reappointed Grand Constable, but at Court was no match for a handsome lover. The new favourite was Giovanni Caracciolo (Sergianni), a cousin of Ottino but his enemy. His ascendancy was long to last, for he had both charm and real ability of its kind. Sforza was prudently dispatched to drive Braccio from Rome, which he now ruled under the title *Almae urbis defensor*. He had ravaged Sforza's possessions in Umbria and the March, the cause of the deadly rivalry which brought both heroes to the grave. Sforza now worked round from Ostia to the Borgo on 27 August 1417, relieved Sant' Angelo, and forced Braccio to withdraw. At this moment Martin's election became known, an event of high importance to both generals.

The favour of Sforza, as possessor of Rome, was essential to Martin. An agreement was soon made that Joanna should retain the guardianship of Rome until Martin's arrival, while she received confirmation of her title. Sforza, on returning to Naples, came into violent collision with Caracciolo, who was forced by nobles and people to withdraw. In the summer of 1419 Martin ordered Sforza to protect Rome. Hard fighting between Sforzeschi and Bracceschi spread from Umbria to Romagna until in the spring of 1420 Martin invited Braccio to Florence and reconciled the rivals, recognising Braccio as Vicar in Perugia. Sforza, always generous, had foolishly allowed Caracciolo to return to Naples, with the usual scandalous results. Martin shared his disgust, and together at Florence they negotiated with Louis III of Anjou, on the understanding that he should become Joanna's heir and expel Caracciolo from the kingdom. Sforza marched on Naples, declared himself the enemy of the government, and attacked the city at the Capuan gate.

Caracciolo meanwhile had prepared a counter stroke. His agent at Rome made proposals to the envoy of Alfonso of Aragon, who was vainly besieging Bonifacio, a Genoese possession in Corsica. The king should be adopted as Joanna's heir, receiving the Castel Nuovo and Castel d'Uovo as pledges on sight of the first Aragonese sails. Alfonso's cousin, Louis III, without any knowledge of this, reached Naples by sea in August 1420. In September arrived Alfonso's Sicilian fleet, the admiral of which received the Castel Nuovo, his troops occupying the town. Alfonso shewed no hurry. On reaching his own kingdom of Sicily early in February 1421, he found his Parliament, his Council, and his brother John, the viceroy, opposed to so dangerous a war. Notwithstanding, Alfonso made for Naples, there finding Braccio, who had received the titles of Prince of Capua and Constable, and had already been hotly engaged with Sforza.

Martin's position was difficult. He had attached himself to Sforza without realising the consequences of his quarrel with Joanna. She was reigning with his consent, and yet she was employing Sforza's deadly enemy, Braccio, whose loyalty to Martin was suspect. During the winter of 1421 he made every effort for peace, but in vain. The real protagonists were not the claimants but the *condottieri*. From them came an unexpected hope of peace. Sforza was now the weaker, and Braccio was tempted by lucrative service in the Viscontean-Venetian war. He persuaded his rival to make peace with Alfonso and Joanna, and then retired from the kingdom, rewarded with the government of the Abruzzi.

Joanna's passion for her lover soon came to Martin's aid. The lovers grew jealous of the masterful adopted heir. Popular feeling rose against the ever-hated Catalans. In May 1423, Alfonso arrested the favourite;

Joanna called Sforza to her aid, while Alfonso summoned Braccio from Tuscany. The latter got no farther than Aquila, which he claimed as governor of the Abruzzi. It was a valuable link between his Umbrian possessions and his recent fief of Capua; but Aquila was stoutly Angevin, and closed her gates. In June Sforza had driven Alfonso into the Castel Nuovo, when the arrival of a Sicilian fleet caused Joanna to escape to Aversa, where Louis III joined her, the Pope and Visconti having reconciled their claims. Alfonso, called away to Aragon by a short Castilian war, left his son Peter in command at Naples, and viciously sacked Louis' town of Marseilles on his way to Barcelona.

Braccio was still besieging Aquila; Sforza, on the march to relieve it, was on 3 January 1424 drowned in attempting to save a trooper's life. His son Francesco retired to Aversa, where Joanna confirmed him in his father's honours. The check had no ill effects on Angevin fortunes. The successes of Louis III's Genoese fleet between Gaeta and Sorrento, and the treason of Peter's chief *condottiere*, the Neapolitan noble, Giacomo Candola, led to the capture of Naples. Peter escaped to Sicily, leaving a small garrison in the Castel Nuovo. In June a papal and Neapolitan force beat and captured Braccio outside Aquila. The savage soldier starved himself to death, but his troops throughout Italy held to his nephew, Niccolò Piccinino, while the Sforzeschi were led by Francesco Sforza. The Aragonese cause seemed lost; the two military companies found full employment in North Italy. Naples enjoyed some years of relative peace under the influence of Martin, whose nephew Antonio was created Duke of Aquila. Nowhere was the Pope's triumph more complete. With masterly opportunism he had allied himself with Joanna against Louis III, then with Louis against Joanna and Alfonso, and finally with Joanna and Louis against Aragon. At his death in February 1431 the supremacy of the Papacy over the feudatory kingdom seemed assured.

Trouble however soon arose at Naples, owing to Joanna's obvious liking for Louis III, whom Caracciolo jealously removed to Calabria. His insolence to Joanna becoming intolerable, she plotted his arrest with his hostile cousin Ottino and the Duchess of Sessa. This they accomplished, and, fearing that the queen might change her mind, mercilessly killed him. The duchess now ruled the Court, keeping Louis at arm's length. Alfonso, seeing an opening, arrived at Ischia, and was well received by her, but lost the duchess' favour by winning that of her husband. So he made peace with Joanna, and sailed to Sicily. The queen, striving to rule through divisions, provoked war between the Sanseverini and the Prince of Taranto, sending Candola and Louis to attack the latter. During the campaign, in November 1434, Louis died. On 2 February 1435 Joanna ended her worthless life, bequeathing her kingdom to his brother René.

It seemed possible that the Colonna might become the ruling house in

Italy. Circumstances were favourable for this. Naples was friendly and dependent; the Florentine aristocracy was tottering; Venice and Milan were at each other's throats; might not Martin pass on to his family the power which he had acquired? The new feeling of nationality alive in Europe, the loss of reverence for the spiritual power, would have aided such a solution. Cardinal Prospero was the obvious successor. But Martin died too soon. The cardinalate proved now, as afterwards, a fatal obstacle. It was easy for a Pope to become absolute in his life, but the stronger he was then, the weaker he was after death. He could prevent the college from being a ruling aristocracy, but not from being an electoral aristocracy. The cardinals could choose their monarch, if they could not govern him.

Gabriel Condulmer owed his election to his comparative insignificance. Born of a wealthy but not noble family of clothiers who had migrated to Venice, he was pushed into the cardinalate under Gregory XII through the favour of a member of the house of Correr. He was genuinely religious, ascetic, and charitable, and did much to reform the Church in matters of detail. But he was obstinate, and at times bad-tempered, perhaps owing to gout, from which, though a total abstainer, he suffered severely in the hands. The restored Papacy, in its tender growth, needed opportunism and adaptability, but Eugenius IV was the greatest inopportunist of the century.

This pontificate was almost contemporaneous with the Council of Basle, which opened four months after Eugenius IV's accession; it dragged on, indeed, until 1449, but his last act was to heal the wound, opened by the Council, by reconciling the larger part of Germany with the Papacy. The difficulty of the reign is to disentangle the Pope's spiritual relations towards Europe from his temporal power in Italy, for they acted and reacted on each other. The former were affected by trivial Italian complications, while the Council's action determined that of his Italian enemies small or great. The secular side of his reign, with which this chapter is concerned, comprises trouble with cardinals, Roman people, baronage, *condottieri*, Italian States, and European powers.

The capitulations imposed upon Eugenius were of unusual stringency. The cardinals were promised complete liberty of speech, guarantees for their offices, and control over half the papal revenues; all important business must be discussed with them; the Papacy must not leave Rome; all feudatories and officials must swear to both cardinals and Pope. The Papacy thus became an oligarchy. Eugenius could never entirely control his cardinals. Two of them sat on the Council till its close, and were cardinals of Felix V. Eugenius began his reign, just as had Boniface VIII, by fiercely attacking the Colonna, whom he accused of secreting papal treasures. He ordered the surrender of all fiefs and fortunes granted by Martin, whose secretary he tortured within an ace of death. The Colonna took up arms, but, after forcing the Appian gate, were driven out of

Rome; their palaces, even that of Martin V, were destroyed. Excommunication and war in Latium followed from mid May till late September. Florence and Venice, whose cause Eugenius supported against Milan, sent contingents, which proved too strong for the Colonna, who surrendered their fortresses and paid an indemnity. Yet Eugenius was to pay dearly for his enterprise, though not so severely as had Boniface, who, in great measure, owed his death to a refugee Colonna.

The Council of Basle and the Pope were soon at issue. The papal legate, Cesarini, and the King of the Romans, convinced that reconciliation with the Hussites was essential to the peace of the Church, summoned Bohemian delegates. Eugenius would have no truck with heretics, and ordered the Council to dissolve and meet again at Bologna. The Council refused obedience. Cesarini remonstrated with the Pope, as did Sigismund, who, on Filippo Visconti's invitation, had received the iron crown in Sant' Ambrogio on 25 November. He was thus in apparent opposition to Eugenius, the ally of Venice and Florence against Milan.

Events in 1432 moved rapidly. It is possible that the appeal of Cardinals Colonna and Capranica, now at Basle, stimulated the personal hostility of the Council to Eugenius, which was early a peculiar feature. Italian temporal and European religious causes already interacted. From January to December the Council successively declared its independence, summoned Eugenius to attend, impeached him, and ordered him to revoke his bull. Fortunately the political atmosphere was clearing. Visconti had offended Sigismund by not receiving him when in Milan, and by entangling him in hostilities with Florence and Venice, whose forces had shut him up at Siena, in his own words, like a beast in a cage. The Council was necessary to him, because peace with the Bohemians was all-important, but he disliked its radical character, resting on elements hostile to the Empire. Eugenius alone could rescue him from the hostility of Venice and Florence; for this and for his coronation he would sacrifice the Council's complete independence. At peace with the Pope and the republics, he entered Rome in May, and, after coronation, stayed in close friendship with Eugenius till August.

This papal-imperial understanding drove Visconti into definite support of the Council. In his service Sforza attacked the March of Ancona, while Fortebraccio threatened Rome from Tivoli, both calling themselves Generals of the Council. The Colonna and Savelli joined Fortebraccio, while it seemed likely that Romagna would fall to Milan or the *condottieri*. By November 1433 Sforza advanced into Papal Tuscany[1]; Visconti was impudently styling himself Vicar of the Council in Italy. These territorial reverses forced Eugenius to concessions. He reinstated the disputed cardinals, and on 30 January 1434 recognised the Council as the highest authority. Sforza was bribed by the Vicariate of the March, with the office of Gonfalonier of the Church. This, like Martin's cession of Perugia

[1] *I.e.* The Patrimony north of the Tiber.

to Braccio, was a sacrifice of the future to the present, for Sforza would be far more dangerous than any ordinary Vicar of local origin. Visconti, however, gave the Pope no rest: he sent Sforza's rival, Piccinino, to help Fortebraccio. Aided by the Colonna, they produced a revolution at Rome. Eugenius was ordered to surrender the temporal power, and hand over Sant' Angelo and Ostia to the people. They stormed the Capitol, and re-established the old republican government of Seven *Riformatori* on 29 May 1434. Eugenius with one companion escaped in disguise to the river bank, where a boat from an Ischian pirate ship at Ostia was awaiting them (4 June). Any visitor to Ostia by road can picture the scene. The Pope lay under a shield, while the mob, who soon realised his escape, pelted the boat with stones and arrows. Some fishermen put out to intercept it, but, finding the pirates preparing to ram, discreetly made for shore. Ostia reached, he sailed for Pisa, and found in Florence a hospitable home in Santa Maria Novella. The revolution was a flash in the pan. The people could not take Sant' Angelo, and Visconti needed his troops in Lombardy. Rome, without a Pope, had no visitors, and, without them, no livelihood. The wires of the nominal republic were pulled by the nobles. When in October Giovanni Vitelleschi appeared with Orsini troops, he was voluntarily admitted. Yet for nine years Eugenius was still an exile.

From Vitelleschi's occupation of Rome, papal territorial history is mainly concerned, for nearly six years, with this soldier-priest, one of his century's most striking figures. Born at Corneto, a hill-town overlooking the Maremma, and now famous for its artichokes, he had, while in Tartaglia's service, destroyed the rival faction in Corneto. He obtained, under the Papacy, clerical preferment, rising to the patriarchate of Alexandria, the archbishopric of Florence, and finally the cardinalate. Before his death he was suspected of aiming at the Papacy in the steps of the quondam soldier of fortune, John XXIII. Though his murderous brutality had driven the March of Ancona into Sforza's arms, Eugenius, attracted by his virility, placed no limits on his actions. From Rome he threw his whole weight upon Jacopo Manfredi, Prefect of Vico, whom he executed. This was the end of a famous Ghibelline brigand house, professing descent from Caesar, or Nero at the least; since Innocent III it had held the office of *Praefectus Urbis*, a title dating from the late Empire. The Prefect was the Emperor's representative, safeguarding him when in Rome; the Manfredi had played this part at the coronation of Henry VII and Lewis IV. They were nominally responsible for the safety of roads leading to Rome, which they intermittently plundered. Holding the *cura annonae*, the control of the markets, they received, as perquisites, rolls of bread, wine, and a sheep's head from bakers, vintners, and butchers respectively. They had now become papal officials, riding before or by the Pope, clad, as was their horse, in magnificent ancient raiment. Nevertheless in the Papal Chancery the term *filius damnatae memoriae* was almost as hereditary as *Praefectus almae urbis*. The dignity of the Prefecture was conferred upon Francesco Orsini, and then generally on a papal *nipote*, but its functions were vested in the papal Vice-Chamberlain, a good example of the absorption of imperial or municipal authority by the curial civil service. Eugenius foolishly alienated the Vico estates to the Counts of Anguillara, who proved scarcely easier to control than the Prefects.

Had Eugenius not refused the petition of the citizens that he should return to Rome, all might have been well. In Vitelleschi's absence, a republican revolution broke out, supported by the Colonna and Savelli. Vitelleschi stormed back to Rome, utterly destroyed the Savelli fortresses on and around the Alban hills, then, turning on the Colonna, captured Palestrina, which was more absolutely destroyed than under Boniface VIII. The old Vitelleschi palace at Corneto, now or lately an inn, is entered between the marble doorposts plundered from the cathedral. Latium for generations to come did not recover from Vitelleschi's devastations. The conqueror re-entered Rome in triumph, had the republican leader, Poncelletto Venerameri, torn with red-hot pincers and quartered on the Campo del Fiore. He reigned as despot, but was popular, for he had suppressed the hated nobles and lowered prices. The Senate and *Parlamento* decreed in his honour an equestrian statue on the Capitol by the hand of Donatello, with the inscription *Tertius a Romulo pater patriæ*. The monument, to the loss of posterity, was never raised.

Vitelleschi's Roman conquests were followed by a Neapolitan campaign, which will receive notice later. Eugenius had claimed Naples as a lapsed fief, the direct lines of Anjou and Anjou-Durazzo having both expired. Alfonso of Aragon's invasion, however, followed by his sensational release, after capture, by Visconti, rendered necessary the recognition of René of Anjou, whom Joanna had adopted, and whose wife was holding Naples during his imprisonment in Burgundy. Vitelleschi, after some successes, was forced to evacuate the kingdom, and joined Eugenius at Ferrara in January 1438. The Pope's arrival here marks a critical stage in his fortunes, both temporal and spiritual. His flight from Rome had encouraged the Council of Basle to take its extremist anti-papal measures. These had estranged moderate opinion, and caused the secession of Cesarini and other leaders. The quarrel over the selection of the site for the Council of Reunion with the Greek Church was closed in the Pope's favour by the Greek Emperor's consent to meet him at Ferrara on 4 March 1438. This Council was transferred to Florence in January 1439, for on the temporal side the Basle Fathers were still the stronger. Piccinino with Visconti had seized Bologna, and Imola, Forlì, and Ravenna revolted from the Papacy. Nevertheless the success of the union with the Greek Church, followed by the accession of the Eastern Churches, indirectly gave prestige to Eugenius on the temporal side, which was not diminished by his deposition on 25 June, by which act the Council of

Basle plunged into schism, and in November 1439 elected Amadeus VIII, the retired Duke of Savoy, to the Papacy as Felix V.

War between Pope and Council was now undisguised. The indispensable Vitelleschi was set the task of recovering Bologna. To protect his rear, he captured Foligno from the despot house of Trinci, putting the dynast and his sons to death. The Abbot of Monte Cassino, commandant of Spoleto, met the same fate. Vitelleschi then organised his troops in Rome for a northward march in the spring. The great soldier's sands were, however, running down. Florence suspected him of an intrigue with Piccinino for the conquest of the city, and the foundation of a *tyrannis* in the Papal States, perhaps even the occupation of the papal throne. The Pope's Chamberlain, Luigi[1], communicated with Antonio Rido, captain of Sant' Angelo, with a view to Vitelleschi's overthrow. The famous bridge beneath the fortress can still recall the tragedy. On 19 March 1441 the papal troops had crossed it en route for Tuscany. Their general had halted in their rear for a few last words with Rido; the drawbridge fell, a chain was drawn behind him, and he was trapped. Dragged fighting and wounded into the castle, he died, or was poisoned, on 2 April.

The Chamberlain Luigi, also a fighting priest, took Vitelleschi's place, commanded the papal troops in Piccinino's decisive defeat at Anghiari in the Upper Tiber valley, and, rewarded with the cardinalate, became the master of Rome, fully as oppressive as Vitelleschi, and less popular. The Peace of Cavriana between Visconti and the two republics relieved immediate pressure, though Sforza's marriage with Visconti's bastard daughter Bianca made his position in the March more dangerous than ever to his sovereign. On 2 June 1442, Alfonso's capture of Naples and René's flight to Provence caused Eugenius to turn a complete somersault in foreign policy. He deserted the two republics for the two monarchies, and declared Sforza a rebel to the Church, while Venice and Florence strove to protect him. The treaty with Alfonso was finally concluded on 6 July 1443. Eugenius made his entrance into Rome, where the Chamberlain had executed all dangerous citizens, on 28 September. His return to Rome was fatal to the Council, and the summons to the Council of the Vatican rang its knell. The Papacy had recovered its centre of gravity. Basle might be on a level with Ferrara and Florence, but what was the Pope at Lausanne to the Pope at Rome? The possession of Rome was nine points of the law.

Absolute peace was not as yet. Sforza lost the cities of the March till Jesi alone was left, but the death of Piccinino, now the Pope's friend, was a serious loss, for Annibale Bentivoglio caused Bologna to revolt and it was not recovered during the Pope's reign. A not unimportant diminution of papal territory was the mortgage of Borgo San Sepolcro to

---

[1] The surname of Scarampo, by which the Cardinal-Chamberlain is usually known, has no authority. See P. Paschini in *Memorie storiche forogiuliesi*, vol. xx. iii.

Florence, in the days of alliance. The mortgage was never redeemed, and so Borgo, a strong position on the high-road to Urbino, and facing Anghiari across the Tiber, is still ungeographically in Tuscany. In 1446 Sforza shot his last bolt. Backed by Florence and the Count of Anguillara, he marched for Rome. The barons did not rise, and he was forced back upon Urbino. Visconti, hard-pressed, and near his death, called his unfilial son-in-law to his aid. Sforza left the March for Milan; thus Eugenius by a stroke of fortune recovered the valuable province which he had so perilously pawned away.

In Italy Eugenius had emerged with fair success from troubles with his rebellious capital, the Campagna nobles, the *condottieri*, and the four greater powers, though Venice and Florence were still estranged. His relations with European powers depended on the vicissitudes of his quarrel with the Council, which belongs to another chapter. Bohemia was still outside the fold, but, in spite of the violent hostility of the French party at Basle, the attitude of the king was friendly. Through the agency of the Emperor the obedience of the greater part of Germany was restored to Eugenius on his deathbed. On 23 February 1447, he died.

Long residence in Florence had widened the intellectual and artistic outlook of the ascetic Venetian Pope. In Tuscany the classical revival was an absorbing interest; the Papal Chancery and the humanistic aristocracy became merged. On the Pope's return to Rome the professional Florentine humanists were tempted to the Vatican. A papal secretariate became a regular reward for classical learning. The union with the Greeks also gave a stimulus to Greek studies, especially to the Platonic side, whereof the chief exponents, Gemistos Plethon and Bessarion, were present. The latter, created cardinal in 1439, was henceforth a centre for Greek learning. The Florentine visit also marks an interesting moment in the revival of the vernacular, and especially the living force of Dante. In 1441 a competition was announced for poems in Italian, for which the humanists of the Curia were appointed judges; they could not decide between the four best candidates, and so declared that the prize lapsed to the Papacy, at which there was much discontent. Tuscan artists also followed Eugenius to Rome. The great iron gates of St Peter's were wrought by Filarete after the model of those of Ghiberti, which Eugenius had seen set up, as he had also witnessed the erection of Brunelleschi's dome. The marvellous papal tiara was the work of Ghiberti. Fra Angelico was employed in the Papal Chapel at the Vatican, while Pisanello continued the frescoes begun under Martin V. Eugenius was buried in St Peter's, but his effigy was removed to San Salvatore in Lauro and set in a later Renaissance monument.

The wish of the Colonna to make the Papacy a family appanage now almost succeeded. One vote more would have made Prospero Colonna

Pope, and Capranica stood second. The aristocracy of the cardinalate was just too strong. Choice fell upon Tommaso Parentucelli of Sarzana, youngest and humblest of the college, to which he had belonged less than three months. He had been tutor to the Strozzi and Albizzi families, had arranged Cosimo de' Medici's library in San Marco at Florence, and then steeped himself in theology at Bologna. Acting as secretary to Cardinal Albergati in his travels, he became one of the European brotherhood of letters. He succeeded his patron in the bishopric of Bologna, and, in his memory, took the name of Nicholas V as Pope. His outwardly simple habits concealed two most extravagant passions, building and book-collecting. Early in life he said that, if he were ever rich, these were the only objects on which he would care to spend. The Jubilee of 1450 soon gave him the wealth he desired, and he spent it to the full.

For the Papal States, with Rome still seething with republican volitions, the Campagna devastated, and Bologna in open revolt, peace was the first essential, and Nicholas was pre-eminently a man of peace and compromise. General political conditions were in his favour. The Visconti succession war drew all fighting forces northwards; Alfonso, who, during the con-clave, overawed Rome from Tivoli, marched on Tuscany. Sforza, having won Milan, lost interest in the March, thus relieving the Papacy from further Venetian encroachments in Romagna. Bologna was pacified by a quasi-republican constitution, and later by the tactful rule of the Greek Bessarion, who had no party prejudices and devoted himself to restoring the decadent university. The despot families in Romagna and Umbria were gratified by vicariates; the turbulent nobles of the Campagna were quieted, the Colonna restored to their possessions, and even Palestrina was once more rebuilt.

Abroad, Frederick III's interests, territorial and imperial, pledged him to complete the treaty signed with Eugenius; the dissident princes, Bavarian, Saxon, and episcopal, returned to obedience. The Concordat of Vienna, thanks to the work of Piccolomini and Cusa, acting respectively for Empire and Papacy, was confirmed at Rome in March 1448. Frederick III had the Council driven from Basle to Lausanne. Charles VII induced Felix to resign, and Nicholas built a golden bridge for his retire-ment. The Council in April 1449 saved its face by electing Nicholas, as though the Papacy were vacant. The last papal schism ended in time for the triumphant Jubilee of 1450.

Nicholas was now free for the work which he had most at heart. His pontificate has the merit of a definite policy, and that not unworthy. The Papacy has won some of its chief triumphs, not by originality of conception, but by adaptability, by turning a current of thought springing from other sources into its own channel, regulating or deepening its flow. Nicholas was no bookworm living in the past; he was eminently modernist. His manhood was spent among the leaders of the new literary and artistic movement. The Papacy must not linger in the stifling atmosphere of

Scholasticism and Canon Law; it must blaze the way to the sunny, airy heights of the new learning. Florence had hitherto been the capital of intellect; Rome must now take her ancient imperial place as the centre of power, at least in art and letters; Rome could only lead by adapting herself to new conditions. This was a reasonable, practical policy, which, but for the want of continuity in the electoral papal system, might have been consistently developed. Nicholas gathered round him artists and scholars whom he had known at Florence.

Eugenius had introduced the humanists into the Curia for the practical purposes of the Chancery or diplomacy, where a florid Latin style was indispensable. Nicholas, rather a scholar than a stylist, required more permanent services than the composition of briefs and speeches. His humanists found their place in the Library; most were utilised for the ambitious series of translations from Greek authors, in which Poggio and Filelfo, Decembrio and Guarino, Valla and Manetti took a part. It was strange that one with so high a religious standard should read and even reward the obscene invectives of Filelfo, stranger still that he should admit into the innermost circle Lorenzo Valla, who in Alfonso's service had pulverised the very foundations of papal temporal power, and shaken essential articles of belief. Valla, however, was no windbag humanist but at once a genuine critic and constructive scholar; the Vatican stall would have been incomplete without him. Nicholas pardoned his principles for his prose, and Valla pocketed them with his perquisites; the temporal power, if theoretically a fiction, was an agreeably remunerative fact.

Less amply rewarded but more interesting for posterity were the artists whom Nicholas brought to Rome. Among them were Fra Angelico, Rossellino, Buonfiglio, Castagno, and Gozzoli, perhaps Piero della Francesca and Bramantino. Leon Battista Alberti formed a link between the literary and artistic groups; to him probably the scheme for the new St Peter's was due. If Rome was to be the world's capital, the Vatican should be its citadel. The Pope would convert the whole much dilapidated Leonine city into a temple, a palace, and a fortress. Three arcaded avenues were to run from a spacious square in front of the Bridge of Sant' Angelo to open out into another facing the Vatican and the new Basilica. The plan was never completed, but Nicholas may claim to be the founder of the new St Peter's, the new Vatican, and its new Library. Old classical ruins were swept away for the sake of their materials, and the dismantling of the old St Peter's was begun. Rome must move with the times, not cling to a cumbrous, sentimental past.

Rome was now ready for the most spectacular event of the reign, the visit of Frederick III for his marriage and coronation. The king, escorted by two papal legates, met at Siena his attractive and well-dowered *fiancée*, Leonor of Portugal. Unable to receive the iron crown at Milan, he begged Nicholas to crown him with it on 16 March. Then followed the royal marriage, and three days later Frederick received the imperial crown in

St Peter's, the first Habsburg and the last Emperor to be so honoured[1]. After a visit to Naples and a short stay at Rome, he was called home by dynastic troubles. Not unimportant in the history of the Papal States was his grant, to Borso d'Este of Ferrara, of the two imperial fiefs, the duchies of Modena and Reggio: the Estensi were long to find it hard to serve two suzerains.

In 1453 the sunshine of Nicholas V's reign was overcast with clouds which never lifted. The conspiracy of Porcaro was the outcome of fermentation under Eugenius; he was intimate with all the men of letters of his day, and steeped in the earlier principles of Valla. Roman humanism took a dangerous direction. Not content with the style of the Classics, it drew lessons from their subject-matter. Pardoned by Eugenius, he had, during the Conclave, inveighed against the government of priests and the slavery of Rome. Nicholas made him governor of Anagni, but his ungovernable tongue caused an honourable exile to Bologna, where he hatched his plot. Rome should be a republic with himself as Tribune. As with Cola di Rienzo, the costumier was a noticeable element in the play. Porcaro carried a golden chain, wherewith to secure the Pope. The Vatican stables were to be fired, the cardinals seized, and, on resistance, killed. Loot was dangled before the less humanistic conspirators. Porcaro's disappearance from Bologna led to the discovery of the plot. His house was surrounded. Sciarra the soldier cut his way out by the front door, Porcaro escaped by the back. He was found in a dowry chest, on the lid of which his sister and a lady friend were sitting. The last scene was tragic, the *mise en scène* still effective; Porcaro was hung, dressed in a neat suit of black velvet, from the parapet of Sant' Angelo. The conspiracy caused more sensation than it deserved. Porcaro had some sympathy. Infessura, Secretary to the Senate, wrote: "So died that lover of Roman weal and liberty, for the freedom of his fatherland from slavery." Machiavelli later took a cooler view: "His intention might be by some applauded, but his judgment will be by everyone condemned." There was an unpleasant strain of the Catiline in the blood of the Cato, from whom Porcaro claimed descent.

The conspiracy alarmed Nicholas to an inordinate extent. Physically timid, he became suspicious and morose, in striking contrast to his previous easy good-fellowship. It is reported that depression tempted him to have recourse to restoratives, which doubtless aggravated his gouty symptoms. The disastrous year, 1453, closed with the capture of Constantinople. This forced Nicholas into prominence; he equipped a fleet and circularised Italian and European powers, but could promote no enthusiasm. Too ill to do more for a crusade, he died on the night of 24–5 March 1455. He was buried in St Peter's, whence Pius V removed his monument to the Vatican Grotto. If the character and work of Nicholas be taken in combination, he may be regarded as the best Pope of the century. The

[1] Charles V was crowned Emperor at Bologna.

irritability and self-sufficiency of the successful scholar are small blemishes to set against the decalogue of virtues with which his friend Vespasiano da Bisticci credits him.

The Conclave of 1455 was unusually international, for, as against seven Italians, it comprised four Spaniards, two Frenchmen, a Greek, and a Ruthenian. Of the absentees two were French, two Germans, and one Hungarian. Once again Prospero Colonna and Capranica were the favourites, but both were baulked by the Orsini cardinal, backed by Neapolitan influence. The cardinals tided over the difficulty by electing a Pope whose age and infirmity would make him a nonentity; they forgot that old men are more selfish and more obstinate than younger ones. Calixtus III, Alonso de Borja, Bishop of Valencia, of Catalan and Valencian origin, was seventy-seven or more, and an invalid. Other qualifications were virtue and legal learning. As a diplomat, he had served Martin V in closing the schism in Aragon, and Alfonso in his settlement at Naples.

Calixtus had two passions, the crusade, natural in a Spaniard, and his family. Both were doubtless exaggerated by senility. If it is a libel that he dispersed the library collected by Nicholas, it seems true that the jewelled bindings were torn off, and the scribes, translators, and literary hangers-on discharged. Calixtus had no use for the Renaissance; his learning was purely legal. Art suffered as did literature. Rome should no longer be Christendom's artistic and literary centre, but its arsenal and dockyard. A considerable fleet was built on the Tiber, with Eugenius IV's fighting cardinal, Luigi, now Patriarch of Aquileia, in command. Its slight successes sufficed only to stir the Turkish hornets' nest. Alfonso's fleet, raised by a crusade tithe, was employed against Genoa; the ships built by Charles VII were reserved for use against Naples. Demands for a tithe from Germany gave the anti-papal party a pretext for insisting on the reforms promised at Constance and Basle. Venice evaded the demand, Florence refused it. France and Burgundy were watching each other, England was absorbed in civil war. Hungary alone stood in the breach at Belgrade, and Skanderbeg in the Albanian mountains. Belgrade at least owed its salvation partly to the Papacy, for its heroic rescuer, Hunyadi, relied on the fiery eloquence of Capistrano and the administrative skill with which the Spaniard, Cardinal Carvajal, organised reliefs at Buda. Hunyadi's death, however, soon after his victory, took the life out of the defence, and the clouds were at their darkest when Calixtus himself died.

Calixtus was right as to the reality of the Turkish danger, perhaps even as to the possibility of conjuring it. But he had neither tact nor sympathy; he would listen to no advice, and therefore got no aid. His nepotism provoked dark suspicions as to his motives. He conferred cardinalates on his young nephews Rodrigo and Luis, and created Rodrigo's brother, Pedro, Prefect of the City and Vicar of the great fiefs, Terracina and Benevento. The Catalans, hated in Italy, as when Dante warned King

Robert against their rapacious poverty, now dominated Rome, held the Castle of Sant' Angelo, and swarmed in all the papal fortresses. One of the reasons for Calixtus III's election had been his close connexion with Alfonso, but throughout his Papacy there was one long quarrel, while in Roman politics he had swung away from the Orsini to the Colonna. When Alfonso died, leaving the kingdom to his bastard Ferrante, Calixtus spurned the engagements of Eugenius and Nicholas, and declared the kingdom lapsed on the ground that Ferrante was a supposititious child. Few doubted that Calixtus meant to bestow Naples on Pedro, just as Pedro's brother Alexander VI coveted it for Caesar Borgia.

The bed on which the old Pope had passed most of his pontificate was now obviously to become his death-bed. Everywhere the populace was rising against the Catalans. Pedro was forced to sell Sant' Angelo to the cardinals, and on 6 August 1458 fled to Ostia, whence a Neapolitan ship carried him to Civita Vecchia, where he died. On the evening of Pedro's flight Calixtus ended his sickly reign. Rodrigo, more courageous than his military brother, had returned to Rome to watch him. In this nephew Calixtus left a *damnosa haereditas* to Italy and the Church.

On Joanna's death in 1435 the Neapolitans resolved to have their say, adding to the Council a committee of nobles and citizens, and hoisting the papal banner. Deputies were sent to René, but found that the Duke of Burgundy had captured him during the Lorraine Succession war. Alfonso at once revived his claim. Many barons, headed by the Duke of Sessa, resenting the pretensions of the Neapolitans, promised support. The Prince of Taranto, having eluded his mortal enemy, Candola, surprised Capua. Alfonso from Ischia joined in an attack on Gaeta, the key position on the coast, as Capua was on the Roman road. The town, held by a Genoese garrison sent by Visconti, was bombed and starved to the last extremity, when a Genoese fleet appeared. Alfonso's squadron put out to meet it, but was annihilated off the Isle of Ponza on 5 August 1435. The king was captured with his brothers Henry and John, King of Navarre, Taranto and Sessa, and most of the Sicilian and Aragonese nobility. Peter alone escaped with two ships. Visconti sent secret orders that Alfonso with Taranto and Sessa should be brought by way of Savona to Milan, and the other captives landed at Genoa. At the first interview Alfonso persuaded Visconti that resistance to French intervention in Italy was their common interest. A treaty was formed; Alfonso's brothers were sent to Aragon to raise troops; Peter was ordered to meet him at La Spezia.

Visconti paid dearly for his generosity. The Genoese, detesting their old Catalan foes, revolted from Visconti, becoming henceforth the main resource of the Angevin dynasty. Peter, sailing from Sicily, surprised Gaeta, almost deserted owing to plague, and brought Alfonso back in February 1436. Meanwhile, in October 1435, René's wife Isabella was rapturously received at Naples. Alfonso was now fighting south of Naples, where the support of the Counts of Nola and Caserta protected his right flank against attack from Apulia. Isabella's fortunes were very low, when help came from an unexpected quarter. Eugenius IV, himself an exile, sent Vitelleschi to her aid. He relieved the faithful Angevin city of Aquila, and reached Naples. Alfonso called on Taranto to join him at Capua. Vitelleschi intercepted the prince and captured him. The Roman Orsini, who formed the flower of Vitelleschi's force, insisted on the release of the head of their house. Taranto promised to serve the Pope, though not personally, owing to his affection for Alfonso. The Angevins must almost have won, had not dissensions played a larger part than arms. Candola quarrelled with Vitelleschi for hoisting the papal flag on conquered cities, on which Vitelleschi made a truce with Alfonso. Isabella reconciled her generals, with the result that Alfonso escaped with a few cavalry from a surprise attack, losing all his treasure and war material. Again the generals quarrelled, Candola retiring to the Abruzzi, Vitelleschi eastwards to amass treasure from the wealth of Apulia. Here Trani, fearing his plundering troops, besieged its own Angevin garrison. Alfonso sent galleys to bombard the castle, while Taranto was secretly raising the province. Vitelleschi, scenting a trap, set sail for Ancona, where later he joined Eugenius at Ferrara. From this moment Aragonese fortunes revived, mainly through Taranto's support, though Candola succeeded to Vitelleschi's troops and stores.

On 18 May 1438 René, released from captivity, arrived at Naples. Henceforth, until Alfonso's final victory in 1442, fighting was continuous, the Angevins usually predominating in the Abruzzi, Alfonso in Apulia and the neighbourhood of Naples. René wandered far and wide to replenish his sieve-like treasury, while Alfonso, in a direct attack on Naples, lost his son Peter. The Castel Nuovo, which had been held for him for eleven years, soon afterwards surrendered. This was more than balanced by the death of Giacomo Candola, whose son had neither his patriotism nor his military genius. Had not Giacomo's service been practically confined to Naples, he would have ranked high among contemporary *condottieri*, from whom he was distinguished by his wide hereditary estates in the Abruzzi, his love of learning, and contempt for titles.

It was a sign of coming defeat that René sent his wife and children home. He himself was holding Naples, when an entrance by an aqueduct was betrayed. After hard fighting he escaped by the aid of Genoese ships on 2 June 1442. Fighting continued in the Abruzzi and Apulia against Antonio Candola and Giovanni Sforza. Alfonso beat their combined forces near Sulmona, and his generous treatment of Candola did much to enhance his popularity. The remaining Sforzeschi possessions in Apulia and the Abruzzi were picked up in detail, Aquila being the last city to surrender. In a Parliament held at Benevento Alfonso was recognised as king, with succession to his illegitimate son Ferrante, who became Duke of Calabria. The Castel Nuovo was allowed to capitulate by René, who retired to Provence, disgusted with his adventure and all concerned in it. Alfonso's entry to Naples in February 1443 took the form of a classic Roman triumph. His reception was exuberant, illustrating the old tradition that the Neapolitans always welcomed the last newcomer. Alfonso's military success profoundly altered his foreign policy. Recognition by his papal suzerain became a necessity. He could no longer use Felix as a stick wherewith to beat Eugenius. The Pope's chief aim was now to eject Sforza from the Vicariate of the March, which, under blackmail, he had conferred upon him, while Sforza had been Alfonso's chief enemy in his contest with the Angevins. Thus Eugenius granted investiture to Alfonso's legitimised son Ferrante, on condition of service against Sforza and abandonment of Felix.

Throughout the confused period from 1443 to the death of Eugenius in 1447 Alfonso stood firm to the papal alliance, which intermittently included Milan. His objects were to prevent Sforza's consolidation of the March, an excellent base for the recovery of his Neapolitan possessions, and also to save Visconti, hard pressed by Florence, Venice, and Sforza, from appealing to René or Charles VII. He could have acted more effectually but for the shifting policy of Visconti, who did actually in 1445 intrigue with René and the French. The Bracceschi were now, as of old, the constant allies of the Aragonese, while Sforza was befriended by Venice and Florence, the latter always faithful to Anjou. Federigo of Montefeltro, who succeeded in 1444 to Urbino, was usually, though not always, for the Bracceschi, while Sigismondo Malatesta favoured Sforza. Twice campaigns alternated with attempts at peace. In 1444 Francesco Piccinino, marching to co-operate with a Neapolitan fleet, which was attacking Fermo, Sforza's headquarters, was totally defeated at Montolmo, a disaster which probably contributed to his gallant old father's death. In 1446 it became clear that Visconti was losing, for in September the Venetians were across the Adda, and threatening Milan. Sforza, on receiving a pathetic appeal from his father-in-law, hesitated between the retention of his remaining possessions in the March and the prospect of succession to Milan. Alfonso was eagerly seeking to promote the reconciliation, when, in February 1447, Eugenius died.

Alfonso, quartered at Tivoli, had kept order in Rome during the Conclave at which Nicholas V was elected. Pope and king were at once on the friendliest terms in their desire for peace. Sforza, having listened to Visconti's appeal, was bought out of his last possession, Jesi, by Alfonso, and marched for Milan on 9 August 1447. Before he reached it, Visconti died. Milan was at once rent between Sforzeschi and Bracceschi factions, which again had their background in Naples. The surprise was a claim to the duchy by Alfonso, under a will executed by Visconti; it is remarkable that the Aragonese flag at once floated from the Castello. The alleged will is one of history's riddles. A summary of the will exists, but even that is not original. In view, however, of Visconti's romantic friendship for his former captive, his hatred for Sforza, and his recent correspondence with Alfonso expressing his wish to abdicate, it would be unsafe unreservedly to reject its existence.

Alfonso naturally became involved in the Seven Years' War for the Milanese succession. The prime enemy was Sforza, whose fortunes must be decided in Lombardy, where the Neapolitan king could not effectively intervene. When, however, Cosimo de' Medici gave support to Sforza, Alfonso directed an attack on Tuscany. He picked a quarrel in 1447 with Rinaldo Orsini, lord of Piombino by marriage with the Appiani heiress. This and the succeeding war of 1452–54 seem to have little importance among larger issues; yet for Alfonso the capture of Piombino had a direct interest. For light-draft galleys the sheltered bays north and south of the peninsula secured a double refuge in a harbourless line of coast. In conjunction with his kingdom of Sardinia, he would have a basis for attack on Genoa, or on Corsica, his old objective, while an Angevin passage from Marseilles to Naples would be endangered. Alfonso obtained aid from Siena, an alliance which remained a recurrent item in Aragonese policy, but the Florentines proved the stronger. Neapolitan galleys entered the port, but the land attack failed, owing to the skill of Sigismondo Malatesta in Florentine service. The net result was the occupation of the Isle of Giglio, off the Argentaro promontory, and Castiglione della Pescaja, a Florentine dependency opposite Elba, together with a vague suzerainty over Piombino. This latter became effective after the death of Rinaldo and his widow, when Emanuele Orsini, one of Alfonso's closest friends, succeeded.

The war fought in 1452, in alliance with Venice against Florence, brought Ferrante, who commanded, no great credit. A disturbing factor in 1453 was the arrival in Lombardy of René, on Florentine invitation. His hope was to promote peace between Venice and Sforza, with a view to an invasion of Naples, but, on finding that this peace was made without his cognisance, he rapidly withdrew. Not a single power really wished for French intervention; all were war-weary. Yet Alfonso refused to join in the treaty of Lodi, because he resisted the surrender of Castiglione. Finally, on Cosimo's assurance that all proposals for French intervention were at an end, he agreed to the treaty in 1455, reserving his freedom of action against Genoa and Rimini. His subsequent attack on Genoa was most unfortunate, for the city was forced to accept a French protectorate, and Charles VII sent René's son, John of Calabria, as governor. It also brought trouble with the Papacy. Nicholas V's successor, Calixtus III, though an Aragonese subject, resented this war as withdrawing Alfonso's fleet from service in the crusade, which was the old Spaniard's monomania. The siege was still in progress when, on 7 June 1458, Alfonso died in Naples of malaria contracted while he was hunting in Apulia.

All deductions made, Alfonso's reign was a great one. He ruled both kingdoms of Sicily; he had added to Naples by papal grant the long-disputed fiefs of Terracina and Benevento. His military career, though chequered, was distinguished by audacity and rapidity of movement; his courage, combined with generosity to the conquered, struck the imagination. A passion for learning and a love of splendour revived the traditions of the Angevin Court at its best; this was calculated to attract the peculiarly centrifugal nobility to the seat of power. The settlement of the kingdom was difficult. Alfonso relied, not only on Catalan mercenaries, but on nobles of rank from his Spanish and Sicilian States, and these must be rewarded. Thus a fresh stratum was superimposed on the conglomerate of Norman, German, and Angevin feudalism. Chief among the newcomers was Indico d'Avalos, who was married to the Marquess of Pescara's heiress, and whose descendants amply repaid the Aragonese dynasty for its founder's generosity. This, however, caused a rupture with the Count of Cotrone in Calabria, whose loyal service raised hopes in him of the Pescara inheritance. His wide estates were confiscated, but his personal wealth enabled him to play a peaceful part at Court, to reappear hereafter. The Prince of Taranto, to whom Alfonso chiefly owed his success, received such accretions to his power that he overshadowed the Crown, causing suspicion in Alfonso and his heir. Another expedient was intermarriage with the higher nobility. Thus Ferrante was married to Taranto's favourite niece, and Alfonso's natural daughter to the Duke of Sessa, with the principality of Rossano as her dower. Alfonso, however, realised that his dynasty mainly rested on international diplomacy; Ferrante's daughter Leonora was engaged to Sforza's third son, and his heir, Alfonso, to Ippolita Sforza. All four were young children, but it was a token of the common interest of the two dynasties in resistance to the house of Anjou and Orleans.

Alfonso's instincts were autocratic, though not so obvious as those of his heir, which caused resentment before his accession. A strong standing army was contemplated, but did not become operative until the following reign. Wide administrative changes were made in favour of centralisation. The old property tax, payable in six rates, which had been farmed, was replaced by a universal hearth tax, in return for a corresponding measure of salt, based upon a census periodically renewed. The toll on cattle moving between the lowlands of Apulia and the upland pastures of the Abruzzi, always one of the Crown's chief resources, was placed under direct control. Judicial reforms brought the subjects nearer to the Crown, though Alfonso was forced to enhance the independence of the greater barons by granting full criminal justice, hitherto very sparingly conceded. For the last three years power was falling into Ferrante's hands, for Alfonso, tired out with campaigns and the supervision of his several kingdoms, surrendered himself to the gratification of his tastes and senses.

The Conclave of August 1458 was short but exciting, for election lay between a French and an Italian candidate, the latter backed by Milan and Naples. Cardinal Estouteville, Archbishop of Rouen, of royal blood and enormous wealth, attended the second scrutiny in possession of eleven promises, one short of winning. He himself had to read the votes drawn from the chalice on the altar. To his horror, Piccolomini headed the list with nine. The method termed Accession was then adopted. After long delay Borgia voted for Piccolomini, and then another acceded. One more vote was needed. The veteran Prospero Colonna rose, whereon Bessarion and Estouteville tried to drag him out, but he shouted: "I vote for the Cardinal of Siena and make him Pope." Thus Æneas Sylvius Piccolomini became Pope, taking the title of Pius II in honour of his classical name-sake, the Pious Æneas.

More has been written on Pius II than on all the Popes of the century together. Of this abiding interest his personality must be the secret. There is a note of tragedy in his death, but there is no striking episode in his career. His reign is of less importance than those of Martin V, Eugenius IV, or Sixtus IV; in the encouragement of art and letters Nicholas V stands high above him. Yet his fascination is always fresh, and biographers jostle round him. The main interest is neither political nor ecclesiastical, but always personal; he was intensely human, a man who might have lived in any age. Posthumous fame he owes, no doubt, to his literary gifts. He was, perhaps, the best man of letters and the best speaker who ever wore the tiara. His versatility was marvellous: he was poet, sacred and profane, essayist on education, rhetoric, and horse-flesh, a novelist so improper that his work was early translated into all European languages, geographer, historian, and, above all, diarist. His baffling character puzzled his contemporaries, and its ingredients have been disputed ever since.

So also is his success a puzzle. Others have climbed from a position equally lowly to St Peter's chair, but have usually been pushed up through one of the great Religious Orders for talents which naturally procure promotion—saintliness, learning, administrative capacity. Æneas had none of these qualifications; the looseness and shiftiness of his earlier life were against him till his very death. He belonged to no Order, he was emi-nently individualist; he won his way by personal qualities. He had not really the genius to mould circumstances, nor, perhaps, even the stuff to fight them. He influenced others by his power of language, but he was rather the receptive medium than the motive force. The impulse came from stronger natures or stronger circumstances. His success was the victory of style, of rhetoric, of the new diplomacy, of unequalled experience in international complications. That his negotiations turned largely on ecclesiastical questions was fortuitous; he complained himself of the obstacles which theology threw in the way of diplomacy; he had in fact reached the Papacy through the *coulisses* of the Imperial Chancery. If impression was the key to his character, expression was his ladder to success.

The interest in the Pope's secular career has exceeded that in his pontificate, but for this the reader must be referred to his biographers. The essentials are, however, his long service for the Council of Basle, in which he rose to the highest secretarial rank, his desertion of its democratic and anti-papal principles for the views of the German neutrality party, and then, in the atmosphere of Vienna, his conviction that the two monarchies, papal and imperial, must lean upon each other. Under the guidance of his friend and patron, the Chancellor Kaspar Schlick, he became the chief agent in the reconciliation of the Empire under Eugenius and Nicholas. At Vienna too he met the two apostles of the crusade, Cesarini, whose friendship he had enjoyed in earlier days at Rome, and Carvajal. From them he derived his passionate belief in the necessity of a crusade, and his close knowledge of East European conditions.

From his election Pius made the crusade his chief object, but for four years was hampered by the Neapolitan succession war, which reacted on the Papal States, connecting itself with raids by Piccinino, revolt of Sigismondo Malatesta of Rimini, troubles with Colonna and Savelli, wild disorder in Rome itself. At his accession Piccinino, inspired by Naples, was occupying Assisi and other places, part of the State once held by his kinsman Braccio. Pius, however, had formed friendship with Sforza and Ferrante when he had accompanied Frederick III on his wedding visit to Naples. Unable to leave for the crusade congress, to be held at Mantua, while Ferrante's succession was unsettled, he recognised his right, but without prejudice to other claimants. René's envoy had to admit that his master could not aid in the expulsion of Piccinino from papal territories, which was at the moment the vital issue. The *condottiere* did by Ferrante's orders withdraw, after Pius had started for Mantua. The bull summoning all princes to a congress had been issued in October 1458. In January 1459 he left Rome, much to the citizens' disgust, and arrived at Mantua on 27 May. Here his reception was hearty, as it was at Perugia and Ferrara, but Siena received him coldly, as he forced the bourgeois government, the Ninè, to admit the gentry, his own class, to office. Florence was polite but non-committal; Cosimo was conveniently ill. The temper of the Bolognese was so ugly that an escort of Milanese cavalry was required. The congress opened on 1 June, but was disappointing from the first. Disaffection, almost amounting to mutiny, spread among his very cardinals. No European sovereign arrived, and only Ferrante sent representatives. At length in August came a brilliant embassy from Burgundy, followed by Francesco Sforza in person. The first real session was held in September, and Pius left Mantua in January 1460. Results were nugatory. The Emperor thwarted operations by land, claiming Hungary from the elected king, Matthias Corvinus. The Germans did endorse a previous promise made to Nicholas, and perhaps the most interesting visitor was Albert Achilles of Hohenzollern. France, offended by Pius' support of Ferrante, refused all aid; René utilised a fleet raised for a crusade to land his son in Naples. Sforza, personally friendly, disliked the project; Venice made impossible conditions for a fleet; Florence, nervous for her Eastern trade, would make no public engagement. The Turk was left to overrun the eastern shores of the Adriatic.

In August 1459, open rebellion (described in detail later) broke out against Ferrante, and René's son John came to the rebels' aid. Next summer the king lost his army at the River Sarno, and Pius' vassals, Federigo of Urbino and Alessandro Sforza, were beaten in the Abruzzi. Pius thought Ferrante's cause hopeless; only Sforza's entreaties and Ferrante's bribes kept him firm. One nephew, Andrea, received Alfonso's former conquests in Tuscany; Terracina, always in dispute, was ceded to Pius and occupied by Antonio Piccolomini, who then married Ferrante's bastard daughter, becoming Duke of Amalfi and Grand Justiciar. In 1460 Sigismondo Malatesta had been added to the Pope's enemies. Pius had reconciled him, when in sore straits, to Federigo of Urbino, mulcting him of Sinigaglia and Mondavio for the papal benefit. Sigismondo now broke out, recovered these towns, and beat Federigo. Pius shewed real determination; he regarded the semi-pagan lord of Rimini as both a spiritual and temporal enemy. His effigy was solemnly burnt at Rome, and Pius fought on until Sigismondo's defeat was complete. He was allowed to recover Rimini, while Novello, his brother, held the other family fief of Cesena; both fiefs were, however, to revert to the Papacy on failure of legitimate male issue.

Rome had never forgiven Pius for his departure; there was no trade and little public order during his absence. A band of genteel hooligans took advantage of the confusion. Their head was Tiburzio, whose father, Porcaro's brother-in-law, had lost his life in the Conspiracy. He gave a political, republican complexion to social unrest. He was in touch with Malatesta and Piccinino, and obtained from the Savelli a base at Palombara in the Campagna. While the Colonna conspired with the Savelli in the south, Everso of Anguillara raided Roman territory from the north. From the Sabina Piccinino threatened Rome, the gates of which Tiburzio was to secure. In October 1460 Pius realised that his long absence must end. Escorted by cavalry lent by Sforza, he entered Rome. Tiburzio, riding in to release a comrade, was greeted with cries of "Too late, Too late." He was captured and executed, but until July 1461 the Savelli held out in Palombara. Whenever Pius left Rome, and he was seldom there, discontent broke into disorder.

If Pius was neither popular nor successful in Rome, he surpassed any other Pope in his knowledge of the territory between Rome and Siena. He loved the country with a quite modern passion; his life at times was a perpetual picnic, which makes delightful reading in his *Commentaries*. His kindliness enabled him to allay the rancorous party hatred which cleft every town in Umbria and Papal Tuscany. His one great artistic feat was the creation of his native village Corsignano into a township, named Pienza, with *piazza*, cathedral, episcopal palace, town-hall, and public well, and the Piccolomini palace commanding all. The cardinals, little appreciative of country life, were expected to build palaces. This little toy town still remains intact, the very epitome of Renaissance structural art.

In 1462–63 the Pope's plans for a crusade took shape. Circumstances were now favourable. The celebrated discovery of alum at Tolfa in papal territory gave prospects of large profits. The Turks now possessed the mines in Asia Minor on which Europe had relied. Small quantities, indeed, existed in Ferrante's dominions, and when Pius requested the Christian powers to give Tolfa the monopoly of supply, some friction was caused. The Neapolitan war was ending to the disadvantage of the Angevins. The Doge Prospero Malipiero, who had consistently promoted peace, was dead; the Turkish attack on Venetian colonies, and their conquest of Bosnia in 1463, were forcing Venice into war. Peace between the Emperor and Corvinus enabled her to conclude an offensive alliance with Hungary against the Turk. Skanderbeg was fighting successfully in Albania, where the little ports would be valuable for a landing. Dangerous illness frightened Philip of Burgundy into engaging to fulfil early promises. Such a combination, with the aid of Genoa and Ferrante, would have been formidable. The Pope's determination to head the crusade excited enthusiasm among the middle and lower classes throughout Europe.

With March 1464 chilling winds set in. Louis XI, always an inveterate enemy, forbade the Duke of Burgundy to fulfil his vow, and Philip, now recovered, was glad of the excuse. Sforza, after long excuses, detached Genoa. The French cardinals, always violently opposed, worked upon their colleagues; in the Papal States themselves tithes and contributions were refused. German crusaders flocked into Italy before arms and supplies were ready. When Pius left Rome, he could rely on no aid whatever except from these crusaders, a Venetian fleet under an unwilling doge, and the possibility of meeting Corvinus at Ragusa. It was a mad enterprise, but the fault was that of Europe at large, for Pius had devoted all his health, wealth, and talents to making the crusade a substantial reality, and of its necessity later European history is the proof.

As a forlorn hope Pius took the Cross; he would shame European princes into following. The actual campaign would be farcical, were it not pathetic. A river barge contained the handful of cardinals and secretaries. The very first night, Pius was too ill to leave it. The drowning of a single boatman upset the champion who was to lead the hosts of Europe to death or glory. Leaving the waterway, the little party struggled over the Apennines under a scorching sun, dropping one and then another from fever or white feather. The curtains of the Pope's litter must be drawn, that he might not see craven crusaders flocking homeward. Arrived at Ancona, from the bishop's palace on the headland Pius saw no Venetian fleet. Below was gathered a riff-raff of crusaders, clamouring for food, selling their arms to buy a passage home, men whom the Pope could only pay with indulgences, which many of them sorely needed. Meanwhile across the narrow sea the greatest soldier-statesman of his age, the Sultan Mahomet II, stretched out his hand against the Christian republic of Ragusa, which cried for help. A septuagenarian cardinal and two ill-found galleys were all that the head of Christendom could offer. Day after day fever fought against the will. At length Pius was carried to the window to see the Venetian fleet sail in, a majestic fleet with the world's first admiral, the doge, on board, but a doge so sceptical that he sent his doctor ashore to discover whether the Pope was ill or only shamming. Pius proved his good faith by dying within the second day.

The crusade was a fiasco, and this was the result of European politics. Pius II's diplomacy, which had won him the tiara, ended in almost general failure. This was, perhaps, due to the impressionable side of his character. His papacy has an antiquarian flavour. He seemed to be playing at being a Pope of old, though he was sufficiently in earnest. Just as his curiosity was excited by every relic of ancient Rome, so his whole nature was impressed by the claims and glories of the Papacy, which, in the words of Hobbes, was none other than the ghost of the deceased Roman Empire, sitting throned upon the grave thereof. For Pius the Papacy was no petty Italian principality, but the world ruler. Nourished in the democratic atmosphere of the Council, he became the stoutest assertor of Papal Supremacy over all powers temporal or spiritual. Of this his bull *Execrabilis* of January 1460, condemning all who appeal to a Council to the penalties of heresy and treason, is the most positive expression. In its own day a *brutum fulmen*, an unexploded bomb, it has since been treasured in the papal armoury among the most effective weapons of the extremest ultramontane claims. With this new idealism he lost his diplomatic acumen, and failed to realise facts. This was the secret of his failure with Louis XI, with George Poděbrady of Bohemia, even of his heroic championship of the crusade. His troubles with these kings concern mainly their respective countries, and can only be touched on here.

Charles VII had protested against the bull *Execrabilis*; his death in July 1461 seemed to give Pius an easy victory. In December Louis XI annulled the Pragmatic Sanction. Rome was triumphant until it appeared that its practical abolition depended upon the Pope's abandonment of Ferrante. Louis conspired with Pius' enemies in Germany, dissuaded Philip of Burgundy from the crusade, coquetted with Poděbrady's idea of a secular crusade, headed by the French king, in opposition to the Pope's traditional supremacy as champion of Christendom.

The relations with Poděbrady were equally disappointing. Both Pope and the elective king were genuinely anxious for conciliation. The latter had been crowned by Catholic bishops, and tendered his obedience. He held that he was no heretic, that his position under the Compacts of Basle corresponded to that of the French king under the Pragmatic Sanction. Pius would be content with nothing less than the abrogation of the Compacts, while Poděbrady realised that this would alienate the majority of his subjects, to whom he owed his crown. One of Pius' last acts was a bull denouncing Poděbrady and his kingdom for heresy and schism.

In Germany alone did Pius meet with any success. This was due to persistency in principles, which lost him the friendship of other States. In these too he had to deal with national ideals and strong rulers. His long German experience had taught him that it was always possible to divide his most dangerous opponents, the great nobles. He had the unfailing support of the Emperor, who had a tenacity and diplomatic sense which were to serve him well in his chequered career. The centres of disturbance were Mayence and Tyrol, which became linked by Gregory of Heimburg, a clever, patriotic, unmannerly German, who, after publicly insulting Pius at Mantua, became attorney and irritant for his enemies in turn, passing from the Pope's former pupil, Sigismund of Tyrol, to Diether of Mayence, and thence to Poděbrady. The quarrel with Sigismund, inherited from Calixtus, was caused by Nicholas of Cusa, Bishop of Brixen, who forced upon his diocese the reforming principles of Basle. He chose as object lesson the aristocratic nunnery of Sonnenburg. Sigismund, as its protector, violently opposed him, in the face of excommunication, appealing to a Council, for Pius the deadliest of offences. This might have been a storm in a tea-cup, had Sigismund not joined the disobedient Elector of Mayence in a revolt which spread through Germany. This lesser quarrel was only closed by the Emperor after the deaths of Cusa and Pius.

The larger conflict arose on a disputed election for the see of Mayence between Diether and Adolf of Nassau; it then became involved in the great war between Hohenzollern and Wittelsbachs. The Pope's legate, the fiery old Bessarion, threatened the princes, creating the impression that the Crusade tithe was compulsory. Both parties joined against Pope and Emperor; all Germany clamoured for a Council, and was ready to revolt against both spiritual and temporal heads. Pius sent agents who discounted Bessarion's wild statements, and played upon the invariable divisions between the princes. He then deposed Diether and recognised Adolf, whose capture of Mayence, in October 1462, was the deciding factor. Rupert of Bavaria, Archbishop-elect of Cologne, negotiated a peace in October 1464. Thus Pius could claim that he had triumphed over his German enemies, though this was mainly due to other agencies.

Pius II is, without question, one of the most living figures in papal history. Yet it cannot be claimed that his was a great pontificate. He added slightly to the extension of the papal territorial authority, and through his incessant intervention in European affairs, and especially in his support of the Aragonese dynasty, left the prestige of the Papacy higher than his immediate predecessors. His nepotism and provincial favouritism have been much condemned. He filled high places with his *nipoti*, as was natural in a Pope always poor and saddled with peculiarly prolific relations. His chief favourite, Antonio, was enriched at the expense of Naples, not of the Church. The cardinalate bestowed upon Francesco Todeschini-Piccolomini was justified by his election to the Papacy in succession to Alexander VI. Posts large and small were monopolised by his fellow-citizens, who were at least superior to the hated Catalans of Calixtus. The Sienese were unpopular, but so were the inhabitants of every Italian State with every other.

Pius, as Pope, is described as a little man with back somewhat bent, and a scanty fringe of hair, prematurely white. A pale face was lit up by smiling eyes, which, however, could flash fire, if his hot temper were aroused. His health had always been weak; gout he described as quite an old companion. Yet in spite of pains in head and feet, or acute agony in the waist, he never shirked work or refused an audience; the only sign was a twitching of the mouth, or the pressure of his teeth upon his lip. Whatever his faults, Pius had real distinction, a brave heart in a feeble frame, and an ideal none the less high for being hopeless.

The cardinals utilised the vacancy to frame capitulations more stringent than ever in limitation of papal autocracy, and then elected Marco Barbo, nephew of Eugenius IV. He was a wealthy Venetian, trained for business, but tempted by prospects of high promotion under his papal uncle. Gossip said that he wished to take the name Formosus, which, however, might be taken to refer to his handsome face and figure, of which he was notoriously vain; so he contented himself with the title Paul II. Lavish in hospitality, kindly in word and deed, shrinking from the suffering of men or animals, he was deservedly popular. Once Pope, he determined to gather into his own hands the threads of curial power, to introduce workmanlike centralisation. He redrafted the capitulations in a monarchical sense, covered the text with his fair, fat hand, and forced the cardinals to subscribe. Bessarion struggled against this, but the stout-hearted Carvajal alone resisted to the end. In spite of this opening, his relations with his cardinals were fairly good, for he was just and generous As a sop, he increased the dignity of the college; the red biretta and the damask mitre, hitherto confined to the Pope, were now granted to cardinals, and the poorer members were subsidised. Paul fully appreciated the work of those who had opposed him, such as Bessarion and Carvajal, the flower of a somewhat blemished flock.

If Paul would not submit to an oligarchy of cardinals, still less would he tolerate a republic of letters. A secretarial bureaucracy had grown up in the College of Seventy Abbreviators. It contained many leading humanists and others who had bought their seats. Paul broke up its independent monopoly, restoring its control to the Vice-Chancellor. This was never forgiven, and has injured Paul's reputation throughout all time, for Platina, who became papal historian, led the counter-attack in a

violent letter and was put to torture. The malcontents organised themselves
in the home of Pomponius Laetus, the most extreme of antiquarian humanists, into the so-called Roman Academy. In view of the actions of Cola
di Rienzo, Porcaro, and even Tiburzio, this affectation of old Roman republicanism might take a dangerous political and anti-Christian complexion. The club, suspected of a conspiracy against the Pope's life, was
raided by police; three of the four alleged ringleaders fled, and the unlucky
Platina again paid the penalty. There was no strong evidence of conspiracy, and the prosecution was dropped. Members of the club bore old
Roman names, vapoured against the government of priests, were pagan
in their cups, making libations to heathen deities, and disbelieved in the
immortality of the soul. They stood outside the shadow of ever-widening
papal power, and were hostile to it. Their heresies were, indeed, affecting
the upper classes throughout Italy, the papal feudatory, Sigismondo
Malatesta, being a striking example. Paul, unable to speak Latin, was
not a man of letters but of business, to whom the conceited humanists
were repugnant in their boast that princely reputations were at their
disposal.

With the Roman people Barbo, as cardinal and Pope, was popular.
A true Venetian, he had the sense for colour and magnificence which was
beginning to make his native city the show-place of Italy. Paul, as
Nicholas V, would make Rome a worthy capital, but with a more popular
aim. His palace, at the bottom of her chief street, if severe without, was
gorgeous in every internal detail. The *piazza* into which the street
expanded was, as that of San Marco at Venice, to be the centre of Roman
life. Lately an open-air garage for the distribution of tramcars, it was then
the scene of Carnival sports and Gargantuan banquets. Paul initiated
the celebrated races down the Corso, since named after them, to the
winning posts by his palace. The huge processions were secularised,
becoming a medley serious and humorous, pagan and Christian. Paul from
his loggia would scatter small coins, and laugh at the games till his sides
ached. Great care was devoted to sanitation, to control of the food supply,
and to the codification of statutes, judicial and financial. This latter was
somewhat at the expense of municipal independence, for, in finance, the
Vatican government was superseding that of the Capitol. Paul's personal
tastes corresponded to his public ostentation. He loved fine clothes, and
was an expert collector of jewels, taking his choicest gems to bed with
him, as a child his toys.

During this reign the Orsini and Colonna were comparatively quiet.
Public security was assured by the overthrow of the house of Anguillara,
which coined false money and kept the Roman-Tuscan frontier in uproar.
Paul was guilty of no secular nepotism. In his hopes for papal expansion
he suffered a serious disappointment. The chiefs of the two Malatesta
branches of Rimini and Cesena died without legitimate male heirs, and
their States should have lapsed to their suzerain. Sigismondo's clever young

bastard, Roberto, who was in papal service, offered to enter Rimini and restore it to the Church, but, once there, he kept it for himself. A general Italian war was only prevented by the panic caused on the Turkish capture of Negropont, but Paul had to submit to a rebuff. Among feudatories his favourite was the genial Borso d'Este, who by a personal visit obtained his heart's long desire, the title of Duke of Ferrara. With the Italian powers Paul was usually on polite terms, except for frequent rubs with Ferrante, once leading to minor hostilities.

European relations were more eventful. The reign began in friction with Louis XI, but the king played fast and loose with the Pragmatic Sanction, which was finally annulled to Paul's great satisfaction. The Emperor Frederick proved his friendship by another visit to Rome, where the rival universal Powers played the somewhat humorous part of twin brothers, walking hand in hand, and changing sides at intervals. Paul contributed largely to the efforts of Hungary and of Skanderbeg in Albania, but the crusade hung fire, in spite of the loss of Negropont, second only to that of Constantinople, as deciding the predominance of the new Turkish navy in Levantine waters. The conflict with Poděbrady was a legacy from Pius II. Paul entered into it without scruple or reserve, finding willing allies in the Emperor and Matthias of Hungary, both of whom coveted Bohemia. Paul's own scheme was the disintegration of the kingdom into principalities. He flooded the country with fanatical or disreputable crusaders, but made no great headway. Poděbrady was, indeed, forced to abandon his ideal of a Czech hereditary kingdom, and to recommend the succession of the Polish prince Vladislav, who, though a Catholic, accepted the Utraquist political system. In March 1471 he died, and Paul was left to decide between Catholic claimants. His sudden death, on 28 July 1471, relieved him from this dilemma.

By Alfonso's death, Naples, though officially styled the kingdom of Sicily, was again separated from the I .nd, as also from Sardinia and the Aragonese kingdoms, which all fell to his brother John. Ferrante's succession seemed insecure. John's son Charles, on hearing of his uncle's illness, had slipped away from Rome to Naples. His claim would find support with the Catalan officials and mercenaries, and from several barons, who feared Ferrante's anti-feudal policy. He, however, rode the towns, finding acceptance with the people, who greeted him as the *re 'taliano*, a proof that in him the Aragonese dynasty was Italianised. Charles sailed away, followed by an exodus of Catalans. Complete recognition ensued, Ferrante remitting taxation and promising to confine offices to Neapolitans. His triumph was only apparent. The Prince of Taranto, disappointed in Charles, turned to John, who, fully occupied with Catalonia and Navarre, supported Ferrante's cause. Calixtus, however, as has been seen, repudiated Ferrante's claim.

Ferrante's general position seemed favourable, for Cosimo de' Medici

and Sforza strongly supported him, disliking the French occupation of
Genoa. Ferrante prudently withdrew his besieging fleet, hoping to reconcile his old enemies, already tired of the French. The issue was
simplified by Calixtus III's death, for Pius II was well disposed towards
Ferrante. Meanwhile, however, baronial troubles had begun. Candola
and the town of Aquila raised rebellion in the Abruzzi. In Apulia,
Taranto played a double game, exacting concessions, and using them
against Ferrante. In Calabria the Marquess of Cotrone, restored to his
possessions on Taranto's petition, stirred up baronial revolt, while there
was a peasant outbreak against taxation. These movements were suppressed by Avalos, Campobasso, afterwards notorious, and by Ferrante in
person. Cotrone's arrest during negotiations was a foretaste of Ferrante's
future methods. All this time Taranto intrigued with John of Calabria,
who, in October 1459, sailed with Genoese ships for Naples. His fleet,
ill-equipped, failed here, and was returning, when John was welcomed at
the mouth of the Volturno by Ferrante's brother-in-law, the Duke of
Sessa. Rebellion blazed up in the Terra di Lavoro, the Abruzzi, Apulia,
and Calabria. Campobasso deserted to the barons; Piccinino, disgusted
by Ferrante's peace with Pius against all his Aragonese traditions, invaded
the Abruzzi; Cosimo's influence alone prevented a large Florentine subsidy
to John.

The war which followed is characteristic of Neapolitan campaigns. The
movements in Calabria and the Abruzzi were generally distinct, while the
main forces manœuvred between the Terra di Lavoro and Apulia. The
objective was often the control of the cattle tolls on the Apulian-Abruzzi
frontier. Thus in 1460 Ferrante thrust himself between these provinces
to secure this source of revenue. Then he counter-marched to Capua to
meet the papal contingent, and crush Sessa. John followed him, and
Ferrante, now the stronger, met him at the River Sarno, east of Vesuvius.
The Angevin fleet was beaten at the mouth of the river; the nobles were
drifting towards Ferrante; in a few days Avalos with his Apulian army would
have joined. But Ferrante, short of money and supplies, risked a surprise;
his troops plundered; the Angevins rallied, and Ferrante's force was
annihilated; the king escaped to Naples on 7 July with only twenty horse.
A fortnight later Piccinino beat Ferrante's allies, Alessandro Sforza and
the Count of Urbino, at San Fabiano, which laid Apulia open. Ferrante's
strongest supporters, especially the Sanseverini, deserted him. John might
have taken Naples, but for wasting time in trying to starve it by occupying
the neighbouring towns. Ferrante and his queen raised money by fair
means or foul. The story tells that the latter sat at the gate or paraded
the streets with a collecting box, and that she journeyed to Taranto,
disguised as a friar, to persuade her uncle to join the royalists. Ferrante
indeed placed reliance on the widening rift between the prince and John.
Yet he was so hard pressed that he thought of surrendering his kingdom
to his uncle, John of Aragon, now only too willing to accept. This

alarmed the Italian powers, who realised the danger to Italy from Spain. Pius was kept true by the territorial concessions and bestowal of family honours, before mentioned; yet he long wavered under pressure from Louis XI, who, succeeding in 1461, offered to annul the Pragmatic Sanction, if he would support the Angevins.

The war now went in Ferrante's favour. Sforza lent him his best general, Roberto Sanseverino. In Apulia Skanderbeg, having crossed from Albania, created a useful diversion. The barons swung from side to side, until the Sanseverini definitely joined the king, which brought over Calabria and the Salerno peninsula. The towns often preferred royal to baronial rule. Sforza rendered signal service in provoking revolt in Genoa against the French; John found it difficult to obtain supplies and naval support. The decisive battle was fought in the autumn of 1462 at Troja in Apulia, where Ferrante and Alessandro Sforza beat John and Piccinino. The Prince of Taranto, long lukewarm, changed sides, and soon after died, whereupon his huge estates reverted to the Crown. Piccinino returned to Aragonese service; Sessa brought the Terra di Lavoro back to obedience. Curiously enough, John's last success was the betrayal to him of Ischia and the Castel d'Uovo. René joined him from Provence, but, on recognising the hopelessness of the cause, both sailed home. The king had profited by his continuous occupation of Naples, whence, acting on interior lines, he could strike north, south, or east, as occasion served.

Ferrante now had twenty-one years of undisputed rule. His first act was to entrap Candola and Sessa, in defiance of the capitulations. He then enticed Piccinino to Naples, and executed him. The *condottiere* had married Sforza's natural daughter Drusilla, but her father, under whose guarantee he went, was suspected of complicity. His guilt is still a subject of dispute. Ippolita Sforza was on her way to marry Alfonso, but her journey was suspended; to outward appearance, the Neapolitan-Milanese alliance was endangered. With the death of Cosimo de' Medici, Francesco Sforza, and Pius II, Ferrante lost his closest friends. Galeazzo Sforza and Piero de' Medici held, indeed, to the Triple Alliance, but Paul II, as usual, reversed his predecessor's policy, insisting upon the Neapolitan tribute remitted by Pius in consideration of civil war expenses. Ferrante, in return, demanded back the county of Sora, temporarily occupied by Pius, and aided the Orsini in holding the city of Tolfa, which commanded the papal alum mines. The Triple Alliance was tested by the mysterious campaign of Bartolomeo Colleone and the Florentine exiles, with the suspected approval of Venice. Ferrante reinforced the Milanese and Florentine forces by a large army under Alfonso. Colleone's progress was checked by the battle of Molinella, near Imola, and Paul brought about a general peace in 1468. Next year, however, he was in actual collision with the allies in his quarrel with Roberto Malatesta over the occupation of Rimini. In this campaign Alfonso supported Paul's enemies. The shock caused by the Turkish capture of Negropont in May 1470 brought peace. Piero de' Medici had died in the previous December, an event destined to alter the relations of the Italian powers. In July 1471 Paul II himself died.

On 9 August 1471 Francesco della Rovere, General of the Franciscan Order, was elected Pope by eighteen cardinals, all Italians, except Bessarion, Borgia, and Estouteville. He was an unexceptionable candidate. Born of humble parents living near Savona, he owed his rise to his own ability as scholar, university lecturer, and preacher. The Eastern question was still prominent, and, to further a crusade, Bessarion, Borgia, and Barbo were dispatched on missions to the several European powers. All three completely failed, Bessarion dying on the way home. Pope Sixtus IV was really in earnest; the sums expended were large, the Papal-Venetian fleet, sailing to the Levant under Cardinal Caraffa, mustered 89 galleys. Early successes were considerable. Smyrna and Satalia in Anatolia, through which contact might be gained with the Turcoman Uzun Ḥasan, were captured. Then followed the invariable dissensions: Neapolitans, having quarrelled with Venetians, sailed away; with winter Papalists and Venetians parted company. A second failure in 1473 and the defeat of Uzun Ḥasan convinced Sixtus that a crusade was impracticable without active support from all Italian powers, and that these, however friendly, despised the Papacy as being weak and non-military. In striking contrast to his previous career, he determined to make it strong, to place it on a level with the four greater powers as an armed temporal State.

To this policy the obstacles were numerous. There was no subordinate expert council, no secular court to dazzle the populace, no sons and daughters wherewith to buy alliances, no reliable generals, such as the Neapolitan princes, to lead potential papal armies. The territories under direct control were scattered and difficult of access. Not only the most important cities, Ferrara and Bologna, were now ruled by families ostensibly independent, but Faenza, Forlì, Pesaro, Urbino and Rimini, Perugia and Città di Castello were held by citizen despots, while Ravenna was in the claws of the Venetian lion. Worse than all, the whole country, north, east, and south of Rome was held by the Orsini and Colonna, or families attached to them. How then was Sixtus to form a consolidated State?

His answer was the adoption of a methodical nepotism; his nephews should personify the princes of a ruling house. Recent Popes had given fiefs and cardinalates to relations, but had not converted nepotism into a regular administrative system, and an engine for expansion. Sixtus would revert to the policy of Boniface VIII, though he lacked the close grip upon his nephews which that masterful Pope exercised. It has been thought that, from time to time, Piero or Girolamo Riario, or Giuliano della Rovere, held the real control; the Pope's inordinate affection for the two former early led to the belief that they were his sons, but for this there is no evidence. Yet Sixtus possessed much intellectual force, he had never been a recluse, and had ruled over his Order.

The first essential was to subordinate the oligarchy of cardinals to the monarchy. This was begun, in defiance of the capitulations, by the elevation of Piero Riario and Giuliano della Rovere, youths without reputation or experience. The college was then packed with seven or eight relations or obscure Genoese satellites. Piero had the congenial task of creating a secular Renaissance Court. The Pope could not yet dine with ladies, nor ride out with a suite of mummers, musicians, race-horses, and sporting dogs. This function Piero, friar though he was, understood to perfection. His entertainment of Leonora, Ferrante's daughter, on her way to marry Ercole d'Este, was a five days' wonder. On Whit-Sunday after mass a drama on Susannah and the Elders was presented as suitable. All Rome delighted in the brilliant spectacles, the lack of which made priestly rule unpopular. Piero publicly flaunted his chief mistress sparkling with jewels from head to slippers. No one could better represent the Papacy abroad. He travelled in princely style to Milan, Mantua, and Venice, always the gay popular spendthrift, with powers of persuasion, personal or pecuniary. Whether he had real ability is uncertain, for his pace was too fast to stay; dissipation killed him at the age of 28 in December 1473. His position passed to his cousin Giuliano, serious, purposeful, and dignified, who could suitably dispense public hospitality, while concealing his private vices.

For marriage alliances Sixtus utilised his lay nephews. Leonardo della Rovere, created Prefect of Rome, wedded a bastard daughter of Ferrante. Girolamo Riario, now the Pope's chief favourite, without any of his brother's charm, was a greedy, brutal vulgarian, brought up in either a grocery shop or a notary's office. To him was given Galeazzo Sforza's illegitimate daughter, the celebrated Caterina. As a marriage settlement Sforza sold to Sixtus his possession of Imola, a papal fief. Giovanni della Rovere made a match ultimately of more substantial value than those of Leonardo and Girolamo; he won the daughter of Federigo of Urbino, whose prestige as soldier and statesman far surpassed his material wealth. As his son died childless, the lowly house of della Rovere succeeded the Montefeltri, who boasted the bluest blood in Italy.

Sixtus at his accession was on the best terms with the members of the Triple Alliance. Papal favour was essential to Ferrante's monarchical authority over his baronage. This explained the gift of his peculiarly plain and stupid daughter to the Pope's nephew. Sixtus remitted the tribute with its arrears, the bone of contention under Paul II, contenting himself with the receipt of the customary white palfrey. Ferrante visited Rome during the Jubilee of 1475; he began to regard papal friendship as even more important than adhesion to Florence and Milan. The rift in the Triple Alliance probably originated in the sale of Imola to Sixtus. Florence had previously arranged the purchase of Imola. She was always sensitive as to the towns on the high road south of Bologna, for the Apennine passes, which led to these, were the outlets for her Adriatic trade. Hitherto Sixtus had showered favours on the Medici, appointing them as papal bankers, and granting special concessions in the alum trade of Tolfa. He had even aided in suppressing the revolt of Volterra. Imola changed all this. Sixtus transferred his banking account to the rival house of Pazzi, which had financed the purchase. Lorenzo refused to admit to the see of Pisa his personal enemy Salviati, whom the Pope had nominated. Mobilisation of Florentine troops at Borgo San Sepolcro, when Sixtus was punishing his recalcitrant feudatories hard by at Città di Castello, was regarded as a hostile act. Finally, Sixtus was drawn by Girolamo into a plot for the overthrow of the Medici. He protested indeed that he would have nothing to do with murder, shutting his eyes to the inevitable consequences of success. Almost insensibly Italy began to split into opposing leagues. Lorenzo turned to Venice, the Adriatic rival of Naples. Milan, much weakened by the assassination of Galeazzo Sforza and the feeble guardianship of his heir by his mother, Bona of Savoy, relied upon Florentine support. Yet there was no general wish for war, which might not have ensued but for the atrocious attack upon the Medici brothers, in which Giuliano was assassinated. For participation in this crime Salviati was flogged and hanged. Lorenzo, having escaped murder, was punished by excommunication, Florence by interdict.

The war which followed broke up the Triple Alliance. Sixtus and Naples took the field against Florence, Venice, and Milan. The chief papal feudatory, the Duke of Ferrara, and the chief papal city, Bologna, sided against their suzerain, Siena, as usual, against Florence. Sixtus had good fortune in securing the services of Federigo of Urbino. Ferrante had little direct interest in war beyond his close tie to Sixtus. He had not, however, forgotten old Tuscan ambitions, and remembrance was quickened by suspected Florentine designs on Piombino. More definite was his hostility to Venice, especially in relation to Cyprus, which she practically ruled through Caterina Cornaro, widow of the last legitimate Lusignan. Ferrante coveted the island for a bastard grandson betrothed to Charlotte, bastard of Lusignan.

Papal and Sienese territory formed an excellent base for attack on Florence, and the papal and Neapolitan troops were on the frontier before defence was organised. Angevin help was not now forthcoming, though Louis XI made strong, if resultless protests. He had ecclesiastical disputes with Sixtus, and rubs with Ferrante over a projected intermarriage, while Ferrante's son Frederick was at the Burgundian Court. The first year's campaign ended in favour of the assailants. Ercole d'Este, Ferrante's son-in-law, in command of the Florentines shewed no alacrity for attack and little for defence. Venice gave little aid, but Milan supplied a fine young general, Gian Giacopo Trivulzio, afterwards so famous. During the winter time, Ferrante employed Galeazzo's exiled brothers, Sforza and Ludovico, and their cousin Roberto Sanseverino to overthrow the Milanese government in Genoa. In command of the sea, they threatened Pisa, and drove Florentine commerce from the Tuscan coasts.

When the main campaign reopened, a promising attack on Perugia was nullified by Carlo Fortebraccio's death, and successes in Sienese territory by quarrels between the Mantuan and Ferrarese contingents. Successive blows then fell on Lombardy. Cardinal Giuliano played upon the pious and predatory instincts of the Swiss, who poured down to Bellinzona. Ludovico Sforza, now Duke of Bari by his brother's death, and Sanseverino passed into the Po valley and raised revolt against Bona. Ercole d'Este and the Marquess of Mantua marched north to stem the tide. Ercole persuaded Bona to restore Ludovico, who soon reduced the regent to impotence. On the very day of Ludovico's entry into Milan, Alfonso and Federigo of Urbino won a decisive victory over the weakened Florentine army, storming its central position at Poggio Imperiale on the Elsa. The rout was only stayed at Casciano eight miles from Florence, which Alfonso could probably have entered, had he not delayed to besiege Colle. The little town's stout defence demoralised his army, while Urbino was invalided home. Alfonso granted a three months' truce in November, with which the war was really over. Lorenzo, still refusing humiliating surrender to Sixtus, threw himself on Ferrante's mercy. His personal charm won a generous peace, published on 25 March 1480 at Florence, Naples, and Rome, though against the will of Sixtus.

Victory lay with Naples. Yet Ferrante had made two grave mistakes in policy. To gain temporary advantage over a former ally, he encouraged the revolt of Genoa, his natural enemy, and then allowed Sforza to overthrow the Milanese regency. Thus he first weakened Milan, and then planted there a clever adventurer, who was to cause his dynasty's ruin. Alfonso, disconcerted in schemes of Tuscan conquest, lingered near Siena, aiding the wealthy citizens to overthrow the popular government, becoming the centre of the pleasure-loving Sienese society, and the favourite godfather of the republic's babies. Siena might have become a Neapolitan protectorate but for the startling news that Otranto had been captured in August by 10,000 Turks, while large supporting forces were gathering in Albania.

Italy was panic-stricken; Sixtus prepared for flight from Rome. But the Turkish numbers were exaggerated, and, when the truth was known, the invariable slackness and disunion reappeared. Alfonso with difficulty raised 3000 men for the siege. Florence insisted on the restoration of places ceded to Siena; Federigo of Urbino's presence at Otranto was urgently required, but he was detained by Girolamo Riario's occupation of Forlì and his designs on Pesaro and Faenza. The siege met with scant success. Otranto was won and Italy saved by the death of Mahomet II and Bāyazīd's disputed succession. The garrison, weakened by withdrawal and disease, surrendered in September 1481 to Alfonso, who enlisted many captured Janissaries in his army.

One war breeds another; the Ferrarese war was the offspring of Sixtus IV's attack on Florence. Venice resented Lorenzo's action in making peace with Naples, while Sixtus could not forgive Ferrante for assenting. In 1481 Girolamo schemed at Venice for the expulsion of Ferrante and the conquest of Ferrara for Venice. Ercole d'Este had married Ferrante's daughter, which the Venetians ill-liked, and a quarrel was picked on the rights of the Venetian consular court in Ferrara, and the manufacture of salt in the Comacchio Lagoon in defiance of Venetian monopoly. The old Triple Alliance, reconstituted, took up the challenge. Venice engaged two first-rate generals, Roberto Sanseverino, who had quarrelled with Ludovico il Moro, and Roberto Malatesta. Federigo of Urbino commanded the allies, who planned an attack on Venice's western provinces, a direct assault on Rome by Alfonso and the Colonna, the restoration of Niccolò Vitelli at Città di Castello by Florence, and the capture of Forlì from Girolamo Riario. Ferrara was soon in difficulties: Federigo of Urbino died there in September, the fertile Polesina was lost; Sanseverino forced the Po, establishing a permanent post at Ponte Lagoscuro; the Stradiots raided to the walls of Ferrara. But the Pope also had his troubles. Vitelli recovered Castello, Terracina fell to the Neapolitans; Cardinal Giuliano's party pressed for peace. Sixtus implored Venice to send him Malatesta. Fortune at once turned. Malatesta on 21 August destroyed Alfonso's army at Campo Morto in the Pontine Marshes. This was, however, a one man's victory; the conqueror died of malaria, contracted in the marshes; the papal coast was still at the mercy of the Neapolitan fleet. It became clear that Venice would be the only gainer by the war, and would be a far more dangerous feudatory in Ferrara than the Estensi. By Christmas Sixtus had come to terms with Ferrante; by February the Quadruple Alliance against Venice was complete, with Bologna and Mantua supporting. Venice did not lose heart. Sanseverino attacked the Milanese, hoping to raise revolt against Ludovico in favour of Bona and her son. Ferrara, bombed and starved, was in dire distress. In July, however, the tide turned again. Alfonso pushed Sanseverino back from the Bergamasque and Brescian provinces to Verona, while Ercole d'Este in person drove the Venetians out of the vital post at Stellata. Venice, almost exhausted, appealed to Charles VIII, Louis of Orleans, the Emperor, and the Turk. Once more her fortunes flickered up. In May 1484 Gallipoli and other Apulian ports were taken, and in July success was won at the very gates of Ferrara, after which Lorenzo de' Medici advised Ercole to surrender.

Peace was already in the air, and on 4 August it was declared. The terms of the treaty of Bagnolo were based on general restitution, with the exception of the Polesina, ceded by Ercole to Venice, who, as was said, had bribed the mediator Ludovico Sforza. Sixtus, who had been left out of the final negotiations, learnt the result on 11 August; he indignantly protested, and died next day. There is therefore some evidence for the tradition that peace killed the Pope who had lived on war.

In the sphere of Art, Rome owes more to the lowly family from Savona than to any other papal house, for Julius II did but continue the work begun in his uncle's reign. The Sistine Chapel, built from 1473 to 1481, and expressly designed for internal decoration, brought together a group of artists such as the modern world has never seen. Tuscany and Umbria contributed Ghirlandaio, Botticelli, Rosselli, Signorelli, and Perugino with his pupil Pinturicchio, while from Forlì came Melozzo. The Chapel walls are the very quintessence of Renaissance art, spoilt only by the destruction of three of the fifteen panels to make room for the writhing nudities of Michelangelo, which replace the key of the whole design, the Ascension with the kneeling figure of the founder, Sixtus. Sixtus also built the admirable churches of Santa Maria della Pace and Santa Maria del Popolo, the latter the family church, with its monuments showing the Rovere emblem, the sprig of holm oak with its acorns. The church of San Pietro in Vincoli begun by Sixtus, and that of Santi Apostoli by Pietro Riario were both completed by Julius II. In the former was the splendid Ascension by Melozzo, burnt in 1711. The right bank of the Tiber was glorified by the rebuilding of the Hospital of Santo Spirito, one of the walls of which described scenes from the Pope's life, by the erection of the Ponte Rotto, and by the broad Via Sistina, leading from Sant' Angelo to the *piazza* of St Peter's. The streets of Rome were widened and paved, its squares opened out in preparation for the Jubilee; the fountain of Trevi once more gave fresh water to the city. In the neighbourhood two of the most interesting Renaissance castles, Ostia and Genazzano, were built by Sangallo for Giuliano.

The Pope's own bronze monument, now in St Peter's, was executed in 1493, on Giuliano's order, by Antonio Pollaiuolo, who, with Verocchio, had employment under Sixtus. His real monument, however, is Melozzo's fresco, removed to canvas and now in the Vatican, shewing Sixtus seated, handing to the kneeling Platina the keys of the Library, and facing his nephews Giuliano, Girolamo, and Giovanni, with a young friar by his side, singularly resembling him, now thought to be his great-nephew Raphael Riario. This collection of portraits, purporting to be such, and not scriptural or classical subjects, in a perfect setting of Renaissance architecture, marks a most important stage in fifteenth-century portraiture.

The new election apparently lay between the three powerful *nipoti* of Calixtus, Paul, and Sixtus. Barbo's Venetian origin went against him, and neither Borgia nor Rovere was quite strong enough to carry his own election. The result was a corrupt compromise to elect a cypher. Battista Cybò was a kindly, self-indulgent Genoese gentleman of fine appearance, but for blinking eyes. As Pope Innocent VIII he openly acknowledged an illegitimate son and daughter of his layman days. Rovere, whose tool he

became, was, it was said, Pope and more than Pope. The reign opened
amid violent fights between Orsini and Colonna. Rovere protected the
latter, and, for a time, the two great families reversed their usual rôles;
the Ghibelline Colonna as the Pope's allies prepared to invite the French
or René, while the Orsini championed the Neapolitan cause, bringing the
Pope into the extremity of danger.

The Neapolitan war was the outstanding event of Innocent's reign.
Rovere had never forgiven Ferrante for his desertion in the Florentine
war. Innocent himself inherited Angevin sympathies, his father having
fought under old René. Ferrante in June 1485 sent the usual white
palfrey to Innocent, but withheld the tribute, on the ground of expenses
incurred at Otranto. The Pope angrily returned the mount, and looked
for allies against the defaulting king. These were easily found in his own
kingdom. Alfonso's military success had turned his vainglorious head.
He urged his father to apply the squeezing of the sponge to his secretary,
Petrucci, and his financial adviser, the Count of Sarno, who had amassed
fortunes at royal expense. On returning to Naples in 1484 he had arrested
the Count of Montorio and the heirs of the Duke of Ascoli. The greater
barons, including the chief Crown officials, Constable, Admiral, Chamberlain, and Seneschal, with Giovanni della Rovere, Duke of Sora, conspired
with Petrucci and Sarno, appealing to Rome for aid. Ferrante himself
was all for peace; his financial straits were desperate, his debts to
Florentine merchants enormous. War would stop the sale of grain to
Rome; Innocent might seize the cattle tolls between the Abruzzi and
Apulia; René of Lorraine would probably press the Angevin claim with
French support. He still trusted his ministers, employing them in negotiations with the nobles in August 1485. His second son Frederick interviewed the barons, who wished him to succeed his father. The Italian
powers were averse to war. Venice merely allowed her general Roberto
Sanseverino to take service at Rome. The sympathies of Sforza and
Lorenzo de' Medici were with Ferrante, but were academic, though Sforza
later allowed Trivulzio and the Count of Caiazzo to give some aid.

On 30 September Aquila expelled the royal garrison, quartered against
the city's privileges. Yet on 2 October Petrucci and Sarno brought news
that the barons had accepted terms, the chief being that Frederick should
marry the Seneschal's daughter and receive the great fief of Taranto.
Aquila returned to temporary obedience. The so-called peace of Miglionico,
nicknamed *Mal Consiglio*, was of service to Ferrante as dividing baronial
interests, just when Innocent was prepared for war. In the ensuing war
the barons played no active or united part. From 30 October it took a
scrambling character. Alfonso with Ferrante's close friend, Virginio
Orsini, fought Sanseverino north of Rome, threatening Perugia, and
joining Trivulzio in Tuscany. The other princes defended Apulia and
the Abruzzi against Giovanni della Rovere, who gained contact with the
barons at Venosa. Genoa declared for Innocent, and in March 1486

Cardinal Rovere went thither to obtain aid from René. His departure and a partial victory by Alfonso at Montorio on 7 May, which laid Rome open, proved decisive. The Romans clamoured for peace, which was urged by Sforza and Ferdinand of Aragon. Cardinal Borgia was now too strong for the French party in the Curia. Aquila revolted from the Pope. Peace was made at Rome on 11 August 1487.

Ferrante had made concessions which he never meant to keep. He engaged to pay the papal tribute; the barons were dispensed from duty of attendance at Court; Aquila might make choice between king and Pope. This last question was decided by Ferrante's occupation of the town and slaughter of the leading papalists. In May 1487 Petrucci and Sarno were executed; the greater nobles, caught in a trap, met a similar fate; Antonello Sanseverino and the heirs of the Prince of Bisignano, almost alone, escaped to Venice. Huge estates were swept into the treasury; the monarchy seemed stronger than it had ever been. Friendly alike with the Colonna and Virginio Orsini, Ferrante seemed to hold Rome in the hollow of his hand. With his son-in-law Matthias Corvinus of Hungary he had threatened a Council for Innocent's deposition, and Matthias was organising an attack upon Ancona. Hard by, a local adventurer, Guzzone, had introduced a Turkish garrison into Osimo, the ancient walls of which were almost impregnable. Rovere was away in France; the feeble, vacillating Pope did not know to whom to turn. Lorenzo de' Medici saved him, partly from a genuine desire for peace, partly from his long-deferred hope of a cardinalate for his son Giovanni. Arrangements were made for the marriage of Lorenzo's daughter Maddalena with the Pope's son Franceschetto Cybò. Lorenzo's bribes, supported by Ludovico Sforza's troops, got rid of Guzzone and his Turks. Alliance with the Medici entailed friendship with the Orsini, so closely connected with them by marriage. All this was deeply resented by Rovere, now bent upon French and Angevin alliance.

Cybò's marriage took place in November 1487, and yet Innocent's position was scarcely improved. In April 1488 Girolamo Riario was murdered in Forlì by his nobles. The Pope wished to annex his fiefs, but Girolamo's widow, Caterina Sforza, stoutly held the castle, and, under Florentine pressure, he was forced to admit her son's succession. Faction fights at Perugia led to the expulsion of the Oddi by the Baglioni, much to papal disadvantage. At Faenza Galeotto Manfredi was murdered by his wife, Francesca Bentivoglio. Florentine aid was again invoked; the Medici were becoming the controlling power throughout Romagna. Bologna in 1489–90 recognised Giovanni Bentivoglio as *princeps et columen* of the republic. Southwards, Ancona was flying the Hungarian banner. The Papal States were falling to pieces. Innocent vainly appealed to Italian and foreign powers, threatening to withdraw the Papacy from Italy. Suddenly he declared for Ferrante, making peace in January 1492, and marrying his grand-daughter Battistina to Alfonso's bastard, Luigi d'Aragona. The price was the guarantee of the succession of Alfonso and his heir, which evoked emphatic protests from the French Crown. On 25 July Innocent died. These two reigns are notorious for the unwholesome growth of the cardinalate, due to the policy of Sixtus and the want of it in Innocent. Sixtus had packed the college with *nipoti* to obtain a secure majority. But the changes in his political alliances necessitated the grant of hats to the Italian or foreign powers in favour. The nominees of Milan, Naples, France, or Spain, would naturally be men of wealth, influence, and a definite foreign policy. Innocent thus succeeded to a cardinalate of contending personalities, each with a clique of poorer and less important colleagues. He increased this body, in defiance of the capitulations, notably by the promotion of Giovanni de' Medici, a boy of thirteen, though not fully recognised till ten years later. The danger now was, not the union of the curial oligarchy against the Pope's monarchy, but the factions between the several groups, over which a feeble Pope had no control. Each great cardinal was a pope in himself, with his own fortified palace and garrison, his own connexions among the Roman nobility, his own foreign policy. They divided among them, in spite of tradition and protest, all the chief Roman benefices, poisoning by factions the life of the populace at large. Rome was rarely in such a corrupt and lawless condition as under Innocent, for the central authorities of the Vatican and Capitol had no power. Secularisation of manners and morals was complete. Innocent added to this by the public recognition of his two children. He was the first Pope to dine with ladies, and this at the marriage of his grand-daughter Peretta Usodimare to the Marquess of Finale. Another wedded Ferrante's bastard grandson, the Marquess of Gerace.

A curious incident in the reign was the purchase of Sultan Bāyazīd's brother Djem, a refugee with the knights of Rhodes. The rulers of Hungary and Spain, the Soldan of Egypt, and Venice, would gladly have bought him from the Grand Master, Pierre d'Aubusson, upon whose French estates he was living. Innocent, however, bribed the owner with a cardinal's hat. This was a profitable investment, for Bāyazīd paid a large annuity for Djem's safe custody, adding a bonus in the gift of the lance reputed to have pierced the side of Jesus, which was received at Rome with much ceremony, and no little scepticism. Innocent was relieved of the responsibility for a crusade, for Bāyazīd promised peace with Christendom during his brother's detention. He made attempts to poison Djem, but the Vatican officials were watchful, and Djem survived his papal gaoler.

Innocent's monument by Antonio Pollaiuolo is in the new St Peter's. Of his interest in Art Rome shews little trace, for his garden house, the Belvedere, was later converted into the Museum of Sculpture. This was decorated by Mantegna and Pinturicchio, the latter's work including the views of Italian cities, which would have been priceless to posterity. The reign of Innocent's successor, Alexander VI, belongs to another book, but for Naples the new era opens with the death of Ferrante. A breach between the Aragonese dynasty and the nephew of Calixtus seemed inevitable, but Ferrante was bent on peace. He bribed Alexander to desert the Milanese alliance by the marriage of Alfonso's daughter Sancia to Jofré Borgia. When the French envoy reached Rome to demand investiture of Naples for his master, he met with unqualified refusal. Yet Ferrante's troubles with Alexander were not ended. In one of his last letters to Ferdinand of Aragon he complained that it was his fate to be harassed by every Pope, and that it was impossible to live at peace with Alexander. Worn out by anxiety and age he died on 25 January 1494. Alexander after all adhered to the Neapolitan alliance, and his refusal to annul Innocent VIII's investiture of Alfonso rendered inevitable the great French invasion, which was to change for centuries the life of Italy.

CHAPTER VI

FLORENCE AND NORTH ITALY
1414–1492.

THE death of Ladislas of Naples (6 August 1414), wrote a contemporary Florentine, "brought release from fear and suspicion to Florence and all other free cities of Italy[1]." For the remainder of the century the unification of Italy under one ruler lay outside the range of practical politics. The treaties by which Filippo Maria Visconti, in the early years of his rule in Milan, recognised the rights of Venice over Verona and Vicenza, and fixed the rivers Magra and Panaro as the boundaries between "Lombard power and Tuscan liberty," are typical of the spirit which inspired the relations between the Italian States for the next eighty years. Florence, Milan, and Venice each pursued a policy of expansion and consolidation within their respective spheres of influence, strong enough to check attempts at hegemony on the part of any single power, and at the same time forced to take account of the clearly defined interests of their neighbours.

Florence at this time was from many points of view at the zenith of her power and well-being. Her banking activities permeated the civilised world; the quantity and quality of her cloth ensured her supremacy in the wool-trade; the acquisition of Pisa (1406) and Leghorn (1421) opened out to her new opportunities for maritime commerce; Ghiberti was at work on his first set of bronze doors for the Baptistery, and Brunelleschi's dome was rising over the Cathedral. Confidence in the regime which had made Florence great, and faith in its capacity to endure, inspired the revision of the statutes which was carried out in 1415. Nothing in the pages of this document suggests that the foundations of the republic were, in fact, already undermined, in that the solidarity of the patrician class, and with it the motive force in the working of the commune, had vanished from the life of the city. For purposes of government Florence was divided into *Quartieri*, which in 1343 had replaced the earlier *Sesti*, and each *Quartiere* was further subdivided into four *Gonfaloni*; the representation of these fractions of the commune in equal numbers formed an essential element in the composition of all councils. The monopoly of political power lay with twenty-one trade-gilds, the fourteen *Arti Minori* and the seven *Arti Maggiori* being represented on the chief magistracies, from 1387 onwards, in the proportion of one to four. This further reduction of the power of the lesser gilds, after the settlement of 1382[2], is one among several instances of a tendency to narrow the basis of government, bred of the fear and suspicions of the leading citizens in

[1] Buoninsegni, D., *Storia della città di Firenze*, p. 7.
[2] See *supra*. Vol. VII, Chap. II, p. 69.

whose hands for good or for ill the destinies of Florence lay. The Signoria, composed of the *Gonfaloniere di Giustizia* and eight *Priori*, were elected by lot from bags (*borse*) filled from time to time with sets of names of those qualified for office and representing *Quartieri* and *Arti* in their due proportions. Save for the check placed upon it by two advisory bodies, the *Collegi*, the authority of the Signoria during its two-months' tenure of office was practically unlimited, and embraced every sphere of government. When serious questions were at issue, it was customary to summon the leading citizens to a *pratica*; the debates which took place at these informal gatherings shew that, whoever might hold office at the moment, the right of a recognised group of *ottimati* to be consulted on the policy of the republic was undisputed. The two principal legislative councils were the *Consiglio del Popolo* and the *Consiglio del Comune*, this last alone among the constitutional bodies not being confined to members of the gilds; their functions were limited to voting without discussion upon the proposals laid before them by the Signoria. On rare occasions a *Parlamento* of all the citizens was summoned to the Piazza by the ringing of the great bell, but the symbol of democracy had become the means by which the party in power obtained authority to impose its will upon the community. The consent of the *Parlamento* was sought for the erection of a *balía*, or commission of reform, and for the delegation to it, for a limited period, of the full powers inherent in the commune. During the lifetime of the *balía* the ordinary constitution was suspended; it legislated without recourse to the Councils, and appointed *Accoppiatori*, who refilled the election bags and usually received authority to nominate the Signoria and other magistracies *a mano* (i.e. not by lot), for a fixed term of years. Outside the main framework of the constitution lay numerous committees appointed, for the most part, by the Signoria. Of these the most important were the *Otto della guardia*, a committee of public safety, the *Sei della Mercantanzia*, a board of trade and court for commercial cases with wide international functions, and the *Dieci di Guerra e Pace*, a temporary committee the appointment of which was tantamount to a declaration of war.

The constitution of Florence as defined by law was a not unworthy embodiment of the ideal of liberty and concord and justice which inspired her citizens. Its most obvious defect, its complication, sprang from an honest attempt to give due recognition to all classes and interests, and, so long as the patrician class remained united, its will prevailed amid changing committees, while short tenure of office enabled each individual *popolano* to contribute his share to the work of government. But Florence, in words which Machiavelli places in the mouth of Rinaldo d'Albizzi, was "a city in which laws are less regarded than persons[1]." Despite much lip-service rendered to public spirit, capitalism was destroying the gild organisation, and rival merchant groups sought

[1] *Istorie fiorentine*, Bk. IV, 33.

to capture the machinery of government in their own interests. The *ottimati* were divided among themselves, and the preservation of unity depended in practice upon the ability of an individual to substitute the authority of a single will for that of the citizen class as a whole.

So long as Maso d'Albizzi lived, the quarrels within the circle of the *ottimati* were not allowed to come to the surface. Rich, able, and attractive, and endowed with the spirit of *civiltà* which enabled him to cloak the substance of power under the manners of a citizen, he ruled Florence in the interests of his family and of the *Arte della Lana*, with which its fortunes were associated. Yet his supremacy was not maintained without drastic purging of the election bags and prolonged persecution of his opponents, the Alberti. With his death in 1417, and that of Gino Capponi four years later, the divisions within the ruling circle became formidable. Niccolò da Uzzano possessed unrivalled authority in the councils and a true patriotism; yet he was growing old, and the only method which he advocated for holding the oligarchy together was to narrow it still further. Of the younger generation, Rinaldo d'Albizzi was a man of high character and conspicuous talent, but he lacked the gifts which had enabled his father to control the city without seeming to do so; an idealist rather than a politician, he disdained to court popularity or to manipulate the constitutional machinery in order to establish his authority, and dreamed of a Florence in which all citizens were equal and offices were awarded according to merit alone. At once touchy and over-bearing, he was inevitably a fomenter of discord, and the friction between himself and Neri Capponi brought strife into the inmost centre of the oligarchy. In 1423 the outbreak of war with Milan made plain the weaknesses of the government, its ineffective diplomacy, its failure to provide a revenue commensurate with its expenses or to convince the majority of citizens that its members were not deriving personal profit from the war. The institution of the *Catasto* in 1427 was an important step towards the regularisation of taxation and its removal from the sphere of party politics. Every citizen was called upon to make a return of his property, movable and immovable, income being reckoned as seven per cent. of capital; after an allowance of two hundred florins for each member of the household and other recognised charges had been deducted, a tax of one half per cent. was imposed on the capital thus assessed. For all its merits, the new system became a source of discord. An attempt to impose it upon the subject cities produced rebellion in Volterra, and, within Florence, the rich were aggrieved by the heavy burden laid upon them while the poor were enraged at the realisation of how lightly wealth had escaped hitherto. During these years the problem of civic unity was prominent in the deliberations of responsible citizens. Gino Capponi was not alone in deploring the practice of carrying on the work of government outside the Palazzo Vecchio, in the business-houses and at the supper tables of influential men, as derogatory to the Signoria and an incentive to faction. Groups of citizens were summoned to the Palazzo to swear on the Gospels that they would lay aside enmity and think only of the honour of the republic, and it became necessary to suppress the religious confraternities as centres of political agitation. Eventually the *Lex contra scandalosos* (1429) provided for a special committee to undertake a biennial denunciation of factious citizens, with power, in conjunction with the Signoria, to impose sentences of exile or disqualification for office. Such a remedy was worse than the disease; as Giuliano Davanzati truly said, in one of the numerous *pratiche* held on the subject, "the root of this evil which torments us is in our hearts[1]."

The war with Lucca (1429–33) sealed the fate of the oligarchy. It began as a military adventure of doubtful honesty in which the voices of those who would have opposed it were drowned amid the popular clamour for conquest. It ended in disaster for the Florentine arms, the day of the final battle being kept by Lucca as the festival of her vindicated liberty so long as the republic lasted. Rinaldo d'Albizzi had been among the most ardent promoters of war, and for three months he was actively engaged in the fighting as one of the Florentine Commissaries. After days spent up to his waist in mud, the miseries of sleepless nights enhanced by accusing letters addressed to him by the *Dieci*, he returned to Florence to find a scapegoat for his misfortunes in the person of Cosimo de' Medici. The precise part played by Giovanni de' Medici and his son Cosimo in the years which preceded the Medicean supremacy cannot easily be determined. It is clear that they were influential, but owing to their deliberate abstention from politics the direction in which their influence was exercised is difficult to trace. The democratic traditions of his family and his own great wealth rendered Giovanni suspect to the oligarchy, yet they found no cause to attack him; indeed their efforts were chiefly directed towards securing his co-operation. His attitude towards the *Catasto* shewed unwillingness to oppose a measure which was popular with those less wealthy citizens who looked on him as their friend, mingled with a natural absence of enthusiasm for an imposition which, with a single exception, fell more heavily on himself than on any other citizen. Before his death (1429) he had won for himself a reputation for wisdom, benevolence, and public spirit, and by strict attention to business he had laid the economic foundations of Medicean greatness. In the course of the war with Lucca the prestige which Cosimo enjoyed in the city became more apparent. His cousin Averardo was a prominent member of the war party, but Cosimo, on his own shewing[2], only supported it because he considered that the honour of Florence had become involved. He won the gratitude of the hard-pressed government by his loans and, as a member of the *Dieci* and of the embassy which negotiated peace, he increased his reputation for states-

---

[1] *Commissioni di Rinaldo degli Albizzi*, III, 507, 23 February 1431.

[2] Letter to Averardo de' Medici, 4 February 1430, *ibid*. 350.

manship. To Rinaldo, eager to be first in Florence, Cosimo's seeming indifference to power and popularity, and the ease with which they came to him, could not fail to be a source of bitterness. After Uzzano's death the two stood out as rivals for supremacy, and in September 1433 Rinaldo launched his attack upon Cosimo in the Signoria. He was accused of being one of the principal authors of the war, and of endeavouring, as his family had endeavoured from 1378 onwards, to bring the city under the Medici yoke, "desiring rather to live according to their own perverse will" than to bow to the laws of the republic[1]. Cosimo returned to Florence from his estates in the Mugello on the summons of the Signoria, and on 7 September he found himself a prisoner in the Palazzo Vecchio. His enemies had the situation in their hands, but they failed to make use of it. A month of delay and discussion followed, in which it was hoped that Cosimo's business would be ruined by his enforced absence, but which he used to buy himself support. When he exchanged his prison for exile in Venice, the prompt intercession of the Venetian republic on his behalf was not without its effect in Florence. Rinaldo took no steps to extend the power of the *balía* which had secured his victory, and on its expiry a Signoria favourable to the Medici was elected. At the eleventh hour Rinaldo attempted to secure himself by means of a *coup d'état*, but Pope Eugenius IV, who was resident in Florence at the time, persuaded him to disband his forces. Meanwhile a *Parlamento* was summoned and a new *balía* received authority to undo the work of its predecessor. The ban on the Medici was removed, Rinaldo and his sons went into exile, and, on 5 October 1434, Cosimo returned to Florence amid the acclamations of his fellow-citizens.

When the miserable reign of Giovanni Maria Visconti in Milan (1402–12) was cut short by his assassination, the great duchy ruled over by his father was in fragments. The chief cities had set up despots from among their own nobility, or had been seized by mercenary captains. Giovanni Vignati was lord of Lodi and Piacenza, Cabrino Fondulo ruled in Cremona, Benzoni in Crema, Rusca in Como; one of the late duke's *condottieri*, Pandolfo Malatesta, was in possession of Brescia and Bergamo, while Facino Cane, the captain-general of the Milanese forces, not only held Alessandria, Tortona, and Novara, but had made himself arbiter of Milan and its duke. The lack of organic unity in what had appeared, ten years earlier, to be the most highly centralised state in Italy received spectacular demonstration. Meanwhile, internal anarchy was fomented by external enemies who sought to make profit out of the misfortunes of Milan. The Swiss descended upon the Val d'Ossola and the Val Levantina; the Marquess of Montferrat made himself master of Vercelli, and the Marquess of Este of Parma and Reggio. Sigismund, King of the Romans, cherished designs for a revival of imperial power in Lombardy, and as a means to

[1] Fabroni, A., *Magni Cosmi Medicei Vita*, Vol. ii, 75.

this end took under his protection the descendants of Bernabò Visconti and other rivals to the authority of the new duke. On his brother's death, Filippo Maria Visconti was virtually a prisoner in his castle at Pavia, while the leading Ghibelline family, the Beccaria, controlled the city in co-operation with Facino Cane. He was not yet twenty, feeble in health and highly nervous in temperament; yet this morbid recluse, who was reduced to a state of panic by a thunderstorm and shunned contact with his fellows, was endowed with strength of purpose and brain-power which enabled him to perform a feat of statesmanship of the highest order. Beginning with Pavia and Milan, he extended his authority over the cities of the duchy one by one, until his dominions stretched from the Sesia on the west to the Mincio on the east; the recovery of Parma and Piacenza brought Visconti power south of the Po; on the north the Swiss were forced to yield up their conquests, and the keys to the Simplon and the St Gotthard passes were once more in Milanese hands. The conquest of Genoa crowned a decade of achievement and, in 1426, Sigismund set the seal of imperial approval on what had been accomplished when he invested Filippo with the duchy of Milan, renewing the privileges which had been enjoyed by his father.

Ability and good luck, force and diplomacy, fraud and legality, all played their part in the work of reconstruction. Facino Cane's death, coincident with that of Duke Giovanni, was a stroke of fortune of which Filippo made full use by marrying his widow, and succeeding through her influence to the control of her late husband's cities. The military successes of these years were largely the work of Carmagnola, whose association with Filippo had begun in Pavia when the former was one of Facino Cane's captains. Carmagnola's part, however, consisted mainly in reaping the fruit of his master's diplomacy. The ducal registers of the period shew the thoroughness and variety of Visconti's diplomatic methods; he treated alternately with the victim of the moment and with his chief enemies, playing on their fears and ambitions and luring each in turn into his net. He was never so dangerous as when he appeared to be conciliatory, and both Giovanni Vignati and Cabrino Fondulo learned that investiture, with the title of count, with the city which owned them as lord was the first step towards the forfeiture not only of their city but of their life. When a city was taken over, procurators were at once sent to receive oaths of fealty from representatives of the commune, and from the leading citizens, while the forces of a strong central organisation were directed towards the conquest of particularism. Communal liberties and individual rights were over-ridden, but Filippo was wise enough not to think himself to be infallible, and to take advice on local questions from those better informed than himself. Although the extent of his dominions made it imperative to delegate power to local officers, trusted servants of the duke watched over their proceedings and checked their extortions. The rural population was protected against the oppressions of cities and feudatories and, if need be, Filippo found favour with his subjects by associating himself with their grievances against his own officials. The party rivalries which were still acute in the majority of Lombard cities often afforded a means for the establishment of ducal authority. When this was accomplished, the central government became a mediator between factions, encouraging marriages between rival families, and providing for the election of an equal number of Guelfs and Ghibellines to the city Councils. In 1440, however, mediation gave place to suppression, and a general decree was issued forbidding the use of party names and ordering elections to be made on considerations of merit alone. Intimate as was his association with the dominion, the duke's first care was for his capital. Under his rule Milan increased in wealth, population, and industry until she became one of the leading cities of Italy. Above all he was an excellent financier, and one of his most conspicuous merits was that of prompt payment for work done. He introduced salutary reforms in taxation, superseding the capricious and interested valuations of special commissions and doing much to mitigate the burden which heavy expenditure and the numerous exemptions, which he found it necessary to grant, undoubtedly imposed upon his subjects. When the Venetians invaded the Milanese, in 1446–47, they were struck with the signs of prosperity which greeted them. Corn, wine, and oil abounded, the people possessed silk and silver, they fared sumptuously and did not know what war was[1]. The testimony of his enemies confirms the general impression derived from internal sources of the beneficence of the rule of the last Visconti.

Amicable relations between Milan and Florence did not long survive Visconti's acquisition of Genoa. His ambitions in Liguria ran counter to the maritime interests of Pisa, and, by an invasion of Romagna, he entered a sphere which was as vital as the western sea-board to Florentine commerce. In 1423 Florence declared war, and from that time fighting was almost continuous up to the peace of Lodi in 1454. These years constitute the heroic age of the Italian *condottiere*. From the victory of Alberico da Barbiano and his Compagnia di San Giorgio over the French forces which were threatening Rome in 1379, native Italian companies rapidly established their ascendancy. Alberico's camp became the cradle of the *condottiere* system; here Braccio da Montone and Muzio Attendolo— nicknamed Sforza—received their military training and formed one of those soldier friendships which persisted through lifelong rivalry in the field; from thence they went out to found the two most famous among Italian schools of soldiery, and to bequeath to future generations of Bracceschi and Sforzeschi their peculiar loyalties, traditions, and methods. As the native profession of arms developed, all classes and all parts of Italy contributed to its ranks. Members of the lesser feudal nobility and younger sons of great houses made up the larger proportion

[1] Da Soldo, C., *Annales Brixiani*, in Muratori, *Rer. Ital. Script.* (1st edn) xxi, 841.

of the *condottieri*, but among them were peasants such as Carmagnola, lords of cities such as Gonzaga of Mantua and Malatesta of Rimini, and ecclesiastics, among whom Cardinal Giovanni Vitelleschi is an outstanding example. Umbria produced Braccio, the Piccinini, and Gattamelata; from Romagna came Sforza, Niccolò da Tolentino, and Agnolo della Pergola, and as the century advanced there was hardly a Romagnol lord who did not hold a *condotta* from one of the larger States. Facino Cane was a Piedmontese, dal Verme and Colleone were Lombards; scions of great Roman and Neapolitan families—Orsini, Colonna, Sanseverini—fought as mercenary captains in North Italy while retaining their character as southern feudatories. Of recent years *condottiere* warfare has been rescued from some of the contempt which tradition has cast upon it. There is abundant proof that the Italian soldier of fortune brought to his profession scientific study of the art of war, technical skill of a high order, and boundless enthusiasm. Among the battles of the period remarkable both for fierceness and heavy casualties is the contest between Carmagnola and the Swiss at Arbedo (June 1422), which demonstrated the superiority of Italian arms over a power whose military reputation stood high. Pusillanimous captains, campaigns fought only in summer, bloodless battles are recognised to be the legendary offspring of Machiavelli's invective rather than the products of history. Nevertheless the system could not fail to be expensive and politically unsound. Forces were multiplied for no other reason than that a ruler could not afford to leave efficient captains free to be bought up by his enemies, and the payment of *condotte* taxed the resources of even the wealthiest of States. Provision of quarters, in the intervals of campaigns, was a serious problem for prince and captain alike. Filippo Maria Visconti, who understood the art of shifting the responsibility for evils which could not be avoided on to the shoulders of others, ordered that troops should as far as possible be assigned quarters in the fiefs of the *condottieri*, in order that they, and not the ducal officers, should have to deal with the complaints of the inhabitants against the depredations of the soldiery. When a *condottiere* acquired a State of his own the problem of quarters found a permanent solution, but from henceforth he had the interests of two States to serve, and, when these clashed, his first concern was not for his employer but for himself. Apart from political considerations, moreover, the system had inherent weaknesses which made its disappearance only a question of time. From the *condottiere* standpoint war was a fine art, an opportunity for the exercise of individual *virtù*; the heavy cavalryman was of its essence and, until late in the century, the use of fire-arms, save in siege warfare, was looked upon with something of the disfavour accorded to shooting foxes in a hunting neighbourhood. Thus the development of artillery and the increasing importance of infantry created a revolution in the art of war to which the system was incapable of adapting itself. It collapsed with the French and Spanish invasions, in common with much else that gave character and distinction to Italian life.

Two campaigns in the Romagna brought disaster to the Florentine forces. Thereupon embassies were sent to Venice to plead that her interests, no less than those of Florence, demanded that the course of the Visconti viper should be checked. Their arguments were reinforced by those of Carmagnola, who had quarrelled with Visconti, chiefly owing to the determination of the latter that he would not be saddled with a second Facino Cane. In the spring of 1425 he came to Venice, there to play what was, in his own opinion, the determining part in her decision to declare war. The hour had struck, however, when Venice could no longer ignore the menace to her mainland dominion created by the growing power of Milan. From the death of Gian Galeazzo Visconti she had been free to conquer and consolidate her territory east of the Mincio without hindrance from her western neighbour. But, although advocates of peace might declare that the hills of the Veronese were the natural frontiers of Venice, it was unlikely that Visconti, who had not hesitated to break the terms of his agreement with Florence when it suited him, would acquiesce in this opinion indefinitely. Thus an extension of Visconti power to the Adriatic came once more within the bounds of possibility, and this for Venice, with a nobility which had invested largely in estates round Padua, a commercial system demanding free access to the Alpine passes, and a population drawing its chief supplies of corn, wine, wood, and fresh water from the mainland, could only mean disaster. Moreover, the subjugation of Genoa had brought Visconti into conflict with Venice in the Levant, where he was active in the promotion of Genoese commercial interests, in alliance with the Turk, to the detriment of the Venetians. Under these circumstances the dangers of peace were at least as great as those of war. The words of the Doge Francesco Foscari turned the scale against the peace party in the Venetian Senate, and on 3 December 1425 an offensive league with Florence was signed.

The two first campaigns of the war resulted in important territorial acquisitions for Venice. In 1426 she won Brescia, and in October 1427 Carmagnola's victory a Maclodio secured for her Bergamo and a frontier which touched the upper waters of the Adda. At this point her advance was checked by Carmagnola's failure to take Cremona, and the conquest of the whole line of the Adda to its conjunction with the Po remained an unrealised ambition for another seventy years. During these campaigns, Niccolò Piccinino, the recognised leader of the Bracceschi, and Francesco Sforza, who had succeeded his father as head of the rival school, fought side by side in the Milanese forces. At their close, Francesco Sforza spent two years in a Milanese prison, while Carmagnola was summoned to Venice for trial and execution as a traitor. The dispassionate progress of Venetian justice, with its sifting of evidence and its ruthless judgment, contrasts with the caprice of the despot who threw Sforza into prison on suspicion, and released him in order to betroth him to his daughter. In 1438, war between Milan and Venice blazed up again with peculiar fierceness. Piccinino led the Milanese, Gattamelata and Colleone fought for Venice, and in 1439 Sforza, twice disappointed of his bride, became captain-general of the Venetian armies. Visconti had at last succeeded in winning over the Marquess of Mantua, and hoped, with his aid, to drive the Venetians from their conquests west of the Mincio. The centre of the fighting was Lago di Garda, a triangle enclosed on two sides by hills and guarded at its southern base by the Mantuan fortress of Peschiera. With the southern route barred to them, the Venetians could only retain contact with Brescia and Bergamo by crossing the lake or by circuitous marches through the northern hills. Their exploits and those of their opponents form the sagas of *condottiere* biographers, which they tell with a wealth of classical allusion and infectious enthusiasm. Both sides launched a fleet on the lake, the Venetian ships being transported on rollers over the hills from the Adige in mid-winter, a remarkable feat of engineering for which a Venetian naval officer—Niccolò Sorbolò—was responsible. Piccinino succeeded in destroying the enemy fleet, and then sailed up the lake to find himself surrounded by Sforza's army near Riva. Thereupon he made his escape through the enemy lines, tied up in a sack on the shoulders of a stalwart German, and carried out a surprise attack on Verona. Sforza followed in hot pursuit and retook Verona three days after its fall.

In the following year, the Venetian fleet established its supremacy on the lake, Peschiera fell, and Brescia and Bergamo were relieved. Meanwhile Piccinino made a diversion on Tuscany in conjunction with the Florentine exiles, to be defeated by a Florentine-Papal army at Anghiari (29 June 1440). Some sixty years later Leonardo's art was engaged to celebrate this victory, which secured Cosimo de' Medici's ascendancy in Florence and led to the incorporation of Borgo San Sepolcro and the Casentino in the Florentine dominion. Piccinino's purpose had been to draw Sforza away from Lombardy, and when this failed he returned to attack him near the Adda. If he had given himself whole-heartedly to fighting, his victory might have been decisive; but his chief concern was to force the Duke of Milan to give him Piacenza, as "a place of his own" in which he might spend his declining years. Other captains made similar requests until Filippo, in disgust, turned to Sforza, offering him the hand of Bianca Maria Visconti with Cremona and Pontremoli as dowry towns, if he would mediate between Milan and Venice. So the long-deferred marriage took place, and the peace of Cavriana was published (10 December 1441). It lasted only until Filippo repented of his action and tried to rob Sforza of the towns which he had recently bestowed upon him. The Venetians rallied in Sforza's defence, and in 1446 they crossed the Adda and came within sight of Milan. Old and ill, with his finances embarrassed, Filippo pleaded for peace; when this was refused, he sought aid of Alfonso of

Aragon and Charles VII of France in turn, and finally threw himself on the mercy of his son-in-law. Despite the quarrels and betrayals of twenty years, both Filippo and Francesco realised that in the last resort their interests were identical. The security and integrity of the Milanese State was vital to both, and neither would allow the other to be ruined. So Francesco gave secret orders that no Venetian soldier was to be allowed inside Cremona, and left his own vanishing dominion in the March of Ancona to come to his father-in-law's aid; on his way he heard that Filippo Maria Visconti was dead (13 August 1447).

The fate of Milan now lay on the knees of the gods. Frederick III claimed the duchy as a lapsed imperial fief. Aragonese troops were in possession of the Castello, armed with a document in which Filippo named Alfonso of Aragon as his successor. Charles VII, eager for Italian adventure, had responded to Filippo's appeal for aid by sending troops to occupy Asti; these proclaimed Charles of Orleans, the son of Valentina Visconti, as the rightful heir. The hopes of all aspirants to the throne were, however, frustrated by the proclamation of the Ambrosian Republic. A committee of twenty-four Captains and Defenders of Liberty were chosen from among the leading families to rule the city, the ancient Council of Nine Hundred confirming the election. Within Milan the republic carried all before it. Visconti's captains threw in their lot with the citizens and drove the Aragonese from the Castello, which was itself destroyed together with many of the ducal registers and tax-books. But the subject cities shewed no inclination to support the new regime, and Venice belied the professions of friendship which she made to the sister republic by occupying Piacenza and Lodi. Faced by the necessity of continuing the war, the Defenders of Liberty invited Francesco Sforza to take service with them. Sforza was naturally ill-pleased with the turn of events in Milan, but his power to take life as it comes stood him in good stead now, as at other crises in his career. He entered the service of the city which he had hoped would receive him as duke, and for the next fourteen months fought with conspicuous success against Venice. When the Defenders of Liberty were about to make peace behind his back, he forestalled them by himself changing sides. Not quite a year later (September 1449), Venice and Milan combined against Sforza in the belief that they would thereby force him to accept their terms, but he defied their expectations and carried on the war single-handed. At this supreme moment of his career he gambled with fortune. He knew that he could not fight Milan and Venice together for long, but he also knew that the Ambrosian Republic was tottering towards its fall. He played high, but he played with judgment and his good luck did not desert him. The Ambrosian Republic failed in respect of two problems of outstanding importance, the maintenance of order and unity within the city and the conduct of the war. A shrunken dominion and a too hasty abolition of taxes rendered the financial problem acute, and the necessity of improvising organs of government, in the place of the ducal council, led to a multiplication of committees which stood in the way of efficiency. Operations in the field were hampered by the mistrust with which the republic quite reasonably regarded its captain-general, yet the reverses which befell Milan after Sforza's desertion shewed that it could not do without him. Within Milan, the root cause of difficulty lay in the lack of cohesion among the citizens. Party feuds divided the nobility; the people were only united in their opposition to the nobles; although individuals had risen to wealth and eminence in commerce, there was no dominant merchant aristocracy or any one group strong and united enough to rule the city. When the tale of misgovernment was at its height, and Sforza's besieging army had reduced the city to the last extremities of want, the mob attacked the Court of Arengo, where the Defenders of Liberty were in session, and drove them from office. On 25 February 1450 the assembled citizens agreed to invite Sforza to enter the city as its lord. Thereupon he loaded his soldiers with bread to distribute to the starving people and rode in at the Porta Nuova to be acclaimed as the successor of the Visconti.

Francesco Sforza's establishment of his authority within the duchy followed naturally and without any real difficulty upon his reception in Milan; the more urgent problem was to secure peace with his enemies and recognition by the Italian powers. His accession was the signal for an offensive alliance between Venice and Alfonso of Aragon, who both saw their ambitions with regard to Milan vanish with Sforza's success. Against this he could set the personal support and friendship of Cosimo de' Medici. Although a considerable section of Florentine opinion would have remained faithful to the Venetian alliance, others, and Cosimo among them, held that during the recent wars Tuscan interests had been unfairly subordinated to those of Lombardy, and that Florentine money had been expended in adding to Venetian territory when the prosperity and security of Florence demanded that the power of Venice should be checked. Even before Visconti's death Cosimo had made up his mind that a strong Milan was the surest guarantee against Venetian domination, and that Sforza possessed the ability to hold the duchy together; so he secretly advised him to come to terms with his father-in-law and gave him financial and diplomatic support throughout his struggle for the throne. The desertion of Venice, to whom Cosimo's personal debt was great, exposed him to the vengeance of his late ally and to the criticism of his fellow-citizens. Yet, in his opinion, the expulsion of Florentine merchants from Venetian and Neapolitan territory, and the heavy expenditure incurred on Sforza's behalf, were not too large a price to pay for the maintenance of a balance of power in North Italy, and Cosimo's opinion was the determining factor in Florentine policy. Owing to Cosimo's mediation, an alliance was effected between Sforza and Charles VII of France, who was persuaded to make the Angevin claims on Naples, rather than those of Orleans on Milan, the object of French enterprise, and sent René of Anjou to Sforza's aid. Francesco's need was too great, at the moment, for him to be able to choose his allies, but he was opposed on principle to the encouragement of French intervention. Milan, as he himself said, was destined to serve both as the gateway of foreign princes into Italy and the barrier which lay across their path. After the removal of René's disturbing presence he was determined that the gateway should remain closed. Thus Cosimo and Francesco each made their individual contribution towards the new orientation of Italian policy which was effected during these years. Cosimo's resolve to stand behind Milan was proof against the war-weariness of Florence and the attempts of Venice to draw him into a separate peace. Francesco, while at one with Cosimo in his determination to maintain friendship with France, was primarily responsible for overcoming the traditional tendency of Florence to combat her Italian rivals by bringing French princes into the field against them. By loyalty to one another, and a readiness to be guided by each other's judgment, they furthered the propagation of a new ideal of national peace and unity in the face of foreign enemies, of which the firstfruits were seen in the proclamation of a general league between the Italian powers in February 1455.

The peace congress which met in Rome during the winter of 1453–4 failed to reach a conclusion, but Venice, to whom freedom to concentrate her whole strength on the Turkish problem was of vital importance, found, meanwhile, a more effective means of settling her differences with Milan. It was apparently at the suggestion of Paolo Morosini, a Venetian *Savio di Terraferma*, that Fra Simone da Camerino, Prior of the Augustinians at Padua, was sent privately to Francesco Sforza to treat of peace[1]. Fra Simone was an enthusiast in his cause and, as a Venetian subject and the confessor of the Duke and Duchess of Milan, he was specially qualified for his task. As a result of three separate visits which he paid to Milan, the vexed question of frontiers was decided by the cession of Crema to Venice, the only substantial addition to her territories after over seven years of fighting. These terms were embodied in the Peace of Lodi (9 April 1454), and in August of the same year a defensive league between Milan, Florence, and Venice was concluded. On its ratification, representatives of the three allied powers journeyed south to carry through the last stage of the negotiations by securing the inclusion of the Papacy and Naples in the league. Alfonso of Aragon proved the most serious obstacle to union. His alliance with Visconti in 1435, when a Genoese naval victory brought him a prisoner to Milan, had been the signal for the revolt of Genoa from Milanese rule, and from that time he had sought to use north Italian dissensions for his own advancement. The solidarity of the northern powers destroyed his hope of becoming in fact what the Milanese ambassador named him—the cock of Italy; only after repeated

[1] Cf. Antononi, F., *La pace di Lodi ed i segreti maneggi che la prepararono.* (*Arch. Stor. Lomb.*, 1930, pp. 233 sqq.)

efforts on his part to divide them did he consent to declare his adherence to the league. The treaty, in the final form in which it was ratified by Nicholas V, bound the five chief States together for twenty-five years against any power, whether Italian or foreign, which might attack them. Each was pledged to contribute specified military forces for mutual defence, and, in case of naval warfare, financial aid was guaranteed to Venice by her colleagues. The allies each named their adherents, with the result that, but for Alfonso's ill-advised refusal to include Genoa and Sigismondo Malatesta of Rimini, the league would have embraced every power in Italy. Questions had arisen with regard to the position of the Emperor, and as to the inclusion of foreign powers, such as France, Burgundy, and the Spanish princes but in the end the league was expressly limited to Italian rulers and Italian territory, a provision which adds some interest to the inclusion of the Swiss Confederation and various Trentino lords among the adherents. A special machinery was set up for dealing with quarrels within the league, each of the five principals appointing representatives to act as conservators of the peace, with power to arbitrate between disputants and to determine the nature of the help to be given to an offended member, if recourse to arms could not be avoided. Both as a genuine effort after peace and in view of its definitely national character the treaty is of considerable significance. If the system which it elaborated only existed on paper, and the peace which it secured was neither absolute nor of long duration, it set up a standard which influenced Italian diplomacy during the next forty years. It bears witness to a factor in the politics of the century which persisted amid deep-seated rivalries, territorial and commercial, to a sense of nationality striving to express itself, and a recognition of common ideals and common dangers transcending the particularist interests of the several States.

Alfonso of Aragon followed up his insistence upon the exclusion of Genoa from the league by a declaration of war which had the effect of throwing his enemy into the arms of France. In spite of Sforza's efforts to preserve her independence, Genoa once more recognised French suzerainty and welcomed John of Anjou as her governor, just a month before the death of Alfonso raised anew the Neapolitan succession question. With Genoa in his hands, Charles VII conceived of conquests which should include the establishment of the Angevin in Naples and the substitution of Orleans for Sforza in Milan. The failure of his schemes is due in large measure to the adherence of the chief Italian powers to the principles of the league. Florence cited her obligations to it, and the fact that her colleagues were pledged to make war on her should she break them, as the reason of her refusal to send help to Anjou; Venice turned a deaf ear to French requests for her support, saying that she wished to be at peace with all the world. Sforza sent his brother to aid Ferrante of Aragon, and himself lent a hand in the overthrow of French rule in Genoa. Faced by this solidarity among the Italian powers, Louis XI decided, soon after his accession, that his path to ascendancy in Italy lay in the conquest not of territory but of men. Already personally friends with Sforza, he determined to attach him to France by investing him with Genoa and Savona. In 1464, Sforza, true to Pius II's conception of him as one who always got what he coveted most, crowned his victorious career by entering Genoa as lord.

Cosimo de' Medici died in August 1464, and Francesco Sforza in March 1466; the disappearance of these two protagonists of Italian peace and unity could hardly fail to create an atmosphere of unrest, especially as the latter was succeeded by a self-willed young man with little of his father's perspicacity and the former by an invalid. The Pope took Galeazzo Maria Sforza under his protection, but Venice, when challenged on her unfriendly attitude towards Milan, replied that the Italian league no longer existed—Sforza had broken it by accepting the lordship of Genoa. In Florence, the question of the renewal of the Milanese alliance was at issue between Piero de' Medici and his opponents, and when Piero vindicated his determination to abide by his father's policy, the exiles fled to Venice to throw their weight into the opposite scale. Some ten years earlier Jacopo Piccinino's attack upon Siena had shewn the power of the unemployed *condottiere* to act as a destroyer of the peace, and the present situation tempted Bartolomeo Colleone to seek a territory at the expense of Milan and Florence. He was officially dismissed from the service of Venice in order that he might serve her the better, while Federigo of Urbino was sent to oppose him in the name of the league. A spectacular but indecisive contest took place at La Molinella on 25 July 1467, when after ten hours' fighting the two commanders shook hands and congratulated each other on coming unhurt out of the conflict. Colleone's ambitions were, however, foiled by his failure to secure a victory in the field, and the general peace which followed marked a further success for the policy of the league. Thereupon Colleone withdrew to his castle of Malpaga to spend the last years of his life in cultivated splendour.

When, in December 1469, Lorenzo de' Medici, Piero's son, assumed the direction of Florentine politics, he found Italy wrapped in profound peace to which the underlying hostility between Milan and Venice seemed to be the only serious menace. In the circumstances, wisdom dictated the cultivation of friendly relations with the latter power, and in 1474 Lorenzo's efforts resulted in a league between Milan, Florence, and Venice, which the Papacy and Naples were invited to enter. But the precedent of twenty years before was not carried to its conclusion: instead of a general league, there followed an alliance between Ferrante and Sixtus IV; Italy was divided into two camps each viewing the other with suspicion, if not with hostility. It is not easy to account for this change of atmosphere nor for the fact that, four years later, a personal quarrel between Sixtus IV and the Medici set all Italy ablaze. Perhaps the most serious cause of tension was the constant activities of France in Italian politics. Louis XI was prompt

either to sow discord between the Italian powers or to act as arbiter
in their quarrels, if his influence could thereby be increased or the circle
of his adherents enlarged; thus the temptation to use France as a weapon
against enemies at home was irresistible, and the knowledge that her
power lay behind some transitory combination of Italian rulers gave it
an importance which it would not otherwise have possessed. During
these years Louis XI's relations with Florence, Milan, and Venice were
peculiarly close; this alone was enough to arouse the fears of Naples, and
to incline Ferrante, who had his own rivalries with Venice in the Mediterranean, to make common cause with the Papacy. For some time past
Sixtus IV's activities in the Papal States had run counter to Florentine
interests, and in particular the establishment of Girolamo Riario as lord
of Imola had been effected against Lorenzo's wishes in a sphere of influence which he looked upon as peculiarly his own. His retaliation took
the form of measures calculated to ruin the Pazzi bankers, who had
financed the sale of Imola, and when to their grievances were added those
of Francesco Salviati, the papal nominee to the archbishopric of Pisa,
whom Lorenzo had prevented from taking possession of his see, the
material for the Pazzi conspiracy was to hand. On Easter Day 1478, in the
cathedral of Florence, Giuliano de' Medici fell a victim to the conspirators, but Lorenzo added to his offences against Sixtus IV the crime of not
being murdered, and the hanging of Archbishop Salviati by the infuriated
mob furnished a pretext for ecclesiastical censures against Florence and
eventually for a declaration of war. Although practically every Italian
State was involved and every soldier of repute had a share in the fighting,
the real issues were decided by the diplomats rather than by the soldiers.
Ferrante helped to bring about a change of government in Milan, whereby
Ludovico Sforza, the friend of Naples, supplanted Bona of Savoy and
Simonetta as regent for Duke Gian Galeazzo. Ludovico's rise to power
was hailed by Lorenzo de' Medici as a stepping-stone towards the reconciliation with Naples which he had come to regard as the salvation of
Florence. Louis XI's diplomacy had been active throughout in support
of his allies, and in November 1479 his agent in Naples reported that the
king was disposed to yield to his plea for peace[1]. Thus Lorenzo made his
famous journey to Naples when the ground was already prepared, and his
persuasive charm, coupled with the logic of the situation, turned Ferrante
from an enemy into a friend. Sixtus IV could not fight on alone, and in
1480 peace was restored, only to be broken two years later by the combined attack of the Papacy and Venice on Ferrara. Once more foreign
intervention exercised a predominating influence on the course of the war.
The Spanish monarchs entered the fray as the allies of their Neapolitan
cousins, who together with Milan and Florence took arms in defence of

---

[1] "Le Roy de Sicile est disposé de complaire au Roy en la requeste qu'il luy a faite
par moy pour la paix d' Italie." Cf. Perret, *Histoire des relations de la France avec
Venise*, vol. II, p. 192.

Ferrara, and their activities were in part responsible for Sixtus IV's change of sides. Finding herself isolated, Venice, who had already taken the Duke of Lorraine into her service, issued a double invitation to France: Louis of Orleans was sounded on his intentions with regard to Milan, and the French Crown was urged to undertake an expedition in support of its claims to Naples. This manœuvre had its desired effect. On 7 August 1484 peace was signed at Bagnolo, and the fertile district of the Polesina passed from Ferrara to Venice.

During the years which followed, the tension between the Italian powers was seldom if ever relaxed. All were aware that the only means of averting foreign intervention lay in ceasing to quarrel among themselves, yet each looked with suspicion on his neighbours and courted opportunities of advancement afforded by another's weakness. The strongest influence on the side of peace was undoubtedly that of Lorenzo de' Medici. When the allied powers met at Cremona in 1483, to lay their plans against Venice, his sound judgment and conciliatory temper won for him golden opinions. Florence, from her character as a small non-military State dependent on her commerce, had most to gain from peace, and to the task of smoothing over quarrels, and isolating them when they could not be prevented, Lorenzo devoted his skill and energy during the years of life that remained to him. But for him the Barons' war in Naples might easily have led to a general conflagration. In 1488, a year of assassinations in Romagna, he constituted himself the champion of the despots—Caterina Sforza Riario, Astorre Manfredi, Giovanni Bentivoglio—determined that rebellion in their cities should not give occasion for the increase of papal or Venetian power. He established complete ascendancy over the mind of Innocent VIII, and did his utmost to restrain Ludovico Sforza, restless and untrustworthy, prone both to give and to take offence. Everywhere and at all times he proved himself the pivot of the Italian State system. Nevertheless, it is doubtful whether, had he lived, he could have saved Italy from catastrophe. The divergence of interests between the chief States was too fundamental to be remedied by diplomacy or to render the balance of power anything but a transitory substitute for political unity. Lorenzo himself did not hesitate to excite the anger of Milan by taking possession of Pietrasanta and Sarzana in the midst of his work for peace. Only deliberate avoidance of armed intervention on the part of Louis XI and Anne of Beaujeu had prevented any one of the quarrels of the last twenty years from culminating in a French invasion, and the breach between Milan and Naples proved fatal, not because it afforded a unique opportunity for intervention, but because Charles VIII was now determined to make use of it. In April 1492, the Florentine agents in Paris and Lyons sent alarming accounts of Charles VIII's hostile intentions with regard to Naples and of his secret understanding with the envoys of Milan. This was a situation with which Lorenzo's foreign policy was not framed to deal; a breach with France would defy the tradition of centuries and deprive the declining

Florentine wool-trade of its best market, yet to aid France in an attack on Naples would be to destroy the unity among Italian powers which Lorenzo had devoted his best energies to maintaining. Perhaps fortunately for his reputation as a diplomatist he died a few days before the letters reached Florence.

With the return of Cosimo de' Medici to Florence in 1434 the republic was destroyed as surely as when in some north Italian commune the citizens, with a semblance of legality, conferred supreme power upon a despot. Here no official delegation of authority took place, and Cosimo, his son, and grandson, while they held Florence in the hollow of their hands, lived and died as private citizens. The task to which they devoted themselves with consummate success was, on the one hand, the evolution of constitutional forms more nearly corresponding with the conditions which in fact prevailed, and on the other, the rendering of their rule acceptable to citizens who gloried in the name of liberty and hankered after their vanished powers of self-government even while they consented to their loss. Cosimo's first care was to break up the oligarchy, and to create in its place a new governing group composed of no one class or interest but of his personal adherents. For the next sixty years the ruling faction in Florence were neither *magnati* nor *popolani*, *Neri* nor *Bianchi*, but *Palleschi*, who made the Medici balls their rallying cry and, unlike the factions of an earlier age, had little to fear from any opposing group. The list of proscriptions which followed Cosimo's return included the leading families in Florence. Rinaldo d'Albizzi and his sons died in exile, as did Palla Strozzi who, although a member of the *balía* which recalled Cosimo, was banished as a potential rival. Prominent patrician families were penalised by being made *grandi*, and others of the *grandi* were granted rights of citizenship. Neri Capponi, who according to Cosimo possessed the best brain in Florence, remained powerful and independent until his death; but the murder of his friend Baldaccio d'Anghiari, a captain of infantry, who was thrown from the window of the Palazzo Vecchio when Neri was enjoying the full flood of his popularity as conqueror of the Casentino, was perhaps intended as a warning that he too was dependent upon Cosimo's goodwill. Later events added to the number of the exiles who went to seek new homes and fresh commercial openings in Italy and abroad, cherishing their hostility to the Medicean regime but impotent to injure it.

Meanwhile, for those who remained in Florence, support of the Medici brought opportunities for money-making, a system of taxation capable of adjustment to their interests, and a virtual monopoly of political power. An increasing number of citizens enlisted whole-heartedly under a leadership which promised fulfilment of the two ends which lay nearest their hearts, the exaltation of their family and of their city. Until 1480, the control of the Medici over the organs of government was maintained through the prolongation, on one pretext or another, of successive *balíe*, which provided for the nomination of the Signoria and other magistracies by a committee. These, however, were emergency measures of limited duration, and the demand for a return to the time-honoured system of election by lot was too insistent to be disregarded. When election by lot was revived, it produced results unfavourable to the dominant party; names of friends of the exiles and lukewarm supporters of the Medici were drawn from the election bags, and proposals were brought forward which hampered despotic control. An attempt to revert to normal methods, after the Italian league of 1455, culminated in the chief constitutional crisis of Cosimo's rule. In 1458 the champions of liberty secured a renewal of the *Catasto*, and a proposal sent to the Councils for the creation of a new *balía* was thrown out. The movement was supported by St Antonino, Archbishop of Florence, who wrote a letter in his own hand, which he caused to be affixed to the door of the cathedral, urging the citizens to cling to their right of voting in secret. A gathering of leading citizens thereupon passed a vote of censure on the archbishop and decided to force through the government proposals. Cosimo, however, contrived to remain in the background and to leave to Luca Pitti the championship of an unpopular cause. A *balía* having been secured by recourse to the *Parlamento*, it proceeded to appoint *Accoppiatori* with the duty of nominating to the chief magistracies for seven years, and to institute a new Council of a Hundred, chosen from the supporters of the Medici, to advise on all matters of State with special responsibility with regard to finance. This victory for the dominant faction was marked by an attempt to add to the dignity of the Signoria; the *Priori delle arti* became *Priori di libertà* when one more stage had been reached in the destruction of Florentine liberty. Lorenzo had to await the reaction which followed the Pazzi conspiracy for his first real opportunity of modifying the constitution in the direction which he desired. The reforms of 1480 set up a permanent *Consiglio di Settanta*, consisting of thirty members chosen by the Signoria of the day and forty others chosen by the original thirty; membership was for life and vacancies were filled by co-optation. Two important committees, the *Otto di Pratica* which conducted foreign affairs and supervised the military forces, and the *Dodici Procuratori* which regulated finance and commerce, were appointed by the *Settanta* from their own number, as were the *Accoppiatori* who selected the Signoria. These changes, says Rinuccini, himself a member of the *balía* which effected them, "contained much that was contrary to the practice of self-government and to the liberty of the people[1]." Although respect for republican principles is reflected in the provision that the powers of the *Settanta* must be renewed every five years, its institution marks the final victory of the new oligarchy; the Signoria itself ceased henceforth to be the most coveted office in the republic, and served rather as a training school for

---

[1] Rinuccini, A., *Ricordi*, p. 133.

the *Settanta*, which was the sole fount of administrative authority. It remained now for Lorenzo to emancipate himself from the control of his own supporters by a further concentration of power. In 1490 the nomination of the Signoria was entrusted to a committee of seventeen of which Lorenzo was a member, and which received wide powers to act in the interests of the State. Rumour was persistent that Lorenzo only awaited his forty-fifth birthday in order to have himself made *Gonfaloniere di Giustizia* for life; this would have placed the coping-stone upon the despotism which had been in process of evolution since 1434, but he died when he was still within a few months of becoming eligible for the official headship of the republic.

The financial administration of the Medici was the aspect of their rule which found least favour with their fellow-citizens. Cosimo's progressive income-tax was arranged with great technical skill, and with respect for small incomes, but the use which he made of it to despoil his enemies overshadowed its merits. Lorenzo, on the testimony of his great-nephew, "was not very good at business[1]"; neither the affairs of his own bank nor public finance held the first place in his interest. His raids upon the state dowry fund earned for him severe condemnation, and his tampering with the coinage, on the introduction of white *quattrini* in 1490, was perhaps the most unpopular act of his government. The financial problem was, however, aggravated by declining prosperity. Florentine pre-eminence in the woollen industry was no longer assured; competition was robbing her of the monopoly of her technical processes, and new industrial centres rivalled her in commercial enterprise. The export of cloth fell considerably during the course of the century, and the *Arte della Lana* employed less labour. A tendency to play for safety and invest in land made capital difficult to obtain for business purposes; trade depression made itself felt in all classes. The acquisition of Pisa and Leghorn did indeed enable Florence to develop her own mercantile marine. Harbour works were carried out and galleys equipped, under the auspices of the *consules maris*, and Florentine ships made successful voyages to England and the Levant. But the opportunity for maritime enterprise in the Mediterranean came too late to be used with real profit, and foreign trade was hampered by restrictions on shipping in the interests of Florentine vessels. In these circumstances, and when the activity of Florence in Italian politics added daily to the expenses of government, it is not surprising that taxation was both heavy and insufficient for the requirements of State. The money spent by private citizens on building and the arts suggests indeed that the burden imposed was not crushing.

The rule of the Medici not only added to the Florentine dominion, but did much to weld the territory together. Pisa was wooed from the contemplation of her economic subjection to Florence by the prospect of winning fresh laurels as the intellectual centre of the Florentine State and

---

[1] "Discorso di Alessandro de' Pazzi," *Arch. Stor. Lomb.* 1, p. 422.

the official seat of the university. Lorenzo was himself a member of the governing body of the university and spared neither money nor trouble upon its development. When a dispute over the ownership of an alum mine goaded Volterra to revolt, it was Lorenzo's initiative which seized the opportunity to reduce the city by force of arms and rob her of the last remnants of communal autonomy. The sack which followed was a misfortune which his wisdom could only deplore; more characteristic of his methods of reducing a subject city to obedience are his purchases of estates in the neighbourhood and the acquisition of a Volterran abbey for his son Giovanni. Giovanni's benefices, scattered at strategic points over the territory, were regarded as a means of accumulating landed property for the maintenance of the family fortunes, and of creating centres of Medici influence where they were most needed. His elevation to the cardinalate, at the age of thirteen, is the crowning instance of the exploitation of his calling in the interests of State. When the young cardinal took up his residence in Rome in 1492, the Medici, like the Sforza and the Gonzaga, had their own representative at the Curia, exhorted by his father to serve as a chain binding the Papacy to Florence, and to use every opportunity of benefiting his city and his house. The inclusion of natives of the subject cities among their personal adherents served a double purpose with regard to the consolidation of Medici power. Devoted servants, like the Dovizi of Bibbiena, created a focus of loyalty to the Medici in their own homes, while they strengthened their control over the governing circle in Florence. The tale of rebellion and loss of territory which followed the fall of the Medici shews the value of the personal link which they created in holding the component parts of the dominion together; at the same time it marks the failure of their efforts to transform it into a single State.

The prestige enjoyed by the Medici, and their friendly relations with the princely families of Italy, contributed alike to the pride and the pleasure of the Florentines. From 1439, when Cosimo as *Gonfaloniere di Giustizia* welcomed Pope, Patriarch, and Eastern Emperor to Florence for the Council, a stream of great people flowed through the city, to lodge for the most part at the Medici palace and to provide occasions for feasting and pageantry in which all had their share. The May revels of 1459, when Pius II stayed in Florence on his way to the Congress of Mantua—the festivities included a tournament, a wild beast show, and a ball, at which sixty young couples chosen from the best dancers in Florence disported themselves in the Mercato Nuovo—helped to dissipate the ill-feeling aroused during the crisis of the previous year. The tournament which celebrated Lorenzo's engagement to Clarice Orsini, and the visit of the Duke and Duchess of Milan to Florence in 1471, which surpassed all previous efforts in magnificence, stand out among a succession of splendid merry-makings. Yet, while they entertained and were entertained as princes, the daily life of the Medici was true to the spirit of *civiltà*. Franceschetto Cybò was struck with the contrast between the banquets which he had enjoyed as a guest and the homely fare which he shared with the family as a son-in-law. The Medici palace in the Via Larga, although already in Lorenzo's day a treasure-house which strangers in Florence sought permission to visit, was not the seat of the government, nor was it a court where men of genius were brought together at the will of a prince. It was one of several no less sumptuous homes of citizen families, in which a group of like-minded friends were given wider opportunities for cultivating the gifts and pursuing the interests which were common to hosts and guests alike. Niccolò Niccoli, Marsilio Ficino, Michelozzo, Donatello, and Fra Angelico were Florentine citizens and Cosimo's personal friends, and it was with and through them that he rendered his chief services to the Renaissance. He chose out Marsilio, the son of his doctor, and provided for his training as the high-priest of Florentine Platonism; he supplied Donatello with models from the antique which inspired his sculpture; Michelozzo was the chief agent for the satisfaction of his passion for building; Niccoli and Fra Angelico represented the scholarship and the mysticism which made their twin appeal to his mind. The work which Michelozzo executed at San Marco includes under one roof the library in which Niccoli's books were available for public use, and the cell to which Cosimo was wont to withdraw from the world and where Fra Angelico has painted the figure of St Cosmas kneeling at the foot of the cross: it is a witness to Cosimo's identification with the fulness of life in the Florence of his day.

Lorenzo grew up in the atmosphere which his grandfather had helped to create; he was the pupil of the scholars and philosophers whom Cosimo delighted to honour. To the men of the Laurentian age, Poliziano, Botticelli, and their fellows, he was less a patron than one of themselves, inspired by a common vision and striving to give individual expression to it in his art. His power lay in the spontaneity and absorption with which he threw himself into every kind of human activity; his poetry has won for him a place among the great names of Italian literature; he was foremost alike in a carnival riot or in a Platonic disputation, a master in the world of imagination no less than in the world of politics. Moreover, his affections spread beyond the walls of Florence to the life lived in the Medici villas dispersed over the Tuscan countryside, where he had his hawks and his horses, where the Medici ladies saw to the oil and the cheeses, and Cosimo talked of farming as if he never did anything else but farm. Steeped in the traditions and prejudices of their fellow-citizens, and sharing their experiences, it was possible for the Medici to direct the government of Florence with the slightest appearance of despotic authority; but unfailing tact and ceaseless attention to detail were necessary in order to keep the balance true. Cosimo must take care that his dearest schemes were put forward in another's name; Lorenzo must receive instructions from the *Otto* when he set out on a diplomatic mission, and address the Signoria in language appropriate from a servant of the State to its official head; Piero's tactlessness and lack of geniality imperilled his position during the five years of his ascendancy. In Italy as a whole, Medicean diplomacy was able, for a time and in a measure, to satisfy the desire for unity without running counter to separatist instinct. Within Florence, Medicean personality made possible the rule of an individual under the forms of a republic. Such a system had in it all the elements of impermanence and compromise. Its achievement was to give, to Florence and to Italy, an interlude of peace in which the spirit of man was set free to create for itself a wonderland of beauty, more enduring than the political framework from which it sprang.

Francesco Sforza and his successors claimed to rule Milan in virtue of powers conferred on them by the people. At the opening of his reign, a general assembly of citizens, composed of one member from each household, invested Sforza with the duchy, and confirmed the capitulations to which he had previously pledged himself. Although the right of the commune to delegate its authority to an individual or group, by the grant of a *balía*, for a limited time and purpose, was universally recognised in Italian law, it is doubtful whether Milan, or any other city, was legally entitled to commit suicide by a permanent surrender of its functions. Consciousness of a defective title explains Francesco's efforts to obtain a renewal of imperial investiture and, when these failed, his suggestion that the Pope should confirm him in his possession of Milan, *negligente imperatore*. His internal government rested upon a system of monarchical centralisation tending towards the destruction of the communal institutions which were in theory the source of his authority. On his accession the two branches of the ducal Council, the *Consiglio di giustizia* and the *Consiglio secreto*, were revived, as were Visconti's two finance committees. For the conduct of foreign affairs, he relied chiefly upon Cecco Simonetta, who had been his secretary during his *condottiere* days; the confidence enjoyed by this upstart Calabrian in matters of State was a constant source of grievance to the Milanese nobility. Francesco was more uncompromising even than the majority of his contemporaries in his vindication of the sovereignty of the State. The capitulations of 1450 provided for the suppression of private jurisdictions and immunities within the duchy, and forbade subjects to accept titles or privileges from Pope or Emperor without the duke's consent. With regard to the Church, he did not hesitate to plead necessities of State as an excuse for helping himself to the revenues of vacant benefices, and he obtained from successive Popes the right of nominating to bishoprics and abbeys within his dominions. In 1460, Pius II consented to the establishment of an office, with its own register and in charge of a bishop devoted to Sforza's interests, to examine applications for Milanese benefices and ensure that the successful can-

didates were acceptable to the secular power. In Milan itself and in
Pavia and Cremona, cities with which Francesco's personal connexion was
close, his rule was popular. Benefactions such as the Ospedale Maggiore
and the Martesana canal, together with the simple family life lived in the
midst of their subjects by the duke and duchess and their eight children,
mitigated the discontent caused by high taxation and the building of the
Castello Sforzesco. In the outlying cities of the dominion, however,
disaffection was rife. An inquiry into the state of the duchy made in 1461
shewed that in the majority of the subject cities the local nobility was
definitely hostile, and that ambitious neighbours, such as Borso d'Este
and the Marquess of Montferrat, were prompt to encourage the malcontents. The fact that Francesco and his son thought it necessary to
maintain an organised system of espionage upon the daily doings of
Bartolomeo Colleone indicates their consciousness of the instability of their
rule. The accession of Galeazzo Maria and his marriage to Bona of Savoy
brought an increase of magnificence to the ducal household, especially
after its migration to the newly built Castello. Galeazzo was a villain,
but he was by no means an inefficient ruler; he spent freely, but he
balanced his budget, and his murder during the Christmas festival of 1476
was prompted by purely private discontents. The vengeance taken by the
citizens upon his murderers suggests that Milan as a whole had no serious
objection to his rule. His seven-year-old son was recognised as duke under
the guardianship of his mother, while Simonetta carried on the real work
of government. Simonetta's tendency to lean on the Guelfs produced a
revival of faction within Milan. The Ghibellines revolted and were supported by the duke's uncles; from their exile they intrigued against the
government, until Ludovico profited by a quarrel between Bona and
Simonetta to win admission to the Castello and to become henceforth
the arbiter of the duchy (7 September 1479).

The ascendancy of Ludovico il Moro saw the complete development of
princely rule. Within a year of his return, Simonetta was brought to the
scaffold, and his fall cleared Ludovico's path for the overthrow of the
instruments of his own rise. Prominent Milanese nobles were deprived of
their seats on the ducal council; Bona went into forced retirement; even
Roberto Sanseverino, the companion of Ludovico's exile, was not permitted to enjoy the fruits of the victory which he had helped to win. The
Consiglio secreto, which had been active under Simonetta, ceased to be the
chief organ of administration. Its members, while holding office at the
pleasure of the duke, were drawn chiefly from the native aristocracy and
possessed some degree of independence. Their place was taken by
secretaries, dependent upon Ludovico alone, each of whom had charge of
one of the various departments of government—justice, finance, foreign
affairs, and the Church. The Council of Nine Hundred met twice under
Galeazzo Maria, and confirmed him in possession of the duchy, but it had
no place in Ludovico's system. In 1494, when the death of his nephew

from natural causes apparently saved him from the trouble of murdering him,[1] he produced the diploma of investiture which he had bought from Maximilian and ascended the throne as a vassal of the Empire. The development of the duchy during the splendid years of his domination is the measure of the power of a single will to transform the State. His unfettered authority enabled him to gather round him the most distinguished of Renaissance courts, and to stamp every side of life and every corner of his dominion with the impress of his personality. He possessed in full measure two of the most outstanding qualities of the Renaissance, the spirit of scientific enquiry and sureness of artistic judgment. His peculiar genius is seen in town-planning and irrigation works, in efforts to stamp out the plague, and in improved methods for the cultivation of the vine and the mulberry. It inspired the promotion of mathematical studies which brought Luca Pacioli of Borgo San Sepolcro to his court. It guided the choice which he made of Bramante of Urbino and Leonardo the Florentine to be his friends and fellow-workers.

Under Il Moro's auspices, Milan reaped in full measure the harvest of her natural resources and of the strong government bequeathed to her by the Visconti. Until the *Arte della Seta* received its statutes from Duke Filippo, the silk industry had been carried on by individuals in their own homes, with a limited output of inferior quality; now it employed 20,000 operatives and formed one of the main sources of revenue. The Milanese armourers, at the height of their fame and prosperity, celebrated Il Moro's marriage by lining the principal street of their quarter with a double row of lay figures clad in specimens of their craft. International commerce was facilitated by the maintenance of consuls at the chief European centres; numerous German merchants had establishments in Milan, and Milanese houses were represented in German cities as well as in London and Bruges. The peculiar contribution made by Milan to Renaissance art is due in large measure to the patronage of the Sforza dukes. From 1450, the two great Visconti foundations of the Cathedral of Milan and the Certosa of Pavia, no less than the Castello Sforzesco, became schools of architecture and sculpture, where native craftsmen gained fresh inspiration from the Florentines introduced by Francesco. Ludovico employed Bramante not only in the capital but throughout the dominion, and in close association with Lombard masters whose tradition he absorbed and transformed. Francesco brought Foppa of Brescia to Milan to become the dominant influence in painting until the advent of Leonardo. Native artists may have suffered from the overmastering effects of Leonardo's genius, but he found here opportunity for the exercise of his manifold gifts, together with an atmosphere of understanding criticism which enabled him to

[1] See Bridge, J. S. C., *A History of France from the death of Louis XI*, Vol. II, pp. 135–40 (Oxford, 1924), for a summary of the evidence with regard to the circumstances of Gian Galeazzo Sforza's death, and the case against Ludovico's responsibility for it.

work at his ease. The chief glory of Il Moro's court is that it provided the setting in which Leonardo's art was brought to perfection. The marriage of Gian Galeazzo to Isabella of Aragon in 1489, and that of Ludovico to Beatrice d'Este two years later, while adding to the gaiety and brilliance of the court, introduced into it a spirit of faction which was to prove the source of its destruction. The two women were first cousins and alike clever and self-assertive, yet Isabella's primacy as duchess was wrested from her by Beatrice. Gian Galeazzo acquiesced readily in his uncle's domination, apparently preferring it to that of his wife, but she, consumed with the desire to rule, filled the Castello with her lamentations and urged her relatives in Naples to come to her aid. Meanwhile the Guelf nobility and all other elements of opposition to Ludovico's rule found in championship of the rightful duke the rallying point of their discontents. Gian Giacopo Trivulzio, a prominent Guelf, had already left Milan for Naples, and his presence enabled foreign foes to join hands with rebels at home. Conscious of his vulnerability to attack, Ludovico turned to France, hoping no doubt that a threat of French intervention would serve, as it had done in the past, to avert a crisis. In so doing, he destroyed the foundations upon which, from the days of the last Visconti, the power of Milan had been built. Milan as a barrier against French invaders was the surest guarantee of Italian liberty. Milan as the ally of Charles VIII opened the flood-gates to foreign domination.

The development of princely rule in Florence and Milan had its counterpart in the smaller Italian States. During the course of the century, Este in Ferrara, Gonzaga in Mantua, Bentivoglio in Bologna, Montefeltro in Urbino, and other lesser lords of cities, modified their constitutional position in a monarchical direction, won for themselves a place in the world of Italian politics by marriage alliances and attention to diplomacy, and vied with each other in the transformation of their courts into splendid homes of the Renaissance. Among these the Este lords of Ferrara occupied the first place. A strategic position, long standing as rulers, and conspicuous ability, gave them an importance in fifteenth-century politics out of proportion to the extent of their dominions. Leonello, the pupil of Guarino and the friend of Pisanello and Leon Battista Alberti, made Ferrara famous in the history of learning and the arts. Borso obtained investiture of his fiefs of Modena and Reggio from the Emperor, and in 1471 was made Duke of Ferrara by Paul II. At home he proved himself a master in the art of government, and won for himself a reputation for justice and benevolence which enabled him to concentrate power in his own person amid the enthusiasm of his subjects. Ercole, through his marriage with Leonora of Aragon and other family connexions, and the resident envoys whom he kept at the chief courts, wielded no little influence over the politics of his day. His daughter Isabella, who went to Mantua as a bride in 1490, was heir to his tradition; there, from her cabinet filled with the artistic treasures of her choice, she manipulated the threads of Italian diplomacy and steered her relatives through the troubled waters of the foreign invasions. The position of the Este was perhaps more stable than that of other Italian rulers, but their hold upon Ferrara was menaced by the pretensions of Venice and the Papacy and by rivals within their own family. Ercole was not sure of his throne until he had sent Leonello's son to the scaffold and made the streets of Ferrara run with blood. When the Castello of Ferrara was at its gayest and most hospitable, the morrow held no certainty for the best loved among Italian princes. In comparison with Ferrara, both Mantua and Urbino were small and poor States; their rulers were soldiers by profession, dependent both ror their revenues and their political importance upon the power to sell their arms to others. It is significant of the opportunities for advancement which the profession of arms afforded that the Gonzaga palace at Mantua, enlarged and beautified out of all recognition by its fifteenth-century owners, and the palace built by Federigo of Montefeltro at Urbino were among the most stately dwelling-houses of the age. Imperial investiture as Marquesses of Mantua and marriages with German princesses gave to the Gonzaga lords of the period a close connexion with the Empire, which they used to augment their authority and influence. Their association with Urbino began when Federigo was a fellow-pupil with Ludovico Gonzaga and his brothers and sisters in Vittorino da Feltre's school, and was strengthened by matrimonial ties and common tastes and interests. Federigo's high character and gifted personality, together with the charm of his mountain home, make him the most perfect representative of the Italian profession of arms; his death during the war of Ferrara marks the close of *condottiere* warfare in its most characteristic phase. The rule of the Bentivoglio in Bologna represented a despotism of a different kind. Giovanni I was recognised as *dominus* when he seized supreme power in 1401, but his successors were only the leading members of a city magistracy; Nicholas V's capitulations (1447) conferred sovereign powers upon legate and commune acting jointly. Nevertheless, Sante and Giovanni II exercised an authority which differed little in practice from that of their neighbours; they carried on an independent foreign policy, often in direct opposition to the Papacy, and within Bologna the position of the legate is summed up in Pius II's aphorism, "*legatus qui verius ligatus appellari potuit*[1]."

Interchange of visits and a steady flow of correspondence kept the ruling families of Italy in close touch with one another, and they acted as a unifying force in politics, which served the interests of the individual citizen. Offices of every kind, from a professorial chair or a post as *podestà* to a bank-clerkship, favours such as facilities for collecting debts or release from imprisonment, were solicited by one lord from another on behalf of his subjects with unremitting energy and eloquence. Although

[1] *Commentarii*, p. 55.

these requests were as often refused as granted, the citizen who had no lord to plead his cause must have suffered under grave disabilities in his dealings with other States. The despot, in short, was an antidote to local exclusiveness, and his activities fostered a belief in his own existence as necessary to the well-being of the community. To this belief the tenets of humanism lent their support. In its reverence for the past and in the homage which it paid to the authority of the expert, it stood for the principles of discipline rather than for those of freedom. The pursuit of learning and the arts offered a means whereby men might be turned from thoughts of self-government, and find fresh forms of self-expression in place of their stifled political activities. Princely rule was exalted as the sphere in which man's manifold powers could alone find complete development. Thus the teaching of current philosophy, no less than the trivial incidents of daily life, enabled despotism to strike fresh roots and to undermine the traditions of liberty. At the same time, the tendency on the part of the despots to seek investiture from Pope or Emperor preserved the conception of the medieval Empire, and threw the aegis of feudal tradition over the evolution of the modern State.

When despotism prevailed throughout Italy, and even the republics of Siena and Perugia fell beneath the control of a single citizen before the close of the century, Venice alone remained a strong and well-ordered republic. Her position at the beginning of the century and her history during its course have been authoritatively treated by Dr Horatio Browne[1]. It must suffice here to indicate the characteristics which separate her from the general trend of Italian political development. Amid the failure of communal institutions to meet the requirements which circumstances demanded of them, the Venetian constitution stands out as an example of efficiency and adaptability which responded to every need as it arose, and allowed no power outside itself to supplement its shortcomings. The *Maggior Consiglio*, since the famous *serrata* of 1297, was limited to the Venetian patriciate, numbering at this time some fifteen hundred members; yet no antagonism existed between its members and those of the plebeian classes, who found adequate scope for their political activities in the civil service, and honoured a government which was carried on in their interests. The *Maggior Consiglio* was the source of all authority in the State, but it understood the art of delegating its powers, and was content to concentrate upon its elective functions, leaving the work of legislation to the *Pregadi* or Senate. The *Collegio* was the executive and initiative body, consisting of the heads of government deparments (*Savii di Terra Ferma, Savii da Mar*) and of six *Savii Grandi*, one of whom performed what were practically the functions of prime minister for a week at a time. Council, Senate, and College were presided over by the Doge and his six Councillors. The Doge could not act apart from his

---

[1] *Cambridge Modern History*, Vol. i, Chap. viii.

Councillors, but he alone among Venetian statesmen held office for life; thus the advice which he tendered was formed by ripe experience and his position as visible head of the State ensured him a respectful hearing. In 1310 the *Consiglio di Dieci* was instituted "to preserve the liberty and peace of the subjects of the republic and protect them from the abuses of personal power[1]." For all its wide discretionary authority, it did not supersede the constitution as the creation of a *balía* superseded it; elected in the Grand Council for six months at a time, it formed part of the ordinary machinery of government and was subject to constitutional control. Admirable as were the constitutional forms of the republic, it was not these which differentiated her most sharply from her neighbours, but rather the spirit which animated her political life. When Savonarola instructed the citizens of Florence on the manner in which they could contribute to the perfecting of popular government, he bade those called to any magistracy or office "love the common good of the city, and laying aside all individual and private interests have an eye to this alone[2]." It was the glory of Venice that she trained her sons to obey this precept and that the whole-hearted devotion of every Venetian to the service of the republic was expected and rendered. The oligarchy was animated by a common will and purpose, and any signs of independence on the part of an individual or group were ruthlessly suppressed. Moreover, the peculiar history and position of Venice contributed to the maintenance of unity between all classes. Isolation from the main current of Italian politics saved her from their devastating factions. The temperament of the people, bred of the soft air of the lagoons and a seafaring life, rendered them amenable to discipline, and turned their skill and energies towards the practical and the technical rather than towards agitating problems of politics and philosophy. The Church was never allowed to become a rival to the authority of the State. The economic interests of patrician and plebeian were centred in a single commercial system which it was the chief concern of the government to foster. Thus the republic drew its strength from the combined energy of its citizens, which constituted a reserve force from which it could meet the heavy demands made upon its endurance.

At the opening of the fifteenth century Venice had reached the full measure of her powers; her constitution was fixed and her commercial and colonial system was elaborated. A period of almost uninterrupted warfare, with the new responsibilities which her conquests brought, formed the supreme test of Venetian greatness, and of the principles upon which the republic was founded. In 1484, the mainland dominion of Venice stretched from the Isonzo and the Adriatic to the Adda, and from the Alps to the Po. The system of government established in the subject territory strove to preserve local autonomy and at the same time to bind the cities to Venice by the benefits which her rule conferred. Each city

---

[1] *Capitolare dei Capi del Cons. X, da leggersi ogni primo giorno del mese.* Romanin, III, 54.   [2] *Trattato circa il reggimento e governo della città di Firenze,* III, 2.

retained its own constitution, its council being presided over by the Venetian *rettore* or *podestà*, who, together with a military officer, acted as representatives of the republic. In Vicenza, where the tradition of liberty was strong, *anziani*, elected by the citizens, had the duty of watching the *rettore* in order to prevent breaches of Vicentine laws and custom. Commissions were sent from time to time to all subject cities in order to enquire into the conduct of the *rettore* and hear complaints. Taxation was light and mainly indirect, and Venice won general respect from what Harrington has termed "her exquisite justice." If the local nobility chafed under her control, and the neighbours who were stripped of their territories thirsted for vengeance, the lower classes were unwavering in their allegiance. The strongest vindication of Venetian rule is that, with a few exceptions and save for a brief interval, the cities which fell to her during the fifteenth century remained under her in peace, prosperity, and contentment for three hundred years. In addition to her pre-occupation with the mainland, Venice was engaged in a losing battle for the maintenance of her supremacy in the Levant. Although her successes in naval warfare against the Turk during the early years of the century enabled her to secure a respite from hostilities and free trade and navigation in Turkish dominions, the fall of Constantinople entailed heavy loss of property and the disappearance of the supremacy which she had hitherto enjoyed in the Black Sea. From 1463–79 she fought the Turk single-handed with a courage which refused to be daunted by reverses. She emerged from the struggle with depleted revenues, and losses of territory for which the acquisition of Cyprus afforded only partial compensation. Despite the prolonged strain to which she was subjected, however, Venice had energy to spare for all that promoted the prestige of the city and the wellbeing of its citizens. She secured the removal of the seat of the Patriarch from Grado to the capital, and further strengthened the control of the republic in matters of ecclesiastical jurisdiction and appointment to benefices. Various improvements were introduced into the judicial system, and a permanent commission was set up to visit the prisons and ameliorate the lot of the prisoners; a ministry of public health was instituted; the arsenal was enlarged. The Venice which Philippe de Commynes visited in 1494 amazed him by its magnificence. Churches, monasteries, gardens, set in the midst of the waters, palaces faced with white marble from Istria, gilded ceilings, carved mantelpieces, gondolas made gay with tapestries, claimed his admiring attention. "C'est la plus triomphante cité que j'aye jamais vue, et qui fait plus d'honneurs à ambassadeurs et estrangers, et qui plus sagement se gouverne, et où le service de Dieu est le plus solemnellement fait[1]." His words bear witness to the worth of Venetian achievement, and to the power of the spirit of the commune which had not ceased to animate the life of the city

Memoires, Bk vii, Chap xvii

CH. VI.

CHAPTER VII

FRANCE: THE REIGN OF CHARLES VII AND THE
END OF THE HUNDRED YEARS' WAR

THE death of Charles VI on 21 October 1422 was an event of little significance in itself, but infinitely important in its consequences. The sovereign who thus disappeared from the stage had for a long time had no personal part to play. But the circumstances attending the succession to him upon the throne of France created an entirely novel situation. In this setting, a wholly gloomy one for France, the third act of the Hundred Years' War opened; from 1422 to 1453 was to be unfolded, amid the changing fortunes of the great struggle, a sequence of events stirring and decisive for the destiny of the West. France was to be the prize of an intensely dramatic contest, in which its existence as a nation was at stake. In a most critical state at first, at one moment almost desperate, it made one of the most marvellous recoveries in history; and, finally, it came triumphant out of this terrible ordeal, the most formidable that it encountered throughout the ages, and emerged from so many misfortunes a new France, bruised and exhausted, but intact in all essentials, organically sound and convalescent, and ready to play in modern Europe an active and a preponderating part.

It is interesting to note, at the moment when the wretched career of Charles VI came to an end, the impression produced by this event on his contemporaries. All the evidence is in agreement on this point. It was one of complete indifference among the princes and nobles; but, on the other hand, of sincere emotion and of dismay among the people. The princes and the lords regarded Charles VI as a useless creature, who had in some sort outlived himself and whose existence was a nuisance, an obstacle to the realisation of the political combinations they had devised. The Court was impatient to see upon the throne of the Valois the little Henry VI, already King of England and heir to France. In fact, "heir to France" (*haeres Franciae*) had been the title borne by Henry V from the time of his marriage with Charles VI's daughter Catherine of France until his death, and from him Henry VI had inherited the title, which gave him formal guarantee for his expectancy of the succession. The Dauphin Charles, son of Isabella of Bavaria and reputed illegitimate, excluded from all right to the crown, banned as the guilty author of the assassination of the Duke of Burgundy, John the Fearless, on the bridge of Montereau, was a wanderer in France, and the late king's entourage considered his cause as adjudged, as lost. While Charles VI was alive, it might still be questioned whether article 6 of the Treaty of

Troyes in 1420 was to be enforced[1]. Now that Charles VI was dead, this extraordinary deviation from the true course of succession was realised with the greatest ease and without resistance. As soon as the funeral of Charles VI was over, the English king, in spite of his tender age, was immediately and solemnly proclaimed.

Thus was accomplished the transference of the crown of France to the house of England. The union of the Lancastrian Henry V with Catherine cloaked this transference with a semblance of legality; but it was none the less a direct contradiction of the decision of the French barons in 1328, and the solemn function of 1422 testified, as the result of the English victory, to the military collapse of France.

Now, while Court, princes, and grandees looked on unmoved at this presumptuous transference of the crown which went so directly counter to past history, it was quite otherwise with the people; the honest masses were strangely moved by the sadness of this grave occurrence. The people of France, of Paris above all, grieved bitterly on the news of the poor mad king's death; at his funeral there were open manifestations of the popular feeling. This was very characteristic of their mood. It must not be looked upon as a mere outburst of emotion; it denoted the strain of apprehension, of anxiety, which gripped the minds of all true Frenchmen at this turning-point in their country's history. What the man in the street at Paris was lamenting as the funeral cortège passed along its way was both the prince who was named " the Well-Beloved" and also the national cause which was felt to have died with him.

There is, in fact, no more sombre date in the history of France than the year 1422. It was not merely defeat, misery, civil war oppressing men's minds; the very soul of the country was in agony. The dread of the unknown hung over the future; there was no longer any certain constitution, any firm idea from which the hope of better things might spring. France, in the course of its monarchical evolution, had come to associate its sentiment of nationality with the tradition of kingship; and now, at this moment of complete change, when, "in spite of all efforts and all the blood that had been shed," the crown of France was united to that of England, the bewildered Frenchman asked himself where he was to bestow that loyalty to a king which was so indispensable for the ease of the individual conscience. Was this English king, thus solemnly proclaimed, the king by right? Or did not the law of succession, standing above the caprice of policy and the chance of military or diplomatic encounters, rather summon to the throne him whom they had long known officially, and whom many still spoke of beneath their breath, as the dauphin, Isabella's son, Charles? As against the answer officially given

[1] It is useful to recall here the actual text of this article: "Item est accorde que tantost après nostre trespas et deslors en avant, la couronne et royaume de France avecques tous leurs droiz et appartenances demourront et seront perpetuelement de nostre filz le roy Henry et de ses hoirs."

by the Court and dictated by the Treaty of Troyes, product of the coalition of the unworthy queen with the Burgundians and the Lancastrians, was there not also another answer, that of the Armagnacs, who abided by the fundamental principles of the "Salic Law" and the person of the dauphin, a prince forsaken, but become king now by his father's death? Opposed to each other stood the partisans of Henry and the partisans of Charles, and among them, on both sides, there were some who were convinced of the legitimacy and right of their cause, others who were perplexed by doubts; while in between came the great multitude of the undecided, the indifferent, and the dispirited. The best minds were afflicted by a problem of conscience. Just as the Church had suffered and still was suffering from its schism, owing to the multiplicity of Popes, so now France was suffering from a duplication of royal authority.

Then, as to the division of the country between Henry VI of England (who should have been Henry II of France) and Charles VII. Territorially, there was no comparison between them. The victories of Henry V, the part played by the house of Burgundy in alliance with that of Lancaster, the apparent validity of the Treaty of Troyes, the title of *haeres Franciae* borne in turn by the husband and the son of Catherine—all contributed to create a position of manifest preponderance for the English party. In 1422, indeed, the English controlled the greater part of French soil. They held Normandy and Guienne, the old Plantagenet fiefs re-won by Henry V; they held Picardy, Champagne, the Île de France, also conquered by the same prince; they profited by the adhesion and support of the house of Burgundy, which possessed, in fief from the Crown of France, Flanders, Artois, and Burgundy proper, not to mention its imperial fiefs, the Low Countries and Franche Comté; they had the suzerainty over Brittany. Paris, at once the head and the heart of the French kingdom, was theirs. The great institutions of State, the Parlement, the University, recognised, like the Court, the authority of King Henry.

On the other hand, the provinces in the centre—Berry, the Orléanais, Touraine, Poitou, Anjou—remained faithful to Charles; and there were others too, here and there, east, south, and west—Dauphiné and Provence in the Empire, Auvergne, Languedoc, and lastly La Rochelle and part of Saintonge. These scattered provinces, forming no coherent group, constituted the sum total that remained to the disinherited prince, who from 1422 onwards, however, may properly be called Charles VII.

It was at Mehun-sur-Yèvre, that noble castle built and beautified by his great-uncle the Duke of Berry, brother of Charles V, that he learnt on 24 October the news of his father's death. At first he made no move. But on 30 October, on information that steps were being taken at Paris to settle the question of the succession to his prejudice, he followed the advice of those who were in his immediate entourage and assumed the title of king at Mehun. In the castle chapel he caused a funeral service to be conducted to the memory of the sovereign who had just passed away; All Saints Day came immediately afterwards, and he was careful to perform with royal pomp the duties prescribed for this great festival of the Church. Thus the new reign was inaugurated. "The king of Bourges," as he was commonly known, stood in the lists against the king of Paris[1]. And the chronicler Jouvenel des Ursins applies the term *Francoys-Angloys* to those who cried: "Long live Henry, King of France and England." "Renegade Frenchmen" became the more usual name for them.

So there were two kings and two obediences—two Frances. Leaving out of account the Burgundian territories, which were spared by the war, and apart from the losses and ravages wrought by physical violence or by the moral upheaval, it would be true to say that the same desolation afflicted the provinces administered from Paris as those administered from Bourges. In short, the two Frances were plunged, to the same depth, in anarchy. Bands of Armagnacs were still at large in the provinces of the English obedience; unemployed mercenaries, known as *routiers* or *Écorcheurs* (a most expressive name, which tells its own tale), were coming and going, heedless of frontiers, robbing, massacring, torturing, and living on plunder. Ruined churches, a devastated countryside, terrorised towns, universal misery, famine, monetary disorder, high prices, unemployment, dislocation of the social framework, crime unpunished and multiplying, inhuman atrocities, a return to barbarism and the evil instincts of the most savage ages—these were the characteristic features of the crisis created by the Hundred Years' War and the troubles which it brought in its train. At the moment when the most grievous stage of this period of prolonged ordeal began, all the causes of suffering were crowding upon one another and reaching the height of their effect; the constant tragedies of this awful time form the material for the stories of the chroniclers. The picture they give is one of the deepest gloom; and the unanimous agreement of all the contemporary literature makes it impossible to doubt that the colouring of the picture is absolutely realistic.

Besides the accounts of the chroniclers there is also the evidence of the charters[2], which are even more eloquent for being impersonal. They reveal the ghastly intensity of the crisis: there are contracts which deal only with waste land; acts of a later date in which the lord enfranchises his serfs in order that after so many lost years they may have a better heart for work; an account-book in which the head of a family has noted down, in matter-of-fact language that is therefore the more impressive, the successive catastrophes which have befallen his home; wills in which the ruin of families can be seen and almost felt by the reader. The ferocity of the nomad bands has left its mark on the language, in that a detail of military equipment has owing to them become the source of the

---

[1] Pierre de Fenin (p. 194). "...Ainsy y avoit en France deux roys, c'est a sçavoir le roy Charles et le roy Henry, lequel roy Henry se nommait roy de France et d'Engleterre."

[2] The most impressive documents are to be found in the collection of Père Denifle.

precise modern significance of the word "brigand[1]." Fortified towns stood out as islands amid the waves of armed men battering upon them, but even they suffered equally with the countryside. Overcrowded with refugees, each of them was transformed into a beleaguered city in which means of livelihood were scarce and precarious, the mortality was terrible, famine and disorder almost incessant. Even in Paris the documents reveal a lamentable situation. The *Bourgeois de Paris*[2] gives us some of its features: " When the dog-killer killed any dogs, the poor folk followed him into the fields to obtain the flesh or the entrails for food...they ate what the swine disdained to eat." And the same author sums up in these words the crisis of which he has been telling the story: " I do not believe that from the time of Clovis, the first Christian king, France has ever been so desolate and divided as it is to-day." These are not the exaggerations of a pessimist, but the expression of one who is meticulously stating the facts. Never, in truth, since the beginning of the French monarchy, had the country undergone a crisis, both material and moral, of such a character.

Exhausting as was the physical crisis, the moral crisis was even more severe a strain. For French patriotism, which had given new life to France at Bouvines, and had restored it to health after its constitution had been vitally impaired by the Treaty of Brétigny, might have been the salvation of the France of 1422. But on what was patriotism to depend in this hour of dismay? Patriotism was inconceivable unless founded upon kingship; loyalty to a prince was the inevitable form for national sentiment to take. Now two princes were at the same time claiming to be the lawful ruler, and between them everyone, before the bar of conscience at any rate, had to make up his mind.

For the modern Frenchman no hesitation is possible. Charles VII, the son of Charles VI, was the true king. But for the men and women of the fifteenth century the situation was much more difficult to resolve. The Burgundian party had spread the report of the possible, or even probable, illegitimacy of the dauphin. Queen Isabella's reputation provided only too good a basis for this, and she herself had justified it by accepting the Treaty of Troyes. Precision was given to the rumour by those who made out Charles to be the son of Louis of Orleans, lover of his sister-in-law the queen; this was affirmed, for instance, by the author of the *Pastoralet*. The act which removed Charles from the succession proceeded from Charles VI, the Well-Beloved. The exclusion of Isabella's son was recognised by the constituent bodies at Paris, by the Parlement and the University; this had a natural effect upon men's minds. Yet, was this action on the part of these venerable bodies the result of conviction and a clear conscience, or was it not rather due to constraint, to resignation, or to submission in the face of force?

---

[1] *Brigandine* was a coat of mail.
[2] *Journal d'un bourgeois de Paris,* p. 153; p. 151; pp. 134–5.

At any rate, the fact that he was recognised as king by the governing classes in Paris, by the Parlement, and by the University, gave Henry a presumptive right which made an impression upon the worthy provincial peasantry. Instinctively, however, they revolted against it. How many, then, were questioning their consciences, anxiously, in perplexity, having lost their bearings in face of this novel and distracting problem of the two kings who disputed the realm between them?

So much for the material and moral picture of the France of 1422. The next task is to shew what sort of men they were who faced one another in the lists, to contrast the kingship of Paris with the kingship of Bourges.

Henry VI personally did not count at all. He was an infant, and a sickly one. Born on 4 December 1421, he was not even a year old when the crown of France by inheritance from Charles VI was placed upon the frail head which already bore the crown of England by inheritance from Henry V. The guardianship had been offered, on Henry V's death, to the Duke of Burgundy, but he had refused it; and it was the Duke of Bedford, Henry V's brother, who took over on the accession of his nephew the regency of the kingdom of France. Bedford was a fine soldier and an able statesman, but in manner he was haughty, hard, and quick-tempered. He made, in truth, a serious and painstaking effort to remedy the evils from which the provinces subject to his authority were suffering; it was his deliberate policy to render the English occupation as mild as possible and not to injure the inhabitants[1]; he laboured sincerely to assure the normal functioning of government, and even to improve it. He suppressed, to the best of his ability, brigandage in Normandy, the typical province of the English obedience; Thomas Basin speaks of 10,000 persons hanged in one year. This figure, however, is evidence both of the duke's severity and of the intensity of the evil. As Basin also shews, the English regent's care for the Normans did not prevent them from cordially detesting the English.

Administratively, Bedford did what he could and deserves that credit should be given to him for the methods he employed. He improved the coinage, simplified and purified the procedure at the Châtelet at Paris, created a faculty of law at Caen, and granted on a considerable scale remissions of taxes to impoverished towns. But his policy was everywhere confronted by a passive resistance; he was tricked by the psychological factor. Though in law subjects of the Lancastrian dynasty, the French served it against their will. Bedford had to exact a strict oath from

---

[1] See the interesting documents published by Miss B. J. H. Rowe, *Discipline in the Norman Garrisons under Bedford*, 1422–35 (EHR. Vol. xlvi, 1931, pp. 194 sqq.). Bedford, moreover, was continuing the policy of the preceding reign. Cf. A. Newhall, *Henry's policy of conciliation in Normandy*, 1417–22 (*Anniversary Essays in medieval history by students of Charles Haskins*, 1929, p. 205).

ecclesiastics as well as from laymen. At every moment he learned of possible, even imminent, defections. He had to make use of threats to obtain the voting of supplies by the Estates of Normandy or Champagne. Now, his task did not consist only in giving life to the conquered provinces and keeping them in their allegiance; he had also to conquer for his nephew the provinces held by those who were called in his camp "the Dauphinois."

Dauphinois was the name given in the English North to the partisans of Charles, who were sometimes also dubbed by their adversaries with the old name of twenty years before, "Armagnacs." Charles' supporters had no objection to the former name, since, as he had not been crowned at Rheims, they still designated him by the title of "dauphin." Indeed, Joan of Arc was herself to greet him at Chinon as "gentle dauphin."

Charles had not the personality to thrill those who adopted his cause, and he displayed none of the attributes of a leader. He is among the least pleasing of historical personages. His character defies exact definition. He acted in a vague and colourless manner at first; though he declared himself king in 1422, it was rather, it would seem, in order to satisfy his entourage than because he had the consciousness of being cast for a great rôle. He was listless, and on the morrow of his proclamation at Mehun-sur-Yèvre, appeared to be sunk in a deep apathy. This young man of twenty, faced with so many difficulties, seemed to be unequal to the task of surmounting them. He was like a child, heedless, letting men and things go their own way; in the absence of a firm hand everything was being allowed to drift.

What, then, is the explanation of this insensibility, which intensified the existing gravity of the situation and cast its gloom over the whole of the first period of the reign? Charles, though he was no man of distinction, was not without capacity. He proved himself, in the second half of his career, to be a capable administrator; and though a large share in this must be assigned to his ministers, he cannot be denied all credit[1]. But he had failings which were very harmful to him, especially in the critical circumstances in which he commenced his reign. One personal characteristic was his lack of any soldierly instincts, in which he resembled his grandfather Charles V; this military defect was a serious matter for a prince whose kingdom was attacked, invaded, and in part occupied by the enemy, at a time when fighting was continuous and force seemed the only arbiter. Besides this, Charles was slow to develop; he was late in reaching maturity. At the age of twenty his character was still unformed; he was naïve, timid, shallow, heedless of the seriousness of his circumstances and the grave duties they imposed upon him; living a hand-to-mouth existence, he was accessible to all comers and became subject to influences often of the most harmful kind. As ill luck would have it, around this inexperienced

---

[1] His surname "the Well-Served" shews, however, that according to general opinion his fellow-workers played the chief part.

youth, deserted by his family, there prowled a troop of low adventurers, who were greedy after their own personal gain and unaffected by the vital issues of the day.

Charles VII has often been accused of premature debauchery and dissipation at the beginning of his reign. It is necessary to make a stand against these unjust accusations, which were the inventions of his enemies. The sources studied by the Marquis du Fresne de Beaucourt[1] give the lie to these malicious rumours. The king of Bourges appears in the sources as a pious and devout prince, much attached to his wife, Mary of Anjou, but somewhat under the thumb of his energetic and imperious mother-in-law, Yolande of Sicily[2]. If we take the evidence of reliable documents only, we find neither luxury nor pleasure dominating his Court; the impression we get is rather of poverty and distress. In 1422, the year of his accession, he had to put his jewels in pawn and in particular his finest diamond, known as "the mirror"; he had to borrow from one of his cooks (*queux*) in April 1423, and he was unable to pay the wages of his servants. Many other equally good examples could be cited to shew the wretchedness of his state[3].

The most serious factor was the absence of a strong personality at the central point of resistance to Bedford. Charles VII was dominated at first by a triumvirate composed of the president Louvet, Tanguy du Châtel, and a petty nobleman named Frotier. Then it was the turn of Arthur de Richemont. Third in order came the too lengthy period of the egoistic La Tremoïlle. To all these men Charles was little more than a cipher. His protracted adolescence, his delayed manhood, was not the only reason for his apathy. There was a deeper psychological cause for his weakness and his repugnance to face responsibility and decision. He was doubtful about his birth, whether he was legitimate or no; this problem which disturbed his subjects was a torment to himself. Besides, the crime of Montereau had broken his spirit; the crushing responsibility laid on his shoulders when he was declared to be the author of the assassination of John the Fearless had deeply impressed itself upon his mind. And the distress of his youth, when he had been renounced by his family, had added to his depression. In him had been extinguished the taste for living and reigning. It needed

---

[1] In his *Histoire de Charles VII*, ii, 177 sqq.

[2] The widow of Louis II, Duke of Anjou and claimant of Naples (Sicily).

[3] Charles had to refrain from buying new shoes, as he was unable to pay his shoe-maker, and to be content with his "vielz honzel" (Quicherat, *Procès*, iv, 325). The poet Martial d'Auvergne (*Les Vigilles du Roy Charles VII*, i, 56) tells how :

> "Un jour que La Hire et Poton
> le vindrent veoir pour festoyement
> n'avoient qu'une queue de mouton
> et deux poulets tant seulement."

It is clear that the resources of the unhappy king of Bourges allowed him an existence that was very modest for a fifteenth-century king. One day it happened that his treasurer Régnier de Bouligny had only four crowns in the chest (Quicherat, *Procès*, iii, 85).

CH. VII.

time to raise him from the depths again. And while he waited for a spark of hope or a ray of truth to lighten his darkness, the king who should have issued his call to France did nothing of any avail. So far from directing events, he let himself be led by them.

It was, indeed, very difficult in the circumstances to react against the English occupation. However, if the impulse was to spring from another than the king, that impulse when it came was to be the more intense, spontaneous, and irresistible. But, in the meantime, the patriotism latent in the French, the national sentiment which was to save both king and kingdom, was displayed in a merely negative form; the only sign that revealed the popular instinct, hostile as always to a foreign occupation, was the stubborn passive resistance of those Frenchmen who inhabited the provinces that were in English hands. Renegade Frenchmen, whole-heartedly attached to the Lancastrians, were the exception; most of the inhabitants shut themselves up, as it were, in their shells, and without committing as a rule any overt act of rebellion, met the conciliatory and well-meaning policy of the energetic Bedford with a blank enmity, a heartfelt antipathy, which denoted a fixed determination never to surrender.

At times, too, the voice of loyalty was already to be heard in the north. Tournai, a Burgundian town, on Charles VI's death sent a deputation to Charles VII[1]. This was a rare, if not a unique[2] instance, but it was symptomatic; one would look in vain for an instance of the opposite, of a spontaneous rally to the English side "par de là la Loire." It is a valuable point to note, for it helps one to understand why, in spite of appearances to the contrary, the future was better assured for the king of Bourges than for the king of Paris. It little profited the son of Henry V that he could boast the more regal state and that the constituent bodies were in his train. He was a usurper legitimised, and the officials were too fulsome in their recognition of him for their sentiments to be sincere. When they sought to give an appearance of reality to the rights of their king, these Parisians were trying to stifle their own doubts; many of them, however, kept thinking of the imprescriptible and inalienable rights of the lawful race of national kings, and it is to be noted that the line in the modern opera, "Never in France shall reign an English king," was no fiction, but an actual utterance of the time. It is to be found in the trial of Guillaume Prieuse, Superior of the Carmelites at Rheims, who was brought to justice for using suspicious language: "he said...that never had Englishman been King of France, and never should be so[3]." What Tournai proclaimed and Rheims was whispering, many were thinking without daring to breathe it

---

[1] "Veut tenir le dauphin pour roi," says the *Chronique de Tournai* (Marquis du Fresne de Beaucourt, *Histoire de Charles VII*, ii, 9).

[2] Later, in the charter granted to Tournai, Charles VII himself recalled the town's loyalty: "demourée comme toute seule des parties de par de là la Seine." See, too, the case cited below of Prieuse at Rheims.

[3] *Ibid.* ii, 56.

aloud, and in the Lancastrian provinces were looking forward to the day when they would have the right to give expression to it. Everywhere, in fact, a latent patriotism was working during the worst years for the king of Bourges, and it was he that already was virtually the true king of the whole of France.

"At this date the English sometimes took a fortress from the Armagnacs in the morning, and then lost two again in the evening. Thus went on the war accursed of God." This passage from the *Journal d'un bourgeois de Paris*[1], an invaluable source for the light it throws on contemporary opinion, admirably sums up the military history of the early years of Charles VII's reign. They are confused years, years of bitter struggle between the two parties who were contesting the possession of France; years marked by trifling episodes which cancelled each other out: the capture and recapture of castles, a company here and there surprising a company of the enemy, warfare of a purely local character but taking place simultaneously everywhere, and with no other result than to increase the general misery and year by year to make the demoralisation more intense. From the accession of Charles VII to the coming of Joan of Arc, a war that lacked any pleasing or redeeming feature may be divided into three periods, all of them quite short. In the first, the English had the advantage; in the second, the cause of the king of Bourges seemed to be improving; finally, in the third period, this fleeting hope vanished and it appeared that the resumption of the initiative by the English must prove decisive.

What gave the English their chief advantage in the first period was their close accord not only with the Duke of Burgundy in the east and north, but also with Duke John VI of Brittany in the west and with Count John I of Foix in the south. John VI of Brittany and his brother the Count of Richemont constituted an important and effective menace to the king of Bourges; and this was the more effective since Charles, though secure in the firm loyalty of the town of Toulouse as well as of Languedoc, had to protect himself in that region against John I of Foix, who was similarly aided by his brother, Count Matthew of Comminges. Dominating Béarn and the territories attaching to it, the house of Foix was a formidable power in the south-west; Charles' partisans had difficulty in maintaining themselves at Bazas. On the other side, the Earl of Salisbury and John of Luxemburg ranged at will over Champagne and the region of the Ardennes. The Count of Aumale, with a small body of adherents of the house of Valois, did defeat the English leader Suffolk in Maine at La Gravelle on 26 September 1423. But this victory had no morrow. For the Count of Aumale was himself overwhelmed and slain at the battle of Verneuil on 17 August 1424.

Verneuil was an unlucky day for the king of Bourges. The striking

[1] p. 190.

victory won by Bedford seemed to signalise the military triumph of the English party. It was the most important English success since Agincourt, and it makes a fourth in the series of great French disasters in the Hundred Years' War. Verneuil almost ranks as an equal with Agincourt, Poitiers, and Crécy.

It was not any sudden outburst of energy on the part of Charles VII that originated the improvement which marks the succeeding period. The reasons were wholly external and fortuitous. The ambition of Bedford's brother, the Duke of Gloucester, who wished to play a part on the Continent[1], provoked a coolness between the Courts of England and Burgundy. At the same moment, the house of Brittany and the house of Foix severed their ties with Bedford. These various events resulted in a revival, though of rather an artificial nature, in the fortunes of the king of Bourges. It was over Hainault that a difference arose between the Duke of Gloucester and the powerful Duke of Burgundy, Philip the Good. Philip in umbrage withdrew his support from the English and dissociated himself from their interests. A similar change of front took place in Brittany also. Richemont, the brother of Duke John VI, went to Chinon and on 7 March 1425 received from Charles VII the sword of the Constable of France. He immediately conducted an active campaign against the Lancastrians in Brittany, Normandy, and Maine. Finally, John I of Foix was won over by the office of Lieutenant-General of Languedoc and changed sides, passing with his brother the Count of Comminges into the camp of Charles VII.

Richemont was now the most influential figure at Charles' Court; he appeared to be an acquisition of the first importance, and his successes were most encouraging for the future. But Bedford had succeeded in settling the dispute about Hainault, and in preventing Burgundy from abandoning the English alliance. The regent was skilful enough to set against Richemont the Earl of Warwick, who was given the high-sounding title of "Captain and Lieutenant-General of the king and the regent throughout France and Normandy." The Béarnais, in the service of the Count of Foix, reached the banks of the Loire; but they contented themselves merely with pillaging the countryside.

Then came the third period, the period of disillusionment. Jealous of La Tremoïlle, Charles VII's new favourite, Richemont confined his activities to Brittany. Warwick took heart again, and achieved the capture of Pontorson on 8 May 1427. Finally, the Earl of Salisbury arrived with an English army to lay siege to Orleans.

It is essential to appreciate the full significance of this siege of Orleans. In the first place, the English were attacking a town whose overlord, Duke Charles of Orleans, had been a prisoner in their hands since Agincourt, his rights being expressly guarded by treaty; therefore the English government was committing a breach of signed agreements. At

See *infra*, Chap. x, p. 353, Chap. xi. p. 390.

the same time, it was disregarding the customary practice of feudal and chivalric behaviour: in the fifteenth century it was regarded as a definite rule that no attack should be made upon the domain of a lord while he was a prisoner. Salisbury was perhaps attracted by the town's importance as the key to the line of the Loire. At any rate, his attack upon it was looked on as a moral outrage, and not only the citizens of Orleans but the people of France also were infuriated by it. This explains both the heroic and impassioned resistance of the defenders, and also the stir that their resistance aroused. Orleans became in everybody's eyes symbolic. Something was needed to quicken the latent patriotism in France into life; and that something was provided by the siege of Orleans.

There were indeed other heroic exploits calculated to maintain the spirits of the Valois party; for instance, the magnificent defence of Mont-Saint-Michel, that proud fortress which never yielded to the English. But there was a great difference between the resistance of Mont-Saint-Michel and that of Orleans: the former excited the feudal element only; in the case of Orleans the emotions of a whole people were aroused. If the English triumphed over Orleans, if the gallantry of its inhabitants who had justice, as it seemed, and right on their side was proved to be vain and useless, then surely it was plain that the King of England was the true King of France and that resistance to him was a crime. In the simple minds of the perplexed Frenchmen the notion of a judgment of God took shape, and in an agony of suspense they looked for the signs of it in all the events that attended the siege of the devoted city. The English felt that the resistance they encountered had a special significance, an exceptional importance, and they redoubled their efforts. Even after Salisbury had been killed and Talbot had taken his place, though the assaults ordered by the new commander failed, as had those of his predecessor, against the invincible heroism of the defenders, the besiegers did not lose heart; they counted on famine to break the valiant resistance of the inhabitants. At the Court of Charles VII also, there was a confused idea of the gravity of the crisis, and that it might possibly be the deciding one. In a vague way they realised that something must be undertaken on behalf of the loyal town in its hour of danger; and a body of troops from Auvergne, under the command of Charles of Bourbon, Count of Clermont, was dispatched against the besiegers.

Charles of Bourbon learnt that a convoy of provisions under the charge of Fastolfe was on its way to the English camp; and he planned to intercept it. But the Auvergnats were defeated on 12 February 1429; the battle is known in history as "the battle of the herrings," because the provision-train attacked, which was saved by the English, consisted mainly of barrels of red herrings destined to feed the English camp during the season of Lent. After "the battle of the herrings" it appeared impossible to save Orleans, and it can be taken for granted that in spite of all the heroism displayed by the inhabitants and by their leader, Jean de Dunois, the most valiant of Charles VII's captains, the courageous town would finally have succumbed, had it not been for the intervention of Joan of Arc.

There is no more astounding or more moving story in history than that of Joan of Arc, the peasant girl who became the commander of an army, saved her country from mortal danger, and herself died a martyr for her religious and patriotic faith.

Joan[1] was born in the hamlet of Domrémy in the duchy of Bar, on the borders of Champagne and Lorraine, a district over which the King of France claimed an absolute right, which, however, was disputed. Whether belonging to Lorraine or to Champagne, Joan regarded herself as a Frenchwoman[2]. Her father, Jacques d'Arc, had by his wife Isabella Romée five children, two of whom were girls; Joan was the youngest, and was known in the family as Jeannette. She was probably born on 6 January 1412, though the actual year is uncertain as the heroine herself was not absolutely sure of her age. The child of lowly but comparatively well-to-do peasants, Joan received no education; she could neither read nor write, but was employed in household tasks, was expert at sewing and spinning, and as the youngest child of the house regularly took the animals to pasture. She was, to use her own description of herself, "a shepherdess." Joan was most sincerely pious. In her environment the misfortunes of France and of its king made a profound impression. Situated on one of the main highways, Domrémy caught the echo of all that was happening. The "great sorrow" of the kingdom was the subject of every conversation. Joan was evidently enveloped in this atmosphere of distress which tortured the soul of France, and naturally the hope of escaping from the haunting dread of irremediable defeat was present in every pious heart. The shepherdess of Domrémy was about thirteen years old when, for the first time, a supernatural voice made itself heard to her in her father's garden, coming from the right, from the direction of the church; the voice was accompanied by a bright light, and it told her to be of good conduct. The child was thoroughly frightened, until she realised that the voice came from Heaven. Afterwards the visions became more frequent, more definite, and more urgent: St Michael appeared to her, as a knight, surrounded by angels; and two saints, St Margaret and St Catherine. The celestial voices bade Joan set out for France, and when

---

[1] The documents of the two *Procès* (her condemnation and her rehabilitation) provide practically our only evidence for the childhood and early life of Joan of Arc.

[2] The *Mystère du siège d'Orléans* makes Joan say:

> "Quant est de l'ostel de mon père,
> Il est en pays Barrois
> Honneste et loyal François."

(Doc. inéd. 1869, p. 398.)

Cf. *La nationalité de Jeanne d'Arc* (*Intermédiaire* Vol. LXXXII, 1920.)

Orleans was besieged they revealed to her that she would deliver the town. Joan resisted, but for five years the visions continued, becoming more and more insistent, to dictate her mission to her. At last she acknowledged that the will of God was irresistible and that she must accomplish it. She held out to her saints a ring given her by her parents which bore the inscription *Jhesu Maria*; the saints touched it, and the young girl, her hands in theirs, took the vow of virginity. Henceforward, her mind was decided, to obey Heaven whatever might befall[1].

But she was at a loss how to carry out the order of Heaven. She went to Burey, near Vaucouleurs, to a cousin of her mother, Durand Lassart, whom she called uncle, and with him she went, in the month of May 1428, to Vaucouleurs to visit the nearest royal captain, Robert de Baudricourt. He only laughed at her, and advised Lassart to box her ears and take her home to her parents.

But meanwhile the war was coming nearer. Enemy scouts appeared in the district, and a panic seized upon Domrémy. Joan went a second time to Baudricourt. The captain in his embarrassment sent her to Duke Charles of Lorraine, who questioned her and made her a small present. She returned to Baudricourt and spoke to him with such ardour and conviction that he decided to send her to the king. He gave her a letter for the king and a sword for herself; some of the people of Vaucouleurs bought her a man's suit of clothes and a horse; an escort of four men-at-arms and two serving-men accompanied her, and she started for Chinon where Charles VII was then residing. This was towards the end of February 1429. The journey lasted eleven days, and at midday on 6 March the shepherdess of Domrémy arrived at Chinon and dismounted at a modest hostelry in the town.

From one of her halts, Sainte-Catherine de Fierbois, Joan had dispatched a letter to the king announcing her coming and notifying him that she "knew of several good things touching his business[2]." Already the rumour had spread in Orleans that a young shepherdess, called *The Maid*, was coming to the king in order to raise the siege and conduct the king to Rheims[3]. An attempt was made to question Joan before admitting her into the castle, but she refused to reveal anything until she had seen the king; and he at last consented to receive her[4]. While

---

[1] She herself declared at her trial: "Puisque Dieu le commandoit, il le convenoit faire; eût-elle eu cent pères et cent mères, eût elle été fille de roi, qu'elle fût parti quand même."

[2] Joan's interrogatory of 27 February 1431 (*Procès*, ed. Quicherat. Vol. pp. 75–6).

[3] *Ibid.* Vol. III, pp. 3, 21.

[4] Charles VII had always hoped for a supernatural intervention in his favour: "toujours espérant avoir aulcun secours de la grâce de Dieu et commemorant que certaines femmes avoient fait merveille, comme Judith et autres" (*Chronique de Tournai*). His hesitation to receive Joan did not denote scepticism. It was derived from mere prudence; he was afraid of being made the victim of some trick or a snare of the Devil (Quicherat, *Aperçus nouveaux sur l'histoire de Jeanne d'Arc*, p. 30).

she waited, full of anxiety, Joan prayed to God to send her "the sign of the king." She came to the castle, and though the king, modestly clad, effaced himself among the lords who filled the vast hall, she went straight to him, saluted him familiarly with the title "gentle dauphin," and at once made known to him the object of her mission: "I am come with a mission from God to give aid to you and to the kingdom, and the King of Heaven orders you, through me, to be anointed and crowned at Rheims, and to be the lieutenant of the King of Heaven who is the King of France[1]."

After a private interview with Joan, the king returned to his courtiers, his face alight with joy. It has been suggested that Joan had shewn him a "sign" of her mission, which has remained a secret. But this supposition does not seem necessary; the truth is no doubt much more simple. Joan had declared to the king, in the name of God, that he was the true son of Charles VI and the lawful heir. On the night of All Saints Day 1428, Charles VII, seeing his kingdom gradually passing away from him, had entered his oratory and had implored God to succour him if he was truly a king's son. Joan gave the answer to the question put by the king to God; and one can imagine his feelings when they were alone together and he heard himself addressed by the inspired Maid in the following words: "I tell you on the part of Messire [Our Lord] that you are true heir of France and King's Son[2]." Momentous words, indeed! For, humanly speaking, the problem of Charles' birth was insoluble. Thanks to Joan of Arc, the problem was solved by divine aid. Mysticism came in as an essential agent in the making of history. To believe in Joan was to believe in the right of Charles VII, and so the paralysing doubt which clouded the minds of Frenchmen disappeared, and the spirit of loyalty, that is to say of patriotism in the only form conceivable in that age, was released from its prison. No longer were there two kings in France. The scaffolding of the Treaty of Troyes was falling down; did a prince of the Lancastrian house continue to call himself "King of France and England," he was only repeating the empty formula of Edward III.

Joan, too, gave formal expression to the political consequences which resulted from her revelation; she issued her famous letter to the King of England and his lieutenants, summoning them to evacuate the kingdom which belonged to the Valois heir. "†*Jhesu Maria*†. King of England, and you Duke of Bedford, who call yourself regent of the kingdom of France; William de la Pole, Earl of Suffolk, John de Talbot, and you Thomas, Lord Scales, who call yourself lieutenant of the Duke of Bedford—give way to the King of Heaven over His royal lineage, render to the Maid sent by God, the King of Heaven, the keys of all the good towns which you have taken and ravaged in France. She is come, too, from God, the King of Heaven, to proclaim the royal lineage; she is full ready to make peace, if you will give way to her, so that you will restore and repay

[1] *Procès, ibid.* III, 103.
[2] Marquis du Fresne de Beaucourt, *Histoire de Charles VII*, II, 209.

France for that you have had her in your hands. As for you, archers, squires, gentles, and others who stand before the good town of Orleans, go you away, in God's name, to your own countries....King of England, if you do not so do, I am a leader in battle, and in whatever place I shall come upon your people in France, I will make them to go out, will they or will they not....And do not have it in your mind that you hold the kingdom of France from God, the King of Heaven, the son of Saint Mary, as King Charles, the true heir, will hold it; for God, the King of Heaven, wisheth it so, and He is revealed by the Maid...[1]."

An ecclesiastical enquiry, conducted at Poitiers by a commission presided over by an archbishop, the Chancellor Regnault of Chartres, had decided in favour of the truth of Joan's mission. She was then sent to Tours. There she formed her household, consisting of a chaplain, Jean Pasquerel, a squire, Jean d'Aulon, her own two brothers, two men-at-arms, Jean de Metz and Jean de Poulengy, two pages, Louis de Contes and Raymond, two heralds, Ambleville and Guyenne. She had a suit of armour made for her, sent to Sainte-Catherine de Fierbois for a miraculous sword, and commissioned a Scottish painter, James Power, to paint her a standard, a banner, and a pennon. Thus equipped and become, as she had said, "a leader in battle," she took over the command of a relieving army, 7000 to 8000 men, the supreme effort of the king of Bourges. Joan succeeded in passing a convoy of provisions into Orleans on Wednesday 27 April, and immediately afterwards she herself entered the town. From this moment the Bastard of Orleans, Dunois, the valiant defender of the valiant city, believed in the Maid's mission[2]. She it was who directed the sorties. She electrified the defenders, spread discouragement among the besiegers, and with the moral and mystical factor on her side won success after success. Feeling that his troops were wavering, Talbot gave the order for retreat, after ninety days of siege. On Sunday 8 May Orleans was delivered.

The deliverance of Orleans, by reason of the symbolic character of the siege, made a profound impression. Predicted and accomplished by the Maid, this liberation appeared as a decisive proof of her divine mission, and henceforward the truth of all that she announced followed logically. Charles VII himself notified the miracle to the towns in official manifestos, and a postcript to the letter preserved at Narbonne makes express mention of the part played by the Maid[3].

---

[1] *Procès*, ed. Quicherat, v, 96.

[2] Joan had said to Dunois: "C'est Dieu qui, à la requête de Saint Louis et de Charlemagne, a pitié de la ville de Orléans, ne voulant pas que les Anglais eussent à la fois le corps du duc d'Orléans et sa ville" (*Procès*, ed. Quicherat, iv, 219); and Dunois recalled it at the rehabilitation: "D'après tout ce qui vient d'être dit, il paraît bien au dit seigneur que Jeanne et son fait, dans ces événements, étaient non des hommes, mais bien de Dieu" (*ibid.* iii, 7).

[3] *Procès*, ed. Quicherat, v, 101–4, with this sentence in the postcript: "La Pucelle qui a toujours été en personne à l'accomplissement de toutes ces choses."

Charles was still to Joan only the "gentle dauphin" so long as he was unconsecrated. To cause the heir of Charles VI to be consecrated at Rheims was to affirm triumphantly his royal right. For the Maid, Rheims, coming after Orleans, was the second and perhaps the last stage of her mission. But it looked like madness to traverse an immense stretch of territory and to go through Lancastrian France in order to accomplish a religious ceremony. Charles and his Court hesitated. Joan, by her resolute conviction and her tranquil assurance, overcame all resistance. The Duke of Alençon, one of the most ardent in her support, collected a royal army and put in train operations designed to "sweep the river Loire." The French army carried the bridge-head of Meung on 15 June, captured Beaugency, and thanks to a fiery charge by La Hire won the brilliant victory of Patay on 19 June; 2000 of the enemy were slain, and among the prisoners were Talbot, Scales, and other English nobles, while, according to the accounts, only three Frenchmen lost their lives. The march to Rheims became a triumphal progress, and on Sunday 17 July, in the cathedral for which this honour was reserved, was celebrated with all the traditional pomp the most moving coronation in history. Joan of Arc stationed herself with her standard at the foot of the altar during the ceremony. "When the Maid saw that the king was consecrated and crowned, she knelt down, all the lords being present before him, clasped him round the legs and said to him, shedding warm tears the while: 'Gentle King, now is fulfilled the good pleasure of God, who willed that I should raise the siege of Orleans and should bring you to this city of Rheims to receive your holy anointing, shewing that you are true king and he to whom the kingdom of France ought to belong[1].'" For the first time, Joan gave Charles the royal title; to every true believer he was henceforward King of France.

It seems certain, in spite of what has been said to the contrary[2], that Joan of Arc at one time considered her mission as accomplished at Rheims. She said to Archbishop Regnault of Chartres: "God will that I may be able to retire, to go to serve my father and my mother, to look after their flocks with my sister and my brothers who would be so happy to see me again." But she had aroused too much admiration, too much enthusiasm[3]. Whether owing to pressure from her comrades-in-arms or to a fresh intervention of her voices—for on this the evidence is obscure

---

[1] *Procès*, ed. Quicherat, iii, 186.

[2] Marquis du Fresne de Beaucourt, ii, 230 sqq.

[3] The people named her *l'Angélique*. The poet Alain Chartier sang her praises in these words: "O fille vraiment extraordinaire! Tu ne viens pas de la terre, tu es descendue du Ciel....Tu es digne de toute louange et de tout hommage, tu es digne des honneurs divins; tu es la lumière du royaume, l'éclat des fleurs de lis, le soutien non-seulement de la France, mais de la chrétienté!" (*Procès*, ed. Quicherat, v, 135). From all sides came proofs of the general trust in her. The *Capitouls* of Toulouse wanted the Maid to be consulted as to the best means of solving the monetary problem which was causing economic distress (Antoine Thomas in *Annales du Midi*, i, 232).

—she decided to remain in Charles' service. Then, however, her misfortunes began. Paris, which had been expected to rise to the occasion and to expel the English on its own initiative, made no move; doubtless Bedford's precautions were too good. Negotiations entered into with the Duke of Burgundy achieved no positive result; his accession would have been decisive, but he held himself open to the best offer from either side. Meanwhile, the prestige of the king after his coronation at Rheims had risen so high that the towns on his route vied with one another in admitting him—Corbeny, Vailly, Laon, Soissons, Château-Thierry, Montmirail, Provins, La Ferté-Milon, Crépy-en-Valois, Lagny-le-Sec, Compiègne, Senlis, Saint-Denis. Bedford certainly was avoiding battle, which the French were offering. But the English cause was very much on the down grade, and Charles penetrated to the immediate approaches to Paris. To win the capital would have been the culmination of his triumph; Joan, backed by the Duke of Alençon and the Count of Clermont, wanted to make the attempt. But in the unsuccessful assault of 8 September she was unluckily wounded in the thigh by a shot from a crossbow. In requital, Charles VII ennobled her, and included in the patent of nobility both her family and the descendants of her sister and brothers. The king, however, was beginning to waver. His strength was overtaxed by so rapid an effort; the acceleration of pace did not suit his temperament. Above all, he was lending too ready an ear to the insinuations of the ignoble courtier, La Tremoïlle, who was basely envious of the ascendancy of Joan. He refused to listen to her counsel of immediate action, and imposed upon her a rest of some days, thereby compromising the success of the campaign which had been so well conducted up to this point. What Joan had feared was coming about. On the way to Châlons, actually before the coronation, she had said to a ploughman from her village who had come to greet her: "I fear one thing only—treason[1]." She took up arms again, however, since she could not resign herself to idleness. She fought minor engagements at Melun and Lagny, and around Compiègne, which the Duke of Burgundy was trying to invest. It was under the walls of this town that, on the evening of 24 May, she was captured in the course of a sortie; she had been beaten back and found herself unable to re-enter within the walls, as the gate had been shut either of deliberate malice or merely thoughtlessly; she was thrown down and taken prisoner, and had to surrender to the bastard of Wandonne, a vassal of John of Luxemburg who was commanding on behalf of the Duke of Burgundy. Taken first to the castle of Beaulieu in Vermandois, and afterwards to John of Luxemburg's castle of Beaurevoir, she was the object of a series of confused negotiations, the principal agent in which was the Bishop of Beauvais, Pierre Cauchon, a tool of Isabella of Bavaria and a devoted adherent of Bedford. Finally, Joan was sold to the English for the sum of 10,000 gold crowns.

[1] *Procès*, ed. Quicherat, ii, 423.

An English escort conducted the prisoner by way of Arras, le Crotoy, Saint-Valery, Eu, and Dieppe to Rouen, where she was shut up in a tower of the fortress of Philip Augustus known as the Vieux-Château. The task of guarding her was entrusted to John Grey, a squire of Henry VI's bodyguard, John Bernwoit, and William Talbot. The Earl of Warwick was in command at Rouen, and Henry VI was brought to the Norman capital as a precaution in case of a rising.

The suit instituted against Joan of Arc was conducted by a tribunal of the Inquisition presided over by Cauchon, in whose diocese she had been taken prisoner. Driven from his see of Beauvais by the advance on Rheims and Paris, he pursued at the same time both his personal revenge and his political ends. The University of Paris, submissive to English and Burgundian interests and hostile to Joan through jealousy arising from the favourable judgment of the clergy of Poitiers, intervened in the suit. The procedure was probably correct in form, but was vitiated by the fixed determination of the court to arrive at a condemnation. The least that can be said is that some of the devices employed were mean and odious; for instance, the trick of restoring to the prisoner her masculine attire in her cell in order to accuse her of clothing herself again in it. Now, in spite of the one-sidedness and the cowardly complacency of the judges, in spite of the frequent duplicity and the insidious nature of the questions put to her, no document is more to the credit of the heroine than this moving record of her examination. Her answers provide the most striking evidence of her sincerity, her nobility of soul, her clear common sense, the purity of her faith, and the ardour of her patriotism; the report of the proceedings is full of those historic utterances on which has been sustained the cult devoted by France to the noblest figure in its annals[1].

A year of cruel captivity did not break the courage of this choice spirit. That she had a moment of weakness on 24 May 1431, the day of the scene at the cemetery of Saint-Ouen, is very doubtful. She was ill at the time and probably did not understand at all the subtle formula which was read to her and to which she had to give her adhesion, couched as it was in deliberately equivocal language. Moreover, it was possibly a mere manœuvre, to justify the ultimate condemnation. However that may be, on the morrow of the abjuration, real or pretended, Joan re-affirmed all her former statements and was then declared a heretic and relapsed, and was condemned to the stake. On hearing this iniquitous sentence, she said: "I appeal to God, the great Judge, on the grievous wrongs and

---

[1] The other members of the tribunal besides Cauchon were either partisans or terrorised. Saint-Avit, Bishop of Avranches, dared to say: "És choses douteuses l'on doit toujours recourir au Pape et au Concile Général"; his opinion was not recorded in the proceedings, and, on the pretext that he had plotted the surrender of Rouen to Charles VII, he was imprisoned the following year. This example will serve to shew how little freedom was permitted to the judges and the corrupt nature of the whole proceedings.

injuries that have been done to me." And she said to Cauchon: "Bishop, through you I am dying....You promised me to put me into the hands of the Church, and you have let me fall into the hands of my enemies." On the pile erected in the old market-place at Rouen, on 30 May 1431, Joan was tied to the stake, bearing on her head a mitre with this inscription upon it: "heretic, relapsed, apostate, idolatress." She endured the awful agony with fortitude, in a spirit of ecstatic exaltation, protesting to the last her innocence and proclaiming that her voices were veracious. She expired with the cry "Jhesu!"

The remains of Joan of Arc were thrown into the Seine. Now, contrary to the expectation of those who had demanded her death, this tragic end did not annul her work; it consecrated it. Joan *l'Angélique* has had the same apotheosis as the saints, men and women, whose story the people heard in sermons, whose heroism they viewed with admiration above the doors and the columns of their churches, and whose adventures they read in the "Golden Legend." To confess one's faith and die a martyr's death was to give the supreme proof of the Christian verity. The execution of Joan of Arc was the demonstration not, as her enemies imagined, of the falsity, but of the truth of her mission. The French people in their multitudes henceforward regarded Joan as a saint[1] and all her words as prophecies.

Charles VII might have taken advantage of this movement of the national conscience; he might have directed it and raised it to a higher plane. This his lethargy prevented him from doing. So long as Joan's enemy, La Tremoïlle, was alive, Charles was little more than a figurehead, incapable of initiative. La Tremoïlle was assassinated in 1433 by a squire of the Constable Richemont. The latter then took charge of the government, supported by the king's mother-in-law, Yolande of Sicily, and by her son, Charles of Anjou. The English by this time had recovered, and Richemont could only proceed by the laborious method of conquering bit by bit the provinces still held by the English. The story of this process, also, is disconnected, intricate, and confused. Further, the means employed were feeble; what the ardent faith of a Joan of Arc would have achieved in a few months, it took a mediocre king and his generals years to accomplish.

The prime factor which decided the fate of the English domination in France was the reconciliation of Charles VII with Philip the Good. The very year of Joan's death, whether or no he was affected by remorse, the Duke of Burgundy entered into negotiations with the king. They were protracted, but they culminated at last in the Treaty of Arras of

---

[1] The Catholic Church did not go beyond the rehabilitation of the fifteenth century (see *infra*, p. 253) until the twentieth century. Joan of Arc was beatified by Pius X on 18 April 1909, and canonised by Benedict XV on 9 May 1920. It was in the twentieth century also that France instituted a national festival of Joan of Arc (by a law of 10 July 1920), celebrated each year on 8 May and carried on to the following Sunday in memory of the liberation of Orleans.

21 September 1435. The duke devised an excuse for abandoning the English: he suggested papal mediation between the claims of the French and the English dynasties, and, on the refusal of the English to accept this arbitration, declared himself released from all obligation to the house of Lancaster. By the Treaty of Arras, Charles VII disavowed the crime of Montereau, offered reparation for the murder, and ceded to the duke Auxerre, the Auxerrois, Bar-sur-Seine, Luxeuil. the "Somme towns" (Péronne, Montdidier, Roye), Ponthieu, and Boulogne-sur-mer; a clause reserved to the Crown the right of repurchasing the "Somme towns"; but the duke was exempted for life from the obligation of homage to the king. The conditions were hard, but no price was too high to pay for such an accession of strength, which tilted the scales completely in favour of the Valois.

From 1435 onwards everything went awry for the English. After the death of Bedford (15 September 1435) a breach arose between Henry VI's surviving uncles, Gloucester and Beaufort. The subject population everywhere was seething with disquiet. No longer, as before the appearance of Joan of Arc, was it a matter of passive resistance; it was now a continual state of conspiracy. Paris was in agitation. Bands of Frenchmen penetrated everywhere. On all sides there were revolts and surprise attacks. Richemont, Dunois, Barbazan, Jean de Bueil, and others too, at the head of small forces, were assisting the inhabitants in each locality, ranging in every direction, even as far as Normandy. The Dauphin Louis went to the help of Dieppe, which was in revolt. Richemont entered Paris on 13 April 1436, and Charles VII could justly write that the Parisians themselves had turned the English "out of the town." And now, as he became more and more convinced of his right and of the truth of the Maid's mission, Charles' courage grew. His mind, slow to mature, was achieving its balance. Possibly his mistresses, each in her turn, Agnes Sorel and then Antoinette de Maignelais, assisted in this evolution; in any case, royalty, gaining in strength and convinced of its ultimate triumph, was launching out upon a laborious task of administrative reform. The series of great *Ordonnances*, the full extent of which will be made evident later, had already commenced.

The exhaustion on both sides was such that they agreed to accept papal mediation and to sign the truces of Tours on 16 April 1444; by successive extensions the truces lasted until 1449. It was arranged that King Henry VI should marry Margaret of Anjou, the niece of the Queen of France[1]. The truces of Tours worked mainly to the advantage of

[1] Margaret was the daughter of René of Anjou, "the good king René," brother of Mary of Anjou, who had married Charles VII. The Angevin marriage was a token of reconciliation between the Lancastrians and the Valois. But in England Margaret was held responsible for the disasters which followed and for the loss of the continental possessions of England. She did, indeed, exercise a dominant influence over a husband who was unfit to reign. The charges against her find an echo in Shakespeare, *Second Part of King Henry VI*, Act i, Scene 1.

France, where, as will be seen shortly, the work of reconstruction proceeded systematically. Hostilities were resumed in 1449 as a result of English intervention in Brittany against the new duke, Francis I, who after his accession in 1442 had done homage to France and taken up arms in its favour. Following on the capture and sack of Fougères by François de Surienne, a captain in the English service, the king revived the tactics of Charles V, allowing his captains to operate against the English in Brittany while making no official breach of the truces. But Normandy was in a continually increasing state of ferment, and its population appealed to the French. An assembly held by the king on 17 July 1449 at the castle of Roches-Tranchelion, near Chinon, decided that this appeal must be answered and Normandy freed. In less than a year the province was conquered; the salient features in the campaign which effected this were the recapture of Rouen (the Duke of Somerset surrendered it on 29 October 1449, and the king made his solemn entry on 10 December), the victory of Formigny on 15 April 1450, and the fall of Cherbourg on 12 August 1450. The conquest of Guienne, the last province remaining to the English, proved to be a more troublesome undertaking. Bordeaux was recovered for the first time on 12 June 1451, and Bayonne opened its gates on 20 August following; but Talbot recaptured Bordeaux on 23 October 1452, and it was only the defeat and death of the valiant Englishman at the battle of Castillon on the 17 July 1453 which made possible the final acquisition by the king of Bordeaux (19 October) and with it the possession of the whole of the south-west. Henceforward, Calais alone remained to the English; and this was inaccessible to the French, because it was surrounded by Burgundian territory, which could not be violated by them.

Now that he was definitely the victor, Charles VII caused commemorative medals to be struck in honour of his troops. These medals, struck at the Paris mint, perpetuate the memory of the reconquest of Normandy and Guienne and the expulsion of the English from France[1]. But Charles did more than this. Once in possession, at Rouen in 1450, of the documents of Joan of Arc's trial, he ordered an investigation, from which resulted the suit of rehabilitation. The verdict was given on 7 July 1456, and annulled the first trial as irregular in its constitution and its procedure; a tardy but a just reparation, and a splendid epilogue to the Hundred Years' War which was now at last at an end[2].

The period occupied by the third phase of the Hundred Years' War is one of exceptional interest in the internal development of France and

[1] These medals, which produced a great effect, as the mention of them by Alain Chartier shews, bore a legend in Latin recalling the military effort that had been achieved and the success that had been won. Examples of them can be seen at Paris in the Bibliothèque Nationale, Cabinet des Médailles.

[2] No treaty brought the Hundred Years' War to an end. For certain consequences of this negative fact, see *infra*, p. 257.

the elaboration of monarchical control. In the epoch of the decisive struggle which rescued it from the English, France came to see in the Valois monarchy the living and concrete personification of itself. Charles VII, to Joan of Arc and her contemporaries, stood for the country. "God wills it so"; and with this all the utterances of the heroine, through whose mouth the voice of France itself was speaking, were in accord. This national character of the legitimate monarchy was consecrated by military happenings and during a struggle for independence. It resulted, accordingly, that, in order to assure the triumph of the king, its champion, no sacrifice was too great for France to make. King and monarchy had the people behind them. There could be no serious question of discussing the respective rights of sovereign and nation, since the one was fighting for the other. There is no disputing the orders of the person to whom you look for salvation. Once Joan of Arc was gone, the Hundred Years' War could only be brought to a conclusion completely favourable to France, provided that the country was willing to consent to a great military effort. So the needs of the war dictated the military reforms of Charles VII, and such reform at such a time must in the main be the expression of the aim of the body politic.

The truces of 1444 are exceptionally important from this point of view. The English king signed them to avoid the loss of all his possessions; he obtained a breathing space for a few years. But Charles VII, who also needed a breathing space, profited by the respite to recover his strength and to prepare the definitive success of his arms. This was the occasion for the commencement of the noble series of *Ordonnances* which will be described in detail. But first it must be noted that the military effort implied financial resources; so financial reform was a necessary accompaniment of the effort. Financial reform in its turn also brought the governmental system into play. In the result, therefore, the monarchy emerged from its great trial far more powerful than it had been at the beginning of the crisis. Such was the general notion underlying the work of internal reconstruction which was accomplished under Charles VII; it is necessary now to describe its essential features[1].

The Constable Richemont appears to deserve the chief credit for the great military reform which marked the reign; at any rate, it was under his direction that it was put into execution. This reform may be regarded as having been accomplished in three stages: the first, which preceded the truces and occurred in 1439, aimed at the repression of the abuses committed by the military; the second, in the year 1445, consisted in the

---

[1] Apart from the rôle played by Richemont on the military side, it is impossible to know what share of the credit must be given to the king or to each of his collaborators in the administrative work of the kingdom. Among the influential personages in the second half of the reign may be mentioned: Dunois, Bueil, Raoul de Gaucourt, Jean d'Estouteville, Pierre de Brézé, Jean and Gaspard Bureau, Guillaume Cousinot, and lastly, until his fall, Jacques Cœur, as will be shewn later.

formation of *compagnies d'ordonnance*; the third, in 1448, was marked by the creation of the *Francs-Archers*.

The *Ordonnance* of 1439 had been tentatively anticipated by the *Ordonnances* of 1431 and 1438, which were limited, however, to a repetition of Charles V's regulations on the same subject. The abuses committed by the military were one of the scourges of the time. But the *Ordonnance* of 1439 had a much wider range than any of its predecessors. It inaugurated, in fact, a regular military discipline. By it the regulations introduced by Charles V were revived and reinforced. The captains of Companies were forced to hand over to the ordinary justice any soldier under their command who was charged with an offence against the law. The right of levying troops or causing them to be levied was henceforward reserved to the king alone. Finally, companies of 100 men were re-established; and, moreover, upon each of these companies was imposed a special garrison-duty, from which it was forbidden to move without royal authorisation. Such was the first stage of military reform. The object was to bar the employment of armed forces by private initiative, to prevent it from being, as it were, a private concern; it had the result of fixing the companies as garrisons in definite places, and so of bringing to an end the scourge of soldiery ranging at will.

The second stage of reform followed upon the truces of 1444. At this date, since the truces were renewable, there was a temporary pause in the conflict between England and France. This fact gave rise to a serious problem—what was to become of the Companies in time of peace? Briefly, the problem with which the government of Charles VII was thus confronted was the same that Charles V and Du Guesclin had had to solve in the previous century; with this difference, however, that in the fifteenth century it was a question not only of preventing the excesses of the idle soldiery, but also of preserving for France an army in preparation for the day, for which due reckoning was being made in advance, when hostilities would be resumed. In these circumstances, it was the policy of the king and his Constable to eliminate the dangerous elements and to preserve those that were sound. In the first case, Charles VII essayed remedies analogous to the famous Spanish expedition of the fourteenth century. He dispatched a force of *routiers*, under the command of the dauphin, the future King Louis XI, with the avowed object of assisting the Emperor Frederick III against the Swiss; in the course of this campaign, the young prince's troops won a victory which caused considerable stir, the victory of St Jakob (26 August 1444)[1]. The Swiss were definitely defeated, but on the French side many *routiers* lost their lives—in both respects a gain to the royal policy. In 1444 also, Charles VII laid siege

[1] See *supra*, Vol. VII, Chap. VII, p. 202. The dauphin's army had as its principal commander one of the best captains in the French service, Jean de Bueil. The battle of the leper-hospital of St Jakob was fought near Basle, but the dauphin took no part in it himself (Marcel Thibault, *La jeunesse de Louis XI*, p. 356; Tuetey, *Les Écorcheurs sous Charles VII*, I, 230–35).

to Metz, and though he failed to capture it, the Companies engaged in this Lorraine adventure were in the course of the campaign purged of their more inflammable elements.

There remained the second of the two objectives—to find a means to preserve in the service of France, instead of sacrificing them in battle or disbanding them, the better elements in the Companies. First of all, in order to purge these heterogeneous troops, the government decided to remove the evil characters. A complete amnesty was granted to all those with a crime on their conscience who retired voluntarily from the profession of arms. Thus the undesirables were eliminated. The remainder—the better, or at any rate the less bad, elements—were retained and were incorporated in companies of a new formation.

The organisation of these new companies—the third stage in the reform—was the object of the celebrated *Ordonnance* of 1445. It is most unfortunate to have to record that this document is lost; the exact date, even, is unknown. All that can be said is that it was published in February or March, at Nancy. It is possible, however, to reconstruct almost completely the text of it, by making use of the subsequent *Ordonnances*, which repeated it with some additions and amendments, and also by means of the information supplied by the chroniclers, notably by Mathieu d'Escouchy and Thomas Basin.

In broad outline, the king appointed fifteen captains, each with the command of a hundred lances; there were in all, therefore, 1500 lances. By "lance" was meant a tactical unit composed of six men and six horses. The personnel of the lance consisted of a man-at-arms, a *coutilier*[1], a page, two archers, and a page or *valet*; in some Companies the last-named was replaced by a third archer. The captain recruited his men himself, but he had to exact from each of them an oath to be faithful to the king and to fulfil the terms of the *Ordonnance*. Every member of the Company had to be present at the inspections (*montres*) held by royal officers. The companies thus organised were officially known as "Compagnies de l'Ordonnance du roi" or, more succinctly, "Compagnies d'Ordonnance."

The principle of the garrison, which had already been adopted, was maintained and in 1445 was put into definite operation. The "Compagnies de l'Ordonnance du roi" were assigned their stations and were distributed among the provinces. So, for example, Poitou received 130 lances, Saintonge 60. Later, changes were made in the original geographical distribution of the Companies, especially after 1453, that is to say, when the conflict with the English had come to an end. Now, though there were garrisons, there were of course no barracks. The soldiers were billeted on the inhabitants, who, however, could free themselves from this burdensome obligation by the payment of money instead, a sort of composition-tax; this was known as the *taille des gens d'armes*. Contemporary chroniclers are unanimous in praising the reform and recording

---

[1] *I.e.* a soldier armed with a knife.

its successful results. Thus Chastellain[1] boasts of Charles VII's work for peace. The reform, indeed, had the double effect of creating internal order and of forging an effective weapon for the purpose of a possible future war[2].

The term "standing army" is usually employed to describe the military force which was created by the *Ordonnances* of Charles VII; it is necessary, however, to be clear as to the exact significance of this term. In enacting the regulations which have been described and the supplementary ones which followed, neither the king nor his Constable had in view the creation of permanent companies, properly so called. Their object was simply to keep mobilised the soundest troops of which they disposed at the time of the truces, so as to have them in readiness at the moment when hostilities should be resumed. But, as it happened, the Hundred Years' War came to an end in 1453 without the interposition of any treaty. No guarantee existed that the war would not be resumed; fresh outbreaks were always possible[3]. That is why the Companies were retained. Henceforward they were to continue indefinitely. Thus the biographer of Richemont, M. Cosneau, could justly write that, if Charles VII did not actually create a standing army, he did at any rate create what became a standing army.

The *Ordonnance* of 1445 only applied to a part of the kingdom, the country of Langue d'oïl. It needed therefore to be completed, and this was done by the institution of 500 lances for Languedoc (*Ordonnance* of 1446); consequently 500 lances in the South were added to the original 1500, bringing the total number of lances to 2000. There were also some additional companies, less well paid or at any rate less well equipped. Little is known as to their organisation; in the texts they are called "petites payes," "mortes payes," or "compagnies de la petite ordonnance."

So far only mounted corps had been instituted. Charles VII and Richemont wished to create an infantry as well. This object was attained in the third stage of reform. By an *Ordonnance* published at Montils-les-Tours on 28 April 1448, the *Francs-Archers* were instituted. The French monarchy already employed companies of archers or cross-bowmen, associations of which were formed in towns. In the fifteenth century the "noble art of shooting with the bow" was all the fashion. Undoubtedly the patriotic ardour aroused by "the English peril" had contributed greatly to the popularity of this pursuit, which became a favourite sport

---

[1] "Fit d'une infinité de meurtriers et de larrons sur le tour d'une main gens résolus et de vye honneste; mist bois et forests, murtrières, passages, asseurés,...toutes villes paisibles, toutes nations de son royaume tranquilles." Chastellain, *Chronique*, Bk. II, Ch. xliii (*Oeuvres*, II, 184).

[2] At the beginning of the reform the wages were paid, in part at least, in kind. This Thomas Basin explains as due to the distressed conditions of the time.

[3] The house of York, no less than the house of Lancaster to which it succeeded, might have renewed the war on the Continent. Cf. Calmette and Périnelle, *Louis XI et l'Angleterre*, Introduction.

with the youth of the towns, whose example was followed by smaller places; a force available for use had thus come into being of its own accord. Naturally the successful employment of archers by Edward III of England could not be unfamiliar to Frenchmen. In 1425 the Duke of Brittany had formed a body of infantry in this way, composed of "folk of the commonalty." Charles VII determined to outdo this Breton experiment, which was of course familiar to Richemont. The king's intention was to operate on a grand scale, and to establish a powerful infantry by mobilising the archers from the parishes. This was the source from which the *Ordonnance* of 1448 drew to produce the *Francs-Archers*[1]. The name of "Free Archers" was derived from the right attaching to them of exemption from taxation. The herald Berry says, in fact, that the king "freed them from paying any of the subsidies current in his kingdom"; and the same chronicler explains the method practised for the recruiting of these foot-soldiers: "it was ordered to all *baillis* in the kingdom, each in his own right, to choose in each *bailliage* and parish and to take therefrom the most skilful and suitable." The *Ordonnance* of 1451 introduced some modifications in the arrangements originally made for the levying of the archers. Instead of the uniform system of one archer from every parish whatever its size, it seemed to be more equitable and practical to fix one archer for every fifty hearths. The equipment of the archer was at his own expense, or, in cases of poverty, at the expense of the parish. The choosing of the archers was done by the *élus* or the *prévôt*. They took an oath, and their names were entered on a roll, a duplicate of which was sent from every *bailliage* to the central authority. At first posted among the feudal levies, the *Francs-Archers* were soon formed into a separate corps; and they were made up into companies, probably one for each *bailliage*. Each company-commander received a salary of 120 *livres tournois*, and was entitled further to 8 *livres* for expenses. The cross-bowmen of the town bands, which had been formed already in the time of Charles V, were united to the archers from the parishes. It is difficult to estimate the exact numbers of the infantry force that was raised in this way. The figure of 8000 men, divided into 16 companies of 500 archers, has been suggested; but no contemporary document makes it possible to arrive at so precise a calculation.

Several acts in Charles VII's reign were designed towards the perfecting of the old, the feudal, army. The most characteristic of the *Ordonnances* issued with this object appeared shortly after the expiration of the Hundred Years' War, dated 30 January 1455. The king instructed the nobles to inform him as to the following they maintained, and announced that he would assign to each a payment proportionate to the importance

[1] "Voulons et ordonnons pour le plus aisé et à moins de charge pour nos subjects, que en chascune paroisse de nostre royaume aura ung archer qui sera et se tiendra continuellement en habillement suffisant et armé de sallade, dague, espée, arc et trousse, jaque ou hougue de brigandine, et seront appellez les Francs-Archers."

of his following. The sums fixed upon, which were not to differ appreciably from the average rates previously in force, were briefly as follows: per month, a man-at-arms received 15 francs, a *coutilier* 5 francs, an archer or cross-bowman 7½. Genoese and Scottish archers reinforced, under Charles VII, the national troops of France. The brothers Bureau had particular charge of the artillery, which by the end of the reign had become a considerable and a formidable arm; there was both light artillery, with its characteristic weapon the piece known as *couleuvrine* or *serpentine*, and heavy artillery, composed of *bombardes*. These pieces, especially the *bombardes*, were christened after the fashion of ships; some of them were of vast size, encircled with strong hoops of iron. The stone cannon-balls which they discharged weighed 100 to 150 lbs. Already in Charles VII's time the cannon were mounted on gun-carriages, and cannon mounted on wheels had also made an appearance. However, the rate of fire was still very slow, and scarcely more than two cannon-balls could be discharged per hour.

The fleet under Charles VII was used to support the army and to protect the coasts. Though France relied in the main on the assistance of the Castilian fleet—there was a traditional friendship between the two countries and, since the accession of the Trastamara dynasty, an alliance which was renewed from reign to reign—Charles VII realised the necessity of having a naval force at his disposal. The French king had ships of war of his own, and he also employed merchant vessels, which he put into fighting trim, acquiring them from their owners in return for the payment of an indemnity.

Jacques Cœur, the greatest man of business of the century, fitted out for the purpose of his own commercial ventures, of which something will be said later, a private flotilla; it was completely equipped, however, and consisted of seven vessels sailing under the flag of the Virgin. He obtained from Charles VII a license to raise crews by pressing vagrants as sailors; they were known as his *caimans*, and he was also allowed to hire convicts. In return for these advantages, Cœur put his fleet at the king's disposal, much in the same way that the captains did with their Companies before the military reforms. Cœur's nephew, Jean de Villages, was in command of his uncle's vessels[1]. Besides the ships belonging to the king or put at his disposal by their owners, the part played in naval matters in the fifteenth century by the corsairs must not be left out of account. Their operations, moreover, were not limited to wartime, although the king could make use of them. In practice, every time that a crime at sea remained unpunished and unrequited by the government responsible for the offender, the injured party received from his sovereign letters of marque authorising him to recoup himself at the expense of any of his aggressor's compatriots, without being liable to an action of law in consequence.

[1] Later, Louis XI purchased Villages' fleet (1478).

The military effort was, as has been seen, conditioned by the problem of finance. The monarchy could only meet the expenses of the national defence by instituting a reorganisation of its finances. So, side by side with the military *Ordonnances* of Charles VII's reign there went a noble series of financial *Ordonnances*[1].

In the course of the civil war in Charles VI's time, the monarchy had surrendered its right to impose taxes; this was the evil fruit of the policy of competition for popular favour which had followed the death of Charles V. Charles VII was not content merely to re-establish the old royal right. He went farther, made royal taxation permanent, and effected a complete remodelling of the financial regime. By tradition a distinction was made in the royal revenues between the "ordinary finances," derived from the domain, and the "extraordinary finances," derived from taxes, dues, and subsidies. Now, war had affected the domain to such an extent that the "ordinary finances," of which it was the source, were almost exhausted[2]. Clearly, in order to bring these ruinous wars to a favourable conclusion, money must be found. It was to the "extraordinary finances," therefore, that recourse had to be made. For this a new financial organisation was indispensable, and it came about as the result of a series of financial *Ordonnances* following one another in succession from 1443 onwards, of which the most important was the *Ordonnance* of Nancy of 10 February 1445. This remodelling left intact the fundamental distinction between the "ordinary finances" of the domain and the "extraordinary finances" consisting of impositions (*gabelles, aides, tailles*). This distinction is clearly marked, and there were two separate budgets, as there were also two financial administrations. The domain itself was composed of two parts, the mutable and the immutable domain; the return from the former was irregular (sealing dues, cutting of woods etc.), that from the latter was fixed (perpetual quit-rents, for instance). To the receipts from the domain were charged not only the costs of the upkeep of the domain, but also general expenses of government, such as the pay of the *baillis* and of other officials of the *bailliages*. The "extraordinary finances" comprised three essential classes of revenue. The *gabelle* was a tax on salt, which was almost analogous to the employment by the modern French State of the monopoly of tobacco, but with this difference, that the Frenchman of to-day is at liberty to refrain from the consumption of tobacco while the purchase of a definite amount of salt was obligatory under the monarchical regime. *Aide* is a generic term to denote dues levied on the sale of

---

[1] The following is the list of the great financial *Ordonnances* of the reign: *Ordonnances* of Saumur, 27 September and 25 November 1443; *Ordonnance* of Nancy, 10 February 1445; *Ordonnance* of Sarcy, 19 June 1445; *Ordonnance* of Châlons, 12 August 1445; *Ordonnance* of Bourges, 26 November 1447; to which must be added those of Mehun-sur-Yèvre, 23 December 1454, and of Chinon, 3 April 1460. The financial *Ordonnances*, like the military *Ordonnances* of which we possess the text, figure in the *Grand Recueil des Ordonnances des rois de France*.

[2] The *Ordonnance* of Saumur of 25 September 1445, referring to the domain, says: "il est venu en ruine et comme en non-valoir."

commodities. *Taille* implies a direct tax assessed on the basis of landed property. It was in regard to *tailles* that Charles VII made his chief innovations.

It can be asserted that mainly by virtue of *tailles* the kingdom raised the sums necessary for victory. The *taille*, which hitherto had retained its exceptional character, was converted into a regular and permanent tax; it was now, in fact, levied every year. Formerly the monarchy had had to assemble the States in order to obtain a vote for what was held to be an extraordinary imposition. Under the cover of one-sided and ambiguous votes, obtained, for the purpose of the war, from assemblies mainly of notables and of local Estates, the annual levy of the *taille* came at last to be made purely and simply by virtue of the royal authority. This usurpation, which brought into being a new right, was accomplished without any difficulty, because the sacrifice imposed by the sovereign upon his subjects had its justification in the public welfare. The point has already been made, that no Frenchman could dispute his gold or his blood when the king, the incarnation of the country, claimed it manifestly for the great cause of the liberation of the realm. So, the formality of a vote from the States General fell into oblivion. The king fixed each year the rate of the *tailles* simply by letters patent decided on in his Council; and it came about that, as the practice went on, he even augmented the rate by "increases of *taille*." Towards the end of Charles VII's reign, the revenue from the *taille* reached the sum of 1,200,000 *livres tournois* while the maximum amount provided by the total of the royal impositions, though it had already grown considerably, never exceeded the figure of 1,800,000[1].

Even more than taxation, the financial administration underwent important reorganisation under Charles VII. Two parallel services functioned side by side, the one for the domain, the other for the "extraordinary finances." The revenue from the domain was known as the *trésor* and its administration was entrusted to four *trésoriers de France*, each of whom was at the head of a district entitled his *charge* (Langue d'oïl with Paris as the headquarters, Languedoc with Montpellier, Normandy with Rouen, Outre-Seine with Tours); there were also territories lying outside these *charges*, the administration of which will be described later. The *trésoriers de France* were overseers or administrators, but with no responsibility for the accounts; they handled none of the receipts and they made no disbursements. These duties were entrusted to *receveurs ordinaires* and to the *changeur du trésor*; this official, with his seat at Paris, acted as a centre for the revenue which came in from the provinces and was assisted by a *contrôleur du trésor*. In the provinces lying outside these *charges*, that is to say, the provinces reunited to the domain after Charles VII's reorganisation, the regime prior to the reunion

---

[1] Commynes, *Mémoires*, ed. Calmette, Vol II (*Les classiques de l'histoire de France*, fasc. 5), p. 220.

was allowed to continue; in practice, however, this regime differed little in its method of functioning from that of the *charges* described above.

For the administration of what were still known as the "extraordinary finances" France was divided into *généralités*. The *généraux des finances* corresponded to the *trésoriers de France* in the domain, and like them were managers and administrators; they also were four in number, and the four *généralités* had the same name and the same areas as the *charges*. The functionaries, however, who corresponded to the *receveurs ordinaires* bore various different names. For the receipt of *tailles* and *aides* the *généralité* was divided into *élections*, each with two *élus* at its head, assisted by a *procureur royal*, a *greffier*, a *receveur de la taille*, and a *receveur des aides*. Further, some provinces had neither *élus* nor *élections*. Those were the ones in which the Estates had survived, as will be shewn later; in these provinces the Estates themselves continued to assess the taxes which in theory it still rested with them to vote. Thus was settled the classic division of France into "pays d'États" and "pays d'élections." The service of the *gabelles* was particularly complicated. As a rule the two principal agents of this administration were known as *grenetier* and *contrôleur*; in Languedoc there was at the head of the service an official with the title of *visiteur général des gabelles*. The returns from the "extraordinary finances" were rendered to the headquarters of each *généralité*, into the care of the *receveur général* (or *général*), who was assisted by a staff similar to that which handled the receipts from the domain.

This financial regime with its duplicated machinery was obviously cumbersome to manage. Actually, from 1450 at any rate, there was an *État général des finances*, and so a measure of co-ordination between the two financial services. This *État* was under the supervision of "le roy et messieurs de ses finances," which meant a kind of superior commission consisting of the *trésoriers* and the *généraux*; from this was to evolve at a later date the unification of the financial system.

There remained the regulation of disputes. Charles VII created a *chambre du trésor* and a *chambre des aides*; finally, he instituted a *chambre des comptes* (*Ordonnance* of Mehun-sur-Yèvre of 23 December 1454), which had the duty of checking and overhauling all parts of the financial machinery. From this sketch it will be seen that Charles VII endowed France with a new and a coherent financial system, just as he also endowed her with an army worthy of the name.

The ecclesiastical organisation was also subjected during this reign to extensive and bold changes, thanks to a celebrated and important act, the Pragmatic Sanction of Bourges (1438). The abuses of the fiscal system of the Papacy, aggravated by the Great Schism, aroused in fifteenth-century France a wide-spread revival of Gallicanism. The Schism at an end, a concordat had been concluded between the French Court and Pope Martin V in 1418, to last for five years. The five years expired in 1423, and as no arrangement had been concluded in the interval, Martin made a one-sided settlement of the problems in suspense by a constitution of 13 April 1425. The chief difficulty arose over the collation to benefices, owing to the rights associated with a vacancy and the choice of a new incumbent; the Pope disposed of vacant benefices during eight months of the year. In spite of the protests of the clergy, Henry VI and the Duke of Burgundy accepted this arrangement. Charles VII was more inclined to Gallican ideas, but, fearing to put Rome on the side of his enemies, he dissembled for some time. Negotiations entered into with Martin V led in 1426 to the signature of the Concordat of Genzano, which was almost identical with the bull of 1425. As soon as Martin was dead, Charles VII reopened negotiations with his successor Eugenius IV. After the recovery of Paris in 1436 the French Court was able to take a firmer line, while Eugenius IV, on the other hand, was in a weaker position owing to his conflict with the Council of Basle. Charles convoked a great assembly of the French Church to meet at Orleans on 1 May 1438; on 5 June its sessions were transferred to Bourges. The Bishop of Castres, Gérard Machet, the king's confessor, played the leading rôle at the sittings, at which twenty-five bishops and numerous other dignitaries were present; the Archbishop of Tours, Philippe de Coëtquis, distinguished himself by his attacks on the abuses of the Curia. The assembly adopted most of the decrees of the Council of Basle, while amending some of them, and a Statute of the French Church was passed in the form of a "Pragmatic" issuing from Bourges and dated 7 July 1438.

The term "Pragmatic," borrowed from the phraseology of the old imperial rescripts, was used in an entirely specialised sense, of a solemn settlement of ecclesiastical affairs by the civil government[1]. No precedent could legally be invoked; the so-called Pragmatic of St Louis was a forgery[2]. By virtue of this statute, the Pope was to have the right only to nominate to those benefices in which a vacancy was created at the Roman Court. Most of the sources of papal revenues from France were abolished; the monarchy established under its aegis a Gallican Church. Eugenius IV naturally resisted, and his successor Nicholas V did the same. But further assemblies of the clergy in 1450 and 1452 confirmed the statute of 1438. It was not until after the death of Charles VII that the Papacy was able to obtain from the French Court the renunciation of the "Pragmatic," which had introduced a system so completely to the advantage of the monarchy.

The other institutions of medieval France did not bear so deeply the impress of the reign of Charles VII as those which have already been passed under review. Their development, however, in the period covered

---

[1] The Pragmatic Sanction figures in the *Recueil des Ordonnances*.

[2] In all probability the forgery must be attributed to Gérard Machet, who wished, after the event, to appease the qualms raised by the act for which he was responsible.

by the third phase of the Hundred Years' War, is of definite importance, and it is essential to outline the changes which took place.

In judicial matters, only one innovation marks the reign, but that was of considerable importance: the creation of the first provincial Parlement, the Parlement of Toulouse[1]. This was the successor to the ephemeral Parlement of Poitiers, which was the actual Parlement of the kingdom with its seat transferred to the provinces by the king of Bourges since he was dispossessed of Paris. The continued existence of the Parlement of Toulouse definitely brought to an end the old concentration of judicial competence in the hands of a single Parlement.

It was during the period covered by this chapter that the monarchy was freed from the tutelage of the States, a fact of extreme significance, since thereby vanished the possibility, which had appeared for a time, of a constitutional monarchy more or less on the English pattern. The States, the assemblies of the three orders of nobles, clergy, and third estate, remained a vague institution. By this vagueness Charles profited to escape from the control which he might well have had reason to fear. Only once after the death of his father did Charles summon an assembly of a general character—the States of Chinon in 1428; at this meeting the deputies from Languedoc expressed the hope that no tax would be levied without a vote. Generally in Charles VII's reign there were separate meetings of the States of Langue d'oïl and of Languedoc. Fifteen sessions of the former have been noted, and four of the latter; so the provincial Estates took the chief place and pushed the States General into the background. In actual fact, Languedoc, Normandy, and Champagne were the only parts of the France of Charles VII's day which were to preserve their Estates. Moreover, as has been seen, the king had everywhere assumed the right of levying subsidies on his own authority.

Thus strengthened, and released from any effective limitation or control, the power of the sovereign was far stronger at the end of the crisis than on the accession of the Valois line. The feudal nobility was bridled. The military reforms of the reign made the king irresistible. Wars between baron and baron were no longer possible: the Dauphin Louis prohibited all private warfare in Dauphiné[2]; Charles VII forbade his vassals to construct or repair any stronghold without his permission. At the same time that he increased the royal taxes, he prohibited the raising of excessive impositions by the lords[3]. The performance of homage, the recognition and enumeration of fiefs, were strictly enforced. In 1435

---

[1] The Parlement of Toulouse was not provincial in origin. It replaced the Parlement of Paris when that was in English hands. Created first by the dauphin in 1420, it continued to exist after the recovery of Paris and was reorganised in 1443 as a court of appeal for the whole of the south-west. The Parlement of Bordeaux, given a temporary existence in 1452, also became permanent under Louis XI and thereby greatly restricted the jurisdiction of Toulouse.

[2] *Ordonnance* of la Tour du Pin 10 December 1451.

[3] *Ordonnance* of 1439.

Charles caused a careful list to be made of fiefs acquired in the last sixty years. Well-served by his *baillis* and seneschals, he exacted respect for royal justice and furthered its development, and he affirmed his exclusive right to tolls from fairs and markets, and his right of granting patents of nobility and of legitimation. More and more the petty nobility tended to develop into a Court aristocracy. In 1440 there was a vain attempt at a feudal reaction, the *Praguerie*, so-called in memory of recent outbreaks in Bohemia; Duke Charles of Bourbon was at its head, the Dauphin Louis took part in it, and even Dunois was compromised. Vigorous action by the king in Auvergne stifled the movement.

The military effort which decided the conclusion of the Hundred Years' War had rendered the monarchy safe from internal dangers; but it did not allow Charles VII to advance the economic prosperity of his kingdom, a task reserved for his successor. There was one figure in the king's entourage, however, who impressed his personality upon French commerce. Born at Bourges about 1395, Jacques Cœur was a typical pioneer of industry. He combined commercial activity with official duties. He was the king's silversmith, royal commissioner in the States of Languedoc, and a member of the Great Council. He enjoyed a practical monopoly of French trade in the Mediterranean and, as we have seen, he had a fleet at his disposal. The principal seat of his business was at Montpellier, where he owned a magnificent mansion; but he also had houses in several towns and his residence at Bourges was a dwelling fit for a prince. Charles VII ennobled his silversmith, but later, in 1451, he lent an ear to Cœur's enemies, and accused him not only of granting monopolies, of which he was certainly not innocent, but in particular of having poisoned Agnes Sorel, who had died in childbirth the previous year (9 February 1450). Finally, he banished him on this trumped-up charge and confiscated his goods. Cœur died in exile at Chio, where he had taken refuge, in the service of the Pope, on 25 November 1456. The great expansion of French maritime commerce in the second half of the century derived from the bold impulse given to economic activity by Jacques Cœur.

So, at the close of the age-long war, there dawned an era of restoration for devastated and ruined France. Already in the last years of Charles VII, even before the final victory of his arms, the renewal of agriculture and the revival of normal activities gave promise of a speedy recovery. The France of the middle of the century that set itself so courageously to work with the intention of repairing its fortunes was a France that was clearly monarchical, loyal and bound by ties henceforward indestructible to the royal dynasty.

One menace alone remained: the power, confronting the France that was the king's, of some great feudal States. Out of the duel between France and England, a few favoured lordly houses were able to make their profit, and emerged from the war with added strength. Of these, in the front rank were Burgundy and Brittany; behind them at varying distances came some princes of the centre—Anjou, Bourbon; or of the south—Foix, Armagnac, Albret. These were the feudal dynasties which were to make the supreme attack upon Louis XI; and to this monarch it was left to break those formidable powers and to assure the definitive domination of the Crown over the united country.

The last years of Charles VII's reign are not merely characterised by the economic and social revival of France after her release from the great war. The monarchy profited by the regaining of its freedom and the strengthening of its authority; it started again upon its traditional policy abroad, at the same time that it caused what remained of the French feudality to feel more and more the weight of the new power of the king upon them.

Actually, France had never ceased, even in its worst days, to look abroad; even before the end of the struggle with England, as soon as the truces of Tours gave the king a breathing space and the prospect of an end to the crisis—in fact, it might be said, from the time of the Treaty of Arras and the recovery of Paris—the monarchy had begun to make its presence felt outside the country and to assume again the rôle of a great power. The manifestations of this activity in the east, in Italy, and in Spain can be clearly detected.

On his eastern frontiers, Charles VII strove to restrict the area of Burgundian expansion. Burgundy, indeed, under Philip the Good had become a powerful and a formidable State[1]. It had been indeed the true beneficiary of the Hundred Years' War, and had grown out of all proportion. Skilful marriage-alliances rounded off an adroit policy, which was continually encroaching and was pursued without pause under cover of the conflict between the houses of Lancaster and Valois. The duke possessed what at the present day is represented by almost the whole of the kingdoms of Holland and Belgium, the departments of the Nord and the Pas de Calais and a part of the Somme, and in ducal Burgundy and Franche Comté and their dependencies the equivalent of twelve modern departments[2]. Wealthy and powerful, the house of Burgundy was the most splendid in Europe; the life of its Court, its art, and its literature were on the same level, and Philip the Good, haughty and magnificent, was already aspiring to the royal crown which Charles the Bold, in the time of Louis XI, was so

---

[1] On the Burgundian State, see the works cited in the bibliography to this chapter, principally, besides Pirenne's *Histoire de Belgique*, the works of Doutrepont, Kleinclausz, and Cartellieri. The great Burgundian chroniclers—especially Olivier de la Marche, Chastellain, and Molinet—provide striking evidence of the splendour and the ambitions of the ducal State. On Philip the Good, cf. Jean Huizinga, *La physionomie de Philippe le Bon* (*Annales de Bourgogne*, 1932, pp. 102–29).

[2] The possession of the towns of the Somme, which were ceded in the Treaty of Arras of 1435, gave Burgundy the strategic key to the Île de France. Charles VII tried in vain to reclaim them in 1452, and his persistence gave considerable offence to Philip.

obstinately to pursue. Charles VII realised the danger to the French State from this other State in process of formation on its very flanks. His eastern policy, then, was first and foremost a defensive policy. The expedition against the Swiss and the siege of Metz were not only designed as a means of employing the *routiers*, but also with the secret intention of interposing a barrier to Burgundian ambitions. In this roundabout way the Valois monarchy was returning to the ideas of Philip the Fair, to the French tradition expressed in the mystic saying of "natural frontiers," to the attraction of the Rhine. Metz resisted, but Épinal, Toul, and Verdun recognised the authority of Charles VII; the king even took the Rhenish domains of Sigismund of Austria under his protection on the occasion of the marriage of that prince with Eleanor of Scotland; and he completed the encirclement of Burgundy by purchasing her claim to Luxemburg from the Duchess of Saxony. The reception given at Tours in 1457 to a Hungarian embassy had the same end in view. Philip the Good had sworn, with great pomp and circumstance, at a banquet at Lille[1], to go to reconquer Constantinople from the Turks, thus representing himself as the leader of the future crusade. The Franco-Hungarian agreement was a step towards the transference to the French monarchy of the direction of Christian policy against the Sultan[2], and up to the end of his reign Charles VII, the heir of the great crusading kings, was appealed to by Rome and by the East, to the great vexation of the Court of Burgundy.

In Italy, too, Charles VII revived a policy which came to him from old tradition; the aspirations of the house of Orleans to Milan, the claims of Anjou to Naples, and the French protectorate over Genoa, created manifold duties for the Valois monarchy. Among the repercussions of the Hundred Years' War must certainly be reckoned the failure of René of Anjou in South Italy and the establishment at Naples of Alfonso V the Magnanimous of Aragon. On the death of the latter in 1458, the house of Anjou hoped for its revenge, and René's headstrong son John of Anjou, the Duke of Calabria, attempted a vigorous counter-offensive against the Aragonese dynasty, represented now by Ferrante, Alfonso's illegitimate son. This counter-offensive received support, both diplomatic and financial, from Charles VII[3].

It was the Hundred Years' War also that prevented France from giving help when it was most needed to Charles of Orleans, son of Valentine Visconti, at Milan, in his rivalry with Francesco Sforza for the domination of

[1] At the banquet (on 17 February 1454) there was brought onto the table a pheasant with a necklace of precious stones, and "Lady Church" came to stir the guests with a recital of her woes. Then the duke and all his guests took an oath to go to the rescue of the Church. This oath was called "the Vow of the Pheasant." The crusade was never actually undertaken, nor did Philip the Good ever go to the East.

[2] With the same object was associated the attempt of French diplomacy to obtain the election to the Bohemian throne of Charles VII's second son, Charles of France and to marry him to a daughter of the King of Poland (Stein, pp. 19 sqq.).

[3] On these Italian events see *supra*, Chaps. v and vi.

Lombardy. The war which began on the death of Filippo Maria Visconti in 1447 ended in 1450 with the triumph of Sforza, who won both the admiration and the support of the Dauphin Louis; the county of Asti, Valentine's dowry, alone remained to the house of Orleans to provide an opening for future claims.

As for Genoa, which was temporarily re-won by John of Calabria at the outset of his campaign in 1458, it was again lost to France while the champion of Angevin rights was performing dazzling but useless exploits in South Italy; the foolish enterprise of René's son ended in the disaster of Troja at the beginning of Louis XI's reign.

Finally, Spain, where once again Charles VII outlined the future policy of expansion which was to be pursued in detail by his successor. Two questions forced themselves on the attention of the French monarchy—the problem of Navarre and the problem of the eastern Pyrenees. In Navarre, which was a meeting-ground of French, Castilian, and Aragonese influences, a particularly difficult situation was created on the death of Queen Blanche, daughter of Charles the Noble and grand-daughter of Charles the Bad. John of Aragon, the husband of the dead queen, asserted a claim to the throne, interpreting his wife's will in his own sense, and disregarding the rights of their only son, Charles, Prince of Viana. So the little kingdom, rent by factions, was bitterly disputed between father and son. The Count of Foix, Gaston IV, the husband of Leonora, one of Charles of Viana's sisters, acted as intermediary between John of Aragon and Charles VII, who, with an eye to advantage to himself in the future, favoured the aims of the house of Foix upon Navarre[1].

At the other end of the Pyrenees, Charles VII, who inherited through his wife, Mary of Anjou, a somewhat dubious claim to the crown of Aragon[2], was planning a revision of the treaty of Corbeil[3], which had fixed in 1258 the Franco-Aragonese frontier at the Pas-de-Salses. A French embassy went to Barcelona in 1447 to claim the payment of the dowry of Yolande of Sicily, to whom the Queen of France was heiress[4]. On their return, having obtained nothing more than vague promises from the regent Maria, the wife of Alfonso the Magnificent, the ambassadors took a significant step. When they came to Perpignan, they demanded an audience from the consuls of the town, and after describing the purpose and the ill-success of their mission, declared that they would hold their hearers

---

[1] On the question of Navarre, see Des Devizes du Désert, *Don Carlos prince de Viane* (Paris, 1889) and Courteault, *Gaston IV* (see bibliography to this chapter).

[2] Mary of Anjou was the grand-daughter of Yolande of Bar, widow of John I of Aragon.

[3] See *supra* Vol. vi, Chap. x, p. 359.

[4] The dowry of 160,000 florins promised to the daughter of Yolande of Bar and John I, Yolande of Sicily, the mother-in-law of Charles VII, had never been paid. Louis XI, in his dealings with Spain, on several occasions raised claims deriving from Anjou.

responsible for the debt[1]. Roussillon was virtually treated as a pledge. This was the first indication of the intention to push the frontier up to the eastern Pyrenees, the historic boundary which Louis XI was to reach and which he was even tempted to overstep.

While these schemes were maturing, Charles VII continued to give his attention as much to Barcelona as to Pampeluna. The death of Alfonso the Magnificent on 25 June 1458, by putting his brother John II on the throne, brought about a definite modification of the political equilibrium in Spain. Charles of Viana became *primogènit* of the principality of Catalonia, and the Catalans were already using this title as an excuse for manifesting their separatist tendencies, which were soon to develop into a tragic revolution[2]. For some time Gaston of Foix had been working unceasingly to bring together his suzerain and his father-in-law, and his policy had resulted in the treaty of Valencia (17 June 1457), actually a defensive alliance between the two monarchies[3]. Moreover, on his accession John II had dispatched to France his Constable of Navarre, Pedro de Peralta, to bind still closer this alliance; while the Prince of Viana, for his part, formed a league with the Dauphin Louis.

To impose obedience on the feudality was the domestic task which Charles VII, delivered from his preoccupation with England, had to bring to a successful conclusion, simultaneously with his conduct of affairs abroad. In this direction, the administrative measures which have been detailed, as well as the consequences of the Hundred Years' War, automatically worked most effectively to the great advantage of the monarchy. During the last years of his reign, the liberator-king had to take serious action practically against only two of his vassals, the one in the north, the Duke of Alençon, the other in the south, the Count of Armagnac.

The Duke of Alençon, John II, handsome, affable, and free-handed, had preserved close relations with the English, whose side he favoured during their domination of Normandy. In 1455, he wrote to the Duke of York inviting him to descend upon the Cotentin. One of his messengers revealed the plot, and John was arrested by Dunois on 31 May 1456. The Court of Peers condemned him to death, but the king contented himself with confiscating the duchy and with imprisoning the traitor at Loches; from this prison he obtained his release on the accession of Louis XI.

Graver still was the case of the Count of Armagnac[4], John V, who had succeeded his father John IV on 5 November 1450. A turbulent feudal baron, ruddy, stout, and short of stature, John V, like Gaston of Foix,

[1] Calmette (Joseph), *Un épisode de l'histoire du Roussillon au temps de Charles VII* (*Revue d'histoire et d'archéologie du Roussillon*, Vol. i, 1900).

[2] Calmette (Joseph), *Louis XI, Jean II et la révolution catalane, 1461–1473* (*Bibl. méridionale*, 2nd series, Vol. viii).

[3] Zurita, lib. xv, cap. lxi.

[4] On the history of the Counts of Armagnac, see the work of C. Samaran cited in the bibliography to this chapter.

was as much interested in Spanish affairs as in French. Like the Dauphin
Louis, he had formed an alliance with Charles of Viana. His designs on
the county of Comminges and his actions at Auch, where he tried to effect
the nomination of an archbishop of his own choosing, brought him into
violent opposition to Charles VII. Further, John V had displayed a keen
and most untimely regret for the defeat and death of Talbot. To this
offence of a political character was soon added the intolerable scandal
caused by his cynical immorality. He was in love with his young sister
Isabella, by whom he had two children, and after their birth he had the
effrontery to apply at Rome for a dispensation to enable him to marry the
partner of his guilt. Pope Nicholas V replied with an excommunication[1].
John promised amendment, but the scandal continued and a third child
was born of this incestuous union. When all means of conciliation had
failed, Charles VII dispatched against him a punitive expedition under
John of Bourbon. The count took refuge first in his stronghold of Lectoure,
which capitulated on 24 June 1455; he had escaped thence, and by way
of Sarrancolin arrived in Spain, whither his sister Isabella had preceded
him. Summoned to appear before the Parlement of Paris, he had the
audacity to present himself; but after having exhausted every conceivable
trick to stay proceedings, he again made good his escape by flight[2], and
was found guilty by default of treason, incest, and rebellion. Like the
Duke of Alençon, John V was rehabilitated by Louis XI.

So, at every turn in the policy of Charles VII there appeared the
disturbing figure of the son who was to succeed him on the throne, the
Dauphin Louis. It was the terror inspired by his heir, so little loved and
so unlovable, that darkened the last days of the king whose youth had
been so unhappy and whose old age was even more unhappy.

The king and the dauphin had from early days been in opposition to
one another. Charles had not forgiven his son for his participation in
the *Praguerie*; still less did he forgive his unpleasant behaviour towards
the favourite, Agnes Sorel, then at the height of her influence. If Louis
did not actually strike his father's mistress, as one story has it, he did at
any rate revile her to her face. In 1447 he was sent off to Dauphiné, and
there he set up his court at Grenoble and took up an attitude of independence. While towards the local nobility he displayed an autocratic
tendency, at the same time he endowed Grenoble with a Parlement in
1453, gave his support to industry, improved the communications, founded
fairs, protected agriculture by a duty on French corn, and provided
facilities for the Jews to practise banking; in a word, he devised an
economic policy which he was to develop later as king, and he simultaneously pursued with great energy an expansive foreign policy, which
took no account of French interests and in fact was usually quite contrary
to them.

[1] Samaran, p. 120.
[2] He went to Flanders (Samaran, p. 129).

With Savoy he had a secret treaty, and he plotted with this power a partition of Milanese territory. Left a widower by the death of his first wife, the unhappy Margaret of Scotland[1], he contracted a second marriage with Charlotte of Savoy, daughter of the Duke Louis, on 9 March 1451, and this marriage, which he carried out in the face of his father's express prohibition, shewed both his ambitions in the direction of the Alps and his growing opposition to his father. And when Charles VII reacted against this by forcing Louis of Savoy into an alliance with himself (treaty of Clappé, 27 October 1452), the dauphin took his revenge on his father-in-law in the following year by laying waste the district of Bugey.

Everywhere the young prince seemed to delight in taking the opposite side to his father. He was now on terms of close friendship with Francesco Sforza, whom he took as his model, while Charles VII, as has been said, supported the Orleanist aims; in Spain, he exchanged messages and presents with the Prince of Viana. Suspecting a punitive expedition, since he was fully conscious of the offence he had given, the dauphin took fright when he learnt that the king was advancing on Lyons in 1456, and on 30 August he abandoned his appanage to take refuge at the Burgundian Court.

While Charles VII took possession of Dauphiné, Louis put himself under the protection of Philip the Good. Philip installed him at Genappes in Brabant, and, in spite of the king's effort to prevent it, granted him a pension of 36,000 *livres*; from this asylum the dispossessed dauphin tenaciously carried on in all directions the policy that he had previously pursued. Beyond the Alps he continued his intrigues, adapting himself in a remarkable way to the practices of Italian diplomacy, in which subtle art he shewed himself to be already a past master; he supported Ferrante of Naples against John of Anjou; he kept in closer touch than ever with Sforza; and he pushed his agreement with the *primogènit* Charles of Viana so far as to conclude an alliance with him, opposing to the league of the fathers a league of the sons[2]. In England also the same opposition manifested itself. Charles VII supported his niece Margaret of Anjou[3], and in August 1457 the Grand Seneschal of Normandy, Pierre de Brézé, took and sacked Sandwich; in retaliation the English threatened La Rochelle and plundered the island of Ré. When Edward IV was victorious over the Lancastrians, Charles tried to raise Wales against him. The dauphin for his part associated himself with the Yorkists, and so closely that his soldiers were seen fighting at Towton and his standard was flown in the battle, under the charge of Philippe de Melun, lord of La Barde. On the very eve of Charles VII's death,

---

[1] This princess, whom Louis never loved, died of consumption on 16 August 1445. Her last words were: "Fi donc de la vie, qu'on ne m'en parle pas!" (Champion, *La dauphine mélancolique*). Cf. Barbé, Louis A., *Margaret of Scotland and the Dauphin Louis* (London, 1917).

[2] Calmette, *Louis XI, Jean II et la révolution catalane*, p. 50.

[3] Calmette and Périnelle, *Louis XI et l'Angleterre*, pp. 3 sqq.

his son's emissaries were encouraging Edward to make an attack upon France[1].

This last episode reveals the intensity of mutual fear and hatred that existed between father and son. These sentiments cannot be doubted in either of them. Impatience to reign had reached such a pitch with the heir to the throne that he had lost all sense of French interests.

In Charles VII, now at the end of his days, this bitter and unnatural struggle had bred imaginative terrors: a sick man, he suspected his son of wishing to poison him. However, Charles VII died on 22 July 1461 not of voluntary starvation but as the result of a necrosis of the jaw which made it impossible for him to take any nourishment[2]. It was in this culmination of moral and physical ill-being that came to its painful end the career of him "who had done so many fine things in France[3]": in his reign, the kingdom of France had not merely escaped from the immense danger of English dominance; it had acquired the definite conception of its independence, its dignity, and its strength; it had linked its destiny with that of the national dynasty; finally, it had made its choice in favour of the monarchical regime and of institutions which, with their solid framework, were to remain as the foundation of the centralised government of modern times.

[1] Basin, i, 304, *Dép. des ambassadeurs milanais*, ed. B. de Mandrot (Société de l'histoire de France), i, 17.

[2] There can be no doubt of the fears of Charles VII, for Commynes obtained his knowledge of them from Louis XI himself. All the evidence on the subject of his last illness, with enlightenment from medical commentaries, is to be found in Brachet, *Pathologie mentale des rois de France*, pp. 72 sqq.

[3] Commynes, *ed. cit.* iii, 260

CHAPTER VIII

FRANCE: LOUIS XI

WHEN Charles VII died, the Valois monarchy had been reconstructed, and the French were living at peace. The greater part of the population was under the orders of the king's officials, and paid taxes in which they had no say but which were, however, not excessive. It was evident that the royal authority had recovered all its old strength. But there remained some questions of capital importance still in suspense. In spite of the great efforts made by the peasantry to put the land back into cultivation and by the merchants to revive their former connexions, France had recovered little from the disasters of the Hundred Years' War. The towns, with their houses often deserted and their monuments in ruins, were yet less desolate than the countryside. The register of the archidiaconal visitations of Josas (1458–70) shews us the region to the south of Paris devastated and lying waste, the parishes often denuded of inhabitants, and a rural society everywhere scanty in numbers and being decimated besides by violent epidemics, in wretched state, sunk in barbarism. An Englishman, Sir John Fortescue, passed through the north of France about 1465 on his way to Paris; his witness, which lies in the pages of his *Governance of England*, agrees with that of the ecclesiastical visitor: the French peasants were ill clothed, ill fed, and lived in a state of utmost poverty. The country was exhausted, and there was plenty to occupy the time of an ambitious king who was anxious to have adequate resources for the great things he had to do.

There were other problems, too, to be faced in 1461. The domain of the Crown, vast and homogeneous though it was, yet comprised only half of the realm. The remainder belonged to great feudal houses. Some of these were of great antiquity—Brittany, Foix, Armagnac, Albret—and jealous of their old independence; others had been offshoots from the Capetian stem, and first and foremost came the powerful dynasty of Burgundy. A conflict was inevitable between the king and the Duke of Burgundy, who claimed complete independence and had in vision the formation of a kingdom lying between France and Germany. Besides Burgundy, there were the houses of Bourbon (Bourbonnais, Auvergne, Forez, Beaujeu, Clermont-en-Beauvaisis etc.), of Orleans, and of Anjou (Anjou and Maine, and, outside the kingdom, Provence, Lorraine, the duchy of Bar, and claims upon the Two Sicilies). These three dynasties, though less dangerous than that of Burgundy, were none the less a permanent obstacle to the development of the monarchy, and the time had come when it could no longer continue to expand unless they disappeared.

With England no peace had been concluded. Public opinion in England was hostile to France; neither the Lancastrians nor the Yorkists had renounced the title of "King of France." Edward IV, who was on the throne in 1461, was, it is true, the friend of Louis, by whom he had been helped to win his victory. But he was of too crafty and fickle a disposition to be relied upon.

The relations of Church and State in France were passing through a critical period. A great cleavage was already in process. The Pragmatic Sanction, arbitrarily enforced by the monarchy, had lowered the vitality of the French Church. The Holy See was pressing keenly for its abrogation.

The tension between king and Pope tended to lessen the rôle and the prestige of the Valois in Italy. The Holy See had entered into the league formed by Milan, Venice, Florence, and Alfonso of Aragon to counter the ambition of the French king and the Dukes of Orleans and Anjou. It was a question whether the era of French expansion in Italy had not come to an end.

Royal diplomacy had shewn itself inert in Spain, where the Aragonese monarchy seemed threatened with dismemberment. Eastwards, however, it was fully alive; its efforts, directed against Burgundy, made war in this quarter inevitable, and dark clouds were beginning to gather over Liège and the Upper Rhine.

The power of Burgundy was asserted even in the domain of arts and letters. The Court of Philip the Good was more magnificent, and gave a warmer welcome to writers and artists, than that of Charles VII. There was a Burgundian literature, and the Flemish-Burgundian art had attained so splendid a position and exercised a hegemony so incontestable that native French art was almost stifled in its growth. The intellectual orientation of France seemed to depend on the fate of the Burgundian dynasty.

Louis XI resolved only a portion of these grave problems. But it is certainly to him, and to his personal initiative, that must be attributed the great advantages gained by the monarchy during the twenty-two years of his most eventful reign; it is similarly to him that must be assigned the responsibility for the faults that were committed. There is not a single king at the end of the Middle Ages who has impressed so strongly the stamp of his personality upon government and policy.

Louis XI, the son of Charles VII and Mary of Anjou, was born on 3 July 1423, at a time when the King of England was ruling over practically the whole of the north of France, from the valley of the Meuse to the bay of Mont-Saint-Michel. He had passed his childhood in Berry and Touraine, in circumstances of great anxiety and distress for the royal family, which sometimes found itself entirely unprovided with money. Brought up by a tutor of good sense, he received a solid education and at an early age acquired habits of simplicity and reflection which played their part in the formation of his individuality. From the age of sixteen he took a large share in affairs, and from 1439 to 1445 was employed on important missions; everywhere he shewed himself active, courageous, and shrewd. But he was of an intriguing and unruly disposition, and in 1440 he took part in the *Praguerie*; the king's counsellors and the king himself distrusted him. After the death of the Dauphine Margaret of Scotland, for whom Charles VII had a warm affection, the differences between them became accentuated. Louis, exiled to Dauphiné, governed there for ten years as an independent sovereign, married, in spite of his father, the daughter of the Duke of Savoy, countered the policy of Charles VII in every quarter, and intrigued with all the enemies of the French royal house; finally, believing that his father desired his death, he fled to the Duke of Burgundy, there to await the death of the king.

When this event, which he was not ashamed to desire quite openly and with a cynical impatience, gave him the throne of France, Louis was thirty-eight years old. He was furnished with a wide experience of life and of men, was accustomed to hard work, and scornful of the futilities of chivalry in which the princes then wasted their time; but he was devoured by endless ambitions and violent rancours, which he purposed immediately to gratify.

One of the people who hated him most, Bishop Thomas Basin, declared that it was very difficult to draw a character-sketch of Louis XI, since he abounded in contradictions. One reason for this complexity of character was certainly his physical constitution; it often played tricks with his judgment and his will. He was ill-favoured and of poor physique, suffered from frequent illness, and was plagued by a skin disease which was rendered more and more severe by his excesses at table. At the end of his life he imagined that he was a leper[1]. It seems proved that he was epileptic and that, at any rate from 1467 onwards, he suffered from malaria and all the ailments which that disease brings in its train. Louis XI, therefore, was a neuropath. His nervous disorder found expression in idle chatter which spared nobody and often cost him dear, or again in a craving for movement, which sometimes launched him on long hunting expeditions, most exhausting for his entourage, and sometimes caused him to undertake at top speed a journey across his kingdom. He was on edge, suspicious, wished to manage everything, and interfered in even the most trifling matters. There was something unhealthy about the extraordinary restlessness of a character so fertile in combinations that his policy was often capricious and confused.

His countless projects were inspired by a high sense of his duties as king. But all means appeared to him to be legitimate. In short, he had no moral sense. Very scrupulous in religious observances, he imagined

---

[1] See my article in *Revue historique*, CLVII, 1928, pp. 85–6.

that his prayers and his gifts of piety were all that were required to put him right with Heaven, and that in order to have God and Our Lady and the Saints on his side it was only necessary to pay the price. To extract himself from a mistake or to confound his enemies, as also to overcome an internal ailment, he bought the intercession of the leading personages in Paradise by presents which were calculated by the rank and influence of the recipients as well as by the importance of the boon to be obtained.

The best way to obtain a real knowledge of Louis XI is to read the voluminous collection of his *Letters*, itself only a fragment of a vast correspondence, and the dispatches of the Milanese ambassadors. Commynes, shrewd and clear-sighted though he was, has concealed or omitted so much; Thomas Basin only played the part of a pamphleteer; Chastellain, for all his effort at impartiality, gives us only fragmentary information. But Louis' letters and the ambassadors' dispatches depict the whole man to us. Revealed in the light of his dealings with his correspondents and with the ambassadors of the Duke of Milan, he did not, nor did he wish to, hold people save by interest alone, and he judged them only by the profit he drew from them. He knew how to cajole, to jest familiarly, to play the "gossip;" but he was suspicious, crafty, cruel. There was in him a real baseness of soul, a disgusting delight in lying, tyranny, and vengeance. And yet, out of these documents, in spite of all the cynicism and the brutality so often displayed in them, there emerges one very forcible impression: the aims of this king were grand in their conception, remarkable for their originality, and usually well-judged, and he devoted to them the striking qualities of a true leader of men. He was wonderfully intelligent, alert, supple, and energetic. As a diplomat, he had assimilated the old methods of the "king's servants," and added to them the finesse and the craft which he had learnt in the school of his friends the Italians. As a soldier, he was fond of repeating that he had given proofs of courage and had risked his life, and that he had thus acquired the right of employing his imposing army only when he felt it to be necessary. As an administrator, he had his hand on every part of the machinery of monarchical government, and no person or thing escaped his searching gaze. His very faults, often as they compromised his position, served his ends. His craze to be on the move, to talk with everyone, gave him the opportunity of seeing everything, knowing everything, hearing everything. Never had king so direct a knowledge of his subjects.

So, then, in spite of his defects and his blemishes, he was well shaped to confront the great tasks that awaited him. He had, besides, the good fortune of having as his adversaries men of mediocre ability. Finally, circumstances worked in his favour: the French had had their fill of anarchy and for the most part put their trust in monarchy alone; the "good towns" were devoted to his cause; and, lastly, the petty nobility had no thought of aiding their greater brethren against the king.

However, the first years of his reign were troubled years, and the king came within an ace of destruction. He owed his set-back to his own faults, to his thirst for vengeance, his passion for changing everything, his vexatious tyranny.

On his accession, he discharged a large number of officials, and caused some of the best counsellors of the preceding reign to be arrested, suspecting them of having prejudiced his father against him, though sooner or later he recognised their loyal devotion and used it to his advantage. Men like Pierre de Brézé and Antoine de Chabannes, heroes of the war with the English, were imprisoned for some time. Louis took away the chancery from the upright Guillaume Jouvenel des Ursins to entrust it to Pierre de Morvilliers, a former councillor in the Parlement who had been dismissed for corruption. He gave the office of admiral to Jean de Montauban, who had had to take flight to evade the Duke of Brittany's justice. Louis' former associate in Dauphiné, Jean de Lescun, bastard of Armagnac, became the principal adviser of the new king. He was held to be the "master" of the king, "a second king," yet all the same a person "of great worth." But to have betrayed Charles VII was often sufficient recommendation for Louis' favour. John V of Armagnac and the Duke of Alençon were restored to the possession of their estates.

In every quarter Louis succeeded in creating distrust. Promises of financial reforms which he was unable to realise deceived the middle classes, and led to outbreaks which he savagely repressed. He "reduced to slavery" the clergy of France; this is the statement of Thomas Basin, and it is hardly an exaggeration. For reasons both domestic and foreign he abolished the Pragmatic Sanction on 27 November 1461, only to restore it in full working order again, when he had fallen out with Pope Pius II; but, whatever his relations with the Holy See, he never ceased to bully the clergy. As for the higher nobility, he offended it by his dictatorial manner and by the encroachments of his officials; he scandalised it by his exhibition of contempt for fashion, Court life, and the code of chivalry, and by his refusal to fritter away the royal revenue in idle munificence. He could be lavish with his money, if need be, but only to attain some particular object. Moreover, he detested magnificent festivities and ceremonial functions, and, in his rare moments of leisure and relaxation, he shewed that his tastes were those of a middle-class citizen or country squire who found his chief delight in drinking deep and exchanging spicy anecdotes with his boon companions. So, he did away with costly entertainments, and even suppressed the payments which with Charles VII had been the means of creating a circle of courtiers. He offended the petty nobility by restricting its hunting rights; he even claimed to dispose of rich heiresses in order to provide advantageous marriages for his dependents, and this was naturally a cause of particularly bitter resentment against him.

Among the princes, there was one who seemed to be insured against the designs of the king, both by his power and by the memory of his recent good offices. The Duke of Burgundy had but lately afforded Louis a refuge, and on his accession to the throne had escorted him with great pomp to Paris and there had given magnificent entertainments in his honour. But Louis XI, though capable of recognising most bounteously the services of those whose master he was, kept no account of kindnesses if they were likely to prove an embarrassment to his policy. He at once determined to wrest from the house of Burgundy the important strategic line of the Somme. Philip the Good was growing old, and in 1462 he all but died; the Lords of Croy, in whom he had a blind confidence, had embroiled him with his son Charles the Bold, Count of Charolais. The moment was a favourable one. Through the medium of the Croy lords, which he obtained at a high cost, Louis was enabled in 1463 to repurchase the Somme towns for the price of 400,000 gold crowns, the sum stipulated in the Treaty of Arras. At the same time, by promises of assistance he stirred into flame the smouldering ashes at Liège, where the national party was hostile to the Burgundian protectorate. In the Lorraine region, on which the house of Burgundy kept a covetous eye, he laid claim to the protectorate of Toul and Verdun, and tried to get possession of Metz. Clearly, when it should come to pass that the young Count of Charolais should be reconciled with his father and take the government into his own hands, the king would no longer find things so easy and would have to beware of an opponent who was thirsting for revenge.

At the other end of the kingdom, another feudal house was also asserting its independence. The Duke of Brittany, Francis II (1458–88), regarded himself as sovereign in his duchy and barred its entry to the king's officials. This roused the wrath of Louis XI. King and duke each gave hospitality to refugees who inflamed their mutual hostility: Jean de Montauban, now the favourite of Louis XI, had his counterpart in Odet d'Aydie, who had lost his post as *bailli* after Charles VII's death and had found an asylum in Brittany, and these two were largely responsible for the incidents which led eventually to war. The chief causes of the conflict between Louis XI and Francis II were the question of the English alliance and the assertion of regalian rights over the Church in Brittany. The king insisted on Francis II abandoning his alliance with England, and maintained his right to fill the bishoprics and abbeys of Brittany with his own nominees. Francis shewed no signs of yielding; he sent a procurator to the Roman Court in October 1462, who declared before the Pope and the Sacred College "that the duke was not a subject of the king, and that he would put Englishmen into his country rather than those who were servants and friends of the king." This, indeed, was what he proposed to do.

The house of Bourbon enjoyed no such independence; it had to allow the royal officials to levy taxes within its territories. It had already shewn that its chief object was to enrich itself by the acquisition of important and lucrative posts; and Louis XI alienated Duke John II, his brother-in-law, by depriving him of the government of Guienne.

With the houses of Orleans and Anjou, it would have been easy for Louis to maintain the relations established by Charles VII. The head of each was an old man, Charles of Orleans and King René, both of whom were engrossed in art and poetry rather than in politics; and Charles' life came to a peaceful end on 5 January 1465. But Louis XI offended the most active members of these two houses, the Count of Dunois, bastard of Orleans, and René of Anjou's son John, Duke of Calabria and Lorraine, by the policy which he pursued from 1463 onwards in Italy—a policy of friendship and close alliance with the Duke of Milan, Francesco Sforza, and of neutrality in the peninsula. To the able Milanese envoy, Alberigo Malleta, who was in no small measure responsible for his change of attitude, he declared in April 1464 that it was no longer proper for Frenchmen to have domains in Italy. He enfeoffed Sforza with Genoa and Savona (December 1463), tried to induce Charles of Orleans to sell Asti to the Duke of Milan, and gave no assistance to the Angevins for the reconquest of Naples. The dispatches of the Milanese ambassadors make it possible to assert that the discomfiture of John of Anjou, his intrigues against Louis XI, and their mutual hatred, form the principal reason for the coalition of 1465.

Louis took no account of the ill-feeling aroused by his abandonment of the traditions of his dynasty and by his arbitrary, abrupt, and change-able policy. Abroad as at home, his personality inspired both fear and dislike. Certainly he was right in refusing any longer to play the game of the houses of Orleans and Anjou in Italy, and in repudiating ambitions which diverted France from the true path whereon her security was assured. Very wisely his ambition was limited to the frontier of the Alps Ever since his marriage with Charlotte of Savoy, he had kept a close watch upon Savoyard affairs, had intervened in them, striven to win over the nobles, and taken pains to strike terror into the hearts of the re-fractory, for instance his brother-in-law Philip of Bresse, whom he held prisoner for two years; however, he publicly announced that he had no intention of annexing Savoy—the time, he felt, was not ripe. In Spain on the other hand, he shewed a lack of prudence. He thought the moment propitious for conquest on a grand scale, and he had a covetous eye on the succession, which might soon be expected, to the aged John II of Aragon. Roussillon and Cerdagne, Catalonia, Aragon, Navarre—all the territories accumulated by John II—seemed to him ready to fall into his hands. But here he was confronted with the King of Castile, who like-wise aimed at despoiling John II, and in this way he compromised a traditional alliance. He was confronted, too, with the spirit of independence of the Catalans, and he attempted to coax them in vain. Above all, he was confronted with the ability and energy of John II, who revealed himself as a statesman of the first order. The audacious cynicism with which Louis employed in turn intimidation, violence, and cajolery, and shifted from one alliance to another, did, indeed, achieve the annexation, under the form of a pledge, of Roussillon and Cerdagne in 1463, but it ruined his influence in Spain. Towards England, too, he shewed a similar lack of prudence. He tried to rekindle the Wars of the Roses. He made an enemy of his former friend, Edward IV, by supplying Margaret of Anjou with a small army. The expedition was a failure: he had hoped at least to recover Calais; his only harvest was a crop of animosities.

Such was the dangerous condition of affairs when the League of "the Public Weal" was formed against Louis XI. An Anglo-German coalition might well have come into being again and joined forces with the coalition of French feudatories, as at the time of the battle of Bouvines; and there was a new peril for France, the Spanish peril, already looming on the horizon. Fortunately, the indolent Edward IV, letting slip the opportunity both to strengthen his hold on the throne and to make conquests in France, granted Louis a truce until 1468; Charles the Bold's alliances with the German princes only produced a few troops of mercenaries; John II of Aragon had his hands full with the Catalan revolt; and the Count of Foix, Gaston IV, heir-presumptive to Navarre, remained faithful to Louis XI and kept the whole of the South at peace. The only foreign prince to intervene effectively was Louis' friend, Sforza; he lent Louis a small but efficient contingent under the command of his own son.

But all the same the League of the Public Weal was a formidable ordeal for the monarchy. The revolt, which lasted from March to October 1465, was, properly speaking, only the beginning of a long struggle which Louis had to maintain against the higher feudality, especially against the princes of the blood, until 1477. But the League of the Public Weal, which included a section of the clergy, of the bourgeoisie, and of the holders of office, was an event of particular significance; it is also rendered especially interesting to us, since light is thrown on it by a mass of documents, which enable us to obtain a clear picture of the attitude of the different classes within the nation.

On both sides appeal was made to public opinion. Manifestoes, letters, declarations of the princes, confessions of prisoners reveal the grievances alleged by the members of the League, their demands, and their political intentions. In the main, the responsibility for "the exactions, oppressions, wrongs, and other countless ills done to churches and nobles as well as to the poor and lowly folk" was attributed to five or six persons who had been in the king's entourage since his accession, who were not acquainted, it was said, with the business of the kingdom, and who had no outlook other than their own personal interest; the people aimed at were those who had been at Louis' side when he was dauphin and whom he had loaded with favours, such as the Bastard of Armagnac. But the king himself, though no one dared openly to say so, was the real object of the hatred of the feudality. He had not only frustrated their ambitions and

galled their pride. He appeared to them as a traitor and an enemy to all
that they held dear. It was at once both the spirit of regional independence
and the spirit of feudalism, of chivalry, that were in revolt against him.
Georges Chastellain, the honest and impartial historiographer of Philip the
Good and Charles the Bold, declared himself to be "a good Frenchman,"
but he held it as intolerable that the noble house of Burgundy should be
threatened with ruin by the monarchy. This same Chastellain regarded
Louis XI as a disloyal lord, who merited no longer the fidelity of his subjects;
in ballads composed on the eve of the war by him and by Jean Meschinot,
the king is depicted as a man treacherous and deceitful, who "loves silver
better than the love of his subjects," is full of vain promises, cannot endure
a powerful neighbour, picks a quarrel with everyone, and respects no man's
right. The illustrious Dunois, in a speech he made to the Paris deputies in
August 1465, openly accused the king of being a tyrant and of aiming at
reducing the nobility to servitude: "he had made alliance with the Duke
of Milan and other foreigners to destroy all the noble houses of France,
especially the houses of Orleans, Brittany, Burgundy, and Bourbon. He
caused numerous persons to be married into an estate unequal to their
own, to the great dishonour and displeasure of the said persons"; he aimed
at controlling everything by himself alone, and refused to convoke the
Three Estates of the Realm. In the manifestoes he was charged with
oppressing and molesting churchmen, with allowing the exactions and
false judgments of the men of law, with levying intolerable taxes from the
poor people. In consequence, it was proposed to prevent him from doing
harm in future. The rumour was current that it was intended to crown
the king's brother Monsieur Charles, the Duke of Berry, at Rheims, that
the king was to be kept in perpetual confinement and allowed to go out
only to hunt from time to time; but the general opinion was that no more
would be done than the putting of order into his government, "for that
he was king and could not be displaced[1]." Various projects were put
forward. There was talk of making the Duke of Berry regent, as a figurehead for an oligarchic government. The dukes were to divide between
them the government of the provinces in the royal domain. They were
to receive large pensions. At the same time there was talk of the abolition
of the taxes, though no explanation was given as to how these contradictions were to be reconciled. Dunois declared to the Paris deputies that
the princes demanded to have "the receiving, the handling, and the control of all the finances of the realm, and to have in their power and
governance all the army of the realm; *item*, they demanded to have the
knowledge and the distribution of all the offices of the realm; *item*, they
demanded to have the person of the king and the governance of the same;
item, they demanded that the town of Paris should be handed over and

---

[1] Interrogatory of the brothers Meriaudeau at Paris in July 1465 (Stein, *Charles de France*, pièce justif. VI).

delivered to them, and that all their demands should be adjudged to them by the Three Estates of the Realm."

The grievances, the demands, the designs for an aristocratic government, the promises to restore its liberty to the Church and to lighten the burden of the poorer classes, recall the very similar attempts of the English nobles to seize power, notably in the time of Henry III. But what the Leaguers lacked in 1465 was a leader. They had not among them a Simon de Montfort or even a Gilbert de Clare. Monsieur Charles, whom they pushed to the front, was a feeble creature who was to die prematurely of syphilis. Francis II of Brittany and Charles the Bold were not anxious so much to share in the government as to be left independent in their own principalities; moreover, they were mediocre statesmen, and the same is true of John of Anjou and the Duke of Bourbon. The men of real ability were not princes and so could not direct the policy of the League: for instance Dunois, Antoine de Chabannes, and the ingenious Odet d'Aydie, whom Louis XI eventually took into his service, in the same year (1472) that he recruited Philippe de Commynes. But what constituted the chief difference between the English revolts in the thirteenth century and the French attempt in 1465 was the fact that the clergy took practically no part in the latter. They confined themselves in the main to organising processions on behalf of the re-establishment of peace. The application of the Pragmatic Sanction and the despotic regime which Louis XI substituted for it had filled the bishoprics with supporters of the monarchy. Only three bishops openly declared themselves against the king: the Bishop of Puy, a bastard of the house of Bourbon, and two bishops of a particularly intractable province, Normandy; the most famous of the two, Thomas Basin, had no pretensions to leadership; he was not a Stephen Langton. The nobility did not have the advantage of the lofty inspiration and the guiding counsels of a great Churchman, capable of a consistent policy and able to hold in check the selfish aims of individuals.

The figure of Thomas Basin, however, and his ideas deserve a brief consideration. He came from a bourgeois family of Caudebec. Made Bishop of Lisieux in the period of English domination, he was the first Norman bishop to hand over his town to the French. He was a counsellor of Charles VII. He composed a memoir for the rehabilitation of Joan of Arc, and another, after Louis' accession, on the reforms that were most urgent, at the request of the king himself, who, however, had no liking for him. The high-handed treatment of the clergy and the arbitrary acts of the king drove him into opposition. There is nothing novel in the ideas expressed by him in his partisan *Histoire du roi Louis XI* and in his *Apologia*, but for that very reason they are thoroughly interesting, for they shew the continuity in the point of view of the Church. They are the same ideas that were formerly expressed by all the great prelates of the Middle Ages, and are imbued with the spirit of the Church's attitude towards the secular power. Kings have no claim to obedience unless they govern in conformity with the divine law, take counsel of the clergy, respect the customs, and in particular the rights of the Church in matters judicial and financial. When Basin speaks of "liberty," he means "privileges." He was horrified by a prince who scoffed at all tradition and wished to have the clergy at his beck and call—in fact, a "tyrant." Insurrection is justified against "a ruler who, so to say, is insane and does not govern by the advice of good and wise men, but destroys and brings all to ruin, despoils the citizens of their patrimony at his pleasure and without lawful judgment, and exiles men who have deserved well of the republic; suppresses the liberty of the Church and the honour due to ecclesiastics; forces women whether of noble birth or not, contrary to all right and against their will and that of their family, to marry the men that he wishes." "It is said that the princes and their adherents are subjects and vassals, and have not the right to take arms against their lord and king. But to those who say this I ask: if they were in a ship the captain of which, through lack of skill or malicious design, was about to lose his ship and run it on a shoal, ought not those who are with him, even though they were his slaves, to remonstrate with him and, if he were so foolish as to scorn their exhortations, to restrain him? We think that, provided they were not themselves insane, they would have to let the crew take the helm from him, and if necessary, for the common safety, tie him up or treat him more rigorously still[1]." Here we have the doctrine of regicide, the doctrine of John of Salisbury in the twelfth century and of Jean Petit in the fifteenth. It contains exaggerations common to speculative writers, it has the tricks of rhetoric and a touch of insincerity. But the murder of Louis of Orleans fifty years before had been justified by similar arguments. It was not quite without reason that Louis XI was all his life afraid of assassination. There would always have been people ready to assert that in the sight of God the act was just and reasonable.

In the ranks of the opposition, it was the holders of office, or some among them at any rate, whose views most nearly coincided with those expressed by Thomas Basin: for instance, François Hallé, who was one of the most important members of the Council. The reign of Charles VII had been a reign of the king's servants. They it was who governed then, and they did so not only in the gratification of their own pride and personal interests, but also with the feeling that they were bringing back the old prosperous traditions, which transcended their private inclinations, and were creating the liberties of the kingdom; they continued to work out a constitution which, uncodified though it was and dispersed among various *Ordonnances* and decisions at law, was a living entity with binding powers. In their eyes Louis XI was a dangerous revolutionary. In the

---

[1] *Histoire de Louis XI*, Bk II, ch. 3 (Tome II, pp. 109–111).

Parlement of Paris, the Châtelet, the Chambre des Comptes, the League found partisans. But the majority of those in office were afraid, and kept their opinions to themselves.

The petty nobility for the most part refused to withdraw their allegiance from the king. The workers in the towns saw that they would gain nothing from having several kings in place of one. The commercial bourgeoisie were not of one mind: Bordeaux, Lyons, and even Amiens, shewed themselves loyalist; other towns, in fear, or perhaps with grudges of their own to settle, opened their gates to the rebels, especially in Normandy. Paris was divided in its sympathies; and it needed all the energy of the Provost of the Merchants, Henri de Livres, to prevent the popularity formerly enjoyed by the Dukes of Burgundy from coming to life once more. During the whole of Louis XI's reign, there was ill-feeling between the king and the Parisians.

The whole issue in 1465 depended on whether the princes would act in unison, and would succeed in laying hands on the capital. They did not begin the war together, and Louis, at the head of a compact army of 30,000 men, was easily able to overwhelm the Duke of Bourbon, who had started too soon. But from July to September the situation became most critical for the king. The Duke of Burgundy, Philip the Good, restrained for a long time by his scruples as vassal, had grown old, worn out by a life of pleasure, and had abandoned power to his son Charles the Bold; and Charles was enraged at Louis' alliance with the people of Liège and wished to bring matters to a head. The two armies met south of Paris, at Montlhéry, on 15 July. Louis failed to crush the Burgundian forces or to prevent their junction with those of his brother, of the Duke of Brittany, and of John of Anjou. He retired back to Paris, where he passed some days in despair, as we learn from the dispatches of the Milanese ambassador Panigarola. He contemplated flight to Dauphiné, where the nobles were faithful to him. His counsellors, terrified, dared give him no advice; some of them turned traitor. Defections increased. At last, he decided to negotiate.

Peace was concluded at Conflans and at Saint-Maur-les-Fossés in October 1465. "Never was wedding-feast so grand," says Philippe de Commynes, "but that some folk dined ill; some had all they wished, and others had nothing." The Duke of Nemours gained practically nothing by his treason, save the hatred of his master. But the king's brother Monsieur Charles and Charles the Bold were loaded with gains. Charles the Bold obtained the Somme towns and the counties of Guines, Péronne, Montdidier, Roye etc., while his friend, the treacherous Count of Saint-Pol, received the sword of Constable of France; the Liégeois, abandoned by the king, were forced to accept a humiliating peace. The king's brother received, in place of his meagre duchy of Berry, the splendid duchy of Normandy, which, lying between Brittany and the Burgundian territories, now intercepted communications between the royal domain and the Channel; this made it possible for the English king, if occasion arose, to come to the aid of the princes against the King of France.

Louis XI was beaten. For a long time peace vanished from the kingdom. Bands of mercenaries remaining under arms were everywhere pillaging the countryside, while waiting for the inevitable re-opening of civil war.

Louis had, indeed, no intention of keeping his word. During the seven years that elapsed before the death of his brother, he strove hard to prevent Monsieur Charles from keeping any dangerous appanage, to wrest the Somme towns from Charles the Bold, and to make head against difficulties of every kind, with an energy and an ingenuity which were sometimes defeated by his excess of self-confidence. The events of this period are extraordinarily complex. Here it must suffice to give an impression of the perils the monarchy had to face and the policy which Louis XI adopted to meet them.

In the month of December 1465 Louis profited by a revival of the old enmity between Bretons and Normans to recover Normandy, "the chief jewel in the Crown." He began to undermine on every side the power of the new Duke of Burgundy (for Philip the Good died on 15 June 1467). The "king's servants" resumed their practice of persistent provocation; they contested the right which the duke had arrogated to himself of judging without appeal and of raising taxes and troops in his domains. Finally, they persuaded the Liégeois to take up arms again. More important still was the question of alliance with the Duke of Brittany and of alliance with Edward IV; for both of these Louis XI and Charles the Bold competed with one another. It was the Duke of Burgundy who won: a Breton army invaded Normandy in 1467, and on 3 July 1468 Margaret, Edward IV's sister, married Charles the Bold. In this grave crisis a speedy stroke was necessary to get the better of the coalition. Louis adopted a principle of strategy which was thoroughly successful on this occasion and again at a later date: he directed his main effort to overwhelm at once the Duke of Brittany, who was easier to deal with, and forced him to accept the peace of Ancenis (10 September 1468). As for Charles the Bold, Louis decided to go himself with a small escort to the place where Charles then was, Péronne, relying simply on a safe conduct from his adversary.

The journey to Péronne is one of the most characteristic facts in the history of Louis XI, and shews clearly that he was not at all the man of unfailing prudence, who chose out every step with caution and calculation, that he has been made out to be in literature. He was of a feverish temperament, and had in him something of the gambler who trusts to his lucky star. He had complete confidence in his ability to submerge distrust in a flood of honeyed phrases, to cajole, and to seduce; was he not known as "the siren[1]"? On the other hand, he despised Charles the Bold, and regarded him, not without reason, as a fool. He said to Malleta,

[1] Molinet, *Chronique*, Vol. ii, p. 61.

mimicking the passionate gestures of Charles: "He is a man of little worth and little sense, arrogant and wrathful; he is only a brute (*una bestia*)[1]." He expected to win him over, if he could have a talk with him. But on his arrival at Péronne, on 9 October 1468, he learnt of the presence of several of his worst enemies, and he began to regret the step he had taken. Negotiations were opened on his behalf by Cardinal Balue, but they met with an obstacle at once in Charles' refusal to recognise the recovery of Normandy. Louis decided that the game was lost, and on 11 October he made preparations to depart. But "the spider[2]," so clever at spinning a web, had made a slip this time. "The king," says Commynes, "in coming to Péronne, had not considered that he had sent two ambassadors to the Liégeois to rouse them against the duke, which ambassadors had already shewn such diligence that they had done great business." The Liégeois had forcibly brought their bishop back into the town, and had killed some of his adherents. The news of these events had been greatly exaggerated, and some distraught folk arrived at Péronne on the evening of 11 October, crying that the Bishop of Liège and the ducal governor had been massacred at the instigation of the emissaries of Louis XI. Charles the Bold, without pausing to verify the facts, caused the gates of the castle where Louis was lodging to be barred. Commynes, who was then in Charles' personal service, was present, and has left us a famous description of what took place. What he does not tell us is whether Balue, who was directed by the king to divide 15,000 gold crowns among the Burgundians who "might be of aid to him," did or did not forget him in the distribution. It is probable that Commynes received 1000 or 1500 crowns, and it is certain that 2000 went to the powerful Bastard of Burgundy, Antoine. The duke let himself be persuaded that he could not violate a safe conduct, and he consented to see the king. He adopted a humble attitude, but his voice trembled with rage. Louis accepted his conditions. The gravest clause in the treaty concluded at Péronne was the stipulation that the "four laws of Flanders," the tribunals of Ghent, Ypres, Bruges, and the district of Bruges, should cease to be within the jurisdiction of the Parlement of Paris. The king made a verbal engagement to give Champagne, which was adjacent to the Burgundian State, to his brother, and he promised to assist the duke in punishing the Liégeois.

On 30 October the Burgundian troops entered Liège. Olivier de la Marche, an eye-witness, describes how Louis XI followed the duke and cried: "Long live Burgundy!" The town of Liège was kept burning for seven weeks; everything except the churches was destroyed. Louis returned to France affecting a calm air of satisfaction and of close attachment to the Duke of Burgundy. In reality, as Chastellain says, "he hated Duke Charles with a deadly venom." Everywhere his humi-

---

[1] *Dépêches des ambassadeurs milanais*, Vol. i, p. 361.
[2] Chastellain, Bk. vii, pp. 207–9 and p. 208 *n*.

liation and the triumph of the house of Burgundy were the common talk.

Louis was not discouraged; he immediately set to work to make the conventions of Péronne as null as the treaty of Conflans. Commynes says that he was the wisest man that he had known "at drawing himself out of a blunder in time of adversity." Louis took as his model his dead friend Sforza, who, he said, "never retreated when he had missed his mark, and put forth all his energy when the flood was up to his chin[1]." For several years he was to exert the desperate efforts of a drowning man. He had enemies everywhere, even in his immediate circle. As he never gave preference to honesty, and willingly employed men with a stain or a crime on their character provided they were men of intelligence, no king was so often betrayed as he. He had to get rid of his friend, Cardinal Balue, and also of another intriguing bishop, Guillaume de Harancourt; an emissary of theirs chanced to be caught when on his way to the Duke of Burgundy. To avoid trouble with the Holy See, Louis did not bring them to trial, but he kept them in prison for several years. The Count of Armagnac, John V, and the Duke of Alençon, who had both of them won his regard by their betrayal of Charles VII, betrayed him also: John V, accused of "pro-Anglicism" and condemned by the King's Council in 1469, was deprived of his estates and fled to Spain; his brother, Charles of Armagnac, was shut up in the Bastille (1471) and made to undergo a captivity atrocious in its severity; the Duke of Alençon was for a second time condemned to death (1474) without the sentence being carried out. Louis XI became more and more distrustful. "He thought," writes Commynes, "he did not stand well with all his subjects...and, if I dared say all, he has told me many a time that he knew his subjects well, and that he would soon be made aware of it, if his business was faring ill."

Louis succeeded, in 1469, in inducing his brother to accept the duchy of Guienne in place of Champagne; he also set to work to obtain the alliance of England. It was a question, in his mind, of nothing less than the restoration of the Lancastrian dynasty and of sharing with it the spoils of the Burgundian house. He profited by the persistent ambition of the dethroned queen, Margaret of Anjou, to reconcile her in July 1470 with Warwick the King-maker, who had recently heaped the vilest abuse upon her. Edward IV, surprised by a sudden invasion, fled to the Court of Charles the Bold. King Louis, says Chastellain, "was bathed in roses." To the unhappy Henry VI, now restored to the throne, he proposed the dismemberment of the Burgundian territories. His troops invaded Picardy and Burgundy (1470–71). The end of the adventure is well known: Edward IV, furnished with ships and men by Charles the Bold, was victorious at Barnet and Tewkesbury; Warwick, Henry VI's son, and lastly Henry VI himself, perished in turn (April–May 1471). Edward IV

[1] *Dépêches des ambassadeurs milanais*, Vol. ii, p. 306.

immediately planned vengeance on Louis. At the same time, the King of Aragon, enraged by the behaviour of Louis XI, who had supported the claims of the house of Anjou to Catalonia (1466–70), formed a coalition against him, and found allies for himself and for the Duke of Burgundy in Italy and in the South of France. Gaston IV, Count of Foix, whom Louis XI had alienated by trying to lay hands on Navarre, gave his daughter in marriage to the Duke of Brittany. John V of Armagnac returned to France, recovered his estates, raised an army, and invaded the Toulousain. Monsieur Charles, who had been warmly received in Guienne, was frightened by the threats of his brother, who surrounded him with spies, and he endeavoured to obtain the hand of the Duke of Burgundy's daughter. Furthermore, a rising fomented by the King of Aragon broke out in Roussillon in April 1472 against French domination.

The death of Monsieur Charles (24 May 1472), the cleverness of Louis XI, who contrived to obtain a succession of overlapping truces from his adversaries, and the military incompetency of Charles the Bold, combined to save the king. The Burgundian campaign of 1472 was characteristic: the Duke of Burgundy was incapable of taking the small town of Beauvais; its inhabitants, women as well as men, defended themselves with fury, for they knew that the inhabitants of Nesle had just been massacred; a girl of the people, Jeanne Laisné, during an assault tore a banner from the Burgundians—at Beauvais they still talk of "Jeanne Hachette." The duke had taken no care to provide himself with supplies, and he was forced to ask for a fresh truce (3 November 1472). The Duke of Brittany, against whom Louis had directed his own forces, was himself obliged to lay down his arms. In the South, the deaths of the Duke of Guienne and Gaston IV had disorganised the coalition. John V of Armagnac, who had entrenched himself at Lectoure, had to capitulate, and lost his life in a minor affray. His lordship was of considerable extent; in order to destroy it for ever, Louis partitioned it among some twenty of his vassals in 1473, retaining regalian rights over the whole. The people of Roussillon did not actually submit until two years later. But, on the whole, the year 1472 marked the end of the period of grave danger. Except for an abortive attempt in 1475, there were to be no more feudal coalitions against Louis XI; practically the issue was resolved into a duel between the monarchy and the house of Burgundy.

It will be told later on[1] how Charles the Bold, particularly from 1472 onwards, strove to create for his house an independent kingdom between France and Germany, to join up the two portions of the Burgundian State, to lay hands on the possessions of Sigismund of Austria in Alsace and on the duchy of Lorraine. As for a crown, he expected to receive that from the Emperor Frederick III; his only child was a daughter, Mary of Burgundy, and he offered her hand to Maximilian, Frederick III's

[1] *Infra*, chapter x.

son; pending the expected union of the two houses, he was himself to have the title of King of the Romans. As far as his relations with the King of France were concerned, his independence was an established fact; after Louis' violation of the treaty of Péronne, Charles no longer acknowledged himself to be a vassal of the king.

To conjure the danger, and to dissolve bit by bit the megalomaniac schemes of the "Grand Duke of the West," Louis XI, with a wealth of experience behind him and with his political genius at its height, adopted a system of playing with his victim, ringing him round, and setting traps for him which his brutish adversary was unable to counter or even to perceive. "He made greater war upon him by letting him go his own way and in secret creating enemies for him," says Commynes, "than if he had openly declared against him." Without compromising himself, he spied upon the relations of Charles with Germany, contracted friendships with the Rhine princes, and contributed to the failure of the conferences at Trèves in 1473 which were designed to arrange for a royal crown for the duke. Finally, he succeeded in forming a coalition against Charles[1]. He had learnt in his youth to appreciate the military value of the Swiss and had long had a pact of friendship with them. Now, though the people of Berne and Lucerne were uneasy at the progress of the house of Burgundy, this uneasiness was not shared by the six other cantons in the Swiss Confederation, who looked on Sigismund of Austria as their one and only enemy; it was Louis' greatest achievement to reconcile them with Sigismund, and to unite the whole Confederation against the Duke of Burgundy. "It was one of the wisest things that he did," says Commynes. In return for a pension from the king, Sigismund recognised the independence of the eight cantons, and they for their part promised him their assistance (*Règlement perpétuel* of 30 March 1474). René II, Duke of Lorraine, the grandson of King René, signed a treaty with the King of France on 15 August 1474, and joined a coalition which included, besides the Swiss and Sigismund, the towns of the Upper Rhine. Louis persuaded the confederates, backed by his troops and above all by his money, to invade the Burgundian territories.

Charles the Bold did not succeed in forming an effective coalition against his adversary. In Italy, Venice was only nominally his ally; Ferrante, King of Naples, and Galeazzo Sforza, two masters in cunning, tacked this way and that; the Duchess of Savoy, Louis XI's sister, would gladly have been revenged on her brother for his treatment of her, but she had not the wherewithal. The King of Aragon, John II, and his son Ferdinand could give no help to the Duke of Burgundy, as they also had to protect themselves against Louis XI. It is true that they got the better of him. The tortuous policy of Louis XI in Spain resulted only in failure. He tried, but too late and without success, to prevent the dangerous marriage of the Infant of Aragon with Isabella,

---

[1] For the relations of Louis with the Swiss, see *supra* Vol. VII, pp. 205 sqq.

sister and heiress of King Henry IV of Castile, in 1469. On the death
of Henry IV in 1474, he hesitated, then recognised Ferdinand and
Isabella, and finally gave his support to the Portuguese claimant, who
failed (1475–76). The mistakes of his Spanish policy were only of indirect assistance to his Burgundian adversary, in that a part of his forces
were absorbed by them. On the side of England, Louis won a great
success. Edward IV and Charles had concluded an alliance for the dismemberment of France on 25 July 1474: the King of England was to
leave Picardy and Champagne in full sovereignty to the duke, and he
himself was to be crowned King of France at Rheims. Edward crossed the
sea without interference, for Louis XI "did not understand the business of
the sea so well as he did the business of the land," and disembarked at
Calais on 4 July 1475; he had a splendid army but no supplies, and he
received no help from either Brittany or Burgundy. Louis made liberal
offers to him, and did not forget to grease the palms of the English
counsellors. For the sum of 75,000 crowns down, the pledge to pay an
annual sum of 50,000 crowns, and the promise of a marriage between the
dauphin and one of Edward's daughters, he obtained a truce for seven
years. The interview at Picquigny on 29 August 1475 was a pattern of
suspicious friendship: the two kings embraced one another through the
openings in a stout wooden grating, on the middle of a bridge.

For Louis XI the English danger was conjured for good, and Charles
the Bold at once consented to a truce for nine years (13 September 1475).
Louis took advantage of this to punish those of his vassals who had
recently betrayed him or whose attitude of neutrality was suspect: the
Duke of Brittany had first to renounce independence of action in his
external relations, and was then made to swear that in future he would
aid the king against his enemies (treaties of 29 September 1475 and
27 July 1477); the Constable of Saint-Pol was executed at Paris on
19 December 1475: the Duke of Nemours was put into a cage in the
Bastille, was tortured, and finally executed in 1477; the Duke of Bourbon
was forced to surrender the Beaujolais, which linked up his domain with
Burgundy, to his brother the Sire de Beaujeu, the king's son-in-law
(April 1476). King René had entered into compromising negotiations with
the Duke of Burgundy; he was summoned to appear before the Parlement
of Paris, and Louis XI talked of having his counsellor, Gaspard Cossa,
"thrown in a sack into the river." To make his peace, the aged King of
Sicily had to swear, in April 1476, never to ally himself with the Duke
of Burgundy.

Louis had promised Charles the Bold that he would not assist the
Swiss or the Duke of Lorraine if they made war on Burgundy. Actually,
he never ceased to support them with his money and his backing. He
prevented the Swiss from coming to terms with Charles, and he was at
Lyons, all ready to intervene, at the time that they inflicted on the duke
the disastrous defeats of Grandson and Morat. Lorraine had been con-

quered by the Duke of Burgundy; Louis provided Duke René II with money to enrol Swiss mercenaries, and thus contributed to the third great defeat of Charles the Bold, who on this occasion perished in the flight, at Nancy on 5 January 1477. On the news of this, Louis had such an outburst of joy that he "hardly knew how to restrain himself."

The Burgundian State was exhausted of men and money. In vain did Charles' daughter and heiress, Mary of Burgundy, the god-daughter of Louis XI, appeal to the "kindness and clemency" of her godfather. He was determined to annex to the royal domain all the French domains of the late duke, and in addition Hainault and Franche Comté, which were held from the Empire. The royal lawyers had long asserted that the Count of Hainault was a vassal of the King of France, and in respect of Franche Comté Louis replied to the protests of Frederick III that Duke Charles had never done homage to the Emperor. Finally, he proposed to hand over Brabant and Holland to German princes who would be his allies. It all seemed quite simple for him. "If he had not thought his work so easy of accomplishment, and if he had relaxed somewhat his passion and the vengeance he desired against the house of Burgundy, without doubt he would to-day be holding all this lordship under his control." This was the very just opinion of Commynes, and he advised the king to consent to a form of protectorate; he was not listened to, and was dismissed into exile in Poitou. Louis conducted the war without pity and with powerful forces at his disposal. Maximilian had assembled a large army, and the battle of Guinegate, near St Omer, on 7 August 1479 was indecisive. Louis raised the *Compagnies d'ordonnance* to the total of 4000 lances, recruited 6000 mercenaries among his friends the Swiss, and organised troops of pikemen on the Swiss model. He created the most powerful artillery force yet known. He established great camps at Pont-de-l'Arche and Hesdin. His military expenses, which did not reach a million livres *tournois* in 1470, now almost exceeded three million. Resistance was overcome with atrocious brutality. The town of Dôle was burnt to the ground. The inhabitants of Arras were all expelled, the town evacuated, and Louis took the step of forcing every town in France to send a contingent of artisans and merchants to people it again; this was one of the most striking examples of the senseless tyranny that he sometimes displayed.

His brutality had one unfortunate consequence for France: Mary of Burgundy, driven to desperation, had bestowed her hand upon the young Maximilian, Archduke of Austria, on 19 August 1477. This was the origin of the establishment of the house of Austria in the Low Countries. Mary died on 27 March 1482, and it was Maximilian who signed the peace of Arras with Louis XI on 23 December following. The Burgundian State was dismembered for good and all. Flemish and Walloon Flanders and the Low Countries reverted to Maximilian, though without any change in the frontiers of the kingdom, since Flanders as far as

Ghent remained a fief of the French Crown and subject to the jurisdiction of the Parlement of Paris. The duchy of Burgundy was annexed to the royal domain. Louis also kept Franche Comté and Artois, though only as the dowry of his future daughter-in-law, Margaret of Austria, who was betrothed to the dauphin. Finally, he recovered Picardy and the Somme towns, and obtained the Boulonnais by exchange. To make sure that the English would not try to take Boulogne from him, he declared, with that mixture of cunning and superstition which was one of his characteristic traits, that he held Boulogne as a fief from Our Lady.

By the death of King René, followed by that of his nephew the Count of Maine (1480–81), the domain of the Crown was further enriched by the duchies of Anjou and Bar, the county of Maine, and finally the county of Provence with Marseilles and Toulon. So little by little the way was being paved for the advancing of the frontier to the Alps. The Holy See held Avignon and the Comtat; but in Louis XI's day the protectorate exercised by the French kings over the Papal States in France had become more and more rigid. Savoy was not annexed, but Louis adopted the tone of a master there; he had overcome the feeble efforts at independence of his sister Yolande, the regent of the duchy.

The absorption of the newly annexed provinces was rapidly on the way to accomplishment by the time that Louis was nearing his end. Even Roussillon, thanks to the prudent administration of Boffille de Juges, made no further move. Louis had learnt wisdom from experience, and he retained in Burgundy most of the officials of Charles the Bold.

Except for the Duke of Brittany, who disregarded his oath and resumed his former attitude of hostility, all the great vassals bowed and trembled before Louis XI. Their pensions, usually of ten to twelve thousand livres, and their fear kept even the princes of the blood from a lapse. "There was no one so great in his kingdom," wrote Jean de Roye, secretary to the Duke of Bourbon, "that could sleep or rest securely in his house." René of Anjou, who in spite of his title of king and his vast domains was no better than a pensioned prince, said in 1476 of his formidable cousin: "the King of France can do all that he wills, and he has the habit of doing it[1]." Louis of Orleans (the future Louis XII) had been constrained by force to marry one of the king's daughters, Joan of France, who was deformed and incapable of bearing children. Louis XI reckoned on the extinction of the house of Orleans and said cynically: "their children will not cost them much to keep." The Duke of Bourbon was deprived of his judicial prerogatives; "Grands Jours" were instituted at Montferrand to try important cases. In the South, Alain the Great, Sire of Albret, a grim old fighter, had long ago been reduced to docility. One of the king's sisters, Madeleine, who had married a son of Gaston of Foix, was regent of the county of Foix as well as of the kingdom of Navarre, and Cardinal Pierre de Foix, an agent of Louis, assisted her in

[1] Arnaud d'Aguel, *Politique des rois de France en Provence*, Vol. II, P. J. no. 4, p. 8.

the government. In the duchy of Alençon, the resistance of the ducal officials to the king's servants was overcome; René, the son of the traitor, was imprisoned in consequence of some youthful misdemeanour and endured a terrible captivity in an iron cage.

Abroad, Louis had surmounted his difficulties or postponed them. He had continued his annual payments to Edward IV and succeeded in keeping England neutral during the Burgundian wars. Neither the English merchants, however, nor the counsellors of Edward IV could look on unmoved when French troops were in occupation of the shores of the North Sea. Louis had, indeed, offered to share with Edward IV the spoils of Charles the Bold. But the offer was not a serious one. To gain time, he kept up the farce for several years. Even the treaty of Arras and Louis' breach of faith when, though he had promised a marriage between the Dauphin Charles and Edward's daughter, he betrothed his son to Margaret of Austria, did not decide Edward to make war. It was, as Commynes maliciously remarks, "the greed for the fifty thousand crowns, paid every year into his castle at London, that deadened his heart." And, later, Louis had caused the Scots once more to invade the Border. The early death of Edward IV on 2 April 1483 and the tragedies which followed made it possible for Louis even to save the expense of the annual payments.

In the east and over the Pyrenees clouds were hovering. Maximilian was only waiting for an opportunity to break the treaty of Arras. Louis started a quarrel with René II of Lorraine by laying hands on the duchy of Bar and by forcibly expelling the troops which the duke had sent to Provence to assert his claim to the succession after King René's death. In Spain, Louis had made peace with Ferdinand and Isabella; but after the death of the aged John II in 1479, the union of Castile and Aragon under two vigorous princes had brought a powerful Spain into being; the question of Roussillon might be reopened; and Ferdinand and Isabella disputed with Louis the protectorate he had assumed over Navarre.

Throughout Christendom, however, the prestige of the King of France stood high. Nowhere was it better assured than in Italy, though it had only been established there by diplomatic measures, except in the case of Venice, which had drawn upon herself a disastrous maritime war (1468–78). The tangle of Italian politics excited a passionate interest in Louis XI, and all his life he enjoyed following its course and putting in his spoke. Since the assassination of the tyrant Galeazzo Sforza he had held the upper hand over the government of Milan. He had succeeded, without the dispatch of a single soldier, in saving the house of the Medici when it was threatened with ruin by Pope Sixtus IV and his ally the King of Naples; he was as practised at reconciling as at creating divisions, and he had reconciled Naples and Florence. The King of France, while abandoning all idea of territorial conquest and sacrificing the claims of his cousins of Anjou and Orleans, had succeeded in wresting from Venice the dominating rôle in Italy. He had become the arbiter and the pacifier of the country.

His policy with regard to the Holy See cannot be detailed in a few lines, so fluctuating was it and so precisely adapted to circumstances. Any account of it must be connected with the history of Louis' general diplomacy and also with the history of the French Church. The king needed papal help to cope with his enemies, and he often found the Pope athwart his plans. Men like Pius II, Paul II, and Sixtus IV were not easy to manage. On the other side, Louis' idea was to have a docile episcopate, to distribute benefices at his pleasure, to oppose the influx of Italian prelates and the outflow of French gold. Neither the Pragmatic Sanction, which he abolished (in 1461 and 1467) and restored by turns, nor an accommodation with the Pope, such as the illusory concordat with Sixtus IV in 1472, gave him complete security. So he constantly intervened in the appointment to benefices, without following any fixed principle. He treated the clergy despotically and used the threat of a General Council to check any move of the Holy See. At the end of his life, he managed to reach an agreement with Sixtus IV upon the collation to benefices; the one was as cynical as the other; they were just the pair to come to an understanding.

A Lancastrian writer, Sir John Fortescue, who wrote in 1468–70 his *De Laudibus Legum Angliae* for the Prince of Wales, then in exile in France, presented the government of Louis XI as a type of despotism. Louis XI, he wrote, oppresses and impoverishes his subjects; he has a standing army which devastates the countryside, he levies taxes at his will, he condemns without form of justice, he has people secretly executed, he commits all kinds of enormities under the guise of the *ius regale*[1].

Louis XI did, in fact, govern as a tyrant; he had the tyrant's disdain for traditional forms and powers, his determination to be obeyed without question by his officials, his hatred of the aristocracy, his care to have servants under him ready to do anything, to have a docile middle class on which to depend, and finally to enrich it so as to become rich through it.

Innovator though he was, however, when it came to the justification of his authority he professed with sincerity the same ideas as his predecessors. "The Kings of France alone," declared an ambassador whom he had sent to the Pope, "are anointed with a holy oil sent by the Father of Lights, and carry on their escutcheon the lilies, gifts from Heaven; alone they are resplendent with miracles manifest." In consequence, said Louis XI, "because of our sovereignty and our royal majesty, to us alone belongs and is due the general government and administration of the realm." In return, the king ought to sacrifice

[1] *De Laudibus,* chap. xxv.

himself for the good of all. In the *Rosier des Guerres*, written by Pierre Choisnet, the king's doctor and astrologer, for the education of the dauphin, it is stated that the prince exists only for the public weal, that he ought to know everything and watch over everything himself. Commynes remarked that in fact, in the life of his master, "there would be found full twenty days of pain and toil to one of pleasure and ease."

One who connected so closely his rights with his duties could not be disposed to isolate himself away from his subjects. It was only at the end of his life that Louis, a sick man, acquired a taste for solitude and for impulsive decisions. Till then he had been careful not to under-estimate the force of public opinion or even the advantage of consulting it. When the League of the Public Weal was formed, he sent skilfully worded and most persuasive manifestoes to the provinces. All his life he kept up an active correspondence with such towns as Lyons; to preserve his popularity with them, he sent them "communiqués" on all the great events, the information being accommodated to his own desires. Like Charles V, he often called meetings of assemblies. He summoned the princes of the blood and a certain number of nobles in 1464, to expose to them his grievances against the Duke of Brittany. He did not negotiate with the Leaguers in 1465 until he had consulted "the great and wise men of all conditions." It was by an assembly of the Three Estates in April 1468 at Tours that he had it decided that Normandy ought not to have been alienated in favour of Monsieur Charles, and that the concession was null and void. At Tours again, in 1470, an assembly released him from the treaty of Péronne. On several occasions he consulted assemblies of merchants and notables. In 1479, for example, deputies of "the good towns" debated at Paris the question of the circulation of foreign currency and the measures to prevent the flight of French money from the country[1]. But the meeting of 1468 alone had the character of an assembly of the Three Estates. It was made up of nobles, of representatives of the clergy, and of laymen elected by sixty-four of the good towns; the official report mentions twenty-eight lords and 192 deputies. In 1470 there were only about sixty participants: a few nobles and loyal prelates, with a majority of counsellors and officials; it was a meeting similar to the *Cours non générales* under the Capetians. The competency of these assemblies was severely restricted to the object of their summons. It was not a question of providing money for the king, since he dispensed with the practice of consent in the raising of taxes. When, in 1468, some deputies wished to formulate their grievances and to speak of the judicial abuses and financial extravagance, Louis came in person to remind them "gently and kindly" that the subject of their conference was the alienation of Normandy. They obeyed, and asked the king to give a less important appanage to his brother, and for the future

---

[1] *Lettres de Louis XI*, Vol. viii, pp. 4, 19; see also p. 20. *Ordonnances*, Vol. xviii, p. 638.

to proceed against the rebels without convoking the Estates, for it was very difficult for them to respond to the summons.

The provincial and local Estates, where they still existed, continued to vote taxes; but Louis XI, pushing to their extreme the arbitrary practices of his predecessors, often refrained from consulting them, on the pretext that it was necessary to save the province expense; anyhow, their deliberations were only a waste of time, for the king would not brook protests, and the increased rates and extraordinary subsidies which he demanded had to be voted. Sometimes, too, he levied sums above the amount to which consent had been given. Even the Estates of Dauphiné, which had for a long time been intractable, were completely subdued by the end of the reign.

In the main Louis did not interfere with the administrative machinery which had been gradually erected by the monarchy during the three preceding centuries. At the beginning of his reign he set out to make great changes. It was only a short flare up, however. He suppressed the *Cour des aides* at Paris and the *élus*, but he had to restore them. He even created a new *Cour des aides* in Languedoc, and restored the one at Montpellier. What was most characteristic of his attitude towards his subjects was not economy or the repression of abuses, but the aggravation of the bureaucratic system, the increased number of officials, and especially the arbitrary power of the king.

It is true that after the War of the Public Weal he allowed an *Ordonnance* (21 October 1467) to be wrung from him, in which he pledged himself not to appoint to an office "unless it was vacant by death, by voluntary resignation, or by forfeiture previously adjudged after sentence in court of law by a competent judge"; and from this it has been concluded that he established fixity of tenure for office-holders. But he did not respect his pledges. He revoked appointments and arbitrarily dismissed officials if he mistrusted them, or even merely out of caprice; he told Commynes shortly before his death "that he spent his time making and unmaking people, for fear that they should look on him as dead." He was obliged constantly to require the collaboration of the great departments of State, *Conseil, Parlements, Cours des aides, Cour des comptes*, and in his *Ordonnances* he often spoke of their "great and ripe deliberations." Sometimes he even put up with remonstrances or opposition from them, if they were justified in the interests of the Crown. But he was continually humiliating them by thrusting new colleagues upon them who had no qualifications other than that they had rendered a service to the king; a long distance had been travelled since Charles V and the system of election he preached and practised.

Louis exacted hard work from his Council; all kinds of matters were deliberated there. The king's counsellors were very numerous, and great lords sometimes attended the sittings. But the real work was done by a few prelates and nobles of assured loyalty, such as Peter of Beaujeu, the king's son-in-law, by newcomers of modest family like Commynes, and finally by legal and financial experts, among whom figured famous counsellors of Charles VII who had been retained by Louis XI at his accession or recalled later on, such as Étienne Chevalier. Further, the Council could be reconstituted in a limited number of sections for special purposes. Under Louis XI there was a Council of secret affairs, a Council of finance, and a Great Council dealing with religious and judicial matters.

Louis XI created royal Parlements in three newly acquired provinces, at Bordeaux, Perpignan, and Dijon. He often spoke of reforming the administration of justice, which was causing many complaints. But what he actually did hardly tended to improvement, since he took upon himself to demand from the judges the sentences that he desired. Affronted by the independent attitude of the Parlement of Paris, he removed from its cognisance most of the political suits, which were numerous throughout his reign, and he would not admit of the councillors in the Parlement, when sitting on extraordinary commissions, following their own inclinations; some of them were dismissed, some even imprisoned. He talked of "purging the Court." To lessen its importance he gave greater weight to the judicial committee of the Council, giving it the competency in all suits in which the Crown had an interest. Finally, he often exercised his right of personal justice, for instance, by instructing his famous Provost of the Marshals of France, Tristan Lhermite, to interrupt a trial for treason and summarily execute the prisoner, or by a brutal repression of rioting.

During this reign, regional and local officials became increasingly numerous and powerful. Governors and deputy governors, seneschals, bailiffs, provosts, *élus*, *receveurs des finances*, and the like, were all formidable personages. The posts were much coveted, and Louis was besieged with applications. The characteristics of office under the Crown, as such offices continued to be up to the French Revolution, tended to become fixed: frequent purchase of offices, security of tenure, retention in the same family, profits made at the expense of the local population, and the privilege of exemption from taxation. The official was both greedy and aggressive; he laboured to ruin neighbouring powers, but he often went too far, with an eye mainly to his own interests; it was necessary to keep a check upon him, and punishments and dismissals were frequent. To keep in constant touch with his servants, "to have careful information from every quarter and to distribute information himself when it seemed good to him" (*Ordonnance* of 19 June 1464), Louis created the *Poste*: on all the main roads in the kingdom were arranged, under the charge of *maîtres de la poste*, relays of four or five good horses, able to gallop. The relays were reserved, and still were so until 1507, for the king's riders. Never had a king been kept so well-informed as Louis XI.

CH. VIII.

In spite of everything, Louis did not succeed in protecting the populace from the abuses of power, and the commissioners of reform sent to put a stop to the abuses often made them worse still. "If he pressed upon his subjects," said Commynes, "yet he would not have suffered another to do so." This is only half the truth.

One of the principal tasks of the local officials of the Crown was to reduce the powers of the municipal officers, to strengthen the king's hold on the towns, and also to protect them from feudal violence. The ancient alliance of monarchy and towns still subsisted, but it had taken the form of a protectorate continually becoming more and more strict; it provided the king with a solid support against the schemes of the feudality, and the bourgeoisie with manifold material advantages. Of municipal liberties there could hardly be any question under such a master. He declared that he could "renew, create, and ordain at his good pleasure both mayoralty and shrievalty, without anyone having a say in it," and he often imposed mayors of his own choosing. He infringed the constitutions of towns or altered them, reduced their financial or judicial privileges, and sometimes suppressed town-councils to replace them by royal commissioners. On the other hand, he assumed the right of granting political liberties to towns outside the domain, and of founding consulates in them, so as to be able to intervene there at will and to deprive bishop or lord of his part in the urban administration. Practically it can be said that the evolution, long ago begun, which transformed the municipalities into organs of royal authority, was completed in most towns during the reign of Louis XI.

The royal officials, with an activity never achieved before, pursued their rôle of termites in undermining the edifice of feudalism. Apart from the house of Brittany and that of Burgundy before its downfall, the nobility lost its prerogatives. The king no longer asked leave of the lords to raise taxes in their territories; at most, as an act of grace, he left them a share. On the other hand, they could not themselves raise taxes, or even set up a fair or market, without his permission. It was only in the years of disorder and as an exceptional circumstance that the lords possessed armed bands comparable with the retinues of the English lords; the king assumed as his own the privilege of raising an army and held the castles at his disposal. The exercise of seignorial justice was continually interfered with and disputed, and there was always an appeal to a royal tribunal. Finally, the towns escaped from seignorial authority. The nobility recognised that it was crushed.

This despotic government was a natural result of Louis' temperament; but it was also dictated by circumstances, the political events of the time. Louis could not make head against his enemies and realise his ambitions, unless he had large sums at his disposal and could impose very heavy burdens upon his non-privileged subjects; for that he needed to make himself everywhere obeyed and feared. Never did a king spend so much on overcoming scruples, on recompensing the services rendered by his representatives or by his celestial protectors, on maintaining agents and spies in France and abroad, on diplomatic missions, on paying an excellent standing army, on building and repairing fortresses, and, finally, on carrying out such great operations as the repurchase of the Somme towns for 400,000 gold crowns, and the purchase of peace from the Duke of Brittany (for 120,000 crowns in 1466) and from the King of England. Even the household expenses of this so-called "miserly" king increased considerably. "He put nothing into his treasury," says Commynes. "He took it all and spent it all." The regular receipts, which amounted to 1,800,000 livres at his accession, had by his death risen to 4,655,000 livres. The revenue from the domain, seriously affected by the general insecurity of the countryside, was only 100,000 livres. It was the *taille* that provided the chief resources: from 1,055,000 livres in 1461 it rose to 4,600,000 in 1481, and in the year of his death (1483) was 3,900,000; under his successors, in spite of the Italian wars, it never exceeded 3,300,000 livres. Finally, the *aides* on articles of consumption and the *gabelle* supplied 655,000 livres[1]. But the revenue was still insufficient. In this difficult situation all sorts of expedients were employed: investigation of fiefs acquired by non-nobles, the sale of offices or patents of nobility, grants of privileges to towns or merchants, fines imposed on Jews "for having practised excessive usury or spoken ill of His Majesty," temporary suppression of the wages of officials, and finally subsidies and

---

[1] Spont, *La Taille en Languedoc* in *Annales du Midi*, 1890, pp. 368–9, 498; corrected figures in *Annales du Midi*, 1891, pp. 489–90. As is well known, the livre *tournois*, divided into 20 *sols*, was only used as a standard. The gold *écu soleil* was worth 1 livre 13 s. *tournois* in the middle of Louis XI's reign. So the livre *tournois* reckoned by the metallic value of its equivalent in actual currency was equal to 6 francs 54 cent. in gold francs of 1914. But these 6 francs 54 cent. had a much higher purchasing power for agricultural produce than in our day: in Poitou a hundred litres of wheat could be bought for 8 or 10 *sols*, and a pair of oxen for 11 livres. Manufactured goods, both relatively and in comparison with modern prices, were much dearer. An attempt has been made, by adding together the average prices of a certain number of commodities, to arrive at a general average for the purchasing power of the livre *tournois* at the end of Louis XI's reign. Mlle Yvonne Bézard has suggested 80 gold francs for the region of Paris, M. Paul Raveau 55 gold francs for Poitou. These arithmetical calculations not only thus produce very different results, but also are quite untrustworthy as a means of estimating either a public budget or the private budgets of the various classes of society. To multiply 4,655,000 livres by 55 or by 80 would not give a proper idea of what Louis XI was able to do with the revenue derived from taxation. Moreover, a fifteenth-century budget has little in common with a twentieth-century one. To the revenue from taxation must be added all the savings the king was able to make by expedients which do not figure among the normal receipts. The expenses of education, poor relief, and the like, fell upon the Church. Officials were underpaid, and recouped themselves at the expense of the public; it often happened that Louis XI did not pay his soldiers, who in that case lived on the inhabitants; and so on. A budget of this kind reminds one of that of a sultan rather than of a European State in the nineteenth century. The figures given in the text are of interest mainly because of the comparisons that can be made between them.

forced loans, to which churches, towns, and individuals had to submit. Towns above all, such as Tours and Lyons, were overwhelmed with demands. The financial officials were worn to the bone. When the Treasurer, Jean Bourré, received an order such as this: "Go to-morrow to Paris, and find money in the magic box, and let there be no lack," it meant that Bourré was to bring pressure to bear on the wealthy citizens of Paris and was to dip into his own resources as well.

The taxes appeared the more burdensome in that they were unfairly apportioned and improperly collected. There was great indignation with the exactions of the *élus*, who sought to compensate themselves for the meagre salaries they received. The privileged classes (the clergy, the universities, nobles, royal officials, *francs-archers* etc.) aroused great jealousy. At Grenoble, more than half of the landed property in the town was exempt from *taille*. The question of this privilege was raised on several occasions. To the magistrates of Lyons the reply was made that nobles ought to be exempt, because they had to go to war and to expose themselves and their horses to protect townspeople and peasants. At Bordeaux the clergy argued that they offered up prayers and held processions for the welfare of king and country.

So the vices in the administration which three centuries later were to lead the monarchy of the *ancien régime* to its fall were already visible in the time of Louis XI; and he must bear his share of responsibility for the aggravation of them.

He had, however, too much sense not to understand that the "magic box" was not inexhaustible, and that in order to extract much money from a country it was necessary to provide means for it to grow rich. Louis was the first of his dynasty to have a reasoned economic policy on which to act, but his only thought was of industry and commerce; a long time was to pass before the government of France turned its attention to agriculture and the lot of the peasants.

Louis found time to give his personal attention to the organisation of labour, the protection of industries, the creation of markets and means of transport. Not only did he wish to increase the general wealth of the country, discover new sources of profit for his treasury, and facilitate the raising of the taxes; he also had the desire of strengthening the class of substantial citizens which provided his chief support against the nobility, and his natural bent led him to extend royal tutelage in all directions, and himself to impose a certain uniformity on the world of labour.

These tendencies, which are the key to his economic policy, were displayed above all by his interference with the organisation of corporate bodies and his participation in industrial development. He had no more interest in the artisan class than in the peasantry; he was not, as he has been very mistakenly described, "the king of the small folk." He mistrusted them, and looked on them as "people of evil mind." Just as he detested democratic constitutions in towns and took steps to put the power in the hands of bourgeois oligarchies, so he concerted with the rich members of corporations to reserve admission to their freedom to the sons of members and to exclude the workers; he crushed independent artisans with fines, created new corporations, and gave the regulations an official character by the sanction of an *ordonnance*. An examination of texts, dates, and circumstances shews the policy underlying them. He recompensed services and strengthened the upper bourgeoisie wherever he had need of it. On the other hand, he followed his natural inclination to direct and to unify. Very characteristic is the *Ordonnance* of 1479; it was copied from the regulations laid down four years previously for the Paris cloth-trade, and it regulated the cloth-trade through the whole kingdom. That he also thought of getting profit for himself by the reforms which he introduced cannot be doubted: he reserved for himself a portion of the fines which he exacted, and of the dues for membership and apprenticeship. Further, as he was not hampered by any prejudices, he did away with the corporative system when he considered it to be disadvantageous for new industries, and he even favoured the immigration of foreigners, from Italy or Germany, to assist in the manufacture of silk or the development of the mines.

In his commercial policy he exhibited the same flexibility and the same breadth of view. He sought means to enrich his subjects and his treasury at the same time, and to prevent the flight of money out of France, sometimes by protectionist measures, at others by allowing freedom of trade. He had formerly been on intimate terms with Jacques Cœur, whose memory he in a way rehabilitated after his own accession by lavishing favours on his sons and on his partner Guillaume de Varye, who was one of the *généraux des finances* and Louis' commercial adviser. The wide sweep of Jacques Cœur's enterprises inspired the king in his commercial policy. His conception was on the grand scale. His achievement in the Mediterranean was as remarkable as Cœur's work before had been. The harbours of Languedoc were in a ruined condition, and Aigues-Mortes, besides being difficult of access, was only of use to the Venetians, who monopolised the trade between the Levant and France. Louis was determined to defeat this monopoly and to find a good harbour. In 1468 he broke with the Venetians, who also stood in the way of his Italian policy, forced them to stop their convoy to Aigues-Mortes, and engaged in a privateering struggle with them lasting until 1478. The admiral Coulon attacked their merchantmen off the shores of Spain, in the Atlantic, and in the Channel. Royal galleys began trading as far east as Alexandria. In order to have a deep-water harbour, Louis, immediately after the conquest of Roussillon, caused work on a large scale to be begun at Collioure. At the end of his reign, in 1481, he at last got possession of Marseilles, and announced that it was to become the emporium at which the merchandise from the East would be unloaded, to be transported from there to all the countries of the West. To bring that about, it was necessary to build the Mediterranean fleet on which he had long set his heart, and first of all to found a great trading company, with a capital of 100,000 livres, in which all the merchants of the kingdom were to participate. This was the scheme he expounded to the deputies of the "good towns" assembled at Tours in January 1482. It was too vast for the minds of his audience, and obtained a chilly reception. Louis died without having the opportunity of reviving his plan. But, at any rate, he had given a great impetus to French trade in the Mediterranean.

In the west, he revived the prosperity of La Rochelle and Bordeaux. But here foreign co-operation was necessary. He granted favours of all kinds to Spanish, Portuguese, and Hanseatic merchants and even to the subjects of the Duke of Burgundy; and into almost every political compact which he concluded he introduced commercial clauses. He was particularly anxious for the renewal of trade with England; this trade had been seriously affected by the recovery of Normandy and Guienne by the French Crown, and entirely ruined by the alliance of Edward IV with Charles the Bold. After the temporary restoration of Henry VI, Louis organised in 1470 a small exhibition of French products in England. But it was only by virtue of the truce of Picquigny that a commercial treaty could at last be concluded.

It was in matters of internal trade that the most marked effects of Louis' despotic character were to be seen. Seventy-six of his *ordonnances* relate to fairs and markets, whether in the royal domain or outside its boundaries. He succeeded in ruining the fairs of Geneva to the advantage of those of Lyons, and he strictly prohibited French merchants from going to Geneva.

At the end of his life, when he had triumphed over his enemies, he became more and more obsessed by grandiose designs, which to his contemporaries appeared fantastic. He wished to empower members of the clergy and of the nobility, whom he looked on as mere idlers, to take part in trade. He announced his intention of abolishing internal tolls and the diversity of weights and measures. In 1480, impressed by the difficulties created in civil life by the diversity of laws, he gave instructions for a collection of customs, "so that a new custom may be made."

Did this king, whose intelligence was so untrammelled and who was curious of everything, also desire to regiment the mind? He shewed no signs of religious fanaticism; he stopped the persecution of the Vaudois. He also thwarted schemes for a crusade against the Turks. Did he think of giving a particular direction to the arts and to letters?

Not to mention the numerous orders he gave to architects and gold-smiths to win the graces of his celestial protectors, he shewed himself able to distinguish the best artists of his day, Jean Bourdichon, Michel Colombe, and Fouquet (to whom he gave the title of "king's painter"). In spite of his close associations with Italy, he gave to French painters and sculptors, especially those who belonged to the Loire region, the preference over transalpine artists. He was well-informed and, to judge from some bantering and satirical letters which he certainly dictated himself, had wit and could express himself neatly. His favours to universities, men of learning, and students are sufficient proof that he had no "scorn for the works of the mind." He did not make use of the new art of printing[1] for political purposes only; he appreciated its intellectual value, and expressed in excellent terms his recognition of " the advantage which can derive from it to the public good, as well for the increase of knowledge as otherwise"; his protection was not unimportant, for the hostility of the copyists and the booksellers was retarding the spread of printing in France. In that way Louis XI rendered good service to the cause of French humanism, then in its infancy, for it could only make progress by the aid of good texts of the classics. But the king's part stopped there. If the age of great poetry was over, and if the cold and mordant literature of the day seems to be a reflection of the mind of Louis, he was not responsible for that; there was, however, something in common between his individual tendencies and the spirit of positivism, of disillusioned irony, which was characteristic of the age. He could not have had much personal influence unless he had played the part of a generous Maecenas. He spent his money in other ways, and it was outside his Court, which was given up wholly to politics and administration, that French humanism had its birth. The school of the " rhétoriqueurs" was developed at the Burgundian Court. Apart from Commynes—and he did not write until several years after Louis' death—the best poets and historians of the age were hostile to the royalist cause. Similarly the king had no extensive influence over artistic production. Of this there were numerous centres. Besides the art of the Loire, there was a Flemish-Burgundian art, a Bourbon, a Provençal. We are only at the dawn of the absolute monarchy. The time had not yet come when it was to bring art and literature under its control, and to make them contributory to its greatness.

Louis XI, at the end of his life, said that he had " well looked after, defended and governed, augmented and increased all parts of his realm, by his great care, his solicitude, and his diligence." Certainly he had defended and increased it. But he had not given France the order and the peace which the mass of the population craved. He had had unceasingly to make or prepare for war. The great disorders and the great miseries of the Hundred Years' War still left their traces during his reign, in spite of energetic and rigorous action to repress them. In the southwest, the local squires continued their fighting with one another and their brigandage. From all sides came complaints of the pillaging and

[1] Louis XI caused at least nine different editions of the Treaty of Arras in 1483 to be printed, in order to circulate a large number of copies in France and Flanders (Picot and Stein, *Pièces historiques imprimées sous le règne de Louis XI*, 1923, p. 286).

violence of the men-at-arms, who were irregularly paid by the king. The misery increased with the burden of the now heavy taxation. There were popular riots, which were always harshly repressed. Epidemics, famine, and the severe winter of 1481–82 took their toll of the population. The last years of the reign were gloomy years indeed.

After 1479 the king's health grew rapidly worse. Though not sixty years old, he felt his life was ebbing. He became more and more irascible and suspicious. He abandoned his incessant journeys throughout the realm and stayed in the province of his choice, Touraine. From June 1482 onwards, he divided his time between his domain at Montils-lès-Tours, where he had built the pleasant castle of Plessis-du-Parc, at Cléry-sur-Loire, where he had set up a noble church in honour of Our Lady, his patron, at Amboise, where he kept the young dauphin shut up, and lastly his " good town " of Tours. It became difficult to gain access to him ; the approaches to his castle were lined with traps. He lived with his chief confidants around him, the Sire de Beaujeu, Commynes, the doctor Coitier, the barber Olivier le Daim, not to mention astrologers, charlatans, and even saintly characters like the hermit Francesco di Paola, whom he sent for from Italy that he might have the benefit of his prayers. Furthermore, he continued to receive embassies, and to give orders which were always obeyed at once. " His great heart bore him up." On the day of his death, 30 August 1483, he was still talking distinctly and in his usual dry tone, "and was constantly saying something of sense."

In conformity with his orders he was buried without pomp in the church of Cléry, that he might lie there under the protection of Our Lady. He had given instructions that he was to be depicted on his tomb, not by a recumbent statue, but " on his knees, with his dog by his side, dressed as a hunter." Had he not all his life been a hunter?

Much has been written upon Louis XI. He has become a figure in literature. He who complained once and again of his life of anguish and tribulation has still been plagued after death; he has become the victim of writers of romance. From reading them the popular imagination has created an absurd picture of Louis XI: he is represented as a miser, a silent man, a torturer, a poisoner who spared neither father nor brother. The most at fault was Casimir Delavigne: his *Louis XI*, which in spite of its platitudes and its ineptitudes still draws an audience, reduced this great king to the level of a villain of melodrama. Victor Hugo, with all his parade of learning, shewed no better judgment. Walter Scott, though his *Quentin Durward* is full of the mistakes of his romanticism, presented a picture with more light and shade and less incorrect, while Balzac (in *Maître Cornelius*) came nearer still to the truth. Finally, there was Michelet, and he with the intuition of genius restored Louis to his place.

All the elements for a just appreciation are now before us in the admirable documents already mentioned and in the works of erudition published during the last half-century. It is now possible for anyone with a desire for historical truth to form an exact idea of Louis XI. Not that this is easy, for he is one of the most complex figures in French history, and those who delight in forming moral judgments run the risk of falling into gross error in his case.

In conclusion, there remain two points which seem to deserve attention being called to them. This singular personage, who did not wish to be buried at St Denis among his ancestors, and who could dare to say " that he didn't know whose son he was," in the line of French kings was indeed an isolated figure. The only one who, from certain points of view, resembles him at all is Charles V, and this is one trait that deserves to be noted. Far more intelligent and industrious than the other Valois kings, Charles V and Louis XI each gave to his reign the stamp of a practical and matter-of-fact mind, of clear-sightedness and sagacity. Look at the few portraits that we possess of Louis XI, and then at the famous statue of Charles V in the Louvre: the profile is the same, there is the same unhealthy leanness, the same long inquisitive-looking nose, the same equivocal and foxy expression on a bland face. Both were fine talkers. Both disdained the practice of chivalry, and to the art of war preferred the art of outwitting the enemy and wearing him down. But what a contrast in their methods of government! Charles V was neither cruel nor devoid of scruple, and his inclination in administration was towards a limited monarchy. Louis XI was a tyrant in the full sense of the word, a tyrant like the Italian tyrants of his day. There lay his affinities, and there in truth was his moral parentage. His Machiavellism, before the days of Machiavelli, was of a fit kind to inspire the author of *The Prince*. The shrewd Malleta wrote: " One would say that he has always lived in Italy[1]."

[1] *Dépêches des ambassadeurs milanais*, Vol. i, p. 362.

CHAPTER IX

THE KINGDOM OF BURGUNDY OR ARLES FROM THE ELEVENTH TO THE FIFTEENTH CENTURY

THE region, whose history from the eleventh to the end of the fifteenth century forms the subject of this chapter, has been known by different names in turn. It was called *regnum Burgundiae* after the people who occupied it at the time of the barbarian invasions; its ruler was known also as *rex Iurensis, rex Austrasiorum,* or even *rex Alamannorum et Provinciae.* It is not until the twelfth century that we meet with the expression "kingdom of Arles" (*regnum Arelatense*), to which "and of Vienne" is often added as well. In the course of this chapter the term "kingdom of Burgundy" will be employed for the earlier period, and "kingdom of Arles and Vienne" for the later.

The history of this kingdom is the history of a part of Gaul which derived extreme importance from its geographical situation. On the south it was bounded by the sea, from the western mouth of the Rhone to the neighbourhood of Ventimiglia. Its eastern frontier, starting from the coast, coincided at first with the modern frontier between France and Italy, except that it included the valley of Aosta, now part of Italy. From there the line ran to the St Gotthard, and thence north to the Aar and the Rhine, thus bringing into the kingdom not only French Switzerland, but also an important stretch of territory with a German-speaking population. Basle marked the most northerly point of this region, in which the principal towns were Geneva, Lausanne, Sion, and Solothurn. Next the line passed through the gap of Belfort to the southern Vosges, and then turned back to the Saône, following its course almost exactly, but relinquishing to France that part of the county of Chalon which lay on the left bank of the river. On the other hand, it crossed the Saône lower down, so as to include the town and county of Lyons and the county of Forez. Farther south, it diverged from the Rhone to embrace Tournon, Annonay, Viviers, and the Vivarais, afterwards following the course of the river to the Mediterranean. The kingdom thus comprised western Switzerland and that part of modern France which corresponds to the Free County of Burgundy, Savoy, the Lyonnais, Dauphiné, Vivarais, and Provence.

It is obvious that this kingdom was composed of two distinct elements: in the West, a region varying in width, made up of the valleys of the Saône and the Rhone and adjacent lowlands; in the East, a mountainous region of the Alps and the Jura, containing the loftiest peaks in Europe. The plain was one of the great arteries of the Western world, thanks to the roads which, from ancient times, followed the course of the Rhone and then continuing north along the Saône brought the Mediterranean into touch with the fairs of Champagne, with North and East France, and with Alsace; to these must be added the transverse routes crossing the great rivers at different points, such as Avignon and Lyons, and linking up southern Gaul and the Spanish peninsula with Italy and with Switzerland. These lowlands by themselves alone appeared a most desirable domain, and, if we can credit Gervase of Tilbury, who wrote at the beginning of the thirteenth century, one quite easy to master. They are, he says, lands blessed by heaven, spreading out in fertile champaigns rich in the gifts of nature, filled with trading towns, inhabited by a population mentally alert and excitable, who are active or listless as the impulse takes them but, when circumstances demand, ready to endure hardship and suffering. These peoples, Gervase adds, need a kind and upright master; for they are prone to submit to any power which will display sufficient energy to make itself feared.

The highlands, however, were a far more difficult conquest. Thanks to their configuration and their rugged character, the inhabitants had been able to retain their independence for a much longer period against the Roman conqueror; while the feudal lords who held sway there in the Middle Ages were not disposed to submit to the authority of a distant sovereign, however great the prestige of his title, and, in spite of the ban of temporal and spiritual authority alike, they were well able to bar their passes against any who refused to pay what they deemed to be an adequate toll.

How powerful, then, would that ruler have been, in the Middle Ages, who could have exercised an uncontested authority over mountain and plain alike! He could have penetrated without difficulty into the lands of the King of France from the north of the county of Burgundy, the traditional route of invaders. He would have had control of the passes of the Jura and the Alps, and the opening of the gates into Italy, France, and Switzerland would have been subject to his pleasure. Master of the Mediterranean ports, he could easily have dominated this sea, in which Latins, Byzantines, and Arabs were to dispute the hegemony of the world, and he could have held at his disposal the routes by which the crusaders went to the attack on Syria and Egypt. On several occasions during the Middle Ages it looked as though such a kingdom was on the point of being established. The following pages will describe how and why this consummation failed of its realisation.

With the break-up of the Carolingian Empire there came into being, as is well-known, two new kingdoms[1]. The one, Jurane or Upper Burgundy, had Swiss Burgundy as its core; the other, Provence, of

---

[1] For further information on this earlier period see *supra* Vol. III. Chap. VI. by Professor L. Halphen; the standard works are those of R. Poupardin, *Le Royaume de Provence*, Paris, 1901, and *Le Royaume de Bourgogne*, Paris, 1907.

which at first Vienne was the political centre, extended over the valley of the Rhone from Lyons to the sea. The frontier between these two kingdoms varied with the change of circumstances and as each was powerful in turn. Now, between 920 and 930, it happened that the King of Upper Burgundy, Rodolph II, and the ruler of Provence, Hugh, were in turn tempted with the prospect of bringing the Italian peninsula beneath their sway. Rodolph II was the first to make the attempt; but after some short-lived successes he had to recognise his powerlessness and to withdraw. Hugh was more fortunate; but, to avoid the danger of a fresh enterprise on Rodolph's part, he bought him off by abandoning to him the greater part of his rights in Provence. After various changes of fortune, the son of Rodolph II, Conrad the Pacific, was able to unite the two kingdoms under his rule. Thus was established a State which was to exist for three-quarters of a century, nominally, at any rate, under the control of Conrad and his son Rodolph III, the Sluggard.

The formation of this kingdom was due neither to geography, nor to ethnography, nor to commercial relations; it was the product of a purely political contrivance. The numerous peoples scattered throughout its parts were united by no permanent bond. So artificial was the structure that, as has been seen, some considerable time elapsed before the kingdom received a definite and regular name. And not only a title, but also the reality of power, was lacking to the monarchy; without an army of its own at its disposal, without financial resources regularly assured, and without an organised and trained body of officials, its existence was half-stifled by the rapid development of ecclesiastical principalities and lay powers. By the side of the great ecclesiastical lordships of Besançon, Lyons, and Vienne—to mention only the most important—there were to be found the domains of secular dynasties, especially those of Otto-William in the County of Burgundy (Franche Comté), of Guigues in the Viennois, of Humbert Whitehands in Maurienne, and of the counts and marquesses of Provence in the valley of the lower Rhone. It was to these local lords far more than to the king that the people looked for protection from the incursions of the Saracens, raiding from their Alpine strongholds or landing upon the Mediterranean shores. The real authority rested with these local rulers, and only the shadow remained to the monarchy.

Wandering up and down their territories, the kings dwelt where they could. Hardly ever were they to be seen at Arles, in spite of the still-surviving tradition which gave this city exalted rank in the hierarchy of the towns of Gaul. On the other hand, they frequently resided at Vienne, the rival of Arles and proud, like it, of its Roman memories, where they long retained domains of their own; also in Jurane Burgundy, where were the best part of the lands belonging to the royal *fiscus*—often they settled in the lake-district of western Switzerland and in Savoy. On different occasions they had lived at Basle, and sometimes too they had taken up their residence in great abbeys such as Payerne; above all, at St Maurice-en-Valais (Agaune), whose history was closely bound up with that of the royal house. These weak kings further aggravated their weakness by grants from their domains to the nobles. In truth, the kingship of the rulers of this kingdom, which had no name and no capital, no treasure and no army, and resembled in many respects that of the later Carolingians, was an illusion rather than a reality.

In the beginning of September 1032, the cathedral of Lausanne received the mortal remains of Rodolph III. This prince left no legitimate issue, and it had for some time seemed that the succession was bound to fall to the Emperor Henry II, who was the nearest relative in the collateral line. Henry, doubtless estimating none too highly the efficacy of an appeal to hereditary right, had taken his precautions during Rodolph's lifetime by occupying Basle; further, Rodolph had bound himself in solemn conventions to bequeath to him the succession. The prospect of the accession to the Burgundian kingdom of a powerful sovereign—the most powerful in Europe—had alarmed many of the local nobles. Possibly they were reassured by the death of Henry, whom Rodolph outlived. If so, their security did not last long. They soon learnt in Burgundy that the German crown had fallen into the hands of an able and determined ruler, Conrad II, who, as his object was to reconstitute the Empire of Charlemagne, could not relinquish the task undertaken by his predecessor in Burgundy; he had all the more excuse for continuing it as he too was a near relative of King Rodolph III. Actually, in the order of affinity, Conrad's hereditary claims were inferior to those of a powerful French baron, Odo II, Count of Chartres, Blois, and Tours. But Conrad had been able in 1027 to persuade Rodolph III to set aside the rights of the next of kin; a convention assured to him the succession to the feeble sovereign. In accordance with this agreement, on Rodolph's death a Burgundian deputation had to bring to the Emperor the emblems of the kingship, the royal diadem and the lance of St Maurice, the patron saint who was as popular in the northern part of the Rhone valley as St Denis and St Martin were in France. On various occasions Count Odo tried to win his heritage by force of arms; but the Emperor Conrad II was able, by diplomacy or force, to foil his attempts and to obtain general recognition as the successor of the last of the Burgundian kings. Legally, then, the kingdom which was ultimately to be known as the kingdom of Arles became in this way united to the Empire, which was to retain it, nominally at any rate, until its own dissolution under the blow dealt it by the victories of Napoleon I.

The uneasiness aroused in the local nobility by the accession of the new king of Burgundy was, in fact, well founded. If we picture to ourselves the juridical position of these nobles, we see that they were either great prelates or counts descended from Frankish officials. In either case, by virtue of their titles they were not necessarily vassals of the king; they were, indeed, bound to him by the general obligation of obedience and fealty which was imposed on all subjects, but there was no other obligation than this. Such a bond was a slender one, as the nobles had clearly demonstrated to Rodolph III and his predecessors; in order to strengthen it, the royal policy aimed at transforming into vassals bound by definite obligations under feudal law those persons who could be ranked in the category of allodial nobles.

The question was whether the Emperors, having become direct rulers of the country, could change this ancient state of affairs to their advantage. Just at the time when the crown of Rodolph III was passing to them, a personage closely in touch with affairs in the Empire, the imperial chaplain Wipo, was stressing the risks that his master's sovereignty had to face in the newly-acquired territories. "O king," he said to Conrad II, "Burgundy has called for you. Arise, come in haste.... Profoundly true is the old saying: Out of sight, out of mind. Though Burgundy now enjoys peace because of you, it wishes to contemplate in your person the author of this peace, and to feast its eyes on the sight of the king." This is to be the appeal, often uttered and almost always in vain, of the imperial partisans in Burgundy: the Emperor was too far off; let him appear at last and take in his own hands the direction of the country's affairs.

If Conrad II formed the design of responding to these appeals, he had not the time to carry it into effect. He died a few years after his acquisition of Rodolph's kingdom. His son Henry III, whom he had caused to be recognised as king in his own lifetime by the grandees of the kingdom, endeavoured to satisfy the wishes of his partisans. Not only did he organise for Burgundy a special chancery, at the head of which he appointed as arch-chancellor one of his supporters, Archbishop Hugh of Besançon; besides this, he visited the country himself on several occasions. In 1042, he was at St Maurice-en-Valais at the head of an army, and there received numerous submissions; on three occasions he held diets at Solothurn; in 1042 he visited Franche Comté, and again in 1043 it was at Besançon that he celebrated his betrothal with Agnes of Aquitaine, who was related to Count Rainald I of Burgundy; in 1044 he repressed by force of arms an insurrection of the Counts of Burgundy and Genevois. Meanwhile he did not neglect to establish his influence over the ecclesiastical principalities. He could, of course, count on the Archbishop of Besançon; after two successive vacancies, he himself nominated the Archbishop of Lyons; finally, in 1046, when he went to Rome to obtain the imperial crown, he was accompanied not only by the Archbishop of Besançon but by those of Lyons and Arles as well. This was clearly significant, and the conclusion could be drawn that the Emperor was basing his power in Burgundy on the influence of the higher clergy;

moreover, this was the line that he, like his predecessors, followed in Germany. It was a course of action imposed upon him; for he could not count on the lay nobles, who were anxious to preserve independence both for themselves and for their descendants. Only Count Humbert White-hands of Maurienne was faithful to him, and he was rewarded for his fidelity by a considerable extension of his domains. The others displayed an attitude of indifference towards the Emperor, when they did not shew themselves openly hostile.

On the death of Henry III, the kingdom of Burgundy passed without trouble to his son, the future Emperor Henry IV. His mother Agnes, who governed during his minority, doubtless distrusted her own capacity to play an effective part in Burgundy. It is to her initiative that is due the first example of an institution which later Emperors were to copy, the rectorate of Burgundy. The rector had to play the part of a viceroy, and Agnes entrusted this duty to a great Transjurane noble, Rudolf of Rheinfelden, who also became her son-in-law. It does not appear that Rudolf's rectorate fulfilled the expectations of the Empress, or that it left any mark on the history of Burgundy.

The policy followed by Henry IV during the early years of his reign differed little from that adopted by Henry III. But since the king relied on the bishops, it was essential that no conflict of principle should provoke a breach between Church and State; it was essential that, while bestowing his favour on the Church, the king should not seek to hold it in thrall, and thereby pave the way for a reaction which would be fatal to his authority. Henry IV was not wise enough to avoid this grievous error; the history of the Investiture Struggle shews how he became implicated in it and with what persistence he pursued it. The consequences were disastrous to imperial authority in the former kingdom of Rodolph III. The lay nobles in general, while refraining from imitating the Count of Burgundy, gave no support to the Emperor. As for the clergy, its leaders shewed themselves for the most part faithful to the cause of the Church. One of them, Hugh, Bishop of Die and later Archbishop of Lyons, was, as legate of the Apostolic See, a devoted auxiliary of Gregory VII and an active worker in the cause of ecclesiastical reform with which that Pope's name is associated. Later, when Paschal II was prepared to concede lay investiture to Henry V, it was in the valley of the Rhone, at a council held at Vienne in 1112 under the presidency of the archbishop, Guy of Burgundy, that the concession was condemned with more vehemence than it had been some months earlier at the council in the Lateran; it is significant that it was this same Guy, Archbishop of Vienne, who in 1119 was elected to the papal throne as Calixtus II. If this was the prevailing opinion in this region, it is not surprising that Henry IV coming to Canossa was looked on rather as a criminal than a king, and that the chancery of Burgundy had become a sinecure. The most important questions, such as the division of Provence in 1125 between the Berengars and the house of Toulouse[1], were settled, apparently, without the parties concerned thinking of obtaining the consent of their sovereign, the Emperor. The habit of referring to the royal authority had been lost; and this was the more dangerous for the Empire as the best part of Burgundy, the Rhone provinces, were attracted towards France, to which they were linked by the ties of custom, of kinship, of language, and of literature. From this time, the current which drew these provinces Francewards, and which had been accelerated by the religious wars, had gathered too much strength to be checked by the feeble measures to which the Emperors were reduced, such as the reconstitution of the Burgundian chancery or the granting of charters which shewed a royal authority more nominal than real.

Perhaps a ruler of considerable energy, personally resident in the kingdom, might have arrested the decline. Such a task presented the gravest difficulties; nevertheless, it attracted the Emperors of the twelfth to the fourteenth centuries who succeeded the Franconian dynasty. The most active in this undertaking were, it is not surprising to find, the princes of the house of Swabia. But they were to have no better success than their predecessors.

Between the houses of Franconia and Swabia came one intermediary reign, that of Lothar III of Supplinburg. Lothar was soon forced to recognise his almost complete lack of authority, when the members of the Burgundian and Provençal nobility refrained from answering his summons. "You have paid no heed to them," he wrote; "you have thus marked in most impudent fashion your contempt for our supreme power." Except for the Archbishop of Besançon, no noble in the kingdom of Arles appeared at an imperial diet or took part in the campaigns of Lothar; moreover, on the occasion of his expedition into Italy in 1136, the Emperor had to subdue one of them, Count Amadeus III of Maurienne, who had been bold enough to make common cause with the enemies of his sovereign. A few years later, it was the turn of Rainald III, who had succeeded William the Child as Count of Burgundy and paid little heed to the imperial rights; Lothar decided to replace him by a powerful Swiss noble, Conrad of Zähringen. He went farther still, following the example set in the reign of Henry IV, and made Conrad, as a loyal subject whom he could trust, not only the successor of Rainald in Franche Comté, but also the governor, with the title of rector, of the whole of Cisjurane and Transjurane Burgundy. Doubtless he hoped to find in him an able and energetic representative, such as his predecessors had never known. But, in spite of Lothar's orders and threats, the scheme was a failure; Rainald maintained his hold on Franche Comté, and Conrad was unable to assert his authority on the western side of the Jura.

[1] This gave rise to the County (the Berengars) and the Marquessate (house of Toulouse) of Provence.

Nothing had been done, then, by the time of the accession in 1143 of Conrad III, the first king of the Swabian house. In the course of his reign, he indicated his policy with regard to the kingdom of Arles in two ways: firstly, he granted privileges to members of the higher clergy, especially Archbishop Humbert of Vienne, whom he thus attached to his cause; secondly, he intervened, without much success, on behalf of the head of an important Provençal family, Raymond of Baux, who on the death of Count Berengar-Raymond tried to make good the claims of his house to the county of Provence, and approached the king to obtain his support. The action of Conrad III was not fruitful in results, but at any rate it revived a twofold policy which his successors did not fail to pursue: of seeking the support of the leading prelates, and of taking the opportunity to intervene in all the dissensions which arose among the lay nobility. This was the old tradition of imperial policy.

Since the death of Rodolph III, the imperial authority had made but feeble progress in the old Burgundian kingdom. Then to Conrad III succeeded Frederick Barbarossa, a young prince of keen intelligence, of active will, eager for fame, and fired with the ambition of re-establishing the universal monarchy of Charlemagne. He was not long in realising that, to attain this end, he must first bring effectively under his control the kingdom of Arles; he turned his attention to this quarter even before occupying himself with Italy.

At the very beginning of his reign, he recognised, as the result of a fresh and again unsuccessful effort, that no useful results were to be expected from the viceroyalty of Berthold, the son of Conrad of Zähringen. So a reversal of Frederick's former policy in this region soon became evident; having given to the house of Zähringen, by way of compensation, the advocacies of the churches of Lausanne, Geneva, and Sion, he came to terms with the comital house of Burgundy and married the young Beatrice, who had recently inherited Franche Comté on the death of Rainald III. At once Barbarossa acquired in Burgundy an advantage which his predecessors had never had—a firm basis and devoted adherents. The fruits of this policy can be seen in 1157. Frederick appeared at Besançon, and held a diet there at which all the magnificence of the imperial court was displayed; among those who hastened to attend their sovereign were, as well as the Archbishop of Besançon, the Archbishops of Lyons, Vienne, and Tarantaise, and a number of bishops and secular nobles. The Emperor was justified in announcing to his faithful minister, Abbot Wibald of Stablo, "the magnificent success" of his affairs in Burgundy. Certainly the imperial chancery distributed numerous privileges, and their general effect was theoretical rather than practical. But the Emperor did not limit himself to this expedient; he did not hesitate to intervene in several disputes which broke out at Lyons or in Provence. In fact, he shewed plainly that he understood how to play the king. The King of France, Louis VII, realised this so clearly that he took umbrage, slipped away from a conference which had been arranged between him and Frederick, and assembled in Champagne considerable forces, so that for some time there was danger of war between the two sovereigns. The fact was that the Capetian monarchy had now become powerful enough to resent the establishment in the south-east of Gaul of a power which was not subject to its influence.

Meanwhile, the Emperor, thinking to follow in the Carolingian tradition, had attempted to establish his authority over the Roman Church. The result of his attempt is well known—his rupture with Alexander III and the election of an anti-Pope, Victor IV. In the struggle which ensued, the Emperor asked for help from his subjects in the kingdom of Arles, and for some years he met with open friendship or at any rate latent sympathy there. This development was only fully revealed when the news arrived of the memorable expedition of 1162, which culminated in the destruction of Milan; the prestige of the Emperor rose to the summit, and with it the terror that he inspired. Several of the prelates, and among them the most important, were won over to the side of Frederick and his anti-Pope. And not only in Franche Comté could Barbarossa reckon on adherents; he could pride himself on having Guigues, the Dauphin of Viennois, in his train, and even, for a time, Raymond-Berengar II, the Count of Provence. Leaving minor nobles out of account, the only personage who eluded his influence was Humbert III, Count of Maurienne. It even seemed in 1162 that the moment had come when he would succeed in associating with his religious policy the King of France, Louis VII.

Once more, at the last moment, Louis withdrew, and refused to abandon the cause of Alexander III. His decision had important repercussions in Burgundy throughout the Rhone district. Louis quite soon found himself the leader of a considerable party in the east and south-east of Gaul; the various elements of discontent rallied round him; he became the recognised protector of that section of the higher clergy which still remained faithful to Alexander III; and, moreover, the members of this party now began to raise their heads once more. A visit paid by the Emperor with his wife Beatrice to Burgundy did not perceptibly improve the situation for him; and it became definitely worse after the disaster which brought his expedition into Italy in 1167 to an end; Frederick himself, on his return, in order to assure his retreat, had to solicit, and to pay heavily for, the goodwill of the Count of Maurienne.

As a result of all this, Barbarossa was destined to see his influence decline in Burgundy; it is not surprising that, during the last years of his struggle with Alexander III, his interference in this region was less frequent and less effective. To attempt to revive his authority, he had to wait until 1177 when he had bent the knee to Alexander III and concluded peace with him; then he thought it necessary to make a fresh and a striking manifestation of his sovereignty in the kingdom of Arles. He went to Arles, attended by a numerous train, and in the cathedral of St Trophimus, which was resplendent with all the brilliance of the court, he had himself crowned king, after the ancient tradition, by the metropolitan, Raymond of Bollène, assisted by the Archbishops of Vienne and Aix and five bishops of neighbouring dioceses. Besides these prelates there were numerous lay nobles, among them Raymond of St Gilles, who held the marquessate of Provence and the French county of Toulouse.

The nobles, lay and ecclesiastical, who came to greet their sovereign, either at Arles or at different points in his progress through the country, were rewarded by numerous grants of various kinds: privileges, confirmation of immunities, grants of the title of prince of the Empire, tolls, guardianship of the Jews, and a general settlement of disputes. The prelates seem to have appreciated these favours. During the last years of Barbarossa's reign, they are often to be found on the look-out for similar grants, and for that purpose hastening to different diets summoned by the Emperor in North Italy. Frederick, moreover, followed the policy of his predecessors in giving his protection to the bishops: he took up the cause of the Bishop of Geneva who was engaged in a contest with the Count of Genevois, and particularly that of the Archbishop of Tarantaise and the Bishop of Sion against the claims of Count Humbert III of Maurienne; also, that of the Bishops of Valence and Die against the Counts of Valentinois. Meanwhile, he did not neglect, whenever possible, to win over the lay nobles; he always preserved a nucleus of loyalty in Franche Comté, he acquired vassals in Bresse, and he strengthened the tie which held the Dauphin of Viennois to his side.

On a general consideration of the facts that have been detailed above, it will be seen that Frederick took his title of king in Burgundy and Provence quite seriously. He employed favourable circumstances to assure the obedience of subjects who had disregarded it hitherto. Furthermore, he laboured to supply the indispensable machinery for his government by reorganising the chancery, over which he placed the Archbishop of Vienne as arch-chancellor, and by sending to the various districts trusty representatives—*legati curiae imperialis, legati domini imperatoris, iusticiarii*— whose functions cannot precisely be stated, but who certainly had as their mission to make the royal government's action and its control felt, a thing unknown before in Burgundy and Provence. A few years before his death Frederick gave a further proof of his care for the royal authority in those districts. On 27 April 1186, when he was holding his court in Milan on the occasion of the marriage of his son Henry, King of the Romans, with the heiress of the Norman kings of Sicily, after Henry, in the basilica of St Ambrose, had received the crown of Italy from the Patriarch of Aquileia, Frederick had himself crowned anew as King of Arles by the Archbishop of Vienne. There was nothing in the repetition of the coronation to appear strange to the Middle Ages; but it is a testimony to the importance Barbarossa attached to the royal authority in those regions.

Henry VI, who succeeded his father Frederick Barbarossa as Emperor in 1190, had been concerned, before his accession, with affairs in the kingdom of Arles. It was he who had arranged the closer alliance of the Emperor with the Dauphin of Viennois; he too who had conducted the campaign which the Emperor had to undertake against Humbert III, Count of Maurienne and Savoy. To be better informed of the state of these regions, he had returned from Lombardy by the Mont-Cenis or the Mont-Genèvre, and had stayed at various places, notably at Lyons. It is impossible to know what impression this journey left upon him. But, since the ambition of his race seemed incarnate in his being, since too he considered himself the universal monarch, allowing no considerations to qualify his pretensions, it is certain that he was prepared to yield none of his rights or of his claims over Burgundy or Provence.

However, the sustained effort which was necessary in order to bind more closely these provinces to the Empire, and so to make good the work of his father, was ill-suited to the temperament of the new sovereign. He preferred to begin and end this task in one stroke by placing at the head of these provinces, as a king dependent upon him, a personage who, he hoped, would subserve his policy. This was a renewal on a grander scale of the Zähringen rectorate which had been so unsuccessful. The person he chose was no other than Richard Cœur-de-Lion.

To explain his choice, it is important to notice that, during the early years of Henry's reign, the King of France had pushed to extremes his attack on England, and so had aroused the uneasiness not only of the Welf party in Germany, but also of the Emperor, who had to take account of this party, although it was hostile to his policy. In 1192, Richard, on his return from the Holy Land, in defiance of the principles of public law in the Middle Ages, was captured and thrown into prison by the Duke of Austria. Henry VI caused the prisoner to be handed over to him, and found him a valuable pawn in the game that he was playing, which was, as at least he hoped, to result for him in the hegemony of the West. His first thought was to turn Richard's captivity to account by rendering a service to Philip Augustus for which he would not have failed to require payment; but in this way he would have irritated the Welfs, the traditional friends of the English sovereigns. By itself this consideration might perhaps not have been sufficient to modify Henry's plans, but he had also taken umbrage at the alliance contracted at about the same time by the King of France with Denmark, an alliance which was consolidated by Philip's unhappy marriage with Ingeborg. Denmark was in Henry's eyes his enemy, because its king had refused to recognise his supremacy.

So the Emperor suddenly veered round and decided to satisfy the Welfs, who threatened him with civil war if he took the side of France against England. At the diet of Worms in 1193, he made Richard surrender to him his kingdom and receive it back as a fief of the Empire. By such infeudations, which thrilled his imagination and which he took pains to effect as often as he could, Henry thought to make himself, in appearance if not in fact, the master of the world. The diet of Worms was followed by a period of complicated negotiations, in which the only detail that concerns us here is that, about the end of 1193, the Emperor, holding to the English alliance, wished after his fashion to mark his favour to his new ally. Perhaps it was due to the suggestion of Savaric, Bishop of Bath, who was related to the house of Hohenstaufen and later became chancellor of Burgundy[1], that he offered to Richard to enfeoff him not only with England but also with Arles, Vienne and Viennois, Lyons, and all the country up to the Alps—that is to say, the kingdom of Arles and Vienne together with the Hohenstaufen possessions in Burgundy. Roger of Howden, to whom we owe our knowledge of this scheme, adds that the infeudation was to extend to other territories situated in Languedoc and not subject to Henry's overlordship, which appears most unlikely. However, it is none the less true that the Emperor was reviving, in a different form, the plan conceived by his predecessor Lothar of Supplinburg on behalf of the house of Zähringen, which had been abandoned by Barbarossa. Had he been able to carry it into effect, he would have been freed from the task of having to govern directly provinces where he was really powerless; the responsibility of governing would have been transferred to a bold and active prince, who would still be his feudal subordinate. Moreover, the scheme entailed a further advantage in that it removed the kingdom of Arles from the sphere of French influence, which was regarded as dangerous to the Empire. Richard, for his part, could not fail to realise that to his possessions in the west of France he would be uniting the valuable and wealthy provinces of the east, and that he would also have the prospect of stifling in his grip the nascent power of his Capetian rivals.

Unfortunately for the Empire, a scheme of this kind belonged, not to the sphere of practical politics, but to the visionary world in which Henry VI was living. It was soon abandoned; contemporary documents have left no trace of any measure destined to carry it into realisation.

The register of Henry's acts shews a great poverty as far as the kingdom of Arles is concerned. He could not hope for any effective assistance from his incapable younger brother, Otto, Count of Burgundy (Franche Comté), and in the course of his short reign he seems to have gradually lost interest in these regions, after he had come to recognise the failure of his plan of entrusting them to Richard as his viceroy.

During the years which followed the death of Henry VI, and which in

[1] This is the opinion of Mr A. L. Poole; see his "England and Burgundy in the last decade of the twelfth century" in *Essays in History presented to R. L. Poole*, Oxford, 1927.

the Empire were taken up with the rivalry between Philip of Swabia and Otto of Brunswick, the first-named was able at certain times to count on quite a considerable number of supporters in the Burgundian territories; Otto's influence, on the other hand, appears to have been very slight. It is not, however, until the reign of Frederick II that the ruler of the Empire is again found to be following a clearly defined policy.

It is not possible here to describe in detail the very complicated policy of Frederick II in the kingdom of Arles and Vienne, but only to denote some of its characteristic traits. In the early years of his reign he followed in the footsteps of his predecessors. He reverted to the practice of viceroys, and nominated two, or perhaps three, in turn: William of Baux, Duke Odo of Burgundy (though there is doubt in his case), and Marquess William of Montferrat. These attempts were no more successful than the preceding ones. At the same time, as the register of his acts attests, he was not sparing in his favours to the prelates. Thus, in a conflict between the bishop and the townsfolk of Marseilles, he took the bishop's side without reserve, and in resounding proclamations he put the town under the ban of the Empire and threatened the freedom and the privileges of its commerce in the Mediterranean world. This threat, coming from a ruler who was master of Sicily and counted numerous adherents in Italy, did not fail to agitate the people of Marseilles; but it did not decide them to abandon the struggle. The Emperor was too much occupied in these years with affairs in Italy and his crusade to the Holy Land, and he could not back his proclamations by effective action. Another sign of this is seen in the cautious nature of his protests when the French crusading army, led by Louis VIII, occupied an imperial town, Avignon, after a siege of several months.

The imperial policy took a different form in 1230. Freed from his embarrassments in Lombardy and the East, and reconciled again with Pope Gregory IX, Frederick took in hand the pacification of the kingdom of Arles, in order to be able to draw from it the contingents and the subsidies which he needed for his Italian expeditions. In the valley of the Rhone his subjects were divided into two camps: at the head of one party, besides the Bishop of Marseilles, was Raymond-Berengar IV, Count of Provence; at the head of the other were the townsfolk of Marseilles and Count Raymond VII of Toulouse. For four years Frederick set himself to support the bishop and Raymond-Berengar. He did not confine himself to action from a distance; he entrusted the duty of representing him in this region, first of all to the Archbishop of Arles, Hugh Béroard, then to one of his intimate counsellors, an Italian by origin, Quaglia of Gorzano. He was able in this way to increase his influence in the Provençal area, but he did not succeed in re-establishing peace. At any rate a proof of this influence was to be seen at the end of 1235, when there appeared at the side of the Emperor, in the assembly of Hagenau, the Counts of Provence and Valentinois and Count Raymond VII of Toulouse, to whom in the previous year Frederick had given a diploma granting him, in defiance of the claims of the Roman Church, the restitution of the Venaissin, which had been taken from him as a result of Louis VIII's crusade.

At Hagenau was clearly betokened the radical change of imperial policy which took place at this time. It is impossible here to investigate the causes of this *volte-face*; it must suffice to say that Frederick had already been irritated by the friendly relations between St Louis and his own intractable son, Henry (VII), King of the Romans, and that he was offended by the marriage of the French king with the daughter of Raymond-Berengar IV. Henceforward he made common cause with Count Raymond VII of Toulouse, and bitterly opposed the Count of Provence. Raymond VII, who was suspected of favouring heresy, was the leader of the anti-clerical party throughout this region; around him were gathered, not only those lay nobles who were hostile to the clergy, but also the associations or confraternities which, in the towns, combated its influence. There were henceforward in the kingdom of Arles two great parties, the one favourable to the Church, the other opposed to it; and with all the forces of which it could dispose the imperial power supported the latter party.

The facts are too complex to be mentioned here in detail. All that can be said is that, in order to sustain the struggle, which he pursued with ardour, Frederick on different occasions sent confidential agents, taken from his Italian entourage, to watch over his interests and rally his supporters: for instance, Henry of Revello, who came in 1237, and later Sopramonte Lupo, Torello of Strada, and finally Count Berardo of Loreto; these agents bore the title either of imperial nuncio or imperial vicar, and none of Frederick's predecessors had taken so much trouble about the kingdom of Arles. Thus, while fortune favoured him, his authority in these regions continued to increase; in 1238 he was able to count, in his army in Lombardy, contingents from Provence, Dauphiné, Valentinois, and Savoy.

At the moment when everything seemed to smile on Frederick, fortune turned traitor. The army failed before Brescia, and the check was anything but fortunate for the Emperor's prestige in the kingdom of Arles. Meanwhile he persisted in his policy; amid all the conflicts which raged in Provence he fought the partisans of the Roman Church; and when in 1245 the Pope, who had taken refuge at Lyons, assembled there the episcopate of the Latin Church, the Emperor, thanks to the assistance of the Dauphin Guigues VII and Amadeus IV, Count of Savoy, prepared an attack by force of arms upon this city. A rising of the Guelfs at Parma, however, prevented him from carrying out his design. About the same time, by the death of Raymond-Berengar IV, the county of Provence passed to his other son-in-law Charles of Anjou, St Louis' brother, who was a far more redoubtable enemy for Frederick than the father-in-law had been. A few years later, in 1249, the death of Raymond VII deprived the Emperor of an ally, and gave him a new adversary in the person of another brother of the French king, Alphonse of Poitiers, to whom was assigned the Venaissin. Frederick none the less persisted in his anti-clerical policy, and up to his death in 1250 he was in Provence as elsewhere the leader of all the enemies of the clergy.

The period of the Great Interregnum which followed the death of Frederick was an age of imperial decadence; and it was particularly so in the kingdom of Arles, where the imperial power, in spite of the efforts of several sovereigns of the house of Swabia, had never become solidly established. If one of the claimants to Empire, Alfonso of Castile, tried to form connexions within the kingdom, he gained no advantage thereby; he could not, still less could his rival, exercise authority there. The bankruptcy of imperial prestige resulted naturally in profit to the France of St Louis and Philip the Bold, as can be seen at this time by what happened in Savoy and Dauphiné, and also by other similar negotiations.

When Rudolf of Habsburg came to Lausanne at the beginning of his reign, he was received there by a few prelates of the kingdom of Arles. These adhesions could not create in him any illusions as to the extent of his influence in the kingdom; for at this time the most important of the lay nobles, starting with the Count of Savoy, Philip, the rival of the Habsburgs in the Swiss territories, were hostile to him; and others were at least neutral. The work essayed by Barbarossa and Frederick II had all to be done over again. It would seem that Rudolf was not attracted by a policy which meant a slow piecemeal recovery of the kingdom of Arles. He preferred a line of action similar to that of his predecessors who had wished to put over the kingdom a ruler bound by close ties to the Empire; it was no longer a question of a rector, a kind of viceroy, but of a vassal king as had been Henry VI's dream. Projects of this kind, formed in the reign of Rudolf of Habsburg and his successors, were to occupy the attention of the chanceries of Europe for half a century.

The first of these plans came into being in 1278 as the result of a *rapprochement* between the Empire and England; this in its turn had arisen out of a negotiation in which Rudolf had shewn himself favourable to the claims of Margaret, St Louis' widow, to the succession in Provence, for at the French court Margaret was the leader of the English party and hostile to that of Charles of Anjou. A marriage was arranged between Rudolf's son Hartmann and Joan, the daughter of Edward I of England. Hartmann was to wear the crown of Arles, and hold it as a fief from the Empire. Apparently, however, none of the parties concerned took any steps to carry this somewhat chimerical plan into execution.

If the crown of Arles was to be revived, it could only be by agreement with the leading figure in that region, who was then playing the chief rôle on the political stage in the West—Charles of Anjou. From the beginning of his rule in Provence he had evinced his ambition of wearing the crown. This is proved by the conventions which he made in 1257 with the head of the house of Baux to yield to him the rights to the kingdom of Arles which that family could base on the grant accorded them by Frederick II in 1215. Later, in 1309, Charles II of Anjou renewed this convention with the Prince of Orange, Bertrand II de Baux. The Angevin dynasty had the idea firmly rooted in their minds that, if the kingdom of Arles was to be revived, it must only be done on their behalf.

During the reign of Rudolf of Habsburg, Pope Nicholas III had been solicitous to reconcile the king with Charles I of Anjou, and so to establish a balance of power which would produce peace in Italy. One of the terms in the arrangement proposed by him, and accepted, was the marriage of Charles Martel, the grandson of Charles of Anjou, with Rudolf's daughter Clementia; the dowry she was to bring with her was nothing less than the kingdom of Arles, which was to be reconstituted for the Prince of Salerno, Charles' eldest son; and he was to pass it on immediately to the young couple, whose marriage was to inaugurate a new system of alliances in Europe. The scheme raised lively alarm in Burgundy and Provence; Count Philip of Savoy, the Count-Palatine Otto IV of Franche Comté, Duke Robert of Burgundy, and others used every effort to make it fail. Whether they would have succeeded, we shall never know. For the catastrophe of the Sicilian Vespers soon put an end to the soaring ambition of the house of Anjou. Henceforward the question for Charles was to maintain his Sicilian kingdom, not to acquire a new one.

A similar project was to be raised thirty years later. Once more it was a question of reconciling Guelf and Ghibelline, the Emperor Henry VII and King Robert of Naples; the reconciliation was by no means displeasing to Pope Clement V, since it would have furnished him with a means of support against the imperious demands of Philip the Fair. One of the conditions of the scheme was the re-establishment of the kingdom of Arles for one of King Robert's sons, who was to marry a daughter of Henry VII. The project seems to have been seriously discussed during the year 1310, both at the court of Avignon and in the chanceries of Naples and the Empire.

It was easy to foresee the opposition this scheme was likely to encounter. It had to reckon with the hostility of divers rulers whose domains formed part of the kingdom; as they were in fact independent, they were not anxious for this new suzerainty to which they were expected to submit. But above all the opposition of the King of France was to be anticipated. The plan of the treaty did, indeed, lay down that any king appointed by Henry VII "ez aisles ou ez frontières du royaume de France" should bind himself by oath to be "bienveillant du roy de France ou allié a lui." This was not enough to disarm Philip the Fair; he was not anxious to see the organisation of a regime which would have the effect of consolidating, to his own detriment, the power of his cousins of Anjou in the south-east of Gaul. We know how vigorously his ambassadors protested at the court of Avignon, towards the end of the year 1310, against the reconstruction of the kingdom of Arles, "if kingdom it be." They did not fail to impress

on the timid Clement V that their king would hold him responsible for
this untoward creation. It was inevitable that the project should be
silently dropped when the Pope declared that he refused his adhesion to
it; moreover, the reconciliation of Henry VII and King Robert was to
remain in the realm of things unattainable. On the other hand, negotiators
on both sides worked for several years to bring about an accord between
Philip the Fair and the Emperor; this also came to nothing, and it seems
highly probable that the policy pursued by the King of France on his
eastern and south-eastern frontiers contributed no little to the failure.

Philip the Fair had not hesitated to declare his opposition to the
accession of an Angevin prince to the crown of Arles. Four years later,
however, he was himself working to place this crown on the head of one of
his own sons, probably the future Philip the Tall. Now, besides the
opposition of the Angevins of Naples, the Dauphin of Viennois, John II,
and Amadeus V, Count of Savoy, forgot their rivalry to make common
cause against this project. What became of it we do not know. For
Philip the Fair died the same year, and his ambitions vanished with him.

Ten years later, the kingdom of Arles became the object of a new
scheme, contrived once again for the advantage not of the Angevins but
of the Capetians of France. The author of this scheme was no other than
Henry's son, John of Luxemburg, the King of Bohemia. He had one end
in view, to win over the King of France, Charles the Fair, to the policy
of restoring the house of Luxemburg to the imperial throne, which at
the moment was in dispute between the houses of Bavaria and Habsburg.
To attain this end, it was necessary to give France something in return;
and the proposal was to hand over the kingdom of Arles to Charles,
Count of Valois, the brother of Philip the Fair and uncle of the reigning
monarch. The misfortune was that this ingenious scheme encountered
the opposition of Robert of Anjou, King of Naples and Count of Provence,
in spite of the tie which linked him with Charles of Valois in the marriage
of Charles' daughter with Charles of Calabria, the heir-presumptive of
Naples. The Angevin king would not renounce, even in Charles' favour,
the hope so long entertained of acquiring the crown of Arles for himself
and his line.

A similar project was put forward in 1332, once again on the initiative
of John of Bohemia. The idea was to obtain the election of an Emperor
favourable to the house of Luxemburg in place of Lewis of Bavaria, and
to establish for John a hereditary kingdom in Italy. In return for these
advantages, which were of the greatest importance to the Luxemburgs,
the imperial authority would invite the King of France, Philip of Valois,
to undertake the government of the kingdom of Arles and Vienne; and
assent to this had already been given by Duke Henry of Lower Bavaria,
who was to be Emperor under the scheme. The plan could only succeed
provided that Lewis of Bavaria would bring himself to abdicate. From
this course Lewis was dissuaded by certain powerful influences: first of

all, Michael of Cesena and his associates, the Spiritual Franciscans; secondly, King Robert of Naples, the head of a house of which several members professed a lively sympathy with this Franciscan sect; and, finally, the aged Cardinal Napoleon Orsini, whose body still lies in the lower basilica at Assisi, and who in his day played an important rôle in the politics of the time. Thus the second of John of Bohemia's schemes was ruined.

These failures had not discouraged the ambition of the King of France; he had his eyes constantly fixed upon the rich domains of Burgundy and the valley of the Rhone. To bar the road to him, Lewis of Bavaria, two years after the essays of John of Bohemia, tried to block Philip's policy by creating a King of Arles who would not be a Capetian. At that time Dauphiné was governed by Humbert II, the last descendant of three lines to which this county had belonged in turn. He had been brought up at the brilliant court of Naples, and his imagination was filled with magnificent dreams that could never come true; to Lewis of Bavaria he appeared to be just the man whose ardent ambition could be tempted. So he dispatched an embassy to offer him, in the name of the Empire, the crown of Arles and Vienne. Humbert's pride was certainly flattered by this brilliant perspective; but, dreamer as he was, he could not fail to realise that he would encounter the energetic resistance of the powerful King of France. Besides, he had also to reckon with the determined opposition of Pope John XXII. The Pope could not be expected to support a project for the creation of a kingdom put forward by a ruler who had been banned by the Church and was in open revolt against its power. Guided by common prudence as well as by religious sentiments, the dauphin had to bring himself to decline the offer of Lewis of Bavaria.

These numerous negotiations, the different authors of which aimed at settling at one stroke the fate of the kingdom of Arles, had continued for half a century without producing any resultant advantage either to the French princes, the Angevin princes, or any other claimants. However, in the course of the same period, the firm and persistent pressure of the policy of the Capetian kings on different parts of the kingdom of Arles had brought some partial, but at the same time quite substantial, advantages to France, which promised a still more successful prospect for the future.

In the last quarter of the thirteenth century, the French monarchy, putting forward the claim that in making war on Aragon it was serving the cause of the Church, had obtained from the Holy See a tenth of the revenues of all benefices; and now, by a special favour, the Popes had assigned the French kings a tenth from various dioceses in the kingdom of Arles, though these were not dependent on the French Crown. It goes without saying that this favour was revoked during the quarrel of Boniface VIII and Philip the Fair; but it remains a fact that for a certain number of years, as far as the payment of tenths was concerned, the clergy of this region had been treated as French clergy.

This assimilation Philip the Fair and his successors were only too anxious to push still farther, as can be seen from the way in which they acted with regard to the temporalities of certain bishoprics in the kingdom of Arles. The temporalities of the archbishopric of Lyons formed an important principality on which the city was dependent. To subordinate this to the royal authority was an aim that had long been pressed by French policy; as is well known, Philip the Fair, assisted by the towns-folk of Lyons, laboured actively to this end, and succeeded, in 1312, in reaching the desired goal, though not without causing grave ill-feeling in the Church as well as in the Empire. Some years earlier, in 1305 and in 1307, conventions made with the Bishops of Viviers gave the king an overriding influence in the domains of that bishopric; he formed a *pariage*, or association, with the bishop, which in the nature of things meant that the royal authority was really dominant. On the other side of the Rhone there extended an ecclesiastical principality of considerable importance, the temporality of the Archbishop of Vienne. The king could certainly not lay hands on this domain; but he kept a close watch on it, and, in order to make his presence felt, Philip VI constructed opposite Vienne at Sainte-Colombe one of those fortified bridge-heads which he regarded as so useful on the French bank of the Rhone. The clergy of Vienne well understood the intentions of their powerful neighbour, and they were anything but pleased by them.

It was not only the ecclesiastical temporalities that stirred the ambition of the French monarchy. At the end of the thirteenth century, Philip the Fair had acquired a dominance over the County of Burgundy (Franche Comté) which no local resistance could shake. By the marriage of his son, the future Philip the Tall, with the heiress to the county, a French dynasty was installed there to the great injury of imperial authority. Farther south, the French king had brought the Count of Valentinois under his influence. Moreover, by skilfully making use of the traditional rivalry between the Count of Savoy and the Dauphin of Viennois, he had made his support necessary to one or other of them, according to circumstances, sometimes to both at once. The time came when the Dauphin Humbert II, having no direct heir and being hope-lessly encumbered with financial difficulties, was prepared to sell his dominions. Philip of Valois, as is well known, bought them from him and put in Humbert's place the eldest son of the King of France, who was to take the title of dauphin without there being any actual change in the subordinate relation of Dauphiné to the ruler of the Empire; although he belonged to the French royal house, the dauphin was to remain, in law, a prince of the Empire.

The negotiations for this cession of Dauphiné were begun during the reign of Lewis of Bavaria, who was not consulted at all; they were concluded during the first years of his successor, Charles IV of Bohemia, whose consent was similarly not asked for. There was nothing abnormal in such a procedure at this time. Charles IV was entirely disregarded in 1348 when Queen Joanna of Provence sold the imperial town of Avignon to the Holy See, and again in 1355 when the French dauphin and the Count of Savoy concluded a treaty which profoundly altered the territorial constitution of their respective States[1]. Meanwhile, in 1350, the county of Burgundy passed to a minor, Philip of Rouvres, who by his mother's second marriage became the step-son of King John. Further, in the course of these years, the French king, having consolidated his position in Dauphiné, tried by a similar arrangement to make himself master of Provence. This ambitious scheme was premature, it is true; but it was certainly the case that from this time, during the second half of the fourteenth century, the royal government and especially its representatives in Dauphiné, the governor and the delphinal council, worked assiduously to transfer the control of Provence from the Angevins of Naples to the French royal house. This was a scheme which must not be lost from sight if the history of the policy pursued by France in these regions is to be properly elucidated.

The situation in the kingdom of Arles during the early years of his reign could not fail to cause grave anxiety to the Emperor Charles IV. Undoubtedly he aimed at recovering the *iura Imperii* which were being seriously compromised by the encroachments, especially of France, but the question was how this programme was to be realised. Charles was not possessed at all of the chivalrous traits which distinguished his father John of Bohemia, the hero of Crécy, and his grandfather Henry VII; his qualities were in the spheres of diplomacy and public business. Meticulous, suspicious, and at the same time cold and calculating by nature, he was endowed with consummate patience, which enabled him to leave to time the solution of many difficulties. To make war on France on behalf of the kingdom of Arles was perhaps in his mind; there is a sign of this in the pact he made in June 1348 with the King of England, Edward III, in which he stipulated to take no part in the struggle between Edward and Philip of Valois, unless he decided to enter into war with France *pro iuribus Imperii nostri*. This eventuality was never realised: it was consonant neither with Charles' own character nor with his relations with the French rulers.

Meanwhile, he renounced none of his claims to sovereignty over a considerable portion of ancient Gaul, and especially over the kingdom of

[1] Amadeus VI, "the Green Count," of Savoy ceded his lands in Viennois and the southern Lyonnais to the dauphin in exchange for Faucigny and Gex and the suzerainty of Genevois. The rivers Rhone and Guiers became the boundary, which lasted until 1601. Thus both States were consolidated, the dauphin obtaining all Viennois to the south and west of the two rivers, the Count of Savoy lands to the north and east round the Lake of Geneva.

Arles. At the beginning of his reign he had manifested this intention by giving his uncle Baldwin, Archbishop of Trèves, the function of acting as his representative, in the capacity of arch-chancellor of the kingdom, a title retained by the archbishops of Trèves up to the seventeenth century. But these claims, which he affirmed at intervals and of which he sometimes liked to make a show, were especially maintained by him in a diplomatic contest, at times somewhat stormy, with intervals of comparative calm, at times displayed in public acts which are as contradictory as the tendencies which inspired them. The present writer has already attempted to disentangle the threads of this story, in a book published more than forty years ago[1]. A detailed account would exceed the limits of this chapter, and it must suffice to denote the main points which mark the conduct of the Emperor in relation to the kingdom of Arles.

Charles viewed himself as being the legal embodiment of all secular sovereignty in the kingdom; it resulted that there were no rightful powers other than those emanating from the plenitude of jurisdiction possessed by him. In the secular world, apart from him, the princes could appeal only to claims that were open to dispute; this was a defect in an age more keenly concerned than our own with the ideas of justice and right. It is not surprising, too, that on various occasions he refused to recognise the validity of important acts which had been carried through without his consent, such as the cession of Dauphiné or the treaty between the dauphin and Savoy in 1355. Nor is it surprising to find a large number of charters issuing from his chancery to ecclesiastical or lay nobles from whom he exacted homage, to religious establishments, or to towns in the kingdom, granting rights of jurisdiction, municipal organisation, coinage, fairs and markets, even the creation of universities. He never ceased to act as sovereign, and he used the language of his part when he claimed feudal homage from rulers such as the Counts of Burgundy, Savoy, and Provence, the dauphin, or the holders of the great episcopal sees; he received it when they had an interest in approaching the imperial court, or wished to regularise their position in the eyes of the law. His diplomas undoubtedly possessed, both for the grantor and for the recipients, a moral and a legal interest; but the beneficiaries were experienced enough to know that the Emperor would not employ force to give them sanction.

So numerous are the manifestations of this that if anyone were to cast a hasty glance over the register of Charles IV's acts he might easily be led to imagine that the author of them enjoyed an undisputed authority in these parts. Two instances will be sufficient to illustrate the point.

First of all, the imperial diet held at Metz in December 1356, a few months after the battle of Poitiers. It was a brilliant gathering, and the Cardinal of Périgord was there to represent the Holy See. The great nobles thronged the court, bringing to the sovereign the unequivocal testimony of their obedience. It was an event quite out of the common

Le royaume d'Arles et de Vienne (1138–1378), Paris, 1891.

in the annals of the Empire when on 22 December 1356 the young Dauphin Charles, regent of France for his father John, who was a captive in English hands, presented himself at the gates of Metz to discharge his duties as a prince of the Empire. He entered the city escorted by a brilliant cavalcade; a period of festivities and negotiations commenced, in the course of which the dauphin decided to yield to the ruler of the Empire what his father John the previous year had hesitated to do. It was undoubtedly under the dauphin's influence that the young Philip of Rouvres paid to the Emperor's representative the homage which had long been demanded for the county of Burgundy; while, for his part, the regent of France personally did homage to Charles IV for Dauphiné, and obtained from him in exchange the investiture of this province and the confirmation of his privileges.

Nine years later the Emperor gave a still more striking display of his rights over the kingdom. In 1365 he went to Provence to revive the solemn ceremony of royal coronation which had lapsed for two centuries. The inhabitants of Geneva, of Savoy, and of Dauphiné gave him a magnificent reception *en route*, such as it was their duty to give to their acknowledged sovereign. After a stay with Pope Urban V at Avignon, where he met the Dukes of Berry and Anjou, he continued his journey and arrived at Arles surrounded by a numerous escort, including the Duke of Bourbon and Count Amadeus VI of Savoy. On 4 June, the basilica of St Trophimus witnessed for the last time the splendours of this ceremony, in which the Emperor received from Archbishop William de la Garde the royal crown of Arles and Vienne. This journey was the occasion of numerous grants of privileges, which were bestowed upon prelates, lay nobles, and the new universities of Geneva and Orange; added to this was the creation by diploma of a special coinage. It seemed that Charles IV, in such circumstances, could perform all the functions necessary to display, at any rate in theory, his sovereignty over the kingdom.

Nor did he limit himself to displays such as these. On several occasions in the course of his long reign he went farther and tried to make his authority more real by delegating it. His method was to create imperial vicars, whom he instituted in the kingdom of Arles as in other parts of his dominions, notably in Italy. In 1349, at the moment when the Capetian dynasty had just acquired Dauphiné, Charles, who bore this with an ill grace, appointed the Count of Valentinois as his vicar in the kingdom; he delegated the supreme jurisdiction to him, and by the same act put him in a position transcending that of the bishops and great nobles who till then had been his peers. Later, by virtue of various diplomas, the first of which is dated July 1356, Count Amadeus VI of Savoy, known as the "Green Count," was deputed, as vicar, to hold sovereign imperial rights not only in his hereditary estates, but also in the dioceses of Lausanne, Sion, Geneva, Belley, Ivrea, Turin, and in various neighbouring districts; it was as though the Emperor, by this act, was wishing to contribute to the formation of a vast territorial sovereignty in favour of the house of Savoy. At the end of this same year, 1356, on the occasion of the diet of Metz, Charles, the son of King John of France, obtained the same favour for the domains which he had acquired from the Dauphin Humbert II.

Now the French monarchy had for a century been striving to expel foreign dynasties, including its kinsmen of Naples, from the kingdom of Arles and Vienne, with the clear intention of acquiring it for itself. The granting of the vicariate, which was common in the second half of the fourteenth century, seemed to members of the French government a means of realising the acquisition, while in appearances safeguarding imperial sovereignty, which would thus become a mere outward show. In 1355, before the diet of Metz, the dauphin's council had claimed for him, not indeed the whole kingdom of Arles, but a delegation of imperial sovereignty over his own domains in Dauphiné, over Vienne and its castles, over the counties of Provence, Forcalquier, Valentinois, and Genevois, over the temporalities of the churches of Valence, Die, Sion, Lausanne, and Geneva, and in addition the advocacy of several important monasteries in those parts. The diploma granted to the dauphin on the occasion of his journey to Metz, since it restricted the vicariate to Dauphiné, was far from satisfactory to the extensive ambitions of the French government. Those who directed its policy, with their characteristic tenacity, were later to take the project in hand again.

In 1365, when Charles IV stopped at Grenoble on his way to Arles for the coronation, the governor who represented the king-dauphin Charles V had the task of requesting, on behalf of his master, from the Emperor a delegation very similar to that asked for ten years previously, but including also the marquessate of Saluzzo on the other side of the Alps. The negotiations that were begun on this point came to nothing. Charles was evidently not prepared to make concessions of this character; they would have seriously compromised his relations with the Count of Savoy, whose vicariate, moreover, he revoked in 1366.

It was a different story thirteen years later, when Charles IV, realising the dangers that threatened his dynasty after his death, wished to form a close tie with his relatives at the French court, and paid Charles V the famous visit which caused such agitation in the chanceries of the western kingdoms. The Emperor, who was a skilful negotiator, certainly neglected no means of winning the favour of his host. We do not know exactly the promises he obtained from Charles V, who was a ruler as discreet as himself. What we can say is that, in the matter of his own concessions to France, the Emperor held out expectations of his support against England, that he consented to recognise the Franco-Hungarian alliance, which was to be cemented by the marriage of the king's younger son Louis of Valois (later Louis of Orleans), with the heiress of Hungary and finally, which is most to the purpose here, that he handed over to the French dauphin the vicariate of the whole kingdom of Arles with the exception of Savoy.

This grant was made effective by various solemn diplomas issuing from the imperial chancery at Paris in January 1378. In the whole kingdom of Arles, from Franche Comté to Provence, except the county of Savoy, the young dauphin, Charles, the eldest son of the King of France, received, with the title of Vicar of the Empire, the delegation of most of the attributes of sovereign power—supreme jurisdiction, the rights of pardon and amnesty, of declaring war, of exercising the ecclesiastical patronage and the feudal suzerainty of the Emperor, of coining money, of instituting tolls, fairs, and markets; in short, practically the sum total of regalian rights. All concessions were revoked which conflicted with the diploma conferring the vicariate for his lifetime on the young dauphin.

Actually this grant did not produce throughout the whole kingdom of Arles the effect which the French court might perhaps have been led to imagine. But it was effective in the Rhone region at any rate. The governor of Dauphiné hoisted the standard of the vicar and, by virtue of the powers which he derived from the title conferred on his master, compelled the allodial lords, especially bishops who had previously relied on the immunities granted them by charter, to recognise the superior authority of the dauphin acting in the Emperor's name; the Archbishop of Vienne, the Bishop of Valence, the Count of Valentinois all discovered this to their cost. To resist with effect the encroachment of the delphinal government required force that they could not muster; but others possessed it and made use of it, for instance the regents of Provence for the children of Louis I of Anjou.

Charles IV did not long survive his grant of the imperial vicariate to the French dauphin. His immediate successor, his son Wenceslas, and after him Rupert of the Palatinate, were too far off and too much occupied with other things; they seem to have paid little heed to the kingdom of Arles. It was different with the Emperor Sigismund, another of Charles IV's sons. During the first part of his reign (which began in 1410), he displayed on several occasions, as his father had done, his claim to sovereignty. The journey he undertook at the end of 1415 to Perpignan to meet Pope Benedict XIII, whose abdication he wished to obtain, gave the peoples of the Rhone valley the opportunity once more to render the honours due to their lawful sovereign. He himself, like his father, was prodigal of grants and diplomas, among which may be mentioned the one that raised Amadeus VIII, Count of Savoy, to the rank of duke[1], and the confirmation of privileges to the towns of Valence and

---

[1] With Amadeus VIII (1391–1440), created first Duke of Savoy on 9 February 1416, and later the conciliar anti-Pope Felix V, the medieval evolution of the State of Savoy, begun by Humbert Whitehands, was completed. The duke's dominions in

Vienne; further, he made the Bishop of Valence his vicar, and renewed the grant again in 1426. The representatives of the King of France in Dauphiné took offence at this. Sigismund certainly was at pains to appease them, for, on the occasion of his journey to Perpignan, he described himself as the fervent friend of Charles VI. This friendship did not survive the visit of the Emperor, a few months later, to the English court, where the glories of Agincourt were still fresh. He made a rapid *volte-face*, characteristic of his fickle temperament, and embraced an alliance with Henry V, becoming his warm partisan. He went so far as to form a plan to unite his forces with those of the victor of Agincourt, and to make France feel his strength, by taking from her the regions which he accused her of having usurped from him. Of these regions he placed Dauphiné in the forefront, claiming that the Empire had never ratified the agreement made between Philip of Valois and the Dauphin Humbert II; and he did not hide his intention of giving it, after he had won it back, to a prince of the English royal family. This design, which caused some uneasiness in France, was not to be put into execution; it was one of those fanciful ideas that one finds on so many pages of the history of the kingdom of Arles.

Later, influenced doubtless by the French victories, Sigismund changed his point of view once more. The grant of the imperial vicariate had been limited to the lifetime of Charles V's eldest son, Charles VI; so, on his

Burgundy now consisted of Savoy proper (round Chambéry), Maurienne, Bugey, Bresse, Gex, Genevois (annexed finally in 1405), Tarantaise, Faucigny, Aosta, Chablais and the Lower Valais, and the Pays de Vaud (first entered by Count Peter II in the thirteenth century), thus encircling the Lake of Geneva and commanding the three Alpine passes of the Great and Little St Bernard and the Mont Cenis. Only the city of Geneva was a real alien enclave nominally under its bishop. Entrenched solidly, as the Counts of Savoy had long been partially, in the western Alps, the duke ruled in Italy, after the extinction of the vassal Princes of Achaia in 1418, the plain of Piedmont, including Turin and Ivrea, to which he added Vercelli in 1427, and Tenda, leading to his Provençal county of Nice on the Mediterranean; he was suzerain of the Marquessate of Saluzzo. Thus, as once before in the eleventh century, the house of Savoy dominated the borderlands of Burgundy and Italy from the Jura to the Mediterranean, and though still looking north as well as south, its greatest opportunities of expansion were in Italy.

This assemblage of fiefs and jurisdictions, gradually put together during four centuries, was already acquiring a certain unity and central administration. There were a ducal council and a *Cour des Comptes*; Estates General of the duchy were occasionally summoned, as well as local assemblies; Amadeus VIII, in this, too, a consolidator, issued the first General Statute of laws for his dominions in 1430. In local government the land was divided into bailiwicks, subdivided into castellanies. In short, Savoy had passed, like other similar principalities of the time, from the purely feudal to the monarchic stage. It was the only independent State in Burgundy, save one or two Swiss cantons and the principality of Orange, which emerged from the Middle Ages. Its ruler still hoped for expansion on all sides, but the growth of the French kingdom and the Swiss Confederation was already checking its ambitions north of the Alps, while its steady advance in Italy amid the wars of Lombardy was already pointing the way to its future destiny.

death in 1422, it legally came to an end. Later on, it became known in the entourage of Charles VII that Sigismund was returning to his father's policy and might be inclined to renew this grant in favour of France. The question whether there was any advantage from such an arrangement was discussed in the royal council and decided in the negative. The monarchy felt itself strong enough in the east and south-east of France to stand on its own feet. It was obvious that the imperial power was getting more and more feeble in those regions, and that it could cause no alarm to France. Another power was growing and needed to be watched with care, and if need be forcibly opposed, by the Valois kings, though in the meanwhile it served a useful purpose on the eastern frontiers by preventing any advance on the part of the Habsburg Emperors. This was Burgundy under its second ducal house, which in the course of the fifteenth century came near to changing the whole future of the Capetian monarchy. The battle of Nancy (1477), as is well known, at one stroke put an end to the life of the "Grand Duke of the West," and also to his ambitious schemes.

Though his chief preoccupation was to combat the policy of Charles the Bold, Louis XI did not abandon the traditional designs of his predecessors upon the kingdom of Arles. While still dauphin, he had retired into his Alpine domains, wishing to emancipate himself from his father's control; having in consequence incurred the wrath of Charles VII, he had taken refuge in Flanders, leaving his principality to come under his father's direct and absolute rule. When he became king, Louis did not dream of making Dauphiné autonomous again. As dauphin and as king, he completed the work begun by his ancestors, and succeeded in finally establishing his suzerainty over the Archbishop of Vienne and the Bishop of Gap, whose allodial position was transformed into one of vassalage. At the end of his reign, in 1481, he was able to acquire the jewel so long coveted in vain—Provence; and from this time its destiny was linked with that of France. Henceforward, the king was master of Lyons, of Dauphiné, to which Valentinois had been added in the first half of the fifteenth century, of Vivarais, and of Provence; he kept a watch over Avignon from his fortress at Villeneuve; and so in the chief part of the kingdom of Arles he was unquestionably the dominant power. Savoy and the districts of French Switzerland certainly remained independent, and for two centuries to come Franche Comté avoided the sovereignty of France. But the French king was master of the fertile valley of the Rhone, of Lyons, a commercial town of the first rank, and of the great port of Marseilles, which introduced French influence into the Mediterranean. A splendid share had come to the kingdom of the fleurs-de-lis; this was the due reward of a far-seeing and patient policy, which made it possible to look forward to the future with confidence and with security.

CHAPTER X

THE LOW COUNTRIES

The territories which it became customary to describe collectively at the end of the Middle Ages as the Low Countries (*Partes Advallenses, Nederlanden*) had not, in fact, any unity, whether geographical, linguistic, or political. Extending from the Ardennes to the shores of the North Sea, the area they covered included practically the whole of the basin of the Scheldt, as well as the basins of the lower and middle Meuse and the lower Rhine. The inhabitants, north of a line drawn from Dunkirk to Maestricht, were of Frisian and Frankish origin and spoke Germanic dialects; those south of this line, although containing a strong admixture of German elements resulting from the invasions of the fifth century, had preserved a language which in its different forms, known usually by the generic name of Walloon, derived directly from Latin. As a contrast to this horizontal division of the country between the two languages, it was divided politically by a line running from north to south. The treaties of partition in the Carolingian age had in effect made the Scheldt the boundary between the kingdoms of France and Germany; to France was assigned the county of Flanders on the left bank of the river, to Germany the duchy of Lower Lorraine on the right bank. So, looked at from every point of view, the Low Countries appeared essentially as a frontier-country; the territory, the race, the language, and the suzerainty of France on the one side, of Germany on the other, were prolonged into it and came thus into juxtaposition. And henceforward in history the Low Countries were destined to be subject to the constant influence of these two great States, though eventually they were to arrive at an independent position of their own between them.

Until the beginning of the twelfth century, the weakness of the French kings left the Counts of Flanders free to develop a feudal autonomy so complete that the suzerainty of the Crown there was reduced to a merely nominal prerogative. In the duchy of Lorraine, however, the power of the Emperors succeeded in preventing the higher nobility from throwing off the yoke which it was the duty of the Bishops of Liège, Utrecht, and Cambrai to maintain. But after the War of Investitures there was a complete reversal of the situation. Absorbed by the internal troubles of Germany and their duel with the Papacy, the Emperors paid no heed to the Low Countries; and the Lotharingian nobles took advantage of this to found in their turn solid feudal principalities, after the example and on the model of their neighbours of Flanders. So, by the side of the episcopal principalities of Liège, Cambrai, and Utrecht, created by the

Ottos in the tenth century to hold the lay nobles in leash, were formed the duchies of Brabant and Limburg, and the counties of Hainault, Namur, Luxemburg, and Holland-Zeeland. From that time their independence with regard to the Empire continued constantly to increase. Lorraine did not revolt against the Emperors; its interests were separate, and, while it continued to belong to them in law, it became foreign to them in practice. The troubles of the Great Interregnum (1254–73) completed the process of detachment, and to this Rudolf of Habsburg had perforce to submit. He dared not intervene when in 1288 Duke John I of Brabant by force of arms conquered the duchy of Limburg at the battle of Worringen; Limburg was henceforward to belong to the Brabançon dynasty. Eleven years later, in 1299, the helplessness of Germany was displayed in an even more deplorable light. In spite of the threats of Albert of Austria, Count John of Hainault (John of Avesnes) took possession of the counties of Holland and Zeeland, to which he claimed the succession; nor did he hesitate to march against Albert, who had advanced to Nimwegen but on the count's approach had to beat a hasty retreat.

While German suzerainty was losing its hold over the Lotharingian nobles, French suzerainty, on the other hand, weighed more and more heavily upon the Count of Flanders. As the Capetian monarchy consolidated its power, one of the clearest objectives of its policy was to compel the obedience of its great vassal in the north, whose position became so hazardous that in self-defence he had recourse to the support of England. The first manifestation of this policy was the intervention of Louis VI in 1127 in the question of the succession to Flanders after the murder of Charles the Good. Under Philip Augustus, Count Philip of Alsace (1157–91) was forced after a long war to surrender to the Crown the territories which were from this time onwards to form the county of Artois. In 1214, Count Ferrand was involved in the disaster of Bouvines and taken prisoner on the field of battle; he was only released after subscribing to the treaty of Melun (5 April 1226), by which his obedience was assured. After him the Countesses Joanna (1202–44) and Margaret (1244–78) accepted a situation of which the French monarchy with its increasing prestige allowed no modification; by their submission they were assured of the goodwill of the king, who looked on them as useful agents of his policy and accorded them his protection against their enemies. During the long contest between the houses of Avesnes and Dampierre, deriving from the two marriages of Countess Margaret and each claiming the succession, the Crown effectively supported the latter against its rival. And this support made Guy de Dampierre, who became Count of Flanders in 1278, an effective instrument of French expansion; from that time the Capetian monarchy used every effort to bring the whole of the Low Countries under its hegemony. In vain did John of Avesnes in 1277 urge Rudolf of Habsburg to come to his rescue against Dampierre, who, thanks to France, was able to ridicule the "blunted sword of the Empire." In fact, the house of Flanders owed the position which it was henceforward to enjoy to the obedience it shewed to its suzerain, whose designs it continued to favour. Through it the French monarchy extended its sphere of influence among the nobles on the right bank of the Scheldt, taking a hand in all their quarrels; and so completely did they submit to its interference that the moment seemed to be approaching when the Lotharingian lands of the Low Countries, which Germany no longer thought of defending, would be added to the territory of the French kingdom.

That this annexation was prevented was due much more to social causes than to political. So, in order to comprehend the sequence of events, it is necessary at this point to envisage the phenomena to which the marvellous effervescence of town life had given rise, from the thirteenth century onwards, in the basins of the Meuse and the Scheldt.

The geographical situation of the Low Countries, which made them dependent on the political fluctuations of the two great States of Western Europe, had also the effect of arousing at an early date a powerful economic vitality. Having a natural outlet to the North Sea by three rivers provided with numerous navigable tributaries, they were possessed of a complete system of communications; owing to this, the commercial movement initiated by the voyages of the Scandinavian peoples at their natural terminus—the confluence of the Rhine, Meuse, and Scheldt— penetrated into the interior during the course of the tenth century. Thielt and Dorestad on the lower reaches of the Rhine appear henceforward as trading points, and their influence was soon felt higher up the rivers. In the basin of the Scheldt it spread to Arras, Cambrai, Douai, Lille, Ypres, Ghent, Saint-Omer, and Bruges; up the Meuse, to Dinant, Huy, Liège, and Maestricht. In all these places a collection of merchants and craftsmen settled round the walls which had been constructed after the Norman invasions to serve as a refuge for the populace of the neighbourhood. To the old military *bourg* there was thus attached the new *bourg* (*novus burgus, portus*), which grew in size as the economic life became more intense; moreover, new needs and a way of life hitherto unknown demanded a profound transformation of law and institutions. Whether they liked it or no, the territorial princes were forced to allow to the newcomers a law conformable to the needs of the life they led. In the midst of a society founded exclusively on agriculture, these newcomers, depending solely on the far more complicated business of commerce and industry, formed a distinct social group; of necessity it had to receive a recognition as a legal group as well. This group is the *bourgeoisie*, a new class, which acquires a definitive legal status in the course of the twelfth century by means of charters obtained from the princes. At this point the trading *bourgs* which it had founded around the feudal *bourgs* are transformed into towns; and in every town the municipal organisation was in the hands of the *bourgeois* who had taken up their residence within it.

Not merely for the official recognition of the *bourgeoisie* does the twelfth century mark an epoch in the history of the Low Countries; it was in this century too that they acquired the essentially urban character which they have preserved to the present day. Nowhere, save only in the Lombard plain, were the towns so numerous, so populous, or so active. While the earliest commercial centres continued to expand, new ones were founded; in Brabant, the towns of Louvain, Brussels, and Antwerp began to rival the Flemish towns. Town law was accorded to a number of lesser localities, which received from the princes the grant of charters imitated from those of their more important neighbours. And this fecundity of urban life has its explanation in the increasing intensity of the economic movement, of which the *bourgeoisie* was the instrument.

In order to explain this remarkable progress, it must be noted that it was the collaboration of industry with commerce that made it possible. The Low Countries enjoyed this extraordinary prosperity, not merely because they possessed means of communication and transit, but also, and perhaps mainly, because they were the seat of a busy industrial productivity. Since Roman times, the metal industry had been extensively pursued in the valley of the Meuse and the woollen industry in the basin of the Scheldt. The invasions of the Northmen and the disorders of the ninth century had brought them to decay but not to total extinction. They were developed anew as soon as the re-birth of commerce gave them a fresh impulse. In the eleventh century the copper industry revived at Huy and at Dinant, and at the same time the woollen industry revived in Flanders. Concentrated in the growing towns, these crafts, thanks to the commercial stream which they fed with their products, at once played the part of exporting industries. They were concerned not only with the home market but with the foreign market as well, and their possibilities of expansion became henceforward unbounded. The merchants carried these products abroad and returned with the raw material. From the beginning of the eleventh century the Flemings sold their cloth at London and furnished themselves there with wool; while from the beginning of the twelfth century the Dinant merchants went to the mines of Goslar to obtain their supplies of copper.

By supplying foreign merchants with goods which soon enjoyed a universal reputation for excellence, the craftsmen of the Low Countries had a large share in attracting the merchants thither. The cloth of Flanders, and soon too that of Brabant, became a principal feature in the export trade, which increased with the increasing expansion of commercial activity in Europe. In the course of the twelfth century the port of Genoa provided a centre for its distribution in the Mediterranean, while in the North it was carried on shipboard along the coasts of the North Sea and the Baltic as far as the fairs of Novgorod. In the fairs of Champagne it formed one of the principal objects of barter and of credit transactions between the merchants of Italy and of the Low Countries. In England the combined traffic in cloth and wool attained such proportions that it gave rise to the formation of the Flemish *hansa* of London, in which some fifteen towns of the county of Flanders participated. Bruges, where vessels were assured of an abundant supply of cloth for their homeward freight, took the place of the older markets of Thielt and Dorestad, and in the twelfth century became the chief port in the country. By about 1180 its busy traffic made it the commercial pivot of the Low Countries, while, in the thirteenth century, owing to colonies of Italians, Germans, Bretons, and Spaniards settled there, it became the chief centre of international commerce in the north of Europe. Along the gulf of Zwyn new quays were built to accommodate the vessels which owing to their increased tonnage could no longer reach the town itself; thus Damme was founded about 1180, and in the thirteenth century Hoeke, Monnikerede, and finally Sluys.

The imposing economic development of Flanders, of Brabant and certain parts of Hainault (Tournai, Valenciennes), of the district of Liège (Liège, Huy, Dinant, Maestricht), and of Holland (Utrecht, Dordrecht) had the effect not only of conferring an extraordinary influence and importance on the *bourgeoisie*, but also of giving rise to social phenomena of the greatest consequence. The practical effect of industries (the cloth and metal industries) which received their particular stimulus from the export trade was to produce on the one hand a numerous class of rich merchants, on the other a far more numerous class of workmen. Quite unlike most towns in the Middle Ages, in which the urban industries had as a general rule no outlet other than the local market, production in these towns depended on the boundless possibilities of the international market, with the result of a continual increase in the numbers of those who were engaged in it. In Flanders, in contrast to the smaller crafts—of bakers, smiths, butchers, and the like—each of which contained only a few dozen individuals, the gilds of fullers and weavers comprised some thousands of members. It has been computed that, in the middle of the fourteenth century, the numbers of the weavers alone at Ghent amounted at least to 4,500, so that we may infer that some 15,000 persons in all were dependent upon their labours. But, besides the weavers, there are the fullers, shearmen, dyers, and others to be taken into account; they were equally concerned in the making of cloth, and it can hardly be an over-estimate to assess the numbers of this group as at least of equal importance. The conclusion, then, is that in this town alone, in which the population at this date cannot have exceeded 50,000, some sixty per cent. of the whole, say 30,000 persons, depended for their livelihood on the great cloth-making industry. The state of affairs is analogous to that in a manufacturing town of the present day; it is evident that conditions which appear to us to be peculiarly modern were already in existence during the Middle Ages in the industrial centres of Belgium. From the thirteenth to the fifteenth century they frequently experienced all the hardships resulting from a stoppage of work. This might simply be caused by war or by some interruption in trade which prevented the arrival of wool or the exportation of cloth. But there was a more frequent cause in the inevitable conflicts which arose from the clash of opposing interests between the capitalist merchants and the wage-earning workmen whom they employed.

The craftsmen in the cloth industry differed in essentials from the normal craftsmen in the Middle Ages. They were not, in fact, petty independent masters, purchasing themselves in small quantities the raw material that they required and selling to their clients the manufactured article. In this industry the raw material, wool, was bought wholesale by the merchants at the fairs in England; the same merchants distributed it throughout the small workrooms of weavers, fullers etc., and it came back to them as textiles all ready to be sold to the foreign buyers. So the relations of the cloth merchants with the workers in cloth were remarkably similar to those of a large-scale employer dealing with home workers. The craftsmen lacked economic independence; or, to put it better, the workers in the cloth industry should be described as wage-earners rather than as craftsmen. In these conditions it was inevitable that the question of wages should soon arise between employers and employed. And it was even more obviously necessary that this must happen, because in all the towns the municipal authority was in the hands of the wealthy *bourgeoisie*, the class to which the wool and cloth merchants belonged. As they possessed the power, they used it naturally for their own advantage. The whole industrial organisation was contrived so as to bring rigidly under their control not merely the technical details of the industry, but all the activities and the pay of the corporations in which the various professions concerned with the making of cloth were grouped.

So it is not surprising to note grave symptoms of social unrest appearing in all the centres of this great industry in the middle of the thirteenth century. Already, in 1245, the *échevins* of Douai had intervened to prevent the formation of "takehans," that is to say, of strikes. At Ghent in 1274, the weavers and fullers, following on an attempt at revolt, left the town in large numbers, to seek refuge in the towns of Brabant; but there the *échevins*, on the request of their Ghent colleagues, promised not to admit them. In 1280 a general movement of insurrection of the "lesser folk" against the "great folk" convulsed all the leading communes of Flanders, and also Tournai and Valenciennes. At Dinant the coppersmiths, whose economic position was exactly similar to that of the cloth workers, rose in open revolt in 1255.

The princes could not remain indifferent to disturbances which compromised so seriously the public peace. They were by no means sorry to see the haughty patricians, who by their inclinations towards independence had already aroused the uneasiness of their overlords, exposed to attacks which must perforce reduce their strength. In Brabant, the upper *bourgeoisie* obtained protection from the duke, and repaid it with a steadfast loyalty. But in Hainault and Flanders, the counts shewed themselves disposed to defend the malcontents against the very real abuses from which they suffered. Guy de Dampierre took advantage of the circumstances to add to his princely prerogatives at the expense of the plutocratic *échevins*, who were openly defying him and by their policy were tending to transform the towns into municipal republics. To thwart his efforts and to preserve their oligarchic authority, threatened by count and commons alike, they applied to a protector who was by no means averse to lend his aid, the new King of France, Philip the Fair.

Nothing could have been more tempting for this sovereign, who was bent on curbing the great vassals under his royal sway, than to have this opportunity both of weakening and of humiliating the powerful Count of Flanders. The favour with which the Crown for half a century had rewarded the submissiveness of the house of Flanders, and from which that house had reaped such great advantage, gave place henceforth to the openly avowed aim of bringing the comital independence to an end. In 1287 the king, at the urgent request of the *échevins* of Ghent, sent them a "sergent," who was instructed to place them under the direct authority of the king; and he hoisted the royal banner on the town belfry. Similar "guardians" were placed in charge of Bruges and Douai, and the *bailli* of Vermandois extended his sphere of control to include Flanders. In fact, the government of the count was at the mercy of his suzerain's pleasure. All who wished to resist his authority knew that they could now count on the approbation of the king.

The brutal treatment of Guy de Dampierre by Philip the Fair was not only induced by the wish to make the Count of Flanders closely subordinate to the monarchy, but also by the desire to secure the county as a base for military operations; hostilities between France and England, of which there had been a cessation since the time of St Louis, were at the end of the thirteenth century on the point of breaking out again. In his dangerous position, the idea of gaining the favour of Edward I must have presented itself to the mind of the count. Since 1293 he had been in secret negotiations with Edward, and in the next year he betrothed his daughter Philippa to the King of England's eldest son. Immediately the hand of Philip the Fair fell upon him; he was made prisoner and sent to the Louvre, and he only regained his freedom by handing over Philippa to his suzerain. Henceforward his position was untenable. The patricians of the towns, to whom the populace gave the name of *Leliaerts* (the party of the fleurs de lis), defied him openly, since they knew that he was under the king's suspicion. The king for his part allied himself with Guy's ancient foes, Count Florence of Holland and the Count of Hainault, John of Avesnes, whose house had been treated as an enemy by France until then. Feeling himself lost, the Flemish count decided to break with his suzerain, accusing him of violating the protection due to him as a vassal. He openly championed the party of the craftsmen against the patricians, and on 2 February 1297 made a formal alliance with the King of England, who promised to come to his help and not to make peace without his concurrence.

It was then too late, however. Deserted by the towns, which were under the control of the *Leliaerts*, and by the majority of the nobles, Guy could not hope to face the army which Philip led into Flanders in the following June. By September it had occupied the greater part of the county. Edward, who had just landed at Bruges, came to terms instead of fighting (October 1297), and then returned to England. His truce with Philip, which was to last until 6 January 1300, was soon turned into a definitive peace (19 June 1299), in which, in spite of Edward's promise, the Count of Flanders was not included. From that time the old count was helpless against his suzerain and was also exposed both from north and south to the attacks of John of Avesnes, who by inheritance had added the county of Holland to his county of Hainault; his fate was therefore a foregone conclusion. A second French expedition occupied Flanders without encountering any serious resistance. In May 1300 the count surrendered to Charles of Valois, and Philip, who refused to admit him to his presence, assigned as his prison the castle of Compiègne.

The king's purpose seemed to have been attained. Flanders lost its feudal autonomy, and as a result of its conquest sank to the position of a dependancy of the royal domain. Philip came to visit it in great pomp in May 1301, and, pending the promulgation of a decision as to its ultimate destiny, placed Jacques de Châtillon in charge as lieutenant-governor.

If the French occupation was greeted with enthusiasm by the patrician *Leliaerts*, whose dominance was thereby guaranteed, for this very reason the workers in the cloth industry, on whom the yoke of the masters weighed more heavily than ever, were driven to despair. The catastrophe which had befallen the house of Dampierre fell on them too; and the King of France, allied to their enemies and to their count's enemies, was doubly hateful to them. Moreover, from their retreat abroad, the sons of Guy were entering into secret correspondence with the leaders of the popular party. So the "commune" identified its cause with that of the dynasty, and against the royal fleur de lys, the badge of the patricians, they adopted the black lion of the count's banner. The *Clauwaerts* (the party of the lion's claw) and the *Leliaerts* confronted one another in a conflict which arose out of the social barriers between them, but which was transformed by circumstances into a political and national struggle. By the strangest of accidents the democratic movement of the workers championed the cause of feudal legitimacy.

The bitterness of party feeling, manifested first in rioting, was to result in an explosion. The hatred against the French was intensified by the arrogant behaviour of the mercenary soldiers of Châtillon and by the difference of their speech from the Flemish dialect. In the night of 17–18

May 1302, when the governor had come to Bruges to punish a revolt there, the people rose, massacred the soldiery as well as a large number of patricians, and gained possession of the town.

This insurrection, known to modern historians as the "Matins of Bruges," was the culmination of the agitation fomented by a popular leader, the weaver Peter de Coninck, who had already been for some time in communication with William of Juliers, the young nephew of Guy de Dampierre. It was the signal for a general rising in the whole of northern Flanders, in which not only the workmen and the lower *bourgeoisie* in the towns took part, but also the peasants of the coastal region, where the nobles had unwisely taken advantage of the French occupation to oppress them. Ghent alone remained in the hands of the patricians. The popular confidence reached its height when first William of Juliers and then Guy of Namur, one of Guy de Dampierre's sons, arrived to take the lead in the insurrection and to share the general danger.

It was to be expected that the king would avenge without delay the outrageous affront which had been inflicted upon him. His army was composed of Genoese mercenaries and of a numerous body of knights reinforced by contingents from John of Avesnes; it seemed that it must inevitably crush all resistance. On 11 July 1302 it met the Flemish troops before the walls of Courtrai. The weavers and fullers of Bruges formed the nucleus of these troops, and added to them were the craftsmen of the lesser gilds, the inhabitants of the smaller towns, and the peasants of the neighbourhood. They were improvised troops, but they were inspired by blind hatred of the enemy, whose victory would have forced them again under the yoke which they had just shaken off. In addition, the young princes who were in command had disposed them very skilfully behind trenches. Victory was finally assured them by the overweering pride of the French knights; these, anticipating an easy success, made a reckless charge which broke on the stout pikes of the Flemings. It was a victory which astounded Europe, and which caused the double triumph of *Clauwaerts* over *Leliaerts* and of the Flemish dynasty over the King of France.

The results of the battle of Courtrai were hardly less important than those of the battle of Bouvines a century before, which they directly reversed. Bouvines had been the commencement of the uninterrupted progress of the French monarchy in Flanders, and by means of Flanders in the whole of the Low Countries; Courtrai brought this development to an end. Certainly Philip the Fair could not tamely submit to the disaster which had just shaken his prestige. But he found himself now confronted by a popular resistance, the more formidable because the people had acquired self-confidence. In 1303, after an expedition which had no result, he concluded a truce and had to resign himself to the return of the aged Guy de Dampierre into his county. A fresh campaign, in 1304, only resulted in the indecisive battle of Mons-en-Pévèle

(18 August). Robert of Béthune, who had just succeeded his father, consented to the peace of Athis-sur-Orge in June 1305, in order to be reconciled with his suzerain; but it could not be made effective owing to the indignation which it aroused among the people. On the death of Philip the Fair, war was resumed, but Louis X failed in a fresh attempt to occupy Flanders (1315). After five years of latent hostility, his successor, Philip the Tall, at last concluded a definitive peace at Paris on 5 May 1320 with the adversary whom he could not conquer. The count surrendered to the Crown all his Walloon lands, that is to say the districts of Lille, Douai, and Orchies; in return for this sacrifice he recovered the rest of his fief. The protracted effort of the monarchy to absorb Flanders had only resulted therefore in the acquisition of a portion of the territory. It abandoned the annexation of the Germanic region in the north, where a territory quite modest in size acquired a wholly disproportionate influence and wealth owing to the international port of Bruges and the two great manufacturing towns of Ypres and Ghent.

The peace of 1320 was a political peace only; it did not restore social peace within the country. The two parties did not come to terms. The patricians, deprived of power by the dominance of the popular movement, which had everywhere been favoured by the recent course of events, were bent on recovering their authority. In all the towns a struggle, concealed or avowed, kept rich and poor at daggers drawn. This unrest was increased by the rivalries which were revealed in the heart of the industrial population among the workmen's corporations, the control of which was disputed between the weavers and the fullers. Between the towns themselves the clash of interests and above all the differences in their governments, according as *Leliaerts* or *Clauwaerts* were in power, produced perpetual disturbances. Finally, in the agricultural districts near the coast, inhabited by a peasantry which had obtained very advantageous conditions from charters granted in the thirteenth century, and which had taken an active part in the war, ill-feeling had been dangerously aroused by the return of the nobles who had been driven out during the recent events. And then, in addition to all this, there was the burden of a heavy indemnity to the King of France, by the terms of the peace of 1320.

Ghent took a line of its own. There the patricians had regained the government, and they tried to make Bruges the scapegoat, accusing it of being alone responsible for the rising against Philip the Fair.

Affairs reached a crisis in 1323, when the popular party at Bruges broke into open revolt against the new count, Louis of Nevers; he was suspected of being a mere tool of King Charles IV, whose niece he had married, and consequently of favouring the party of the *Leliaerts*. This was the starting-point of a civil war which threw Flanders into confusion for five years, and in its atrocity revealed the intensity of social hatred which had for so long been brewing. The country was divided into two camps: on the one side, the craftsmen of Bruges, who were joined by their Ypres colleagues, by the smaller towns of western Flanders, and also by the peasants of maritime Flanders; on the other, Ghent, the rallying-point of the *Leliaerts*, was allied with the nobles and the count. In the maritime districts, the brutalities of the peasant mobs reached incredible heights of cruelty. Nobles and rich men were forced to put their own relatives to death under the eyes of the mob. The Church itself was threatened: priests had to take to flight or else were forced to say Mass in spite of the interdict laid on the country by the bishops. The count was surprised by the rebels at Courtrai and handed over to the people of Bruges; by them he was compelled to surrender the government to his uncle Robert of Cassel, a dangerous intriguer, who pretended to support the revolt in the hope of deposing his nephew.

No sooner was Louis at liberty again than he begged the new King of France, Philip of Valois, to grant him the protection due from a suzerain to his vassal. His request could not be refused; and it was a great satisfaction for the Crown to have the grandson of Robert of Béthune soliciting its support. The king knew, besides, that the burgomaster of Bruges had just offered Edward III to recognise his claims to the throne of France and to accept him as the lawful sovereign of Flanders. Philip himself took the field at the head of his troops. On 23 August 1328 they met on the slopes of Mt Cassel bands collected from the castellanies of Furnes, Bergues, Bourbourg, Cassel, and Bailleul, led by a peasant of Lampernesse, Peter Zannekin. The battle was short but bloody. It ended in a massacre of the untrained bands, who were incapable of manœuvring and were broken by the charges of the French knights. The disaster of Courtrai was avenged, and the self-confidence the rebels had acquired was immediately dissipated. Bruges and Ypres opened their gates to the conqueror without resistance. The burgomaster of Bruges was taken to Paris, and there drawn and quartered. As for the count, his vengeance was on a par with his rancour. He confiscated all the charters and privileges of the rebel towns and castellanies, and condemned Bruges and Ypres to the demolition of their ramparts, the exile of the most guilty of their citizens, and the payment to him of an annual tribute in perpetuity.

It might seem strange that the King of France did not take advantage of his victory once more to break down the autonomy of Flanders. It is well-known, however, that, since the death of Philip the Fair, the power of the monarchy had considerably weakened; above all, the imminence of a fresh conflict with England prevented the Crown from undertaking an enterprise which would have dissipated its forces. Philip was convinced, besides, and rightly so, that by the service he had just rendered to Louis of Nevers he had secured the count's loyalty and obedience. Such gratitude, in fact, did Louis henceforth display that it extended even to the sacrifice of his own life. In the diplomatic campaign which Edward III inaugurated in the Low Countries to gain allies, before launching the

Hundred Years' War, the count refused, with an obstinacy that was as creditable to his character as it was disastrous to his people's interests, to listen to any suggestions that he should take sides against his suzerain and saviour.

In the same year as the battle of Cassel, Edward III married at York the princess Philippa, daughter of William I of Avesnes, Count of Hainault and Holland. This marriage was the reward for the assistance given by the count to Edward in 1326, when he put at his disposal the splendid chivalry of Hainault for his use in the war against his father; and William became in consequence the king's right-hand man in the Low Countries. It was through his mediation, powerfully seconded by the bait of English gold, that the Duke of Brabant broke off the alliance he had recently concluded with Philip of Valois and promised his adhesion to Edward. The collaboration of the Count of Flanders, the master of Bruges and the North Sea coast, would have been much more valuable from the military point of view; but neither to solicitations nor to promises would Louis of Nevers pay any heed. Edward then resolved to employ a method which had already more than once brought success to his predecessors in their conflicts with Flanders: he prohibited the exportation of wool to that country. This struck a blow at the heart of the cloth industry, and a terrible crisis broke out in the towns. Enforced stoppage of work brought ruin to the merchants and starvation to the working classes. Since the regular entry into the country of the raw material was a necessity of existence, the needs of the public welfare obviously dictated a *rapprochement* with Edward, who alone could bring back its prosperity. In this all parties were in agreement; patricians and people alike condemned the policy of the count, who was sacrificing his subjects to his loyalty to the King of France. Ghent, which had defended the cause of Louis in the previous crisis, was now the first to abandon him. Under the pressure of necessity, the *bourgeoisie* organised in the town an administration of Public Weal entrusted to the charge of five captains (*hooftmannen*) and the deans of the weavers, the fullers, and the lesser crafts. The captain of the parish of Saint-Jean, James van Artevelde, was by common consent placed at the head of this organisation, over which he soon acquired the preponderating influence of an actual dictator.

This man, the most celebrated of the burgher politicians who are so numerous in Belgian history, came into power solely in order to put an end to the crisis which was racking his fellow-countrymen. Very different from the demagogues who have previously been mentioned, he belonged to a patrician family, and his power can only be explained by the common catastrophe which, falling alike upon rich and upon poor, had for the moment welded them together. He was able to act in the name of them all, and that probably accounts for the confidence he received immediately from Edward III. In 1337, ignoring the impotent rage of the count, he entered into negotiations with Edward, and obtained from him the re-entry of the wool. This first success won all Flanders to his policy. Ghent, where he was supreme, was, until his death, itself supreme over the towns as a whole. The prestige he enjoyed proved to be so irresistible that even the King of France was prepared to recognise the neutrality of Flanders during the war, provided the King of England would do the same. But, in the great conflict which had just broken out between the two Crowns, neutrality was impossible. From Antwerp, where he had landed in July 1338, Edward directed all his efforts to draw the Flemings into an alliance with him. If they had no part, however, in the ineffectual expedition which he launched against France in October 1339, they were soon obliged to take the decisive step. The flight of the count, who had taken refuge in France to escape from the tutelage of Ghent and Artevelde, facilitated events; besides, Artevelde could not hesitate long about declaring openly for Edward, whose support made his own influence secure. On 26 January 1340 he had him recognised at Ghent, by the delegates of the three great towns of Flanders, as the lawful heir of St Louis and the true King of France.

The effect of so striking an insult to Philip of Valois did not correspond with the expectations of Artevelde and his supporters. The siege of Tournai (July–September 1340), to which the Flemings sent contingents to assist the troops of Edward, resulted in a check, and soon afterwards hostilities were suspended by the truce of Esplechin. When they were resumed in October 1342, the scene shifted to Normandy. Edward was not to appear again in Flanders, where his presence was indispensable if the ascendancy of Artevelde was to be maintained. For prosperity had returned with the wool, and the temporary harmony, which had been the result of the common distress, gave place again to internal dissensions. The greater towns profited by the count's absence to oppress the smaller and to ruin their industry; while Ypres and Bruges endured with impatience the hegemony of Ghent. In Ghent itself, the powerful craft of the weavers aimed at getting the control of affairs and upsetting to its own advantage the equilibrium established in 1338 among the various groups of the population. On 2 May 1345, an open struggle broke out between them and the fullers, who were cut to pieces. From that time the fall of Artevelde was certain. His patrician rank made him suspect to the victorious faction, and only the intervention of the English king could have saved him. But Edward could not abandon his military designs for the sake of Artevelde; all that he would grant him was a rapid interview at the port of Sluys. On his return to Ghent, about 22 July, the celebrated tribune perished in the course of a riot stirred up by his adversaries. In the following year Louis of Nevers also met his death on the battlefield of Crécy (26 August 1346).

The weavers' party, since the death of Artevelde in possession of Ghent, strove to obtain the mastery in all the towns, and so provoked a fresh civil war. Under the lead of its mortal enemies, the fullers, there was a rising in every town against the extreme form of democratic government which it aimed at introducing everywhere. At Ypres and at Bruges the people massacred the weavers, and appealed to the young Louis de Maële, who had just succeeded to the county by the death of his father. On 13 January 1349 the capture of Ghent, the last refuge of the weavers, brought the whole of Flanders under his authority.

The fate of his father would have been sufficient to deter Louis de Maële from following his example, and his ambitious and practical mind fully realised the danger. It was evident that the power of the towns made it impossible to govern Flanders contrary to their interests. The problem consisted, then, in avoiding a fresh rupture with England without at the same time openly violating the feudal obligations by which the count was bound in his capacity as vassal of the French king. Over a long period Louis was able, with a reasonable measure of success, to preserve a balance between the two sovereigns, so that, though neither of them trusted him, they both had to keep on terms with him. It was the more important for them to avoid a breach, since the succession of his mother to the county of Artois and the county of Burgundy (Franche Comté) in 1361 guaranteed to him at no distant date a territorial power such as none of his ancestors had possessed. In 1351 the question had been raised of the marriage of his daughter and sole heiress to an English prince, and later of a fresh betrothal, when her hand was promised to a French prince. But the unexpected death of the latter caused negotiations to be reopened which would have resulted in her marriage with Edmund, Earl of Cambridge, had not the King of France, Charles V, put forward a counter-proposal still more flattering to Louis' ambitions. Accordingly, in 1369, Margaret of Flanders married the king's own brother, Philip the Bold, Duke of Burgundy. The marriage-settlement contracted for the return to the county of Flanders of the territories of Lille, Douai, and Orchies, which had been separated from it in 1320[1]. This, however, did not prevent Louis from making a new move towards England, and he soon became regarded as openly on its side. He was, however, like his father and for the same reasons, to be forced to appear as a suppliant at the French Court.

The weavers' party, beaten in 1349, was not long in recovering its position. The rise in the cost of living, which had been the sequel to the Black Death everywhere in Europe, had caused the spread of mystical tendencies, imbued with communistic aspirations, which added new elements to the existing social discontent. The contrast between rich and poor was emphasised more violently than before and rekindled the old hatreds. The weavers did not fail to turn this to immediate account. In opposition to "the Good" (*Goeden*)—the capitalist and conservative

---

[1] By a secret agreement Philip the Bold was to return these territories on his succession to Flanders—a promise he did not carry out. See *supra*, Vol. VII, p. 371.

bourgeoisie—they put themselves at the head of "the Bad" (*Kwadien*), the name given by contemporary writers to that section of the people which was inspired by vague aspirations after social reform. The count's authority formed a natural rallying-point for all those who were frightened by such ideas, and it became the more hateful to the reformers as he more and more openly gave his backing to the cause of "those who have something to lose," a characteristic expression applied to all who had possessions—nobles, merchants, craftsmen—in contrast to those who lived from day to day on their pay. Flanders, then, became actually the theatre of a class-struggle, every phase of which was watched with excitement by the outside world. At Paris in 1358 Étienne Marcel relied on the aid of popular leaders, and soon the cry "Long live Ghent" was raised in the streets of the French capital to celebrate the triumph of the weavers. For, after risings which were pitilessly repressed, they succeeded in 1379 in again getting control of the chief town, and their example caused their comrades in Bruges and Ypres immediately to rise. For a few months their domination over the whole county was maintained by a reign of terror. Governors (*beleeders*) were appointed to replace the count's *baillis*, and the peasantry were compelled, whatever their views, to send contingents to the revolutionary forces. But the excesses of the weavers provoked the resistance of all the interests they were so brutally trampling under foot. In May 1380 Bruges paved the way for a reaction which spread rapidly to the other towns; and the count, supported by the nobles, assumed the direction of the movement. As in 1349, the weavers, nothing daunted, made Ghent their refuge and defied the coalition against them. Philip van Artevelde, son of the great tribune who had met his death at their hands in 1345, put himself at their head[1]. Too little is known about him to discover the motives underlying his action. Perhaps the explanation lies in his desire to emerge from the obscurity in which he had lived up till then, perhaps in his adhesion to the social dreams of Lollard mysticism; or perhaps he hoped, with the prestige of his name, to be able to renew the alliance of Ghent with England. He solicited her intervention, but in vain. In the desperate situation in which he found himself, he determined to cut the knot by a bold stroke. On 3 May 1382 the forces of Ghent marched straight upon Bruges and captured it after an easy victory which temporarily restored the fortunes of the weavers.

The count in his humiliation had no resource but to implore the aid of the King of France, to whom until then he had paid such scanty heed. His son-in-law, Philip the Bold, had no difficulty in persuading the young Charles VI to take this opportunity of brilliantly asserting his suzerain rights over Flanders, and of crushing at the same time a revolt which threatened to infect France as well. On 27 November 1382, the French army won a decisive victory at West-Roosebeke; Philip van

---

[1] He received the name Philip from Queen Philippa of England, who had stood godmother to him on the occasion of her stay in Ghent in 1340.

Artevelde was among the slain. However, "the horrible weavers," with
heroic persistence, clung to the hope of revenge. The King of England
decided to come to their aid, and in 1383 the Bishop of Norwich landed
at Calais and then laid siege to Ypres. The resistance of the town and
the approach of a French army forced him to retreat[1]. But Ghent, which
received some assistance in troops from Richard II, continued to resist
and to fight. Louis de Maële died on 30 January 1384 without witnessing
its capitulation. But Philip the Bold, who at last entered into his inheritance, was determined to bring matters to a conclusion. The skilful
diplomacy, of which he was later to give so many proofs, succeeded where
force had failed. On 18 December 1385 the people of Ghent made peace
with their new overlord, on condition of the maintenance of all their
privileges and the granting of a general amnesty. A new era was opened,
over which the house of Burgundy was to preside; so this house brought
to an end a period of political and social upheaval which had lasted for
more than a century.

As Flanders, so the prince-bishopric of Liège, Brabant, the episcopal
cities of Tournai and Utrecht, and the town of Valenciennes in Hainault
were agitated throughout the whole of the fourteenth century by the
conflict of "the great folk" and "the lesser folk," "the Good" and "the
Bad," rich and poor. But it is unnecessary to deal as fully with them,
because in no case were the antagonists as powerful, and particularly
because no outside power played a part in their quarrels. The Emperors
were too weak and were too completely dissociated from the territories on
the right bank of the Scheldt to think of intervening, as we have seen
the French kings continually did in Flanders. Moreover, neither princes
nor towns asked for their aid, knowing full well that it would be useless
to make the appeal.

In all the industrial towns of the Low Countries, the battle of Courtrai
had provoked a popular rising which was almost exactly analogous to the
upheaval of Liberalism throughout Europe after the Paris revolution of
1848. In Brabant, where the duke actively supported the patricians, the
revolt was quite easily crushed; it was not until 1378 that the craftsmen
at Louvain were admitted to a share in the municipal government, and
Brussels had to wait until 1421 before obtaining a similar régime. In the
principality of Liège, on the other hand, the weakness of the prince-
bishop helped "the lesser folk" as against "the great folk"; and, to
maintain themselves, the latter had to ally with the nobles. Passions were
roused to such an extent that in 1312, after a battle in the streets, the
people drove their antagonists into the church of St Martin, and there
pitilessly did them to death by setting the building on fire. After that
the struggle went on unceasingly until at last, in 1384, "the great folk"

[1] This expedition is usually called a Crusade. The pretext given for it, indeed, was
to support the Flemings, who like England recognised the Pope of Rome, against
the French, who remained faithful to the Pope of Avignon.

had to recognise their defeat and surrender to the 32 crafts the right of choosing exclusively from among themselves the members of the communal government. This constitution, giving the power to the craft-gilds and dividing it equally among them, was made possible by the fact that Liège, unlike the Flemish towns, had no branch of industry powerful enough to claim a distinctive position. It was therefore possible to establish a regime in which the whole *bourgeoisie* was distributed among the crafts and these were all placed on an equal footing. The result was an extremely vigorous political life, but it was disturbed during more than two centuries by the jealousies of the 32 privileged bodies, so that the general concord was continually being broken.

In all the towns, however, where an exporting industry prevailed, the organisation which was ultimately established aimed at giving representation to all the prevailing interests. At Dinant, for example, from 1348 onwards the administration of the commune was divided between "the good folk" (the well-to-do *bourgeoisie*), the copper-smiths, and the group of smaller crafts. In Flanders and Brabant, the preponderance of the cloth industry led to similar arrangements. Political power was to be shared by the various social groups, which were divided in the different towns either into "members" (*leden*) or "nations" (*natien*). But, as has been made sufficiently clear already, the demands of the workmen very often upset the delicate equilibrium of these structures. They did not take permanent shape until the end of the fourteenth century, when the decline of the urban cloth trade reduced the strength of the powerful corporations which owed their former vigour to its prosperity. From that time they were maintained almost unchanged for centuries, and in several towns it even happened that the constitution continued, down to the seventeenth or eighteenth centuries, to give the crafts in the cloth industry a special place in the urban council, while in fact those crafts were so much reduced that they counted no more than a few dozen members.

It may appear somewhat strange that towns as powerful as those of the Low Countries never achieved the position of free towns, which was achieved by the German towns though they were inferior both in wealth and population. The explanation of this fact must, it would seem, be found in the attitude of the territorial princes in the Low Countries. These, as a general rule, were careful to avoid refusing the towns the autonomy which was indispensable to their development, and were satisfied with maintaining their own right of oversight which meant little real interference. The social conflicts of the fourteenth century, in which they were forced to intervene, strengthened rather than diminished their authority by identifying it with the cause of the anti-revolutionary elements in the ranks of the *bourgeoisie*.

Moreover, since the end of the thirteenth century, the territorial princes had been obliged, owing to the increasing expense of their courts, their governments, and their wars, to appeal for larger and larger subsidies from the towns. Their treasuries were mainly fed by the supplies which they demanded under the form either of aids (*beden*) or of loans. The leading communes naturally took advantage of this to obtain a share in the direction of affairs. Already in the course of the thirteenth century, we find their representatives appearing in the prince's council, hitherto reserved for members of the clergy and nobility. From the beginning of the fourteenth century their share in the government of the principality became not only regular but preponderating, and it was guaranteed by charters. In Brabant, Duke John II, on the verge of bankruptcy, paid for the financial assistance of the towns by instituting, on 27 September 1312, a council composed of representatives from the towns and the nobility, which was to assemble every three weeks in order to see to the privileges and the customs of the duchy being observed. Two years later, in 1314, the towns obtained the right of ratifying the appointment of the high officials of the duchy, of giving consent to all alienations of the demesne, and of overseeing the coinage. In 1356, Duke Wenceslas swore to abide by the terms of the famous document known as the *Joyeuse Entrée* (*Blijde Incomst*), which remained until the end of the eighteenth century as the basis of the Brabançon constitution[1]. It established a political régime by which the prince was bound not to declare war, coin money, or conclude an alliance without the consent of the country represented by the three privileged orders of clergy, nobles, and towns; the delegates from these formed the assembly which was known, from the fifteenth century onward, as the Estates of Brabant.

The constitution of the principality of Liège was different from that of Brabant; it was derived out of the peace-treaties of the fourteenth century, which were the result of the internal discords in this turbulent principality. The most famous of these, the Peace of Fexhe in 1316, bestowed on "the country's opinion," that is to say, the decision of the canons of the cathedral (representing the clergy), the nobility, and the towns, the right of determining on the customs, which meant that these classes were associated with the bishop in legislation. Adolf and Engelbert of Mark sought in vain to shake off this tutelage; their reigns were in consequence one long struggle. The next bishop, John d'Arckel, at last accepted, on 2 December 1373, the Peace of the Twenty-Two, which placed all the episcopal functionaries under the supervision of a tribunal of twenty-two persons—four canons, four knights, and fourteen burgesses; it met every month to enquire into the conduct of the officials, and its decisions were final. This left the prince with only the semblance of power, so that it is not surprising to find in the sequel that the bishops, whenever they possessed the means, strove to rid themselves of this yoke. The Peace of Fexhe and the Peace of the Twenty-Two continued, however, to be regarded by the Liégeois as the most precious guarantee of political liberty.

[1] Its name is due to the fact that the dukes had to swear to it when they made their formal entry into the town of Louvain after their accession.

In 1789 these venerable survivals from the Middle Ages were used as a pretext for the revolution—in reality inspired by the Declaration of the Rights of Man—which they launched against their bishop.

In the counties of Hainault and Holland, where the power of the towns was limited, equilibrium was easily established between the three orders of clergy, nobility, and *bourgeoisie*; there too they were summoned by the princes, from the fourteenth century onwards, to give their consent to demands for subsidies.

In Flanders, on the other hand, Bruges, Ypres, and Ghent exercised a preponderating influence, so that no such collaboration was possible. They boasted of being "the three pillars on which the country is supported," and the characteristic expression, "the three members of Flanders" (*de drie leden van Vlaenderen*), which this triumvirate assumed, well depicts their ambition to subordinate the whole country to their interests. The count was continually being forced to negotiate with them; and if he did not come completely under their control, it was because their continual discords prevented them from forming a coalition against him. Moreover, the clergy, the nobles, and the smaller towns supported him against the dominance of the three great communes. In such circumstances, there was no possibility of establishing a constitutional regime which should define, as in Brabant and the bishopric of Liège, the share of the country as a whole in the settlement of its political affairs.

Chance, which so often decides the fate of dynasties, was responsible for the introduction from abroad of new houses into the Low Countries during the fourteenth century; and the ultimate destiny of them was to be the reunion, within less than three-quarters of a century, under the sceptre of the dukes of Burgundy, of all the Lotharingian principalities on the right bank of the Scheldt with the county of Flanders. In 1345 the house of Avesnes became extinct with the death of William II[1], and his heritage—the counties of Hainault, Holland, and Zeeland, and the Frisian territories which the counts were actively engaged in conquering—passed to his sister Margaret, the wife, since 1324, of the Emperor Lewis the Bavarian. Ten years later, on the death of John III (1355), the duchies of Brabant and Limburg became the property of his eldest daughter Joan, who in 1347 had married Wenceslas of Luxemburg, the brother of the Emperor Charles IV. Finally, as has been already stated, in 1384 Margaret, daughter of Louis de Maële, inherited Flanders conjointly with her husband Philip the Bold, Duke of Burgundy.

Two, therefore, of these three dynasties were of German and imperial origin, while the third was closely related to the French royal family. But the Empire was unable to take advantage of the opportunity offered it to regain its lost suzerainty over the Low Countries. Lewis IV, absorbed in his struggle with the Papacy, had died in 1347 without having

[1] As Count of Holland he is known as William IV.

made any effort on his wife's behalf; in fact, he left her at daggers drawn with her son, William of Bavaria, who fiercely disputed with her the possession of Holland and Zeeland. As for Charles IV, the marriage of his brother Wenceslas with Joan of Brabant meant a most fortunate increase in the domains of the house of Luxemburg; but he was content with this advantage, and made no attempt to exploit it in the interests of the Empire. So, in their political outlook, the princely houses just established in the Low Countries turned their backs on Germany, since Germany had given them no support. With surprising rapidity they assimilated the manners and speech of their subjects, and their political horizon was bounded by the frontiers of the rich territories they had just inherited.

The house of Burgundy, on the other hand, was assured of the support of France. Charles V had considered the securing of the succession to Louis de Maële for his brother as a striking political success. There was every indication that Philip the Bold in his capacity as "prince of the fleurs de lis" would restore the prestige of the Crown in Flanders, and would definitely wrest that country from English influence. Never had any prince in the Low Countries possessed a power comparable with his. To his duchy of Burgundy were added the counties of Burgundy, Artois, and Flanders, which he held from his wife, and as the minority of the young king, Charles VI, had made him one of the regents of the kingdom, he was able also to employ to his own advantage the military and financial resources of France. His far-sighted ambition led him to recognise at once the splendid prospects that lay before him in the Low Countries. In 1384, the same year that he took possession of Flanders, he succeeded in winning the good graces of the old Duchess of Brabant, who had recently been left a widow; and a few months later he contrived to unite the houses of Burgundy and Bavaria by a double marriage, which weaned the Wittelsbach house from the alliance it had been contemplating with England. Shortly afterwards, under cover of promoting French interests, he won a still more considerable success. In 1387 he persuaded the counsellors of Charles VI to send an army to the assistance of the Duchess of Brabant when she was being attacked by the Duke of Guelders, who had just taken an oath of fealty to Richard II. Joan repaid this service by tearing up the testament in which she had bequeathed her duchy to the house of Luxemburg in default of issue of her marriage with Wenceslas. She recognised Philip as her heir, in spite of the feeble protests of the wretched King of the Romans, Wenceslas of Luxemburg, whose rights of suzerainty and dynastic interests were alike infringed. The Estates of Brabant, however, hesitated to accept a count of Flanders as their prince. To avoid hurting their susceptibilities, Philip transferred his rights to his second son, Antony; for the moment it was enough for him to have introduced the younger branch of his house into the Brabançon territories.

The progress of Burgundian influence in the Low Countries might have been taken as synonymous with the progress of French influence in the time of Philip the Bold. But after his death (27 April 1404) it became evident that this would no longer be the case. John the Fearless was, in fact, the most dangerous engineer of the anarchy which afflicted the kingdom during the long madness of Charles VI. No adequate study of his policy has yet been made, so that it is not possible to follow his motives or to explain apparent contradictions. But there can be no doubt that his chief purpose was to settle the Burgundian power on a solid foundation in the basins of the Meuse and the Scheldt. It was there that his mortal enemy at the French Court, the Duke of Orleans, sought to strike at him. The rights in the duchy of Luxemburg which Louis of Orleans caused Jošt of Moravia to cede to him, and also the alliance which he negotiated in 1405 between the Duke of Guelders and Charles VI, gave just cause to fear that he was planning to lend his dangerous aid to the hitherto quite ineffective protests of the Kings of Germany. The cowardly assassination of his rival on 23 November 1407 naturally forced John the Fearless to take a leading part in the civil war, for which he was himself responsible, between the Armagnacs led by the house of Orleans and the Burgundians, as they significantly called themselves. He was careful, however, not to entangle himself in this struggle to the extent of endangering his interests. When war was resumed between France and England in 1415, he maintained a dubious neutrality. While his brother Antony, faithful to his duty as a member of the house of Valois, went to his death at Agincourt (25 October 1415), he himself entered into negotiations with Henry V, which prevented the latter from assisting the attempts of the new King of the Romans, Sigismund, to wrest Brabant from the Burgundian dynasty. Antony's son John was recognised as their rightful prince by the Estates of Brabant, who could be certain of the support of John the Fearless. Not long afterwards, the young Duke of Brabant was married by his uncle to Jacqueline of Bavaria, who had just succeeded to the counties of Hainault, Holland, and Zeeland, so that the house of Burgundy replaced the house of Bavaria in those regions. The enraged Sigismund in vain assigned these territories as fiefs to the Bishop of Liège, John of Bavaria; but, to be successful in this, he needed the support of England, and England remained neutral. In view of the imperial claims, this neutrality was so valuable to the duke that he took steps to make it more certain. Without declaring himself openly, he drew nearer to Henry V, so that in France, among the partisans of the dauphin, he was regarded as a public enemy; and on 10 September 1419, in an interview with the dauphin on the bridge at Montereau, he also fell a victim to assassination.

This murder necessarily drove his son and successor, Philip the Good, into the English camp. Henry V had no more dependable ally in the war in which the French kingdom all but came to an end. Just as James van Artevelde had recognised Edward III in 1340 as the true King of France, so Philip in 1420 signed the Treaty of Troyes which declared the dauphin deprived of all his rights; and, after the death of Henry V on 31 August 1422, it lay with him to direct the government of France during the minority of Henry VI. That he abandoned it to the Duke of Bedford, with whom he was on terms of the closest confidence, was due to his political insight which saw the magnificent prospects of aggrandisement in the Low Countries. His collaboration with England was not merely imposed on him by the duty of avenging his father; he reckoned on making it impossible for Charles VII to interfere with his aims, and with fortune on his side he was able to realise them with surprising rapidity.

In 1422, Jacqueline of Bavaria left her husband John IV of Brabant, the son of Antony, and, without waiting for the annulment of this marriage, contracted another with Duke Humphrey of Gloucester, the brother of the regent of France, Bedford. This bold *coup* threatened to deprive the house of Burgundy of the Bavarian inheritance, but it was foiled by the energetic action of Philip. While he obtained from the Pope the promise to annul Jacqueline's marriage and from Bedford that he would abandon Gloucester to his fate, he drove the latter from Hainault and seized the person of Jacqueline, whom he kept prisoner at Mons (1424). The escape of the adventurous princess upset the situation once more; and the Emperor Sigismund also took advantage of the death of John of Bavaria to renew his claims to Hainault, Holland, and Zeeland. Philip, however, having induced his cousin John IV to surrender to him the administration of Jacqueline's territories, invaded Holland. During two years (1426–28) he waged war on his rival, defeating Gloucester's troops at Brouwershaven and winning the assistance of the *bourgeois* party of the *Kabiljauws* against the noble party of the *Hoecks* who supported the countess. Finally, by the Treaty of Delft on 3 July 1428, he obtained recognition as governor (*ruwaert*) and inheritor of the districts of Hainault, Holland, Zeeland, and Friesland. The last scene in this drama was brought about by a final piece of folly on Jacqueline's part. In spite of her promise not to enter into another marriage, she wedded Frans van Borselen in 1436. To save her husband from execution, she had to consent to abdicate in favour of Philip.

While he thus seized by force of arms the territories of Jacqueline, he entered peacefully into possession of Brabant and Limburg. The death of the miserable John IV on 17 April 1427, followed by that of his brother and successor, Philip of Saint-Pol, on 4 August 1430, brought the younger branch of the house of Burgundy to an end in the two duchies. Disregarding the persistent claims of the Emperor Sigismund, who was as obnoxious in words as he was inoffensive in deeds, the Estates of Brabant pronounced unanimously for Philip the Good. His hereditary rights were too manifest for them to take any account of imperial suzerainty, which was barred by lapse of time; the Empire had for a long time been only a name to the small feudal States of Lorraine, nothing, in fact, but a geographical expression. Confident in the attitude of his new subjects towards him, Philip could disregard the alliance concluded against him in 1433 by Sigismund and the King of France. He only replied to it by an insolent manifesto, in which he accused the Emperor of having been bought by the "dauphin's" gold; by allying himself with the murderer of Philip's father, he had lost all rights over the son.

However, since he was now in possession of Brabant, Limburg, Hainault, Holland, Zeeland, and also of the county of Namur, which he had purchased in 1421, his position in relation to the Empire, of which all these territories formed part, became embarrassing. He could not conceal the fact that he held them simply by virtue of occupation and in constant defiance of public law. Also, as he was now master of the Low Countries, in which he had only possessed Flanders and Artois at the beginning of his career, the English alliance was no longer indispensable to him. In 1435, he obtained dispensation from the Pope for the oath he had formerly taken to Henry V, and on 21 September recognised Charles VII as the lawful King of France and concluded with him the Peace of Arras, the clauses of which he dictated himself. The king was quite content to pay the price of the humiliating terms exacted for the murder of John the Fearless, in order to detach the duke from the English alliance. He restored to him a large amount of territory and revenue in Burgundy, exempted him from the feudal duty of homage during his own lifetime, and ceded to him, though indeed with the right of redemption, the Somme towns which formed a powerful military barrier for the Low Countries against France. The treaty, in fact, recognised Philip as virtually sovereign, and afforded him the expectation of securing some day for his dynasty the actual title, which was not yet accorded to himself.

He had undoubtedly foreseen that England, weakened by the discords in its government, would be unable to take any revenge for a treachery which was as disastrous for it as it was profitable to France. After vain attempts to detach the Flemings and the Dutch from the duke, and after hostilities in which its commerce suffered as much as that of the Low Countries, it gave way, and signed a commercial treaty in 1439 which was afterwards regularly renewed. Things might have turned out differently if a last attempt of the Emperor Sigismund, who hoped to profit by the Anglo-Burgundian rupture to wrest Brabant from Philip, had not resulted in a miserable failure. The Brabançons declared themselves ready to risk their lives and their possessions on behalf of "their true and lawful master"; however, they had no need even to take up arms. Rich in llusions as he was ill-provided with means of fighting, the Emperor magined that a mere demonstration would be enough to rally the usurper's subjects to his side. The Landgrave of Hesse, who was given the task of carrying out his design, had only 400 lances at his disposal. A rising of the peasants in Limburg was all that was needed to throw them back in disorder on Aix-la-Chapelle (1437).

Sigismund only survived this last discomfiture a few weeks, and his death left Philip free to enter into possession of Luxemburg, the succession to which he had bought from its heiress, Elizabeth of Görlitz, in the year of the Peace of Arras. The King of the Romans, Albert of Austria, did not succeed in preventing this further advance of the Burgundian power to the detriment of the Empire, and his successor Frederick III, taught by experience, judged it prudent not to continue to treat the duke any longer as an enemy. He raised no opposition when the Estates of Luxemburg took the oath to Philip in 1451, and looked on with indifference when Philip assumed the protectorate, one after the other, of the episcopal principalities of Cambrai, Liège, and Utrecht, into which he succeeded, during the years 1439–57, in introducing members of his own family.

By the middle of the fifteenth century, then, thanks to favourable circumstances and to the energy and dexterity of its head, the house of Burgundy had succeeded in raising itself to the rank of a great power. It had realised to perfection the plans conceived by Philip the Bold. Between France, England, and Germany the provinces of the Low Countries formed a compact block, and the duke, who had dictated the Peace of Arras to Charles VII, had triumphantly resisted Henry VI, and had made advisable the self-effacement of the Emperor, enjoyed a prestige which none of these kings could rival. The vow which he took in 1454, in a scene of dazzling festivities, to lead a new crusade against the Turks, seemed to prove that his ambition soared to the rôle of defender of Christendom. But his constant good fortune had given him illusions about himself; actually his position was brilliant rather than secure. Though Frederick III dared not imitate the attitude of Sigismund towards him, yet he carefully refrained from investing him with the numerous fiefs which he had occupied in spite of imperial protests; and he obstinately refused to grant Philip the title of king which would have given the final sanction to his success. But, more important still, since France had regained the upper hand in its long duel with England, Charles VII was openly preparing to take the offensive against this house of Burgundy which in his eyes was nothing but a traitor vassal. He sought to stir up the German princes of the Rhine valley against Philip, he bought up the claims of Ladislas of Hungary to Luxemburg, and he spoke of making the Burgundian territories which held from the French Crown subject to the decisions of the Parlement at Paris. The accession of Louis XI on 22 July 1461 aggravated still more the already strained relations. Philip, grown old, allowed himself to be duped by this Machiavellian genius, and himself did away with the most advantageous clause in the treaty of Arras when he restored to the king the Somme towns. At last, however, he realised the danger of the direction in which he was being led, and two years before his death he handed over to his son the reins of government (1465).

There is hardly a more striking contrast than that between Louis XI and Charles the Bold[1]. Their portraits by Philippe de Commynes, which have become classic, have given later ages a fixed impression of them; but he certainly seems to have exaggerated the ambition and the imprudence of the latter, to whom indeed he turned traitor, in order to throw into higher relief the wisdom of the former, who was his benefactor. Whatever Charles may have wished, he could only, in face of the fixed intention of his adversary to ruin the house of Burgundy, have maintained himself by force of arms. From the time of his accession, war was inevitable, and at first he only undertook it in self-defence. But, goaded on by Louis XI, as Napoleon was goaded on by England, he allowed himself to be drawn into enterprises beyond his strength, and, finally, at Nancy he met his Waterloo.

The revolt of the high nobility of France against Louis XI in 1465 (the War of the Public Weal) gave Charles an opportunity of weakening his enemy which was too good to be missed. On 15 July the king was defeated at Montlhéry and surrendered to him that bulwark of the Burgundian domains, the Somme towns, which Louis' diplomacy had contrived to redeem from Philip the Good. Then Charles turned against the Liégeois. The extremely democratic nature of their institutions had led them to revolt at once against their new bishop, Louis of Bourbon, whom they rightly suspected of plotting against their liberties in agreement with Burgundy. Charles VII was not slow to offer them his protection, and Louis XI had just concluded a formal alliance with them. Believing that this gave them complete freedom of action, they had expelled their bishop, set up a "mambourg"[2] in his place, and invaded the duchy of Limburg. Their punishment was the complement of Louis XI's defeat; on 22 December 1465 they were compelled to recognise the Duke of Burgundy as their "guardian" in perpetuity. The following year, a revolt at Dinant was savagely repressed by the sack and burning of the town (25 August 1466). This cruelty, so far from intimidating the Liégeois, merely embittered them. It was only too easy for Louis XI to use them again as the instruments of his designs, or rather to sacrifice them to his political ends. Their defeat at Brusthem on 28 October 1467 forced them to accept a sentence which revealed the pride and the wrath of their conqueror. The constitution of the country was repealed, the privileges of the city were abolished, Roman Law was substituted for the national customs, and the "perron," the ancient symbol of the communal liberties of Liège, was removed to Bruges to adorn the Place de la Bourse. The old episcopal principality was at an end; it was, in fact, no more now than an appendage to the Burgundian domains.

In crushing so decisively the Liégeois, Charles was punishing particularly the instruments of Louis XI. A new war with this implacable adversary was an unavoidable necessity. To get the better of him, the duke returned

---

[1] "Le Téméraire," i.e. "the Rash," but "the Bold" has become the established English form.

[2] "Mambourg" was the title of the governor of the principality *sede vacante*.

to the alliance with England, which was sealed on 12 July 1468 by his marriage with Edward's sister Margaret of York. He was preparing to take the field when Louis, counting on keeping him in check by negotiations, proposed an interview at Péronne. There Louis almost became the victim of his own intrigues. He had forgotten, says Commynes, that he had just instigated the indomitable Liégeois to a new revolt. It broke out too soon, and, in order to deliver himself from the hands of his enemy, the king did not hesitate to sacrifice his sovereign rights as well as his personal honour. He consented to remove Flanders from the jurisdiction of the Parlement at Paris, and made no scruple about attending at the vengeance which Charles took upon the too-trusting Liégeois; "as a splendid example," the duke ordered the burning of the city to last for a space of seven weeks.

So the first passage of arms between king and duke had ended to the latter's advantage. Elated by the prestige he had won in the eyes of Europe from his easy victories, he began from this time to give the rein to his ambition. His end undoubtedly was to make Burgundy into a great power; to achieve that, a necessary preliminary was to get hold of the territories which separated the county and duchy of Burgundy from the Low Countries. So, in 1469, he bought Upper Alsace from Sigismund of Austria. The possession of this district brought him into contact with the Swiss. At once, the idea of utilising these warlike mountaineers in place of the ruined Liégeois came into Louis' mind, and in 1470 he concluded a treaty of alliance with them. The civil war, which his *protégé* Warwick was starting in England against Edward IV, made him hopeful that the moment had come when he could take his revenge for the humiliation of Péronne; and he cited Charles to appear before him on the charge of high treason. However, the ensuing hostilities only resulted in truces (October 1471, November 1472) which settled nothing. On the other hand, the conquest of Guelders and of the county of Zutphen shortly afterwards (1473) increased still further the power of Burgundy. Charles thought that he would then obtain from the Emperor the royal title which his father had already coveted. But Frederick III slipped away at the critical moment, and Charles, who had come to Trèves on purpose to receive the crown, was in the most exasperating of all situations for a man of his character: he was left looking ridiculous (September 1473).

From this foiled coronation dates the series of reverses which the hatred of Louis XI awaited as the fruits of his own devising, but which his adversary, blinded by pride and passion, could neither foresee nor escape. To humiliate the Emperor, he persisted in the siege of Neuss in 1474, undertaken at the request of the Archbishop of Cologne against the Chapter who were supported by Frederick. He was so certain of immediate success that, when he started on the enterprise, he promised Edward IV to rejoin him in a year's time at Calais and to assist in reconquering the kingdom of France. But when after eleven months' effort he was forced to raise the siege, he found that the French expedition had come to nothing, as Louis had managed to come to terms with Edward IV. Charles made up for this disappointment by marching against Lorraine[1], where Duke René, relying on the support of France, had just declared war upon him. The annexation of this duchy in November 1475 filled the gap which still remained, after the conquest of Alsace, between the Low Countries and Burgundy. It was Charles' last success. The expedition which he led the next year against the Swiss, the allies of Louis XI and the enemies of his own allies, the Duchess of Savoy and the Duke of Milan, failed in front of the castle of Grandson on 3 March 1476. To restore Burgundian prestige without delay, the duke decided on a fresh campaign. Ill-prepared and ill-conducted, it ended in the crushing defeat of Morat (22 June). Charles ought then to have resigned himself to peace. But he was blinded by a desperation which bordered on madness, and wasted valuable time in impossible schemes for revenge. At last, when René of Lorraine had returned to his duchy and blocked the road to the Low Countries, he reassembled his shattered forces and moved northwards again. But, instead of making all possible haste, he halted in front of Nancy, his mind centred on its capture. It was before the walls of this town that the Swiss attacked him on 5 January 1477. Two days later his body was discovered on a frozen pond, half-eaten by wolves and bearing the marks of three mortal wounds upon it. The power of Burgundy, so glorious four years before, seemed to be irretrievably ruined. Louis XI invaded Artois, the Liégeois resumed their independence, and the sole heiress of the duke, his daughter Mary, was a prisoner in the rebel town of Ghent, terrified lest she should be handed over to the King of France.

The rapid accomplishment of the union of all the territories of the Low Countries under the Burgundian sceptre was undoubtedly due to two main causes: the ability of the princes and the favourable circumstances they enjoyed. But it must be recognised that it would have been impossible without the consent of the various peoples. The Liégeois who under the feeble government of their bishops had practically created a petty republic and were very jealous of their independence, were alone in offering resistance to the duke, and moreover its obstinate character was largely due to the intrigues of Louis XI. Everywhere else, as we have seen, the attempts of the Duke of Orleans, Sigismund, Henry VI, to win over the inhabitants resulted in dead failure. In Brabant and Limburg, as in Hainault, Holland, and Zeeland, the Estates recognised Philip the Good as their prince. The insurrections of Bruges (1436) and Ghent (1450–53) against him had none of the character of national risings. They were the last attempts of the two great towns to defend

---

[1] This is the duchy, once known as Upper Lorraine; it was limited to the actual fiefs of its dukes round Nancy, and retained the name of Lorraine, which was lost by Lower Lorraine in the Low Countries.

privileges which no longer corresponded to their real interests. It is sufficient to remark that the rest of Flanders left them to fight alone; this shews that they were only fighting for an out-of-date parochialism.

In truth, the work of the dukes of Burgundy was done just at the proper moment and corresponded to the needs of the time. The sub-divisions of the Middle Ages could not have been continued into the fifteenth century without causing the Low Countries to be dissolved in a medley of dynastic wars and municipal struggles, or without involving them fatally in the last phase of the Hundred Years' War, which would have ruined and dismembered them. It was their good fortune, thanks to the power of Philip the Good, to have been able to preserve the blessings of peace in the midst of the formidable conflict between France and England. The alliance of their prince with England from 1419 to 1435 guaranteed to them a period of rest and prosperity. And the benefits they obtained from this contributed greatly to bind them to the dynasty which had created for them a situation of such advantage.

The social and political conditions of the period also favoured the house of Burgundy. The decay of the cloth industry in the towns during the second half of the fourteenth century led to the migration of the working classes who had for so long been keeping up a revolutionary agitation within them. So, with political peace came social peace also, and both the well-to-do *bourgeoisie* and the nobility looked upon the prince as indispensable for its continuance. He was able, for the good of his subjects and the increase of his own influence, to turn to advantage in other directions the changes which were transforming the economic equilibrium of the country. Philip the Good encouraged with all his might the extension into the country-districts of the cloth industry, which was no longer a monopoly of the towns; he protected, in spite of the protests of Bruges, the development of the port of Antwerp which was to have so brilliant a future; he supported, against the hostility of the Hanseatic League, the steady progress of the Dutch shipping. Further, it must be noted that the uniting of all the territories of the Low Countries under the authority of a single dynasty allowed a freedom to commerce and general intercourse such as had not existed before. From 1433 onwards the duke was able to issue coinage which had legal currency through the whole of his dominions.

From all this there resulted a prosperity which astonished the rest of Europe. The dazzling luxury with which the dukes liked to be surrounded was the counterpart to the wealth of their subjects. And it was in its artistic efflorescence that this period, which was distinguished for painters like the Van Eyck and Van der Weyden, architects like Jean de Ruysbroeck and Mathieu de Layens, sculptors like Claus Sluter, musicians like Jean Ockegem and Josquin des Prés, received its loftiest and noblest expression. Philippe de Commynes called the Low Countries a "promised land", and the expression does not seem exaggerated when we look at the smiling champaign and the charming town-views which form the background in the paintings of the time. At the present day, it is still to the Burgundian age that Belgium owes the finest pieces in its museums and the most characteristic monuments in its streets.

The Low Countries, after they had been united into one territorial whole, still remained quite separate from the ancestral domains of their princes, the duchy of Burgundy and the free county (Franche Comté); they were too far apart from one another in distance, and quite different in history, race, and interests. For political reasons, as we have seen, Charles the Bold sought to gain possession of Alsace and Lorraine, and thus to extend his dominions continuously without a break from the shores of the North Sea to the Jura. But neither he nor his father had any thought of extending to their Burgundian lands the system of government they had established in their northern territories. The most they did was to admit into their council and to attach to their service a number of jurists and military and other officials, who came originally from Burgundy properly so called; these, being strangers to the Low Countries, were the more pliant instruments of ducal authority.

The way in which the unification came about explains the characteristics of the State which the dukes created. It was not, as we have seen, due in any way to conquest; it was simply the result of the recognition by the Estates of the different territories in turn of the rights which Philip the Good acquired by inheritance himself or by purchase from their hereditary ruler[1]. The duke, therefore, did not impose himself on his subjects as an alien ruler; he appeared, to each of the regions into which the Low Countries were historically divided, as its "natural prince." To the Flemings he was merely Count of Flanders, to the Brabançons Duke of Brabant, to the people of Hainault or of Holland he was Count of Hainault or Count of Holland, and so on. By these diverse titles he ruled over the whole, and each of the districts which in turn were united beneath his sceptre preserved its own peculiar constitution. In the full meaning of the term, the Burgundian monarchy was a federal monarchy.

But the association into one body politic of so many principalities, which had for so long been separate, put them in an entirely new relation both to one another and to the reigning dynasty. Their conjunction went far beyond the level of a merely personal union; it reached to that of a political union. Above the regional constitutions the dukes built a framework of institutions, which extended their competence throughout the whole country. The Great Council, presided over by the Burgundian chancellor, in which representatives of all the provinces had a seat, took cognisance of all matters of general interest; and, little by little, it imposed its authority over all the spheres which were outside the local constitutions. The financial organisation, which was put under the supervision of the three *Chambres des Comptes* of Lille, Brussels, and the

---

[1] An exception must be made, in the time of Charles the Bold, for the principality of Liège and also for the duchy of Guelders, both of which were annexed by force of arms.

Hague, achieved its complete shape as it gained in centralisation. In 1471, the institution of *Compagnies d'ordonnance* established a standing army recruited from the whole country. In judicial matters, a special Chamber of the Great Council, which was separated off from the parent body in 1473 to become the Parlement of Malines, acted as a court of appeal and extended its jurisdiction over all the ducal domains. The process of unification was not manifested only in the sphere of government properly so called. In 1430, the creation of the Order of the Golden Fleece indicated the clear intention of the duke to attach the high nobility of the Low Countries to his own person and policy. Much more important was the summons by Philip the Good in 1463 of representatives of all the local Estates in his dominions to a single assembly at Bruges, which borrowed from France the name of Estates General. But the Estates General of the Low Countries were to play a much more important rôle than those of France. Without their consent it was impossible to raise taxes, since in each of his territories the duke had to ask for them from its particular Estates, and these Estates General were in fact a congress of local Estates. Their financial importance gave them at an early date a political importance which resulted, during the revolution of the sixteenth century, in their becoming the organ of national opinion.

It can be seen, therefore, that the Burgundian monarchy was a monarchy doubly tempered, firstly by its federal character, and secondly by the political tradition which had obliged the princes, from the end of the thirteenth century onwards, to keep on good terms with the Estates. There can be no doubt, however, that the dukes, like all the princes of their time, looked on personal government as the ideal form of government. The wise opportunism of Philip the Good avoided any open display of this. But Charles the Bold never managed to control his absolutist tendencies; and they were largely responsible for the dangerous revolt which broke out on the news of his death.

It must be recognised, besides, that this personal rule, of which contemporary opinion was so apprehensive, did initiate certain excellent reforms, which proved so beneficial that they won acceptance. In 1386 Philip the Bold established in Flanders a "Chamber" which was the origin of the Councils of Flanders, Brabant, and Holland for justice, and also of the financial organisation already mentioned. The opposition aroused at the outset by these innovations is not hard to understand. It was the natural consequence of the social transformations which were setting up the modern State, the organ of the "common weal," against all the champions of outworn privileges, who in effect were championing their own "private weal."

To sum up, then. The Burgundian State, while it laid between France and Germany the foundation on which the kingdoms of Belgium and Holland stand at the present day, at the same time caused these countries to pass from the civilisation of the Middle Ages to that of modern times.

CHAPTER XI

ENGLAND: THE LANCASTRIAN KINGS, 1399—1461

THE revolution of 1399 placed on the English throne a man in several ways well-fitted to rule. Henry of Lancaster was handsome, brave, and energetic; his knightly exploits in the lists and against the heathen, his liberality and his affable manners had made him widely popular abroad and at home; he was besides a devout churchman, free from any taint of his father's anticlericalism, an accomplished musician, and a discriminating patron of letters. His education, for his time and class, was also considerable; from surviving records in his hand we know that he could write both French and English and on occasion quote a Latin tag; while he was famed for the ease with which he argued difficult problems in casuistry with the scholars of his court. There can be no doubt, therefore, that he was endowed with many royal graces; unfortunately the tasks before him demanded sterner qualities than these, qualities such as patience and circumspection which he did not possess. The office which he had so lightly seized was passing through a crisis; yet he shewed little appreciation of its difficulties. Of one of them in particular, the inadequacy of the royal revenue, he was so far from being aware that on his march south from Ravenspur he had made extravagant promises which he could not possibly keep as king. During the fourteenth century, the monarchy had carelessly wasted its resources. Not only the machinery of the Exchequer, but the whole administrative system had been dislocated to pay for expensive wars. It was the first duty of a prudent usurper to restore and to maintain financial stability. Hardly less urgent was the need to reassert the lost authority of the Crown in local government. Here the policy of allowing the maintenance of order and the administration of justice to be engrossed by private persons—as marked a feature of "bastard" as of true feudalism—had already proceeded to disastrous lengths. Lack of justice was becoming one of the most fruitful sources of popular unrest. It is to the credit of Richard II that he had realised these dangers, but the weapons with which he had chosen to meet them had been unwisely used and were in any case blunted by his failure. To levy arbitrary taxes and to combat private armies by enlisting a private army of his own required more tact than he was master of. The violence and uncertainty of his fiscal methods and the lax discipline which he permitted his retainers contributed largely to his downfall. His successor was pledged to find other means; yet, in spite of frequent warnings, Henry did nothing. Under his rule the royal debt was swollen to unmanageable proportions by a series of annual deficits; hardly a year passed without fresh evidence of administrative weakness, while the many baronial rebellions of the reign derived support and justification from the fact of widespread discontent. Those who had looked for much from the change of kings were quickly disillusioned. It was not that they had expected the impossible; the fault lay with the man. In so far as Henry IV fell short of Henry VII in parsimony, caution, and reforming zeal, he was unfitted for his task. In other respects, he was not an unsuccessful king. Tenacious of his rights, unflagging, until disease incapacitated him, in his attention to public business, tireless in his efforts to defeat his many enemies, he managed to retain the throne which he owed to Richard's errors rather than his own deserts. But because he took too narrow a view of his responsibilities, his failings outweighed his merits, and if his dynasty was shortlived and its end inglorious the blame in the first place must be attached to him.

For these reasons it is impossible to regard the revolution of 1399 as a landmark in English history. Its outstanding importance was as a precedent. A dynasty with a weak hereditary title had usurped the throne; it had merely been the business of a popular assembly to ratify what had been achieved by force and to recognise a *de facto* king, one indeed who never fully abandoned his first intention of claiming England by conquest. This was a lesson easily learned, and it is not surprising that it was often imitated during the coming century. But otherwise—except for the persecution of Lollardy by the State—there is little to distinguish the period after 1399 from that before it. Under the Lancastrians the same constitutional battles were fought as under Edward III and Richard II; this was inevitable, since Henry IV came in, like Charles II, "without conditions," and nothing was settled about the powers and composition of the council or the control of royal expenditure. Already in the first parliament of the reign, the old issues were joined; in the commons the extravagance of the new king's grants were criticised; and while Archbishop Arundel put the traditional baronial case for government not by "the voluntary purpose or singular opinion of the king," but by "the advice, counsel, and consent" of "the honourable, wise, and discreet persons of his realm," Henry was at pains to accept for himself all the liberties which his predecessors had enjoyed. Richard doubtless had erred, but that was no reason why the rights of the Crown should be diminished. On this point Henry took his stand, and was so far from yielding that he risked civil war before at the very close of his life he finally gained his way. From the first he revealed a determination to rule, as Richard had done, by the help of servants of his own choosing, and to resist any attempt to impose upon him that aristocratic or "natural" council which was to be the principal aim of baronial policy. Lancastrian knights like John Cheyne and Thomas Erpingham, esquires like John Doreward and John Norbury, clerks like John Scarle and John Prophete, were the men in whom he put his trust. In this he was assisted by divisions in the ranks of the baronage, personal feuds and jealousies

arising out of the late king's attempt to pack the upper house. There
was little chance of common action so long as the victors of 1399 only
desired to settle old scores with the Appellants of 1397. At first Henry
succeeded in protecting Richard's favourites from the vengeance of their
enemies, inspired perhaps by a wish to preserve some counterpoise to
those powerful families which had helped him to attain the throne—the
Percies, the Nevilles, and the Arundels. If this was his object, he failed.
In January 1400, fear drove the Appellants to risk all in an ill-planned
rebellion. Richard's tyranny was not, however, yet forgotten and many
of his friends now met their deaths at the hands of the common people.
Kent and Salisbury perished at Cirencester, Huntingdon at Pleshey, and
Despenser at Bristol; many men of inferior rank were afterwards executed
by the royal command. The alarm this outbreak excited was sufficient to
seal the fate of Richard II; by the end of February he was dead at
Pontefract in circumstances which leave little doubt that he was murdered.

The first attempt at counter-revolution had failed; there still remained
the possibility of armed interference from abroad. Although England
had demonstrated her loyalty to the new dynasty, France and Scotland
were in no hurry to extend their recognition. But the fact that both
kingdoms had their own internal difficulties prevented them from making
any serious effort to oppose the English revolution. Richard's French
queen was in Henry's custody, and the government of Charles VI had
therefore to proceed cautiously until she was safe. The Scots, however,
had not the same motives for restraint. Their truce with England expired
at Michaelmas 1399, and under cover of half-hearted negotiations for its
extension Scottish raids over the border recommenced. On hearing this,
Henry told parliament on 10 November that he proposed to invade
Scotland in person. Yet it was not until Robert III had made it clear
that he had no genuine intention of coming to terms that on 14 August
1400 the English marched into the Lowlands with the king at their head.
A fortnight later, after failing before Edinburgh Castle, they were obliged
to beat an ignominious retreat. This expensive fiasco brought peace no
nearer, but when in August 1402 the Scots in their turn invaded England,
it fell to the Percies to regain the credit which Henry had lost, by defeating their army decisively at Homildon Hill. Four earls were among the
prisoners. Domestic strife in Scotland prevented any attempt being made
to avenge this disaster. Finally, the capture of Robert's heir, James, at
sea on his way to France in 1406 put an end to all further danger to
England from the north. The French were not so easily disposed of. In
the first place Henry was obliged to surrender Isabelle without receiving
very much in exchange. Preliminaries of peace were signed at Leulighen
near Calais on 3 August 1401, but many details were left over for
discussion; and although definite hostilities were for the time avoided,
the conversations dragged on until the French saw in Henry's troubles
at home a favourable opportunity for adding to his embarrassments.

For no sooner had he returned from his Scottish expedition than he was greeted by news of a Welsh rising. Its leader, Owen Glyn Dŵr (Glendower), was a descendant of native princes and a landowner of some importance in North Wales. It is possible that he had been denied legal redress for wrongs done to him by the king's friend, Lord Grey of Ruthin, but whatever the cause of his disaffection, his countrymen responded with enthusiasm when he had himself proclaimed Prince of Wales at Glyn Dyfrdwy on 16 September 1400. During the following week Ruthin and several other English settlements were plundered and burnt. An ugly situation was saved by the prompt action of a Shropshire magnate, Hugh Burnell, who collected the local levies and forced the rebels to take refuge in the mountains. By the time the king reached Shrewsbury all occasion for anxiety seemed over, and Henry contented himself with a progress round the outskirts of Snowdonia. But the lull was deceptive. Next year Glyn Dŵr appeared in South Wales, and as time passed it became evident that he had inspired a genuine national revival which it would take long years and much campaigning to overcome. In October 1403 a French fleet made a descent on Kidwelly; although the damage done was slight, the way was prepared for a Franco-Welsh alliance. Had Henry had undisputed command of the narrow seas, this development might have left him unmoved, but in fact he was badly prepared for a maritime war. Any advantage which an enlarged navy might have given him was thrown away when he permitted—perhaps even encouraged—his subjects to prey on neutral shipping, for this immediately involved him in disputes with Brittany, Flanders, and the Hanseatic League. Between 1400 and 1403 English privateers wrought great havoc in the Channel, capturing scores of rich prizes and making themselves feared and hated from Danzig to Finisterre. Their most active captains were Mark Mixtow of Fowey, John Hawley of Dartmouth, and Henry Pay of Poole, but even the royal admirals were not above taking a part in the game. This inevitably led to reprisals and to the persecution of English merchant communities abroad. In a short time the narrow seas were the scene of a bitter privateering war. Buccaneers of various nationalities from bases on the coast of Brittany threatened the principal trade routes. The English ports themselves were not safe from attack. In August 1403 Plymouth was burnt by the Counts of La Marche and Vendôme; in the following December a landing was made on the Isle of Wight by a force under the command of the Count of St Pol; and during the summer of 1405 considerable damage was done at Looe, Poole, and elsewhere by a Castilian, Don Pero Niño. All this time the pretence of a truce was maintained between England and France, surviving even when in July 1404 Charles VI promised to give military assistance to Glyn Dŵr against "Henry of Lancaster." French help was long in coming and, though it came at last in August 1405, it proved of small use to the Welsh. The allies advanced into England as far as Woodbury Hill near Worcester,

but they were obliged to retreat when Henry threw himself into the city.
Although the back of Welsh resistance was not yet broken and the
struggle continued for some years after the failure of the French invasion,
it was only a question of time before the English were successful. Under
Prince Henry, the king's eldest son, they recovered castle after castle,
and when at length Harlech fell in 1409 Glyn Dŵr again became a
fugitive in the woods and mountains. Meanwhile, as a result of the
murder of the Duke of Orleans in 1407, France was rapidly falling into
anarchy, and at the same time peace was being restored with the maritime
powers. After long negotiations a commercial truce was arranged with
Flanders in March 1407. This was followed in July by a similar agreement with Brittany, and finally at the beginning of 1408 friendly relations
were re-established with the Hanseatic League. Europe had been forced
to accept the house of Lancaster.

A usurper's greatest enemies are often those to whom he is most
indebted for his success. As the repentant kingmakers of 1399 discovered,
Henry's gratitude had its limits; he proposed to rule as well as reign.
The ease with which one revolution had been achieved fascinated and
demoralised the greater barons, and it was not long before the youth of
Richard's heir, Edmund Mortimer, Earl of March, began to suggest to
the more ambitious and discontented of them the advantages which might
follow for those who placed him on the throne. To the Percies, allied
with the Mortimers by marriage, even a Percy king did not seem an
impossible dream. From a situation full of danger, Henry could derive
one consolation. This preoccupation with treason rendered the nobility
incapable of a common policy. Those who should have led the constitutional opposition in parliament were busy plotting isolated rebellion
in the country. This gave the king his chance. So long as common
advantage was abandoned for private ambition, he could hold his own
by playing one family off against another. But for the ancient feud
between Percy and Neville his cause might have been lost more than
once during the first half of his reign. One after another the plots against
him misfired. That of 1403 probably came nearest to success. Henry
Percy, Earl of Northumberland, his brother Thomas, Earl of Worcester,
and his son the famous Hotspur, had been amply rewarded for their share
in the revolution, but they were dissatisfied at not being allowed to ransom
the prisoners they had taken at Homildon Hill. If they had reasonable
grievances, they made no attempt to obtain a hearing for them in parliament. Instead, asserting the king's faithlessness to the oath which, they
said, he had sworn to them at Doncaster in 1399, only to claim his duchy
of Lancaster, they took the field at the beginning of July 1403. Hotspur
raised the standard of revolt at Chester on the tenth, and, followed by
men from Cheshire and the March to whom the name of Richard was
still dear, set out with his uncle, Worcester, to surprise the young Prince
of Wales at Shrewsbury. The king heard the news at Nottingham on the

13th, and with all the speed of which he was capable in an emergency, hastened to forestall them. He entered Shrewsbury on the 20th, and on the following day defeated the rebels outside the town both before they could make a junction with their Welsh allies and before the old earl could come to their assistance from the north. Hotspur died fighting; Worcester and other captured leaders were executed after the battle. Northumberland, threatened by a Neville army, drew off, pretending that he had taken no part in the rebellion. On 11 August he submitted to the king at York, and was promised a pardon in return for the surrender of his castles. His constables nevertheless refused to admit the royal officers, and he seems to have been kept in custody until he was brought to parliament on 6 February 1404. The lords showed their sympathy with his designs by refusing to convict him of treason; his fault, they said, was nothing more than a trespass against the Earl of Westmorland, and the king was obliged to set him free.

If this was parliament's attitude, it is not surprising that fresh insurrections shortly took place. In February 1405 a successful attempt was made to carry off the Mortimer children from Windsor, but the plot was discovered and they were recaptured at Cheltenham before they had time to reach safety in Wales. Several lords were implicated, including the Duke of York and Thomas Mowbray, the Earl Marshall; even the Archbishop of Canterbury did not escape suspicion. The duke was imprisoned and his lands confiscated, the earl pardoned, and the archbishop's protestations of innocence accepted. Northumberland, although he held aloof from this conspiracy, was meanwhile preparing a new enterprise. On 28 February he entered into an agreement with Glyn Dŵr and Edmund Mortimer the elder, uncle of the Earl of March, to divide the kingdom between them. The Earl Marshall and Lord Bardolf consented to join him and the mild and saintly Richard Scrope, Archbishop of York, was also drawn in. The latter's proclamation aimed at giving the rebellion a popular basis. But again the rebels were too slow in massing their forces. The Earl of Westmorland captured Scrope and Mowbray by treachery at Shipton Moor near York on 29 May, while the king was still on his way north. When he arrived, he was in no mood for mercy and in spite of the prayers of Archbishop Arundel, who had followed him, he ordered the execution of the captives. After a hurried and irregular trial by the Earl of Arundel and Sir Thomas Beaufort, they were beheaded under the walls of York on 8 June. It says much for the strength of Henry's position that it was so little shaken by the execution of an archbishop. Pope Innocent VII was too weak to avenge his servant; so low was his credit among Englishmen that it was thought that his mouth had been stopped with gold. But if God's vicar was powerless, men believed that it was God's direct judgment on the murderer of a saint that immediately afterwards Henry was stricken by a mysterious disease. From 9 to 16 June he lay ill at Ripon, we are told with leprosy. Whatever it was, it was not this, for he was soon healthy again and able to set about the systematic reduction of the Percy castles. The royal artillery proved irresistible and by the end of August all the rebel garrisons had submitted. The earl and Bardolf fled to Scotland at the king's approach. From here they made one last desperate attempt early in 1408. But the weather was against them; it was the coldest winter in living memory and, after a futile effort to raise the north, they were brought to bay and slain by Sir Thomas Rokeby, sheriff of York, at Bramham Moor on 19 February. With them died the selfish policy for which they had stood. Its chief effect had been to paralyse the endeavours of the more moderate among their peers to criticise and control the royal administration. Freed from this embarrassment the loyal majority were shortly to find a leader in the Prince of Wales. But it was not until he had mastered the Welsh problem, not, that is to say, until 1409, that Henry of Monmouth was able to devote his energy to politics. For more than half the reign, therefore, the main brunt of opposition fell upon the parliamentary knights, who did not prove themselves altogether unworthy of the trust.

Custom, as well as their own reluctance to assume new burdens, for long excluded the commons as a body from any active share in the government of the country, although it must be remembered that one or two of their members were generally of the king's council. But nevertheless the lower house was being driven by its wish to restrain the royal extravagance into adopting a more aggressive policy than that of mere criticism; it claimed and was beginning to exercise an effective control in certain administrative matters which was far from welcome to the king. Its power was derived in the last resort from its command over supply. Henry could no longer hope to "live of his own"; he had begun his reign by repudiating the illegal exactions of his predecessor; therefore, so long as he was refused a grant of taxation for life equal to his needs, he was bound to come regularly to parliament for money. His opponents' policy of making supply conditional upon the redress of grievances, though he might reject it in principle as he did in 1401, was in practice very difficult to circumvent. Thus the commons were able to impose conditions upon the expenditure of their grants and to attempt at least in questions of finance to secure the responsibility of the executive to parliament. The progress of their demands can be traced in the early parliaments of the century, reaching their culmination in that of 1406. Each step was contested or evaded by the king, whose chief advantage lay in the want of continuity between successive parliaments. But it is the mere existence of this initiative on the part of the commons, premature and unfruitful though in the main it was, which makes the period one of great constitutional importance.

Controversy, following traditional lines, slowly developed over the composition and functions of the king's council. At the beginning of the reign Henry had been tacitly permitted to appoint his advisers without any formal nomination in parliament. In spite of this he displayed a marked unwillingness to submit his acts to their approval. When in 1399 he was petitioned by the commons to make no grant save by the advice of his council, he returned a temporising answer "saving his liberty," and during the first year of his reign many minor offices were filled and pensions awarded upon the royal authority alone. In 1401 the commons returned to the attack with a request that they might know the names of the king's councillors, and that these might then be charged in their presence to hold office until the next parliament. Although there were good precedents for this request, it was, it seems, refused by the advice of the council itself.[1] The opposition was more successful three years later when on 1 March 1404 after a troubled session the king announced that "at the strong instances...made at divers times in this parliament by the commons, he had ordained certain lords and others to be of his great and continual council." The list contained no new names and the point of this surrender is lost if it is regarded as in any sense a change of ministry. Unfortunately, the considerable speculation to which it has given rise in modern times receives no assistance from contemporary sources, since these are uniformly silent as to the object of the commons in making this demand. But it is clear that they attached far greater importance to the act of publication than to the contents of this list, which must indeed have been already well-known to them, and it is therefore not unreasonable to assume that their purpose was rather to underline the doctrine that the council was answerable to parliament than to impose on the king men who were not of his own choosing. The direct assault on Henry's freedom of action had recently failed; his critics may well have hoped to gain their object by fastening responsibility for his mistakes upon those whom he had publicly acknowledged as his advisers. The fact that they had in impeachment a ready-made procedure for dealing with unpopular ministers must have added point to their claim. How this was circumvented by the king will shortly be seen.

On the other hand, the financial arrangements made in the first parliament of 1404 succeeded at least temporarily in curbing the royal power. For some time there had been serious grumbling at the prodigal expenditure of the government and especially of the household. Now it was said that the knights and officials of the king's court had since 1399 enormously enriched themselves at the public expense. The resentful commons expressed their surprise that the revenues were so suddenly diminished and, having characterised the treasurer's proposals for meeting this deficit as "most outrageous," for some days obstinately refused to make the necessary grants. The king's retort was to keep them in session until they changed their minds.

[1] Exchequer, Council and Privy Seal, E28/28/39 and 58. These documents are misdated by Professor J. F. Baldwin (*The King's Council*, p. 154); since the Earl of Worcester is mentioned as Steward of the Household, they cannot be later than 1403, and 1401 is therefore the only year which fits.

At length, worn out by this treatment, they surrendered so far as to vote an extraordinary tax of one shilling in the pound on land-rents. But so anxious were they that this should not be accepted as a precedent that they made it a condition that all record of their vote and of the subsequent collection of the tax should be afterwards destroyed. Further, determined to safeguard the proceeds from being squandered in the usual way, the commons insisted on appointing four special treasurers to control expenditure under the direct supervision of the council and later to render an account of their office to parliament.[1] The king consented, but it is said that, though the necessary documents were prepared, they were not sealed when parliament was dissolved. Nevertheless, it was the existence of these four men—three London merchants and a clerk from Rutland—standing between the king and his normal carelessness in matters of finance, which made necessary the early summons of another parliament. In the summer of 1404, Henry withdrew to his Lancastrian estates in the north midlands, whence a large number of warrants were issued *par commandement du Roy* without the advice of the council. He was so short of money that on 5 July payment on all pensions and annuities was suspended. At a great council at Lichfield on 25 August it was decided to hold a parliament at Coventry on 6 October. The king made no secret of his determination to convoke an assembly from which all troublesome elements had been excluded; for not only did he forbid the return of any lawyers but actually pointed out to the sheriffs those whom they were to have elected. In view of this, it is not surprising that next year the rebels included in their manifesto a demand for the free election of members as in former times. Henry had undoubtedly chosen his ground well, since Coventry was in the heart of his private duchy and undisturbed by those influences for which the capital had already begun to be famous. As the proceedings soon demonstrated, it was his intention to reverse the acts of the previous parliament. In the first place the council was not reappointed; in the second, the four independent treasurers were replaced by two royal servants, Lord Furnival and Sir John Pelham, the former of whom became shortly afterwards Treasurer of England. But though the commons were timid and deplored their inexperience, they were by no means uncritical. Their suggestions for financial reform, while comprehensive enough, were scarcely practicable, and the fact that they were too sweeping gave the king the excuse he desired for shelving them. An equally rash attack upon the wealth of the clergy brought down upon the commons the abuse of Archbishop Arundel, so that in the end they were obliged to drop their proposals and to vote instead a very substantial grant. When parliament broke up, Henry might well have congratulated himself on having outmanœuvred his opponents.

[1] The accuracy of Walsingham's well-known account of this incident is proved by the terms of a commission of 24 March 1404 (*Calendar of Fine Rolls*, xii, p. 251–64); note especially "that all payments that the said treasurers shall make of the said subsidy be made by warrant of privy seal directed to them by order of the great council."

His success was, however, illusory. In spite of the liberality with which he had been treated, the expenses of the next critical year drained the exchequer, and the government was hard put to it to maintain forces in the field sufficient at the same time to cope with foreign attack and domestic rebellion. Its unpaid creditors were becoming impatient; it was losing the confidence of the people, and when it essayed to borrow money, the response was so disappointing that by the end of 1405 there was no alternative but another parliament. It seems that Henry attempted to repeat his previous triumph, for on 21 December writs were despatched summoning members to Coventry for 15 February. But the meeting-place was changed, first to Gloucester and at the last moment to Westminster, for reasons which leave little doubt that the Londoners, supported by certain members of the council, brought pressure to bear upon the king. This was to prove a costly change of plan for the government. It was probably not unconnected with the estrangement from the regime of a powerful but moderate group of councillors of which the three Beauforts, sons of John of Gaunt by Katherine Swynford, became the active nucleus. In February 1405 Sir Thomas Beaufort was removed from his post as Admiral of the North to make way for the king's second son, Thomas, a youth of eighteen years, who was later prominent as the rival of his elder brother and the enemy of the Beaufort family. It is clear from the demand for the better keeping of the seas, brought forward early in the new parliament and urged insistently by the English merchant community, that this appointment was not popular. It was quickly followed by the resignation of Henry Beaufort, the ablest of the brothers, who had been Chancellor since 1403. This foreshadowed the emergence of an opposition party within the council itself, loyal to the dynasty but critical of the king's methods, which was soon to make its importance felt. The balance of political forces was therefore altering when on 1 March 1406 the estates met at Westminster and the government came face to face with a hostile and determined house of commons.

The "Long Parliament" of 1406 lasted with two adjournments until 22 December. It was characterised throughout by the activity and outspokenness of the king's critics, and its great length was due solely to their obstinate refusal to vote taxes until the king had conceded their demands. The keynote was struck when on 23 March the Speaker made a solemn request for "good and abundant governance." This somewhat colourless phrase, frequently repeated in the debates which followed, embodied all the aspirations of the reforming party, and the zeal with which the commons sought to give it a practical meaning justifies Stubbs's description of this parliament as "an exponent of the most advanced principles of medieval constitutional life in England." Very little time seems to have been spent in condemning the past shortcomings of the government, though the extravagance and inefficiency of the civil service came in for some very pointed criticisms. But while the greatest efforts were devoted to safeguarding the future, in one respect Henry's former good resolutions were not forgotten. In 1404 he had promised that the special treasurers should present their accounts to parliament for audit. He was now asked to fulfil this promise. At first he gave an uncompromising reply: "Kings were not wont to render account"; and every sort of obstruction was resorted to by ministers. But knowing how hard pressed he was for money, the commons remained obdurate; their firmness was rewarded when on 19 June, in return for a slight increase for one year in the rates at which poundage might be levied, they were allowed an audit by parliament. This was a notable victory; not only did it encourage the opposition to continue the struggle but it was a clear vindication of the policy towards which it was feeling its way, the policy of appropriating supplies and of holding ministers personally responsible to parliament for their expenditure.

It may well have been this demonstration of its value which now prompted the commons to extend the use of their principle by enforcing it not merely in the case of an extraordinary tax but in that of all taxes, and not merely upon treasurers appointed *ad hoc* but also upon the regular officers of the Crown. With this in view they were far from satisfied by the king's action on 22 May in nominating a council in parliament, but began to demand stricter terms of reference. Yet Henry, giving his ill-health as an excuse, had already made one very important concession. It had long been his habit to make his wishes known directly to the chancery and exchequer by means of letters under the signet and bills countersigned by one of his chamberlains; he was thus able to short-circuit the council and to incur expenditure without its supervision. Now he agreed to submit all such direct warrants to the council for endorsement, only reserving for himself the right to pardon criminals and to appoint to offices and benefices which were actually void. These reservations, it will be noticed, involved no power to put fresh charges on the revenue. But although such an arrangement would have contented parliament in 1399, it fell very short of the desires of 1406. At first it seemed as if nothing would soften the extreme reluctance of the commons to authorise any fresh taxation; in spite of the king's obvious intention to prolong parliament until they yielded, it was only on the night of 22 December, when it was no longer possible for many of the members to reach their homes by Christmas, that their resolution melted and a grant was made. It was, however, a grant on conditions,[1] and in order that these conditions might be fulfilled, it was suggested that certain lords who were still present in parliament and therefore probably members of the council should bind themselves to refund out of their own pockets any part of the tax which should be misappropriated. It is not surprising

---

[1] These are possibly contained in a draft preserved among the records of the council (Nicolas, N. H., *Proceedings and Ordinances of the Privy Council*, 1, pp. 283–7); they include a provision that no gifts, annuities, or pardons for debt should be granted for two years, and another that any patent contrary to this should be void.

that these lords joined with the king in angrily rejecting this revolutionary proposal. But although the commons were forced to withdraw it, they only capitulated on terms. In the first place they insisted that councillors should publicly swear to obey thirty-one articles which were drawn up by parliament for their guidance; and secondly that this oath, together with the articles, should be put on record on the parliament roll in order that no doubt should be allowed to exist as to the terms on which the appointments had been made. Experience had convinced the government's critics that they could not rely upon the spontaneous willingness of the councillors to impose economies on the king unless they in their turn were obliged to assume public responsibility. How far the commons were from trusting the king's good faith is revealed by a petition that at least six of their number should be present when the roll was engrossed. Immediately afterwards parliament was dissolved. In it the knights, with little or no help from the lords and actively obstructed by the council, had secured the humiliation of the Crown and a recognition of the fact that England was governed not by the king alone but by a king acting on the advice of a council which was ultimately accountable to parliament.[1]

In view of what had happened in 1404 it was not likely that Henry, now that he had obtained the necessary supplies, would loyally respect the constitutional scheme which had thus been thrust on him. Once again he compelled a submissive parliament to loosen his bonds. Ten months after the Long Parliament had dispersed, another met at Gloucester to reverse its acts. Meanwhile the king had found a minister who was to serve him faithfully until his death. The Archbishop of Canterbury had never shown himself over-scrupulous. In 1386 and after, he had worked with the Appellants to humiliate Richard II. Ten years later he was ready to betray his former associates to the king until the fate of his brother, the Earl of Arundel, opened his eyes to Richard's duplicity. As was generally the case in that sordid period, he rarely hesitated to put his own interests before those of his class. At the beginning of the new reign he seemed to stand with the Percies and other noble supporters of the revolution for the preponderance of the baronage in the affairs of the realm, and on one occasion at least was, as we have seen, under suspicion of sharing the Percies' treasonable designs. But from 1405 there are signs that he was drawing closer to the king. In this year he was allowed to have his way in the election of Walden to the vacant see of London. His desertion of the aristocratic cause may have been due to his dislike of the Beauforts who were beginning to champion it; perhaps he was alarmed by the enterprise of the commons and by the envious eyes cast by some of them on the wealth of the Church; probably personal ambition was the deciding

[1] Here and elsewhere I have been able to make full use of the longer version of Walsingham's History contained in Bodley MS 462 by the kindness of Mr V. H. Galbraith, who placed his transcript at my disposal.

factor. Already in the parliament of 1406 he had in the name of the
council put obstacles in the way of reform. Shortly afterwards, on
30 January 1407, he accepted office as Chancellor, in the words of an
ecclesiastical chronicler, "against the will of those who loved his honour."
A patent confirming the legitimation of the Beauforts, dated ten days
later, which contained a new proviso "*excepta dignitate regali*", has been
regarded as proof of Arundel's hostility to the king's half-brothers. But
there was as yet no open breach.

At the short parliament which sat in St Peter's Abbey at Gloucester
on 20 October 1407, Arundel as Chancellor was the natural spokesman
of the government. His choice of text for the opening sermon, "Honour
the king," set the tone appropriate to the meeting. As Henry boasted
to a Hanseatic agent, this was to be a parliament which would do his
bidding. Proceedings had scarcely begun before the Chancellor, anticipating criticism, went in person to the commons' house to inform them
how the taxes granted in 1406 had been spent. This apparently
did not satisfy the commons, but when on 9 November their Speaker,
Thomas Chaucer, cousin and partisan of the Beauforts, tried to reopen
the discussion, Arundel plainly told him that the council had laboured
diligently to perform its duties and declined henceforward to be bound
by the oath which its members had sworn in the previous December. The
king was graciously pleased to excuse them, and thus the matter was terminated. In the same fashion, an attempt by Chaucer to raise the question of illegal purveyance was successfully postponed. But before long
the government overstepped wise limits and provoked a display of spirit
even from the feeble commons. On 14 November, in response to a petition,
seven lords—including the Chancellor and the two elder Beauforts—had
been permitted to confer with the members about taxation. But a week
later, before any grant had been reported, the king approached the lords
and invited them to state what they would regard as a suitable provision;
on receiving their reply, he then commanded the lower house to endorse
it. Loud was the outcry against the lords and great the clamour that
ancient liberties had been infringed. The king hastened to reassure the
members; nothing had been farther from his thoughts than that of which
they complained. The "altercation" was settled on 2 December when it
was recorded that each house might in the absence of the king debate the
country's needs, provided that neither should report until both were agreed
and that the report should always be made by the commons' Speaker. It
can hardly be claimed that this established save in a very limited sense
the right of the lower house to initiate a grant, but it certainly prevented
a novel, and if it had been successful, a very damaging invasion of its
hard-won privileges. Here ended, however, the commons' success. For
although they were promised that no precedent should be thereby created,
they went on immediately to vote the same taxes as the lords had recommended. In return the king promised solemnly not to ask for any more

money until 23 March 1410, and gave to each returning member a copy
of this promise to show to his constituents.

The ensuing two years are for us the most baffling in the history of the
reign. There is every sign that events were moving towards a crisis, but
the unexplained absence of conciliar records at this critical period is a
serious obstacle to its understanding. The king was dangerously ill; in June
1408 he had a seizure at Mortlake and for a time was thought to be dead,
"but after some hours the vital spirit returned to him." In the following
winter he lay sick at Eltham and Greenwich for many weeks; his children
were summoned and on 21 January he made his will. Yet by 6 April he
was able to write in his own hand "of the good health that I am in" to
his friend the Chancellor. There has been much dispute about the nature
of his disease; contemporaries called it leprosy, but the symptoms point
rather to some form of embolism, probably cerebral, complicated by other
less destructive ailments.[1] Both his mental and physical powers suffered
from these attacks. Although he was still capable of occasional spurts of
energy, these were of brief duration and quickly succeeded by renewed
visitations of weakness. His belief that his illness was a divine judgment
on his sins may explain his tendency to lean more and more upon the
support of his spiritual adviser, Arundel. Certainly the Chancellor was
little less than his vicegerent during these years. But the heir to the
throne, who may perhaps have felt that he had a better claim to this
position, was beginning to assert his rights. Prince Henry, advised by the
Beauforts, was resentful of the government's incompetence and anxious to
begin his reign. Already, if we are to believe Monstrelet, the Bishop of
Winchester had in 1406 informed the French court of the impending
abdication of the king in favour of his son; be this as it may, there is no
doubt that at a later date the prince lent his ear to such a suggestion.
When his father was on the point of death, he may have been willing to
wait, since it seemed that his time was not far distant, but with the king's
recovery in the spring of 1409 inaction no longer contented him. The
outcome of this period of tension was the fall of Arundel at the close of
the year. The sequence of events leading up to this can only be inferred.
When on 26 October a parliament was summoned to meet at Bristol in
the following January, no unusual difficulties appear to have been
anticipated. Soon afterwards, however, a council, called to deal with the
financial crisis, reached decisions which seem to have been unwelcome to
the king.[2] Discharging Sir John Tiptoft from the office of Treasurer,

---

[1] In view of Gascoigne's statement about the death of John of Gaunt (*Loci e Libro
Veritatum*, ed. Thorold Rogers, J. E., pp. 136-7), syphilis cannot be entirely ruled out.
We have it on the authority of the contemporary English translator of John Arderne's
Treatise on Fistula-in-Ano [ed. Power, D'A., EETS. Orig. ser. cxxxix (1910) pp. xii
and 74] that Henry also suffered from a prolapse of the rectum. I have to thank
Mr H. W. S. Wright and Sir D'Arcy Power for their kind assistance with these
medical details.

[2] *Calendar of Close Rolls, 1409-13*, pp. 25-6.

Henry ordered the collectors of customs by signet letter to ignore the council's orders. His defiance was nevertheless shortlived. On 18 December Westminster was substituted for Bristol as parliament's place of meeting, and three days later Arundel resigned the great seal. But although the two great offices were vacant, the king was either unable to find or unwilling to accept new ministers. It was not until 6 January that Lord Scrope became Treasurer; on the 19th orders were given to carry out the council's suspended financial regulations. There was no Chancellor for more than a month; when necessary, Henry himself superintended the sealing of documents, keeping the great seal by him for that purpose and giving instructions *viva voce* to a clerk.

In the absence of a chancellor, the opening sermon on 27 January was preached by the Bishop of Winchester, the Speaker again being Thomas Chaucer. Four days later the great seal was conferred on Thomas Beaufort. That the king himself had in no sense quarrelled with the Archbishop of Canterbury is proved by the fact that he spent the greater part of the session not in his own palace at Westminster but across the water at Lambeth. Parliament was adjourned for Easter on 15 March, but before that the commons had created great scandal by presenting a Lollard petition, which proposed to solve the country's financial difficulties by confiscating the estates of the Church. The king—and not his son, as has been generally supposed[1]—refused to consider it, and his faithful servant, Sir John Norbury, pleased at least one monastic chronicler by urging the primate to launch a crusade against these English heretics. Unabashed, the followers of Wyclif continued to make their voices heard in parliament, but in vain. In the second session the commons turned their attention to the only less controversial matter of administrative reform. On 23 April, they offered a series of remedies for the better and more economical government of the realm. In its forefront appeared the inevitable nostrum that the king should "ordain and assign in the present parliament the most valiant, wise, and discreet lords to be of his council" and that these along with the judges should be publicly sworn. In response to a similar request of 2 May, Henry replied that certain lords had for good reasons excused themselves, and then produced a list of seven names. Now the extent of the prince's triumph was revealed. Not only were his friends strongly represented along with himself on the new council, but even more significant was the omission of Arundel and of the usual curialists. It was in fact a small aristocratic body, from which both the king's friends and the members of the commons were excluded. The Earl of Somerset had recently died, but both his brothers were nominated, along with the Earl of Arundel, whose quarrel with his uncle, while dating back to his share in Richard Scrope's execution, had since been aggravated by a mass of

---

[1] The "*serenissimus Princeps*" of Walsingham's *Historia Anglicana*, ii, p. 283, is abbreviated from "*princeps catholicus et ortodoxus rex ipse*" which appears in Bodley MS 462, f. 300ᵛ.

litigation over their respective rights in Sussex.[1] When the councillors were sworn, the prince declared that they could not be held to their oaths unless sufficient funds were provided. After rejecting the suggestion that they should give the king an annual tax for the remainder of his life, the commons proceeded to vote a subsidy and a half, its collection to be spread over three years. Just before the dissolution, Bishop Langley and the Earl of Westmorland were excused attendance at the council on account of the necessity for their presence in the north, and, at the prince's request, the names of two more of his friends, the Earl of Warwick and Bishop Chichele of St David's, were added to fill their places.

The new councillors threw themselves into their task with energy. For the rest of the year, they virtually governed the country in the king's name, while Henry, visiting his palaces at Windsor, Woodstock, and Kenilworth, was content to leave affairs at Westminster in their hands. During June and July they met frequently, mainly to discuss finance. A genuine attempt seems to have been made to discover the government's liabilities and to meet them by borrowing and by ordinances for the better collection of the revenue. These researches evidently brought home to them the gravity of the situation, for on 19 March 1411 a great council was held at which the Treasurer placed a financial statement before the lords in the king's presence. Budgeting for the year Michaelmas 1410 to Michaelmas 1411, Lord Scrope estimated the probable deficit at over £16,000, even before any provision had been made for annuities payable at the exchequer or for the salaries of councillors. It appears that the half-subsidy due at Midsummer 1411 had already been assigned to the king's creditors, and the Treasurer referred to the debts of the household, wardrobe, and other spending departments as " amounting to a huge sum." There is no evidence that the lords had any remedy to offer for the unsoundness which this statement revealed. The fact was that all this financial activity was occasioned by a desire to find means for fresh expenditure. That Prince Henry's thoughts were already turning towards the possibility of military intervention in France, where the feuds of Burgundy and Armagnac offered a tempting bait, is suggested by estimates drawn up at this time for the cost of Calais in time of war. Notwithstanding the fact that the ancient debts of this fortress alone were more than £9,000, he was ambitious to raise and equip a new expeditionary force. In this he does not appear to have had his father's approval, but nevertheless in September 1411 a small English army under the Earl of Arundel was despatched to the assistance of Burgundy. On 9 November they took part in the victory of St Cloud, but were shortly afterwards sent home.

Meanwhile in England the prince's ascendancy was drawing to an end. Following the arrest in October of six knights, including the steward of his household, on an unnamed charge, he made a progress through the

[1] *Calendar of Close Rolls, 1405–9*, p. 525 and *1409–13*, pp. 59 and 183–5.

country in search of popular support. It was said that his advisers, led by Henry Beaufort, were openly proposing that the king should be deposed in his favour, and apparently a formal demand to this effect was made in the parliament which began at Westminster on 3 November. It does not seem that this propaganda was at all favourably received by the people as a whole or that Henry IV had any difficulty in countering its effects. The latter bided his time. At his side was Arundel, fresh from his triumph over the prince's friends at Oxford, where in the face of obstinate resistance he had succeeded in humbling the University. The king did not attend the opening of parliament, but when on its second day the Speaker was presented to him he told him sharply that he wished on no account to have any manner of novelty but intended "to stand as free in his prerogative as any of his predecessors." Nothing was heard for the moment of his abdicating, but a statute of the last parliament was annulled because it improperly limited the rights of the Crown. Before the end of the session, the council was thanked for its services and discharged, Thomas Beaufort and Lord Scrope were removed from office, and the Archbishop of Canterbury again entrusted with the great seal. No council was formally nominated, but the Prince of Wales and Henry Beaufort were excluded from that which met for the remainder of the reign. It was a cowed and anxious parliament which, hearing that the king's heart was heavy against its members, begged and secured from him a declaration of his faith in their loyalty before they returned home.

In the matter of finance, the commons had not been generous. The government's insolvency did not, however, prevent it from planning a fresh expedition to France, this time to succour the Armagnacs. It is difficult to explain this change of policy on any other ground than that the king desired to mark his disagreement with his son, though the possibility of recovering Aquitaine no doubt had its influence in determining his choice. This decision produced a domestic crisis, the facts of which are by no means clear. Henry was persuaded that the Prince of Wales, who was raising troops in the northern midlands, contemplated rebellion with a view to seizing the throne and preventing the betrayal of his former Burgundian allies. In reply the prince issued a public statement at Coventry on 17 June, asserting his innocence; he explained that his only object in mustering an army larger than his quota was his desire to assist his father to reconquer Aquitaine with all the means in his power, that he had acted as he believed with the royal permission, and that the king had been listening to the calumnies of certain sons of iniquity by whom he was surrounded. With protestations of filial obedience, but "with much people of lords and gentles," he then marched to London and took up his residence at the Bishop of London's inn. For several days the city and suburbs were full of armed men, while the king and council hurried on their preparations for the French voyage. In an interview with his father the prince demanded the punishment of those who had slandered him; "the king seemed indeed to assent to his request, but asserted that they ought to await the time of parliament that these might be punished by the judgment of their peers." The reconciliation would therefore seem to have been incomplete. But at length the tension was relieved when it was settled that the prince and the king, who had meant himself to lead the expedition, should remain at home, while Thomas of Lancaster, now created Duke of Clarence, and the other lords went to France. The army set out from Southampton on 11 July, but it had not been long in Normandy before the French parties temporarily sank their differences and bought the invaders off. While this was taking place, the prince continued to act in a fashion that did much to justify his father's suspicions. For again on 23 September he "came to London to the council with a huge people," this time to defend himself also against a charge of misappropriating the wages of the Calais garrison. Leaving his followers in Westminster Hall he forced his way alone into the royal presence, where after an emotional scene the king embraced and forgave him. An enquiry conducted by the council into his government of Calais resulted, as was inevitable, in his complete exoneration. Henry IV's health was now rapidly failing; in December he was again for a period unconscious, but recovered sufficiently to take part in the Christmas celebrations at Eltham. He died after another seizure at Westminster on 20 March 1413. For nearly fourteen years he had struggled doggedly and with some measure of success, not only to preserve his usurped throne against enemies at home and abroad, but to maintain in the teeth of baronial pressure and popular criticism what he believed to be the rights and prerogatives of the Crown. Arundel did not long survive his master. Dismissed from the chancellorship on the first day of the new reign, he withdrew from political life and died within a year.

It was remarked by contemporaries that on his accession to power Henry of Monmouth underwent a species of conversion; "in all things at that time he reformed and amended his life and his manners." The lawless and high-spirited youth became, as it were overnight, a bigot and a disciplinarian. There was no room in his nature for compromise, and by this abrupt change he expressed his conscious dedication of himself to what he regarded as the supreme purpose of his being. If in the past he had been riotous and addicted to low company, this was only because his enormous energy, denied adequate scope in politics, had been compelled to seek another outlet. Once the curb imposed by his mistrustful father was removed and he was free to give unfettered play to his imperial designs, he abandoned his disreputable courses without hesitation or regret. The same thing had happened when Thomas Becket went to Canterbury; Henry threw himself with an ascetic zeal equal to that of St Thomas into realising a highly exalted conception of the duties of his station. It was his dream, having first conquered France, to lead a reunited Christendom against the Turk and, as he confessed on his death-bed, to "build again the walls of Jerusalem" in a last Crusade. To this Napoleonic task he was prepared to devote his life and fortune—and the lives and fortunes of his less idealistic countrymen. But large as were his schemes, there was nothing in the least visionary about his methods. A soldier of genius and resource, he owed his success almost as much to his diplomatic skill as to his victories in the field; while no medieval statesman grasped more fully the importance of sea-power or set himself more actively to win for England the undisputed command of the Channel. Imperious, untiring, and single-minded, Henry was a cruel enemy and a harsh master, brooking no opposition to his will; yet though he renounced all those qualities which make a monarch popular, he achieved the remarkable feat of inspiring Englishmen with a patriotic enthusiasm and a community of aims in marked contrast with their bitter disharmony during the previous age. He found a nation weak and drifting and after nine years he left it dominant in Europe.

The whole-heartedness of this response to Henry's lead made one thing clear: in spite of many superficial indications to the contrary, Lancastrian England was by no means decadent; the source of its troubles lay less in its own rottenness than in the futility of its governors, unsettled by an economic revolution which they did not understand. A young and vigorous civilisation had failed to obtain the authoritative guidance of which it stood desperately in need. Its political unrest, though it often served the ends of ambitious nobles, was not mere factiousness; it sprang rather from the efforts of a new class to break through the cracking shell of traditional medieval society. For more than a century, the country had been waxing rich from the sale of its staple commodity, wool, which for its unsurpassed quality was in steady demand on the markets of Flanders. No amount of royal interference, of regulation in the interests of foreign policy or of public finance, could hold up the progress of this traffic. Nor did it stand alone; for alongside it had grown up the cloth industry: the products of English looms were beginning to be carried in native bottoms to foreign parts. The legend of the commercial backwardness of medieval England dies hard. Yet during the fourteenth century, latecomers though they were, needing to force their way into the closed markets of the continent, the English were laying the foundations of their mercantile greatness. It was of no exceptional shipman that Chaucer wrote:

> "He knew wel alle the havenes, as they were,
> From Gootlond to the Cape of Finistere;
> And every cryke in Britayne and in Spayne."

By the reign of Richard II, English merchants had planted a factory at Danzig and won recognition of their privileges there from the reluctant Hansa. In the early years of the fifteenth century native ships sailed adventurously from Lynn "by nedle and by stone...unto the costes colde" of Iceland and established a profitable trade with the inhabitants. All efforts to penetrate into the Mediterranean were, however, repulsed. When in 1412 William Walderne of London and his partners shipped £24,000 worth of wool to Italy, it was seized by the Genoese authorities. Thereafter, apart from occasional privateering ventures, no further attempt was made to challenge Italian monopoly beyond the Straits of Morocco. In spite of this defeat, which was in any case unparalleled, the time was one of increasing material prosperity. It is hardly surprising that Italian visitors, though they considered the English intellectually backward, were deeply impressed by the high standard of comfort, amounting often to luxury, which they found everywhere prevalent. Their observations are confirmed by the monuments, perhaps only a tithe of those erected, which have survived into our own day. It is a striking fact that the magnificent castles at Tattershall, Wingfield (co. Derby), and Bolton in Wensleydale were built by men of lesser baronial rank, and those at Caister and Hurstmonceux by no more than simple knights. Nor was this splendour confined to domestic architecture. The scores of lofty perpendicular churches still extant in East Anglia bear witness to the thriving trade of Ipswich, Yarmouth, Lynn, and Boston; while their counterparts in Somerset and the Cotswold area tell a similar tale about the western ports. Most districts profited directly, all were ultimately fertilised, by this new wealth. For its benefits were enjoyed not merely by that numerous middle class which was engaged in the transport, sale, and manufacture of wool and cloth, but equally by those landowners, great and small, from whose sheepfolds the raw material was drawn. The capital thus accumulated was not suffered to lie idle; it was often reinvested, so that territorial magnates became sleeping partners in business and in some cases even possessed their own merchant-ships. The result of all this financial dealing was to place too great a strain upon that ancient theological doctrine by which Christians were forbidden to practice usury. In spite of the fact that this prohibition was reinforced by the law of the land, it was rapidly becoming a dead letter. But because steps were taken to circumvent it by legal fictions, these unspectacular beginnings of modern capitalism for long escaped the notice of historians. Nevertheless we find Sir John Fastolf advancing large sums to London tradesmen *"ad mercandizandum"* at 5 per cent. per annum. The truth is that loans at interest were common, and even ecclesiastics did not hesitate to swell their incomes by committing *" l'orrible et abhominable vice de Usure."* By far the largest borrower was the government, which, since Edward III had defaulted to his Italian creditors, was obliged to rely in this matter mainly if not wholly upon native capitalists. Fortunately for it there were several individuals and many corporations rich enough to take the places of the Bardi and Peruzzi. But the king's credit was so bad that, as we are informed by Sir John Fortescue, he had to offer a premium of 20–25 per cent. before he could raise the necessary sums. It is small wonder that acquisitiveness was the predominating characteristic of Lancastrian England. Yet the mercenary spirit which has often been taken for proof of its degeneracy was the outcome of a boundless vitality and optimism.

It was inevitable that these developments should profoundly modify the structure of medieval society. In feudal England a definite limit had been set to the free play of these competitive tendencies. It is of course true that a man of gentle birth, given enough military skill, might rise from landless poverty to affluence, and that both Church and law had always offered the chance of high preferment to those whom the profession of arms did not suit. But the underlying conception was one of static order, dependent upon an established military caste. Yet once fortunes could be made by trade and invested in land, the boundaries which had hitherto separated class from class rapidly disintegrated and in a short time the old feudal aristocracy was itself invaded by the *nouveaux-riches*. Already in the fourteenth century its highest ranks had been entered by the son of William de la Pole, a Hull merchant. This was still unusual enough to excite resentment, but a little later no one minded when Chaucer's grand-daughter became a duchess or thought it odd that the grandson of Sir Geoffrey Boleyn, who was mayor of London in 1457, should be an earl and the father of a queen. Mixed marriages were quite common; thus William Stonor, an Oxfordshire knight, took as his first wife the widow of a mercer, as his second the daughter of a marquis. Several of the most famous Tudor families, who throve on the purchase of monastic lands, owed their importance in the first place to their mercantile ancestors in the fifteenth century. Many ancient institutions could not survive in this changed atmosphere. The process of adaptation radically altered the external structure, if not the essence, of feudalism itself. In the fifteenth century military service was no longer merely an incident of tenure but also a commodity to be disposed of by sale. The army of the Hundred Years' War was a mercenary army, consisting not of vassals but of hired retainers who were by no means always the tenants of the man they served. The bond which united them to him was a contract voluntarily entered into by both parties and not an indissoluble hereditary tie. An enterprising magnate could therefore reach out beyond the frontiers of his fief, and by indenting with his neighbours for their services bring whole districts, sometimes an entire county, under his control. The " bastard feudalism " thus begotten approached nearer to its continental prototype than to the revised version which had been introduced into England by William I. By substituting a few great areas of influence for the dispersed honours of the Norman period, it raised the problem of " the overmighty subject " in a new and more acute form. Another factor was also at work to the same end. Estates scattered in half a dozen shires could not be managed economically; administrative convenience would in any event have dictated some measure of consolidation, and the feudal geography of England had already been profoundly modified in this direction by three and a half centuries of grant, purchase, marriage, and exchange. But although this tendency threatened the stability of the central government, it only produced a crisis when the enlistment of retainers gave baronial ambition a wider range. Its corrupting effect on local institutions was soon apparent. To attract retainers the baron had to be able to find patronage for them and their dependants, to maintain their quarrels in the royal courts, and to reward their loyalty in many other ways. Sir John Fortescue has admirably described the result: " this hath caused many men to be such braggers and suitors to the king for to have his offices in their countries to themself and their men that almost no man in some country durst take an office of the king but he first had the good will of the said braggers and engrossers of offices. For if he did not so, he should not after that time have peace in his country; whereof hath come and grown many great troubles and debates in divers countries of England." As his father's reign had shewn, civil strife was already imminent when Henry V temporarily resolved all discords by proclaiming war on France.

Although his enthusiasm was for the moment infectious, it may be doubted whether many of the king's subjects really shared his dream of a continental empire. For one thing the merchants were becoming dimly conscious that England's destiny lay not in France but upon the seas, a suspicion which a few years later deepened into certainty. If they hated the French as traditional enemies, they hated the Flemings, the Hansards, and the Italians still more as commercial rivals. Yet Henry's policy rested upon a close understanding with Flanders as a first step towards a military alliance with Burgundy, and upon the neutrality of the other maritime powers in order to isolate France at sea. In neither case was he absolutely successful, but by 1415 his diplomacy had accomplished enough to permit him to cross to Normandy in safety. Anglo-Flemish relations had been put on a surer footing by an agreement of 7 October 1413, which provided for the appointment in each country of " conservators of truces" to punish breaches of the peace, to investigate charges of piracy, and to restore stolen goods to their lawful owners. In pursuance of this a Statute of Truces and Safeconducts was passed by the Leicester parliament in the following year. Do what he would, however, Henry could not induce the Burgundians to throw in their lot definitely with the English, and it was not until Duke John the Fearless was murdered in 1419 that the longed-for Anglo-Burgundian alliance became a fact. The negotiations had on the other hand secured the absence of the duke from the French army of Agincourt and after, a service which contributed largely to Henry's chances of success. The isolation of the French at sea presented few difficulties. Only the Genoese, whose seizure of the Londoners' wool in 1412 had created bad blood, were persuaded to come to the assistance of France. In 1416 some twenty ships, commanded by Giovanni Grimaldi, appeared in the Channel to join in the French blockade of Harfleur; but on 15 August they were attacked by a hastily collected fleet under the Duke of Bedford and decisively beaten in the Battle of the Seine. While Henry lived the English command of the narrow seas was never again disputed. His policy nevertheless was not altogether popular. The only interest to which it appealed strongly was the Staple. For it meant allowing Flemings and Hansards to trade unmolested in England and some restriction of native enterprise in the Baltic ports; since, though the king maintained his subjects' claim to fair treatment in Danzig, he was not prepared to jeopardise Hanseatic neutrality by embarking on those wilder courses which some extremists were already urging. It meant also putting down English piracy, a great source of profit for the seafarers of the western ports. Again and again Henry wrote to the home government from France pressing for stern measures against native privateers, "that no man have cause hereafter to complain in such wise as they do for default of right doing nor we cause to write to you always as we do for such causes, considered the great occupation that we have otherwise." Though all this resulted in more security for English shipping, since it diminished reprisals, it did not go nearly far enough for those whose views found clear expression some twenty years later in the *Libel of English Policy*. For the anonymous author of this pamphlet the conquest of Normandy was not a stage in the conquest of France but a means of dominating the Straits of Dover. He was a militant nationalist, but his nationalism was economic not political, and though he praised Henry V generously for his naval victories, he makes it clear that he would have put them to a different use. The English Channel was, he realised, the high road of Western European trade. Along it passed Italian carracks laden with "thynges of complacence" from the South and East, silks and spices and oil, wine-ships from Lisbon and La Rochelle bound for the Low Countries, and fleets carrying salt from the Bay of Bourgneuf to the Hanseatic towns. England had therefore, he argued, only to "kepe thamyralte" to be able to hold this traffic to ransom and to extort favourable terms for its merchants in the continental markets. By blockading Flanders, suspending the export of English wool, and compelling aliens in England to submit to drastic regulation, he thought to give his countrymen the economic mastery of the northern seas. It was an ambitious scheme, but it is doubtful whether England, for all the advantages of its geographical position, was strong enough to risk an encounter of this magnitude with all the naval powers at once. In any case it never had a fair trial; Henry V, the one man who might have realised it, had other, more medieval, ideas. It is the tragedy of his reign that he gave a wrong direction to national aspirations which he did so much himself to stimulate, that he led his people in pursuit of the chimera of foreign conquest, an adventure from which they recoiled exhausted and embittered after more than thirty years of useless sacrifice. When the war ended, not only were they ignominiously defeated, but as a consequence of this defeat, their commercial expansion was postponed for nearly a century.

Henry did not live to deal with the troubles to which his large project gave rise. Though by 1420 there were beginning to be signs of popular discontent with the cost of the war, on the whole national enthusiasm survived his death. Before, however, he had silenced criticism by his brilliant Agincourt campaign, he had been faced by two recurrences of the domestic factiousness which had so frequently disturbed his father's peace. Of these the Lollard rising was the more serious. The infection of Wyclif's teaching had spread widely since the heresiarch's death, especially among the middle and artisan classes, where its assault on clerical pride and covetousness was naturally most popular. Many poor parish priests as well as unemployed and ambitious clerks from Oxford had good reason for envying the princes of the Church. But its appeal had reached also the more serious-minded among the educated laity, who were disturbed by the continuation of the Schism and by the worldliness of an episcopate more zealous for discipline than for the Christian life. Such men as Sir John Cheyne, Sir Lewis Clifford, and above all Sir John Oldcastle (Lord Cobham by right of his wife) had embraced the new doctrines. At the opening of the century the University of Oxford was still the centre of the movement, but, as we have seen, the house of commons contained a formidable body of sympathisers. Nevertheless the Church was bent on persecution, though whether it was as much shocked by the doctrinal heresies as by the anticlericalism remains doubtful. The passage of the Statute *De Haeretico Comburendo* in 1401 ensured it the co-operation of the lay arm in its attempt to stamp out the heretics. During Henry IV's reign a small number of obstinate Lollards were burnt, and at Oxford Archbishop Arundel cowed the authorities into recognising his rights of visitation and correction. In 1413 everything turned on the new king's attitude to the religious question. Hitherto this may well have puzzled contemporary observers. He had, it is true, in 1410 exhorted John Badby, a convicted heretic, to save his life by recantation and, on his refusal, he had suffered him to be burnt; but on the other hand, he had championed his old university against Arundel, and he was the friend of Sir John Oldcastle. All doubts were set at rest early in his reign, when it became clear that he was ready to abandon Oldcastle along with the other disreputable associates of his youth. Old-castle was arrested by the royal officers and on 23 September 1413 brought before his ecclesiastical judges at St Paul's; when he declined to abandon his errors and firmly reasserted his faith in them, sentence of condemnation was passed upon him. On 19 October, however, he made his escape from prison and began in secret to rouse his co-religionists to armed rebellion. It was his intention, the government asserted, to capture the king and to establish a commonwealth with himself as protector, but this does not sound a likely story. The rising was planned to take place at St Giles' Fields, London, on 10 January 1414, but the conspiracy was betrayed to the king, who took immediate steps to forestall it. As the insurgents were making their way in bands to the scene of action during the night of the 9th, they were surprised and scattered by the royal forces. Many were captured and promptly executed, but Oldcastle again escaped. Though the Leicester parliament in May 1414 gave its consent to fresh statutes for the extirpation of Lollardy, it was not until the end of 1417 that he was apprehended in Wales and hanged on the site of his rebellion. The subsequent history of the sect is obscure; persecuted and hunted unmercifully, it went into hiding, but there is no evidence that it was ever completely eradicated.

It was to an informer also that Henry owed his timely knowledge of a mysterious plot to assassinate him in July 1415, on the eve of his departure for France. The principals in this affair were Richard, Earl of Cambridge, Sir Thomas Gray, and Henry, Lord Scrope of Masham, the last-named being one of the king's most trusted servants. Their object was to restore Richard II, whom some believed to be still alive, or, failing that, to enthrone his heir, the Earl of March. The wretched March, to whom they rashly confided their secret, was so afflicted by scruples that he went and unburdened his conscience to the king. He thereby earned forgiveness, but his three companions were speedily arrested and put to death as traitors. This done, Henry sailed from Portsmouth, leaving his brother Bedford to rule a peaceful country in his absence.

His expedition had been carefully prepared. For months beforehand artificers had been employed constructing siege-engines, pontoons, and pieces of artillery; vast quantities of war-material, armour, and weapons of every type had been assembled by the royal purveyors and stored in casks at Pountney's Inn in London. It was a comparatively small, but an unusually well-equipped, army which landed near Harfleur on 14 August. With its achievements and those of its successors we are not concerned, since they have already been described elsewhere; here it is only necessary to speak of the effects of the war upon the English Exchequer. Like many conquerors, Henry does not seem to have bothered his head overmuch about the financial soundness of his enterprise; he needed money, but was quite indifferent as to the means by which it was procured. In spite of heavy taxation, it was impossible to pay for the Agincourt campaign out of current revenue, still less for the piecemeal reduction of Normandy which began in 1417. Income was therefore deflected from its normal uses and huge loans were raised upon the security of the Crown jewels. Even so, many soldiers and more civilians went unpaid. Death no doubt settled many accounts. But as late as 1454 that veteran warrior, Sir John Fastolf, was still claiming the arrears due to him for services rendered at Harfleur in 1415. In a very short time the strain became intolerable. Modern estimates, based upon an imperfect under-standing of the principles of medieval book-keeping, have unfortunately disguised the real gravity of the position. Much more reliance can be placed in a contemporary statement drawn up and laid before the council by the Treasurer on 6 May 1421. Not only was a gigantic deficit expected, but every department was shown to be heavily in debt. Yet a considerable proportion of the Treasurer's estimated revenue of nearly £56,000 had in any case no real value, since it had long ago been assigned in advance to the king's numerous creditors. The malady, that is to say, which was already present in 1399, neglected year by year and recently aggravated by Henry's wild extravagance, had made and would continue to make rapid strides. Loans staved off a crisis, but the cumulative effect of such a policy was bound to be disastrous. We should be careful, however, not to talk loosely about the country's financial exhaustion in 1421; it was not the national wealth which was exhausted, but that small fraction of it upon which the king could lay his hands. At first the commons had been remarkably free with taxation, but in the parliaments of 1420 and May 1421 no grants were made. Henry retaliated by extorting forced loans and popular enthusiasm waned still further. Adam of Usk's well-known description of the smothered curses with which the royal com-missioners were greeted, however much it may exaggerate, cannot be dismissed as pure rhetoric. Dissatisfaction was also spreading among the soldiers in France; thus one complains of " the long time that we have been here and of the expenses that we have had at every siege...and have had no wages since that we came out "; while another prays earnestly that he may soon depart " out of this unlusty soldier's life into the life of England." It would not be long before such men grew mutinous. The national effort had been too great to be long sustained; it was visibly weakening when Henry himself succumbed to camp-fever at Bois-de-Vincennes on 31 August 1422 in his thirty-sixth year.

As the king lay dying, his thoughts were busy with the future. In addition to the fact that his work was but half-finished, there was also the prospect of a long minority to fill him with concern. For he was leaving behind him as heir a son, Henry, not yet nine months old. In his third will, drawn up on 10 June 1421, when he knew his queen to be with child, he had bequeathed the regency of England in the event of his premature death to his younger brother Gloucester; but there is reason to believe that he changed his mind more than once during his last ill-ness. Owing, however, to the violent disagreement of our authorities, we do not know for certain what he finally decided. In any case it was not carried out; for, as soon as he was dead, his wishes lost their binding force and were set aside. He had long ruled the barons with a firm hand; they joyfully reasserted their independence. Above all they were quite determined that Gloucester should not step into his brother's shoes. The prime mover in their resistance to the duke's advancement was Henry Beaufort, whose royal blood, forceful personality, and ripe experience well qualified him for leadership. Though only forty-seven years of age, he had been a bishop, first of Lincoln and afterwards of Winchester, for nearly a quarter of a century. Not content with this, he had looked higher, to Rome itself, but Henry V had forbidden him to desert the royal service for the Curia. Yet, in spite of this discouragement, he cultivated the friendship of Martin V, whose gratitude he had earned at Constance in 1417, and waited for a suitable opportunity to turn it to account. Meanwhile his knowledge of domestic politics was unrivalled. He had first held the chancellorship in 1403, and since that date there had been few periods when he was not officially employed. But for all his statesmanlike qualities, Beaufort was an arrogant and grasping man. He had accumulated from various sources an immense fortune, which enabled him to wield great influence. The sum total of his loans to the Crown between 1417 and 1444 exceeds £200,000; he was owed more than £20,000 by Henry V at his death[1]. These transactions have been generally regarded as proofs of the bishop's disinterested patriotism, as though it was glaringly obvious that by lending he had no thought of his own profit. But such a view of his character has little to commend it. On the other hand there can be no reasonable doubt that in 1424, under cover of such a loan, he defrauded the king of some £10,000 by converting Crown jewels to his own use[2].

When Beaufort set himself to undermine Gloucester's pretensions, the latter was no match for him. Equally overbearing and unscrupulous, the duke lacked his rival's administrative talents and political sagacity. For, while he inherited his father's affable manners and cultivated tastes, he inherited also his financial incompetence and his rash ungovernable temper. He was rescued from political insignificance by his birth and by the success with which he courted popular favour. This latter gift saved his reputation after his death. Posterity for centuries accepted the legend of " good Duke Humphrey," overthrown and finally murdered by the machinations of that " pernicious usurer" and " presumptuous priest," the Cardinal Bishop of Winchester.

The first victory in their long duel went decisively to Beaufort. This took place in the parliament which met at Westminster on 6 November 1422. On the day before, Gloucester was given permission to open the proceedings and to continue them as long as should be necessary "*de assensu consilii.*" Nothing was decided at this stage about his future status, but the duke immediately objected to the use of these conditional words, on the plea that when he had had similar powers from Henry V there had been no such limitation. The council refused to omit the offending clause;

---

[1] Receipt and Issue Rolls, 1417–1446 *passim*.

[2] This was first pointed out by Gloucester in 1440 (Stevenson, J., *War of the English in France*, ii, ii, p. 443), and is substantiated by the records of the Exchequer.

that is to say, they already drew a distinction between the authority delegated to Gloucester as Regent by an absent king and the authority to be exercised by Gloucester as the spokesman of a king too young to rule. In this the ultimate settlement was foreshadowed; during the minority there was to be a council of regency in fact if not in name. This did not content the duke, who imagined that his brother's death was a reason for augmenting rather than reducing his share in the government. When parliament assembled, he made haste to state his claim; as soon as the commons desired to know what the lords proposed, he came forward to request "the governance of this land, affirming that it belongeth unto (him) of right, as well by the mean of (his) birth as by the last will of the king that was." In reply, the lords appealed to history; in the minority of Richard II, the king's uncles had been associated together to "survey and correct the faults of them that were appointed to be of the king's council." Gloucester was not the only uncle of Henry VI; besides Bedford who was abroad, there were two Beauforts. But if they had hoped to silence the duke by this historical argument, they reckoned without his bookishness, for he countered their example by the case of William Marshal, who had been *Rector Regis et Regni* during the minority of Henry III. Thereupon the lords fell back on the constitutional rights of parliament; Gloucester's proposal was "against the freedom of the estates"; Henry V "might not by his last will nor otherwise alter...the law of the land...without the assent of the three estates, nor commit nor grant to any person governance or rule of this land longer than he lived." But not wishing to drive the duke into open opposition, they decided that in Bedford's absence he should be chief of the king's council and "devised therefore (for him) a name different from other councillors." They rejected a number of names such as Tutor, Lieutenant, Governor, and Regent for the very significant reason that any of these would "import authority of governance of this land," a suggestion which they were particularly anxious to avoid, and chose instead "the name of Protector and Defensor, the which importeth a personal duty of attendance to the actual defence of the land" and nothing more. With this Gloucester was for the moment forced to rest content. A council was then appointed in parliament and it was enacted that the Protector was to take no steps without its advice. With a few trifling exceptions it was to retain control of all official appointments and all royal patronage. No controversial business was to be transacted in the absence of a majority of the councillors, none at all unless four were present in addition to the three officers.

This arrangement, in spite of Gloucester's attempts to upset it, remained virtually unchanged for seven years. It was a thoroughly practical solution of the constitutional question which, while denying Gloucester the authority he craved, gave him titular rank and vested all real power in the hands of an aristocratic council. But though the lords treated the Protector as they had desired but failed to treat Henry IV, it is wrong to see in this a

victory for the principles of 1406. In the first place there was no suggestion
that the constitutional checks imposed on the Protector were to apply to
the king when he came of age, though naturally enough by the end of
the long minority councillors had become too deeply attached to their
new privileges to surrender them without regret; and secondly, nothing
was said or hardly even implied about the responsibility of ministers to
parliament. In spite of the reference to the three estates, the aspirations
of the commons, as formulated in 1406, were passed over in silence. It is
difficult at first sight to understand why the lower house did not grasp so
obvious a moment for asserting its rights. Yet though for some years all
direct taxation was withheld, only the burgesses showed any disposition
to criticise the government. It was as if the knights of the shire who had
led the attack on Henry IV trusted the council to make a better use of
the royal authority than had the king and his curialists. Everything
points in short to a closer identification of outlook between the baronage
and the knights than the exceptional events of 1406 had seemed to
suggest. The strength of those local ties which still bound the small
landowners to their greater neighbours was felt as soon as the latter gained
control of the royal patronage. The council filled offices and settled
disputes in deference to the predominant territorial interests; it is not
unreasonable to see in this the explanation of the commons' inaction.
The one danger to be feared was a division among the lords themselves;
though this ultimately occurred, it was temporarily averted by the
obviousness of Gloucester's ambition; the need to make common cause
against him kept the lords united when every consideration of private
profit was drawing them apart.

Between 1422 and 1425 the Protector gave very little trouble. The
government was on the whole popular and he had no following in the
country. The vigilance of his opponents was such that he was driven to
employ his energies elsewhere. When the parliament of October 1423
confirmed its predecessor's settlement, he was already playing with the
idea of seeking his fortune abroad. The presence in England of Jacqueline
of Hainault, who had deserted her husband the Duke of Brabant, offered
him a favourable opening. Notwithstanding the knowledge that his
purpose endangered the Anglo-Burgundian alliance, he went through the
ceremony of marriage with Jacqueline and in October 1424 departed in
her company to invade Hainault. During his absence the protectorate
was in abeyance, and his place at the head of the executive was taken by
Bishop Beaufort, now again Chancellor. The expedition was a failure,
Jacqueline was soon discarded, and for the future all Gloucester's hopes
were centred in England. He returned in time for the parliament of
April 1425, to find his colleagues at issue with the city of London over
the protection which they wisely insisted on according to foreign
merchants. By fanning the passions which it was his duty as Protector to
extinguish, he made himself in a short time the idol of the middle class.

His period of political isolation seemed at an end. Yet Beaufort chose this moment to provoke an open quarrel by some tactless references to the futility and dangers of the Hainault escapade. Thenceforward Gloucester's ambitions were bound up with a desire to humiliate his critic. The support of the Londoners made him so formidable that for a few weeks in the autumn of 1425 he was able to shake off the council's control. Beaufort went in fear of his life, and on the morning of 30 October an armed affray actually took place on London Bridge. Gloucester's victory was, however, of brief duration. The Chancellor at once called in the Duke of Bedford to redress the balance, and when on 20 December his brother landed in England, Duke Humphrey's days of freedom were at an end. In dudgeon he withdrew from the council and declined to meet his enemy; it was only after several interviews that the lords persuaded him to agree to a formal reconciliation. He and Beaufort shook hands before parliament at Leicester on 12 March 1426. Owing to the recent disorders it was thought best to avoid the capital and, as an additional precaution, members were forbidden to come armed. Bedford made no secret of his sympathies. On his arrival he had treated the men of London with marked coldness, and when the commons charged the government with bad faith in the matter of tonnage and poundage, he made short work of their complaints. But Gloucester's inaction had been dearly purchased. Bedford was anxious to return to France, and it was soon known that the Chancellor would accompany him. The time was ripe for Beaufort's long-contemplated entry into the larger field of Roman politics. Martin V was willing to make him a cardinal and to give him employment. A short delay, however, was necessary to save his pride and to enable him to collect his debts. On 14 May he resigned the great seal and soon afterwards obtained permission from the council to undertake a "pilgrimage." He left the country in March 1427, and on Lady Day at Calais received his red hat at Bedford's hands.

If Gloucester thought to have things his own way after Beaufort's removal, he deluded himself. On 24 November 1426 the councillors drew up a series of articles which left no doubt that they intended to maintain the *status quo.* Not content with this, they took steps just before Bedford's departure to obtain from him and his brother an emphatic recognition of their rights. On 28 January an impressive ceremony was staged at Westminster; Duke John, in response to an appeal from Archbishop Kemp of York, the new Chancellor, swore solemnly to abide by the decisions of the council so long as he should be in England. Duke Humphrey, who was absent ill, was rumoured to have said on hearing this: "Let my brother govern as him lust while he is in this land, for after his going over into France, I will govern as me seemeth good." Next day, however, Kemp visited him in his inner chamber to ask for a similar assurance; thus confronted, Gloucester found it expedient to agree "to be ruled and governed by my said lords of the council…and so sub-

mitted him unto their governance." Nevertheless within a year he had
forgotten his promise. Finding his claims ignored at the beginning of
1428, he refused to attend parliament until they were satisfied. But his
desertion of Jacqueline and her cause had lost him popular support and
it was no longer necessary to spare his feelings. In a crushing rejoinder,
the lords justified the arrangements which they had made in 1422 and
exhorted him "to be content...and not to desire, will or use any larger
power" than he had been granted then. At last Humphrey admitted
defeat; for the remaining months of the protectorate, he did not once
question the council's right to command his service[1].

This same year which witnessed Gloucester's submission was also
memorable for the victory of the government in another quarrel. Soon
after his election Martin V had revived the ancient controversy over
Provisors. But although he again and again pressed for the withdrawal
of the offending statute of 1390, his representations fell on deaf ears. At
length in 1427 his patience was exhausted. Accusing Archbishop Chichele
of lukewarmness, he ordered him to use his influence more actively in the
Church's cause. When this too proved fruitless, he suspended the Primate's
legatine commission and threatened England with an interdict. His bulls,
however, were seized by the royal officers and not permitted to take effect.
In January 1428 Chichele besought parliament to comply with Rome's
demands. It would nevertheless be wrong to assume that he therefore either
sympathised with the Pope's campaign or was intimidated by his threats.
Since he must have known that the commons would reject his plea, it is
more likely that he wished to ease Martin's retreat from the humiliating
position into which his offensive tactics had got him. Thus the Pope was
able to accept this evidence of his servant's zeal and to let the proceedings
against him drop. But though in future Rome adopted more diplomatic
methods to gain its object, the statutes remained in force. All that this
dispute had done was to make Martin extremely unpopular in England.

Cardinal Beaufort therefore chose a most inauspicious moment to
return home on papal business. After a futile crusade against the
Hussites, he arrived in August 1428 to collect men and money for another
invasion of Bohemia. His reception was far from cordial. Only one bishop
—his creature, Neville of Salisbury—was present at his state entry into
London, while convocation declined to vote him any funds. On the other
hand, although the government formally protested against his use of his
legatine authority in England, it allowed him to recruit half the numbers
for which he asked. He might still have escaped unscathed had not events
in France now taken a serious turn. Before his preparations were complete,
the English were obliged to raise the siege of Orleans and to fall back

---

[1] On the strength of a council warrant, Professor Baldwin (*The King's Council*,
pp. 181-2) argues that "in 1428 Gloucester evidently won a victory in the council."
But this document in fact proves the opposite (Chancery Warrants, C. 81/1545,
8 December, 1427).

towards Paris. News of Talbot's defeat at Patay, arriving just as the crusaders were about to leave for Bohemia, startled the council from its preoccupation with domestic issues. Bedford wanted reinforcements at once, but it had none handy; and so on 1 July 1429 it persuaded Beaufort to lead his crusading army against the French. It is not clear what induced him to obey. But whether he acted under duress or from motives of patriotism, his obedience cost him the favour of the Pope. Martin set great store by the Church's neutrality and, when he heard what his legate had done, he refused to accept his excuses. So grave was his displeasure that there was no question of his employing the cardinal again.

The resurrection of French nationalism discovered the weakness of Bedford's hold on the conquered provinces. His seven-years' rule had been tactful and conciliatory, but it could not avoid being burdensome; for he had had to rely too much on his own resources with only meagre and intermittent support from home. Although Beaufort's 3000 men had arrived in time to save Paris from capture, a great deal of ground had been meanwhile lost and the confidence of the army was badly shaken after its hurried retreat. The Regent therefore decided that his best hope of putting new heart into his followers was to send for the king. Henry's presence would also help to counteract the growing prestige of Charles VII among the inhabitants of northern France, while another advantage of this plan was that it compelled the English government to assume responsibility for the war and to provide a retinue worthy of the occasion of the king's first voyage. For once the councillors did not shirk their duties; half of them consented to accompany the king; even parliament acknowledged the need for heroic measures by voting a double subsidy, and everything possible was done to make the expedition a success. In readiness for his departure, Henry was belatedly crowned at Westminster on 6 November 1429; he crossed the Channel with a numerous and impressive company on St George's Day 1430.

The king's coronation served as a pretext for removing Gloucester from office. Regrettable as the experiment may well have seemed to the lords, his appointment as Protector with carefully defined, indeed almost negligible, powers had undoubtedly minimised his capacity for mischief. His struggles to upset the constitution of 1422, though a frequent source of anxiety, had eventually ceased. For nearly two years he had behaved with propriety and restraint, submitting himself to conciliar control. Now the abolition of the protectorate once more unmuzzled him. The unwisdom of this did not disclose itself immediately, for two reasons. In the first place the duke had himself at length grasped how much he stood to gain by caution; instead of harping on his rights as of old, he conducted himself with unusual forbearance while he awaited a suitable moment for an offensive. Secondly, he was no sooner free than his hands were again tied, although only temporarily, by the scheme of government drawn up in anticipation of the king's absence from the country. At a council, held at Canterbury on 16 April 1430, it was decided *inter alia* that nothing controversial should be done by the councillors in England until their colleagues in France had expressed their concurrence; it was therefore impossible for Gloucester, even if he succeeded in winning over a majority of those who remained at home, to dismiss any of the great officers of State or to alter the composition of the council; and neither the Chancellor, Archbishop Kemp, nor the Treasurer, Lord Hungerford, could be trusted to fall in with his plans. In consequence it was necessary to await the king's return. The interval was employed by Gloucester in living down his unfortunate reputation. One liberty he did allow himself, that of harassing Cardinal Beaufort. The latter's anomalous legal status offered an easy mark, attacks on which were well calculated to arouse the sympathy not only of the laity but also of the bishops, who in the absence of many lords at the war usually outnumbered their secular colleagues on the council. Gloucester's championship of English liberties threatened by papal encroachment probably did more than anything else to deflect suspicion from his own designs and to create a party favourable to him among the lords. Already in the spring of 1429 he had called in question, inconclusively but not entirely without success, Beaufort's right to hold the see of Winchester *in commendam*. In January 1430, on the ground that no man could faithfully serve two masters, he criticised a proposal to invite the cardinal to resume his seat in the council; in deference to his objection, the reappointment was made conditional upon Beaufort's taking no part in discussions which touched the relations of Church and State. But for the fact that Beaufort was contributing largely to the expenses of the royal voyage, it is unlikely that he would have emerged from these encounters so comparatively unscathed. Whatever its sentiments, the council could scarcely proceed to extremes against one who in little over a year put nearly £24,000 at the government's disposal. Moreover, in spite of his being regarded with jealousy and suspicion in many quarters, Beaufort was far from friendless. On the other hand, his loans are no evidence of his desire to recover his lost influence in English politics. His thoughts were still elsewhere. For notwithstanding his dismissal in 1429, he had not ceased to entertain hopes of further work at Rome, and when he sailed with Henry VI in 1430 it was to be nearer at hand and secure from interference in the event of a papal summons. His expectations were not disappointed. Martin, it is true, remained implacable, but Martin's successor, Eugenius IV, elected in March 1431, did not pursue the quarrel. Letters of recall arrived early in 1432. The cardinal, with the permission of those councillors who were with the king in France, hastened to obey. But as he was making ready, a fresh attack by Gloucester, delivered with unexpected force, left him no choice but to abandon his preparations and to return to England to defend himself.

It would have been far better for Gloucester had he suffered his enemy to depart in peace. His clearest chance of success in the *coup d'état* which he was then plotting lay in the prolonged absence of his only serious rival from the scene. With Beaufort safely out of the way, no one stood between Duke Humphrey and his objectives; by compelling Beaufort to reside in England, he made the one serious blunder in an otherwise well-laid plan. Until the autumn of 1431 nothing had occurred to disturb the harmony of his relations with the English council. In May of that year he had been employed to stamp out a Lollard conspiracy which was discovered at Abingdon, a task which he performed without mercy and which seems to have given him confidence for what he had in hand. It was on the strength of this cheap triumph that a great council in November was called upon by Lord Scrope, his warmest supporter, to grant him a largely increased salary for life, though the motion was only carried in the teeth of a considerable opposition under the leadership of Kemp and Hungerford. An attempt to persuade a similar assembly to condemn Beaufort in his absence for a breach of the Statute of Praemunire did not, however, meet with enough support. Gloucester had better fortune with the privy council; yet although it agreed on 28 November to the sealing of writs of *praemunire* against the cardinal, it persuaded the duke to suspend their execution until the king landed. The threat of these proceedings would probably have sufficed to bring Beaufort to England; but in addition a vast quantity of his portable wealth was seized by Gloucester's orders on 6 February 1432 as it was being smuggled from Sandwich to the continent. Beaufort, who had parted from the king at Calais to go on a visit to the Burgundian court, was in Flanders when news of his peril reached him. From Ghent on 16 February he wrote to his friend the Chancellor requesting his good offices and appointing attorneys to answer the charge of *praemunire*. From Ghent also on 13 April he addressed to the citizens of London what was virtually a manifesto, in which he proclaimed his innocence, denounced his accusers, and intimated his intention of confronting them in person as soon as parliament assembled. He had not long to wait. Writs had already been sent out summoning members to meet at Westminster on 12 May, and it was there shortly afterwards that he presented himself for trial.

Meanwhile Henry VI's entry into London on 21 February had been Gloucester's cue. In the space of a few days he brought about a complete change of government. The Archbishop of York was relieved of the great seal on 25 February; next day Scrope succeeded Hungerford at the exchequer; and on 1 March Lords Cromwell and Tiptoft, together with some lesser officials, were removed from the household. At the same time writs ordering Beaufort to appear before the king's justices at Westminster, which had been held in readiness, were sent to the sheriffs, while the repayment of his loans was interrupted. There followed a lull; but the existence of an order to certain lords, including the aggrieved Cromwell, forbidding them to come to parliament with more than their customary retinues, proves that trouble was anticipated. As soon as the session had been formally opened, Gloucester hastened to disarm criticism by a declaration that, although his birth entitled him in his brother's absence to be the king's chief councillor, he would nevertheless act in co-operation with the council and not "*ex suo proprio capite*." This assurance was well received, and Gloucester had no difficulty in snubbing Cromwell when the latter sought to raise the question of his summary dismissal. Duke Humphrey's position was for the moment unassailable, and Beaufort on his return wisely confined himself to his own defence. At what stage in the proceedings he made his appearance is uncertain; but it was not until 3 July that he succeeded in obtaining redress. On a motion of the commons, the charges against him were quashed, while Gloucester graciously consented to admit that his loyalty was not in question. Some sacrifices, however, were necessary to produce this result. In order to recover his property, which the court of the exchequer had adjudged on 14 May to be forfeited to the Crown[1], he had to make a deposit of £6,000; this was not to be restored to him unless he could satisfy the king of his innocence within six years. And the repayment of his loans was only resumed when he had agreed to lend another £6,000. Lastly, some sort of promise was extracted from him that he would not attempt to re-enter papal service without the government's consent. If therefore he had been able to repulse Gloucester's attack, it was only at the expense of his most cherished ambition. For another year even his prospects in England remained far from bright. He was not summoned to the council, over which his adversary held undisputed sway, so that for want of employment he was thrown back on the affairs of his neglected diocese. But, as in 1425, the intervention of the Duke of Bedford in July 1433 again rescued him from his isolation.

Bedford came to England neither to take sides nor to apportion blame, but to compose the dissensions which threatened the cause which he had most at heart. His sole concern was with the increasing gravity of the military outlook in France. The Burgundian alliance, upon which English security depended, was becoming strained. A resolute offensive would therefore be necessary in 1434 if disaster was to be avoided, and Bedford knew that he could only achieve this in co-operation with the ministers at home. To a limited extent he gained his purpose. He seems, that is, to have shamed the English leaders into sinking their differences and consenting to work together in outward amity. But it was easier to restore "good and abundant governance," to get Beaufort and Gloucester to share responsibility, than to overcome the financial obstacle and to place another army in the field. Duke Humphrey had perhaps not been unusually liberal in his awards to himself and his partisans, but the exchequer was practically

[1] Exchequer K. R. Memoranda Roll, E 159/208, *Communia Recorda, Pasche.* memb. 2 *et seq.,* and Exchequer K. R. Bille, E 207/14/4.

empty.[1] One of Bedford's first actions was to dismiss Scrope and to make Cromwell Treasurer. In his campaign to extract supplies he was to find in Cromwell an energetic and resourceful collaborator. Under his guidance the permanent officials were immediately set to investigate the nature and extent of the Crown's resources and commitments. The result was the fullest and probably the most accurate financial summary which has survived from the medieval period. This was laid before parliament on 18 October by the new Treasurer, who brought out its implications in an accompanying gloss. Excluding the war from his calculations and dealing only with the requirements of the home government, he estimated that receipts fell short of normal expenditure by at least £35,000 per annum. Yet even these receipts were not available, since they had already been pledged to creditors for more than two years in advance. He was daily compelled to refuse payment on countless warrants which were brought to him, and these went to swell a debt which at that moment amounted to over £168,000. Even therefore if Bedford's military needs could be met wholly out of special taxation, not in itself a likely event, the domestic problem would remain unsolved. The stinginess of the commons finally shattered any hope that survived of a large-scale offensive in France in the following year. Something, however, was gained by the report. The lords swore to support Cromwell in his unpopular duty of curtailing grants, while the councillors under Bedford's leadership set an example to others by consenting to forgo the whole or part of their salaries in the national interest. Thus encouraged, the Treasurer agreed to continue in office. But although, during the next few years, he revealed determination in opposing thoughtless extravagance, tried his hand at manipulating the wool trade to the royal profit, and applied novel methods of taxation, he scarcely touched even the fringes of the problem. Meanwhile commissioners of loans reported a steady deterioration of the royal credit, and the yield of taxation itself began to be affected by a decline in national prosperity. Peace, the first condition of financial recovery, proved unattainable, and as the war dragged on the policy of repudiation with all its ruinous social consequences was forced more and more urgently upon a desperate government.

Bedford took no pains to conceal the bitterness of his disappointment. But not unnaturally he was beginning to tire of exertions which brought him neither credit nor reward, and when both lords and commons urged him to prolong his stay in England as Chief of the King's Council, he yielded with a good grace. A peasant rising in Normandy, however, soon recalled him to a sense of duty. Under no illusions as to the hopelessness of his task, he took his leave early in July 1434. His premature death at Rouen just over a year later was an irremediable misfortune for the Lancastrian dynasty. Not that even his courage and unselfish devotion

---

[1] It contained only £175 when Cromwell assumed office on 11 August (Receipt Roll, E401/735).

CH. XI.

could have much longer staved off the inevitable in France. But as the
one adviser of Henry VI whose character commanded universal respect, he
might have exercised a moderating influence in English politics which
would be sorely missed during the coming critical years. A few days
before his death another event, almost equally calamitous, had sealed the
fate of Paris. At Arras on 21 September 1435, as a result of the breakdown of negotiations for a general peace, Duke Philip the Good forgave
his father's murderers and was reconciled with Charles VII. If not entirely
unexpected, Burgundy's defection created a profound impression in
England. For some time the cause of peace had been gaining ground
there. The more far-sighted among the councillors were definitely in its
favour, provided that it could be achieved without sacrifice of territory
or of national pride. The attitude of the country as a whole was non-
committal; most men grudged the cost and effort inseparable from war
and yet were noticeably lukewarm in their desire for peace. It was as
though they had awakened from the dream of cheaply-won military glory
but not to a full realisation of the possibility of outright defeat. All this
was now changed. Within a year of Arras the people's jealous hatred of
the Flemings, which had been with difficulty restrained for a quarter of
a century in the interests of Anglo-Burgundian friendship, gathered such
force that the government was reluctantly stampeded into war with its
recent ally. At the same time Englishmen began to harden their hearts
in an angry determination to surrender nothing voluntarily, to denounce
all concessions as treasonable and, if they could not have peace on their
own terms, to relieve their feelings by making scapegoats of their leaders.

At home the political truce which Bedford had imposed was outwardly
maintained, but it only thinly disguised the transfer of power into the
hands of a group headed by Cardinal Beaufort who, once he had been
readmitted to the council, made short work of the rival pretensions of
the Duke of Gloucester. The stages by which this group captured control
are now obscure; but the factor which assured its permanence was undoubtedly the favour of the king. The reappointment of the council on
12 November 1437 marks the formal termination of the minority. But
for at least two years before this Henry VI had been enjoying a share in
the administration. He had not yet celebrated his fourteenth birthday
when he began to minute state papers with his own hand, while 1436 saw
the signet and other "immediate" warrants again in general use. Apart
from this precocious interest in public affairs, the king's childhood would
seem to have been normal and healthy. Hardyng's oft-quoted assertion
that he was from the first so simple as to be unable to distinguish between
right and wrong, cannot be accepted; for, whatever may have been Henry's
shortcomings, it is hard to believe that a defective moral sense was ever
one of them. There is as little reason for supposing that he was physically
backward. In 1432 he was described as so "grown in years, in stature of
his person, and also in conceit and knowledge of his royal estate, the

which cause him to grudge with chastising," that it was thought wise to arm his "master," the accomplished Warwick, with more authority to correct him. This early promise, recalling his father's youth, was not to be fulfilled. Henry grew up a delicate and studious recluse, not merely without military ambition but with a pious horror of all bloodshed, morbidly devout and wholly incapable both in peace and war of giving his distracted realm the leadership it craved. We do not know anything to account for this breakdown; it is probable, however, that between 1432 and 1435 he prematurely overtaxed a constitution in which the faulty strains of Lancaster and Valois were united. The alternative, that his spirit was broken by harsh treatment, seems scarcely worth considering. It was not until many years later that his brain definitely gave way, but at fifteen he was already a nervous invalid, whose feeble will rendered him the easy victim of those who sought to use him. Although the council affected to lament his pliancy and more than once rebuked his open-handedness, its members for all their joint protestations were not the men to be deterred from exploiting such attractive qualities to the full. For a year or two Henry distributed his favours with a generous impartiality, but this heyday of the office-seeker was soon over. Before long the flow of patronage was regulated and the Beaufort faction came to be its sole conduit. In denying others access to the source, the cardinal was greatly assisted by the king's ill-health, which made it advisable for the latter to reside out of town and therefore deprived him of direct and frequent contact with his council. Beaufort had only to secure the loyal co-operation of the Household to achieve his end. In this he was entirely successful. He had many well-wishers among the officials; of these the staunchest was the Steward, William de la Pole, Earl of Suffolk; but he could also rely on the assistance of Sir William Phelip the Chamberlain, Sir Ralph Boteler, Sir John Stourton, Sir John Beauchamp, Robert Rolleston, and the brothers Roger and James Fenys (or Fiennes), the majority of whom were eventually raised to the peerage in recognition of their services.

But what perhaps most facilitated this transition from conciliar to curialist government was the constant presence at the king's side of an additional clerk of the council. Designed in all probability as a link between the central administration and the court, this office, in the able hands of Adam Moleyns, a devoted adherent of the new regime, was soon turned to a very different use. By 1438 Moleyns was in all but name the king's principal secretary, discharging his duties under the eyes of a few officials and household knights, often in the presence of Suffolk alone. And yet his endorsement on a bill, with or without the royal sign-manual, was a sufficient warrant for both the great and privy seals. Outside the household, Beaufort's warmest supporters were, among the baronage, his two nephews Somerset and Dorset, the Earl of Stafford, and Lords Cromwell, Beaumont, Tiptoft, and Hungerford; among the bishops, Kemp of York and Lumley of Carlisle. The cardinal, however, was aging, and when in 1443 he finally retired from public life Suffolk stepped into his shoes. Consciously or unconsciously the king was their willing instrument. It is possible, indeed, that he was deliberately kept in ignorance of the real state of popular sentiment; for, according to Gascoigne, he was guarded with such care that those invited to preach before him had either to undertake to say nothing "against the actions or counsels of the king's ministers" or else to allow their sermons to be censored in advance by the officials of the court. On the other hand, the favourites were quick to shelter behind the royal name and to attribute many of their most controversial decisions to the exercise of the king's personal authority alone. By these and other means, the council was gradually stripped of its importance, devitalised rather than suppressed outright. As a purely advisory body, without control over the seals, meeting at a distance from the court and communicating with Henry only through his ministers, it continued to debate such questions as were referred to it, but its inability to take action on them caused the atmosphere of its meetings to become increasingly unreal. As Gloucester himself said, what was the use of their wasting their time when the cardinal would have his way in any case. It is not surprising that barons who were out of sympathy with the regime found attendance unprofitable and began to stay away. Duke Humphrey, it is true, still came to criticise, but even he lost patience when his utterances were ignored. Although several attempts were made to revive its effectiveness, notably in 1444 during Suffolk's absence abroad, the council was in eclipse until the eve of civil war.

These developments seemingly excited no comment in parliament. The commons may have been deceived by the very gradualness of the change, but in any case they were preoccupied with other issues. If they had any quarrel with the king's treatment of his council, it was for the moment overshadowed by their concern for the future of international trade. Their plain-speaking on this topic proves at least that their apparent indifference to the need for constitutional reform did not spring from timidity. Profiting at every turn from the crippled state of the royal finances, they gave the government no rest. In their view its unenterprising naval policy was responsible for the fact that the high seas and many continental ports were no longer safe for English merchantmen. Although their strictures were not undeserved, they forgot how much this insecurity was due to the excesses of their own privateers whom they themselves had encouraged in the teeth of ministerial opposition. For twenty years the Statute of Truces and Safeconducts had acted as a reasonably effective deterrent, but isolated cases of piracy were from time to time reported to the council. In the parliament of 1430, however, an agitation was begun for the repeal of the statute. This came to a head in 1435, when in the hope of coercing Burgundy the ministers, acting probably under the stress of poverty, agreed to relax its operation for a period of seven years. They soon had reason to regret their decision. No sooner were the seamen unleashed against the Flemings than they turned to prey on the shipping of other nations with a total disregard for safeconducts and neutrality. Reprisals only led to fresh excesses, and in a short time all the worst features of 1403 were again rife. Too late the government endeavoured to repair the damage by negotiating commercial treaties with Flanders and the Hanseatic League. But they were running counter to popular prejudices, they were not strong enough to put down piracy, and the treaties were still unratified when parliament met in November 1439 in a mood of bellicose nationalism which destroyed all chances of peace. Instead of blaming the irresponsibility of such shipmen as John Mixtow and William Kyd, the commons interpreted the situation as yet another argument for their favourite thesis—the injustice of permitting aliens to trade in the home markets. That the king both protected these unwanted competitors and at the same time failed to "keep the seas" increased their sense of grievance. For a whole session the court resisted this attack. But it could not afford to maintain an attitude which threatened to deprive it of the necessary supplies. After failing to weaken the resolution of its opponents by transferring parliament from Westminster to Reading, it at length capitulated in January 1440. Not only was it obliged to impose "hosting" regulations of an unusually irksome kind, but to accept a poll-tax on foreign residents as a fraction of its reward. Two years later another parliament re-enacted these measures, and made the want of order in the Channel a convenient excuse for entrusting the policing of the coasts to a body of private traders. At the same time the Statute of Truces was suspended for another twenty years. These acts completed the reorientation of English mercantile policy and the substitution of anarchy for order. Such exploits as the capture of the Bay Fleet by Robert Winnington in 1449 were a doubtful gain when set alongside the interruption of ancient trade-routes and the loss of foreign markets which this reversal of policy involved. Nor did the government derive any lasting benefit from a surrender which only too clearly had not been accompanied by a change of heart; on the contrary, it was still suspected of lukewarmness in its championship of native interests and allowed scant credit for having its hands full elsewhere.

Meanwhile Beaufort and his friends had not entirely lost sight of the fact that their own safety as much as the nation's welfare depended upon the cessation of hostilities in France. To seek peace, however, was one thing, a totally different thing to agree to the humiliating price at which it was offered by a confident foe. Even when the English representatives had at length brought themselves to abandon Henry VI's claim to the French throne, they still clung obstinately to the hope that he would not be required to do homage for his continental lands. It was because Charles VII proved unaccommodating on this point that the conversations between Beaufort and the Duchess of Burgundy, held near Calais in the autumn of 1439, were broken off with a general peace as far away as ever.

But the failure of Somerset's expedition in 1443, on the success of which much had been staked, and the gradual loss of ground in the north during York's lieutenancy finally convinced Suffolk for one that the only thing that now mattered was the preservation of what remained of Henry V's conquests, even if this implied a sacrifice of title and a confession of defeat. The earl had a better right to express an opinion on the military situation than any other of the king's ministers. For like his grandfather, the hated favourite of Richard II, he had seen long service in the wars before he turned courtier and advocate of peace. Experience had also well qualified him to act as an ambassador; apart from the diplomatic knowledge which he had gained at Arras, as Dunois' prisoner after Jargeau, and for four years the amiable gaoler of Charles of Orleans, he had become intimate with several of the French leaders. Unfortunately, he did not possess the courage of his convictions and was unwilling to identify himself publicly with a course of action which might become unpopular. For ten years he had enjoyed great backstairs influence without attracting hostile notice, when Beaufort's retirement forced him out into the open. But though he was bent on self-aggrandisement, he had no taste for the kind of prominence which had been fatal to his grandfather. Foreseeing that he might be accused of betraying his country's interests if he assumed the responsibility of treating in person with Charles VII, he tried to shift the burden to other shoulders; the mere rumour of his appointment had been sufficient, he alleged, to provoke an ugly growl from the citizens of London. He was, however, overborne by his equally nervous colleagues and, on the explicit understanding that he should incur no individual blame for what he was about to do, he consented in February 1444 to head an embassy to the French court. Although no impartial record of his mission survives, his own account, if only because it reveals him as shirking all the major issues, bears the stamp of truth. According to this, he secured the hand of Margaret of Anjou for his master and a general truce for two years without committing England definitely to anything in return. As he told parliament in 1445, 'he neither uttered ne communed of the specialty of the matters concerning in any wise the said Treaty of peace, nor of what manner of thing the same Treaty should be"; he left all this to be determined later by the king himself in consultation with ambassadors from France. His audience was so relieved at the ease with which he had obtained this breathing-space that they were blind to the possibility that a final settlement might not be won as cheaply; their subsequent disillusionment and anger were all the more extreme. For the moment everything seemed to be going well for Suffolk. He returned from Tours with a greatly enhanced reputation. His report was enthusiastically accepted by both lords and commons and Gloucester himself seconded the Speaker's vote of thanks. But on 22 December 1445, Henry VI, acting apparently under the influence of his sixteen-year-old queen, wrote to his father-in-law, René of Anjou, agreeing to the surrender of Maine. He had reckoned without the effect of his promise in England. Owing to the refusal of his captains to obey orders, the province had to be taken by force in March 1448. Meanwhile, although the truce was renewed, the occurrence of frontier incidents and the rising temper of the English had killed all prospects of a stable peace. Finally Charles VII declared war in July 1449.

The news of the proposed delivery of Maine annihilated Suffolk's brief popularity and stamped him in most eyes as a traitor. It became an article of common belief that he had already promised it secretly when negotiating the king's marriage, but for this there is not a scrap of evidence. Many stories of his criminal incompetence as a general, his Francophil sympathies, and his treasonable ambition were soon being freely circulated. Although the majority of these were unfounded, his detractors were on firmer ground when they criticised his covetousness. There was no gainsaying that he had profited from his situation at court to a degree unusual even in those times; when the commons put the number of his patents at more than thirty, they were guilty of no exaggeration.[1] And not content with amassing lands and offices, he and his business partners made use of royal licences to circumvent the regulations of the Staple and to forestall their competitors in the Flemish wool market. While privileges like these set the middle classes against him, his territorial designs excited the jealousy and alarm of his own order. In East Anglia, where his ancestral estates lay, he was a grasping and unscrupulous neighbour; and Sir John Fastolf was not the only landowner to find himself "vexed and troubled...by the might and power of the Duke of Suffolk and by the labour of his council and servants." Such notorious malefactors as Sir Thomas Tuddenham and William Tailboys were encouraged to terrorise the countryside and were shielded from justice in the royal courts. In this way Suffolk made a host of enemies, including his former colleague, Ralph, Lord Cromwell, and the young and powerful Duke of Norfolk. His example was naturally followed elsewhere by other members of the government; in no district more ruthlessly than in Kent, where the tyrannies and extortions practised by Lord Say and Sele with the aid of his son-in-law, sheriff William Crowmer, led to Cade's Rebellion in 1450. It is not surprising that the regime did not last.

At the moment when his reputation was becoming tarnished, Suffolk

---

[1] In 1446 Suffolk was Steward of the Chiltern Hundreds, Constable of Wallingford, Steward of the Honours of Wallingford and St Valery, Chief Justice of Chester, Flint, and North Wales, Chief Steward of the Duchy of Lancaster North of Trent, Steward and Surveyor of all mines in England and Wales (taking a $\frac{1}{15}$ of their annual yield), to mention only the more important of his grants. He held also the reversion of the wardenship of the New Forest and of Gloucester's earldom of Pembroke, together with the castles and lordships of Pembroke, Llanstephan, Tenby, and Kilgarren. In 1447 he became Chamberlain of England, Warden of the Cinque Ports, and Constable of Dover Castle; in 1448 Captain of Calais. Raised to a marquisate n 1444, he was made Duke of Suffolk in 1448. The heiresses of Warwick and Somerset were among his wards.

involved himself in fresh difficulties by making a martyr of the Duke of Gloucester and by alienating the even more formidable Duke of York. In his dealings with York he would appear to have been gratuitously offensive, but with regard to Gloucester it is more than likely that he could not help himself. For Duke Humphrey had ceased to be a harmless spectator with the veering of popular opinion against the truce. The difference was clearly marked in his bearing during the parliament of 1445–46; at its beginning he joined with the estates in congratulating Suffolk upon his diplomatic triumph; before its close he had denounced the government's peace policy in unmeasured terms. This "Long Parliament," with its protracted debates and numerous adjournments, severely tried the ministers' patience and opened their eyes to the danger of allowing Gloucester to remain at large. They therefore decided upon his impeachment and, in order to lessen the risk of a miscarriage, to hold the trial at Bury St Edmunds, where Suffolk's influence was strong. The latter's adherents were mustered in large numbers about the town when parliament met there on 10 February 1447, less than a year after its troublesome predecessor had been dissolved. Gloucester justified these precautions by making a show of resistance, but was easily outmatched. As soon as he had arrived, on 18 February, he was placed under arrest in his lodgings. Five days later he was dead. Although foul play is improbable and in fact was not at first suspected, a removal so opportune was bound to give rise to unpleasant conjectures. Embroidered with much contradictory detail, the murder of "the good Duke Humphrey" became before long part of the stock-in-trade of every Yorkist pamphleteer. Even Cardinal Beaufort, then himself dying far away at Winchester, was eventually made to play a part in this fictitious tragedy.

Unlike Gloucester, York had had no quarrel with Suffolk or his colleagues before 1443. In that year, however, the appointment of the Duke of Somerset to be Captain-General of France and Guienne had given him, as the king's Lieutenant in Normandy, just cause for protest. Scarcely had this storm blown over than he began to nurse another and more rankling grievance. It was being openly said in England and, as he hinted, with the connivance of the ministers, that he had "not governed the finances of France and Normandy so well to their weal and profit as he might have done." In 1445 he came home to attend parliament, and was so far successful in clearing himself that by 20 July 1446 his accounts had been examined and approved. This did not, however, silence his traducers. He therefore decided to pick a quarrel with Suffolk's right-hand man, Adam Moleyns, by this time Bishop of Chichester and Keeper of the Privy Seal, whom he regarded as the source of his ill-fame. Moleyns, he told the council, had bribed soldiers from the Norman garrisons to complain to the king that he had defrauded them of their pay[1]. The in-

---

[1] For the Articles of the Duke of York against Adam Moleyns and the latter's Replies, see British Museum, Harley MS. 543, ff. 161–3.

sulting terms in which Moleyns flatly denied the truth of this accusation still further widened the breach between them, put an excessive strain on York's loyalty, and made 1447 the turning-point in his career. By treating him as an enemy, the court had made him one. Though time would disclose his want of judgment, no one could have been better suited by rank and fortune for the leadership of what was now certainly the popular cause. He had become in 1447 by the death of Gloucester heir presumptive to the throne; through his mother he had already inherited the rival Mortimer claim, and as the representative of the three noble houses of York, March, and Clarence he was far and away the largest landowner among the king's subjects. Suffolk's reasons for wishing to be rid of him are clear. After prolonged hesitation, it was decided not to send him back to France, where he was beginning to win the affection of the army, but to virtual exile as King's Lieutenant in Ireland. His appointment was dated 29 September 1447, but he was so reluctant to obey that nearly two years elapsed before he betook himself to his new post.

Yet even with Gloucester and York out of the way, Suffolk can hardly have felt himself secure. His government, enjoying neither the respect of the people nor the co-operation, outside certain districts, of the landed gentry, found it almost impossible to preserve order. Tyranny at the centre was therefore diversified by anarchy on the fringes, where the king's writ ran to little or no purpose. In many parts of England, but especially in the more lawless north and west, magnates were beginning to settle their disputes in the field rather than in the royal courts. Even when the forms of law were outwardly respected, justice was perverted by corruption and "maintenance," for although judges were as a rule superior to bribery or intimidation, this was most certainly not the case with sheriffs, juries, and witnesses. A legal quarrel often ended in an encounter between rival bands of men-at-arms. In 1441, for example, Devon witnessed the first of a series of "wars" between Courtenays and Bonvilles, in which, it is said with perhaps some exaggeration, "many men were hurt and many slain." Yet when the parties were called to account, they made the merest pretence of obeying and were soon again at one another's throats. It was the knowledge that he could not count on redress in Star Chamber which prompted Archbishop Kemp to garrison Ripon "like a town of war" when threatened by Sir William Plumpton and the inhabitants of Knaresborough Forest. That the king's ministers from weakness tolerated such breaches of the peace sapped their remaining authority and brought them into universal contempt. For a decade the country had been slowly getting out of hand; by the autumn of 1449 it was ripe for revolution and civil war.

What finally destroyed Suffolk was the French invasion of Normandy, for it precipitated the long-impending financial crisis. Since 1433 the royal debt had risen from £168,000 to £372,000; the land was full of disappointed creditors and of unpaid and mutinous soldiers; and now a new expeditionary force was wanted. Although the Winchester parliament of 1449 had only just been dissolved when war broke out, another immediately became necessary. This met at Westminster on 6 November, to be greeted on its arrival by news of the fall of Rouen. The Speaker, William Tresham, who was an adherent of the Duke of York, was not long in proving himself a resolute champion of administrative reform. The hour had come for the rats to leave the sinking ship; the Treasurer, Bishop Lumley of Carlisle, had in fact already resigned in September rather than face the wrath of the commons; his example was followed by Bishop Moleyns on 9 December and by the Chancellor, Archbishop Stafford, on 31 January. Cardinal Kemp, who had for some time wisely held himself aloof, now accepted the great seal and displayed considerable ingenuity in steering a moderate course under difficult circumstances. The new Treasurer, Lord Say, who had the more exacting task, was less skilful. What looked suspiciously like an attempt by William Tailboys to murder Lord Cromwell, in Westminster Hall on 28 November, produced the first trial of strength. Although defended by Suffolk, Tailboys was committed to the Tower to await trial at the request of the lower house.

When parliament adjourned for Christmas, the future of the unpopular favourites was still in doubt. But during the vacation, on 9 January, Moleyns was assassinated at Portsmouth "for his covetousness" by a mob of angry seamen; as he died some sort of confession was wrung from him which fatally incriminated Suffolk in the loss of Maine. The duke's impeachment was now inevitable. But although Cromwell was working assiduously against him among the members, he was still secure in the royal favour. Moreover, when the estates reassembled on 22 January, "there was great watch about the king and in the city of London every night. And the people were in doubt and fear what should fall, for the lords came to Westminster and to the parliament with great power as men of war." Hoping to steal a march on his critics, Suffolk rose on the first day of the new session to ask to be heard in his own defence; he recited his past services and challenged anyone to find any evidence of his disloyalty. The commons, however, were not to be intimidated; their answer was to request his arrest pending a detailed indictment. This was at first refused by the lords. But when the commons asserted that the duke had sold England to Charles VII and had fortified and victualled Wallingford Castle in readiness to assist the invaders, he was ordered to the Tower. On 7 February he was formally impeached under nine heads. These amounted to little more than a repetition of current gossip about his treasonable correspondence with the French, the supposed object of which was to place his son, John de la Pole, on the English throne, after marrying him to the Beaufort heiress, Margaret of Somerset. This was unconvincing enough, but even more wildly improbable was the suggestion that he had deliberately prevented peace with France. When the indictment was read over to Henry VI in council on 12 February, he ordered the matter to be reserved for his own decision. This was generally interpreted as an acquittal. "The Duke of Suffolk is pardoned," Margaret Paston wrote from Norwich a month afterwards, "and hath his men again waiting upon him and is right well at ease and merry." But already her news was out of date. On 7 March the lords ordered the impeachment to proceed and two days later the commons presented a fresh bill of charges, far weightier than their first. The duke, they argued in the course of eighteen articles, had been the "priviest of the king's counsel" since 1437, and during this time had impoverished the realm, broken its laws, sold offices to the highest bidder, and enriched himself mightily at the Crown's expense. The prisoner in reply stoutly maintained his innocence and described these new counts as "false and untrue." But during the ensuing argument some damaging points were made against him[1]. The lords still hesitated to deliver their verdict, and meanwhile the court was working behind the scenes to achieve a compromise. This was announced by the Chancellor in the king's name on 17 March; no judgment would be passed on the accused, but he would be banished from the country for five years. Soon afterwards he was set at liberty. At the same time parliament was adjourned to Leicester in an attempt to save his friends. Narrowly escaping capture by the infuriated Londoners, Suffolk made his way to Ipswich, where he solemnly swore to his innocence in the presence of the county and bade farewell to his heir. On 1 May he embarked for Calais. He was, however, intercepted in the Channel by a mutinous royal ship, the *Nicholas of the Tower*, and beheaded without further trial by a nameless Irishman with six strokes of a rusty sword. Mysterious as was his end, his character and aims are hardly more intelligible. To one historian he is a statesman, farsighted, loyal, and misunderstood, to another an unscrupulous and blundering tyrant. The truth, as so often, lies probably somewhere midway between these opposite extremes. For good or ill, he was no figure of heroic mould; ambitious yet timid, corrupt yet well-meaning, he was the inevitable scapegoat who atoned for the sins of others as much as for his own.

The fall of Suffolk was the signal for which the country had been waiting. While his trial was in progress, riots, routs, and unlawful congregations were reported from various quarters. Kent especially, for long the playground of Lord Say and his band of extortioners, was in a ferment, inspired by wandering agitators known as "the Queen of the Fair" and "Captain Bluebeard." The authorities dealt promptly with a danger so near the capital, and Captain Bluebeard, alias Thomas Cheyney, a fuller of Canterbury "feigning himself a hermit," was caught and executed. For a while all was quiet. Then at the beginning of June a large and disciplined force, commanded by one Jack Cade, who called

---

[1] Suffolk's detailed answer is lost, but the commons' reply to it will be found in *Historical MSS. Commission, 3rd Report,* App., pp. 279–80. This document was overlooked by C. L. Kingsford in his *Prejudice and Promise in XVth Century England,* pp. 146–76.

himself John Mortimer, a cousin of the Duke of York, marched unexpectedly on London and encamped at Blackheath. No contemporary
document gives a clearer picture of the hardships with which the lower
and middle classes were afflicted than the restrained and skilfully drafted
manifesto in which the rebels set forth their grievances. These were
partly economic, partly administrative. "All the common people, what
for taxes and tallages and other oppressions, might not live by their
handwork and husbandry." The Statute of Labourers, which had been
re-enacted with new provisions in 1446, and excessive purveyance were
singled out for separate mention, while grave unemployment was said to
have been caused in the weaving industry by the interruption of overseas
trade. The courts, whether central or local, offered no help to the poor
litigant; "the law serveth nought else in these days but for to do wrong."
As for the traitors about the king, it was through them that he "hath
lost his law, his merchandise is lost, his common people is destroyed, the
sea is lost, France is lost (and) the king himself is so set that he may not
pay for his meat and drink." Among the reforms desired were an act of
resumption, the dismissal and punishment of Suffolk's "false progeny and
affinity," the recall of York, the formation of a new government of "true"
barons, and the repeal of the Statute of Labourers. This was a popular
programme, and it is not surprising that a London chronicler thought
its contents "rightful and reasonable." Its moderation was calculated to
set at rest the fears of property-owners and to win new recruits to the
army on Blackheath. With the same objects in view Cade kept his men
well under control and dealt severely with those who disobeyed his orders
against plundering. Nevertheless the government accused him of advocating communism. The baselessness of this charge is exposed by the
recorded occupations of those afterwards pardoned for their share in the
insurrection. More than half were yeomen, husbandmen, and craftsmen,
and over a hundred were of gentle birth. The presence of 98 constables
may explain how the host was collected and why it was so orderly. Far
from being a rabble of peasants and labourers, it was a well-organised
body drawn from all classes of society below the rank of knight. That
these men should have wished to "hold all things in common" was
absurd.

Parliament was sitting at Leicester when the court was informed of
what was afoot. No time was wasted in raising an army since the lords
were already attended by the bulk of their retainers. Having hastily
adjourned the session, the king set out for London in their company.
From his camp in Clerkenwell Fields, he opened negotiations with Cade's
men on 15 June. But two days later he rejected their demands and
peremptorily ordered them to disperse. They withdrew overnight towards
Sevenoaks. Here on 18 June the vanguard of the royal army came into
conflict with them and suffered a defeat; whereupon the main body,
which had remained inactive at Greenwich, became mutinous and began

to clamour for the heads of the king's ministers. The arrest of Lord Say and William Crowmer came too late to appease its wrath. By this time it was completely out of hand and engaged in sacking the houses of courtiers in the city. After some days of indecision, the king retreated to Kenilworth, leaving the citizens to fend for themselves with the help of the Tower garrison. His departure coincided with a general outbreak of disorder in the southern counties. On 29 June at Edington in Wiltshire Bishop Ayscough of Salisbury was dragged from the altar and stoned to death, while other household officials narrowly escaped like fates elsewhere. Cade, who had employed the interval in rounding up supporters from Kent, Surrey, and Sussex, marched into Southwark at their head on 2 July; on the same day the men of Essex, with whom he had established contact, advanced as far as Mile End. Although the rebels had many friends among the Londoners, a majority of the aldermen were justifiably reluctant to admit them within the walls. Treachery, however, next day enabled Cade to obtain possession of London Bridge and to make himself master of the city. His difficulties were vastly increased by the narrow streets and by the excited condition of the London mob, but so well did he maintain discipline that only a few houses were pillaged and no extensive rioting took place. Saturday, 4 July, was occupied in bringing Say and Crowmer to justice. The former, delivered up to his enemies by the commandant of the Tower, was tried at the Guildhall and summarily executed in Cheapside, when he declined to plead; his son-in-law met his death at Mile End. Cade and his followers then passed Sunday quietly in their lodgings on the south bank of the Thames. This gave the city authorities a chance to take the offensive. That night the royal troops sallied forth from the Tower and attempted to recapture London Bridge. But they failed to surprise the sentries, and after a battle which lasted until daybreak they were glad to withdraw under cover of a truce. This encounter, however, had also cooled the ardour of the insurgents. They had less to fight for since their principal oppressors were dead and the others out of reach. When therefore Cardinal Kemp, Archbishop Stafford, and Bishop Waynflete opened negotiations, Cade was ready to come to terms. On 8 July, less than a week after their entry into the capital, the rebels marched home bearing with them full pardons for all that they had done. No sooner were they dispersed than the ministers began to regret their initial clemency. The amnesty which they had granted did not of course apply to any fresh acts of rebellion, and therefore, when Cade made a wholly gratuitous though fruitless assault upon Queenborough Castle in Sheppey, they were within their rights in proclaiming him a traitor. Pursued by the new sheriff of Kent, he fled to hiding in Sussex, where he was mortally wounded on 12 July while resisting arrest. Eight of his accomplices were condemned to death by a royal commission which sat at Canterbury during the following month. For the moment popular indignation had spent its force, and when two other "Captains of Kent" came forward, they failed to raise the commons and were easily suppressed.

The government was still reeling under the shock of these events when Richard of York landed uninvited at Beaumaris. To meet this new danger, Edmund Beaufort, Duke of Somerset, was hurriedly recalled from France and made Constable of England. His presence at the king's side emphasised the dynastic issue already raised by York's return. For although his family had been debarred from the royal succession by Henry IV, Somerset was, after the king, the sole surviving male member of the House of Lancaster and therefore, so long as the queen continued barren, the only man who could dispute with York the title of heir to the throne. If, on the other hand, the latter chose to prefer his descent in the female line from Edward III, he had a better right to be king than Henry VI himself. But, whatever may have been at the back of his mind, York, like Bolingbroke in 1399, assumed an air of injured innocence and simple loyalty. It is unlikely that he deceived anyone, except perhaps the unsuspecting king. For some time the name of Mortimer had been in people's mouths and now its representative, himself the son and nephew of traitors, had returned from banishment without permission to set the realm to rights. Many therefore flocked to his standard, and in spite of several attempts to arrest his advance, he succeeded in reaching Westminster with 4000 men-at-arms. Here, towards the end of September, he forced his way into the royal presence. The household was "afraid right sore" at this intrusion, but the king received his cousin with fair words and accepted without demur his assurances of good faith and allegiance.

From now onwards Henry devoted his energies to the vain task of trying to reconcile the warring elements in his kingdom. It is impossible to doubt his honesty, but had his efforts as peacemaker been the result of guile, they could hardly have played more completely into the hands of Somerset and the courtiers. Again and again York was outwitted. Thus, when he opened his attack by submitting a programme of necessary reforms, he was answered that it was unseemly for the Crown to take one man's advice alone. This was such sound constitutional doctrine that he could not question it without putting himself openly in the wrong. Nor could he object to the proposed appointment of a "sad and substantial council," including others besides himself and his friends. His success was no greater in the parliament which met at Westminster on 6 November, even though he spared no pains to prejudice its verdict in his favour. The influence which he brought to bear on the elections doubtless helped to procure him a more sympathetic hearing from the already friendly commons, but he had badly miscalculated the reactions of his fellow peers. Headstrong and self-centred, he neither possessed their confidence nor had exerted himself to secure it; his call to his partisans to be with him during the session in their best array was therefore foiled by the presence of his opponents in equal or superior numbers. He had now lost the advantage of surprise. His royal blood and the pretensions which it nourished were to handicap him as they had handicapped Gloucester. He could not rely upon the support of the barons as a class, because their interests as a class were not served by his elevation to the first place in the State. For them the choice no longer lay, if it had ever lain, between good government and bad government, but between York and Somerset, ultimately between York and Lancaster. In the absence of a common motive, each man would choose as his private ambitions and opportunities dictated. The upper classes were already in any case too much divided by local and family feuds to align themselves solidly on any one side. These lesser loyalties now governed their conduct in the wider field of national politics; if Courtenay was for Lancaster, then Bonville was for York. Duke Richard was, apart from the king, the lord of more acres than any man in England; he could depend upon the assistance of his nephew, John, Duke of Norfolk; and his other kinsmen, the Earls of Salisbury and Warwick, cadets of the powerful house of Neville, were soon to become his close allies. Those who hated or feared these families as neighbours wanted no stronger motive for drawing closer to the court. Thus, as the issues became clarified, the opposing forces revealed themselves as more evenly matched than at first seemed probable. Yet it was not in York's nature to draw back, even though he saw the promise of a decisive victory slipping from his grasp. Instead of waiting for a more favourable opportunity, he merely displayed his impotence by appealing Somerset, who soon regained his freedom. The commons fared no better. Their petition, that some thirty men and women, accused of "misbehaving" about the royal person, should be expelled from the court and brought to justice, was treated by the king with almost contemptuous levity. And when Thomas Young, M.P. for Bristol, asked for York's recognition as heir presumptive to the crown, he was sent to the Tower for his pains, while parliament was immediately dissolved. This was at the end of May 1451. In the previous February, York had further damaged his cause by taking a conspicuous and, it seems, a willing part in the so-called "Harvest of Heads," that bloody assize by which the last traces of the popular movement in Kent were extinguished. He was soon given cause to repent his harshness. For when he was next hard-pressed, the gates of London were barred against him and the men of Kent remained sullenly unresponsive to the call of Mortimer. It is not difficult to account for the indifference of the middle and lower classes during the Wars of the Roses. Bitter experience had taught them that they could look for little help or gratitude from either party, and they were therefore content except on rare occasions to be idle spectators of a barons' quarrel. In this battle of kites and crows they only shewed their good sense by their neutrality.

The parliament of 1450–51 had concluded nothing. The government, though badly shaken, had outlived the crisis; it had even succeeded to some extent in entrenching itself afresh; but its most formidable critic was not disarmed and only temporarily discouraged. The struggle therefore continued, in and out of parliament, with increasing violence for another ten years, the result being in doubt up to the very last. Until the autumn of 1453 the tide ran strongly in favour of the Lancastrians. When in February 1452 Duke Richard again took up arms, they were already preparing to strike. He was promptly cornered at Dartford in Kent, induced to disband his forces, and tricked into an ignominious capitulation. In the following year the return of a parliament with strong royalist leanings enabled Somerset to push home his advantage. During the course of two sessions, the one at Reading from 6 to 28 March, the other at Westminster from 25 April to 2 July, an unusual harmony prevailed between the commons and the court. Thus the king was desired to resume all royal grants to York and the other "traitors assembled in the field at Dartford" and to "put in oblivion" that petition of 1450 which had aspersed his choice of household servants. Sir William Oldhall, Speaker in the last parliament and one of York's trusted councillors, was attainted for his share in the recent disturbances, and a statute was passed condemning all who in future neglected to appear at the royal summons to the penalty of utter forfeiture. Needless to say, so loyal a body lent a favourable ear to the king's request for money; not content with voting one and a half tenths and fifteenths, it granted him the wool-subsidy and certain other taxes for life, and authorised him to raise 20,000 archers at the expense of the shires and boroughs for six months' service if and when they were required "for the defence of the realm." Parliament was then adjourned until 12 November. In the interval, however, on or about 10 August, the king, whose strength had been overtaxed, lapsed without warning into a state of imbecility. At first the news was not allowed to leak out. But on 24 October a gathering which is described as a council, though neither Somerset nor the Chancellor was present, met at Westminster, and resolved to send for York "to set rest and union betwixt the lords of this land." By 21 November he had assumed control. Shortly afterwards Somerset was appealed by Norfolk and committed to the Tower. The situation had, however, been complicated by the birth of a son and heir to the queen on 13 October, an event which destroyed York's hope of a peaceful succession to the throne on Henry's death. He met this new blow with commendable calm. If there were those who cast doubts on the boy's paternity, he gave their insinuations no official countenance. On the other hand, motherhood wrought a violent change in Margaret's position and behaviour. Whereas she had hitherto rested content with a subordinate place at her husband's side, interfering only to obtain small favours for her personal dependants, she now became the resolute and implacable defender of her son's rights. The Lancastrian cause had at length obtained a mettlesome if uncompromising champion. As soon as the adjourned parliament reassembled at Westminster on 14 February, she laid claim to the regency. It is probable that she received some support from the commons; even the lords were loth to decide against her, but after much hesitation York was named Protector on 27 March. It is nevertheless clear that many did not relish his elevation and that the spirit which had vexed Gloucester was not dead. He was able to abridge the royal household "to a reasonable and competent fellowship," to ensure the appointment of new ministers, chosen from his own kin, and to restore a measure of conciliar government; he was equally successful in subduing a Lancastrian rising in the North. But the infant Edward was recognised as Prince of Wales, and though Somerset continued in prison, it was not thought expedient to bring him to trial[1].

These arrangements did not endure, for about Christmas 1454 the king returned to his senses. At the beginning of February Somerset was reinstated and York dismissed. Although for a time moderate counsels prevailed and some attempt was made to effect a last-minute compromise, this was imperilled by the open preparations of the courtiers to avenge their wrongs. By March the prospect was so threatening that York withdrew in dudgeon to the North and with the support of the Nevilles began to collect an army. This done, he marched on London. Arriving outside St Albans on 22 May, he found the town occupied by the king and a royal host commanded by the Dukes of Somerset and Buckingham. Barricades had been hastily constructed, but the defenders were out-numbered by five to three[2]. After an abortive parley, York, without waiting for the arrival of the Duke of Norfolk, who was at hand with reinforcements, gave the order to attack. The engagement in the streets and gardens of the town lasted less than an hour; for, thanks to their superior numbers and to the skill and dash of the young Earl of Warwick, the Yorkists soon carried the day. But although the casualties were few, the deaths of Somerset, Northumberland, and Stafford gave rise to blood feuds in the ranks of the nobility which were not assuaged for many years to come. After the battle, King Henry, who had received a slight wound in the neck from an arrow while standing idly beneath his standard, was respectfully conducted back to Westminster by the victors. There he agreed to summon a parliament. In spite of the fact that the Yorkists openly rigged the elections, the proceedings were interrupted by rancorous quarrels and "many a man grudged full sore" an act of indemnity which was passed to absolve the rebels from the consequences of their treason. In the autumn, however, the king's mind again gave way, and York

---

[1] Even Somerset's captivity was protective rather than punitive; "it was done," as he himself told James II of Scotland, "by the advice of the Lords of the King's Council, which, as I understand, was most for the surety of my person." (Nicolas, *Proceedings*, vi, p. lxiv n.)

[2] York's advantage lay in his more numerous rank and file. He was accompanied by the Earls of Salisbury and Warwick and by Lord Clinton. The king had with him the Earls of Pembroke, Devon, Northumberland, Wiltshire, Dorset, and Stafford, and Lords Clifford, Roos, and Dudley.

became Protector for the second time on 17 November. But the lords only consented to his appointment after they had been thrice petitioned by the commons, while they carefully safeguarded the rights of the Prince of Wales and insisted on the ultimate authority of the council to exercise "the politic rule and governance of this land." York did not enjoy his position for long. For after Christmas Henry once more recovered. He was, it seems, at first in favour of keeping the duke as chief councillor, but the queen spared no pains to undermine their good relations. Although an open breach was somehow averted, in August 1456 she carried her husband off to the midlands, where the Lancastrian estates afforded them better protection than the capital. On 7 October a council took place at Coventry, attended by York and his friends, at which Buckingham essayed the rôle of peace-maker. But after taking an oath of obedience to the king, the malcontents again withdrew from the court. Nothing happened for a year or more. Then on 25 March 1458, a hollow pacification or "loveday" was staged at St Paul's in London, although this did not interrupt the preparations which each side was making for civil war. York spent most of his time in the Welsh Marches, Salisbury was at Middleham in Wensleydale, and Warwick was at Calais, biding their chance, while Margaret kept "open household" in Cheshire and set herself to court its gentry on her son's behalf. Warwick's naval successes, sheer piracy though they were, helped to revive Yorkist credit. In November 1458, therefore, he was ordered to resign his command and, when he declined, an attempt was made to waylay him as he left the council-chamber. Meanwhile Duke Richard was strengthening his hands by means of a family alliance with the house of Burgundy. There can be little doubt that he had by now set his mind on the throne, but he wisely kept his own counsel and not even his own allies were aware of the direction of his thoughts. By the spring of 1459 both parties were ready. The court had the advantage of interior lines, and it was in its interests to prevent the Yorkists from combining forces. But Salisbury slipped past an army sent to intercept him, defeated Lord Audley at Blore Heath on 22 September, and joined York at Ludlow. Warwick arrived from Calais with a part of its garrison shortly afterwards. When, however, the royalists advanced into Shropshire, York's followers melted away at the "rout of Ludford," and their leaders were obliged to beat a hasty retreat. Duke Richard and his second son, the Earl of Rutland, retired first into Wales and later to Ireland, where they were received with enthusiasm by the inhabitants of the Pale; his heir, Edward, Earl of March, accompanied the Nevilles to Calais; at the close of the year only Denbigh held out against the king.

The royalists celebrated their triumph in the Coventry parliament of 20 November–20 December 1459, an assembly hastily convened and unscrupulously packed. The lords found the leading Yorkists guilty of treason in their absence, and swore to uphold the Lancastrian succession.

But the government cast aside discretion by the oppressive fashion in which it sought to repair its crumbling authority. Its forced loans, purveyances, and commissions of array, rendered it generally obnoxious and prepared the country to accept a revolution. When, therefore, Salisbury, Warwick, and March landed at Sandwich on 26 June 1460, they were welcomed with every sign of joy by the men of Kent. Thus fortified, they entered London on 2 July. To curry popular favour and to justify their invasion, they proclaimed the misdeeds of the king's advisers and even accused them of preaching that his will was above the law. Their task was simplified by the fact that the royal forces were scattered; for while Henry and a number of lords were at Coventry, some were in the south-west and others had gone north with Margaret to search for reinforcements. Leaving Salisbury to guard the capital, Warwick and March rightly decided to strike at once. Outside Northampton on 10 July they came up against the main body of the enemy and won a battle in which the king was captured and several of his closest supporters, including Buckingham and Shrewsbury, were slain. This done, they returned to London to await York's arrival and to call a parliament in the name of Henry VI. It met on 7 October. Three days later Duke Richard appeared, and without waiting to test the temper of his allies strode to the throne in Westminster Hall as if he intended to occupy it. He was, however, stopped by Archbishop Bourchier, who asked him pointedly whether he desired to interview the king. His reply, "I know of no person in this realm the which oweth not to wait on me rather than I on him," filled his audience with consternation. Obstinately though he pressed his claims, the lords stood firm. A fortnight's deadlock ended in a compromise by which Henry was to retain the crown for life on the understanding that York was to succeed him to the exclusion of the Prince of Wales. But precious time had been wasted in argument while the Lancastrians were massing afresh in Yorkshire. It was not until the beginning of December that Richard, now again Protector on the grounds of the king's incapacity, set out to cope with these new enemies. After spending Christmas at his castle of Sandal near Wakefield, he issued forth only to be overwhelmed and killed by Northumberland and the young Somerset before its gates on 30 December. Rutland was stabbed to death soon afterwards by Lord Clifford, whose father had lost his life at St Albans; Salisbury was beheaded by the men of Pontefract. Margaret's absence in Scotland, where she succeeded in obtaining help from the queen-mother, delayed the Lancastrian advance; but in February 1461 she put herself at the head of a mixed band of English, Welsh, and Scots, and marched south along the Great North Road. Her wild border levies struck terror among the inhabitants by plundering houses and churches on their route. At St Albans, Warwick tried to head them off, but he was decisively defeated and forced to leave the capital unguarded (17 February). King Henry, who was with him, escaped to join his wife. It was probably owing to his influence that she was persuaded not to lead her undisciplined troops into the city, where they would almost certainly have got out of hand. By this clemency he threw away his one remaining chance of keeping the crown. For Edward of York, after crushing the Earls of Pembroke and Wiltshire at Mortimer's Cross, was approaching from the west. On 26 February he rode with Warwick into London where he was "elected" king by general acclamation. Too late, the Lancastrians retreated northwards, but he pursued and overwhelmed them with great slaughter at Towton on 29 March. Henry, Margaret, and their son fled towards Scotland, while Edward returned to Westminster for his coronation.

It is only too easy to convey a distorted impression of Lancastrian England by dwelling exclusively upon the story of its political failure. The continued existence of a government which had abdicated its primary function of maintaining order and impartial justice, the abuse of power by turbulent vassals, and the clash of baronial factions could not but leave their mark upon the lives of ordinary men and women. Yet in describing the hardships inflicted by this "lack of governance," there is a very real danger of exaggeration. Such incidents as the cold-blooded murder of William Tresham by a private enemy in 1450 or that of Nicholas Radford five years later had few contemporary parallels. In some districts and at some times, conditions were admittedly bad and growing worse; this was, for example, the case in Yorkshire, Norfolk, Kent, and Devon throughout much of the last two decades of Henry VI's reign and over a wider area during the years 1450 and 1459-61. But if the rights of property were often infringed, the forms of law misused, juries and witnesses bribed and intimidated, some allowance must be made for the fact that these evils were at least to some extent common to all medieval periods. For the rest, the customs accounts show a decline in overseas trade, taxation was by normal standards high, and the king did not pay his debts. That as a result both town and country were less prosperous goes without saying. But for any blacker picture of universal desolation the evidence is slight and untrustworthy. It would never do, for instance, to accept at their face value the *ex parte* statements of those engaged in litigation. And after all even the war at sea had its compensations, since it brought no small gain to innumerable native privateers.

There are, however, other things for which these sixty years deserve to be remembered, namely for their artistic achievement and their bright promise of intellectual growth. It is true that in painting and illumination Englishmen had fallen well behind their continental neighbours, though critics have perhaps been over-ready to attribute to this or that foreign artist everything of value which time and Protestant iconoclasm have spared. It is also true that the architecture of the fifteenth century was often wanting in inspiration and mechanical in its detail. But no one can question the splendour of its bell-towers, the rich perfection of its

wood-carving, stained glass, and metal-work or the occasional excellence
of its figure sculpture. Civil disturbance did not impair the mastery with
which these arts were practised; the traditions of native craftsmanship
survived the wars undamaged. As much if not more can be claimed for
English scholarship. Under the enthusiastic patronage of Humphrey
Duke of Gloucester, the "new learning" took root, especially at Oxford,
and began to flourish. William Grey, Chancellor of the University in
1440, and the infamous John Tiptoft, Earl of Worcester, were among the
first humanists to study in Italy and to correspond with foreign scholars.
The ancient ways, on the other hand, were not deserted. Lyndwood's
Provinciale and the controversial writings of Thomas Netter of Walden
repel the charge of intellectual stagnation frequently brought against this
period. One book deserves more special mention: *the Repressor of Overmuch Blaming of the Clergy*, by Bishop Pecock of Chichester, a defence
of reason against Lollard "fundamentalism," was the first considerable
work of learning to be written in the English tongue. Everywhere the
vernacular was gaining ground. Between 1400 and 1450 it completely
ousted French as the language of the upper class and even made inroads
upon the conservatism of the government departments. It had already
triumphed in poetry with Chaucer; and if after his death it proved a
clumsy instrument in the hands of Hoccleve and Lydgate, the ballads of
John Page and others shew that there were still men who could turn it
to robust and graphic use. Finally, education was being more widely
spread by the foundation of new grammar schools. In short a low degree
of public security was not incompatible with a vigorous national life.

CHAPTER XII

ENGLAND: THE YORKIST KINGS, 1461–1485

In October 1460 Richard, Duke of York, confronted Henry VI's parliament with a petition which set out his claim to the throne. It was a short document, not very interesting to read. It was, in fact, merely a genealogical table. But it had a weighty thesis, for it purported to shew how the duke could trace back his rights to the crown through Philippa, daughter of Lionel, Duke of Clarence, third son of Edward III, to Edward I and beyond. Against their wishes, and after vain efforts to push responsibility upon the judges and serjeants-at-law, the lords gave their considered opinion in a carefully graded series of objections. They could not approve the duke's claim, because they were bound by oath to Henry VI; because acts of parliament were of greater authority than arguments drawn from chronicles; because entails of the crown destroyed the Yorkist case; because the science of heraldry disproved it, inasmuch as Richard bore the arms of Edmund Langley, whereas—if his assertions were true—he should be bearing those of Lionel, Duke of Clarence; because, finally, the Lancastrians were kings of England not by conquest, but by lawful right descending to them from Henry III. The duke answered these challenges in a replication of sound medieval dialectic. His claim was just; therefore by the laws of Holy Church the lords were absolved from their oaths, since oaths sworn to the prejudice of the just rights of another were void. If need be, he would take the decision of a spiritual judge on this point. As for acts of parliament—and the same held good of entails of the crown—if Henry IV had so just a claim, why did he want to bolster it up with such devices? As for the laws of heraldry, for reasons not unknown to all the realm, he had refrained from using Lionel's arms; but "though right for a time rest, and be put to silence, yet it rotteth not, nor shall perish." The Lancastrian title from Henry III was false; no more needed to be said of it.

Instead of following the sequel to this play of dialectic until we see Parliament nominating the Duke of York heir-apparent, let us turn to another series of objections. Between 1461 and 1463 Sir John Fortescue, sometime Chief Justice of the Court of King's Bench, and at that time an exile in Scotland, sharing in the meagre hopes that still kept together the remnants of the Lancastrian party, exercised his wits—and they were tolerably sharp—upon those same Yorkist claims. He arrived at some conclusions that should interest us. Lawyer-like he sought the weakest link in the chain, and he found it in the reference to Philippa. Think on the inconveniences that would follow if a woman ruled. To Fortescue they were many and obvious. How could she collate to prebends in the voidance of bishoprics, or give a death sentence in criminal cases? How act as God's medium as a healer? The king's touch derived virtue from the coronation rite of anointing the king's hand, and no woman could be so anointed since she was unable to bear the sword. And what of disadvantages more practical in kind? What of the risk that a king might have several daughters, so that the English realm, like a feudal estate, would descend to co-parceners? And what of graver possibilities? A queen might marry a foreign ruler, or (prescient Fortescue) might take so long to choose a husband that her subjects would not know where they stood. It could not be. Woman was under subjection to man. There was no place for her as ruler. And if so, how was she to pass on to another any rights to the crown? No man—it was a principle of the common law—had power to transmit greater rights than he himself possessed. *Ergo* this Yorkist claim was impossible. It was also revolutionary. For it upset an arrangement accepted by the Yorkists, whereby Lancastrian kings had ruled in England for over sixty-three years, and by so doing had acquired a prescriptive right. There seemed nothing more that needed saying.

Here was pretty argument, but not the constitutional theory needed to keep abreast of the facts of politics. For behind York's petition lay at least ten years of history, years steadily productive of impressions upon his mind. If he looks to us like a conspirator, we ought not to forget the stimulus provided by Lancastrian ineptitude. It was not so much the unexpected birth of Henry VI's son (13 October 1453), nor the openly avowed hostility of Margaret of Anjou, nor the rivalry between him and Somerset, nor even his attainder after defeat at Ludford (12 October 1459) which finally decided York's course. Behind all these lay a logic of events forcing him towards one conclusion. Even before 1450 York, like many other subjects of Henry VI, looked critically on that king's occupation of the kingship (to call it misgovernment would be to impute too much activity to that "puppet of a king"), and before 1460 York was holding strong opinions which he shewed himself capable of expressing in manifestos more cogently political than the petition in which he sued for the crown. The weakness and extravagance of Lancastrian administration, the poverty consequent upon reckless alienation of Crown lands, the failure of the war in France, ending in the complete inability of the government to protect the south coast-towns from the raids of French pirates, above all, hatred of the foreigner which was finding—not perhaps without some reason—a butt in Margaret of Anjou, these were the realities of politics. They brought home to one kept out of the king's counsels by the machinations of evil advisers the imperative need for action. It would have to be action strong and far-reaching; but when it came it must be justified in language plain men could understand. Ideas gathered from legal antiquarianism were grafted on to a feudal conception of kingship to serve as a solution of problems of practical politics. So York propounded his subtleties, and Fortescue shuffled his quotations from the Scriptures, the Fathers, the Schoolmen. And each in a vague way must have known that the problem lay elsewhere. The lawyer, indeed, lived to say so, was induced to take back his arguments, and—more important—struck right down to the bed-rock of the political troubles in an analysis of the government of England so masterly in its realism that it yet remains an indispensable guide.

We have arrived, surely, at the crux of the Yorkist dilemma. For a movement which began as a bid for reform was soon linked to a theory unworthy of it, which hampered the Yorkist achievement. Legitimism was something of a novelty, but it contributed nothing worth while to constitutional theory. It pointed into the past. Intended as a solution of Yorkist difficulties, it was to prove a *damnosa haereditas*. It led, however, to some consequences that are instructive.

The legitimist argument implied—it is seen clearly enough in Fortescue's thought—an analogy between the kingship and a private estate governed by the rules and principles of private law, and that analogy, characteristic as it was of the medieval approach, was not adapted to solve the problems of an age bristling with real, new difficulties. For these legitimism had nothing to offer. The right to the crown was made to read like the pleadings in an action on a deed of gift. It was all very well, but consequences would sooner or later have to be met. True, they were not obvious in 1460 when Richard, Duke of York, seemed successful. They were, indeed, even less clear in 1461, after Richard had met his fate at Wakefield, and his head, decorated with a crown of paper and straw, had been placed upon the walls of York. His young son Edward succeeded to claims having the colour of a greater right by virtue of the grievous wrongs done to his house. So the full implications still remained hidden. But they were looming large in 1483 when Edward IV was no more, and men were bringing his young son Edward, a child of thirteen, across the English shires towards his father's throne. We need not seek to know, at this point, what happened in those weeks of June and July 1483, when Richard, uncle of the king elect, was taking charge of affairs. We need only notice Richard's justification of what he was about to do. It was so commonplace, so familiar an episode in the medieval court of law. He nullified the prince's right by imputing against him the stigma of bastardy. We have not reached the depths. When Henry Tudor turned his attention towards Richard and the English throne in 1485 he went one step farther. Henry's novel disseisin upon the Yorkists was followed by a marriage—into the family whose possessions he had seized.

To an age not yet removed from the crudities of legal procedure the peculiar emphasis that was being placed upon claims, rights, possessions, and family trees suggested an obvious solution. "...incontynent after the pitouse and dolorouse Deth of that noble and famous Prynce and oure Right honorable Lord of worthy memorie youre Fader the Duc of York....It pleased your high Mageste...to procede of Princely prowesse...

in Bataille: uppon whom it pleased Almyghty God to graunt unto youre seid Mageste the hande of victorye...." It is war, but war under the eye of the Supreme Judge, and that is trial by battle. And as we watch the demeanour of Englishmen living under the sudden changes of kingship during the Wars of the Roses, and preparing to accept whatever comes, may it not perhaps be helpful to keep in the front of our explanations a suggestion of this special cast of thought? It has unexpected results. When a Lord Rivers, like many of his contemporaries, could change over to the Yorkist side in 1461, and could tell a foreign observer that Henry's cause was lost irretrievably, one begins immediately to search for epithets like disloyalty or double-dealing. Is it necessarily what such behaviour implied to contemporaries? Was indifference to the political situation the reason why the country acquiesced in the change? Men had much to lose and gain by what was happening; but who were they to adhere to a king deserted by God?

Now, as in many other problems of this difficult period, men have held divided opinions about the real meaning of the Wars of the Roses. We cannot afford to be uncertain. For some years now we have been hearing some challenging questions, and their import is great. Was the struggle between Lancastrians and Yorkists, it has been asked, the simple affair it was once fashionable to depict? Was it a protracted civil war, an almost unbroken series of bloody battles, which sapped the resources of the country, decimated the families of the nobility, and engaged the energies of contemporaries to the exclusion of practically all else, leaving behind a trail of desolation easily traceable in the social, political, and cultural life of the community? Or was it, on the contrary, an aimless—some would even go so far as to say a meaningless and futile—faction-fight that it is not worth while trying to understand? Was it a struggle with no interest for the country generally, the concern of few save the rival family groups of great lords, who joined gladly, impelled by no real political predilections, but finding in it an easy means of gratifying that taste for military ventures stimulated by war with France though doomed to find outlet elsewhere after the disastrous failure of the English enterprise across the Channel? If the first of these views be correct, then it would seem that the wars are at once the beginning and the end of Yorkist history. If the latter is to be accepted, then clearly it becomes necessary to look more closely at the other features of the period. The alternatives are embarrassing; an incident from Edward's reign may suggest an approach.

In April 1465, the ladies at court amused themselves with a pastime that should remind us we are still in the Middle Ages. Their hero was Lord Scales, the queen's brother. They tied around his thigh a collar of gold and pearls, and pushed into his cap a parchment roll. Opened by the king, this proved to be articles for a tournament in which the ladies' champion was to engage against a noble adversary. How it all fell out, how Scales challenged the renowned Antoine, Bastard of Burgundy, what preparations there were for the jousts at Smithfield in 1467, and what knightly prowess was shewn before a brilliant court, all these things and more may be read in the elaborate surviving account. This, surely, is the generation that will appreciate what Sir Thomas Malory will be writing in 1469: "Then was the cry huge and great when Sir Palamides smote the neck of Sir Launcelot's horse that it died. For many knights held that it was unknightly done in tournament to kill a horse wilfully— except it were done in plain battle, life for life." But it is this generation, too, of which it will be said: "And aftyrwarde thei [the Earl of Oxford, Aubrey, Tuddenham] were brought before the Erle of Worscetre and juged by lawe padowe that thei schuld be hade to the Toure Hylle where was made a scaffolde of viii fote hyzt and ther was there hedes smyten of, that alle men myght see." This is the dualism to be encountered in the period. Before we become involved, it will be well to make some play with chronology.

Subsequent to the challenge whereby the Duke of York brought his discontents into the open with the first battle of St Albans (1455), there was a lull in active hostilities. Then began the period of sustained conflict, though not of continuous warfare. An examination of the events shews that the military engagements fall into four well defined phases: the first runs from 1459–61; the second from 1462–64; the third from 1469–71; and the fourth includes the events of 1484–85. The first phase was, as might be expected, one of considerable activity, with several heavy engagements. If the Yorkists were successful at Blore Heath (23 September 1459), they were beaten at Ludford (12 October 1459), largely because of the refusal of the men Warwick had brought over from Calais to fight against their king. But York's party was avenged at Northampton (10 July 1460), when Henry VI was captured. They were routed at Wakefield (30 December 1460), but the Lancastrians besmirched their reputation by breaking the Christmas truce, and—worse than this—by shewing after the battle a vindictiveness which set an evil precedent. The death of the Duke of York was a staggering blow for his party. He was not of the stuff from which great leaders are made, but he was no mere conspirator for a crown. However much motives of self-interest influenced his actions, there was mingled with them a genuine zeal for administrative reform, and a love of justice in all probability nobler than would have been his achievements had he lived to translate into royal decrees the ideas of his manifestos. If responsibility for the beginning of war must be laid on his shoulders, then at least it should be counted to him that his opponents did less than nothing to help him keep the peace. And in removing him they did not right the evils he wished reformed. His party, left without a leader, was not crushed. Of the battles of 1461, Mortimer's Cross (2 February), second St Albans (17 February), and Towton (29 March), the second was a Lancastrian victory, but the other two proved that the young Earl of March had military ability, and could take his father's place. The first phase, then, was decisive. It gave the English crown to a Yorkist.

The second phase (1462–64) was of altogether different quality. Its events were only of local significance, its military engagements minor affairs in northern England, where Edward IV's supporters dealt with attempts made by the remnant of the Lancastrian party to win a foothold on the border. The main activities recorded were sieges of the castles of Bamborough, Dunstanborough, and Alnwick, a minor engagement at Hedgely Moor (April 1464) which went to the Yorkists, and another Lancastrian rout at Hexham (15 May 1464).

There followed four years of peace, and then the third phase (1469–71) began. It was short, but full of incident. In reality the period comprised three separate movements. The first, covering the months of June and July 1469 and the battle of Edgecote (26 July), put Edward in Warwick's hands. The second, with the rebellion in Lincolnshire, the defection of Warwick to Henry VI's side, led to the expulsion of Edward IV (September 1470). The third movement began in March 1471 with Edward's return. After the battles of Barnet (14 April) and Tewkesbury (4 May) he was again king, this time firmly established, and until his death (9 April 1483) he reigned in peace.

The disturbances after his death were unsettling, but they did not amount to war, and the fourth and last phase of the Wars of the Roses opened in October 1483 when the Duke of Buckingham raised rebellion against Richard III. It was to have been an ambitious enterprise, with risings in Brecknock, Kent, and the south, and with help from Henry of Richmond. But by 2 November Buckingham had been caught and beheaded at Salisbury. On 7 August 1485 Henry of Richmond landed at Milford Haven, and the last challenge to the Yorkists was made. The struggle was brief. On 22 August 1485 the Battle of Bosworth made Henry VII king.

A description of the incidents confirms some impressions concerning the real nature of the struggle. It is evident that the military events were sporadic, that we are not concerned with a country suffering under thirty years of constant fighting, that there were, on the contrary, long periods of peace. Estimates of the effects of the military campaigns must, accordingly, be temperate. The results could not have been as serious as they have sometimes been described. Closer examination confirms this opinion. The last word on such a matter must rest on what can be discovered about the military events themselves, and the vagaries of medieval writers when handling figures are now well known. Modern research finds it difficult to take seriously their statistics of troops engaged in any campaign, and in some conflicts—the first battle of St Albans is an instance—it is content to label them as mere skirmishes. Nor are the chroniclers' estimates of casualties now regarded without scepticism. That combatants, especially the nobility, were killed during and after battle is certain, but whether in such numbers as chroniclers state is doubtful. And there are other questions. There is, for example, the charge that troops inflicted heavy damage in the towns and villages through which they passed. On this count, certainly, the northern troops employed by the Lancastrians were severely criticised by contemporaries, and it goes a long way towards explaining Margaret's failure to win support in the south. But the modern scholar looks for facts, and legal records have been searched on the assumption that they should yield evidence of robberies, lootings, assaults, and like offences committed in areas occupied by troops. Such have not been found in significant quantity. Thus, the old picture of an England devastated by civil war is not borne out, and modern writers are inclined to regard other features in the life of the century as those deserving greatest attention.

All this is to the good, provided reaction does not go too far. To put the Wars of the Roses in proper perspective is one thing; to write the history of the period without them is another. They have to be explained, not explained away. It can be argued, for instance, that the absence of evidence in legal records is natural, due not to any absence of lawlessness, but to the plain fact that victims would be unlikely, in such times of disturbance, to expect much from due process of law as a means of satisfaction for wrongs done. A striking estimate of the dislocation due to the wars is revealed from the trade statistics for those years. At the crucial periods, 1460 and 1470, trade at the ports came virtually to a standstill. This was not due to material destruction. In the years immediately following, figures leap up, in many cases, to an abnormal height. The trading returns register the shock due to political disturbance. There can be no doubt that the struggle between the two parties for political control must be taken into account in dealing with the period. The Wars of the Roses were in the background affecting the life of the times, and affecting it for evil. What this really meant will be better appreciated when other features have been noticed.

Where are we to look, if not at military events? The question raises a problem, that of the nature of the available historical material. For if we were content to view the period through sixteenth-century writings we should see what their authors intended us to see, an England languishing in misery, awaiting the Tudor dynasty that would put all things right. And this is assuredly where we should begin were it not that everyone now discredits the legend about the lack of contemporary material for the Yorkist period. There is no dearth of evidence, though all is not easily accessible, or simple to use when found. And, certainly, all has not yet been forced to yield up its secrets. If we lack, with a few poor exceptions, the monastic chronicles which were the pride of an earlier age, that fact is in itself a matter of history; and the town chronicles which take their place, imperfect though they may be, are memorials to that civic consciousness whose growth is one of the most hopeful features of the period. It was an age when ordinary men and women were beginning to make use of pens, and from the sets of family letters surviving much history can be written. Nor is that all. Intensive study has exploited plea rolls, chancery proceedings, wills, customs accounts, local records—to mention only some of those recently used—and the work has as yet only skimmed the surface. What it promises can be suggested by some examples.

It has been the opinion of some that the inhabitants of the great merchant towns, including London, were violent partisans in the wars, consistently Yorkist in their sympathies. Others have spoken of them as actuated throughout by downright motives of self-interest, ready to desert either party if there was anything to be gained. Others, again, have suggested that the townsmen carefully refrained from shewing any preferences and completely ignored the wars. Considered opinion favours the view that in the main the attitude of the citizens was one of cautious moderation. They could not fail to be interested in the changing fortunes of the political parties, for whatever happened bore ultimately on the question nearest their hearts, the hope of a government firmly established, strong enough to give England peace, far-sighted enough to refrain from interfering with their trading interests, if not wise enough to encourage their enterprise. From the immediate events they had normally little to fear. Both parties in the wars needed support; so policy constrained them to be careful. Thus, although many of the towns figured in the conflict by lending either arms or men, they were not the scenes of battles or sieges, which is another argument against too serious an estimate of the material damage done. Some towns—Coventry is an example—suffered financial losses. Some gained. London, for example, won two charters, and the confirmation of a third, from Edward IV. Canterbury, Colchester, Ludlow are other instances of charter-gaining towns. But, on the whole, the citizens took no really important part in the dynastic struggle. That is not to say that they did not feel the effects of what was happening. They could not stand completely aloof. Some suffered as did Southampton. In 1460, when Warwick was expected, the Earl of Wiltshire descended upon the city, seized five Genoese trading vessels riding in the harbour, filled them with sailors, and drew upon the town for their provisions. When Edward IV came to the throne, Southampton had to make a payment to the treasurer of the household, and also find an annuity of £154 for the Earl of Warwick as Constable of Dover. In the troubles of 1469–71 Warwick demanded, and seems to have obtained, payment of his annuity. But when Edward returned, and a new Constable of Dover was appointed, the town was charged with another pension for him. Not all towns were as unfortunate. Some—Bristol is the best example—seem to have been almost untouched. Others, the majority, had a history for which Nottingham will serve as type. That city began by being well disposed towards Henry VI until Edward gained ground. Then, by the gift of a few troops and money, the citizens won a confirmation of their charter. In 1464 they sent some troops to Edward at York. In 1471 they spent about sixty pounds on soldiers and liveries for him. When Richard III came to the city he was royally received; but when news of Bosworth reached them, the citizens hurried to cultivate Henry VII. It was the common story. At Henry VI's restoration in 1470 the University of Oxford sent their felicitations; the hand of Providence was at work. But some months later they were sending up infinite thanks to a most merciful God whose divine wisdom had seen good to restore Edward IV. They rejoiced with Richard III at his accession; but they hailed Henry VII in words which placed him somewhat higher than Hannibal and Alexander. So the towns, on the whole, played for safety. Their preference, when they shewed it, seems usually to have been for the Yorkists, and that choice was not haphazard. What they wanted above all else was peace, and a strong government able and wishful to give trade and industry a chance to flourish. They thought they saw a hope in the Yorkists; at any rate, they knew how little they could expect from Henry VI. So they bided their time in caution, and went on with the work that lay to their hands.

There was much for them to do, and most of it took them far from politics. They, like their fathers before them, were alive to the possibilities of trade, and at home and abroad they were busy making use of their opportunities. The scope was wide. Their ventures took them far afield. Yorkist merchants in Iceland fought strenuously to retain trading interests in danger of being lost. Yorkist ships sailed into Irish harbours in quest of the commodities that rich land could produce. They journeyed regularly to the ports of France and Spain, and there were adventurers among them ready for greater risks. Nor was trade limited to the commodities their own ships brought. The more seasoned traders of the Italian cities brought to these shores the luxuries of the Mediterranean and the East: there was scope for trade at home as well as abroad. In such enterprises much of the energy of Yorkist England was being spent, and it was with those engaged in such tasks that the future lay. To write their names is to chronicle the fifteenth century, and provide, as well, the clue to more than half the history of the sixteenth century. There is a crowded gallery of portraits from which to choose, in the main (thanks to letters) self portraits. The Celys form a link between the wool of the Cotswolds and the merchants of Calais and Bruges; experts in all matters pertaining to credit and trade and exchange; shipping goods to Zeeland, Flanders, Bordeaux; skilled in the lore of markets; not always very scrupulous in their dealings, and yet, on the whole, not an unattractive set of business men. There are the Midwinters, the Busheys, the Forteys, dealers in wool, scouring the Cotswold villages for the commodity their packhorses would carry to the busy ports. There are the Springs of Lavenham, the Tames of Gloucestershire, the Wottons, Boleyns, Jocelyns, shrewd men of business, generous builders of churches, speculators in landed estates on which the next generation of their families would live veneered with Tudor honours, the new nobility around the throne. There are the Canynges of Bristol, busied with the cares that crowded in upon the owners of so large a fleet of ships, but not too busy to leave their memorial in Bristol's most beautiful church. These, and others like them, were the men into whose hands trade and industry had been entrusted, and the results of their enterprise would be known in the days when the Yorkists had long passed from the scene. They had much to do, a great deal to gain. But with all their commercial interests and cares, they never forgot the towns where they had made their homes. They played their part in gild and local government, sharing in civic feuds and festivities, lending their patronage to town pageants, building and decorating churches and halls. They lavished their wealth upon beautiful homes, combined sternness and charity in their treatment of the less fortunate and more improvident members of the community, cultivated with discreet gifts the lawyers and judges and gentlefolk whose favours might advantage themselves and their towns. Men with many faults, but not without inestimable virtues, learning to handle wealth, gaining experience in self government, and benefiting their towns with much of that wealth they must leave behind them when their trading cares would trouble them no more. Little wonder if national politics had few attractions for them: they had so much else on hand.

If the merchants were intent on their own lives and advancement, so too were the country gentry with whom they had some dealings, and into whose homes their daughters were permitted sometimes—a little superciliously—to bring welcome dowries and powerful connexions with the world of trade. Here, too, there is no lack of types. Pastons, Plumptons, Stonors, Timperleys, Debenhams—we know the family portraits, and the public records often flash an unexpected gleam on to careers it would sometimes be kinder to leave in the dark. The impressions to be gathered are all of one kind. We see these country gentry living strenuous lives in a world that is very real, very hard; fighting many difficulties, surrounded by foes. They play their part in local government as sheriffs, justices of the peace, commissioners appointed to do work for the Crown. Sometimes they are members of parliament. They are to be found in the wars, serving in the company of nobles whose protection and favour they seek. But their real loyalty is not here. What interested them above all else was the family to which they belonged. They were consecrated to its conservation; to its well-being they gave up their lives. To further its prosperity they fought the countryside. In its interests there was no trick to which they would not stoop. They were capable alike of fraud or of taking a hand in a trading venture. They were not above a little smuggling, or the risks and gains of piracy. Theirs was a cynical view of life, especially in matters pertaining to law. Usually up to the eyes in litigation, they were for ever in the law courts. They would use any means to gain their ends: bribe a juror, intimidate a sheriff, flatter a nobleman, knock a rival on the head. They were past masters in the finesse of writs and legal procedure, experts in filing a bill of complaints against an enemy. But it was all done in the greatest of causes: for the furtherance of the family fortunes. Marriage was a matter of business, for when such interests are at stake there can be no place for sentiment. And yet it seems to have worked very satisfactorily. These Stonors and Pastons were well served by their women-folk, fit mates for such men, efficient rulers of large households, stern mothers, shrewd housewives, and yet not devoid of the finer graces, quite able to appreciate a gift of ribbons or seek news of London fashions.

The country gentry knew what they were about in being ambitious for their families. The nobility had often sprung from lowly origins, and what had happened before could be repeated. It was worth the effort, for the nobles were still powerful, despite their experiences in the French wars, and although the dynastic struggle was leaving its mark upon the resources of most of them. Vast landed estates accumulated in few hands by a skilful policy of marriage alliances made the heads of great houses, like the Nevilles, the leaders of politics. Their household establishments were modelled on, or challenged comparison with, the royal household; their hospitality was lavish, their retainers were numerous. But they were living on their capital, and not all of them would have the staying power needful if they were to survive unimpaired. As yet they were not feeling the full effects of the social changes, or of the political quarrels in which they were involved. But the future would not lie with them. It was reserved for the wealthy middle class now rising to importance. Meanwhile, the most sinister influence of the Yorkist nobility was its deliberate encouragement of the forces of lawlessness and the spirit of turbulence. By their participation in the Wars of the Roses, their employment of large bands of retainers, their failure to collaborate with the government in any policy of repression of lawlessness, they were in no small measure the creators of the problem which lay at the root of the Yorkist failure. When the time came for a ruthless eradication of these evils, the nobility were found so inextricably involved in them that they had to suffer.

Whatever remains to be said of Yorkist England, few will now accept as true a judgment which would dismiss it as a scene of decay, or exhaustion of national vitality. Here was exuberant life, but what is difficult to determine is the exact quality of that life. So far we have been thinking largely of material things. Before we can feel sure that we have all we need for interpreting the age we must try to probe things pertaining to the mind. It is a venture in which unprovable generalisations do not help. The existence of private correspondence is interesting; it is not enough to justify the looser statements of Gairdner and Kingsford to the effect that literacy and education were widespread, and that most people could express themselves in writing, with ease and fluency. There is no proof of this. All we know is that Yorkist society shews some surprising signs of education, and that—however it was done—facilities for rudimentary instruction seem to have reached a wider sphere than the houses of the nobility or the business circles in large towns. To say that is, of course, to concede much; but there is no great claim to be made for the second half of the fifteenth century in the history of literature. It was no golden age. The best list that could be drawn up for it is a strange assortment, not one to thrill with admiration: Malory's *Morte d'Arthur*, Fortescue's works, Littleton's treatise on *Tenures*, Capgrave's English works, Ripley's *Compound of Anatomy*, Hardyng's 'poetical' *Chronicle*, the Latin poem of Peter Carmelianus. And yet, it was a matter of no small significance that a goodly few of the ordinary folk of Yorkist England were not ignorant of letters. Some day—it was not so far away—there would be material for them to use, and their demands would dictate supply. It is worth a thought that when, after 1477, William Caxton began his great work in England, some of the first products of his press were a *Book of Courtesy* (1477), *The Canterbury Tales* (1478), and *Chronicles of England* (1480). Was he forming public taste or catering for it?

How such things were made possible takes us into the history of English education. We have no need, and no business, to say over again what others have said of Henry VI's services to that cause. But we have the right to ask whether the Yorkists did anything to continue his work. And the answer is unexpectedly encouraging. Not even the political uncertainty could stop the movement entirely, and even though they were not the equals of their predecessor, both Edward and Richard did some things of which they had no need to be ashamed. True, Edward started badly. In 1463 his enthusiasm for St George's Chapel, Windsor—and perhaps the fact that he had not as yet seen how to combine a continuation of Henry's work with the elimination of Henry's name—led him to annex the properties of Eton College for his own foundation. For a while Eton's progress was checked, if its definite retrogression was not encouraged. But in 1467 wisdom prevailed, the school received back its privileges, this time with Edward as founder. His wife, too, gave generously to Queens' College, Cambridge, the foundation of Margaret of Anjou. Even Richard III and Anne were mindful of the universities. They gave lands to Queens' College, found money for fellowships, and granted—from the forfeited estates of the Duke of Buckingham—property to Magdalen College, Oxford. What they did, private donors like Thomas Rotherham, Chancellor of Cambridge University in 1475, imitated.

Nor did the earlier movement for the foundation of schools die out. Between 1465 and 1475, Stillington, Bishop of Bath and Wells, founded Acaster. In 1472 Margaret, widow of Lord Hungerford, obtained a royal licence to carry on the work of her father-in-law by founding a grammar school at Heytesbury in Wiltshire. In 1480 Waynflete made statutes for his college of Magdalen, Oxford, and the school attached. In 1483 Rotherham founded Jesus College, Rotherham.

Here were the channels of education. They were being used. Shrewd families like the Pastons knew the value of learning, for their fortunes rested on money borrowed by old Clement Paston for the education of his son William, who rose to be a judge. The tradition lingered on in the family; the sons went to Eton, Oxford, Cambridge, or the Inns of Court. For we must not forget these last, although their fifteenth-century history is almost a blank. There is more than a suspicion that education there was construed in fairly liberal terms. But to what extent they were doing anything to educate beyond the standards of a highly skilled profession is as yet uncertain. The connexion of the sons of country gentlemen with them is a subject that would bear investigation.

The day will come when someone will venture to put together what can be known of the intellectual life of Yorkist England. Of the fascination of the subject there is no doubt: but an exacting equipment will be required. For this period in the story of English humanism will be mainly a study of origins. Data yet to be collected will consist mainly of human relationships, contacts of minds, influence of teacher on student, fashions in thought. Intangible things, and yet important. Beyond a few letters, some translations, scraps of poetry, and the manuscripts they so assiduously collected, these early humanists do not seem to have left much on which we may work. To discover their secrets will be a delicate task demanding patience in piecing together unexpected and faint clues, discrimination in analysing facts, subtlety in interpretation, skill in handling evidence so gossamer-like that only the deftest of fingers may touch and yet keep it intact. But the results, if we are not mistaken, will justify the work. For the first time the real nature of the Yorkist achievement will be seen. Already there are encouraging signs. We have, at any rate, been told enough to teach us this is a subject on which we dare not be dogmatic, and that is more than some earlier writers knew.

The older theory provided two well defined phases into which most of what was known of English humanism could be packed. The first, ending in 1448, saw the dawn of the Renaissance, with Humphrey, Duke of Gloucester, as its leader. Then came the period of darkness, 1448–88, when humanism was killed, presumably by the Wars of the Roses. Then in 1488 the full Renaissance opened with the work of the Oxford reformers. That tidy theory needs examination. The work of the first phase is now scrutinised more closely, and although its importance is fully appreciated, it is seen that there were shades in what is too glibly described as humanism. Humphrey and his contemporaries were humanists, but not to the same degree or in the same way as the more finished products of later years. These forerunners, enthusiasts for Italian culture, wealthy book-collectors, ready patrons, were only beginning to be touched by Italian ideas; and were only partially changed by the contact. Their successors were more thoroughly imbued with the new spirit. There is, too, a different opinion of those years between 1448 and 1488. In that apparently sterile period something seems to have been happening. What exactly it was cannot as yet be told; but some facts are known. For one thing, it is certain that throughout those years contact with Italy was maintained. The known dates when some of these Englishmen went to Italy is evidence of continuity. In 1442 Grey went; in 1451 Flemming; in 1455 Free and Gunthorpe; in 1458 Tiptoft; in 1464 Selling and Hadley; in 1469 Selling again. Further, there is a distinct development discernible in the humanism of these men. They go to Italy to some extent equipped. They are accepted as equals by Italian humanists. Their culture is richer than that of the first generation. Some, like Free, may well be called professional scholars. They begin to leave specimens of their work and we can judge its quality. In a word, humanism is gathering strength as it moves through these years. Like earlier visitors to Italy these men were also book-collectors, and they, too, bequeath their collections to English colleges, thus preparing the way for those who followed them.

Quite as interesting, but a more involved story, is that concerned with England. Not much is known, but exchequer records have been brought to light which note payments made to Greek scholars in England in 1465–66, while the study of manuscripts has revealed a group in English collections written—almost certainly by one of these same Greeks—to the order of an English archbishop in 1468. In 1475 Cornelio Vitelli was praelector of New College, Oxford. One recalls that Grocyn became a Fellow there in 1465, that Linacre went to Oxford in 1480, and was a Fellow of All Souls in 1483. These are precious links: they stress the continuity of development. Men did not return to England to forget what they had learned, and most of them came back to important offices in Church and State. And what of places nearer home than Italy? Yorkist foreign policy had close contacts with Burgundy, and although this is not the place for a description of that Court as a home of art and letters, it may be profitable to recall that Caxton was employed by Margaret of Burgundy, that the monochrome paintings in Eton College Chapel (1470–83) shew a revival of English painting under Flemish and Burgundian influences, that similar contacts can be traced in English illuminations. The historian of the English Renaissance may well extend his search if he is to do his work thoroughly. But the last word on the subject must rest with him.

When a young king of twenty-two, more than tolerably good looking, popular because of his skill and courage in war and the promise he shews of developing into a strong ruler, decides to marry, we shall judge rightly that his subjects will be interested. When we learn that his bride is a widow, five years his senior and the mother of two sons, we may be a little apprehensive of his choice. And when we gather that on May-day of 1464 Edward IV married Elizabeth Woodville in strictest secrecy, with no intention of letting the news be made public—it was only forced from him in a council on 4 September of that year—we shall fancy we have found a topic of some note. To probe all Edward's motives is not possible; but that here is a masterful, if not wise, personality is certain. And we have the advantage of being able to track some of the results of his action.

For four years, ever since the death of the Duke of York, Richard Earl of Warwick had been by the king's side. A foreigner writing from England in March 1464 said there were two rulers here. One was the Earl of Warwick; the name of the other he could not remember. Whoever it was, this was not quite a fair judgment on Edward, but it does no more than justice to Warwick, and certainly expresses what the earl would have liked men to feel. Here was a worthy representative of the baronial class, wealthy, powerful, able, the leader of a family group owing position and power to the number of its offspring and the skilful policy of marriage alliances in which its members specialised. He had all the requisites, and not a little of the ambition, wherewith to take the lead in affairs. From 1459–71 he is never negligible in English politics. Indeed, one may say that Edward's reign falls into two distinct periods (1461–69: 1471–83), and that Warwick was primarily responsible for that division. In the first phase it is not an exaggeration to say that the reaction of these two personalities one to the other provides a key motive to Yorkist history. From 1458–64 there can be no question of Warwick's whole-hearted devotion to the Yorkist cause, and his effort to keep the party together after Wakefield was the work to which Edward owed his throne. Throughout his career Warwick's aim was to maintain and increase his power, and to govern the king's affairs. Edward's marriage suggests that Warwick underestimated the young king.

In 1460, when the Yorkist leaders were sheltering at Calais, a supporter of Henry VI who had gone out to find them was captured, and brought into their presence:

"and there my lord of Salisbury rated him, calling him knave's son, that he should be so rude to call him and these other lords traitors, for they shall be found the king's true liegemen when he should be found a traitor &c. And my lord of Warwick rated him, and said that his father was but a squire, and brought up with King Henry the Fifth, and sethen himself made by marriage, and also made lord, and that it was not his part to have such language of lords being of the king's blood. And my lord of March rated him likewise."

By May 1464 the Earl of March was king; the prisoner, Richard Woodville, Earl Rivers, was his father-in-law. Another family had jostled its way a little too near the throne, and a crowd of greedy relatives intrigued with the queen for rich wives, titles, estates. To suggest, as some have done, that Edward married in order to make an opposition party to Warwick is to rationalise unduly the follies of youth. The

Woodvilles never exercised much influence over the king. He certainly did not throw off the domination of Warwick to deliver himself captive to second-rate men for whom he never seems to have shewn feelings other than those akin to contempt. But policy or not, the results were all one. The new arrivals soon found Warwick and his friends their deadly enemies, whose memories were not so short as was the king's. While Edward lived, the Woodvilles did not have to be taken very seriously as politicians. But as soon as one of their number became a queen it must have occurred to some far-sighted Englishmen to ponder anxiously what would happen if Edward should chance to die. For the moment we need not look so far ahead. What we see is that Edward's marriage, something of a *mésalliance* despite his mother-in-law Jacquetta of Luxemburg, was also something of a gesture. It told Warwick that, although he and the king might still work together, it could never again be on the old terms. Thus, a man whose very ambition was a pledge that he would have been Edward's strongest supporter in the years between 1461 and 1469, when the king was honestly trying to govern well, was given a grievance to nurse. There was in France one who would know how to awaken it when he judged the moment opportune.

Louis XI succeeded Charles VII on 22 July 1461. Ties of sentiment had bound Charles to the Lancastrian cause—was not Henry VI the son of his sister, and Margaret of Anjou the niece of his wife? With Louis XI no such fond ideas would be given any play. His problems were too serious. There was the great task of keeping intact, and adding to, the powers of the Crown. There were the Dukes of Burgundy and Brittany to watch, and, if possible, to crush. And with Edward IV as a party to whom they might apply for help, that king would have to be controlled; not because Edward was likely to be as clever as Louis, but because anything he did would have reactions for France. Louis would not have deserved his reputation for diplomatic subtlety had he not seen how to use his advantages. So Edward and Warwick were soon involved in his schemes. Thus it is that foreign policy played a large part in Edward's reign, but it is not due to that king's ability. Through all, it is Louis' master-mind that is at work. And the tragedy, from the Yorkist standpoint, was that this concentration of energy upon foreign politics hindered internal reform that was so essential to stability. It helped, too, to produce the theme of the first phase of Edward's reign, the slowly widening breach between the king and Warwick.

The first four years of Yorkist supremacy shewed the dangers of Lancastrian plots abroad. In April 1461 Margaret of Anjou had crossed to Brittany to get support for a projected invasion of England. Louis also lent 20,000 marks with the promise of Calais as security. But by 1463 Edward was known to be mastering his kingdom; so Louis stopped spinning this web. He was in need of English help. He would cut his losses, abandon the wretched Lancastrians, consider seriously Edward's claims to Normandy and Guienne, if only England would help him against Burgundy. Warwick, the powerful subject, seemed worth cultivating. He and Louis explored together the possibilities of a marriage between Edward and Bona of Savoy, the sister-in-law of the French king.

As we have seen, Edward had other plans. And thus it was continually between 1464 and 1469. Edward's eyes strayed in the direction of Burgundy. Warwick was charmed by the master diplomat in France. Edward had reasons. English merchants were anxious about their trade with Flanders; there was still the glamour of old memories—it would be so good to win again in France what the Lancastrians had won and lost. Louis had to work hard, and by 1467 his need of the English was so great as to cause him to raise his bid. He promised to place Edward's claim to Normandy and Guienne for arbitration before the Pope. Edward was right to be suspicious, but his subsequent policy went farther. On 1 October 1467 his sister Margaret was betrothed to Charles, Duke of Burgundy. By the middle of 1468 a definite alliance with Burgundy was followed by an agreement with Brittany. It shewed Louis that Warwick's influence was less than he had thought.

Ever since the beginning of his reign Edward had shirked the issue whether the Hanse merchants should be given renewed trading privileges. There was history behind that question, but the present politics is all we need note. Until a clear understanding with Burgundy had been reached it was unwise to take a strong line. So in 1461, 1463, and 1465 temporary renewals were granted. The truce with Burgundy freed Edward. In 1468 when an English trading fleet was seized by the King of Denmark, Edward retaliated by confiscating the goods of Hanse merchants in England. The council upheld the legality of this act. Thus a serious commercial dispute was opened.

So the years passed between 1464 and 1469. Towards the end Warwick began to realise where he stood. Others were as disillusioned as he. In January 1468 there were tales of mob attacks on the Rivers' estates in Kent. In July the trial of Cornelius and Hawkins for treason revealed Lancastrian plots, and worse, shewed that the government stooped to torture in order to ferret them out, and that wealthy merchants like Sir Thomas Cook might be implicated, to satisfy Woodville vengeance, and be mulcted of their wealth. In November there were more plots. Sir Thomas Hungerford and Henry Courtenay paid with their lives. In April 1469 the mysterious Robin of Redesdale was massing troops in the North, and when Edward went against him in June he was surprised at the strength of this malcontent's following.

There were deeper depths. On 11 July 1469, Warwick was at Calais, marrying his daughter to Edward's brother, the Duke of Clarence. That weak, ineffective, yet troublesome young man, tempted by a rich dowry and perhaps encouraged to dream greater things, had thrown in his lot with the earl. The day after the marriage they sent to England to say they would shortly arrive to support Redesdale. Before the end of July Edward's army had been defeated at Edgecote and soon the king was in Warwick's hands. His plans did not as yet include the substitution of Clarence for Edward. As always his aim was control of the king and dismissal of the Woodvilles. They were not plans easy to realise. Whatever feeling ran against Edward, there was no enthusiasm in England for two kings in prison and Warwick supreme. So the earl walked circumspectly. Edward was freed to go to London, but he soon discovered that freedom was not release from his captor. He was too weak to punish Warwick and Clarence; so he had to pardon them. There was even a scheme for a marriage between Edward's four-year-old daughter and George Neville, the nine-year-old son of the Earl of Northumberland, Warwick's nearest male heir. It looked as if the earl would win. But the Lincolnshire rebellion of 1469–70, when a private quarrel between local gentry spread into a serious rising, shewed that behind the ostensible leaders were Clarence and Warwick. By April the two were in flight for Calais.

Warwick had failed, but he was not yet beaten. Was it subtle, coldblooded Louis XI who thought of the next move, the diplomatic revolution? At any rate, there it soon was: nothing less than a proposal to replace Edward IV by Henry VI, and a marriage alliance between the earl's daughter and Edward, son of Henry VI. It is not surprising that Margaret of Anjou was slow to give consent. About 23 June 1470 Louis broached the new scheme to her. She took a month before she could bring herself to meet Warwick; but in the end she gave way. By September, Warwick and Clarence were in England. By October, Edward IV was across the water at Alkmaar, a king without a kingdom.

After the release of Henry VI his "re-adeption" began, with Warwick in command. The problems before him were many, their solution was not obvious. A country alarmed at this fresh political upheaval wanted peace, firm government, relief from taxation, and perhaps it still thought of war with France. Warwick could not work miracles. He could not prevent a young, determined, and chastened Edward from planning a return. On 11 March 1471 the king sailed from Flushing, landing at Ravenspur. It should not escape notice that he crossed in boats supplied by the Hanse merchants. At Barnet when his forces met those of Warwick it was not Edward who was left dead on the field.

If Warwick's career was finished, the second phase of Edward's was beginning. It was not like the first. From 1471–83 a different Edward was in control, one whose rivals had been removed from his path. The death of Warwick was followed by that of the young son of Henry VI, killed after Tewkesbury. And on 21 May 1471 Henry VI himself ended his unhappy life. Contemporary gossip thought his death too opportune to be altogether natural, imputing a share in it to Edward and Gloucester.

Whether that was so or not, Edward was at last secure in the possession of his crown; but the results were not wholly beneficial. Security brought out the least attractive features in his character. His companions were of lesser calibre than his earlier friends, and some ugly traits, not altogether absent formerly, now became intensified. Cruelty, avarice, lack of grip on affairs, absence of sustained purpose amounting at times almost to idleness, extravagance, extreme dissoluteness, these are predominant. He is said to have retained the affections of the populace to the end, but there were signs that men no longer expected much from Yorkist rule. These twelve years cannot be dismissed as uneventful, but many of the happenings were of a kind unlikely to do England any good.

The end of the main struggle between Yorkists and Lancastrians ought to have been seized as an opportunity for giving England peace, and the solution of some of those problems so much in need of attention. Instead, Edward returned determined to seek revenge, and war with France was assured. In July 1474 a treaty of perpetual friendship with Charles of Burgundy pledged the duke to help Edward against Louis. The early part of 1475 was big with preparations and by July he was in France leading as fine an army as had ever left England for that country. Despite grumbling at taxation the idea of war was popular in England, but what was really in Edward's mind when he exploited this traditional sentiment it is hard to see. In August he met Louis at Picquigny; but it was in order to talk peace. They agreed that the dauphin should marry Edward's daughter, that Louis should pay 75,000 crowns and a further annual pension of 50,000 crowns for the rest of Edward's life, and another 50,000 crowns for the ransom of Margaret of Anjou. In return, Edward promised to take his troops home. By 28 September Edward's great expedition was over and he was back in London. The fact that after such a shameless failure to take the offensive he survived his return is a measure of England's weariness with civil strife.

Meanwhile, those Hanse ships had not been lent by philanthropists. Edward had promised redress of the wrongs complained of by the merchants. In 1474 a conference met at Utrecht. The merchants were in no mood for compromise. They asked for complete restoration of privileges, reversal of the council's decision of 1468, heavy compensation, and a clause exempting them from English taxation. They had their way. It was no victory for English commerce. Within the year the Hanse merchants were back in England, and English merchants had to yield to them the monopoly of trade with central Europe.

For the rest of the reign Edward's foreign policy can be dismissed briefly, provided it is remembered that although results were negligible foreign affairs still absorbed much of the king's time, and caused him to squander energies which might with profit have been used in domestic politics. The years 1475–83 are dominated by Louis XI. Although the regular payments of Edward's pension suggest that the English king had made a good bargain, in reality Louis was not throwing money away, and time shewed that he knew best what he was doing. The key to the tangled politics was the death of Charles of Burgundy in January 1477. Henceforth Louis' object was the acquisition of Burgundy. Mixed motives tempted Edward to join Maximilian, who had married Charles' heiress, Mary of Burgundy; but his desire to make marriages for his children, unwillingness to forfeit his French pension, and increasing laziness held him back. On the other hand, Louis kept him busy by scheming with James III of Scotland, until in 1482 England and Scotland drifted into war. Louis' superiority was manifest in the treaty of Arras (23 December 1482), by which he agreed that the dauphin should marry Maximilian's daughter. At last Edward realised Louis' duplicity and the futility of his own work, but death overtook him before he could retaliate. The short reign of Richard III does not centre around foreign politics. Richard was too uncertain of the chances of invasion by Henry of Richmond to be able to take a strong line. His fears made him keep on good terms with France and Brittany, and in 1484 even the Scottish war was brought to an end.

Must a puzzle of personality for ever prevent us from understanding Richard's brief career as king? It would seem so, because of the peculiar nature of the materials available for study; and yet, if we can agree that grey is a better medium with which to paint him than either black or white, there is hope of a tolerably credible portrait. Among contemporaries, Warkworth would seem to acquit Richard of the murder of Henry VI's son after Tewkesbury, but his insinuation that the duke was at the Tower on the night Henry VI died may be read to mean that even during his own life-time Richard was suspect. The Croyland narrative, written about 1486, is hostile. Its author clearly believed Richard put to death the two young sons of Edward IV. Certainly, such talk was going the rounds in France in July 1484. The too ingenious theory that would discredit this Croyland source by making it a composite work by two writers of opposite views has been completely disproved. But as yet we are only on the threshold. The Tudor writers are the source of the controversy. They have to be weighed, because the best of them did probably obtain information from Richard's contemporaries; but they could hardly avoid prejudice in dealing with what was for them very recent politics rather than ancient history. And one took one's politics seriously, as seriously as Rous did when he thought he could make men believe in a Richard who began life as a monster, born after two years of gestation, with a complete set of teeth, hair down to the shoulders, and the right shoulder higher than the left. More's Richard III is of different stuff; but it is not devoid of guile. Whether More or Morton wrote it has been canvassed, and serious study would have to explore the relation of the Latin and English texts. "*Aut Morus aut nullus*" thinks one who has spent time on the problem, and his verdict can be accepted. Certainly the work is of great interest, a contribution to English historiography, a landmark in the history of English prose. But is it history? There are things in it we cannot accept as fact, and it must remain for historians a secondary authority. To a far greater degree is that true of what other Tudor writers like Polydore Virgil, Hall, and Fabyan have to say.

But what can be substituted for such works? The obstacle before those who try to acquit Richard of the charges Tudor writers levelled against him has been the scarcity of material. No contemporary writer refutes them; so all that can be done is criticism of the details of their statements. The subject is treacherous. Those who try to take sides are soon in a sea of speculation upon human character and motives, for the interpretation of Richard's personality varies with the degree of emphasis placed upon the facts. Take an example in the theories of the way Richard's accession was achieved. Opposite schools will agree, to a point. Both accept some things without question: that Edward IV before he died (9 April 1483) meant Richard to protect his son's interests; that Edward left the prince with his mother and her family; that the Woodvilles and Richard had no love for each other. Both will say that by 4 May 1483 Prince Edward was in London in Richard's care; that on 13 May Richard summoned parliament; that by 14 May Richard was calling himself the king's dearest uncle, Duke of York, and Protector of England; that Richard pushed on preparations for Edward's coronation; that on 9 June a prolonged council was held. But here is the parting of the ways. One school, accepting wholly, or at any rate leaning towards, an unfavourable interpretation of Richard's character, sees all later events as a calculated plot which had been present in Richard's mind from the start, involving the execution of Lord Hastings (13 June) because he opposed Richard's plans, the publication of a fictitious story of a pre-contract of marriage between Edward IV and Lady Eleanor Butler which made the Woodville marriage illegal, and the execution of Anthony, Earl Rivers, his nephew Richard Grey, and others of the Woodville party at Pontefract (25 June). The other school prefers to stress the legitimacy question. They depict Richard anxious, in the early days after Edward's death, to be scrupulously fair to his son, preparing for the boy's coronation with no idea of usurpation in his mind. Then, about 8 June, Dr Robert Stillington revealed the secret of the pre-contract. An astounded Richard faces the facts, sees the dangers that would follow the coronation of a bastard, and in a difficult situation decides that the only solution is for him to take the throne.

Neither interpretation satisfies. An explanation of Richard's action is possible, but not on these lines, nor in a manner acceptable to those who take back into the fifteenth century standards acquired in a later age. Some of the facts are clear enough, and there can be no doubt that Richard had the acumen and self-interest to appreciate them. Edward IV settled his son's fate by raising the Woodvilles to power. For the key problem of politics after his death was bound to be that of the custody of the royal minor, and the candidates were the Woodvilles and Richard. Whichever was in power, neither could be safe. There is no need to depict a Richard steeped in crimes, the murderer of Henry VI and his son, and the destroyer of Clarence. There is no reason, even, for thinking of him as a man of one idea, and that his own advancement. There was room in his mind for many conflicting ideas. Indeed, the more we visualise him as a man of his own times the more satisfying that view will appear to be. He could be fearful for his own safety and yet at the same time anxious to act loyally by his nephew, ambitious and yet resigned to bide his time, starkly realist and yet sufficiently Yorkist to be absurdly credulous of gossip affecting legitimism. There was room for all these things in his mind, but for one thing there was no place. Sentiment was not a fifteenth-century virtue, and neither Richard nor his contemporaries cared much about the fate of those whom business or politics threw in their way. The dualism of the century was in Richard's personality. He was not lacking in some of the finer qualities. His career as Duke of Gloucester reveals a loyalty to Edward IV which compares favourably with the attitude of Warwick or Clarence; his private life, though not without reproach, was infinitely better than that of Edward; his grief for the death of his son Edward (died 9 April 1484) was very genuine; to the end, his reputation in the north country stood high. But contemporaries found it hard to forget the suspicion that "he also put to death the ij children of Kyng Edward for which cause he lost the hertes of the people," and rumours of his projected marriage to his niece made them wonder what he had done to his queen, so that Richard found it necessary to denounce publicly the story of an engagement. No amount of apology can remove all the suspicions, but many of them may perhaps be understood, if not condoned, when thought of in relation to the age in which he lived.

Who shall say what heady brew was in the cup of knowledge Renaissance Italy was handing around so freely? There are some, at any rate, who drank and were never again the same. What happened to John Tiptoft, Earl of Worcester, to change him from an earnest seeker after Italian culture into the savage butcher and beheader of men? Only the most pronounced pathological case plays with death for a whim, and Tiptoft's unswerving loyalty to Edward IV until his execution at the "re-adeption" (18 October 1470) suggests there was some logic behind his remorseless treatment of those taken in rebellion, and that it must be explained by something other than mere lust for blood. He had travelled widely, and had been an honoured friend of scholars and statesmen in Italy. Had he learned something more seductive than humanistic reverence for the classics? Had he, perchance, caught the whisper of some new-fangled ideas of politics, a new doctrine, for instance, that the State was right as well as might, that resistance to authority must be crushed no matter what the means employed, that the necessity of the State knew no

law? His opinions are not easy to glean, but the speech he is supposed
to have made when condemning Sir Ralph Grey suggests that in his eyes
disloyalty to the king was a breach of feudal obligations and a challenge
to authority besides which death was as nothing. Behind the cruelty we
fancy there was purpose. Had Richard III heard the same voices? He
had opportunities. After 1470 he was Edward's close adviser, and there
had been some ugly incidents. Clarence had been no friend to him or to
Edward. Forgiven for his past with Warwick, he had learned nothing.
To the end he remained futile, restless, shifty, quarrelsome. He hated
Gloucester because of his desire to marry Anne Neville, and Clarence
wanted the Warwick estates for himself. He quarrelled with Edward
because the king would not allow him to pursue a marriage with Mary
of Burgundy. He defied the king by interfering in the treason trial of
Stacy and Burdett. It could not go on. At last there was a bill of
attainder, and on 18 February 1478 a mysterious death in the Tower.
What part, if any, Gloucester played is not known; but he must have
heard Louis XI's cynical advice to Edward to put Clarence out of his
way. It is useless to speculate on Richard's motives. What is clear
enough is that his ruthlessness, cruelty, lack of the moral or sentimental
ties that might stand between him and what he sought, are all traits for
which we shall not look in vain in the politics of France or of Renaissance
Italy. And assuredly they will be met again in the England of the
Tudors.

What Richard would have done with power we can hardly judge. He
had so little time in which to work out a policy. But there are signs of
ability, a desire to do stern justice, a generosity towards the dependants
of those who fought against him, some qualities of leadership which
suggest he might have achieved something greater than his crimes. The
whole problem of his career lies in its brevity. It is more than likely that
in the eyes of his subjects much—if not all—would have been forgiven
him had he reigned twenty years and given England peace. But in the
Duke of Buckingham he had his Warwick, and even though this rebellion
could be stamped out and Buckingham beheaded (October 1483), behind
him was a more sinister and more fortunate conspirator. From Henry
Tudor there was no escape.

When all has been said of the personalities of these kings, the real
significance of the Yorkist period is still elusive. An account that
dismisses the subject with some comment that inadequate kings failed
to maintain their position because of their weakness does less than justice
to the work of Edward IV and Richard III. For these kings had some
contribution to make to general development. If they were not Lancastrians, neither were they Tudors. They stand apart. Their reigns have a
quality of their own.

The secret may be revealed if the period is viewed from another angle.
To approach it through official records rather than narrative sources is to

make discoveries. We shall find—but it is a fact over which one need not be greatly disturbed—that there are some inconvenient gaps in such sources. For this it is likely that antiquarians, rats, and carelessness are more responsible than the government departments, and historical arguments to the effect that the machine of government was not functioning are inconclusive if based wholly on the absence of records. Allowing for such gaps, there remain materials sufficient in quantity to provide a picture of the Yorkist government at work. Not much of the machinery has the attraction of novelty, and the constitutional historian has only a few opportunities to study fresh expedients of government. The main framework remained what it was before 1460, departments of chancery, exchequer, household, courts of common law, parliament, and council. The Middle Ages had devised a system competent to administer the country even in a period of political disorganisation. There was no call for a revolutionary policy, no need for reconstruction. Not even the Tudors, when they came, needed to make many alterations. They merely adapted existing institutions to new needs. And perhaps there will be found the heaviest indictment of the Yorkist kings. They realised, but only partially, the nature of some of their problems, and on the whole shewed little skill in adaptation. It was not that they shirked responsibility. "My Lord Chaunseller, thys must be don." Such notes are sometimes found in Edward's hand on warrants. They give a truer picture of Yorkist kingship than that suggested by generalisations about failure due to weak leadership. Far from being inefficient both Edward and Richard did much, but it is doubtful whether they knew what they wanted to do. Neither had the dogged purpose, ruthless power of concentration, dominating motive, of a Henry VII. But the criticism must be tempered. Twenty-four years span the reign of Henry VII, years fully occupied with the preliminaries making it possible for five members of the Tudor dynasty to call the crown of England theirs over a period little short of one hundred and twenty years. In the same length of time three members of the house of York made more or less fleeting contacts with that same crown; then a house that was scarcely a dynasty was transformed from a political fact into a historical problem. Perhaps there is some excuse if a deep and consistent policy is not discernible in their actions.

Of one thing we can be certain. The challenge to the Yorkists sprang from the prevalent lawlessness. It is worth exploring, for it reveals the subtleties of their task. That the country recognised the seriousness of the problem the most superficial glance at the rolls of parliament will reveal. The Yorkists came to power because of their implicit promise to restore law and order. Edward IV, in his first parliament, was greeted by a petition revealing what men hoped. It was for peace and good government. When we meet parliament again in 1483 they are still hoping in almost identical phrases. So, too, private individuals. "God for Hys holy mersy geve grace that ther may be set a good rewyll and a sad in this contre in hast, for I herd nevyr sey of so mych robry and manslawter in thys contre as is now within a lytyll tyme." Margaret Paston was not alone in her prayer. But peace and security did not come. The reason is not found on the surface. Lawlessness was directly connected with rapid changes in the whole structure of society, and the Yorkist failure to cope with it was due not to indifference but to the inability of the legal machine to adapt itself sufficiently quickly to new needs. Both Edward and Richard knew the urgency of the question, as may easily be proved. In the Easter term of 1462 Edward actually sat in King's Bench—an unusual incident for the later Middle Ages—and in several years he can be followed in various parts of the country in company with his judges making a judicial progress in an attempt to stem the tide of disorder. Wholly admirable work, but it did not touch the roots of the problem.

Arrangements for the administration of law in the country felt the impact of changing conditions, and the main difficulty was for law to deal with men who held its forms in contempt, and were too familiar with its limitations. For the paradox of those years, when it was imperative to keep the country gentry in order, was that the responsibility for administering the law was put into their hands. The justices of the peace were the chief agents of local government. They were the most sufficient knights and esquires in the country. They were also, very often, the leaders of armed bands and retainers of the nobility.

The problem went deeper. To understand it there must be kept in mind the close relation between social and economic movements, and the development of the forms and doctrines of law. If society is to stand the strain of progress in the former, it must be equipped by constant development in the latter. And as we watch the working of the common law system at the end of the Middle Ages there comes a conviction that the relationship was not sufficiently close. Throughout those years clerks were writing their records, their plea rolls come regularly from King's Bench and Common Pleas, the Year Books report cases. All is done so formally that we can hardly tell that the party conflict developed into war. Yet a study of these records leaves a doubt. Theoretically, all is well. In fact, a legal system, centuries old, was overburdened with archaic survivals and highly technical formalism, so that it offered to the unscrupulous countless opportunities ranging from essoins to bribery, from perjury to legal quibbles, from pardons, benefit of clergy, and sanctuary privileges to pedantic insistence on procedural forms, whereby the ends of justice might be defeated. It is not that lawyers were corrupt, but rather that a stereotyped, highly technical, and over-elaborate structure was unable, though its agents had the best will in the world, to respond to the fresh needs of the age. Indeed, the more scrupulously the common law judges did their work according to the procedure and principles they knew, the more clearly they revealed the deficiencies of the system, and confounded confusion.

Men were blindly feeling their way towards the truth. Proof is provided by developments outside the common law. This is not the place to write the history of conciliar jurisdiction, or the growth of equity in the chancery. But these things had their place. It is from 1474 that we date the first extant case in which a chancellor made a decree on his own authority without the council, and it is certainly after that date that the independent equitable jurisdiction of the chancery was fully exploited. That result was due to developments going back earlier than the Yorkist period, but the forces increased in impetus after 1460. The failure of the common law to meet new needs came out clearly as fifteenth-century commercial enterprise increased the complexity of business relationships. Trade implied contracts, ties between native merchants and aliens, disputed agreements needing legal decisions. The common law did not always provide remedies; when it did they could only be arrived at through involved technique and slow process. Some more elastic method of settling such questions was needed. It was found in the chancellor. The exercise of his discretion in settling disputes was not unquestioned by the common lawyers, and the Year Books contain opinions which shew they were in fighting mood. But the chancellor's conscience was too useful a device to be checked by academic protests, and the growth of this new court is one of the most significant features of the late Middle Ages.

In a similar way earlier ideas combined to give the council sitting in the star chamber importance in criminal cases when the common law courts failed to do justice. Activity here was checked because of the council's unreliability when such matters had to be decided; but the fact that such process was possible was important. The court of Star Chamber of the early Tudor period cannot be understood unless it is linked to ideas current in the Yorkist period.

In examining other elements in the system of government there is something to be said for another glance at the ideas of Fortescue. Those thoughts of his prophetic of Tudor policy have become a little hackneyed, and the maxims in his writings which seventeenth-century writers were to use have been often noted. But enough is not always made of the medieval cast of his thought. And that, rather than the novelties, is of greatest value, for it shews us that the political and constitutional thought of his day had not yet fully emerged from the Middle Ages.

For Fortescue, the fundamentals of English politics lay in the special quality of the kingship. Elsewhere there might be the rule of kings, but it was *dominium regale*, the rule of one who makes the law. In England it was *dominium politicum et regale* whereby the king rules with laws to which his subjects have assented. It is doubtful whether Fortescue meant more than a concept of a king under the law, and the emphasis he is making is not intended to exalt parliament. His king has two duties: to defend his people from external foes, and to do justice. In the most famous of his works Fortescue applied his ideas to the English system. The Lancastrians had failed because they were weak; was it possible to prevent a recurrence of the tragedy? It is unfortunate that the dating of this work should have to depend upon the interpretation of a passage in one manuscript, for we are left to guess whether it was written as a programme of reform for Henry VI in 1470, or for Edward IV after his return, though the presumption is in favour of the latter theory. In any case, the hope of connecting it with the Yorkist system of government is slender; but its ideas suggest a true line of approach.

He saw the root of the matter in the poverty of the Crown. A poor king will have to borrow; creditors will be usurers, and if unpaid, men with a grievance. Payments have to be made by the extravagant method of assignments on revenues, and the king's needs may tempt him to adopt "exquisite" means of screwing money from his subjects. His heavy expenses demand a large income, and if it is not forthcoming, there is a danger that his subjects may desert him for a richer man. Subjects richer than he are a menace. So Fortescue concentrates on means for increasing royal revenue: by acts of resumption of Crown lands, by stern refusals to alienate any royal demesne. The overmighty subject must be curbed by preventing the accumulation of large estates under one man, by hindering marriage alliances between great families, by the seizure of lands for treason, by heavy fines for permission to alienate estates. Against these great subjects, too, is aimed his reform of the council. The great lords have been so busy looking after their own affairs, even in the council, that they have had no time to spare for the king's business, and their relationships with retainers militated against the preservation of secrecy in matters of State. Fortescue's council would consist of twelve clerics and twelve laymen, sworn of the council to serve during pleasure, but not to be dismissed save by a majority vote, and bound to none save the king. There would be an afforcement of four spiritual and temporal lords appointed yearly, and the office holders, the chancellor, treasurer, privy seal, and smaller men would also be members. Councillors would be paid, there would be a president—probably the chancellor—and the council would have a register. This scheme had something in common with the Yorkist council.

Despite generalisations that absence of council records for this period implies absence of conciliar activity, there are reasons for suggesting that the subject will bear closer investigation. In chancery warrants, signed bills, petitions, chancery rolls, teller's rolls, year books, the archives of the Hanse towns, and other sources there is a quantity of scattered material. Brought together, it suggests an impression of a council working less sporadically than has been supposed, in matters of diplomacy, trade, administration, domestic policy, and judicial business. To some extent the personnel seems to fit Fortescue's proposals. Under Edward and Richard the tendency seems to have been for a small group of ecclesiastics, clerks, and officials, with a sprinkling of nobles attached to the king by their official posts, to form the nucleus of the council at Westminster. Apparently, here as elsewhere, Henry VII worked out a policy not of revolutionary innovation, but of development to a logical conclusion of the ideas and institutions of his immediate predecessors. Another feature should be noticed. There is some evidence of a division of the council, with a group at Westminster and another with the king. Here, too, was an idea to be more fully utilised by the next dynasty. There is work still to be done, but when the Yorkist period is probed for signs of conciliar activity, some threads will be found that make connexion with the conciliar development so emphatically associated with Tudor rule. It will not be ignored, for instance, that a Council of the Marches of Wales—even though it was not made a permanent institution until the reign of Henry VII—certainly originated under Edward IV; that it was Richard III who, improving on Edward's ideas, organised the Council of the North; and that if the title of the Court of Requests was only evolved after Henry VII and Henry VIII had dealt for some years with "poor men's complaints," there was in Richard III's reign a special clerk of the council whose duty it was to deal with such cases. Faint origins, it is true; but their existence strengthens the impression that in constitutional matters the Yorkist period was not without experiments. The merit of the early Tudors lay in the skill with which they worked out the details.

What Fortescue thought of parliament is suggested by the care with which he kept his council free from its control. What the Yorkist kings made of it is best read in its history. In a reign of twenty-two years Edward IV called seven parliaments, but as the writs for one were recalled, only six actually met. At the "re-adeption" Henry VI issued writs for a parliament. It seems to have assembled, but there is no official record of its proceedings. Richard III summoned one parliament. Kings whose justification lay in legitimist doctrines could not, in the nature of things, be expected to champion parliamentary authority; but they found the institution useful for passing acts of attainder against their enemies, and they could not afford to ignore it as long as they needed money. It is noteworthy that after 1475, when in receipt of his French pension, Edward called only two parliaments, one in 1478, almost exclusively busied with Clarence's attainder, and another in 1483 when the Scottish war made finance a pressing question.

Yorkist parliamentary history has yet to be written, and there are formidable difficulties in the way, unless materials now missing are brought to light. But some work has been done which shews there are discoveries possible. They are worth mention if only to suggest the lines on which fresh investigation is likely to run, and what modification of older views such work is likely to produce.

Of first interest is the composition and personnel of parliament in those years. For the lords this is not difficult. A clear decline in numerica strength indicates the reaction of politics upon the nobility. In 1454—

the last parliament before the outbreak of war—the number summoned was 53. In 1461 the total was 45. In 1485 only 29 came to Henry VII's first parliament. The decrease was only temporary, but it suggests the effects of deaths, attainders, and non-attendance during the period of party strife. It is, however, the representation of the commons which attracts greatest attention, and presents most difficulty. For here, unfortunately, we have full returns for only three parliaments, so that generalisations must necessarily be tentative. Some striking facts, however, can be perceived. Shire representation remained constant at 72, but it is not easy to learn much about the members chosen. More can be said of the boroughs. The highest number making returns under Henry VI was 96 in the parliament of 1453; the lowest being 77 in that of 1425; while the average was 87. For Edward's parliaments the figures were about 96 to the parliament of 1467, 97 to that of 1472, and 101 to that of 1478. Study of the personnel also suggests that something was happening to make parliament less insignificant than some writers have been prepared to admit. Borough representation changed its character. It was no longer the monopoly of merchant burgesses. Others competed with them. The younger sons of great families, professional men, civil servants, and lawyers, the smaller gentry retained by great nobles, were stepping into their places. Further, the nobility were manipulating elections. The Duke of Norfolk, for example, seems to have controlled elections at Lewes, Shoreham, Bramber, Reigate, Gatton, Horsham, and probably exerted authority in some Suffolk elections as well. Other cases shew that he was not exceptional. Now, the full meaning of this will only be clear when more is known of the part parliament was playing in political life. But it seems safe to conclude that parliamentary representation was seen to have advantages, it may have been because of the dynastic struggle, it may have been because of the opportunities it offered of a political career. In any case, the history of the Yorkist parliaments does not suggest that they fostered any sturdy opposition to royal policy. Perhaps when more is known of their activities we shall learn that already the Crown had found the way to control parliament in its own interests, and for its own purposes.

Such is, indeed, suggested by other known facts. Edward IV undoubtedly interested himself in elections, and—it has been suggested—controlled the commons through their Speakers. Certainly in this period that official, accidentally or by design, can usually be shewn to have court connexions, and that must have had some weight. Possibly these facts help to explain a phenomenon recently emphasised which suggests a profitable field of study. Investigating the forms and procedure of parliament in the late Middle Ages, a recent study has drawn attention to some striking tendencies[1]. Most notable is the suggestion that under Edward IV and Richard III some changes occurred in the method of

---

[1] H. L. Gray, *The Influence of the Commons on Early Legislation* (Harvard Hist. Ser. xxxiv, 1932).

initiating legislation. After 1465, instead of the commons taking the lead, the government began to do so. It began with the framing of acts of resumption, but the process was extended until by the time of Richard III official activity in legislation was so marked as to deserve the epithet "epoch-making." Now the full meaning of this will only be caught when it can be linked more closely to the personnel of these parliaments, for we must see the reactions of party divisions. But if this theory has any meaning it most assuredly is that earlier views on the nature and function of parliament in the Yorkist period need revision.

Coupled with this subject is another of equal importance. Whatever has been said in disparagement of parliament during this period, there has been no question of its participation in financial matters. But in relation to Edward IV the non-parliamentary financial activities of that king have usually excited more interest than his dealings with parliament. Even here, however, attention to detail suggests subtleties. Between Edward's parliaments and his own financial policy there is an interesting connexion. The financial event of 1474–75, usually regarded as the peak of Edward's arbitrary policy of raising money without parliamentary sanction, must be set in perspective with parliament in the background. There can be no question that between November 1474 and March 1475 there was exacted from wealthy subjects a new form of tax on income and property. Contemporary sources describe how Edward personally interviewed likely subjects to make them promise payments. The official accounts shew that such "gifts" were described as "benevolencia," and that the proceeds amounted to a considerable sum. But the proceedings, while novel, were not entirely without precedent. The parliament of 1472, to which Edward announced his intention of recovering the lands in France, made a grant of 13,000 archers for a year. The money produced by a tax on lands, tenements, rents, and annuities was insufficient; so a fresh expedient was devised, which fell most heavily on those not seriously touched by this taxation. This new tax was not collected, but it probably inspired Edward's benevolence. This was to be a tax to yield about two-thirds of a fifteenth and tenth, and was to be paid by those who would otherwise escape taxation. The incidence of the benevolence was largely on the south-eastern counties—London alone contributed 28 % of the whole—and these parts were precisely those where trade and industry flourished. It would appear then that Edward's benevolence may fairly be regarded as one of a series of attempts to reform an antiquated system of taxation, and that it was designed to include those who were growing rich in trade and industry, but who escaped equitable taxation under the old forms of assessment. In 1484 Richard's parliament, in a statute whose preamble grossly exaggerated the effects of this taxation, abolished benevolences. But a year later, when Richard's generosity to those who had helped him had practically depleted the resources left by Edward IV, he was compelled to use a very similar expedient. True, he kept strictly to the letter of his law, by calling such contributions loans and giving pledges of repayment; but in effect there was little difference. The failure to keep the spirit of his own legislation may have reacted on his popularity.

Yet another problem connected with parliament cannot, in the present state of our knowledge, be solved. It has to do with the content of legislation. In this period the commons concerned themselves largely with matters economic, and statutes deal with a variety of subjects, prohibitions from using foreign shipping, regulation of the staple for wool, orders for the bringing of bullion to England, acts to encourage the home manufacture of cloth, regulations for the silk industry, limitations on the import of wheat, sumptuary legislation, and similar measures. Unwin's destructive criticism of attempts to read into Edward III's legislation an economic policy makes it hazardous to insinuate that these Yorkist measures were framed in the interests of an economic nationalism. But the consistency of parliamentary activity, and stray examples which have come down to us indicative of English opinions suggest that a case might well be made out for the existence of such ideas.

In one sphere the Yorkist kings certainly expressed self-sufficient, independent, not to say nationalist ideas, and that was in their relations with the Church. In 1461 the chances were against this. For if the papal legate Coppini had been as great as he thought he was, there would have been considerable ecclesiastical activity in English politics. The Lancastrians ruined his reputation at Rome, and Edward soon shewed he had no intention of allowing ecclesiastical interference with his plans. His relations with the Papacy were friendly but independent. Pius II in 1464 asked for assistance against the Turks, and when the English clergy might have granted a tenth, Edward refused, authorising a subsidy of sixpence in the pound provided the money were sent through his hands. Much of it seems to have remained there. With Paul II his relations were not happy, since that pontiff dabbled in Warwick's schemes, but in 1482 Pope Sixtus IV sent Edward the sword and cap of maintenance. Richard III's views coincided with his brother's, and although Innocent VIII was not pleased with news of sequestration of ecclesiastical property and violation of church privileges, on the whole there is not much to be said of the king's relations with Rome.

With the Church in England the Yorkists cultivated close relations, and the support given to the party in 1461 by the leaders of the Church was maintained fairly consistently. Main interest in ecclesiastical history— as in so many other matters—is to be found in the curious mixture of new and old ideas, problems, and institutions from the clash of which, in the fulness of time, was to spring that grave issue of State *versus* Church that dominates the Tudor period. Of the old problems, the most important are the existence of the Church as a privileged institution whose immunities challenged the secular power; and the signs that ecclesiastical institutions were failing to maintain the standards of an earlier age. The first of these questions means primarily the continued existence of benefit of clergy and the institution of sanctuary. The second is largely concerned with the state of the monasteries. Of the new, the most significant is the existence of opinion hostile to the doctrinal teaching of the Church, and attacks upon its members for their failure to meet the needs of the age. Of all these cross currents there are indications, but Yorkist policy lacked direction and there is little to shew that the real nature of the problems was grasped. In the matter of ecclesiastical immunity, for example, Edward IV, by a charter of 2 November 1462, granted complete exemption from all lay jurisdiction in cases of felony, rape, treason, and trespass committed by clergy. How far such a grant was realised is difficult to discover. The Church, under Edward and Richard, certainly complained that it was not. On the other hand, legal records and Henry VII's act against benefit of clergy suggest that the privilege was grossly abused, and was one of the contributory causes of the criticisms levelled against the Church. And the abuse of sanctuary was such as to make that institution one of the first to be attacked when the Tudors began their onslaught on ecclesiastical immunities.

The state of the Church is a more difficult question. That there were grave abuses is certain, and some of the visitations, evidence from legal records, and other sources suggest that some of the clergy were no better than they should have been and often not as good. But the lack of sufficient evidence makes it hard to tell how far degeneration had set in. The attacks on Church teaching emphasise again the Yorkist period as one of continuity. Edward IV was a zealous opponent of new doctrines and his reign supplies several examples of punishment, the cases of James Wyllys (1462), William Balowe (1467), and John Goose (1474) being the best known. They shew that teachings derived from Wyclif and Pecock were doing their work; but we are dealing with a thin stream. Interest lies not in the strength of the movement but in the fact that it exists. Slowly, as we move on towards the sixteenth century, heretical opinion gathers force; the Yorkist contribution was important because it maintained continuity.

Here this survey of Yorkist England may well end. It is wisdom not to be dogmatic about a quarter of a century in which there was so much life, but not so much self-assurance or conviction. Men hardly knew whither they were going, and to try to suggest the opposite is to lose the really essential quality of the period. If it had been otherwise, if there had been some deep, invigorating purpose to give direction to their energies, these Yorkist monarchs would have left a more abiding influence for good or ill upon the national development. As it was, they failed. They lacked something. It was not courage, nor opportunity, nor ability. The difference between them and their Tudor successors—and it was a vital difference—was that the latter knew what they wanted to do, and did it. Because of this the new dynasty ruled over a new England.

CHAPTER XIII

IRELAND, 1315-c. 1485

ROBERT BRUCE followed up his victory at Bannockburn, not only by directing raids into the northern counties of England, but also by organising an invasion of Ireland under the leadership of his brother Edward. Ireland had formed an important recruiting ground for previous campaigns against Scotland, and a diversion there would hamper the English king and prevent him from obtaining further aid from that quarter. Moreover it is probable that Donnell O'Neill, King of Tirowen, was already in correspondence with Bruce and had promised him assistance, though the *Remonstrance of the Irish to Pope John XXII*, sometimes cited as proof of this correspondence, was not written until at least two years later.

On 26 May 1315 Edward Bruce landed at Larne Haven with about 6000 men. With him came Thomas Randolph, Earl of Moray, who had played a leading part at Bannockburn, and a number of knights. Having overcome the opposition of the local lords and left a force to besiege Carrickfergus, the Scots, accompanied by Donnell O'Neill, marched southward, plundering many a prosperous homestead on the way. On 29 June they reached Dundalk, where they took the town and plundered and burned the neighbouring country. About 22 July Edmund Butler, the justiciar, with the feudal host of Munster and Leinster, and Richard de Burgh, Earl of Ulster, with levies from Connaught, including an Irish force under Felim O'Conor, King of Connaught, assembled together in the plains of Louth. Bruce, however, avoided a regular battle and began to retreat northwards through Irish territories west of the earl's domains. The earl, leaving the justiciar to guard Leinster, undertook to deal with Bruce, whom he followed northwards, but through his own territory east of Lough Neagh. Thus Bruce reached the district between the Bann and Lough Foyle and broke down the bridge at Coleraine before the earl arrived there. While the two armies were at opposite sides of the river Bann, Bruce secretly offered Felim undivided power in Connaught if he would desert the earl, and at the same time encouraged his rival, Rory O'Conor, to attack the English in Connaught. Felim accordingly withdrew with his forces, only to find himself supplanted in Connaught by his rival. The earl, seeing himself deserted by Felim, moved a little southwards towards his base at the town of Connor. Bruce then crossed the Bann in boats and surprised and completely routed the earl in a battle near Connor on 10 September. William de Burgh, the earl's cousin, was taken prisoner, and the earl retreated to Connaught where sheer anarchy prevailed. This was Bruce's first important victory. It left Ulster at his mercy, and it was the signal for risings of the Irish in Connaught and West Meath.

On 13 November Bruce, having received some reinforcements, marched south again into Meath. Here at Kells he defeated Roger Mortimer, lord of Trim, who had assembled a large but untrustworthy force. Bruce made no attempt against the strong castle of Trim, but burned Kells and many places in the western half of the lordship of Meath. Early in 1316 he passed through Irish Offaly to the FitzGerald districts about Rathangan and Kildare. Here about the upper waters of the Barrow in Clanmalier must have occurred the incident, misplaced by Archdeacon Barbour, when O'Dempsy, chieftain of that district, tried to drown Bruce's army by turning the river into his camp. Bruce went south as far as Castledermot, plundering and destroying everything in his course, and meeting with little opposition until on 26 January, near Ardscull, he encountered a formidable force under Edmund Butler, John FitzThomas of Offaly, and Arnold le Poer, seneschal of Kilkenny. What happened is obscure. Discord, it is said, arose among the commanders and they dispersed in confusion leaving the field to the Scots. Thus the third attempt to defeat the invaders failed. There was no "unity of command." A more formidable foe to the Scots was the widespread famine which prevailed owing to the failure of the harvest of 1315. In the third week of February 1316 Bruce led back his forces, thinned and weakened by hunger, to his camp in Ulster.

Some sporadic risings of the Leinster clans were suppressed by the justiciar, and in Connaught Felim O'Conor, assisted by Richard de Bermingham of Athenry, succeeded in recovering his throne from his rival. Afterwards, however, he made a great combination of the Irish with the object of expelling the English from the province, but at Athenry on 10 August he was killed and his army cut to pieces by the English under William de Burgh (who had been released from Scotland) and Richard de Bermingham. The O'Conors never recovered their former power.

Edward Bruce did not again in this year venture out of Ulster, where he was crowned King of Ireland early in May, but though some opposition was made to him there by the local lords, and it was not until September that the heroic defenders of Carrickfergus were starved out, no combined effort was made to expel him. About Christmas King Robert Bruce himself joined him with reinforcements, and about 13 February 1317 the two brothers appeared without warning at Slane in Meath. The Earl of Ulster tried unsuccessfully to cut off their rear-guard by an ambuscade, but his forces were dispersed and he fled to Dublin. The citizens, now thoroughly alarmed, imprisoned the earl whom they suspected (but seemingly without valid grounds) of complicity with Bruce, hastily strengthened their walls, and fired the suburbs. Bruce, seeing their determination and not being prepared for a lengthened siege, came no nearer than Castleknock, and the campaign, like that of the previous winter, resolved itself into an uninterrupted progress of devastation. The Scots marched through County Kildare and across County Kilkenny and the Butler territory in Ormond to the confines of Limerick, the English magnates hanging about their rear, but not staying their course. Presumably Bruce expected the Irish of the west to rise in his support, but the battle of Athenry had crushed the Gaelic clans. When about 11 April intelligence was received of the landing of Roger Mortimer with a force from England, the Scots, weakened once more by hunger and hardship, slipped back to Ulster, and on 22 May King Robert, seeing that nothing more could be done, returned to Scotland. These two winter campaigns, though they wrought incalculable damage to Ireland, so far from establishing Edward Bruce on his throne resulted for the Scots in the wasting of two armies. There was no Bannockburn in Ireland. Not a single important town or castle except in Ulster was taken and held, and the Irish, though they rose sporadically to plunder their neighbours, were only half-hearted in supporting Bruce. Finally, at the close of the year, Pope John XXII pronounced excommunication against the invaders and all who supported them.

Meanwhile Mortimer released the Earl of Ulster, outlawed the de Lacys who had assisted the invaders, and forced the border clans into submission, but made no attempt to recover Ulster. It was not, however, until October 1318 that Edward Bruce once more came south, with apparently a smaller Scottish force than before but attended by an unwieldy body of Irishry and some disaffected Englishry including the outlawed Lacys. He took up a position on the slopes of the hill of Faughard a little north of Dundalk, and here on 14 October he was opposed by John de Bermingham of Tethmoy at the head of a force composed of the local levies of the neighbouring counties and some of the townsmen of Drogheda. Disregarding the advice of his knights to await some expected reinforcements, and in spite of the frank warning of the Irish that they would not "stand in plane mellé," Bruce in his "outrageous succudry" determined to fight that day. The Scots, apart from their Irish followers, were probably outnumbered by their opponents and appear to have been overpowered by a rush of footmen. Edward Bruce and all who stood their ground were slain, while the remnant protected by the Irish fled. Thus ended the Scottish invasion to the general relief of both Anglo-Irish and Gael. "No better deed," says the Irish annalist, "for the men of all Erin was performed since the beginning of the world than this deed, for theft and famine and destruction of men occurred throughout Erin during his time for the space of three years and a half."

The Scottish invasion marks the beginning of the ebb of English influence in Ireland, but its immediate effects were a general impoverishment, a weakening of the moral fibre of the settlers, and a growing turbulence no longer confined to the Irish. Except in Thomond, where in May 1318 Richard de Clare was killed and English supremacy received its death-blow, there was little immediate change in the relative positions of the two races, but both Irish chieftains and English lords were everywhere weakened and began to lose control over their subordinates. The conflicts of the period between the court and the baronial parties in England had also their echo in the feuds that arose in Ireland between the Geraldines, Butlers, and Berminghams on the one side, and le Poers and de Burghs on the other. As a means of keeping the peace it was ordained in 1324 that "every chieftain of great lineage should chastise the felons of his own family" and their adherents, and this inept plan was persisted in though the magnates always preferred to chastise each other's felons. In the end, under the Mortimer régime, Arnold le Poer was left to die in prison (whither he was flung on a trumped up charge of heresy), while in 1328 Maurice FitzThomas was created Earl of Desmond and in the following year James Butler was made Earl of Ormonde.

An example of the lengths to which the spirit of insubordination led the Anglo-Irish may be seen in the murder of John de Bermingham, the victor at Faughard, who had been created Earl of Louth in recognition of his services. On 10 June 1329 he and a large number of his relatives and dependents were massacred by members of the oldest families in the county, and in the view of contemporaries their motive was their unwillingness "that he should reign over them." But a more fateful snapping of the feudal tie was the murder of William de Burgh, the young Earl of Ulster. When Earl Richard died in 1326 his vast domains passed to his grandson, William, then in his fourteenth year. In 1331, when Edward III was for the first time his own master, he appointed Anthony de Lucy, already noted for his severity, as justiciar and the young Earl of Ulster as king's lieutenant, and at the same time issued a mandate to the justiciar to resume all grants of lands and liberties made since the king's accession. These were in fact grants made under the influence of the late Roger Mortimer, and the principal person affected would seem to have been the Earl of Desmond. The justiciar imprisoned Desmond and also William de Bermingham, brother of the late Earl of Louth. William was a turbulent baron and had assisted the Earl of Desmond in his feud against the Poers and de Burghs, and in July 1332 the justiciar caused him to be hanged. This unwonted act of severity caused a great stir, and in November De Lucy was superseded by John Darcy. Desmond was released on mainprise, and a milder regime was instituted. Meantime, in November 1331 the Earl of Ulster, in pursuance of the ordinance to chastise wrongdoers of his lineage, imprisoned his kinsman Walter, son of William de Burgh, who had acted in a very high-handed manner against Turlough O'Conor, King of Connaught, and, like his father before him, was said to have been aiming at the sovereignty there. In the course of the year 1332 he died in the earl's prison, and vengeance for his death is said to have been the motive for the murder of the earl. Certain it is that on 6 June 1333 the earl was treacherously killed near Carrickfergus by some of his Ulster feudatories. He is described as a man *subtilissimi ingenii, reipublicae et pacis amator*, and he received the full confidence of the king, but it is clear that his attempt to control the aggressive action of his kinsmen in Connaught was deeply resented.

Though it does not appear that the De Burghs of Connaught were directly implicated in the earl's death, they certainly took advantage of it for their own ends, but their action was neither so sudden nor so dramatic as generally represented by modern writers. The main facts seem to have been shortly as follows: The custody of the Connaught lands during the minority of the earl's daughter and heiress Elizabeth was given to Edmund de Burgh called 'the earl's son' (*i.e.* son of Earl Richard), but differences soon arose between him and another Edmund de Burgh, called "Albanach," brother of the late Walter de Burgh. For two generations this last-mentioned branch of the family had exercised virtual control in Connaught, and a state of war soon existed between the two Edmunds. Finally in 1338 Edmund "the earl's son" was taken prisoner by Edmund Albanach, and while the Archbishop of Tuam was trying to reconcile the kinsmen, the earl's son was drowned in Lough Mask by the Stauntons. Edmund Albanach could not hope to escape liability, and he fled to the Scottish Isles. The King of England, however, was too much engaged with his designs on the French crown to exert his authority in Connaught; so he granted Edmund and his brother Raymond "sufferance" for two years, and then on 10 April 1340, apparently as a reward for their obtaining troops for him against France, he pardoned them for the death of Earl Richard's son. This practically amounted to the abandonment of the rights of his ward, and indeed resulted in the extinguishment of the authority (never very great) of the Crown in Connaught. There was, however, no renunciation by the De Burghs of their allegiance, nor any immediate adoption of Irish customs. After this the supremacy of Edmund Albanach was recognised by most of the English settlers in Mayo and Sligo, and from time to time he fought to establish his supremacy over Clanrickard (Galway) also. He was called by the Irish "Mac William," and the patronymic became a title, but it was not until after his death in 1375 that there were two recognised Mac Williams, viz. the Mac William *Lochtar* (the Lower) in Mayo, held by his descendants, and the Mac William *Uachtar* (the Upper) in Clanrickard, held by the descendants of his brother William or Ulick, while the descendants of Edmund the earl's son had to content themselves as lords of Clanwilliam in Counties Limerick and Tipperary.

In the earl's domains in Eastern Ulster great changes also took place, but not immediately. There were dynastic disputes in Tyrone between the descendants of Donnell O'Neill, who died in 1325, and the descendants of Hugh Boy (Aedh Buidhe) O'Neill. The latter, called the Clannaboy O'Neills (Clann Aedha Buidhe), were eventually driven out of Tyrone and settled in the Irish districts east of Lough Neagh and the Upper Bann.

In 1354 they were supported by the English against the O'Neills of Tyrone, but about the year 1360 they began to encroach upon the English, who were eventually confined to the littoral of Counties Down and Antrim.

In Leinster too the area of English rule was beginning to shrink. Lysagh O'More, who died in 1342, took Mortimer's castle of Dunamase, and henceforth the O'Mores practically dominated the district of Leix up to the time of the Protector Somerset. The clans about the fringes of the Wicklow mountains became more turbulent and began to combine in their attacks on the Anglo-Irish of the plains. To meet these the plan was adopted of employing a Mac Murrough to control the rest. In the Great Roll of the Exchequer of Ireland for 1334 there is entry of a payment to Donnell son of Art Mac Murrough for his good service in fighting against O'Tooles and O'Byrnes, rebels to the king, and from a subsequent entry for 1336 it appears that by an agreement with Roger Outlaw, deputy of John Darcy, an annual payment of 80 marks was to be paid to the said Donnell "for expediting certain business of the king[1]." This appears to be the earliest record of that annual payment to Mac Murrough which eventually became a "black rent" exacted under threats.

In 1341 the king, presumably attributing the decreased revenue of Ireland and the ill-success of the Irish government to the corruption and self-seeking of Anglo-Irish officials, ordered John Darcy, the justiciar, to remove "all officers beneficed, married, and estated in Ireland and having nothing in England," and to substitute "other fit Englishmen having lands and benefices in England," and at the same time ordained the resumption of all Crown grants made by himself or his father. The former measure was the beginning of that distinction between "English by blood" and "English by birth" which naturally incensed the older settlers, and both it and the high-handed resumption of Crown grants caused widespread disaffection amongst them. Consequently, when John Morris, Darcy's deputy, summoned a parliament to meet at Dublin in October, the disaffected Anglo-Irish did not attend, but headed by the Earl of Desmond met at Kilkenny and drew up a long petition to the king in French under twenty-seven heads setting forth in moderate language the evil state of the country, the causes of the reduced revenue, and the grievances, including the said resumption of grants, under which the loyal inhabitants suffered. The king made conciliatory replies and, with reference to the resumed lands, ordered that they should be delivered to the owners on giving security to restore them to the king if the grants should be found on enquiry to be rightfully revocable. On the strength of this concession the king urged the Irish lords to bring him troops for his intended expedition to Brittany.

But some of "the old English" were not conciliated. This was apparent when Ralph d'Ufford arrived as justiciar on 13 July 1344, accompanied

[1] Compare the entry in the roll misplaced in the printed *Calendar of Patent and Close Rolls (Ireland)* as 10 Edward II, p. 20, No. 26. The roll clearly belongs to 10 Edward III.

by his wife, Maud of Lancaster, widow of the murdered Earl of Ulster. In the following February the Earl of Desmond tried to convene another irregular assembly of the notables at Callan in County Kilkenny. This was prohibited and failed, but when the justiciar summoned a parliament in July, the earl held aloof. Thereupon the justiciar marched into Munster, took Desmond's castles at Askeaton and Castle-Island, hanged after trial three of his knights who defended them, and confiscated his lands and those of some of his former mainpernors. He also entrapped and imprisoned the Earl of Kildare. Ralph d'Ufford is given a black character by the Anglo-Irish annalists, but he died in office on 9 April 1346, and a milder regime followed. Kildare was released, and in May 1347 he joined the king with a contingent at the siege of Calais. Desmond also went to England under the king's protection and was eventually restored to favour.

In the winter of 1348–9 the Black Death reached Ireland and many fell victims to it. As in England it resulted in a great scarcity of labour, decay of learning, and a further relaxation of the bonds of society. The Statute of Labourers, already passed in England, was ordered to be enforced in Ireland. Its objects were to compel labourers to work at the rate of wages accustomed in 1346 and to secure that victuals should be sold at reasonable prices. But economic laws cannot be permanently evaded by legislative devices, and in spite of the statute labourers were not forthcoming except at wages which rendered landlord cultivation no longer profitable. Owing, too, to the frequent raids and consequent insecurity, many freeholders gave up the struggle and migrated to England, and the great agricultural prosperity which had followed the introduction of the manorial system into Ireland was at an end.

In 1358 the situation in Leinster became alarming. Art, son of Murtough Kavanagh, who, it appears, had been "recently created Mac Murrough by the justiciar and Council," and had been in receipt of payment for service against the rebels of Leinster[1], now turned against the king and headed the rebels. Subsidies were hastily raised and defensive measures taken, and in the summer of 1359 expeditions were made under James, second Earl of Ormonde, against Mac Murrough and "Obryn"[2]. (This was seemingly the occasion of the capture by the O'Byrnes of Henry Cristall, who in 1395 gave to Froissart an account of the expedition of Richard II in that year.) About this time the castle of Ferns was finally lost and with it all English control over the northern part of County Wexford. In March 1361 the king announced that he was sending his son Lionel to Ireland, where he declared his dominions were in danger of being totally lost if his subjects there were not immediately succoured.

Lionel, who had been created Earl of Ulster and given in marriage Elizabeth, daughter and heiress of the last earl, landed at Dublin on 15 September with a goodly retinue. Actual records concerning his

[1] Great Roll of the Exchequer (London) $\frac{242}{}$, for 1356–8.
[2] *Calendar Close Rolls, Ireland*, 32 and 33 Ed. III, pp. 68 and 77.

military achievements are few. Art Mac Murrough, King of Leinster, and Donnell Reagh, his expectant successor, were captured by him—it is said by treachery—and died in prison. He had in his pay some of the Kavanaghs and even Sheeda (*Sioda*) Mac Conmara of Thomond[1]. Niall O'Neill also submitted to him[2]. There appears to have been a comparative respite from Irish raids in his time, and it was thought safe to transfer the sittings of the Exchequer and Common Pleas to Carlow.

But the viceroyalty of Lionel, now Duke of Clarence, is chiefly remembered for the Statute of Kilkenny passed in 1366. This act has been much misrepresented. Its aims were two-fold: (1) to preserve the allegiance of the dwindling number of loyal subjects of the Crown in Ireland and keep them from falling, as others of English descent had already done, into the turbulent ways of the Irish and their lower plane of civilisation; (2) to remove as far as seemed possible the occasions of conflict between the two races and of dissension among the English themselves. The clause which has especially been stigmatised prohibited all alliances by marriage, gossipred, fostering of children, etc. between English and Irish. This provision was not new. A similar clause appears in an act of 1351 and again in an ordinance of 1358, where the reason is given that through such alliances, "by warnings and espials on both sides of the Marches, infinite destructions and other evils have hitherto happened" and expeditions in war and peace have been impeded. There were other provisions with the same object: such as enjoining in English districts the use of the English language, and prohibiting, as between Englishmen, the adoption of the Brehon law and the making of any difference between English born in Ireland and those born in England. Such attempts to preserve the loyal remnant from becoming merged among the wild Irishry were indeed a poor substitute for the bolder policy of enforcing order and even-handed justice over the whole of Ireland, but they were presumably all that the statesmen of the period were prepared to undertake. These clauses were moreover welcomed by the loyal inhabitants, were often re-enacted, and probably did help to keep in being some of the higher culture, the political organisation, and the wider outlook which had been inherited from England.

In the twenty-eight years that elapsed from the departure of the Duke of Clarence to the arrival of King Richard II in person there were twenty-four changes in the office of chief governor. It was difficult to get anyone to accept the thankless task of trying without adequate resources to defend the sorely harassed land. The king chafed at being called upon to pay for defending territories in Ireland, from which on the contrary he sought subsidies for his foreign wars, while on the other hand the Anglo-Irish pleaded inability to grant subsidies for either purpose. Recourse was again had to paying pensions to Irish chieftains to induce

---

[1] Great Roll of the Exchequer (London), aᵒ 38 Ed. III (1364).
[2] *Calendar of the Register of Archbishop Sweteman*, p. 283.

them to keep the peace. Thus in the last year of the reign of Edward III Art, son of Dermot Mac Murrough, of Okinselagh (North Wexford) undertook for himself and his following that they would fight on the king's side against the insurgent Irish of Leinster, he receiving 40 marks for the ensuing year, and about the same time "Art Kavanagh [*i.e.* Art Og, son of the Art executed by Lionel], who pretended to be chief of the Irish of Leinster," claimed 80 marks a year from the king as his fee, and having assembled a great number of Irishmen committed divers outrages in Leinster and would not come to peace unless paid that sum. Whereupon the justiciar, James, second Earl of Ormonde, was authorised to retain Art for one year at that rate. But 'buying off the Goths' has always proved a policy of the worst example, and in the following year Murrough O'Brien of Thomond came into Leinster with a great force threatening devastation, and a parliament at Castledermot was obliged to raise a subsidy of 100 marks to stay his hand. This was somewhat exceptional, but this Art Kavanagh, commonly called "Mac Murrough," during his long chieftainship of forty-two years, broke out again and again, probably because his retaining fee was not regularly paid, and in his time the greater part of the County Carlow, which had been dominated by Raymond le Gros and his feudatories and successors since the twelfth century, was lost to the English. Other border Irish chiefs, too, soon followed Art's example.

There were moments when the tide of the Irish resurgence was stayed. In May 1380 Edmund Mortimer, who had married Philippa, daughter and heiress of Lionel, Duke of Clarence, landed in Ireland as King's Lieutenant. "The nobles of the Gael," we are told, "came into his house headed by [Niall Og] the heir of the King of Ireland, Niall O'Neill," but when Mortimer took prisoner Art McGuiness (who had defeated the English and slain their ally O'Hanlon earlier in the year, and had slain Mortimer's seneschal, James de la Hyde, in 1375[1]) the Gael held aloof from him. He rebuilt the bridge at Coleraine and advanced far into Tyrone. He also recovered and fortified the castle of Athlone, and during his brief term of office Ireland enjoyed comparative peace, but he died unexpectedly at Cork on 26 December 1381. After Mortimer's death the Irish again became aggressive. O'Brien was attempting to make "a general conquest" of the south-west, and O'Neill was plundering and burning English towns in the north-east, while in Connaught the insecurity that followed on the decay of English government reduced both English and Irish to nearly the same level of disorder and consequent poverty. In 1385 the Sil Murray clans became permanently divided into two bodies under O'Conor Donn and O'Conor Roe respectively, and were often at variance with one another, while the English, already grouped under the two Mac Williams, often joined in the fray and in general on opposite sides. In this year the Irish

---

[1] See *Chartularies, St Mary's Abbey*, Vol. II, p. 283; and compare the *Four Masters* a° 1375, where the editor, followed by other writers, misunderstands the name.

parliament besought the king to visit Ireland in person to save the land which was in peril of being in great part lost, but the young king had too many troubles to contend with both at home and abroad to think of complying at the time, and though John Stanley in 1390 obtained the submission of O'Neill, there was no marked improvement in the state of Ireland until at length, on 2 October 1394, the English king landed at Waterford with a large army.

Richard II met with no serious opposition except at first from Art Mac Murrough, as he is now usually called. This formidable chieftain, who claimed to be King of Leinster, had a new grievance. In 1391 the lands of his wife, Elizabeth Calf, heiress of Sir Robert Calf of Norragh in County Kildare, were forfeited, not because (as often stated) she had married an Irishman, but because her husband "was one of the principal enemies of the king[1]." According to the *Four Masters* in 1394, but probably before the king's arrival, Art burned New Ross which had been the most prosperous town in Leinster, "and carried away from it gold silver and hostages." Richard's army attacked Art in his woody fastnesses called Garryhill (*Garbh-Choill* near Myshall) and Leverock (*Leamhrach* near Clonegall) and burned his fortresses, but failed to capture him. Afterwards he submitted and was admitted to the king's peace on the terms of an indenture (still extant) made between him and Thomas Mowbray, Earl of Nottingham, and dated 7 January 1395: viz. that he would faithfully serve the king and obey his orders, and would surrender all lands of which he or his followers "had recently taken possession in Leinster" (*que nuper occupata fuerunt*); while the king would treat Mac Murrough as his liegeman, and on performance of the terms would provide him and his heirs with 80 marks a year and his wife's inheritance in Norragh, and that all his armed warriors should leave Leinster and go with him and receive the king's pay for warring against the king's rebels elsewhere, and should hold of the king all lands which they might so acquire. These terms having been approved by the king, Mac Murrough and his *urriaghs* on 16 February and following days did homage and swore to observe the covenants in the said indenture, and in default to pay large sums to the Papal Chamber. To understand this arrangement it must be remembered that the present County Wicklow formed no part of the fief of Leinster, as granted to Strongbow, and that even in Leinster so understood it was only from the "recently occupied districts" that the fighting men (*homines armati bellatores seu guerrantes*) were to clear out. Presumably the various enclaves which the Irish had always been allowed to retain in parts of Okinselagh, Leix, and Offaly were not to be disturbed, and certainly no great clearance of the native population was contemplated. To the king the arrangement must have seemed a pacific and even a generous way of procuring the disbandment of the rebel armies as such, but he little understood the Irish mentality if he thought they would willingly carry it out.

[1] *Calendar Patent Roll, Ireland,* 15 *Richard II,* p. 148, No. 27.

As the *Four Masters* observe, "although Mac Murrough had gone into the king's house he did not afterwards keep faith with him."

Meanwhile the king went to Dublin which he reached on 6 November, and at Drogheda on 16 March Niall Og O'Neill, captain of his nation, submitted to the king in person and undertook to restore all lands which he had "unjustly seized" together with the *buannacht* (military service) of the Irish of Ulster. The submissions of Turlough O'Conor Roe of Connaught, Brian O'Brien of Thomond, Teig MacCarthy of Desmond, and of some fifty of the lesser chieftains, and also of some rebels of English descent, followed during the course of the king's stay in Ireland[1]. Froissart recounts how a certain squire of England named Henry Cristall, who had been for seven years (probably 1359–65) in captivity with a chieftain named "Bryn Costerec" (probably O'Byrne "the victorious," *Coscorach*) and had learned the Irish language, was employed by the king to teach the four "moste puyssaunt" Irish kings, namely O'Neill, O'Brien, Mac Murrough, and O'Conor, the usages and customs of England preparatory to receiving the order of knighthood. This he did to the best of his power, though they were "ryght rude and of grose engyn," and on Lady Day in March in the cathedral of Dublin they were made knights "with great solempnyte."

Having thus won over the Irish chieftains to his "obeysaunce," Richard made a peaceful progress through Leinster, holding pleas and receiving submissions at various places. He was at Kilkenny for most of April and reached Waterford on the 28th of that month. Here on board the king's ship O'Conor Donn submitted and was knighted. He had previously written to warn the king against his rival O'Conor Roe, who, "though base-born, sought to appropriate to himself the title of O'Conor," and in fact was one of the four chief kings already knighted. At the same time the king knighted William de Burgh, the Mac William of Clanrickard, and Walter de Bermingham of Athenry. On 11 May he was back in Dublin, whence he left for England on the 15th, having been upwards of eight months in Ireland. Whatever we may think of the wisdom of taking Irish submissions at their face-value, Richard II among English sovereigns deserves special credit for his personal efforts to pacify Ireland.

Roger Mortimer, Earl of March and Ulster, grandson through his mother of Lionel Duke of Clarence and heir presumptive to the throne, was left behind as King's Lieutenant. But the royal army once gone, it soon became manifest that the Irish had no intention of observing the terms of their submissions. In 1396 and again in 1398 the O'Tooles and O'Byrnes broke out, and on 20 July in the latter year Roger Mortimer was slain by them at Kellistown in County Carlow. To avenge this disaster and punish Mac Murrough and his *urriaghs* was the object of King Richard's second expedition to Ireland. On 1 June 1399 he landed,

---

[1] Notarial instruments embodying the terms of these submissions, or enrolments thereof, and other connected documents are still extant in the Public Record Office in London and have been edited by Professor Curtis.

as before, at Waterford. We have a circumstantial account of this expedition from an eye-witness, a Frenchman named Jean Créton. After waiting a fortnight at Kilkenny for succour that never came, the king on 23 June set out against Mac Murrough. His route seems to have been across the County Carlow and by the woody valley of Shillelagh to Arklow. The Irish feared the English arrows and did not oppose the main force, but they harassed the vanguard and cut off stragglers. Mac Murrough's uncle came with a halter round his neck and sued for mercy, but Mac Murrough himself scorned to follow his example. He knew that the English could get no provisions, and in fact they suffered great privations until three ships with supplies came from Dublin to a port close by (presumably Arklow). But now Mac Murrough craved an interview to treat for peace. The young Earl of Gloucester met him, each at opposite sides of a stream between two wooded hills some distance from the sea (presumably in the vale of Ovoca). The interview, graphically described by Créton, was abortive. The earl charged Mac Murrough with the breach of his sworn fealty and the killing of Mortimer, but Mac Murrough insisted on pardon without any penalty (*i.e.* without surrendering his possessions in Leinster). When Richard heard this, he swore that he would not leave Ireland until he had Mac Murrough, alive or dead, in his power. But the army had to be fed, and they went on to Dublin. Three companies were made ready to go in quest of Mac Murrough, but when about the middle of July tidings came from England, "the redeless king" learnt that he had a more formidable foe to meet in the person of Henry of Lancaster, and with the departure of Richard II the prospect of a pacified Ireland became more visionary than ever.

During the reigns of the three successive kings of the house of Lancaster, in spite of some active viceroys, the condition of Ireland went in general from bad to worse. Henry IV was too much engrossed in securing his own position against revolts and conspiracies of his English subjects, Scottish raids, and Welsh guerrilla warfare, to pay adequate attention to the unhappy state of Ireland. Henry V wasted his energies in splendid but futile victories in France, which only left a heritage of woe to his successor; and when at last the claim to France was abandoned by Henry VI, the long struggle between the Houses of York and Lancaster forbade all unity of action. Again and again border Irish chieftains entered into agreements to be liege subjects henceforth and even to war against the king's enemies, but these agreements had at best only a temporary effect. Thus in April 1400 Art Mac Murrough was again admitted to peace, his annuity and his wife's lands restored to him, but he more than once plundered the English of Carlow and Wexford and attacked their walled towns before his death in 1417. In 1401 when the king's son, Thomas of Lancaster, was lieutenant, Mac Mahon, O'Reilly, and O'Byrne entered into similar agreements. Between 1414 and 1420 John Talbot, Lord Furnival, afterwards famous as leader in the wars with France, brought all the border Irish into temporary submission, and actually "caused in many places every Irish enemie to serve upon the others." But Talbot had to create and maintain his forces, and being supplied with insufficient funds was unable to pay for the victuals which he commandeered from the impoverished liege people. They were therefore faced with the alternative of being either plundered by their enemies or despoiled by their defenders. In 1421, when the fourth Earl of Ormonde was justiciar, articles of complaint were drawn up and sent to the king, and these show the pitiable state of the loyal English owing to "unceasing wars" on them and the "hateful coignes" levied by some lieutenants and the great men of the land.

During the whole period from 1414 to 1449 the chief power in the government continued, with some exceptions, to oscillate between the Talbots (Sir John and especially his brother Richard, the Archbishop of Dublin) and the Butlers, and there was much enmity between the two families. Both the fourth Earl of Ormonde and Sir John Talbot, however, did their best to resist the encroachments of the border clans and to bring them to submission. Thus in 1425 Talbot induced Calvagh O'Conor Faly to free all English lands from "black-rent" and to make many promises of redress and of good behaviour in future, and later in the same year Ormonde caused Owen O'Neill to enter into an elaborate indenture acknowledging the rights of the young Duke of York to whom, as heir to Roger Mortimer, the earldom of Ulster had descended, and to make similar pacific promises. But in 1430 and following years Owen burned Dundalk and exacted tribute, and with O'Conor Faly plundered West Meath, and afterwards he expelled Mac Quillin from the Route in County Antrim, while Donough Mac Murrough, recently released from captivity, raided County Kildare. These and other outbreaks caused the Irish council in 1435 to write to the king that "Ireland was well nigh destroyed," so that "in the nether parts of Counties Dublin, Meath, Louth, and Kildare, there were scarcely 30 miles in length and 20 in breadth where a man may safely go to answer the king's writs."

At this time indeed the fortunes of the few remaining English in Ireland were nearly at their lowest ebb, and just when England was about to lose her last possessions in France she seemed to be on the point of losing her last hold on Ireland also. English statesmen at the time paid little heed to Ireland, but that some in England with clearer vision saw how vital it was for her to control the neighbouring isle appears from the *Libelle of Englyshe Polycye* published in 1436. In a passage which deserved to be remembered the writer says:

> "Nowe here be ware and hertly take entente,
> As ye wolle answere at the laste jugemente,
> To kepe Yrelond, that it be not loste;
> ffor it is a boterasse and a poste
> Undre England, and Wales another.
> God forbede but eche were othere brothere
> Of one ligeaunce dewe unto the Kinge."

The extreme weakness of the loyal Anglo-Irish in the fifteenth century was no doubt a consequence of the long-continued failure of the government to perform its primary functions of keeping order and dispensing equal justice, and thereby gradually winning the confidence—no easy matter—of the Gaelic clans. The loyalists, always a small minority, had become fewer in number and economically weakened. Many had migrated to England and others had become Hibernicised. The Irish in military efficiency were no longer their inferiors. All the great chieftains had strengthened themselves with regular bodies of Galloglasses (*gallóglaigh*), or professional soldiers, originally imported from the isles and of the race of "Mighty Somerled," such as the the Mac Donalds, the Mac Dugalls, the Mac Sweeneys, and the Mac Sheehys. They had learned the importance of discipline and there was no great disparity of weapons. What saved the remnant of the old English settlers and the semblance of English organisation was the lack of unity, nay the utter discord, that prevailed over Gaelic Ireland. Not only were neighbouring clans frequently warring against each other, but the ruling families of the old clan-groups were splitting up into rival factions. This was particularly the case with the O'Conors and the O'Neills, but others shewed the same tendency. Even the Leinster clans, since the days of Art Kavanagh, never united all their forces. Each preferred to plunder the English for his own hand. The spirit which caused this fissiparous tendency, whether we regard it as love of independence or mere jealousy and self-seeking, prevented Gaelic Ireland from combining under any one chief to expel "the foreigners."

In July 1449 Richard, Duke of York, came to Ireland as King's Lieutenant, to which office, "as to an honourable retirement," he had been relegated for ten years in December 1447. He was well received not only by the Anglo-Irish, but also by the Irish chieftains of Leinster and Ulster, towards whom he adopted a conciliatory policy resulting in many indentures of peace. He held parliaments in 1449 and 1450, but early in September in the latter year he returned to England determined to claim at least his rightful share in the councils of the kingdom. The contest now brewing between the Houses of Lancaster and York had its pale counterpart in Ireland, where it soon embittered the longstanding jealousy between the Butlers and the Geraldines. James, the fourth Earl of Ormonde, was, however, trusted by the Duke of York as well as by the Lancastrian kings, and the duke appears to have left him (and not, as stated by many writers, his son, the Earl of Wiltshire) as deputy when he departed for England. Ormonde held two parliaments as the duke's deputy and made a successful martial circuit through the border territories before he died in August 1452[1]. Edward FitzEustace, a Yorkist, was then appointed the duke's deputy, probably by the Irish council. On 12 May 1453, however, the new Earl of Ormonde and Wiltshire, who had

[1] See Duald MacFirbis's *Annals*, aᵒ 1452.

thrown in his lot with the Lancastrians, was appointed lieutenant by the king, thus superseding the Duke of York; but this appointment led to great disturbances and was not accepted in Ireland, which was pre-dominantly Yorkist, and FitzEustace appears to have acted up to his death in October 1454, when Thomas FitzMaurice, seventh Earl of Kildare, was appointed by the council, and afterwards, as the duke's deputy, held parliaments up to 1459.

After the dispersal of his followers at the Rout of Ludford on 12 October of that year the Duke of York fled for refuge to Ireland. In England he was attainted as a traitor, but he was well received in Ireland, "for he had exceedingly tyed unto him the hearts of the noblemen and gentlemen of that land." In a parliament held before him in 1460 he sought by several enactments to protect himself against his opponents in England and to gain favour in Ireland, but the contest, which had now become a dynastic one, could only be settled in England, and the duke accompanied by several Anglo-Irish lords and their retainers left about September to join the victorious Earl of Warwick and claim the crown. When he seemed on the eve of success he fell in the fight at Wakefield on 30 December. But the triumph of the Yorkists was only deferred, and on 4 March 1461 the duke's son was enthroned at Westminster as Edward IV.

The new king confirmed the Earl of Kildare in his office and rewarded the Barnwalls, FitzEustaces, Prestons, and others for their services to the Yorkist cause. The Earl of Ormonde and Wiltshire had been beheaded after the battle of Towton, but his kinsmen still caused disturbances in Ireland. They were, however, defeated by the forces of the Earl of Desmond in 1462, and in the following year, in reward apparently for this service, Thomas, Earl of Desmond, was appointed deputy, while Kildare was made lord chancellor. Desmond had the characteristics of an Irish chieftain and relied greatly on the support given to him by the Irish and the "degenerate" English, but was regarded with distrust by the English lords of Meath and Fingal. They accused him of "extorting coigne and livery, and of being advised, ruled, and governed by the king's traitors and rebels." At the time he was supported by the king, but his rule ended in disaster. In 1466 he was taken prisoner along with some Meath lords by O'Conor of Offaly, and though the prisoners were afterwards rescued, marauding parties devastated Meath unchecked. More ominous still, O'Brien of Thomond led a host—"the greatest since Brian Borumha was conquering Ireland"—into Desmond, and was only bought off from Leinster by the earl "making sure to him" the territory of Clanwilliam in County Limerick (which did not belong to the earl) and a tribute of 60 marks from that city.

Next year Desmond was superseded by John Tiptoft, Earl of Worcester, and by the parliament held before him on 4 February 1468 both Desmond and Kildare were attainted of treason in respect of "alliance fosterage and alterage with the Irish enemies, and in giving them horses and harness and arms and supporting them against the King's faithful servants." Desmond was beheaded on 14 February, but Kildare was pardoned and restored in the following July. The Gaels of Ireland lamented the death of the Earl of Desmond, whom they regarded almost as one of themselves, and contemporary evidence indicates that he was suspected of using his influence with them to further his own ambitions and against the interests of the loyal English. The unwonted severity of his punishment, however, may be ascribed to the character of the Earl of Worcester, who earned the name of the "grim butcher" for his ruthless executions of those who intrigued against the king. It was at any rate bad policy, and it led to the complete estrangement and ultimate ruin of the house of Desmond.

During the brief restoration of Henry VI in the winter of 1470–71 Tiptoft—"the wreck of the maledictions of the men of Ireland"—was himself beheaded. The Irish council now again appointed the Earl of Kildare as justiciar, and he was continued as deputy under the Duke of Clarence. In short, he and his successors in the earldom, the eighth and ninth earls, gradually made themselves indispensable to the government, and whoever was named King's Lieutenant, an Earl of Kildare for the next sixty-four years, with brief exceptions, was the real governor and source of power in Ireland.

CHAPTER XIV

SCOTLAND, 1328–1488

THE treaty of Northampton (1328) surrendered the Plantagenet claim to the suzerainty of Scotland. But the tender years of Bruce's son David II (1329–71) and an opportune revival of the Balliol candidature afforded occasion for provocation which English policy was willing to exploit. The circumstances were largely of Bruce's making. After Bannockburn he declared forfeiture upon many between whom and himself Red Comyn's murder raised a blood-feud. The treaty of 1328 provided for the restitution of some thus dealt with. But its stipulations were not fulfilled, and the "disinherited" set their hopes of restoration upon foreign arms. Among the disaffected were Henry de Beaumont, whose wife was niece and heiress of John Comyn, seventh Earl of Buchan, Gilbert Umfraville, also a Comyn by maternal descent, who claimed the earldom of Angus of which his father had been deprived, and the forfeited Earl of Atholl, whom marriage connected with the same stock. A Balliol restoration promised to promote their own, and, with Edward III's secret encouragement, Balliol having died in 1313, his eldest son Edward returned to England from France in 1330. Two years later, accompanied by the "disinherited," he landed in Fifeshire (1332), demanding "the lands which are our own by right," dispersed a force under the incompetent Regent Mar at Dupplin Moor, and mastered Perth. In September he was crowned at Scone as "Edward I." But before the end of the year he was over the Border, expelled by as sudden a turn of fortune as won his first success. Like his father, he had bartered Scotland's independence for English support, and with English auxiliaries returned in 1333 to make another bid for the throne. Defeat at Halidon Hill, near Berwick, drove David Bruce to France for security, and Edward III exacted from his *protégé* renewed acknowledgment of his suzerainty, along with the surrender of Berwick and Lothian (1334). Bruce's work was undone. But Balliol's authority depended wholly on his suzerain's aid, and Edward III's ambition inconveniently veered to another purpose. In October 1337 he published his claim to the throne of France. Scotland consequently was spared; her English-held strongholds were slowly recovered; Balliol was recalled to England, and in 1341 David was again among his people. Bound to France by ties of hospitality, he was now invited to strike a blow on her behalf. Defeated at Neville's Cross (1346), he was carried into captivity, recovering his liberty eleven years later (1357) upon an undertaking to pay 100,000 marks in ten annual payments. By a subsequent agreement the rigorous terms were somewhat abated. But when David died in 1371 Scotland was still deep in debt to England, in whose hands

Annandale, Berwick, Roxburgh, and Lochmaben also remained. A century passed before she was expelled from Scottish soil.

Unworthy in other aspects, David's reign may be counted the cradle of vernacular Scottish literature. Among his subjects were John Barbour, archdeacon of Aberdeen, author of *The Brus*, an epic of David's heroic father, and Andrew of Wyntoun, a canon regular of St Serf's, whose metrical *Original Chronicle* records history from the Creation to the accession of James I in 1406. Contemporaries of Chaucer, their remoteness from the Renaissance spirit reveals the relative backwardness of Scottish culture in a period calculated to brace rather than refine the national character. On the other hand, the Bruce reigns placed Scotland on the path of constitutional progress. Already in 1291 the voice of the Crown's lesser vassals had been heard in a national crisis, though an organised system of county representation was not planned till the reign of James I. Unlike England, where the development of borough and county membership was simultaneous, the Scottish burghs preceded the counties as an established estate in Parliament. Bruce's Parliament at Cambuskenneth in 1326 must be counted their earliest association with the Estates. Needing money to finance a costly and persisting warfare, his summons of the burghs was not disinterested. But, as with the English Third Estate, the date of their first appearance may not be regarded as the beginning of an uninterrupted attendance. In the course of the following hundred and thirty years they frequently were not summoned; only after 1424 their attendance seems to have been regular. The reign of David II also supplies another detail of constitutional development. At the Scone Parliament in 1367 the majority returned home *causa autumpni*, leaving a commission to watch the interests of their constituencies. At Perth also, in 1369, *propter importunitatem et caristiam temporis,* the majority departed, leaving the remainder to hold the Parliament. A few months later the practice was repeated. Alleging the impropriety of divulging matters of State to the whole body, a commission was set up, which, in 1424, was constituted specifically to consider "articles" of business submitted by the Crown. Thenceforward, till the seventeenth century, the Committee (or Lords) of the Articles virtually usurped the deliberative functions of Parliament. Whether it was the natural outcome of circumstances, or the convenient device of the Crown or another dominant interest, or modelled on French precedents[1], the Committee made the Scottish Parliament the pliable instrument of the Crown. From a similar committee, appointed specially to deal with litigation (*ad deliberandum super iudiciis contradictis*), developed the judicatory which at a later time became the Court of Session[2]. Still, the circumstances of the two reigns put in the hands of Parliament powers which considerably curtailed the sovereign's prerogative—regulation of the coinage and

---

[1] Cf. Rait, *The Parliaments of Scotland.*
[2] Cf. Hannay, *The College of Justice.*

currency, determination of war and peace, and the supervision of executive acts.

In David's reign also the inferior clergy had direct representation in Parliament, though there is no appearance of such a *praemunientes* clause as Edward I addressed to the English bishops. At the Scone Parliament in 1367, besides the bishops and their proctors, priors, and abbots, certain of the lower clergy were placed upon the commission *ad parliamentum tenendum*. In 1369 and 1370 a similar course was followed, while in the latter Parliament a few inferior clergy (*pauci de inferioribus cleri*) were condemned for absence *per contumaciam*, a term which predicates a special summons. Throughout the fifteenth century the number of inferior clergy present was always small, in some degree for the practical reasons that deterred their secular colleagues[1]. But a few ordinarily sat upon the Parliamentary committees, while the association of the Spiritual Estate with Parliament explains its frequent trespasses upon the domain of ecclesiastical authority. During a period of pestilence in 1456, the Estates directed the bishops to organise open-air processions in their dioceses, and to grant indulgences to the clergy conducting them. Other notable examples are Parliament's attempts to restrict the immunities of criminous clerks, curtail the abuse of sanctuary, and oppose the system of papal provisions.

In the thirteenth and fourteenth centuries France and Scotland both suffered interruptions of a hitherto unbroken male succession in the reigning house. The experiences of 1292 and 1306 were repeated upon David II's death in 1371. His heir was his nephew Robert Stewart, son of his half-sister Marjorie (*ob.* 1316) and Walter the High Steward (*ob.* 1327). Of Breton stock, the Stewarts were established in Shropshire early in the twelfth century and thence migrated to Scotland under David I's patronage. Walter FitzAlan (*ob.* 1177), first of the Scottish line, received estates in Kyle and Renfrew and the High Stewardship of the kingdom, a dignity which became hereditary till a higher superseded it; from it the family took its name[2]. Robert, sixth in descent from Walter FitzAlan, was the first of a line of sovereigns who reigned, but rarely ruled, for more than 300 years. In a period when a strong hand was needed to curb feudal arrogance, it was Scotland's misfortune that, with few exceptions, the Stewarts were ill-equipped to accomplish their task. From 1371 onwards to 1488 the arresting fact in Scottish history is the challenge offered, especially by the house of Douglas, to the new dynasty. Supported by a private competence relatively trivial, the Stewarts were hard put to it to hold their own.

When Robert II (1371–90) received the crown, the lordship of Douglas had recently (1358) been raised to an earldom. Faithful service to Bruce

---

[1] Principal Rait (*Scottish Hist. Rev.* xii. 116) concludes that those who attended were generally officials or clerks.

[2] The form "Stuart" came from France with Mary Stewart.

brought it much property in Moffatdale, Jedburgh, Ettrick Forest, Lauderdale, Teviotdale, and Eskdale, while the Wardenship of the East Marches and Justiciarship below the Forth, augmenting its private jurisdiction, made its authority almost royal in a situation whose proximity to England afforded opportunities for spectacular service which constantly exalted it in popular estimation. William, first Earl of Douglas, significantly contested the succession to the throne with the first Stewart, and no less than six children of the first and third earls married into the royal house. James, second Earl of Douglas (*ob.* 1388), husband of Robert II's daughter Isabella, placed his name upon the pinnacle of popular regard at Otterburn, the one heroic event of the first Stewart reign. Almost upon its second anniversary Robert II laid down his undistinguished sceptre.

His successor, Robert III (1390–1406), inherited his father's character and, like him, came past middle age to the throne. Called John at the font, the unhappy associations of this name clung to him persistently. Crippled, irresolute, he stands in the background in turbulent years whose chief disturbers were his own family. The wanton burning of Elgin Cathedral (1390) was the act of his brother, fittingly named "Wolf of Badenoch," whose clumsy effigy to-day is incongruously housed in Dunkeld Cathedral. Such acts as those that made his nephew Alexander Earl of Mar, and brought the earldom of Ross to the Stewarts, display a lawless spirit in the royal house which called for Parliament's reproof in 1397. The king's eldest son, David, Duke of Rothesay[1], dissolute and reckless, provoked a claim to suzerainty by the newly established house of Lancaster, and in 1400 a King of England for the last time campaigned on Scottish soil. Two years later Archibald, fourth Earl of Douglas (*ob.* 1424), Robert's son-in-law, retaliating, was defeated on Homildon Hill, and, supporting Hotspur's blusterous challenge at Shrewsbury (1403), passed into Henry IV's custody till 1408. Meanwhile, after an act of characteristic violence, Rothesay died (1402) in confinement, probably at the instigation of his uncle Robert, Duke of Albany. Anxious to preserve his heir, James, a boy of twelve, the king sent the prince to France. Off Flamborough Head he was intercepted by English privateers, who conducted their prize to London (March 1406). The disaster broke Robert's declining spirit.

Till his death in 1420, little concerned to procure his nephew's release, Albany ruled as Regent in his name, and by a characteristic act of self-seeking provoked an enemy in a new quarter. For a century and a half the allegiance of the Western Isles to the Scottish Crown had been perfunctory. John of the Isles (*ob.* 1387), balancing his course between Bruce and Balliol, was with difficulty brought to an oath of fealty. Donald his son (*ob.* 1423) flung down the gage at Harlaw. Alexander, Donald's

---

[1] In 1398, along with his uncle Robert, Earl of Fife (Duke of Albany), he received the dignity of a dukedom. The title was new to Scotland.

successor (*ob.* 1449), was twice imprisoned as a rebel. John, last Lord o the Isles (*ob.* 1503), suffered attainder. The record ranks the Macdonalds of the Isles with the Douglas as types of the feudal license of their generation. Donald's quarrel with Albany was provoked by the duke's dealing with the earldom of Ross, which devolved in 1402 on the late earl's heiress Euphemia, Albany's grand-daughter. Euphemia was induced to take the veil and resign the dignity to her uncle, Albany's son, to the prejudice of her legal heir, Mary, wife of Donald of the Isles[1]. Asserting his wife's claim, Donald demanded the earldom, and, offering England his "allegiance and amity," led his caterans to defeat at Harlaw (1411) a few miles from Aberdeen.

Otherwise Albany's regency was marked by events which reveal the stirring of intellectual forces elsewhere at work in Europe. The voices of Hus and Wyclif already echoed in Scotland, where, in 1407, James Resby, an English Wyclifite, was burnt for challenging the Pope's authority. A quarter of a century later (1433) Paul Crawar, a Bohemian, testified at the stake for similar heterodoxy. Equally significant is the foundation of the first Scottish university. The apparatus of learning as yet was confined to the cathedrals and monasteries, whose libraries, as, for instance, those of Aberdeen and Glasgow, contained the works of the Fathers, the treatises of the schoolmen, Latin translations of Aristotle, and remains of pagan antiquity. With meagre opportunities at home, Scottish students sought instruction elsewhere. Oxford and Cambridge in the infrequent intervals of peace received them in their halls. And when that avenue to learning closed, the Ancient League opportunely invited them to France. In 1326 a Scots College, restricted at first to natives of Moray, was founded at Paris. But the zeal for learning, as well as the need for an educated clergy competent to confound heresy, demanded a university on Scottish soil. In 1413 Pope Benedict XIII sanctioned a *studium generale* at St Andrews. Forty years later (1451) a second was established at Glasgow, and, after a similar interval, a third was founded (1495) at Aberdeen. In all three the university was the daughter of the Church whose interests it was designed to serve.

Albany's son Murdoch, his successor as Regent, was more sensitive than his father to the national dishonour involved in the sovereign's prolonged captivity, and the death of Henry V in 1422 facilitated an agreement. In 1423 "perpetual peace" was covenanted between the two realms, Scottish men-at-arms were recalled from French service, and James obtained his release. Delaying his return to marry Lady Joan Beaufort, the "milk-white dove" of the *Kingis Quair*, he arrived in Scotland in the spring of 1424 and took up his heavy task. Succeeding two sovereigns of indifferent health and vitality, James came to the throne, at the age of thirty, in full physical vigour. At peace with England, save for a vain effort to recover Roxburgh (1436), his purpose bent

[1] See Pedigree Table xxiv in Terry, *op. cit.*

unrelaxingly to one absorbing task. "Let God but grant me life," he is said to have promised, "and there shall not be a spot in my kingdom where the key doth not keep the castle and the bracken the cow." The crises through which the kingdom recently had passed—the war with England, his own minority and captivity, and the accession of a new dynasty undistinguished as yet by ability or public service—had permitted the Crown to be overshadowed by its feudatories, whose addiction to private vendettas, contempt of royal authority, and subordination of national to selfish interests, constituted a serious menace to the public welfare. James held it his mission to restore to the Crown the authority others had usurped, and if he was little scrupulous in the means he employed, the circumstances called for drastic action.

James' activity was tireless, his vengeance unrelaxing. Within two months of his return he seized Murdoch's eldest son Walter, his brother-in-law Malcolm Fleming of Cumbernauld, and Thomas Boyd the younger of Kilmarnock, one of an aspiring family. Early in 1425 he laid hands on Murdoch's father-in-law, the aged Earl of Lennox, and arrested Murdoch himself, his wife, and their younger son Alexander. If their fate was ever in doubt, Murdoch's remaining son James More decided it. Descending upon Dumbarton, he gave the place to the flames and slew the garrison. James hesitated no longer: in May Murdoch's eldest son was executed at Stirling; Murdoch, his son Alexander, and his father-in-law Lennox met the same fate. The ruin of the house of Albany requited James' long captivity and Rothesay's death. Till the end of his reign James retained the Lennox earldom. He dealt as summarily with three other fiefs. On the plea that it was a male fee he attached the earldom of Strathearn and sent its holder to England as a hostage for the royal ransom. The Earl of March, whose father had leagued with England in the late reign, suffered forfeiture. Putting aside the legal heir, James also seized the earldom of Mar. As summarily he dealt with Alexander of the Isles, son of Donald of Harlaw, who, with other chiefs, was seized and imprisoned. But though the most formidable of his associates went to the block, Alexander was spared, and in 1429 was again in arms, till, marching upon the lowlands, he was intercepted and made submission. Of the highlands, as of the lowlands, James was the master.

As tireless was the king's legislative activity. Parliament empowered him to summon his vassals to produce their charters and justify possession of their lands, forbade pursuit of private vendettas and the maintenance of excessive feudal retinues, and secured the Customs to the Crown for a "living." His enactments reveal James' close observation. He prescribes the arms and armour at military musters, instructs all males above twelve years to "have usage of archery," recommends the provision of practice grounds for the purpose conveniently "near paroche kirks", proscribes the competing game of football under penalty of fine, instructs in the sowing of peas and beans, imposes penalties on negligent farmers entertaining destructive rooks "biggand in treis," insists upon honest sporting tackle for the lure of salmon, orders vigorous hunting of wolves, and threatens poachers and unlawful slayers of the red deer. He regulates the costume of his lieges and the price of their victuals, devises precautions against the outbreak of fire, regulates weights, measures, and the coinage, ordains an inquisition of idle men, provides for hospitals, and requires ale and wine houses to close on the stroke of nine.

James was as masterful in his relations with the Church. The first act of his first Parliament assured its accustomed liberties and privileges, and in 1425 the law was enacted under which Paul Crawar suffered. James was as firm with the orthodox as with the heretic. He admonished the Church to use its wealth in the service of religion, bade the monastic fraternities put their houses in order, and gave them an example in his Carthusian foundation at Perth, the only house of that rule in Scotland. He instructed the ecclesiastical synod to modify the procedure of the Church courts, and involved himself in a dispute with the Papacy by his fearless invasion of the spiritual province. At the Council of Basle he was represented in the effort to uphold the liberties of Christendom against papal usurpation. In the constitutional development of the kingdom his reign holds a place no less important. From an early period freeholders of the Crown below baronial rank had the right to attend Parliament. In fact, they did so either perfunctorily or not at all. To give the Crown the support it needed against its baronage, James desired to establish the country lairds in Parliament alongside the burgesses. To that end, by an act of 1428, he permitted their order in every sheriffdom to send up two[1] or more of their number competent to speak in their behalf. But he failed to overcome the indifference of the county gentry, and more than a century passed before county representation was satisfactorily regulated. As clearly grounded upon his English experience was James' injunction to the county freeholders to elect "a common speaker of Parliament" competent to "propone all and sundry needs and causes pertaining to the Commons in the Parliament or General Council." The innovation failed to commend itself and was not pressed.

The tragedy that cut short James' strenuous career was invited partly by his rapacity, partly by the ambition of his kinsmen, descendants of his grandfather Robert II's second marriage with Euphemia Ross, of whom James' half-uncle Walter Earl of Atholl, only surviving son of their union, was head and representative. James himself was descended from Robert II's first marriage with Elizabeth Mure, which, though legalised by papal licence, remained canonically irregular on grounds of consanguinity, of the previous contraction of Elizabeth to another spouse, and of her irregular cohabitation with Robert before matrimony. Atholl's hopes of succession, advantaged by James' destruction of the house of Albany, were further encouraged by the fact that James' heir was not

[1] Clackmannan and Kinross were restricted to one.

born till 1430, after six years of wedlock, and was still an infant when his father's murder gave him the throne. The active contrivers of that deed were Sir Robert Stewart, Atholl's grandson, whom James had admitted to his household, perhaps with an eye to naming him heir-apparent should his own marriage remain barren, and Sir Robert Graham, whom he had arrested and released upon his return to Scotland, a man whom his brother's marriage attached to Atholl, and whom James' treatment of Strathearn provoked. Early in 1437 Parliament was summoned to Perth to receive a papal legate. The castle not being in repair, James quartered the court upon the Black Friars outside the city. On the night of 20 or 21 February, Stewart, in service as Chamberlain, admitted Graham and a band of Atholl's retainers. James was about to retire, when a sound of tumult warned him of danger. Seeking to bar the door of his apartment, he found the bolt withdrawn, and, raising a flag in the stone floor, dropped to a vault below. Graham, with others, entering the hall, found it empty of all but the queen and her women. But a noise from below revealed the king's hiding-place, and there the assassins did their work.

Aeneas Sylvius Piccolomini, afterwards Pope Pius II, who visited Scotland in James' reign, found it a rugged, inhospitable land, where the winter sun "illuminates the earth little more than three hours." The towns were open and their houses for the most part constructed without lime. In the country the roofs were of turf and the doors of ox-hide. Bread was a luxury, flesh and fish the principal diet of the poor. The crops were meagre and the country ill-supplied with timber. Hides, wool, salted fish, and pearls were exported to Flanders, and the native oysters were superior to those fished in English waters. The common people lacked refinement, and their women, though comely, were not distinguished for chastity. Scotland appeared to Piccolomini "a barren wilderness," and not until he reached Newcastle on his southward journey did he "once more behold civilisation." Froissart, who visited the country in David II's reign, tells a similar story: Edinburgh could not vie even with Tournai or Valenciennes. The French who campaigned in the country declared they had never known till then the meaning of poverty and hard living. On the other hand, Pedro de Ayala, who visited Scotland *c.* 1500, found populous towns and villages, hewn stone houses, glass windows, excellent doors, good furniture, a prosperous trade in salmon, herring, and dried fish, and a considerable and growing public revenue. Scotland's economic development in and after James I's reign was considerable.

From the accession of James I to that of Charles I in 1625, a period of two hundred years, every sovereign came to the throne as a minor. James I's English widow was the first of a succession of queen-mothers left to guard a juvenile king, a circumstance of which the baronage took advantage. In no other country had their order so prolonged an opportunity to exhibit the evils of a feudal society. James II's reign (1437–60) passed in circumstances with which Scotland was to become familiar. His mother, after her second marriage to Sir James Stewart, Knight of Lorn, vanishes out of Scotland's story, leaving James in the control of minor notables—Sir William Crichton and Sir Alexander Livingstone of Callendar, both of whom had enjoyed his father's favour. In collusion the two planned a crime which, whether inspired by fear or by the traditions of their dead master's policy, put a feud between Douglas and Stewart which only the ruin of one or the other could compose. In the autumn of 1440, William, sixth Earl of Douglas, a boy of fifteen, was invited with his brother David to Edinburgh, where the young sovereign was in residence. Douglas was related to those who had planned the late king's murder, and actually was heir to the pretensions of the house of Atholl. On these or other grounds his death was determined. The brothers were seized as they sat at meat with their royal host, and, after a swift and mock trial, were hurried to the scaffold. Both were without issue and the vast Douglas heritage was broken up. Annandale, a male fee, reverted to the Crown. The French duchy of Touraine, which dated from 1423, lapsed to the Crown of France. Only the unentailed portions of the inheritance descended to the dead earl's sister Margaret, the Fair Maid of Galloway. No sentence of forfeiture having been declared, the title passed to James the Gross (*ob.* 1443), great-uncle of the murdered earl.

William, eighth Earl of Douglas (*ob.* 1452), set himself to exact the vengeance his father had been careless to demand. Uniting with Livingstone he procured Crichton's outlawry and his own appointment as Lieutenant of the Realm. A papal dispensation in 1444 permitted him to marry his cousin the heiress of Galloway, and about the same time he entered into a "band" with the Earl of Crawford, the most formidable noble north of the Forth, who inherited the wrongs of the fallen house of March, and also with John, Lord of the Isles and Earl of Ross (*ob.* 1503). The termination of the truce made with England in 1438 gave him opportunity for service in a familiar field, and a notable victory near Gretna on the banks of the Sark in 1448 revived the prestige of the Douglas name throughout Scotland. James, now in his twentieth year, had in his cousin and chancellor, Bishop James Kennedy of St Andrews, an able statesman concerned to maintain the Crown's authority against baronial leagues and ambition. In the summer of 1450 Douglas was dispatched to Rome on a diplomatic mission, and in his absence James made a formidable demonstration of authority on his territories. In February 1452, either unsuspicious or contemptuous of danger, Douglas obeyed a royal summons to the court at Stirling. His retinue found quarters in the town below. Douglas was housed in the castle, and on the morrow of his arrival supped with the king. The topic of the Crawford–Ross "band" was broached and the king demanded its dissolution. Douglas refused, and James flung himself upon him, shouting "False traitor, since you will not, this shall," dirking him as he spoke. The crime demanded a conclusive trial of strength between the Crown and its most powerful vassal. Parliament attainted

Crawford in June 1452 and applauded James' recent violence upon a traitor. Lavish grants of property drew a formidable army to the Crown's support, and before the summer was over the new Douglas and his brothers made their submission, while Crawford yielded to the king's lieutenant, Alexander Gordon, first Earl of Huntly. For the moment James was content, permitted Douglas' marriage with his brother's widow, and named him a commissioner to England to negotiate a truce. Douglas probably used his opportunity to promote disloyal ends. Whatever the provocation he received, James took the field again in March 1455, wasted the Douglas lands, and drove the earl and his brothers to England, where they became pensioners of the English court. Meanwhile, in Scotland, the earl was attainted, his property forfeited, his Wardenship of the Marches recalled. Once or twice he made futile efforts to trouble Scotland, and, so engaged, was captured in 1484. He died without issue in 1488, and the greatness of his house with him.

That a subject should so long have menaced the Crown was due in large measure to the poverty of the royal house. This disability was now removed. Douglas' attainder forfeited to the sovereign a rich property, while in 1455 opportunity was taken to attach to the Crown in perpetuity lordships which the public interest forbade to pass into the hands of subjects—Galloway and Ettrick forest, sometime Douglas property; the castles of Edinburgh, Stirling, Dumbarton, with their domains; the earldoms of Fife and Strathearn; and others of less importance. James outdistanced his father in the extent of his appropriations and enrichment of the Crown. He died master of the kingdom and in the moment of his last success. Excepting Berwick, Roxburgh remained the last fortress in English hands. It fell in August 1460, but cost the king his life. While watching the practice of one of his great pieces, "mair curious than became the majestie of ane king," the monster burst and killed him on the spot. He was only in his thirtieth year and had reigned twenty-four Something he owed to Kennedy's sagacity, most to his own character.

The new king, James III (1460–88), a boy of ten, inherited none of the vigour and resource of his father and grandfather. In him the royal authority was as impotent as under the first two Stewarts, the Crown once more became the sport of contending factions, and treason, abetted by England, shewed itself within the royal house. The rivalry of York and Lancaster also affected Scotland. Allied to the Beauforts, James II's sympathies inclined to the Lancastrians, and though his widow, Mary of Guelders, influenced by her relationship to the Duke of Burgundy, favoured the Yorkists, her son's advisers, alarmed by the exiled Douglas' collusion with the White Rose and the latter's disposition to revive English claims to superiority, supported their late sovereign's preference. In 1461, after their rout at Towton, Margaret of Anjou and her husband besought assistance and offered Berwick as a bribe. With intervals it had remained in English hands since 1296. In April 1461

Henry restored it and recruited a considerable force in Scotland in his behalf. Edward IV, retaliating, promised Douglas reinstatement and John of the Isles possession of Scotland north of the Scots Water (Firth of Forth), provided they gave him faithful and effective service as lord paramount. John of the Isles took arms, Douglas and his brother harried the marches, and Kennedy, gauging the weakness of the Lancastrian cause, at length turned Henry VI adrift. In 1463 a truce was made with Yorkist England, prolonged by mutual agreement to fifteen years.

The deaths of the queen-mother and Kennedy, first of Scotland's ecclesiastical statesmen, delivered James in his fifteenth year to an aspiring family whose fall was as sudden as its rise was swift. The chief actors in a rapid drama were Robert Lord Boyd and his brother Sir Alexander, the latter of whom was both governor of Edinburgh Castle and the king's instructor in martial exercises. In February 1466 the Boyds banded with others to secure the king's person. In July James was kidnapped and carried to Edinburgh, where, in October, a submissive Parliament named Lord Boyd sole governor of the realm, keeper of the king and his two brothers, and custodian of the royal fortresses. Whether or not he acted in collusion with the Yorkist government, Boyd's chief purpose was to advantage his family. His son received the earldom of Arran and the hand of James' sister Mary (1467). If selfishly inspired, Boyd's rule performed one first-rate service to Scotland. Her failure to pay the "annual" for the Western Isles since 1426 had accumulated considerable arrears, and even before James II's death Norway declared her dissatisfaction. French mediation suggested a match between Christian I's daughter and the Scottish king to compose the difficulty, and in 1468 Arran was sent to Norway to arrange it. His mission was successful: James' proposal for Margaret of Norway was accepted; of her jointure one-sixth (10,000 florins) was to accompany her to Scotland; for the balance (50,000 florins) the Orkneys were pledged and full acquittance was given for the "annual." In fact the princess brought but two of the promised ten thousand florins; her father therefore pledged the Shetlands too. Neither group was ever redeemed, and in 1472 both Orkneys and Shetlands were annexed to the Scottish Crown. The king's marriage extinguished the Boyds' supremacy. Arran's presumptuous union with royalty excited the jealousy of his peers. His father and uncle, impeached of treason, suffered forfeiture and Sir Alexander went to the block. Arran passed a roving life in Europe until his death. His wife, divorced from his fortunes, gave her hand to the first Lord Hamilton (*ob.* 1479), to whom she took the Arran title.

James at this point could look back upon a reign not undistinguished. Berwick, Roxburgh, Orkney, and Shetland had been recovered, St Andrews had been constituted an archbishopric, John of the Isles had been brought to submission, and his earldom of Ross augmented the domains attached by forfeiture. But within the royal house dissension had been growing. In tastes and temperament James had little in common with his brothers, Alexander Duke of Albany and John Earl of Mar, who shared the contempt of his lords for what they held their sovereign's unkingly occupations. Albany, ambitious and disloyal, sold himself to England in a treaty signed at Fotheringhay in 1482, and, joining Edward's brother Gloucester, gave siege to Berwick. The crisis brought the barons' quarrel with the king and his plebeian counsellors to a head. Accompanied by his favourites, James encamped at Lauder Bridge, where Archibald 'Bell-the-Cat,' Earl of Angus, speaking for the malcontents, threatened to retreat unless the king's minions were dismissed, and, on James' refusal, hanged them forthwith. Opposition to Gloucester and Albany collapsed, and, Berwick having fallen, the dukes entered Edinburgh in triumph. Returning to England, Gloucester mastered the castle, as already he possessed the town of Berwick (1482). It passed finally from Scotland's possession.

Meanwhile, James and his brothers seemed reconciled. In December 1482 Albany received the Lieutenancy of the Realm and the earldom of Mar and Garioch. But he was still in league with England, where his agents in February 1483 confirmed the Fotheringhay compact. Suspecting his treason, James, in March, banished him from court, and Parliament, in May, visited his treason upon his head. Attainted, he fled across the Border, threw a last stake with exiled Douglas in 1484, and passed to the Continent, where he died (1485). Three years later James closed an uneasy reign. His favour of men "of the lowest description" remained a grievance with his nobles. His employment of ecclesiastics in the public service equally displeased them. In 1488 the storm long threatened broke. Provoked immediately by James' intention to attach the revenues of Coldingham Priory to his Chapel Royal at Stirling, a confederacy was formed by the Homes, but agreement was reached upon the king's undertaking to choose as his counsellors none but "prelates, lords, and others of wisdom." Yet his sincerity was doubted, and the confederates kept the field. In June the armies faced each other at Sauchie Burn, near Bannockburn. Carried from the field by a charger beyond his management, James was tracked by his enemies to a distant hovel and dispatched in cold blood (1488). The circumstances of the murder were never divulged. The king, the curious were told, "happened to be slain."

Thus the fifteenth century closed for Scotland in depressing conditions. The careers of Douglas and Albany, and of lesser men, Boyds, Crichtons, Livingstones, and others, reveal the imperfect degree to which, after more than a century of rule, the Stewarts had tamed their intractable baronage. On the other hand, the apparatus of an ordered State had been set up; Parliament functioned in a form it never lost; the outlying islands had been recovered to their natural allegiance; and though English enmity was still to inflict a disaster greater than any Scotland had experienced, English imperialism, working indirectly through a Balliol, Douglas,

Albany, or Lord of the Isles, had been firmly resisted. With France an alliance existed which drew Scotland into the current of European politics and advanced her cultural progress. Two universities promoted learning, and cultivated thought found expression in a hardy vernacular literature which possessed, in Robert Henryson, a poet whose outlook and style bespeaks Scotland's closeness to the Renaissance, though his contemporary Blind Harry's *Wallace* glances backward at an enmity which had tested and established the foundations on which Scotland's natural existence was laid. She awaited the Reformation to draw her into a new world of thought and action from which her geographical isolation and concentration upon the problem of national preservation as yet held her somewhat aloof.

CHAPTER XV

SPAIN, 1412–1516

THE political history of fifteenth-century Spain may be taken to begin in Castile in 1406 with the accession of John II, the son of Henry III; in Aragon in 1412 with the election to the thrones of Aragon and Catalonia of an Infant of Castile, Don Ferdinand *el de Antequera*, the son of John I of Castile and grandson of Peter IV of Aragon.

The history of Castile in this century is lacking in political importance until 1474. It is merely a record of the persistence of internal discord, due to the lawlessness of the nobility and the efforts made by the kings to dominate this class and to recall it to a state of subordination and submission to the laws. Unfortunately, the two kings who succeeded Henry III—John II and Henry IV—were lacking in the qualities necessary for the achievement of this end.

John II came to the throne when he was only two years old. His minority, however, was a period of tranquillity and good government, thanks to the statesmanlike and disinterested character of his uncle Don Ferdinand *el de Antequera*, who not only mastered the nobles, but also boldly pushed forward the work of reconquest from the Muslims. He achieved the capture of the town of Antequera, in the north-east of the district of Málaga, in 1410. Unfortunately, his election to the throne of Aragon, of which more will be said hereafter, caused the regency to fall into the hands of the Queen-mother Catherine, and she was entirely devoid of the qualities that were essential for success. When John II attained his majority in 1419, he proved to be no better fitted for the task. His tastes were for literature, and for the pastimes and spectacles of courtly chivalry, rather than for the grave cares of government; and he left the management of public affairs in the hands of a nobleman, Don Alvaro de Luna, nephew of the Archbishop of Toledo, who became Constable of Castile.

Don Alvaro was fully capable of pitting himself against the lawless nobility and gaining the mastery over them, in spite of their incessant attacks upon him, in which they were assisted by members of the royal family. But, in order to succeed, he needed the constant support of the king; and this was often lacking, since the king had not the strength of mind to resist the palace intrigues. On several occasions Don Alvaro was banished from the Court, only to be recalled again. This continual alternation of fortune proved too great a handicap for the establishment of his political aims, so that they were doomed to failure. The end came when the king's second wife, Isabella of Portugal, who had obtained a complete ascendancy over her husband, sided with the enemies of the

Constable. Won over by his wife, King John caused Don Alvaro to be arrested, regardless of the fact that the Constable, whatever his personal defects—and they were characteristic of the governing class of his time— was his best friend and the only person capable of defeating the nobility. Don Alvaro was brought before the Council and condemned to death on the charge of attempting by sorcery to gain a hold over the king's mind. He was executed in July 1452, and this event marked the triumph of the lawless spirit among the nobles and of the intrigues and factions of the Court.

This was clearly demonstrated when John II's son Henry IV succeeded him on the throne in 1454; for he was even weaker than his father, and, moreover, he was psychologically abnormal. The nobles profited by these disastrous traits, and the tale of intrigues reached its height. The reign of Henry IV, which lasted for twenty years, was one continuous record of scandals of all kinds, emanating from the gossip cleverly exploited, and probably invented by one of the Court factions, that Henry IV's daughter Joanna was in fact a bastard. On this depended the manœuvres of the rival adherents of Henry IV's brother Alfonso and of his sister Isabella; each party sought to have its own candidate declared successor to the throne, though the Cortes had already decided in favour of Joanna. The culmination was reached at an assembly held at Avila by the rebellious nobles, where, after a mockery of a trial lacking in all legality, the king was deposed and driven from his throne in a grotesque ceremony, the part of Henry IV being taken by a lay figure which was stripped of crown and sceptre and cast to the ground. The assembly then proclaimed the Infant Alfonso (*ob*: 1468) as king.

This outrage produced a strong reaction in favour of Henry, and his troops won a victory over those of the nobles. Instead of profiting by this, the king came to terms with the rebels, recognising his sister Isabella as heiress to the throne, which was tantamount to a definite affirmation of his daughter's illegitimacy. Isabella had refused to be elected queen when this was proposed by the nobles, but, believing in her right to the succession, she accepted the king's recognition of her as heiress to the throne. Henry, however, changed his mind again, taking offence at Isabella's marriage with the Infant Ferdinand of Aragon in 1469. Consequently, he revoked his decision in favour of Isabella, and made another in favour of Joanna. It failed of its purpose, since neither Isabella nor her supporters would accept this new royal judgment. Five years later (1474) the king died, and civil war immediately broke out.

The nobles were divided, some supporting Joanna, others Isabella. Joanna tried to avoid war and to refer the matter to arbitration by a commission composed of members of the Cortes. This, however, came to nothing. Then the King of Portugal, who was offered Joanna's hand in marriage by her supporters, took sides with her; while Isabella's party was joined by Henry's old favourite, Don Beltran de la Cueva, who was reputed by public opinion to be the actual father of Joanna[1]. The issue of the war was favourable to Isabella, whose troops were victorious at Toro and Albuera. Peace was signed with Portugal at the treaty of Trujillo in September 1479, which had an important bearing on the relations of Castile and Portugal in the Canary Islands and on later expeditions and conquests in West Africa[2]. As a compensation to Joanna, an attempt was made to marry her to the son of Isabella and Ferdinand, Don John. But Joanna returned a dignified refusal to this proposal, and of her own accord entered into a convent, and remained there until her death, never ceasing to style herself Queen of Castile.

While these events were happening in the Castilian kingdom during the reigns of John II and Henry IV, Aragon was entering upon a new phase in its political history, which was marked externally by the accession of a dynasty Castilian in origin. Not that the previous kings of Aragon had been of pure Aragonese or Catalan race. Actually, they had frequently married Castilian princesses, and rarely Catalan ladies, after Catalonia had been linked under Raymond-Berengar IV with Aragon. So, much Castilian blood had mingled with the old Aragonese strain and with the newer but distant Catalan strain which derived from the marriage of the Count of Barcelona and the princess Petronilla, niece of Alfonso I of Aragon, in 1137[3].

The change of dynasty took place in the following circumstances. The existence of various claimants after the death of Martin I caused the menace of civil war, since public opinion was very much divided in its choice. After two years of hesitation and procrastination, the Cortes of Catalonia in 1410, and those of Aragon and Valencia in 1412, decided to settle the question by arbitration. A mixed commission was appointed, consisting of three delegates from Aragon, three from Catalonia, and three from Valencia; Majorca, Sicily, and Sardinia were not represented. This commission acted as a court deciding the question on the basis of private law, that is to say as a matter of family inheritance, following the precedent set a century before by Alfonso X of Castile in deciding the succession to the throne.

The two most important claimants from this point of view were the Castilian Infant Don Ferdinand *el de Antequera*, who has been mentioned before in connexion with the minority of John II of Castile, and who was, through his mother, the nephew of Martin I; and the Count of Urgel, the son of a cousin of Martin I and great-nephew of Peter IV. From the point of view of degree of kinship the advantage lay with Ferdinand. It

---

[1] In consequence of this rumour Joanna was called La Beltraneja by her contemporaries.

[2] See *infra*, Chap. XVI, p. 523. There were two treaties, one of Alcaçovas on the succession to Castile, the other of Trujillo on the Canaries etc., and they were confirmed at Toledo in March 1480.

[3] See *supra*, Vol. VI, pp. 405 sqq.

is very probable, too, that his personal qualities, which had been demonstrated in his regency of Castile and in the war with the Muslims of Granada, played an appreciable part in helping the commission to their decision. Moreover, within the commission the candidature of Ferdinand was ardently supported by the famous Valencian preacher, Vincent Ferrer, who had great prestige among his contemporaries. The commission decided in accordance with Ferrer's view, six votes being definitely in favour. To these may be added the vote of the Archbishop of Tarragona, who declared the election of Ferdinand to be "the most useful," though from the point of view of kinship he preferred the Count of Urgel or the Duke of Gandía; the Catalan Vallseca also supported the view of the archbishop. The decision of the parliamentary commission was known as the "Compromise of Caspe," from the town where the sittings were held.

The election, which was proclaimed on 28 June 1412, was well received by public opinion in Aragon, but with some discontent in Valencia and more still in Catalonia, where feeling was in favour of the Count of Urgel, himself a Catalan. However, this did not lead in either case to open opposition. The Cortes of Catalonia even sent to Ferdinand a deputation authorised to recognise him as king and to obtain from him a general amnesty, which was to include the Count of Urgel provided that he too would recognise Ferdinand. The new king granted even more than they asked, proposing a marriage between the count's daughter and his third son, Don Henry, to whom he promised to grant the duchy of Montblanch as well as a large sum of money.

The Count of Urgel, however, was induced by the injudicious advice of his mother and of the Lord of Loarre to refuse his assent to the decision of Caspe, and to embark upon a civil war, which only lasted for a short time in spite of the assistance he received from English, Gascon, and Navarrese knights and men-at-arms, and the moral, though secret, support of the Duke of Clarence, the King of England's son. Ferdinand soon triumphed over his rival, who surrendered at Balaguer on 31 October 1413. The king spared his life and confined him in a castle, allowing him the right of having his own servants, of receiving visitors, and other kindnesses, which considerably softened his captivity. Shortly afterwards, the war was ended by the surrender of the Lord of Loarre and the count's mother.

Meanwhile, a section in Catalonia remained hostile and distrustful towards the new king. This attitude seems to have derived from two sentiments: the one, which may be called a national feeling, based on the fact that Ferdinand was neither Aragonese nor Catalan by birth, though in fact through his mother he had Aragonese blood in his veins; the other proceeding from the fear that Ferdinand, owing to his Castilian origin, would be a despotic ruler. This was a very questionable hypothesis, for the Aragonese kings, so far as in them lay, had taken as strong a line as the kings of Castile in their struggle with the lawless nobility and the burgher oligarchies, and had been no less careful to strengthen as much as possible the powers of the ruler against the feudal tendencies which made for the decentralisation of political and administrative functions in the usual medieval manner.

Ferdinand, indeed, though he was certainly cognisant of this Catalan prejudice, was probably not sufficiently careful to preserve a show of respect for the traditional rights and customs of Catalonia; these did not, in fact, constitute a formidable danger to the sovereignty of the king as had those of the Unión which had been crushed so relentlessly by Peter IV of Aragon[1]. He accordingly had some friction with the Catalans over certain parliamentary formalities in the Cortes of Montblanch in 1414, and over the payment of a toll at Barcelona. Ferdinand maintained the view, which was subsequently to prevail in public law, that the king was exempt from this payment. The authorities at Barcelona, on the contrary, maintained that payment was obligatory even upon the king. The king ended by yielding, owing to the popular excitement which was aroused over this question; and, fortunately, nothing worse occurred than a few minor affrays. Ferdinand, moreover, did not interfere with the political and administrative autonomy which Catalonia enjoyed in the kingdom of Aragon.

He had another much more serious problem to settle, international in character and closely affecting Spanish sentiment and interest—the Great Schism of the West. The Avignonese Pope at this time was Benedict XIII, an Aragonese of the powerful family of Luna; consequently he was called the anti-Pope Luna, though in fact the circumstances of his election were perfectly legal. He had assisted Ferdinand to win the crown of Aragon, and might logically have expected to receive the king's support. But Ferdinand was won over by the instance of the Emperor Sigismund, who was anxious to end the schism and had secured the abdication of the other two Popes, John XXIII and Gregory XII, to pave the way for a new election; so he brought pressure to bear on Benedict XIII to obtain from him his abdication also. Benedict, however, would not hear of it. Strong in his legal position, and to that extent justified in his attitude, since he had been elected in accordance with the canonical regulations then in force, he refused to abdicate and, shutting himself up in his castle of Peñiscola in Valencia on the Mediterranean coast, continued to bear the title of Pope up to his death in 1423. And even this event did not, as was anticipated, provide a final solution of the schism.

Ferdinand I was succeeded in 1416 by his eldest son, Alfonso V, who inherited together the united States of Aragon, Catalonia, Majorca, Valencia, and Sicily. Sicily was governed at the time by Ferdinand's other son, John, whom the Sicilians, in their desire to be independent, tried to elect as king. To avert this danger, Alfonso recalled John to Spain. He himself was soon drawn into the vortex of Italian affairs, especially owing to the problem of the old dispute between Aragon, Genoa, and Pisa over Sardinia and Corsica.

[1] Cf. *supra*, Vol. VI, p. 591.

Alfonso was actually in Sardinia when he received an embassy from the Queen of Naples, Joanna II, asking for his support against the numerous enemies who were trying to deprive her of her Neapolitan realm[1]. She promised Alfonso the title of Duke of Calabria and the succession to the kingdom of Naples on her death. Her most formidable enemy was the French duke, Louis III of Anjou, who, like his father Louis II before him, maintained his claim to the Neapolitan throne. Alfonso responded to Joanna's appeal and accepted her conditions. He despatched a squadron against Louis who was threatening Naples with a fleet, and won a striking victory over him; and he himself captured the castle of Cena near the city of Naples.

But Joanna was quite inconstant, and once more changed her mind; under the influence of her lover, the Grand Seneschal Caracciolo, she deprived Alfonso of the inheritance and transferred it to Louis of Anjou. Alfonso refused to submit to this cavalier treatment, and began a struggle to make good his rights. This provoked a fresh war in 1423 between the kingdom of Aragon and the house of Anjou, which supported the queen; and she remained in possession of her kingdom up to her death in 1435. In her will she bequeathed the throne of Naples to the surviving son of Louis II, René of Anjou. Alfonso determined not to accept this, but to conquer the kingdom which had been promised to him. The war at the beginning went most unfavourably for him: he was captured by the Genoese at Gaeta in 1435 together with his brother John, who was then King of Navarre, and was handed over to the Duke of Milan, Filippo Maria Visconti. The duke was won over by Alfonso to render him his liberty without ransom and even recognised him as King of Naples. Fortune then changed in Alfonso's favour, and he entered Naples in triumph on 26 February 1443. René of Anjou judged it hopeless to continue the struggle and returned to France. Alfonso was careful to enter into good relations with the Pope, Eugenius IV, by assisting him against the *condottiere* Francesco Sforza. The Pope granted him investiture with his new kingdom on 15 July 1443, and this was confirmed by the next Pope, Nicholas V. Thus Alfonso completed the work begun in South Italy 161 years before by King Peter III of Aragon, and fulfilled too the political aims long cherished by the counts of Barcelona.

From 1443 onwards Alfonso V resided at Naples, and was rather an Italian than a Spanish monarch; for, despite the frequent appeals, backed by all the notables of the realm, of his wife, Queen Maria, who governed Aragon and the other provinces during his absence, he never returned to Spain. Of the 42 years of his reign, he spent 29 in Italy, 26 of them without a break. It used to be thought that this voluntary exile was due to disagreement with his wife, but since the monograph of the Spanish

---

[1] For these events and Alfonso's reign in Naples see *supra*, Chap. v. pp. 164–5, 176–80.

historian Giménez Soler in 1898, this hypothesis can no longer be maintained. Probably the real reason for his permanent stay at Naples was the fear that he would lose it if he returned to Spain. Naples was to him a conquest of the greatest importance and worth the sacrifice he made for it; his Spanish subjects were not of his mind, and to them there was no justification for their king's absence.

Alfonso was not only endowed with great political and military qualities, but he was also highly cultured; at Naples he shone as a Maecenas of the sciences, of the arts, and of letters, and he was inspired deeply with the spirit of the Renaissance. He was justly called the Magnanimous. His court was the most brilliant centre for philosophers, linguists, men of letters, and artists of his age, Spaniards as well as Italians. He enriched Naples with architectural monuments, some of which remain to the present day. He paid a compliment to the Catalan part of his Spanish kingdom by making its language the official language of his court at Naples, a proof that the kings of the Castilian dynasty were able to assimilate the spirit of their new country.

At his death in 1458, Alfonso divided his territories, giving Naples to his natural son Ferdinand (Ferrante), and the remainder to his brother John, who had been for some years, as has been said, King-consort of Navarre. The queen, Blanche, died in 1441. From his marriage with Blanche John had a son Charles, Prince of Viana, and a daughter Leonora, betrothed in 1432 to Count Gaston of Foix and married to him a few years later. So the heir to the throne of Navarre was the Prince of Viana, who was bound by an undertaking given to his grandfather not to adopt the title of king during his father's lifetime; actually, he frequently took over the government of the country owing to the absence of his father, who was more concerned with the intrigues at the court of Castile, the struggle of the nobles with Don Alvaro de Luna, than with the interests of Navarre.

John's second marriage, in 1447, with Joanna Enriquez, daughter of the Admiral of Castile, connected him still more closely with affairs at the Castilian Court, especially in opposition to Don Alvaro, a bitter enemy of the Admiral. Don Alvaro tried to make peace and to obtain the alliance of the Navarrese; and he applied to the Prince of Viana with this object. The prince welcomed the proposal, but his father was hostile to it. Opinion in Navarre was divided between the two views, not from any real interest in the quarrels of the Castilian Court, but because these provided a convenient excuse for the feuds of the great aristocratic houses of Navarre and for the lawless tendencies of the nobles. So the rival factions ranged themselves in two parties: the one, known popularly as the *Béarnais*, supporting the prince; the other, known as the *Agramontais*, on the side of the king, or more truly of the queen, Joanna. Civil war soon broke out, aggravating the situation in Navarre, which was already complicated by the intervention in Castilian politics against Don Alvaro. At the beginning, fortune so favoured the *Agramontais* that the

Prince of Viana had to leave the country and take refuge in Italy. His father tried to disinherit him, and to this end made a pact with his son-in-law, Count Gaston of Foix, the husband, as has been already mentioned, of Charles' sister Leonora. The Prince of Viana, for his part, succeeded in gaining the support of his uncle Alfonso V, King of Aragon and Naples, and of the Pope, both of whom favoured the regular succession to the throne of Navarre. Unfortunately Alfonso V died shortly afterwards (1458), and as a result Don John found himself possessed of the kingdom of Aragon, both legally and actually, while at the same time he was *de facto* ruler of Navarre as well. In the trial of strength Charles seemed to be hopelessly overmatched. As soon as he returned to Spain, he was arrested by his father's orders, and his cause seemed to be irremediably lost. But then a new element entered into the situation. Public opinion in Catalonia was stirred by the injustice of the king's attitude; and the imprisonment of the prince provoked so serious a revolt that the king had to give way, and not only set his son at liberty, but even sign a formal recognition of him as successor to the throne of Navarre (Agreement or Concordat of Villafranca, 21 June 1461) and also as the acting governor of Catalonia with the title of Lieutenant (*Lugarteniente*).

The sudden death of the prince three months afterwards caused a fresh outbreak of civil war, for public opinion attributed his death to poison and assigned the guilt of it to the queen, Joanna. So, the Catalans were ranged against king and queen. The army of the *Generalitat* (*Diputación General*), which directed public affairs in Catalonia, marched against the queen, who was then in Gerona. The town was besieged, but was courageously defended by Joanna and her adherents, so that the king was able to come to the rescue and forced the Catalans to raise the siege. John was determined to crush the revolt, and had collected an army composed of Aragonese, Castilian, and French troops. The Generalitat then issued a manifesto declaring the king and queen enemies of Catalonia and as such to be expelled from Catalan territory (11 June 1462). At the same time the government sought for a new monarch to aid them in their struggle with the treacherous king. In turn, Henry IV of Castile, the Constable of Portugal, and John, Duke of Calabria, René of Anjou's son, consented to help the Catalans. René of Anjou was even named Count of Barcelona, in spite of the old enmity of the Dukes of Anjou to Catalonia, which had been so strikingly evinced in their rivalry with Alfonso V for the throne of Naples. But Henry IV's help was only transitory; that of the Constable of Portugal was limited to himself alone, since he brought no troops, and was soon ended by his death; while John of Calabria, whose arms won fortune in the field, fell a victim to poison on 15 December 1470. The war was then in its eighth year. King John II at last ended it by offering peace on favourable terms in 1472; he was indeed forced to this by necessity, for he had become afflicted with blindness and he was left desolate by the death of his second wife.

Catalonia and Aragon thus reunited, joined forces against the King of France[1], to whom John II had imprudently ceded Roussillon; this province was attached to the crown of Majorca, which had been incorporated with that of Aragon from the time of Peter IV. Seven years later John died (19 January 1479), and the thrones of Aragon, Catalonia, Valencia, and Majorca passed to the son of his second marriage, Ferdinand II, who in 1469 had married the Infanta Isabella of Castile and on Henry IV's death had been proclaimed, with his wife, King of Castile on 13 December 1474. So, at the beginning of 1479, the two great monarchies which emerged from the struggles of the Middle Ages in Spain were united under the sceptre of the royal pair, Ferdinand and Isabella. This opened the period, so fruitful for the history of the Peninsula, known as the age of the Catholic Kings, as a sequel to which a single monarch was to reign over the whole of Spain.

Navarre remained for the time apart, as it had been inherited by John II's daughter Leonora, Countess of Foix. As a result, this kingdom fell under the preponderating influence of France and so remained for some years.

To understand properly the structure of political life, both in Castile and Aragon, during the age of the Catholic Kings—that is to say, from 1479 to the death of Isabella in 1504—it is necessary to realise the political relations existing between the two sovereigns, Ferdinand and Isabella. These relations had been fixed first of all by their marriage-contract (*Capitulaciones*), and later by the regulations drawn up by the Cardinal of Spain and the Archbishop of Toledo as arbiters of the dispute which arose between Isabella and Ferdinand after 1474, owing to the claims of the latter to be regarded as actual sovereign of Castile. His claims, which were supported by some Castilian nobles and by opinion in Aragon generally, were based partly on the fact that Ferdinand was nearest of kin to the dynasty which had reigned in Castile from the time of Henry II, partly on the Aragonese custom which recognised female rights of succession to the throne but always preferred the ruler to be a man rather than a woman.

The above-mentioned regulations created a kind of dyarchy, in which justice was to be exercised conjointly when they happened to be together in the same place, or by either of them independently if they happened to be separated. Royal charters were signed by them both, and the coinage bore both heads upon it, while the seals also contained the arms of both kingdoms. Apart from this the administration of Castile was reserved to Isabella in her own right. Ferdinand raised some difficulties about accepting this arrangement, but eventually he gave way. The principle of equality between the two spouses which resulted from this system is expressed in the well-known formula, "Tanto monta, monta tanto, Isabel

[1] See *supra*, Chap. VIII, pp. 279–80, 288, 292.

como Fernando," which is found so often on contemporary monuments; there is a magnificent specimen on tapestry still to be seen in the cathedral of Toledo. On the other hand, Isabella was not recognised to have any rights in the government of Aragon; she never interfered in the concerns of her husband's kingdom, which remained completely distinct from those which affected Castile.

In Castile the problems were of two very different kinds. The one was of an international order—the constant possibility of war with the Muslims of Granada, and the rivalry with Portugal over Africa. The other was an internal matter—the contest between the monarchy and the nobles, which raised the question of public order, of the maintenance of the central authority of the State, and of social and political discipline. The Catholic Kings confronted all these diverse problems with equal energy, and ended by solving each of them successfully.

The war against the Muslims, the continuation, that is to say, of the Reconquest, was pursued with a deliberate persistence aiming at the absorption of the kingdom of Granada. At the death of Henry IV, with the exception of Gibraltar which had been ceded by the King of Granada, Ismāʿīl III, there had been no farther advance upon Muslim territory since that won by Don Ferdinand during the minority of John II. The brilliant campaign of Don Alvaro de Luna and Henry IV, and the victory of La Higuera (or Higueruela) near Granada in 1431, which is depicted in the magnificent frescoes in the cloisters of the Escurial, had had no positive result.

Ismāʿīl III had acknowledged himself as a tributary of the King of Castile, but his successor ʿAlī Abū-l-Ḥasan, also called Muley Hacen, broke this dependence and took by surprise the castle of Zahara in 1481. The Castilian forces replied to this attack by capturing Alhama on 26 February 1482, a stronghold seven leagues from Granada, the loss of which was lamented in a famous Moorish ballad of the time. The war, once started, lasted for eleven years. In view of the determined attitude of the rulers of Castile, it is remarkable that the Moorish kingdom, weakened as it was, still preserved sufficient strength to oppose a long and desperate resistance to the Christian armies. Moreover, these armies, backed by the diplomatic skill of Ferdinand and Isabella, were further materially aided by the rivalries which broke out in the royal family of Granada, especially after 1483, between Abū-l-Ḥasan and his son Boabdil, and also between Boabdil and his uncle Abū-ʿAbd-Allāhī Muḥammad ("Az-Zaghal").

In 1482 the war went unfavourably for Castile. Ferdinand besieged the town of Loja, south-east of Granada, but was defeated and pursued by the Muslims as far as Cordova. He suffered a similar disaster shortly afterwards in the Ajarquia hills near Málaga, where "Az-Zaghal" was in command of the victorious Muslims. But in the spring of 1483 fortune changed. While the town of Lucena, south of Cordova, was being besieged

by a Muslim army commanded by Boabdil and his father-in-law, the
general 'Alī 'Aṭṭār, a Castilian force under the Count of Cabra arrived on
the scene. In the battle that ensued, 'Alī 'Aṭṭār was killed and Boabdil
taken prisoner (23 April). Then the diplomatic skill of the Catholic
Kings and their advisers, the Marquess of Cadiz and the Count of Cabra,
was brought into play. By the pact of Cordova, Boabdil was released on
condition that he would assist the Castilian troops against that part of
the kingdom of Granada which was ruled by "Az-Zaghal" (he had
recently dispossessed Abū-l-Ḥasan), the rulers of Castile promising him
their help in return.

So began a new period of civil war among the Muslims, with the
throne of Granada as the stake. Father, son, and uncle (Abū-l-Ḥasan,
Boabdil, and "Az-Zaghal") fought out their triangular duel, and thereby
assisted still further the purpose of the Castilians. At one point Boabdil
had to take refuge with the Christians, and once again he was set at
liberty. Then Abū-l-Ḥasan died, but the struggle continued between
Boabdil and "Az-Zaghal."

The Castilian troops profited by these circumstances to carry on the
war and to capture towns and fortresses in the neighbourhood of Granada.
Zahara, Álora, Setenil, Cártama, Coin, Ronda, Marbella, Loja, Velez-
Málaga, and finally Málaga itself fell in turn into their hands between 1483
and 1487. The year 1487 marked a critical stage. Most of the Muslims
followed "Az-Zaghal," in disgust at Boabdil's open attitude of submission
to the Christians for the sole purpose of maintaining himself at Granada.
"Az-Zaghal" himself and his followers maintained their resistance with
a splendid courage. They succeeded in raising the siege of Almería, and
in prolonging inordinately the defence of Baza, an important fortress to
the west of Granada and close to "Az-Zaghal's" headquarters at Guadix.
Queen Isabella even sold her jewels to expedite military operations, and
Baza was at last taken at the end of 1489. The result of this triumph
for Castile was the submission of "Az-Zaghal" and the surrender to the
Catholic Kings of the territory he ruled, namely the eastern portion of
the province of Granada and the district of Almería.

Only Boabdil and the town of Granada now held out. Boabdil refused
to open the gates of the capital to the Catholic Kings as he had formerly
promised to do, and the Castilian army besieged the town in 1491. The
camp of Ferdinand and Isabella, which was pitched close to the town on
its south-east side, in the farm of Gozco, was destroyed by fire; it was
then decided to construct an entrenched camp, with buildings, walls,
ditches, and the like—a military town, in fact, after the fashion of the
old Roman encampments. This town was called Santa Fé, and it is still
in existence to-day.

The result was easily to be foreseen. Negotiations for the surrender of
Granada were opened at the end of the year; the town capitulated, and
the Catholic Kings made their triumphal entry into the fortress-palace

of the Alhambra, which commanded the town, on 2 January 1492. The principal conditions of the surrender were: a complete guarantee for the persons and property of the Muslims who wished to remain at Granada; liberty to all who wished to leave the country to depart, and to take their possessions with them; the preservation of Muslim religion and law; and the freeing of prisoners. The Moors of Granada were substantially placed under the same conditions as the Mudéjares of old.

Thus was completed the Reconquest of the Spanish territory which had fallen into the hands of the Moors at the beginning of the eighth century. Granada was regarded as a new kingdom attached to the Castilian monarchy. In the final stage of the war, besides the Marquess of Cadiz and the Count of Cabra who have already been mentioned, the following distinguished themselves on the Christian side: the Duke of Medinaceli, Gonzalo de Córdoba, whose prowess shortly afterwards in Italy won him the title of the Great Captain, the artillery-commander Francisco Ramirez, and several other officers and soldiers whose deeds of daring can still be read in the ballads of the time. There were also foreign volunteers, like Lord Scales, who came with an English troop, and Gaston de Lyon.

The national glory and pride in its definitive victory over the Muslims were soon tarnished by the failure on the part of a section in Castile to observe some of the terms of the surrender. Cardinal Cisneros (Ximenes), who earned an illustrious name in the organisation and support of learning and letters, took upon himself to contravene the royal pledges, after the manner of Archbishop Bernard of Toledo five centuries earlier. His Christian zeal caused him to ignore the religious liberty promised to the Muslims; and he endeavoured to enforce baptism upon them. The result was a general rising of the Muslims in Granada and its neighbourhood, in the Alpujarra, Baza, Guadix, Ronda, and the Sierra of Filambres (Filabres) to the north of Almería. This second war was long and bloody; and it resulted not in the reversal of Cisneros' policy, but in the adoption of it by the Castilian government, making of no account the terms signed at Granada and the long and ancient tradition with regard to the Mudéjares. A royal decree of 11 February 1502 gave the Muslims of Castile and Leon the alternative of abjuring their religion or leaving Spanish soil. It was rigorously enforced, in spite of the disorders it provoked in various parts, even in the Basque lands.

This decree was not enforced in Aragon. At the request of the Cortes, and especially of the nobles who had Muslims among their vassals, the ancient privileges of the Mudéjares were left practically intact. King Ferdinand forbade the Inquisition to force these vassals to change their religion, which was thus preserved by the economic interests of the richer classes. Those Muslims who submitted to conversion were termed *Moriscos*. Their social and religious life up to the time of their expulsion in 1609 forms an interesting study, upon which modern research has thrown considerable light.

In the very year, 1491, in which Granada was on the point of falling into the hands of the Castilians, there occurred the prelude to another great event, and one far more important in its consequences for Spain and for the whole world—the discovery of America. It would be out of place here to describe the causes and the genesis of Columbus' enterprise, or to give the details of his biography and his travels in Portugal, France, and Spain to obtain the support and the means necessary in order to undertake the voyage on which he had set his heart, and which he expected would bring him by the Western route to the lands of Eastern Asia. Even in Spain, in spite of the support he received from the very start, there were difficulties to overcome. At last, owing to his insistence and to the steps taken on his behalf by some ecclesiastics and members of the nobility, of whom the most noteworthy were Fray Antonio of Marchena, Fray Diego of Deza, Fray Juan Pérez, prior of the monastery of La Rábida, the Duke of Medinaceli, the queen's treasurer Alonso of Quintanilla, the king's chamberlain Juan Cabrera, and the royal notary Luis de Santangel, he succeeded in arousing the interest of Queen Isabella and in gaining acceptance for his project. A contract (*capitulaciones*) between the Crown and Columbus was signed at Santa Fé on 17 April 1491. In this were laid down the rights and obligations of both sides, and also the principles to be adopted in the government and the development of the lands to be discovered by Columbus.

To provide for the voyage, the sovereigns ordered the authorities at the port of Palos (Huelva) to put ships and all necessary equipment at Columbus' disposal; but this end was achieved, not so much by the royal order as by the good services of the Andalusian sea-captains Martin Alonso Pinzón and his brother Vicente, and by the Catalan captain Pedro Ferrer of Blanes. The financing of the expedition was arranged almost entirely by the notary Santangel and the Genoese Francesco da Pinedo. The sum Columbus had agreed to provide was guaranteed by Pinzón and other Spaniards and also by Genoese residents in Spain. Three vessels (*carabelas*) were employed on the voyage, two of them, the *Pinta* and the *Niña*, being the property of Pinzón and his brother. The third, which was also the largest, the *Santa Maria* (*Gallega, Mari Galante*), belonged to the sea-captain Juan de la Cosa, who became famous subsequently for his map of the regions first discovered and of the voyages in general. The *Santa Maria* was the flagship, and from it Columbus directed the expedition. The crews were mainly composed of Spaniards drawn from different parts of the Peninsula.

The start took place on 3 August 1492, from the port of Palos. Two months and a few days later, on 12 October 1492, the expedition arrived at the first point of American soil, one of the Bahama islands, called by the natives Guanahani and by Columbus San Salvador; conjecture has ranged over various islands of the group, but it cannot certainly be identified. Between this date and 16 January 1493, Columbus discovered other islands of the same group, and also both Cuba and Haiti (*la Española*). Though he was not yet aware of it, he had, in his projected voyage to Asia, discovered the archipelago of the Antilles, adjacent to the mainland of America. He returned to Palos on 15 March 1493, and in April was magnificently welcomed by the Catholic Kings at Barcelona. After this first voyage Columbus carried out three others, the last in 1502, in the course of which he reached the mouth of the Orinoco and the coast of Honduras, that is to say, the mainland both of South and Central America. Shortly before the end of the third voyage, in 1499, an expedition undertaken by Juan de la Cosa, in company with Alonso de Hojeda and Amerigo Vespucci (an Italian in the service of the Castilian sovereigns), availing themselves of a general permit from the Crown, in an order dated 10 April 1495, to make discoveries, to trade, and to colonise, began the great series of discoveries which followed those of Columbus; these, ranging over the lands and seas of America and Oceania, were due to Spanish enterprise and to the powerful States of the Spanish peninsula, which were shortly afterwards united under the rule of the grandson of the Catholic Kings, Charles I of Spain.

It was not only in the discovery of America that the reign of Ferdinand and Isabella left its mark on American history. In the same reign the foundations were laid for the organisation of the new countries added to the Castilian Crown, and a beginning was made, as will be seen later, in the solution of the novel and difficult problems of all kinds to which these discoveries gave rise.

As to Columbus himself, it remains to add that he was involved in political misfortune, arising from his administration of the Antilles and the rivalries among the first colonists of *la Española*; and that he died at Valladolid, seven months after his return to Spain from his fourth voyage. He was in easy circumstances at the time of his death, and not in the wretched conditions so often depicted. He, and his brothers with him, had enjoyed the advantages granted to him by the *capitulaciones* of Santa Fé, and he had also profited by the financial results of his enterprises. Though the sovereigns tried—solely for reasons of State—to reduce the privileges originally granted to Columbus, yet the lawsuit that followed resulted in the granting to Diego, the son and heir of the great navigator, the title of Admiral of the Indies, which brought with it corresponding advantages. The story of the ingratitude of Spain to Columbus can therefore be dismissed as legend. Finally, the attempt has been made to prove that Columbus was not a Genoese but a Spaniard of Galician, or even of Castilian, race, though no adequate historical evidence for this thesis has yet been adduced. However, there are still considerable lacunas in our knowledge of the life of Columbus.

Columbus' success in his first voyage aroused the jealousy of the Portuguese, who had already discovered Madeira and were continually pushing their expeditions along the coast of West Africa, in search of an eastern route to the Indies and also in the acquisition of trade, both in slaves and other merchandise. At the beginning of the reign of Isabella, as we have already seen, a treaty in 1480, followed later by others, had decided some of the issues arising from the navigation along the coasts of north-west Africa, and the respective rights of Spaniards and Portuguese. The latter had had the foresight to obtain by papal bull the monopoly for their own expeditions. The Catholic Kings followed their example after Columbus' first voyage, and obtained from the Pope, the Spaniard Alexander VI, four bulls, the most important, to judge by the protests of the Portuguese, being that of 4 May 1493, which drew a vertical line from the North to the South Pole to divide the actual and the future discoveries and conquests of the two countries. The objections raised by the King of Portugal to this division, and the indefiniteness of the line drawn by Alexander VI, led to so much ill-feeling as almost to produce a state of war. Fortunately the differences were settled by the treaty of Tordesillas on 7 June 1494, which fixed a new line of demarcation: for future discoveries this was taken to be 370 leagues west of the Cape Verde Islands, but 250 leagues west for discoveries already made or to be made by 20 June 1494. As is well-known, the Portuguese expeditions along the coast of Africa culminated in that of Bartholomew Dias and Vasco da Gama (1497–99), which discovered the eastern route to the Indies at the same time that Columbus, in the course of his third voyage, arrived at the Gulf of Paria, that is to say, the north-east coast of Venezuela.

Besides the new lands in the West, Spain had important interests also on the coast of North Africa. It was realised in Castile, and Queen Isabella was deeply convinced of the point, that to assure the success of the Reconquest which had been so happily completed in 1492, it was necessary to preserve Spain from fresh African invasions. To this anxiety had been added, since 1453, the fear of what might result from the victory of the Turkish Muslims and their entry and establishment in south-eastern Europe. The Catholic Kings, and Isabella in particular, exerted every endeavour to control North Africa; for the majority of the Muslims of Granada who had refused to abjure their religion had taken refuge there. By the treaty of 1480 Castile had already acquired a littoral zone in Magrab; she also acquired the right to the Canary Islands, but in order to obtain actual possession military operations were necessary. Accordingly, the town of Melilla was captured in 1497, and after the last descendants of the original conquerors had renounced their rights in favour of the Castilian Crown, the Canary Islands were completely and definitively conquered by Spanish troops, assisted by the native princes, Guanarteme and Anaterve de Guimar. The work of converting the islands into a Spanish possession was speedily accomplished, the native *Guanchos* being given equal rights, both legal and social, with the Spaniards.

With regard to the Turks, nothing of importance happened at the time. But the Catholic Kings were justified in adopting a watchful attitude; later, on the personal initiative of Charles I and Philip II, there was a change, and military enterprises on an important scale were undertaken.

While the international activity of Castile was directed to America and North Africa, Aragon was pursuing the route traced out for it by the rights and interests of its kings, by those of the counts of Barcelona, and also by its agelong rivalry with the kingdom of France.

This rivalry was temporarily lulled by the treaty of Barcelona in 1493, when Charles VIII restored to the Crown of Aragon the districts of Cerdagne and Roussillon, which had been lost in the time of John II; while Ferdinand the Catholic pledged himself to give no assistance to the enemies of the French kingdom, the Pope alone being excepted, and to form no marriage-alliance with the royal houses of England or Naples or with the imperial house of the Habsburgs. But once again the question of Naples arose to trouble the good relations established by this treaty. Charles VIII, listening to appeals from a section of the Neapolitan nobility and from other parts of Italy as well, in spite of the weighty opposition of several personages at his court, decided to undertake his enterprise in Italy[1]. Ferdinand the Catholic protested against the King of France's attack upon Naples, arguing that this kingdom, being a fief of the Papacy, was logically included in the provisions of the treaty of Barcelona. Charles VIII paid no heed to this protest, and after gaining possession of Naples he had himself crowned king there, in February 1495. The result of this was the formation of an alliance, known as the Holy League, between Ferdinand, the Pope, the dethroned King of Naples (a descendant of Alfonso V), Germany, the Duke of Milan, and Venice. The armies of the League were for the most part composed of Spanish officers and men, Castilians as well as Aragonese, a further proof of the close association of the two kingdoms brought about by the marriage of Ferdinand and Isabella. Moreover, the commander of these armies was the Castilian general Gonzalo Fernandez de Córdoba, who had already distinguished himself against the Muslims of Granada.

In the war that ensued there were, from the point of view of Spain, two main phases. In the first (1495–98), the French and their allies were defeated, and Naples was reconquered. Hostilities were suspended after the death in 1496 of the King of Naples, Ferrante II, who was succeeded by his uncle, Federigo; and peace was made with Charles VIII, and renewed afterwards with his successor Louis XII. The terms of this peace were laid down in the secret treaty of Granada (1500): King Federigo was deposed and the kingdom of Naples divided, Apulia and Calabria being assigned to Aragon, and Naples, the Abruzzi, and the Terra di Lavoro to France. The Pope and Venice approved the treaty. But its

[1] For the Italian wars, see the *Cambridge Modern History*, Vol. i.

execution raised difficulties as to the assignment of the districts known as Capitanata, Basilicata, and Principato. The war broke out again, and brought to the Spaniards striking successes in the land-battles of Cerignola and Garigliano and the naval battle of Otranto (1503). As a result, the kingdom of Naples was restored to the domains of the Aragonese Crown. Gonzalo de Córdoba, the great hero of these two wars, in which he was aided by subordinates who were to make their names still more famous in America, was not only the outstanding general of his age but also a skilful administrator of the Spanish possessions in South Italy.

The Catholic King was famous not only for his military achievements but also for his diplomatic skill, for he was a master in the cunning and the treachery that were the stock-in-trade of the statesmen of his day. He shewed too, as did his wife, a careful forethought for the future in planning matrimonial alliances for his children with those royal houses that were most likely to advance the international position of Spain and its political future. Isabella was married to the Infant of Portugal, Dom Afonso, and after his death to King Manuel. The only son of this second marriage, Miguel, was recognised, after the death of John, the only son of the Catholic Kings, as heir to the two crowns (1498–99). The purpose behind this recognition was to unite the two parts of the Peninsula, Spain and Portugal, into a single monarchy; but the plan failed, as Miguel died when only two years old. Joanna married the Archduke of Austria, Philip the Fair, son and heir to the Emperor Maximilian, and heir to Burgundy as well. This was the second marriage which the Catholic Kings had arranged with the imperial house; the first had been between John and a daughter of Maximilian. Their second daughter, Catherine, became the wife, first of Prince Arthur, heir to the throne of England, and then of King Henry VIII. These two marriages had fatal consequences in the future. Joanna's caused a profound change in the political orientation of Spain; it drew Castile into the current of general European politics from which it had held aloof for centuries, and which was not its natural sphere. Combined with the association with Italy and the south of France, which was the tradition of Aragon and Catalonia, this fact diverted the districts of central, southern, and western Spain from their own tradition of isolation.

Queen Isabella died in 1504. This broke the personal bond which had caused the two Spanish kingdoms to direct their efforts and their policy to the same united purposes in the many enterprises that marked the period from 1479 to 1504. The bond was not to be maintained, for the evil fate which dogged the lives of the children of the Catholic Kings willed it otherwise.

Joanna, the heiress to the crown of Castile, being afflicted with a mental malady, was incapable of governing the kingdom, and had to be kept in disguised restraint. Queen Isabella in her will had named King Ferdinand as regent of Castile, and the Cortes gave their assent at Toro in 1505. This roused the jealousy of Philip the Fair and caused frequent quarrels among the royal family. At last Ferdinand renounced the regency and retired to Aragon. Philip I did not long enjoy the authority which Joanna's condition imposed upon him, for he died the same year that he came into Spain. A short provisional regency followed, in which Cardinal Cisneros played the chief part, and then Ferdinand was again invited. He accepted, and retained the regency until his death.

This new period of government by Ferdinand, as king in Aragon and regent in Castile, was as crowded with political happenings as the years 1474–1504 had been. First, in point of date, came Africa; there the policy pursued by Queen Isabella, described above, was continued. The inspiration of this period came from Cardinal Cisneros, who even took part himself and actually financed one of the expeditions. For some years all went favourably for the policy of the Spaniards. Peñon de la Gomera (1508), Oran (1509), Bougie (1510), and Tripoli (1511) in turn fell into their hands. The taking of Bougie resulted in the submission of Algiers and the recognition of Spanish sovereignty by the Kings of Tunis and Tlemcen. But the same year, 1511, saw a grave check to Spanish arms at the island of Gelves, which postponed for long any further progress in the conquest of North Africa.

Shortly after the defeat of Gelves, Ferdinand engaged in another enterprise, having for its objective the Spanish kingdom of Navarre, which had been under French influence since 1479. The Catholic Kings had tried on two occasions to conclude a marriage alliance with the royal house of Navarre; but both times the negotiations had failed owing to the intervention of Madeleine of Foix (Viana), the mother of the Queen of Navarre. The effective cause of the war which resulted in the conquest of Navarre and its annexation to Castile was the perfidy shewn to Ferdinand by Queen Catherine and her husband John d'Albret; on the one hand they appeared to favour Ferdinand, on the other they signed treaties with France that were definitely hostile to him. One of these treaties, at Blois in 1512, pledged Catherine and John to refuse the Spanish troops passage through Navarre. Ferdinand, who was cognisant of this agreement, asked leave from the Queen of Navarre to pass through her territory with an army in order to enter France; and, as he expected, his request was refused. Accordingly he declared war. It proved to be a simple matter, as it lasted only two months and terminated with the submission of John, who took refuge in France. Having conquered Navarre south of the Pyrenees, Ferdinand did not intend to annex the kingdom, but only to retain it during his war with France. To this end, he proposed a marriage between the Prince of Viana, the heir to the throne of Navarre, and an Infanta of Spain, on condition that the rulers of Navarre abstained from assisting the King of France. Once again this proposal was received unfavourably by Catherine and John, who shewed the extent of their animosity by their insult to him in imprisoning his ambassador and handing him over to the French. Ferdinand then decided to annex Navarre to Castile, and carried this into execution, after an unsuccessful attempt by Louis XII and John d'Albret to recover the kingdom. Thus was the territorial unity of Spain, begun in 1492 in the south at the expense of the Muslims, completed in the north by the incorporation in the Spanish structure of the ancient kingdom of Navarre. Following the tradition practised in the other parts of the Aragonese kingdom, Ferdinand loyally respected the laws and the institutions, political and civil, of Navarre, including the Cortes, which continued to exist until the end of the eighteenth century.

An interesting factor in the conquest of Navarre was the justification of it both by Ferdinand and by the Pope. A few days before the entry of the Spanish troops into Navarre, which took place in July 1512, the Pope, evidently at Ferdinand's instigation, published a bull excommunicating Catherine and John and depriving them of their territories and dignities. Six months later, on 18 January 1513, a second bull confirmed the provisions of the first relating to the deprivation of territories, which were assigned by the Pope to the person who should achieve their conquest. This had already been accomplished by Ferdinand some months previously, but all the same the Pope's bull gave him a legal warrant, though, even by the ideas of the time, it was of doubtful validity. Ferdinand's own justification took a different form. It was expressed in the book written by the Castilian jurist, Palacios Rubios, on "*The justice and lawfulness of the acquisition and retention of the kingdom of Navarre*," published at Salamanca in 1514. The arguments of Palacios Rubios were little different from those of the Pope; they were almost exclusively religious in character, and were concerned principally with the schism from Pope Julius II led by some cardinals supported by the King of France. Ferdinand, however, as has been shewn, had been influenced in his decision to conquer and annex Navarre solely by political motives, which were stated in his manifesto of 31 July 1512. Moreover, Navarre during its independent existence had been fundamentally a Spanish kingdom, and for the greater part of its history it had been united, or at least linked, with Castile or Aragon.

In the meanwhile, affairs in Italy continued their complicated course. Julius II, who did not lose sight of the general interests of Italian policy, such as he conceived it, had formed against Venice the League of Cambrai (10 December 1508), which included Ferdinand the Catholic. Shortly afterwards, the Pope became jealous of the success of the French king and substituted the League of Cambrai by another, known as the Holy League (October 1511); in accordance with the facility with which States changed sides at that time, Venice, formerly the enemy, was now one of the partners in the League as well as the King of Aragon. The King of France, who remained outside it, sought the alliance of the Emperor

Maximilian, and war began afresh. It opened favourably for the French side, but shortly afterwards a victory won by the League at Novara in 1513 forced Louis XII to abandon Milanese territory, and to conclude a truce with Ferdinand regarding Italian affairs (December 1513). The result of this war was to consolidate the position of Spain in Italy, and to this the incessant rivalries of the States which played the leading part in Italian politics considerably contributed.

Two years after the truce signed with Louis XII, Ferdinand the Catholic died (23 January 1516). In his will he named as regent of the kingdoms of Castile, Leon, Granada, and Navarre his grandson Charles of Ghent, the son of Joanna and Philip the Fair; and he also bequeathed to him the throne of Aragon. The union of Spain under one ruler dates from this point, which marks the political end of the Middle Ages.

Charles was not only born at Ghent; he had also been brought up in Flanders, and had never set foot in Spain. During his absence, which only lasted until 19 September 1517, the regency of Castile was in the hands of Cardinal Cisneros, Queen Joanna being incapacitated by the increasing severity of her mental disorder.

The reign of the Catholic Kings was not only important for the political incidents hitherto recorded, and for the discovery of America which resulted in the conquest and annexation of such vast territories. It was also important both for institutional, legal, and social facts influencing most deeply the internal life of Castile and Aragon, and for other facts belonging to the domain of literature, the arts, and the sciences.

As far as Castile was concerned, the most important of all was the definitive solution of the formidable problem of aristocratic lawlessness, which had been so grievously manifested in the two reigns—of John II and Henry IV—preceding that of Isabella. The Catholic Kings applied to this problem energetic remedies, which were fully in keeping with the character of Isabella and her idea of royalty, and also with the political temperament of her husband. They made a direct and speedy attack upon, and reduced by force of arms, the lords who dared to brave royal orders, and did not hesitate to employ the sternest possible measures. At the same time they weakened the financial position of those nobles who had received grants from the previous kings to the impoverishment of the resources of the Crown, by causing the Cortes in 1480 to revise these grants and annul such as were inequitable; they deprived the nobles of the possibility of using the Orders of Chivalry as a means of gaining for themselves a dominant position, by attaching these Orders directly to the Crown and thus making the king the Grand Master of them all (1487–94); they rigorously prevented the lords from building castles, and caused a number of those in existence to be dismantled; they reorganised the administration of justice, putting it into the hands of men of middle-class extraction trained at the universities, thereby interposing a solid barrier against the arbitrary power of the nobles. In short, they attempted, and with success, to transform the nobility which dominated the provinces and the countryside into a courtier class whose political influence was henceforward to depend on the favour and will of the sovereign. So they succeeded in dislodging the old aristocracy from the castles and palaces whence it had dominated towns and country-side, by flattering its vanity and giving its members honorary posts at Court. It remained, therefore, tied to the monarchy without being a source of danger. One of the forms of this disguised subjection was the organisation (in 1512) of a palace bodyguard of 200 gentlemen chosen from the noblest families of Castile, Aragon, and Sicily. The position was not only an honour highly-coveted, but it carried with it a salary as well; and this was the beginning of the standing army, which was shortly afterwards to be organised in detail by Cardinal Cisneros, and perfected on its technical side by Gonzalo de Córdoba.

The municipal administration also, which had a tradition of practical independence but at that time was much disturbed by political and social factions, experienced the intervention of the central authority, which, in order to direct both local finance and government, dispatched *veedores de cuentas* (inspectors of accounts), *corregidores,* and other officials. Thus the Catholic Kings, while they rendered a real service to the municipalities by giving them order and discipline, at the same time fostered the development of a centralising tendency characteristic of absolute monarchy. This tendency, too, was significantly manifested in relation to the Cortes, which were seldom summoned after the reforms of 1480. One form that this centralisation took, not only in Castile but in Aragon and Catalonia also, was the nomination of municipal councillors by the Crown, and the strengthening of the representation of the upper middle-class in the Council of the Hundred Jurats at Barcelona (1493).

From the social point of view there were also important changes. Actually we know little as to the effects on the peasantry of the absentee landlordism consequent on the concentration of the nobility at Court, or as to the differences produced in the economic sphere by the transference, already noticeable, from agriculture to industry and commerce. But we do know of certain legislative reforms on the social side, such as the law of 28 October 1480, which, following the lines of the charter of 1285, authorised the peasants in the kingdom of Castile to change their residence (in other words, to remove from a seignory) and to take their possessions with them. On the other hand, there is also evidence to shew that the situation of the Christian peasants underwent no marked change, and that the abuses and the narrow dependence on their lords continued still to be the rule in most districts; and this in practice prevented any general conversion of the peasants as a whole into free tenant-farmers or small free-holders. It seems, however, that the general condition of the peasant classes in Castile was already easier and more fortunate than in the various parts of the kingdom of Aragon. That seems to be demonstrated by the frequent revolts of a social character which broke out in those parts at the end of the fifteenth and the beginning of the sixteenth centuries.

Ferdinand the Catholic tried to put a stop to these conflicts by limiting the seignorial rights, especially with regard to money dues and forced labour. But the nobles put up a firm resistance, and the king had in great measure to renounce his aims. He was more fortunate in Catalonia: following a formidable rising of the peasants known as *pagesos de rameneça*, who were kept in the closest subjection by the land-owning class, he issued an arbitral judgment, the Decree of Guadalupe, by which the *pagesos* were relieved of certain payments and services to their lords, the so-called "evil usages" (*mals usos*). By the same decree all *pagesos* could become free on the payment of an indemnity to the lord.

At the other end of the social scale, on behalf of the wealthy middle class in particular, the Catholic Kings deferred to a custom already of long standing in Castile and elsewhere, and, in one of the laws passed at the Cortes of Toro (*Leyes de Toro*, 1505), sanctioned the institution of *majorats*, that is to say, the entailing of an estate, usually in favour of the eldest son. This fostered the creation or continuance of great aristocratic or middle-class patrimonies. The laws of Toro are also important in other respects in the domain of private law; they mark quite definite drift away from the older laws and customs and towards Roman law.

Another fact of great importance from the social and economic point of view also happened at this time. It is well known how heterogeneous was the racial composition of the population in all the Spanish kingdoms. This was brought about, during the Middle Ages, by the grafting on the original Spanish-Latin stock of a succession of new strains, Visigothic, Jewish, Muslim from different sources (Arab, Syrian, Berber), not to mention other European elements, the amount of which, though appreciable, may be disregarded, except perhaps the Frankish strain in Catalonia. We shall probably never know to what extent racial admixture took place between the Spanish-Latins and the Germans at the end of the seventh century, but we do know that there was considerable admixture of Spaniards with their Muslim conquerors and still more with Jews. Documents of the late Middle Ages speak quite explicitly of the large amount of Jewish blood that was to be found in most Spanish families, even in the most highly placed. When full allowance has been made for the fact that these statements were definitely depreciatory in character, and exaggerated by passion and malice, there still remains much truth in them.

This heterogeneity attracted the attention of the Catholic Kings and of many of their contemporaries, but they looked on it as a political rather than an ethnical question. And they were much more concerned with the Jewish than with the Muslim aspect of the problem, owing to the existence from the fourteenth century onwards of a growing movement of acute anti-Semitism. Moreover, the facts shew clearly the difference in sentiment towards the two races, for while in the case of the Muslims it led no farther than the imposition of baptism upon them, in the case of the Jews it led to their expulsion.

It seems clear that the principal reason for this measure was the desire on the part of the Catholic Kings to bring about religious unity, as a means, in their view, to internal peace, the realisation of which was being frustrated by the existing hatred towards the Jews. Undoubtedly, too, they knew that the expulsion of Judaism, whether brought about directly, or indirectly by forcing the Jews to change their religion, would bring with it evil economic consequences for Spain. These consequences, which were later to be responsible for saving the Muslims in Aragon from the harsh measures adopted against their co-religionists in Castile, were apprehended at the time by contemporaries; in spite of their Christian sentiments, they did not overlook the danger of the expulsion from the point of view of industry, commerce, and other branches of the economic life of the nation. Notwithstanding, the expulsion was ordered during the years 1483?–86, but it was not then carried into execution. It was repeated on 31 May 1492, in the same terms that were to be used in the case of the Muslims in 1502. By the ordinance of 1492 the Jews had to be baptised under pain of banishment from Spain within four months.

It is not possible to obtain exact statistics of the numbers who were baptised or who chose to leave the country; estimates vary from 200,000 to half a million. It was from the Jews who then left Spain and took refuge in different parts of Europe or in North Africa that the Sephardim are descended; for *Sepharad*, from which their name is derived, was used by them to designate Spain. The economic effects which had been anticipated did in fact happen. One of these, which historical research is now bringing to light, was the fact that rich Jewish merchants among the exiles from Spain gave assistance, especially in regard to America, to other countries; and they as a result were able to vie with Spain in the control, the commerce, and the colonisation of the New World.

The expulsion, moreover, did not settle the Jewish problem in Spain. The people, and the clergy of course in particular, distrusted the sincerity of the converted Jews in their new beliefs. There is definite evidence to prove that this suspicion, if not always, was sometimes at any rate well-founded. Nor is there anything surprising in this, considering the manner in which the change of religion was brought about.

It was in order to deal with these *Judaising* Christians that the Catholic Kings established in Castile a special tribunal against heretics, the Tribunal of the Inquisition, which was already in existence in Aragon since the thirteenth century. In Castile these offences came within the ordinary episcopal jurisdiction, and their treatment was based on the penal legislation of the State. The Inquisition, on the other hand, was absolutely independent of the bishops, but was closely connected with the civil authority of the king. Its organisation and administration were highly developed, all the details being precisely elaborated. It owed its foundation to a royal decree issued at Seville in 1477, and it was recognised and accepted by Sixtus IV in bulls of the years 1478, 1482, and 1483. In 1483 the Supreme Council of the Inquisition was created by papal bull. The tribunal was presided over by a Grand Inquisitor, nominated at first by the king; but the third (the famous Torquemada) and subsequent ones were nominated by the Pope. It was Torquemada who drew up the original rules of the new Inquisition, and these were put into force in 1488. Four years earlier the old Aragonese Inquisition was reorganised on the model of that set up in Castile in 1477, though the change met with some opposition. In 1487 it was also introduced into Catalonia, where the opposition was much stronger, for reasons other than religious. When it was finally established at Majorca in 1490, the Catholic Kings had attained uniformity in jurisdiction and procedure in this department, a most important one at a time when the storm-clouds of religious revolt were already lowering over Christendom. Another novelty was the requirement of "purity of blood" (*limpieza de sangre*) as a condition for admission into public posts, the ranks of the clergy, and the Orders of Chivalry; this definitely isolated the converts or new Christians, and kept the original Christian element in the Spanish people uncontaminated.

As to the internal organisation of the Church, the Catholic Kings paid particular heed to the religious Orders and the purging of the morals of the clergy; vigorously supported by Cisneros, they boldly took in hand the work of reform, which was in part satisfactorily accomplished.

In the American countries where Spanish rule was beginning to be established there also arose problems both social and religious. The former, so far as they concerned the union of the races and equality of treatment, were soon decided in the affirmative by the administration, in accordance with the natural bent of the Spaniards; intermarriage between the white and the coloured races was allowed, and the Indians were granted political liberty and equality under the law by a manifesto of Queen Isabella of 20 June 1500, which was repeated in later decrees. As to the religious question, it is well known that the aim of converting the infidels and pagans figured as one of the foremost reasons for expeditions to non-Christian countries, and that it was laid down as an essential condition in the papal bulls which granted the conquered lands to the Portuguese or the Spaniards. The Catholic Kings tried to produce and to maintain religious unity in their new territories, both by the preaching of the gospel and the conversion of the Indians, and by prohibiting non-Catholics or the descendants of Muslims or Jews from going to the Indies. These were not the only points in which the Catholic Kings shewed their concern for their American lands. They elaborated so completely the organisation of the new territories added to the Crown that, except for the institution of viceroyalties which came a little later, of the universities, and of governorships (*intendencias*) which belong to the eighteenth century, all the essential elements in the political, administrative, religious, and social structure of Spanish America can be said to have been introduced, and even to some extent perfected, during the twenty-four years of the joint reign. Evidently, from the very beginning, the sovereigns and their counsellors in the government of the country visualised very clearly the problems arising from Spain's position as mother-country to the rulers of the Indies.

Finally, it was in the age of the Catholic Kings that the Spanish genius in letters, the arts, and the sciences came into flower; at this moment it began to shew its originality and to lay the foundations for the great development of the sixteenth and seventeenth centuries. The literary Courts of John II in Castile and Alfonso V at Naples—the latter a product of the Renaissance having all knowledge for its aim, the former more truly medieval in character—foreshadowed the Court of the Catholic Kings, wherein the most striking features were the devotion to study and the protection of culture. As formerly Alfonso X of Castile, and again as Alfonso V of Aragon more recently, the Catholic Kings attracted to their palace teachers and persons of eminence, women as well as men, foreigners and Spaniards alike; they gave their protection to the art of printing, newly-introduced into Spain; and, by a law of 1480, they gave authority for all books that could be of use to the national culture to be freely imported into the country.

CHAPTER XVI

PORTUGAL IN THE MIDDLE AGES

PORTUGAL takes her name from the city near the mouth of the Douro which we call Oporto, and from the tenth century the names *Portugal, Portugalis, Portucale,* and *Portugale* are applied in Latin documents to it and the surrounding lands. The kingdom of Leon and Castile, to which they belonged, was divided into provinces ruled by counts, and in the reign of Ferdinand I the county of Portugal and the district of Coimbra to the south appear among these provinces. Though their exact boundaries are unknown, the first seems to have included the territory between the Minho and the Douro with part of the modern province of Tras-os-Montes, while the second comprised the territory from the Douro to the Mondego; in documents of the eleventh and twelfth centuries the *terra portucalensis,* which embraced both districts, sometimes figures as a distinct province, at others it is considered as part of Galicia.

On the death of Ferdinand in 1065 the monarchy was divided between his three sons, and Galicia with the *terra portucalensis* fell to García, but it was again reunited under Alfonso VI, who in 1093 extended his frontiers to the Tagus by capturing Santarem from the Muslims and making Lisbon and Sintra tributary to him. In the following year, however, he handed over Galicia and the districts already mentioned to a French knight, Raymond, son of William, Count of Burgundy (Franche Comté), who had come to the Peninsula in or about 1087, and married Alfonso's only legitimate daughter, Urraca.

Raymond's cousin Henry, a great-grandson of King Robert II of France, followed him to Spain, and at the beginning of 1095 he was married to Teresa, one of the two illegitimate daughters of Alfonso; either then or some months before he obtained the government of the county of Portugal and the district of Coimbra under Raymond. This subordination was, however, ephemeral, and perhaps because the defeat of Raymond in the same year, followed by the loss of Lisbon and Sintra, convinced Alfonso that the frontier could not well be protected by the ruler of distant Galicia, he dismembered the territory south of the Minho from that to the north and entrusted the former to Henry to hold as an hereditary fief. Thus the county of Portugal, extending from the Minho to the Tagus, became a distinct entity.

For the next few years the strife between Christian and Muslim seems to have been suspended, so that Henry was able to absent himself from his county; in the winter of 1097–98 he made the pilgrimage to Compostela, in 1100 and 1101 he was at the court of Alfonso VI, and in 1103 he set out for Palestine as a simple knight; afterwards we find him either residing at court, or at Coimbra, occupied in the work of administration.

In the meantime family disputes arose, in which he intervened and revealed qualities as a politician and an ambition for independence. Raymond considered that he had a right to succeed to the crown of his father-in-law, and in 1107, encouraged by Hugh, the powerful Abbot of Cluny, who was his near relation and had given three bishops to Portugal, he entered into an agreement with Henry by which the latter was to support him, in exchange for the gift of part of the treasure of Toledo and the government of the city and district; in case Raymond could not carry out this cession, he was to hand over Galicia to Henry, when he obtained possession of Leon and Castile. The death of Raymond in 1107, two years before that of Alfonso, rendered the pact nugatory, and Henry then sought to realise his designs by persuading the king to leave him a part of the monarchy; in this he was disappointed, for on his death-bed Alfonso declared Urraca his sole heir. The choice displeased the magnates, who naturally desired a ruler capable of carrying on the war against the infidel, and they induced the new queen to espouse Alfonso I of Aragon, a young man famous for his military prowess; but strife soon arose between the pair and led to civil war, in which they were alternately allies or ranged on opposite sides, while a revolution broke out in Galicia in favour of Urraca's son by her first marriage, Alfonso Raimundez.

The accession of Urraca irritated Henry. In the autumn of 1110 he proceeded to France to enlist troops, and on his return to the Peninsula the next year he entered into a treaty with Alfonso I for the deposition of the queen and the division of the monarchy. A temporary reconciliation between the consorts frustrated his hopes, and in 1111 he lost Santarem, but was able to renew his league with Alfonso, and in November they obtained a victory at Campo d'Espina. However, the Castilian magnates succeeded in separating him from the king, by promising to induce Urraca to hand over a part of the kingdom, and in 1112, joining his forces to hers, he besieged Alfonso in Peñafiel. On this occasion Teresa arrived at the camp and persuaded him to press for the fulfilment of the promises he had obtained; his compliance, and the fact that the Portuguese soldiers treated her sister as queen, revealed their ambitions to Urraca and angered her so far that she entered into secret negotiations with her husband to counteract them; nevertheless she agreed in public to a division of her States, but when Henry went to take possession of Zamora and Sahagun, which with other places had been allotted to him, the inhabitants, by order of the queen, refused to admit him. Cheated of his expectations once more, he resolved to carry on the war against both king and queen, but died in his town of Astorga in May 1112 or 1114, without having been able to realise them; he left an only son, Afonso Henriques, two or three years of age.

On hearing of his death, Henry's widow, whom the chroniclers describe as beautiful and astute, hastened to court to press the rights which had descended to her, and lacking force, she had recourse to intrigue, informing the king that his wife intended to poison him. The allegation seems not to have been without foundation, and Alfonso caught at so good a pretext to separate from the queen without losing her possessions; he expelled her from Astorga, but the nobles and burghers of Leon and Castile rallied to her side and he had to retreat to his own country. Teresa was now exposed to the vengeance of her sister, but found safety in submission and probably also in the support of Diego Gelmirez, Bishop of Compostela, a man of great influence in Galicia on account of his ecclesiastical rank and estates, whom Urraca dared not offend; moreover, though in her husband's lifetime Teresa had rarely used the titles of Countess or Infanta, she now styled herself Infanta and Queen in the charters she gave; her subjects also called her by that title and even spoke of the county as a kingdom. It is true that at the Cortes of Oviedo (1115) she figured after the queen and her elder sister Elvira and merely as Infanta, but while Elvira signed on behalf of her children and subjects, Teresa only spoke for the former; she recognised Urraca as her superior, but the absence of the Portuguese magnates, and the omission of any reference to them, suggests that they had already gone far on the road of independence.

In the following year a fresh revolution broke out in Galicia in favour of Alfonso Raimundez, the leaders being his tutor Pedro Froylaz, Count of Trava, and Bishop Gelmirez, and Teresa was induced to take their side, because like them she aspired to overthrow the queen's authority. Though apparently unsuccessful in the field, she obtained from the count as the price of her support the districts of Tuy and Orense, north of the Minho, to add to her county, but had almost immediately to return to Portugal to meet the Muslim invaders, who had captured the line of castles covering Coimbra; thus exposed, the city itself was besieged in June 1117 for twenty days, but, inspired by the presence of Teresa, the garrison made a successful resistance. The next three years were tranquil; her troops took no part in the renewed war between Urraca and Alfonso, though nearly every other part of the monarchy was represented in it, and her barons by their aloofness seem to have wished to mark the growing separation between them and Leon and Castile. In 1121, however, they were drawn into the general conflict, and the occupation of Tuy, if not the motive, served as the pretext, though the ambition of Gelmirez to liberate his see from dependence on that of Braga was a contributory cause; Gelmirez obtained his wish and promotion to the rank of archbishop from Pope Calixtus II, in exchange for the promises he gave to help in securing the crown of Galicia for Alfonso Raimundez, who happened to be the Pope's nephew. Urraca perhaps learnt of the plot to replace her by her son, and in any case she determined to attack Teresa, who adhered to the league. Accordingly in the summer of 1121 she invaded Portugal, overran the country as far as the Douro, and besieged the castle of Lanhoso, to which Teresa had retired. The latter probably had with her the Galician noble Fernando Peres de Trava, reputed to be her lover, whom she had made Count of Oporto and Coimbra; he was a friend of Gelmirez, therefore of the party hostile to Urraca, and the destruction of Teresa would have been fatal to the success of their plans. How they were able to prevent it is a mystery; all we know is that Urraca suddenly made a peace-treaty with her sister, and gave her dominion over the districts of Zamora, Toro, Salamanca, and Avila, in subordination to herself, in exchange for an offensive and defensive alliance. The territories thus ceded to Teresa appear to have been those which were allotted to her husband in 1111, but while he was to possess them independently, she only received them as her sister's vassal. Nevertheless she had reason to be satisfied with the agreement, since her cause had been saved when on the brink of ruin and her possessions almost doubled.

During Urraca's lifetime Teresa made no attempt to assert the independence of Portugal, but shortly after the accession of Alfonso VII she formally refused to fulfil her obligations under the treaty of 1121, with the result that the king declared war in the spring of 1127, and after a campaign of six weeks forced her to recognise his supremacy. An episode of the siege of Guimarães is still remembered; the garrison, unable to hold out, undertook on behalf of the young Afonso Henriques that he would consider himself in the future a vassal to the Crown of Leon and Castile, and his tutor, Egas Moniz, one of the principal nobles and a man of high character, went surety for the fulfilment of the bargain. On this the siege was raised, but when in the following year the government came into the hands of Afonso Henriques, he ignored the promise made in his name; whereupon Egas Moniz accompanied by his wife and children went to court, and presenting himself to the king unshod and with a rope round his neck, asked leave to redeem by his death the broken word. This noble action earned him freedom and its incidents are engraven on his tomb.

After the check her ambitions had received, Teresa had to face an internal revolt, directed against the predominance of her lover and the influence of other Galician barons in the administration of the county. It was largely an anti-foreign movement, justified by the feeling that they were opposed to the general desire for independence; indeed it is probable that Fernando Peres induced Teresa to submit to Alfonso, since the chief author of the pacification was his friend Gelmirez. In Afonso Henriques the Portuguese magnates, including the Archbishop of Braga of the powerful family of Mendes de Maia, found a natural leader; he had reached the age of seventeen and according to a contemporary was a handsome youth, a keen soldier, prudent in all his actions, and possessed of a clear intelligence. In 1125, as if in pursuit of the plan realised only much later, he had knighted himself in the cathedral of Zamora, "according to the custom of kings," and now needed no incitement to head a movement against the small clique which his mother had raised to power. Early in 1128 at Braga he published his intentions, the province of Minho rose in his favour, and when three months later Teresa reached Guimarães with a Galician-Portuguese force, she found him encamped with his partisans at St Mamede outside the walls. In the battle that ensued she was defeated, and two years afterwards died in exile, the victim, not merely of her moral lapse and of the ambitions of others, but of the sentiment of nationality which she had worked to develop during a rule of fourteen or sixteen years.

The rebellion of Portugal against Teresa was a challenge to the king who had just reduced her to submission, but internal difficulties and the incessant war with Aragon forbad him to take it up. In 1130, encouraged by this inaction, Afonso Henriques invaded Galicia. He had a pretext in the conventions made with his father and the possession by his mother of the south of that province; the raids were repeated in the following years with varying success, and it is significant that the little county in the west continued its defiance while the rest of the Peninsula gradually recognised the supremacy of Alfonso, who was acclaimed Emperor of Spain in 1135. Two years later the King of Navarre sought to free himself and made a pact with the discontented barons of Galicia and Afonso Henriques for mutual action; while the former began hostilities in the East, the Portuguese count with his allies defeated the royal forces at Cerneja, and, but for a diversion, would have extended his conquests to the north of Galicia. The capture by the Muslims of the great castle of Leiria, which he had only just founded, and a disaster near Thomar, compelled him to return and defend his southern frontiers and, when he was thus occupied, Alfonso VII, having temporarily disposed of the King of Navarre, marched rapidly across his states to Tuy and there began to collect an army to invade Portugal. The count had to submit, and by the peace of Tuy (4 July 1137) he and 150 of his barons swore to help the Emperor against any foe, either Christian or Muslim, and to restore any territories he might receive, when so required. Alfonso was now free to direct his arms against the common enemy, and in 1138 he advanced as far as the river Guadalquiver and in the following year besieged the strong fortress of Aurelia; at the same time, by arrangement with him, Afonso Henriques led his troops across the Tagus for the first time and overthrew the Muslims under Esmar at Ourique (25 July 1139), and as a consequence Aurelia surrendered. According to an old tradition, Our Lord appeared to him on the eve and promised victory, while his men acclaimed him King on the field of battle; actually in a document of the previous March he had used the title. The success must have restored the self-confidence the Portuguese had lost by the humiliating conditions of the Peace of Tuy, and early in 1140 Afonso Henriques felt strong enough to break the pact and invade Galicia once more. When they met at Val de Vez, the Emperor was satisfied with a truce, instead of risking a battle against his disobedient cousin; it would seem that he considered the subjection of Portugal too difficult an enterprise. Its count was henceforth absent from the political assemblies of the monarchy, and Alfonso VII never enumerated Portugal among his dominions, though he may perhaps have considered it as part of Galicia, to which it had lately been attached.

In 1143 Afonso I, as we shall now call him, met the Emperor and Cardinal Guido, legate of Pope Innocent II, in conference at Zamora, and a definite peace between the cousins was arranged: Alfonso VII recognised the title Afonso I had taken and the latter received the lordship of Astorga in vassalage. Even in his capacity as King of Portugal, he doubtless remained in some sort of dependence on the Emperor, but it was a frail tie, and the meeting with Guido may have suggested how it might safely be snapped. While the Roman See exercised considerable authority in all Christian kingdoms, it had a special and immediate dominion in Spain, so that, if the Pope extended protection to the new State, that State's existence was assured; Afonso I therefore did homage to the legate and wrote to Innocent offering his realm to the Holy See under an annual tribute of four ounces of gold. The conditions of the homage were that he and his successors should pay this sum in perpetuity, and in exchange receive support and not recognise any superior authority, save that of Rome in the person of its legate. In May of the following year Lucius II replied, praising the king's resolution and promising protection, but addressing Afonso I as *dux portugallensis* and called his realm *terra*; nevertheless the acceptance of the king's offer meant confirmation of the independence of Portugal, though his royal dignity was only recognised by Alexander III in 1179, probably owing to the papal desire for an undivided Spain as a barrier to the Muslim. The Emperor protested, but made no further attempt to recover his authority, while the king seems to have abandoned the idea of extending his territory to the north and east and to have lost Astorga, of which Alfonso VII naturally deprived him; henceforth he directed his efforts of expansion southward, and the subsequent disputes with his cousin refer to the limits of Portugal on that side.

The death struggle between Almorávides and Almohades in Africa, and the consequent confusion in Spain itself, gave him his opportunity, and in 1146, allying himself with Ibn-Kasi, Wali of Mertola, he issued from his base at Coimbra, crossed the Tagus, leaving Lisbon and Santarem on his flank, and penetrated into the districts of Beja and Merida; his devastations led the authorities of Belatha, the province lying between the Mondego and the Tagus, to offer their submission and tribute. He followed up this success by surprising and taking by escalade the strong castle of Santarem, and next cast his eyes on Lisbon. In June 1147 a fleet of some 200 sail carrying 13,000 men, Anglo-Normans, Germans, and Flemings, entered the Douro on their way to Palestine; and the leaders were persuaded to put in at the Tagus and join him in an attack on the city, which was starved into surrender after a four months' siege. Thereupon the almost inaccessible castle of Sintra submitted on terms and the garrison of Palmella fled, while many of the crusaders obtained grants of land and remained in Portugal. In the tract of country liberated from Muslim rule, the Military Orders, cathedrals, and monastic bodies were also given a share; near Leiria the monastery of Alcobaça was founded about 1153, and its monks reduced to cultivation a large district which had been a desert. These corporations established villages and towns with colonists attracted from the north, and the king divided up among his soldiers the estates belonging to the Muslim inhabitants of Lisbon who had died or fled, though the survivors who accepted the Christian yoke continued to enjoy their property under the name of *mouros forros*. He made two attempts in the next few years to capture the strongly fortified town of Alcacer do Sal with the aid of soldiers recruited in England, and though these failed, it fell on 24 June 1158, and in 1159 he appears to have taken and abandoned Beja and Evora.

The reputation he had gained is shewn by the fact that Alfonso II of Aragon sought his daughter Mafalda in marriage, and that in 1165 another daughter of his, Urraca, became the wife of Ferdinand II of Leon; and though he suffered a serious defeat in 1161 at the hands of the Almohad Emperor of Morocco, 'Abd-al-Mumin, a body of municipal troops acting independently won back Beja in 1162, and, some years after, a guerrilla band under Giraldo the Fearless took Evora, Serpa, Juromenha, and then striking north-east seized Cáceres and Trujillo, in modern Spain. In 1163 the king himself had entered Leon and occupied Salamanca to avenge the injuries his subjects received from Ciudad Rodrigo, refortified by Ferdinand in 1161, and when defeated at Arganal he sought compensation by invading Galicia and seizing Tuy and the territory of Limia which had once been in the hands of his mother. Good fortune made him reckless; and, while the King of Leon was engaged in expelling the Portuguese from Galicia, he proceeded in 1169 to besiege the castle of Badajóz, at the summons of Giraldo, who had already captured the town. Ferdinand hastened back to oppose him and the besieger became the besieged, the Portuguese were driven from the place, and in the flight Afonso fractured a leg and was taken prisoner. The King of Leon behaved with extraordinary generosity, for when Afonso confessed his fault and offered to hand over all he had in exchange for freedom, he is said to have replied: "Restore what you have taken from me and keep your kingdom." Afonso was only too glad to accept these terms; he handed over twenty-five castles and a large sum of gold and after two months' imprisonment returned home. Incapacitated by his injury from bearing arms for the rest of his life, he provided for the defence of the Alemtejo by granting to the Templars a third of all they could acquire there, on condition that they used the revenues in the royal service. Two years later he was besieged in Santarem by an Almohad army and again saved by the prompt arrival of his son-in-law; since the affair of Badajóz he no longer inspired fear in his foes.

He now made a truce with the Muslims which lasted a decade; his

reign as chief of a military nation had virtually come to an end, and
on 15 August 1170 he knighted his son Sancho and gave him a share
in the administration and in the control of military affairs; as Portugal
had no rules of succession, it was advisable to accustom his subjects and
foreigners to treat Sancho as king before his own death. In 1174 the
prince married Dulce, sister of Alfonso II of Aragon, and four years later
he recommenced the war by a raid against Seville, where he burnt one of
the principal suburbs; his boldness in penetrating as far as the capital of
Andalusia stirred up Yūsuf, Emperor of Morocco, who resolved to reduce
Portugal, but a naval expedition against Lisbon in 1179 had no result
and a serious invasion by land required time to prepare. However, in
May 1184 the invading army from Africa arrived and shut up Afonso in
Santarem and, though Sancho was able to hold the enemy at bay,
Portugal owed its salvation to the aid of the Archbishop of Santiago de
Compostela, who brought an army of 20,000 men on 26 June, and to
that of the King of Leon, who arrived a month later. The sudden death
of the Emperor and the dispersal of his host, followed by the failure of
a fresh attack on Lisbon from the sea, completed the almost miraculous
deliverance, and Afonso could die in peace on 6 December 1185 after a
rule of forty-five years. Often unscrupulous in his methods, he succeeded
by courage, persistency, and good fortune in making a nation, increasing
its boundaries, founding a dynasty, and securing its recognition abroad.

Succeeding to the throne at the age of thirty, Sancho devoted himself
to rebuilding towns, founding new ones, and erecting castles, and earned
the name of *Povoador* for his work in repopulating the territories devastated by the long wars. To add to the defences and revenues of the
kingdom, he encouraged the Military Orders, who in the field possessed
the discipline lacking in the royal troops and in those of the communes,
and by their strongholds protected the frontiers and the settlers under
their walls; these Orders included the Templars and Hospitallers and the
newer ones of Calatrava and Santiago. At first Sancho kept aloof from the
quarrels between his brother sovereigns, and for some years intestine
strife in Africa prevented Ya'qūb, the new Emperor of Morocco, from
repairing the disaster of 1184 and, when he attempted it in the spring of
1189, he met with no permanent success. This encouraged Sancho to take
the initiative, but instead of pushing south-east to recover Beja and the
Guadiana fortresses, which had been lost in the last years of his father,
he secured the aid of two crusading fleets on their way to Palestine, and
sailing together down the flank of Muslim territory to the Algarve, where
the Portuguese had never penetrated, the allies took Alvor and Silves,
a city larger and richer than Lisbon, in 1189. The barbarities practised
by the crusaders at the fall of Lisbon and their accusations of bad faith
against the King of Portugal were repeated, but the prospect of booty
never failed to secure their co-operation. This naval expedition, the first
in Portuguese history, brought the submission of the western part of the

province, and the king marched back through Muslim territory and reconquered Beja, but in the spring of the following year he had to meet a
fresh invasion from Africa; Ya'qūb proceeded first to Silves and, leaving
a force to besiege it, he traversed the Alemtejo plains, crossed the Tagus,
took Torres Novas, and sat down before the Templar fortress of Thomar,
while some of his troops got as far as Coimbra.

Sancho now found himself in a critical position; the enemy was established in overwhelming force in the heart of the country and might enter
his capital; but once again Providence came to its aid, in the shape of
crusaders, who entered the Tagus and were persuaded to reinforce him.
Moreover, a pestilence broke out in the Emperor's camp and led him to
offer terms; if Silves were restored, he would give back Torres Novas,
retire, and make a seven years' truce. Though the terms were refused, the
Emperor none the less broke up camp and led his army to Seville, but in
the following year he not only retook Silves and the other conquests of
Sancho, but got possession of Alcacer, Palmella, and Almada, so that the
Muslim frontier came up again to the Tagus. Evora held out, and the
Muslims abandoned Palmella and Almada, but the king had to resign
himself to his other losses, and during the next four years he sought to
provide against a similar calamity by establishing strongholds of the
Military Orders along the right bank of the Tagus, by peopling the
province with colonists from the north, and by restoring the castle of Leiria.

In 1195 the prowess of Alfonso VIII of Castile provoked another
invasion of the Peninsula by Ya'qūb, and a Portuguese contingent shared
in the defeat of Alarcos. In the following year war broke out between
the Kings of Portugal and Leon; the former overran the southern part
of Galicia and captured Tuy, which he held until 1199, but he suffered
a defeat in front of Ciudad Rodrigo; though hostilities appear then to
have ceased, he founded the city of Guarda on the eastern frontier as a
protection against Leon and made it the seat of a bishopric. He also re-
occupied the north of the Alemtejo by members of the Military Orders,
and the number of foreign settlers along the estuary of the Sado justified
the grant of a charter to Cezimbra. The loss of life caused by the great
famine of 1202 compelled him to greater efforts, and in the ensuing years
he travelled over his kingdom, and established many new towns and districts in the centre, and even south of the Tagus. These acts rather than
his exploits as a warrior, which were inferior to those of his father, are his
true title to fame, and he was able to practise them by the peace he
preserved with his neighbours, Christian and Muslim; on the other hand
a breach with the Church and a grave malady clouded his last years.

A conflict broke out between Martinho Rodrigues, Bishop of Oporto,
member of a noble family, and his Chapter, during which the populace
rose against and imprisoned their overlord and the royal officers seized his
goods and those of the see. Sancho took sides against the bishop, but was
compelled by Innocent III to make restitution, while the citizens were

adjudged to be vassals of the Church in accordance with the grant made by Teresa to Bishop Hugo in 1120, notwithstanding their charter. Before this peace came, long-standing differences between Sancho and the Bishop of Coimbra came to a head; when reproved for his personal misconduct and placed under an interdict, Sancho retorted with acts of violence and imprisoned the prelate, and to a papal protest he sent a violent reply, doubtless penned by his chancellor Julian, a lawyer who shared the ideas of Arnold of Brescia. However, before his death in 1211 he became reconciled with both bishops and left the country better defended, cultivated, and peopled, if no larger, than he had received it, but the sum total of his legacies, £266,000 in gold, suggests fiscal extortion.

On ascending the throne in 1211, Afonso II summoned Cortes at which it was decided that canon law should form part of the law of the realm, and that any civil enactment running counter to it should be void, the clergy were exempted from many forms of taxation, a concession which their maintenance of schools and hospitals justified, and in exchange they accepted a law forbidding ecclesiastical corporations to purchase more land. The king gained the favour of the Church by these measures, and Innocent III confirmed his royal title. Doubtless inspired by Julian, Afonso then felt strong enough to refuse to carry out the provisions of his father's will in favour of his brothers and sisters, on the ground that Crown lands were inalienable. This led to civil war and an invasion by the King of Leon, who took Coimbra, but the King of Castile intervened, out of gratitude for the help rendered by Portuguese troops at the battle of Las Navas de Tolosa (July 1212), and after five years of litigation the conflict was settled in Afonso's favour by Innocent III, who received twenty-eight years' tribute owing to the Papal See. Nevertheless, the former national unity had been broken, and the efforts of the king to remove the hostility of the nobles by a general confirmation of their title-deeds did not bear fruit; for as it suggested a right of revocation, many refused to accept it. Afonso was too much occupied with internal questions and too lacking in military spirit to seek to extend his frontiers, and he was absent when his troops won back Alcacer with the help of another crusading fleet, led by the Counts of Holland and of Wied, after a two months' siege on 18 October 1217. In the following year he made the bishops a present of tithe on the revenues of the royal lands in each diocese, which had hitherto been exempt from the tax. This step seems to have been taken mainly on the advice of the dean of Lisbon, but shortly afterwards a dispute between the latter and the bishop, in which the king supported the dean, led to a change of policy. Gonçalo Mendes, Julian's successor, and the Lord High Steward, Pedro Annes, supporters of the supremacy of the civil power, incited Afonso to violate the immunities of the Church and the privileges granted to the clergy by the Cortes of 1211; the law against mortmain enacted at that time had not been observed, and land had continued to pass into the hands of the clergy to the detriment of the exchequer. The

33

Archbishop of Braga convoked an assembly of prelates, and after condemning the public acts and adulterous life of Afonso excommunicated him and his ministers. About the same time a general inquest into titles to landed property, ordered in 1220, raised up enemies among the nobles, who were generally not heard in their defence, and Afonso's bastard brother Martin Sanches and the King of Leon invaded Portugal and took Chaves. Though the energetic intervention of Honorius III in favour of the archbishop had not moved the king from his purpose, these events and the papal threat to release his subjects from their allegiance induced him to make peace with the Church some months before his death from leprosy in 1223.

By making reparation to, and a concordat with, the Church Sancho II, who came to the throne at thirteen, obtained the removal of the interdict which had been laid on the realm, but the hatreds provoked by the events of the last reign continued, and were reflected in perennial civil strife. To heal these divisions, the king, who had crusading in his blood, renewed the war against the Muslims in co-operation with the King of Leon and took Elvas (1226), but did not attain his end; noble contended with noble, Templar with Hospitaller, bishop with bishop, the monastic Orders suffered persecution from the prelates, who met the robberies and usurpations committed by the royal officials with spiritual weapons. The Cardinal of Abbeville, sent in 1228 by Gregory IX, secured a temporary pacification, during which new towns were founded on the eastern frontier, while Elvas, which the Muslims had reoccupied, and Juromenha were definitely conquered. The captures of Moura, Serpa, and Aljustrel followed in 1232–34, but Sancho's weak government and his continual changes of ministers neutralised these victories, and the kingdom gradually fell into anarchy. In 1237 the Bishop of Oporto drew a terrible picture of its condition when he invited the Dominicans to establish themselves in the city, yet the Order contributed to the evils by its own dissensions, by evading the mortmain law, and by admitting to the priesthood men who only sought to evade taxation or military service; moreover, the clergy of Lisbon commonly compelled testators to leave part of their property to the Church under the threat of deprivation of the Sacraments. There was reason for extending the law of 1211, which forbade the purchase of land by ecclesiastical corporations, to the acceptance of gifts and bequests, as these had become excessive through the piety of the people; but the continual breaches of ecclesiastical immunities, the expulsion of the Bishop of Lisbon in a grossly sacrilegious manner by Sancho's brother Ferdinand, and similar deeds by his uncle in the north, could not fail to provoke papal intervention, even against a crusading monarch. The king yielded and gave full satisfaction to the prelates, though the citizens of Oporto continued for two years the struggle with their bishop which they had inherited from their forbears; but in the midst of these contentions Sancho found time to pursue the Holy War, and he reduced the castles on the Guadiana from Mertola to the sea, together with the western part of the Algarve (1238–40) and confided them to the Order of Santiago.

Records are lacking for the next few years, and all we can be sure of is that the public disorder continued and that the king did nothing to check it; in consequence, the prelates presented at Rome a catalogue of the wrongs of the Church and the misdeeds of Sancho and his ministers, including toleration of heretical opinions, and to strengthen their case they detailed the injuries done to the State. The accusation that he had let the castles fall into disrepair and failed to defend the frontiers was well calculated to deprive him of the credit he had gained from Gregory IX for his campaign and, whether true or not, his recent indolence gave it colour. The intention of the prelates was to shew that he was incapable and ought to be deposed; in that case the Pope had a special right to take action, because Portugal was a papal fief. As Sancho had no children, his brother Afonso, Count of Boulogne, was the natural successor, and some of the bishops and nobles, apparently with the approval of the new Pope Innocent IV, had already invited him to play the part of saviour of the country. Early in 1245 the Pope commissioned the Bishops of Oporto and Coimbra to require the king to repair his past offences and give pledges for the future, and on their arrival at the Council of Lyons they reported his obduracy, whereupon Innocent appointed Afonso curator of the realm and ordered the authorities to obey him, though he declared that he had no intention of depriving Sancho of the crown. In September, at a meeting in Paris, Afonso accepted the conditions imposed by the Archbishop of Braga and the Bishop of Oporto, which referred mainly to the Church, and at the beginning of 1246 he proceeded to Lisbon, which declared for him in the first of its many revolutions. Though Sancho defended himself and called in the aid of Spanish troops, led by Alfonso, son of Ferdinand III of Castile, he was finally vanquished and died in exile at Toledo in 1248, whereupon the Count of Boulogne took the title of king.

In 1249–50 the forces of the Military Orders conquered the rest of the Algarve, but Ferdinand's son claimed the province under a grant from the Wali of Niebla, invaded Portugal, and compelled Afonso III to yield it to him; however, in 1253 the latter, intent on its recovery, and though his wife was living, agreed to marry Beatrice, illegitimate daughter of the former, who had become King of Castile and Leon under the title of Alfonso X, and it was arranged that the Algarve should revert to Portugal when the first child of the union reached the age of seven. In 1263, after conflicts over its ownership, Alfonso X ceded it to the Infant Dinis, son of Afonso III, with certain reservations, on condition that he served him in war with 50 lances; the irregular marriage of the King of Portugal was validated by Urban IV on the death of the Countess of Boulogne; and finally in 1267, by the convention of Badajóz, all restrictions on Portuguese sovereignty were removed, and the Guadiana became the boundary between the two countries. Since then the frontiers of Portugal have hardly varied, a fact unique in European history. In internal affairs the policy of Afonso III was to strengthen the Third Estate as an ally against nobles and clergy, to recover the Crown property alienated by himself under compulsion at the beginning of his reign and by his predecessor, and to increase the revenue which these grants and the civil war had considerably diminished. The presence of representatives of the towns at the Cortes of 1254 for the first time shewed their increasing importance, the provision for the payment of tributes in money and not in kind benefited the people as well as the king, who was the chief landowner, and the Inquest of 1258 enabled a correct schedule of Crown property to be prepared and revealed how far it had been alienated in favour of private persons and corporations, often fraudulently to avoid taxation. In 1261 the Cortes disputed the ancient right of the monarch to raise money by debasing the value of the coinage every seven years, and for a consideration Afonso had to renounce it and agree that he and his successors would accept instead a fixed sum payable once only in each reign; the principle that a new general tax could only be imposed by the consent of the nation was thus established. Notwithstanding this check, instructions were issued in 1265 to the judicial authorities for the recovery of lands held from the Crown which had been sold by the grantees to the loss of its rights; they were to be purchased at the price paid by the present owners and, if the latter refused to sell, they were to be confiscated, and lands abandoned or uncultivated were also to be seized. In no case was a Crown estate to be divided up between members of a family, unless one became responsible for the whole rent, and those granted to the Military Orders were in future to be subject to taxation.

If these revolutionary measures, which were carried out in part and without hearing the parties interested, failed to relieve the treasury, we may attribute this to the lavish expenditure of the king and to the rapacity of his courtiers, especially the Lord High Steward, Dom João Peres de Aboim, and the Chancellor, Estevam Annes; but as they affected thousands of the nobility and clergy, this issue offered an excellent occasion for the leaders of the latter to open a campaign against the king they had helped to set up and who had abused their confidence. Five of the bishops went to Rome and presented a list of grievances, those of the clergy being in 43 articles. They contained the old charges of infringement of ecclesiastical immunities, interference in the appointment of bishops and clergy, robbery of the Church, and ill-treatment of clerics, but for the first time the municipalities appear as abettors of the monarch; the accusation that Afonso threatened the bishops with death to secure his ends, and had their servants castrated and killed and priests stripped naked, accords with his violent temper and the barbarity of the times. He met the storm by presenting a declaration of the towns in his favour and by enlisting for a new crusade promoted by Clement IV in 1267, and by his own efforts and those of his agents in Rome he succeeded in neutralising the representations of the prelates for some years, until the acts of violence and the illegalities grew worse and drove them to present fresh complaints. In 1273 Gregory X endeavoured to bring the king to reason, whereupon Afonso summoned the Cortes and had a committee consisting of his friends appointed to examine the matter, with the result that it reported in his favour. This further subterfuge did not avail him, for by a bull of 4 September 1275 the Pope required him to swear to carry out the obligations he had contracted in Paris and the resolutions contained in the bulls of Honorius III and Gregory IX, failing which he threatened him with excommunication and interdict, and in the last resort with deposition. The king remained obdurate and, now as before, changes in the occupancy of the Papal See favoured him by causing a delay in the execution of the threats, but in 1277 an apostolic commissary published the bull in Lisbon and intimated its provisions to the king, so that they became effective in due course. No revolution followed, because no pretender existed, and Dinis, a capable youth of sixteen, already shared in the administration; however, on his death-bed in January 1279, Afonso took the oath required of him without reserve. The tenacity of the clergy and the patience of successive Popes had won after a struggle of nineteen years.

The interdict continued for some time, because Dinis, following in the steps of his father, did not carry out the provisions of the bull of Gregory X, in the hope that they would be modified; and though he entered into negotiations at Rome, the short reigns of several Popes and differences between him and them delayed a settlement until 1289. The concordat then made and its sequels represented a fair compromise, and regulated the relations of clergy and Crown so as to preclude further disputes on questions of principle. By means of a declaration of war against Castile in 1295, the king obtained the restitution of the towns of Serpa and Moura and the cession of those of Aroche and Aracena on the east to which he laid claim, and by an invasion in the following year he annexed the district of Riba Coa between the river of this name and the Douro. On the suppression of the Templars by Clement V, he endeavoured to incorporate their property in that of the Crown, but as the Pope refused his consent, it was agreed that they should be transferred to a new Order, the Order of Christ, which was founded in 1319. After the conquest of the Algarve, the older Military Orders, through lack of occupation, fell into decay, of which we have evidence in the complaints of the Cortes in 1361, 1472, and 1481, but the Order of Christ played an mportant part in the voyages directed by Prince Henry the Navigator, which were financed out of its revenues. Notwithstanding the war with Castile and the rebellion of the king's eldest son Afonso, which disturbed the whole reign, it was one of moral and material progress, shewn in the peaceable settlement of the conflict between Crown and clergy, in the foundation of the university, and in the development of letters, agriculture, industry, and the navy. A college had been founded in Lisbon in 1286 by Dom Domingos Jardo, one of the king's tutors, under his protection and that of the monks of Alcobaça, and in the previous century schools existed in the cathedrals and monasteries, but Portuguese who aspired to a degree had to go abroad. To remedy this the clergy suggested the foundation of a university, offering to pay the teachers, and in 1290 the king founded it in Lisbon, but owing to the conflicts between students and citizens he transferred it to Coimbra in 1308. In imitation of his grandfather Alfonso X of Castile, he substituted Portuguese for Latin in judicial procedure, and caused that king's code, the *Siete Partidas*, to be translated; his court, like that of his father, who had lived for many years in touch with French culture, was one of the literary centres of the Peninsula, and Dinis himself, beside being a protector of letters, left a large number of lyric poems which are contained in the *Cancioneiros*. To benefit agriculture and the revenue, he sought to increase the number of small proprietors and prevent further land from falling into mortmain. Following in the trend of previous legislation, a law of 1286 forbade corporations from acquiring real estate by purchase, and ordered what had been bought since the beginning of the reign to be sold within a year, under pain of confiscation; in 1291 another law provided that the landed property of those who entered religious Orders should not pass to the latter but only to laymen; moreover, to induce the upper class to farm, it was decreed that *fidalgos* by so doing should not lose their nobility, and steps were taken for the division and leasing of uncultivated land. Marshes were drained and the pine forest of Leiria planted to provide wood for constructions and prevent sand from the sea-shore being thrown by the wind over the fields round the city; these measures gained for the king the title of *Husbandman*, while his reorganisation of the navy under the Genoese Emanuele Pezagno enabled the Portuguese in the next reign to commence the ocean voyages and reach the Canaries. The queen, St Isabel, contributed to the civilising work of her husband and ministers by the example of her life devoted to good works, by constant efforts to promote harmony between her husband and turbulent son, and by her charity in the great plague of 1333.

Happier than Castile, which was a prey to constant civil disturbances, Portugal during the forty years following the death of Dinis enjoyed internal peace, save for a conflict between Afonso IV and his bastard brother, Afonso Sanches, and the brief rebellion of his son Peter, consequent on the execution of the latter's mistress Ignez de Castro by royal order. In spite of the war with Castile (1336–39), which had no tangible results for either side, Afonso helped its King Alfonso XI to repel the great Muslim invasion of the Peninsula from Africa in 1340, and shared in the Christian victory of the Salado (4 April). The foreign policy of his successor Peter I was one of neutrality, while at home he devoted himself to the stern administration of justice and to the increase of the Crown revenues, and amassed a large treasure which was squandered by his son Ferdinand; the ideal of equality of all men before the law was realised, and afterwards the people said that there had never been such ten years as those of his reign. We have an echo of the former quarrel between the monarchy and the Church at the Cortes of Elvas (1361), when the prelates complained without success of the exercise of the royal *beneplacitum*; they raised the point again at the Cortes of 1427 and 1477, and in 1487 John II renounced the right.

On the accession of Henry II of Castile, Ferdinand claimed the throne as great-grandson of Sancho the Brave, and at the invitation of certain magnates he invaded Galicia in 1369, but retired at the first sign of opposition, and a Castilian army entered Portugal and captured several strong places. A Portuguese naval expedition against Seville had to retreat with loss, and in the following year peace was made; Ferdinand agreed to marry Henry's daughter, but with the volatility which characterised him, he ignored this promise and married Leonor Telles, wife of a vassal, in spite of the protests of his subjects, and he entered into an alliance with John of Gaunt, Duke of Lancaster, who claimed the crown of Castile in right of his wife Constance. In December 1372 Henry II invaded Portugal and reached Lisbon, while Ferdinand remained shut up in Santarem, waiting for English aid which never came, and in March 1373 he had to accept Henry's terms, abandon the English alliance, and hand over six towns as security for his good faith. He then set about to build a new circuit of walls for Lisbon, a great work which was completed in two years by forced labour, and at the same time made preparations to renew the war with Castile at the first opportunity. This came with the death of Henry II in 1380. Having secured the assistance of an English expeditionary force under Edmund, Earl of Cambridge, the Portuguese opened hostilities on the eastern frontier, but a Castilian fleet entered the Tagus and laid siege to the capital (March 1382). It held out, though the king made no serious effort to relieve it, and in August he made peace without informing the earl, who had to return to England in September. Being a weak man, Ferdinand's change of policy may be ascribed to the clash of interests and influences around him, and in any case the enactments in favour of agriculture and shipping shew that he had capable ministers; they included the *Lei das Sesmarias*, described later on, and two others, which granted privileges to builders and buyers of ships, and established a maritime insurance company, whose regulations influenced the formation of sea law in the Mediterranean. At this time Lisbon was already a great trading port, frequented by merchants of all nations, and, according to the chronicler Fernão Lopes, 400 to 500 cargo boats lay in front of it at once, many employed in the export of salt and wine.

On the death of Ferdinand in October 1383, the crown passed to his daughter Beatrice, who had been espoused to John I of Castile in the previous April, while Leonor Telles became regent and by the marriage contract was to hold office until a son of Beatrice completed the age of fourteen. These arrangements were generally resented, because Leonor had earned the fame of an adulteress by her relations with João Fernandes Andeiro, Count of Ourem, and because the crown of Portugal would pass to the King of Castile if Beatrice predeceased her husband. The great majority of the nation set its hopes on the Infant John, Grand Master of the Order of Aviz, bastard son of Peter I by Teresa Lourenço, as the champion of independence. The agitation against the scandalous life of the regent, coupled with the fear of foreign rule, grew until a group of nobles led by Nuno Alvares Pereira and by Alvaro Paes, one of the tribunes of Lisbon, with the support of the citizens, resolved on the death of Andeiro and persuaded John to carry it out. The latter was then proclaimed Defender of the realm by the populace of the capital, though the burgesses hesitated at first to join his party, through fear of the power of Castile and of the nobles, who were legitimists. Thereupon Leonor summoned her son-in-law to invade the realm, while John and his friends sent ambassadors to London to seek leave to recruit volunteers; this they obtained, but few came. In January 1384 the King of Castile reached Santarem, and Leonor found herself compelled to hand over the government to him; and, though Nuno Alvares Pereira defeated a Castilian force at Atoleiros, the main body arrived before the capital on 8 February and began the siege. Oporto had adhered to the nationalist cause, and after repelling a Galician attack directed by the Archbishop of Compostela, it sent a squadron to the relief of Lisbon which forced the Castilian blockade of the Tagus. The city continued to resist, plague worked havoc among the besiegers, and, when in September his wife fell ill, John I broke up his camp and returned home. After reducing some places which held out for Castile, the Master of Aviz and Nuno Alvares Pereira proceeded to Coimbra, where the Cortes had been summoned to settle the succession to the crown; some favoured the former, others another John, son of Peter I by Ignez de Castro, but the arguments of Dr João das Regras, afterwards chancellor, persuaded the assembly to elect the Master of Aviz (6 April 1385).

Though the King of Castile had retired, nearly all the north and centre of the realm with 70 towns and castles obeyed him, so that the nationalist cause remained in jeopardy; and though the King of Portugal and Nuno Alvares Pereira, now Constable, succeeded in reducing Vianna, Guimarães, and Braga, and the Castilians lost a battle at Trancoso, their fleet of 63 vessels entered the Tagus in the spring of 1385 and blockaded Lisbon. In June John of Castile invaded Portugal with 32,000 men, and to meet this large army the King of Portugal could oppose only 6,500, including 200 English archers, when the two armies met at Aljubarrota (14 August 1385). Yet the Portuguese host, though small and fasting, for it was the eve of the Feast of the Assumption, had the advantages of position and desperation, and fighting on foot it routed the chivalry of Castile and their French allies in less than an hour; the allies lost 3,000 men killed, the royal standard of Castile, and the ornaments of the king's chapel. So decisive was the victory that the Constable was able to invade Castile, and he defeated the Master of the Order of Alcántara and his army at Valverde (15 October). On his election to the throne, John I had sought an alliance with England, and on the news of the battle of Aljubarrota, the Duke of Lancaster decided to pursue by arms his claim to the crown of Castile, while the treaty of Windsor was signed between the King of Portugal and Richard II (9 May 1386). In July the duke landed at Corunna, and after over-running Galicia met John I and gave him his daughter Philippa in marriage; but the Anglo-Portuguese campaign proved a failure, and in May the duke accepted the terms of peace offered him, under which he received an indemnity for his expenses, while his daughter Catherine was betrothed to Henry, heir of the King of Castile. The war between this country and Portugal had virtually terminated, though frontier incursions continued, and in 1387 a three years' truce was made, and renewed for fifteen years in 1393; in 1396 hostilities broke out afresh, followed soon by another truce for ten years, and finally the conflict, which had lasted since 1383, was ended by a definite peace treaty (31 October 1411).

The long war had drawn large numbers of men from their usual occupations and accustomed them to fighting and plunder or to a life of idleness and crime; to employ them abroad, to satisfy the chivalric ideas of his sons, to check piracy, and to continue the crusade against the Muslims which was a Portuguese tradition, the king was persuaded to undertake the first of the overseas expeditions, which resulted in the capture of Ceuta (21 August 1415) and its retention. His son Prince Henry the Navigator had previously sent ships down the west coast of Africa, but the methodical explorations he directed, which were inspired by religious and scientific ideas and based largely on the information obtained in that city, date from then. To supervise the expeditions, Henry fixed his abode in the Algarve and applied himself to the study of mathematics and cosmography, selected pilots, and had them instructed; moreover, he sent to Majorca for Master Jacome, a noted Jewish cartographer, who taught the Portuguese to make maps. In 1418–19 his captains rediscovered Madeira and Porto Santo, which were settled and cultivated so as to become sources of wealth in his lifetime. They made various attempts to conquer the Canaries from 1425, rounded Cape Bojador in 1434, and by 1436 had reached the Rio do Ouro; but the voyages were then interrupted for some years, first by the disastrous expedition against Tangier in 1437, where Henry had to leave his brother Ferdinand in the hands of the Moors to save his army, and secondly by a dispute over the regency.

To gain adherents and reward services in the war of independence, John I had made extensive grants of Crown lands to the Constable and others, so that, when peace came with Castile, the royal patrimony was exhausted and he had nothing for fresh claimants on his bounty and for his growing sons; by the advice of Dr João das Regras and others, he bought back part of the lands and took their tenants into his service, and in 1433 he made a further attempt to restore the position of the Crown by the *Lei Mental*. Promulgated by his son King Edward (1433–38) in 1434, it provided that lands granted by the Crown could only descend to the eldest son of the grantee and his successors, excluding females and collaterals, and that they could never be divided up nor alienated. This enactment and the preparation of a new code, published by Edward's successor under the name of the *Ordenações Afonsinas*, together with a literary movement, in which he was foremost, mark the reign of the philosopher king; Fernão Lopes, the greatest of Portuguese chroniclers, in whose pages an epoch comes to life again, received his commission to write in 1434, and was succeeded by Gomes Eannes de Zurara, Ruy de Pina, and Garcia de Resende. When Edward died in 1438, he left the queen, Leonor of Aragon, regent for his son Afonso V who was a minor, but his brother, the Infant Peter, by force and intrigue succeeded in getting himself elected in her stead at the Cortes of 1440, and notwithstanding opposition from the queen and the nobles, he held the post until 1448, when at the instigation of the Duke of Braganza and others, Afonso took the government into his own hands. Thereupon the pent-up hatred against Peter broke out; he allowed himself to be driven into rebellion, and was defeated by the royal forces and killed at the battle of Alfarrobeira (20 May 1449).

The Henrician voyages recommenced in 1441, and the profits attracted adventurers and led to the formation of companies to exploit the trade of the new-found lands; already by 1446 as many as 51 caravels had left Portugal and penetrated 450 leagues beyond Cape Bojador, but after that date there is a gap in our information. In 1455–56 Antoniotto Usodimare and Alvise da Cá da Mosto explored the Senegal and Gambia, and then, or later, with Antonio da Noli, they discovered five of the Cape Verde Islands, while Diogo Gomes made two voyages in 1456 and 1460 with orders to reach the Indies, and he carried an interpreter in case he succeeded. Henry died in this year, and the Portuguese had then penetrated as far south as Sierra Leone, while the Azores had been known at least since 1439. In 1461 Pedro da Sintra went on to Cape Mesurado, and in 1469 Afonso V leased the royal rights in the Guinea trade to Fernão Gomes on condition that he discovered yearly 100 leagues of fresh coastline, with the result that the Equator was crossed and Cape Catherine attained between 1469 and 1471. The king did not therefore neglect maritime exploration, but he attached more importance to extending Portuguese dominion in Morocco, and in pursuit of this aim he captured Alcacer Ceguer in 1458, attacked Tangier and Arzila in 1462, and gained them in 1471; these strongholds served as schools of arms, but their maintenance drained the country of men and money it could ill afford to lose.

On the death of Henry IV of Castile in 1474, leaving an only child Joanna, the partisans of the latter invited Afonso V to invade the country and marry the princess, who was his niece, promising to recognise him as king, though Isabella, Henry's sister, married to Ferdinand of Aragon, was already in possession of the crown. As Louis XI of France desired to recover Roussillon, which the Aragonese had annexed, Afonso proposed an alliance to him, which was accepted, and while Louis invaded Biscay, Afonso entered Castile in 1475 to uphold Joanna. After nine months, occupied with frontier raids and fruitless negotiations, the Castilian and Portuguese armies met at Toro (February 1475) and fought an indecisive battle, for while Afonso was beaten and fled, his son John destroyed the forces opposed to him. Nevertheless the king's partisans in Castile grew fewer and fewer, and he decided to apply to Louis XI for help; but his journey to France proved fruitless, and he had to make peace with Ferdinand and Isabella at Alcaçovas (4 September 1479). This was followed by the treaty of Toledo (6 March 1480), the value of which to Portugal lay in its recognition of her right to the lands and islands to the south and to the conquest of Morocco; in exchange she ceded her claims to the Canaries, which had led to friction between the two countries at least from 1425. The wars and liberalities of Afonso left the treasury in debt, and under his easy rule the Braganza family had come to regard itself as almost equal to the sovereign. The energetic character of John II (1481–95) fitted him to grapple with these problems, and the general movement towards absolutism in other countries pointed out the way. Immediately after his accession, a question arose at the Cortes of 1481 as to the form in which the nobles should do homage; they considered the one suggested by the king too rigorous and the Duke of Braganza invoked his privileges and sent to his palace at Villa Viçosa for his title-deeds. The royal officer who accompanied the duke's agent in the search found a treasonable correspondence with Castile, in which the duke and his brother the Marquess of Montemor were implicated, and he took and shewed it to the king, who waited for two years before striking at his greatest and richest subjects. At the same time the Third Estate asked John to examine the grounds on which the nobles held a number of towns under their jurisdiction and, if these proved invalid, to revindicate them for the Crown; they also demanded protection against the injustices they suffered at the hands of the great lords and their officials, and suggested a number of financial reforms. In seeking to promote their own interests, the municipalities facilitated the king's absolutist policy, and he proceeded to act on their requests. In 1483 the

Duke of Braganza was arrested, tried and sentenced to death, and executed at Evora (30 May); all his goods were confiscated, and the Marquess of Montemor only escaped by flight. The queen's brother, the Duke of Viseu, who was involved in the conspiracy, received a pardon on account of his youth, but soon afterwards entered into a plot with some of the nobles to assassinate the king, who thereupon slew him with his own hand (28 August 1484), while some accomplices suffered imprisonment or death. Thenceforth John II provided himself with a personal guard, which his predecessors had not needed, for, unlike most other countries, Portugal did not suffer from regicide, and her sovereigns appear to have been esteemed by their subjects. John shewed a like ruthlessness to the Jews expelled in 1492 from Spain. He allowed some 90,000 to enter Portugal and stay eight months on payment of a poll tax of eight *cruzados* each, and agreed to supply vessels to take them wherever they wished to go; many were robbed and others slain by the people, who had suffered from the extortions of their own Jews and attributed the plague which broke out to the presence of the aliens, and when the time came for the latter to leave, the king ordered them to proceed to Africa. Those who went were treated even worse by the Moors; those who did not go were reduced to slavery. Previous to this, the Jews had no reason to complain of their lot in Portugal, as their own historians admit.

Afonso V had handed over the administration of the forts and factories on the African coast to John in 1474, and as soon as the latter came to the throne he took up Henry's work, the search for a sea route to India, with Henry's zeal. In 1482–83 Diogo Cão reached the Congo and Cape St Mary, in 1485 Cape Cross; in 1482 Diogo de Azambuja built the fort of St George at Mina, and in 1488 Bartholomew Dias rounded the Cape of Storms, renamed by the king Good Hope from the expectation that India would soon be attained, and discovered 1250 miles of fresh coast, but the death of Prince Afonso and a dispute with Spain caused delays, and the prize fell to John's successor, Manuel the Fortunate; it was not until 1498 that Vasco da Gama anchored off Calicut and realised the union of East and West of which Henry had dreamed. To supplement the voyage of Dias, John had endeavoured to obtain information about the route to India by means of land travellers; an expedition went up the Senegal, which was supposed to be connected with the Nile, while Pedro da Covilhan and Afonso de Paiva proceeded to Cairo and Aden, where they parted company. Paiva died, but his companion went on to India and East Africa and, after returning to Egypt, sent home an account of what he had learnt. His information combined with that of Dias led to the voyage of da Gama, which the king planned before he died in 1495.

The Portuguese failed to discover America, but John II had good reasons for rejecting the project Columbus submitted to him of a western passage to India, after its careful examination by his mathematicians and cosmographers; the eastern route proved to be far shorter. When the navigator returned from his first voyage in March 1493, the king was advised that the new-found lands were in his sphere, and the rumour arose in Spain that he had sent a caravel thither and was equipping others for the same destination; thereupon King Ferdinand proposed that the matter should be settled by negotiations, but without waiting for these he persuaded Alexander VI, a Spaniard, to issue the bull of 4 May 1493 by which all lands west and south of a line drawn at 100 leagues from the Azores and Cape Verde islands were to belong to Spain; then, still not content, he induced the Pope to issue another bull on 26 September, enlarging the previous concession to the prejudice of Portugal. John had then to choose between a war and negotiations; he chose the latter, and by the Treaty of Tordesillas (7 June 1494) succeeded in getting the line between the Portuguese and Spanish spheres moved, so as to run at 370 leagues west of the Cape Verde islands. The king yielded to Spain the supposed route to the Indies discovered by Columbus, obtained control of the true way to the East, and secured possession of Brazil. This diplomatic victory was due to his skill in the conduct of the matter and to the ability of his plenipotentiaries. Duarte Pacheco, one of these, wrote of John: "his judgment and intelligence have been unequalled in our time," and his opponent, Isabella the Catholic, spoke of him as "the man."

When the history of the monarchy begins, the population was of Hispano-Arab stock with a landed aristocracy of Gothic origin. Portugal had a relatively well-endowed Church, whose prelates were men of culture, communes representing the middle class, possessing an internal administration, guaranteed by their charters, as independent as that of the nobles and clergy on their estates, and in the country districts freedmen and serfs; by the end of the thirteenth century personal servitude disappeared. The Muslims and Jews formed groups apart, and in the towns, where they usually lived, they had their own quarters, enjoyed certain privileges, and paid a special tax.

The monarchy was hereditary and, according to a doctrine inherited from the Visigoths and founded on Biblical texts, the king represented God, from whom he received his authority; but in practice the privileges and immunities of each class and local customs restricted it, and Sancho I and his successors, inspired by their chancellors trained in Roman Law, strove with success to escape most of these restrictions. Their efforts were directed to secure the supreme administration of justice, the limitation of baronial and ecclesiastical privileges and properties, the control of local administration, and untrammelled exercise of the legislative function. In 1317 Dinis, following in the steps of Afonso II, proclaimed that by the law and custom of the realm the right of judgment in the last instance was understood as reserved to the Crown in all royal grants, in recognition of its overlordship, and the people defended this doctrine in the Cortes of 1372. Though monarchs sometimes renounced this right in their grants, the Third Estate supported it and the *Ordenações Afonsinas* confirmed it; moreover, in this code the royal judges (*Corregidores*) were ordered to visit every place twice yearly. This was a direct challenge to the nobles, whose lands called *coutos* and *honras* were by custom exempt. In the Cortes of 1398 the nobles had complained that their privileges were not respected, and in the Cortes of 1434 the people asked Edward to assume the entire jurisdiction, but he refused; the time had not come for so sweeping a reform. Fiscal considerations, even more than the point of authority, were at the root of the war waged by the monarchs with the Church and nobility, because the lands of the latter were usually free from taxation, and they explain the Inquests and the laws against mort-main, which have already been mentioned. In their policy of aggrandise-ment, the kings often shewed the same lack of respect for the rights of others which was commonly imputed to nobles and clergy, as for instance in the seizure of six towns belonging to the abbey of Alcobaça in the reign of Afonso IV, which were restored by Peter I. The struggle between the Crown and the prelates, in which the former was usually the aggressor, ended by a compromise under Dinis, and subsequent disputes between the two were amicably settled, while the revocations of grants, the restrictions imposed by the *Lei Mental*, and the confiscations under John II, by de-stroying fraudulent titles and recovering property which the kings had been constrained to part with in times of difficulty, broke the power of the landed aristocracy. With the abasement of the privileged classes, the support of the communes was no longer necessary to the Crown. In the past it had been regularly given; in the Cortes of 1472–73 the people told Afonso V that it was his duty to use his "absolute power" to repair the injuries done them and not to wait for their complaints. Moreover, a town considered it a calamity to be given to a magnate, when civil and criminal jurisdiction accompanied the grant, and some, like Oporto, counted among their privileges that a noble could not reside in them, in order that their womenfolk might be secure from outrage. Nevertheless, when in the Cortes of 1475 the Third Estate asked that its approved laws and customs should be maintained and royal orders and judicial decisions to the contrary be cancelled, Afonso V replied that the general request was ill-made, but that any special injury would be repaired.

In the course of time, legislative power became the chief attribute of royal authority. The early Portuguese kings based their ordinances on their own good pleasure and on the consent of the magnates, but in the fourteenth century this style was replaced by the will of the monarch, either with or without the consent of his Council, and in the middle of the same century documents attribute to the king unlimited power. Some of these emanating from Peter I speak of "our free will and certain know-ledge," but this changes in the reign of his son Ferdinand to "our knowledge and absolute power"; the last formula becomes increasingly frequent and at the end of our period it corresponds to a fact, notwith-standing the institution of the Cortes. This assembly had its origin in the old *Curia Regis*, or Royal Council, which existed among the Visigoths; though in theory under no obligation to consult it, the kings did not fail to do so when they had to take important resolutions. The *Curia* acted in two distinct ways, as an ordinary assembly, or in extraordinary sessions, in which matters of great moment were discussed. Both were attended by members of the royal family, court officials, magnates, lay and ecclesiastical, and certain nobles and prelates in whose lands the meetings were held, or who happened to be at court. As lawyers grew in political importance, they began to have seats on the Council. At extraordinary meetings the nobility was represented, not only by the usual members, but by all the magnates, who were specially summoned, and the Church sent its prelates, secular and regular. The Masters of the three Military Orders also attended, and later on procurators of the cities enjoyed the right to be present. The king called the Council, and those summoned were bound to attend, because the duty of giving advice was one of the obligations of a vassal.

As thus described, it was an organism suited to the administrative and political conditions of the country in early times, but when these became more complex it necessarily underwent a transformation and the two forms of the assembly, the ordinary and extraordinary, became separate bodies with different functions. The Royal Council, a continuation of the ordinary sessions of the *Curia Regis*, directed the life of the State in its political, administrative, legislative, and judicial spheres, while the Cortes, as the heir of the extraordinary Councils, dealt only with general questions of an economic or legislative nature and with grave political matters.

This evolution was slow and may be said to have begun in the middle of the thirteenth century. It was marked by the following stages:

1. The presence of representatives of the towns, at the Cortes of Leiria in 1254.

2. The convocation of the Cortes to deal with finance and taxation, which originated in the practice pursued by monarchs, in times of pecuniary stress, of renouncing for a number of years, usually seven, the right to debase the coinage, in consideration of the grant of a sum sufficient to meet the needs of the treasury. Afonso III obtained a capital sum by these means at the Cortes of Leiria, as he could raise money in no other way; however, two centuries later Ferdinand dealt with the coinage as he thought fit, and a hundred years afterwards John II did not think it necessary to consult the people about it.

3. The right of representation thus acquired led members of the Cortes to attend with the object of watching over the administration and of defending their privileges, and the assembly thus came to act as a check on the king.

4. Little by little the idea of the representation of various classes as a fixed principle arose, and their duty to attend developed into a right to be summoned and to take part in these assemblies.

5. Finally, to the privilege of giving advice, their only business at first, was added the right of petition, formulated in articles requesting the removal of abuses, which the king accepted or rejected.

The time of convocation remained dependent on the king's will and the mode of summons was by royal letter, sent to all who were entitled to sit in the assembly, stating the reasons for which the Cortes were called, the matters to be discussed, and the date and place of meeting. Each of the Three Estates was represented, but this title does not appear until the fifteenth century; they consisted of nobles, clergy, and procurators of the cities and towns. The choice of persons and their number depended on the king, but certain individuals owing to their high position could not be omitted, while the right of cities and towns to send members depended on custom, or on their charters. The voters consisted of the most important citizens, voting took place by signed lists, and one or two persons of position and wealth were elected, but rarely more. When the municipal spirit declined, nobles and prelates were often chosen by the Third Estate, and in this case they sat among the representatives of the people; sometimes the king wrote to recommend the choice of men in whom he had confidence. The members chosen were given procurations, in the form of an instrument written in a notary's book, which contained their powers; they could not exceed these, and their expenses were paid by the municipality.

The Estates conferred separately and each communicated with the others by means of *Definitors*, elected on the ground that business could be dispatched more speedily by a few, and this committee did the real work. The written proposals submitted to the king had the name of *chapters*; the replies, signed by the sovereign or his secretary, were issued in the form of a letter, and together with the *chapters* they constituted legislative acts. Each class fought for its own interests, and divergent economic needs often led to discord even among members of the Third Estate. Moreover the latter objected to sharing its power with the common folk, and in the Cortes of 1481 it petitioned against the intervention of the trading gilds, even in municipal administration, on the ground that it was not the business of the lower class to rule, but to work and serve. The Cortes rarely lasted longer than a month, but, if necessary, the king was requested to continue them, which he generally did; he could, however, dissolve them before the term had elapsed. One of the most important attributes of the Cortes was taxation. In early times the revenue from Crown lands and the usual contributions were sufficient for the current expenses of the administration, and a further general tax was only needed on an extraordinary occasion; in that case a levy was made, and the Cortes would be called together to sanction it. The right of the assembly to a voice in the imposition of taxes obtained recognition at the end of the fourteenth century; in 1372 it refused to grant Ferdinand a general excise; in 1387, however, this was voted, but only for a year; and John I, when planning the attack on Ceuta, declared that he would make no levy, so as not to be obliged to summon the Cortes.

By customary law the king should have consulted the Cortes before declaring war or making peace, but he did not always do so. They first claimed to be heard on these matters with a view of ending the conflict upon which Ferdinand had embarked with Castile, and he promised to attend to their representations, but forgot his promise. In the Cortes of 1385 similar demands were made on John I with more success, for at least once, when he was negotiating for a peace with the neighbouring country, he called the Cortes at Santarem to consult them. Afonso V, however, never asked the consent of the people to his African expeditions; it is true that in 1475, when about to invade Castile, he summoned the Cortes to obtain a subsidy, and they gave it without questioning his project. The monarch could require the people to fight, but could not oblige them to contribute money without their consent. Nevertheless, this and other foreign wars would have been impossible had the nation been opposed to them.

It was one of the privileges of the Cortes to receive the oath of the sovereign on his accession and to do homage to the heir to the throne, and in addition to their ordinary attributes they had others on extraordinary occasions, such as the election of a king on the extinction of a dynasty, his deposition, the alteration of fundamental laws, and the appointment of a guardian or regent when the king was a minor. By their representations they provoked legislation, which, however, was more often carried out in the Council than in the Cortes, but they did not constitute a legislative assembly; their resolutions had not the force of law unless sanctioned by the king, and he claimed and exercised the power to make laws without their intervention.

The value of the Cortes as a means of obtaining the redress of grievances and other benefits may appear to us to have been slight, and the repetition of their complaints shews the small effect they had, but the Third Estate attached great importance to them and continually asked that they should be summoned periodically and often; its members could only find in union the force that the nobles and clergy possessed individually by rank and wealth. John I was requested to call the Cortes annually and consented to do so, but though a record of all the assemblies that were held has not come down to us, we may none the less be sure that the promise was not kept. In the Cortes of Torres Novas in 1438, amid the agitation about the regency, an annual convocation was actually decided upon, but not carried out. Down to 1385 we have notice of twenty-seven Cortes and from 1385 to 1580 of fifty-six; the fifteenth century was that in which they met most frequently. After the consolidation of the royal power under John II, they met only on ten occasions in a hundred years; they were replaced satisfactorily by the various

Councils, composed of nobles and lawyers, who represented public opinion and had more power than the Cortes ever enjoyed.

The policy of centralisation was maintained by John's successors and enabled Portugal to complete the discoveries, create an overseas dominion, and colonise and hold Brazil, the largest country in South America, achievements which give her a place in world history; only by the combination of the national resources under the direction of the monarch could a small, poor, and undisciplined people have achieved so immense an undertaking.

The ordinary revenue of the State was derived mainly from the royal lands and from direct or indirect taxation; the most lucrative impost in the last category was the *sisa*, payable on sales and purchases, at first purely municipal, next granted to the kings on special occasions for a year, and finally converted by John I into a regular tax, from which no one was exempt. The extraordinary revenue came from alterations in the value of the coinage, already referred to, "requests" (being a levy on private fortunes), forced loans, and the product of monopolies, such as the export of salt and hides. From the beginning of the fifteenth century, the revenue did not cover the expenditure and the deficit became permanent; the main causes were the war of independence, the African expeditions of Afonso V, his generous grants to the nobles, and attempts to win the crown of Castile. The exemptions enjoyed by the privileged classes and the faulty system of collection, entrusted largely to Jews in spite of popular protests, prevented an expansion of receipts sufficient to meet the growing needs. The net of taxation was cast so widely and frequently over the lower class that it formed a heavy burden, and may have been partly responsible for the agricultural depression which prevailed from the middle of the fourteenth century.

Agriculture was and still is the chief occupation and source of wealth in Portugal; it had reached a high level under the Muslims, and after the Reconquest the Cistercians carried on and even improved upon their traditions. The monks of Alcobaça made farming implements in their own forges with iron extracted from the mines they worked, and such was their skill on the land that they were employed to drain marshes and superintend the royal granaries. A law of 1252, fixing prices and the salaries of labourers, mentions all degrees of men employed to-day on a large estate and shews the progress realised at that date. The kings were the chief landowners, and all of them enacted agrarian laws and protected agriculture in the interests of the revenue, yet for reasons that are not quite apparent Dinis alone earned the name of the *Husbandman*. When the population was small and scattered, the land produced sufficient to feed it, but as the people and their needs increased, any irregularity in the season and harvest led to famine; the export of corn was forbidden in 1272 and afterwards on several occasions, but it could not be entirely prevented and, like cattle, it was often smuggled over the Spanish border.

The *Lei das Sesmarias* only imitated previous legislation in the same sense: uncultivated lands were to be confiscated and granted to such as would till them, and idle persons were to be arrested and compelled to work. It was followed by similar enactments of John I, Edward, and Afonso V intended to increase the production of breadstuffs, but none of them achieved their purpose, and corn had frequently to be brought from abroad to make up for the shortage at home. The depression had many causes. The first was the scarcity of labour, owing to the mortality from plagues and famines and because labourers fled to the towns, where they found greater security and freedom, or adopted an easier mode of life in the service of noble or prelate, or took to begging as a profession. Hence wages and the cost of animals and tools rose, farmers could not pay them, and from the middle of the fourteenth century the land under cultivation gradually diminished; while in the fifteenth century the ocean voyages and the new-found islands took more and more men from the soil, especially in the Algarve, and their places were filled with slaves from Africa. The multiple taxes which the agriculturist had to pay and the oppression he suffered at the hands of the magnates and their servants were only contributory causes, for these burdens existed before and there is no reason to suppose that they grew worse.

Next in importance to agriculture came sea and river fisheries, followed by the raising of live stock and horses, which the kings took a prominent part in and encouraged by numerous enactments. The chase was pursued, not only as a preparation for war and as a diversion, but to obtain skins for home use and export; the quantity of wild animals in the forests which then covered a large part of the land made the occupation lucrative. Industries were entirely domestic, and wearing apparel, except some rough cloth, articles of luxury, manufactured goods, and minerals, save salt, came from abroad in exchange for the products of the soil—oil, wax, cork, honey, fruit, wine, and occasionally cereals. The population increased very slowly, and at the end of the fifteenth century probably did not much exceed one million; from the end of the fourteenth century the towns grew at the expense of the rural districts. The Cortes of 1481 give a sad picture of the internal state of the country, but though their *chapters*, like those of previous assemblies, abound in complaints of the wrongs from which the people suffered, the absence of revolts by towns or peasants, and even of literary tirades against kings and barons, suggests that conditions were not beyond endurance; a sunny climate, religion, pilgrimages, dancing, song, and the recital of folk poems, lightened the yoke of the peasantry, who had the hardest existence. The leisured classes sought recreation and acquired dexterity in the use of arms, in chess, riding, games of ball, jousts, tourneys, and *jogos de cannas*, while bullfights formed part of the programme on great occasions and even ecclesiastics took part in them until forbidden to do so.

Lisbon and Oporto were the chief commercial centres, and foreign trade was carried on mainly with the countries of the north and the Mediterranean. Portuguese merchants possessed a factory at Bruges and frequented Marseilles in the twelfth century, and in the thirteenth they were established in the French channel ports. In 1226 more than one hundred safe conducts were granted to them in England, and in 1352 Edward III made a commercial treaty for fifty years with Afonso Martins Alho, representing the Portuguese maritime towns, which was the precursor of the still existing alliance between the two countries; it contained a novel clause authorising Portuguese fishermen to carry on their industry on the coasts of England and Brittany.

In the fifteenth century the islands discovered and settled under the directions of Henry the Navigator and also the west coast of Africa sent their products to Portugal and to other countries; Madeira supplied wood for the building of houses, wheat, wax, honey, and sugar; the last article appears in the Bristol Customs Accounts from 1466 in increasing quantities, and it competed successfully with that of Sicily and the Levant. The Cortes of 1472–73 and 1481 complained that its export had fallen into the hands of foreigners, who in 1480 loaded twenty large vessels and more than forty smaller ones with it. The sugar industry gave Madeira its first importance and spread thence to the Azores and Cape Verde Islands. The Malvoisie grape, introduced from Crete, was used to make the famous Malmsey wine, while the raising of cattle and the export of dragon's blood flourished in Porto Santo. West Africa sent to Portugal slaves, ivory, and pepper, and the large profits derived from the gold of Mina enabled John II to build up the maritime organisation by which the discoveries of his reign and that of his successor were made possible.

CHAPTER XVII

THE SCANDINAVIAN KINGDOMS DURING THE FOURTEENTH AND FIFTEENTH CENTURIES

THE fourteenth and fifteenth centuries are above all the period of feudalism in the Scandinavian countries. At the beginning of this period, the feudal nobility had fixed itself firmly in the saddle, and it overrode proudly all other powers. In particular the Danish nobility shewed, during this period, a robust and high-handed vigour that easily made it the master and arbiter of the country and even of the lands beyond. There appeared, however, very little of a national spirit in the ranks of the nobles; they simply looked on themselves as nobles, as the naturally privileged class of society, and, inspired by this feeling, in the struggle for their privileges, they combined with their fellows beyond the national frontiers as well as inside them. Herein is to be found the chief factor which caused these centuries to be also a period of Scandinavian union. But a political union of formerly independent kingdoms was not possible without the intermediary of the royal power, and although the king, in principle, was at the head of the nobility, he at this very time began the attempt of building up a self-relying power, representing the nation and deriving its strength from non-feudal sources. He too, then, seized upon the idea of uniting the Scandinavian kingdoms under a single sceptre, seeing in this policy a chance of increasing his own power; and so it happened that Scandinavianism in these centuries became an instrument to be employed equally by the rival powers which came to the front at different moments.

It was the natural outcome of social and economic conditions that feudalism and nobility still had the upper hand in all conflicts; Scandinavian society still was so predominantly agricultural, the economic units so small, that the government could only be decentralised and rest upon the landed proprietors, vassals of the Crown. But, outside this feudal society, there was developing a commerce tending to create new economic relations; and here the king could see possibilities of a new financial foundation of his power. As a matter of fact, we find him beginning to utilise the means that thus presented themselves, striving to acquire revenue which would be at his free disposal. The assistance of the commercial capitalist appeared, however, a two-edged weapon; giving his money as a loan to the king, he really made the king his servant, indebted and pledged to him for life, and this was the more dangerous to the Scandinavian king because the merchant from whom he had to borrow was a foreigner. Indeed, the commerce of the Scandinavian countries during these centuries was wholly in the hands of the cities of northern Germany, of the rich and powerful Hansa; and, when the king tried to consolidate a national royal power, he was faced by the alternative danger, the loss of national independence.

So, in all directions, we meet conflicting tendencies of development. The three great powers of Scandinavian history in this period were the Nobility, the King, and the Hansa. The fourth leading element in society, the Church, had consolidated itself but was no longer an aggressive force; essentially, however, it ranged itself on the side of feudalism. The three other powers were still struggling for expansion, and the possibilities of conflict were widely varied. The history of the conflicts is abundant in dramatic events, and some imposing personalities emerge from the whirlpool. It is a pity that no contemporary historian has pictured to us the men and their doings. The days of the sagas and other historical writings were at an end; all national literature faded away and vanished. Only Sweden, previously without any literature at all, produced some works of religious, political, and even historical content, some rhymed chronicles which provide some glimpses of the personalities in action. Isolated events that were fitted to impress themselves upon the mind of the people were celebrated in popular ballads which were preserved by oral tradition, mainly in Denmark, and which enable us to catch at least the moral effect of certain acts upon general opinion. But mostly we are compelled to study these centuries from dry annals and documents, too often disconnected and full of gaps, where we have to guess at motives and characters.

The murder of the Danish king, Eric Clipping, in the year 1286, led up to a crisis in the history of all Scandinavia. His widow, as guardian of the new infant king, Eric VI Menved, succeeded in bringing home to the leaders of the nobility the responsibility for the murder and effected their exile. But they immediately found support in Norway, where, at that moment, with a barely adult king, the nobility was in power, and where, besides, the queen mother, a Danish princess, had a common interest with the exiles, who from their own feudal interests had sustained against their own king her claims on Danish territory. The war that resulted from these claims now turned into a struggle between feudalism and royal power. The coalition of nobles of the two kingdoms proved successful, and by the truce of 1295 the Norwegian princes as well as the Danish exiles obtained acknowledgment of their territorial claims in Denmark, while—a provision still more characteristic of the progress of feudalism—two Danish castles, erected by the exiles during the war, were to be kept under the suzerainty of the King of Norway. King Eric of Denmark by no means intended to accept this truce as a final settlement of the questions involved, and he immediately sought an alliance with the young King of Sweden, who just at this date became free from the guardianship of his council of vassals. The following decades witnessed a series of changing alliances, in which the Kings of Norway and Sweden supplied a continually unstable element, sometimes dominated by the influences of the nobility, sometimes trying to make themselves independent, throwing themselves on the one or the other side in the incessantly renewed inter-Scandinavian wars.

One of the most remarkable expressions of the conflicting tendencies of the period was the royal ordinance issued in the year 1308 by King Hakon V of Norway. Apparently this king looked on Philip the Fair of France as the model for his internal policy, and he really succeeded in making the clergy an instrument of royal government. Now, probably alarmed by the crushing defeat of the King of Sweden by the nobles with whom he was allied, King Hakon proclaimed the resumption of all fiefs granted and the abolition of baronial powers, in fact the introduction of absolute monarchy. This sweeping ordinance had no practical results; King Hakon shewed no power of persistence in a policy of such monarchical centralisation.

The only Scandinavian king who steadily kept up the struggle for royal power was King Eric of Denmark; but he spent his forces, economic as well as military, in far-reaching plans for extending his power even over the German duchies of Mecklenburg and Pomerania with the wealthy Wendish towns. In spite of some brilliant moments of victory, he was in the end defeated, and his real power even at home was declining. He was forced to recognise the autonomous position belonging to the Duke of Schleswig and to give away a province at the other end of the kingdom, Northern Halland, as a fief to the King of Norway; in order to pay his debts he had to mortgage the whole island of Funen to the Counts of Holstein and to pledge the incomes of other fiefs and castles. As a matter of fact, Denmark was rapidly becoming feudalised, and when, in the year 1319, King Eric died leaving no children, his brother Christopher, who himself had been fighting on the side of the nobility against the king, was forced to accept the crown under the conditions presented to him by the nobles. He was the first Danish king who at his election (1320) was obliged to submit to a capitulation, pledging himself to govern the kingdom under the absolute control of the parliament of nobles, and to make no wars and to demand no taxes without their consent. It was the complete victory of the new feudalism.

While King Eric of Denmark was vainly fighting the ascendancy of the nobility within and without his country, feudal tendencies obtained a brilliant champion in Sweden and Norway in the person of a brother of the Swedish king, named Eric, Duke of Södermanland, supported with never-failing fidelity by his younger brother Duke Waldemar. The two dukes really became the leaders of the nobles of Sweden in their fight for feudal privileges. Eric, the hero of the first Swedish rhymed chronicle, is presented to us as the most charming knight of the age, but in his acts he appears as a type of the most unscrupulous noble imaginable, by every method pushing his personal interests, greedy for power and land, breaking his oaths whenever it suited him, betraying friend and foe alike.

After many vicissitudes, his activities resulted in creating a unique position for him in Scandinavian politics. He married the daughter and only child of King Hakon of Norway, thus winning the prospect of power in that country; he obtained as a fief the south-eastern province of Norway with the new castle of Bohus and also the Danish province of Northern Halland; and having gained as his share of Sweden Western Gothland and other western provinces, he was finally the master of a compact territory, composed of contiguous parts of all the three Scandinavian kingdoms, an omen of the future union of Scandinavia. At the same time he was the representative and ideal of the whole Scandinavian nobility, which was the more strongly bound together in the fight for common interests.

An end was put to the intrigues of Duke Eric by a piece of treachery of the same kind that he was himself wont to use. In the closing days of 1317, he and his brother were captured by the King of Sweden and committed to a prison from which they never emerged; it was rumoured that they were starved to death. But the consequence was a general rebellion of the Swedish nobles; the king could get no effective assistance from his friend the King of Denmark and was forced to flee the country; and in the year 1319 an assembly of the Estates of the realm elected the three-year-old son of Duke Eric, Magnus, to be King of Sweden. By inheritance, owing to the death of King Hakon, Magnus had just before become King of Norway, and so the two kingdoms found themselves united under a common king, the essential fact being that in each country the nobility was in control of the government.

From 1319, feudal principles dominated in all the Scandinavian countries, though they had not developed to the same extent in each of them. In Iceland, a truly feudal system was always out of the question, merely because there was no need of a military organisation. In Norway and Sweden, the holders of fiefs never acquired rights of jurisdiction in their districts. In none of the kingdoms did the fiefs ever become hereditary, except in the Danish duchy of Schleswig, which held a position peculiar to itself. The dominating fact in all the kingdoms was that the nobility had grown up into an organised class that possessed the monopoly of the local government, the leading part in the central government, and the control of the economic resources and the military forces of the nation. In all three countries the Church stood outside the feudal organisation, in the sense that the bishoprics and abbeys never became fiefs of the Crown; but from this very time there was an increasing tendency to give the high offices of the Church to members of noble families, and, since almost all landed property belonged to the Crown, the Church, and the nobles, these latter really had almost exclusive command of territorial wealth. In Norway and Sweden, and in some parts of Denmark, particularly Jutland, there was still in existence a class of yeomen; but feudal influences from abroad, strengthened by the influx of German nobles, stimulated the greed of the native nobility, and, chiefly in Denmark, feudal privileges over the peasants were steadily extended.

The victory of feudalism in Denmark almost seemed destined to dissolve completely the unity of the kingdom. The weak King Christopher, stripped of all military and financial authority, vainly tried to defend the royal power against the nobles whom he himself had formerly helped to resist the king. The Danish nobles obtained a vigorous leader from abroad, one of the Counts of Holstein, the high-handed Gerhard, who became the tutor of his nephew, the young Waldemar Duke of Schleswig. Together with his cousin, another of the Counts of Holstein, he made himself the real ruler of Denmark. King Christopher possessed no other means of getting money to arm himself against his powerful rival than that of pledging away his lands, and after a few years he had hardly any land left, and not a single castle in his own country. Virtually all Denmark was divided between Count Gerhard and his allies; for some years King Christopher was a fugitive in Germany, while the count made his nephew the nominal King of Denmark. When Christopher died (1332), Denmark was without a king for eight years; Count Gerhard ruled with absolute power the whole of Jutland north of Schleswig as well as the island of Funen, while his cousin ruled Sealand and most of the other islands. This same cousin sold Scania to King Magnus of Norway and Sweden, who assumed the title of King of Scania, keeping at the same time Northern Halland, while Southern Halland with some other parts of Denmark were in the hands of his mother, who had married a Danish noble. The kingdom of Denmark seemed only a name, and the old frontiers between the Scandinavian countries were disappearing.

But the rule of the Counts of Holstein, demanding heavy taxes and putting new feudal burdens on the inhabitants, roused an opposition that combined with the jealousy of the lower nobility to make an end of their dominion. Count Gerhard was murdered (1340), and the son of King Christopher, Waldemar, who lived in exile in Germany, was recalled and elected King of Denmark; by shrewd negotiations he was able to make use of the situation to create for himself a position of power which was a sufficient starting-point for a restoration of the monarchy. Waldemar (IV) received the surname of *Atterdag*, the original sense of which, like that of several other surnames of Danish kings, is uncertain and disputed, but in popular tradition it is surmised that it originated from a customary phrase of his: "To-morrow is a new day," expressing his never-failing patience and hope. Indeed he proved to be a statesman who incessantly worked to strengthen the royal power. In agreements and promises he was just as unreliable as his father had been; but he was also as systematic and obstinate in pursuing his aims as his father had been unstable and weak. He started by marrying the sister of the Duke of Schleswig; he induced the Counts of Holstein as a preliminary measure to exchange northern

Jutland for the duchy of Schleswig, and gained for himself a part of
northern Jutland as the dowry of his queen. From this beginning he
gradually succeeded in redeeming the peninsula bit by bit, utilising all
his revenues for this purpose, and persuading his subjects to grant him
taxes to restore peace and justice.

For the same purpose he received important assistance from the Church,
which had suffered seriously from the lawlessness of the interregnum.
Immediately on his accession the Bishop of Sealand handed over to him
the castle and city of Copenhagen, and from there he could begin to
redeem the whole island. He exploited the weakness of the Papacy in
order to make the Church of Denmark an instrument of royal government,
and so he laid the foundation of a durable gain to national organisation.
He realised a large sum of money by selling Esthonia to the Teutonic
Order, parting with a province that had been conquered in the crusade
of Waldemar II more than a hundred years earlier, but had never been
other than a burden to the kingdom. By means of this treasure he was
able to start a series of proceedings with a view to recovering the Crown
lands that had been lost during or even before the interregnum, and he
enjoyed the advantage of the low price of land that was the consequence
of the Black Death. The nobility, led by the Counts of Holstein, did
not allow the king to increase his power in this way without resistance,
and they took up arms repeatedly against him, but never in perfect accord;
in each war Waldemar had the upper hand, and in the year 1360 they were
compelled to make their peace with the king. By that time almost the
whole kingdom was reconquered, and in a parliament of the realm a
charter was sealed which was in fact an agreement between king and people
for the defence of peace and justice as well as for the mutual maintenance
of rights and privileges; an important advantage for the king was the
formal confirmation of the royal courts of justice. It is true that in other
respects he would have to govern the country through his faithful
vassals; feudalism was still the reigning principle, but the kingdom of
Denmark was again a reality.

At the same time, in Sweden and Norway, the national government
was becoming ever more feudalised. While King Magnus was a minor,
the representatives of the nobility and clergy were ruling in both countries,
and they were not willing to give up their power after his coming of age.
We may observe how the king himself was under the domination of the ideas
of feudalism: when, in the year 1335, he married Countess Blanche of
Namur, she received as her marriage portion certain districts in both kingdoms to administer and tax—a complete novelty in Scandinavia. These
districts after some years were consolidated into a Swedish-Norwegian
dominion on both sides of their southern frontier, following the example set
by Duke Eric, the king's father. When the queen had given birth to
two sons, one being named Eric after his Swedish grandfather, the other
Hakon after his Norwegian great-grandfather, King Magnus and the

nobility of both countries agreed to make each prince the heir of one of the two kingdoms; the younger, Hakon, even succeeded to the government of Norway as soon as he came of age, though King Magnus retained some provinces of Norway. So we see the two kingdoms treated without regard to national traditions; the only point of view seemed to be the personal interests of the members of the dynasty.

An exception to this policy may, however, be found in the work, set on foot by King Magnus, of combining all the different district-laws of Sweden into a national code, as had been done at an earlier time for Norway; and he succeeded in accomplishing such a codification for Sweden in the year 1347. This national law did not mean, however, the strengthening of the royal government; on the contrary, it enacted, what formerly was but customary, that the king could only exercise his authority in collaboration with the Council of Peers. In spite of this concession on his side, the nobility in both kingdoms felt jealous of his natural tendency to take decisions on his own account, particularly with regard to his third "kingdom," Scania. Several times there was friction between the two parties, and the feelings of the Swedish nobility are expressed in the "revelations" of Saint Bridget, a lady of one of the greatest families of her country, who in her holy discourses reviled the king and queen in most venomous and foul terms, and at least succeeded in blackening their fame to posterity.

To a certain degree, in Sweden and Norway we meet with the same tendency towards a dissolution of national unity as manifested itself in Denmark somewhat earlier. But even the political separation of the two kingdoms could not stop the welding together of the upper classes that had set in from the closing years of the thirteenth century. A particular event came to further this development: the Black Death, which devastated all the Scandinavian countries during the years 1349–50. Only Iceland escaped the plague, because it interrupted the navigation from Norway to that distant island; but this first great plague was followed by others in the course of the same century, and these reached Iceland as well, so that all peoples of the Scandinavian race had to bear the consequences of their devastations. In popular tradition the Black Death, in these countries called the Great Death, was said to have depopulated them almost completely. Statistics on this point are highly discordant, and the consequences of the plague are much disputed. Economic values, particularly those of land, seem likely to have been depreciated through the loss of a large number of the cultivators, and for that reason the wages of labourers and the conditions of peasants may possibly have improved. More certain is it that the incomes of the land-owners must have diminished. In Denmark the king appears to have taken advantage of these conditions to win back much land for the Crown. In Sweden and Norway we see nothing of that kind. But the Norwegian land-owners were hard stricken by the effects of the plague, and the consequence was an increasing denationalisation of both nobility and Church. It became necessary in Norway to fill ecclesiastical offices to a great extent with incumbents from Sweden, and the number of noble families was manifestly dwindling. We observe at this time an avowed tendency of men and women of noble birth to marry only persons of their own rank, and the consequence was that inter-marrying of Swedish and Norwegian great families became increasingly frequent. In both countries there resulted a concentration of landed property in relatively few hands, some single families rising to hitherto unknown wealth. But necessarily this mingling of nationalities was more to the disadvantage of the nobility of Norway, which was easily outnumbered by that of Sweden. If on the whole the Black Death weakened the national and economic forces of Norway in relation to those of Sweden and Denmark, this was most marked in the case of the nobility, and so it pushed on the development which was already in progress and was undermining the national independence of Norway.

Without respect to national policy, the Swedish nobles went on fighting for their class privileges. When, in 1355, the younger son of King Magnus ascended the throne of Norway as King Hakon VI, a party of the Swedish nobles egged on the elder son Eric to rebel against his father, and they did not hesitate to accept foreign assistance. On this occasion a new power entered actively into Scandinavian politics, that of the Duke of Mecklenburg, Albert, the very fox of foxes, the match even of the "wolf" King Waldemar of Denmark. Twenty years earlier he had married the sister of King Magnus; and in pledge of her dowry he had received the control of the herring staples of Scania. Now he saw the opportunity of extending his power and his revenues; when, by his intervention, King Magnus was forced to divide Sweden, leaving the southeastern part to Eric, Duke Albert received his reward in the possession of several castles and districts in the country. For his defence, Magnus sought the alliance of King Waldemar and had his son King Hakon betrothed to Waldemar's younger daughter Margaret, promising to cede the principal castle of Scania, Helsingborg. But he gained no advantage from the bargain; when, in the same year (1359), the young King Eric was removed by death, Waldemar attacked and conquered the whole of Scania, thus uniting again all the old Danish provinces (1360). The following year he even conquered the island of Gotland with the rich city of Wisby.

He had entered upon this policy of conquest with the connivance of Duke Albert, giving his elder daughter Ingeborg in marriage to the duke's elder son Henry. But by taking Gotland he went beyond the limits that the duke could well tolerate, and he also renewed his alliance with King Magnus, causing the marriage between his daughter Margaret and King Hakon to be celebrated. Duke Albert took his revenge by an alliance with the nobles of Sweden, who willingly deposed King Magnus and elected the duke's younger son Albert as King of Sweden (1363);

Magnus only succeeded in keeping some of the western districts of the country. In the war that followed, King Albert was not able to maintain himself in Sweden without the support of the nobility, and finally he was compelled to grant a charter or capitulation (1371), the first in the history of Sweden, by which he pledged himself to govern the country only by the consent of the council of lords, the lords themselves getting the right to nominate to the council and to appoint the governors of castles and fiefs. This meant the absolute power of the nobility.

With the increasing feudalism, which took away from the Crown much of its revenues and transferred the military control to the vassals of the realm, the kings had to look for new means to maintain the royal authority, and in the course of the fourteenth century the Scandinavian kings began borrowing money in order to have armies at their disposal. But the state loans became a new danger to their power; for, in most cases, they had no other way of paying their debts than by embarking upon new loans or pledging lands and revenues. The first state loans seem to have been supplied by the Pope and by the wealthy princes of northern Germany, the Counts of Holstein or the Dukes of Mecklenburg, and we can easily realise the political effects of the borrowing from the latter. But soon we see emerging another financial power, which in virtue of its economic superiority came to be a dominating element of Scandinavian politics for about two centuries; that power was the towns of the German Hansa, in particular the so-called Wendish towns, *i.e.* those of the Baltic.

Their wealth and power were due to their control of the great export trade of the Baltic countries, the rye from the plains of the Oder and Vistula, the furs from Russia, and so forth[1]. By their commerce they built up important funds of mobile capital, by which they were able to control the export and import trade of all the Scandinavian countries, the herring-fisheries of Scania, the production of iron in Sweden proper, the exporting of cod from Norway, making themselves at home at Wisby, at Stockholm, at Bergen, and elsewhere. Starting in the thirteenth century by obtaining protection for their navigation, they were able to extend their privileges by agreement, by prescription, and by force, fighting with success all attempts to keep them to the strict letter of the original treaties; and gradually they became one of the great political powers of the North, particularly after uniting in the celebrated Hanseatic League, a name that appears in the midst of their disputes with the Scandinavian governments towards the middle of the fourteenth century.

When King Waldemar ventured to conquer Wisby, they felt their position highly endangered, and a coalition of towns under the leadership of Lübeck declared war against Denmark. The war developed into a general Scandinavian war after the Duke of Mecklenburg had made his son King of Sweden. On the one side were the Kings of Denmark and

[1] See *supra*, Vol. VII, Chap. VIII.

Norway, on the other side, not only Sweden and Mecklenburg but also the Counts of Holstein, the Duke of Schleswig, and finally (1367) an alliance of seventy-seven North-German towns, reaching from the Netherlands to Prussia, called contemptuously by King Waldemar "hens." The "hens," however, proved strong enough to defeat the over-confident king, capturing the castles of Copenhagen and Helsingborg, ravaging the open plains of Denmark as well as the coast of Norway, and cutting off the foreign commerce of both countries. While Waldemar was absent in Germany, trying to win allies among the princes there, the Danish Council of the Realm made peace with the Hansa, which, on its side, found it profitable to treat on its own account without regard to its allies when it was offered an important extension of its commercial privileges. According to the terms of peace (1370), the German towns obtained not only full protection for all their commerce, but in addition a considerable lowering of the customs' tariff, and even in certain cases entire exemption from duties; and, as reparation for damages, they were granted the dominion for sixteen years of the chief castles and market-places of Scania with two-thirds of the revenues. The transformation of economic into political interests was expressed in the treaty by the humiliating provision that the successor of King Waldemar should not be nominated without the consent of the Hansa towns. In the same year Norway made a truce for five years with the Hansa towns, confirming all the rights and privileges they had won in that country.

King Waldemar was obliged to accept the situation as determined by the treaty; returning to his country, he agreed to be reconciled with Duke Albert of Mecklenburg, to whom he gave the assurance that the grandson of them both, the infant son of Henry and Ingeborg, named Albert, would be elected King of Denmark on his death. By these agreements he at least was able to expel the Counts of Holstein completely from northern Jutland, and to limit their power in Denmark to the southern part of Schleswig. With Sweden alone the state of war subsisted, although the Norwegian kings on their side concluded a treaty of peace by which they recognised the younger Albert of Mecklenburg as King of Sweden.

The situation envisaged by the treaty with the Hansa towns in 1370 was realised on the death of King Waldemar in 1375, and the question arose whether the Danes would allow a Mecklenburg prince to mount the throne of Denmark, and so in fact make the Duke of Mecklenburg the master of Denmark and Sweden alike. The Hanseatic towns of Mecklenburg could not very well oppose the wishes of their sovereign, but they contrived that the Hanseatic League as such did not make use of its right of intervention and held aloof from the election in Denmark. So the matter rested with the Danish lords, and among them two parties formed.

At this moment, there entered the scene of Scandinavian history one who was quickly to become the most remarkable personage in these countries during the later part of the Middle Ages. This was a woman,

Queen Margaret of Norway, the younger daughter of King Waldemar. Born in Denmark, and from the time of her marriage at the age of ten educated by a great Swedish lady, a daughter of Saint Bridget, probably in the part of Sweden that obeyed King Magnus, she was now Queen of Norway and therefore presumably dowered, like Queen Blanche, with the frontier fiefs of all three kingdoms. She thus represented more than any-one else the idea of a Scandinavian policy, which had been prepared by the preceding development. Her character proved her a true daughter of her father, only still more clever in dealing with men, using kindness, art, or force according to circumstances, always self-controlled and clear-headed, keeping firmly in view her ambitious plans. At this date she was aged twenty-two, and five years earlier she had given birth to her only child, her son Olaf, whom she made the first instrument of her desire for power.

At the news of her father's death, she hurried to Denmark with young Olaf, soon followed by her husband King Hakon, and there she proceeded to win votes for her son. She immediately acted as if the royal power were hers, granting fiefs and donations to the Danish nobles. While the Mecklenburgs allied themselves with the Counts of Holstein and received the support of the Emperor, Margaret delivered the decisive stroke in sending a communication to the Hanseatic towns, informing them that she would reconfirm all their privileges in Norway if they allowed Olaf to be elected King of Denmark. Having thus secured her position, she succeeded in gaining for Olaf the homage of the parliament of Denmark. In return, together with King Hakon, she signed the charter that defined Olaf's obligations as king. A consequence of the election was war with the Mecklenburgs of Germany and Sweden, but it was a rather tedious affair, since the nobles on both sides had but little interest in carrying on feuds with one another. Queen Margaret stayed in Denmark, governing there as the guardian of her son, and four years later, at the death of King Hakon VI (1380), when her son inherited the crown of Norway, she became the virtual ruler of that country also. The chronicles of Lübeck have preserved the impression of wonder made upon her contemporaries by her "great prudence," her wisdom and strength, and they tell how she made the nobles obey her will, sending the vassals from one castle to another, "as the superior sends the monks from one monastery to another." It is true that she only obtained peace with the Counts of Holstein by granting them the duchy of Schleswig as an hereditary fief (1386). But on the other hand, in the same year, she regained the castles and markets of Scania from the German towns. In Norway she strengthened her power by having two of the clerks of her household made in succession Archbishops of Nidaros, first a German, and then a Swede; the brother of the latter was the chancellor of the realm. It was a sign of still farther-reaching plans that she made King Olaf, when he came of age (1385), take the title of "true heir of Sweden."

Then, at a blow, all her plans and all her power seemed to fall to ruins, when King Olaf, in whose name she governed, suddenly died in Scania in the summer of 1387. At this critical moment, she shewed to the fullest measure the energy of her character; she proved strong enough to overthrow all the traditional rules of government and to make herself in law as well as in fact the head of her kingdoms. King Olaf left no direct successor; the nearest and only heirs by the law were the descendants of the sister of King Magnus, the Dukes of Mecklenburg, either King Albert of Sweden or his nephew, the now reigning Duke Albert, who had been the rival of Olaf in the Danish election of 1376. Neither Queen Margaret nor the nobles of Denmark and Norway could have the slightest idea of admitting either of the dukes to the succession. On the other hand, neither law nor practice allowed the crown of any of the Scandinavian kingdoms to be conferred on a woman. Examples had, however, been recently given by foreign nations: during the forty years that ended in 1382, a queen of the house of Anjou, Joanna I, had reigned in the kingdom of Naples, and, in the same year that she met with her death, a princess of the same house was made "king" of Hungary, reigning there till 1387, while her sister Hedwig for a couple of years was "king" of Poland. Such a title Queen Margaret could not assume; but within a week after the death of King Olaf, the members of the Danish Council present with her in Scania consented to elect her regent of the realm, and in the weeks following she received the homage of nobles and people in all the provinces of Denmark as "mistress and ruler with full authority as guardian of the realm." Immediately afterwards she went to Norway, where the Norwegian Council met at Oslo. She had been fortunate in having the new Archbishop of Nidaros, who had been in her service, with her in Scania when King Olaf died, and he summoned the spiritual and secular lords of the realm to meet. They had no legal authority to nominate the new king, but, in the beginning of 1388, they decided to elect Margaret regent of Norway for the rest of her life, denying the Mecklenburgs any right of succession inasmuch as they were enemies of the kingdom. By this act Margaret became the source from which the future succession was to be derived, and the Norwegian Council, passing over her nephew, the young Duke Albert, declared her grand-nephew of the same line, the infant Duke Eric of Pomerania, the nearest heir to the crown.

It is worth while noting that many of the lords who participated in this irregular election were Swedes married to Norwegian heiresses or otherwise land-owners in Norway, and at the same time we may observe the influence of the intermarriages between the noble families not only of Norway and Sweden, but of Sweden and Denmark as well, which created common economic interests particularly in the frontier provinces. Exactly at the same date that King Olaf died, many Swedish nobles had openly rebelled against King Albert because he tried to win back for the

Crown the fiefs of his greatest vassal, who had just died; they allied themselves with their kinsmen beyond the frontier, and, in the spring of 1388, their delegates met with Queen Margaret in one of her Swedish castles, acknowledging her as the rightful ruler of Sweden and promising to accept a successor at her choice. War followed, and in the battle of Falköping, 24 February 1389, King Albert was defeated and captured. The whole of Sweden submitted to Margaret, and so she became the ruler of all three Scandinavian kingdoms.

Her first object now was to regularise her position and establish a durable Scandinavian union. She immediately obtained the recognition of young Eric as her successor in Denmark and Sweden, and he even received homage as king, first in Norway, later in the two other kingdoms, while she kept as her personal dominion a combination of Swedish, Norwegian, and Danish provinces. When Eric came of age, she summoned a joint Scandinavian assembly of lords at Calmar in Sweden for the summer of 1397, with the object of having him crowned as the king of the Union and of making an agreement between the kingdoms that would seal their union. It was an unusually magnificent assembly that met at Calmar; the only serious disappointment was the complete absence of the prelates of Norway, which was probably to be explained by their reluctance to accept the abandonment of their ancient privilege in the election of kings in Norway. King Eric, at the age of fifteen, solemnly received the crown at the hands of the Archbishops of Lund and Upsala, and he created more than a hundred knights from all his kingdoms. But the negotiations for a real act of union ended in failure. A document was drawn up, confirming the perpetual union of the three kingdoms, establishing the right of succession of the king's sons in all of them, and providing for a common election in the absence of surviving sons; in this way a compromise was made between the constitution of Norway on the one side and that of Denmark and Sweden on the other. Further, the document established rules about mutual assistance in case of war, but the government of each kingdom was to be conducted according to its own laws. This agreement never obtained legal validity; the representatives of Norway refused to sign it, perhaps because it did not afford sufficient guarantees against neglect of their interests (there is no evidence in favour of the generally accepted hypothesis that Queen Margaret induced them to stay away because her desires were not met by the agreement), and no attempt was made to obtain its ratification by the councils of the separate kingdoms. So the Scandinavian Union was not placed upon a stable legal basis; its future was at the mercy of the conflicting interests of the royal power and the nobility and of national jealousies.

Margaret remained the virtual ruler of all the Scandinavian kingdoms until her death in 1412, and she kept the reins firmly in her hands. It is characteristic of her position that, on one occasion, the delegates

35

of Lübeck referred to her as "Lady King." As long as she lived, King Eric exercised no real power; she instructed him never to decide anything by himself, but always to adjourn all matters until she could be present. After she was dead, he continued the government according to her principles, only carrying them still farther, following out their consequences with decision and energy.

Both Margaret and Eric strove to make a permanent unity of their kingdoms. In Sweden and Norway, even in Iceland and the western islands belonging to Norway, they adopted the ecclesiastical policy started by Waldemar IV in Denmark. By means of papal provisions they enthroned their personal servants or friends in all vacant sees, and, as most of these were naturally Danes, they became instruments for denationalising the Church of their adopted country. In Sweden, Margaret began intruding Danish nobles into the fiefs, and Eric extended this policy to Norway. Both of them omitted to fill the high offices of administration in Sweden, and they partly did the same even in Norway, where, at last, the king made the Danish Bishop of Oslo his chancellor. In fact, the administration of all the kingdoms was united in Denmark. Sometimes, members of the Swedish or the Norwegian Council of the Realm came to Denmark to assist at deliberations over matters concerning their countries, and occasionally common meetings of all three Councils were held. But, generally, decisions were taken with the assistance merely of Danish councillors or even by the royal chancery alone. On the part of the king, there was a demonstrable tendency to unify the administration in central bureaux, and Copenhagen tended to develop into the capital of an empire in the modern sense of the word. It would not be right to characterise all this as the expression of a truly Danish imperialism or nationalism; in Denmark itself, queen and king took into their service many German nobles, and thence they spread even to Sweden and Norway; their recommendation was their fidelity towards the king. But it must be added that these German immigrants brought with them a feudal spirit that in the end would be dangerous to the royal power.

On one particular point Queen Margaret maintained a tenacious struggle against the feudal principles that from Germany threatened to get a foothold on Scandinavian soil. This was the question of the succession in the duchy of Schleswig. When the Count of Holstein, to whom, in 1386, she had felt forced to grant this Danish duchy as a hereditary fief, died in the year 1404, leaving only children under age, she succeeded in making King Eric their formal guardian, and she began to seize lands and castles of the duchy for the direct royal administration. When, accordingly, in 1410, the eldest son of the former duke at last proclaimed himself Duke of Schleswig, Eric protested, claiming that according to Danish law no heredity in fiefs was allowed. War broke out, and, with interruptions of negotiations, law-suits, and judgments, it lasted for more than twenty years. King Eric went so far as to contend that fiefs in the

European sense could not legally exist in Denmark, and appealing to the Emperor Sigismund, who was his cousin, he obtained in 1424 an imperial sentence in his favour. But the Counts of Holstein did not submit to a decision even of such an authority. They allied themselves with the Hansa towns, they were able to conquer Schleswig by arms, and finally, in 1432, Eric was forced to leave the duchy in their possession; his fight over this matter ended in defeat.

On other points too he brought himself into conflicts which he could not control. The war of Schleswig was an expensive affair, and he had to seek for money wherever it was to be found. He tried to extort as high duties as possible from the German merchants, limiting their liberties and exemptions as far as he was able, and this policy was the reason why the Hansa too went to war against him. In this war he was more successful, and in any case he was able to establish, from the year 1428, a royal revenue of a new kind, the Sound dues on all ships passing through the straits between Sealand and Scania. But the extension of the war meant still more expense, and he was obliged to tax his subjects more heavily than they had been accustomed.

Queen Margaret had continued her father's policy of regaining lands, castles, and fiefs for the Crown, and, in particular, she had pursued the same object in Sweden in order to increase the royal revenue; in all her countries as far as possible she appointed her own bailiffs in place of the feudal lords. In this way, the peasants came as it were between the upper and the nether millstone. If, after the Black Death, their condition had improved, now the reaction set in more and more strongly, king, bailiffs, and landlords vying with one another in heaping upon them all kinds of taxes and imposts. For the peasants, both feudalism and the development of royal power led to the same result—increasing oppression. But another consequence was dissatisfaction and disquietude, and from about 1420 we notice a tendency to riots and rebellions among the peasants, particularly directed against the foreign bailiffs and fief-holders. Of these there were most in Sweden, in all probability because the lands and fiefs there were richer and more attractive than those of Norway, and so, naturally, the movement in Sweden became more important than that in Norway. For the same reason, the native nobility of Sweden was more irritated in its national particularism than that of Norway; but in both countries, even among the nobility, dissatisfaction and opposition to the royal policy made themselves increasingly felt. The intrusion of foreign clerics into the sees created a certain uneasiness in the Church of Norway as well as of Sweden, and from 1432 a sharp conflict arose between King Eric and the chapter of Upsala regarding the nomination of a new archbishop. So, in Sweden, quite an army of different forces united to oppose the government of the king. Besides, a new social force entered the field, strengthening the movement; this was the growth of an independent merchant and industrial class, based chiefly on the export trade of Stockholm and the iron-smelting of the province of Dalarne (Dalecarlia). From this province came the leader of the movement.

His name was Engelbrecht, son of another Engelbrecht, a mine-owner of knightly rank. Personal interests were involved in his rebellion: heavy taxes burdened the mining industry, and wealthy nobles were busy shouldering out the original owners. But the noble character of Engelbrecht raised him above egoistic considerations, and his far-sighted views made the rebellion a revolution in the history of Sweden. After appealing in vain to the king for the removal of the oppressive Danish bailiff of the province, he put himself at the head of the dissatisfied peasants and yeomen, who, perhaps, were encouraged by the reports of the Hussite rebellion in Bohemia. In the summer of 1434 he marched with his army through the eastern and southern provinces of the country, everywhere calling men to arms against foreign masters, capturing the castles, and expelling the bailiffs. Some of the higher nobility joined the rebellion; but the Council of the Realm met at the order of the king, fearing to lose its privileges and anxious to repress the people. Engelbrecht, however, forced the Council to throw off, in the name of all Sweden, their allegiance to King Eric, and a general parliament was called for the next year (1435) in the town of Arboga, near the home of Engelbrecht. With this parliament, something new was created in Sweden; there met not only the old orders of the realm, secular and spiritual lords, but besides them the burghers and the yeomen, thus forming an assembly of four orders and thereby establishing an institution destined to remain for more than four hundred years an important element in Swedish politics; for centuries it was the most democratic body in any European country.

The Parliament of Arboga elected Engelbrecht regent of the realm. The Council looked for means of annulling such revolutionary proceedings; it negotiated with King Eric with the object of acquiring the government of the country and the transference of the fiefs to itself, and it appointed a man of the higher nobility, Karl Knutsson, regent along with Engelbrecht. In the first place, the popular rebellion was defeated by the murder of Engelbrecht in the spring of 1436. His ideas and his example, however, were kept alive in the tradition of the new classes he had called to power, and one of his friends composed songs about the little man raised by God to save the people, praising liberty as the finest thing in the world.

In the meantime, the rebellion of Engelbrecht had infected the people of Norway. Some weeks before his death, yeomen and peasants in the districts around Oslo rose against the foreign bailiffs under the leadership of a noble, Amund Sigurdsson. The Council of the Realm assembled and made an agreement with the rebels, prudently securing their adhesion to a purely national programme, which included provisions that all fiefs were to be given to natives and all high government offices to be filled up. Such was the policy of the Swedish Council too, and it succeeded in crushing new risings of the farmer class. When the peasants of Denmark likewise rebelled, the Danish Council joined its Swedish colleagues and would not obey King Eric any longer. Now the whole movement against the king had passed into the hands of the nobility, fighting for its class interests. When Eric fled the country in the year 1438, the Danish Council summoned from Germany his nephew Christopher, son of the Count Palatine of the Rhine (Pfalz-Neumarkt). He was made King of Denmark in 1440, and later in the same year King of Sweden. When the Norwegian Council, whose requests had been complied with by King Eric, found itself deserted by its lawful ruler, it last of all, in 1442, saw no other way open but to elect Christopher King of Norway as well.

The accession of King Christopher to the throne of the Scandinavian kingdoms meant the defeat of the aspirations for monarchical power that had animated the government of his immediate predecessors. In all three countries the nobility took the undisputed control. The Church rose again from its former subordination and freed itself from the encroachments of the kings upon the episcopal elections, only indeed to drift under the dominion of the nobility. The nobles took advantage of the decisions of the Council of Basle which dissolved the alliance of king and Pope, and in Sweden and Norway alike native bishops of noble families filled the sees. At the same time, the interests of the rising national burgher class were sacrificed; the powerlessness and poverty of King Christopher made him dependent on the financial assistance of the Hanseatic towns, and he confirmed their commercial privileges to the widest extent in spite of the protests of the native burghers; he himself jestingly declared that the Hansa had more privileges and liberties in his countries than the king. He even gave up the dues on shipping in the Sound.

When, after a short reign, he died in 1448, the nobility saw no limits to their power. In Sweden, a party of the nobles elected one of themselves king, the regent during the former interregnum, Karl Knutsson (Charles VIII). In Denmark, the nobles offered the crown to the greatest of their order, the Duke of Schleswig, who was at the same time Count of Holstein. He refused, however, being probably not at all desirous of falling under the influence of his Danish compeers; but he recommended to them a German nephew of his, Count Christian of Oldenburg, who was accordingly elected King of Denmark with a capitulation that left all power in the hands of the Council of the Realm. In Norway two parties formed, which favoured respectively the Swedish and the Danish candidate. At first, the Swedish party, led by the Archbishop of Nidaros, had the upper hand and caused King Karl to be crowned, on which occasion he signed a capitulation corresponding to the Danish one. In fact, earlier in the same year (1449), King Christian had already agreed to a capitulation for his election in Norway, the first act of this kind issued for that country; and, when the archbishop died shortly after, the Danish party carried the election of its candidate, making Christian King of Norway. Now a formal act of union was signed by representatives of the Councils of Denmark and Norway at Bergen on 29 August 1450, laying down the principle that both kingdoms should always obey the same king, and providing for a common election by the two Councils on the death of the reigning monarch. As a matter of fact, this agreement was a copy of a similar agreement signed by representatives of the Councils of Denmark and Sweden a few months before, and, after a war of some years, King Karl was forced to flee the country, Christian I being crowned as King of Sweden as well (1457).

The reign of Christian I marks the lowest point in the decline of royal power in the Scandinavian kingdoms. Apparently, his position was a brilliant one. He not only united the crowns of three kingdoms, but he added to them the dominion of Schleswig and Holstein, succeeding his uncle there in the year 1460, on the condition, however, of granting new privileges to the nobility of both provinces, thereby confirming the famous provision that Schleswig and Holstein should for ever remain linked together, a provision that was originally drawn up to protect the interests of the landed nobility, but later became a kind of national programme. Some years later, Christian gave his daughter Margaret in marriage to King James III of Scotland; but for the payment of most of the dowry he pledged the Norwegian islands of the Orkneys and Shetlands (1468). Still later, he undertook with great splendour a journey to Rome, obtaining from the Pope the authority to found a university at Copenhagen and from the Emperor the elevation of the county of Holstein into a duchy. For all such things he had to pay dearly. In order to win the two duchies he was obliged to give other claimants 123,000 florins in all; he loved to hold a splendid court, and he always travelled in great state. But he was always in straits for money, and in Swedish tradition he received the surname of "the leaking purse." He was obliged to borrow, and he incurred large debts, particularly with the nobles of Holstein and the Hanseatic towns; they became his real masters. Of course, he could not avoid confirming all Hanseatic privileges in his kingdoms, and he even tolerated it when the German merchants of Bergen slew the castellan of the city who tried to limit their control.

What characterises the national development of the latter half of the fifteenth century is the eclipse of Norway and the rise of Sweden. In Norway, the only authority that remained a bulwark, however weak, of its independence, was the Church; the fight for ecclesiastical freedom became identified with that for national independence. The nobility, too, had chiefly their class interests in view; but the national demands which they had been driven to put forward in 1436 had very soon lost their hold upon them. The immigration of Swedish nobles had been followed by that of Danish, and about 1450 most of the leading families of the country were in fact essentially foreign; it is characteristic that the last appeal sent by the Norwegian Council of the Realm to King Eric, in 1440, was written in the Danish language, thus foreboding the supersession of

Norwegian as the official language of the nation. A Council of the Realm with such a foundation could have neither the will nor the ability to maintain a strong national policy, and patently the government of the kingdom was continually growing weaker. The pledging of the Orkneys and Shetlands in 1468 really meant the final loss of the islands. Already before the end of the fourteenth century the administration of the earldom was left to the Scottish family of St Clair; from this time the bishops were Scots; both earls and bishops gave offices to their fellow-countrymen, who acquired land in the islands, and about 1440 the judge of the Orkneys gave his decisions in English. Now, from 1472, the Bishop of the Orkneys and Shetlands was made a suffragan of the Archbishop of St Andrews, and from that time the Norwegian character of the people of the Orkneys began rapidly to disappear, although in Shetland the Norwegian language still lived on for three more centuries. The national resistance of the Shetlands could be so durable because of the continual commercial intercourse with Norway. But, as a matter of fact, the active commerce of Norway was, towards the end of the Middle Ages, at its lowest ebb. Obviously, that was one reason why the traffic with far-off Greenland came absolutely to an end about the middle of the fifteenth century; and the government neglected its duties toward the colonists, so that, left without assistance from the mother country, they died out in starvation and degeneration.

Since the thirteenth century, the export trade from Norway was almost completely in the hands of the Hanseatic capitalists, and such a condition was not exclusively to the disadvantage of Norway, since they were able to make Bergen a great staple for fish, selling the Norwegian cod to the whole of northern Europe. One of the consequences was the development of fisheries in the northern parts of the country, and during these centuries Norwegian fishing-folk spread in settlements along the coast of Finmark as far east as the Varanger fjord, thus making this part of the kingdom truly Norwegian. But the economic superiority of the Hansa merchants was an almost insuperable obstacle to the growth of a native burgher class; at Bergen the merchants of Lübeck, at Oslo those of Rostock formed a power against which the natives vainly tried to rise. It was the chief weakness of Norway that, in an age when the nobility had lost all national force and spirit, the country could not produce a burgher class that might take over the task of a national policy. In the fjords and the valleys there lived a sturdy race of farmers who kept up the national traditions of law and language, and there are signs that, during these centuries of national depression, a popular literature of folk-songs developed among them, in part founded upon the sagas of the thirteenth century. But yeomen and peasants here had no political interests or aspirations, and so no powerful class was left to defend the independence of the nation.

In Sweden, on the contrary, commercial and industrial activities created a burgher class that was able to comprehend intellectual and political interests, and at the same time was strong enough to animate with new ideas both the lower ranks of the nobility and the higher ranks of the yeomanry, thus uniting them into an efficient body able to express a national will. For some decades it might seem as if Swedish politics were nothing but the rivalry of different sections of the higher nobility, using for their egoistic purposes alternately Christian I and Karl Knutsson. During a period of twenty years, until his death in 1470, Karl was thrice made King of Sweden without ever having any real power; wars were fought with changing success, and great families joined one or other party for merely personal reasons. But beneath the surface of ignoble ambitions we are able to observe the new life awakening. The struggles of Engelbrecht and Karl were told in rhymed chronicles, imitating those of the age of Duke Eric, and in these chronicles we meet with a really national spirit, proclaiming the idea of independence. Other authors strove to build up complete histories of the kingdom of Sweden, trying in this way to rouse a national consciousness.

Finally, upon the death of King Karl, the programme of Engelbrecht was revived again by the king's nephew Sten Sture. Against the majority of the Council of the Realm, chiefly with the assistance of burghers and yeomen, he was proclaimed regent of Sweden, and he kept this position for almost thirty years. In a hard battle just outside Stockholm, on a hill that now forms a part of the city, he won a decisive victory with his army of burghers and yeomen over the forces of King Christian (1471). The burghers of Stockholm had rushed against the enemy, singing the song of St George, the patron saint of their city; and as a token of gratitude for the victory Sten Sture made a German artist carve a magnificent sculpture of St George killing the dragon which still adorns the Great Church of Stockholm, an expressive witness to the burghers' pride. Immediately after the victory, the citizens of Stockholm, assisted by representatives of other towns, forced the Council of the Realm to expunge from the law the provision that half of each town council should be Germans; this was the declaration of independence of the Swedish burgher class. The new spiritual life of the nation manifested itself by the foundation of the University of Upsala (1477), preceding by a year that of the University of Copenhagen, and in the following decade the new art of printing was employed for the national propaganda.

At the same time, Swedish population and Swedish power were spreading northward and eastward. Merchants and farmers of Swedish and Finnish nationality settled on both sides of the Gulf of Bothnia, and the whole of Finland was brought more and more closely under Swedish administration. At the easternmost point of the Gulf of Finland, the town of Viborg obtained its chartered privileges in 1403, and in the decade from 1470 to 1480 it was strongly fortified by the same castellan, a relative of King Karl and of Sten Sture, who, a little farther to the north, founded the strong castle of Olofsborg. At this part of the frontier, the Swedes met rivals for commerce and power in Russian cities and princes. This was a rivalry which, as early as the middle of the fourteenth century, had led to war, but which received a more dangerous and important character after the erection of the dominion of the Tsars of Muscovy. As a matter of fact, under the rule of King Karl and the independent regents who succeeded him, Sweden entered upon the policy of conquest that aimed at extending its power over the lands of the Teutonic Order east of the Baltic. As yet, these plans did not produce durable results, but they inaugurated a momentous feature of future Swedish politics, and they already played a part in the relations of Sweden with Denmark.

In Denmark and Norway, King Christian I, who died in 1481, had been succeeded by his son Hans. On the part of Norway, there had been some vacillation, the Archbishop of Nidaros desiring to unite with the Swedes; but, finally, the two Councils of the Realms met together and elected Hans as common king of both countries (1483), obliging him to sign a capitulation that confirmed the absolute authority of each Council over the royal power; it even stated the duty of resistance on the part of the subjects in the event of the king not keeping its provisions. It testifies to the increasing closeness of the union of the two kingdoms that on this occasion the royal capitulation was issued in common for both of them. On the other hand, in the duchies of Schleswig and Holstein, King Hans was obliged to divide power with his younger brother Frederick.

In the reign of this king, two opposite tendencies were clearly manifested. On the one side, he was the creature of the nobility, dependent on the will or the consent of the members of the Council for all his actions. On the other side, he appears as a kind of burgher king, almost on a par with his contemporary, King Louis XI of France, finding his friends and associates among the wealthy burghers of Copenhagen, even having his son and successor educated in the house of one of them; and he was able to reverse the weak policy of his immediate predecessors in regard to the Hansa towns. This task was facilitated for him by the discords inside the Hansa League and even inside the single towns, particularly in Lübeck. But the essential factor was the development of a native class of merchants and artisans in the Danish towns, while in eastern Norway Dutch merchants began an active competition with the Wendish towns, coming there to buy and export on an increasing scale a new commodity, timber. King Hans dared to engage in a privateering war with the Hanseatic towns, and they were forced to acquiesce in the grant of equal commercial privileges to their rivals. It was an omen of a new age for Norway too when his son Prince Christian, as viceroy of this country, in 1508 issued new privileges for the city of Oslo, by which all those of the German merchants were revoked and the retail trade was made a monopoly of the burghers of the city.

When, however, King Hans schemed to renew the Scandinavian policy of his father by winning the crown of Sweden, he had to consider exclusively the interests of the nobility. In fact, already in the year 1483, the Swedish Council of the Realm had agreed with the Councils of Denmark and Norway to acknowledge him as their king, accepting with pleasure the provisions of his capitulation in favour of the nobility. But the regent Sten Sture, supported by the lower classes, succeeded in putting off the realisation of this promise from one year to another, and even papal excommunication could not induce the people to abandon him. He roused the enmity of the higher clergy by interfering in the nomination of bishops and abbots, and the nobles complained of not receiving the fiefs to which they thought themselves entitled. He threatened them with a social revolution, with "another Engelbrecht;" but at last they organised a rebellion, and at the same time King Hans made an alliance with the Russian Great Prince Ivan, who invaded Finland. Arriving at Stockholm with a strong army, Hans forced Sten Sture to capitulate and was crowned as King of Sweden (1497).

This renewal of the Scandinavian Union lasted only for a few years. King Hans had the misfortune to be completely defeated when, with his brother Duke Frederick and a strong force of knights and German mercenaries, he attacked the yeomen of the Ditmarschen in Holstein; the battle (1500) ended in a disaster, similar to that of so many other conflicts between feudal knights and yeomen towards the close of the Middle Ages. In the same year, a man of a new type began to agitate for a rising in Sweden; his name was Dr Hemming Gadh. He was an ecclesiastic by education, a diplomat by his talents, a revolutionary by instinct. For twenty years he had lived in Rome as representative of Sten Sture and had been able to obtain the removal of the regent's excommunication. On returning, he succeeded in reconciling Sten with one of his bitterest enemies among the Swedish nobility, a distant kinsman, Svante Sture, and, being himself nominated bishop to a vacant see—a nomination, it is true, that was never confirmed by the Pope, but, instead, drew down on him the papal excommunication—he became a member of the Council of the Realm. As such, with both the Sture and a few other members, he proclaimed the deposition of King Hans (1501), accusing him of oppression of the people and of alliance with the Russian enemies of the land. At the same time, he instigated a rebellion in Norway, led by a noble of mixed Norwegian and Swedish descent. This rebellion, however, was unsuccessful, the leader being murdered by a personal enemy, one of the Danish nobles in Norway; his widow fled to Sweden and married Svante Sture. In Sweden, the rebels had the upper hand against both the nobles' party and the Danish armies.

Upon the death of Sten Sture (1503), Svante Sture was made regent, to be succeeded in 1512 by his son, the younger Sten. Under the regency of these two Hemming Gadh was the dominating spirit, agitating for an increasingly democratic and national programme. He had to give up his episcopal see and was made a military commander; recalling the former extortions of Danish bailiffs, he excited the hatred of the people against the Danes and the higher nobility alike. Meanwhile the representatives of the nobility addressed an appeal for assistance to their fellow nobles in Denmark. "We speak the same tongue, and almost all of us are kinsfolk." So, more and more clearly, the antagonisms of home politics were deciding the dividing lines in the fight for independence.

Hemming Gadh achieved his greatest success when, as a delegate to the Hansa assembly at Lübeck, he induced the Wendish towns to declare war against Denmark. This war, however, impelled King Hans to appeal to the Dutch and English rivals of the German merchants and to build up a strong Danish fleet for the defence of his own burghers. In fact, when he died in the year 1513, he was victorious on the sea, breaking the predominance of the Hanseatic power, and at home he had strengthened the royal authority so far as to give the Council of the Realm occasion to complain that he had broken more than half of the articles of the capitulation granted at his accession, particularly in conferring high positions on non-noble persons.

In Denmark, as well as in Sweden, the result of the development was the decline of the political importance of the nobility. In both countries a burgher class was rising that was able to reconquer the national independence, both economic as against the Hansa and political as against its Scandinavian neighbour. In part leaning upon this burgher class, the royal power organised itself more firmly, thus preparing the creation of truly national kingdoms. Only Norway was lagging behind, because the growth of an independent burgher class came more slowly there; for that country, then, the sixteenth century meant the climax of the power of the nobility and, as a consequence, the loss of national independence.

For all three countries, the crisis began with the accession of King Christian II (1513). His government meant the sharpening of all social and political conflicts, and led, through much bloodshed, to the establishment of new conditions for the classes and the nations of the Scandinavian North.

CHAPTER XVIII

POLAND AND LITHUANIA IN THE FOURTEENTH AND FIFTEENTH CENTURIES

On the extinction of the Přemyslid dynasty in 1306, the restoration of the Polish monarchy by a Piast prince became at last practicable. Vladyslav the Short had been a claimant to the throne of Cracow ever since the death of his elder brother Leszek the Black in 1288. The elder or Silesian branch of the Piast dynasty was divided into numerous princely families, which presented the objection from the Polish point of view of being both partially Germanised and politically without strength or prestige. The second and third branches, which had ruled in Greater and Lesser Poland, had become extinct; so that the Kujawian branch, to which Vladyslav belonged, had an hereditary claim to the throne which had won for him the support of Pope Boniface VIII. Vladyslav was hereditary Prince of Brest Kujawski; he had inherited his brother's principalities of Sieradz and Lenczyca; and during the reign of Wenceslas II he had obtained by conquest a considerable part of Lesser Poland. In 1306 he was recognised as Grand Prince by the magnates of Lesser Poland, Kujawia, and Polish Pomerania. The Princes of Silesia and Mazovia, however, continued to be hostile, while Greater Poland remained faithful to his old rival Henry, Prince of Glogów, until his death in 1307. The most obstinate resistance was offered by the German elements in the country and by the pro-German princes of Silesia, who realised that the advent of so strong a ruler as Vladyslav involved a Polish patriotic revival against the powerful German communities which had established themselves in the towns and countryside. The crisis became acute in the year 1310 when a rising of the German citizens of Poznań (Posen) in favour of the Silesian princes was followed in the next year by a still more formidable rebellion of the Germans of Lesser Poland headed by the *Wojt* and the Bishop of Cracow. Both movements were crushed by the energy of the new Grand Prince, and the leaders were severely punished. Far more serious for Poland was the new attitude of the Teutonic Order. Securely established in Prussia, the Order did not confine its activities to the continuance of its crusade against the pagan Lithuanians, but began to extend its territory at the expense of its neighbour and former ally—Poland. It had acquired the district of Michalów from an impecunious Kujawian prince; but a greater opportunity for aggrandisement presented itself when Vladyslav requested the Order to assist him to recover the province of Pomerania from the Margrave of Brandenburg who had seized it in 1307. The Knights, who had long coveted the region of the Lower Vistula, responded to the prince's summons with alacrity, seized Danzig, where they massacred the Polish garrison, overran the whole province, and settled down in permanent occupation of this important Polish territory. In the same year, 1309, the Grand Master, who had hitherto directed the affairs of the Order from Venice, transferred his residence to Marienburg in Prussia, and took over the direct control of the formidable organisation which had established itself on the Baltic seaboard. Vladyslav, indignant at this unexpected act of aggression and treachery, appealed to the Pope in the first instance, but soon began to realise that an armed struggle with this dangerous neighbour would inevitably be forced on Poland. In the meantime he attempted to strengthen the position of Poland externally by a series of alliances. It was natural that he should first invoke the aid of the Holy See, to which both Poland and the Teutonic Order owed allegiance; and the friendship for Vladyslav so strongly shewn by Boniface VIII in the past was now maintained in the firm support given to Polish claims by his successors, whose assistance was unfortunately moral rather than material owing to the weakness of their position at the time. The new rulers of Bohemia of the house of Luxemburg began to claim the Polish throne as successors of the Přemyslids. Against this new foe Vladyslav sought the help of Charles Robert of Hungary, in whom he gained both a son-in-law and an ally, and through whom he attracted to Poland that cultural influence by which the Angevin dynasty was beginning to restore Hungary from the disorder into which she had been plunged since the Tartar invasion. Against another enemy, Brandenburg, he made an alliance with the Scandinavian kings in 1315; and finally, by a brilliant stroke of political originality and foresight, he suggested an alliance with the Lithuanians who were, like the Poles, the victims of Teutonic aggression. The able ruler of Lithuania, Gedymin, welcomed his overtures and sealed the alliance by the marriage of his daughter Aldona to Vladyslav's only son, Casimir. Having in this way established his power at home and abroad, the Grand Prince, with the consent of the Papacy and in spite of the angry protest of John of Bohemia, had himself crowned as king at Cracow in 1320 under the name of Vladyslav I.

Meanwhile the appeal of Vladyslav I against the Order had been heard by a papal commission, which in 1321 made an award in favour of Poland. The Order, however, refused to abide by the decision and remained in Pomerania, so the Polish king decided to resort to arms. The first war between Poland and the Teutonic Knights was a severe ordeal for the weak divided State, in which Polish sentiment had only just begun to assert itself against the German element. Apart from the military prestige and the religious character of the Order, which brought it recruits from among the best elements in Western Europe, the support of Brandenburg and of Bohemia made it almost invincible, the more so as John of Bohemia was himself a claimant to the Polish throne and could count on the assistance of Vladyslav's enemies in Silesia and Mazovia. Against such formidable allies the assistance given to Poland by Hungary and the Lithuanians was scarcely adequate. King John won over most of the Silesian princes and the Prince of Plock in Mazovia, and, though his activities were partly checked by the Polish and Hungarian armies, and though Vladyslav won a great victory over the Order at Plowce in 1331, the terrible invasions of the Knights devastated not only the frontier province of Kujawia but even Greater Poland, where many ancient cities such as Gniezno (Gnesen), Lenczyca, and Sieradz were reduced to ashes and never recovered their former significance; and the end of the war found the Order in possession not only of the district of Dobrzyn, but of all Kujawia. But before this Vladyslav had died at the age of seventy-three, urging his son with his last breath to prosecute the struggle against the Order and to recover Pomerania. Vladyslav, reared in the petty provincialism of the thirteenth century and forced to struggle against insuperable obstacles, had displayed a tenacity of purpose and a patriotic idealism that was unusual in his age, and by the singleness of his aims and his indomitable courage he had successfully revived the Polish State and the Piast monarchy. He proved himself a great king not only in actual achievement, but in laying so firm a foundation on which others might build.

Casimir III, subsequently called "the Great" (1333–70), succeeded his father without opposition, and was crowned king in Cracow in 1333. Growing up with the self-assurance of a prince born in the purple, he had not had to experience the uncertainties and bitterness of exile like his father. His political education was guided rather by the spacious ideas and enlightened ideal of kingship of the Angevin court of Hungary than by the petty quarrels and provincialism of the Kujawian house from which he had sprung. A statesman by disposition, he had very different views from those of his father, and was prepared to sacrifice ideals to expediency. He determined to abandon his father's warlike policy, to husband the resources of the State, and by graceful concessions in matters of less importance, to attempt to secure what he considered to be the essential needs of his country. He realised that in any case Poland had neither the means nor the organisation to wage a successful war against the Teutonic Order or to dispute the ascendancy of the house of Luxemburg. The root of the problem was the necessity of a closer union of the Polish provinces to avoid such disasters as the defection of Silesia and Mazovia. Apart from the pressing need for other domestic reforms, it was essential to weld the remaining provinces into an organic whole. In pursuance of this aim, Casimir, by the mediation of the King of Hungary, opened negotiations for peace with the King of Bohemia, and agreed to the Treaty of Vyšehrad by which John renounced his claim to the Polish throne, while Casimir paid him an indemnity and recognised his suzerainty over the princes of Silesia and the Prince of Plock, hoping by these wide concessions—which were, in any case, inevitable—to gain the support of Bohemia against the Teutonic Knights. The attempt to settle the questions at issue between Poland and the Order was unsuccessful, and the case was again submitted to the Holy See; but the negotiations with Hungary and Bohemia continued, and at the second Treaty of Vyšehrad in 1339 the question of the succession to the Polish throne was settled. Casimir had no sons, and he wished to secure the succession for the Angevin house of Hungary with which he was so intimately associated. It was agreed that on Casimir's death he should be succeeded by the son of his sister and of Charles Robert, Lewis. This agreement, which was confirmed in 1355 by the Treaty of Buda, imposed certain conditions on the future king, namely (1) that he should attempt to regain the lost Polish provinces, particularly Pomerania; (2) that he should confer offices exclusively on Polish magnates; (3) that he should respect all previous charters and impose no new taxes. Meanwhile, the dispute with the Order dragged on interminably. Pope Benedict XII refused to accept the decisions of the negotiators at Vyšehrad, and set up a special commission in Warsaw, which again pronounced in favour of Poland. The Order once more protested against this verdict, and soon Casimir himself, desiring to turn to the new problem of Russia, found it advisable to terminate the protracted negotiations, and consented by the Treaty of Kalisz in 1343 to abandon in favour of the Order the Polish claim to Pomerania, Chelmno (Kulm), and the district of Michałów, receiving in return Kujawia and the district of Dobrzyn. As compensation for these serious losses to Poland in the west, Casimir had for some years been seeking fresh acquisitions in the east—a policy which had brought him into competition with the powerful ruler of Lithuania, and drawn Poland into close relations with the Lithuanian and Russian principalities which became of primary importance to her political position.

The early rise of the Lithuanian people to political importance under Mindovg had been checked by the dissolution of their State through lack of internal cohesion. But towards the end of the thirteenth century, the pressure of the two German Orders on the north and west had forced the princes of Lithuania to unite under a new dynasty. The new Lithuanian State was the more formidable in that it not only comprised Lithuania, Samogitia, and Black Russia, but was rapidly overrunning the extensive principalities of Western Russia, which preferred Lithuanian rule as the only alternative to the Tartar yoke. Moreover Gedymin (1315–41), the real founder of Lithuanian greatness, had at his disposal the remnants of the fierce Jadźwing tribe and the fugitives from Prussia, most of whom he settled in Black Russia. He built a new centre for his principality at Troki in Lithuania, but later he transferred his capital to the new city of Vilna. It is not difficult to account for the amazing extension of Lithuanian power. A long tradition of military activity, from local raids in search of plunder to great aggressive campaigns of the whole people, had created a warlike spirit and a rude discipline to which must be added the despair and thirst for vengeance of the Prussian emigrants and the patriotic fervour of a people menaced with the destruction of their liberty and beliefs by the hated German invader. With the exception of the Order, all their neighbours were weak. Poland, in her days of weakness, offered the chief field for plunder in men and material, and since her recovery had been an ally. The Russian principalities had come to look upon Lithuania as their saviour from Tartar rule, since the Lithuanian princes, behind their impenetrable barrier of marsh and forest, could defy the Khan of the Golden Horde with impunity. Thus Polotsk, long under Lithuanian influence, became subject to Lithuania in 1307; Vitebsk soon followed. Podlasia with Brest[1] was seized by Gedymin in 1315; Minsk was occupied soon after. By his victory on the Irpen in 1320 Gedymin conquered the princes of the Kiev region, though Kiev itself, since the departure of the Metropolitan to Vladimir in 1300, had lost the last shred of its political and commercial predominance, its place having been taken partly by Lemberg (Lvov, Lwow) and partly by Gedymin's new city of Vilna. Gedymin had thus brought under his rule all White Russia and a large part of Little Russia, and had established a loose union of Russian principalities not unlike the Kievan union of an earlier age. The main thread of Russian history runs in North-Eastern Russia, where Moscow was rising to importance under Gedymin's contemporary Ivan Kalitá. But the real successor of Kievan Russia, as historians have now realised, was not Moscow, alien partly in race and wholly in political ideas to Kiev, but the new Russo-Lithuanian State. To complete the union of Western Russia, it remained only to occupy Red Russia (Ruthenia), as the principalities of Volhynia and Galicia may most conveniently be called. The question of the succession to this important State came up in 1324 when the princes of the house of Roman, Andrew and Leo, perished in battle with the Tartars. There were several claimants to their heritage. The Khan of the Tartars, the powerful Uzbeg of the Golden Horde, claimed the land as suzerain lord of all Russia. The Kings of Hungary had since the beginning of the thirteenth century called themselves rulers of Galicia and Lodomeria (*i.e.* Galich and Vladimir, the ancient capital of Volhynia). Gedymin's son Lubart was married to a daughter of the late prince. The boyars, however, called in the nephew of the late princes, Boleslav of Mazovia; but his tyranny and support of Catholic propaganda resulted in his assassination in 1340, whereupon Lubart proceeded to occupy Volhynia, while Casimir III, as a relative of the last prince, claimed Galicia. He invaded the principality with a large army, and after some resistance the boyars were won over to recognise Casimir as king, while the son of the King of Hungary, being the heir to Casimir's kingdom, was persuaded to postpone the assertion of his claims. But with Lithuania a war broke out which lasted with intervals for twenty-six years. Gedymin died in 1341, and was succeeded after a period

---

[1] Subsequently called Brest Litewski (Lithuanian) to distinguish it from the town of the same name in Kujawia.

of civil war by his son Olgierd (1345–77). After a long struggle, Lithuania successfully held Volhynia, while Poland retained Galicia. Peace was made in 1352, whereupon both rivals united to extend their power over the southern steppe which the decline of Tartar power after the death of Uzbeg threw open to foreign conquest. Casimir's expedition to the new Roumanian principalities, which he claimed as a former dependency of Galicia, resulted in failure. But Olgierd overthrew the Tartar Khans of Podolia at Sine Vody, annexed Podolia and the Ukraine, drove the Tartars into the Crimea, and extended Lithuanian rule to the Black Sea. The sons of his brother Koryat governed in Podolia, which began to recover from Tartar devastation and to prosper through Polish co-operation. One of the same family even became ruler of Moldavia. Despite a renewal of the struggle with Lithuania, Casimir remained in possession of Galicia till his death, and Polish influence remained strong in the neighbouring province of Podolia.

The results of Casimir's diplomacy were of the highest significance for the future of Poland. Without offering serious resistance, he had given up Silesia, the most wealthy and advanced province of Poland, which, despite the pro-German policy of its princes and the preponderance of the German element in its towns, still contained in the main a Polish agrarian population. He had surrendered Pomerania to the Teutonic Order and with it the sole link between Poland and the sea. Under the rule of the Order and the influence of the Hansa League, Danzig lost its Slav character and became a German town, subject to none of the influences which made the Germans of Cracow or Poznań good subjects of Poland; and, together with Thorn, it secured a monopoly of the foreign trade of Poland with the Baltic area. In exchange for the loss of these Polish lands, Casimir had gained in Galicia a country that was rich and extensive and offered a field for Polish expansion, but which contained a foreign population, politically backward and professing a different form of religion. The occupation of this province entailed new responsibilities and direct contact with the Tartar world. The general result was that the Polish population, pressed back from the Oder and Lower Vistula regions and already spreading in dense masses over the plateau of Lublin, Eastern Mazovia, and the Carpathian uplands, began to pour over the Vistula and the San into the Russian provinces, and together with the Russians to colonise Podolia and the deserted lands of the Ukraine. It may be pleaded in defence of Casimir's actions that he could not have done otherwise than surrender Silesia and Pomerania. His real intentions and those of the Polish magnates are clear from the continual appearance in the treaties with the Angevin kings of the clause concerning the recovery of the lost provinces, especially Pomerania. Casimir himself made persistent efforts to carry out this policy. It was obvious that the recovery of these lands was not abandoned, but postponed. In the war with Bohemia in 1343 he reconquered two border districts of Silesia. In 1351 he reasserted Polish suzerainty over the princes of Mazovia, who became formally vassals of the Polish Crown. The princes of Kujawia, too, bequeathed their small provinces to Casimir, who found himself by 1364 in possession of the whole of that province. Moreover, the decline of Brandenburg after the extinction of the Ascanian dynasty enabled Poland to recover part of the frontier district at the confluence of the Noteć and Warta. Yet Casimir's foreign policy, while securing the position of Poland among its neighbours, was forced to recognise a definite advance of the Empire and the Teutonic Order at the expense of Poland. His reign marks a permanent withdrawal of the Polish ethnographical frontier in favour of the Germans, and the undertaking of new and onerous tasks by the annexation of a Russian province which brought Poland into Eastern politics, into contact with the Tartars, the Roumanians, the Lithuanians, and ultimately the Muscovites.

While Casimir was forced by the difficulties of his position to postpone rather than to solve the greatest problems of foreign policy, he was able to grapple effectively with the important domestic questions which confronted the restored monarchy—problems of equal difficulty, on the solution of which his title to greatness would depend. Chief of these problems was the local independence of the different provinces of Poland. The early Slavs, with their strong tribal separatism, had adhered tenaciously to the idea of a tribal prince. The early monarchy, which with its crust of Western ideas and institutions had been superimposed on the tribal system, had only temporarily succeeded in checking this idea, which reappeared in 1138 and gained strength during the Partitional period. Even apart from the retention of separate princes by Silesia and Mazovia, Casimir was by no means ruler of a united Polish State. He was simply Prince of Greater Poland, Prince of Lesser Poland, and suzerain Prince of Mazovia, and with each of these provinces he dealt quite independently of the others. Each former principality preserved the shadow of an independent ruler in the person of its *Wojewoda* or Palatine with his hierarchy of officials. Vladyslav I and his son began their task of centralisation by restoring and developing the institution of the Starostaship originally introduced by Wenceslas. Thus over each of the provinces of Greater Poland—Lenczyca, Sieradz, Inowroclaw and Brest Kujawski (the two parts of Kujawia)—a *Starosta* was appointed, with an additional *Starosta* for Galich after its annexation. Since the *Starosta* was regarded as the king's deputy, no such office was created in Lesser Poland till later times. There, as the duties of the ruler grew in volume, special officials were entrusted with the functions of the post. The *Starosta*, like the *bailli* in France, was the king's deputy and chief administrative officer in the provinces; he was also given control of military and judicial matters. The office gained in power at the expense of the older offices of *Wojewoda* and *Kasztelan* which came more and more to be held by local magnates as representatives of the province rather than of the royal power. From the *Wojewoda* the *Starosta* took over the duties of royal deputy and judge, while from the *Kasztelan* he took the management of the castles and military affairs in general, together with the administration of the royal domain, leaving to the *Kasztelan* in each case sufficient land to support the dignity of his office. The increase of royal power in the provinces was thus accompanied by a material accession of wealth to the royal revenue, owing to the resumption of the royal lands by the Crown and their more efficient exploitation by the *Starostas*. Together with this development of the king's power over the country went a gradual expansion of the central administration, by which the greater officials of the province of Cracow were transformed into king's ministers, whose sphere of operations covered all the *Wojewodztwa*[1] of the kingdom. The Chancellor, the Deputy Chancellor, and the Treasurer of Lesser Poland became important royal officials, while similar posts in other provinces became merely titular. The king was still the real link between the greater provinces. By the new central institutions his officials were able to bring a certain systematisation of local government and a greater concentration of important common affairs in the hands of the new officials. In the provinces the royal prestige had grown through the permanent subdivision of the great tribal units owing to the need in the previous century of finding thrones for the junior princes. Thus the king had not always to deal with a large tribal unit like Greater Poland, but with the two princedoms of Poznań and Kalisz, each with its *Wojewoda* and lower officials. Lesser Poland was divided into the provinces of Cracow and Sandomierz. Kujawia, in particular, had lost its unity and consisted of the two *Wojewodztwa* of Inowroclaw and Brest and the district of Dobrzyn. But with the union of many provinces under one ruler, direct contact of the ruler and the ruled had been lost. The king found it more and more convenient to summon the officials and magnates of a province to discuss the affairs of that province on some important question of State. At such a *Wiec* or assembly, whether convoked by the king or his local official the *Starosta*, the *Wojewoda* appeared as head of the territorial officials and the magnates of the province. Thus, with the new importance of the local *Wiec*, the territorial officials gained a new dignity in compensation for the administrative and judicial power which they had lost.

One great defect, which had long been a source of confusion for the Polish community, was the chaotic condition of the laws. Each province had hitherto preserved its own customary laws, which differed widely from province to province. On this mass of custom there had been superimposed the decrees of the princes and of the two kings, a growing volume of legislation which was uncoordinated and contradictory. The king called together a Council of advisers, chief of whom were Skotnicki the Archbishop of Gniezno and John Strzelecki the Chancellor, to co-ordinate into

[1] For administrative titles see *supra*, Vol. VI, Chap. XIII (B), p. 447.

a common code the laws of Greater and Lesser Poland. For the systematisation of the laws advantage was taken of the existing statutes of the ecclesiastical synods, which offered a model for the legal phraseology, Latin style, and formal arrangement of the new code. The Statute of Wiślica was issued in 1347 as a code for the whole of Poland. It was in reality, however, based on the laws of Lesser Poland, and the king published a separate statute for Greater Poland. The original and successful work of the codifiers was of permanent value in clearing away a mass of cumbrous material, in giving lawyers an authoritative legal handbook, and in bringing as far as possible into harmony the legal conceptions of the different parts of Poland. Constitutionally the reigns of Vladyslav and Casimir were a continuation of the preceding age and were also characterised by the practice of granting charters conferring privileges and immunities. But in the fourteenth century such charters tended to affect large groups rather than individuals, and the crystallisation of definite classes was completed in this period, culminating in the Charter of Koszyce in 1374. As the result of these privileges, in contrast to the difficulties and dangers threatening the State from outside, internally the reign of Casimir was a period of unprecedented prosperity for all classes of the community, and the great Casimir as "peasant's king," protector of the Jews, conqueror of Russia, with a court of brilliant, if licentious, splendour, has remained in popular tradition as a magnificent, legendary figure like Charlemagne, Barbarossa, or St Vladimir. The knights, though overshadowed by the small but powerful group of magnates, were emerging as a definite class basing its position on noble birth as symbolised by a coat of arms and on the possession of an hereditary estate. Whether magnate or humble squire, the gentleman "bene natus et possessionatus" was beginning to assert himself. This class had played a patriotic part in the revival of national sentiment and of the Piast monarchy. It was becoming more and more conscious of its rights under numerous charters and of its duties to the State as well as to one particular province. By the charter granted at Koszyce, the *Szlachta* (as it came to be called) received formal confirmation of its detailed liberties and of its existence as a class. For the peasantry, the liberties granted by "German law" in the last hundred years had been universally imitated and had profoundly modified the position of those who remained under Polish law. For the rural population the fourteenth century was an age of great prosperity. The villagers, whether managing their own affairs under their hereditary *Soltys*, or dependent on some great landowner, had the right to migrate at will and the right of appeal to the royal courts. The new economic improvements introduced by the Germans and the colonising movement over all the country contributed to the progress and well-being of the agrarian class, which was now, under favourable conditions of unity and order, able to develop its land secure from interruption by external and internal foes; and the foreign colonists were gradually absorbed into the Polish peasantry. Even more than for the gentry or the peasants, the age of Casimir saw the rise of unusually favourable circumstances for the development of the towns. It has been seen that the influx into the towns of German immigrants had created a serious political problem. On the other hand, it had given them great industrial and commercial prosperity. Not only did the industrious German artisans and their Polish fellow-citizens produce important articles for home consumption and for export, but the Polish towns became centres of trade, ready to take advantage of the opportunities offered by the annexation of Galicia. Trade routes from Danzig through Plock and from Breslau and Poznań through Cracow converged on Lemberg, and there met the great trade route from the Genoese colonies on the Black Sea through which so much of the Eastern trade was carried. Russian towns like Lemberg received charters under Magdeburg law, and their population was swelled not only by Poles and Germans, but by Jews from the Crimea and from Western Europe and by Armenians. The burghers of the Polish cities became wealthy and prosperous, so much so that a rich Cracow merchant was able to entertain royalty with a magnificence impossible for a country gentleman. The development of the towns owed a great deal to the care and tact of Casimir, who was a zealous protector of their autonomy and was careful to tolerate the creeds and customs of the non-Polish elements, while at the same time he put down with a firm hand any signs of the political separatism which had shewn itself so dangerous to his father in 1310–11. To cut the links which bound the Germans to their native land, he established a supreme court of municipal law in Cracow and forbade all appeal to the courts of the German cities. As the result of his prudent policy, the growing Jewish and Armenian colonies settled down to live contentedly under Polish rule, while the German citizens became, if not Poles, at any rate good citizens of Poland. It was not till the sixteenth century that the German burghers became finally assimilated.

In dealing with Galicia or Red Russia, while the mixed population of the towns received the Magdeburg municipal organisation, Casimir prudently abstained from any attempt to impose Polish institutions too abruptly on the Russian population. The former principalities were in many cases retained by the Russian princes of the Rurik dynasty or were granted to those Lithuanian princes like Lubart or the sons of Koryat and Narymunt whom the Russian boyars had come to consider as natural rulers. The leading boyars were summoned to the royal council to debate matters concerning Russia. Moreover, Casimir was consistently tolerant towards the Orthodox Church to which the majority of his Russian subjects belonged. He retained the existing Orthodox bishoprics and supported the efforts of the Church to have the bishopric of Galich raised to the position of a metropolitan see, since the departure of the Metropolitan of Kiev to the North in 1300 had left Western Russia without a direct head. An Armenian bishopric was established at Lemberg (Lwow) in 1367. At the same time the king supported Catholic propaganda which had begun to penetrate Russia long before the annexation. Catholic bishoprics were established at Przemyśl, Vladimir, Chelm, and Galich, while an archbishopric was subsequently established at Lemberg, Casimir's favourite city. In the great expanses of Eastern Galicia and Podolia Polish colonisation was encouraged: in particular, the magnates of Lesser Poland began to form large estates in Red Russia. Throughout his reign Casimir bound the Russian province to Poland by this prudent policy of toleration and peaceful penetration. Besides his domestic reforms in Poland and Red Russia, Casimir did much to encourage education and the arts. He protected learned men like Janko of Czarnków, who chronicled the events of his time and country and rose to be Deputy Chancellor. He founded the Academy of Cracow in 1364, which became a centre for the study of law and was modelled on Bologna. Henceforward Polish learning had a centre to rival the older Czech university at Prague. Above all, Casimir was a great builder, and the saying that he found Poland made of wood and left it a country of stone merely expresses the truth. Beloved in Poland and respected abroad, Casimir died in 1370 at the age of sixty as the result of an accident in the hunting-field.

The compact and prosperous State which Casimir had so wisely and successfully ruled for thirty-seven years passed by his own wish not to a Piast but to Lewis of Hungary. By a deliberate desire to raise the throne above the petty rivalries of the native princes of Silesia and Mazovia, he gave Poland into the hands of the Angevin dynasty which had brought strong rule and enlightenment from Naples to Hungary. But, however statesmanlike this policy may have been, the king failed to foresee the great change it was destined to bring about. His plan failed, not only because Lewis had no male issue and was occupied with the affairs of Hungary and in his own dynastic ambitions rather than with the administration of Poland, but because it brought about a political revolution which gave the Polish magnates a predominant position in the State. Lewis, after being crowned at Cracow, returned to Hungary leaving Poland under the rule of his mother Elizabeth, who did not find favour with the Poles. He then proceeded to alienate the Poles still more by uniting Red Russia to Hungary, nominating as his viceroy there Vladyslav, Prince of Opole[1]. His lack of male issue made the selection of husbands for his three daughters of paramount importance to him and the two kingdoms, while it also forced him to revise the terms of the treaties of Vyšehrad and Buda. On the death of his eldest daughter, he arranged a marriage for her sister Mary with Sigismund, son of the Emperor Charles IV, thus planning that she would inherit Poland and Brandenburg. The youngest daughter, Jadviga (Hedwig), was to be betrothed to William of Austria and was to inherit Hungary and Red Russia together

[1] To-day Oppeln in Silesia.

with Austria. Lewis met the Polish magnates at two congresses in Hungary and concluded with them in 1374 the Pact of Koszyce, which not only determined the succession to the Polish throne, but conferred on the *Szlachta* the fundamental rights which thenceforward regulated its relations with the Crown. This epoch-making agreement comprised the following main clauses: (1) On the death of Lewis, one of his daughters, to be chosen by himself or his queen, should succeed to the Polish throne; (2) The king pledged himself not to diminish the territories of the Polish Crown, and to attempt to regain the lost provinces; (3) The king formally exempted the *Szlachta* from all taxes and dues with the exception of the payment of two groschen per hide annually which was obligatory for all; (4) Territorial offices should be held by the gentry of the province concerned and not by foreigners. The chief significance of the Pact of Koszyce was its recognition of the privileged position of the *Szlachta*. It was the first Charter granted to the whole of the *Szlachta* as a class. Secondly, it limited the resources of the monarch by compelling him to support himself from the royal domain and by depriving him of the right to tax the gentry. Lastly, by the very procedure of the congress, it constituted a precedent for the election of the king by the *Szlachta*, a custom which eventually became permanent.

Meanwhile matters were going very badly for the new king in Poland. Piast claimants for the throne appeared in Vladyslav, the last surviving prince of the Kujawian house, and Ziemovit of Mazovia; the Lithuanians invaded Red Russia, and the Magyar nobles made themselves so unpopular in Cracow that a massacre took place. After the death of Lewis in 1382, still greater confusion followed, and an Interregnum ensued which lasted for two years. Sigismund claimed the Polish throne for his wife Mary, but the magnates of Greater Poland, followed by the Lesser Polish leaders, insisted that no daughter of Lewis could reign in Poland who had not taken up her residence in the country. Parties were formed, one of which put forward Ziemovit of Mazovia as a candidate for the throne; but the power of nomination according to the Pact of Koszyce rested with Lewis' widow. She designated Jadviga, but did not at first allow her to come to Poland. The claims of Ziemovit were resisted by Sigismund, who devastated Mazovia in terrible fashion. At last Jadviga appeared at Cracow where she was crowned as "King" in 1384. Soon after a suitor for the hand of the new ruler appeared in the person of the Grand Prince of Lithuania.

Since the death of Gedymin, his son Olgierd had continued his conquests in the south and east. To his younger son Kiejstut (Keystut) fell the more difficult task of defending the north of Lithuania against the Teutonic Order. Under its greatest Grand Master Kniprode (1351–82) the Order was then at the height of its power. By the occupation of Esthonia in 1346, its possessions extended from the Narva nearly to the Oder. Its attacks on Lithuania had become so formidable that most of Samogitia had fallen to the knights, and Kiejstut had almost decided to leave his country in despair. Olgierd was succeeded in 1377 by his son Yagaylo, or (to use the common Polish form) Jagiello, who had for some time wished to adopt Christianity. This aim brought him into opposition to his uncle and civil war broke out which ended in the death of Kiejstut, whose son Vytautas (called Vitovt by the Russians, Vitold by the Poles) fled to the Teutonic Knights and with their help invaded his own country. The situation was favourable for a revival of the alliance made with Vladyslav the Short in 1325. Jagiello sought an ally who would help him to convert his people to Christianity and to fight the Order. Such an ally he could find in the Poles, who had been great apostles of the Christian religion and who were bound to resume their struggle against the Order. Now that the ruler of Poland was an unmarried princess he had the opportunity to seal such an alliance by a marriage which would unite both States. To Poland the proposal of Jagiello offered still greater advantages. Besides ending the incessant Lithuanian raids, it held out the prospect of union with a State of enormous resources in which the more advanced Poles would be the dominant element. They would be able to introduce civilisation and Christianity into a great pagan community. The Polish magnates gave their strong support to a project for which they were probably responsible. By a treaty at Krevo in 1385 the Grand Prince pledged himself to accept baptism, to convert his people, to unite Poland and Lithuania, and to recover the lost provinces. In return he was to be married to Jadviga and to become King of Poland. Jadviga, against the dictates of her heart, gave up the friend of her childhood, William of Austria, and sacrificed herself to the interests of her country in accepting the barbarian prince as husband. In 1386 Jagiello entered Cracow in state, was baptised as a Christian according to the rites of the Catholic Church, married Jadviga, and was crowned King of Poland under the name of Vladyslav II (1386–1434). His first act was to confirm and amplify the privileges conferred by the Charter of Koszyce. Thus by a brilliant stroke of diplomacy the Polish magnates achieved one of the greatest triumphs of the Middle Ages, by which they secured their own political predominance and brought about the union under one ruler of Poland, Lithuania, and a great part of Russia.

The dynastic union of Poland and Lithuania caused a complete change in the external relations of Poland. The last two Piast kings had based their foreign policy on the alliance with Hungary against the house of Luxemburg and the Teutonic Order. Now that a scion of the imperial house was on the Hungarian throne, the situation was quite different. Secure on her Lithuanian frontier, Poland was able not only to recover Red Russia, but to open relations with the Roumanian principalities which had just emancipated themselves from Magyar rule. In 1387 Jagiello found himself master of Galicia and received the homage of Peter of Moldavia. The rulers of Wallachia and Bessarabia followed suit and not only enhanced the prestige of Poland, but gave fresh commercial advantages to Lemberg. The first act of Jagiello in Lithuania was to convert his pagan people to Catholicism and to create an ecclesiastical hierarchy under a bishopric in Vilna. The fierce Samogitians still remained pagan, while the large Russian population adhered to the Orthodox faith. But internal difficulties soon disturbed the Grand Principality, and were intensified by the intrigues of Sigismund and the Teutonic Order. The king had set up his brother Skirgiello as viceroy of Lithuania, thereby exciting the jealousy of Vitold, the ablest of the descendants of Gedymin. A brilliant soldier and an able diplomat, Vitold possessed in a high degree the martial character of his dynasty, which gave him better qualifications for the esteem of his countrymen than the Polish innovations of Jagiello. To his natural talents he added an overwhelming ambition which aimed at the creation of a great Eastern Empire in which not the Poles but the Lithuanians should dominate the Tartars, West Russians, and Muscovites. He set himself at the head of the Lithuanian national party, connived at rebellions in Polotsk and Smolensk, and lent an ear to the intrigues of Sigismund and the Teutonic Knights. With the help of the latter he overthrew the incompetent viceroy and forced Jagiello to give him the office for himself, whereupon he soon crushed the rebellion and drove out the troops of the Order. He felt himself strong enough to be proclaimed as Grand Prince, placated the Order by the cession of Samogitia, and set out to realise his Eastern scheme. Lithuania already ruled the whole of the Dnieper basin and only needed to annex Moscow and Novgorod to restore Russian unity. The great Northern republic was not unwilling to intrigue against Moscow, but Moscow was a serious rival for the leadership of the Russians, especially after the victory of the Don over the Tartars in 1380, which had brought her great prestige. Further, the Tartar overlord of Moscow had first to be reckoned with. The Tartar world, like Russia, was at this time in a fluid condition. The leadership of the Golden Horde had been seized by Tuqtāmish, ruler of the White Horde, who had reasserted Tartar rule over Moscow in 1382. He had rebelled against his overlord, the mighty Tīmūr, and had been expelled from his dominions. He now appealed for aid to Vitold, who seized the opportunity for attacking the Golden Horde and assembled at Kiev a great army of Lithuanians, Russians, Poles, and even Western crusaders which was joined by the Tartars of Tuqtāmish. Unfortunately, Vitold permitted the new Khan of the Golden Horde to effect a junction with Tīmūr's general, Edigey; and in 1399 on the banks of the Vorskla he suffered a terrible defeat in which many Lithuanian and Russian princes together with eminent Poles like Spytek of Melsztyn were slain. Vitold's great scheme was frustrated, and though he annexed Smolensk and made the Ugra his frontier with Moscow, it was obvious that Lithuanian expansion had reached its limit. Realising his failure and fully aware that his own capital was perpetually menaced by the Germans, Vitold decided to seek a better understanding with his cousin. At the congress of Vilna in 1401, with the consent of Jagiello, Vitold was proclaimed Grand Prince, on condition that at his death Lithuania should return to Jagiello or his successor, and that Lithuania should remain a vassal of the Polish Crown. The Poles pledged themselves for their part not to elect a successor to Jagiello without consulting the Lithuanians.

This agreement, the first of many acts leading to the union of the Grand Principality with the kingdom, made possible the co-operation of the two States in the matter of the long-deferred settlement with the Teutonic Knights. The Order was now a powerful State which regarded the tradition binding it to the Empire and the Papacy as an advantage to be manipulated to its own profit rather than as a tie of allegiance. It ruled a large and wealthy country, well able to maintain the most redoubtable military force in Europe, while its prestige as a crusading institution attracted the most enterprising knights of Europe, including such celebrities as John of Bohemia and Henry of Lancaster. The dismay of the Knights may be pictured when the news reached them that Poland had accomplished by peaceful means what they had failed to do by force— the conversion of the pagans whom they regarded as their natural prey and whose paganism was the sole reason for the continued existence of the Order. The absence of a religious stimulus was bound to affect the flow of recruits. Moreover, the recovery of Samogitia by Vitold in 1404 cut off the eastern from the western portion of its territories. To Lithuania, revenge on the Order was almost a sacred duty, and for the Lithuanians, still pagan at heart, the Order had none of the majesty which filled the true Catholics with awe. The antagonism of the Poles to the knights was based partly on political history, partly on national sentiment. The Order had seized and kept the Pomeranian seaboard. It formed an outpost of Germanism which had been untouched by the Polish revival of the last century. National sentiment in Central Europe, where the acceptance of medieval institutions and ideas generally entailed submission to Germany, was a far stronger force than in the West. Though German feudalism had triumphed in Pomerania and to a great extent in Bohemia, and though Silesia while retaining a Polish population had accepted German institutions and Czech suzerainty, Germany found herself confronted in the fifteenth century by a strong Slavonic reaction which found expression in the war between Poland and the Order and in the Hussite movement. Jagiello, like his predecessor Lewis, had sworn to recover the lost provinces of Poland, and he found it politic to ingratiate himself with his new subjects by a struggle against the Order. The peace party in Poland lost its influence after the death of the saintly Jadviga in 1398. The peaceful policy of the Grand Master Conrad von Jungingen was reversed after his death by his brother who succeeded him in 1407. The immediate cause of war was a frontier dispute. The Order had purchased the Neumark from Brandenburg and had seized the border town of Drezdenko which was claimed by the Poles. The impetuous Grand Master wished to regain Dobrzyn and Samogitia, and was spurred on by the support of Wenceslas of Bohemia and Sigismund of Hungary who were jealous of the growing power of Jagiello. The year 1409 saw the outbreak of a series of wars which only terminated with the fall of the Order in 1466.

Overshadowed though it was by the Hussite wars, the great Northern War was important no less for the enormous forces that were brought into the field than for its political results. The first year saw merely frontier raids. Both sides were organising their forces for the decisive encounter. The Knights had the support of the Kings of Hungary and Bohemia; of the princes of Western Pomerania who sent a large force under Prince Casimir; while they drew great numbers of crusaders and mercenary soldiers from all parts of the Empire. Jagiello and Vitold were dependent mainly on their own resources and were only able to obtain an inconsiderable force of mercenaries from Bohemia and Silesia, among whom was John Žižka, the future leader of the Hussites. The plan of campaign appears to have been settled by Jagiello and his Deputy-Chancellor Tromba with Vitold at Brest in December 1409. Mazovia had been chosen as the base of operations on account of its convenient situation between Poland and Lithuania and on the route to Marienburg, the goal of the invaders. The food supply for the armies was prepared by great hunting expeditions in the forests of Belovezh and Kozienice. The meat was salted, packed, and sent down the Narev and Vistula to Plock. The *Starosta* of Radom had a pontoon bridge constructed and floated down the river to Czerwinsk, where an island made a more suitable point for crossing the Vistula than Plock. Vitold, by one of the rapid mobilisations for which the Gedymin princes were famous, assembled his army at Vilna. Besides Lithuanians, Russians and Tartars flocked to his standard. He marched to the Narev to join Jagiello on the Vistula. The mobilisation in Poland was more complicated. The general levy had not been summoned for fifty years, and many nobles preferred to fight in their clan groups. However, at the call to arms the levy of each province assembled under its *Wojewoda* and *Kasztelans* and, together with various clans, met the Czech and Silesian mercenaries at Wolborz (near Piotrków). The united army marched north, took three days to cross the bridge at Czerwinsk, and joined the Lithuanian army under Vitold and the Mazovian force under its princes Janusz and Ziemovit. The complete army was of imposing size and unusual diversity. Alongside the Polish knights and the clan groups, each with its common arms and slogan, rode thousands of Tartars under Soldan, soon to be Khan of the Golden Horde. Martial Lithuanians marched side by side with sturdy Czech mercenaries who were destined to astonish the world. The model of Polish chivalry, Zawisza the Black, was in striking contrast to the turbulent Russian boyars or the rude skin-clad Samogitians. A division of Poles had been left in the south against Sigismund, while a large force had been detached to guard the long Kujawian frontier. The latter first came into contact with the enemy, and impressed the Grand Master with the idea of a Polish invasion of the coveted province of Pomerania. Sending Henry von Plauen with 3000 men to protect that province, the commander himself with his main army remained near the Vistula to await news of the enemy. It was only when the Poles had crossed the Wkra and the Tartars began to plunder the countryside that he realised from which direction the attack would come. He hastened to oppose the Poles at the crossing on the Drwenca. The Poles withdrew, whereupon he crossed the river himself, and the two great armies met on 15 July in the great battle which is called Grunwald by the Poles, Tannenberg by the Germans, from the names of the two nearest villages. The numbers on both sides were enormous, but were exaggerated by the credulity of contemporary Europe. Yet even a moderate estimate gives about 83,000 troops for the Order and nearly 100,000 for the Polish-Lithuanian army apart from the Tartars. The army of the Knights was led by the Grand Master in person, Ulrich von Jungingen. On the other side, though Jagiello was in supreme command, Zyndram of Maszkowic commanded the Poles and mercenaries in the centre and on the left, while Vitold who led the Lithuanians and Russians on the right wing seems to have played a great part in the direction of the whole army. The Polish army sang the ancient hymn of St Adalbert, after which the battle began by a cavalry engagement, at first with lance, then with sword and axe. The first part of the battle ended favourably for the Teutonic Knights, who routed the Lithuanians and Czechs. The battle was equalised, however, as fresh Polish troops entered the fray, and the threatened right wing was gallantly held by three Russian detachments from Smolensk. Meanwhile the Deputy Chancellor, Tromba, rallied the Czechs, and the battle became fierce and prolonged. At length the Grand Master decided to advance with his sixteen banners of reserves, but the Polish army swung round and withstood the attack, while the Tartars rode round his flanks. The Grand Master, whose sacred person was held in awe by the Poles, was killed in the dense mob of Lithuanians and Tartars, and the remnant of the Knights fled, leaving over 18,000 dead on the field, and 14,000 prisoners and all their fifty-one standards in the hands of the victors.

The victory of Grunwald was the chief triumph of the Slav reaction against the Germans, and was as important as the later Hussite successes. All praise is due to the Poles whose patriotic spirit and military prowess was largely responsible for the victory, while due respect must be given to the wisdom of Jagiello and the valour of Vitold, undoubtedly the greatest figure in the battle. No people but the Lithuanians could have mobilised and equipped such vast forces as were necessary to defeat the mighty Teutonic Order. Their primitive qualities and simplicity of organisation made them expert in handling large masses of men such as feudal Europe could hardly equip, move, or maintain. Nor, on the other hand, could the Lithuanian army have ventured to invade Prussia without the military knowledge and discipline and the intelligent organisation of the Poles. But these qualities, while enabling the two peoples to win victory in the field, did not help them to exploit their victory. They marched through Prussia and commenced the siege of the capital. But von Plauen threw himself into Marienburg and defended it heroically, while fresh troops came to his aid from Livonia and from Germany. The great army began to disperse. Vitold returned to Lithuania and the Mazovian princes withdrew their troops, while Sigismund invaded Poland in the south. The Order was saved, and Jagiello reluctantly made peace in 1411 on condition that he received Samogitia and an indemnity. In the next year, by the Peace of Buda, Sigismund surrendered his claim to Red Russia and Moldavia in favour of Jagiello. As a pledge for his debt to Poland, he leased to Jagiello thirteen towns in the Spiz district of Hungary, which remained Polish till 1769. In domestic affairs the war had two important results, the conversion of the Samogitians to Catholicism under the new bishopric of Miedniki, and the Union of Horodlo between Poland and Lithuania in 1413. This agreement confirmed the previous treaties of 1387 and 1401 by which the Poles and Lithuanians gave mutual guarantees as to the election of rulers after the death of Jagiello and Vitold. The right to bear Polish coats of arms was extended by the Polish *Szlachta* to the Catholic boyars, who were granted privileges similar to those of the Polish nobility. Lithuania was divided into *Wojewodztwa*, and an official hierarchy was established on the Polish model. Common Councils were to be held at Lublin or Parczów. The Union of Horodlo was an important step towards the closer association of the two States, but it failed to conciliate the non-Catholic element in Lithuania. It encouraged the Poles to resume the war with the Order. The Knights, however, had learned the dangers of a pitched battle, and the Second War (1414–22) was a campaign of starvation and devastation which was interrupted by the important developments in Bohemia. By the Treaty of Melno in 1422 the Order renounced all claims to Samogitia and ceded Nieszawa and other frontier towns.

The great religious and social upheaval in Bohemia had drawn Poland into the vortex of European politics. John Hus had corresponded with Jagiello, and Jerome had preached in Cracow. The similarity of the Polish and Czech languages made the Hussite doctrines accessible to the Poles, while the anti-German element in the Czech revolution evoked a sympathetic response from the victors of Grunwald. The Polish ecclesiastical leaders were naturally opposed to the new doctrines, and they took an important part in the Council of Constance under Nicholas Tromba, who was now Archbishop of Gniezno. After participating in the general questions discussed by the Council, particularly the Hussite question, in which the secular members of the Polish delegation supported the Hussites, the Poles were most interested in two other matters. They made a formal protest against the activities of the Teutonic Order. Paul, the Rector of Cracow Academy, wrote a treatise on the one side, while the pamphlet of Falkenberg expressed the views of the Order. But a still more important problem raised by the Poles concerned an older group of dissenters, the Orthodox subjects of Lithuania. For over a century the decline of Greek power and the remoteness of Russia after the Tartar invasion had lessened the importance of the Eastern Church for the Western world. But the incursions of the Ottoman Turks into the Balkans and Hungary, the occupation of Red Russia by Poland, and the entrance of Lithuania into the European system, had not only awakened the Catholic Church to the problem of its relations with the Eastern Church, but had given it an unusually favourable opportunity for effecting a union on its own terms[1]. While the Orthodox prelates of Greece and the Balkans were ready to make wide concessions to gain assistance against the infidel, Jagiello and the Polish clergy were burning to bring the Russian schismatics within the fold of the Church—an achievement which would facilitate the political as well as the religious settlement of Lithuania. A deputation of Russian bishops under the Metropolitan, Gregory Tsamblak, was sent to support the petition for a union with the Catholic Church. For the moment, however, no union was achieved, as the Hussite problems excluded all others. Stimulated by the Polish support of their doctrines, the moderate Hussite leaders, desiring a Slav union, offered the Czech throne to Jagiello, and on his refusal in 1420 to Vitold. But the Polish ecclesiastics under Zbigniev Oleśnicki had resolved to oppose the Hussite doctrines in any form. The new leader of the Polish oligarchy owed his rise to his rescue of the king from danger at the battle of Grunwald. His position was at first difficult, because he had not only to face the opposition of many secular magnates and a majority among the lesser *Szlachta* who were in revolt against the ecclesiastical hierarchy, but he had to dissuade Jagiello and Vitold from the favour which they shewed to the new doctrines. But when Sigismund, fearing a Polish-Czech alliance, began to hold out hopes of the restitution of Silesia to Poland, the clerical party were able to dissuade the magnates from their inclination to join the Czechs, and the Statute of Tromba in 1420 restored Church discipline and enacted severe penalties against heresy. Vitold, however, still anxious to mediate between the Church and the Hussites, accepted the Bohemian crown; and in 1422, Jagiello's nephew, Zygmunt Korybut, with 5000 men was sent to assist the Czechs. This policy of irresolution soon proved futile. Not only did Korybut prove a poor soldier and diplomat, but the expedition aroused the wrath of the Papacy as well as the Empire. If the Poles could ignore the threat of their old enemy Sigismund to incite the neighbouring States to a partition of Poland, they could not afford to alienate the Papacy and European opinion in general in their dispute with the

[1] See Vol. IV, Chap. XIX.

Teutonic Order, nor could they relinquish an opportunity of regaining Silesia by negotiation. In fact their national interests drew the Poles away from the Hussite cause. The Czechs were their ancient enemies and had weakened the Slav cause by a compromise with the Germans, becoming members of the Empire and adopting German institutions far more readily than the Poles, whose interests were more bound up with those of Hungary, which, like Poland, had preserved its independence, its national institutions and customs. Moreover, Bohemia was in possession of a Polish province, Silesia, which every Polish king was pledged to recover. The Polish lesser gentry and clergy had grievances against the ecclesiastical oligarchy, but these churchmen were Poles like themselves. The Czechs were in rebellion against their overlord, the Emperor, who had no status in Poland. The Poles felt that they had struggled for Slav liberties at a time when the Czechs had not only compromised with Germany, but taken advantage of their stronger position to deprive Poland of its wealthiest province. The religious and social struggle was not acute in Poland, and it was a prudent policy to sacrifice the vague ideal of a struggle on behalf of Slavdom for the support of the Papacy and Emperor in the national struggle against the Order and the chance to regain Silesia by negotiation. So Jagiello made peace with the Emperor in 1423, and by the Edict of Wieluń in 1424 imposed severe penalties on the Polish Hussites.

Oleśnicki, having successfully checkmated the efforts of Vitold to support Hussitism, had next to oppose his threats to the Polish union with Lithuania. Frustrated in his attempt to effect a religious union in the Grand Principality, Vitold devoted his energies to the task of making himself King of Lithuania. A zealous advocate of Catholicism and Western civilisation, at the same time he wished that Lithuania rather than Poland should be the leading State in Central Europe, and his ambitions were secretly encouraged by Sigismund and the Order. At the famous Congress of Lutsk in 1429 Vitold entertained a brilliant gathering of princes, ostensibly to discuss the question of defence against the Turks. Besides his son-in-law, the Grand Prince of Moscow, the chief guests were the Emperor Sigismund, Jagiello, the King of Denmark, the Grand Masters of both Orders, the papal legate, the ambassador of the Byzantine Emperor, the Khans of the Volga and Crimean Tartars, the Hospodar of Wallachia, Princes of Silesia, Pomerania, and Mazovia together with all the nobility of the province of Volhynia. At this picturesque assembly, where the guests and their retinues, according to the chronicler, consumed daily 700 oxen, 1400 sheep, and 100 bisons and boars, and drank 700 barrels of mead besides wine and beer, the Turkish question was used as a pretext to cover the attempt of the Emperor to persuade Jagiello to consent to the coronation of Vitold. This intrigue was frustrated by the determined opposition of the Polish magnates under Oleśnicki, and the proposal was dropped on the death of Vitold in 1430. The tortuous diplomacy in which his position involved him, his failure against the

Tartars, and his soaring ambition cannot obscure his greatness as a man. He was the last brilliant soldier of the house of Gedymin, an able diplomatist, and a great influence for progress in a backward area of Europe. He ruled his vast principality with ideals that could never merit the approbation of Polish or Russian patriots, and while enhancing the prestige of Poland, his main work was devoted to his own principality and entitles him to be considered as one of the great men of his age.

Vitold's greatness was revealed by the ferment into which the country was plunged by his death. His project of a religious union with the Orthodox Church had been intended to entail an equalisation in status of the Russians with the Catholic Poles and Lithuanians. Its failure left a cause for discontent among the Russian boyars. The Lithuanians, desirous of reasserting their independence, joined the malcontents, who found a leader in the king's brother Swidrygiello, already notorious as a rebel against Vitold. The king was forced to consent to his election as Grand Prince. But his ambition was not satisfied and was fostered by the Emperor, the Grand Master, and Alexander of Moldavia. The action of Sigismund was particularly treacherous in that Polish troops were helping him in his Turkish campaigns, in one of which the model of Polish chivalry, Zawisza, had perished. The Teutonic Knights invaded Poland and began the third period of the Northern War (1431–35). Jagiello acted promptly, deposed his brother, with whom the Lithuanian boyars were soon disillusioned, and in 1432 raised Zygmunt, Vitold's brother, to the position of Grand Prince. By the Act of Grodno he conferred on the Orthodox Russian boyars all the rights and liberties possessed by the Catholics. At the same time Red Russia received an organisation similar to that of Poland, and Russian magnates there were invited to sit in the royal council. The attacks of the Teutonic Knights were met by the employment of Hussite troops. At the same time as the Hussite mercenaries plundered Pomerania, Zygmunt defeated Swidry-giello at Oszmiana, while the Poles routed his supporters in Podolia. The war was ended in 1435 by a decisive victory over the combined forces of the rebels and the Livonian Knights at Wilkomierz. The Grand Master made peace in the same year.

Meanwhile Jagiello had died in 1434 at the age of eighty-six, as the result of a chill caught while listening to the nightingale in the woods at night, as was his custom. He left two sons by his fourth wife. The eldest son, aged ten, was elected king as Vladyslav III (1434–44), under a regency consisting of the great magnates of Lesser Poland, the Tenczynski and Oleśnicki families, with Zbigniev, now Bishop of Cracow, at their head. The Jagiello dynasty had now reached the height of its power. The religious zeal of Jagiello had won new regions for Catholicism, and he had proved, under the guidance of Oleśnicki, a staunch supporter of the Church, while at the same time he had won the respect of Hussite heretics and Orthodox dissidents alike for his moderation.

With the death of Sigismund in 1437, the great Luxemburg dynasty came to an end, leaving vacant the thrones of Bohemia and Hungary. It was a testimony to the moderation of the Jagiellos when the Czech throne was offered to the young Casimir, as it was to their military prestige when the Hungarian throne was offered to Vladyslav. The Polish oligarchy refused the former offer and continued to persecute the Polish Hussites—a policy which involved them in a struggle with the opposition under Spytek of Melsztyn in 1439. The Hungarian offer was accepted, and Vladyslav III became, like his predecessor Lewis, ruler of both kingdoms. Casimir was made Grand Prince of Lithuania on the death of Zygmunt. On his departure to his principality and in the absence of the king in Hungary, Poland was left in the hands of the regents. Their interest was now concentrated on the Council of Basle, which ended the Hussite schism in Poland in 1433, and before which they once more raised the question of the Orthodox Church in Lithuania. The Greek Church at this time was appealing for union with the Western Church and soliciting help against the Turks. The Metropolitan Isidore voiced the views of the Russians of Lithuania, and at the Council of Florence in 1439 a union of the two Churches was concluded which failed of its objects because of the subsequent fall of Constantinople, but which lasted longer among the Russians despite the opposition of Moscow. Oleśnicki, who had by this time realised a great part of his political programme by the suppression of Hussitism in Poland, the Union of the Orthodox Church, and the maintenance of Polish control over Lithuania, now turned his attention to the crusade against the Turks and the recovery of Silesia. But the Turkish campaign ended in disaster, and in the defeat of the allies at Varna in 1444 the young King Vladyslav disappeared. The Poles were unwilling to credit the news of his death and an interregnum followed (1444–47), after which his younger brother was elected king.

The new king, Casimir IV, was the first Jagiello in Poland who needed no political tutor. His position in Lithuania was secure, and he shewed resentment and impatience at the influence of the ecclesiastical magnates in Poland. His long reign of forty-five years (1447–92) was marked by sweeping changes in the political and economic fabric of the Polish State. The policy of the great leader of the oligarchy had been based on the traditional Polish attitude of resistance to the Empire and zealous support of the Church, from which Poland drew its cultural ideas and through which it maintained ties with Western Europe. This policy had given the Polish clergy a leading position in the government, and had brought the Poles into prominence in Europe. It had won Poland for the Church in the Hussite struggle, in the union with the Eastern Church, and in the crusade against the Turks, but it had drawn Poland away from the Slav sympathies felt by the lesser *Szlachta*, and especially from the war against the Order, which to a man like Oleśnicki was a religious rather than a German institution. The failure to regain Silesia and the calamity in the

Balkans had weakened the power of the Bishop of Cracow. The new policy of the king was to overthrow the oligarchy by concessions to the lesser *Szlachtu*, to abandon the Turkish war, and to resume the national war with the Order. Casimir resembled in his methods the European rulers who were evolving the " New Monarchy," but he differed from them in seeking help from the gentry rather than from the middle class, which in Poland was relatively small and of foreign origin. He triumphed over the ecclesiastical party in the question of the nomination of bishops. To secure the support of the *Szlachta* for the forthcoming war, he consented to the Statutes of Nieszawa, by which he bound himself not to pass any new laws or to summon the armed levy without consulting the *Szlachta* through their *Sejmiki* or local assemblies. Casimir was able to recover by purchase the Silesian principality of Oswiencim in 1457 and the district of Rawa from Mazovia in 1462. To these were added the Mazovian principalities of Sochaczew and Plock and the Silesian principality of Zator in 1495. The rest of Mazovia did not return to Poland until 1529.

But the great event of Casimir's reign was the final settlement with the Teutonic Order. A new situation had arisen in the lands of the Order. The population, becoming discontented with such an anachronism as the ascendancy of a religious Order, began to look longingly towards the growing freedom of the neighbouring realm with its political prestige and commercial prosperity. A number of rebel groups were formed, of which the chief, the Prussian Union, in 1454 sent a petition to the Polish king for the incorporation of Prussia and Pomerania with Poland. The declaration of incorporation was opposed only by Oleśnicki, now a cardinal, who felt the loss of his power acutely and died in the next year. The war lasted for thirteen years. It was impossible in a long war against fortresses to depend on the clumsy levy of the *Szlachta*, which had not the skill to combat the new type of soldiers that had been evolved by the Hussite wars. The campaign, therefore, was carried on by mercenary troops. The decisive battle of Puck was fought in 1462 and was followed by the capture of the chief fortresses of the knights. By the Peace of Thorn in 1466 the Order surrendered to Poland Pomerania, the western part of Prussia with Marienburg, Warmia (Ermeland), Chelmno, and Michalów. East Prussia was retained by the Grand Master with his capital at Königsberg, as a vassal State of Poland. He pledged himself and his successors to recognise no suzerain but the Pope and the King of Poland, to contract no alliances and to wage no wars without the permission of the king. He was also given a seat in the Polish Senate. The annexed territories were organised as three *Wojewodztwa*: Pomerania, Chelmno, and Marienburg. Poland thus recovered her lost province and acquired the lower Vistula with Thorn and Danzig, while East Prussia, which was secularised in 1526 under Albert of Hohenzollern, became an insignificant German vassal State. The Slav reaction in Central Europe had triumphed. Casimir refrained from interfering in Turkish affairs, but

in 1475, by the occupation of Kilia and Akkerman, Lithuania was cut off
from the Black Sea. The king concentrated his energies on the defence
of his realm from the Tartars, who were wont to invade the Ukraine by
the three Tartar routes or *Shlakhi* leading from Perekop to Red Russia.
Abroad, Casimir extended the power of his dynasty and obtained for his
eldest son Vladislav the crown of Bohemia in 1471 and of Hungary in
1490. His second son, John Albert (1492–1501), succeeded him as King
of Poland, but the Lithuanians elected the third son, Alexander, as Grand
Prince. Another son, Frederick, became a cardinal, while the youngest
son, Zygmunt, was appointed by his brother to rule Silesia and Lausitz.
Thus the end of the century saw the Jagiello dynasty attain a predominant
position in Central Europe.

The great empire ruled over by the Jagiellos was not a unitary State.
Their dynastic relations with Hungary and Bohemia led to no close
association of those States with Poland. Their own possessions consisted
of three groups: the kingdom of Poland, the Grand Principality of
Lithuania, and the vassal States of Mazovia, Ducal Prussia, and Moldavia.
Poland comprised: (1) Greater Poland, which had come to include the
Kujawian provinces as well as Sieradz and Lenczyca, (2) Lesser Poland,
in which Lublin had been made into a province together with Cracow
and Sandomierz, (3) Royal or Polish Prussia, *i.e.* the provinces annexed
by the Peace of Thorn, and (4) Red Russia. To these should be added
Podolia, the subject of dispute with Lithuania, and the small parts of
Silesia recovered from Bohemia. Mazovia remained a vassal State till its
incorporation into Poland in 1529. All these provinces were held together
by a common monarch, common officials, and similar institutions, which
sent representatives to a central assembly. Of the vassal States, Mazovia
was soon to be incorporated, Moldavia to fall within the sphere of Turkey.
Ducal Prussia remained a vassal State till the seventeenth century. The
Grand Principality of Lithuania was ruled by a Grand Prince who was
not necessarily King of Poland, but was usually under the supreme
authority of the king. It contained (1) Lithuania, *i.e.* the provinces of
Vilna, Troki, and Samogitia; (2) the Russian provinces in process of
organisation on the Polish model, but retaining many small principalities
under princes of the lines of Rurik and Gedymin. The Grand Prince was
still an autocrat, but he took the advice of the Lithuanian magnates
of the Gasztold, Holshanski, Radziwill, and other families, while the
southern provinces were mainly in the power of the great magnates, of
Russian or Lithuanian origin, of the families of Ostrogski, Czartoryski,
Sanguszko, Sapieha, and others. It was not till 1569 that Lithuania was
united to Poland by an organic union and fully adopted Polish institutions.

At the head of the Polish State stood the king. His power had undergone considerable modification on account of the change of dynasty.
While the succession of Lewis and his male descendants (if he had any)
was fixed by Casimir the Great, Lewis, in order to secure the succession

for one of his daughters, was forced to grant the Charter of Koszyce. But this daughter, Jadviga, herself had no children, so that not only had Jagiello to earn and keep the favour of the Polish magnates during his own reign—he was no mere Prince Consort—but he had to grant concessions in 1425, 1430, and 1431 to secure the succession for his sons. Thus by pure chance—the accident that neither Casimir nor Lewis nor Jadviga had sons—the throne of Poland became elective. The fact that it was in practice hereditary for nearly two hundred years in the family of Jagiello was due to the importance of maintaining the union with Lithuania, where it was hereditary by custom. In theory the whole body of the *Szlachta* elected the king. In practice he was chosen by the chief dignitaries of the realm. His election was followed by his coronation in Cracow by the Archbishop of Gniezno, after which he usually confirmed the rights and privileges granted by his predecessors. But although he was elected, the king was responsible to no one save in so far as he was bound to observe the terms of the charters. He was chief legislator. The Sejm was encroaching on his legislative powers, but did not seriously curtail them till the next century. The king was also chief judge, commander of the army, and supreme administrator. He governed the provinces through the *Starostas*, whose functions have been described. The central administration was carried on by ministers and officials whose numbers and importance were constantly growing: the Marshal who managed the Court, the Hetman who commanded the army in the field, the Treasurer, and—most important of all—the Chancellor and Deputy Chancellor who conducted all diplomatic correspondence, published all royal acts, received petitions, and spoke for the king in the parliament.

Alongside the administration, there grew up in the fifteenth century a parliamentary system, important not only as a system of representation, but as a close bond between the different provinces. The Polish Sejm or parliament in its final form consisted of a Senate and a House of Deputies. The origin of these two bodies was quite separate. In each *Wojewodztwo* there had been for some time a *Wiec* or council, composed in the main of the officials of the province. But as general matters began to interest all the provinces, it became the custom, after the death of Casimir III, for general councils to meet to discuss the question of privileges or the succession to the throne. Such general councils became more frequent in the fifteenth century. Such a general council was summoned by the king and consisted of the Bishops, *Wojewodas*, *Kasztelans*, and for a time members of the *Szlachta*. With them sat the king and his ministers, and the body thus constituted came to be called the Sejm. Quite different was the origin of the House of Deputies. The ordinary *Szlachta* began to take a lively interest in the great questions of the fifteenth century, particularly the struggle with the Church, the Hussite question, and the war with the Teutonic Order. At first they began to combine in "Confederations", *i.e.* temporary unions for a specific purpose, sometimes in support of the Government, more usually in opposition to it. The towns had formed such a Confederation in 1310, and the *Szlachta* in 1352 had combined against the king. Though the rise of parliamentary institutions superseded the Confederation, it always remained as an extraordinary Polish institution. The *Szlachta* found a better medium for the expression of their views in the Council of Justice held in each province by the *Starosta*. Here, besides the transaction of legal business, it was customary for the gentry to meet and discuss local affairs. In the middle of the fifteenth century these councils split up into two parts, the Court of Justice and the *Sejmik* or Little Sejm, an assembly of all the *Szlachta* of the province under their *Wojewoda*. The constitutional importance of the *Sejmiki*, which originated in Greater Poland, dates from the time when the king, who was pledged to impose no new taxation on the *Szlachta* without their consent, found it expedient to refer matters of this kind to these assemblies. The Polish parliament was at first composed of the original Sejm, which came to be called the Senate, and the whole body of *Sejmiki* in the provinces. It was soon found convenient for the *Sejmiki* to send their deputies to the Sejm, and thus the House of Deputies was formed. But the actual power of the *Sejmiki* remained unchanged. They continued to meet, to make their decisions, and the deputy sent to the central Sejm was merely a delegate bound by the mandate of his *Sejmik*. As regards the clergy, the king dealt with questions of taxation at the synods, so that they were never represented in the Sejm. The towns were asked to send representatives, but though from time to time such delegates appeared, it was customary for Cracow only to send a deputy to the lower House. As the gentry had full representation in the House of Deputies, the Senate was limited to the Bishops, *Wojewodas*, *Kasztelans*, and the Ministers, numbering eighty-seven in all at the end of the century. Since there were no titles in Poland, save the honorary title of Prince given to descendants of Rurik and Gedymin, a seat in the Senate was esteemed a high honour and the offices of *Wojewoda* and *Kasztelan* were generally held by the great families in each province. The Sejm met in time of necessity at the summons of the king at no fixed place, but usually at Piotrków. The procedure was for the Senate to assemble and greet the king. The House of Deputies met separately and elected its Marshal. The king, through the Chancellor, then addressed the united Houses and presented the business for discussion. Then followed the vote of the Senate, which in early days decided the matter. But as the influence of the Deputies grew, the lower House too deliberated apart and voted. The two Houses could combine for common discussion. In the House of Deputies unanimity must be secured to pass a measure, since each Deputy had a mandate from a *Sejmik* representing the *Szlachta* of a whole province, which had already decided on its policy. Further, in matters of taxation which rested on fundamental charters, only the whole *Szlachta* of a province could agree to a change of policy. The right of one Deputy to stop the business of the House by his veto was thus inherent in the parliamentary system, and resulted from the power of the *Sejmiki* over the Sejm. It was not its use but its abuse which became so disastrous in later times. To pass a bill, the consent of King, Senate, and House of Deputies was necessary. The Polish Sejm, which thus developed as a legislative and representative institution, represented chiefly the *Szlachta* and its legislative activities were confined to matters which interested them as a class.

Besides the political predominance which the gentry were gaining by the parliamentary system, a great economic change began towards the end of the fifteenth century—a change which also contributed to overthrow the balance between the classes. The period of peasant prosperity reached its height in the reigns from Casimir III to the death of Jagiello. But in the middle of the century, for economic and other reasons, the gentry began to find rents derived from their peasants insufficient. The fall in the value of money, and the increased standard of living due to contact with the nobles of Western Europe, caused the land-owners to increase their rents. Further, the revolution in military tactics had displaced the levy of the *Szlachta* as a military force by professional mercenary soldiers. The knight found his vocation gone, and he settled down on the land as an agriculturalist. In order to find labour for the expansion of his small farm into a large estate that would pay, he began to demand more work from his dependants, and the small burden hitherto laid on the peasant began to grow into the formidable *panszczyzna* or forced labour which became the economic basis of the serfdom which grew up in the next century. The new intensive agriculture of the *Szlachta* found specially good fields in Red Russia and Podolia. Later on, the export of corn through Danzig to Western Europe began, and gave the land-owners a market for their products. This economic change was followed by a tendency to limit the autonomy and civil rights of the peasant class. Their autonomy was brought to an end by the purchase of the office of *Soltys* or headman by the local squire, who took over with the office the rights attaching to it. Further, by legislation in 1493 and 1496 completed in the next century, the peasant was forbidden to leave his village unless he obtained the consent of the squire. The curtailment of the peasant's right of appeal to the royal courts gradually brought him under the jurisdiction of his lord. Thus, though the peasant remained a landholder, his burdens were increased and his economic and political position considerably weakened.

The prosperity of the towns also received a severe blow. The German population after 1311 had ceased to present a political problem. Content to avail themselves of the advantages of the rising power of Poland and the autonomy based on past charters, they developed their wealth particularly by the Eastern transit trade. They occasionally sent deputies to the Sejm, but generally were not interested in national questions except in so far as they affected trade, when they found it simpler to deal directly with the ministers. But their prosperity suffered from the occupation of the Black Sea coast by the Turks, the rise of the Crimean Khanate, and the ruin of the Genoese colonies. At the same time the discovery of the sea-route to India altered the whole system of trade routes. The same causes which created the commercial prosperity of Spain, Portugal, Holland, and England, ruined the cities of Poland and Red Russia. Eastern products were imported by sea to Danzig. Further, the landowner began to envy the wealth of the burghers and to compete with them, and to deal directly with the merchants of Danzig through their own agents who were often Jews. Danzig, which benefited enormously by the fall of Novgorod, rose to great wealth and power at the expense of the other cities.

The *Szlachta*, on the other hand, steadily increased their political power during the fifteenth century. Their rights as a class were based on a series of concessions granted by the Jagiello kings, from the Charter of Czerwinsk in 1422 containing the important clause "Neminem captivabimus nisi iure victum," and the Statutes of Nieszawa in 1454 which raised the *Sejmiki* to constitutional importance, to the important "Nil Novi" Act of 1505 which legalised the position of the Sejm. These concessions gave the *Szlachta* a privileged position above other classes and at the same time gave it a dominant place in the government of the State. It must be remembered that the Polish *Szlachta*, often incorrectly described as an aristocracy, was a very large body which had been recruited freely from many sources, and contained, besides the element which was elsewhere called the nobility, elements which were known in other countries as knights, lesser gentry, or yeoman farmers. All these elements had been merged in the *Szlachta*, in which in legal theory strict equality existed. No distinction was made between magnate and small farmer, rich and poor, Pole, Lithuanian, Russian, and German. There was no peerage, and the highest dignities were in theory open to the humblest *Szlachcic*. Moreover, at the end of the century the *Szlachta* were placing their position on a firmer economic basis by settling down to farm their own estates. They also began to assume family names. An individual usually formed his family name by the addition of the suffix *-ski* to the name of his estate. Having in every way established its position as a class, the *Szlachta* proceeded to close its ranks. Thenceforward admission to the class was strictly limited and was only possible in cases of adoption by the clan or the conferment of nobility by the king. As a result of this increase in the privileges of the *Szlachta* the balance of classes, which had been stable since 1374, began to be seriously disturbed, and by 1505 the *Szlachta* had risen to be the predominant body as against the peasants, burghers, the Church, and even the King. This phenomenon can only be explained by the weakness of the other classes. There was no class strong enough to be a counterbalance to the *Szlachta*. The peasantry were sinking into serfdom, the middle class was partly foreign and politically indifferent, while the gentry were patriotic, politically conscious, and rapidly absorbing from the humanism of the time the ideals of ancient Rome. The monarchy had no traditions of Roman law to support its dignity; there was no social or religious struggle of which a king might take advantage to strengthen his position; there was no national class except the gentry who by their power of election and of legislation in the Sejm could control the power of the monarch. Poland was about to enter an age, in which monarchy was to be almost universally supreme in Europe, under the rule of a democratic gentry and a representative parliament without parallel save in Hungary and England. The tolerance with which Poland had admitted great bodies of religious dissidents to her State, and extended a share in all her institutions to foreigners who were politically far behind the Poles, was destined to cause great danger in the future. But such danger was scarcely visible on the horizon in the fifteenth century, when the royal power was still considerable, and the prestige of Poland abroad was equalled by her vigorous political life at home. The fifteenth century was an age of astonishingly rapid developments in Poland, and marked a great triumph for all the Northern Slavs. Though the Czechs, the Poles, and the Muscovites were acting quite independently—even with hostility to each other—each of these nations achieved success in its own way; and Slavdom, which in the thirteenth and fourteenth centuries had been crushed between the Tartar hammer and the German anvil, rose not only to liberty, but to power, and was able to inflict severe blows on its former German and Tartar oppressors.

The political development of Poland was reflected in its intellectual advance. The Academy established in Cracow by Casimir the Great had not survived the troubled times of Lewis. By the zeal of Jagiello and Jadviga, the University of Cracow was founded again in 1400; and besides the study of law, the teaching of theology, mathematics, and astronomy was established. The university played its part both in the education of the Polish youth and in the theological controversies of the time. Among its professors was the astronomer, Wojciech of Brudzewo, one of whose pupils was the famous Nicholas Kopernik. The language of science and literature in Poland continued to be Latin. For many reasons—the difficulty of adapting the Latin alphabet to Polish phonology, the use of Latin by the Catholic Church and all the early educators of the Poles—the Polish language was not adopted as a literary medium, as Russian was in the Kievan period, until the Reformation. Some works in Polish have come down from earlier periods, but the annals, the lives of saints, and the chronicles are in Latin. A successor to Gallus and Kadlubek appeared in the chronicler, John of Czarnków. In the fifteenth century appeared the great figure of John Dlugosz. Son of a knight who fought at Grunwald, Dlugosz became secretary to the great Cardinal Oleśnicki, under whose patronage he maintained close touch with the high politics of his time. Casimir IV chose him to serve on various embassies and entrusted to him the education of his sons. Among his many important works, his title to fame rests on his *History of Poland* in twelve volumes, modelled on the style of Livy and combining a mastery of the Latin tongue and style with a great power of graphic narrative and a masterly handling of his subject. His book remained the standard history of Poland until the eighteenth century, and even to-day it is one of the leading authorities for the history of the fifteenth century. The chief intellectual movement of the time was due to the influence of the revival of humanistic studies in Italy. Many Poles were wont to visit Italy for their education and to bring back the new knowledge to Poland. This contact was made closer after the Council of Basle, and it found its chief exponent in Oleśnicki, whose style and oratory excited the admiration of the papal court. Foreigners like Callimaco Buonaccorsi came to settle in Poland and influenced the natives. Callimaco himself wrote the life of one of the leading Polish humanists, Gregory of Sanok, Archbishop of Lemberg, who lectured on Virgil at Cracow. The movement brought the Poles into the intellectual stream of Europe, and it was not limited to mere subtleties of style or theological controversies. In John Ostroróg, *Wojewoda* of Poznań, appeared a really original thinker. He compared Rome with Poland, supported the idea of the emancipation of the State from the Church, and offered quite modern views as to the organisation of the State. He displays a strong sense of nationality in his attitude towards the Germans. "Let everyone", he writes, "who dwells in Poland learn the Polish language." He represents both the nationalism of his country and the keen interest in political science which became so prominent a feature of Polish literature. The humanistic movement undoubtedly brought an interest in Roman history to the *Szlachta,* and contributed to that view of a patrician republicanism which was becoming the ideal of the Polish gentry.

GENEALOGICAL TABLE OF THE PIAST DYNASTY

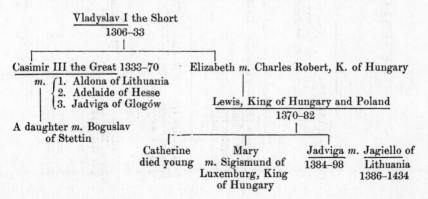

Vladyslav I the Short
1306–33

Casimir III the Great 1333–70   Elizabeth *m.* Charles Robert, K. of Hungary
m. 1. Aldona of Lithuania
2. Adelaide of Hesse
3. Jadviga of Głogów

Lewis, King of Hungary and Poland
1370–82

A daughter *m.* Boguslav of Stettin

Catherine died young   Mary *m.* Sigismund of Luxemburg, King of Hungary   Jadviga 1384–98 *m.* Jagiello of Lithuania 1386–1434

586

GENEALOGICAL TABLE OF THE DYNASTY OF GEDYMIN

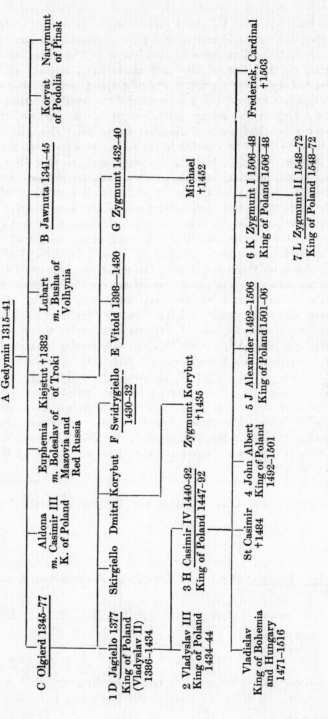

A Gedymin 1315-41

C Olgierd 1345-77   Euphemia m. Boleslav of Mazovia and Red Russia   Kiejstut †1382 of Troki   Lubart m. Busha of Volhynia   B Jawnuta 1341-45   Koryat of Podolia   Narymunt of Pinsk

Aldona m. Casimir III K. of Poland

1 D Jagiello 1377 King of Poland (Vladyslav II) 1386-1434

Skirgiello   Dmitri Korybut   F Swidrygiello 1430-32   E Vitold 1398-1430   G Zygmunt 1432-40

Zygmunt Korybut †1435

2 Vladyslav III King of Poland 1434-44   3 H Casimir IV 1440-92 King of Poland 1447-92

Michael †1452

Vladislav King of Bohemia and Hungary 1471-1516   St Casimir †1484   4 John Albert King of Poland 1492-1501   5 J Alexander 1492-1506 King of Poland 1501-06   6 K Zygmunt I 1506-48 King of Poland 1506-48   Frederick, Cardinal †1503

7 L Zygmunt II 1548-72 King of Poland 1548-72

Names underlined with letters are Grand Princes of Lithuania.
Names with numbers are Kings of Poland.

CHAPTER XIX

HUNGARY, 1301–1490

THE Magyar nation, which at the close of the ninth century migrated from the Bulgarian-Chazar culture-zone north of the Caucasus and the Black Sea to the heart of Europe, made its new home in a territory adjoining three different spheres of civilisation. Settled at the point of contact between communities—the Western Latin-Germanic, the East European Greek-Slavonic, and the Nomad Turkish which had penetrated as far as the Carpathians—differing from one another (even antagonistic to one another) in race, natural endowments, culture, and political organisation, it became the chief problem of Magyar history to balance the forces of West and East and to secure a peaceful habitation between them. The Magyar State had to decide very early which of these civilisations to choose as the basis for its own.

The choice between Asia and Europe had been already made by the Magyars in their original home, when the Onogur ancestors of the race joined their Bulgarian kin in separating from the nomad Asiatic group of peoples; under Iranian and Greek influence they adopted settled life, changing from nomad shepherds into half-nomads practising agriculture as well. This separation was widened by Duke Árpád, the leader of the Magyar conquerors who occupied Hungary[1], when he made an alliance with Leo, Emperor of Constantinople, and Arnulf, Emperor of the West, against his eastern Patzinak and Bulgarian enemies, and then in his new country assumed a defensive attitude of complete isolation from the East. At the end of the tenth and beginning of the eleventh century the nation also made its choice between Byzantium and Rome. By creating permanent peaceful connexions with the West, providing for the conversion of their people, and establishing the Hungarian Catholic Church and the Christian kingdom, Duke Géza and St Stephen, the first King of Hungary, paved the way for the spread of Western culture and Western modes of life, and definitively brought the Magyars into the Latin-Germanic civilisation. A century later St Ladislas and Koloman (Kálmán) completed the organisation of the State and Church administration of their patriarchal kingship. Reaching the natural frontiers, they created the geographical unity of historical Hungary, and established the long-lasting union of the Magyar and Croatian peoples which lived amid similar conditions at the meeting of East and West. After the lapse of another half-century, Géza II and Béla III, who had been brought up in the highly cultured court of Manuel, Emperor of Constantinople and ambitious to add the West to his Empire, strengthened the ties binding their nation

[1] See *supra*, Vol. IV, Chap. VII.

to the West by establishing family relationships with the Western—
French, Spanish, English—dynasties, by the settlement in Hungary of
French monks and German, Flemish, and Walloon farmers and craftsmen,
by sending Hungarian priests and Court knights abroad for their education, and by creating fresh political connexions. Obtaining suzerainty
over the Balkan States, which were engaged in dividing among themselves
the inheritance of the Byzantine Empire then falling to pieces, Béla III
established the Balkan hegemony of the Hungarian kingdom; and his son
Andrew II was actually able to enter the lists with some chance of success
as a candidate for the crown of the Latin Emperors of Constantinople.
This endeavour was wrecked on the opposition of the Holy See of
Rome; but Hungary became one of the leading powers of Western
Christendom at the gateway of the East. In the days of Andrew II, the
ideas of Western feudalism and the spirit of the age of chivalry penetrated
into the country; and the spirit of the patriarchal kingship was gradually
supplanted by the triumphant advance of the system of Estates. The
Hungarian kingdom was transformed into a complete Western State, and
Hungarian society into a society of Estates organised on a Western model.
But this transformation, which took two centuries and a half, was not
effected smoothly or without upheavals.

The Christian faith had to fight a bitter contest against the pagan inclinations of the orientally conservative section of the Magyar people;
the opposition of the latter was enhanced by the bitterness felt against
the domination of the foreign elements—mostly German priests and
feoffees—who had acquired a position of authority in the Court and
administration of the first kings of Hungary; while the situation was still
further aggravated by the aggression of the Romano-Germanic Empire
in the eleventh century, which even threatened the independence of the
country. The immigrations encouraged by the Hungarian kings for
military and economic reasons gave rise to racial antagonisms. The
original elements of the nation—the Finnish-Ugrian and Onogur-Turkish
(Bulgarian) sections—had long been welded into a single race by many
centuries of common life; but the Chazars (Kabars), who had joined
the Magyars during the period immediately preceding the conquest of
Hungary, as also the Patzinaks, Uzes (Guzes), Cumans, and Turkish-
Bulgarian and Arab immigrants who were continually making their way
into the new home of the Magyars, together with the Pannonian Slavs,
Slovaks, and Bulgarian Slavs, whom the Magyars found in Hungary at the
time of its occupation, the Slavonians, Croat-Dalmatians, Bosnians, Serbs,
Bulgarians, Cumans, Wallachians, and Russians subjected to Magyar rule
by conquests made in the south and north-east, and the immigrants from
the west and south—dense swarms of Germans and Flemings, scattered
groups of French (Walloons) and Lombard-Italian colonists—all these
elements composed a motley crowd which sowed the seeds of fresh racial
antagonisms in the Magyar State. There was a continnal struggle between

the Western political and social organisation introduced by the royal power and the forces of the older social system. With the overthrow of the clan chieftains the older political organisation came to an end; but the tribal organisation of society remained unimpaired, and the clans of the free Magyars (nobles) fought for a very considerable period before yielding place to the new social communities based upon feudal ties. For centuries the original social system of clans existed as a living force side by side with the royal power established in Hungary on the model of the Frankish imperial organisation and under the influence of feudal ideas.

The first national dynasty did the country yeoman service in gradually eliminating these antagonisms. However, in the middle of the thirteenth century the strife broke out again. Immigrations from East and West, the settlement of large masses of Cumans in the Tisza district, together with the German influence prevailing as a result of the settlement of German feoffees—an influence enhanced by the autonomy enjoyed by the Saxons who had settled in compact masses on the northern and south-eastern frontiers—revived the racial antagonism between the Eastern and Western elements of the population. Under the influence of pagan Cuman and other Eastern (mostly Muslim and Arab) immigrants, the pagan movement began once more to make headway, while Islām appeared as a fresh influence making for disintegration. Whereas on the one hand the activity of the monks and especially in the thirteenth century of the friars, who enjoyed the support of the Court, led to gratifying symptoms of a deepening of religious life, on the other hand there were signs of the growth of complete religious apathy and of anti-clerical and even anti-religious tendencies. The ecclesiastical and secular owners of great estates, which had come into being as the result of enfeoffments on a large scale involving the transfer to private ownership of a considerable proportion of the once enormous Crown lands early in the thirteenth century, began in feudal fashion to organise themselves as an order in the State. This was followed immediately by a movement aiming at counteracting the power of the great estates, *viz.* the territorial organisation of the military freemen (nobles possessing small estates, royal *servientes*, and *milites castri*) and the establishment of the autonomous (noble) county assemblies (shire-moots). The crystallisation of the classes of prelates, magnates (*barones*), and lesser nobility naturally led to the Estates making endeavours to ensure their privileges and obtain political rights. The result of these endeavours was the Golden Bull of 1222—issued by King Andrew II within a few years of the Great Charter of England and in respect of constitutional law pointing to Aragonese influence—which, like the other charters of similar purport dating from the thirteenth century, survived the Acts of the years 1231, 1267, 1291, and 1298, and in 1351 was re-confirmed. From that date it remained in force—apart from the abrogation of the *ius resistendi* in 1687—as the fundamental law of the privileges of the nobility and of the constitution benefiting the Estates, or rather the noble classes, as late as the middle of the nineteenth century.

The Golden Bull was merely one symptom of the great evolution— the break-up of the older organisations and institutions and the gradual formation of new ones—which had begun in the white-hot atmosphere of social, economic, and political movements. There could not be any question now of hindering the dissolution of the older patriarchal kingship and of the institutions of the ancient social organisation which had lived and co-operated with that kingship. The transformation was indeed retarded and the final dissolution postponed during the reign of Béla IV (1235–70) by the strength of the royal power and the social organisation; but the catastrophe that followed in the wake of the Mongol invasion released the forces of dissolution; and during the reign of the infant king Ladislas IV (1272–90), whose mother was a Cuman, and who himself betrayed decided pagan inclinations, there ensued complete anarchy. As a result of the destructive action of personal, social, economic, political, and racial antagonisms the edifice of State and society suddenly began to totter; and by the close of the century, despite the well-intentioned endeavours of the last king of the house of Árpád, Andrew III (1290–1301), there was a general collapse.

Great landed barons eager to possess power seized the reins of government. The barons holding the highest offices in Court and State began to exercise their official power as a species of private authority: the counties and provinces were treated as private property; and, binding the populations of whole provinces to their service by means of feudal ties, these magnates strove to establish hereditary feudal principalities modelled on those of the West. At the opening of the new century neither the central power, nor the prelates of the Church, nor even the lesser nobility organised in counties, succeeded in effectively resisting the might of the usurpers. The first family dynasty of the new oligarchy was established about 1275 by the Counts of Kőszeg (Ban Henry and his sons), descended from the German Heder clan which had migrated to Hungary in the twelfth century. These magnates subjected to their direct or indirect rule the district lying on the right bank of the Danube, as far south as the line of the Save. To the south of the Kőszegis, in the part of the trans-Save Croatian province stretching north from the Kapela range, the Counts of Vodicha—ancestors of the Blagais of later days— acquired supreme control. The northern section of the Croatian seaboard and the islands of Veglia and Arbe were the hereditary province of the Frangepán family. In Croatia beyond the Kapela range the Counts Subich of Brebir—Ban Paul and his sons—ruled as independent princes, extending their influence at times to the Dalmatian towns and Chulmia (Hum) and Bosnia as well. In like manner to these dynasties of German and Croatian origin in the western and southern marches, in the north and east autocratic power was acquired by Matthias Csák, Ladislas Kán, and

Amadé Aba, descendants of the Magyar dukes who had taken part in the occupation of the country, and by Stephen Ákos and Kopasz Borsa, also scions of ancient Magyar clans. Matthias Csák defied the authority of the king as lord of the north-west highlands, Amadé as lord of the north-east highlands; Kopasz ruled over the district between the Upper Tisza and the Kőrös; the Ákos clan shared the rule of the northern half of the region between the Danube and the Tisza, together with the hilly districts stretching above it, with the Rátolds, a family of French origin; while Ladislas Kán ruled supreme as voïvode of Transylvania. In the territory of the South Cumania of former days the voïvode Basaraba laid the foundations of the future Wallachian principality. In the trans-Save provinces embracing the northern part of the Bosnia and Serbia of to-day —the districts flanking Mačva and Belgrade—a member of the Serbian Nemanja dynasty (Stephen Dragutin, who had wedded a member of the house of Árpád) acquired princely authority; while the eastern half of the Szerém district and of the region between the Drave and the Save was under the sway of Ugrin Csák, a kinsman of the lord of the north-west highlands. On both banks of the middle Tisza an autonomous clan organisation of nomad Cumans had developed into an important power. Apart from the family estates of the royal house lying between Fehérvár and Buda, the only part of the country which remained independent of the influence of the various over-mighty magnates was the territory between the Maros, the lower Tisza, and the lower Danube.

With the extinction of the national dynasty the key to the situation passed into the hands of the great barons, who claimed royal authority; combining in leagues, these magnates endeavoured to secure the throne for their own candidates. There were several pretenders to the throne, all basing their claims on descent in the female line from Árpád, seeing that the great nobles now at feud all agreed that the new king must be chosen from the descendants of the first duke of the country, as provided in the ancient covenant made with him. From the very outset the candidate who had the best chance of success was Charles Robert (Carobert) of Anjou, grandson of Charles II of Naples and Mary of Hungary, who stood nearest to the throne in the order of inheritance in the female line. For years, however, the victory of his claim was hindered by the support of the Pope, who had granted Hungary to his *protégé* as a fief without consulting the Hungarian Estates. He was acknowledged by the Croatian nobles, with Ban Paul Subich at their head, and by a few Magyar nobles in the south. He was indeed actually crowned by them; but his coronation was declared invalid by the majority of the nation. All the prelates and large numbers of aristocrats and lesser nobles, under the leadership of the most powerful oligarchs, determined to support the claim of Wenceslas, prince of Bohemia, the chosen son-in-law of the last king of the house of Árpád, whose father was the great-grandson of Béla IV and had claimed the Hungarian throne at the time of the accession of Andrew III. Nevertheless, the papal legates—Cardinals Nicholas Boccasini and Gentile—succeeded by skilful diplomacy in winning the prelates to the side of Charles Robert, and later also gained over the over-mighty barons. After this change in the public temper neither Wenceslas nor Duke Otto of Bavaria, who made an attempt to secure the throne after his departure, was able to hold the field.

When Gentile had acknowledged in the Pope's name—though only tacitly—the right of the Estates to approve the succession and elect their king by acclamation, the Estates on their part acknowledged the right of the Pope to confirm the election; and in 1308 the young Angevin prince was acclaimed the lawful hereditary King of Hungary, to reign under the name of Charles, and was subsequently crowned with the Holy Crown of St Stephen.

With the accession of Charles I (1308–42) we enter a fresh and a brilliant period of Hungarian history, which closed with the death of Matthias Hunyadi in 1490, and may be called the period of Hungary's greatness as a medieval power. During this era Hungary played just as leading a rôle in the direction of affairs in the eastern region of Western Christendom as France and England did in the western region. The monarchs who laid the foundation of this position as a Great Power were the native kings Géza II and Béla III. But its full development was due to the branch of the French Capetian dynasty which had found its way to Hungary—to the Hungarian branch of the house of Anjou, and in particular to Charles I, who, after finally breaking the power of the provincial dynasts, against whom he fought unceasingly for a decade and a half, created the economic, military, and administrative substructure of this power by dint of a quarter of a century of skilful organising work.

It was out of the question to restore the older political organisation—the immense royal domains and the patriarchal power built up on that organisation; and Charles, being a practical politician, never attempted to do so. During the era of internal struggles and of the rise of magnate oligarchs, the older institutions had fallen into decay and the older ties had been severed. The royal boroughs had to a large extent come into the possession of the provincial dynasts and their adherents, some of them falling into the hands of the lesser nobility, which had grown into a separate class by the inclusion of all the freemen doing military service. The parts of the country left in the immediate possession of the Crown took the form of small farming establishments grouped round the numerous royal castles built for purposes of national defence after the Mongol invasion. The most important constituent elements of the former royal army—the battalions of the *milites castri* and the *servientes*—had been dispersed, or had been absorbed in the private armies of the provincial magnates, and from being the organs of the central power developed into instruments of the centrifugal forces serving the ambitions of the local dynasts. Extensive organisations for the exercise of political power came into being round the persons of single over-mighty barons. The victory of the king did indeed result in these provincial organisations falling to pieces; but their remains came into the possession, not of the king himself, but of the landowning class which had maintained its loyalty to the Crown—of the new aristocracy which had taken part in the overthrow of the great dynasts, and of the landed gentry who had been delivered from the pressure of those barons' power. Numerous economic, social, and military units and corporations quite independent of one another—privileged members of the landed class and autonomous counties—secured an existence of their own; and in Hungary in the abeyance of the central power the economic and military forces had been in the hands of these units and corporations. Had the older tribal organisation of society been in existence, this state of things would have involved a great danger to the royal power. That organisation was, however, already defunct. During the interregnum the ancient clans followed the institutions of the kingship and fell into decay; and the consciousness of tribal interconnexion disappeared among the branches of the original clans. During the internal struggles the branches of the clans, which had become estranged politically and disunited geographically, formed into independent families and became antagonists; and the separation became complete after the victory of King Charles. The clan-names (*e.g. de genere Csák*)—which denoted tribal interconnexion and expressed the economic, legal, and cultural community uniting the members of the several clans—lost their vogue; and the new families which had separated from the clans adopted independent family names of their own. The place of the older society resting on the basis of tribal connexions and feudal relations was taken by a new society of Estates based upon class ties. Among the lesser nobility there had been signs of a process of unification as far back as 1222—a process expressed in 1351 in the unification of the law of inheritance for the nobility. The property-law of the clans which occupied the country, under which allodial freehold passed from branch to branch within the clan and was completely inalienable until the extinction of descendants in the male line, was extended by the law of "entail" (*avicitas*) to those sections of the nobility—the descendants of the original feoffees, of *servientes, milites castri*, etc.—which had formerly under the feudal law been able to inherit only in the line of the original feoffees and their brothers; these sections had already, under the Golden Bull of 1222, acquired the other privileges of nobility. The adoption of the principle of "entail" had eliminated all legal differences between the various members of the landed nobility (great and small proprietors); and it had also removed the former motley character of the society composed of the free military elements differentiated according to the character of the service. Great landed baron, noble official, noble with a medium-sized estate, and lesser noble in the service of some lord whose service was based upon feudal relations—all alike were now legally members of one and the same class (*una et eadem nobilitas*). But the differences in respect of wealth and social position still remained. Accordingly, the owners of great estates who enjoyed immunity from the county administration still continued to play the part of an independent aristocratic class (*barones et proceres*); and this magnate class organised itself in its turn, so that despite the equality of the nobles before the law there was still a clear differentiation between the prelates, magnates, and lesser nobility as distinct classes of society—a differentiation which found expression in a bitter political struggle between those classes. In the new organisation of society the class next below the lesser nobility was that comprising the bourgeoisie, provided by the foreigners (*hospites*) of the town communities and settlements, and the elements (partly foreign— German, French, and Italian—and partly Magyar) of the free merchants, craftsmen, and agriculturists living in the autonomous parish organisations. The innumerable fractions of the lower stratum of society, divided according to the character and measure of their previous feudal service, which were subject to baronial jurisdiction and did not possess either privileges of nobility or civil rights—the descendants of freemen, freedmen, and slaves—were now welded into one large uniform peasant class. This class had previously been the highest among free dependents on the king and the lords; it inherited the name of *jobbágy*, which came to correspond to the English villein[1]; but in respect of imposts it was on a level with the former lower classes of *servientes*.

King Charles used every means to further the advance in wealth and power of the new landed families which owed their origin to the break-up of the older clans; for he desired to build up the new political organisation of his kingdom, in keeping with the change of conditions, on the basis of the economic strength of his subjects, above all of the new landed aristocracy. In 1324, when the power of the insurgent dynasts had been completely shattered, he followed the example set by the older kings of the house of Árpád and allotted the chief offices of State—formerly the objects of barter between the king and the owners of the great estates—to his most trustworthy personal adherents, who, being put at the head of the counties and of the Transylvanian, Slavonian, Croatian, and other provinces, laboured systematically to create order and to augment the authority and the military and economic resources of the kingship.

The new military organisation was based on the power of the new landed classes, which, while they could not vie in wealth and political strength with the provincial dynasts who had been overthrown, as a whole represented the united strength of the country, and on the economic strength of the great ecclesiastical and secular landowners and of the county nobility; this organisation was called "banderial," the name being taken from the military banner (*bandiere*) which now came into fashion. In contrast to the army of the house of Árpád based upon the military tenants of the royal

[1] By derivation it originally meant a free member of the Magyar host; cf. the Lombard *arimannus*, who likewise suffered degradation in the course of time.

estates, this new army was composed of the armed bands (*banderia*) of the landed classes—*i.e.* of king, prelates, great barons, and lesser nobility—which were thus the private forces of the Estates. The strength of a *banderium* ranged from 300 to 400 (later, in the fifteenth century, it had only 50) mounted knights or soldiers; while the troops of the land-owners supplying a smaller number of armed men were included, together with the lesser nobles who took the field in person, in the county bat-talions—in the subordinate provinces, in the provincial battalions—also called *banderia*. The peace footing of the royal *banderium* was 1000 horsemen; but in times of war it was supplemented and reached a far larger number. An important complementary element of the royal army was supplied by the garrisons serving under castellans in the castles scat-tered all over the country, which played a significant rôle in securing the peaceful administration of the provinces and ensuring the maintenance of order and consolidation.

The new army—the origins of which, despite its having been organised on French and Neapolitan models, reach back to the days of Béla IV—possessed a distinctively feudal character. The *banderia* were to a very large extent private armies; and even the county and provincial *banderia*, which represented the political element, were not without certain feudal features. This military system based upon feudal foundations made the royal power to some extent dependent upon the great landowner class which provided the bulk of the *banderia*. The danger inherent in this cir-cumstance was, however, counteracted by the *banderia* of the king, the queen, and the prelates, and by the county forces of the lesser nobles, who for two centuries consciously opposed the owners of great estates, as well as by the battalions of the Cuman and Saxon settlers directly dependent on the king, of the Siculians (Széklers) of Transylvania, and of the Slavonian nobles, which were under the control of the county sheriffs (*comites*) and other high officials owing their positions to the confidence of the sovereign.

However, Charles also provided another counterpoise. He followed in the footsteps of Andrew II and Béla IV and built up a new organisation of the public finances, which had been deprived of all income from the demesne; he drew upon economic sources independent of the landed baronial class. Such sources were provided by the remnants of the royal demesne and the royal dues and tolls, and in connexion therewith by the taxation of those free elements of the population which were independent of the great estates—in particular of the burghers of the towns who were developing into a professional, industrial, and commercial class. The in-come from the demesne was made more lucrative by the organisation of the small farming establishments referred to above, the possession of which converted the king once more into the wealthiest landowner in the country, though this property was nothing like so enormous as the exten-sive demesne-lands of the kings of the house of Árpád had been. Charles succeeded in augmenting the revenue obtained from the royal customs by a complete re-organisation of the administration of the customs (*regale*), which at the close of the twelfth and beginning of the thirteenth century had provided 44 % of the royal revenue but had subsequently been utterly exhausted. His object was to exploit as far as possible the wealth of the country and to increase his revenue on a large scale. He knew that this object could not be attained by overburdening his subjects, but rather by enhancing their capacity to pay and by increasing the number of contributors through a circumspect economic policy. Behind all his financial reforms there were grouped economic measures aiming at increasing the general welfare of the country. Now that the policy of agricultural settlements followed by the house of Árpád was comparatively of less importance, the king found the chief expedient of his economic policy to be the organisation of industrial and commercial settlements and the foundation of towns. The provision of agricultural settlements was, indeed, still of far-reaching consequence in a country as thinly populated as Hungary, and was effected by the private farming establishments of the landed classes themselves. The prelates, the new aristocracy, and the king himself in his character as a land-owner, did all in their power to encourage immigration. Large numbers of Czech, Polish, Russian, and German settlers entered the highlands of northern Hungary from the adjoining countries and from the more densely inhabited parts of Hungary itself, mostly under the direction of German contractors or factors (*Schultheiss*). And it was at this period that there began, under the direction of Cuman, Bulgarian, and Serbian factors (*Knyaz*), the immigration of Rumanians or Wallachs on a large scale into the wooded districts of Transylvania and the trans-Tisza region.

However, the king attached far greater importance to strengthening the bourgeois element which could be taxed by means of customs and fiscal imposts; and this endeavour was accompanied by the foundation of a whole series of towns (including Bártfa, Eperjes, Kassa, Körmöcbánya, Kolozsvár, Brassó, Beszterce, and Mármarossziget) and by the conferment on others (*e.g.* Buda, Komárom, Pozsony, Sopron) of fresh privileges. Abandoning the system of internal duties, which abuses had made the object of universal hatred, he built up the system of frontier duties which had been developing so strikingly since the beginning of the thirteenth century; he increased the foreign trade of the country by granting various privileges which would enhance the yield of that system, and concluded customs and road agreements with Venice, Bohemia, and Poland. He made an alliance with the King of Bohemia against the Duke of Austria who was exploiting the right of detaining goods in Vienna (*ius stapuli*); and through the mutual acknowledgement by Buda and Brünn (Brno) of the staple right exercised by them he ensured the unbroken course of the trade of the two countries going west and south by diverting it from the Vienna route.

With the new system of mining law, modelled on that of Bohemia, he paved the way for the Hungarian gold mines—the richest in medieval Europe—to increase their production. At the same time he put an end once for all to the system of an annual renewal of the coinage which had been in vogue for centuries; he minted *denarii* and groats of permanent currency, and restored the credit of the Hungarian coinage; and he began the minting of the Hungarian gold florin which continued of the same weight down to the nineteenth century, thus putting into circulation a means of payment in international trade. This measure, by means of the monopoly in the precious metal put into force simultaneously, ensured the Treasury and the mining and trading communities a considerable permanent revenue. At the close of the thirteenth century, owing to the shrinkage of the revenue from the demesnes and customs (*regale*), practically the only reliable source of income was the extraordinary tax (*collecta, subsidium*). After the re-organisation of the customs (*regale*), this lost much of its importance; nevertheless, Charles resorted to the source of income provided by the extraordinary tax, still imposed at this period without consulting the Estates, and fixed its scale at one-quarter or one-eighth of a silver mark per house. By introducing the regular town tax (*census*), originating from a fusion of the tenement rent (*terragium*) and the extraordinary tax, he exploited to an increased degree the taxable capacity of the burghers and the inhabitants of the tenement lands. In connexion with the collection of the papal tithes the king did not shrink even from taxing the Church revenues; he made the licence to collect the tithes subject to the payment to the Treasury of one-third of the revenue accruing, thereby taxing revenues which according to the view then dominant were exempt from taxation. Along with the re-organisation of the customs (*regale*) he placed the fiscal administration upon a new basis—on the lines of decentralisation subject to a business management by tax-farmers who were strictly controlled—under the direction of the royal treasurer (*magister tavarnicorum*).

Whereas the development in national policy, in the military organisation, in the administration, and in the management even of the public finances, was of a feudal tendency, Charles' financial policy developed in a decidedly political direction; this was shewn, not only in the domanial revenues being replaced by revenues obtained on the basis of the *ius regale*, but also in the method of utilising the rights involved therein. The new constitutional State protected itself against the complete feudalisation of the royal power and its reduction to dependence upon private law, by availing itself of economic resources based upon legal relations founded upon public law. The vitality of the new State organisation rested on the two chief pillars of the banderial military system and the customs (*regale*) administration, and the predominance of the central power was secured by distributing the military and economic burdens between two different classes whose interests were divergent, the power of the Crown serving to balance the two. The devolution of the military burdens upon the landed nobility and of the public revenue burdens upon the bourgeoisie meant a proportional and balanced distribution of political functions—at all times the characteristic endeavour of the sovereigns of feudal States who possessed a strong personality.

Along with the re-organisation of the military and financial systems, there was effected a transformation of the administrative and judicial systems too, this being done on the lines of local self-government, although provision was made to secure the intensive influence of the royal power. It was in the days of Charles and with his assistance that the autonomous territorial organisation of the Hungarian landed nobility was fully developed; this noble *comitatus* (county assembly), with its extensive administrative functions and its political rights, is the most character-istically Magyar institution of the feudal State, and has succeeded in a modified form in surviving the latest changes. It was at the same period that the judicial system of the royal *Curia* (Supreme Court of Justice), which has been in existence for centuries since, came into being. The prominence of feudal features in the political organisation and the domi-nance of a spirit of self-government in the provincial administration meant the triumph of the ideas of feudal constitutionalism. In the national policy, however, the royal power stood in the way of the complete pre-dominance of this spirit. There was a break in the constitutional develop-ment which had begun with the Golden Bull and had advanced rapidly at the close of the thirteenth century; there was indeed a reaction. Charles was not inclined to share with his subjects the royal power he had had such difficulty in acquiring, and from 1324 did not even hold a parliament. Though the Estates assembled in Székesfehérvár once every year, on St Stephen's Day (20 August), their assembly did not exceed the dimensions of the royal judicial moots (assizes) of the eleventh and twelfth centuries. The private powers which had obtained a share of the govern-ment had to come to terms with the might of the Crown now reviving in a new form out of the wreck of the kingship established by St Stephen; and it was the union of these two factors that gave birth to the new State organisation of constitutional Hungary, based upon the balanced co-opera-tion of the monarchic and feudal forces, and to the greatest achievement of that co-operation—the position as a great power enjoyed by Hungary in the fourteenth and fifteenth centuries.

The kings of the house of Árpád created two conceptions of foreign policy of a practical value—(1) a defensive alliance with the Holy Roman Empire to meet any eventual danger from the East, and (2) an alliance between Poland, Hungary, Croatia, and the Papal See. This latter alliance was designed to unite the peoples living on the eastern fringe of the Western sphere of civilisation, and be defensive towards the power of Germany and expansive towards the Balkans and the north-east; it also en-visaged a possible *entente* with France. Since the Mongol invasion the foreign policy of Hungary had been based upon the former system; and in the early part of his reign Charles, too, adhered to it. However, as soon as he had succeeded in restoring internal order, he began to look elsewhere. Making succession treaties and a political alliance with his uncles, Casimir and Robert, then reigning in Poland and Naples, he revived the foreign policy of Géza II and Béla III, a policy of which his son Lewis the Great, a king possessing eminent qualities as a man and great capacity as a ruler, also became a most important champion.

At the time of the accession of Lewis the Great (1342–82) the position of Hungary in international politics was an extremely favourable one. The Eastern and Western powers—the two Empires and the Mongols—whose ambitions of expansion had caused so much anxiety in previous centuries, had fallen into utter decay. The only powers of any significance in comparison with or in opposition to the kingdom of Hungary, which had been so enormously strengthened by the reign of the first Angevin king, were the three neighbouring countries of Bohemia (now a kingdom under the half-French house of Luxemburg), Poland, and Serbia. In the case of Poland, however, Lewis, besides being connected by ties of kinship and alliance with its king, was acknowledged as the heir to its throne. Ties of friendship and kinship connected him with the Bohemian Crown Prince too, who barely four years later, as Charles IV, obtained the German and imperial crowns, and was, like Lewis himself, a member of the great French coalition which at this period was master of practically the whole of Europe. Both Lewis and Charles of Bohemia were associated with the French imperialism called into being at the close of the thirteenth century—the schemes of the European hegemony of the Capet-Anjou houses and the dynasties related to them—which resulted in members of these families after 1346 occupying the thrones of most Latin-Christian countries (with the exception of the Scandinavian States) and acquiring also the dignity of Holy Roman Emperor and the empty title of Latin Emperor of Constantinople. As a consequence, there was no danger threatening from east or north or west. There was, however, a serious rival to the south of Hungary: Serbia had, under the rule of Stephen Dušan[1], a gifted and ambitious king of the Nemanja dynasty, made an alliance with Venice (which for two decades had kept the Dalmatian towns under its control), with the Croatian nobles of the south who were discontented with the rule of the Hungarian king, and with the malcontents of the decaying Byzantine Empire, and had achieved the position of a great power. Extending his frontiers on the south as far as the Gulf of Corinth and the Rhodope range, and causing himself to be crowned Tsar, Dušan claimed the inheritance of the Eastern Empire and proposed to extend his power to the north as far as the Save. Against the growing Serbian power, however, Lewis found valuable allies in the lord of the feudal Bosnian province which stood in the way of Serbian

[1] See *supra*, Vol. IV, Chap. XVII.

expansion to the north, as also in the kingdom of Naples, which was in
control of the Albanian seaboard and the Morea. Stephen, Ban of Bosnia,
was a near relative of the Hungarian king; later on, the ties of kinship
were drawn closer still by the marriage of Lewis (after the death of his
Bohemian fiancée) to Stephen's daughter. At the time of Lewis' accession
his younger brother, Andrew, Prince of Salerno, was husband of Joanna,
the heiress of the kingdom of Naples.

In this situation Lewis the Great saw that the first thing he had to do
was to check the movement of the Croatian malcontents, to recover the
Dalmatian coast towns, and to weaken the power of Serbia. The armed
expedition to the south for this purpose was, however, unexpectedly
stopped by the change that took place in Naples in the autumn of 1345.
The Angevins of Naples—the Princes of Durazzo and Taranto, and also
Joanna, the young, ambitious, and inordinately passionate Queen of
Naples herself—looked askance at the efforts to obtain the power made
by her husband Andrew, who claimed a share in the royal authority[1].
At first they merely tried to prevent his coronation; but, when their
efforts failed, they had him murdered by hired assassins. The murder,
which to all appearance was committed with the knowledge of Andrew's
wife and of Louis, Prince of Taranto, was a profound outrage on Lewis
the Great's fraternal feelings and also on the claim to the throne of Naples
inherited from his father, who had been deprived of his inheritance in
favour of the younger branch in the person of King Robert, Joanna's
grandfather. When he heard of the deed of horror, Lewis applied to
Pope Clement VI, the suzerain of Naples, for redress, and requested the
assistance of his father-in-law, Charles IV of Luxemburg, who was on the
friendliest terms with the Pope, his whilom tutor. He sent ambassadors
to the papal Court at Avignon to demand the severe punishment of the
guilty persons and the recognition of his own claim to the Neapolitan
throne. However, all he got from the Pope, who was influenced by Naples
and Paris, was courteous words, his demand for action being met with a
rigid refusal; so in 1347, and again in 1350, he sent a punitive expedition
against Naples. And he did succeed—the Italian towns and princes who
sympathised with him observing a benevolent neutrality—in occupying
the kingdom of Naples at the head of his Hungarian troops and German
mercenaries, and in linking it for three years by a personal union with
Hungary. Yet the Pope, as suzerain, refused to acknowledge the
legality of Lewis' rule; and, as the majority of the Neapolitans regarded
the Hungarian regime with dislike, at the end of 1350 Lewis evacuated
Naples and led his army home. In connexion with these events, his relations became strained with his fiancée's father, the Emperor Charles IV,
who, though to all appearance supporting his son-in-law, remained on
the side of the Franco-Papal alliance which supported Joanna and was
hostile to the King of Hungary. Though it did not lead to a diplomatic
conflict or to any more serious complications than petty warfare carried

---

[1] See *supra*, Vol. VII, p. 62.

on in the interest of Poland, this tension resulted in a final breach between Lewis the Great and the French political combination referred to above. The scheme for a union of the Neapolitan and Hungarian thrones and for the creation of a vast Angevin dominion embracing Italy, the Balkans, Hungary, and Poland had miscarried. The eastern link of the conception of a system of States under the Capet-Anjou houses inaugurated by the French King Philip the Fair and Charles of Anjou, King of Naples, had been torn from the chain of French alliances encircling and dominating the whole of Western Europe. The dynastic schemes of the Hungarian royal house, so far as they were connected with the ambitions of the French dynasties, had failed; and their place was taken by a policy of expansion based upon the foreign policy of the kings of the house of Árpád.

After the failure of the attempt to acquire Naples, Lewis the Great concentrated all his forces on an endeavour to develop to full completion the political conception of the kings of the house of Árpád, to secure the hegemony of the Balkans, to overcome the Serbian, Bulgarian, and Vlach principalities, and to obtain the crown of Poland, which included the former Galician and Lodomerian provinces of Andrew II. In 1358, after a campaign lasting two years, he recovered the Dalmatian towns from Venice, and made the republic of Ragusa, which had not previously been subject to Hungarian rule, acknowledge his suzerainty. Twenty years later Lewis was compelled once more to take up arms in defence of Dalmatia; but after the desperate struggle with the Genoese at Chioggia, Venice, under the Treaty of Turin, renounced all claim to the possession of that province. After securing Dalmatia, Lewis turned against Serbia; and upon the death of Tsar Stephen Dušan he did eventually succeed in making the weak Tsar Stephen Uroš acknowledge his overlordship[1]. He once more conquered and organised the provinces on the right bank of the Save which had belonged to the house of Árpád, the banates of Mačva and Kučevo, and the stronghold of Belgrade. About the year 1360 he annexed to his country as a separate vassal kingdom the northern part of Bulgaria, which had been split into sections. By obtaining possession of Croatia, Dalmatia, Bosnia, Mačva, North Bulgaria, and the two new Vlach principalities of Cumania, the Hungarian kingdom at this period attained its greatest expansion. In 1372, after the death of King Casimir, the crown of Poland too fell to the Hungarian sovereign. With the personal union between Hungary and Poland the Polish-Hungarian-Croatian federation which originated in the eleventh century during the reign of St Ladislas, and had subsequently been frequently revived, was for ten years consolidated into a personal union of States.

The internal government of Lewis the Great was accompanied by results similar to these military and diplomatic successes. The king's noble qualities, which were so highly praised by his contemporaries—his love of justice and his fairness, his chivalry and reverence for law—secured

---

[1] Cf. *supra*, Vol. IV, Chap. XVIII.

him an unprecedented authority. It is characteristic of him that during the forty years of his reign—barely a decade or two after the cessation of the gravest internal disorders—not a single attempt was made by the barons (who were certainly not deficient in tendencies to insubordination) to rebel or incite any political discontent. Great credit is due to Lewis for his revival of the chivalric forms of life, ceremonies and customs which had been introduced at the beginning of the thirteenth century but had subsequently sunk into oblivion in the coarse age of party warfare. There was a formal chivalric court of honour (*curia militaris*) for the maintenance of the laws of honour interpreted in the sense of the age of chivalry. This court, and the Order of the Knights of St George, which was under strict statutes of its own, rendered signal service in refining the forms of social intercourse and in softening the manners which had been made ruder in the age of club-law. The age of the Angevins generally, and that of Lewis the Great in particular, was the golden age in Hungary of respect for the chivalric ideal in the noblest sense of the word and for the spirit of chivalry. In older Hungarian history this spirit of chivalry was expressed in the intensive cult of the figure of the Hungarian king St Ladislas, who was depicted as the ideal chivalric knight—a cult which Lewis himself and later on his son-in-law King Sigismund did everything in their power to foster.

The spirit of the French age of chivalry was manifested also in the support accorded to chivalric poetry, arts, and science. It was the churches erected by Charles and Lewis the Great that raised the Gothic architecture of Hungary—an art abounding in French influences—to its zenith. In the manuscripts belonging to Lewis' library which have come down to us we find the first important products of Hungarian miniature painting; and the taste of his Court is reflected also in the creations of the eminent sculptors, Nicholas Kolozsvári and his two sons Martin and George, one of these creations, the statue of St George in Prague, being among the finest products of contemporary art. There was a noteworthy revival in the production of precious metals in Hungary; and its abundance enabled the silversmith craft of Hungary, which had begun to come to the fore as far back as the days of the Árpád kings, and had subsequently reached a very high level, to make a great advance. A noteworthy cultural creation owing its origin to Lewis the Great was the University of Pécs, which was founded by him in 1367, only two years after the second German university, that of Vienna. In the field of legislation special attention is due to the Act of 1351, by which Lewis the Great confirmed the Golden Bull of 1222, fixing the rights of the nobility for centuries to come and raising the guarantees of the new constitution to the status of a permanent law. It was this same Act that for the first time regulated the feudal obligations of the new peasant class; while in the field of criminal law it broke with the previous practice and forbade the punishment of children for the sins of their fathers.

Since Lewis the Great died without male issue, his death was followed by a fresh period of struggles for the crown. Though the Estates acknowledged his daughter Mary (1382–95) as his heir, Charles of Durazzo, who claimed the throne by right of the male line of the house of Anjou, opposed Sigismund of Luxemburg, Mary's betrothed, who had been designated to share her authority as king, and successfully invaded Hungary. After the tragic murder of Charles in 1387, Sigismund, the younger son of the Emperor Charles IV, was crowned king, though after the death of Queen Mary in 1395 a section of the aristocracy advanced the claims of Charles of Durazzo's son, Ladislas, King of Naples, to the throne. Ladislas based his claim upon his right of succession, while Sigismund based his upon the election of the Estates; and Tvrtko, King of Bosnia, a nephew of Lewis the Great's consort, taking advantage of the chaos that ensued, attempted to wrest the Bosnian and Croat-Dalmatian provinces from Hungary.

The struggle finally ended in favour of Sigismund; but as a result of the feuds the dominions of Lewis the Great had shrunk considerably. Poland had separated from Hungary on the death of Lewis. The throne of Poland was given to Hedwig (Jadviga), Lewis' youngest daughter; and after her premature death the Polish crown came into the sole possession of her husband, Jagiello, Grand Prince of Lithuania, who adopted the name of Vladyslav II, and of his successors. Dalmatia was re-occupied by Venice, while the provinces of the Balkan vassals were conquered at the end of the century by the Ottoman-Turkish hosts which, coming from Asia and surrounding Constantinople, had penetrated into Europe and made a permanent settlement there. Sultan Murād in 1389 annihilated the Serbian forces; in 1396, at Nicopolis, Sultan Bāyazīd gained a bloody victory over the huge army of King Sigismund, which had been reinforced by French, Spanish, German, and Italian auxiliaries[1]. The eastern danger had revived again in the gravest form; and for the next three hundred years the Turkish question became the central problem of Hungarian policy.

The mighty kingdom of the Árpáds and Angevins would have had little difficulty in resisting the Asiatic power, which had at its disposal forces far inferior to those of the Mongol empire of yore; but Sigismund and his successors had not the strength of their predecessors. The succession wars which followed on the extinction of the Angevins combined with the weakness of female rule to bring about events almost the exact counterpart of those which had preceded and followed the extinction of the House of Árpád. The great landed magnates belonging to the aristocracy of the Angevin age were insatiable of wealth and power; and, taking advantage of the situation, they seized the reins of government. A few leading aristocratic families formed leagues and fought bitterly against one another; they did not hesitate during these struggles even to throw their sovereign into prison. And, though the lesser nobility was already

[1] See *supra*, Vol. IV, Chaps. XVIII and XXI.

better able to resist the ambitions of the great land-owners, since the self-governing counties provided them with a fully developed organisation, Sigismund was nevertheless driven to submit to a compromise with the great barons. Being king by election, and the once rich material resources of the Crown being now completely exhausted, the king was dependent upon the support of the landed nobility. He therefore entered into a family alliance with the league of the most powerful lords; and he chose his second wife, Barbara of Cilli, from among them. Besides securing his power in this way, he was, however, set upon strengthening the class of noble freemen which was independent of the great land-owners. During his reign the county organisation of the nobles (*comitatus*) developed into an active political factor; and at the parliaments—now, as a consequence of the triumph of the constitutional spirit, held regularly—the lesser nobility became a serious political power capable of counteracting the influence of the barons.

While on the one hand he secured the lesser nobility as political allies, Sigismund's objects in developing the county organisations (*comitatus*) and extending the rights of the bourgeoisie were of a financial character. His luxurious habits and far-reaching political ambitions involved him in enormous expenditure; and he acquired the necessary funds from the industrial and commercial classes—burghers and Jews—whose resources were drained in a measure far in excess of that of normal taxation. He later, in 1405, shewed his gratitude and esteem outwardly by inviting deputies of the craftsmen too to attend Parliament. This did not, however, confer any political advantages upon this class; for they had only collective votes, one for each corporation, whereas the nobles were entitled to attend in person. There was a financial motive also behind the struggle with the Holy See over the appointments to high offices in the Church; at the outset we find a political reason too, the support given by Pope Boniface IX to Ladislas of Naples against Sigismund, because the latter, in 1404, had issued a *Placetum regium* claiming the right to fill bishoprics and thereby—in the face of the unceasing protests of the Holy See—converting into an effective law the Hungarian king's supreme right of advowson derived from the privileges conferred upon St Stephen. In view of the constantly increasing menace from the Turks, Sigismund also developed the military system considerably. In 1435 the banderial system and its organisation were regulated by law; and Sigismund created the new militia (*militia portalis*) for active service comprised within the limits of the banderial system, the landed nobles being required to provide one well-equipped mounted soldier for every 33 villein holdings, thus bringing the strength of the regular army of Hungary up to some 120,000. However, the new militia imposed fresh serious charges upon the feudal villeins, the mass of the population, who had been excluded from all political rights, though the burdens devolving upon this class at this period were almost intolerable already.

The scale of the contributions in kind payable by the villein class—which came into being in the fourteenth century and remained in existence until its enfranchisement in 1848—had been fixed in 1351 by Lewis the Great at the amount of one-ninth (*nona*) to be collected for every tithe paid to the Church, thus creating a second tithe of each product of the soil. This charge undoubtedly involved a relief as compared with the contributions in kind devolving on the lowest class of agricultural labourers (the *servi*) of the earlier Middle Ages, which amounted to one-third, and indeed even to one-half, of the produce. But it exceeded the measure of the former feudal contributions of the free peasants absorbed into the villein class, who paid their taxes in cash, as also of the classes of freemen and *servientes* who had been required to contribute various imposts or to perform customary labour-services. And the land-owners, even after the systematic introduction of contributions in kind, still formulated a claim both to the previous monetary contributions from the higher classes of the people (the amount of these contributions being a quarter silver mark = 1 gold florin) and also to the various labour-dues, whether performed by men or by their animals. All these burdens were laid upon the villein class as a whole, which was required already to pay two-tenths of its produce. In addition it was compelled to pay the extraordinary royal tax, which had previously been a charge on freemen and freedmen but had not been imposed on the serf classes; this amounted usually to 1 gold florin, though in more than one year it exceeded double, or even quadruple, that amount. The establishment of the new militia (*militia portalis*) further involved the obligation to supply one active soldier for every 33 villein families. Seeing that the members of the peasant class, which possessed no political rights whatsoever, were subject in justice and administration to their feudal lords, they were entirely at the mercy of those lords; and in the period of territorial expansion the lords did not shrink from exploiting the situation. As a result, after the end of the fourteenth century, there was a constant increase in the number of complaints against the encroachments of the prelates, who illegally demanded the payment of their tithes in money, and of the land-owners, who demanded labour-dues in excess of the customary scale and special contributions in kind. Seeing that the government during the reigns of the successors of the Angevins depended exclusively upon the economic resources of the landed classes, the villeins could not hope for any assistance from that quarter. They were indeed granted the right of free migration, and were no longer legally bound to the soil as formerly; but in practice, owing to reasons of an economic nature, this right was hardly capable of being enforced, and offered but little compensation for the constantly increasing charges imposed upon them. All these causes contributed to impoverish the peasantry; and the tendency to increase the public taxes, due to the extravagance of Sigismund and the Turkish wars, rendered the burdens of that class practically intolerable. Its situation had become far worse than that of its forerunners in the thirteenth century, so that it was natural that familiarity with the idea of the literal equality of men, which penetrated into Hungary and Bohemia with the teaching of the Hussites, stirred the peasants to demand a mitigation of their burdens; and when they met with a rigid refusal from ecclesiastical and secular land-owners alike, their discontent found vent in bloody revolt. The first peasant rebellion broke into flame in the last year of Sigismund's reign, and was followed eighty years later by a series of partial revolts culminating in the general peasant rising of 1514, which resulted in the revocation of the villeins' right of free migration and in their complete subjection.

Sigismund's power was made stable and his popularity increased when, after the death of his brother Wenceslas, he inherited the throne of Bohemia; and both had been earlier enhanced when in 1410 he was elected King of the Romans. His struggle against the heretics of Bohemia and his activity in the field of ecclesiastical politics do not come within the scope of Hungarian history, although these movements indirectly affected Hungary, since the followers of John Hus, after his condemnation to death at the stake by the Council of Constance, organised marauding bands and for two decades devastated the Hungarian highlands in repeated incursions. On the other hand, again, the Hussite teachings, though only in secret, struck root in Hungary also.

In warlike operations Sigismund was not lucky. Though he succeeded in suppressing the rebellions in Hungary and the Bosnian-Croatian revolt as well, Dalmatia came again into the possession of Venice, the expedition which he sent in 1412 failing to recover that province. Sigismund was also unfortunate in his campaigns against the Turks: in 1428 he was defeated a second time on the Lower Danube; and it was only in the last year of his life, at the castle of Smederevo (Semendria), that he was able to win a victory due to the strategy of John Hunyadi, the triumphant hero of the subsequent Hungarian-Turkish warfare, who here made his first appearance at the head of his battalions[1].

After the reign of Sigismund the politics of Hungary were dominated by two great problems: the defensive struggle against the Turks, and the political feud (constantly increasing in bitterness) between the two landed Estates, the great land-owners and the lesser nobility.

The Ottoman Sultans[2], during the fourth decade of the fifteenth century, established a footing on the line of the Lower Danube and the Drina facing the kingdom of Hungary and the small Balkan principalities under Hungarian protection—the provinces of the despot George Branković, who then ruled over the remaining fragments of the Serbian people, of the King of Bosnia, and of George Castriota (Skanderbeg), Prince of Albania. The other inhabitants of the Balkans—Serbians, Bulgarians,

[1] Cf. *supra*, Vol. IV, Chaps. XVIII and XXI.
[2] See for these Balkan events *supra*, Vol. IV, Chaps. XVIII and XXI.

and even the Wallachians living on the north bank of the Danube—were driven to submit, so that the difficult task of hindering the inevitable advance of the Ottomans devolved upon the kingdom of Hungary.

The revival of the eastern danger necessarily involved a change in the tenor of Hungarian foreign policy. The headway made by the Turks resulted in completely frustrating the Balkan expansion of the Árpáds and Angevins. Feudal Hungary lacked the strong central power which had enabled the Árpád and Angevin dynasties to make such mighty displays of strength. The banderial army, consisting of private bands of troops, and the foreign mercenaries were far inferior to the royal army of the older kingdom which had been under central control; nor was the royal treasury able to procure the supplies required for the prosecution of warfare out of its own resources (the revenues of the royal domains and customs—*regale*). The strength of the army and the amount realised by taxation alike depended upon the decision of the Estates, now that the voting of both had been converted by the advance of the constitutional spirit into a parliamentary prerogative of the nobility. Under such circumstances the success of a conflict with the Turkish army, which was highly disciplined and splendidly trained, was inconceivable without foreign aid; so that the consciousness of the need for a military alliance with the German neighbours of Hungary grew continually stronger and stronger in the public opinion of the country. The consequence was the abandonment of Lewis the Great's conception of an alliance between Poland, Hungary, Croatia, and Italy and the revival of the defensive policy adopted by Béla IV as a means of protection against the Mongols. The idea of an alliance with the Holy Roman Empire had come to the fore already in the closing years of Lewis the Great's reign, when he had designated the son of the Emperor Charles IV to be his daughter Mary's consort. With Sigismund's accession to the thrones of Bohemia and of the Empire this alliance assumed the more concrete form of a personal union; and the idea of an alliance of the same kind appears also during the reigns of Sigismund's immediate successors. His son-in-law and heir, Albert of Habsburg (1437–39), was King of the Romans and Duke of Austria; Albert's son Ladislas (László) V (1444–57) was also Duke of Austria and King of Bohemia; and both were elected to the throne by the Estates to ensure the alliance with the Empire. The election of Vladyslav I (1439–44), King of Poland, was the last attempt to revive the policy of Lewis the Great; but the lamentable defeat and death of this king at Varna resulted in the definitive triumph of the idea of a German-Bohemian alliance. Matthias Hunyadi himself—the national king raised to the throne by the reaction against the rule of foreign princes—was compelled to adopt this line of policy; it was by the conquest of provinces of the Empire and by entering the lists as candidate for the imperial crown that he endeavoured to secure the aid of Germany against the Turks. It was the national desire to secure effectual protection against the Turkish advance that after the death of Matthias raised the weak Czech Jagiellos to the throne of St Stephen; and it was the same consideration that after the disastrous rout on the field of Mohács induced the Hungarians to offer the crown to the house of Habsburg.

This change of tendency in foreign policy, sanctioned by the will of the Estates, which their right of electing the king had converted into a decisive factor, shews quite clearly that the Hungarians of the fifteenth century regarded the Turkish danger as the vital problem of their national life and indeed of their national existence, and looked upon the task of driving back the Ottoman power as a historical mission and a duty which they owed alike to their own nation and to the lands of Western civilisation as a whole. In the first—twenty years'—phase of the protracted struggle which began with the relief of the castle of Semendria in the year of Sigismund's death, the leading rôle was played by John Hunyadi (Hunyadi János), a member of the lesser nobility who rose eventually to the dignity of Governor or Regent of the country.

The first ancestors of the Hunyadis known to history—Radoslav and Serbe—belonged to the ranks of the Southern Slav factors (*knyaz*) who organised the Wallachian (Rumanian) shepherds of the province of South Wallachia in village communities and also aided in settling them in Hungarian territory; but Serbe's son Vajk was a knight in the Court of Sigismund, receiving the castle of Hunyad in Transylvania, together with the adjacent demesne, as a reward for his knightly prowess. Vajk Hunyadi, created a Hungarian noble by the grant of this fief, wedded a Magyar woman; their eldest son, John, also began his career as a knight in the Court of Sigismund. After the victory at Semendria he rose rapidly. In 1439 King Albert placed him at the head of the banate of Szörény (Severin) on the Danube in Wallachia, a position destined to be of the utmost importance in the struggle against the Turks. Vladyslav I made him captain of Nándorfehérvár (the Hungarian frontier-fortress standing on the site to-day occupied by Belgrade, the Serbian capital), and later appointed him voïvode of Transylvania, in which capacity he was made commander-in-chief of the armies operating against the Turks. After the death of Vladyslav in the disastrous battle of Varna, Hunyadi became a member of the national government (Committee of Seven) elected by the Estates to act during the absence of the king, who was presumed to have been taken prisoner; then, when Albert's posthumous son was acknowledged and accepted as Ladislas V, at the Parliament held at Rákos in 1446, Hunyadi was elected to act as Governor or Regent of Hungary during the minority and absence from the country of the young monarch. In his capacity as Regent Hunyadi enjoyed a power which but for slight restrictions was that of a king; and even after the assumption of royal power by Ladislas V (in 1452) he remained in possession of the real supreme authority in his capacity as Viceroy and Captain-General. His enormous power and universal authority rested upon the undivided confidence of the lesser nobility and upon the position ensured by the extensive estates acquired by him in recognition of his military services to the country, estates which provided him with resources enabling him to equip an army vying with that of the king himself.

Though he took his due share in every field in the direction of national policy, he regarded the driving back of the Turkish power and the securing of the southern frontiers of the country as the primary task of his life. In 1442 he inflicted a double defeat upon the army of Mezid Bey which had invaded Transylvania; and then, on the bank of the Lower Danube, he dispersed the vast host which was hurrying under the command of Sehab-ad-dīn Pasha to the assistance of Mezid Bey. In the autumn of 1443 he crossed the Danube into Bulgarian territory, and, after taking the fortresses of Niš, Pirot, and Sofia, conducted his army over the Haemus range as well. A year later Vladyslav I made a treaty at Szeged with the Sultan, whom the news of the defeats inflicted upon his armies had impelled to offer to make peace; but, encouraged by an absolution from his oath granted by the papal legate, Cardinal Cesarini, the Hungarian king broke his compact and began to wage war against the Turks on Bulgarian soil. Hunyadi joined his sovereign at Nicopolis; but the troops promised by the Christian princes of Europe never arrived, and the Hungarian army was defeated at Varna. Vladyslav fell; and Hunyadi himself had the greatest difficulty in escaping from the clutches of Vlad "the Devil," the double-faced Voïvode of Wallachia. During the years which followed, Hunyadi was engaged in the direction of the internal affairs of the country, which had been left without a king; and in 1448 the treachery of his Wallachian and Serbian allies involved him in a fresh defeat—on the Field of Blackbirds or Kossovo—at the hands of the Turks. Five years later (1453), by the capture of Constantinople, the new Sultan, Mahomet II, became master of the whole Balkan peninsula; and in 1456 he started to attack Hungary at the head of an army said to have numbered nearly 200,000 men. While besieging the fortress of Belgrade, however, this army was decisively beaten by Hunyadi, assisted by Giovanni Capistrano, the Franciscan friar who had put himself at the head of the European crusaders; and the fortress was relieved. The victory at Belgrade stemmed the tide of Turkish expansion for a long period; and in commemoration of the triumph of the Christian arms the Pope ordained that a bell should be rung every day in all churches in Christendom. Unfortunately, however, Hunyadi fell a victim to the plague which had broken out in the Christian camp.

John Hunyadi's rapid rise to power was largely due to the bitter struggle between the magnates and the lesser nobility. According to the new political conception which developed after the extinction of the house of Anjou, the lesser nobility, which was in a numerical majority in Parliament, endeavoured continuously to increase its influence upon the direction of the affairs of the nation. John Hunyadi was the leader of the party of the lesser nobility; the great land-owners despised him, but they feared him too; and during the period when he was acting as Regent he made Parliament invite six lesser nobles to sit on the National Council attached to his person as an advisory body, which contained two prelates and four secular magnates, his object being thereby to ensure the predominance of the lesser nobility in politics and in government. His appointment as commander-in-chief and his election as Regent was therefore a victory of the lesser nobility over the haughty and imperious aristocracy; and this was the reason why the great conqueror of the Turks, who on his father's side was of foreign origin, became the hero of the knightly order of Hungarian nobles and the darling of all classes of the nation alike.

The internal problem of the period was indeed the struggle between the Estates. During the days of the Árpád kings down to the reign of Béla IV, and during the reigns of the two strong Angevin sovereigns, the royal power had appeared personified in the person of the reigning king. During the reign of the minor, Ladislas IV, however, power passed from hand to hand and came successively into the possession of the various party governments, the result being that the royal power came eventually to be regarded as impersonal. It was at this period that the use of the words *corona* and later *corona sacra* came into vogue in place of the words *rex* and *regnum*, this change being accompanied by the cult of the Holy Crown presented originally to St Stephen by the Pope—which had originally been an ecclesiastical symbol—as a symbol of the royal power. This cult had reached such an importance by the accession of the first Angevin king that a coronation performed without the Holy Crown was not regarded as valid. And now, in the days of Ladislas V, also a minor, when the reins of government were in the hands of Hunyadi, a lesser noble elected to the office of Regent by the Estates, the conception of the Holy Crown received a wider interpretation in public law: that Crown was raised from a mere symbol of the royal power to the political symbol of the nation corporate embracing the sovereign himself and the Estates endowed with political rights. Under this interpretation, which was systematised half a century later by Stephen Verböczy, the great jurist responsible for the scientific codification of Hungarian private and public law, power is possessed, not by the king, but by the Holy Crown, the members of which are the king and the nation—in other words, the Estates endowed with political rights, or the *totum corpus sacrae coronae*—that power being enjoyed and exercised as a trust by the king crowned with that Crown. The doctrine of the Holy Crown in the form in which it has existed in the legal system of constitutional Hungary is without doubt the conception of Verböczy; but its roots reach back to the political conception of the lesser nobility in the days of Ladislas V, while the foundations of the historical development of this thesis may be traced as far back as the thirteenth century, to the reign of Ladislas IV.

The conception of the central power latent in this political interpretation was an instinctive move on the part of the lesser nobility for self-
defence against the encroachments of the aristocracy; and it is owing to
this move that the oligarchs of the fifteenth century were unable to obtain
a power equal to that exercised by their predecessors two centuries previously, when the national assembly of the prelates and lesser nobles had
had to submit its resolutions for approval and ratification, not to the king,
but to the king and barons who jointly represented the royal power or—
to use the expression then in vogue—the power of the Crown. It wa
this same political conception that the nation relied upon later, in the
days of the Habsburgs, in its struggle against the anti-constitutional
endeavours of the foreign princes. The conception of the division of the
power between king and Estates comprised in constitutional law is reflected
also in the elections to the throne made in the fifteenth century. The
successive dynasties—Luxemburgs, Habsburgs, Jagiellos—had at all
times proclaimed and considered the transfer of the crown by right of
heredity to be the only legal method. The nobility, on the other hand,
regarding both lines, male and female, of the ancient dynasty ruling
by hereditary right as extinct with the deaths of Lewis the Great
and his daughter, insisted upon their right to elect their king. The
conflict of the two principles usually resulted in a solution by compromise, as may be seen in the cases of Sigismund, Albert of Habsburg,
and Lewis II. However, after the death of King Albert in 1439 the
conflict led to a civil war between the Habsburg party, which stood for
the right of that king's posthumous son Ladislas on the ground of
legitimate inheritance, and the adherents of the right of free election—
the Jagiello party—who raised Vladyslav, King of Poland, to the throne
by election. Out of this struggle, which when repeated in 1526 resulted
in the country becoming divided into two opposing sections and thus
indirectly in the advance of the Turks into the heart of Hungary, the
nation was led, in the middle of the fifteenth century, into smoother waters
by John Hunyadi and his son King Matthias Corvinus.

The struggle between the aristocracy and the lesser nobility (gentry)
for the possession of power, which John Hunyadi, with the aid of his
paramount authority, succeeded for a time in restricting within narrow
limits, after his death broke out again with renewed violence. The
aristocratic league which had secured a predominant influence over the
helpless young king Ladislas, under the direction of Ulrich of Cilli, the king's
cousin, incited the monarch against Hunyadi's sons; and the rivalry of
the two parties degenerated into implacable hatred when the adherents
of the Hunyadis cut the conspirator Cilli to pieces, and when the king,
breaking the promise he had given, threw the responsibility upon Ladislas
Hunyadi and had him executed, while he took his younger brother
Matthias prisoner and dragged him off to captivity in Prague. The
treatment meted out to the sons of the national hero provoked great

bitterness all over the country among the lesser nobility ; and when, barely a year later, news came of the death of Ladislas V, the public opinion of the Hungarians espoused the cause of the surviving son of the great Hunyadi with irrepressible enthusiasm.

Two members of the aristocracy possessing great power—Ladislas Garai, Count Palatine, and Nicholas Ujlaki, Voïvode of Transylvania—themselves aspired to the throne. Others again endeavoured to obtain the kingship for one of the sons-in-law of King Albert of Habsburg—for Casimir, King of Poland, or William, Duke of Saxony. Though at the outset he supported the claims of the King of Poland, the Emperor Frederick of Habsburg would have liked to secure the Hungarian throne for himself, having the Holy Crown, entrusted to his keeping during the minority of Ladislas V, still in his possession. However, not one of the claimants was able to hold his own against the Hunyadi party. The lesser nobles stood in serried ranks behind Michael Szilágyi, the organiser of young Matthias' party, and his sister, John Hunyadi's widow; and they enjoyed the support of a section of the prelates too, who were under the direction of the great humanist, John Vitéz, Bishop of Nagyvárad. Seeing how things stood, the most powerful of the magnates changed their attitude and perforce joined Matthias' party. Then the Parliament convened by the Count Palatine early in 1458 elected Matthias Hunyadi king, appointing his uncle Michael Szilágyi as Regent; this was done both because Matthias was a minor and in order to ensure the influence of the lesser nobility on the conduct of affairs.

This was the first time since the extinction of the house of Árpád that a national king had occupied the throne of St Stephen. The lesser nobles, however, dictated severe conditions to the young king who had been chosen from their own ranks. Regarding Matthias as a party king, they made every effort to ensure their influence on his conduct of the government, and at the same time to mitigate the burdens of military service, of which the Turkish wars had compelled Hunyadi to take full advantage. One of the conditions governing the election (*capitulationes*) stipulated that the king was to defend the country with his own soldiers and at his own expense, being entitled to call the *banderia* of the magnates to arms only in the event of great danger and the levies of the lesser nobility only in extreme urgency as a last resort. Szilágyi accepted these conditions, agreeing also to the stipulation of the league of magnates which required Matthias to wed the Count Palatine's daughter. But King Matthias (1458–90) frustrated all these calculations. He returned from his captivity in Bohemia as the betrothed of the daughter of George Poděbrady, who had been raised to the throne of Bohemia by the Bohemian Estates, and with an energy and earnestness that belied his youth (he was only eighteen) seized the reins of power, compelling his uncle to resign his office as Regent. Hereupon, a section of the aristocracy got into touch with the Emperor Frederick III and invited him to occupy the Hungarian throne. However, Matthias compelled these magnates to yield one after another, and, after defeating the imperial armies, made peace with Frederick: the Emperor agreed to surrender the Holy Crown, while Matthias on his part undertook that in the event of his not having a male heir Frederick and his successors should, by virtue of the right handed down by Albert and Ladislas V, be entitled to succeed to the Hungarian throne.

After having secured his throne, Matthias turned against the Turks. He once more reduced Wallachia and Serbia to the position of vassals of the Hungarian Crown, victoriously compelled the Turks to withdraw also from the fortress of Jajce in Bosnia, and, in order to ensure the success of his further efforts, without delay began the work of reforming the military and financial organisation. The banderial system, as a result of the negligence of those under obligation of military service, did not represent such a force as it had a hundred years previously. With the object of further developing the militia (*portalis*) established by Sigismund, the Parliament of 1458 itself required the nobility to provide one mounted soldier for every 20 villein-holdings (*sessiones*), separate county battalions being organised out of the *portalis* cavalry and placed under the command of captains appointed by the king. Later, in 1465, Matthias, with the consent of Parliament, required nobles possessing fewer than ten villein-holdings to do military service in person, and compelled the more wealthy to provide one mounted soldier each for every ten villein-holdings. In addition to these measures, which amounted practically to universal conscription, Matthias established a standing army which, except for the smaller mounted army of Charles VII of France, was the first of its kind in Europe. Matthias' standing army comprised both cavalry and infantry. By these measures the peace footing of the military forces of Hungary advanced to some 40,000, and the war footing to 150,000 or 200,000 men. Simultaneously with the abolition of the land tax of 18 dinars which had been introduced instead of the coinage tax (*lucrum camerae*)—the seignorage—he established a Treasury tax of 20 dinars, extending the obligation to pay this tax to all the villeins, poor nobles, and privileged settlers (Saxons and Cumans) alike. More than once he imposed the extraordinary tax without it being voted by Parliament, fixing the amount at 1 gold florin a year. The new system of taxation increased the revenue of the treasury, the same object being served also by re-organising the customs duties on foreign trade and by intensifying the activity of the mines.

Whereas his military and financial reforms were directed by considerations of foreign policy, Matthias' important reforms of administration and justice were inspired by a desire to restore internal order and to improve the situation of the lower classes oppressed by the selfishness of the landed Estates. The reform of the administration of justice carried out towards the close of his reign aimed at a re-organisation of the courts and at a simplification of legal procedure. The lowest court—the county court with a bench consisting of four justices representing the county nobility and ten *homines regii*—was re-organised into a court holding public trials on fixed dates, against the judgments of which appeal could be made to the judicial commissions of the royal Curia. In the field of legal procedure the king introduced an important measure providing for the abolition of trial by combat, as well as completely abrogating the system of compositions; thus the penal code was developed in the direction of public law. In the Court administration—probably under the influence of Italian models—the king broke with the older feudal organisation and laid the foundations of the professional central bureaucracy, in this point anticipating many States of Western Europe.

Matthias' reforms in administration and justice reflect that spirit of fairness and that strong sense of justice which, together with the unrivalled energy of his personality, were the most typical features of his character. In the administration of justice he did not permit any secondary consideration. His hand fell heavily on the privileged classes; yet there is hardly a name which has been the object of such universal praise—or worshipped for so long a period with such fervour—in Hungary as his was. Though he did not formally commit any breach of the constitution, and had his laws passed by Parliament, he nevertheless had but little respect for the privileges and constitutional rights of the mighty lords. All the greater was his understanding for the troubles of the lowly, the oppressed, the petty nobles, and the villeins; and he did all in his power to relieve them. This was the secret of his great popularity and the source of the epithet "the just" conferred upon him by posterity. He was one of the great Renaissance princes who were the harbingers of modern absolutism, princes who, by relying upon the support of the lower classes of their subjects, were able to assert their power to the full.

An impressive manifestation of the personality of this great Renaissance prince was the foundation of his famous library in Buda, the *Bibliotheca Corviniana*, which according to the evidence of his contemporaries vied both in quantity and in quality with the wealthy Renaissance libraries of the Vatican and of Urbino. The library, which the Hungarian Estates, in the agreement made with John Corvinus after Matthias' death, declared to be inalienable national property, thereby converting it into one of the first public libraries in Europe, fell after the capture of Buda in 1526 partly into the hands of the Turks, the remainder being carried off by Mary of Habsburg and Ferdinand I and scattered all over the world; but the remains which are still in existence—some 160 volumes decorated by the most famous miniature painters of the fifteenth century—are eloquent evidence of the artistic leanings and taste of the great king and bibliophile. It is to this artistic taste that we owe the advance made by Renaissance architecture, which flourished in the age of Matthias side by side with the Gothic architecture now at the zenith of its development. The earliest important monument of this style of architecture in Hungary was the palace in Buda, of which only fragments have survived. The court of Matthias offered a home and a generous livelihood to the humanistic artists and scholars who had accepted his invitation to come to Hungary; these artists and scholars obtained Hungarian pupils and founded schools; but all this was swept away by the days of chaos and upheaval which followed his death. Humanism had found its way to Hungary already in the days of Sigismund. Later on, John Vitéz, Archbishop of Esztergom (Gran), the personal friend of Hunyadi who acted as tutor to young Matthias, became the leader of the humanistic literary circle in Hungary. It was Vitéz who had awakened in Matthias a desire to encourage science and scholarship; and the latter welcomed to his court the humanistic historians Bonfini, Galeotti, and Ranzano, the founders of the humanistic school of Hungarian historiography, who enjoyed his constant patronage. Regiomontanus too, the eminent astronomer, came to Hungary; and it was with his co-operation that Matthias founded the *Academia Istropolitana* at Pozsony (Pressburg) to replace the university founded by Lewis the Great at Pécs, which had been destroyed. A large number of Hungarian humanists were active, under the direction of John Vitéz, furthering science and poetry. The most eminent of these humanists was John Csezmiczei, Bishop of Pécs, who under the name of "Janus Pannonius" attained distinction among the neo-Latin poets. It was with the co-operation of these savants that, after the death of Matthias, the first scientific association was formed (the *Sodalitas Litteraria Danubiana*). And it was in the age of Matthias (in 1473) that the first Hungarian printing press—that founded by Andrew Hesz of Nuremberg—began its operations in Buda, the first product of this press being the *Chronicon Budense*, which offers such striking proof of the revival of historical research in the days of the great king.

The remarkable revival and rapid development in Matthias' reign of science, scholarship, and art was almost overshadowed by his signal success as a general. However, while his father had practically confined his attention to the Turkish campaigns, Matthias made the adjoining provinces of the Romano-Germanic Empire (Austria and Bohemia) the primary objects of his wars. In 1468 he had a conflict with his whilom father-in-law, George of Bohemia, who had maintained secret relations with the discontented Hungarian magnates conspiring against their king, and who by his Hussite leanings and Hussite policy had at the same time provoked the bitter hostility of the Holy See. Pope Paul II prompted Matthias to undertake a crusade against Bohemia, the Hungarian king being encouraged also by the Emperor Frederick III, who was delighted to see that the relations between his Czech and Hungarian neighbours had cooled. Not that Matthias needed much encouragement: the war against Bohemia fitted into his political schemes; so he invaded Moravia, occupied Brno and Olomouc, and penetrated into Bohemia, whereupon the Czech-Moravian and Silesian Estates, at a Parliament held at Olomouc in 1469, elected him King of Bohemia, crowning him at Brno. In answer to this move George Poděbrady induced the Bohemian Estates to elect as his successor Vladislav, son of the Polish king Casimir, thereby creating a breach between Matthias and Poland. After the death of Poděbrady in 1471, the Emperor too acknowledged Vladislav as King of Bohemia, while at home there was discontent owing to the failure to carry on the war against the Turks and to the heavy burdens involved by the taxes imposed for the purpose of carrying on the Bohemian contest; and the insurgent magnates invited Casimir, Prince of Poland, to occupy the throne. Prince Casimir actually entered Hungary with an army; but Matthias had meanwhile disarmed the disaffection of the magnates, and the Polish claimant was compelled to retire without having achieved anything. Then in 1474 Matthias led a fresh expedition against Bohemia, this time with the approval of the Hungarian Estates; and, anticipating the proposed Austrian-Czech-Rumanian offensive against Hungary, he entered Breslau in triumph. After an armistice of four years, the Treaty of Olomouc (1478) finally put an end to hostilities; under this treaty Bohemia was left to Vladislav, but the subordinate provinces—Moravia, Silesia, and Lusatia (Lausitz)—came into the possession of Matthias, who also retained the title of King of Bohemia.

By this time Matthias was at war with the Emperor Frederick too, whose double-dealing in the conflict with Bohemia had forced the Hungarian king to resort to armed intervention. Between 1477 and 1485 Matthias conducted three campaigns against the Emperor's Austrian hereditary provinces; the result of these campaigns was the fall of Vienna and the subjection of Lower Austria and Styria to the Hungarian king.

By acquiring possession of these Bohemian and Austrian provinces Matthias had paved the way to the imperial throne. He first made a peaceful attempt to obtain it; and in 1471 he did succeed in securing from the Emperor Frederick a promise that the latter would recommend the Electors and the German Reichstag to accept Matthias as his successor. About the same time Matthias opened negotiations with the Electors themselves, one of whom—Albert of Hohenzollern, Margrave of Brandenburg—declared his willingness to support him, while the others refused to entertain the suggestion. Failing to achieve his object in this manner owing to the duplicity of the Emperor, in 1474 he invited Charles the Bold, Duke of Burgundy, to make an alliance for the purpose of breaking the power of the Habsburgs. Charles, however, turned a deaf ear; and after his death in 1477 this scheme too came to nought. Then Matthias concentrated his forces on the work of securing the possession of the neighbouring imperial provinces of Bohemia and Austria, in order to be able in the event of the election of a new king on the death of Frederick to enter the lists in the struggle for the crown as the mightiest prince of the Empire.

Matthias Hunyadi has been very severely reproached, both by his contemporaries and by posterity, for departing from the path marked out by his father, and, instead of energetically continuing the struggle against the Turks, squandering the forces of his country and his own eminent military capacity in campaigns of conquest in the West. However, this reproach is not quite just; for in the years 1475–76 and again in 1479 and 1481 he began campaigns for the purpose of freeing the frontier zones of Bosnia and harassing the Turkish frontier district in Bulgaria; and the records of these campaigns shew that he never lost sight of the Turkish danger, and that the ultimate object of his policy in the West was the organisation of an eventual expedition on a huge scale for the expulsion of the Ottomans. Experience had taught Matthias, as it had taught his father before him, that all he had to expect in the struggle against the Turks was the papal subsidy, which came to take the place of the auxiliary hosts the West had undertaken to send to his aid; so it had become evident to him that he could not reckon upon the assistance of Western Europe except in the event of a close political connexion based upon a German-Hungarian federation. Despite her undoubted power, Hungary seemed to him too weak to oppose the oriental enemy which was disciplined by the Asiatic despotism of the Turks; even as national king he paved the way for a personal union with the east German provinces and, if possible, with the whole Empire, thereby resuming the foreign policy of Béla IV and Sigismund. Owing to his death, which ensued unexpectedly at the early age of fifty, and to the weakness of his successor, his policy proved a failure; but his conception— to revive Sigismund's personal union of German, Czech, and Hungarian —appears in the light of results to have been the only one calculated to provide the means of checking the advance of the Turks and averting the national catastrophe of 1526. The conquest of a large section of Bohemia and of the Austrian provinces was a masterly achievement and a signal feat of generalship; and the conception of foreign policy expressed in these conquests is eloquent proof of Matthias' sound practical appreciation of the situation.

In the last year of his life the question of the succession caused Matthias the greatest anxiety. His married life with both his consorts—Catherine Poděbrady and Beatrice of Naples, both of whom he had wedded for political reasons—had been unhappy; and both marriages remained without issue. His only child was his illegitimate son, John Corvinus, whose mother was the daughter of a Breslau burgher. Though at his death he was only fifty years of age, he had already made every effort to secure Prince John's succession to the throne. The result of these efforts was the so-called *Lex Palatini* (Law of the Palatine), which later on acquired such importance in constitutional law. Under this law the Count Palatine became Captain-General of the country, second only to the king as head of the judicature, guardian of the king during his minority, regent of the country during the king's absence or during an interregnum, intermediary between king and nation in the event of any quarrel between the two; at royal elections it was his privilege to proclaim the assembling of Parliament for the purpose and to record the first vote. At a later period this law put into the hands of the Estates electing the Count Palatine a strong constitutional guarantee against the absolutist tendencies of their Habsburg sovereigns. By this law Matthias had desired to ensure the succession of John Corvinus to the throne; for simultaneously with the promulgation of the law he had made one of his most devoted adherents—Imre Szapolyai, a man who had been advanced from the obscurity of a poor lesser noble to the dignity and wealth of a magnate—Count Palatine. Nevertheless, he failed to achieve his object. Szapolyai died before him; and when, in April 1490, the king too passed away unexpectedly, the palatinate was vacant, so that Prince John lacked the official support which his father had desired to secure him. But the young prince lacked also the energy essential for obtaining the crown; and he lacked his father's authority too. Though he had followers among the lesser nobles whom the Hunyadis had exalted and by the grant of estates had advanced at the expense of the aristocratic families, public opinion was not on his side. The Estates had had enough of the glorious but severe rule of the Hunyadis. They preferred to put themselves under the rule of Vladislav Jagiello, the prince who had abandoned the kingdom of Poland for Bohemia. They hoped that they would find him to be a weak king yielding to their will and respecting their rights. This anticipation proved to be correct. Vladislav II (1490–1516) was a weak ruler, during whose reign there was a renewal of the troubles which the Hunyadi regime had for half a century kept in check; and Hungary began to approach her doom to the accompaniment of bitter internal feuds on the one hand and an unceasing heroic defensive struggle against the Turks on the other.

The aristocracy and the gentry, nobility and villeins, prelates and towns, the court favourites—some of whom were foreigners—and the provincial Hungarian nobility jealous of their liberty, the political feuds of all these several factors with one another and with the weak power of the Crown, in a few short years destroyed the results achieved by the rule of Matthias. It was only by selling the finest of the Corvin manuscripts and of the artistic gems of the royal collection, and by the aid of loans obtained from subjects allowed to make havoc of the royal property, that this successor of Lewis the Great and of Matthias Hunyadi was able to maintain his unpretentious household. And this financial decay was only one of the many symptoms of the utter decline of the central power and of the royal authority, and of the collapse of the constitutional State, which was accompanied by signs of anarchy; and as a result, despite the heroic bravery of her soldiers, thirty-six years after the death of Matthias Hungary was brought to the field of Mohács, where in 1526, with the death of King Lewis II and the annihilation of his army, two-thirds of her territory were lost and remained for a century and a half under the Turkish yoke.

CHAPTER XX

POLITICAL THEORY IN THE LATER MIDDLE AGES

DANTE was not the last medieval thinker to dream of unity as the most splendid of political ideals; but he was the last to whom that dream might reasonably have presented itself as instinct with hope. After his time circumstances compelled the onset of plurality, and if men repeated the old dogmas, it was without conviction and as a tradition already in defeat. For the existence of separate and right-claiming nationalities had become (or was becoming) an inescapable fact. *Praemunire* and *Provisors* in England, the Pragmatic Sanction in France, were the index to a modernity which had escaped the swaddling clothes of medieval thought. Once the Pope had been at Avignon, even more, once he had left it, the world as a single Christian society could hardly be preached as reality; and if there remain men like Augustinus Triumphus, the federalism of Nicholas of Cusa shews that even the splendour of unity had come to have a new connotation. Our task is to analyse the decay of the idea of the *Respublica Christiana* as a system of ideas, and to discover the outlines of the new system by which men sought to replace it. The decay, of course, was not a matter of one moment or of one thinker. It took at least until the French Revolution for the self-sufficiency of the secular State to be recognised as practically beyond repeal; and, even then, the *Du Pape* of de Maistre and the *Syllabus* of 1864 stand as protests against its advent. But the indestructible pluralism of the facts was already, even in Dante's time, becoming finally evident. Once there had been the captivity of Avignon, the Great Schism, and the Councils, pluralism in government was only a matter of time. The Reformation only set the seal upon ideas that an earlier generation had made inevitable.

The later Middle Ages are occupied, for the most part, with three great problems. There is the problem of the position of the Papacy in the Church. Can a power, it is asked, be absolute and irresponsible that is used for ends either dubiously good or certainly bad? Men, thereby, are driven back to search into the foundations of authority, and from such an enquiry no institution has ever emerged unscathed. What, secondly, is the relation of the Church to secular society? That question is asked from two angles. It is asked by men like the supporters of Lewis of Bavaria, and by the simple Parliamentarians at Westminster who do not like good English money to fill the pockets of Italian churchmen. It is asked, also, by men like the Spiritual Franciscans, who are convinced that the true Christian life is one of humble poverty, and are distressed at the spectacle of a Church devoted to worldly ideals. And, thirdly, what are the internal relations of secular society? How measure the meaning of imperial lordship when an English king, as with Richard II, can claim to be *entier empereur dans son roialme,* and lawyers like Bartolus are driven, almost despite themselves, to recognise that *civitas* and *regnum* have all the marks of the original world-State, the Empire itself?

These are the problems, and, at long last, they shatter the medieval unified commonwealth into the fragments we to-day call sovereign States. They do not do so, let it be insisted, upon general principle. Until at least Machiavelli, there is no thinker who does not somehow feel that Christendom is a single people in which there may be different kingdoms but in which, at least ultimately, there must be a single *imperium.* For some, that power is papal; for others, it belongs to the Emperor; for others, again, it is built upon the Gelasian model of a harmony that is one in its duality. And the modern conception of the sovereign State could not, in this time, come into full birth because all medieval thinking was penetrated by the idea of a legal order which reflected the principle of nature and controlled thereby the legality of particular laws. "Right" in the medieval time is a blend so cunningly compounded of ethics and theology that the notion of something justifiable merely because it was ordered would have struck most minds with horror. Whatever contradicted natural law contradicted that which reflects the declared will of God; it cannot, therefore, possess validity. With such an idea suffusing the whole of medieval life, it is only with difficulty that we pass to a power in the prince to interpret natural law, and thence to a law which is binding upon all because it is his will. Yet, even then, not only does the older doctrine persist, as with Marsilio and Gregory of Heimburg, but the modern idea of the ruler's sovereignty has to struggle also with the idea of law as the mandate of the people. The lawyers may argue that there has been *translatio* of power from people to prince, and that in perpetuity. But *populus maior principe* is a rule that dies hard; and even in the triumph of its mighty opposite it is not forgotten. For with the religious nonconformity of the sixteenth century it arises, phoenix-like, from what were deemed its ashes. The natural law of the Middle Ages is the parent of the natural rights of the eighteenth century.

The pontificate of Boniface VIII marks a real epoch in the history of the Papacy. Logically, doubtless, he made no claims that were not already implicit in the proud challenge of the Hildebrandine Papacy; and his dogmas had already been enunciated, if with very different emphasis, by men so different as John of Salisbury and Thomas Aquinas. But the theses of Boniface were announced in a very different atmosphere. The Empire was ceasing to count as a pivotal force in European affairs. The Papacy itself, confronted by the new nationalism of England and France, was less administratively than doctrinally paramount. The struggle with Philip the Fair on the one hand, and with Lewis of Bavaria on the other, only brought into the more striking prominence at once its physical impotence and its moral degeneration. Yet at no time in its

history were its claims so splendidly displayed. Merely to suggest duality
of power, says Boniface, is heresy; his opponents, who posit that principle,
put themselves out of court. Therefore to the Papacy belongs the lordship of the world; and the contrast is striking between the power substantially achieved and the claims it is thought legitimate to advance.

In the period before the Conciliar Movement, no one stated the papal
case with either the power or the insight of Thomas Aquinas. The
arguments have little of novelty either in substance or in statement.
The point of departure is the historic one of the need for a unified
world, reinforced by every argument that scriptural text and imaginative
metaphor can suggest. Thence it is inferred that unity needs a visible
embodiment on earth, and it is a short step therefrom to argue that the
Pope has *utrumque gladium*. The temporal power may be administratively in the hands of secular princes, but, as of right, it is an ultimately papal prerogative. For since it originates in sin, it is necessarily
inferior in spiritual authority. "Princely power," says Alvaro Pelayo,
"is ordained by the spiritual power." Ultimately, at least, all States are
ecclesiastical institutions, for they have merely the care of those antecedent
ends which are the threshold of that greater eternal end of which the
Church is the appointed guardian. Metaphor emphasises the relationship
of subordination. The Church is heaven to the earth of the secular power;
it is the sun to the moon, it is gold to lead, or soul to body. Temporal
rulers are the mere executors of papal will; their offices, argues the clerk
in that best of medieval dialogues, the *Somnium Viridarii*, are *gradus in
ecclesia*. And temporal exercise of authority is a trust subject at every
point to papal interpretation of its fitness. A theory which, as late as
Innocent III, had distinguished between the Pope's spiritual power to
correct the misdeeds of princes and his extraordinary intervention as a
temporal sovereign, already, by the middle of the fourteenth century, is
unable to see effective difference between them. History, or what passes
for history, is invoked in papal support. The *Donation of Constantine*
becomes a restoration to the Pope of an authority originally his own.
The electors to the Empire are, accordingly, his agents; and the imperial
title is dependent upon his confirmation. So, if the throne be vacant, the
Pope is its natural guardian. And as he confirms, so may he nominate
and depose; the fealty of subjects is a function of his pleasure. We have
moved far from the earlier Gelasian view of Church and State as co-
ordinate powers. The *duplex directivum* of Dante ceases to have a place
in a world where the majesty of Rome is alone paramount and legitimate.

It is a tremendous doctrine, the more noteworthy in its amplitude when
it is remembered that he in whose name it was made was either the virtual
partisan of France at Avignon or struggling with difficulty, after 1378,
to win back his hold of Rome itself. The greater, indeed, the decline of
papal power, the more far-reaching are the claims of its partisans; the
trappings of royalty are more eagerly displayed that the shrunken body

may be the better concealed. All civil legislation may, as the priest argues in the *Somnium Viridarii,* be at bottom Canon Law; but there is no ecclesiastical text which sanctions the Statute of Praemunire. The medieval Pope is a true Austinian sovereign, but, like most species of that genus, he cannot get his will enforced. The claim is there, but it is an index to conflict rather than a lever of action.

Nothing, perhaps, illustrates so well the ambit and the environment of papal theory as the treatise *On the Power of the Pope* by Augustinus Triumphus. Written, almost certainly, before 1325, it was dedicated to John XXII and intended as a weapon in the great struggle against Lewis of Bavaria. With a single exception, it sees no limit to the power of the Pope. He is the vicegerent of God with plenipotentiary authority. He is to be worshipped as a saint, and so vast is his prerogative that, even if he be a sinner, yet his power is of God. Neither the Emperor nor the laity can interfere in his choice, nor can he be deposed. If, indeed, he be a heretic, a general council has the right of deposition; but in that event it is the heresy, and not the will of the council, by which his authority is terminated. That apart, he is entitled to absolute obedience. His will is the will of God, and from his decision neither prince nor peasant may appeal; nay, to venture to do so is to rebel against God, since papal authority is of divine institution.

Nor is this all. Since the Pope has a power which clearly transcends all earthly rivalry, the superiority of the Papacy to the Empire is manifest. Indeed, granted the nature of his office, the Empire, in the view of Augustinus, shrinks to a pale figment of reality. For the Pope may depose the Emperor. He may set aside an election. He may transfer the power to choose from the constituted electors. He may alter the actual constitution of the Empire. And these rights apply similarly to all other secular governments since the Pope acts on earth as the vicegerent of God. Temporal authority, Augustinus argues, has no validity save as it conforms to the will of the priesthood. The *Donation of Constantine* means the restoration to the Pope of direct sovereignty over all earthly kingdoms. It means that the forms of government exist by his permission; that the property of princes is his property; that neither royal nor imperial law is valid save as he consents to it. And this, be it noted, is not a theory set above the battle which had been joined. It is the necessary weapon of a Papacy which had abandoned the pursuit of spiritual right and sought to control the world by immersion in the world. It is the voice of imperialism using for its purpose weapons it had neither the moral right nor the physical power to wield.

Inevitably it met with challenge, and it is with the outline of the case against its claims that the faint shadow of modern political doctrine appears on the horizon. For, as Frederick II pointed out to his fellow-princes, the papal theory was not only an attack upon the Empire; it laid the axe at the root of all secular independence. Nor did it fit the facts of European life. If the Empire was a declining power, the new nationalism of England and France was an index of growth. And such claims could only have made their way if they had been supported by a moral vigour which made men eager to respect the Papacy. That was not the case. The popular literature of the fourteenth century is nothing so much as a contemptuous account of the ethical degradation of the Church. Chaucer has no good word for any ecclesiastic save the poor parson; Langland strikes the same note with even greater emphasis; Gascoigne's sombre picture is later attuned to the same key. The dislike of Rome is evident on every hand. It is shewn, for instance, in the refusal to allow Henry Beaufort, the Cardinal-Bishop of Winchester, to take part in the business of the Privy Council once he had been elevated to the purple. It is shewn in Archbishop Chichele's response to Martin V when ordered to set aside the Statute of Provisors: only he himself, wrote the archbishop, in all England would venture to raise the question; and it was hard to be blamed for what he could not avoid. What, indeed, Rome and its partisans failed to understand was that the rise of national States was even more fatal to their claims than the existence of the imperial power; and when, as with Wyclif in England and Hus in Bohemia, the condition of Rome made possible the synthesis of national feeling and the demand for religious reform, the maintenance of those claims had become impossible.

Not the least interesting evidence of their unreality may be found in a treatise, written in 1300, which was almost certainly the work of one Pierre du Bois, a royal advocate in Normandy, and an eager partisan of Philip IV in his struggle against Boniface VIII. The treatise is a curious mingling of medieval and modern ideas. It is medieval in its insistence on the need for unity of world-direction, in its confident appeal to astrology, in its admission as historic of the *Donation of Constantine*. But it is modern in its pride in the national power of France, and in the somewhat naïve realism with which it analyses the real facts of the papal position. The purpose of his book, says du Bois, is to enable the King of France to avoid making war; and the method he proposes is the domination of the world by his sovereign. His reasons are two-fold. First, there is the inherent superiority of the French character: the French have a wiser judgment than other nations, they do not move without thought, they act as right reason would dictate. This emphasis upon national superiority is a new note in political literature. Nor is there less of novelty in his advice to the Pope. The latter, he admits, has the right to all the lands granted to him by Constantine. But he is usually old and weak, and he cannot—du Bois did not foresee John XXIII—be a soldier. Not only, therefore, can the Pope not enforce his rights, but, also, his very weakness stirs up the ambition of sinful men. This leads to war, which, in its turn, leads to the condemnation by the Pope of innumerable persons whom it is his real function to safeguard against danger. Let him then surrender his temporal power, and an effective source of conflict would be removed.

The rights thus relinquished could be transferred to the King of France in return for a pension; and the latter, partly by conquest and partly by treaty, could soon bring Europe to submission.

The scheme is not the less important because it is impractical. It shews how far men's minds had already gone in rejecting both the suzerainty of Pope and Emperor. The Ghibelline view of Dante was at least reconcilable with a great historic past; it was the ruins of old Rome he sought to restore. But du Bois has no hesitation in breaking with that past; and he has an emphatic sense of the papal claims as no more nor less than a source of mischief. Not less noteworthy is the clear view, emphasised throughout his treatise, of the right of the civil ruler to unexcepted allegiance; if Lombardy, he says, will not give obedience to the King of France after the arrangement with the Pope has been made, every method may lawfully be used to force it into subjection. Not less interesting is his argument, in a treatise upon the power of the Papacy, that while the Emperor must acknowledge, as the right of confirmation and coronation makes manifest, the overlordship of the Pope, no such acknowledgment is necessary from the King of France. This emphasis upon national independence is clear proof of a new temper; and it lends, both to English and French political speculation before the Conciliar Movement, a freedom in opinion which was much more difficult to the partisans of the Empire. That is evident, for example, in the examination by John of Paris of the question whether the clergy are entitled to worldly goods. He does not accept the view of the more radical party that they explain the moral degradation of Rome; but, with equal vigour, he denies that they are the inherent right of the Pope as the Vicar of Christ. He takes his stand upon the simple fact that princes in particular, and the laity in general, have been eager to purchase their salvation at the expense of their property; and clerical possessions result from grants in the same way as any other. This rationalisation of vaster claims is, of course, a basic attack on papal pretension; and it is accompanied, both with du Bois and John of Paris, by the insistence that the phrases of Scripture have no significance outside their historic context. The denial of the mystical interpretation of Scripture already points the way to the scepticism of the Renaissance.

Yet, significant as these protests are, they are not less unreal than Dante's epitaph upon the Empire. For they do not answer the papal claims in their own terms: and the unity they seek to substitute therefore is built upon expediency. The plea is an inadequate one. The papal doctrine, whatever its weakness in fact, is a doctrine of universal right, and it could be shattered only by the overthrow of its own postulates. Men like du Bois arrest us rather by the temper they reveal than the theory they represent; and the central challenge to the Papacy was still to be the work of imperialist partisans. The radicalism of a pamphlet like du Bois' *De Recuperatione Sanctae Terrae* with its suggestions of monastic disendowment and international arbitration, of women's enfranchisement and a French Emperor at Constantinople, is not less fanciful than the conservatism of Augustinus Triumphus. The real attack came from men who were driven to rejection of the papalist assumptions, to acceptance, therefore, of secular independence, not by the desire to erect kindred assumptions in its place which would merely have served an alternate despotism, but by the observation of the difference between the ideal end the Church sought to serve, and the ends in practice achieved. They judged the Church not by what it claimed to be as a vision but by what its actual life shewed that it was. On that ground only could a reasonable alternative have been erected.

Much the most brilliant exponent of the true case against Rome was Marsilio of Padua. He was born at Padua about 1270 of middle-class parents, and little of his early life is known; but his appearance, in 1312, as Rector of the University of Paris is evidence that he had already attained no small intellectual distinction. At Paris, it is possible that he came into contact with the great English schoolman, William of Ockham, whose defence of nominalism had made him the outstanding thinker of the time; and if, as is not unlikely, he listened also to the teaching of the French radical John of Paris, his own intellectual powers would have been strengthened by contact with the two great sources of fourteenth-century innovation. After 1312, a silence again enshrouds his career; and its next stage is marked by his appearance with a colleague, John of Jandun, in the camp of Lewis of Bavaria. This was in 1327. Three years before, by midsummer of 1324, he had already written, with John's help, his great work, the *Defensor Pacis*; and, with such ideas already in his head, his resort to Lewis is natural enough. The latter's sudden access of glory in Italy resulted in Marsilio's appointment as Papal Vicar in Rome. But the triumph of Lewis was short-lived. His adherents were denounced as heretics, and he himself was compelled to offer submission to the Pope. Marsilio, however, remained recalcitrant; and he died, perhaps early in 1343, professing the opinions in which he had lived.

For Marsilio, the historic struggle between Empire and Papacy was probably but an aspect of a wider conflict. The true mainspring of his ideas is the antagonism between Rome and the Spiritual Franciscans, to whose supporters he, with Ockham and John of Jandun, belonged. It was the insistence of his party upon the literal significance of the poverty preached by their founder which brought them into conflict with Rome. A doctrine of rigorous apostolic simplicity was not likely to be acceptable in the luxurious ease of Avignon; for it would have deprived the Papacy of every material weapon at its command. It was condemned by John XXII, and the condemnation enforced amid circumstances of great brutality. The defeated party did not acquiesce in silence. They denounced John as a heretic, and appealed against him to a general council. Their general, Michael of Cesena, in a treatise against the errors of the Pope, made criticisms of far-reaching import. A Pope, he argued, can err both in faith and morals; infallibility belongs only to the Universal Church. The final announcement of faith is, therefore, the prerogative of the latter. The Pope is no more than the minister who executes its will.

It is easy to see that there was a real relation between these ideas and the doctrine embodied in the Ghibelline view. Lewis was struggling to free the Empire from the Papacy; the Spiritual Franciscans were seeking to free the Church from the sordid absolutism of which the Pope had become the representative. It was not difficult to assume that an imperial victory would set the Emperor free to effect a reformation of Rome; and the Spiritual Franciscans who devoted themselves to that cause never lost sight of the larger and nobler aim. Their effort naturally drove them back to the foundations of authority. They confronted a Church which had given itself the organs of a State, and was seeking to make of secular authority no more than an instrument for its own material advancement. They had to shew that this whole conception rested neither upon legitimate history nor ethical foundations. More, they had to discover an alternative view which would not only recall the Church to what they conceived its original and nobler purpose, but would also safeguard the secular authority, whose power they would thus advance from the poison inherent in the nature of that power.

It was a gigantic task; yet the *Defensor Pacis* is not unworthy of its underlying aim. To understand it, we must remember that it is written by a man whose grasp of the *Politics* of Aristotle—which Aquinas had made an essential part of the medieval tradition—was invigorated by contact with the eager life of the Italian cities. Civil Society, it argues, is a community aiming at a common life. It is composed of classes each of which has some specific function; that, for example, of the priesthood is "to teach and discipline men in those things which, as the Gospel lays down, must be believed or done or refrained from, to attain eternal salvation." The ruling power of the community belongs to the judicial class who enforce the law. Law is defined as "knowledge of the just or useful to compel observance of which a command with a sanction attached has been issued." The sole legislator of a community is the people as a whole, or a majority of them. They only, in their general assembly, can say what men, under sanction of general punishment, must do or refrain from doing. It is from the people as legislator that the prince, or other ruler, derives his power. His task is himself to observe the laws, and to see that others observe them. But he is the servant, and not the master of the laws; if he sets himself above them, he must be controlled by the legislative power of which he is no more than minister. And it is important that the power of the community should belong to all its citizens. If it is in the hands of a few, there is no safeguard against error and selfishness. Only the whole people can know its wants; and that it may be protected against an ambitious prince, Marsilio insists that monarchy must be elective and not hereditary. While he himself believes that monarchy is the best form of government, he admits the argument for other views; nor does he urge, like Dante and the orthodox Ghibellines, that a universal monarchy is necessary. For him the essence of kingly rule is the popular right of deposition. He is concerned at every point, especially, for example, in his discussion of the place of the army in the State, to see to it that the will of the majority is the effective power in the State. And the axiom upon which the whole argument rests is that the State is itself a *societas perfecta* having within it all the means of sufficient and independent life.

The first book of the *Defensor Pacis* reads not unlike an eighteenth-century treatise the author of which has learned from Locke the importance of majority rule. By majority, indeed, Marsilio did not mean a mere counting of heads; he has rather in mind that "maior et sanior pars," the men of worth and substance, who appear so often in medieval thought. Numbers are to count; but they are not to outweigh quality in the making of decisions[1]. Particularly striking is Marsilio's insistence that the priesthood is not essential to the existence of the State. At the outset of his treatise he is thus able to free himself from what, until Machiavelli, was the outstanding feature of political science. With rare detachment, he is able, that is to say, to conceive of the Church as an institution made by men for purposes defined by them. But the Church has departed from the path laid down for it. So far from devoting itself to the eternal welfare of men, it has usurped other functions with which it has no true concern. It asserts its power over all manner of secular persons, especially the Roman Emperor; and in this assertion of its temporal authority Marsilio finds the real cause of medieval disturbance. It is, therefore, essential to discuss the true character of the priesthood and its relation to the secular community. Here Marsilio is as radical as he is original. He anticipates not only the views of Wyclif and of Hus, but the essential claims of the Reformation itself. For to him the only possible definition of the Church is that it is the whole body of believers. Layman and ecclesiastic alike are churchmen; and the prerogative of the Church cannot, therefore, be restricted to a single class of its members. No priest, for example, has the right to excommunicate; that power belongs either to the congregation to which the sinner belongs, or, on appeal, to the Church as a whole. The spiritual functions of the clergy do not comprise whatever actions ecclesiastics may do; whenever they step outside the narrow limits of ecclesiastical duty, as in holding property, they are as much laymen as the ordinary citizen. When they commit crimes, they have no right to a special jurisdiction. They are merely

---

[1] Dictio I, Chap. xii, Pars 3, "Valentiorem inquam partem considerata quantitate personarum et qualitate." Clearly the conception of a majority is intended to combine numbers and status in the community; it is not based on the equality of citizens.

ordinary members of Society entitled to no peculiar rights. The prince, indeed, would be wise to limit the number of ecclesiastics in any State, if they appear likely, through their growth, to threaten the peace of the kingdom.

This is already a thoroughgoing defiance of the orthodox papal doctrine. It assumes that the clergy have power only in spiritual matters; and Marsilio assumes that they can effect their purpose only by spiritual means. To temporal penalties they have no right whatever. These are unconnected with the Gospel which is not, in the legal sense, a law at all, but a code of conduct. Men are not compelled to obey it by a temporal sanction and its injunctions are, therefore, purely ethical in character. For Marsilio, therefore, the priest is like the King of England to-day—he may advise and encourage and warn, but he cannot himself act. Even over heresy he has no jurisdiction. The sole judge herein is Christ, and His sentence is awarded in the life to come. If the heretic offends the civil law, he may be tried by the civil law for disobedience to it; but the Church, as such, can have no part in his trial. Error of opinion in religious matters is outside the competence of spiritual organisation. And it follows, from these views, that Marsilio must reject altogether the contemporary view of papal power. For the clerical hierarchy he can find no scriptural warrant; and the Papacy itself is no more than a convenient centre of unity, of which the historical growth is proof that it has no origin in the plan of Christ. He denies that Peter had any primacy over his fellow-apostles, or, if he had, that there is any reason to suppose that the Pope of Rome inherited it. Peter never was Bishop of Rome, so far as we can certainly say, and the pre-eminence of the papal office is an accidental function of Roman prestige. From this Marsilio concludes that the governing organ of the Church is the Church itself, acting through a general council composed of clergy and laity. Only the civil State can convoke it, since only the civil State has authority to judge and to legislate. So convoked, the general council has not only power over the Pope himself; it may decide all spiritual questions even so far as to excommunicate princes and issue interdicts. For the general council speaks in the name of the Universal Church and is thus the voice of the whole Christian Commonwealth. The Pope is thus no more to Emperor or prince than an adviser in spiritual matters; he no more rules them than the Archbishop of Rheims rules the King of France. Nor has he, or any other of the clergy, the power of forgiveness. His keys may open the door, but forgiveness itself depends upon the will of God who acts by his knowledge of the sinner's penitence. If this is absent, no priest has the power to absolve.

No summary can do justice to the brilliance with which these gigantic theses are laid down. The conceptions they involve foreshadow almost every point of modern political philosophy. The substitution of the people for the ruler as the true source of power; the insistence upon religious toleration; the reduction of the clergy from a hierarchy dominating the lives of men to a ministry serving them; these, laid down in detailed precision, are a prophecy as daring as anything in the history of human speculation. Of their influence, both immediate and prospective, there can now be no question. Marsilio, doubtless, was far in advance of what his own age would attempt. But the horror he inspired in the papal camp, the constant references to him in the literature, the recollection of him in the Reformation as the greatest of its precursors, are all testimony to the fact that he stated boldly and in detail what was already implicit in the minds of thousands dissatisfied with the moral conditions of the Church. He does not suffer from the narrow scholasticism which, with Ockham and Wyclif, makes his contemporaries seem remote from ourselves. He was unhampered by tradition either in method or in conclusion. To his friends, his radicalism may have seemed as Utopian as it seemed iniquitous to his enemies; yet it is difficult, in the long range of medieval philosophy, to find any thinker with a deeper insight into the conditions of human association.

It is, of course, probable that Marsilio's very originality made him less influential to his contemporaries than a thinker like Ockham who was content to travel the wonted path. However much the foundations of Marsilio's thinking were affected by the general philosophy of the English scholar, it is difficult not to believe that the latter's political thought was, in the main, derived from the Italian innovator. Marsilio had written the *Defensor Pacis* before he left Paris; his association with Lewis of Bavaria was its consequence and not its explanation. But Ockham did not write on behalf of the anti-papal view until he had been some years with Lewis; and it is, accordingly, natural to assume not only that his treatises are an apology for his actions, but also that they were written in the background which Marsilio had already drawn. Yet Ockham has qualities that are all his own, and a real independence of view; and his treatises are thrown into a form which, repugnant as they are to ourselves, probably contributed to the influence they exerted upon his generation. He rarely writes as one who has attained certainty. His business, whether in the *Dialogus* or the *Quaestiones*, is to throw out difficulties in the environment of a general scepticism. The very massiveness of his work probably explains no little part of his authority, for it enables him to explore the whole field in the terms of those subtle distinctions and counter-distinctions so dear to the medieval mind. In two ways, moreover, he was more attuned to the thought of his own age than was his great contemporary. He was, throughout his work, primarily engaged as a theologian doing battle for his own party; he has nothing of that air of aloofness which often makes Marsilio seem apart from the actual conflict. And he is much more aware than Marsilio of the complexity of the problems with which he has to deal. Marsilio, by a superlative effort of detachment, is able to outline a political philosophy almost in the terms of modern speculation; Ockham is more conscious of the long road men have to travel before that result may be attained.

Yet the general direction of the two thinkers is identical; where they differ is in the emphasis they offer. Ockham, not less than Marsilio, is hostile to papal sovereignty; but he has no desire to transfer that sovereignty elsewhere. Like Marsilio, he agrees that the Pope can err, but he does not suggest that even a general council is infallible. He is as sure as any man that the truth of the Christian faith is eternal; but he is uncertain how, in an imperfect world, its survival may be safeguarded. He denies that either the Decretals or the Roman accretions to Scriptural doctrine have a character particularly sacred; but when he searches for the limits of Revelation, his speculations wear an air of doubt and even bewilderment. He is not even convinced of the need for unity; for he suggests that there are conditions under which both ecclesiastical and temporal sovereignty might well be pluralistic. And even while, as an adherent of the Empire, he is prepared to concede to it a certain shadowy supremacy, he hints that institutions made by men are constantly subject to change; so that even the imperial power is, as it were, merely a moment in time. The one thing of which he seems to be confident is the self-sufficiency of the temporal power. That enables him to assert its complete independence of papal authority, and to insist that the power of the latter, as also its functions, are purely spiritual in character. And for him, of course, as for Marsilio, while the Pope may be the active, representative organ of the Church, he speaks always subject to its decision through a general council. With Ockham, indeed, the latter is even more universal than it is in the pages of Marsilio, since he argues, with much cogency, that women are equally entitled with men to represent the laity upon it.

No one can read far into medieval political philosophy without being greatly impressed by its abstract character. There is little therein of that obvious pragmatic urgency which is the typical feature of modern speculation. No one would imagine that John of Salisbury's *Policraticus* is a weapon in the conflict over investitures; no one would say, at first blush, that the *Defensor Pacis* is in essence a plea for the Spiritual Franciscans. There seems a deliberate effort on the part of writers to make the actual conflict in which they are engaged an incident in the eternal. It is this, perhaps, which explains the vastness of the claims on either side. Boniface VIII can never have hoped to give the substance of reality to the principles set out in the bull *Unam Sanctam*; the partisans of Lewis of Bavaria cannot have supposed that the scheme of the *Defensor Pacis* was an immediate ideal. But the willingness to write in terms of an ideal remote from immediacy gives to medieval speculation some of its essential characteristics. It enables them, after the period of Thomas Aquinas, to write as though Aristotle were a contemporary, and the features of the Greek city-State the natural situation of the medieval community. It permits the use, or rather the distortion, of scriptural texts as arguments

to which there is no answer save through the medium of counter-quotation.
It allows them, even when they write in England with a legal system
incapable of reference to classical models, to discuss the meaning of law
as though the jurisprudence of Rome were the only system to which attention may be paid. The basic feature of the Middle Ages is feudalism;
yet the classic political philosophy of the time hardly takes account of
feudal assumptions in its scope. That is the more curious since many of
the ideals for which the medieval publicists were striving, above all, their
notion that impersonal law is superior to personal desire, would have been
profoundly helped by the aid that inference from feudal theory might
have given. Not, of course, that there is absent a great feudal jurisprudence; but it cannot be said to influence seriously the main stream of
political thought, and so far as its impact on Canon Law is concerned it
need hardly have existed. The result, of course, is to give all medieval
doctrine an air of unreality. It does not seem attuned to its chronological
perspective. It moves, but it moves circuitously rather than directly, with
its epoch. There is nothing like that immediate impact of events on
doctrine which marks the religious wars of the sixteenth century in France,
the Great Rebellion in England, or the synchronisation of socialism with
the Industrial Revolution.

Yet when a theory of society in feudal terms comes to be written, it is
even more remote from the facts about it than the classical ideas.
That Wyclif's theories exercised a profound influence is obvious, especially
in the domain of theology. That they represented, in their general outline, the ideal for which men like Marsilio and Ockham were striving is
not less clear. They were hardly less nationalist in ultimate temper than
the writings of du Bois, different as may be their method of giving expression to nationalism. But they are as repulsive in form as they are
remote from the real. They are, on the one hand, an interesting effort to
reconcile Catholicism with national feeling, a reverence for Rome with a
realisation, common to all Englishmen of his time, that reform was urgent;
and, on the other, a highly idealised theory of communism as difficult to
apprehend as it was impossible to realise in practice[1].

The Wyclif who sought the means of papal reform does not go much
beyond the typical Ghibelline argument against the Roman claims. It is
significant, in this connexion, that the nineteen conclusions from his works
condemned by Gregory XI, in May 1377, are all political in character;
and most of them might have come directly, so far, at least, as their
substance is concerned, from Marsilio or Ockham. The original thought
of Wyclif is to be found in the two treatises on Divine and on Civil
Dominion, which seem to have been published about twelve years before
their author's death. Their main thought is the notion of dominion and
service. They are the terms of an eternal order which links up the lowliest
being of creation to its maker. God, so to say, is the supreme possessor

[1] Cf. *supra*, Vol. VII, Chap. XVI, pp. 495–507.

of all things, and the process of subinfeudation is continuous throughout the chain of creation in terms of reciprocal rights and duties. It is the performance of these which legitimises power; without them a man may have possession, but he cannot have dominion, which is possession justified by right. But the relation of God to his creatures is not precisely that of an overlord in the feudal scale. All hold of him directly and owe supreme allegiance to him; there is, so to say, an Oath of Salisbury, which makes the eternal feudalism built upon the English and not upon the Continental model. And since the individual is thus directly dependent upon God, it follows that the position of the Church is one of convenience and not of prerogative. Its mediation is not necessary to salvation, since every man may treat directly with his Maker. All men are, therefore, priests, and the rights of the ecclesiastical hierarchy are demolished at a stroke. Already, that is to say, we have reached the fundamental starting-point of the Reformation. The Church becomes, not a necessary, but a voluntary, organisation of men, and the way lies open to the dogma of territorial sovereignty.

No more radical blow at ecclesiastical privilege was struck in the Middle Ages. The remainder of Wyclif's political philosophy is special to himself and interesting less for its influence than for the ability with which it is argued. The righteous man, he urges, has all the riches of God, both in fact and in right; the unrighteous, the man not in grace, has no title to any of his possessions. For, as the *Book of Proverbs* says, "the faithful man hath the whole world of riches, but the unfaithful hath not a farthing." There can be no right without grace, since that is proof of God's favour; and possession by the wicked cannot be just, since it cannot be supposed that God would permit those who do not enjoy His favour to own by a just title. If the unrighteous have in fact the possession of power, they may, therefore, be legitimately deprived of it, since they have failed to perform that service to their overlord by which alone true dominion may be acquired. It may then be asked why it is that the evil man has in fact earthly possessions. Wyclif's answer is that the Church may be regarded either as the bride of Christ, or as a human community, in which bad and good are alike compounded. It is to that ideal Church, the bride of Christ, that God's grant of property is made; the possession of it by evil men is the accident which results from their seeming member-ship of the Church. But their possession is, in truth, unreal since it is not founded upon grace. Their title is temporary only, since they are wicked, and cannot, therefore, have dominion; and we know from Scripture that "whosoever hath not, from him shall be taken even that which he seemeth to have."

There is a certain scholastic abstractness about this doctrine; but it is grim reality itself compared to the consequences Wyclif draws from it. Since, he argues, the righteous man truly possesses the whole universe, all things work together for his good; and since there are many righteous and each must, therefore, possess the whole universe, only a communistic scheme of property is justifiable. "Charity," said St Paul, "seeketh not to be a proprietor but to have all things in common," and Wyclif, equating charity with grace, assumes that this is, therefore, the only scheme of things with divine sanction. All other rules of life are made by man, and are, therefore, so Ockham noted, transitory and indifferent in character. To discuss whether one form of government is better than another, whether one form of inheritance is better than another, exercises such as these are purely idle; for we are given the divine plan and our business is to seek its realisation. In an imperfect world, the governance of society by judges, as in ancient Israel, is perhaps best; though, so sinful is mankind that monarchy may be preferred, since its unity gives strength to restrain evil. That monarchy, moreover, should rather be hereditary than elective, since an electing body is bound to be infected with sin. In any case, no earthly title is adequate; only the favour of God as proved by grace can confer legitimacy. Rulers, indeed, are responsible to God; "By love serve ye one another," said the Apostle, and the title of the Pope, *servus servorum*, shews that they are stewards of the divine will. And their stewardship again implies communism, since all righteous men are at once lords of the world and servants of their fellows.

From this would seem to follow a doctrine of revolution which would aim at the establishment of the ideal commonwealth. That, indeed, was the conclusion drawn, not entirely without relation to Wyclif's teaching, by such men as John Ball in the revolt of 1381. But it must be emphasised that it was a conclusion to which Wyclif's own teaching lent no countenance of any kind. Whatever is, is for him of God; therefore the use of violence is incompatible with His laws. To resist is, thus, to disobey His will, which is sinful. Possession by the righteous does not mean temporary possession on earth, but ultimate possession in the Kingdom of God. The ideal scheme is for the world of the spirit; men must not seek by force to assure themselves its enjoyment. And the whole plan is applied by Wyclif to the ecclesiastical sphere. The Church lives in the realm of the ideal; if it concerns itself with temporal things, it abandons the law of its being and may be controlled by the temporal power. Wyclif, indeed, is even prepared to suggest that the Church may one day dispense with the Papacy itself. But in this realm, save in the form involved by his philosophy, Wyclif has little to add to the views already adumbrated by his continental predecessors.

Taken as a whole, the significance of Wyclif is, of course, theological rather than political. In the latter sphere, the system of which he was the advocate was too remote from the life about him to be important. He had none of Aquinas' insight into the naturalness of human institutions, nor of Marsilio's power to predict the polity of the future. Yet his doctrine is important if only because it shews so clearly how the ideas of the Middle Ages were being directed into new channels. With him, as with

Ockham and his compeers, the separation of ecclesiastical affairs from the State not only implies that the life temporal destroys the spirit; it is also evidence of the dawning sense that the secular world must be left un-hindered to manage its own concerns. In his over-subtle fashion, as befitted a doctor of the schools, he outlines with lavish detail his philosophic Utopia, and, in the discovery of its boundaries, he is already, by unconscious implication, outlining the frontiers of the modern world.

Yet we must not fail to notice that Wyclif's radicalism is deceptive unless we remember that it is steeped in a conservative temper. Wyclif is by nature an evangelical; for him reality is that inner light by which a man is led to intimate contact with his Maker. The knowledge of that contact, the prospect it offers in the life to come, are, for him, far more important than the grim facts of the existing world. There is, therefore, a conflict between the ultimate goal at which his philosophy aimed, and the methods by which he desired to reach that goal. The first may have given comfort to men like John Ball, the Abbé Meslier of his generation; the second was an assurance to the statesman that Wyclif was on the side of the established order. For, like Wesley and Wilberforce in a later age, he was so sure that the godly man had all the means of a rich life as to be undisturbed by the spectacle of a world in which the earth seems the inheritance of the sinner. To him, the glory of the life to come is too real to make the temporary evil of the present order seem worth assessment. It must be endured because it is the will of an Omnipotent God, a part, however difficult, of His mysterious plan. What must be looked at is less the actual situation than the purpose which informs it. We have assurance that the purpose is splendid. We derive from that assurance the duty of acquiescence in the *status quo*. Here, clearly, Wyclif lays down the elementary principles of philosophic conservatism. His tactic links him with those who, however radical in ultimate aim, have refused to admit the legitimacy of methods which seek directly for its realisation.

The anti-papalists of the fourteenth century are in much the same position as those who protested against the *ancien régime* prior to 1789. In both cases, there is a clear sense of the impossible results of unlimited autocracy. In both cases, there is the realisation that administrative corruption lies at the heart of the evils it is desired to cure. Marsilio, Ockham, and Wyclif can produce their ideal schemes of constitutional reorganisation in much the same way as Rousseau, D'Argenson, and the Abbé St Pierre. But, in each case, the opposition to the system has the fatal weakness that the system, degenerate though it is, represents too great a tradition to be overthrown by merely intellectual protest. It cannot be said that the fourteenth-century Papacy was popular any more than it can be said that, after 1754, there was enthusiasm for the *ancien régime*. Yet in neither case was it possible, until a final crisis arose, to find a lever of action whereby definitive change became possible. In the case of France, that lever was provided by the bankruptcy precipitated by the American war; in the case of the Papacy, it was the Great Schism which made inevitable a reconsideration of the Pope's authority. In each case, a revolution was attempted; and in each case, as is the historic nature of revolutions, the result was to recreate in what seemed a more powerful, because purified, form the centralised autocracy against which the revolution had been a protest. For the outcome of 1789 was Napoleon, as the outcome of the Conciliar Movement was Eugenius IV. The failure to realise the larger purpose of change meant, inevitably, a further disruption. Just as 1789 was a link in a chain of which 1830 and 1848 are other links, so the Conciliar Movement is the necessary prelude of Luther and of Calvin. And just as the principles of 1789 draw new life from each effort at their restatement in novel terms, so do the principles of the Conciliar Movement lie at the root of all subsequent effort at ecclesiastical reorganisation.

The Papacy suffered much in prestige by its seventy years' captivity at Avignon; but no one thought that its removal from Rome would serve as the occasion for a break in the unity of the Church. Yet the death of Gregory XI in 1378, after he had brought the Papacy back to Rome, was followed by a schism not healed for nearly forty years. The French cardinals realised that residence at Rome implied the destruction of their influence, they hated Urban VI, and they elected an anti-Pope. Thenceforward Europe was scandalised by the existence of two and even three Popes. The schism, naturally enough, emphasised to the full the need of general reform. It was clear that the prestige of the Church would be destroyed unless men bent themselves seriously to the task of reorganisation. Already, in Bohemia, the Hussite movement had shewn the implications of anarchy; and the failure of the Council of Pisa in 1410 to do more than accentuate differences involved a European effort. In 1414, at the instigation of the Emperor Sigismund, the Council of Constance met; and its attempt to grapple with the issues confronting it raised problems so large both in magnitude and consequence, that we are entitled to regard it as the real watershed between medieval and modern politics.

The Council of Constance was summoned to deal with three urgent problems. It sought to end the schism in the Church; it attempted to arrest the Hussite movement in Bohemia; and it desired to reform the Church in head and members. In the third of these, little or nothing was effected. Minor concessions were made by the Papacy in such matters as annates and provisions, and the decree *Frequens* laid it down that a new council should be summoned every ten years; yet, broadly speaking, the only permanent result on this side was the Pragmatic Sanction of Bourges (1438), which may be said to have given the Gallicanism of Gerson and the University of Paris a quasi-legal foundation. The Hussite movement was broken in pieces, but only after a long and bloody struggle in which the defeated party made plain how strong was the new nationalism of which the fourteenth century had seen the beginnings. The Council achieved the papal unity Europe so ardently desired; and though the Council of Basle seemed to threaten a new schism by its election of Amadeus of Savoy as anti-Pope, the rapid abdication of the latter consolidated the position of the Papacy in a final way. Since that time, there has been no anti-Pope in Europe; and though the notion of conciliar action lingered on until the early years of the sixteenth century, it is practically true to say there has been no possibility of effective challenge to papal supremacy within the confines of the Church. Those who have sought to combat Rome have been ultimately driven to do so from without its boundaries.

The literature of the Conciliar Movement is immense, for its impetus is European in character. Nor can it be divided into categories upon any simple plan. There are the treatises of the reforming party who seek for radical changes in ecclesiastical organisations. Of these, the most important are the French, and, in particular, Gerson, the Chancellor of the University of Paris, and Pierre d'Ailly, the Bishop of Cambrai. Their interest in reform is, broadly speaking, mainly structural in character; and their sense of ecclesiastical nationalism is everywhere emphatic. But hardly less notable are the Germans, among whom Nicholas of Cusa, Gregory of Heimburg, Henry of Langenstein, and Dietrich of Niem, are the outstanding figures. The chief characteristic of the Germans is their profound zeal for moral improvement. It is not untrue, for instance, to say of Nicholas of Cusa that he sees in institutions the main road to a recovery of religious well-being. For him, they are always a means, and never an end. In the Conciliar Movement proper, the only writer of real importance on the papal side is Aeneas Sylvius, who became, in 1458, Pope Pius II. But he had already written with equal ability for the conciliar schemes; and his writings are interesting less for their insight into the problems they confront than for the skill with which they are written, and their complete absence of religious enthusiasm. They are the work of a brilliant journalist adapting himself to the changing currents of popular opinion rather than of a man who felt deeply the meaning of events. A little later, however, the Papacy secured an advocate of great ability and profound conviction in Turrecremata, whose *Summa de Ecclesia* and *De Potestate Papae* expressed with great power the case for papal centralisation. Middle ground is occupied by the Italian cardinal Zabarella, whose *De Schismate* is an able attempt at compromise. Zabarella sees all the weakness of the papal cause; but he is not less capable of grasping the administrative difficulties presented by conciliar schemes. So, too, with the German, Dietrich of Niem, in his *De modis uniendi ac reformandi ecclesiam*. Dietrich has no doubt that reform must come; but he realises that reform must make its bargain with tradition.

It is important, however, to realise that no single thinker, or group of thinkers, represents at all adequately either the sweep or the impetus of the movement. Its theories, both in their strength and weakness, are seen most vividly in the acts and debates of the Councils, in chronicles like that of the learned Spanish canonist, John of Segovia, or in schemes of practical reform like the sixteen points drawn up by the Oxford theologian, Richard Ullerston, for discussion at the Council of Pisa. The real centre of conciliar discussion is the nature of sovereignty in the Church. Popes have to be deposed if unity is to be achieved; it is, therefore, essential to regard the Church as itself a sovereign and perfect society with the means and right within itself to correct what deficiencies may be discovered. And the experience of papal supremacy involved the search for means whereby it could be kept permanently in leading-strings. The conciliar thinkers were thus led back directly to the foundation of authority. They were compelled to argue that power is a trust and that only its proper use can justify its exercise. But "proper use" means that which benefits the Church as a whole; and only the Church as a whole can decide what is for its benefit. At the very outset, in fact, the thinkers of the movement are driven to discuss the Church as though it were a State, and to settle the primary relations between its government and its subjects. What, accordingly, they construct is not merely a theory of ecclesiastical organisation, but a whole armoury of civil principle. The road from Constance to 1688 is a direct one. Nicholas of Cusa, Gerson, and Zabarella are the ancestors, through pamphlets like the *Vindiciae Contra Tyrannos*, of Sidney and Locke.

For they are concerned with the ultimate principles of obedience in a State. What, they ask, is a valid law? Is it simply a command issued by a competent lawgiver which must, by the mere fact of being issued, be obeyed? It would not have been difficult to take that attitude when the lawgiver was the Pope. For centuries of tradition seemed to authorise his primacy, and therein men could discern that centre of unity so necessary to the medieval mind. It was, moreover, impossible to deny certain legal rights to the Pope; he was the recognised depository of an authority it had long seemed not only traditional, but also right, to obey. Yet the movement is able to rise above these difficulties. At the base of its doctrine lies the all-powerful concept of natural law. Positive law is legal only when it reflects the substance of natural law; the human lawgiver must be obeyed, then, only when his commands are consonant with that substance. It follows at once that the Pope is not a sovereign but a minister. He has power upon conditions. He is the executive authority of the Church. But as he is made by it, so the Church has the power, also the right, to unmake him. Otherwise, clearly, the Church would be his slave, and since *orbis maior urbe*, the Church must have the means within itself of asserting its supremacy. Power wrongfully used may be destructive of the very purpose of the society, and, when so used, that supreme law which popular well-being demands must come into play. All government is thus ultimately built upon consent, and it cannot, without consent, be a righteous government.

These general principles are explosive in their results. They destroy, for practically every writer in the period, the notion of right built upon prescription. The only ultimate source of right is the need of the Church; and the only authority capable, or even justified, in interpreting the need of the Church is a council representative of its members. The Pope has therefore no plenitude of power. He is never *legibus solutus*. His primacy is built only upon consent; and, since, so Nicholas of Cusa argued, the *Donation of Constantine* is a forgery, it could be transferred to whatever centre the Church might select. A council alone can define and enforce ultimate rights. It may meet whether the Pope summons it or no. It may, after papal summons, continue even when the Pope has ordered it to terminate, if a majority of its members so ordains. If the Pope will not summon it, it may meet under imperial authority. It is this profound sense that the nature of the Church demands representative institutions which led to the famous decree *Frequens* of the Council of Constance. Implied in that decree is a complete ecclesiastical constitution. It regards the Pope as a prime minister, whose delegation is from the supreme assembly of the Church. Therefrom are derived the principles within which his powers are laid down. He is flanked by a privy council of cardinals by whose advice and consent he should act. They represent the guardians of the Church in the period when its council is not in being. Their business is to curb the exercise of papal authority, since the wrongful use of power may be fatal to the life-principle of the Church. The cardinals, moreover, should represent the constituent-nations of the Church, for its ultimate unity is expressed through a diversity which requires expression. No one doubts that unity, but it is, so to say, essentially feudal in its character. In this way an end may be made of autocratic power, and the will which receives effectiveness can be built upon the consent of the ecclesiastical organism as a whole.

No book in the period of the Councils so well expresses the temper of this thought as the *De Concordantia Catholica* of Nicholas of Cusa. It is a passionate plea for unity, but a unity which expresses itself in the manifestation of difference. It emphasises the need of a power built upon a wide basis of consent. It sees the need everywhere for a rigorous limitation of authority. It makes large concessions to that ecclesiastical nationalism which the discussions of Constance and the Bohemian wars had shown to be inescapable. It is hostile to clericalism in the same way that Marsilio and Wyclif were hostile, without their ruthless refusal of all attempt at compromise. It sees not less clearly the need for civil reform, the necessity of equitable taxation, the creation of a representative parliament for the Empire, the limitation of imperial power by some form of council. Nicholas, moreover, may be said to have learned something from the martyrdom of Hus, for he is clear that persecution is rarely effective and he pleads for religious toleration in matters of minor importance. Throughout, the book is a protest against the narrow legalism of temper which used prescription as a weapon against necessary change. Nicholas wrote with a sweetness of temper, an eager desire to conciliate hostile opinion, an anxiety, at all points, to attain largeness of view, which give his book something of the breadth and insight of Hooker. But whereas Hooker was the prophet of a reform to be achieved, Nicholas of Cusa, like Dante a century before, was writing a *credo quia impossibile*. The facts had already destroyed his solution when he propounded it, and the end he sought had to seek realisation along very different paths.

The Conciliar Movement was the one universal expression to which medieval constitutionalism attained. The men who guided it were seeking to give institutional form to experiments, like those of the English Parliament or the general assembly of the Dominicans, which were the effort to make the will of a group the embodiment of the full purpose implied in its existence. They sought to make law the expression of consent and not merely the vehicle of power. They tried to limit authority by mechanisms which would compel it to labour within an area of competence previously defined and rigorously controlled. If the atmosphere in which they worked was consistently medieval, the temper they brought to their effort was definitely modern. The aims are precisely similar to those who sought the correction of a despotism like that of Charles I or Louis XIV. Pym and Prynne, Saint-Simon and Fénelon, these and thinkers like these we can parallel without difficulty from the earlier time. Just as the doctrinaires of the Civil Wars in England based their claims on a fundamental law to which power was necessarily subject, so the medieval doctrinaire built his attack on papal autocracy on the supremacy of natural law. The Parliamentarians were aided by the bankruptcy of the Crown; the conciliar thinkers were assisted by the Great Schism. In each case, probably, the nature of the crisis led men to theories far more drastic than they would have dared to formulate at its outset; opposition in a revolutionary epoch is the obvious nurse of radicalism. And in each case, the movement, broadly speaking, failed because the administrative mechanisms necessary to give these theories reality were lacking to those who announced them.

For the Conciliar Movement was a gigantic failure. There was never behind its leaders a public opinion wide enough or informed enough to make possible the success of its schemes. The grounds of its failure are obvious enough. Once it had reunited Christendom, it lacked all singleness of aim. It dispersed its effort in a multiplicity of plans, many of which—as the Council of Basle made clear—would simply have recreated the schism it was its purpose to terminate. The princes who blessed Constance had no interest in its continuance once reunion had been effected, and they only could have provided a vigorous opposition to the concentrated power of Rome. The movement produced only one great leader in Cesarini; and he was driven to abandon it by the recalcitrance of men without importance in the Church. It produced only one thinker of the first importance in Nicholas of Cusa; and his schemes were fruitless because they were already too late when he devised them. No conflict can be waged by a committee when its opponent is a single will that needs merely to wait to be victorious. The movement illustrated brilliantly the essential truth that in social life men will only obey when their allegiance is grounded in an ability to revere, which is also a basis of self-respect. But it shewed also the danger of thinking out the purposes of a revolution when its occasion had passed.

Another cause of its failure must not be omitted. The constitutionalism which the Conciliar Movement sought to make real was the application to the Christian Commonwealth as a whole of views already in part applied to the secular society founded on feudal principles. But, as the effort was being made, those principles were becoming obsolete in feudal society itself. The reverence for natural law, the right to choose a ruler, the sense that what touches all must be approved by all, the insistence upon the right to depose a bad ruler—these ideas, which are the foundation upon which the conciliar thesis was built, were already decaying in the secular world when men sought to transfer them to the ecclesiastical. The history of the Middle Ages is so much a conflict between Church and State that it is difficult to escape the tendency to make the theologian its typical political thinker. There is a sense, of course, in which that is true; but there is a sense in which it is important to remember that the typical thinker is a secular lawyer concerned pre-eminently with the secular commonwealth. We may emphasise the significance of Marsilio and Ockham, of Wyclif and Nicholas of Cusa. But we must not thereby obscure the importance of Baldus and Bartolus and Sir John Fortescue.

It is, of course, true that no medieval lawyer ever lost the sense of natural law as a system of eternal principles by which all positive decrees were to be tested. It is the will of conscience, the motivating principle of right, the will of God Himself. Jurisprudence is for him essentially, if ultimately, a branch of ethics, and might has always to run in the leading strings of moral principles. The idea never dies that at the back of phenomena may be discovered eternal right to which all political conduct must conform; and few would have dared to deny the illegitimacy of action which ran contrary thereto. But the work of the lawyers, in their effort to revive the art of jurisprudence, is an attempt to discover what precisely natural law is. It needs to be interpreted. Its meaning is not always obvious in the particular occasions where it must be applied. Gradually, particularly as the fourteenth century develops, there comes a vigorous insistence upon the idea of positive law as something made by the State and deriving the weight of its authority merely from its source. The prince is *legibus solutus*; his will has the force of law. These great texts seem to enshrine the notion of law as embodied in the person of a ruler. There grows up a strong division between *ius publicum* and *ius privatum*. The one takes precedence of the other. The rights, for example, of positive law are regarded as at the disposal of the sovereign. Bartolus clearly feels that the incidents of the imperial office are inalienable; the knight in the *Somnium Viridarii* develops the notion of a *raison d'état* which places legislation at the royal mercy. The prince is *lex animata*; he gives to positive enactment the principle of its being. The influence of classical jurisprudence naturally strengthened this view. It drives even the philosophers to recover the need for a unity in the State which involves a supreme organ for the expression of its will. Phrases creep into the books which begin to foreshadow Bodin and Hobbes and Rousseau. *Imperium*, says Gregory of Heimburg, is *indivisibile et inalienabile*; and Bartolus argues that things like the right to tax can never be given to a private person even if the profits therefrom are surrendered to him.

Nor is this all. The invention and the triumph of the concession theory of corporations inevitably meant the victory of princely power. The group is put in fetters; it is, because a superior will has permitted it to be. *Civitas* may mean a city as well as a kingdom, but Bartolus is clear that a true State is a body which does not recognise a superior. Anyone who studies the history of gild or burghal franchises in England will realise the influence of this notion. In public law the group is derived from the State, and it has no will save that permitted to it by lawyers who are seizing every occasion to exalt State-power. They dare not resist. There is no appeal, says Aeneas Sylvius in his Germanic days, from the fiat of the Emperor; even to think of such a thing is *lèse majesté*. Petrus de Andlo says roundly that all power is derived from the State. Albericus de Rosciate refines away the difference between natural and positive law until, for practical purposes, it is non-existent. Baldus preaches with eloquence the duty of passive obedience. The joint result of legal and philosophic effort is two-fold. It makes the State identical with the community, and, thereby, transfers to the State the power which the medieval need for unity implies. And since the State is recognised as the supreme corporation, it follows that its representative organ, whether prince or assembly, is entitled to speak absolutely in its name. That absoluteness is marked in striking fashion. It means, for example, that, *a priori*, contracts which diminish the power of the State are void. It means that a right of expropriation in the ruler is recognised which, even if accompanied by remarks on the wisdom of justice, is broadly unlimited in extent; indeed there is hardly a thinker on the radical side in the ecclesiastical controversy who does not say forthright that public well-being permits, and may even demand, the confiscation of Church property.

It is, indeed, true, and it is important, that for the great glossators in an absolute sense, the only true State is the Empire as a whole. Their recognition of a quasi-independence to *regna* and *civitates* is a grudging one; there is something private about them, and to accord them such status is at bottom incorrect. But the concession is in fact made and it has in fact to be made. For the actual events of the fourteenth century made any other attitude impossible. It is the inference from all the English anti-papal statutes of the fourteenth century, as from the attitude to Henry Beaufort in the fifteenth, that England is an independent State with all the means within itself of a sufficient life. If the test of Statehood is *superiorem non recognoscere*, as it is for Baldus, the English lawyer would have asked no more. So, too, with France. The first chapter of John of Paris assumes without discussion that the realm of France is the abstract State of metaphysics. The *Somnium Viridarii* argues definitely that the need for unity is satisfied by its existence within a definite realm. Marsilio is, similarly, prepared for secular plurality. There are, it need hardly be said, not less emphatic views on the other side; and men as keenly nationalist as Gerson were dubious in this regard. But it is in general emphasised that the State is no longer the Empire, and that separation adds to the sense of a State which makes the law for the community of which it is the ultimate legal embodiment.

It is worth while to emphasise some of the results of this evolution. Broadly, it means that the way is being laid open for the emergence of the Reformation State. The *Respublica Christiana* of the Middle Ages is giving way before the exclusiveness of nationalism. And nationalism is coming to involve the idea of a centralised State which, in its turn, claims to represent and embody the total social interest of the community in all its varied aspects. That tendency is strengthened by the failure of feudalism to find a place in either juristic or philosophic politics; had it done so, its underlying notion of bilateral contract might have made the history of sovereignty very different. Had office, for example, remained a subject of proprietary right it would not have been very easy for the prince to treat his officials as merely the creatures of his will. So, also, with the rights of corporations. There was a period when it did not seem unlikely that jurisprudence would recognise them as at once original and real. What, instead, occurs is the emergence of an attitude which sets State against individual as the only true subjects of law. The corporation, or fellowship—and medieval life is nothing so much as a complex of fellowships—becomes, accordingly, a mere grantee of the State in public law and in private law that *persona ficta* the consequences of whose artificiality we are to-day but slowly removing from the Common Law. Generally speaking, it may be said that by the end of the fifteenth century everything is ready for the modern theory of the State except that crisis the needs of which will make it explicit. The Emperor, says Petrus de Andlo, can give to any fellowship what powers he will, and revoke them as he pleases in defiance of their tradition. It only required the demands Luther was driven to make upon the secular authority to transform such a creed into a philosophy of power by which Europe has been governed to our own time. The thinkers of the fifteenth century make a direct high-road to Luther; and, perhaps only half consciously, it is from the wants he fashioned into dogmas that men like Hobbes and Hegel took their weapons.

Nor have these ideas merely the insubstantiality of theory. The famous attempt of Richard II to found a despotism upon the basis of a *lex regia* which becomes, in his hands, the notion of indefeasible prerogative is proof that they had reality. When the Bishop of Exeter preached to the Parliament of 1397, his text (*Ezek*. xxxvii. 22) is the need for the incarnation of power in the prince lest anarchy supervene. In the end, of course, Richard failed. But the grounds upon which he stood, and, as the Articles of Deposition shew, the grounds upon which he was overthrown, were in England three centuries in the examination before they were finally rejected. For, after all, the Revolution of 1688 is only a repetition, upon surer territory of conflict, of the Revolution of 1399; and more than a century longer was needed before the continent of Europe was won to the general acceptance of the victorious philosophy.

If we enquire into the causes which explain the downfall of the typical notions of the Middle Ages, we shall have to find them in all the varied characteristics of the period. In part, they are to be found in the decline of the Papacy; that which claimed divine power was proved unworthy to apply it. In part, also, the unity of which the Empire was an attempt at secular embodiment never achieved administrative success; and the emergence of nationality was fatal to its claims. Within the new nation-State, a predominant cause is doubtless an economic one. The absence of enforceable unity in social organisation meant a multitude of petty tyrannies; and, as in France in the fifteenth century, the merchants were glad to make common cause with the Crown that, in its exaltation, they might escape from their thraldom. Beneath the high-sounding dicta of lawyers and theologians, in short, it is not difficult to discover the will of ordinary men to live under a common rule which may permit of enforcement equally upon all. The unified and sovereign State triumphed, in the first place, because it was an obvious convenience in general administration. It made certain what was before uncertain. It built order where, before, there was chaos. Later, of course, it may receive justification in terms of the divine right of its ruler, and passive obedience may become, as with Tyndale under Henry VIII, so much the customary view that men will receive with horror the theories of the Monarcho-machic writers. Yet, in its origin, the unified State simply appears as an avenue to peace; and it is intelligible enough that an age weary of internal strife should have received its coming, as in Tudor England, with gratitude.

But it is important to remember that the true medieval doctrine never dies. Not merely to the end of the Middle Ages does the notion persist that the State is built upon the idea of law. How strong it was can be seen from the fact that a secular judge like Fortescue is prepared, amongst other reasons, to admit the supremacy of the Pope over a secular ruler in order that the latter may be compelled to do justice to his subjects. Natural law, for the Middle Ages, has the primary force of modern enacted legislation; and no State would, in its view, have been entitled to obedience which did not assume its power to take rise therefrom. Even the thinkers who, on classical precedent, oppose positive law to natural law, have a sense of discomfort in making the opposition; for positive law is clearly the creature of expediency and its sanctions are hardly felt to be sufficient. Medieval politics, in fact, are a philosophy of universal right; and that, in its turn, is a theory of ethics, which is a part of theology. Men, accordingly, may not transgress it, since they dare not transgress the will of God. It is thus the ultimate criterion by which all human action must be judged.

The idea is a vital one; for it is at once the cause and the demonstration of the continuity of political thought in the Western world. The contribution of Greek Stoicism to Roman Law and to Christianity, that twofold sanction gives it new vigour and authority for over a thousand years. In the sixteenth century it encountered the antithetic notion of *raison d'état*; and the form given to it in the Hobbesian philosophy started a counter-tradition from which it has never fully recovered. Yet, even in the age of its decline, its roots are deep in human experience. International law traces its origin to its influence; men like Alberico Gentili, Grotius, and the great Jesuits wrote confessedly in its terms. "Ubi in re morum consentiunt," says Grotius of the schoolmen, "vix est ut errent." It is one of the factors by which the Common Law is moulded, as in the hands of Mansfield, to new needs. Freed from its ecclesiastical environment, it becomes, in the doctrine of the Rights of Man, one of the creative forces in modern time. And even when Benthamite dogmatism on the one hand, and Hegelian subtlety on the other, had made the rights of man an unacceptable conception, the thesis of a State to be judged by the purposes it achieves bore testimony to the power it embodies. There is a sense, in fact, in which the basic idea of natural law is a necessary part of any political philosophy which seeks to be more than a doctrine of immediate expediency. It was the glory of the medieval thinkers not only to have grasped that truth, but so to have stated it as to make it an integral part of the heritage of mankind.

CHAPTER XXI

THE ART OF WAR IN THE FIFTEENTH CENTURY

THE ancient supremacy of heavy cavalry, as has been shown in an earlier chapter, had been destroyed in the fourteenth century. In different parts of Europe different tactics had proved fatal to the ascendancy of the feudal knight. The burghers of Flanders at Courtrai (1302) and the Scots of Robert Bruce at Bannockburn (1314) had shewn that the pike-phalanx on favourable ground and with its flanks covered might prove invulnerable to the fiercest charge of horse. The Switzers at Morgarten (1315) had demonstrated the helplessness of cavalry in an Alpine defile; and at the less remembered—but more tactically important—battle of Laupen (1339) they had repeated the lesson of Courtrai, and beaten off the chivalry of Lesser Burgundy on an open hillside. These were victories of the pike and halberd over the horseman's lance; but far more important for the history of the future was the other group of battles in which it had been proved that "combined training" of the bowman and the dismounted knight might produce a form of tactics fatal alike to the column of pikes and to the charging squadron. This group starts with the obscure fight of Dupplin Moor (1332), where for the first time an Anglo-Scottish army formed itself in the combination which was to rule for more than a century—a central and steady mass of fully armoured men-at-arms, and long wings of archery. The much more numerous Scottish army was shot to pieces on its flanks, while held at bay in front by the spears of the dismounted chivalry. The same lesson was repeated against the same army at the better-known battle of Halidon Hill in the following year (1333). It remained for Edward III, the victor of Halidon, to make the great experiment of trying the new tactical combination which had beaten the Scottish infantry upon the French cavalry. Crécy (1346) showed that it was fully as effective against the onset of successive waves of charging horsemen as against the slow-moving column of pikes. This decisive battle had an immense moral effect all over the continent, far greater than that of Laupen or Courtrai. It set the feudal lords—in France at first, but soon after in Germany and other countries also—searching for new methods of tactics by which the power of the bow might be discounted. But the first experiments were not—as might have been expected—in the direction of raising a numerous infantry armed with missile weapons, who might suffice to oppose and 'contain' the archery.

The first experiments for use against the English combination of bow and spear were in the line of dismounting the greater part of the men-at-arms and throwing them in column against the English centre, while a small proportion of the cavalry kept their horses and tried to turn the

English flanks by a rapid encircling movement. This perhaps may have been inspired by a knowledge of the effective use of Sir Robert Keith's squadron against the archery of Edward II at Bannockburn, for there were always Scots adventurers in the French hosts. But at the first two occasions on which it was tried, the combat of Saintes (1351) and the battle of Mauron (1352), it failed—in one case the encircling did not come off, in the other it broke one of the two English archer-wings, but did not succeed in cutting in on the flank of the main body. At Poitiers (1356) John of France varied the device: while dismounting the mass of his cavalry, he sent 300 chosen knights to ride in ahead of the columns of attack, and to endeavour to distract the archers by a very rapid charge pushed home with desperation, under cover of which he hoped that his front line might come up unmolested. The plan was hopeless: the whole of the forlorn hope were shot down, and never succeeded in closing with the archers. The main column had to fight its own battle without cavalry aid.

After Poitiers the French seem to have despaired of the event of all experiments on the English "combined tactics," and allowed the whole of the rest of the first period of the Hundred Years' War to pass by without attacking a fully equipped English army. Cocherel and Auray (1364) were cases in which their enemies were mainly of their own race, and had with them only a few hundred auxiliary archers from overseas. Even so it is to be noticed that the French regularly dismounted all or almost all their knights and fought on foot at both battles. So did the French contingent at Navarete (Nájera) (1367), though their Spanish allies operated against the English wings with clouds of light horse. Both alike failed lamentably against the Black Prince's combination of bow and lance. In the end the 'counsel of despair' of Bertrand du Guesclin—the avoidance of all pitched battles—was destined to bring relief to France. He proved that a war might be won by harassing an enemy superior in battle-tactics, while denying him the chance of employing them. The English raiding armies found the French either elusive, or else so protected by stone walls or entrenchments (as at St Malo in 1378) that they could not be got at. But when the invading army had passed by, its enemies overran outlying English provinces of Aquitaine, and captured isolated towns and castles before another great force could be scraped together to retrieve them.

The first half of the Hundred Years' War ended with a truce in 1388, by which Richard II gave up the idea of reconquering the lost regions, and secured for himself only the narrow coast-strip from Bordeaux to Bayonne. Hostilities ceased, but the definitive treaty of peace, ratifying the *status quo*, was not signed till 1396.

Meanwhile the conclusion drawn by all continental captains after Poitiers and Navarete, that cavalry charges were useless, was working all over Europe. It was shown equally at Sempach (1386), where Leopold of

Austria dismounted his knights to attack the Swiss phalanx, and at the large-scale battle of Castagnaro in Italy (1387), where the Paduan leader dismounted all his men-at-arms, under the advice of the English *condottiere* John Hawkwood, and received at a stand and behind an obstacle— a broad water ditch in a marshy meadow—the attack of the much heavier force of the Veronese tyrant Antonio della Scala. But the Veronese also, it is to be noted, sent their horses to the rear, and attacked on foot, only to be soundly beaten. There is but one notable victory to be recorded for the column of dismounted men-at-arms in these years, that of Roosebeke (1382), at which Charles VI and his chivalry trampled down the less heavily armed pikemen of Philip van Artevelde, the leader of Flemish revolt. But here it was the tactics of Mauron and Navarete—mailed men in the centre, encircling movements by detached bodies of horse on the flanks—that turned the day against an enemy unprovided with any proper proportion of missile-bearing infantry. Had van Artevelde owned 5000 competent archers, the battle would undoubtedly have gone otherwise.

The only part of Europe in which during the last years of the fourteenth century the noblesse still fought on horseback was the East, where against Turk and Tartar the Hungarians, Poles, and Yugo-Slavs kept to the old methods. In each of these nations the strength of the State consisted in masses of light cavalry, and their enemies were also essentially fighters on horseback. When the French and Burgundian crusaders of 1396 went to the aid of Sigismund of Hungary against the Ottoman Sultan, they fell in with the system of their allies, kept their mounts, and charged the Turkish light horse, whose leading squadrons they rode down, but whose system of reserves, rallies, and successive attacks was too much for them in the end. Tired to death after several desperate mêlées, they finally succumbed when their horses could no longer be spurred to a trot, and their sword-arms were too weary to strike. Against an enemy composed mainly of light horse heavy cavalry is as useless for the offensive as is the phalanx of pikemen for the defensive. The only proper counter is the combination of large masses of missile-bearing infantry with a proper proportion of cavalry fit for the shock, or of heavy infantry able to protect the archers or bowmen from outflanking and encirclement. The first method was that employed by Richard I at Arsūf (1191) against the Saracen, the second that used by the Black Prince at Navarete against the Spanish *genetours* and their oriental tactics. Each was effective.

Probably the cavalry-battle fought on the largest scale in this epoch was that of Tannenberg (1410), where the united hosts of the Poles and Lithuanians beat and almost exterminated that of the Teutonic Order, the conquerors of Prussia and Livonia. The Knights of the Order, always engaged with the Polish enemy, and out of touch with new military developments in the West, had kept to the old system of war, and fought with squadrons of light horse supported by reserves of fully mailed men-at-arms. They had with them a certain number of cross-bowmen, but these apparently were used only for preliminary skirmishing; we hear of them at the commencement of the battle but not in its main clash. The Poles and Lithuanians were all mounted, the former with a certain proportion of heavily armed knights, but the latter mainly as semi-Oriental light horse. Hence the battle was a long and desperate cavalry scuffle, in which the larger army finally overcame the less, though at the left end of the line the Germans at the beginning of the engagement drove off the ground a large part of the Lithuanian light horse. It is rather odd to find that both sides had brought a few cannon to the field; but, as in so many engagements of this age, they only got off two or three rounds and had no influence on the day. Artillery, as has been mentioned in a previous chapter[1], goes back to the first quarter of the fourteenth century, about seventy years after the mention of gunpowder by Roger Bacon. There are indisputable references to guns shooting missiles in 1324–26, and the first contemporary picture of a cannon may be seen in an Oxford manuscript of 1327. A few years later they were quite common, but remained for a long time very ineffective except for siege work and the defence of places, the idea of mounting them on wheels having come much later. In their early days they were fitted upon "gun stocks", or large beams, and taken about on waggons. They could be set down and trained on a given spot, *e.g.* the gate of a town, or some weak spot in its *enceinte*, but change of position or of aim was a lengthy matter. The smaller ones were so ineffective, and the larger ones so cumbrous, that it was long before they could be used to any effect in the shifts of battle. At the most they could be set in fixed places in an entrenched position, if an army was resolved to accept a purely defensive action, and was certain of being attacked frontally.

In the middle years of the fourteenth century an attempt was made to secure volley-firing by a number of very small gun-barrels clamped together, and with their touch-holes so arranged that one sweep of the linstock would discharge them simultaneously. These primitive *mitrailleuses* were clamped to a beam with a mantlet to shelter the gunners, and sometimes mounted on wheels, so that they are called occasionally 'carts of war'. But generally they are named *ribaulds* or *ribauldequins*. Their fatal defect was the impossibility of quick reloading: after giving one blasting discharge, they would take an intolerable time to be got ready for a second. Hence, after enjoying some vogue for two generations, they dropped out of use early in the fifteenth century.

Their disuse was mainly due to the discovery of the fact that a number of single tubes of very small dimensions, carried on a wooden stock and each managed by a single man, were a more effective battle-weapon than a clumsy *ribauld*. The original "hand-gun" was nothing but a toy cannon strapped to a staff, and fired by the application of a match to a touch-hole. It was some time before men learnt to shorten the staff into a butt-

[1] See *supra*, Vol. VI, Chap. XXIII.

end, and to fire the weapon from the shoulder. We begin to hear of 'portative bombards,' only a foot long and fired from the hand, as early as 1365; but it does not seem to have been before the fifteenth century had begun that they grew quite common, assumed somewhat the shape of the later arquebus, and were used by organised units of soldiery. The first army that made them well-known were the Bohemian bands of the Hussite general Žižka and his successors (1421–34). The invention gradually killed the *ribauld*, because the latter could only be fired in one direction and was intolerably slow to load, while the hand-gun could be rapidly changed from one mark to another as its bearer chose, and could be loaded with much greater rapidity. It was never popular in England in the fifteenth century, because the national long-bow retained for many generations the advantage of very rapid discharge, and its arrow was, when shot by a competent archer, almost as penetrative as the pellet of the hand-gun. In fact the advantages which the long-bow held over the cross-bow in the fourteenth century it still retained over the primitive fire-arms of the fifteenth—it was both quicker in shooting and more certain of aim. But in the greater part of Europe archers trained to the English level of competence could not be found. Hence the cross-bow survived till it was finally superseded by the improved hand-gun during the great Italian wars of the Renaissance. There were cross-bowmen in the Spanish ranks as late as the battle of Pavia (1525), though bands of hand-gunners had been familiar to most armies ever since the days of the Hussite Wars.

The perfection of the cannon was as slow as that of smaller firearms. "Bombards" had been known, and regularly used, first in siege-work and then tentatively in the field, since the second quarter of the fourteenth century. But they had been so slow in technical development that armies well provided with siege guns did not triumph over the defensive so rapidly as might have been expected. This is well shewn by the length of early fifteenth-century sieges, in which towns attacked by the best artillery of the day could hold out for six months or more, like Rouen in 1418–19 or Meaux in 1421–22. The first case in which a very heavy train of artillery made unexpectedly rapid havoc of a formidable ancient system of fortification was at the capture of Constantinople by the Ottoman Turks in 1453. Sultan Mahomet II had got together the largest accumulation of big guns yet known—62 pieces throwing balls of 200 lbs weight or even more. These in six weeks completely broke down several points of the ancient triple wall of the imperial city, and made the storming of the breaches easy.

From the peace of 1396 down to the invasion of France by Henry V in 1415 there was no conflict on a large scale between the English and their continental neighbours. Though small bands of French auxiliaries came to the help of Owen Glyn Dŵr's rebellion in Wales, and though Henry IV lent a modest contingent to the Burgundian faction in their strife with the Armagnacs in 1411, no serious collisions took place, and the two countries went on each in its own line of military usage. There was, however, one battle on English soil which deserves a word of notice—that of Hately field by Shrewsbury (1403). This was the first fight in which two armies both trained in the school of Dupplin and Halidon, each operating with a central mass of dismounted men-at-arms and wings of bowmen, met each other in action. The good archery on both sides made the fight very deadly, and, tactics being equal, it was finally numbers which settled the day, the army of Henry IV being decidedly larger than that of the rebel Percies.

Henry V was already by 1415 a veteran soldier, but his experience had been all in the mountain wars of Wales; the protracted sieges of the castles of Owen Glyn Dŵr, and the long hunting down of his irregular and elusive bands, were a very different matter from the tackling of the forces of the great French kingdom. The experiment of his invasion of Normandy was therefore a very interesting one. Unlike those great raiders, Edward III, the Black Prince, and John of Gaunt, he was a strategist with limited and definite objectives, carrying out a plan for the slow subjection of Normandy by a series of sieges, each dealing with the key-town of a region. There is only one exception to this line of strategy in all his campaigns—the battle of Agincourt (1415). There is no doubt that he was convinced of the tactical superiority of the old English "combined training" of bow and lance, and he was anxious to court a pitched battle at all hazards. The French had made no attempt to disturb his siege of Harfleur; so he resolved to force them to action by marching at large through Picardy and challenging them to a fight. Only this intent can explain the apparent rashness of his Agincourt campaign, in which he ran many risks, not so much from the enemy as from the abominable weather, which left his army in danger of ruin from autumn cold and starvation. He finally obtained the battle which he wanted; the enemy got across his line of march to Calais, and after some hesitation attacked him. The tactics on both sides were precisely those of Poitiers repeated: the French sent in front of their great column of dismounted men-at-arms a vanguard of picked horsemen, who were to ride down the English archery, and cover the advance of the main body. Henry arrayed his army in the normal national formation—three bodies of dismounted knights, each provided with wings of archers thrown somewhat forward, covered with stakes planted in their front, and with orchards and villages covering the flanks. As at Poitiers the French advanced squadrons were shot down helplessly. But Agincourt saw a new modification of tactics: finding the enemy's main body slow in coming on—the recent heavy rain had made the fields into a slough, and the French could only shuffle forward at a snail's pace in their heavy armour—Henry took the offensive. He advanced against the enemy, halted long enough to let his archers riddle the front line with arrows, and then ordered a general charge, in which the lightly equipped bowmen joined in with their hand-weapons.

The chroniclers express their surprise that an onset of troops, many of whom wore little armour, should have rolled over in helpless confusion masses of dismounted knights. The explanation apparently is that the French line had been well shot about with arrows, was embogged from a weary trudge in the mud, and was tired out by long waiting in impracticably heavy armour. But of the result there was no doubt, and the rear lines presently shared the fate of the vaward division.

Henry could never get the French to oblige him with another pitched battle, and the rest of his series of campaigns is a record of sieges, the deliberate conquest town by town of Normandy, followed by encroachment farther inland after he had been taken into alliance by the Burgundian faction, and saluted as heir to the crown of France. His enemies of the dauphin's party refused to meet him in the field, the superiority of the English national system of tactics being taken for granted, as it had been after Poitiers seventy years back. If anything was required to prove this admission, it was the one English disaster of the period—the combat of Baugé (1421)—in which the Duke of Clarence, having outridden his archers, was surprised, overwhelmed, and slain, because he had given battle with his men-at-arms alone.

After the death of Henry V the French obviously considered that the change of commanders might bring them luck, and twice ventured to face the Duke of Bedford at Cravant (1423) and Verneuil (1424). But it was the system that was beating them, not the general; at each of these battles the English fought with the normal array of lances flanked with archery, their enemies with masses of dismounted men-at-arms and detachments of mounted men told off for sudden strokes. The event was the same as at Agincourt, and once more the French gave up in despair all hope of beating an English army in the field, and fell back on the defence of their innumerable towns and castles.

This was a reversion to the policy by which Bertrand du Guesclin had saved France fifty years before; but it was not by mere passive resistance and the avoidance of general actions that the second and more dangerous English scheme of conquest was to be foiled. On this occasion the change of fortune was caused by a moral and psychological factor—the appearance of Joan of Arc to rally French national and religious sentiment to the side of Charles VII. We are not here concerned with spiritual things, and must only point out that the military side of Joan's activity was appreciable. She not only put a new energy into the French generals, but shewed them that the English force was too small for the great task that it had taken in hand, that detachments might easily be cut up, and—this was most important—that the way to tackle an English army was to surprise it before it could get into array and throw out its archer-wings. For the credit of the battle of Patay (1429) was hers; coming on with headlong speed she caught Talbot's force before the line was formed, or the archers had time to fix their stakes, and scattered it. Whether her *coup* was inspired by a true military instinct or by a mere eagerness to get to handstrokes, we cannot be sure.

Joan stopped the progress of the English invasion, and dissipated the prestige of English invincibility. But, owing to the grudging and pusill-animous policy of her king's ministers, she did not finish her task, and perished unrevenged. The war lingered on for another twenty-three years, spent in the slow recovery of the fortresses which Henry V had mastered in 1415–22. It was essentially a war of sieges, but ended with two pitched battles of high tactical interest, whose details shew that we have arrived at a new epoch in the art of war, for in both field-artillery played a notable part. At Formigny (1450) the English army in Normandy had taken up one of its usual defensive positions, and seemed likely to hold it with success, when the French brought up two culverins to their front, and placed them on a spot from which they enfiladed the hostile line. They were outside archery range, and did so much damage that at last the English charged out from behind their line of stakes to capture the guns. This led to a hand to hand fight, which was undecided when a newly ar-rived French detachment rode in from the flank and rolled up the English line. Almost the whole force was exterminated. In consequence the few remaining English strongholds in Normandy surrendered with small delay.

In the final battle of the war, which lost Guienne as surely as Formigny lost Normandy, artillery was also prominent. Lord Talbot led the last levy of the English in the south to raise the siege of the loyal town of Castillon. The French faced him not in the open field, but behind a line of entrenchments, part of the contravallation which they had drawn around the besieged place. Talbot saw no way of reaching Castillon save by a frontal attack on the lines; the enemy, being completely "dug in" and under cover, could not be effectively reached by archery. All along the entrench-ments their numerous artillery had been placed. Talbot formed his men, both lances and bows, in a column, and dashed at the weakest point of the lines. The guns opened upon him with a concentric fire, the head of the storming party was blown to pieces, and he himself was mortally wounded by a ball which shattered both his legs. A few of the English got inside the lines, but were soon expelled, and the French then sallied out and made an end of the shattered column (1453).

It is worth noting that this intelligent use of artillery by the French distinguished all the later years of the war; the two master-gunners of Charles VII, the brothers Bureau, established a great reputation by their siege-craft—it is said that in the years 1449–50 they reduced as many as sixty castles and towns, small and great, in Normandy, after sieges of no great length, which contrasted strongly with the six months or more of leaguer by which Henry V had won many of these same places thirty years before. Obviously artillery was now a growing power, and could even be used effectively in the field, though as yet only under certain limited conditions.

CH. XXI.

All through the last years of the Hundred Years' War the English were still fighting wherever possible with the old tactics of the bows flanking the dismounted lances. The French shewed a growing tendency towards the use of cavalry for its proper purpose, but the merits of the two systems were hotly debated. When the Burgundians fought René of Bar at Boulgneville in 1431 there was long debate whether their knights should dismount or no; they chose the English system, and were victorious. At Montlhéry thirty years later, Commynes tells us of a precisely similar discussion, which ended in Charles the Bold bidding nearly all his men-at-arms take to their horses, only a few being left to stiffen his infantry. His French enemies all fought mounted, and succeeded in getting in some effective charges upon the Burgundian foot. This was in 1465; ten years later at Grandson Charles is found using all his men-at-arms as cavalry against the Swiss phalanx, which beat them off with ease. Nevertheless, except in England, where every battle of the Wars of the Roses was fought on foot, the knighthood was tending to resume its old methods of action over the rest of Europe. The fact was that the English system depended in essence on the possession of a very large force of trained archers of high efficiency, and no country save England could produce them. The continental infantry were still inferior in the field, with the exception of the Swiss, whose pike-phalanx was immune against cavalry, and could only have been dealt with in this age by the use of masses of missile-bearing infantry properly supported by cavalry. But the Italian, Burgundian, and German enemies of Switzerland had not as yet any such infantry. And when the Swiss in the next century met their first checks, it was not from the bow or the hand-gun, but from the German Lanzknechts—pikemen trained in their own style—or from the combination of cavalry with field artillery, as at Marignano (1515).

In parts of Europe where the English archer had not penetrated, the fifteenth century shewed some curious tactical developments. The most interesting was that of the Hussite armies in the long Bohemian War (1420–34). This was the result of an improvisation by a general of talent, who had to face the feudal forces of Germany at the head of a raw but fanatical national levy, inspired at once by religious enthusiasm and by hatred for the Teutonic invader. Žižka's device was the tactics of the *Wagenburg* or moveable *laager* of waggons combined with the use of masses of hand-gun men. It was as essentially defensive as the original English combination of archery and dismounted men-at-arms, but was less easy to handle, because its strength lay in the array of war-carts which sheltered the missile-bearing infantry. If there was leisure, not only were the carts chained together, but a ditch was dug in front of them, and the earth from it thrown up round the wheels. There was always a broad exit for sallies left in front of the *Wagenburg*, and another in the rear. But till the moment of counter-attack arrived these were closed with posts and chains. The hand-gunners mounted upon the carts, men irregularly armed with pikes, halberds, war-flails etc. were stationed in the narrow gaps between them. As the war went on the Hussites acquired cannon, which they mounted on specially built carts placed at intervals along each side of the fortification.

In the first years of the war the Germans repeatedly attempted to storm the *Wagenburgs*, sometimes by cavalry charges, more often by columns of dismounted men-at-arms, but they were invariably repulsed. When the attack had been shattered by the effect of the fire-arms, the Hussites habitually charged out, the counter-attack being led by the small proportion of cavalry which they possessed. Hence came many victories against an enemy who seemed unable to learn anything from his defeats. At last the Germans refused to attack a *Wagenburg*, and the Hussites took to invading Bavaria, Meissen, and Thuringia, where they wrought great havoc. Obviously the tactics that should have been used against them were those of refusing to assault a prepared position, and of only attacking when the Hussites were on the march, and the *Wagenburg* not yet formed. Or when it had been formed, artillery placed at a safe distance should have been used against it *en masse*, so as to force the defenders either to suffer unrequited slaughter, or else to sally out and lose the advantage of their defences. As a matter of fact the defeat (Lipany, 1434) which ended the Hussite wars was inflicted by their own countrymen of the Calixtine or moderate party on the "Taborites" of Prokop. After the failure of a real or simulated assault on their *Wagenburg*, the Taborites sallied out against an enemy who was not really beaten, but waited till they had come far forward in pursuit, and then faced them in the open and charged their flank with cavalry. The pursuing horde was cut up, and the victors then stormed the inadequately manned *Wagenburg*. The main legacy which the Hussites left behind was the multiplication of small fire-arms: during the next generation bands of hand-gun men—Bohemian, or trained in the Bohemian wars—were to be found in most of the armies of Eastern and Central Europe.

The military history of fifteenth-century Italy shews no such interesting experiment as that of the Hussites. While Sir John Hawkwood and other *condottieri* trained in the wars of Edward III, who had many bowmen in their ranks, were the most noted figures in Italy, the English system was for a time employed—*e.g.* we have already noted it at the important battle of Castagnaro. But as the influence of the Transalpine bands and generals faded away, and was replaced by that of native captains of fortune, the decisive use of infantry was forgotten, and cavalry tactics once more became predominant. Machiavelli and Guicciardini ascribe this to the decaying military efficiency of the civic infantry militia of the great towns; when mercenaries had been hired on a great scale, they forgot the valour of their ancestors, who had fought sturdily enough in the wars of the thirteenth century. When tyrants, the inevitable result of faction, grew common in Italy, they habitually discouraged the native *levée en masse*, preferring to rely on mercenaries. But the cities which never fell into the hands of a tyrant, such as Venice, were no less given to the employment of foreign bands than were the lords of Milan, Verona, or Padua. These mercenaries, hired out by their *condottieri*, or contractor captains, were from the early days of the fifteenth century onward nearly all heavy cavalry. Machiavelli remarks, with perfect truth, that in an army of 20,000 men there were often only 2000 or 3000 properly equipped infantry. A horseman naturally wishes to get the advantage of his horse, unless some overruling condition of war forces him to dismount, and the Italian battles of the fifteenth century were essentially cavalry fights.

But mercenaries fighting for profit, and hired one year by one prince and the next year by his rival, had neither patriotism nor fanaticism to excite them. To them war was a matter of business, and they were much more set on making and ransoming prisoners, or on extorting contributions from captured towns, than on killing their employer's enemies. Why should a thrifty captain slay the men-at-arms of the opposite party, who were capable of paying good ransoms, and perhaps were old comrades who had been serving along with him in the last campaign? And since war was his trade, was it wise to put an end to war by a crushing and conclusive victory over the enemy of the moment? And so, as Guicciardini says, "they would spend the whole of a summer on the siege of one fortified place, so that wars were interminable, and campaigns ended with little or no loss of life." When in 1428 the great *condottiere* Carmagnola captured nearly the whole army of the lord of Milan, at the battle of Maclodio, he disgusted his Venetian employers by ransoming all the chiefs and officers next day for his private profit.

The consequence of leaving the conduct of war in the hands of the great mercenary captains was that it came often to be waged as a mere tactical exercise or a game of chess, the aim being to manœuvre the enemy into an impossible situation, and then capture him, rather than to exhaust him by a series of costly battles. It was even suspected that *condottieri*, like dishonest pugilists, sometimes settled beforehand that they would draw the game. Battles when they did occur were often very bloodless affairs, ransoms rather than killing being the object of the players. Machiavelli cites cases of general actions in which there were only two or three men-at-arms slain, though the prisoners were to be numbered by hundreds.

This insincere and absurd form of war—long cavalry manœuvres ending sometimes in an almost bloodless tilting-match—continued in Italy down to the moment when the French came over the Alps to conquer the kingdom of Naples in 1494. These Transalpines, and the Swiss hired to fight in the Milanese quarrels, shocked Italian military opinion by winning unscientific battles after they had been out-manœuvred, and by slaying the routed enemy wholesale—*cosa nuova e di spavento grandissimo a Italia, già lungo tempo assuefatta a vedere guerre più presto belle di pompa e di apparati, e quasi simili a spettacoli*, as Guicciardini cynically remarks. The history of Italian fifteenth-century strategy and tactics ends with the coming of the bloodthirsty hordes of Charles VIII, and the introduction of the new forms of war which marked the period that was to endure for the next two generations.

The complicated and interesting battles of the great Italian wars between 1494 and 1558 only concern us here because it is necessary to shew that the elements of their tactics were already to be found existing as separate phenomena, not yet correlated, in the wars of the later fifteenth century. We have already noted the commencement of the practical use of field-artillery, and the multiplication of the smaller fire-arms which dated from the Hussite Wars. The cavalry charge, a thing almost extinct in Western Europe about the year 1400, had already been seen again at Montlhéry and in the wars of Charles the Bold with the Swiss. It was to emerge on a larger scale at Fornovo, Marignano, and many another bloody Italian field. Above all, the use of the heavy column ot pikemen, as a thing immune against the cavalry charge, had been seen in all the earlier Swiss victories, and had reached its culminating point ot victory at Grandson and Morat. The simultaneous employment on one field of fire-arms great and small, of the column of pikes, and of the onset of the heavy *gendarmerie*, was to be the characteristic of the sixteenth-century wars. But into these struggles we have not here to enter.

It was, in the end, to be the development of small fire-arms, capable of rapid discharge, which was to drive armour from the battle-field. But the hand-guns of the fifteenth century were still very imperfect weapons, not yet able to hold their own against good archery. Plate-armour had developed mainly as a defence against the long-bow[1], and defensive armour was at its prime during this period, for workmanship and for complicated ingenuity—we may add also for picturesque and artistic appearance; and the scalloped and fluted panoplies that are generally named after the Emperor Maximilian are certainly the most graceful armour ever known. But the man-at-arms paid dearly for the complicated defences which the smith forged for him. All through the century we hear complaints of the drawbacks of a complete harness. During the period when fighting on foot still prevailed, rapid advance was difficult, and retreat generally fatal. At Agincourt the French chivalry were wearied out, and finally almost embogged, by a mere march of a mile over newly-ploughed and rain-sodden fields. By the time that they got into collision with their enemy they were wellnigh exhausted. And the dreadful proportion of casualties among the higher ranks to be found in the Wars of the Roses was undoubtedly due to the fact that in a routed army the bowmen and billmen could make off rapidly, but the knights and nobles were doomed, unless they possessed exceptionally trusty pages to bring up their horses from the rear. In normal fights on the continent the slowly moving vanquished were captured and held to ransom. But

---

[1] See *supra*, Vol. vi, p. 796.

when a party blood-feud was prevalent, as during the latter part of this great English series of campaigns, we find commanders like Edward IV giving orders to spare the commons, but to cut down every man wearing golden spurs. In such a struggle complete armour was a death-trap. When horse-fighting came back into favour the drawback was not quite so evident, since the wearer of a heavy panoply might escape, if his horse were not disabled. Masses of fully-armed horse were still seen during the great Italian wars which covered the period where the fifteenth and sixteenth centuries join. But when cavalry once more became the dominating arm, as the sixteenth century wore on, it was a much lighter cavalry, which had begun to discard great part of its armour, and to aim at rapid movement rather than at mere massive impact.

Only one more point of importance remains to be dealt with before we have done with the fifteenth century and its art of war. This is the beginning of the national standing army, as opposed to mere royal guards or small permanent garrisons of castles, with which the world was already familiar. Of royal guards the largest and most formidable existing in 1450 had been the Janissaries, the slave-soldiery of the Ottoman Sultan, a force of disciplined infantry armed with the bow, which by the time of Mahomet II had reached a total of some 10,000 or 12,000 men. No Western power could shew any equivalent for it in numbers or efficiency; the personal retainers of Christian sovereigns never exceeded some few hundreds of men in permanent pay. And the existence of the Janissaries as a formidable unit of infantry had, all through the fifteenth century, given the Turks a great advantage over the irregular hosts of their Yugo-Slav, Polish, and Hungarian enemies—as witness Varna (1444) and the second Kossovo (1449).

But a permanent standing army had appeared in Western Europe, on a modest scale, in the year 1445, and was to be the first symptom of a general movement toward the creation of modern military organisations. This force was the *Compagnies d'Ordonnance* of Charles VII, a body of 20 units of horse and foot combined, which the King of France kept under arms when he disbanded after the truce of 1444 the greater part of the heterogeneous troops whom he had been employing in the English war. Charles's old levies had been *Écorcheurs* for the most part, ill paid bands often hard to distinguish by their conduct from robber-gangs, working for the benefit of themselves and their captains. At the great disbanding in 1444–45 the king selected from the mass of his officers a score of professional soldiers, some of them great nobles, others *condottieri* mainly of French blood, only a very few foreigners being chosen. To each of them was given the task of selecting and organising into a "company" a limited number of trustworthy and efficient troopers and archers.

Each of the twenty companies—fifteen for Langue d'oïl and five for Languedoc—consisted of a hundred *lances fournies* or *lances garnies* as they were sometimes called. The "lance" was composed of one fully equipped man-at-arms, a *coutilier* who acted as his squire, a page, two archers, and a *valet de guerre*. All were provided with horses for transport, but the two archers and the *valet* were intended to act as infantry, and it is doubtful if the page was a combatant. Thus the companies ran up to six hundred men apiece; they were each officered by a captain, a lieutenant, an ensign, and a "guidon." The total made up a standing army of 12,000 men, quite a considerable force for the fifteenth century. The man-at-arms received ten *livres tournois* a month, out of which he had to provide for his horses and the page. The other members of the lance had four or five *livres* apiece. That they were royal troops, and not mercenary bands hired from their respective captains, was shewn by the fact that the king nominated all officers, paid the men individually, and had a staff of inspectors, who reviewed the companies at reasonable intervals. They were not kept about the king's person, but garrisoned at strategic points all over France, and in their earliest years one of their chief duties was to keep the roads clear of highway-robbers, the legacy of thirty years of war.

It will be noted that the proportion of men trained to serve as infantry in the *compagnies* was small. To provide greater numbers, if of less valuable material, Charles tried the experiment of establishing a sort of local infantry militia, the *Francs-Archers*. In each parish or similar unit an able-bodied man was designated, who, in return for receiving immunities from taxation, was always to be ready to turn out with a bow or cross-bow, a steel-cap, and a "jack" or brigandine, when summoned to the field by the king. The archers of each district were to be assembled for inspection by royal officers four times a year, and were ordered to keep themselves efficient by regular practice at targets. The experiment was a failure, no arrangements for keeping the men organised in regular units, or accustomed to discipline, having been provided. Only long periods of embodiment could have made them a useful force. They turned out, when mobilised, to be little better than a peasant-levy, and though assembled in considerable numbers by Charles VII and by Louis XI in his earlier years, were gradually allowed to drop into obsolesence. The real origin of the infantry corps of the French standing army was to be found in the bodies of Swiss, whom Louis XI first hired, and who became under his successor a permanent part of the French military organisation. Regular infantry of native origin were not raised and kept on foot till the great Italian wars had begun, after our period has come to an end.

But from 1445 Europe had before its eyes the type of the modern standing army—the tool of Renaissance monarchs—as embodied in the *Compagnies d'Ordonnance*. Feudal armies are beginning to disappear, mercenary bands under *condottieri* or contractors are destined to follow them into oblivion, and in short the military organisation of the Middle Ages is about to give place to that of the modern world, though the hired adventurer, and the feudal man-at-arms doing his stipulated turn of service for his fief, were yet to be found for many a year on the rolls of the armies of the West

CHAPTER XXII

MAGIC, WITCHCRAFT, ASTROLOGY, AND ALCHEMY

THE Middle Ages received from previous periods and civilisations a rich inheritance of magic, divination, occult science, and demonology. Egypt and Babylonia bequeathed their long-accumulated stores of superstition. The one offered its elaborate mortuary ritual and charms for the dead, its scarabs and amulets, its wax images and mannikins, its polypharmacy and divining dreams. The other added its incantation tablets, omens, liver divination, prediction from the stars, and varied magical paraphernalia. Both bestowed their sorcery and demons. Greek philosophy had introduced a more rational attitude towards nature, but the Greeks had not abandoned magic and divination. From the Persian Empire came Zoroastrian dualism, in which the struggle of the prince of this world against the other offered possibilities for both terrestrial and celestial magic. During the Hellenistic period astrology developed its elaborate technique. The mysteries and oriental cults that flooded the Roman Empire were accompanied by kindred philosophies: Gnosticism, with its close relations to astrology and magic as well as to Christianity, and Neo-Platonism, with its divination and theurgy. In the literature of the Roman Empire, whether scientific or popular, historical or suppositious, magic and astrology were prominent and were passed on to the Middle Ages in such authoritative works as Pliny's *Natural History* and Ptolemy's *Quadripartitum*. Finally, there was the primitive magic and folklore of the less civilised peoples who lived in or near the Roman Empire, such as the Celts, traces of whose Druidic lore already appeared in Roman authors, or the Germans, which were to affect popular belief and custom of the medieval period.

As that period opened, however, the Western world, so far as it comes within our ken, was predominantly Christian, and the authorities, clerical or secular, were displaying systematic intolerance towards other forms of religious belief or of popular superstition. Paganism, as the word suggests, became relegated to the rural and backward districts. The Christian Emperors since Constantine, in their edicts preserved in the Theodosian Code, had forbidden magic and divination as well as idolatry and heathen worships. Various Church Councils of the early medieval centuries legislated against this or that popular superstition. How far did this policy succeed in wiping out the magical beliefs and practices of the past? To what extent did Christianity substitute an analogous magic of its own? To what degree did the old superstitions reappear in slightly changed forms or under new names?

The Old Testament contains prohibitions of divination and sorcery but also instances of their employment. In the Roman Empire the Jews were often regarded as charlatans, enchanters, and conjurers of spirits. The early Christians were similarly accused of magic by their adversaries, and the apocryphal and heretical writings, at least, of the early Christian centuries provided some evidence to substantiate the charge. The situation was not unlike a war in which either side hotly charges the other with employing illicit methods, weapons, or gases. But as with gases, so with magic. There is the kind that one indignantly prohibits and condemns, and, on the other hand, the kind that one practises and condones. This is a distinction to be kept in mind throughout the medieval period, that a prohibition of magic does not necessarily imply disapproval of all forms thereof.

If Christianity at first tended to simplify and purify religion and daily life, there soon grew up again the institutions of sacraments, priesthood, and ritual which had an affinity with the ancient order of religious ideas. On the other hand, the personification of things in nature was frowned upon as too closely approaching nature worship. This in turn brought into disfavour the belief that magic power is inherent in natural objects and in rites of nature. God must be given all the glory. But sooner or later the suggestion was made that all these marvels of nature were God's gift to man, that God had endowed gems with their extraordinary powers, that the stars—although not to be worshipped as gods—were His signs in the sky or instruments and secondary causes manifesting the future, that there was no harm in plucking a potent herb at dawn if one simultaneously repeated a paternoster. Thereby was saved the conception of occult virtue, fundamental in natural magic, and practically the entire pseudo-science of astrology.

The early Christians lived in an atmosphere of prophecy, vision, and miracle, and were keenly sensitive to what the Apostle Paul would have called the "pneumatic" world, or realm of spirits. This continued to be the attitude of the average monastery, and was inculcated by such literature as the lives of the saints and the sermons of popular preachers, or by such practices as the cult of relics, exorcisms, and holy water. The early Christians had been accused of atheism by their opponents, but, instead of denying the very existence of the pagan gods, they generally classed them as evil spirits, thereby swelling the ranks of demons, a class of beings already recognised by pagan antiquity, and increasing the possibility of magic.

Throughout the medieval period theologians repeatedly discussed the nature of demons and their capacity to perform or assist in the performance of feats of magic. Did these spiritual beings possess bodies at all, and if so, were these aerial and transparent to the point of invisibility? Could they assume any bodies they pleased, or did they delude the human senses or imagination into fancying that man perceived such bodies? Could they enter human and other bodies? Could they penetrate and pass through solid bodies? Could they move or transport through the air with extreme rapidity to great distances heavy bodies such as the prophet Habakkuk or witches on their way to the sabbat? Free from bodily limitations, immortal or very long-lived, and possessed as they were of extreme guile, had they acquired so intimate an acquaintance with the secrets of nature and so prolonged an observation of signs and sequences, causes and effects, contingencies and probabilities, that they could perform any marvel required by magicians and enchanters, and could predict with reasonable certainty the outcome of almost any event? Could they speak with the tongues of men and of angels? Could they produce impotency and prevent the consummation of marriage? Did they merely affect dreams and the imagination, or were they capable of intercourse with either sex? Such were the questions debated—in no small measure, it is true, in terms of what classical authors like Plutarch and Apuleius had said already concerning demons. While such questions were variously answered at different times and by different persons, enough preternatural power and subtlety was always allowed the demons—at least by theologians; medical men were more sceptical—to account for the success of a vast amount of divination, sorcery, and other occult arts. This was diabolical and forbidden magic in distinction from the natural and less objectionable variety.

Just as there is a fundamental resemblance between the charm which kills and the charm which cures, so it was no easy matter to draw a hard and fast line between diabolical and natural magic, or, for that matter, between natural magic and natural science. Even Augustine, an exponent of the demoniacal theory of magic, in his *Confessions*[1] censures "the vain and curious desire of investigation" through the senses, which is "palliated under the name of knowledge and science," but is apt to lead one "into searching through magic arts into the confines of perverse science." Overmuch stress has been laid upon the diabolical magic of the Middle Ages. Magic, according to those who believed in it and practised it, could be performed merely by human agency, without invoking spirits, by use of fitting materials, whether natural or artificial, due rites and ceremony. This sort of magic was related more closely to learning and science, to medicine, technology, and the arts than it was to religion or demonology. For this reason we must somewhat qualify the generalisation of Hansen that faith in magic grows as interest turns away from empirical study of nature to religious speculation, since it obscures the close historical connexion between the empirical study of nature and magic. Empiricism is often another name for superstition, while magic—and still more astrology and alchemy—may be characterised by experimentation and associated with research. All the Pauline "pneumatics," all the Christian personification of evil in place of the previous pagan personification of nature, failed to eradicate the underlying connexion of magic with nature. Magic may have striven to transcend, perturb, and upset nature, instead of being content to interpret and utilise it as modern science does. But it made

[1] x, 35: Migne, *Patrologia Latina*, xxxii, c. 802.

much use of natural objects and relationships; it had its own characteristic view of nature, its own fixed laws and well-observed rules.

Theologians and canonists might argue that demon activity was concealed in this sort of magic too, by implied pact or otherwise; their
strained contention does not seem to have carried general conviction.
Even an incantation was not necessarily spoken to a spirit; it might
address itself directly to herb or wind, to drug or human being. It was
a command or cue to be obeyed by the thing directly concerned. Moreover, the theologians were perhaps none too well advised in granting to
the demons so great a sway over this attractive field. If those evil spirits
knew so much and could do so much, why should not adventurous and
heroic individuals risk soul and body to snatch some of these secrets for
the benefit of humanity and posterity? The theologians would reply
that demons are by nature deceivers, whose prime object is to lead men
astray, and that no dependence is to be placed upon them. Yet men
could read in professed histories, or even in professed scriptures, that all
useful arts and sciences had been revealed to early man by fallen angels,
and men might insist that, while certain arts of divination had originally
been learned from demons, they were now workable independently of any
diabolical aid or pact. Apart from the standing temptation to invoke
a spirit and try to extract some desired information or service from him,
there was another flaw and seduction in the arguments of the Church
Fathers and schoolmen. If the demons' ability to work marvels vying
with divine miracles and to predict the future was in large measure
explainable by their long lives and close acquaintance with nature, why
might not mankind, by long-continued observation and experiment, by
building on the results believed to have been already obtained by Moses
and Solomon, or by " the divine men of Egypt and Babylon," keep
developing the powers and enlarging the sphere of natural magic until
men would have little need or temptation to solicit the dangerous assistance of spirits? Thus, at least, the matter would be apt to present itself
to a person of superior intellect such as Roger Bacon or Albertus
Magnus.

The ordinary man, of course, employed the one or two charms which
were known to him personally and of whose efficacy he had somehow
become convinced, or paid an occasional visit to a diviner or astrologer
under the urge of some selfish motive or curiosity. A preacher might
spiritedly exhort the peasant to let all his cows die rather than consult
a witch for a charm to cure them; the rustic was apt to try to save his
cattle first and his soul afterwards. For we must guard against inferring
that prohibitions of magic by Church Fathers or ecclesiastical synods
and councils would make much impression on the superstition of the
common man. Magic had always been more or less prohibited and
practised *sub rosa* in classical times and pagan antiquity, and the requirements of logical consistency which a trained intellect would draw from a

monotheistic faith were not much taken to heart by the populace. Consequently in the Coptic period of Egyptian history we find popular magic remaining unchanged save for an added Christian tinge, such as the use of Christian divine names with which to conjure. There is little reason for supposing that the barbarous Celtic and German West under the influence of declining Rome would prove more enlightened.

Standing out on the watershed between ancient and medieval times and thought is the tremendous figure of St Augustine (A.D. 354–430), "the greatest of the four." As the sun of classical culture and oriental religion set behind it, it cast a long shadow over the centuries to come. Undoubtedly St Augustine's credulity concerning tales of sorcery and the many passages in his writings against magic and astrology were very influential. But he had too little sympathy with scientific investigation to carry much weight with those interested in nature. Even in the fifth century he still found it advisable to defend Christians and Christianity from the imputation of magic. That his own opposition to astrology was not universal, or even typical, is shewn by the uncompromising astrological manual of Julius Firmicus Maternus in the fourth century, written almost certainly after his intolerant attack on other religions than Christianity, and by Augustine's fellow African bishop and contemporary, Synesius of Cyrene, who was a student of the occult and of divination, and perhaps author of a work on alchemy. Even Augustine shared the faith in mystic numbers of his Neo-Platonic contemporaries, Macrobius and Martianus Capella.

Alchemy, which we just mentioned, is thought of as especially connected with the Middle Ages, and not without some justification, since the earliest extant manuscripts of alchemical writings date from about the third to the fifth centuries of our era. That ascribed to the historian Zosimus appears to be genuine. Alchemy continued, however, to flourish in early modern Europe and is still practised in Egypt and the Orient. The earliest alchemical treatises are closely associated with magic papyri and are themselves full of magic. Their tone and style are even more mystical and oracular than those of later productions in the same field. These earliest extant treatises are written in Greek; alchemical compositions in Arabic can hardly be traced farther back than the Abbāsid dynasty.

From the early medieval period, when literature, learning, and the arts were in a state of decline in the Latin West, there nevertheless have come down to us documents attesting the continued interest in magic and astrology. A few may be mentioned by way of illustration. Medieval epitomes of the fourth-century work of Julius Valerius on the legend of Alexander set forth the story of Nectanebus, Egyptian magician and astrologer and natural father of Alexander, and were thus precursors of the magic motif in the later vernacular romances of Alexander. Other characteristic works were the *Herbarium* of the Pseudo-Apuleius with its conjurations of herbs and other magical procedure; the *De medicamentis* of Marcellus Empiricus with its very superstitious remedies; the Latin translation of Alexander of Tralles, a Greek physician of the sixth century, with its ligatures and suspensions, incantations and characters; the translation by the Venerable Bede of a treatise on divination from thunder. The *De natura rerum* of Bede likewise comprised several chapters on presages from moon, stars, clouds, fires, and birds, which Hauréau justly censured the printed edition included in Migne's *Patrologia latina* for having expurgated. Boethius strengthened the position of astrology in the Christian world by his discussion of fate, free will, and the stars in *The Consolation of Philosophy*. Isidore of Seville blew both hot and cold on the subject, stating that astrology was partly superstitious, partly a natural science. For a brief definition, however, it is doubtful if this can be bettered. Isidore also gave a definition of magic and a catalogue of occult arts which was much utilised by subsequent writers—Rabanus Maurus, Hincmar of Rheims, Burchard of Worms, Ivo of Chartres, Gratian in the *Decretum*, Hugh of St Victor, John of Salisbury, and others after him. We may not affirm with absolute certainty that the naïve and simple schemes and methods of divination which are found scattered through the extant manuscripts from the ninth to the twelfth century and still later were equally in use earlier, but everything seems to point towards this conclusion. The *Sphere* of Apuleius or Pythagoras, which was used to determine whether the patient or person otherwise in danger would live or die by a numerical calculation based upon the letters of his name and referred to a table, was but a continuation of the Greek *Sphere* of Democritus or Petosiris. The lists of unlucky Egyptian days for each month go back to a Roman calendar of A.D. 354 and were mentioned by St Ambrose and St Augustine. Other common methods of divination were prognostication of the character of the coming year according to the day of the week on which it began, a method supposed to have been divinely revealed to the prophet Esdras, and prediction from the day of the moon. These moon-books in the earlier manuscripts are either anonymous or attributed to the prophet Daniel. Thus scriptural names were used to sanction questionable superstitions, which are furthermore apt to occur on the fly-leaves of ecclesiastical calendars.

The customs of the Germanic peoples were not reduced to writing in the form of Latin *leges* until the early medieval centuries, after their practitioners had long been on Roman soil and under Christian influence. Their redaction was probably the work of ecclesiastics who omitted traces of heathenism and primitive magic or at least covered them with a Christian veneer. An example is the method of proof by ordeal, over which Christian priests presided until Innocent III at the Fourth Lateran Council of 1215 forbade participation of the clergy on the ground that the procedure was superstitious.

A larger amount of primitive folklore appears to have survived in Celtic law, witness the introduction of the Senchus Mor, and in Celtic culture generally. When St Columba expelled the evil spirits from a magic fountain in Scotland, he sanctified it by bathing in it and blessing it, so that it continued to heal diseases as before. The *loricae* of Gildas, Patrick, and others seem to be Christianised charms. St Patrick had feared the incantations and prodigies of the Druids, but some of the practices of their successors, the *fili*, were tolerated in the medieval period. Christianity forbade two of their methods of divination, but permitted a third by one's finger-ends. Prognostications were also made from the howling of dogs. Moreover, such satires or maledictions of the *fili* as the following were as dreaded as had been the incantations of the Druids: "I'll make a satire against you; I'll make one against your father, your mother, and your grandfather. I'll sing magic words on the waters of your realm, and there'll be no more fish caught therein. I'll sing magic words on your trees, and they'll bear no more fruit. I'll chant against your fields, and they'll never yield crops again." Or the *fili* would kill a man by taking hold of his ear with two fingers. Especially characteristic of the Celtic peoples was the belief in fairies or underground beings. Other reported details of Celtic magic, such as magic shields or swords, wands of yew or rods of hazel, enchanted caves and draughts, the virtues or voices of winds and waves, may for the most part be duplicated in the similar lore of other peoples and in later medieval romance. Astrology does not appear to have been highly developed among the Celts, but they observed the waxing of the moon.

Of popular superstitions of the early Middle Ages we are also informed by such documents as the *Indiculus superstitionum*, the decrees of Church councils, and the capitularies of the Carolingians. These denounce the making of offerings at trees, stones, fountains, and cross-roads, or the lighting of fires and candles there, or the addressing of vows and incantations to such natural objects. They forbid the worship of groves, stones, wells, and rivers. The sun and moon are not to be called lords. Wizardry and tempest-raising, divination and dancing, choruses and orgies, are prohibited. Among these laws against nature-worship and magic is one noted for its sceptical character, the so-called *Canon episcopi*, a regulation of uncertain provenance, first given in the legal collection of Regino of Prüm about 906. It brands as a mere dream the delusion that women ride at night with Diana. Agobard, Archbishop of Lyons from 814 to 841, attacked the belief in magic weather-making in his *Liber contra insulsam vulgi opinionem de grandine et tonitruis*. But such rare instances of scepticism stand out against a background of general credulity in magic in the early medieval period. At its close the Northmen were firmly convinced of the reality of wizards, ghosts, and other preternatural phenomena and forces, and of the magic of strange peoples, especially the Lapps. Of their own primitive magic as well as pagan mythology there is still some reflection in their literature as written down about the twelfth century.

The Anglo-Saxon Leech-Book of Bald and Cild contains a large amount of magical procedure with much Christian colouring which may often replace a previous pagan equivalent. For example, a man stung by an adder is cured by drinking holy water in which a black snail has been washed, and the bite of a viper is smeared with ear-wax with three repetitions of "the prayer of St John." For another type of poisoning is prescribed an application of butter churned on a Friday from the milk of "a neat or hind all of one colour," with nine repetitions of a litany, paternoster, and an unintelligible incantation. Much fear is shewn of witchcraft, enchantment, and ills from evil spirits. Other medical manuscripts from the ninth to the twelfth century abound similarly in charms, incantations, and characters, with Christian tags and prayers to certify their unimpeachability or to reinforce their healing virtue. Even the medicine of Salerno was free neither from magic and empiricism nor from lunar and astrological superstition. Latin treatises on the arts from the eighth or ninth to the twelfth century are marked by quaint procedure dependent on the conception of occult virtue and by an occasional bit of magic or incantation. Two of the foremost minds of the tenth century, both in intellectual history and in ecclesiastical and political activities, Gerbert and Dunstan, gained reputations for magic, the one posthumously, the other already as a studious youth.

The Arabic world until the twelfth century was more civilised and learned than Western Christendom. It produced far more men of science. But it was hardly less given to the occult, since magic and necromancy, astrology and alchemy, flourished there apace. Supposititious and apocryphal literature multiplied; various superstitious works were fathered upon famous philosophers and physicians of antiquity. We must not, however, lay too much stress upon a supposedly orienta tendency to vagaries, fantasy, and occultism. The worth of astrology was questioned by Fārābī and others; alchemy was not without its critics. The accomplishments of Arabic medicine, mathematics, and astronomy have won general recognition, but Berthelot pronounced Arabic alchemy inferior to the Latin alchemy of the thirteenth and fourteenth centuries. He regarded the genuine writings of the Arabic Geber (Jābir ibn Ḥayyān) as of little worth compared to the Latin treatises ascribed to Geber but for which no Arabic originals could be found. More recent research has found additional Arabic manuscripts which go far towards rehabilitating Geber's reputation, while the eleventh-century work by Abū'l-Ḥākim Muḥammad Ibn 'Abd-al-Malik aṣ-Ṣāliḥī al-Khwārazmī al-Kati contains matter corresponding to some of the inventions credited to the later Latin alchemists. Abū'l-Ḥākim also emphasises the importance of quantitative relations and of scientific instruments and apparatus. Indeed the contribution of Arabic alchemy to experimental method may not be gainsaid.

But this is not to say that Arabic alchemy was entirely scientific and free from taint of magic and the occult. Nor was the scepticism to which we referred above sustained and consistent. The philosopher Kindī might deny the possibility of the transmutation of metals and write on *The Deceits of the Alchemists*, but he believed in astrology to the full and in the magic force of words, figures, characters, and sacrifice, as his *On Stellar Rays or The Theory of the Magic Art* makes plain.

The occult science of the Arabic writings would not have made such an impression upon the Western Latin world, had it not been intertwined with chemical, medical, and mathematical knowledge of real value, had it not come in under great names which were as often genuine as apocryphal, and had it not formed an integral part of the prevailing *Weltanschauung* or general scheme of things. This may be briefly yet sufficiently illustrated by the case of Avicenna, whose *Canon* constituted the chief medieval textbook in both medicine and surgery, and who had further influence as a commentator on Aristotle. Yet he introduced a mystical and magical factor into science which was rather foreign to Peripateticism. He was repeatedly cited in medieval Latin works as a supporter of fascination and incantations, as holding that nature would obey thought, that a strong effort of the human will and imagination might move phenomena, "that souls can in so far conform to the celestial intelligence that it will alter material bodies at their pleasure, and then such a man will work wonders." Another doctrine of an astrological cast which was constantly ascribed to him by Latin writers was that the power of the stars was so great that their virtue would generate another race of men, should the present population be wiped out by a universal deluge. Alchemical works were also ascribed to him.

Whenever we may choose to date the first beginnings of the medieval revival of learning in the Christian Latin West, it had at any rate become pronounced by the twelfth century. With the increase of schools and studies, of written literature and learned works, the amount of natural magic intermingled with the science and medicine of the time, and also the number of professedly magic books, became more abundant. This was especially true of the numerous translations from the Arabic, and probably in no field was Arabic influence greater than in astrology. Yet the voluminous writings of the Arabic astrologers would not have been so eagerly sought out and translated had there not already been existent in the Western Christian world a very lively interest in that subject. Comets were feared, and even bishops and abbots were not unknown to pore over the pages of Manilius or Firmicus. The process of translation from the Arabic perhaps began as early as 984, when Gerbert asked a Lupitus of Barcelona to send him a book on "astrology" of which he had made a version. *Astrologia*, however, might mean astronomy, just as *astronomia* in medieval Latin may denote judicial astrology. Gerbert himself may have been the translator of other works not wholly free from the astrological interest, and the *Mathematica Alhandrei* (or, *Alchandri*), a confused miscellany of astrological detail, which certainly shews Hebrew—and probably Arabic—influence and names, if not a direct translation, is found in manuscripts dating back to the tenth or eleventh century. But the bulk of Arabic astrology appears to have been translated in the course of the twelfth century, when such authors as Albohali, Haly Heben Rodan, Messahala, Abenragel, Alcabitius, Kindī, Albumasar, Zael, Thebit ben Corat, Aomar, and Almansor were put before the Latin-reading public. These works remained in use long after the invention of printing, when they appeared in early editions or old collections of astrological works. The twelfth century also saw the Greek *Tetrabiblos* of Ptolemy turned into the Latin *Quadripartitum* through the medium of the Arabic. Indeed, the translation of this astrological work preceded that of the astronomical *Almagest*. Moreover, the very translators promptly began to write astrological manuals of their own, such as John of Spain's *Epitome*, consisting of an introduction to astrology and four books of judgments.

The prevalence of an astronomical interest may be further inferred from such works of the first half of the twelfth century as the *Philosophia* or *Dragmaticon* of William of Conches and the *De mundi universitate* of Bernard Silvester. John of Salisbury essayed an attack upon astrologers in his *Policraticus*; but it had so little effect even upon his own countrymen that in the second half of the century we find Daniel of Morley defending both astrology and the Arabic learning of Toledo, and Roger of Hereford writing astrological treatises in several parts. Early in the thirteenth century Michael Scot composed an elaborate but confused and cumbrous introduction to astronomy and astrology at the request of Frederick II. Leopold, son of the Duke of Austria, made a long astrological compilation for which different dates between 1200 and 1260 have been suggested; it was later printed.

Let us note the character and content of astrology as accepted in the Middle Ages. According to the then prevailing Ptolemaic or geocentric theory, the earth was the centre of the universe to which all matter gravitated in order of its grossness and heaviness, just as, according to the Aristotelian physics, earth, the heaviest of the four elements, was covered with water, which in its turn was enveloped with air, beyond which came the sphere of fire. Then followed in succession the spheres of the moon, Mercury, Venus, the sun, Mars, Jupiter, and Saturn, and outside these the eighth sphere of the fixed stars. Things on or near the earth within the spheres of the four elements were known as inferiors, while all bodies from the orb of the moon upwards were called superiors. For in one way or another the stars, planets, and celestial spheres were preferred to terrestrial creation; whether as of longer or eternal duration, a more refined substance, a more regular and purposive motion than inanimate objects—so that they must needs be either themselves animate beings or at least guided each by its ruling Intelligence—or whether as secondary causes closer to the First Cause in the chain of causation than were other phenomena. It followed that other natural phenomena were produced by them as instruments of the First Cause. In other words, inferiors are ruled by superiors.

This may be regarded as the fundamental hypothesis not merely of astrology but of the entire medieval view of nature. Moreover, it was more universally accepted throughout Christian society than is, for example, the theory of evolution at the present time. The most sceptical or pious opponent of the astrologers would hardly venture to call it in question. This may serve to explain why the Copernican doctrine was so slow to be formulated, why it seemed so revolutionary at the time, and why it so long failed of anything like general acceptance. The astrological hypothesis was also closely related to the Peripatetic conception of form and matter, and more particularly to the notion of matter receiving form at a certain moment and thus becoming a composite or individual. Inferiors are the matter which receives form from the superiors. Hence, so long as men continued to think of everything as composed of matter and form, it was unlikely that the belief that terrestrial phenomena are ruled by the celestial movements and figures would be seriously shaken.

Everything on earth was thought of as related to some force in the sky. From the enclosing spheres potent influences concentrated upon the earth's surface, and as the errant planets in the circle of the zodiac wove their intricate pattern of approach and recession, epicycle and eccentric, stationary and retrograde, conjunction and opposition, the course of nature altered to correspond. It was plausible to connect three of the twelve signs into which the zodiac divided with each of the four elements, qualities, humours, winds, and the like; to divide the human body into twelve sections from top to toe, each under the control of one of the signs; to relate the seven planets to the days of the week, the chief metals, the ages of man and of the world; to suppose that fluids in vegetation and animals were affected like the tides by the waxing and waning of the moon. Winds and weather, all gems and minerals, herbs and trees and medicinal simples, all animal life even to the human body, were believed to be governed by the stars. Hence no one could go far in zoology, botany, mineralogy, alchemy, or medicine without knowledge of this astral rule of inferior nature.

But then arose the disputed question: how far was man as a part of nature subject to the decrees of superior bodies, and how far was he, as a conscious, intelligent, and self-willed being, the master or wrecker of his own destiny? What events in human life and history might be classed as necessary and predictable, what as contingent and only conjecturable? Ptolemy, in a passage cited by almost every later writer, whether *pro* or *con*, had granted that the wise man rules the stars, but his meaning was that it is necessary to know astrology and the future in order to make the best of it or to avoid it. Similarly the prevailing medieval view would seem to have been that, while an astrologer might make mistakes or try to predict something beyond his ken, he was so likely to tell one something true and valuable that it was the safer procedure and part of prudence to consult him beforehand. Some were even so bold as to urge that horoscope and ascendent kept step with divine prescience and providence without violating human freedom, and that God regulated the moment of an individual's birth to conform to the fate which He foresaw was in store for him.

Astrology in this narrower sense of the prediction of human character and fate divided into four sections. Nativities were the determination of a person's temperament and life from the position of the constellations at the time of his birth. Revolutions and conjunctions determined general events—including the weather, crops, pestilences, and other natural phenomena as well as historical occurrences—for the ensuing year in the case of a revolution, or for the duration of the influence of the conjunction of the planets or eclipse of sun or moon. Interrogations were answered by the astrologer on the basis of such considerations as the questioner's horoscope and the time when the question was put. Elections were the art of selecting the favourable astrological moment for the initiation or performance of any undertaking, from planting a cucumber vine to electing a Pope. As an adjunct to this fourth branch we find the science of astrological images, in which the fundamental idea was to engrave or construct the image at the right moment when the prevailing constellations would be most favourable to the end sought. Thereby it was supposed that the virtue of the stars could be transferred to the image, which thus became a potent talisman for future use. It was by such channels as elections and images that astrology ceased to be mere divination and fused with operative magic. Two popular treatises on these astrological images were those of Thebit ben Corat and Thetel or Zael; another was ascribed to Ptolemy.

Geomancy ranked next to astrology in popularity as a method of divination. From the twelfth century onwards geomancies occur with great frequency in the manuscripts. Many of those in Latin bear the names of Arabic authors or of twelfth-century translators. Probably the most elaborate Latin work on the subject was that composed in 1288 by Bartholomew of Parma for a bishop-elect. Even a humanist like Pomponius Laetus late in the fifteenth century copied a geomancy with his own hand. Strictly speaking, geomancy should be divination from the element earth, just as pyromancy is prediction from fire. Actually, the method of these medieval geomancies is to obtain a figure by jotting down at random four lines of dots and then cancelling dot for dot in either pair of lines until only one or two dots remain in each line. Presumably the marks were originally made in dust or sand with the four fingers of one hand. By this chance procedure one of sixteen possible figures is obtained which serves as a key in referring to a set of tables for the answer which is sought as to the future. Since a number obtained by chance would serve as well for this purpose, we have analogous methods such as revolving a wheel until a pointer comes to rest upon a number, as in the treatise assigned to the physician of King Amalricus (Amaury) or the *Prenosticon Socratis Basilei*. These geomancies usually claim at least an astrological basis, but often determine the prevailing constellations by the same chance method. Sometimes, however, not only are the sixteen figures related to signs, planets, houses, and other astrological details, but prognostication is based upon general instructions instead of fixed tables of answers.

Divination from dreams found a certain amount of support both in Aristotle's *De somno et vigilia* and in the Bible, although theologians warned men to beware of the illusions of demons in dreams. The work of Achmet or Ahmed ben Sirin, in over three hundred chapters, was translated from the Greek by Leo Tuscus in the twelfth century. The briefer Latin dream-books which were common from the tenth to the fifteenth century were generally attributed either to Joseph or Daniel, and usually consist of an alphabetical arrangement of things seen in dreams with a line of interpretation for each: for instance, "Aves in sompniis apprehendere lucrum significat." There were also fuller treatments, such as that of William of Aragon, who endeavoured to relate dreams to the constellations and to find an astrological basis for oneiromancy.

Other arts of predicting the future were for the most part prohibited or disapproved, possibly because of the prominence of divination in pagan Greece and Rome. Necromancy was reckoned especially reprehensible, although some Arabic writers had classed it as a department of natural science, notably Fārābī in *De ortu scientiarum*, and this classification was repeated even by some Christian writers such as Gundissalinus in *De divisione philosophiae*, and Daniel of Morley. Pyromancy was suspected of involving fire-worship. Treatises on it are scarce and those on hydromancy and aerimancy still more so. Divination by gazing into lucid surfaces, such as the blades of swords, crystals, basins, mirrors, or finger-nails, was much practised and even by the clergy, but was suspected of demon aid and condemned by ecclesiastical councils. Chiromancy was less open to objection, since it seemed to have a physical basis in physiognomy, or the relation of personality and character to physique, upon which a treatise was ascribed to Aristotle. Lot-casting seemed to have scriptural sanction, but Aquinas gave the warning not to tempt God unduly in this practice in his opusculum, *De sortibus*, addressed possibly to the Duchess of Burgundy. Opening the Psalter at random was a common method.

Like astrology, alchemy received an impetus from translation from the Arabic. *The Book of the Composition of Alchemy of Morienus* purports to have been translated in 1144 by Robert of Chester, but Ruska has questioned its authenticity. By the middle of the next century, if not earlier, such works as the *Lumen luminum* and *De aluminibus et salibus* were well known. These two titles suggest the contrasting sides of alchemy, the mystical and the practical. Other much-read medieval treatises were *The Book of Seventy Precepts* and *The Book of Perfect Mastery*, the *Turba Philosophorum*, and the *Summa* attributed to Geber. Works of alchemy were later ascribed to Albertus Magnus, Roger Bacon, Thomas Aquinas, and other prominent philosophers and students of nature of the thirteenth century, as well as to mere men of letters like John Garland and Jean de Meung. However, the works of undisputed authenticity of such natural philosophers, observers, and experimenters as Albertus Magnus, particularly his five books on minerals, and Roger Bacon give a fairly good picture of the status of alchemical theory, practice, and literature at that time. Alchemy met with more scepticism than astrology, partly because the transmutation of metals seemed more contrary to the course of nature as then understood, and partly because it could be better put to the test of immediate and repeated experiment, and because persons lost more money by it.

The conception of occult virtue was generally held by medieval encyclopedias, treatises on animals, herbs, and stones, and medical works. Such virtues were marvellous, producing results that seemed almost divine and could not be accounted for by the component four elements in natural objects or by their qualities of hot and cold, moist and dry. Most of these reputed virtues seem fictitious: for example, the power of a gem to make its bearer invisible, of the heart of a vulture to make him popular and wealthy, or of the eye of a tortoise, taken internally, to clear the system of vapours and make possible illuminating visions. The carcass of an animal may yield some acid or drug useful in industry or pharmacy. But when Bartholomew of England affirms that "there is nothing in the body of an animal which is without manifest or occult medicinal virtue," we cannot but feel that he is overstating the case, however commendable his desire to utilise waste products. Nevertheless some occult virtues were true, such as the power of the magnet to attract iron. Because there were certain remarkable natural properties which medieval science could not explain, men assumed the existence of many others which do not exist. How far shall we classify this attitude as superstition, how far as mistaken science? Certainly it was closely related to both magic and astrology. The magnet is especially employed in magic, Marbod and other medieval writers tell us. And occult virtues which could not be accounted for from the elements and qualities were explained as produced by the influence of the stars. Pliny was probably right in suggesting that the *Magi* were both the great employers and the discoverers (or rather, imaginers) of these occult virtues. They were apt to be associated with magic procedure, and it was easy for defenders of superstition against criticism to adduce the existence of these occult virtues as an unanswerable argument in favour of the occult and marvellous. Their existence was accepted by men of the highest scientific attainments then possible. The most extreme claims in the way of occult virtue were made for gems, so that even the advocates of such virtues recognised that there was an opposing scepticism. Yet there seems to be no purposive attack upon the occult properties of gems extant from the medieval period.

Poisons, with their mysterious action, were commonly confused with sorcery in times past. The Greek and Latin languages employed the same words, φαρμακεία and *veneficia*, for both. The fact of poisoning supported the supposition of sorcery, and conversely the belief in sorcery encouraged an exaggerated credulity as to distant and far-fetched action of poisons and drugs. We therefore find the theory of occult virtue carried to great lengths in the numerous medieval works on poisons, such as that of Peter of Abano, which was perhaps addressed to Pope John XXII, that of William de Marra to Urban V, that of Christopher de Honestis, and those of Francis of Siena, Antonio Guaineri, professor of medicine at Pavia, and John Martin of Ferrara to three different Dukes of Milan. In such treatises we read of venomous animals that kill by mere glance or hiss, of poisons which act at a distance or whose effects are felt only after a long lapse of time, and of amulets like the foot of a vulture which betray the presence of secret poisons or prevent their operating. Akin to poisoning was the supposed human power of fascination or the evil eye.

There was more doubt felt and expressed as to the efficacy of immaterial things, like words, figures, and characters, in altering either natural phenomena or human nature. This scepticism was often extended to astrological images even by those who accepted the influence of the stars upon nature, man, and society. It was not merely that those who called magic diabolical insisted on crediting to the agency of demons what might otherwise have been ascribed to the power of words, characters, and images. There was also a rational objection to assigning any motive force to incorporeal entities without power of physical contact.

On the other hand, by the twelfth and thirteenth centuries there were in circulation numerous books of magic, some of which went to the length of necromancy and the invocation of spirits. William of Auvergne, Bishop of Paris from 1228 to 1249, cited many of these in the discussion of magic and demons in his *De universo*. Later in the same century Albertus Magnus wrote the *Speculum astronomiae* to distinguish unobjectionable works of astronomy and astrology from other treatises contrary to the Christian Faith and concerned with necromancy, but making a false pretence of possessing an astronomical basis and character. To this end he gave a critical bibliography with titles, names of authors, and incipits. Not only were such magic books cited in other medieval writings, but many survive in manuscript. The *Liber lune* ascribed to Hermes, the *Book of Venus* of Toz Grecus, and the *Book of the Spiritual Works of Aristotle or the Book Antimaquis* associated spirits with the stars and planets. Still more elaborate works, dealing with various kinds of magic, were *Picatrix*, which emanated from Spain and the Arabic, the *Liber vacce* or *Liber Anguemis*, which pretended to be a work of Plato revised by Galen, and *The Sworn Book* of Honorius. Of the Notory Art, which sought illumination from God by use of mystic diagrams, magic words, and invocation of angels, there are treatises ascribed to Solomon and to Apollonius.

We may illustrate the character of these works a little further. The *Liber lune* associates fifty-four angels with outlandish names with the twenty-eight mansions of the moon, employs suffumigations and repetitions of names of spirits, and instructs in the engraving of images to effect such results as injury to a personal enemy, the rout of an army, or the destruction of a given place. *Picatrix* tells how to work almost every conceivable marvel, from walking on water, becoming invisible, or appearing in animal form, to impeding the erection of buildings or rendering them safe and stable. The magician must meet certain personal requirements, go through the most complicated procedures, and use a vast number of natural substances. The pages are also thickly sprinkled with incantations, characters, and adjurations. Sorcery and sacrifice are prominent and often attended with great ceremonial. In the *Liber vacce* the animal to be sacrificed must commonly be of a specified colour and physique, and is then confined for a period before being killed and is subjected to a strict regimen or diet. For example, a crow without a speck of white on it is to be drowned. An equally black dog is imprisoned in a dark kennel and on the third day is to eat the crow and drink the water in which it was drowned. On the eleventh day when only the whites of the dog's eyes shew and it cannot bark, it is to have some of the juice of a certain small tree, after taking which it will be enabled to bark loudly. But it is then to be bound so that it may not struggle and to be boiled in a big pot. The broth which is thus obtained is to be used in producing rain.

Among less objectionable works, not open to the charge of dealing with spirits, was the *Kiranides* of Kiranus, King of Persia, which was translated from some Oriental original into Greek in 1168–69, and into Latin not very long afterwards. Its four books deal with the virtues of trees, birds, stones, and fish for medicinal and magical purposes. Of the same category are the *Secrets* or *Experiments* and the *De mirabilibus mundi*, which were attributed to Albertus Magnus. While these treatises were probably not by Albert, his genuine works on nature sometimes contain parallel passages, and he was not unfavourable to what we have earlier defined as natural magic. In one passage he even speaks of the three sciences of magic, necromancy, and astrology. But he regarded natural magic as essentially different in method and results from the Aristotelian "physical science." William of Auvergne also accepted the existence of a natural magic which was not concerned with demons, but he called it a part of natural science. The attitude of Roger Bacon was similar, although he was more timid about giving the word "magic" any favourable connotation. These men also leave us with a strong impression of the empirical and experimental character of magic. The "experimenters" to whose activities they allude or whose writings they cite are as apt to appear charlatans, quacks, and empirics in our eyes as they are to represent the forerunners of modern scientific investigation. An "experiment" then might be a successful prescription or cure in medicine, the discovery of a new occult virtue of a stone or a part of an animal, the finding of a herb of potent quality, the working of a magic illusion, or any other marvel attested or supposed to be attested by experience. William of Auvergne repeatedly cites *experimentatores* and books of experiments for feats of magic, especially of natural magic. Just such books of experiments have come down to us: the *Experimenta Alberti* already mentioned, several treatises of medical experiments and secrets ascribed to Galen or Rasis, collections of chemical and magical experiments such as the *Liber ignium* of Marcus Grecus or the twelve experiments of John Paulinus with pulverised snakeskin. While all this so-called experimental literature smacks strongly of magic, yet it leads on to the experimental method of modern science. The alchemists in particular were assiduous experimenters, just as the astrologers were frequent observers and measurers of the heavens. Works of alchemy consist largely of directions for processes, and the modern laboratory may be regarded as the lineal descendant of the medieval alchemist's workshop. Roger Bacon has been given great credit as a forerunner of modern scientific ideals and procedure because of the section in his *Opus maius* entitled, "Experimental Science." But when we come to analyse its spirit and content, what else is it than natural magic and alchemy?

All books of magic, however superstitious, unscrupulous, and immoral they may seem, were almost certainly the work of educated authors and make at least some pretence to science and learning. Vulgar witchcraft may be said to have left practically no written records of its own. Old wives, enchantresses, and ordinary diviners were mere practitioners or imposters, not authors. Witches had no libraries. We learn of their doings from the tales with which chroniclers endeavour to enliven or lighten their pages, from the hostile diatribes of preachers and theologians, from the caustic comment of members of the medical profession who lost their patients to such quacks and charlatans, from adverse legislation or the accounts of trials. As a rule such vulgar witchcraft was of a dull and sordid character, simple and restricted in its procedure, inferior in interest and variety to the magic of the learned which could give it points even in such matters as sex appeal.

As for adverse legislation, for some centuries it seems to have been more ecclesiastical than secular. Even in the later Middle Ages most Italian cities had no specific legislation against magic in their statutes. This was likewise true of French *coutumes* of the thirteenth and fourteenth centuries, and of German law of the same period. These municipal statutes and local customs seem tacitly to have continued the attitude of the Roman Law, that a magician, witch, or sorcerer was to be punished only if he or she could be shewn actually to have done someone injury, in which case he or she would be liable anyway by ordinary process of law. Somewhat similar but not quite identical was the attitude of the Spanish code, *Las Siete Partidas*, of Alfonso the Learned in the thirteenth century. Those who invoked evil spirits, or made wax images of other persons with the intent to injure them, were to be punished by death, but those who employed incantations with kindly purpose and good results were pronounced deserving of reward rather than penalty. Here credulity in the power of witchcraft had reached a point where sorcery with intent to injure was punished rather than actual injury, while on the other hand no objection was made to the employment of magical procedure for good ends.

The closing years of the thirteenth and opening years of the fourteenth century saw some further development of Latin astrology and astrological medicine. Guido Bonatti, an astrologer of Forlì, in the defence of which against the papal troops in 1282 he played a prominent part, wrote a voluminous *Liber astronomicus* in ten tractates. The famous Catalan, Arnold of Villanova, who served a number of kings and Popes as physician until his death in 1311, in his numerous medical writings included ligatures and suspensions, incantations and fantastic procedure, astrological medicine and images or seals. In the *Libellus de improbatione maleficiorum* he questioned the power of sorcerers to invoke demons and the extent of diabolical magic, but in his *Remedia contra maleficia* he repeated old counter-magic against both sorcerers and demons. Many works of alchemy were ascribed to Arnold, and recently Pansier has argued that he believed in transmutation. Peter of Abano, in his celebrated scholastic work of medicine, the *Conciliator*, finished in 1303, and in his other writings, shewed a credulous interest in dreams, fascination, incantations, and every variety of astrology. Far from limiting himself to astrological medicine, he interpreted the course of history, religious as well as secular, by the theory of conjunctions of the planets. In 1320 Firminus de Bellavalle added his treatise on weather prediction by astrology to similar works by Arabic authors, and in 1325 the same theme was discussed in a work composed at York by an author who in one of the manuscripts is called Perscrutator and who has sometimes been identified with a Robert of York, to whom have been further ascribed a *Correctorium alchimiae* and a treatise on ceremonial magic. The Alfonsine Tables, completed about 1272, seem to have become known outside of Spain rather slowly, but led in the first part of the fourteenth century to a very considerable output of astronomical tables, canons, and commentaries in Latin, which often had as their prime purpose to shorten the labours of astrologers in finding the positions of the heavens in making their judgments and predictions.

The poet and astrologer Cecco of Ascoli was burned at the stake in Florence in 1327, after being condemned by the Inquisition as a relapsed heretic for having violated the terms of a previous lighter sentence imposed upon him at Bologna in 1324. The event was apparently unusual and sensational, and aroused much subsequent interest. It is mentioned by later medieval writers, while numerous manuscripts contain what purport to be summaries of the sentence on Cecco by the Inquisition or accounts of his life and death. Unfortunately, these various sources of information are open to suspicion as of late date, some being of the seventeenth or eighteenth century. Moreover, they do not agree as to the nature of Cecco's heresy either with one another or with Cecco's works as they have come down to us, since these contain no denial of freedom of the will, no subjection of Christ to the stars, and no palliation of necromancy, which are among the leading suggestions made as to the nature of his heresy. However, these same suggestions are already present in the nearly contemporary chronicle of Giovanni Villani. It is true that Cecco displays undue curiosity as to necromancy and that he quotes from books of magic or astrology passages which might well be regarded as heretical, but he is always careful to express disapproval of them. This may, of course, have been only a subterfuge on his part.

If Cecco was executed as an astrologer, it was an isolated instance rather than part of a general policy of persecution of that pseudo-science by the Church and Inquisition. It was at the very time when Pope John XXII was taking measures against sorcerers and alchemists, but we have no decree by him against astrologers, although his penitentiary, Walter Cato, is said to have written a treatise against them which does not seem to be extant. Such Christian scholars as Albertus Magnus and Thomas Aquinas had allowed all except the more extreme tenets of astrology, granting a considerable influence of the stars over men as well as nature, since most men obey impulse rather than resist it. Guido Bonatti had, on the one hand, assumed an attitude of defiance towards theological critics of astrology, and, on the other hand, had addressed an audience in which members of the clergy were evidently not his least frequent patrons. Arnold of Villanova more than once found himself in theological difficulties, but this was because he, a mere layman, presumed to discuss mysteries of the Faith and to urge Church reform, and not because of his astrology. Peter of Abano has been represented by some historians as one whose astrological doctrine was held to be heretical and who escaped the stake only by dying during his trial. The existing evidence rather shews that, while his views had met with some theological objection, he had successfully defended himself and had been acquitted. The same late medieval writers who depict Cecco's heresy as meeting a merited fate either tell how Peter ably defended himself before a council, or praise his learning in such a way as to indicate that no stain rested upon his memory.

No interruption of astrological activity is manifest following upon Cecco's execution. Although the astrological writings of Andalò di Negro of Genoa have not been exactly dated, he appears to have been as devoted to astrology after 1327 as before. Galfredus de Meldis (Gaufred de Meaux), who had made predictions from the comet of 1315 and the conjunction of Saturn and Jupiter in 1325, lived on to make a prognostication from the eclipse of 1341[1] and to discuss the astrological causes of the Black Death in 1348 after the event. This last treatise has been confused with other predictions made at the time of the triple conjunction of 1345 by Leo Hebraeus, Jean de Murs, and others. In 1331 John of Saxony did not hesitate to write a commentary upon the judicial astrology of Alcabitius as Cecco had done before him. The Oxford school of astronomy at Merton College engaged also in astrological prognostications, of which John Eschenden may be mentioned as a leading author. Besides predictions from conjunctions and eclipses in 1345, 1349, 1357, and 1366, there is extant by him a ponderous *Summa iudicialis* which he brought to a conclusion during the terrible year of the Black Death. It was later printed, and in 1379 John de Ponte made an abbreviation of it which cut away much of Eschenden's verbosity.

Even stronger evidence that religious opposition to astrology was slight and ineffectual is the fact that members of the Dominican and Franciscan Orders, from whose ranks inquisitors were drawn, themselves composed astrological treatises. Only three years after Cecco's death, in 1330, the Dominican Niccolò di Paganica (also called de Aquila) compiled a compendium of astrological medicine. Petrarch, whose criticisms of both medical men and astrologers have been taken too seriously by some of his modern expositors and biographers, treasured a copy of Niccolò's work in his celebrated library. Some of the Oxford school of astronomers and astrologers were Franciscans. Dionysius de Rubertis de Burgo Sancti Sepulchri, who was praised by Petrarch and called by King Robert to Naples on account of his astrological predictions, was an Augustinian. He died in 1339; a prediction for the following year was made by another member of the same religious Order, Augustine of Trent, who lectured at the University of Perugia. In 1359 a Dominican of Magdeburg, John of Stendal, "at the instance of the reverend masters and students of Erfurt," where he was "censor," commented, like Cecco, upon Alcabitius. Passing on to the next century, we find the Dominican Nicholas of Hungary, in his *Liber anaglypharum* written in 1456, accepting astrology in all its ramifications, even to the use of images, giving a horoscope for Christ which he ascribes—I think incorrectly—to Albertus Magnus, and affirming that "all astronomers are agreed in this, that there never was any conjunction of these two planets (*i.e.* Saturn and Jupiter) without great change in this world." A remarkable instance of good relations between the Inquisition and astrology is provided by a treatise of 1472–73 by Franciscus Florentinus, a Franciscan and inquisitor, entitled: *De quorundam astrologorum parvipendendis iudiciis pariter et de incantatoribus ac divinatoribus nullo modo ferendis.* Despite the title, Francis always speaks

---

[1] Otto Hartwig, *Henricus de Langenstein dictus de Hassia*, Marburg, 1857, p. 27. Hartwig called him Gaufredus de Mellis and could find nothing more about him.

with respect of the astrology of the learned, and even recounts with approval Peter of Abano's doctrine of the influence of conjunctions on the course of history and religious change. Similarly, Jean de Murs addressed a memoir to Clement VI pointing out that the approaching great conjunction of Saturn and Jupiter on 30 October 1365, in the eighth degree of the sign Scorpion, would be critical for Islām and offer a great opportunity to Christendom to strike a telling blow against the Muslims and perhaps to convert them. The canonist and supporter of the temporal power of the Papacy, John of Legnano, in his treatise on war written in 1360, questioned whether wars ever could be abolished, since the constellations would require them in the future just as they had brought them in the past.

The Black Death of 1348 stimulated the literature of astrological medicine, if it did not indeed encourage a more fatalistic attitude in general and, by the shock it gave to society, foster the growth of vulgar witchcraft. Gui de Chauliac not only manifested belief in the influence of the stars in his great surgical work of 1363, but composed a separate astrological treatise. We see a like union of surgery and astrology in the writings of Leonard of Bertipaglia in the next century. His *Cirurgia*, which was several times printed, concludes with a discussion whether wounds will heal or are fatal according to conjunctions of the sun and moon in the twelve signs, and with other astrological matter. A few years later he composed a *Judgment of the Revolution of the Year 1427* which has remained unprinted. A leading work of astrological medicine in the fifteenth century was the *Amicus medicorum or Directory of Astrology Made Medical*, a clear and well arranged manual written in 1431 by Jean Ganivet, a Franciscan of Vienne. That it continued in use for two centuries may be inferred from the appearance of editions at Lyons in 1496, 1508, 1550, and 1596, and at Frankfort in 1614.

An anonymous writer against astrology in the second half of the fourteenth century stated that the citing of the Fathers of the Church against astrologers had become ineffectual; one must combat them with their own science. Astrology and magic encountered such technical and rational opposition in a notable series of treatises written in the latter half of the fourteenth century by Nicolas Oresme, known for his French translations of Aristotle and his contributions to mathematics and economics, and by Henry of Hesse, who from Paris went to the new University of Vienna about 1382–84 as professor of theology. In several treatises in Latin and French Oresme tried to dissuade princes from consulting astrologers, demonstrated the difficulty and uncertainty of prediction from the stars, and rejected much of astrological technique and rules as unreasonable. He did not, however, reject astrology entirely. Even less did Henry of Hesse, although while still at Paris he belittled the significance of the comet of 1368 and attacked the theory of conjunctions of the planets with especial reference to fantastic predictions made in 1373. In the next century Cardinal Pierre d'Ailly, who was much enamoured of astrology, accepted some of Henry's criticisms but rejected others. Oresme's attack was remembered as late as 1451, when John Lauratius de Fundis, doctor of arts and medicine at the University of Bologna, composed a defence against it. In a collection of miscellaneous questions or *Quodlibeta*, Oresme also tried to shew that apparent works of magic could be explained on natural grounds without resort either to miraculous power, the influence of the stars, or the interference of demons. Somewhat similar were the works of Henry of Hesse, *On the Reduction of Effects to Their Common Causes* and *Of the Habitude of Causes and the Influx of Common Nature with Respect to Inferiors*. These were, however, almost too abstract and subtle in their scholastic reasoning to have any very general influence. More humanistic were the arguments of Coluccio Salutati in the closing years of the fourteenth century.

Eymeric (1320–99), Inquisitor-General of Aragon, wrote against alchemists and divination as well as invokers of demons, but still left to astrology about the usual field of activity that it was accorded by stricter Christian opinion. This was likewise the position of Jean Gerson (1363–1429), who was also primarily a theologian and less given to astrology than his master, Cardinal d'Ailly. Gerson was unusually severe against superstitious observances and went to the length of endeavouring to impose his point of view upon members of medical faculties and of the medical profession by reproof or advice. For instance, he censured a physician of Montpellier for employing an astrological image. Gerson became Chancellor of the University of Paris in 1395, and three years later its theological faculty condemned twenty-eight errors connected with the magic arts[1]. Popular superstitions, whether magical or religious, were opposed in a number of fifteenth-century works, of which may be here mentioned the *De superstitionibus* of Nicholas Jauer, Jawor, or Gawir, composed in 1405 and extant in a large number of manuscripts but often ascribed to other authors, and the later *Contra vitia superstitionum* of Dionysius the Carthusian (1402–71), which was printed in 1533. Other names are Thomas Ebendorfer of Haselbach and Henry Gorichem. The work of Franciscus Florentinus, which has already been mentioned, also contains much material concerning popular superstitions, among which this inquisitor classed the observance of birthdays other than those of Christ and the saints. These later discussions of popular superstition were apt to borrow a good deal from the thirteenth-century work of William of Auvergne. Noteworthy, however, is the defence of vulgar superstition ascribed by Gerson and others to its practitioners. They insist, we are told, that similar practices may be found in medical and other learned books, and that the Church tolerates similar usages in its rites. Our authors deny that the Church does so officially or as a whole, but are inclined to grant that many practices, which it would be better to omit, have been introduced under the guise of religion among the laity and have even been permitted or sanctioned by some of the clergy.

[1] For the text of this censure see the *Chartularium Universitatis Parisiensis*, IV, 32–35.

Despite the Extravagans of John XXII, *Spondent quas non exhibent*[1],
which decreed that alchemists must give as much real gold to the poor as
they had produced of the artificial variety, while those who coined it into
money were to suffer severer penalties, treatises on alchemy continued to
multiply during the fourteenth and fifteenth centuries. Nor were the alchemists, any more than the astrologers, exclusively laymen. John XXII,
in his decretal, had been careful to provide that if the offenders were clerics,
they should in addition to the other penalties lose their benefices and be
disqualified from holding any in the future. As Brother Elias, one of the
first Generals of the Franciscans, had been charged with alchemy in the
thirteenth century, so to another Minorite, John of Rupescissa, noted also
for his prophecies and imprisonments by his Order and the Popes at Avignon in the middle of the fourteenth century, is ascribed a work of some
importance on the fifth essence. In some manuscripts the text is simple,
direct, practical, and business-like; in others and even more in the late
printed versions it has grown verbose, rhetorical, fuller of pious cant, and
in general sounds less genuine. Other interesting fourteenth-century alchemical writings are the letter of Thomas of Bologna, father of Christine
de Pisan, to Bernard of Trèves—not Trevisan, or of the march of Treviso,
as the printed editions represent him—and the latter's longer reply. In
this and other late medieval alchemical treatises may be traced the influence of philosophical and scientific conceptions and phraseology then
current among the schoolmen. There is also much citation of previous
medieval literature on the subject. A favourite theory at this time was
that the elixir was to be obtained from mercury alone. There was much
speculation as to the constitution of the four elements from the first
four qualities and as to their relative weights, and much experimentation
seeking to separate them. There are many anonymous works and many
authors, presumably of this period, whose names have as yet scarcely been
identified: for example, Jacobus de Garandia, Geraldus de Morangia of
Aquitaine, Friar Osbertus de Publeto, Tankardus, Antonius de Abbatia.
This is even true of some of those whose works were printed in the alchemical
collections of early modern times, like Petrus de Silento or Zelento or
Zeleuce. Two frequently-encountered English names in alchemy are John
Dastin in the fourteenth, and George Ripley in the later fifteenth century.
For the most part the fourteenth century seems more productive of
alchemical writing in Latin than the fifteenth, but the numerous alchemical treatises current under the name of Raymond Lull are found
almost exclusively in manuscripts of the fifteenth century or later and
seem to have been composed long after his death.

The Middle Ages had always been given to visions, revelations, and
prophecies, especially of the coming of Antichrist, but these seem to have

---

[1] Eymeric states that John issued this decretal only after holding a disputation
between representative alchemists and natural scientists to determine whether transmutation was in accordance with nature.

reached their height, both in number and fantasticalness, in the troubled times of the Hundred Years' War, the Black Death, and the Great Schism. Were these revelations authentic and orthodox, it would not be appropriate to mention them here. But if they were considered as the work of evil spirits, they might have a close relation to magic and to prohibited divination. There was much doubt on this point in the minds of men at the time, so that Henry of Hesse wrote an *Epistle concerning False Prophets* and another treatise *De discretione spirituum*, Gerson composed a work with a similar title, *De probatione spirituum*, and Joan of Arc was regarded as a witch by her enemies. When brother Theolophorus based his *Book of Great Tribulations in the Near Future* in part upon the prophecies of Merlin, he might be regarded as treading close to magic ground. John of Bassigny claimed no divine afflatus but based his prediction of ills, especially political, to come in the years 1352 to 1382, on reading of the Bible and other previous predictions and upon information picked up during his travels: what a Syrian had told him in Cadiz and a Chaldean in Bethsaida—both through an interpreter—as to events to happen in 1336, and what a Jew had prognosticated about the year 1342. It is not clear whether John's forecast had any astrological basis, but Cardinal Pierre d'Ailly believed that the coming of Antichrist could be foretold astrologically. He also predicted a great change for the year 1789, and vast alterations in the Church within a century. John Nannis or Nannius of Viterbo, a Dominican friar who is better known for his forgery of the lost Annals of Fabius Pictor, in 1471 or 1481 combined an interpretation of the *Apocalypse*, whose first fifteen chapters he held applied to the period before the fall of Constantinople in 1453, with ten conclusions derived from astrology as to future triumphs of the Christians over the Saracens. He addressed his predictions first to Cardinal Niccolò Forteguerra and subsequently to Pope Sixtus IV and various States of Europe.

This combination of divine revelation and astrology would not seem incongruous at that time, since the advocates of astrology held that it was one form of divine revelation, and since it was not uncommon in medieval classifications of the sciences to rank astronomy next to theology. Cardinal d'Ailly's *Vigintiloquium* had for the rest of the wording of its title, "Of the Concord of Astronomical Truth with Theology," while Gerson in 1429 addressed to the dauphin his *Trilogy of Astrology Theologized*. But the best illustration for our purpose is the treatise of Curatus de Ziessele near Bruges, who composed a *Compendium of Natural Theology Taken from Astrological Truth*.

Astrology was also strongly entrenched in the universities. In those of Italy it was the practice for one of the professors, either of astronomy or medicine, to make an annual forecast for the ensuing year. A number of these are extant. Often the prediction was divided into four parts, treating separately each of the four seasons of the year. The arrangement was furthermore topical, taking up one after the other such matters as the weather for the coming year, any general catastrophes like earthquakes and floods, the diseases and pestilences that would be prevalent, economic matters such as crops and prices, the lot of the clergy and other social classes, the prospects for war and peace, and particular political pronouncements for the leading States of Europe and cities of Italy. Sometimes the author gave the astrological grounds for his conclusions in each case, sometimes not. If the University of Paris did not go to such lengths of astrological prediction of human affairs as this, we at least have evidence of a controversy there in 1437 as to what days were favourable for bloodletting and the taking of laxatives. Roland Scriptoris and Laurens Muste, the one master of arts and medicine, the other master of arts and bachelor of theology, had disagreed on this matter, and the university authorities appointed two arbitrators, John de Trecis, master of theology and minister of the Order of the Holy Trinity, and Simon de Boesmare, prior of St Jean Beaumont, to review the astrological arguments of both parties and decide between them. In general these umpires took middle and conciliatory ground. But they further insisted that every physician and every surgeon should possess an astrolabe and a copy of the large Almanac and not merely the small one, in order that he might observe with accuracy the exact position of the moon in the signs. One more example may be given of the place of astrology in the universities in the fifteenth century. The great mathematician Regiomontanus, when called in 1467 to a chair in the new university about to be established at Pressburg in Hungary, was commissioned with a colleague to select a horoscope or favourable moment of foundation for the university which would assure it a splendid future. However able an astronomer Regiomontanus may have been, he proved an indifferent astrologer on this occasion, since the new university was of brief duration and a failure almost from the first. Astrology was also made the theme of their lays by learned poets, such as Pontanus and Lorenzo Buonincontri of San Miniato.

How scant success Oresme's treatise had in dissuading monarchs from astrology may be inferred from this precept of the humanist Aeneas Sylvius, later Pius II, in his *De liberorum educatione*: "A prince must not be ignorant of astronomy, which unfolds the skies and by that means interprets the secrets of Heaven to mortal men." Nor was this attitude limited to Italy. In the later fifteenth century Louis XI of France, Henry VII of England, and Frederick III of Austria and the Holy Roman Empire were all patrons of astrology. An interesting example of the court physician and astrologer was Conrad Hemgarter or Heingarter of Zurich, whence his further appellation of Thuricensis. His writings, as represented by five distinct manuscripts in the Bibliothèque Nationale of Paris, comprise a commentary upon the *Quadripartitum* of Ptolemy addressed to John, Duke of Bourbon; a nativity and treatise of astrological medicine written in 1469 for Jean de la Gutte, an official at the Bourbon court; another work of astrological medicine composed in 1477 for the Duke of

Bourbon himself; and a Judgment for the year 1476 addressed to Louis XI. In print by him is a treatise on comets.

Simon Phares was another astrologer who was in the service of John of Bourbon until the duke's death, but preferred botanising in the mountains of Savoy and Switzerland to entering the service of Louis XI. Charles VIII none the less visited him at Lyons, where his successful predictions had attracted much attention. But then he was condemned by the archiepiscopal court for the superstitious practice of astrology, and appealed to the Parlement of Paris. That body referred the two hundred odd volumes of his library to the theological faculty of Paris for examination. The faculty condemned some of them and took up a very strict attitude towards astrology. That this condemnation was not very effective may be inferred from the fact that some of the treatises condemned are still well-known incunabula; that the king's physician presented a manuscript of one of them to one of the colleges of the University of Paris; and that Simon himself is found in the last year of Charles' reign composing and addressing to the king his *Recueil des plus célèbres astrologues*, an important source for the history of astrology, in which he implies that his accuser had been put to shame and confusion.

Meanwhile what was the attitude towards magic? Michele Savonarola, medical writer of the middle of the fifteenth century and uncle of the Florentine reformer, had a favourable opinion of magic. Ficino, who revived Neo-Platonism at Florence, was a believer in both astrology and natural magic. Benedetto Maffeo addressed to Lorenzo de' Medici a treatise on agriculture filled with belief in signs and astrology, and with bits of agricultural magic. In 1482 Bernard Basin, a canon of Saragossa, arguing against a *vesperiatus* at the University of Paris who had contended that the study of magic arts aided the salvation of the faithful, referred to the audience as "most attentive in listening to discussions of the magic arts." But Basin urged that magic was diabolical and should not even be studied. Presently the youthful Pico della Mirandola promulgated his nine hundred theses at Rome. A number dealt with magic and the Jewish cabala; several were favourable to natural magic; perhaps the most startling was the proposition that no science yields more certainty of Christ's divinity than magic and the cabala. Innocent VIII, who in 1484 had issued his bull against witches, condemned certain of Pico's theses. When Pico attempted to defend and explain his position, he further excited the ire of the Pope, and it was only under Alexander VI that Lorenzo de' Medici succeeded in having his disabilities removed. Meanwhile Peter Garsia, Bishop of Usellus (Ales) in Sardinia, had addressed to Innocent a reply to Pico's *Apology* which was printed in 1489. Garsia insisted that all magic was alike evil and diabolical, and explicitly censured the views of such past Christian authorities as William of Auvergne and Albertus Magnus, to say nothing of Peter of Abano.

Pico, much upset by his difficulties with the Church, devoted the latter years of his brief life to devout meditation, asceticism, and the composition of an elaborate work in twelve books against astrology. Thus he who began proudly by defending magic and cabala ended penitently by attacking even astrology, but one cannot escape a feeling that this onslaught was something of a *tour de force*. The reformer Savonarola was so pleased with the work that he composed a popularisation, abbreviation, and paraphrase of it in Italian. Defenders of astrology replied to Pico's attack, and the pseudo-science had by no means as yet received its death-blow. But further consideration would carry us beyond our period. Let us merely add that natural magic, which Garsia had flouted, found an exponent in a representative of the Christian Renaissance, Jacques Lefèvre of Étaples, whose treatise on natural magic sometimes approaches closely to incoherent occultism.

The witchcraft delusion, with its holocausts of victims, extending as it did from the fifteenth to the seventeenth century, lies in large part beyond our period. Only in the closing decades of the fifteenth century, by "Popes of the Renaissance" such as Sixtus IV and Innocent VIII, was cognisance taken of the supposed existence of witches as a sect in parts of Germany. Only in the opening decades of the sixteenth century did Alexander VI and Leo X recognise the spread of witchcraft into northern Italy. The historian Hansen had difficulty in comprehending how such a degradation of the human intellect and so prolonged and cruel a persecution could coincide in time with Renaissance, Reformation, and the rise of experimental science. He tried to explain it as a survival of the medieval spirit, Church control, theology, and Inquisition. But his argument is unconvincing and is sometimes contradicted by facts uncovered by his own researches. It is possible to over-emphasise the somewhat tenuous connexion between magic and heresy. The witch was probably to some extent a scape-goat for the ills which then oppressed society. When we reflect that by the fifteenth century medieval culture was declining; that economic prosperity, political freedom and self-government, chivalry, and public charity were waning; that the fourteenth century had been marked by the terrible Black Death which demoralised society and never ceased its visitations thenceforth during the entire time of the witchcraft delusion, and by the perhaps worse pest of mercenary soldiers who, aided by artillery and fire-arms, made all wars from the Hundred Years' to the Thirty Years' so cruel, devastating, and financially exhausting—when we consider this, we may incline to regard the witchcraft delusion as in congenial company, and to view it as a sociological rather than theological or intellectual phenomenon, produced largely by popular fear and superstition, and by an undiscriminating wave of "law-enforcement" which swept over the secular more than the ecclesiastical courts, and raged in lands where the Inquisition had hardly functioned.

According to Hansen's own findings, the collective conception of witchcraft prevalent during the delusion did not yet exist in the thirteenth century, indeed is still absent from early fifteenth-century works on magic, and inquisitors of that century were surprised at the existence of this new sect. Hansen found no case of a magician's being charged with sexual relations with demons until the thirteenth century. The German word for witch, *Hexe*, rarely appears in literature until the fourteenth century. In secular trials nothing is said before 1400 of demon lovers, transportation of witches through the air, and the sabbat. Among the many records of early trials by the Inquisition which have been preserved there are practically none for magic until Pope John XXII (1316–34), alarmed by attempts against his life made through sorcery and wax images by Hugh Géraud, Bishop of Cahors, the Visconti, and others, started the persecution of magicians in southern France which was continued by Benedict XII. But before this Philip the Fair had preferred charges of abominable magic against the Templars; Guichard, Bishop of Troyes, had been imprisoned in the Louvre for years on like grounds; and sorcery had been among the accusations trumped up against Hubert de Burgh in England under Henry III; so that there is no reason for giving the Papacy precedence in magic-baiting. During the years from 1230 to 1430 the number of trials for magic before secular judges was large and ever growing. That malicious and diabolical magic was increasing during the fourteenth century was the opinion of John XXII and his anonymous commentator at its beginning, of an Archbishop of Cologne and a Bishop of Utrecht in its mid-course, and of the theologians of Paris at its close. One French writer ascribed its growth to the many foreigners whom the Hundred Years' War had brought into France. There were numerous trials of persons, often of high rank, who had made wax images of others with intent to injure them. We may agree, however, with Hansen that in so far as the witchcraft delusion was led up to by previous writings, it received countenance from works of theologians, canonists, and inquisitors rather than from medieval writers on nature or medicine, who were far more inclined to account for the supposed magical activities of demons by natural causes or human imagination.

CHAPTER XXIII

EDUCATION IN THE FOURTEENTH AND FIFTEENTH CENTURIES.

THE educational needs of a predominantly agricultural population such as existed in Western Europe in the later Middle Ages were necessarily few and simple. Positive, organised institutional instruction was not needed by the many; for the great mass of the people knowledge was traditional, the lore learned by the child from its parents, by the workman from his master and fellow-labourers, by the Christian from his spiritual superiors. School-learning was not necessary for field-work, and in the country-side, therefore, schools were not numerous. Although exceptions were not infrequent, schools were generally confined to the cities and towns, where the needs of life were more complex, where a concourse of people helped to raise the standard of general culture, and where a few had the leisure requisite for the pursuit of knowledge. With the growth of urban life, facilities for education were naturally made available for more people, and this, together with the increase in the numbers of the clergy, helps to account for the steady growth in literacy which is apparent during the later Middle Ages.

For the educational history of these years we are not notably obliged to speculate about origins or to fill up considerable gaps by analogy or deduction from evidence of a later date. The scaffolding of national and international educational organisation had been erected during the two preceding centuries: by 1300 the system was to a considerable degree in working order; the scholar already occupied a defined position in society. The reformers of the twelfth century had done their work so well that their ideals had crystallised into institutions, the later Middle Ages forming an educationally homogeneous period. Apart from the new ideals which accompanied the spread of humanism, there are few unexpected developments. The nearest approach to a cataclysm, the Black Death, seems to have affected the methods and perhaps also the standard of education even less than it affected other forms of contemporary activity. Teaching and study, based mainly upon the scholasticism which so manifestly dominated the universities, went on, almost unchanged, during the whole of this period.

Throughout the Middle Ages education naturally remained the especial concern of the Church. Both the subjects and the methods of instruction were under clerical supervision; educational disputes were settled before ecclesiastical tribunals; even in the rare cases in which schoolmasters were not themselves in holy orders, they were still subject in a peculiar degree to bishop and archdeacon. In practice, too, the boundary between clergy and laity was exceedingly ill-defined, many persons being given the privileges and exemptions of clerks who were for all practical purposes laymen. Yet even so, a notable educational feature of the fourteenth and fifteenth centuries was the rise of a class of lettered laymen, some specifically called *laici literati*, who never had any intention of taking orders. There is much evidence to shew that, in England at least, the number of lawyers and gentlemen who received an education similar to that of the Pastons was considerable and that ability to write was widespread. Really learned, as distinct from just literate, laymen were, however, distinctly uncommon north of the Alps; it is difficult, for example, to name an English layman before Sir Thomas More who could be compared for learning with Dante.

Considering its needs, Western Europe after 1300 was comparatively well-provided with schools which the sons of the laity might attend. Every cathedral church was required by Canon Law to have a grammar school attached to it in which Latin was taught and, after the beginning of the thirteenth century, this law was generally obeyed. Entrance to such a grammar school could be obtained normally only by boys who had already received a certain minimum of instruction. They would usually be expected to be able to write the letters of the alphabet and to read, not necessarily intelligently, but at least to spell out the words placed before them.

This preliminary knowledge was obtained in various ways. There was much sporadic and unorganised elementary instruction by well-disposed priests, by parish clerks, and even by women able to teach mixed classes of small children. Further, every cathedral, and most collegiate churches, supported a song school intended primarily for the training of choir-boys but certainly not limited to these. Unlike the grammar-school master, the master of the song school could as a rule not hope to obtain a monopoly. His work finished where the grammar-school master's began, the teaching of Latin grammar proper being left entirely to the grammar school. At such a song or elementary school, children were taught the elements of their faith, the *Ave Maria*, the Lord's Prayer, and the Creed, a few anthems and psalms, singing and spelling. The children often learned to read Latin without being able to understand it, while if there were no grammar school available close at hand, the song-school master might expound the meaning of the little Latin that he taught, although the proximity of a grammar school with a master who was vigilant to maintain his monopoly of teaching grammar would mean that the song-school teaching would be narrowly confined to the limits indicated. To these song schools small children often came in fairly considerable numbers, and many of those who were not hoping to adopt a definitely professional career went no farther. Small and often ephemeral institutions that have left few records of importance, the song schools none the less accounted for most of the education that many humble folk in the Middle Ages ever received.

The grammar schools were more permanent and significant institutions. Obligatory in every cathedral city and frequently met with elsewhere, they held the key to the gateway of knowledge, Latin grammar. Because of this, they are fundamental to the educational history of the Middle Ages. The Latin for whose teaching they existed had become specialised and distinctive by 1300, a language based upon a few classical texts, upon the Vulgate, and upon the Fathers, adapted for oral conversation, public disputation, and legal and business communications. Medieval Latin was certainly not bad, in the sense of ungrammatical, Latin. The quality of the grammar of most medieval chronicles is distinctly good, although naturally not classical, while even the most involved of scholastic philosophers are usually careful not to depart from the ordinary rules of grammar, even if they do invent special words and constructions of their own. In substance, the same language was used among scholars and traders over the whole of Europe, and adequate knowledge of it was essential to any one whose interests or ambitions were more than merely local. Its general use gave an impress of unity to the learning of Western Christendom that was to fade slowly after the Reformation. The medieval student was an international phenomenon, able to transfer himself without difficulty from one country to another and to be understood wherever he went. For not only was Latin the common language, but also the methods of teaching it were substantially the same all over Europe.

Together with Rhetoric, the art of speaking, and Dialectic, the art of logical argument, Grammar completed the *Trivium*, the first group of the seven liberal arts, and was by far the most important subject of the group. The grammar text-books almost universally used were based upon Priscian's *Grammar* of 18 books (books I-XVI on accidence and XVII and XVIII on syntax) or on Donatus, *De partibus orationis*. The commonest of these, the *Ars Minor*, was an abridgment of Donatus, written in prose. It was short enough to be learnt by heart from beginning to end, the master alone usually possessing a copy and dictating it section by section to the class. Occasionally a fortunate schoolboy may have had a grammar of his own, but this would be distinctly unusual. Memory, it must be remembered, necessarily played a very large part in medieval education, and, outside the monasteries, cathedrals, collegiate churches, and universities, access to books of reference was usually difficult.

The *Ars Minor* was a very elementary book, and the need for something more advanced and at the same time easy to learn led to the production, in 1199, of the *Doctrinale* of Alexander of Villa Dei. This compilation possessed the great merit in medieval eyes of being metrical. The story runs that Alexander, while studying at Paris with two friends, Ivo and Adolphus, was too poor to buy text-books of grammar and therefore invented a metrical version of Priscian, which he later reduced to writing. Much of it was not taken direct from Priscian but was Alexander's own invention. The three parts into which it was early divided are Etymology,

Syntax, and Prosody, the latter being the most original part of the work and an invaluable aid in the rage for versifying that distinguished the fifteenth century. The *Doctrinale* was not intended to supersede Donatus, for some knowledge of elementary Latin grammar was clearly implied in it. It is interesting to notice, however, that the author definitely expected the master to expound his work in the vernacular, as the line "Atque legens pueris laica lingua reserabit" bears testimony. A good deal of space is taken up by exceptions, further evidence that the *Doctrinale* was written as an adjunct to Donatus and was not intended as a complete corpus of grammatical knowledge.

Explanations, often somewhat fantastical, of Greek and Latin words, mainly those of the Vulgate, were introduced, and the whole, because of the ease with which its leonine hexameters could be learnt by heart, was most acceptable to its age. Its popularity throughout the later Middle Ages was remarkable; over 200 surviving manuscript copies have been enumerated, and the list is by no means complete. The need supplied was obviously real, and the *Doctrinale* was almost universally used for teaching purposes in France, England, and Germany. Important changes and modifications were early introduced. As was also the case with Donatus, the text was treated as a peg upon which to hang innumerable explanations and comments, many of the manuscripts and early printed editions consisting of a thin rivulet of text running through an overwhelming mass of gloss. In the sixteenth century the grammar was much criticised, although considerable parts of it were copied by those who were loudest in its condemnation, but for the later Middle Ages it is not too much to say that the *Doctrinale* lies at the basis of all advanced grammar teaching.

Compared with Donatus and the *Doctrinale*, other grammars, although fairly numerous, were unimportant. The *Grecismus* of Everard of Béthune (so called because it included some explanations of Greek words and their pronunciation), for example, was written soon after the *Doctrinale*, but never rivalled it in popularity, while most of the later grammars were simply adaptations of preceding works. Even during the Renaissance, when it became everywhere the fashion to abuse the *Doctrinale* as "barbarous," the new works which superseded it were often largely derived from it without acknowledgment.

Dictionaries were even rarer than grammars; a master of an important grammar school was fortunate if he had acquired, or had made for himself, a copy or adaptation of one of the many etymological vocabularies based on Isidore, such as the *Vocabularium* of Papias, the *Liber Derivationum* of the canonist Uguccio (Hugutio) of Pisa, or, best known of all, the *Catholicon* of the Dominican, John Balbi of Genoa. The latter, as full of ingenious and far-fetched derivations as the others, yet made what would now be considered an advance in that it introduced an alphabetical arrangement—a method which, however, was by no means fully appreciated at the time.

As soon as the elements of grammar were mastered, some simple text-books were read, such as the *Fables* of Aesop, the exceedingly popular *Distichs* attributed to Dionysius Cato (a series of moral maxims), or the *Eclogues* of Theodulus (*i.e.* Gottschalk). Some classical authors were sometimes studied as well, parts of Virgil, Ovid, and Horace in particular, although it was rare for any classical text to be read thoroughly or completely. Apart from Virgil, who was regarded as semi-Christian, specifically Christian authors such as Prudentius, Lactantius, Sedulius, or Juvencus were preferred, Lactantius being particularly popular in the fifteenth century.

In addition to much learning by rote and repetition, attempts were made in some grammar schools to enforce Latin speaking at all times, although this can seldom have been very effective. But a certain easy fluency in talking Latin was usually acquired, and skill in disputation was highly esteemed. In a large city, such as London, where there were several grammar schools, representative scholars of the different schools sometimes held public disputations with one another on the model of the disputations at the universities. Indeed, just as some of the song schools did work that belonged normally to the grammar school, so the curriculum of the better grammar schools overlapped that of the universities. At such schools the *Quadrivium*—Arithmetic, Geometry, Astronomy, Music—figured as well as the *Trivium*, although none of these four subjects received anything like the same amount of stress as was laid on grammar. Arithmetic, the art of calculating with Roman numerals, simplified by the use of the abacus, was probably, after grammar, the most useful subject learnt by a city boy, although it is not likely that any school gave any very advanced teaching in the subject.

A few exceptional schools might go even farther. Starting from declensions and conjugations in the lowest class, the boys (who were not admitted until they could read and write) would proceed to learn the parts of speech and some syntax, followed by elementary exercises in composition and translation of extracts from approved authors. The next stage might start with dialectic and rhetoric, followed by some very elementary theory of music, the method of calculating dates, and some simple astronomical facts. In rare instances advanced scholars might be introduced to the *Organon* of Aristotle, to the elements of Euclid, and even to a little law or theology. Oral work and frequent disputations favoured intellectual agility, and the scholastic form into which most of the instruction was necessarily cast made learning more repellent in appearance than in reality.

The grammar schools attached to the cathedrals were the chief but by no means the only grammar-teaching institutions that existed. One of the commonest ways in which medieval piety found expression was in the foundation of chantries at which chantry priests said mass for the souls of the founder and his relatives. Testators, however, soon realised that a priest could be expected to do more with a reasonable endowment than say a daily mass for the soul of his benefactor, and it thus became common for the gratuitous teaching of boys to be added to the duty of saying masses. Thus a school might be founded, sometimes in quite a small village, as a kind of appendage to, or part of, a chantry. The endowment of education was equally recognised by the Church as a good work, and schools were founded with the chantry element absent or subordinate, just as chantries were founded with free teaching as a minor addition. We find schools endowed not only by kings and great magnates, spiritual and temporal, but also, on a small scale, by humble merchants and citizens. Schools thus founded were usually "free" grammar schools, the boys, or some of them, paying no fees. In some cases, however, chantry priests who were not obliged to teach very often found that the money they received from the endowment for masses was insufficient for a permanent livelihood and they therefore frequently tried to supplement their income by teaching. Thus, directly and indirectly, the amount of education for which un-beneficed secular priests were responsible was considerable. The position of schools conducted by such masters was, however, distinctly precarious. There might not be enough boys to make it worth while to continue; the priest might obtain a benefice or he might be engaged to say a sufficient number of masses to make it unnecessary for him to teach.

The best schools, therefore, would be those in which separate masters and mass-priests were provided and in which the masters were given reasonable salaries and security of tenure. Such schools were, in some cases, so well provided for and so permanently established that the education given in them could be linked directly with that of a university. The ideal relation of school and university, in the fourteenth century, was that planned by William of Wykeham. This notable pluralist, one of the wealthiest men in England, devoted much thought as well as money to the foundation of Winchester College. His primary object was to ensure a sufficient supply of learned clerks for the Church, the number of clergy having been reduced by the Black Death and other epidemics, while provision for masses for the repose of his own soul was duly included in his plan.

The foundation charter of Winchester College was executed in 1382 and the school opened ten years later. The methods of teaching there were the same as elsewhere and, apart from the extensiveness of its endowments and the provisions made for the removal of an unsatisfactory master at three months' notice, its most notable feature was its close connexion with the University of Oxford by the parallel foundation of New College in direct contact with it. For New College, the rule of Walter de Merton was accepted with slight modifications, and the double foundation proved a marked success. In the fifteenth century this was so apparent that the experiment was copied at Eton and at King's College, Cambridge (1440), with such greater endowments and wider privileges as befitted a royal foundation. These colleges, it may be noted, were founded for the benefit of the sons of small land-owners or merchants and not for the very poorest class, the provision for the choice of "pauperes" in many medieval foundations being inserted only in order to ensure the exclusion of the really wealthy.

Besides foundations by individuals, schools were also founded by gilds, or occasionally other corporations, or placed under the control of gilds, the gild usually being immediately anxious for the provision of masses for the souls of its members and willing that the chantry priests employed should teach in addition. Towns, likewise, made provision for the instruction of the children of their townsmen. Particularly in South Germany and the Rhine valley, town-schools were common, every town of importance possessing a grammar school. In France, also, at the beginning of the fourteenth century every great town had at least one grammar school, and a knowledge of grammar, dialectic, and rhetoric was widespread. Unfortunately, education there suffered severely from the Hundred Years' War, and it was not until the second half of the fifteenth century that the French nation had the opportunity to resume the great intellectual advance of the thirteenth century.

The part of Northern Europe in which the most marked educational progress was made during the later Middle Ages was the Low Countries. This area was more highly industrialised than any other, and populous towns were in relatively close proximity to one another. The social life of such a district was predominantly urban, the peasantry being kept in something like subjection to the weavers, while in the towns there was a steady demand for clerks who could write and calculate, and a leisured class existed which was not exclusively feudal.

The ecclesiastical organisation was inadequate for the population; grammar schools attached to cathedrals would have been insufficient in any case, and, where they existed, they were unimportant. Heresy, or at least heterodox thought, was common, partly the result of the comparative rarity of religious instruction. The situation was met by the Brethren of the Common Life, the institutional embodiment of the exertions of Gerard Groote (1340–84) and Florent Radewyns (1350–1400). Groote, before his conversion, had been well educated at Paris and elsewhere and never lost the interest in scholarship that he early acquired. When he returned to the Netherlands as mission-preacher and ascetic, he continued to add to his large collection of books and employed a number of copyists to transcribe works of devotion for him. Some of these scribes followed their employer in his renunciation of the world, so that the Brethren of the Common Life from the first included a number of good scholars.

The Brethren practically revolutionised the education of their day. In some places they opened up schools of their own; in others they took charge of the existing schools, while to others again they sent some of their members as teachers. Even when they had no direct contact with a school, it was often, as at Deventer and Zwolle, completely changed owing to their influence. Thus the Netherlands could claim better school-masters than any other country north of the Alps, and something of the high standard of civilisation for which the country was famous was due to this.

Generally speaking, however, the schoolmasters of medieval Europe occupied no very conspicuous or honoured position in society. Those who lived by teaching in grammar schools were usually neither well paid nor very highly esteemed. In most cases the boys, or some of them, paid fees, the average in England being about 8*d.* a quarter. There were some customary gifts in addition but, even so, the schoolmaster paid by fees can seldom have received more than the schoolmaster paid by private endowment and required to teach freely, the average annual salary of such an endowed schoolmaster being (again in England) about £10. In a fair number of cases schoolmasters were married and in a few instances testators expressed a preference for married men, although normally unbeneficed priests would be chosen. In Germany we occasionally find schoolmasters keeping little shops or making small gains by the sale of school books; elsewhere they would sometimes act as a kind of subordinate town clerk, while they are also to be found among the early printers. In a great number of cases the schoolmaster worked alone, the existence of an assistant or usher suggesting either an unusually large school or an exceptionally adequate endowment.

There were no regular school holidays, apart from the feasts of the Church, and, provided fees were forthcoming, teachers were always willing to be on duty. Attendance at school was thus chiefly a matter for the parents, who obviously could allow their sons to be absent when they wished. In fact, there are more records of complaints by townsmen of trouble caused by schoolboys who should have been at school than of undue length of school terms or pressure of school work. Games of any sort were usually forbidden, partly because they were supposed to detract from the higher aspirations of the soul, partly because of the violence and disorder to which they invariably gave rise. Football, for example, was a free fight rather than a game. One outlet for high spirits was, however, generally recognised. This was the popular feast of the Boy Bishop, which we find kept all over Europe on St Nicholas' Day (6 December). A boy was chosen as Bishop, dressed to suit the part, allowed to lord it over his superiors, to levy contributions, and to entertain his schoolfellows (who had been allowed to run riot all day) to an evening banquet.

The fact that schoolboys behaved like ruffians whenever they had the chance was not due to any lack of corporal punishment. The rod or birch was the invariable symbol of the schoolmaster, and in every country it was applied relentlessly. The Church made no attempt to make matters easier for the boys; the text so frequently quoted in the Middle Ages, *qui parcit virgae odit filium suum*, was decisive, and plenty of flogging characterised every school, and even, at the end of the Middle Ages, spread to the universities. Public opinion saw nothing wrong in brutality in the schoolroom, and harsh as schoolmasters often were, they were not harsher than the majority of parents. In the Middle Ages, very few men indeed can have regretted the end of their schooldays.

Yet there were always those who were prepared to make real sacrifices for the sake of knowledge, the hard lives of boys who, like Butzbach and Platter, had to wander over Europe in order to pick up a precarious education being sufficient evidence of this. Although it would be a mistake to suppose that these boys formed the majority of school, or even of university, students, yet there were always many who were thus constantly on the move, seeking learning restlessly and painfully wherever it might best be found. Their efforts were not helped by the existence of the Mendicants who, if they had made both journeying and begging respectable, had also made them considerably more difficult.

The earliest stages of teaching, particularly of grammar, were very much the same for all classes and for the whole of Europe, but, naturally, special provision had to be made for the vocational instruction of special classes of society. The Church, which made itself responsible for the learning of the West, was obliged to take especial care to secure adequate education for the clergy. The monasteries which, in earlier times, had been such important *foci* of scholarship and instruction, were, in the later Middle Ages, of less general importance. They remained self-contained communities where the professed were expected to study and were assumed to know enough Latin to understand the Vulgate, the services of the Church, and the Rule, and also to speak Latin among themselves. Thus arrangements had to be made for ensuring that a certain minimum standard of scholarship was maintained by all. Further, the novices, many of whom were quite young, had to be taught the meaning and implications of the life they were proposing to live. This, in practice, often involved the ordinary teaching of Latin as given in a good grammar school with specifically religious instruction in addition. A special novice-master was normally appointed for this work, which was probably seldom onerous, since the numbers to be taught were usually very small. The novice school was, of course, strictly exclusive; the admission of children from outside would have been opposed to the first principles of monasticism.

Some of the larger monasteries also maintained a separate almonry school, chiefly for the training of choristers when musical services became customary. These choristers, together sometimes with a few other children, were placed under the control of the Precentor, while their maintenance was part of the duties of the Almoner. Singing, naturally, was the chief subject of instruction, but the teaching of singing was generally accompanied by the teaching of reading, while some elements of Latin grammar were often added as well. Usually a secular priest was employed to teach the boys freely, and by this means a certain number of boys in the immediate vicinity of a great house might learn to read and write. But the number so educated in any country was very small, and the almonry schools can hardly be claimed as contributing seriously to the learning of the West.

The professed monk was under no obligation to study or to teach, although some intellectual as well as manual labour was theoretically required of him. The general standard of scholarship and of intellectual interests within the monasteries necessarily varied greatly in different countries and different houses. Large monasteries were expected to maintain a lecturer in theology within their walls, although this requirement was frequently neglected. They were also under the obligation (by the Constitutions of Benedict XII, 1336) of sending one monk in twenty to a university. At all the larger universities there were special halls or colleges for the reception of monks, who were placed under the charge of a *prior studentium*. The colleges, however, were seldom full. The papal constitutions were frequently neglected or evaded; very few monasteries sent their full complement of scholars, and during the fifteenth century the numbers steadily dwindled.

The educational work of the Mendicants, on the other hand, was of real importance.[1] The Dominicans, in particular, were intensely interested in scholarship; they were an Order of preachers, formed for the express object of combating heresy, laying special emphasis upon the study of theology. This implied a very considerable knowledge of other subjects, for theology was the "Queen of the Sciences," only to be approached by those who had undergone a long and arduous apprenticeship.

The Franciscans, at first, laid much less stress upon intellectual attainments than did the Dominicans, St Francis himself being distinctly suspicious of book-learning. But scholarship could not be excluded, and the Franciscans soon counted as many distinguished university graduates and teachers among their numbers as did the Dominicans. Particularly in England, Franciscan learning became traditional. Unless forced by necessity, however, the Mendicants made no attempt at formal school teaching; they lectured, as they were obliged to do, at the universities, and they communicated much knowledge to the people in their sermons, but their importance for the history of education lies chiefly in the elaborate organisation which they built up for the instruction of their own members.

Mere boys were often accepted by the friars as novices, although, normally, these were not admitted until they had learnt at least the elements of grammar. They were then trained by stages in logic, natural philosophy, and theology, their most eminent members becoming exceedingly influential (and, frequently, exceedingly unpopular) at the universities, particularly at Oxford and Paris. The high standard of the thirteenth century, however, was not maintained during the two following centuries, and although the friar was almost always better educated than the monk, his direct contributions to education at the end of the Middle Ages were not much more noteworthy.

[1] Cf. Vol. vi, Chapter xxi, especially pp. 741–748.

With the highly organised Regulars the secular clergy could scarcely hope to compete. Every parish priest was expected to attempt to teach his parishioners, old and young, the truths of the Christian religion, while some gave direct religious instruction to the children in a way that was almost that of the schoolroom, assisted, sometimes, by the parish clerk. Technically, anyone who had received first tonsure was a cleric and, since this did not prevent a man from marrying or pursuing his ordinary daily work, and often brought substantial legal advantages, most scholars were "clerics." In this way the clergy, particularly in earlier days, provided practically all the trained minds of the West, and their monopoly of learning was long maintained. But the clergy, in the narrower sense of those who had taken higher orders and were following an exclusively ecclesiastical career, and particularly the secular clergy who served the parishes, were at no time highly educated on the average and, indeed, were frequently little better instructed than some of their neighbours and parishioners. Visitation records shew a surprising amount of sheer ignorance; ordination examinations must have been exceedingly simple when we find priests unable to construe or explain the opening sentences of the Canon of the Mass, and sometimes even scarcely able to read. It is true that we frequently find orders in episcopal registers for priests to study at "the schools," while university students were readily granted dispensation from residence in their parishes if, as was often the case, they were beneficed. But apart from the universities there were, of course, no special seminaries for the education of the clergy, and it was the exception rather than the rule for a priest to be a university graduate.

In spite, then, of the constant efforts of Councils and bishops, in spite of the fact that most parsons had at least learnt the elements of Latin at a grammar school, the standard of knowledge amongst the rural clergy as a whole was not a high one. Even when a priest had been well educated, according to the standard of the times, the loneliness, the lack of books and of contact with cultured society in a remote village must have made it only too easy for him to forget the knowledge that he had acquired. Conditions necessarily varied widely, but the tendency during the later Middle Ages was for the clergy to fail to maintain the marked educational superiority that had been theirs in earlier times. During these years, while the general standard of lay education was steadily improving, that of the clergy did not advance with anything like commensurate rapidity.

For the clergy, as for the laity, the universities remained to the end of the Middle Ages almost the only centres for higher education. The history of their origin and development has been told in a previous volume,[1] but the history of education in the later Middle Ages, and particularly the education of the clergy, would be incomplete without a reference to them. A primary purpose of their existence was the training of the clergy; a very considerable proportion of the students and masters

[1] See *supra*, Vol. vi, Chapter xvii.

were in holy orders, and those who were not beneficed hoped that their names would be included in the next *rotulus* that went to Rome or that their merits would soon attract the attention of a patron. It is true that neither civil law nor medicine, both of which subjects claimed considerable numbers of students, were normally studied by ecclesiastics, but outside Italy universities were not founded principally for the study of either of these subjects.

At the universities, no special provision was made for instruction that might be useful for parochial duties. Only a minority of those who matriculated proceeded to a degree, while still fewer remained as students of theology—the only subject for which a thorough knowledge of the text of the Bible was indispensable. Many of the wealthier students enrolled themselves in the Faculty of Canon Law (Decreta), for an expert canonist could always be sure of lucrative employment and often of promotion to high office in the Church. Of the "artists," many came to a university too ignorant of Latin to be able even to follow the ordinary lectures, so that special arrangements were made at some universities for the teaching of grammar and even for the granting of degrees in grammar, sometimes with accompaniments which clearly indicated that the recipient expected to spend his life teaching schoolboys.

One of the reasons that so many left without graduating was the length of the degree courses. Even allowing for the fact that, judged by modern standards, the undergraduates were often very young, few could afford, or would care, to stay the fourteen years that were required (unless some exemption was obtained) for the much-coveted recognition as master or doctor in the Faculty of Theology. Length of residence and the fulfilment of the prescribed formalities, indeed, were more important than industry or intellectual distinction. A man might gain a reputation that would be very useful to him later for mental subtlety and agility in the disputations that formed so prominent a feature of university life, but written examinations as tests of knowledge were almost unknown. Provided a man were of reasonably good character, could swear that he had "read" the prescribed authorities, was of sufficient standing, and had paid the proper fees, admission to a "degree" was practically automatic, carrying with it the right to teach in any other university.

After the thirteenth century, the triumph of scholastic methods in university education was complete. Departure from traditional forms of presentation of knowledge became increasingly difficult, while the disputations too often degenerated into meaningless word-play or were made into public and elaborate quodlibets. There were, naturally, some who could use even the most unpromising media for the expression of real philosophical thought, but the most fertile and suggestive writers were often those most vehemently suspected of heresy. The remarkable increase in the number of universities during the fifteenth century is in itself evidence that education was more widely diffused and that the number of educated men in Europe was growing. This, in itself, helps to compensate for the absence of striking originality or notable writing; it was an age of glosses, epitomes, and commentaries, during which the advances of an earlier period were accepted, tested, and assimilated. Only when this process was complete could further advances be made.

Grammar schools and universities, usually founded for clerics, used also by some who had no intention of taking orders, did not cater for the educational needs of the whole of the population. Two classes—the sons of the nobility, and girls—were almost invariably absent from these regular teaching institutions. The former, if they had only careers of fighting and administration before them, had seldom any considerable acquaintance with book-learning. They received, however, a specialised training of their own which was essentially the same in most countries. Before the age of seven, the young noble was left in the charge of the women of his father's household, largely to play, to learn manners, and (in England) perhaps to speak French. He then often went as a page to the castle of a neighbouring lord, every noble being expected to maintain a court which incidentally served as a training-ground for boys and young men of good family. There, in addition to the performance of a certain amount of menial work, he learnt the manners and customs of gentle society and might receive some instruction in reading, writing, and religion from the ladies of the court or from a chaplain or chantry priest.

From page, at about fourteen, he became a squire, at which stage his outdoor education began in real earnest. He learnt to ride, shoot, hawk, jump, throw, swim, and fight. The method of instruction was largely one of emulation, for the chief merit of such a household was considered to consist in its bringing together youths of the same class and age. The young squire would now be expected to understand French fairly well, this being almost as much the common language of the courtly class as Latin was that of the clerical class. The minstrel was a regular feature of this society and his craft was the more appreciated because many of the knights could themselves play on the harp and improvise songs.

Although examples of literate and even of well-educated knights are not unknown, they are exceptional and are usually found among families with some particular administrative as well as military experience. The specialised chivalric code of the class placed a low value on scholarship. Clerks educated clerks and knights knights, and their spheres did not over-lap; nevertheless the international character of chivalry, common language, common interests, and much association in wars and crusades made a certain minimum of culture inevitable.

In theory the code of chivalry which the knight was taught and expected to practise, combined with the steady increase in the reverence paid to the Virgin Mary by ecclesiastics, should have led to the assignment of a high place in society to women. There is, however, much to suggest that the wife and daughters of a knight were often treated in a way that did not correspond with the chivalric code of the romances and courtly treatises. The Church, too, in spite of much praising of the Virgin Mary, tended to treat women as agents of evil rather than of good and to persuade men that the physically weaker sex was worthy of little consideration. It is thus scarcely surprising that no systematic provision was made for the education of girls of any class. Even the suggestion that any regular instruction for girls should be provided is met with only in speculators such as Pierre Dubois, Christine de Pisan, or William of Ockham, whose alarming originality disturbed rather than enlightened their age.

Occasionally little girls were taught together with boys in the song-schools or by casual teachers. Froissart, for example, has left a delightful picture of his early schooldays and of his child-love for his girl companions. From the grammar schools, however, girls were rigidly excluded. There was no place for women learned in grammar in medieval society, while it was assumed that their very presence in a grammar school would corrupt master and boys alike. Apart from what they learnt in the song school or its equivalent, girls were taught chiefly at home, learning, naturally, mainly matters of domestic utility, it being assumed that every girl who did not enter religion would be married, usually while still very young. Those of the higher classes would chiefly aim at cultivating polished manners, personal beauty and charm, and skill in dress—these being considered their essential attributes. In a large household they would have, if they wished it, opportunities for learning to read and write from the chaplain or from some visiting ecclesiastic. That some made use of such chances is clear, since we find among the nobility occasional examples of ladies with real intellectual interests and administrative capacity, able to read, write, discuss affairs, and manage estates. Women like Margaret or Agnes Paston, whose activity on behalf of their absent husbands and general interest in affairs were so considerable, cannot have been very exceptional, for a great land-owner would frequently be away from home, sometimes for long periods, through wars, crusades, and service at court, leaving much responsibility to his wife. What learning such ladies had was, however, except in very rare cases, not that of the scholars. The literature in which they were interested was written in French rather than in Latin and was concerned with different (and less edifying) matters from that read by clerks.

For a girl of quality who willingly or otherwise remained unmarried almost the only refuge was the cloister. Within the nunneries, as within the monasteries, opportunities were offered for learned leisure, while the daily lives of the inmates necessarily implied a certain minimum of religious knowledge. But in the later Middle Ages the requirements were not considerable. It was frequently assumed by visiting bishops that nuns did not possess sufficient knowledge of Latin to be able to understand summons, injunction, or sermon in that language, so that the vernacular had to be used when addressing them.

CH. XXIII.

Like the monasteries, most nunneries were expected to maintain a
school for the novices, but this meant very little. Admissions of novices
were not frequent, seldom more than two or three annually, often none
at all, while the age and position of many novices did not make them
particularly amenable to instruction. On the other hand, many nunneries
were poorly endowed and were therefore willing to add to their income
by means of teaching. In spite of official prohibitions by bishops and
others, who consistently disapproved of any dealings with the "world,"
some regular teaching was available for girls in many nunneries. Children
of the upper classes were received as boarders, taught some reading and
perhaps spinning, needlework, and embroidery, for which the nuns received
fees. There is, however, no evidence that in any country in Europe
gratuitous or even cheap education for the poor was habitually provided
by the nunneries, just as there is little to suggest that most nuns possessed
any particular capacity for teaching.

Yet apart from the nunneries and the households of the magnates very
little was done anywhere for the direct teaching of girls. Most girls had
to be content with what they learnt at home. "I received no other
instruction," said Joan of Arc to her inquisitors, "save only from my
mother, from whom I learnt my *Pater Noster*, *Ave Maria*, and *Credo*."
A similar answer would have been given by the majority of girls in most
countries.

There was still a third class, in England at least, for which the educational system of the day did not completely cater. This consisted of the
lawyers, who evolved a system of their own, since the two English universities offered no facilities for the study of common law. An adequate
knowledge of Latin being indispensable, the future lawyer would learn
this at home or from a chantry priest or at a grammar school. The high
centralisation of English law at the time made it almost essential for the
young man who would succeed to go to London. Here were established
the Inns of Court where the men of law lived and worked. These institutions thus became, almost accidentally, places for legal education as well,
offering the only facilities in the country for the study of common law.
The teaching there was mainly oral, and public disputations were frequently held, although not many formal lectures seem to have been given.
Civil Law was, of course, always taught at the English universities, though
not very adequately. It was not until 1535, when lectures on Canon
Law had been officially forbidden, that professorships of Civil Law were
founded at Oxford and Cambridge, contemporaneously with an increased
interest in Civil Law on the continent. Before that date men had had to
go to North Italy if they wanted to obtain the best instruction in Europe
in this subject.

There was much else, however, besides Civil Law to be learnt in Italy.
The Italian Renaissance, indirectly at least, had important effects on
the theory and practice of medieval education, helping to bring about

changes that were to alter the educational outlook of the world. Italian political conditions were in many ways different from those of the rest of Europe, and Italian education was affected by such conditions. The memories of the former greatness of Rome, the existence of the Papacy, the high repute of the universities of Northern Italy for the study of Civil Law, the character of the Italian people, the existence of a fairly large class of learned laymen, all made a departure from the educational methods and traditions of the rest of Europe likely. This departure was not noticeable, however, until the fourteenth century, when Petrarch launched an open attack on logic. This subject, which included dialectic and much of what we should call metaphysics, had hitherto formed the basis of medieval education. After the reconciliation of Aristotle with the Bible, completed by St Thomas Aquinas, the authority of Aristotle was accepted almost without reservation. Dante, who died in 1321, regarded him as "the master of those who know." Petrarch, however, born in 1304, challenged the acceptance of the supreme authority of Aristotle and never failed to shew his unqualified aversion for academic logicians themselves. For Petrarch, logic and dialectic were methods of study and means of intellectual advancement and nothing more; the idea of making them an end seemed to him fantastic. He consistently ridiculed the notion of limiting the scope of metaphysical speculation to Aristotle and his commentators, considering their ideals to have noteworthy limitations and in any case to be distinctly inferior to those of Plato. To some extent, Petrarch's diatribe against Aristotle may have been due to dissatisfaction with the inadequate and obscure translations that were current and to the ascription of a common authority to text and gloss alike, but it represents a new point of view none the less.

Part of this attack on the methods of logic and the authority of Aristotle was caused by a desire to escape from the fetters laid by the medieval Church upon the expression of individual personality. For the Italian, the restoration of the Greek and Roman ideals of the place to be assigned to the individual in society, expressed, in part, by the word *virtù*, was to be brought about by copying the ancient methods of training youth. Education was felt to provide the key to a coming new age, and a right standard for this, they thought, could be found in the works of the classical authors. In this connexion the two writers who attracted almost exclusive attention in Italy were Quintilian and Plutarch. Practically all the educational thought of the Renaissance springs from the *Institutio Oratoria* of Quintilian, and in this respect the Renaissance was a real "revival of learning." Almost the whole of the treatises on education written in the fifteenth century that have come down to us are plagiarisms, some selective, some copying almost the exact words of the original. The few new creative ideas that emerged were accidental and the result of practical experience in the attempted application of ancient theories.

Quintilian's treatise on the education of an Orator was rediscovered by Poggio at St. Gall in 1416, and although it had not previously been unknown in monastic libraries and elsewhere, it was the knowledge of the possession of this complete text which Poggio assiduously circulated that was directly responsible for the attention that was paid to its contents. In 1421 the entire text of Cicero's *De Oratore* had been likewise discovered at Lodi, and was eagerly studied by the few who were already appearing as the forerunners of the Ciceronian revival.

The Roman ideal orator as outlined by Cicero and Quintilian was primarily a good man and a philosopher. Quintilian started with the assumption that most, though not all, children were capable of higher education and that therefore care in selection of nurses and teachers was essential. He was well aware of the evils inculcated by the public schools of his day, wherein the morals of the pupils were too often spoilt; yet he insisted that in them alone could the normal boy obtain the maximum amount of benefit to be derived from friendship on the one hand and emulation on the other. Memory and imitative instinct must be cultivated, as well as music, astronomy, and literature (*eloquentia*). Praise and reproof should be sufficient to maintain discipline, flogging being fit only for slaves. Careful attention must be given to grammatical details, and the praise of etymology has an almost medieval flavour. Reading and speaking correctly are important in themselves and the pupil must understand what he reads, beginning with Homer and Virgil, proceeding to the tragedians, lyric poets, and comedians. The study of music and dancing is justified by its effect upon the movements and bearing of the body. All these subjects can easily be included within the work of a school, the juvenile mind being sufficiently elastic to be capable of assimilating several subjects simultaneously. Above all things, adequate care must be taken to see that the moral character of the teacher is of the highest, capable of perfect harmony and sympathy with his pupils. The result of this teaching will be the emergence of an Orator, a man of the highest ideals, whose ability is so sharpened that it may be of the greatest use to his fellow-citizens, something of the combination of philosopher and statesman whom Plato had long before desired to rule his Republic.

Very intimately connected with, and indeed dependent upon, Quintilian's *Institutio Oratoria*, is the treatise attributed to Plutarch, περὶ παίδων ἀγωγῆς, which Guarino translated in 1411. It differs from Quintilian's work mainly in the meagreness of the details of intellectual education, most attention being devoted to moral training. To these two treatises the humanists added little, if anything, that was really new, the creative genius lying in the skill shewn in the adaptation of these recommendations to the circumstances and ideas of their own day. In order to understand the educational bequest of the revival of learning to modern times, in spite of all the reservations stated above, some attempt must be made to trace the progress of the new theories which came into prominence, and this can be done only by means of an account of some of the writers who dealt directly with them.

Petrus Paulus Vergerius (1349–1428), Doctor of Law and Medicine at Padua, made a resolute attempt to abandon scholastic methods in his teaching of logic. Either as early as 1392 or as late as 1404, he composed a treatise, *De Ingenuis Moribus et Liberalibus Studiis*, for the use of Ubertino, son of Francesco da Carrara, the lord of Padua. A spirit of classical enthusiasm and of Christianity pervades the book, and it was diligently studied (*e.g.* by Bembo), containing as it did a systematic exposition and defence of new subjects and methods of instruction. Quickly following on this, came Guarino's rendering of Plutarch's περὶ παίδων ἀγωγῆς and Leonardo Bruni's version of St Basil's treatise on the advantage to be gained from the study of the ancient poets. Vergerius has a noble ideal of "liberal" studies as those which call forth the highest gifts of body and mind in the pursuit of goodness and wisdom. His order of preference would be history, moral philosophy, eloquence (the art of letters, including grammar, logic, and rhetoric), poetry, music, arithmetic, geometry, astronomy in all its branches, to be followed by the three professional courses of study, medicine, law, and theology. Boys of limited capacity must work at congenial subjects, and no one must so entirely surrender himself to scholarship as to forget his duties as a citizen. Mere desultory reading is condemned in favour of some degree of specialisation, to be helped by regular revision, discussion, and exposition. Lastly, athletic training in a mild form is admitted as of value.

In 1404 the Florentine Dominican, Giovanni Domenici, in his *Regola del Governo di Cura Familiare*, protested against those students of the classics who ventured to cast doubts upon the doctrine of the fall of man, therein expressing the ideas of many of his clerical brethren, including his pupil Antonino, later Archbishop of Florence. The torch, in spite of them, was handed on to Leone Battista Alberti (1404–72), who summed up a brilliant youthful career by abandoning his legal studies at Bologna in favour of humanism. A skilful architect, employed by Nicholas V, he never lost his early interest in classical literature and about 1432–33 outlined the preparation best suited for the governing class of his native Tuscany in his *Trattato della Cura della Famiglia*. Instead of medieval intellectual and physical asceticism, he boldly insisted upon the universal obligation of public service, helped by a disciplined and robust body. He declared himself in favour of free will and human progress through the development of individual personality. His model of parental authority was Cato the Censor, supplemented by a tutor of high moral character who should teach "letters" rather than professional requirements. The details of his scheme of work are familiar: Priscian and Servius for grammar, Cicero, Livy, and Sallust for Latin prose, Homer and Virgil for poetry, Demosthenes for oratory, and Xenophon's *Œconomia* for the needs of the home. Arithmetic, geometry, astronomy, the latter including physics, geography, and meteorology, added to the fine arts, would produce the satisfactory citizens that he desired. A few years later (between 1435 and 1440) Matteo Palmieri (1406–75), a friend of Alberti, composed a treatise called *Della Vita Civile*. As an adherent of Cosimo de' Medici, he wished to produce the statesman-scholar, now again a possibility owing to improved methods of teaching and an increased respect for antiquity. The scholar, he argues, will pursue truth for its own sake, but his active life must be passed in society—virtue must be learnt in the home and in the daily task of administration of public affairs. For details of the subjects to be taught Palmieri follows Quintilian, supplemented by Vergerius and Guarino's translation of Plutarch, with a considerable debt to Cicero's *De Officiis*. Moral philosophy must precede natural history, and those children whose talent is apparent at an early age should include both of these in the many subjects that they must pursue.

The next writer on education who caught the imagination of his age was the celebrated Aeneas Sylvius Piccolomini (1405–64), later Pope Pius II. This many-sided product of the Renaissance, in 1450, while Bishop of Trieste and in the service of the Emperor Frederick III, addressed an essay, *De Liberorum educatione*, to the Emperor's ward, Ladislas, King of Bohemia, then ten years old. This academic exercise on the training of a prince is, as we should expect, taken almost entirely from Quintilian and Plutarch. A knowledge of the elements of Christianity is assumed, while the Christian doctrine of immortality can, Aeneas explains, be found in many authors of antiquity. Grammar, in its wider meaning of literature, eloquence, composition, and the *ars dictaminis*, receives a full measure of attention, although Aeneas Sylvius is more concerned with securing harmonious and approved phraseology, to be obtained by wide reading, than with the matter and content of any writings. He proceeds to justify the reading of pagan authors by the example of the Fathers and names Virgil, Lucan, Statius, Ovid's *Metamorphoses*, Claudian, Valerius Flaccus, Horace (to be read, like Ovid and Juvenal, in expurgated editions) for style and Plautus and Terence for diction. Cicero's *De Officiis* is essential, supplemented by parts of the works of St Ambrose, Lactantius, St Augustine, St Jerome, and Gregory the Great. Livy and Sallust represent the historians. Rhetoric and dialectic are useful enough, but, since the prince must become a man of action, logical subtleties can be avoided. Geometry, arithmetic, and astronomy have their uses, but are subordinate to philosophy as expounded in the writings of Cicero, particularly *De Senectute* and *De Amicitia*, in the letters of Seneca, and in the *Philosophiae Consolatio* of Boethius.

The general principles used by Guarino of Verona in his teaching at Ferrara were outlined in 1458 or 1459 by his son Battista, whose treatise, *De ordine docendi et studendi*, written at the age of 25, was directed to Maffeo Gambara of Brescia. It is almost exclusively devoted to an insistence upon the importance of the study of ancient literature, particularly Greek, which is claimed as one of the primary necessities of an educated gentleman. For grammatical rules the text-book of accidence compiled by his father, the *Regulae Guarini*, is recommended, as well as the *Doctrinale* of Alexander of Villa Dei because of its metrical form. The elements of Greek grammar should be learnt from Chrysoloras' Ἐρωτήματα in the original or in Guarino's abridgment of it, and history should begin with general writers, such as Justin or Valerius Maximus, its importance lying in the practical value of its examples to statesmen. Virgil still maintains priority of place among the poets, the *Aeneid* being followed by the *Thebais* of Statius, the *Metamorphoses* and *Fasti* of Ovid, the *Tragedies* of Seneca, and selections from Terence, Plautus, and Juvenal. Geography rests upon Pomponius Mela, Solinus, and Strabo. Rhetoric can be learnt from the pseudo-Ciceronian *Rhetorica ad Herennium*, Cicero, and Quintilian. Logic comes next, including the *Ethics* of Aristotle and the *Dialogues* of Plato, the *De Officiis* and the *Tusculans* of Cicero, followed by the elements of Roman Law. Careful note-taking and consultation of all available authorities are recommended and, in order to obtain a sound general knowledge by wide reading, such authors as Aulus Gellius, Macrobius, and Pliny are suggested as well as St Augustine's *De Civitate Dei*. Greek texts ought to be studied with a Latin translation, and both here and elsewhere stress is laid upon the value of reading aloud. Poetry contains many profound truths, and by following such a course as has been outlined the scholar will learn to converse with the mighty minds of the past and thereby fulfil the finest impulses of his nature. Mankind progresses in learning and virtue by means of the humanities.

The foregoing account of the educational writers of the Italian Renaissance is illustrative rather than exhaustive, since the treatises themselves all shew a marked similarity and are based on classical models. It remains to give some account of the actual teaching that was introduced as a result of these changes of idea and outlook. This involves a sketch of the life and work of one who was one of the most successful and the most famous of the many who sought to apply these ideals, Vittorino da Feltre. Born in 1378, the son of a scribe or notary, he entered the University of Padua in 1396, just as the classical revival was beginning, and remained there for twenty years, apparently making sufficient money as a grammar-school master to enable him to complete the course in arts. He then studied mathematics under a series of teachers not officially recognised by the university, and later taught it himself with great success. His Latin style was immensely improved after 1407 by his acquaintance with the new Professor of Rhetoric, Gasparino Barzizza, who, more than any other, was responsible for the cult of Cicero which marked the later stages of the Italian Renaissance. In 1415, he left Padua for Venice, where he studied Greek under a fellow-teacher, Guarino, the pupil of Chrysoloras, and one of the very few Greek scholars then to be found in Italy.

After he had thus given himself an adequate training, he returned to Padua, where he obtained a great reputation for his skill in moulding the minds and morals of the students whom he received in his house as boarders. In 1422 he succeeded Barzizza as Professor of Rhetoric but resigned in the same year, possibly in disgust at the unhealthy moral condition of the university. At first he went back to Venice, but he soon accepted the invitation of Gianfrancesco Gonzaga, tyrant of Mantua, to go to Mantua as tutor to his family. The Gonzagas of Mantua were very little different from the rest of the Italian tyrants who surrounded them, princes in every sense supreme within their dominions, occupying a position of enormous possibilities for good or evil. Before bargaining about his salary, which was a matter of indifference to him (being unmarried), Vittorino insisted upon being given a free hand, and this was always allowed him. The fact that he was able to rely upon the support of Gianfrancesco Gonzaga and his wife Paola Malatesta in all his measures alone made his success possible. His work was to teach the sons of the Marquess Gonzaga, Ludovico, Carlo, and Gianlucido, Alessandro and his sister Cecilia being added later. He also received the sons of other noble families of the neighbourhood and a number of poorer boys of notable ability. These latter he always insisted upon keeping, making his richer patrons pay for practically the whole of the education of a few of his best pupils. Vittorino realised to the full the influence of environment on the lives of children, and he therefore chose the most pleasant spot in the neighbourhood of Mantua for his school house which he named La Giocosa. Here, surrounded by playing fields, he exercised a vicarious parental authority over his charges, removing their bad companions and winning their affection by his devotion to duty. The causes of his success, which made Mantua renowned throughout Europe, spring from the personality of the man working on the ideas of his time. He was entirely absorbed in his work, personally charming, gifted with a musical penetrating voice, able to enforce his authority with quiet persistence and without passion or harshness, strong, indefatigable, and persuasive. He remained a convinced Christian at a time when many of his fellow-scholars were tending to question the fundamentals of Christianity, and he never wavered in his faith. It is such lives as his that prove that the Italian Revival of Learning was not in essence anti-Christian or opposed to morality; in some wilder spirits it naturally took strange turns and produced an effusive exuberance of irresponsible wantonness, but too much attention can be paid to such examples. For his pupils, Vittorino strongly insisted upon the necessity of regular compulsory daily exercise in the open air. In doing so, he proved himself one of the first teachers of his age to recognise that the mind could act properly only if the body was in good working order and that this was best secured by games and physical training. In this he was really a very considerable innovator, for he thereby threw over the essentially medieval conception of the worthlessness of the body in favour of an attempt to secure a harmony of the claims of flesh and spirit. An ascetic himself, he took up a position opposed in principle to the meaning of ascetic ideals. His task as teacher was complicated by the condition of his chief pupils—Ludovico was lazy and fat, Carlo full of the zest of life but constitutionally weak. Therefore, with that careful individual attention that marked his whole teaching, Vittorino proceeded quietly to induce Carlo to eat more and Ludovico much less, in which, by forbidding all pure luxuries and stimulants, he was most successful. To his pupils he endeavoured to teach something of all the knowledge available to his age, the classical authors naturally bulking most largely. So far as possible, the subjects taught were widely varied, ancient literature being interspersed with lessons in music, natural sciences, mathematics, and other subjects. He insisted upon the value of the cultivation of the memory at all times and upon the educative effect of frequent reading aloud and of declamation. The range of authors studied included Virgil, Livy, and Cicero, for whom he had a particular reverence, Lucan, Ovid, Terence, Plautus, Horace, Juvenal, Seneca, Valerius Maximus, Caesar, Sallust, Quintus Curtius, Pliny, Quintilian, and St Augustine, thus covering practically the whole field of ancient knowledge. It is noteworthy that we have no evidence that he had recourse to such specifically Christian writers as Lactantius, who made such an appeal to Vittorino's northern contemporaries.

Using Gaza's grammar, he taught Greek thoroughly and systematically, and the scholarship of some of his pupils, such as Ognibene de' Bonisoli da Lonigo, Niccolò Perotti, and Lorenzo Valla, bears the best testimony to his ability as a teacher of Latin. Yet, obviously, far more important than the details of his methods or books was the personality of the master, his real genius for education, coupled with his untiring zeal. Instead of confining his attention to lofty theories as did many of his contemporaries, he tried the educational theories of his day by the test of the class-room itself. It is, of course, foolish to suggest that his great merits did not also imply real limitations. Thus, the range of subjects that he taught, judged by a modern standard, was narrow and circumscribed by the humanist conviction that all knowledge was to be found in its most perfect form in the writings of the great Greek and Latin authors. Study was therefore limited to these and a reverence paid to their opinions and methods of expression that almost precluded any personal originality and in less capable hands degenerated easily into mere slavish imitation.

Vittorino himself wrote nothing that has survived and we cannot be certain how far he was prepared to adhere rigidly to the ideas of his class. We know, however, that he despised the vernacular and rejected its claims to be considered as a serious medium of literary or scientific expression. Latin alone was to be the language of scholarship and even of personal intercourse among scholars, and this Latin itself was to be the purest possible imitation of that of Cicero, not the debased language that served the workaday purposes of medieval Italy. He based his work so largely upon the production of the classical ideal of the orator that any historical or critical methods of reading the texts of the authors whose writings he expounded, or any attempt to analyse their ideas scientifically, was impossible. Even his principles of teaching spread slowly. His direct personal influence was almost entirely confined to the small corner of Italy bounded by Padua, Venice, and Mantua; it was only very gradually, and mainly after his death, that his pupils spread his renown, and his mode of teaching obtained general acquiescence.

In some respects Vittorino looked back to the past. His Christianity, true and pure as it was and free from pantheism or rationalism, was thoroughly medieval. Not only did he make his life accord with the best ascetic ideals, but also he used all his influence successfully to induce his able pupil, Cecilia Gonzaga, to forsake the world and become a nun. With all his insistence upon the value of a trained mind and body in every individual, he had little appreciation of the social nature and tendencies of man. The salvation of the individual soul and the moulding of the individual character were his highest ambition; we have no evidence that he recognised any claim of the community as a whole upon the time and abilities of the educated class. At heart, Vittorino was a monk and an aristocrat; he was also the exemplar of all that was best in the combination of these qualities with those of the humanist pure and simple. He shewed that Renaissance education need not involve self-conceit, profligacy, or irreligion, that not every humanist cared solely for fame and for the chance of the posthumous survival of his writings and letters, and that personal faith and devotion could be combined with exact scholarship and real appreciation of classical literature.

One important innovation in the education of Renaissance Italy was the greater advantages offered to girls. Although there was not, here as elsewhere, any general desire to give all girls, even of the leisured classes, the same education as was given to boys, nevertheless exceptional opportunities of instruction were open to them. The result was that there were women like Isotta Nogarola and Olympia Morata who could hold their own in matters of scholarship with the best of their male contemporaries and who were accepted and even acclaimed everywhere. Unfortunately, however, such women were very rare, as few took advantage of the facilities thus made available. While every city boasted its quota of male humanists, well-educated women were throughout a small minority. No preparations were made for maintaining the supply, and when the day of reaction dawned they almost disappeared. Thus the promise of a succession of highly educated women, which might have been expected of the educational revival in Italy, remained unfulfilled.

In Northern Europe, Italian conditions were in certain respects parallelled by those of the Netherlands, and it was with this area that the most conspicuous figures of the revival of learning in Germany were most closely connected. Mention has already been made of the activities of the Brethren of the Common Life as teachers and scholars. Their libraries were celebrated for the number of their books and, although it was long before specifically "classical" authors were conspicuously studied and still longer before Greek or Hebrew became known, there was much active thought and interest in intellectual matters among the Brethren and their friends. The suggestion that their teaching was heterodox was indignantly repudiated, although some of the theories of mystics such as Ruysbroeck (1293–1381), who through his friendship with Groote helped to influence the Brethren, were suspected by some good Churchmen.

The teaching of some of the later adherents of the Brethren did not lessen this suspicion. Gerhard Zerbolt (1367–98) demanded a vernacular Bible; John of Goch (c. 1401–1475) had the courage to oppose the teaching of Aquinas upon several points; Wessel Gansfort (c. 1419–1498) became widely known as an original and fearless theological preacher—all three men whose opinions were regarded by many as savouring of heresy. Others, such as St Thomas à Kempis, who devoted themselves mainly to mystical speculation and writings, were more fortunate in their reputation and helped to save the Order from the condemnation that was more than once sought by its enemies.

The influence of the Brethren on the education of the cities in which they worked was remarkable. Schools directly or indirectly connected with them were founded at Deventer, Zwolle, Windesheim, Amersfoort, Schoonhoven, Harderwijk, Grammont, Hoorn, Delft, Gouda, Hertogenbosch, Doesburg, Groningen, Utrecht, Nijmegen (Nimwegen), Malines, Cambrai, Louvain, Ghent, Brussels, Antwerp, and Liège, while the important work of Wimpheling at Strasbourg was consciously based on his observations and knowledge of what was being done farther north.

This success was partly due to the principles which underlay the educational activities of the Brethren. With them education was a means to an end—the development of better moral and spiritual qualities in the people as a whole. They aimed at training the character of the boys whom they taught rather than at turning out excellent scholars, although they often succeeded in doing the latter as well. They cared for the physical as well as the moral welfare of their pupils, and their schools were distinguished from others by the use of means other than flogging for maintaining discipline. All this they were able to achieve largely because they took great care in the choice of teachers and particularly of headmasters. It was, for example, mainly owing to the personalities of men such as Hegius at Deventer and Cele at Zwolle that these particular schools achieved the marked success that they did. Further, they welcomed really poor boys, whom they taught in every way as well as their richer schoolfellows.

Although the Brethren could shew no one whose ideas were as markedly new as those of Vittorino da Feltre, yet the masters appointed through their influence were highly successful in their endeavours and certainly

taught a better and purer Latin than had been current previously. Text-
books, particularly of grammar, were improved and rewritten, while care
was taken to see that the boys could understand and apply what they
had learnt. Considerable stress was laid upon the actual reading of the
texts of classical authors, and frequent oral tests were made of the knowledge thus acquired.

It is therefore not surprising that the Renaissance in Germany, once
started, made rapid progress and soon developed distinct characteristics
of its own. Men like Agricola (1444–85) and Erasmus (1466–1536), who
both had connexions with the schools of the Brethren, found Italy had
little to teach them. The scholars who came from the north, Langen
(1438–1519), Hegius (1433–98), and Wimpheling (1450–1528) in particular, while quite as good Latinists as those from South Germany, were
far more interested in the theory and practice of teaching. Agricola,
whose influence on the school at Deventer, though indirect, was considerable, visited the school in later life when he was the most renowned
scholar in Germany. He lectured for a short time at Heidelberg,
but steadily refused all offers to teach in a school, preferring a life of
greater leisure which allowed him to cultivate his mind and quietly to
influence his neighbours. He left one short essay on education, a long letter
written in 1484, usually entitled *De formando studio*. This consists of a
tirade against unnecessary verbal subtleties and a demand that "philosophy" (interpreted as the possession of a good Latin style, a knowledge
of the liberal arts, and the art of conduct) should be the aim of all
teaching. Conduct he considered to be the most important of all, proficiency in it to be obtained by a study of the great authors of antiquity,
particularly Aristotle, Cicero, and Seneca. Ancient writers, he insisted,
must be read with great care and attention, for in them almost all secular
wisdom was to be found.

It was Agricola's friend and pupil, Hegius, who put his ideas into practice, chiefly at Deventer, where he was headmaster probably from 1483 to
1498. Hegius divided the school (which was reported to number over 2,000
boys) into eight classes, exercised the greatest possible care in the choice
of masters, and made himself personally responsible for the methods of
teaching and the subjects taught, the latter including a little Greek for
the older boys. His success was considerable, and the great affection with
which he was regarded by his pupils is the best testimony to his fame.

One of these pupils, John Butzbach (c. 1478–1526), became in later
life prior of the Benedictine monastery of Laach and has left an auto-
biography which describes in some detail his early life before he made his
way to Deventer. Acting as the attendant of an older scholar who had
promised to teach him and take him to a university, but who never fulfilled his promise and instead treated him with the utmost cruelty,
Butzbach was forced to lead that life of wandering and begging which
was the lot of many aspirants after learning. After visiting several south

German cities, he made his way to heretical Bohemia, where he stayed for five years, returning to learn grammar at Deventer and finally becoming monk, novice-master, and prior at Laach. The hardships of his life as wandering scholar, however, he never forgot, and there is much evidence to suggest that his experiences were common to many similarly situated youths in the later Middle Ages.

The most distinguished of the boys at Deventer under Hegius was, of course, Erasmus. This famous scholar, the greatest product of the Northern Renaissance, came to Deventer in 1475 after learning some Latin at Gouda and at the cathedral song school of Utrecht. Under Hegius and Sintheim he received a thorough grounding in Latin, although in later life he wrote some hard words about his schooldays at Deventer. From Deventer he moved in 1484 to Hertogenbosch, where he remained until he entered the Augustinian monastery of Stein in 1487, so that during all the most impressionable years of his life he was under the influence of the Brethren.

At Deventer he did not go beyond the third class and therefore did not benefit by the better teaching of the upper part of the school, a fact that must be allowed to discount his later unfavourable reminiscences. When he was able to enter the College of Montaigu at Paris in 1495, he conceived while there an even stronger dislike for the teaching of what was still the greatest university in Christendom. The hardships of his early life ruined an always delicate physique, and, having learnt a little Greek and made the acquaintance of Gaguin, he came to England in 1499. There he obtained the friendship of Warham, Colet, and More, but he soon returned to Paris and Louvain. For the rest of his life he was constantly travelling—to Italy, where he found that there was little money available and that he could study almost as well elsewhere, to England, Flanders, and the Rhine valley, living most of the latter years of his life at Basle, where he died in 1536.

Erasmus thus had ample opportunities for knowing what was the condition of education in Europe at the end of the fifteenth century, while his eager interest in everything that concerned learning made him give some direct attention to educational theories. He was unsparing in his denunciations of the worst aspects of the teaching that his age had inherited—the cruelties, the ignorance of many professional schoolmasters, the futile sophistries and subtleties into which learning frequently degenerated, the obscurantism and prejudice of many of the higher clergy. Like other humanists, Erasmus was the champion and partisan of a cause; he would allow no virtues in the old learning, whose exponents he wholeheartedly abused. Even his own teachers were included in his condemnation, in which connexion, however, it must be remembered that the rapid expansion of printing (itself evidence of a wide demand for books) made transcription, for which the Brethren of the Common Life were renowned, no longer necessary and hastened the decay of the Order.

In his criticisms of schoolmasters and teaching methods, Erasmus relied more on abstract theory than on personal knowledge. Like some other great scholars, he had no wish to teach; occasionally, in his younger days, he acted as tutor to a young nobleman in order to earn money, but as soon as his reputation as a writer was sufficiently established, he ceased to take pupils or to lecture. His gentle nature and persistent ill-health made him unfitted for the strenuous life of the schoolroom, while he was wise enough to realise that his life-work was to write and to edit the books that were to shape the thought and expression of his century.

Two formal treatises on education, however, came from his pen, *De ratione studii* (1511) and *De pueris statim ac liberaliter instituendis* (1529), while there is much about the same subject in his *Christiani Matri- monii Institutio* (1526). From these, and from his letters and allusions else- where, we can obtain a fairly clear conception of the kind of education he considered to be best suited for his age. In the *De ratione studii*, he claims that the study of both Greek and Latin is essential, the best authors to be read as early as possible, for all necessary knowledge is to be found in them. Logic is to be learned from Aristotle alone, with no superfluous commentary, while methods of instruction can be obtained from Quintilian. Composition, style, and criticism are to be taught by the texts of the great classical writers, these being more important than the comments of even the best qualified of masters, although much depends upon the guidance and knowledge of the teacher.

The treatise *De pueris statim ac liberaliter instituendis*, addressed in 1529 to the Duke of Cleves, is more ambitious and definite. After explaining the duty of parents to instruct their children from the earliest years and the need to adapt the subjects, methods, and occasions of in- struction to the temperament and capacity of the child, he emphasises the vital importance of early training and the need for the exercise of the utmost care in the choice of a master. The character of the latter is of vital importance; if kind, attractive, sympathetic, and wise he can work wonders, whereas the popular opinion that any one is good enough to rule a grammar school is very wrong. Above all, and to this Erasmus returns again and again, the school to which a boy is to be sent must be public, not monastic or even semi-monastic like some of those of the Brethren of the Common Life. He then protests against violent corporal punishment, which was still very common, and discusses the subjects most suitable for the early stages in education, giving first place to elocu- tion and pointing out that not all boys can equally easily master grammar and rhetoric. These first stages must be smoothed over by pleasurable methods of instruction and by rousing the sense of emulation. After some more generalities about the need for patience in meeting difficulties and for avoiding unnecessary haste, the treatise ends with an eloquent appeal for the choice of the best possible teachers and for the care of the child's education from birth.

In all his writings on educational subjects, Erasmus shews a refreshing originality of outlook. He had, as was the custom of the age, studied Quintilian carefully and adopted a good deal of material from him without acknowledgment, but when he wishes to depart from Quintilian's opinions, he readily does so. Thus the memory of his own schooldays prevents him from recommending common school-life for boys as Quintilian does, and in his text-books he sometimes plainly dissents from Quintilian's judgments about rhetoric.

These text-books, particularly the *Adagia*, the *De copia rerum et verborum*, the *De conscribendis epistolis*, as well as his editions of texts and grammars, helped much more than his abstract speculations to improve the teaching in the schools. One of these latter, for instance, St Paul's School, London, was, when re-founded by his friend Colet, based almost entirely on Erasmus' ideas. Critical habits of thought, previously very rare, now became more common, while Erasmus helped considerably to emancipate the scholars of Europe from the bondage to Cicero into which they were in danger of falling, boldly advocating a Latin style that would be pure without Ciceronian affectation. His personal religious orthodoxy, combined with the freest outspokenness, added to his constant insistence that action and not contemplation must be the end and aim of all instruction, made his life an educational crusade. Even the cause of the higher education of woman was notably favoured by him, while his frequent reiteration of the great importance of the schoolmaster helped much to improve the status of the latter and even to foster an enduring national respect for scholars and teachers in Germany.

The career of Erasmus indicates clearly that the year 1500 forms no landmark in the history of education; arbitrary in any case, it is even more unsatisfactory for this than for other aspects of the human story. Thus, in England, for example, the ideals personified by Erasmus had hardly found admission before his death. The precursors of the Renaissance, Humphrey, Duke of Gloucester (1391–1447), Cardinal Beaufort (*c.* 1370–1447), Whethamstede (*ob.* 1465), Free (*c.* 1420–1465), Tiptoft, Earl of Worcester (*c.* 1427–1470), Flemming (*ob.* 1483), Selling (*c.* 1430–1494), Shirwood (*ob.* 1494), Gunthorpe (*ob.* 1498), had scarcely yet influenced the universities, still less the general educational methods of the country. It is not until the second decade of the sixteenth century that we can see some signs of educational reform. Bishop Fisher, who became Vice-Chancellor of the University of Cambridge in 1501 and Chancellor in 1504, was well disposed to humanist studies, although no great scholar himself; the Lady Margaret's foundations of Christ's (1505) and St John's (1511) were portents of a new spirit. Erasmus himself was Lady Margaret Professor of Divinity in 1511 and in residence at Queens' from 1511 to 1514, working at his *Novum Instrumentum* and teaching a little elementary Greek. At Oxford the struggles between the "Greeks" and the "Trojans" were decided in favour of the "Greeks" by royal intervention in 1519, while Colet had re-endowed and given new statutes to St Paul's School in 1512. The Dissolution of the Monasteries and the Protestant Reformation naturally threw the educational machine temporarily out of gear, but the damage was rapidly rectified, as the achievements of the reign of Elizabeth indicate, and before the end of the century the educational ideals of the humanists had been generally adopted.

The higher education of the fifteenth century, in so far as it was controlled by the Church, had been too clerical and obscurantist, tending to degenerate into increasingly useless formalism. The new nation-states, created by the energies of Ferdinand and Isabella, Louis XI, and Henry VII, needed an educated governing class emancipated from clerical control and secular in outlook and ideals. There were thus political reasons why the aims and methods of education should undergo marked changes after the end of the fifteenth century, and these changes were certain to be linked on to the new ideals which the humanists learned from ancient Rome. The new teaching, secular in spirit, practical and scientific in its methods, even if restrained in scope by reverence for the writings of antiquity, was certain to triumph in the new conditions of Europe, even in those countries in which the religious innovations were most decisively rejected.

The education of the fourteenth and fifteenth centuries, however, has been unfairly traduced by writers who have taken too literally the diatribes of enemies such as the compilers of the *Epistolae Obscurorum Virorum*. That there was much of real worth in the teaching of medieval schools and universities is now admitted by all; a great deal of honest hard work was done, and men learnt to think with wonderful rapidity and clarity. The pre-eminence of logic and oral disputation did at least lead to a high standard of deductive reasoning and acute argument. The right use of definitions was understood and followed, while the mental training involved in the ready application of fine distinctions and subtle differences was at once severe and salutary. If the medieval teacher was not allowed to question many of his premises, he was allowed considerable latitude in reasoning from them; religion was honoured, philosophy and theology were esteemed more highly than ever since.

Scholarship was international from its elements. French, German, and English children were taught the same grammar from the same textbooks; the universities had consciously similar courses leading to the conferment of the *ius ubique docendi*, opening their doors to each others' *alumni*. Medieval scholars had common ambitions, largely centring in Rome, a common language and common methods of teaching, all of which helped to emphasise the essential similarity of their work and simplified the transmission of knowledge. This implied a society that was mainly static and class divisions that were seldom altered. The poverty of medieval scholars can be exaggerated; educated men who sprang from the serf-class were few and the teaching profession was seldom recruited by really new blood. This the humanists did little to remedy, although men like Vittorino da Feltre were prepared to teach poor boys of ability, and Erasmus desired to see a literate peasantry.

A literate peasantry could not be expected to be made up of good Latinists, and the emancipation of education from scholasticism and from ecclesiastical control was followed by a growth in the use of the vernacular in every country such as the humanists never contemplated. When they succeeded in substituting classical Latin for the jargon of the schoolmen, so far from making Latin a better and more employed vehicle for the expression of thought, in reality they brought the vernacular into its own. When that typical humanist, Sir Thomas More, wished to expound his opinions on subjects that he believed mattered most in the world, he wrote in his native tongue instead of in Latin, as also did Luther in Germany. At the same time, while men were thus made freer to express their thoughts in the way that suited them best, the appreciation of the masterpieces of Greek and Roman literature was greatly enhanced. In 1500 Europe had much to learn about science, law, history, and philosophy from the ancient world; and it was the teaching and the preservation of texts during the Middle Ages that had made it possible for this knowledge to be assimilated rapidly as it became widely available, and therein lies part of the value of medieval education for the modern world.

To sum up: the fourteenth and fifteenth centuries cannot be claimed as a period of great general educational advance. The high hopes which the achievements of the best scholars of the two preceding centuries raised were not fulfilled, but knowledge was made much more accessible and many more boys were taught to read and speak Latin. Considerable intellectual progress is not apparent; indeed, in some respects, there are signs of retrogression. Ultimately, the triumph of humanist ideals was certain; yet, while it must be admitted that a good deal of the humanists' contempt for their predecessors was justified, it was the education that these had provided that made the rapid advance of the sixteenth century possible and the success of the Renaissance ideals so complete.

CHAPTER XXIV

PAINTING, SCULPTURE, AND THE ARTS

THE term Gothic, as now used in relation to Art, has neither historical nor etymological significance. It is merely a convenient label, sanctioned by long use, for a mighty outpouring of the creative impulse in man, which developed and took shape in Western Europe during the twelfth century, crystallised to achieve its greatest triumphs during the thirteenth, and languished into decay during the fourteenth and fifteenth centuries. Yet the label has the justification that only in countries swept by the Teutonic invasions, in which a Teutonic people built up a civilisation, did Gothic Art flourish; in Italy, where classical traditions persisted more strongly, it never found a permanent home. The influence of classical art upon Gothic is not indeed to be neglected. To some extent by direct contact, but mainly owing to filtration through Byzantine and Romanesque art, Greece and Rome gave a starting-point for the development of Gothic Art, and by their very decay had enriched the soil from which Gothic Art was to spring. But primarily it was the genius of the Northern peoples combined with influences from the East which gave birth to the first coherent and distinctive style in art which Western Europe had seen since the days of Rome[1].

This genius found its most complete and characteristic expression in architecture. It has been well said that the people of the Gothic age "had fallen in love with building"; and round their houses, their castles, their monasteries and convents, and above all their churches and cathedrals, centred their activity in the other arts. Not only did painting, sculpture, and the applied arts find their chief scope in the adornment of buildings, but articles of everyday use, psalters and books of hours, devotional and secular ivory carvings, jewellery, seals, furniture, even clothing, were in design or decoration mirrors of the architectural enthusiasm of the age. Consequently the character of Gothic architecture profoundly influenced activities in the other arts. With development of the pointed arch and the ribbed vault, the Gothic church and civic hall became virtually skeletons of stone, which unlike the basilicas of Italy gave small opportunity to the painter on walls, but unrivalled scope for the worker in stained and painted glass to fill the great spaces between the ribs of the structure. The castle of the great nobleman, and the house of the wealthy citizen, provided walls enough; but here lack of light discouraged the painter, and a cool climate made tapestry a more suitable method of decoration. So, apart from glass, Gothic painting found its best

---

[1] Theories and arguments concerning the share of Hellenistic and Eastern Art in the development of Christian Art, both in the East and West, are conveniently summarised in Dalton, *East Christian Art*, 1924.

opportunities in decorating the service books of the Church and books of private devotions. Sculpture in the same way conformed to limitations set by architecture. The great portals of a Gothic church, and its façade, provided a magnificent field for decoration with sculpture, both in the round and in relief. But there was little room for the development of a free-standing figure-sculpture such as flourished in Greece and Rome; and the sculpture of a Gothic church was organised not only to a decorative end, but with a very definite doctrinal purpose, which practically forbade treatment of the nude. It is only with the decline of Gothic, and a divorce between architecture and sculpture, that free-standing sculpture of the nude emerges again.

The chief centre of this remarkable burst of artistic activity was the North of France, and in particular the Île de France; whence by the end of the thirteenth century influence radiated throughout Europe. But this influence varied greatly in extent. In countries such as Italy, with a Mediterranean population and a classic cultural inheritance, it was comparatively slight; and even in countries where it was profound, local conditions combined with it to create a local style. The standardising influence of the Church may easily be exaggerated, also that of the travelling artist. The work at any great church or monastery was often executed by an atelier staffed largely by natives of the district or permanent residents there, and the lay patron utilised local talent side by side with foreign employees. The local styles thus created were largely independent of political boundaries, the main determinants being race, local tradition, and geographical situation.

The main characteristics of Gothic are in clear contrast to those of the Romanesque which preceded it. In Romanesque, majestic forms of mingled classical and Byzantine origin combined with abstract decoration inspired from the East and North to express a mystical, subjective view of religion. By the thirteenth century, Western Christianity was hardening into an intellectual and dogmatic system, as finally expounded in the *Summa Theologiae* of Thomas Aquinas; and the analogous and corresponding change in art is the realism of Gothic. Both in his treatment of the human figure and of decorative details, the Gothic artist found his chief inspiration in nature. Definitely Northern types appear, with prominent foreheads and wavy blonde hair; drapery ceases to be treated as an arbitrary arrangement of folds, and is made to hang naturally from its point of support, expressing the movement of the figure beneath. Methods of representing biblical scenes or incidents with moral or religious significance were fixed within narrow limits by doctrine and custom. But in details the artist never hesitated to use material drawn from daily life to enrich and diversify ordained and established themes. Similarly, the decoration which enriched a great Gothic building, or the initials and borders of a manuscript, found new life and energy in the naturalistic use of plants, animals, and human beings.

But this naturalism extended neither to scale nor to setting. Not until the early fifteenth century does the aim emerge of representing an event as it might actually have happened. This came about partly because the moral or doctrinal bearing of an event mattered more than historical accuracy, partly because the Gothic artist was primarily a decorator. In the late thirteenth and early fourteenth century, realism in scale and action were not suffered to disturb the structural harmony of a cathedral façade, nor to break up the decorative unity of the written page; and in its system of undulating curves, based upon the contour of forms and the swing of draperies, Gothic art revealed its inheritance not only from the geometric patterning of the North but from the arabesque of the East.

The two main characteristics of Gothic, realism in detail and decorative aim, became accentuated in its decline. During the fourteenth century, characterisation in figures becomes more marked, action more emphatic, realism more exaggerated. The inevitable loss of decorative unity the artist sought to overcome by developing decorative devices, such as pleating and folding draperies into arbitrary patterns, which became almost as much a formula as those of Byzantine art. At the same time, a romantic element perceptible in earlier work develops into search for picturesqueness, exaggeration for dramatic effect, and sentimentality.

In these characteristics Gothic art incorporates the ideas and ideals of its time. The intimate connexion of art with the revival of learning and the development of scholasticism in the twelfth and thirteenth centuries appears in the restraint and intellectual force which mark earlier work; while the growing spirit of romanticism and chivalry finds correspondence in the drama and sentiment of later phases. Changes in social organisation also find reflection. The view put forward by Victor Hugo, and enlarged upon by Viollet-le-Duc, that Gothic art embodies civic opposition to feudal and ecclesiastical authority, has no foundation in fact. But Gothic is primarily an art of the city, of a close-knit community with a sense of common interest and organised for common ends; of a society passionately interested in new ideas and vigorously critical of old forms and theories.

The individual artists through whose hands Gothic art took shape are for the most part unknown. The once popular idea of certain social reformers in the nineteenth century, that in some undefined way Gothic art was born of communal effort, has to yield before the growing evidence of strict professional organisation in the arts and of direction by individuals. But to connect the names of these with surviving work is rarely possible, and so the artistic personality of their owners remains obscure.

That in broad outlines and in many details the iconographical schemes of Gothic religious art were regulated by the Church, there can be no reasonable doubt. Their planning is too uniform, their subtlety and elaboration too great, their correspondence with writings of the time too close, to imagine them devised by artists. The principle laid down by the Second Council of Nicaea in 787 still held, that "The composition of religious imagery is not left to the initiative of artists, but is formed upon principles laid down by the Catholic Church and by religious traditions[1]." How control was exercised is uncertain. Cases are known of special instructions, detailing the arrangement and treatment of subjects; and possibly manuals were provided for general purposes. On the other hand, artists had their own traditions; and a few examples survive of medieval pattern books, which would ensure in particular workshops adherence to definite types and methods of presentation. But that the regulation stifled or hampered the artist, there is little evidence. The variation possible between localities, permitting the incorporation of local traditions and legends, was considerable; and in decorative detail the artist threw aside the borrowed and traditional motives which formed the staple of Romanesque decoration, and based his work upon direct study of natural forms. But the artist's freedom had a firmer foundation than this. The outward form of his work might be settled for him; but the animating spirit came from the artist alone, so that contemporary versions of the same subject, designed in the same way, may yet be quite distinct.

In sculpture, the first great manifestation of the Gothic style in France is the triple west portal of Chartres, which dates from between 1145 and 1170. Earliest are the nineteen great standing figures, representing the royal ancestors of the Virgin, which form a continuous band along the jambs of the doors. Byzantine and Romanesque influence appears in the hieratic rigidity of the figures, their frontal position, their symmetrical pose, and in the conventions of the drapery, elaborately arranged in parallel or radiating pleats, with sharply crumpled folds at the bottom. But these characteristics of an older style cannot conceal the life and individuality which mark the stirring of a new spirit. The Christ of the central tympanum, with his hand raised in blessing, adds to the statuesque majesty of Romanesque Art the naturalistic movement of Gothic, effectively expressed by the arrangement of his drapery.

Tendencies thus made manifest soon found more complete expression at Chartres itself. The almost contemporary development in the cult of the Virgin gave artists a wealth of new material; and since the cult was mainly fostered by the secular clergy in opposition to the monasteries, it favoured the supersession of the monastic atelier by the lay craft gild. It is therefore not surprising that representations of the Virgin and of incidents from her life should reflect very completely the growth of Gothic. The speed of that growth is witnessed by the central tympanum of the north portal at Chartres, dating from the first years of the thirteenth century, in which is represented the death and coronation of the Virgin.

[1] For an admirable exposition of the facts see E. Mâle, *L'Art religieux du xiii*^e *siècle en France*, 1923; though the author implies a consistency of practice which did not fully obtain outside Northern France. Cf. Coulton, *Art and the Reformation*, 1928.

The Virgin of Romanesque art, a remote, almost abstract figure, has gone; she has become a woman, though a woman crowned queen of heaven. Gone is the rigid frontality and symmetry of pose; the figure moves freely, with a slow dignified rhythm emphasised by the folds of the drapery. So it is with the lovely groups of the Annunciation and Visitation, on the jambs of the lateral doors. A columnar dignity still marks the figures; their features are still generalised and impassive; but the suggestion of adapted bas-relief, apparent in the Ancestors of the west portal, has disappeared, and the figures are conceived and executed in the round, while the dramatic significance of the scenes is fully expressed in the diffident joy of the younger woman, the calm confidence of St Anne, and the kindly majesty of the angel. This union of emotional expression and harmonious design is pushed still farther in the northern tympanum of the façade of Notre Dame at Paris, dating from the early thirteenth century, and in the south door of the west front of Amiens Cathedral, completed with the other two doors shortly after 1225. At Amiens the statues of the jambs differ notably from their predecessors at Chartres. They retain dignity and simplicity, with the columnar character which preserves their place in the structure of the building; but their treatment is more naturalistic, and characterisation is more emphasised. The Virgin of the different scenes is no mere repetition of the same type. Her timid joy in the Annunciation is replaced in the Visitation by sober consciousness of approaching maternity indicated by the change in her figure, and in the Presentation by the serenity of proud motherhood.

At Rheims, the influence of Chartres and Amiens is combined in the sculpture of the west portal, completed about the middle of the century. Here French Gothic sculpture attains a ripe maturity. The figures are less well related to the structure than in earlier work; already the artist has begun to think of his figures as separate creations, and not as part of a building. The Virgin of the Annunciation is sister to her of Amiens; but in the Angel is revealed a new strain in French art. Lifting his voluminous robe with a dainty gesture, he bends his elaborately coiffured head, to glance sideways at the Virgin with a half-ironic smile. He is among the latest of the great company of angels which surround Rheims; and in his vivacity, elegance, and self-possession embodies the spirit which was to destroy Gothic art, but was to give French eighteenth-century art its characteristic quality. The equally remarkable group of the Visitation in sentiment and treatment is singularly close to early Hellenistic work; and its sophistication has even provoked attribution to an eighteenth-century hand. It does not stand alone at Rheims; and with other figures raises a presumption of direct influence from antique art, which the numerous fragments of antique sculpture found in east and north-east France make reasonable, though the possibility of parallel growth cannot be excluded.

The development traced above is typical. To the Christ in Judgment of the Chartres west portal succeeds the figure on the central door of the Amiens west front, the famous "Beau Dieu," in which remoteness and austerity is replaced by human feeling and tenderness. Similarly, the Virgin of the central door at Rheims is a great lady, somewhat mincing and affected in pose, not greatly interested in the child she holds; while the famous "Vierge Dorée" of the south transept door at Amiens, executed about 1288, is a girl smiling coquettishly and extending her forefinger as much to attract the passer-by as to amuse her baby.

Sculpture in England and Germany followed a similar course to that in the Île de France, though local influences and traditions produced characteristic differences. In the earlier Gothic cathedrals of southern and eastern England and the great abbeys of the north, where Cistercian influence was especially powerful, sculpture was used sparingly, rather as emphasis on constructional lines and points than as decoration; and when, as in the nave of Lincoln and the choir of Ely, there is rich carving, it is rarely of the figure. In the west, however, an older tradition of more luxuriant decoration persisted, and flourished, notably at Wells. Even when sculpture later found more scope, little comparable to the portals of the French cathedrals was produced. The English aim was rather to treat the western front as a great screen with niches on which sculpture was displayed, though only at Wells, Lincoln, and Exeter was that aim realised with any completeness. Elsewhere, as at Peterborough, Salisbury, Lichfield, and York, great arcades, doorways, and windows were obstacles. There were, however, opportunities for the sculptor in other parts of the building. Heads carved to serve as string stops or as corbels were much used in England, though rarely on the Continent; and relief carvings in the spandrils of arches, such as the angels at Westminster and Lincoln, are distinctively English. The angels in the transept of Westminster, executed between 1250 and 1255, stand with one wing displayed, the other furled, swinging censers. Admirably designed to fill the space they occupy, with a flowing rhythm of forms in harmony with that of the architecture, they reveal a grace of personality and a lyrical charm rivalling those of the famous figures which give the Angel Choir at Lincoln its name, and putting them among the finest of medieval works of art. In the fourteenth and fifteenth centuries, the increasing use of panels and tracery on the larger surfaces of the buildings continued to limit the field for the figure sculptor, who found occupation in the alabaster retables of the fifteenth century, the angel carvings which mark the ends and bosses of roofs, and the elaborate wood carving of misericords and bench ends.

The stylistic development of English Gothic sculpture is similar to that of France, though the work at any given period in the two countries is often markedly different. In the treatment of the head, English sculptors of the thirteenth century attained mastery earlier than those of the Continent, while in ability to express the structure and movement of the human body they are inferior to their contemporaries in France. The thirteenth-century figures at Wells are less accomplished, more naïve, and less majestic than those of Amiens or Rheims; though they possess a tender and intimate quality, lyric rather than dramatic, which is peculiarly English. They escaped the direct French influence, which appears in the thirteenth-century sculpture of Westminster, was transmitted to Lincoln, and perhaps lies behind the statuesque, severe figures of the Lincoln Judgment Porch. In the earlier part of the fourteenth century, York became the centre of a Northern School, whose work has affinities to German sculpture at Bamberg and Naumburg; a London School, from which the sculpture of the Eleanor Crosses probably came, exemplifies growing French influence; in the west, the lower tiers of figures on the façade of Exeter Cathedral carry on the tradition of Wells. All exemplify the tendency of the age towards dramatic emphasis and decorative mannerisms. After the Black Death and the ruinously expensive wars of Edward III local characteristics became merged in a uniform and mannered style mainly derived from abroad, which culminates in the figures of Henry VII's Chapel at Westminster. These though executed about 1510, when the art of Renaissance Italy was flooding Europe, are still Gothic in feeling. But they are less sculptural than pictorial and descriptive; and the note of realistic genre which they strike is far removed from the gracious dignity of earlier work.

In Germany, as in England, the earlier sculpture falls into groups which embody different local traditions; but, more quickly and more generally than in England, these traditions were modified by French influence, mainly in proportion to the nearness of different areas to France. In the Carolingian period, the metal workers of North Germany had been famous, and such masterpieces as the baptismal font of Hildesheim witness the persistence of their technical skill into the Gothic period. In stone, however, it was not until the middle of the thirteenth century that anything so accomplished was made. The twelfth-century sculpture of the Rhine valley mainly repeated motives from the remains of Roman sculpture, and from manuscripts or ivories; and it was in Saxony and the adjacent regions extending up to the Harz Mountains that the new style definitely appears. Typical are the stucco bas-reliefs of the choir enclosure of St Michael's Church at Hildesheim, representing the Virgin and Child with the Apostles and dating from the end of the twelfth or the beginning of the thirteenth century. The figures preserve a Romanesque dignity, and Romanesque conventions in their drapery; but there is a vivacity and variety of movement which is Gothic. Intermediate between such work as this and fully developed German Gothic, is the sculpture of the Golden door at Freiburg and of the north porch at Magdeburg, both executed *c.* 1230 to 1240. In these the figures are more elegant, the drapery more flowing and responsive to movement. At Freiburg, mingled with motives apparently derived from Chartres and Rheims, are Germanic types of head; at Magdeburg, the exaggerated attitudes and facial expressions of the Wise and Foolish Virgins reveal the sentimentality which was later to be a dominant note in German art. In its maturity at Bamberg and Naumburg German Gothic was influenced from France, and especially from Rheims, primarily through the visits of German craftsmen to France. The six famous figures (*c.* 1250) on the embrasures of the south door at Bamberg are a case in point; though for the grace and dignity of the French work are substituted an almost *farouche* quality and a suppressed energy, which give them distinct character. At Naumburg, twelve standing figures of benefactors of the church have a massive dignity, unspoiled by extravagance of gesture or needless elaboration of drapery, though each figure has its independent and unstudied pose and is vigorously characterised. The powers which made Holbein great are here revealed in another medium. A Crucifixion with the Virgin and St John, which is on the screen separating nave from choir, foreshadows another great German painter. The heads of the St John and the Virgin are bent, their bodies are twisted, their features are contorted, their hands clutch their robes in an agony of grief. There is the same abandonment to dramatic emphasis which marks the work of Matthias Grünewald.

In the Rhine district, French influence becomes still more evident, notably at Strasbourg, where the earlier work is modelled on that of Chartres, though the later figures of the western façade are more Germanic in character. That towards the end of the thirteenth century French influence in the Rhine district was waning appears also from a Last Judgment in the portal of Freiburg-im-Breisgau, executed between 1273 and 1316. The short figures with large heads, for which the local peasantry were apparently the models, are extravagantly realistic; the treatment is dramatic or anecdotal by turns; breadth and unity of design are lost in vivacity and variety of detail and incident and in emphatic contrasts of light and shade. These characteristics mark contemporary German sculpture in other areas, and dominate it during the fourteenth and fifteenth centuries, as exemplified in the popular anecdotal carvings which decorate the Nuremberg churches.

The work of the Gothic sculptor was not, however, limited to the decoration of buildings. With the relaxation in the thirteenth century of the rule against the burial of lay persons in churches, tomb effigies in metal or stone became common throughout Northern Europe, especially in England. These were either laid flat or placed against the walls. The earlier examples consist of slabs engraved, sculptured, or decorated with mosaic; later, the tomb was treated as a sarcophagus or cenotaph, surmounted by a figure of the deceased. In thirteenth-century effigies, there is little, if any, attempt at portraiture, and the drapery is treated as though the figure were standing upright, the majority of the folds running parallel to the length of the body. In the fourteenth century, however, individual character appears in the heads, and the drapery falls more naturally over the body. Only in rare cases, indeed, can the effigies be assumed to be portraits. In England especially, they were more probably conventional types manufactured in large workshops and sent all over the country. Related in character to these tomb effigies are the rare equestrian monuments of the period. Here Germany was supreme, the so-called Conrad III (more probably St Stephen of Hungary) in Bamberg cathedral and Otto the Great in the market-place at Magdeburg being worthy forerunners of the great equestrian figures of the Italian Renaissance. Another sphere of activity for the sculptor was the production of carvings in ivory or bone. Great activity up to the twelfth century had been succeeded by a cessation of production in Western Europe, perhaps due to failure in the supply of the material. Late in the thirteenth century came a revival, followed by a prodigious output, with France as the main centre. In the earlier period the subjects were mainly religious. The cult of the Virgin caused statuettes of the Virgin and Child to become popular; in diptychs, scenes from the Passion were frequently represented. In the fourteenth century, with the spread of the Romantic movement, secular ivories appear, notably circular mirror cases, and boxes carved with scenes of love and chivalry or incidents from romances. For the most part the ivories are the work of craftsmen rather than independent artists, and draw their inspiration either from large scale sculpture or from illuminated manuscripts to whose stylistic development they conform, proceeding from simplicity, dignity, and restraint to complexity, elegance, and anecdotal exuberance. The ease with which they could be transported made them a powerful agency in spreading French influence over Western Europe, and in particular of enabling it to affect the development of Italian sculpture. In England, ivory was comparatively little used, and the characteristic English *petite sculpture* is the alabaster relief of the later fourteenth and fifteenth centuries. These are mainly workshop productions of small artistic value; but they were exported in considerable numbers, and played some part in establishing English influence in the lower Rhine valley, whose art in the late fourteenth century was to some extent founded on English example.

It should be clearly realised that Gothic sculpture was not only an art of form. There is ample evidence, from the sculpture itself and from literary sources, that colour and gilding were freely employed. Traces still survive in monumental sculpture of red, green, blue, and yellow draperies picked out or diapered with white, black, and gold, set against blue or red backgrounds; sepulchral effigies keep the remains of realistic colour; and a few ivory carvings survive with much of their original colour and gilding intact. Such material as this is an essential element in trying to reconstruct the appearance of a great Gothic building in the first flush of its beauty. Colour, indeed, was an essential and integral part of Gothic art. The work of the architect, no less than that of the sculptor, was completed by the painter. Mouldings were picked out; geometrical and floral patterns surrounded arches and filled their soffits; vaults might carry medallions, linked by flowing tracery; walls were diapered with a variety of designs in many colours. The Gothic painter, however, was more than an adjunct to sculptor and architect. In the painting of windows, in figure subjects on walls, in the illumination of manuscripts, and in panels for altarpieces, stalls, and screens, he had a field for independent work. The relative importance of each type of painting differed according to place and period. The main determinant was the extent to which the Gothic church became a stone skeleton which formed a setting for stained glass, so depriving the painter of wall space, creating a formidable competitor with his work on panel, and encouraging him to turn to manuscript illumination or to glass painting. Thus, the manuscript and stained glass play a far more important part in the painting of North Europe than in that of Italy, where small windows were the rule. But whatever the relative importance of the various types of painting in Northern Europe, their stylistic development was similar. This was partly because they sometimes came from the same workshop; partly because they were all, in the thirteenth and fourteenth centuries, subject to ideas and conceptions derived from architecture; and partly because of their influence on each other. The interdependence of the different types of painting appears from the use, in mural work, of emphatic outlines and masses of strong colour, which were necessary if it was not to be eclipsed by the bold design and vivid hues of medieval glass; and in manuscripts of the thirteenth century, in the arrangement of figures within medallions, as in windows, set against gold backgrounds. In reply, the illuminator of the thirteenth and fourteenth centuries sometimes supplied designs to the painter in glass, wall, and panel. Finally, in the fifteenth century, when the painter had shaken off the dominating influence of architecture, the panel painting comes into prominence, and is imitated in windows and in manuscript miniatures.

The development of painting on glass was largely dependent on technical considerations. Medieval windows were made of pot metal, *i.e.* glass coloured in the course of its manufacture. This was cut into appropriate shapes, in which the artist put in details and modelling with opaque enamel. The pieces were then bound together by grooved lead binding and fixed in position by the help of an iron armature. This method forbade the subtleties attained in the sixteenth century by the use of transparent enamel on clear glass, but was the source of the brilliancy and jewel-like quality of medieval work. The arrangement of the windows in a great medieval church, like that of the sculpture, generally conformed to a settled plan, at the east end being represented the Life and Passion of Christ, on the north the foreshadowing of the Word in the Old Testament, on the south its fulfilment in the Apostles and Saints. In very early glass, such as certain windows at Le Mans (*c.* 1090), the figures are large compared with the size of the window, and are definitely Byzantine in character. The typical thirteenth-century window, such as those in the choir at Chartres, consists of medallions of varying forms, each containing an incident or figure, the intervening spaces being filled with floral or geometrical designs. Windows containing single figures also occur, chiefly in clerestories where it was desired to admit as much light as possible. In the earlier thirteenth century, white glass was little used, the usual colours being crimson and blue, picked out by smaller pieces of green and yellow. The drawing of the small figures of the medallion windows is more naturalistic and vivacious than in earlier work, but is still controlled by the character of the material; and in the larger figures Byzantine reminiscences persist. Similarly in the ornament, the remote influence of classical antiquity appears in the floral forms used. Later in the thirteenth century, despite the development of the mullioned and traceried window, the use of medallions continued in France, though in England they were in places superseded by the "white windows," touched here and there with colour, such as the famous Five Sisters at York. By the end of the century definitely new types of window were appearing in both countries. The enlargement of bays encouraged the use of large areas of grisaille glass, plain or patterned. One form of these, popular in England, was the outcome of greater realism in the treatment of ornament. Plant forms were freely adapted and copied to make running patterns; and with double lines painted to emphasize the leading, the appearance was given of plants growing on a trellis, whence the windows have been called trellis windows. More usually, into the grisaille background was inserted a coloured medallion or figure, and these in windows with several lights formed a belt of colour across the window, giving rise to the name belt windows. In another type, the light was filled by a figure beneath a canopy, and as the lights of windows became longer, the canopies became higher and more elaborate. A variant which first appeared on the Continent was the triptych window, in which the chief subject occupied the three middle lights under one canopy, and was flanked by smaller designs; a development which was succeeded in the fifteenth century by the extension of the canopy over several subjects, or by a single subject occupying the whole window without a canopy. In the fourteenth and fifteenth centuries, also, technical discoveries increased the translucency of the glass, though diminishing its brilliance of colour. Meanwhile, the treatment of figures and incidents became more realistic. Features and drapery are more fully modelled, poise and movement more studied. The glass painter was approaching the outlook and technique of the panel painter, and only awaited the invention of transparent enamel painting to seek to rival him.

The development of mural and panel painting in Northern Europe is so closely connected with that of manuscript illumination that the two are best considered together. In painting, unlike sculpture, England disputed with France for leadership in achievement and influence; and at times the productions of the two countries are so closely related as to justify their being regarded as an English Channel school. In English ecclesiastical buildings of the thirteenth century, the competition of stained glass was less severe than in France, and the wall space available for the painter greater. The development of mural painting was further assisted by a well-established tradition in the illumination of manuscripts. After the Norman conquest the Saxon style was replaced by one more heavy and splendid, with richer colour and more emphatic outlines, which peculiarly lent itself to adaptation by mural painters. Such master-pieces as the Great Bible executed in the twelfth century at Winchester evidently provided inspiration to the painter of the Descent from the Cross and other scenes from the Passion on the walls of the Chapel of the Holy Sepulchre in Winchester Cathedral, executed about 1230. It was, however, in the Eastern Counties and in London that English Gothic painting was chiefly to flourish. In the early thirteenth century, a new wave of later Byzantine influence reached Western Europe, probably as a result of the Fourth Crusade, and stimulated a tendency to replace agitated movement and grotesque conventions by simpler and more naturalistic treatment. This found expression in the work executed at the greatest artistic centre of the time in Western Europe, St Albans. Here was active Matthew Paris, from whose hand perhaps came the admirable drawings in outline occasionally tinted with colour which illustrate his *Chronica Maiora* (in Corpus Christi College, Cambridge) and his *Historia Anglorum* (1250–59) and *Collections* in the British Museum. The last contains a drawing of the Virgin and Child, in which a dignity inherited from the Romanesque is tempered by human feeling and grace of draughtsmanship; making it a worthy forerunner of the lovely Virgin and Child on the wall of the Bishops' Chapel at Chichester, where almost for the first time in Northern art the Mother of God becomes also the Mother of Man. The sensitive and expressive use of outline in these paintings is characteristic of English work, and appears also in con-temporary manuscripts such as those of William de Brailes, one of the few illuminators of the day whose name is known. During this period, the first half of the thirteenth century, English influence abroad was considerable. Peculiarly English are a group of bestiaries, which gave a stimulus to the study of nature in detail, and so hastened the transition from Romanesque to Gothic. Another group of manuscripts illustrating the Apocalypse served as patterns throughout Europe for treatment of the subject; and in Scandinavia, a school of painting on panel arose, which was virtually an outlying part of the schools of Peterborough and St Albans.

In France, meanwhile, painting had taken a somewhat different course. Mural decoration, common in the eleventh and twelfth centuries, during the thirteenth century still appears in districts such as the South-West and South where the use of arch and vault did not attain full development, but usually retained Romanesque-Byzantine character. In the Île de France, it was limited to the emphasis and enrichment of architectural features or to the introduction of small figure-subjects into the spandrils of arches or on the surface of vaults, as in the Sainte-Chapelle and at Petit-Quévilly, where roundels enclosing scenes from the early life of Christ imitate stained glass. Panel painting was little practised; and consequently even more than in England the earlier history of French medieval painting chiefly centres round the illuminated manuscript. Basing themselves at first on imitation of the stained glass window for the design of their page, and on English example for the treatment of the figure, the French illuminators in the course of the thirteenth century developed an originality and skill which produced those exquisite works of art which inspired Dante to speak of "l'onor di quell' arte Ch' alluminar è chiamata in Parigi." Among the causes of this advance were the expansion of the University of Paris, which greatly increased the demand for the services of writers and illuminators and encouraged the rise of the workshop staffed by professional lay artists, and the patronage of painters by members of the royal house, especially by St Louis himself. For him and for his sister Isabelle were produced, among other manuscripts, two psalters, one in the Bibliothèque Nationale, the other in the Fitzwilliam Museum at Cambridge. In these, the influence of architecture has replaced that of the stained glass window in the design of the page. Gothic porticos, whose delicate tracery and mouldings recall those of the Sainte-Chapelle, enclose the figures. Backgrounds of plain gold are replaced by geometric patterns or arabesques; the colours are more delicate and varied than in earlier work; the drawing is more supple and expressive, the figures more elegant, and the realism in detail greater. Thus were laid the foundations of a style, ultimately to extend its influence throughout Europe, and to lie at the root of an international Gothic style which attained full development at the end of the fourteenth century, and whose essential elements were search for decorative effect combined with vivid narration and realism in detail.

In its earlier phase, this style exercised considerable influence in England, where the decline of Winchester and St Albans saw the rise of Westminster as the chief centre of the arts, under the inspiration and control of Henry III. The palace there, with its decorations, has disappeared, but the Abbey still stands as a living monument to the art of his age. To Henry's court came craftsmen from all over Europe. The king's relations with St Louis were especially close; and so nearly do the styles of Westminster and Paris come together at certain points that the provenance is still doubtful of the famous retable in Westminster Abbey, one of the chief monuments of the age. Recent researches tilt the balance in favour of French origin and make the retable a starting-point of French influence in England. The chief work of Henry's reign which was undoubtedly of English origin was the decoration of the Painted Chamber in the Palace, first carried out by "The King's beloved Master William, monk of Westminster," as the Close Rolls of 1256 describe him. A fire in 1262 damaged his work, and there is no record of his being employed in the repainting. But probably his designs were retained, and are those known to us by copies made in the early nineteenth century before the Palace was burnt in 1834. From these it appears that they were painted with six tiers of warlike episodes from the Old Testament and the Apocrypha, above a dado painted to represent a green curtain, and separated by white bands with black inscriptions. Over the fireplace appeared the Labours of the Months, in the jambs of the windows the Virtues and Vices, and dominating the whole was a great painting of the Coronation of Edward the Confessor. During the reign of Henry also were made at Chertsey Abbey the tiles which pave the floor of the Chapter House at Westminster. Their decoration with hunting scenes and incidents from romantic stories, such as that of Tristram and Iseult, marks the rise of the secular subject, parallel with the displacement of the monastic studio by the secular craftsman of the gilds. Surviving paintings in the Abbey belong to the end of the century. Among these are the figure of St Faith in the Revestry, the figures of two kings on the choir stalls, and an Annunciation on the back of the stalls, all marked by a freedom and swing in draughtsmanship closely akin to contemporary French work. The last great enterprise of the Westminster School was the decoration of St Stephen's Chapel, built by Edward III, begun by Hugh of St Albans and finished by William of Walsingham. The Chapel was burnt in 1834, but copies made by Smirke and some fragments in the British Museum indicate the character of the paintings. They include representations of Edward III and Philippa, with their sons and daughters; with incidents from the Old and New Testaments, in which the descriptive and narrative elements triumphed over the monumental and decorative.

By the side of the Westminster painters, and in some measure influenced by them, flourished a great school of manuscript illumination. The delicate and graceful precision of the drawing in the late thirteenth-century Tenison psalter in the British Museum, and in the Windmill psalter of the Pierpont Morgan collection, is in the full English tradition, whence derives also the early fourteenth-century Queen Mary's psalter in the British Museum, the masterpiece of a well-defined group. In this, below the tinted miniature is a series of marginal illustrations: a running commentary on the life and thought of the time, serious, satiric, fantastic, and humorous by turns, which reached its fullest development in England, and is a forerunner of English caricature of the eighteenth and nineteenth centuries. By itself stands the psalter of Robert de Lisle in the British Museum, whose magnificently dignified miniatures suggest connexion with the School of Westminster and the inspiration, if not the hand, of a mural painter. That the Eastern Counties had become, by the early fourteenth century, a great artistic centre is witnessed not only by a notable group of wall paintings in Northamptonshire, but by a magnificent series of psalters, among the finest being the Gorleston psalter of the Dyson Perrins collection, marked by bold and expressive figure drawing and by extraordinarily rich decoration, especially in the borders of foliage crowded with grotesques, heraldic shields, and portrait heads. The margins of the Louterell psalter in the British Museum, latest of the group, are an invaluable source of knowledge concerning contemporary manners; but technical dexterity has corrupted taste and imagination.

This outburst of activity saw not only complete assimilation of French influence, but reassertion of English influence abroad. The political connexions of Edward III favoured the export of English manuscripts, embroidery, and carvings to the Rhineland, where fourteenth-century art took on a markedly English cast; while in Paris in the early fourteenth century a number of English illuminators were active, whose influence was sufficiently strong almost to bring English and French illumination together into a single school. Such fine manuscripts from the School of Paris as the Breviary of Philip the Fair, written before 1297, and tentatively associated with the name of Honoré, a leading painter of the period; a religious treatise known as the *Saint Abbaye*, in the British Museum, written and decorated about 1300; and a Life and Miracles of St Denis, in the Arsenal Library, written about 1317, with genre scenes from daily life in Paris freely introduced, all reveal English influence in the elaboration of ornament, the use at times of figures and grotesques in the borders, the attitudes and gestures of the figures, and the treatment of drapery. This influence also appears, though less obviously, in a group of manuscripts from Lorraine, among them the splendid Metz Pontifical in the Fitzwilliam Museum at Cambridge. Shortly, however, the two schools fell apart. In England, the wars of Edward III drained the country of men and money, and, with the Black Death, dried up the springs of creative activity and patronage. Painting thenceforward became a provincial and derivative art, and France became the main centre of activity in Northern Europe.

To France, on top of English influence, had come direct influence from Italy, partly through Italians such as Filippo Rusuti employed by Philip the Fair, mainly through Italian artists working at Avignon. From 1339 until his death in 1344 Simone Martini, one of the greatest painters of the Sienese School, was settled there; under Clement VI, Matteo da Viterbo, a painter influenced from and perhaps trained at Siena, decorated various chapels in the Papal Palace, assisted by other Italians, Frenchmen, and a German; and the chapel of the monastery at Villeneuve-lès-Avignon, founded by Innocent VI in 1356, was decorated by painters of the same circle. This Sienese influence found congenial soil on which to work, since Sienese painting itself owed much to French Gothic of an earlier period, and so brought to France methods and ideas which were readily acceptable.

Despite restriction of opportunity, the mural painter in France continued to be active, chiefly in the feudal castle, where wall space still remained for the painted decoration which preceded the tapestries of a later and more luxurious age. Generally, figure subjects occupied the upper part of the wall, a painted representation of a curtain the lower, as in the Painted Chamber at Westminster. Surviving examples are crude, but effective, combinations of bold outline and simple vivid colour, and usually represent some scene of chivalry or romance. In Provence, Languedoc, and the Auvergne, the architectural style permitted also the decoration of churches, and here Sienese influence at once made itself felt in the compositions, the types, and the colour. Of greater importance is Sienese influence on the School of Paris. Head of a large studio there was Jean Pucelle, the first French painter to emerge with a recognisable artistic personality. The first mention of him is in 1319; in 1327, assisted by other artists, he decorated a Latin bible, copied by Robert de Billyng (Bibliothèque Nationale Lat. 11935); and a marginal note in the Belleville Breviary in the Bibliothèque Nationale (Lat. 10483–4) records that he directed the work on that manuscript. About 1350 his activity appears to have ended. In the work associated with him, compared with that of the previous generation, the figures are more slender and elegant, the ornament more intricate and varied, with the aim of enriching the decorative effect of the page. At the same time an increased desire for realism appears in the attempt to use light and shade both to give solidity to objects and to create a feeling of space. The results are as a rule unconvincing, but they are an early sign in Northern Gothic art of a breach with decorative conventions, which was to produce remarkable results in fifteenth-century Flemish painting. Apart from the character of these changes, the work of the Pucelle school contains definite evidence of contact with Italy. The architectural backgrounds of their miniatures have Italian features, and in the rare landscape backgrounds rocks and hills occasionally are introduced which are evidently imitated from Italian painters.

The arts in France owed much to encouragement from the House of Valois, which reached its culmination in the lavish patronage bestowed by Charles V and by his brothers Louis of Anjou, Philip of Burgundy, and John of Berry. Artists were attracted to their courts from many parts of Europe. With the traditions of French illumination mingled to an increasing extent ideas and methods derived from Flanders, Italy, and Germany, until among the welter of influences a new style was born, which in its developed form was to change the face of painting in Northern Europe and exercise a powerful influence in Italy. But despite the immense activity of the period, only a few panel paintings, a score or so of illuminated manuscripts, and a few pieces of sculpture and tapestry survive. From these, the transitional character of the age appears. A conspicuous example of older ideas and methods is the "Parement de Narbonne," painted between 1374 and 1378, discovered in Narbonne in the early nineteenth century and now in the Louvre. In the treatment of the Crucifixion and the scenes from the Passion which form its main themes it descends direct from the School of Pucelle; but in the realistic treatment of the heads of Charles V and his queen is a hint of future change. Compared with the Parement Master, Jean de Bandol, sometimes called Jean de Bruges, is an innovator. In 1371 he painted a frontispiece to a bible now in the Meerman-Westreenen Museum at the Hague, in which Charles V is represented receiving from the hands of one Jean de Vaudetar the book for which the miniature was made. Despite the small scale, the portraits are almost brutally realistic, and the bold simplified modelling of the figures and drapery contrasts oddly with the conventional patterning of the floor and of the flat background.

To a later generation belong André Beauneveu and Jacquemart de Hesdin, both probably natives of the Franco-Flemish border, who found their chief employment under the Duke of Berry. Beauneveu first appears as a sculptor, and in 1365 was employed in making effigies for the tombs in St Denis, of some but not outstanding merit. Of greater interest is the one piece of painting which can be attributed to him with reasonable certainty, twenty-four pages of a Latin and French Psalter now in the Bibliothèque Nationale (Lat. 13091), on which are represented twelve prophets and twelve apostles. The little pictures reveal all the miniaturist conventions of the time, but that they are executed by a sculptor accustomed to work on a larger scale is suggested by the solidity of the figures and the attempt at monumental quality. In contrast, also, to the work of illuminators, is the realistic treatment of the heads, and especially the vivacity of the eyes. By Jacquemart de Hesdin and his assistants are the miniatures in the *Grandes Heures* of the Duke of Berry, in the Bibliothèque Nationale (Lat. 919), more directly in descent from the School of Pucelle than the work of Beauneveu, but with some breaking away from convention in the characterisation of the heads and in the realism of the settings.

More decisive evidence that the leaven of new ideas was working appears in a group of panel paintings made for Philip of Burgundy. An example is the wings of an altarpiece painted in 1392 for the abbey of Champmol by Melchior Broederlam of Ypres, which is now in the Dijon Museum. The slender figures and flowing draperies are in the old tradition; but there is novelty in the treatment of the scenes as historical events and their placing in realistic surroundings of an Italian type, in which there is a definite attempt at study from nature. Changing aims found more definite expression in the famous *Très Riches Heures*, now at Chantilly, the last manuscript ordered by the Duke of Berry, and left unfinished at his death in 1416. The painters employed by the duke were one Pol

de Limbourg and his brothers, who were responsible for more than half
the miniatures. Of these, some are purely in the French tradition. A
magnificent example is a Coronation of the Virgin, in which the slender,
graceful figures of Christ and the Virgin with their attendant saints and
angels are woven into a sweeping linear design, formed in the shape of an
S and made the basis of a lovely pattern in colour, wherein massed blue
and gold contrast with yellow, lilac, and scarlet. In contrast is a group of
miniatures in which the main inspiration is Italian, one of them actually
copying the design of the Presentation of the Virgin by Taddeo Gaddi
in Santa Croce at Florence. In these, the solidity of the figures, feeling
for space, and realism in setting are greater than in purely French work.
But the fame of the book chiefly rests on a series of miniatures with
landscape backgrounds, representing views of Paris, of Bourges, and of
various castles belonging to the Duke of Berry. The majority of these,
and the finest, decorate the Calendar, preceding the Hours proper. Most
remarkable of all is the December picture of a boar hunt. In the foreground dogs attack the fallen boar, against a background formed by the
forest of Vincennes with the castle rising behind it. The drawing of the
dogs, as they strain and tear at their quarry, is singularly accurate and
expressive of action; and the tracery of bare boughs in the forest, faintly
seen through the lingering autumn-tinted foliage, is painted with exquisite delicacy. In this series of views, naturalistic landscape makes virtually
its first appearance in European art. Yet for all the keenness in observation and the accuracy of record, the naturalism is in detail only and the
parts do not build up into a visual whole. Nevertheless, the *Très Riches
Heures* exercised considerable influence; and the compromise between
realism and decoration there established was especially useful to Flemish
miniature painters at the end of the fifteenth and the beginning of the
sixteenth centuries. For example, the makers of the great Grimani
Breviary, now in the library of St Mark's at Venice, paid the *Très Riches
Heures* the tribute of practically reproducing many of its miniatures.

Painting east of the Rhine had meanwhile taken a similar course to
that in France and England. But the transition from Romanesque to
Gothic came considerably later than in those countries and was primarily
due to direct influence from foreign sources. Change at the end of the
twelfth century took the form of renewed imitation of Byzantine models,
stimulated by the close connexion of the Empire with Italy. This
Byzantine revival was most marked and persistent in Saxony; and in
West and South Germany about the middle of the century it began to
yield to the influence of French Gothic. The effects of this, however,
were delayed by the fact that in thirteenth-century Germany the illumination of service books and books of hours, for which French models were
plentiful, was rare compared with the illustration of chronicles, law books,
novels, and poems, of which French examples were less usual. Thus, by
the end of the thirteenth century, painting in Germany was represented

by two types of manuscript. In religious works, French influence was paramount; in secular works, a native instinct to illustrate rather than decorate found freer expression, and a native love of exaggerated realism found full scope.

Full development of the Gothic style was attained in the later fourteenth century, the main centres being Bohemia and the lower Rhine Valley. In Bohemia artistic activity owed much to the patronage of the royal house, which reached its height during the reigns of the Emperor Charles IV and his successor Wenceslas. The transition in the earlier part of the fourteenth century, from a style based on Byzantine example to one derived from imitation of French and Italian work, is revealed in a small group of panel paintings, conspicuous among which is a *Coronation of the Virgin* at Klosterneuburg near Vienna, painted between 1322 and 1329. In its linear emphasis and neglect of considerations of scale, the painting gives the impression of an enlarged miniature; and these characteristics, with the facial types and drapery treatment, relate it to the work of the early fourteenth-century school of Paris. The main lines of the composition, however, and the architectural detail come from Italy, possibly directly, perhaps through Paris or Avignon. Under Charles IV, political circumstances increased the strength of foreign influences. Owing to his Luxemburg possessions, Charles spent a large part of his time in the Rhineland, and was in touch with the French Court and with England; while his relations with the Papacy at Avignon and with Italy were frequent. Thus, the school which centred in Prague was increasingly assimilated to those of Northern France, England, and the Rhine Valley, and came to form an outpost of the international Gothic style. In work of the early years of Charles' reign, Northern and Italian borrowings play an equal part; later, Italian influence declined compared with that of Northern France. An outstanding example is a group of panels of scenes from the Passion in the Rudolfinum at Prague, painted late in the fourteenth century by the Meister von Wittingau. In these, insistence on contour has been replaced by more sculpturesque treatment, and flat patterning by an effort to express space. The slim figures, with their long, slender hands and feet, have taken on an exaggerated elegance which verges on the fantastic, and there is a movement towards realism and dramatic expression similar to that seen in the painters of the Franco-Flemish school. Complete assimilation of the French style, in a formalised and exaggerated form which gives it local character, came during the reign of Wenceslas, and is exemplified in two bibles, one produced for Wenceslas himself and now in the Vienna Library, the other for Conrad de Weckta in the Plantin Museum at Antwerp. The first of these, in richness of ornament and variety of illustration, is almost unsurpassed in European art. Into borders of luxuriant and elaborately intertwined foliage are introduced animals, figures, grotesques, and coats of arms, bewildering in their variety. Each initial letter encloses one or more miniatures, the first letter of Genesis containing over thirty, in which, and in the full-page illustrations, there is a lively mixture of realism, fantasy, and drama. The bible is the work of several hands, of unequal merit; but everywhere there is a straining after effect, an elegance become almost ludicrous, and a sentiment both melodramatic and affected, marks of an art almost entirely derivative and academic.

In the lower Rhine valley, by the beginning of the fourteenth century, French influence had almost entirely replaced that of Byzantium. This is evident not only from manuscripts but from mural paintings, such as those in St Cecilia at Cologne. Within a few years, however, the strengthening of political and economic connexions with England brought with it the influence of English art, exercised through manuscripts and embroideries at first, and later through monumental brasses and alabaster carvings. This appears in two groups of work, one including the wall paintings in St Andreas at Cologne, and panels in the Cologne and Berlin Galleries; the other, later in date, consisting of the series of paintings over the stalls in Cologne Cathedral, finished after 1322. Both groups were evidently based on paintings in manuscripts. This is particularly clear in the wall paintings, where the division into tiers and compartments, and the use of decorated bands or architectural canopies to separate them, reproduces the practice of illuminators, and parallels the practice of workers in stained glass. Closer examination makes it highly probable that the source of the borrowings was English work. The compositions, the types, the proportions of the figures, the drapery treatment, even the decorative detail, are closely related to those of such English work as the Robert de Lisle Psalter, the Gorleston Psalter, and Queen Mary's Psalter. Similar dependence on English example appears in the case of manuscripts, a notable example being the illustrations to the epic poem *Willehalm* by Wolfram von Eschenbach, written in 1334 for Landgrave Henry of Hesse.

In the second half of the fourteenth century, this English phase of Cologne painting was succeeded by one of assimilation towards the international Gothic style of the late fourteenth century, with retention of a very distinct local character. During the fourteenth century in the Rhine valley, Eckehart, Tauler, and others were preaching the renunciation of the world and the attainment of salvation for the individual soul by direct communion with Christ, through meditation upon His Life and Passion. The necessary spiritual state might be encouraged by the contemplation of works of art; and so the artist was definitely encouraged to develop the mystical aspect of his work. Thus was bred the lyrical and idyllic quality in Cologne art which marks its crowning achievement in the fourteenth century, the altarpiece of St Clara, which came from the convent dedicated to that saint, and is now in Cologne Cathedral. A central tabernacle to hold the Host is decorated with sculpture, and has double wings painted with scenes from the early life of Christ and from the Passion. It used to be customary to ascribe these paintings to the half-legendary Master Wilhelm of Cologne; but they are certainly by two hands of different date, neither of which can be identified, the earlier one reflecting the influence of English art, the other of Franco-Flemish work.

In Northern Germany there is no steady and continuous development traceable in the art of painting during the fourteenth century. But in the later years of the century, there was an outburst of sporadic activity, which produced a considerable mass of work allied in type to that of contemporary Franco-Flemish, Cologne, and Bohemian painters. At Hamburg, the work of Meister Bertram, exemplified by a panel in the Victoria and Albert Museum, is characteristically German in its vivacious narration and coarse realism. At Soest, the leading figure in a considerable school was Meister Conrad, whose altarpiece of 1404 at Niederwildungen in Waldeck has similar vivacity and realism tempered by Italian influence in composition and settings.

In England paralysis at the main centres had checked any development comparable to that in France and Germany. A renaissance came towards the end of the century, but it centred mainly round the court of Richard II and was primarily of foreign inspiration. The marriage of the king with Anne of Bohemia strengthened the connexion between England and the territories of the Emperor, including the Rhine valley and Prague, whence craftsmen appear to have come to England; and his marriage with Isabelle, daughter of Charles V, put him in close touch with the court of France. There is also some evidence of contact with Italy, through Avignon. As a result, the principal paintings of the period which survive are so complete an embodiment of the continental style that in some cases their English origin is gravely open to question. The remarkable full-length portrait of Richard in Westminster Abbey has been reasonably, if not convincingly, attributed to André Beauneveu, and the famous diptych from Wilton House, now in the National Gallery at London, has been at different times ascribed to an English, Bohemian, Italian, and French artist, though recent research favours a French origin. Similar difficulties arise in the case of illuminated manuscripts. A fine example is the Sherborne Missal in the collection of the Duke of Northumberland, executed about 1400 by a number of painters of whom the chief was a Dominican friar, John Siferwas. Whether Siferwas was an Englishman is uncertain. But the Missal was executed for Sherborne Abbey, and was probably written and decorated there; and despite the continental origin of its style it may be fairly described as an English variant of an international Gothic style.

In the preceding pages, the rise, the full development, and the decadence of Gothic art in Northern Europe have been traced. Within limits set by decorative and expository purposes, narration and dramatic expression had been substituted to an increasing degree for the symbolic exposition of doctrine in Romanesque art; and the study and reproduction of natural appearance had replaced the conventions of an earlier period. The realism of Gothic art, however, even in its earlier and more intense form, was realism in detail. In the assembly of those details the facts of vision were to a large extent ignored, the governing consideration being decorative effect; and during the fourteenth century the detail itself of Gothic art became largely a matter of skilfully applied recipes. But by the side of this reiteration of formulas, a new spirit had manifested itself. The artists' activity became one aspect of an awakening curiosity as to the nature of man and the universe, which was the central element of Renaissance thought. The decorative and expository aims of art continued, but were mingled with a renewed interest in external reality and its reproduction not only in detail but as a whole.

Political and economic circumstances facilitated this change of attitude. The Church as the principal patron of the arts was being replaced by great princes and noblemen, by wealthy merchants, and by civic bodies with very varying demands and standards; while the monastic craftsman had been superseded by the lay artist organised in gilds. So the way was opened for the various arts to develop an independent existence, and for the personality of the artist to become more fully recognised. Also, with the decay of feudalism and the appearance of centralised monarchy, nationalism in art makes its appearance. Gothic art largely ignored political boundaries; but once the personal alliances of princes which had helped to give the art of the late fourteenth century its international character were broken, the process of differentiation was rapid.

The first artist to give tolerably complete expression to the new ideals was the sculptor Claus Sluter, who appears in 1385 in the service of Philip of Burgundy. One of his first pieces of work was to assist Jean de Menneville with the sculpture on the portal of the abbey of Champmol; and in the part known to be by Sluter the breach with late Gothic work is complete. The figures are broad and bulky, standing free from the surrounding architecture with little relation to its design. They wear voluminous draperies cut into deep folds, well designed to express the movement beneath; and in the heads the characterisation is fearless. The motif of the famous *pleurants* on Philip's tomb, now in the Dijon Museum, is not new, but the treatment is entirely original; and the figures swathed in great cloaks, each with its individual and expressive gesture varying from the tragic to the almost comic, is a remarkable achievement. But the work that absorbed Sluter's main energies was the group of statuary completed in 1403 to cover the well in the courtyard of the abbey of Champmol, with the crucified Christ above and round the base massive figures of Moses, David, and four prophets. Sluter's Christ (of which the head alone survives) is neither the King of Heaven of the thirteenth century nor the agonised sufferer of the fourteenth, but a man who has met death bravely and in death has found peace. The prophets are not creatures of celestial inspiration, but great men of this world, each one proclaiming his individuality in feature and gesture. In his combination of intense realism with monumental dignity, Sluter is nearer to Michelangelo in certain of his phases than to the great Flemings of whom he was a precursor. His influence on the rise of the Flemish School is still obscure, but his art sums up all the forces which were to bring that school into being.

Some years after the completion of the Puits de Moïse another work appeared which marks even more decisively the rise of a new art. A great Book of Hours, begun for the Duke of Berry, was partially completed between 1415 and 1417 for his nephew William of Bavaria. Of the additions, six complete pages and five large miniatures formed an outstanding group, of which now only two pages and three miniatures survive in the Trivulzio collection at Milan, the others having been destroyed in a fire at the Turin Library. That this group is the work of either Hubert or Jan van Eyck or of both of them is not now contested, only the distribution between the two being in dispute. The question of authorship, however, is less important than the character of the paintings. In them, the conception of a picture as a window opened upon the real world first takes shape. A piece of space is represented, in which figures and objects are placed in scale with each other, surrounded by light and atmosphere, to which the local colour is subdued. To this change in outlook is added one of technique. Linear pattern is abandoned for construction in terms of tone, and for the expression of form by means of light and shade. In a large miniature of the Birth of St John the Baptist there is as complete a mastery of illusion as was ever attained by Vermeer or Pieter de Hooch. In landscape the artist reveals the same power. Below the miniature of the Birth of St John is represented the Baptism of Christ. Behind the tiny figures in the foreground a river with wooded banks winds into the far distance. Over all falls an evening light, breaking the smooth water with delicate reflections. Every detail is subtly observed, skilfully recorded; but all are subordinated to expressing the solemn calm of late afternoon with its presage of night-fall.

With the emergence of the van Eycks, the artistic centre of gravity in Northern Europe passes definitely to Flanders. There a great commercial aristocracy had developed, whose patronage, added to that of the great nobles, gave the arts in Flanders a firm economic foundation; while no deep-rooted and powerful artistic tradition existed to dictate to artist and patron. When a distinctive Flemish art appears, it is born full grown in the work of the van Eycks, whose origins lay in Franco-Flemish and Burgundian art, and not in Flanders itself.

Study of the van Eycks must take as starting-point the altarpiece of the *Adoration of the Lamb* in the Cathedral of St Bavon at Ghent, which, according to a partly effaced inscription on the outside of the wings, was begun by Hubert and finished by Jan to the order of Jodoc Vyt in 1432. It is the only surviving painting with which Hubert is certainly known to have been concerned, and it contains the earliest recorded work by Jan. Here in one stupendous whole is summed up the main artistic achievement of fifteenth-century Flanders. In aim and method the *Adoration of the Lamb* foreshadows or forestalls almost everything in Flemish painting until the coming of Quinten Massys. In the panel which represents the Lamb and his worshippers, from which the altarpiece takes its name, each figure is a personality, carefully studied from life; yet each takes its place as a unit in a great company, inspired by one aim, moving towards a common goal. The scene is set in a landscape, whose every detail is an extraordinary piece of observation; yet so just are the relations in tone and scale that these details combine to form a visual whole, a piece of space filled with light and atmosphere. But the limitations of Flemish painting are also exemplified. Individual figures are massive and dignified; but as a whole, the altarpiece lacks the monumental quality at which it aims, and is a collection of pictures rather than a single work of art.

The shares of Hubert and Jan in the altarpiece cannot be settled exactly without further documentary evidence; but it is a widely accepted view that the design and the greater part of the painting are by Hubert. On this basis, a considerable group of work has been attributed to him, in which the *Three Marys at the Tomb*, in the collection of Sir Herbert Cook, is outstanding; but the ascription is no more than a hypothesis, of which the validity is denied by Friedländer, who gives the whole group to Jan van Eyck[1]. Jan is a less mysterious figure than his brother, though, apart from his share in the Ghent altarpiece, the only paintings certainly by him belong to his maturity. The basis of these is an unflinching realism which came as a revelation to Northern Europe, but carried with it inherent weaknesses. In Jan's largest and most ambitious work, the *Altarpiece of Canon George van der Paele* in the Bruges Gallery, dated 1436, the development of detail and the rendering of textures are amazing in their accuracy; but the observation is piecemeal throughout, and the various parts are held together by the frame and not by the design or by the dramatic relations of the figures. In only one painting, the portrait of *John Arnolfini and his Wife* in the National Gallery at London, dated 1434, does Jan reveal power to make a monumental design, to subordinate detail and local colour to enveloping light and atmosphere, and to create emotional unity. In this miracle of observation and record those who prize such qualities will never tire of examining the way in which the textures are imitated, nor of tracing correspondences between the interior and its reflection in the mirror which hangs in the background. But the painting has greater merits. For once, Jan van Eyck has allowed each exquisitely wrought detail to fall into its proper place, so that each form has its main structure clearly defined, yet is duly related in space

[1] *Die altniederlandische Malerei*, Vol. I, 1924.

to the others and set in a light whose quality contrasts with the glimpse of open air through the window. The design is simple, but bold and effective; and if there is little dramatic emphasis, a very intimate and human relation between the two figures is established, while Arnolfini's character, secretive and slightly sinister, is forcibly expressed.

The work of the van Eycks also marks an epoch in the technical history of painting. The story, which had its origin in an account given by Vasari in his life of Antonello da Messina, that they invented painting in oil, is entirely legendary. Oil in combination with other substances had long been known and used as a varnish and a medium in Northern Europe, and as a varnish in Italy. That the van Eycks introduced great improvements in its use is, however, certain. The exact nature of these improvements is unknown; but evidence points to their having invented a tolerably colourless and quick-drying oil varnish, which was used not only to cover the surface of the picture, but was mixed with the colours and applied in the form of transparent glazes over a painting laid in with tempera; a method which permitted greater freedom and delicacy of handling, and gave increased brilliancy of colour, thus greatly extending the power and resources of the painter.

Though the influence of the van Eycks was profound and widespread, they created no definite school. The only painter whose work suggests that he may have been a pupil of theirs is Petrus Christus, who was born shortly after 1400 and settled in Bruges in 1443. The chief characteristic of his work is a bold simplicity in light and shade, which gives the main forms sculpturesque quality, and secures a coherence among them unusual in early Flemish painting. Despite some coarseness in detail and emptiness in the forms, this characteristic unites with bold design and deep feeling to make his *Mourning over Christ* at Brussels a masterpiece of the period. Historically, Petrus Christus is important, since his employment in 1456 by the Duke of Milan may have provided a channel through which the van Eyck improvements in technique became known in Italy, where they played an important part in the development of the Venetian school.

Contemporary with the van Eycks, ultimately influenced by them but in his origins independent, is the painter of a well-defined group of work, formerly known as the Master of Mérode, now generally called the Master of Flémalle, from the fragments of an altarpiece painted for the abbey of Flémalle, now in the Frankfort Gallery. A brilliant piece of reasoning by Hulin de Loo[1] identified him with one Robert Campin, a painter of Tournai, who is known to have settled there about 1406. Recently, however, this identification has been seriously, though not convincingly, challenged[2], and it is now suggested that the Master of Flémalle is in fact the young Rogier van der Weyden. In any case, his early work has some affinity with that of

[1] *Burlington Magazine*, xv, 1909, 202 sqq.

[2] Jamot, *Gazette des Beaux Arts*, Nov. 1928; Renders, *Burlington Magazine*, LIV, 1929, 285; and *La Solution du Problème van der Weyden-Flémalle-Campin*, 1931.

the later Franco-Flemish miniaturists, though it is bolder in handling and more rustic in quality. Throughout, he is primarily a genre painter, with a delight in domestic and landscape detail and an interest in human character which inspired several vivid though brutal portraits. His later work reveals increasing power to construct the human figure and to organise design, probably under the influence of sculpture, of which Southern Flanders was an important centre; and in an altarpiece in the Prado, of 1438, the painter's only dated work, the influence of the van Eycks appears both in the details and a suggestion of atmospheric suffusion.

An attempt to make the Master of Flémalle the starting-point of a Walloon school of painting, distinct from the Flemish school of the van Eycks, has its roots in modern nationalist feeling; but it is clear that he is a partially independent derivation from the Franco-Flemish school of the late fourteenth and early fifteenth century. This independence of origin also marks the work of Rogier van der Weyden or de la Pasture. Concerning his beginnings there is still doubt. Those who accept the identification of the Master of Flémalle with Campin hold that Rogier is the Rogelet de la Pasture who was apprenticed to Campin in 1427; those who argue that Rogier is himself the Master of Flémalle say that he and Rogelet are distinct. In any case, Rogier's earliest certain work, the *Descent from the Cross* in the Escorial, is closely related in its realistic detail to the later work of the Flémalle Master, another link with whom is the treatment of the painting as though it were a piece of sculpture in high relief. But there is a pathos and a dramatic power greater than in any work of the Master of Flémalle. In Rogier's later work realism and sculpturesque treatment are less evident. The handling becomes more suave, the forms more slender and elegant, and the emphasis on contour greater, while the feeling becomes increasingly sentimental and languorous, as in the great *Last Judgment* altarpiece at Beaune, and in the *Seven Sacraments* in the Brussels Gallery. A visit to Italy made no change in Rogier's outlook or methods, as the altarpiece in Berlin commissioned by Peter Bladelin indicates; and the profound emotion which inspires a little *Pietà* at Brussels is exceptional. More characteristic are a group of half-length Madonnas, sometimes associated with portraits of patrons to form diptychs, whose popularity led to their being imitated by a considerable group of Bruges painters at the end of the century. Rogier's portraits are primarily transcripts of the sitter's face in terms of linear decoration, tinged with a slightly melancholy refinement; but they are exquisite examples of types recorded in terms of the artist's own temperament.

Though Rogier found many imitators, he is to be regarded as perpetuating old traditions rather than breaking new ground. In the work of Dierick Bouts, a contemporary of Rogier's who was born at Haarlem and worked mainly at Louvain, a temper and technique appear which were to be more fruitful. Bouts' realism in detail, pursued in the spirit of an in-

ventory maker, is as unwearying and uncompromising as that of Jan van
Eyck; and like Jan van Eyck, it is rare for any common sentiment to unite
his figures, while he lacks Rogier van der Weyden's power of linear design.
But above all Netherlandish painters Bouts has a feeling for the modulation
of form and colour by light and air, which enables him to create a spacious
and atmospheric world round his puppets, and joined to his keen observation
makes him a great painter of landscape. At the same time his taste and
invention in harmonies and contrasts of colour give his paintings great
beauty as decoration. The altarpiece of the *Last Supper*, painted for the
Cathedral of Louvain between 1464 and 1468, reveals almost every aspect
of Bouts' genius and its limitations. It is clumsy in design, and in each
panel the individual figures seem scarcely conscious of each other's existence. Yet each head is full of vitality, and the treatment of landscape
and setting is masterly. It is, however, in the portrait of a man in the
National Gallery, dated 1462, that Bouts displays all his strength. The
characterisation is vivid, yet restrained; the figure is set in light and
air, which floods in through a window opening on a spacious landscape;
and the colour is an exquisite harmony of silver greys, cool browns, and
murrey, with one decisive touch of blue in the landscape.

Under Bouts' influence there was active in Holland in the middle and
later half of the century a group of painters whose work is marked by
naïve and sometimes awkward realism in the treatment of the figures, and
by exceptionally sensitive and skilful treatment of landscape and architectural settings. The outstanding figure among these is Geertgen tot
Sint Jans—little Gerard, who lived with the Knights of St John in Haarlem. He is a secondary master, but rich in invention. In his hands, landscape becomes increasingly rich and varied, as in the *St John the Baptist*
in Berlin, with a background like the park round some great English
house; and in the little *Adoration of the Child*, in the National Gallery at
London, Geertgen breaks new ground, by painting the scene as happening
at night, the enveloping darkness broken only by miraculous light
emanating from the child and from the angel appearing to the shepherds
in the background. In the vivid contrast of light with mysterious shadow,
Geertgen found a new means of intensifying and revealing the dramatic
aspect of his theme—means which Rembrandt was later to employ with
unrivalled mastery.

Despite this activity in Holland, the principal centre of the arts in
Northern Europe remained in Flanders. There, of the generation which
followed Bouts and Rogier van der Weyden, the chief figure was the
Ghent painter, Hugo van der Goes, a mysterious and tragic figure, who
died insane in 1482. The only painting by him authenticated by documents is the famous triptych painted for Tommaso Portinari of Florence,
now in the Uffizi. Hugo's art is marked by a passionate and intense feeling,
for whose expression he never discovered adequate means. His instinct was
to work on a large scale, in which he stands alone among the early

Flemings. In his early work, he appears cramped by the necessity of conforming to the fashion for small work; later, when he could indulge his taste for size, he was limited by using the customary Flemish medium, admirably adapted for delicate and precise detail, but difficult to use rapidly and broadly. So it is that Hugo often achieves monumental dignity in a single figure, but rarely in a whole composition.

In the wings of the Portinari triptych—the figures of the donors with the children and patron saints—strong and subtle characterisation is combined with dignity and breadth of treatment to produce a truly monumental effect; while the landscape backgrounds are among the most delicate and spacious in the whole history of Flemish painting. But in the Nativity which forms the central panel, despite the strong underlying emotion and its dramatic concentration, the seduction of local colour and accessory detail has destroyed unity. In a magnificent *Adoration of the Kings* in the Kaiser Friedrich Museum, however, Hugo has come near to full realisation of his aims. The individual figures have his characteristic nobility, especially the young king on the right, who might have been inspired by Piero della Francesca. At the same time, despite some failure to use fully the unifying influence of light, the main masses are united into an imposing design, in which the elaborately wrought detail finds its just and subordinate place.

It is curious that personalities such as Hubert van Eyck and Hugo van der Goes did not found any considerable school of painters in Ghent. In contrast, Bruges in the later fifteenth century developed one of the most flourishing and active schools of painting in the Netherlands. But no considerable personality appeared until Hans Memling settled there at some date before 1467. He was a German, born in the principality of Mayence, probably between 1430 and 1435. His earliest known work is a triptych, in the collection of the Duke of Devonshire at Chatsworth, painted about 1468 for the English knight, Sir John Donne. This is the work of a fully matured master, and in essentials does not differ in any way from Memling's latest work. Here he gives all that he has to give—a summary of conventions and methods, worked out by two generations of original painters, modified and co-ordinated to produce a decorative and descriptive art. Memling reveals no new aspect of the external world, creates no new and convincing reality of his own, and never conveys, if ever he experienced, an intense or passionate feeling. But in his work there is superb craftsmanship, great taste in the decorative arrangement of forms and colours, and an atmosphere of tender and idyllic sentiment. This last quality gives Memling his distinctive position among Flemish painters, and is a source of charm as unfailing as it is apt to become monotonous. It relates him to the group of painters active in Cologne about the middle of the century which centres round Stefan Lochner, and forms the one definite link between Memling and his native country. Despite his limitations, however, Memling takes high rank as a painter of portraits. Finest of all, perhaps, is the diptych in the Bruges Hospital, painted in 1487 for Martin van Nieuwenhoven, with the Virgin and Child on the left side, the donor on the right. With the wings open the painting is like a page from an illuminated manuscript, so delicate and gay is the pattern of lines and colours. The Virgin has all the idyllic charm with which Memling was able to invest her; and the portrait of the donor, weak and foolish though he appears, is painted with insight and patient sympathy.

The influence of fifteenth-century Flemish art made itself felt throughout Europe. In Italy, though the painters of Lombardy and Piedmont on occasion adopted Flemish designs and motives, and Venetian painting owed much to Flemish technique, Italian traditions were too powerful to be more than superficially affected. Elsewhere, Flemish influence ultimately wove itself into the very texture of the national art. In England, a few illuminated manuscripts and panels of the early fifteenth century reveal an intensified realism which marks a breach with the conventions of late Gothic art; but any development parallel to that in Flanders was frustrated by political and religious disturbances, which left art in the hands of provincial craftsmen who found their patrons mainly among the rising merchant class, and their chief field of activity in the parish church. From their hands came the rood screens of East Anglia and Devonshire, the great Dooms which surmounted the screen, and the crude but lively paintings on the walls, representing incidents from the Bible, from the lives of saints, and from popular moralities and mystery plays. In these, local traditions persist, with elements from Flemish and Low German sources grafted on to them. The production was large, but the quality almost without exception mediocre. When English patrons wanted work of fine quality, they usually turned to Flanders. A notable exception is the paintings which decorate the walls of Eton College Chapel, painted between 1480 and 1488 by one William Baker and his assistants. These are in monochrome, with occasional touches of colour, and reveal considerable inventive and technical skill. They are shot through with Flemish influence; but the grace and breeding of the figures, and the linear emphasis, distinguish them from the work of any Flemish painter and link them to the best traditions of English medieval art.

In Germany, and especially in the Rhine valley, native character persisted longer. In the north, Meister Francke at Hamburg worked in the tradition of Meister Bertram and Conrad of Soest with greater naturalism in lighting and setting. In Cologne and its neighbourhood, the idyllic, lyrical temper of the St Clara altarpiece inspired a considerable group of later paintings, such as the *Garden of Paradise* at Frankfort, and the *Virgin with the pea blossom* in the Cologne Gallery, and found its final and most complete expression in the work of Stefan Lochner, who first appeared in 1430 and died in 1451. Variety in character, action, and the gesture of his figures embody the realistic tendencies of his age, also his power to suggest a third dimension by the use of light and shade; but these characteristics are only so much material for the creation of a dainty fairyland, radiant with gold and colour, where human drama and passion have no place. The *Adoration of the Kings* in Cologne Cathedral reflects a temperament nurtured by the mystical side of medieval Christianity, remote from the materialism underlying contemporary Flemish art. In this respect, Lochner carries on not only Cologne tradition, but that of the upper Rhine valley, of which he was a native. There worked Lucas Moser, more naïve and rustic than Lochner, with a greater interest in realistic landscape detail, but equally tender and poetic. Konrad Witz, born probably in Switzerland in 1398, preserved beneath borrowings from Flanders a distinctive lyric and bizarre quality. In contrast, Hans Multscher developed realism to the verge of the savage and grotesque, a characteristic which combined with increasing subservience to Flemish example was to mark German art until the coming of Dürer.

In France, the long-maintained supremacy of Paris disappeared during the English wars and the struggle of Burgundians and Armagnacs. Nevertheless, a considerable school of miniaturists flourished there working in the tradition of the de Limbourg brothers; and later in the century a number of painters found employment under Louis XI. But the chief centres of activity were elsewhere. In the North, painters such as Simon Marmion (*ob.* 1489) were mainly reflections of contemporary Flemish practice. In Anjou and Touraine however, largely under the patronage of René of Anjou, a more distinctive school developed. Prominent in this is Jean Foucquet, who visited Italy, worked in Paris, and finally settled at Tours, where he died in 1481. By him are the celebrated illustrations to a Josephus in the Bibliothèque Nationale (MS Fr. 247) and to the *Hours of Étienne Chevalier*, forty of which are at Chantilly. On the basis of these a number of panel paintings have been attributed to him, among them a celebrated diptych, with Étienne Chevalier and St Stephen on one wing (in Berlin) and the Virgin and Child on the other (Antwerp Museum). These and the miniatures reveal the tempering of Flemish by Italian influence in a largeness of design, a structural grasp, and an incisive sweep of line, which brings realistic detail into unity. In this Foucquet is a precursor of the French painters of the seventeenth and eighteenth centuries, who were to cast elements of Northern origin in the mould of Italian tradition to produce a distinctive national art. To the generation after Foucquet belonged the Master of Moulins, so called from a triptych in the cathedral of that city, painted about 1498; also known as le Peintre des Bourbons, from a notable group of portraits of the Bourbon family. In his work the influence of Hugo van der Goes is predominant, with Hugo's feeling for design and drama replaced by a search for elegance which often degenerates into triviality and prettiness.

In the South of France, Avignon continued to be a point of convergence for artists from every direction, and the work produced reflects a corresponding mixture of influences. A *Coronation of the Virgin* at Villeneuve-lès-Avignon, painted in 1453 by Enguerrand Charenton of Laon, is Northern in its types, Italian in its schematic and decorative design, and Provençal only in the landscape which fills the bottom of the panel. In the work of Nicholas Froment, painter of *Moses and the Burning Bush* in the cathedral at Aix-en-Provence, Flemish influence, notably that of Bouts, is dominant, joined to Italian elements in design. The outstanding work of the Avignon school, however, is a *Pietà* from Villeneuve-lès-Avignon, now in the Louvre, by an unknown painter; a masterpiece of monumental design, structural treatment of form, and poignant feeling, in which currents of alien influence are fused into a highly personal and original art.

Painting in Spain has hitherto been left unmentioned, as during the Middle Ages it was little more than a distorted reflection of the art as practised elsewhere. Until the fourteenth century, the main centre of activity was Catalonia; but as province after province was reconquered from the Moors, so gradually local schools of painters appeared. Catalonia in the thirteenth century was first a French fief and then part of the kingdom of Aragon; so that as an artistic centre its influence extended considerably beyond the borders of the modern province. At the same time, Barcelona was one of the greatest commercial cities of the age, in close touch with Italy, and in particular with Florence; while the conquest of Sicily by Peter III in 1282, and contact with Byzantium, increased the opportunity for foreign influence to affect Catalan art. The few surviving examples of thirteenth-century work are little more than imitations in cheaper materials of Byzantine mosaics, used to decorate church walls and altar frontals. In the fourteenth century, however, Italian influence made itself felt. An early example is an altarpiece from the cathedral at Huesca, doubtfully ascribed to Bernat de Pou, a painter of Barcelona. It takes the traditional form of two figures of saints flanked by small scenes from their lives; but in the types there is a tentative and halting realism, and in the small scenes a hint of Giottesque influence. Later, this Italian influence became paramount, as is evident in the work of Ferrer Bassa (active 1315–48), in whose decorations of the convent of Pedralbe (now in the Barcelona Museum) Sienese and Giottesque types and compositions are mingled. Towards the end of the century mural painting in churches was abandoned, and the principal place for the employment of the painter was the great carved and gilt *retablo* of the altar, divided into many compartments, each decorated with a scene painted on a gold ground, the whole surmounted by a painting of Christ on the Cross. These *retablos* were often the work of two or three generations of artists; and the necessity of keeping the later panels in harmony with the earlier work stereotyped both ideas and methods. A brilliant combination of scarlet, green, and dark blue with gold gives the work of such painters as the brothers Jaime and Pere Serra and Luis Borrassá its best claim to distinction. In types, backgrounds, and composition Italian influence is predominant, mainly due to the presence in Spain of Starnina and other Italian painters. At the same time, intercourse between Spain and Northern Europe was considerable; and so the work of Borrassá and his contemporaries is related in some degree to contemporary work in France, Germany, England, and Bohemia, though far behind it in skill, containing the same elements of realism, drama, and decorative exuberance, which were bred from the contact of Northern mind with Italian example, and had resulted in the formation of the international Gothic style of the late fourteenth century. Later, as in Northern Europe, Flemish influence became dominant in Spain, and inspired work such as that of Luis Dalmau, painter of a *Virgin and Child Enthroned* in the Barcelona Museum, faithfully modelled on a van Eyck pattern. Spanish painting, however, still retained some elements of an almost barbaric splendour, which give it some independent character.

The revival of art in Italy after the Dark Ages came somewhat later than in Northern Europe. As in Northern Europe, impact of the arts brought by the migratory peoples upon the survivals of classical art was mingled with Byzantine influence in producing the art of the Middle Ages; but the relative weight of the forces at work was sufficiently different to create an art of distinctive character. The contrast between the arts North and South of the Alps has in the past been overstressed. Again and again, influences from France, Flanders, and Germany entered Italy, and gave a definite turn to artistic production there, while as often Italian influence travelled north and profoundly affected Northern artists. But always any tendency towards assimilation was checked by a difference in origin and local conditions. One factor that marked off Italy from the rest of Europe was the strength of the classical tradition. The number of monuments known was few and increased but slowly. Even at the period of the High Renaissance, the differences between Greek and Roman Art, between the Republican and Imperial epochs were scarcely understood, and conceptions of the art of antiquity were almost entirely based on late and decadent Roman work. But there was nevertheless continuity in classical conceptions and forms. The makers of the Christian sarcophagus took over the design of their Roman forerunners, and in drapery, proportions, types, and mouldings re-echoed, even though faintly, their standards. Similarly, the activity in Rome during the twelfth and thirteenth centuries, mainly displayed in the construction of tombs and altar canopies, and in their decoration with polychrome mosaic, was less a revival than an intensified persistence in Roman adaptations of *opus alexandrinum*. Moreover, in language, literature, economic and social life, and political ideas, the influence of Rome persisted; so that when artistic activity quickened, ideas inherited from antiquity were ready to shape it. A second factor which helped to give Italian art characteristic form was that Italy was more closely and constantly in touch with the Byzantine Empire than was

Northern Europe; and that in Italy itself were great centres of Byzantine artistic activity, notably in Ravenna and the South, whose monuments continued to be a living source of inspiration long after the Empire had retreated from Italy. The influence of Byzantine art in its earlier phases was to formalise both conception and method. Used mainly to give expression to dogmatic religious ideas, it restricted employment of narrative or dramatic elements, and fostered the use of schematic and non-realistic forms. Story-telling propensities and love of naturalistic detail were encouraged by an independent current of influence from Asia Minor, but had less free play in Italy than in the North; and when the artist broke away from Byzantine models, he found freedom chiefly in the classical tradition, with the result that interest in form and its balanced, harmonious treatment have always been a dominant element in Italian art.

It was not until the end of the thirteenth century that these various influences combined to produce a distinctive Italian art. In the twelfth century, the influence of Byzantine art in its more abstract forms was powerful, and in certain areas supreme, though signs of another spirit at work appear. In Rome, for example, the revolt of 1143 and the establishment of the commune were symptoms of a new enthusiasm for classical example, which bore some fruit in mosaic and painting; in Umbria, a number of painted crucifixes and some wall paintings reveal a variation in facial expression and a dramatic energy foreign to contemporary Byzantine work; in Tuscany and North Italy, hieratic symbolism begins to yield to narrative. The sculpture of Benedetto Antelami at Parma marks an epoch in the effort to attain naturalism in movement and gesture, to design in space, and to infuse the whole with dramatic feeling. During the thirteenth century this loosening of bonds continued. The fall of Byzantium in 1204 caused a considerable influx of Greeks into Western Europe and an increased importation of examples of late Byzantine art. This new wave of Byzantine influence was felt strongly in Italy, and especially in Tuscany, owing to the close connexion at that date of Pisa with the East. It gave a new lease of life to Byzantine conventions, but at the same time brought with it the themes of a new iconography, in which the human and realistic side of the life of Christ and of the Virgin held an important place. The influence of these themes was reinforced by the rise of the Franciscan movement, which not only quickened the demand for works of art, but especially welcomed those in which interest in man and nature was mixed with symbolic expression of dogma. Side by side with the Crucifix, images of St Francis were produced, flanked or surrounded with scenes from his life which gave full scope for dramatic narration.

In Tuscany, the chief centres of artistic activity were Pisa, Lucca, Florence, and Siena, in each of which the reaction in favour of Byzantine methods and the impulse towards a more human and naturalistic art reached a different balance. Many names of artists have come down to us; but to attach works to all but a few of these names is impossible. In

Pisa, however, records and two signed crucifixes establish the importance
of Giunta Pisano. In general character these crucifixes conform to the
Byzantine type; but in detail they differ markedly. Christ is not only
dead, but represented as having died in agony, and this dramatic emphasis
is reinforced by the expressions and attitudes of the Virgin and St John
at the ends of the cross bar. In Lucca the Berlinghieri family was
prominent. A full-length figure of St Francis, with three scenes from his
legend on each side, by Bonaventura Berlinghieri, is the earliest known
example of a large group of similar paintings, of which the unusual number
signed by Margaritone of Arezzo has given their author a reputation
beyond his merits. In Siena the breach was less with Byzantine ideals
than with Byzantine methods. The most important painting of the
period is a large *Madonna and Child* in the Palazzo Pubblico at Siena,
which bears a repainted inscription giving the name of the artist, Guido
da Siena, and the date 1221, which competent critics argue was originally
1271. In any case, the work is one of a considerable group, in all of
which the influence of Byzantine models is present, but modified by a
feeling for the movement of line, for delicate decoration, and for strong
realism in detail, which were to mark later Sienese work. In Florence, on
the other hand, the presence of Greek artists and commercial intercourse
with Rome helped to maintain Byzantine influence, as is suggested by a much
repainted *Virgin and Child* in the Servite Church at Siena, which is recorded
to have been signed by Coppo di Marcovaldo of Florence and dated 1261.

In Rome and the neighbouring districts, the influence of mosaic helped
to keep the Byzantine tradition alive, a contributory factor being the
popularity of painted images of Christ and of the Virgin and Child,
which were held in special veneration and were probably in some cases
imported from the East. In the work of Jacopo Torriti, who signed
towards the end of the century the fine mosaics in the apse of St John
Lateran in Rome, and the even more magnificent decoration of the apse
in Santa Maria Maggiore, the design, the types, the gestures, the drapery,
and the ornaments are so purely Byzantine that, but for the inscriptions,
their authorship and date could scarcely be determined. But by the side
of such works others were being produced which broke with Byzantine
ideals. Such are the mural paintings by one Conxolus in the Sacro Speco
at Subiaco, in which narrative power, a liveliness in action, and a realism
in detail, including an attempt at landscape background, mark the painter
as an innovator. Far more important than Conxolus is Pietro Cavallini,
the leading figure in Rome of a classical renaissance. Two groups of work
only can be attributed to him with any certainty: a set of mosaics in
Santa Maria in Trastevere, which appear to have been originally signed
and dated 1291, and a series of frescoes in Santa Cecilia in Trastevere,
which can be established by documents to have been executed about 1293.
One of the most remarkable of the mosaics represents the birth of the
Virgin, in which a singularly human and intimate note is struck. The

figures themselves are stately and dignified, modelled in three dimensions, with drapery falling in simple, easy folds, while their proportions and attitudes recall those of antique statues. The influence of classical antiquity is still more evident in the Santa Cecilia frescoes, of which the only tolerably complete part is the upper half of a Last Judgment on the west wall. In the centre is Christ enthroned and surrounded by angels; to the left stands the Virgin, on the right St John the Baptist; and on each side are seated six apostles. The mighty figures, in attitude, gesture, and facial type, have an individuality evidently based upon direct observation of nature; while the simple and restrained handling gives monumental dignity and a sense of power. The figure of Christ dominates the whole scene, acting as a dramatic focus for the varying emotions aroused. Yet were it not for such details as the emblem of the apostles, it would be difficult to realise that a culminating event in the history of the world as taught by the Church is represented; rather, the conception is that of the Gods of Olympus sitting in judgment upon mortals. The influence of classical art has passed beyond inspiring the full, fused modelling of the heads and hands and the heavy, naturalistic swathes of the drapery, to influencing the basic conception of the subject.

No other works certainly by Cavallini are known. But it is clear that he was the central figure of a considerable school, of which the most notable productions are frescoes in Santa Maria di Donna Regina at Naples, and on the upper part of the wall in the Upper Church of San Francesco at Assisi, representing scenes from the Old Testament and from the life of Christ. The authorship of the latter is a matter of controversy[1]; but they reveal beyond dispute how great was the influence of Cavallini at Assisi, and indicate one of the channels through which it helped to shape the course of Florentine painting.

Another remarkable manifestation of the classical revival was in the sculpture of Southern Italy. An early example is the bronze gates of the church at Ravello, dated 1179; but it was under the patronage and deliberate encouragement of the Emperor Frederick II that the revival reached its height. On the famous gateway of Capua, built by him, was a statue of the Emperor, with busts of two of his ministers and of a woman symbolising Imperial Capua, remains of all of which are now in the Capua Museum. The statue of the Emperor appears to have been modelled on that of a Roman Caesar, the figure of Capua on that of a Roman goddess, while the busts of the judges, both in tolerable preservation, are imitations of the busts of Roman sages or philosophers. They do not stand alone as evidence of a considerable activity. On the pulpit of San Pantaleone at Ravello is the life-size bust of a woman, crowned with a diadem from which hang long tassels, thought to represent *Mater Ecclesia*; and a similar bust from near Amalfi is now in the Berlin Museum.

[1] See Toesca, *Florentine Painting of the Trecento*, 1929, pp. 60–61 for a summary of views.

In both, the types and technique are those of Roman sculpture, with a high polish, deep cutting, and use of the drill hitherto unknown in medieval art.

The significance of this Southern classical revival is, however, less in the remnants of its achievement than in its having been in all probability the training ground of Niccola Pisano, one of the great formative influences in Tuscan art. Claims once made that Niccola was a native of Tuscany are now generally disregarded. Not only is he referred to in a contemporary document as *de Apulia*, but his work is so closely connected in style with Southern sculpture, and is in such marked contrast to earlier Pisan work, as to make a Pisan origin almost incredible. What is certain, however, is that he was in Pisa before 1260, the date inscribed with the artist's name on the pulpit of the Baptistery there. In this, there is practically nothing which recalls the art of Byzantium, the bas-reliefs and statuettes which ornament it being all directly derived from late Roman art, and in particular from the Roman sarcophagus. In the panel representing the Annunciation and the Nativity the figures are modelled in the round, almost detached from the background, with the features, drapery folds, and other details deeply cut; they are crowded together into an irregular pattern covering the whole surface; and the facial types, the proportions, and the drapery are all classic, the Virgin a Juno, the angels Roman Victories. Into the next great work with which Niccola was associated, however, new elements enter. In the pulpit of Siena Cathedral, finished in 1268 with the help of Niccola's son Giovanni, Arnolfo di Cambio, and others, the reliefs are more naturalistic; the figures have lost their Olympian stolidity and are more lively and human; their draperies fall in finer and more graceful folds; and the dramatic and narrative interest is more evident. One explanation alone is possible: that in the period between the execution of the two pulpits, Niccola and his helpers had come under the influence of Northern Gothic. This conclusion is reinforced by study of the figures which separate the bas-reliefs and the arches. Some of them might, except for their size, come direct from the façade of a Northern cathedral. In the great fountain in front of Perugia Cathedral, completed by the same group of artists in 1278, the influence of the North is even more dominant, though the parts attributable to Niccola himself still retain a strong classic flavour.

In the work of Niccola's immediate followers, the main elements of his art persist, but with a different emphasis. Classical art, from being the principal inspiration, becomes for the most part a source of reminiscence; while Northern Gothic becomes an increasing influence. The work of Fra Guglielmo is little more than a skilful pastiche on Niccola's later phase; but Arnolfo di Cambio and Giovanni Pisano are independent artists of the first rank. It has been argued that this Arnolfo is distinct from the Arnolfo who later in life designed Santa Croce and the Cathedral at Florence; but the weight of evidence favours identification of the two. As an independent sculptor, his earliest known work is the signed monument to Cardinal de Braye in San Domenico at Orvieto, which probably dates from shortly after the death of the cardinal in 1282. Despite mutilation, the monument is an admirable combination of dignified design with graceful and delicate detail, in which the influence of Niccola Pisano and of Roman art mingles with that of Northern Gothic. In the ciborium of San Paolo fuori le mura at Rome, dated 1285, Gothic influence is more evident in the architectural forms than in the de Braye monument, but the sculpture retains classic traits. An Eve seems to have been modelled upon an antique Venus; the angels are flying Victories; a prophet holding a scroll is like the figure of a Roman orator. Yet they pass beyond mere imitation by virtue of a well assimilated naturalism and an easy grace. Perhaps as the result of a longer stay in Rome, the influence of Roman art is more evident in the ciborium of 1293 in Santa Cecilia in Trastevere. The mounted figure of St Tiburtius at one of the corners definitely recalls the equestrian figure of Marcus Aurelius on the Campidoglio, though the artist's naturalistic instinct keeps the work personal and living.

The work of Giovanni Pisano, in contrast with that of Arnolfo, reveals growing domination of Gothic influence. He never worked in Rome, and so was denied first-hand contact with the classical revival, while Tuscany was in direct touch with the North. An early work by him is the half-length *Virgin and Child* which stands in the Campo Santo at Pisa. The proportions, the simplicity of outline, the rigidity of pose, and the absence of deep cutting in the drapery combine to produce a monumental and massive quality, which with the facial types reflects the influence of Niccola. The sculptor's own personality finds expression in the intimate emotional relation between the Mother and Child. In a later Madonna over the eastern portal of the Baptistery the figure still retains the massive proportions of Niccola's work; but its swing and the deep-cut flowing drapery are Gothic; and in the sculpture of the façade of Siena Cathedral, of which his was the controlling mind, there is a freedom and variety of movement, a vivacity of characterisation, and lively rhythms in the drapery, which mark further assimilation of Northern influence. This reaches its highest point in an ivory *Virgin and Child* in Pisa Cathedral, an admirable combination of dignified grace and tender human feeling. Decisive separation from the work of Niccola appears in a pulpit in Sant' Andrea at Pistoia, begun about 1299. This, rather than the later and recently reconstructed pulpit in Pisa Cathedral, gives complete expression to the genius of Giovanni. The design is similar to that of Niccola's pulpit at Siena, but is throughout inspired by a different spirit. In the architecture, the slenderness of the columns, the sharply pointed arches, and the lightness of the horizontal mouldings combine to give the vertical emphasis and sense of upward movement which is a mark of Gothic. Everywhere, movement, individual character, dramatic emotion are emphasised. The eagles which support the central column seem to be sweeping round its base; the figures between the arches and at the angles of the pulpit stand almost detached, poised and gesturing; in the evangelist symbols at the corner which support the lectern is an agitation bordering on the fantastic; the prophets in the spandrils of the arches seem to swell beyond the space for which they are designed; while in the reliefs the characteristics of individual forms are picked up and emphasised by the energetic rhythms of the design.

The importance of Niccola Pisano and his immediate followers in the history of Italian art is difficult to exaggerate. They gave inspiration and suggestion to artists in North Italy which helped to break the bonds of tradition and set men free to achieve the triumphs of fourteenth-century art. Their influence was felt not only in style but in content. Niccola was among the first Italian artists to introduce the full complement of personages into the biblical scenes he depicted, with appropriate accessories; and his use of the nude, under stimulus from classical art, created a precedent of widespread importance. The Northern influence which had shaped their work came mainly through religious houses and commercial channels. Apart from the movement of individual monks or friars, a number of Cistercian monasteries were established in Italy; and Italian merchants, especially those of Siena and Florence, frequented the great fairs of Northern Europe, while pilgrimages added to the number of Northern visitors to Italy. Gothic influence on Italian architecture probably came chiefly through Cistercian example; while sculptors and painters would see such easily transportable works as ivories and manuscripts, of which a certain number are known to have come to Italy. Later, these casual contacts were given a more permanent character by the removal of the Popes to Avignon. But the tide was then beginning to turn. For the time being, Italy had little more to learn from the North, and in the fourteenth century the flow of influence is from rather than towards Italy.

Meanwhile, painting in Tuscany was moving on a similar path to that of sculpture. Almost exactly contemporary with Giovanni Pisano is Duccio di Buoninsegna of Siena, whose work marks development from the modified Byzantinism of the thirteenth-century Sienese School to a definitely Italian style, by force of a genius inspired from the North and untouched by the classical revival. Among Duccio's earliest works is a little *Virgin and Child* adored by three Franciscan friars, in the Siena Gallery. The types are Byzantine; but the arrangement of the figures, the very human child and the graceful, flowing linear pattern made by the contours point to Northern influence transmitted through a marked personality, while the diapered dossal of the background suggests a Northern miniature as prototype. Closely related is the famous *Rucellai Madonna* in Santa Maria Novella at Florence, once universally accepted as the painting by Cimabue round which Vasari wove the well-known story of its triumphant passage from the artist's studio to the church. Documentary research and stylistic analysis, however, have demolished the legend, and substituted a likelihood that the *Rucellai Madonna* is in fact one which in 1285 Duccio contracted with the fraternity of Santa Maria Novella to paint. Yet, combined with many characteristics found in the work of Duccio are Florentine elements, which prevent wholehearted acceptance of Duccio's authorship, and raise the possibility of it being the work of an independent master influenced by both Cimabue and Duccio.

In Duccio's later work, a recrudescence of Byzantine influence is combined with fuller and more delicate modelling and greater feeling for space; a development which paves the way to Duccio's crowning achievement, the great *Maestà* in the Opera del Duomo of Siena. This was commissioned in 1308; and its completion in 1311, and its installation in the cathedral, aroused that very excitement and enthusiasm of which Vasari's Florentine bias had made the *Rucellai Madonna* the occasion. Despite the loss of five panels, and the dispersal of seven others among museums and private collections, the *Maestà* still retains substantially its original form. On the front is the Virgin and Child enthroned, surrounded by angels and saints; on the back is a series of panels containing scenes from the later life and Passion of Christ; and in the predella and cornice are represented incidents from childhood and early manhood, the appearances after the Crucifixion, and scenes from the life of the Virgin. In its emotional power, its accomplishment, and its influence, the *Maestà* must be regarded as the Sienese equivalent of Giotto's decoration of the Arena Chapel. As never before, the devotion of Siena to the Madonna is given outward and visible form with singular intensity; and the life of Christ is revealed as a profoundly human as well as a divine drama. Within the framework of a strictly Byzantine iconography, figures have taken on a new naturalism and expressiveness in gesture and movement; there is a new sense of space, and a nascent feeling for landscape; the buildings in which a scene is enacted are no longer oriental abstractions, but are based on those of Siena itself; there is a vividness in narration, with dramatic unity gained by the skilful relating of individual action to the central theme; and throughout delicate and subtly varied colour is combined with graceful linear rhythms to produce a magnificent piece of decoration.

Duccio cast a lustre upon Siena which Florence could not for the moment rival. But there also the leaven of new ideas was working. The sharp dividing line between art in Florence and Siena which it used to be the fashion to trace has largely been obliterated by modern research. Despite a bitter rivalry in politics and commerce, cultural intercourse between Siena and Florence was close. Duccio and other Sienese worked in Florence; and the still undecided controversy over the *Rucellai Madonna* illustrates how nearly Florentine and Sienese painters were linked. With the coming of Giotto, a breach in ideals and methods definitely appears; but for nearly a century after his death, the tendency is again towards fusion. Giotto himself had some influence in Siena, while Sienese influence in Florence was strongly marked. In Florence, at the end of the thirteenth century, appears the half-legendary figure of Cimabue. That he existed is certain; that he was of some note is probable from the well-known lines in the *Purgatorio*:

Credette Cimabue nella pittura
Tener lo campo, ed ora ha Giotto il grido.

But of his work only one certain example remains. From August 1301 to January 1302 he was director of the mosaic work at Pisa Cathedral, and worked upon the still intact mosaic of Christ enthroned, attended by the Virgin and St John the Evangelist, of which the St John and part of the Christ are reputed to be entirely his work. This scarcity of authenticated work has produced very different conceptions and estimates of Cimabue, one party regarding him as among the chief precursors of the Renaissance and author of a large body of extant work, another denying that any painting by him survives and that he was little more than a mediocrity. To-day, opinion halts between these extremes, accepting a conventional Cimabue, whom it regards as author of a tolerably coherent group of works, related in some degree to the Pisa mosaic and sanctioned by a considerable tradition in some cases. Prominent in this group are a *Virgin and Child* enthroned and surrounded by angels, formerly in Santa Trinità at Florence, and now in the Uffizi, and a series of frescoes which decorate the apse and north transept of the Upper Church at Assisi. That their painter was still under strong Byzantine influence is evident; but differences from Byzantine work appear in more marked and varied expression of character and feeling, in greater grace and variety of attitude, and above all in the treatment of form. Outline ceases to be a simple boundary line, and is related to the interior modelling to assist in creating a feeling of a third dimension. There is contrast also with the method of Cavallini, who modelled in soft and gradual transitions of tone and colour.

Whatever view be taken concerning the authorship of these and similar works, it is beyond argument that in Florence and at Assisi a painter or group of painters were active in the late thirteenth and early fourteenth century who broke the spell of Byzantinism and gave a vigorous impulse to new achievement. It was into an atmosphere thus created and onto a soil thus prepared that Giotto was born. Controversy may be acute concerning his training and early work; uncertainty may obscure some periods of his activity; but there remains a solid core of indisputable achievement, whose influence and intrinsic character make him one of the supreme artists of the Western world. Giotto was probably born in 1266, near Florence. According to long tradition his first master was Cimabue; and both documentary evidence and certain characteristics of his earlier work raise the presumption that he visited and worked in Rome, probably before 1300, though nothing remains that can be regarded as certainly the result of this stay. About his work at Assisi opinion is still sharply divided. None of the work in the Lower Church which used to be attributed to him has survived recent criticism; while competent opinion has even denied to him the famous St Francis series in the Upper Church. Of the twenty-eight scenes which compose this, it is generally agreed that the last three and part of the first are by a follower. The rest, despite the use of assistants, are the product of one mind, and in many cases of one hand. There is no mention of their painter in early documents; and despite a long tradition that they are by Giotto, style must determine the issue. In favour of Giotto's authorship is a series of marked and fundamental characteristics which are to be found only in the undoubted work of Giotto and nowhere else; and if the paintings are denied to him, a genius must be invented who developed on exactly the same lines as Giotto and disappeared in early manhood. Most remarkable in the St Francis series is the attempt to give structural character to the forms, and to give a feeling of depth and recession. It has been truly said that Giotto was the first mural painter to knock a hole in the wall. With him painting is less the decoration of a surface than a means of creating three-dimensional space, within which solid forms may be organised into an architectural unity. Corresponding to this conception is his treatment of human emotions and their interaction. His individual figures are full of vitality, expressing in gesture and action a wide range of feeling, controlled always by a deep-lying tranquillity of spirit; while these varying emotions are directly related to the central event depicted, leading up to or reinforcing the psychological issue. Thus, the pictorial and the dramatic are roads leading to the same end, the creation within the picture of a living reality. In no sense, however, is Giotto an illusionist. In details he reveals the keenest power of observation, and on occasion delights in some piece of looking-glass reproduction; but the reality he creates is of the picture and not of the external world.

The power to achieve this end was not fully developed in the St Francis series. It reaches maturity in Giotto's next great undertaking, the decoration of the Arena Chapel at Padua, completed shortly after 1305. In design, the Chapel is little more than an oblong box, its inside covered with painting. Assistants were responsible for the decoration of the roof, and later followers for the painting of the choir. But the scenes from the story of Joachim and Anna, from the life of the Virgin, and from the life and Passion of Christ, which decorate the north and south walls of the nave and the choir arch, the figures of Virtues and Vices below them, and the Last Judgment on the entrance wall, are either by Giotto himself or painted directly under his inspiration. In these every characteristic of the Assisi paintings is seen developed and brought into greater harmony with the others. A power of psychological analysis and a pitch of emotional intensity is attained, rarely equalled by any artist, yet without a trace of exaggeration or sentimentality; the expression of space is more complete and the relation of objects therein is more assured; and by the subjection of individual colours to the control of a general tone a suggestion of enveloping light and air is given.

Between his stay at Padua and his death in 1336, Giotto worked not only in Florence, but at Naples, probably at Bologna and Rimini, and at Milan. Possibly also he visited Avignon, and he is said to have gone to Paris. Of all this varied activity, however, practically nothing remains except in Florence. There, at some date after 1317, he decorated the Bardi chapel in Santa Croce with scenes from the life of St Francis, and at about the same period the Peruzzi chapel in the same church with scenes from the lives of the two St Johns. Of these, the Peruzzi chapel paintings have been so restored as to make them almost valueless. Those of the Bardi chapel are much better preserved, and in them may be seen certain developments in Giotto's art. The fundamental characteristics of the Paduan series are all present, but receive a different emphasis. The psychological analysis is even more subtle and varied, but the dramatic oppositions are less strong and the action more restrained. The expression of a third dimension is as complete as formerly, but the influence of light plays a larger part. For the first time in the history of painting, light is used not only as a means of defining individual forms, but as an element pervading the whole scene, establishing unity of time and place and defining the relation of individual forms one to another. This is completely exemplified in one of the most impressive and moving of the frescoes, the Death of St Francis. No violent chiaroscuro is used; the light has a gentle ambient quality, appropriate to the delicate restraint with which the subject is treated. But there are definite cast shadows, and the lights are modulated according to their relation to one source, so that the sense of one place and one atmosphere is firmly established.

On Giotto's artistic personality the rare panel paintings by him throw no additional light, nor do his activities as architect and sculptor. In 1334 he was appointed chief architect of the cathedral of Florence, and he is traditionally credited with the design of the famous campanile. But how far the present form is due to him is unknown; and equal uncertainty surrounds his share in the reliefs which decorate its lower storey. After his death, the main centre of artistic influence passed to Siena, where Simone Martini had developed an art whose main inspiration came from Duccio and Northern Gothic. The earliest fully authenticated work by him which survives is the large fresco of the *Virgin and Child* enthroned and surrounded by saints, in the former Council Chamber of the Palazzo Pubblico at Siena, signed and dated 1315. The design derives from Duccio's *Maestà*, and the principal saints represented are the same. Even more explicitly than that work, the painting marks the supremacy in Siena of the cult of the Virgin. It carries inscriptions exhorting to justice and righteousness, the Virgin being conceived as presiding over the deliberations of the city government. The isolation of the enthroned Virgin and Child, and the distinguished bearing and dignified gestures of the attendant figures, create an atmosphere of courtly elegance, and witnesses the influence of that aspect of the Northern Gothic spirit which found expression in the feudal hierarchy and the courts of chivalry. Gothic influence also appears in the emphasis on the vertical lines of the design, in the pinnacles and delicate tracery of the throne, and in the flowing lines of the drapery. In Simone's later work Ducciesque and Gothic elements are more completely fused into a personal style, marked by pensive, gracious figures, more human and consciously elegant than in Duccio, and by a keen feeling for the decorative beauty of line and colour. The most ambitious surviving work by Simone, the decoration of the chapel of St Martin in the Lower Church at Assisi, reveals little of Giotto's psychological penetration and dramatic power, despite the carefully studied realism in action and expression. Yet by virtue of Simone's special gifts, it is more completely satisfactory as decoration of a wall within a given architectural setting than any work by Giotto. These special gifts found their full expression in an *Annunciation* in the Uffizi, dated 1333, in which Simone's brother-in-law, Lippo Memmi, collaborated with him. In the central panel by Simone himself the Sienese tradition and the influence of Northern Gothic have met in perfect union, to produce one of the most exquisite works in the history of Italian art. The problems of space and movement which Giotto raised and solved, and which later generations of Florentines were to develop and overcome, are here set aside in favour of bold and subtle linear rhythms, delicious harmonies and contrasts of colour, and delicately wrought detail; all inspired by a mystic, contemplative spirit, remote from the ordinary passions of mankind.

In 1339 Simone settled at Avignon, where he died in 1344, the central figure of a considerable group of painters. His influence, if less widespread and subversive than Giotto's, was profound in the channels within which it ran. It powerfully affected the course of Sienese art in the fourteenth and most of the fifteenth century; it is stamped upon the Trecento painters of Naples and Pisa, where Simone had worked; and as mentioned earlier it travelled north from Avignon to give a new orientation to Northern Gothic painting, and to lay the foundations of the international Gothic style of the late fourteenth century. On his immediate followers it is unnecessary to dwell. Some were accomplished painters, with distinct individualities, notably Barna of Siena; but substantially their ideas and methods did not pass beyond those of Simone. The case is different with two younger contemporaries of Simone, the brothers Pietro and Ambrogio Lorenzetti. Their work owes little to Simone Martini or to Gothic art, and is mainly a direct development from Duccio, modified by the influence of Giotto and the Pisan sculptors. This appears in the earliest signed work by Pietro, a polyptych in the Pieve of Arezzo, the contract for which is dated 1320, and in an altarpiece painted in 1329 for the Carmelite Church in Siena, which marks the transition to

Pietro's mature style, characterised by an admirable balance of decorative claims with monumental design and by poignant though restrained emotion. A celebrated example is the fresco of the Virgin and Child between St Francis and St John the Evangelist in the south transept of the Lower Church at Assisi, in which an unusual strain of tenderness softens the painter's natural austerity. This austerity, however, reasserts itself in a Crucifixion and a Descent from the Cross, part of a series of scenes from the Passion near at hand in the same church; and joined with profundity of feeling and grandeur of design makes these paintings comparable with the work of Giotto. But a Sienese instinct for decoration has prevented the breaking up of the wall surface, the painting being treated as a great bas-relief, with a rhythmic sweep of contour as the painter's chief pre-occupation. A similar successful adjustment of the claims of dramatic action, of the third dimension, and of surface unity is revealed in the latest known painting by Pietro, an altarpiece signed and dated 1342, representing the Birth of the Virgin, now in the Opera del Duomo at Siena. The figures are admirably disposed in space and all play their part in the little domestic drama, their dignity relieved by delicate touches of realism in expression and gesture; while the whole builds up into an imposing linear pattern.

The earliest accepted work by Ambrogio Lorenzetti is a *Virgin and Child* at Vico l'Abate, dated 1319, which reflects in its types the influence of Duccio, and in its sculpturesque treatment that of Niccola and Giovanni Pisano. In later work a more free and rhythmic play of contour suggests contact with Northern Gothic, and an increasing mastery over space-expression and dramatic narrative the influence of Giotto.

To Ambrogio's maturity belongs the famous altarpiece at Massa Marittima, with the Virgin and Child enthroned and surrounded by saints and angels. This third *Maestà* of the Sienese Trecento differs strikingly from its predecessors. In contrast with the gracious dignity of Duccio's figures and the courtly elegance of Simone Martini's is the massive construction and vigorous action of Ambrogio Lorenzetti's; while a note of gaiety is struck, which has a counterpart in the decorative effect of the delicate, clear colour and the rich gilding. Similar characteristics mark Ambrogio's best known work, the three frescoes in the Palazzo Pubblico of Siena, completed in 1339, one containing elaborate symbolical representations of Good and Bad Government, the others showing their consequences. Individual figures in the first fresco are among the finest Ambrogio ever produced, akin to fine classical sculpture in their dignity and the understanding of construction they reveal. But, in general, pictorial effect has been sacrificed to didactic and allegorical needs; and disproportion in the figures, and their alternate isolation and crowding, confuse the design. In the *Consequences of Good Government*, the architectural and landscape setting is skilfully constructed, and the little figures at work or play are delightfully alert and naturalistic. But neither this nor the almost ruined *Consequences of Bad Government* contain

anything to compare with the majestic figures in the adjoining fresco; and
they owe their charm mainly to the tapestry-like pattern they make upon
the wall.

The race of great painters in Siena came to an end with the disappearance of the Lorenzetti. They had few immediate followers and their
limited influence on the next generation was soon displaced by that of
Simone Martini and of Northern Gothic, which shaped the later work of
such painters as Lippo Vanni and Bartolo di Fredi, and dominated that
of Andrea Vanni and Taddeo di Bartolo. From these painters in turn
descended another group, who were practically indifferent to the problems
of form and movement which fascinated their Florentine contemporaries;
and who gave themselves up to the creation of lovely Madonnas and to
vivacious story-telling, enriched with every possible refinement of pattern
and colour they could devise. Sassetta, Giovanni di Paolo, and Sano di
Pietro, enchanting as they can be, entirely lack the imaginative force and
large rhythms of the Lorenzetti. Their work may titillate the senses, but it
never stirs the blood. So, the seed of the Renaissance found but sterile soil in
Siena; and such fruit as it produced there in the late fifteenth century was
little more than an imitation and adaptation of the greater art of Florence.

Meanwhile, in Florence, Giotto's dominant personality had bred a
succession of increasingly feeble imitators who perpetuated the outward
form of his work, though incapable of assimilating its informing spirit.
Yet even during his lifetime, ideals and methods different from his were
evident; and the history of Trecento art in Florence is largely that of
artists in whose work influences from Siena and from the North modified and even transformed the Giottesque tradition. In this process
imitation played a larger part than independent thought, and few outstanding personalities emerged. Quite apart stands the sculptor Andrea
Pisano, whose work, derived directly from Giovanni Pisano, was touched
by the influence of Giotto, and received high distinction through his own
personality. Only one work certainly by him survives, the bronze doors
of the south entrance to the Baptistery at Florence, decorated with
reliefs of scenes from the life of St John the Baptist and of personifica-
tions of the Virtues. These are signed and dated 1330, the date when
the model was finished; the doors themselves being finished and in
position by 1336. The designs fill their allotted spaces admirably and
combine dignified simplicity with extraordinary variety. The relief is
never unduly accentuated, and no extravagant feats of foreshortening or
recession are attempted; yet space in which the action can take place is
adequately suggested. The figures themselves in proportions and drapery
occasionally suggest classical prototypes, and are marked by a restrained
naturalism which never degenerates into triviality; while the dramatic
feeling, though vigorous, is kept well under control. The same elements
are present that make up the art of Giotto; but the sculptor has greater
feeling for grace and charm than the painter.

Upon the immediate followers of Giotto it is unnecessary to dwell at length. Names such as Stefano, Buffalmaco, and Puccio Capanna have come down to us, with which no work can be securely associated; while there is a large group of paintings directly inspired by Giotto, such as the St Nicholas and St Mary Magdalene series in the Lower Church at Assisi, and the allegorical representations of the Franciscan virtues in the vault of the crossing, whose painters are unknown. Attempts to attach recorded names to anonymous works have been frequent, but have so far yielded no convincing results. Among distinguishable artistic personalities are the master of the St Cecilia altarpiece in the Uffizi, who completed Giotto's St Francis series, and Jacopo del Casentino, both of them minor artists. Of greater interest is Taddeo Gaddi (*ob.* 1366), a prolific painter whose decoration of the Baroncelli chapel in Santa Croce with scenes from the life of the Virgin is an unconvincing compromise between the aims and methods of Giotto and the claims of decorative effect varied by occasional invention in the treatment of light.

Among later painters directly influenced by Giotto an outstanding figure is one Maso, painter of the scenes from the life of St Sylvester in Santa Croce, a mysterious figure whose identity has become almost inextricably confused with that of another painter, Giottino. His spacious dignified designs, in which colour defines form and suggests light, and his psychological insight and dramatic power, make him worthy of comparison with Giotto; but Sienese influence has given his individual figures greater grace and elegance and encouraged a more anecdotal realism. In contrast, the work of Bernardo Daddi (active *c.* 1317–48) was increasingly dominated by Sienese and Gothic ideals, and in his late work everything is directed towards creating a richly decorated surface. Similarly, Andrea da Firenze (active 1343–77), now securely identified as painter of the well-known frescoes in the Spanish chapel in Santa Maria Novella, whole-heartedly adopted Sienese conventions in his vivacious epitome of the cultural and religious ideas of his day.

A distinct and intermediate group is formed by Andrea di Cione, called Orcagna, his brothers Nardo and Jacopo, and their immediate followers. Two certain works by Orcagna himself survive: an altarpiece in Santa Maria Novella at Florence, signed and dated 1357, and the tabernacle in Or San Michele at Florence, completed according to an inscription in 1359. In the altarpiece, sculpturesque heads and the dignified types reflect Giotto's influence, but mate unhappily with the linear elaboration of the drapery folds and the multiplication of surface ornament. In the Or San Michele tabernacle Orcagna achieved a successful combination of Italian Gothic design with mosaic and with sculpture which reveals the influence of Andrea Pisano. Dramatic action is subordinated to securing grace in movement and design; but dignity and simplicity are well preserved. The famous painting of the *Last Judgment* in the Strozzi chapel in Santa Maria Novella was once universally considered as by

Orcagna; but the difficulty of reconciling its style with that of the signed altarpiece has led to its being attributed to Nardo di Cione, though no work by him has yet been identified.

Outside Florence, Giotto's influence had made itself felt chiefly in North and North-East Italy. In Lombardy, Italo-Byzantine conventions ruled until about the middle of the century, when a small group of Giottesque painters appeared, with Gothic influence modifying the proportions of their figures and their treatment of draperies and giving their work a marked genre character. On the Venetian mainland, Giotto's influence was felt at Padua in the work of Guariento and Altichiero of Verona, together responsible for the charming frescoes in the chapel of San Giorgio. In Venice itself, looking towards the East, Byzantine designs and methods held sway until modified by influences direct from the North; while in Rimini, painters such as Giuliano da Rimini and his follower Baronzio owed emancipation from Byzantine convention primarily to Cavallini, though a number of paintings by unknown hands also witness the influence of Giotto.

Meanwhile Gothic influence had made itself felt to some extent in all the more important artistic centres of Italy. The connexion between France and Lombardy at the period was particularly close, and had its effect in Lombard miniature painting of the period. An early example is the work of Giovannino dei Grassi (*ob.* 1398), sculptor and architect, best known by a remarkable book of drawings of birds and animals in the Municipal Library at Bergamo, which are an exact parallel to the drawings with which Northern artists illustrated bestiaries and treatises on hunting and enriched other works. From Verona and Venice, the main roads to the north ran over the passes into Austria and Southern Germany; and Northern influence on their art came chiefly through those countries, as is evident in the work of Stefano da Verona (active 1425–38), a master of dainty realism and delicate decoration. In Venice itself, the presence of Gentile da Fabriano combined with Northern influence to produce painters such as Jacobello di Fiore (active 1415–38) and Giambono (active 1420–62), who, with Antonio Vivarini of Murano and Giovanni d'Alamagna, are minor figures in the transition from Byzantine to Renaissance art in Venice.

Gentile da Fabriano himself is a far more important product of Northern influence in Italy. Of Umbrian origin, he worked in many places, especially in North Italy; and in his earlier work contact with Gothic art is evident. To his maturity belongs an *Adoration of the Magi* in the Uffizi, dated 1423, in which linear pattern and exquisite detail are so enriched with gold and colour as to make it one of the most delightful pieces of decoration produced in Western Europe. Virtually, the painting is a miniature from a manuscript, on a vast scale. Considerations of space, movement, individual psychology, drama, play no part. It is a scene from a gorgeous pageant of medieval court life, frozen into immobility for the spectators' perpetual delight. It is the culmination of a phase in painting, so perfect within its limited range as almost to deny the possibility of farther progress save by a change in ideals. That change is foreshadowed in Gentile's latest work, in which a dawning interest in human personality and its embodiment reflects the influence on a purely medieval painter of humanist ideas.

In Jacopo Bellini, a native of Venice, these ideas wrought a greater change, and made him the chief precursor of the great age of painting in Venice. In 1423 he seems to have been assistant to Gentile da Fabriano in Florence, where a turmoil of eager experiment and creative activity set its mark on his work. His chief monument is two volumes of drawings in the British Museum and the Louvre. His medieval origins are revealed in numerous detached and realistic studies of animals and genre scenes; but a new orientation appears in his compositions, both from the Old and New Testament, in which decorative and realistic trivialities are disregarded in favour of broad sweeping design and dramatic emphasis. The direct influence of classical art appears in drawings of classical architecture and sculpture, and in the choice of classical subjects; human anatomy, the nude, and movement are investigated; and elaborate studies in perspective and foreshortening are made. New sources of inspiration, humanism and scientific curiosity, are at work; and new weapons are being forged to express new ideas. Jacopo's paintings are less remarkable; but all reveal a feeling for noble design and for human emotion which foreshadows the triumphs of his great sons, Gentile and Giovanni.

In the work of Antonio Pisano, called Pisanello (*ob.* 1455), the parting of the ways is even more clear. As draughtsman and painter, he belongs mainly to the Middle Ages; as medallist, he is in the full stream of the Renaissance. His art, even more than that of Gentile, is one of pageantry and courtly display. Almost entirely it was devoted to the service of the great princely houses of Italy, for whom he not only executed paintings and medals, but designed jewellery and costumes. For these purposes he made a large number of drawings, which combine such extraordinary acuteness of observation with power and delicacy of craftsmanship that it has needed the evidence of camera and cinematograph to verify some of the movements and attitudes recorded. In these drawings, which Pisanello made throughout his career, descent from the Northern illuminators and their Lombard followers is clear; in the paintings, which belong to the earlier part of his life, the emphasis on linear pattern and the elaboration of decorative and genre detail are equally witness to Northern influence. In contrast are the medals, of which the earliest is one of the Emperor John Palaeologus, probably executed about 1438. The medal, as commemorating human personality and achievement, was a fit vehicle for embodiment of the spirit of humanism, and so Pisanello used it. His portraits of the great figures of his day are among the most vigorous and living memorials of them which have come down to us. It is, however, on the reverse of his medals that Pisanello's genius finds complete scope. Heraldic devices, *imprese*, incidents serious or humorous referring to the sitter, with or without lettering, are used singly or in combination to construct designs of singular perfection, admirably filling the allotted circle, exquisite in detail but monumental in effect, whose degree of relief is perfectly adjusted to the area they occupy.

In Florence the Gothic ideal found its last and greatest exponent in Lorenzo Monaco, and in his work took on a definitely Tuscan character. His elegant and slender figures, and the elaboration and swing of their draperies, do not prevent the sculpturesque character of the forms being maintained; and in thus establishing a balance between the claims of decorative effect and of the third dimension, Lorenzo Monaco preserves in some degree the Giottesque tradition and is related to the Lorenzetti. In his later work a simpler treatment of the draperies and a more carefully studied relation of the forms in space appear: a development which reaches a climax in a *Coronation of the Virgin* in the Uffizi, dated 1413, and reveals that, after temporary eclipse, the leaven of methods and ideals akin to those of Giotto if not directly inspired by him was again working in Florence. An even more striking example of this is the work of Masolino da Panicale. Among the few fully authenticated works by him are two sets of frescoes at Castiglione d'Olona, near Varese; one in the choir of the Collegiata, representing scenes from the Life of the Virgin and from the early life of Christ, painted *c.* 1425, the other in the Baptistery, representing scenes from the life of St John the Baptist, painted in 1435 according to a renewed inscription. In the earlier work, Gothic influence has inspired the attenuated figures, frail and insubstantial, with draperies falling in flowing decorative curves. In the interval between this and the later work, the genius of Masaccio had stamped itself on Florence; and primarily under the influence of this, Masolino's figures have taken on a new solidity and a new vigour of action, together with a new unity in an adequate three-dimensional space.

The change mirrored in the work of Masolino is the change from medieval to renaissance art. From the early fifteenth century onward, medieval conceptions and methods might still find favour with certain artists, or leave their imprint on men inspired by other ideals; but they appeared as survivals from an earlier age, unconnected with the main currents of thought and action. This fundamental change had its principal centre of radiation in Florence. Discussion of its causes belongs to the general cultural history of the period. Here, it is only necessary to emphasise that the revival of classical learning and of enthusiasm for classical literature and art was less a cause than an effect. Primarily, the Renaissance was a change in attitude towards life, which seeking for a touchstone found it in classical antiquity. Knowledge of the ancient world had never been lost during the Middle Ages, but in the fifteenth century that knowledge acquired a new use and value, which in turn stimulated its growth.

In art, this change in attitude towards life affected both spirit and form. The development of humanistic ideas took God away from the centre of the cosmos and put man in His place. The Christian religion continued to supply the majority of themes to the artist, but the human element was given increasing grandeur and significance, while the divine became more and more human. At the same time, subjects drawn from classical mythology became more common, in which anthropomorphic instincts found full scope, while historical events and incidents from secular literature provided material in which man occupied the whole stage. The development of portraiture is another aspect of the same tendency, reflecting the increased importance of human personality and the growth of self-consciousness. In form, change came chiefly through the spirit of scientific enquiry which was abroad. Imitation of detail and conventional formulas for the reproduction of appearance no longer satisfied artists. They became interested in problems of basic structure, and so the study of human anatomy developed and the increased use of the nude figure, while action, gesture, and facial expression became the objects of elaborate analysis. In this search for a more penetrating realism the antique provided both an incentive and a restraining force. With classical art in the eyes and minds of artists, Gothic standards became discredited, while feeling for harmony, balance, and proportion was inculcated, which saved Italian art from following the same path as the art of Flanders. At the same time, the problem arose, especially in painting, of so adjusting the relative size of individual forms and their relation in space as to give the appearance of the scene as a whole; and towards its solution was directed the study of perspective, and of light and shade. The one provided a logical framework, within which the problems of relative size and distance were automatically, if arbitrarily, solved; the other not only helped to give individual forms three-dimensional character, but joined perspective in securing unity, partly by enabling the artist to give emphasis at decisive points, partly by its power when adjusted with reference to one source of light to establish identity of time and of place throughout a scene. Here also, though less directly than in the case of individual forms, the influence of the antique played a part, in stimulating search for harmony, balance, and monumental character in design.

In all essentials, the aims and methods of Renaissance artists had been anticipated by Giotto; and it is from him and Andrea Pisano that the sculptors and painters of fifteenth-century Florence descend, rather than from their immediate predecessors. The first decisive manifestation of revival was in sculpture. In 1401 a competition was held for the design of the north doors of the Baptistery of Florence. Among the seven competitors were Filippo Brunelleschi, Lorenzo Ghiberti, Niccolò d'Arezzo, and Jacopo della Quercia, a constellation of extraordinary brilliance, in which every aspect of the early Renaissance spirit is represented. The subject set was a design for the Sacrifice of Abraham, within a panel of the same size and shape as those on the doors by Andrea Pisano. Ghiberti was the winner, and his panel is to-day in the Bargello with that of Brunelleschi.

Brunelleschi, perhaps because of his failure in the competition, abandoned sculpture for architecture, and became one of its greatest masters. In his competition panel the design is less skilfully planned and the technique less accomplished than in Ghiberti's; but the figures have greater nobility and grandeur, evidently due to study from the antique, and are united by a more intense dramatic feeling.

Ghiberti, whatever his limitations as an artist, ranks among the finest craftsmen in metal that the West has produced; and by virtue of his writings ranks as one of the most important and reliable sources for the history of art in Florence. The works on which his reputation rests are the bronze doors for the north entrance of the Baptistery, which were completed in 1424, and a second pair of doors for the east entrance, commissioned in 1425 and finished in 1452, which Michelangelo pronounced worthy to be the gates of Paradise. The main decoration of the north doors consists of reliefs representing scenes from the life of Christ. In the figures, Gothic treatment of the drapery mingles with classic reminiscence in attitude and gesture to produce a studied elegance. Realistic and descriptive detail help to make the narrative vivid, though the dramatic effect is often weak. In the design, surfaces are broken up and planes put in recession to produce a pictorial effect, in sharp contrast to the concentration by Andrea Pisano on the frontal plane, inaugurating methods which Donatello was to use with unrivalled power. In the east doors, carrying reliefs of scenes from the Old Testament, increased influence of the antique is evident in greater suavity of form, while skill in modelling and casting has developed to yield an amazing variety in depth and angle of relief. In the interval between the completion of the two sets of doors, Donatello had reached maturity and Masaccio had been at work, and their influence is traceable in Ghiberti's increasing effort to attain the effect of a painting and his consequent sacrifice of the qualities which give sculpture monumental and decorative character.

In contrast is the work of Jacopo della Quercia, born in Siena but singularly little affected by current Sienese fashions. In his work, the exquisiteness and pictorial elaboration of Ghiberti is replaced by monumental forms and large rhythms, which anticipate and, indeed, inspired Michelangelo. In his earliest known work, the sepulchral monument in Lucca Cathedral to Ilaria del Carretto, simplicity and breadth combine with delicacy to make the recumbent effigy one of the most spiritual creations of the Renaissance. Of the Fonte Gaio, designed for the Campo in Siena in 1419, only fragments remain; but in these the proportions of the figures, the balanced contrasts of plane and mass, and the massive sweep of the drapery, are those of the Cinquecento. The font of the Baptistery of Siena, designed by Jacopo and executed jointly with Donatello, Ghiberti, and others, is more Gothic in character; but nothing Gothic remains in Jacopo's most famous work, the portal of San Petronio at Bologna, on which he worked from 1425 until his death in 1438. This it was that fired the mind of Michelangelo when, as a comparatively young man, he visited Bologna, chiefly through the ten bas-reliefs on the pilasters, representing scenes from the Creation to the Sacrifice of Abraham. In these, no concession is made to the picturesque or the anecdotal. The figures fill most of the frontal plane, background and accessories being of the simplest, the relief low, the masses broad and simple. With no traceable imitation of the antique, they have all the grandeur and restraint of early Greek work. The gestures and attitudes are natural and unforced, yet intensely dramatic and expressive; and from their combination has arisen a series of designs, each with its own character but all alike monumental, all mingling subtlety in detail with breadth of statement, all conceived in three-dimensional space. Behind them lies a creative imagination comparable to that which covered the roof of the Sistine chapel.

But an even greater figure among sculptors of the period was Donatello. In him is concentrated every aspect of the Florentine feeling for form, and from him radiated influence throughout Italy. He greatly widened the range of sculpture. His bronze David was the first free standing nude figure cast in bronze since classical times; his equestrian statue at Padua to the *condottiere* Gattamelata, though not the first of its kind, created a type whose influence is not yet exhausted; and his were the earliest portrait busts made in Italy. Similarly, to established forms he gave new life. The pictorial possibilities of the relief he pushed almost to breaking point; the wall tomb was given a new dignity and a wider range; and his use of *putti* was little short of a new invention. Moreover, he was architectural designer as well as sculptor; and into such structures as the ciborium in St Peter's at Rome, and the framework of the Annunciation relief in Santa Croce at Florence, he introduced combinations of decorative motives, mainly derived from the antique, treated with a new freedom and boldness. In technique, Donatello likewise opened new paths. His work was sometimes coarse and hasty, but always spontaneous and direct, definitely divorcing sculpture from the work of the goldsmith; and in the adaptation of work to the position in which it was to be seen he was an innovator. Finally, behind this originality and resource lay deep and passionate emotion. In Donatello, the Renaissance spirit of scientific observation and enquiry was incarnate, driving him to a penetrating realism, saved from the sordid and commonplace by a dominating sense of man's dignity and by a lyric or dramatic instinct.

He explored not only the possibilities of form but of movement; and, both in single figures and in compositions, there is a poise, a suggestion of capacity for change, which gives a vitality whose exuberance anticipates baroque sculpture.

To Gothic art, Donatello owed little. Such early work as the marble David in the Bargello has Gothic swing and proportions, but in the slightly later St George from Or San Michele these have almost disappeared. The literal realism of the Poggio Bracciolini in the Cathedral of Florence and of the Zuccone on the Campanile is soon tempered, in such work as the magnificent bronze David of *c.* 1430 in the Bargello. After a visit to Rome, deliberate recollection of the antique is discernible in his work for a time, but soon becomes so merged in the artist's own technique as to become part of his own personality, expressed in such masterpieces as the Annunciation relief in Santa Croce, the singing gallery from the Cathedral, and the bronze doors and the figures in the Old Sacristy at San Lorenzo. During his visit to Padua from 1443 to 1453, Donatello was at the height of his powers. There he executed the statue to Gattamelata and the bronze figures and the reliefs which glorify the high altar in the Santo, works which changed the whole current of art in Northern Italy and laid the foundations of the art of the Cinquecento there. That art was anticipated in Donatello's work on his return to Florence. The reliefs on the pulpit of San Lorenzo, designed if not carried out by him, the Judith and Holofernes in the Loggia dei Lanzi, the St Mary Magdalene in the Baptistery, and the St John the Baptist in Siena Cathedral, have passed far beyond the limits of quattrocento ideas both in spirit and method. The stage is prepared for Michelangelo and, ultimately, for Bernini.

Expression of the Renaissance spirit in painting took much the same course as in sculpture. The relations of the two arts were so close that movement in the one almost inevitably produced corresponding movement in the other. Among the painters who mark the transition from Gothic to Renaissance art outstanding figures are Fra Angelico and Paolo Uccello. In Fra Angelico, a medieval spirit clothed itself in a Renaissance dress. Humanism as an attitude towards life scarcely touched him. He became a realist in his statement of the external facts of nature and their relations; but with human emotions and human drama he concerned himself little. His imagination created a world remote from all the passions of mankind, a mystic's ecstatic vision of a perfect state, in which earthly events took on a heavenly significance. For him pain and sorrow cease to exist, and even Hell becomes only a fantastic dream. In the character of his imagination, Fra Angelico changed little; only in its outward expression do the Middle Ages and the Renaissance meet. His earlier work is in the full late Gothic tradition, and suggests the influence of Lorenzo Monaco. Later, as in such paintings as the *Descent from the Cross* in San Marco at Florence, the figures are more fully characterised and

better constructed, problems of the third dimension receive more attention, and the introduction begins of a remarkable series of landscape
backgrounds in which subtlety of observation is joined to breadth and
atmospheric quality. At the same time, exquisite taste is shewn in the
construction of a colour pattern. In this, Fra Angelico remained throughout faithful to Gothic ideals. He uses light and shade mainly to give
individual forms solidity, not as a means of constructing a design,
and never allows it to obscure the brightness and purity of his tints. The
lovely *Annunciation* at Cortona closes the phase in Fra Angelico's art in
which Gothic influence still plays a considerable part. In the decoration
of the cells and cloisters of the monastery of San Marco with a series of
frescoes representing scenes from the Life and Passion of Christ, which
was carried out with the help of assistants between 1437 and 1445, the
Gothic elements are subordinate. There is a suggestion of them in the
upward swinging design of the monumental *Transfiguration*, in which
the figure of Christ has the solemn dignity of primitive sculpture; but
they are completely absent from the half-length figures of Christ and of
great Dominicans in the lunettes of the cloisters, in which Fra Angelico
more nearly than in any other work expresses a humanist conception of
his subject.

In contrast with Fra Angelico, Paolo Uccello to the end of his career
retains Gothic mannerisms in his forms, though from the beginning
he approaches his work in a scientific and humanist spirit. In his early
work, the slender figures, the decorative emphasis on outline, and a
fantastic element in the forms, witness Gothic influence, and possibly
that of Pisanello, with whom Uccello might have come into touch during
a visit to Venice. In the much repainted equestrian effigy of Sir John
Hawkwood in the cathedral of Florence, successful mimicry of sculpture
does not prevent the main emphasis being on profile; and this holds true
of Uccello's best known work, the three battle scenes representing the
defeat of the Sienese by the Florentines at San Romano in 1432, distributed among the Uffizi, the Louvre, and the National Gallery. In
these, in the frescoes telling the story of Noah in the cloisters of Santa
Maria Novella at Florence, and in a predella representing the story of the
Profanation of the Host, executed in 1468 for the Confraternity of Corpus
Domini at Urbino, the intention to use line and colour primarily for
decoration is evident, combined with a passionate interest in problems of
foreshortening and perspective. Uccello's attitude towards these latter has
often been misunderstood. That they are used to create illusion is highly
unlikely, since all other means to that end are neglected. Rather they
seem directed towards giving a firm and logical framework to the picture,
so that in constructing a pattern problems of recession and proportion
should automatically be solved. In Paolo Uccello there is nothing of
Fra Angelico's mystic vision; his passion is rather that of the scientist
absorbed in a problem whose solution will remove all difficulties. His
modern counterpart is Seurat, with his calculated pointillism; and like

Seurat, his greatness as an artist depends more on such imponderable matter as design and colour than on the machinery he uses.

With the rise of Masaccio, a figure comparable in stature to Donatello appears among painters. In his brief life—he was born in 1401 and died between 1427 and 1429—he gave expression to every aspect of Renaissance thought, and set Florentine painting upon the road it was to travel until its decay. In his case, the question of origins is unimportant beside that of achievement. His early work, such as the *Virgin and Child with St Anne* in the Uffizi, reveals him as a follower of Masolino. His subsequent relations with that painter are obscure; and there is a well-marked group of work, certainly by the same hand, which some writers regard as by Masolino working under the influence of Masaccio, and others as early works by Masaccio himself. Fortunately, to understand and appreciate Masaccio, decision on the matter is needless, since paintings indisputably by him exist. Among these is the altarpiece of 1426 painted for the Carmine Church at Pisa, the centre panel of which, representing the Virgin and Child enthroned with angels, is in the National Gallery at London. Not since Giotto painted had so massive and imposing a figure as the Madonna, conceived and carried out in three dimensions, been seen in Tuscany. Distinction, elegance, and grace have been disdained in favour of robustness and vitality. Mother and Child alike are heroic but not divine; made in a larger mould than humanity but of the same clay. Yet for all its qualities, the Pisa Madonna is gauche and immature when set beside the frescoes which decorate the Brancacci chapel, in the Carmine Church at Florence. Those undoubtedly by Masaccio are the Expulsion from Paradise, Christ and the Tribute Money, St Peter distributing the goods of the community, St Peter baptizing, St Peter's shadow healing the maimed, and the Resurrection of the Prefect's Son, of which part was executed by Filippino Lippi. In these, human personality is given an emphasis and a dignity such as it had rarely received before in Christian art. Each figure is searchingly characterised, firmly constructed, given its appropriate and significant action or attitude; each seems to stand by itself, a complete being conscious of itself, of its own weaknesses and strengths. Yet individuality has not meant isolation, and in each fresco the forms are brought into unity. Grasp of perspective has provided a firm scaffolding on which to hang construction in space, and almost for the first time in the history of painting every part of the picture is seen and treated in definite relation to a given source of illumination. In this, Masaccio reveals his grasp of the mechanism of painting; in the noble rhythm of his design, and in his power not only to express human emotion but to give it a point of dramatic concentration, he becomes a great artist. His art is founded on intense observation and knowledge of men and nature, inspired by a vivid imagination, guided and controlled by a profound feeling for pictorial and dramatic construction; an art that picked up the torch lighted by Giotto, and handed it on to Leonardo, Raphael, and Michelangelo.

CHAPTER XXV

THE RENAISSANCE IN EUROPE

In an eloquent letter Gregorius Tifernas expressed the regret felt by
the whole humanist world at the death of Nicholas V (1455). He was
very nearly succeeded by another humanist, Cardinal Bessarion, but at
the last moment the Conclave fought shy of a Greek who wore a beard.
So they elected in his place a Spaniard, who was of high character, sound
learning, and political capacity, but whose chief recommendation was his
age of seventy-eight. The new Pope, who took the title of Calixtus III,
devoted his whole energies, which were still considerable, to the furtherance
of a crusade against the Turks and to the advancement of his Borgia
nephews. In 1458 he was succeeded by Aeneas Sylvius Piccolomini, and
the hopes of the humanists revived. But Pius II was a man of letters
rather than a scholar, and he was far too intelligent to rate the pretensions
of the humanists at their own value. The greatest of them, Valla, died the
year before his election, and Poggio the year after. Filelfo still was left,
but, when he clamoured for preferment, the Pope put him off with courteous answers and a few small presents. He shewed, however, that he could
appreciate real learning by appointing Niccolò Perotti, the disciple of Valla
and the author of the first large Latin grammar of the Renaissance (1468),
Archbishop of Manfredonia and by treating with marked consideration
Flavio Biondo, who, probably on account of his ignorance of Greek, had
been neglected by Nicholas V. It was possibly under the influence of his
Roma instaurata that the new Pope issued his brief, *Cum almam nostram
urbem*, for the preservation of those ancient monuments which his predecessor, Nicholas V, for all his love of Rome, had freely used as a
quarry.

Pius II represents the critical and inquiring side of the Renaissance.
He wrote history in a really critical spirit and he took a keen interest in
geography. His *Asia* was a favourite book in the early days of geographical discovery, and was read by Columbus. Like Petrarch he was a
lover and careful observer of nature. There are some charming descriptions
of scenery in his *Commentaries*—of the fields of flax at Viterbo "which
imitate the colour of heaven," of the lakes of Nemi and Albano, and
especially of his native Siena and its beautiful neighbourhood.

His successor, Paul II (1464–71), was equally disliked by the humanists,
and with better reason. For when Pomponius Laetus (1425–98), as he
called himself, a pupil of Valla and a man of sound learning, made his
nursling, the Roman Academy, a centre of childish and reactionary protest
against the Christian religion, the Pope, taking these proceedings too
seriously, suppressed the Academy and threw its leading members into

prison. Platina, indeed, who was one of them, says in his malicious biography of Paul II that many of them died under torture, but his statement is not supported by evidence. Paul II was in fact a truer representative of the Renaissance than Platina and his friends, for he loved beauty as few men have loved it and his superb collections included bronzes, pictures, tapestries, medals, coins, and every conceivable form of art. After his death the Academy was revived by Sixtus IV. Platina became his librarian and Pomponius Laetus the literary dictator of Rome.

A similar Academy, but literary rather than antiquarian in its aims, was founded at Naples by Antonio Beccadelli under the auspices of King Alfonso shortly before the latter's death in 1458. Il Panormita, who died in 1471, was succeeded by Giovanni Pontano (1426–1503), who, as the best writer of Latin verse and prose of his century, fully sustained the literary reputation of the Academy. His betrayal to the French of Ferrante II, whose grandfather, Ferrante I, he had served as chief minister for ten years, and who had loaded him with favours, is at once a blot on his fame and a sign of that lack of patriotism which was one of the chief causes of Italy's decadence. On the other hand, his fellow-humanist, Jacopo Sannazaro (1458–1530), who edited his works, remained faithful to the house of Aragon and accompanied his friend and protector, Frederick, the successor of Ferrante II, into exile. His famous *Arcadia* was first published in a correct and complete form at Naples in 1504, but a considerable part of it was already written in 1490. Sannazaro also wrote six *Piscatory Eclogues*, in which fishermen take the place of shepherds, and a long Virgilian poem on the birth of Christ (*De partu virginis*), upon which he spent twenty years.

The Platonic Academy of Florence had a far wider influence than those of Naples or Rome. Founded by Cosimo de' Medici in 1459, with Marsilio Ficino (1433–91), the son of his physician, who had been carefully trained in Greek philosophy, for its first head, it rose to great importance under Cosimo's grandson Lorenzo. Its meetings were held at the farm near Careggi which Cosimo had given to Ficino, and it counted amongst its members the chief representatives of Florentine culture. As its name implies, its object was the cult and study of Plato, and it was thus the outcome of the movement which had been inaugurated by Gemistos Plethon at the time of the Council of Florence. In Plethon's philosophy the teaching of Plato was blended with that of Plotinus and was further corrupted by fantastic interpretations of his own. Bessarion freed himself from his master's extravagances and did much to restore the pure doctrine of Plato, but Ficino followed rather in the footsteps of Plethon. To the blend of Platonism and Neo-Platonism he added Christian mysticism, and he was thus led to the conception of a "common religion" of which Christianity and other religions were varieties. If this philosophy was but a generous ideal resting on frail foundations, he at any rate did good service by contributing to the spread of spiritual thought in an age of increasing scepticism and materialism, and by his Latin translations of Plato and Plotinus.

His famous disciple, Giovanni Pico della Mirandola (1463–94), surpassed him in learning, originality, and even in influence. To Plato and Plotinus he added Arabic writers, the Schoolmen, and the Kabbala. His philosophy was founded on the belief that man is made for happiness, relative in this world, absolute in the next. With Reason and Will to guide him he must ever strive upwards towards his Heavenly Home. As Pico grew in saintliness—"from his face," says his friend Politian, "shone something divine"—his philosophy became simpler and his religion more definitely Catholic. Yet ritual and outward observance meant little to him; he was wholly absorbed by the love of Christ.

The munificence of Nicholas V and Alfonso I had attracted many humanists to Rome and Naples, but after the death of these patrons Florence speedily regained her primacy as the chief centre of humanism. This was especially marked under the rule of Lorenzo de' Medici (1469–92), one of whose closest associates, Angelo Poliziano (1454–94), represents a higher type of classical scholarship than had hitherto been reached in Italy. Uniting the critical faculty of a Valla with the literary feeling of a Pontano, he brought to the interpretation of a wide field of Greek and Latin literature a rare combination of learning, critical method, taste, and insight. He lectured on Homer and Virgil, and the Latin writers of the Silver age; he translated Herodian, Epictetus, Hippocrates, and Galen. Claiming to be neither a dialectician nor a jurist but only a *grammaticus* or *literatus*, he lectured on Aristotle's logic, and he edited the *Pandects* after a systematic collation of the manuscripts.

At the age of sixteen he began his career with a translation of the *Iliad* into Latin verse, and ten years later (1480) he obtained the chair of Greek and Latin eloquence. So great was his fame that students of all nations thronged to hear him and were held spell-bound by the charm of his voice, the fire of his delivery, and the inspiration of his rhetoric. Each course of lectures was preceded by an introduction illustrating the whole branch of literature of which the author in question was a type. This often took the form of a Latin hexameter poem, for Politian, like Pontano, wrote Latin verse and prose as correctly as Valla and with the ease and freedom of Poggio and Pius II.

If the revival of learning was a stimulus to the invention of printing, the rapid spread of printing contributed greatly to the diffusion of learning. When Politian began his translation of the *Iliad* in 1470, there were only two towns in Italy, Rome and Venice, which had a printing press. By 1500 the number of towns with presses had reached seventy-three, and many of these presses were devoted almost exclusively to the printing of classical works.

The art of printing was introduced into Italy in 1465 by two Germans,

Conrad Sweynheym and Arnold Pannartz, who set up a press in the
Benedictine monastery of Santa Scolastica at Subiaco. They began with
a *Donatus pro puerulis*, but no copy of this is known; the first book from
their press of which copies exist is Cicero's *De Oratore*, and their first
dated book the *editio princeps* of Lactantius (29 October 1465). Then after
printing an edition of St Augustine's *De civitate Dei*, which was finished
12 June 1467, they moved to Rome, where they carried on their work
under the able supervision of Giovanni Andrea, the learned Bishop of
Aleria, who was secretary to the Vatican library. But in spite of great
industry they could not make their business pay, and in 1472 the bishop
wrote in their names to Pope Sixtus IV, giving an account of their labours
and imploring him for assistance. Their last venture, they say—a noble
edition of Nicholas de Lyra's Commentary (*Expositiones*) on the Bible in
five volumes—had left them without the means of subsistence. The letter
is especially interesting from the fact that the printers give a list of their
productions and of the number of copies of each work. Of the twenty-
eight works enumerated, more than two-thirds are Latin classics. With
one exception—the *Epistles* of St Jerome, of which they issued 550 copies
—an edition consisted of 275 or 300 copies.

The next Italian town to follow the example of Rome was Venice, where
John of Spires printed Cicero's *Epistolae ad Familiares* in 1469. He died
in the following year, and his press was carried on first by his brother
Wendelin and afterwards (from 1473) by a syndicate. They had formidable rivalry in the press of the distinguished Frenchman, Nicholas Jenson,
who, first as sole owner and then as chief partner, issued a large number of
Latin classics from 1470 to 1480, the earlier ones being printed in a roman
type which has never been surpassed for beauty. Of all the Italian towns
Venice was the most active in the cause of printing; between 1470 and 1480
at least a hundred presses were at work there, and by the end of the century
this figure had risen to 151.

In 1470 printing was established at Foligno. In 1471 the new art
reached Florence, Milan, and seven other towns, and from this time spread
rapidly over the rest of Italy. The first printer at Milan was Pamfilo
Castaldi with Antonius Zarotus for his assistant. At Florence Bernardo
Cennini, the celebrated goldsmith, was till recently regarded as the pioneer
with Servius' Commentary on Virgil—his only known production—but
he has been displaced by an anonymous printer. The earliest book in
which decipherable Greek type appears is the Subiaco *Lactantius*, but the
first book entirely printed in Greek is the *Grammar* of Constantine Lascaris,
printed at Milan in 1476. Florence made a notable contribution to Greek
printing in 1488 with the first edition of Homer, and in 1494 the distinguished Hellenist, Janus Lascaris, established there a Greek press under
the management of Lorenzo di Alopa, a Venetian, for which he himself
designed the types, consisting at first wholly of capitals. From 1494 to
1496 he issued no less than five *editiones principes* of Greek classics:

the *Anthology*, four plays of Euripides, Callimachus, Apollonius Rhodius, and Lucian.

In the same year, 1494, in which Janus Lascaris set up his press at Florence, the most famous of Italian printers, Aldus Manutius (1450–1515), a native of Bassiano near Velletri, began printing at Venice. After studying Latin at Rome and Greek at Ferrara under Guarini, he went in 1482 to Mirandola, because its lord, Giovanni Pico, as he wrote to their common friend, Politian, "loved men of letters." Thence he proceeded to Carpi to become tutor to Pico's nephew, Alberto Pio, and it was through the latter's munificence that he was able to carry out his project of settling at Venice as a printer with the special object of printing Greek books. He made a beginning in 1495 with the *Grammar* of Constantine Lascaris, and in the same year he issued the first volume (the *Organon*) of the *editio princeps* of Aristotle. This work, of first-rate importance in the history of learning, was completed in 1498. In 1501 he introduced his famous italic type for a pocket edition of Virgil, the first of those cheap and convenient editions of the classics which were not among the least of his services to humanism. In the same year he founded his Neacademia for the encouragement of Greek studies, and during the remaining fifteen years of his life he was continually adding to his editions of Greek classics and Greek works of reference. They included no less than twenty-five *editiones principes*.

There is a note of irony in the fact that Aldus' Greek texts and cheap editions, which did so much for the new learning in general, helped to destroy the primacy of Italy. But so it was. Erasmus indeed spent three years in Italy (1506–9) to perfect his knowledge of Greek, but Budé, Vives, and Melanchthon all learned their Greek north of the Alps.

In art Florence retained her primacy till near the close of the fifteenth century, but as regards Italian art in general there is only space here to call attention to certain features of it which it owed to the inspiration of the Renaissance spirit.

Firstly, there was a marked increase in the influence of classical art. In architecture this was largely due to that remarkable and many-sided man, Leone Battista Alberti (1404–72), whose first important work was the transformation by order of Sigismondo Malatesta of the Gothic church of San Francesco at Rimini into the outward semblance of a classical building (1447–50). For instance, in the façade, unhappily left unfinished, we see the principle of a Roman triumphal arch, of which there was a fine example at Rimini, applied to a Christian church. Some two years later (*c.* 1452) Alberti published his famous *De re aedificatoria*, the first modern scientific work on the theory and practice of architecture, in which he corrected and added to Vitruvius by the light of his own observations and studies. In 1460 he built the Palazzo Rucellai at Florence, in which for the first time the pilasters of the façade were used as mere ornament, without serving any structural purpose. Finally, in 1470 he designed for Ludovico Gonzaga the great church of Sant' Andrea at Mantua, which became the type of an ecclesiastical building for nearly three centuries.

From this time Renaissance architecture, which had hitherto been almost confined to Florence, began to develop rapidly in other Italian cities—especially at Rome—where the court of the Palazzo di San Marco, better known by its later name of the Palazzo di Venezia (built for Paul II), is evidently inspired by the Colosseum.

Roman architecture and Roman decorative work in its various forms were studied eagerly by painters as well as by architects, though naturally their influence was confined to backgrounds and accessories. When Domenico Ghirlandaio (1449–94) was summoned to Rome by Sixtus IV in 1475 to paint frescoes for the Vatican library, he made drawings, says Vasari, from the various antiquities of the city; and the same writer tells us that Filippino Lippi (1457–1504) studied these antiquities with unwearied diligence. In the *Triumph of St Thomas Aquinas*, which he painted with other frescoes for Cardinal Caraffa in 1489 in the Dominican Church of Santa Maria sopra Minerva, not only is the classical architecture a prominent feature, but the whole picture is composed in a spirit of classical symmetry.

In Andrea Mantegna (1431–1506), who painted chiefly in Northern Italy, this cult of antiquity became a veritable passion. Its first symptoms were displayed in the frescoes which he painted from 1455 to 1460 in the Church of the Eremitani at Padua, and during the last twenty years of his life it dominated him so completely that in the end his art suffered. The great series of the *Triumph of Julius Caesar* at Hampton Court (1484–92) is remarkable for grandeur of conception and mastery of execution, but in the *Triumph of Scipio* (National Gallery), painted in the last year of his life, the artist is so completely obsessed by the spirit of classical relief that he has abandoned colour for monochrome.

It was inevitable that this exaggerated cult of antiquity should bring with it a decline of Christian sentiment. Ghirlandaio and Filippino Lippi, with few exceptions, painted Christian subjects, but they often treated them in a thoroughly secular fashion. Their frescoes, for instance, in Santa Maria Novella are merely pretexts for the portrayal of Florentine social life and the introduction of numerous portraits. Similarly Mantegna's religious pictures, as might be expected from his devotion to classical antiquity, are often purely pagan in sentiment.

In 1460 Mantegna entered the service of Ludovico Gonzaga, lord of Mantua, and at Mantua he remained, under three generations of its princes, till his death. The Italian despots were now fast becoming rivals of the Church as patrons of art. Sandro Botticelli (1444–1510) was the favourite painter of Lorenzo de' Medici; Melozzo da Forlì (1438–94) was for three years at Urbino in the service of Duke Federigo; Cosimo Tura (1420?–1495) was employed by Borso d'Este, the first Duke of Ferrara, and his brother Ercole I for the greater part of his life.

Piero de' Franceschi (1416?–1492) was employed in turn by Sigismondo Malatesta, Federigo Montefeltro, and Borso d'Este. It was natural that these lay-patrons should give commissions for mythological subjects and portraits, but on the whole religious subjects still greatly preponderate. Botticelli painted for Lorenzo de' Medici two masterpieces, *Spring* and the *Birth of Venus*, but his non-religious pictures only amount to about a third of his work. A very small proportion of Mantegna's work is pagan in subject. Cosimo da Tura painted only religious pictures, and, except for the famous portrait group which commemorates the opening of the Vatican library by Sixtus IV and the ruined fresco of *Pesta-Pepe*, the same may be said of Melozzo da Forlì.

It was at Venice, in the last decade of the fifteenth century, that the emancipation of painting from the control of the Church definitely began. The Vivarini, Carlo Crivelli (1430?–1493?), and Giovanni Bellini (c. 1429–1516), during the greater part of his career, painted religious subjects with genuine religious feeling; but later the demand arose for the representation of pageants and processions, and in Gentile Bellini (c. 1428–1507) and Vittore Carpaccio (1450–1522) the Venetian State and the "Schools" or Confraternities found men to provide them with pictures instinct with joy and colour. But it was Giorgione (1476 or 1477–1510), a pupil of Giovanni Bellini, who, uniting a rare sense of beauty with a romantic imagination, made mythological and other non-religious subjects an increasingly important feature of Venetian art.

A third Renaissance feature of much of the Italian art of this time is its scientific spirit. We saw in the last volume how zealously the Umbrian painter, Piero de' Franceschi, applied himself to the technical problems of his art. He had disciples in Melozzo da Forlì and Luca Signorelli (1441–1523), of whom the latter was a precursor of Michelangelo in the study of the nude, while both, like Mantegna before them, were masters in the art of foreshortening. But the chief home of this scientific spirit was still Florence, and its chief exponent was Antonio Pollaiuolo (1432–98). He "treated his nude figures," says Vasari, "in a manner which approaches more nearly to that of the moderns than was usual with the artists who had preceded him; he dissected many human bodies to study the anatomy, and was the first (i.e. painter) who investigated the action of the muscles in this manner, that he might afterwards give them their due place and effect in his works." A good example of the result of this anatomical study is the small picture of *Hercules and Antaeus* in the Uffizi, in which the muscles of Hercules stand out with the effort he is making to crush his antagonist. But Pollaiuolo was a greater sculptor than painter, and his superb tomb of Sixtus IV in St. Peter's testifies to his unsurpassed knowledge of the human form and to the freedom and certainty of his execution. Yet the absence not only of religious sentiment but of all religious emotion shews that the scientific spirit had stifled in him the more vital principles of art. With less genius than

Pollaiuolo, Andrea Verrocchio (1435–88), whose many-sided proficiency was remarkable even among the many-sided artists of Florence, shewed equal devotion to the study of artistic problems. His influence was widespread, and it is not his least title to fame that he was the master of Leonardo da Vinci.

Those who hold that the Renaissance was something more than the normal development of civilisation have their justification in Leonardo (1452–1519). In the whole history of the human race has any man appeared who was more variously or more splendidly gifted? Supreme as painter and sculptor, yet ever haunted by an elusive ideal of perfection, he solved as if by instinct the problems upon which his predecessors had laboured so assiduously. His first important painting was *The Adoration of the Magi*, which he left unfinished at Florence when he entered the service of Ludovico Sforza in 1483. But unfinished though it is, it marks an epoch in painting—the beginning of the High Renaissance. To begin with, it introduced an arrangement in the composition of a picture—the triangular one—which has held the field for more than four centuries. Of a higher order of importance is the fact that Leonardo broke with tradition by placing the Virgin and the Child in the central foreground and by directing towards them the eager looks and gestures of the many figures with which he surrounded them. Thus the psychic interest of the scene receives its true importance, and the *Adoration of the Magi* becomes no longer a processional pageant or an occasion for the glorification of the artist's patrons, but an act of the deepest significance—a true adoration. The same principle, though with greater knowledge and greater mastery of execution, governs the miraculous *Last Supper*, completed in 1493, but begun many years earlier. Upon the central figure of Christ are focused the movements, the gestures, and, except for the group on the extreme right, the looks of all the Apostles. The consternation which followed the "One of you shall betray me" is seized at its supreme moment of passionate intensity. After the downfall of his patron Leonardo left Milan, and during his residence at Florence with short intervals from 1500 to 1506 he painted the *Virgin and St Anne* and the haunting portrait of Monna Lisa. Wonderful though he was as an artist, he was even more wonderful as a man of science. He was famous as an engineer and some of his greatest achievements were in mechanics. In astronomy, physics, physiology, human and comparative anatomy, physical geography, geology, and botany (especially as a branch of biology), he anticipated many modern researches. Above all things he believed in the scientific spirit. He regarded the senses as the only road to scientific knowledge and experience as the only test of truth.

Leonardo's discoveries, except so far as they took a practical shape, were little known in his own day, being confided to his note-books, which have only been printed, and not yet in entirety, in quite modern times. The most celebrated Italian man of science of the fifteenth century was the Florentine, Paolo del Pozzo Toscanelli (1397–1482), the friend of

Brunelleschi and Alberti, of Nicholas of Cusa and Regiomontanus. He wrote treatises on perspective and meteorology, but he was chiefly famous as an astronomer and geographer; and he left behind him a flourishing school of geography. Of this school was Francesco Berlinghieri, a member of Lorenzo de' Medici's circle, whose maps of France, Spain, Italy, and Palestine were the first modern maps to be printed, and thus mark an epoch in cartography. The story that Toscanelli encouraged Columbus to proceed upon that momentous voyage from the East to the West which had so profound an influence upon modern thought is now regarded as of doubtful authenticity. Italy also furnished eminent explorers in Ca da Mosto, John Cabot, Amerigo Vespucci, and Giovanni Verrazzano. In pure mathematics the most eminent Italian was Luca Pacioli, one of Leonardo's few intimate friends, whose mathematical treatise, the first ever printed, appeared in 1494, forty years before that of Regiomontanus. The study of anatomy also began to revive in the last decade of the fifteenth century. Marc' Antonio dalla Torre, another friend of Leonardo, though he was only twenty-nine when he died in 1511, was regarded as the greatest anatomist of his day, and Giacomo Berengario of Carpi, who was professor of surgery at Bologna from 1502 to 1527, had also a high reputation as an anatomist. This scientific spirit, whether it manifested itself in actual discovery, of which as yet there was very little, or in the advance of art as the result of observation and experiment, or in the historical criticism of a Valla or a Flavio Biondo, is a side of the Renaissance which must not be left out of account. For it is the fruit of that freedom of thought, of that questioning of tradition and authority in the light of personal experience, which justifies us in defining the Renaissance as the transition from the medieval to the modern world.

The spirit of free inquiry naturally made itself felt also in the domain of religion. But at the close of the fifteenth century rationalism was neither widespread nor aggressive. Its centre was the University of Padua, where, in opposition to the Platonists of the Florentine Academy, the professors of philosophy studied Aristotle—but with the exception of Ermolao Barbaro (1454–93), who was an orthodox Catholic—on heterodox lines and with special attention to one topic, the nature of the soul. The majority, with Alessandro Achillini (1463–1512) at their head, adhered to the old pantheistic teaching of Averroes. On the other hand, Pietro Pomponazzi (1462–152?), who championed the materialistic views of Aristotle's commentator, Alexander of Aphrodisias (c. 200), had great influence both in Italy and later in France and is regarded as the father of modern rationalism. But his chief work, the *De immortalitate animae*, did not appear till 1516, well beyond the limits of this survey.

We must now go back fifty years and trace the first beginnings of the Renaissance in the countries on this side of the Alps.

In France, Charles V and his brothers, with their munificent patronage of art and learning, their many palaces, their libraries, their collections of gems and precious stones and tapestries, were like Renaissance princes, and their courts at the close of the fourteenth century vied with those of Italy in splendour and extravagance. Charles V himself was a real lover of learning, and his library, which numbered about 1100 volumes, reflected his tastes. It contained Latin versions of the *Timaeus* and of the principal works of Aristotle, nearly the whole of Seneca's prose works, Ovid's *Heroides, Tristia, Epistolae*, and *Ex Ponto*, Lucan, and Frontinus. There were also French translations of Aristotle, Seneca, and Ovid. Charles, like his father, John the Good, took a keen interest in the work of translating ancient authors. In particular he employed Nicole Oresme to produce French versions through the Latin of Aristotle's *Ethics, Politics, Economics, De caelo*, and *De mundo*.

The Duke of Berry cared more for art than for learning. About half of his three hundred manuscripts were richly illuminated by the best artists of the day. Among them were a Terence, Virgil's *Eclogues*, and a book of Pliny, all authors unrepresented in the royal collection. He had even a Greek book, but as to its author or its contents his cataloguer is silent. In the next generation the same munificence and the same patronage of art was shewn by Charles' younger son Louis, Duke of Orleans, who married Valentine Visconti, the daughter of Gian Galeazzo.

There were also at this time a few real students of classical literature, chief among them being the three distinguished *alumni* of the College of Navarre, Pierre d'Ailly, Nicolas de Clamanges, and Jean Gerson. As a precursor of the Renaissance the more important of the three is Nicolas de Clamanges, for he was the initiator of a French humanist movement independent of Italy. He possessed a complete Quintilian, discovered in France twenty years before Poggio's discovery at St Gall; he knew many of Cicero's speeches, which he may have found in the monastery at Cluny; and he had certainly explored the library at Langres and the various libraries at Paris. In a letter to an Italian friend he says: "I have lectured on Tully's *Rhetoric* in the Paris University, and sometimes on Aristotle, and there are often lectures on those great poets Virgil and Terence." His correspondence reveals a fairly wide knowledge of Latin classical literature, including so rare an author as Tibullus.

But like Pierre d'Ailly and Gerson he was in the first place a theologian; indeed during the latter part of his life he gave himself up entirely to the study of theology. On the other hand his friend Jean de Monstereul, though in Orders, was a humanist pure and simple, who got his humanism from Italy. He was a great admirer of Petrarch and Salutati, and his enthusiasm for Virgil and Cicero was doubtless inspired by their writings. He had an almost equal enthusiasm for Terence, but there are few Latin authors with whom his letters do not shew some acquaintance. He was also a successful searcher after manuscripts, many of his finds coming from Cluny. He introduced into France Plautus (eight comedies), Cato *De agri cultura*, Varro *De re rustica*, and Vitruvius, and he knew the *Bellum civile*, which was unknown in Italy, and fragments of Petronius. In 1412 he was sent on a mission to Rome, where he made friends with Leonardo Bruni. Six years later he perished in the massacres of the Armagnacs by the Burgundians at Paris, and the movement which he represented withered away under the anarchy, disunion, and foreign conquest which harried France for the next thirty years. Even when the kingdom began to recover from its wounds, humanism was slow to make a fresh beginning. In 1458, indeed, the distinguished Italian humanist, Gregorius Tifernas, was appointed professor of Greek in the University of Paris, but he only held his professorship for a year and a half.

Louis XI did much to promote intercourse between France and Italy by diplomatic missions, and the men whom he chose for his work were generally sympathetic towards humanism. Indeed, one of these, Jean Jouffroy, Bishop of Albi, who had lectured on canon law at Pavia for three years and in later life had resided in Italy, was fairly well read in Latin literature and had some knowledge through Latin translations of Greek authors.

But the chief event, from the point of view of humanism, of the reign of Louis XI was the introduction of printing into France. In 1470 Guillaume Fichet, a native of Savoy, and Johann Heynlin, a German, both doctors of the Sorbonne, induced three Germans, Michael Friburger, Ulrich Gering, and Martin Krantz, to set up a press within the precincts of the Sorbonne. Both Fichet and Heynlin were zealous humanists and with few exceptions the books printed by the new press were of a humanistic character. The first was the *Epistolarum opus* of Gasparino Barzizza, and among the twenty-one other works were eight editions of Latin classical authors. But before the end of 1472 Fichet went to Italy with his friend Cardinal Bessarion, and at the beginning of 1478 Friburger and Krantz also left France. For the next sixteen years the books printed at Paris entirely lost their humanistic character. Romances, devotional works, and the text-books of the old learning entirely took the place of Latin classics and treatises on rhetoric.

Meanwhile Robert Gaguin, General of the Trinitarians, who had attended the lectures of Gregorius Tifernas, carried on as best he could the work which his friend Fichet had laid down. He himself lectured on Latin rhetoric at the Sorbonne, and Guillaume Tardif, a native of Le Puy, gave lectures on the same subject at the College of Navarre. From 1476 to 1478 Filippo Beroaldo of Bologna, a scholar of wide learning, also lectured at Paris, and in 1476 there arrived a native of Greece, George Hermonymos, who, though an incompetent teacher, did good service as a copyist of Greek manuscripts. He remained at Paris till at least as late as 1508. Rather later arrivals were the two Italians, Girolamo Balbi and

Fausto Andrelini, men of second-rate ability and third-rate character, but who by virtue of a certain facility in the writing of Latin verse and prose became highly popular as lecturers and were regarded by their uncritical audiences as miracles of learning. In the memorable year 1494 in which Charles VIII crossed the Alps humanism in France had not reached beyond the stage of Latin rhetoric, a stage which Italy had reached just a hundred years earlier.

Considering the short time—less than fourteen months—that Charles VIII spent in Italy, it may be thought that historians have exaggerated the importance of the journey to Naples. But if Charles and his nobles had no time, except at Naples, for more than hurried glances, certain features of the Italian Renaissance seem to have strongly impressed them, particularly the spacious palaces, the well planned gardens, and the beautiful sepulchral monuments. They noted too the growing fashion for portraiture. Moreover, if the majority were rude soldiers of little or no culture, there were a few who shewed their appreciation by trying to reproduce what they saw in their own country. Charles himself in his unbalanced fashion had a genuine love of art and literature, and he gave practical help to the introduction of the Italian Renaissance into France by establishing at Amboise a small colony of twenty-one Italian artists and workmen. Among their number was the distinguished architect, Fra Giocondo of Verona, and a younger architect, Domenico of Cortona, surnamed Il Boccadoro, who had been a pupil of Giuliano da San Gallo. Sculpture was represented by Guido Mazzoni of Modena, called Il Paganino, whose crudely realistic *Entombment* at Naples with contemporary portraits had made a great impression on the French king, and by Girolamo Pachiarotti, who did much excellent work as a decorator.

France possessed a great national tradition in architecture and her master-masons were men of much skill and long experience. The Italian influence was, therefore, naturally slow in making itself felt. Though the château of Amboise has suffered so much from successive demolitions and alterations that it is difficult to make out its history, it is clear that it owed little to Italy—practically nothing but the great spiral staircases of the two towers, which were made with so gentle an incline that a horse could be ridden up them, and the ornamentation of the pendants of the vault in the southern tower. We have even less knowledge about the château of Le Verger, which Pierre de Rohan, Maréchal de Gié, began to build in 1495 on the site of a former building. The château itself has been totally destroyed, but it appears from some seventeenth-century engravings that the only Renaissance features were the general symmetry of the plan and the symmetrical arrangement of the windows in one of the blocks. Of Mazzoni's activity in France before 1500 there is no record, and with two or three exceptions no Italian sculptor who executed commissions in France before the death of Louis XII seems to have been allowed a free hand. France, indeed, possessed in Michel Colombe a veteran sculptor of high merit who was decidedly superior to Mazzoni and the other Italians in France in both conception and execution.

There were no painters in the Italian colony at Amboise, and the only foreign influence to which at this time French painting was subject was Flemish. The only work of art of the period—its date cannot be later than 1503—which clearly reveals in the idealism of its treatment and the forethought of its design the inspiration of the Italian Renaissance is a triptych of the Virgin in Glory in the sacristy of Moulins Cathedral. The painter is unknown, but he is provisionally called the Maître de Moulins and on the evidence of style eight other pictures have been ascribed to him. Only one of these, however, the portrait of a young girl from eight to ten—presumably Suzanne de Bourbon—has any look of the Renaissance.

We may now return to humanism, and here we find that in the six years which elapsed between 1495 and 1501 some progress was made. In 1495 Robert Gaguin, who, as we have seen, was the leader of the humanistic movement at Paris and whose high reputation as a diplomatist and man of affairs was of great value to the movement, produced, under the title of *De origine et gestis Francorum Compendium*, a history of his country, in which the style, however defective, was at any rate modelled upon the chief writers of Latin prose. Among his fellow-workers in the cause of humanism were Charles Fernand and his brother Jean and Pierre de Bur or Bury, a writer of Latin verse, whom his friends proclaimed to be almost the equal of Horace. All three were natives of Bruges. Guy Jouennaux, better known as Guido Juvenalis, was born at Le Mans; his commentary on Terence and his abridgement of Valla's *Elegantiae* were favourite text-books in the French universities.

From 1494 onwards a change in the direction of humanism began to take place in the productions of the Paris press. Many of the chief Latin classical authors were printed in whole or in part, Virgil being by far the most popular; and grammars and aids to Latin composition by Italian humanists began to supersede the time-honoured Donatus, *Doctrinale*, and *Grecismus*. This latter reform was chiefly the work of a Fleming, Josse Badius Ascensius of Ghent (1461 or 1462–1535), who had studied first in the school of the Brethren of the Common Life at Ghent, then at Louvain, and finally in Italy, where he had learnt Greek at Ferrara from the younger Guarino. In 1492, after holding a professorship at Valence, he migrated to Lyons and early in 1499 settled permanently in Paris, where he acted as general adviser to Jean Petit, the leading publisher and bookseller of that city, prior to setting up a press of his own. Before leaving Lyons he had edited various classical authors with notes for the use of young students, and this work he continued at Paris. With regard to grammars he proceeded in a conservative spirit, contenting himself for a time with preparing a revised edition of the popular *Doctrinale*. The first Italian text-book on the art of writing Latin to be printed at Paris, where it soon became popular, was Dati's *Elegantiolae*, and students were encouraged to read the collected letters of distinguished Italian humanists. Badius edited such a collection, made by Politian, in 1499.

Other universities besides Paris gave the new studies a more or less favourable reception. Chief among these was Orleans, where Reuchlin was a law-student from 1478 to 1480 and gave lessons in Greek and Hebrew. At Poitiers, during the last five years of the fifteenth century, several books of a humanistic character were printed, and at Caen, where there was a close connexion between the printing and bookselling trades and the university, a beginning was made. Lyons, which came nearest to Paris in intellectual activity, had no university, but it had a college at which Badius was professor of Latin from 1492 to 1499. Moreover, Trechsel's press, which was under his management, and other presses in that city issued editions of a few selected Latin classical authors, chiefly for educational purposes.

But up till now humanism in France was almost confined to rhetoric, that is to say, to the reading of Latin authors and the practice of composition in Latin verse and prose. The entry, therefore, of Janus Lascaris (*c.* 1445–1535?), a Greek who was also a thoroughly competent Greek scholar, into the service of Charles VIII towards the close of 1496 was an event of first-rate importance. His preoccupation with public affairs prevented him from giving regular instruction, but he was always willing to help serious students. Such a student was Guillaume Budé (1468–1540), who had begun his Greek studies about the year 1494, and who with some valuable help from Lascaris made such progress that the fame of his learning reached the ears of Charles VIII. By 1505 he had translated four treatises of Plutarch into Latin.

Unlike Budé, Jacques Lefèvre of Étaples in Picardy (*c.* 1455–1536) never became a great Greek scholar, but he earned the right to be called the *doyen* of French humanists, as he was the *doyen* of French Reformers, by his successful reform of the study of Aristotle in the university. He effected this partly by introducing into France the new translations made by Italian humanists, and partly by writing greatly improved text-books.

In 1495, the greatest man of the Northern Renaissance, Erasmus (1467–1536), began his connexion with Paris, residing there almost continuously till May 1499, and again from February 1500 to May 1501. But when he arrived he was an unknown student, nor during his first residence at Paris does he seem to have taken much part in its humanistic life. It was not till his return in 1500 that he applied himself seriously to the study of Greek, and published at Paris the first edition of his *Adagia*. His real influence on French humanism is of later date, but it was all the more powerful because it fell upon congenial soil. His sense of the importance of education, his appreciation of the moral seriousness of the best pagan literature, and generally his conception of the new learning as an instrument of life, found a ready response from the Paris humanists. Gaguin and his friends, of whom the majority were ecclesiastics, were seriously minded men. They led exemplary lives; they were good citizens and true Christians. They were also thoroughly convinced of the need for reform in the Church, and, when Lefèvre of Étaples, who devoted himself more and more to theological studies, initiated a conservative movement in the direction of reform, it was only natural that his evangelical teaching should at first find a warm welcome with the great majority of his fellow-humanists.

If in the last five years of the fifteenth century humanism made a distinct, though slow, progress in France, literature remained stagnant. It was something perhaps that Octavien de Saint-Gelais (*c*. 1465–1502), Bishop of Angoulême, the author of a long allegorical poem, *Le séjour d'honneur*, should make verse translations of the *Heroides* and the *Aeneid* and so introduce them to a larger circle of readers, but the style of his work was far too humdrum to give any idea of the classical spirit. The only French writer before Marot who came under the influence of the Renaissance was Jean Lemaire de Belges (1472 or 1473–*c*. 1515?), and his first work of any importance was not published till 1504.

The Renaissance in the southern provinces of the Netherlands developed on similar lines to the Renaissance in France and more or less looked to Paris as its centre. Robert Gaguin and Josse Badius were Flemings by birth. Charles Fernand of Bruges (*c*. 1460–1517) and his brother Jean (alive in 1494) were professors in the Paris University, and Pierre de Bur (1430–1504), also of Bruges, who had spent seven years in Italy, was a canon of Amiens and resided chiefly in Paris. Arnold Bost (1450–99), however, who was a man of wide learning as well as a Latin scholar, remained in his Carmelite monastery at Ghent, from which he corresponded with humanists of all nations. The two Flemish cities in which printing was the most active were Antwerp and Louvain, but at Antwerp Gerard Leeu (1454–93) out of over 130 books only produced two classics, a Persius and a Seneca. At Louvain John of Westphalia (1474–96) has to his credit a Virgil, an Ovid, a Cicero, a Seneca, and a Quintilian. He also printed Dati's *Elegantiolae*, while another Louvain printer produced an edition of Perotti's Latin grammar.

In the northern provinces of Holland, on the other hand, there was a close connexion with Germany, and Deventer, where Geart (Gerard) Groote (1340–84) established a community of clerks, who came to be known as the Brethren of the Common Life, may be regarded as the common cradle of humanism for both countries. The schools in which the Brethren taught, and which spread rapidly through Holland and Germany, combined the study of the Latin classics with that of the Bible. But their attitude towards their authors was purely medieval, and not till 1483, when Alexander Hegius (1433–98), of Heck in Westphalia, became headmaster of Deventer, can humanism be said to have penetrated their schools.

But before we come to Hegius we must go back to a man, who, according to a widely accepted tradition, received his early education at Deventer, and who is the greatest name, before Erasmus, of the Northern Renaissance. This was Nicholas of Cues (1400 or 1401–64), a small village on the Moselle, later known as the Cardinal of Cusa. Much of his great and various activity lies outside our province. With the champion of the conciliar movement, who afterwards became the strong supporter of Pope Eugenius IV, with the philosopher who wrote the *De docta ignorantia*, with the mystic who wrote the *De Visione Dei*, we have nothing to do. But Nicholas claims our attention as a humanist who had very few predecessors in Europe north of the Alps. After a year and a half at Heidelberg he studied law—chiefly canon law—for six years at Padua and received there his doctorate (1423). Then he visited Rome, studied theology at Cologne, and became secretary to Cardinal Orsini—a step which brought him into close relations with the Italian humanists. His famous discovery of twelve new plays of Plautus in 1429 has been related in the previous volume, but he was always a diligent searcher after manuscripts and during his embassy to Constantinople in 1436 he collected many Greek ones. Most of these latter were dispersed, but his library, which he left to the hospital founded by him at Cues, was a considerable one and in spite of many losses is still represented by about 270 volumes. Conspicuous among them are translations, made by the Italian humanists of his day, of the Greek philosophers, historians, and patristic writers. Nor was Nicholas only a humanist. He was keenly interested in various branches of science. Like his friend Toscanelli, whose acquaintance he made at Padua, he was a geographer and an astronomer; he made the first map of Central Europe, and in his belief in the earth's motion he was a forerunner of Copernicus. He wrote several treatises on mathematics and a remarkable dialogue on statics, to which Leonardo da Vinci, who was one of his chief admirers, owed not a little.

We may now return to Hegius. He was a born teacher and he had already had a long experience in teaching, first at Wesel and then at Emmerich, when he came to Deventer, in 1483, and breathed into the old studies the new spirit of humanism. His reforms are closely reflected in the productions of the Deventer press, which, established in 1477, shewed at this time in the hands of its two printers, R. Paffroed and J. de Breda, the same remarkable activity as the Deventer copyists who had preceded it. Educational texts of a humanistic tendency—Virgil's *Eclogues*, Horace's *Ars Poetica*, Cicero's *De Senectute* and *De Amicitia*, Baptista Mantuanus, Dati's *Elegantiolae*, Filelfo's Latin letters—were produced in increasing numbers. Greek, too, which Hegius, when past forty, had learnt at Emmerich from Agricola, became a regular part of the teaching, at least in the highest forms.

Among Hegius' pupils, who before his death numbered 2200, were many who became men of mark. The greatest was Erasmus, but there was also Hermann von dem Busch (1468–1534) of Minden, who wrote Latin verse and commentaries on the Latin poets.

Deventer's nearest rival, hardly less flourishing, was Zwolle. Among its students was Johann Wessel (1419 or 1420–1489) of Groningen, known as "The Light of the World," who, after three years at Cologne, where he managed to learn Greek and Hebrew, studied theology at Paris. About 1475 he returned to his northern home, where, except for a brief interval of lecturing at Heidelberg, he lived for the remainder of his days, dividing his time between a house of nuns at Groningen, of which he was head, and the monastery of Mount St Agnes. But he also paid frequent visits to the Cistercian abbey of Adwert near Groningen, which became a centre for the meeting of scholars. Here he met Hegius and Rudolf von Langen (1438–1519), whose knowledge of Latin, when he was sent on a mission to Rome, won the admiration of Sixtus IV, and who established a school at Münster which rivalled those at Deventer and Zwolle, and, greatest of all, Rudolf Agricola (1444–85).

Agricola wrote little, but he made a profound impression upon his contemporaries. He impressed them by his splendid personality, his eager pursuit and rapid mastery of learning, his artistic gifts—he was an accomplished musician and a skilled draughtsman—and his athletic prowess. More than any northerner he answered to the Italian conception of an *uomo universale*. Born in a village twelve miles north of Groningen, he studied in turn at Erfurt, Louvain, and Cologne, wasting (as he puts it) six years over scholastic philosophy in the last-named university. Then followed a fruitful residence of ten or eleven years in Italy, during which he studied law and rhetoric at Pavia and Greek under Theodore Gaza at Ferrara. In 1479 he returned to his home and for four years held a post under the municipal council of Groningen, a post which involved employment on various official missions. Then in 1484 he accepted an invitation from the Bishop of Worms, Johann von Dalberg (1445–1503), who had been his pupil at Pavia, to become a member of his household and to give such teaching as he pleased at Heidelberg. A year later he died in the bishop's arms.

Johann von Dalberg, who was a man of learning as well as a patron of it, was Chancellor to Philip the Count Palatine, and it was largely owing to him and his master that Heidelberg became a centre of humanism. Even in the time of Frederick the Victorious a beginning had been made. In 1456, Peter Luder, a wandering "poet," who had studied in Italy, was engaged by Frederick to lecture on the Latin poets, but after struggling for four years with the "wild beasts" (as he calls them) of the university he moved to Erfurt, where he met with a much more favourable reception, thence to Leipzig and finally to Basle, where we last hear of him in 1474. Luder was followed at Heidelberg by Wimpheling, who lectured there from 1471 to 1483, Wessel (*c.* 1477), and, as we have seen, Agricola. Then, in the last decade of the century, came Celtes, Reuchlin, and, for a second time, Wimpheling. All three were of considerable importance in the history of German humanism.

Conrad Celtes (1459–1508), of Wipfeld on the Main, whose real name was Pickel, studied for seven years at Cologne, and then, having learnt some Greek from Agricola at Heidelberg, spent six months in Italy to improve his knowledge of that language. It does not appear that he ever became a really competent Greek scholar, but he was distinguished as a writer of Latin verse, and in 1487 Frederick III conferred on him the poet's crown at Nuremberg. From that time he devoted himself with untiring energy to the spread of humanism. He spent two years at Cracow, he visited Silesia, Bohemia, and Hungary, he founded humanistic societies in Hungary and Poland, and, returning to Heidelberg in 1491, founded "The Literary Society of the Rhine" with Mayence for its head-quarters and Dalberg for its president. Among its members were not only the Heidelberg humanists, Reuchlin and Wimpheling, but Trithe-mius, the Abbot of Sponheim, Peutinger of Augsburg, Pirkheimer of Nuremberg, and the distinguished jurist, Ulrich Zasius (1461–1536) of Freiburg. Celtes' stay at Heidelberg was a brief one. From 1494 to 1497 he held a professorship at Ingolstadt, and in the latter year, as will appear later, he was summoned to Vienna. Though he had no greater love of Italy than the other members of the Rhenish society, Celtes belonged to a type of humanist more common in Italy than in Germany. He was an assiduous writer of Latin verse, regarding himself as the German Horace, and both in his philosophy and in his life he was largely guided by semi-pagan ideas.

Johann Reuchlin (1455–1522), who came to Heidelberg in 1496, was a man of higher character and sounder learning. He had studied at Freiburg, Paris, and Basle, in which last university he learnt Greek from a Greek and took his Master's degree. From 1478 to 1480 he studied law and taught Greek and Hebrew at Orleans. In 1482 he became secretary to Eberhard I, Duke of Wurtemberg, who took him to Rome. After a second visit to Italy in 1490 and a third in 1498 he returned to Stuttgart, where he spent the next twenty years. His main interest was now in Hebrew, which he had studied in Italy, and it was as a Hebrew scholar that he was attacked by the obscurantists of his day. But this memorable struggle between the forces of conservatism and those of progress, between medieval theology and humanism, lies outside our limits.

Jakob Wimpheling (1450–1528), who was more theologian than humanist, is chiefly famous as an educational reformer. A native of Schlettstadt in Alsace, he received his early education in the famous school of his native town which Ludwig Dringenberg, a pupil of the Brethren of the Common Life, had recently reorganised with great success on humanistic lines. Having studied at Freiburg, Erfurt, and Heidelberg, he taught for twelve years in the last-named university. Then for fourteen years (1484–98) he held the post of Preacher in the cathedral of Spires. During his second visit to Heidelberg, he wrote his famous *Adolescentia* (1498–1501). For the rest of his long life he rang the changes between Basle, Freiburg, Heidelberg, Strasbourg, and his native Schlettstadt. Thus, except for a year's residence at Erfurt, he was never far from that Rhine which he loved as a symbol of the German nation.

The friendship between him and Johann of Trittenheim, or Trithemius, (1462–1516) began at Heidelberg, where the latter was studying Latin and Hebrew. In 1482 he entered the Benedictine abbey at Sponheim, near Kreuznach, and sixteen months later was elected abbot. Here he devoted himself to learning and to the welfare of his abbey, giving special attention to the library. In 1502 it numbered 1646 volumes and three years later 2000 volumes. It possessed works in many languages, ancient and modern. The Greek patristic writers were well represented by manuscripts; the printed books (purchased in Italy) included the *Iliad* and the *Odyssey*, Theocritus, Apollonius Rhodius, both of Theophrastus' works on Plants, and the *Theogony* ascribed to Hesiod. Trithemius was a voluminous writer; his *De scriptoribus ecclesiasticis* (1494), dedicated to Dalberg, is, in spite of inaccuracies, an important source of information for the early days of northern humanism, and his *Catalogus illustrium virorum Germaniae* (1495) has two prefaces, by himself and Wimpheling, which eloquently express their patriotism and their jealousy of Italy.

We have seen that Wimpheling after his second departure from Heidelberg spent some time at Basle and Strasbourg. Both were important centres of humanism. At Basle, which was a free city of the Empire till 1501, a university was founded in 1460, and almost from the first it had the advantage of the sage and enlightened guidance of Johann Heynlin of Stein (*c.* 1430–96), otherwise known as Johannes a Lapide. At once a schoolman and a humanist, he came to Basle from Paris in 1464, taught there for two years, returned to Paris, where, as we have seen, he helped Fichet to set up the press in the Sorbonne (1470), came back to Basle for four years (1474–78), and finally after ten years of wandering spent the rest of his life first at Basle itself and then in a neighbouring Carthusian monastery. Here he edited Latin Fathers, worked at Aristotle and Cicero, and continued to be the central figure of humanism in the university.

His most intimate friend was Sebastian Brant of Strasbourg (1458–1520), the famous author of *The Ship of Fools* (1494), who matriculated at Basle in 1475—the year after Reuchlin—and lectured there (latterly on law) from about 1480 to 1500. He was a pupil and friend of Heynlin, and he had in turn as a pupil Jakob Locher (1471–1528), surnamed Philomusus, who translated *The Ship of Fools* into Latin. Brant had some repute as a writer of Latin verse, but he was surpassed as a humanist by his pupil, who travelled in Italy, lectured at Freiburg and Ingolstadt, and edited the first German edition of Horace (1498).

In 1500 Brant left Basle to become clerk to the Council of his native city, Strasbourg. The appointment was made at the suggestion of the famous preacher, Johann Geiler of Kaisersberg (1445–1510), whose classical culture, patristic learning, and noble character not only made him the leading spirit in Strasbourg, but gave him a far-reaching influence.

From the Rhine we may pass eastward to the two greatest and wealth-iest of the free cities, Augsburg and Nuremberg, in each of which there was a highly cultivated society ready to welcome every manifestation of the new movement. At Augsburg the leader of the humanist circle was Conrad Peutinger (1465–1547), who in his early years had gone through a long course of study in Italy and who, returning to his native town after 1490, was employed by the Emperor Maximilian on various embassies, but found leisure to promote learning in many ways. He encouraged historical research, founded a library, and especially devoted himself to the collection of coins and inscriptions. The map of the roads of the Roman Empire, known as the *Tabula Peutingeriana*, was bequeathed to him for publication by its discoverer, Conrad Celtes.

Chief of all the free imperial cities, and a centre not only of European trade but of all that was best in German culture, was Nuremberg. Its first humanist of distinction was Hartmann Schedel (1440–1514), who, after seven years at Leipzig, where he profited by the lectures of Peter Luder, and three years in Italy, where he studied medicine and copied in-scriptions and the drawings of Ciriaco of Ancona, returned to his na-tive town in 1466. Five years later came Regiomontanus, attracted by the fame of Nuremberg's instrument-makers. He worked there till 1475. A later celebrity was Wilibald Pirkheimer (1470–1528), the friend of Dürer, whose house still stands in the Aegidien-Platz. He spent seven years in Italy and did not return to his native place till 1497, so that his chief activity as a humanist lies outside our limits. His wealth and his political experience gave him a wide influence and he formed an important library, partly of manuscripts, and partly of printed books which he had bought in Italy. Even its last relics, when they were finally dispersed by our Royal Society, contained such treasures as the Florence Homer and Greek Anthology, and the Aldine Aristotle, Aristophanes, and Euripides.

Nuremberg not only played a leading part in German humanism in the second half of the fifteenth century; it was also the capital of German art. But the churches, the domestic buildings, the sculptures, the wood-work, the metal-work, the stained glass, the painting, which form the glory of its golden age, were almost wholly medieval and national in their inspiration. In fact it was only towards the very close of our period that the great bronze-founder, Peter Vischer (1455–1529), and the great painter and engraver, Albert Dürer (1471–1528), began to shew in their work the influence of the Italian Renaissance.

The Emperor Maximilian, to whose versatile if superficial intellect the German Renaissance owed not a little, was a friend of Pirkheimer and

Peutinger and had close relations with both Augsburg and Nuremberg. But it is in connexion with Vienna and its university that he rendered the greatest assistance to humanism.

In 1450 the University of Vienna was one of the strongholds of scholasticism, but as early as 1454 the distinguished mathematician and astronomer, George von Peurbach (1423–61), who had spent three years in Italy and had lived in the house of the Cardinal of Cusa, began to lecture there on the Latin classics and continued his lectures for four years. In 1460 he was persuaded by Cardinal Bessarion to accompany him to Italy, where he died in the following year. The main object of his journey was the restoration with Bessarion's help—for he himself did not know Greek—of the text of Ptolemy's *Almagest*. His work was completed by his pupil, Johann Müller (1436–76) of Königsberg, near Coburg, better known as Regiomontanus. Like Peurbach he lectured at Vienna on Latin poetry, but he left that city soon after his master's death and spent seven years in Italy, perfecting himself in Greek and giving frequent lectures on astronomy and mathematics. At the height of his fame he settled, as we have seen, at Nuremberg and established there a flourishing school of mathematics and astronomy (1471–75). Among other activities he set up a printing press and printed the first edition of Manilius' *Astronomica*. In 1475 Sixtus IV made him Bishop of Ratisbon and summoned him to Rome to help in the reform of the Calendar. But in the following year (1476) he died of the plague at the early age of 40.

After the departure of Regiomontanus from Vienna only occasional lectures on Latin classical authors were given in the faculty of arts. The university had now fallen on evil days, and, when the Emperor Frederick III died (1493), the number of its teachers and students had greatly dwindled. Almost Maximilian's first act as Emperor was to reorganise his university and to divert it from scholasticism to humanism. In this work he was greatly helped by Celtes, whom, as we have seen, he summoned from Ingolstadt in 1497, but who had great difficulty in holding his ground against his scholastic opponents. It was in order to strengthen the humanist position that he transferred the headquarters of the Literary Society of the Danube from Buda to Vienna and that he instigated the Emperor to found the *Collegium poetarum et mathematicorum*. The latter, however, did not survive Celtes' death in 1508.

The University of Ingolstadt, founded in 1472, shewed from the first, under the impulsion of Lewis of Bavaria and his Chancellor, Martin Mair, a leaning towards humanism. But it was not till the advent of Celtes, first in 1492 as a private teacher, and then in 1494 as a regular professor, that the new studies began really to flourish. Celtes' successor was Jakob Locher (1498–1503).

On the whole the German university which in its corporate capacity has the best record before 1500 in the matter of humanism is Erfurt. Peter Luder and a Florentine who called himself Jacobus Publicius Rufus lectured there in the sixties, Celtes in 1486. Agricola and Rudolf von Langen matriculated there in 1456, Dalberg in 1468. But the humanist to whom it owed most was Conrad Muth, better known as Mutianus Rufus (1471–1526). A student from 1486 to 1492, and afterwards a lecturer, he left for Italy in 1495 and did not return to Germany till 1502. In the following year he was appointed to a canonry at Gotha, where he made his house the gathering-place of Erfurt humanists and exercised an influence far outside his old university. But of his wide learning and his peculiar and unorthodox religious views (founded largely upon Florentine Neo-Platonism), which however did not preclude a strong attachment to the Catholic Church, it is not the place to speak here. Under his inspiration humanism flourished at Erfurt for the next fourteen years. Yet when he returned to Germany there was a student at Erfurt who was destined to give a wholly new direction to German humanism. The student was Martin Luther.

In the growth of German humanism during the fifteenth century the German printing press played an insignificant part. A small percentage of classical texts, among which Cicero's ethical works, Seneca, and Horace greatly preponderated, Bruni's translations of Aristotle, and some epistles and orations by other Italian humanists, make up the sum of its contribution to the movement. A few printers in the Rhenish towns like Fust and Schoeffer at Mayence, Zel and one or two others at Cologne, and Mentelin at Strasbourg, made a brave beginning, but they gave up the attempt in 1470, deterred by the fierce competition of the two Venetian presses of Jenson and Wendelin of Spires. It was not till the last decade of the century that a fresh start was made, notably by Koberger of Nuremberg, the biggest printer and publisher of his time, who printed in 1492 a Virgil with Servius' *Commentary*, and by Grüninger of Strasbourg, who produced in 1498 the first German Horace, edited, as we have seen, by Jakob Locher. The Virgil can boast of a few sentences printed in Greek, but throughout the fifteenth century Greek type was so rare in Germany as to be practically non-existent.

In Hungary the great soldier, John Hunyadi, had sufficient sympathy with humanism for Poggio to write to him and to send him copies of his works. But the founder of classical studies in that country was John Vitéz (*ob.* 1472), Archbishop of Gran, who had continuous relations with the humanists of Florence and even persuaded some of them to visit his country. Moreover, through the agency of the Florentine bookseller, Vespasiano da Bisticci, who is eloquent in his praises, he formed an excellent library of Latin classical authors. He also promoted the study of Greek by sending young Hungarians at his expense to Italy. Among them was his nephew, Janus Pannonius (1434–72), who spent seven years in the house of Guarino at Ferrara and translated works of Demosthenes and Plutarch. He also acquired considerable fame as a writer of

Latin verse and had, like his uncle, whom he predeceased in the same year, a good library.

The work of these two was continued by Matthias Corvinus (1443–90), who by inviting Italian artists and scholars to his court contributed to the general spread of the Renaissance. His library at Buda, in which he certainly incorporated some of Vitéz' books and probably also those of Pannonius, had a great and not undeserved reputation. On the Latin side it included most of the recent discoveries, while the Greek collection, though only seven of its manuscripts can be identified, was regarded as important by his contemporaries.

Casimir IV of Poland (1447–92) is credited with some taste for art and literature. In 1473 he appointed the Italian historian, Filippo Callimacho Esperiente, as he called himself—his real family name was Buonaccorsi—tutor to his children and later made him his secretary. In this post Callimacho obtained considerable influence, and he continued in favour under Casimir's successor, John Albert (1492–1501), until his death at Cracow in 1496. Another contributor to the spread of the Renaissance spirit in Poland was Conrad Celtes, who, as we have seen, lectured at Cracow for two years between 1487 and 1491. From 1482 to 1500 the number of matriculations in the university nearly quadrupled. We also hear of Celtes' activity in Bohemia, but during the long reign of Vladislav II (1471–1511) there was little sign of intellectual progress in that country, and the decline of the University of Prague, which had thrown in its lot with the Utraquists, was not arrested till the beginning of the sixteenth century. No less backward were the Scandinavian countries. All that there is to record is that a university was founded at Upsala by the regent, Sten Sture, in 1477, and one at Copenhagen in the following year. Of the six books printed at Stockholm in the fifteenth century and the four printed at Copenhagen none were of a humanistic character.

The restorer of classical studies in Spain was Antonio de Nebrija (1444–1522), better known as Nebrissensis, who after ten years passed in Italy returned to his native country in 1473 and filled the chair of Latin successively at Seville, Salamanca, and Alcalá, touching and adorning a wide range of topics. His Spanish-Latin dictionary crowned his reputation as a scholar. In Greek scholarship he was surpassed by the Portuguese, Arias Barbosa (*ob.* 1530), who, like Nebrija, studied for many years in Italy, Politian being one of his teachers. In 1489 we find him at Salamanca, where he lectured on Greek for twenty years. Salamanca was at this time the leading university in Spain, but its fame was soon rivalled by that of Alcalá, founded in 1499. Here Cardinal Ximenes conceived and carried to a triumphant conclusion the idea of his great Polyglot Bible. Another university, Valencia, was founded in 1500.

In Spain as in other countries Italian humanists helped to spread the movement. Prominent among them was the well-known Peter Martyr,

who came to Spain in 1489 and found great favour with Isabella the
Catholic. She encouraged him to open schools in various towns for young
Catholic nobles and in 1492 had him appointed tutor to her son, Prince
John. She herself was a fair Latin scholar and the new learning had in
her a generous and enlightened patroness. Largely at her instance some
half-a-dozen translations of classical authors formed a feature of the scanty
contribution to humanism made by the Spanish press in the fifteenth
century. About as many original classical texts were printed; it is
curious to note that neither among these nor among the translations was
there anything of Terence or Cicero or Horace.

In Spain, as in France, Renaissance art was heralded by the substitution of Italian influence for Spanish. But neither in architecture nor
sculpture is there any Renaissance work by a native artist earlier than
1500. In painting, the work done at Avila by Pedro Berruguete·
from 1499 to his death in 1506 and a *Pietà* at Barcelona by Bartolomé
Vermejo, dated 1490, may be claimed as representing the transition.

Poggio's visit to England, where he spent three and a half years, from
the end of 1418 to the middle of 1422, in the service of Henry Beaufort,
Bishop of Winchester, was a grievous disappointment to him. It brought
neither preferment nor the discovery of fresh manuscripts. It has been
said that his search for the latter was neither long nor exhaustive. It is
true that in the larger libraries, such as Glastonbury, St Albans, Bury
St Edmunds, Peterborough, Durham, Norwich, St Paul's, and the two
libraries of Christ Church and St Augustine's at Canterbury, he could
have seen more than "a few volumes of ancient authors," but it is doubtful
whether he would have found any important classical work that was unknown in Italy.

He might have fared better if he had made the acquaintance of his
patron's nephew, Humphrey, Duke of Gloucester (1391–1447), who,
whatever his sins, must be regarded with gratitude as the restorer of
classical learning in this country. He brought about this revival mainly
by establishing relations between this country and Italy, where he became
well-known as a scholar and a patron of scholars. At his suggestion
Leonardo Bruni translated Aristotle's *Politics*, and Pier Candido Decembrio dedicated to him his translation of Plato's *Republic*. He also invited
Italian humanists to England, among them Tito Livio Frulovisi,
a schoolmaster at Venice and a writer of Latin comedies, whom he
made his "poet and orator," and who at his command wrote a Latin
life of Henry V. His library, which was considerable for his day,
bore witness to his humanistic tastes, and from it he made noble gifts,
129 volumes in 1435 and 1439, 17 in 1441, and 135 in 1444 (N.S.), to
the University of Oxford. Its fate after his death is not known, but it is
a fair conjecture that it passed into the hands of his nephew, Henry VI,
and that we have a record of part of it in the catalogue (made about 1452)

of the original library of Henry's college at Cambridge. But, except for about sixteen volumes, all these manuscripts have vanished, and only the inventories of them are left to tell their tale. Each collection contained an elementary Greek book and each a copy of Decembrio's translation of the *Republic*. Bruni's translation of the *Politics* went to Oxford, as did translations of a speech of Aeschines, of five of Plutarch's *Lives*, and of the *Cosmographia* of Ptolemaeus. The *Phaedrus* of Plato, formerly in the library of King's College, was doubtless the twelfth-century translation by Aristippus of Catania. Cicero was well represented in the gifts to Oxford, among his works being the recently discovered *Epistolae ad familiares*. The less common Latin authors included Apuleius, Varro's *De lingua latina*, and Vitruvius. A noteworthy feature of the Oxford books was seven works of Petrarch, five of Boccaccio, and the *Divina Commedia*.

Among Duke Humphrey's English *protégés* was Thomas Beckington (c. 1390–1465), who gave up his fellowship at New College to enter the duke's service. He rose to be king's secretary (1439) and Bishop of Bath and Wells (1443). His published correspondence shews that, as might be expected, he was a man of humanistic sympathies and that he cultivated relations with scholars who were closer in touch than himself with the centres of Italian humanism. His chief Italian correspondent was Flavio Biondo, proctor to Eugenius IV, who sent him a copy of his history of Italy. Among his English correspondents were Adam de Moleyns, Bishop of Chichester (*ob.* 1450), to whom Aeneas Sylvius wrote in 1444, praising his Latin style and dwelling on the debt which England owed to the Duke of Gloucester; and Andrew Holes (born *c.* 1395), Archdeacon of Wells and like Beckington a Wykehamist and a Fellow of New College, who, having been sent to Florence as envoy to Eugenius IV, remained in that city for a year and a half after the Pope's departure, consorting with the leading humanists and collecting so many manuscripts that they had to be sent to England by sea. He was a client of Vespasiano da Bisticci, who has commemorated him in one of his charming and vivid biographical sketches.

A closer friend of Beckington than any of these, though a much younger man, was Thomas Chaundler (*c.* 1418–90), Dean of Hereford, who from about 1460 to 1475 was the most prominent figure in Oxford. His Latin style, though diffuse and without individuality, is correct and elegant. He also knew some Greek, and when Warden of New College (1455–75) appointed an Italian humanist, Cornelio Vitelli, to a Prae-lectorship. Though Vitelli was of no distinction as a scholar, he was competent to teach the rudiments of Greek, and he seems to have lectured at Oxford till 1488, when we find him at Paris.

William Grey, Bishop of Ely (*ob.* 1478), and John Tiptoft, Earl of Worcester (1427?–70), both Oxford men and both clients of Vespasiano, were in a sense Duke Humphrey's successors. Grey seems to have resided in Italy from 1442, when he ceased to be Chancellor of Oxford, to 1454, when he was appointed to the see of Ely. After visiting Florence and Padua he settled at Ferrara to study Greek under Guarino. Thence he went to Rome as king's proctor. In all these cities he collected manuscripts, of which 152 are still in the possession of his college, Balliol. Among them are numerous occasional writings by the chief Italian humanists, Petrarch's *Letters* and *Secretum*, Bruni's translations of the *Ethics* and *Politics* and that of the *Timaeus* by Gregorius Tifernas, Lactantius, and the *Apology* of Tertullian. John Tiptoft, whose cruelties earned for him the title of the Butcher of England, was revered in Italy as a scholar and a patron. Like Grey, he visited the chief centres of humanism and spared no expense in collecting manuscripts. Unfortunately his collection, which he bequeathed to his university, never came into its possession. Another Balliol man who collected manuscripts and generally favoured the new studies was George Neville (*c.* 1433–76), brother of the king-maker, Chancellor of Oxford, Lord Chancellor, and Archbishop of York (1465). We owe to Dr James the discovery that he employed a Greek scribe, Emmanuel of Constantinople, to make copies for him of classical and other Greek manuscripts. Emmanuel was one of four Greeks who made their way to England soon after the fall of Constantinople, the well-known scholar, Johannes Argyropoulos, being among them. He was also employed by Bishop Waynflete and he has altogether nine, or possibly ten, manuscripts in this country to his credit. Some years later—between 1489 and 1500—we find another Greek of Constantinople, John Serbo-poulos, writing several Greek manuscripts at Reading Abbey.

The connexion between Balliol and Ferrara was kept up by John Free (*c.* 1430–65), who was sent to Italy at the expense of his patron, Bishop Grey, and by John Gunthorpe (*ob.* 1498). Both became good writers of Latin, and Free was even commissioned by some Italian friends to write an epitaph on Petrarch. He did not confine himself to classical learning, but studied law and medicine and taught the latter with such success that he acquired a large fortune. He accompanied Tiptoft to Rome, where the Pope formed so high an opinion of him that he appointed him to the see of Bath and Wells. But he died at Rome before consecration. John Gunthorpe, who held several ecclesiastical appointments, including the Deanery of Wells and the Wardenship of King's Hall at Cambridge, collected manuscripts, many of which he bequeathed to Jesus College, Cambridge; but all these except about ten, dispersed over various Cambridge libraries—only three are of a humanistic character—have disappeared. The most interesting is a literal prose translation of the *Odyssey*, which he bought at Westminster in 1475 for a mark. The smaller collection of 38 manuscripts, which Robert Flemming (*ob.* 1483) presented in 1465 to his college of Lincoln, of which his uncle Richard Flemming was the founder, has fared better, for it remains in its original home. It includes six volumes of Cicero, one of which contains the *Epistolae*

ad familiares, Traversari's translation of Diogenes Laertius, and two works
by Boccaccio. The same library also possesses a Greek manuscript of the
Acts of the Apostles, St Paul's Epistles, and the Catholic Epistles, which
Flemming gave the college shortly before his death. He was made Dean
of Lincoln in 1451, and, like his Balliol contemporaries, studied at Ferrara
under Guarino. After visiting other Italian universities he settled at Rome,
where he formed a friendship with Platina, the librarian of the Vatican.
He was appointed a protonotary to Sixtus IV and dedicated to him a
volume of Latin verse entitled *Lucubrationes Tiburtinae.*

Hitherto we have been concerned with collectors of manuscripts. John
Shirwood (1431 or 1432–93), of University College, afterwards Bishop
of Durham, whose first visit to Rome was made in 1474, seven years after
the introduction of printing into that city, collected printed books. His
Latin books were secured for the library of Corpus Christi College, Oxford
by its founder, Richard Fox, his successor in the see of Durham, and still
remain there. The more recent rediscoveries are represented by Statius'
Silvae (Rome, 1475), the twenty extant plays of Plautus (Venice, 1472)—
both *editiones principes*—Cicero's speeches (Rome, 1471) and his *De
Oratore.* Of Greek historians there are Polybius (five books) in Perotti's
translation (Rome, 1473), Dionysius of Halicarnassus in that of Lapo
Birago (Treviso, 1480), and Plutarch's *Lives* by various translators,
edited by Gianantonio Campano, the friend of Pius II, and beautifully
printed at Venice by Jenson in 1478. Landino's *Disputationes Camal-
dunenses,* Platina's *Lives of the Popes,* and Alberti's *De re aedificatoria*
stand for Italian humanism. Architecture is also represented by a copy
of Vitruvius. Shirwood had the reputation of being learned in Greek as
well as Latin, but whatever Greek books he bought in Italy must have
been manuscripts, and the only one that Dr Allen has been able to trace
is Theodore Gaza's Greek grammar, now in the University Library at
Cambridge. Shirwood made many visits to Rome from 1474 to 1487,
chiefly on matters of legal or diplomatic business. Thanks to his influential patron, Archbishop Neville, he held several ecclesiastical
benefices, including a golden stall in York Cathedral, and after his
patron's fall he was employed on various duties by Edward IV, Richard III,
and Henry VII.

Besides Shirwood there were other well-endowed ecclesiastics who
proved themselves good friends to the new studies—for example, the two
Bishops of Winchester, William of Waynflete (1395 ?–1486), Provost of
Eton and Lord Chancellor, who founded Magdalen College, Oxford in
1457, and Thomas Langton (*ob.* 1501), Fellow of Pembroke College,
Cambridge and Provost of Queen's College, Oxford; Thomas Millyng
(*ob.* 1492), Prior of Westminster, and afterwards Bishop of Hereford, who,
according to Leland, knew Greek; Richard Bere (*ob.* 1524), Abbot of
Glastonbury; and the three friends of Erasmus—William Warham
(*c.* 1450–1523) of Winchester and New College, who in 1504 became

Archbishop of Canterbury and Lord Chancellor; Christopher Urswyk (1448–1522), Henry VII's confessor, who held successively the posts of Warden of King's Hall, Cambridge, Dean of York, and Dean of Windsor; and St John Fisher (1459–1535), President of Queens' College, Cambridge, and Bishop of Rochester, who brought Erasmus to Cambridge.

All these men were employed at one time or another on diplomatic missions, of which one especially calls for notice. It was the mission sent to Rome in 1487 (N.S.) to offer Henry VII's obedience to the Pope. At its head was Bishop Millyng, and among its nine other members were Bishop Shirwood and William Tilley, Prior of Christ Church, Canterbury, who acted as "orator" and who was accompanied by a young Fellow of All Souls, named Thomas Linacre.

With Tilley and Linacre we enter on a new stage of the revival of learning in England. The earlier generation of Oxford humanists had been men of wealth and position. They had patronised scholars, both Italian and English; they had collected books and had given or bequeathed them to their colleges; some of them were men of scholarly attainments, and one or two had even known some Greek. But they were not teachers; they did not hand on the torch of learning. William Tilley (*ob.* 1494) of Selling (a village about six miles west of Canterbury) became a monk of Christ Church, Canterbury, about 1448. He was sent by his prior first to Canterbury Hall, Oxford, and then (in 1464) with a brother monk, William Hadley, to Italy, where he remained three years, learning Greek and collecting Greek and Latin manuscripts. In 1469 he again visited Italy, apparently on business connected with his monastery, and in 1472 he was elected prior. In 1490 he accompanied Bishop Fox on an embassy to Tours, and there made the acquaintance of Robert Gaguin, the leader of French humanism, who was one of the French plenipotentiaries. Like his predecessors, he collected manuscripts, but these alas! with few exceptions were destroyed by a fire just before the dissolution of the monasteries. He proved his Greek scholarship by translating a sermon of Chrysostom, and, greatest service of all, he introduced the regular teaching of Greek into his monastery.

His most distinguished pupil was Thomas Linacre (1460?–1524), a native of Canterbury, who, after continuing his studies at Canterbury Hall, became a Fellow of All Souls in 1484, and, as we have seen, accompanied Tilley to Rome in 1487. On his return journey he was left at Florence to sit at the feet of Politian and Chalcondylas. He remained twelve years in Italy, studying medicine and taking his M.D. at Padua (1496), and making friends at Venice with Aldus, the printer. For the latter he edited and translated Proclus *On the Sphere*—printed in 1499 in the *Astronomici veteres*—and he took part in the production of the great *editio princeps* of Aristotle (1495–98). In 1499 he returned to England, and about a year later was summoned to court and appointed tutor—at least nominally—to Prince Arthur. Another English

scholar who helped Aldus with his Aristotle was William Grocyn
(*c.* 1446–1519) of Winchester and New College. He became a Fellow of
the latter in 1467, when Thomas Chaundler was Warden, and he probably
learnt Greek from Vitelli. When he was over forty he joined Linacre at
Florence and remained in Italy till 1491. Then he returned to Oxford,
rented rooms in Exeter College, was appointed Divinity reader at
Magdalen, and lectured daily on Greek. In 1496 he was appointed to
the living of St Lawrence Jewry, and three years later took up his
residence in London.

Grocyn was an Aristotelian; his friend John Colet (*c.* 1467–1519)
studied Plato and Plotinus in Ficino's Latin translations. He too
travelled in Italy (1493–96) and learnt there the rudiments of Greek. On
his return he resided in Oxford, of which university he was an M.A. His
lectures on St Paul's Epistles, in which he dwelt on St Paul's character
and ethical teaching, attracted men of every standing in large numbers.
It was mainly owing to his influence that Erasmus, who found him at
Oxford in October 1499, took up the serious study of theology and made
it his business to free it from the fetters of medieval dialectic. In 1504
Colet was appointed Dean of St Paul's and joined his friends Grocyn and
Linacre in London. When Erasmus, who now, thanks to his studies at
Paris, had become a competent Greek scholar, paid his second visit to this
country (1505), he declared that "in London there are five or six men who
are sound scholars *(exacte docti)* in both languages." These would be
Grocyn, Linacre, William Latimer (*c.* 1460–1555), a former Fellow of All
Souls, who had just returned from Italy after a residence of six or seven
years, William Lily (*c.* 1468–1522), who was to become High Master of
St Paul's School, and probably Cuthbert Tunstall (1474–1559), the future
Bishop of Durham. Both the last two had studied in Italy before 1500.
Colet and Erasmus' other chief friend, St Thomas More (1477–1535), had
only a smattering of Greek.

All these men, except More, took Orders, and More had at one time a
strong desire to follow their example. All, without exception, were men
of high character and principles, and three—Grocyn, Latimer, and Colet
—were theologians as well as scholars. This will help us to realise that in
England as in France the Renaissance at the close of the fifteenth century
had a profoundly serious and ethical bias, which turned it in the direction
of theology and Church reform. But we must not be misled by Erasmus'
enthusiasm into forming an exaggerated estimate of English humanism.
In 1505 there may have been in this country five scholars who could not
be surpassed, even in Italy, but they were all busy men, occupied with
the work of their several professions. The teaching of Greek took no
firmer hold in London than at Oxford. When Erasmus came to lecture
at Cambridge, at the invitation of Fisher, in 1511, he chose for his
text-books two grammars, and he soon abandoned his lectures altogether.
When Richard Fox founded Corpus Christi at Oxford in 1516 with

the view to provide a complete humanist education, the new college was greeted with a storm of opposition. It was not till 1519, when Richard Croke of King's College was appointed Greek Reader in the University of Cambridge, that the teaching of Greek can be said to have been securely established in England.

Thus humanism in England during the fifteenth century was confined to a comparatively few individuals. Even after the introduction of printing students even more than in Germany had to depend on Italy for such books as they required. Terence and the *Grammar* of Sulpitius were the sole contribution of Wynkyn de Worde and Pynson to the new learning. No printer had enough Greek type to print a Greek quotation. No Greek book appeared till 1543.

We see from this account of the Renaissance in the countries on this side of the Alps that its positive results were practically limited to the field of Humanism. Here the advantage was with France, which was helped by having an effective centre of learning in Paris and two influential leaders in Fichet and Gaguin. But, as regards art, except for one or two doubtful instances, we can point to no work in France that can be claimed definitely for the Renaissance. But, as in other fields, the influence of Italy was making itself felt, and before long was to bear fruit that was not mere imitation, but in which native idiosyncracies and traditions found an adequate expression. In vernacular literature on this side of the Alps there was even less sign of the Renaissance than in art. Jean Lemaire de Belges, the earliest French writer who shews definite Renaissance characteristics, though he was twenty-seven in the year 1500, published no work of any importance till 1504. The memorable meeting between Boscan and Navagero at Granada which so deeply affected Spanish literature did not take place till 1526. In England Barclay and Skelton were both versed in classical literature and Skelton had an admiration for Cicero almost equal to Petrarch's, but the poetry of neither shews in the slightest degree any trace of classical influence. In Germany there was no Renaissance literature before the seventeenth century; in its place they had a great national work—Luther's Bible.

EPILOGUE

THE close of the Middle Ages has been placed by the general consent of historians at the end of the fifteenth century after Christ, with which the narrative portion of this concluding volume mainly deals. Although this date is arbitrary and conventional, and suggests a sudden transformation remote from reality, it is yet the fittest at which to make one of the artificial divisions between the great periods of history, for it was the eve of the religious disruption, the conscious rivalry of national States, the complete supremacy of the State within its boundaries, the enfranchisement of capitalism, the enlargement of the known world, the accompanying translation of commerce into its "oceanic" stage, the diffusion and amplification of learning, the awakening of critical induction and scientific investigation—those potent forces which were to be the mainsprings of the modern age. That the date, however, with all its importance, is artificial is shewn on the one hand by the slowness with which medieval conditions, ideas, and preoccupations faded from Europe after it, and on the other by the long period of preparation for change before it, in which the fifteenth century, perhaps, holds the most significant place.

With but few exceptions, indeed, and those mainly in Italy, the men of the fifteenth century by no means appeared to themselves the harbingers of revolution. They were so, not so much because they invented new things, as because they failed in maintaining and revivifying the old and resigned themselves discontentedly to their failure. They hardly recognised that, beside the ideals they accepted and betrayed, other instincts and motives were leading them towards fresh modes of thought, a fresh outlook on life, and a fresh direction of society. In reality, in the very attempt at defence and conservation the fifteenth century was full of marked changes, which undermined the social structure and the dominant ideas inherited from earlier times and fostered the development of younger conceptions which were to replace them.

First among the older ideals we may take that of the unity of Christendom derived from classical times, made for a moment a physical reality by Charlemagne, and brought to some degree of permanence and organisation by the spiritual autocracy of the Papacy. But the unity of Western Christendom had not only always been a shell for incessant feudal and local anarchy, it was rent more and more by the swelling force of national union and national aversions within it, and, more than all, had been weakened and deprived of its spiritual appeal by the cumbrous, unhealthy functioning and frequent corruption, both increasing with the years, of the ecclesiastical hierarchy on which it depended. The Great Schism made apparent to all men that the government and system of the Church were out of gear. The Councils were the conscientious endeavour of the piety of Europe to restore that system of unity, to reform and lead back to efficient working Papacy and hierarchy together. But the Councils strove to restore more than had ever existed, to give the unity achieved by papal autocracy what was in fact a new basis in a representative synod, and they forgot, as reformers forget, that the vices they attacked were due in large measure to natural human tendencies which were ingrained in the Church's system. The champions of unity at Constance and Basle entered on a duel with centralisation; those foes of autocracy attempted to stereotype thought and institutions in a partly bygone, partly imaginary mould. Themselves both conservative and revolutionary, they dreaded revolution.

Thus the Conciliar Movement hoped to keep the Pope, a permanent monarch, subject to an intermittent assembly of shifting, jarring individuals, to keep a bureaucracy while abolishing taxation, to prevent the diversion of uncoordinated local endowments from local needs to that maintenance of learning, eminence, and favouritism to which each single member owed his livelihood. The task was formidable from its inherent contradictions, and to them were added the incalculable influence of personality and the steady current of nationalism. The Council of Constance ended in separate national Concordats. Pope Martin V, strong in the prestige, the authority, and the organisation of his office, embedded in law and habit, naturally yielded no foot of defensible ground, and was also determined to fortify the Papacy, threatened in revenue and independence, by the secular rule of the Papal States which in law belonged to him. He bequeathed to his successors the stubborn retention of profitable abuses and the purely worldly policy of an Italian prince denuded of scruples. The Popes were aided not only by the inevitable dissensions of moderates and extremists, doctrinaires and self-seekers, in the Council of Basle, but also by the facts that the Conciliar Fathers were drawn from different nations, unsympathetic and often hostile to one another, and that national and State governments were at the same time playing for their own ends not for those of the universal Church. France and England were at grips in the Hundred Years' War; the German princes and the Spanish monarchs were all engrossed by problems of their lands. The mastery over the Church in their own dominions was their only real aim in matters ecclesiastical. That it was then impossible to segregate effective Church Reform from national self-assertion and policy was shewn by the extraordinary strength and theological innovation of the Hussite movement which broke the unity of the Church throughout the fifteenth century. In Hussitism the vivid national consciousness of the Czechs and their hatred of their German neighbours found their outlet and expression in religious revolution which practically broke with the idea of the Universal Church. It was a true transition, hybrid because transitional, from the medieval towards the modern age. Religion in this isolated territory of Bohemia behind the rampart of its mountains and its language became the badge of a nation; and in the shelter of the alliance novelty of thought, once the singularity of stray thinkers and scanty, surreptitious communities, could take firm root and grow.

To sum up, the fathers of Constance and Basle typify the failure to maintain and reinspire older conceptions which is one mark of the fifteenth century. Throughout they strove for fixity of doctrine, for ecumenic Christendom, and for co-operative government by discussion. Yet these things were then incompatibles. Only the papal autocracy had held the Catholic Church in some sort together. It was still a living force allied to the contemporary trend towards despotism. Conciliar government was growing steadily obsolete in secular life, and in the Church gave a field for the separatist, national impulse. Allied with monarchs, rigid against heresy, the Councils provided a stage for national dissidence, and yet— for they represented Western Christendom—naturally shunned the separatist thought of individuals which found its home in nationalism. They cut themselves off from the growing life their efforts nourished. Their failure to produce conservative reform was the prelude to later revolution. Small bands of fiery innovators were to be given their opportunity by the tepid inertia of the existing order.

It is something of a paradox to introduce here the increasing persecution of the Jews, which began and was in theory justified by the fact that they were the enemies of Christianity, an excrescence in Christian society. Yet hatred of the Jews had always largely been a racial hatred of aliens in manners and in laws, and it took on a more national complexion as the nations formed. Mere segregation, prescribed by the Church, and fanatical massacres were succeeded by systematic expulsion in the interests of national uniformity in the several States. Edward I drove the Jews from England in 1290, Philip the Fair from most of France in 1306, the German towns and nobles with more prolonged and terrible violence from Germany. Finally, Ferdinand and Isabella expelled the Jews from Spain in 1492 with the definite aim of national consolidation. It is significant that the persecuted race found refuge in the loosely constructed territories of Poland and the Ottoman Empire[1]. Thus what seemed to be an effort of the expiring unity of Christendom was really a symptom of a new exclusive force—nationality.

As the efforts of united Christendom came to open failure in the attempt at the reform and reorganisation of the Church, so did they in the latter Crusades, the defence of Europe against Asia and Islām. Those efforts were at times serious enough, yet they were always sporadic, partial, and halting. The Papacy made the Crusade against the Ottoman Turks a permanent policy, but among other policies and more heartfelt objects nearer home; it was only the superfluous energies of Western knights which were spent in the defeats of Nicopolis and Varna; even Hungary, Venice, and Genoa, whose vital interests were at stake, seldom

[1] See *supra*, Vol. vii, Chap. xxii, and Vol. viii, Chap. xv.

if ever flung their whole weight into the war; the pathetic fiasco of Pius II at Ancona was an emblem of the impotence of Europe in face of the common peril; and the fall of the Roman Empire of the East published the collapse of the Crusading ideal[1]. When the Catholic Kings unified Spain by the conquest of Granada from the Moors, it was the triumph of a nation, not of Christendom.

In the preceding volume of this history it has been seen that Western Europe, most especially France and England, in the fourteenth century reached the last stage of feudal monarchy as a political system. A centralised government by the king and his bureaucracy was superimposed on a class of feudal nobles great and small, who either as in France still retained in large measure their feudal franchises or as in England were no less powerful by reason of their armed retinues and their influence on the royal administration. Beside the nobles two other strata of society possessed political importance, the clergy held separate by their celibacy, their unique privileges, and their international organisation, and the bourgeoisie characterised by their trading vocation and their town-dwelling communities. By these classes of men and their rights, by the representative assemblies of them which met round the king for consent and counsel, and by the law or custom handed down from the past and inherent in each human society, the kingship was limited and controlled. Government might be monarchic, yet the king's powers were circumscribed and shared; he was fettered by hereditary or official counsellors, by local privileged potentates and corporations. Similarly, in Germany the Emperor was but the chief of the teeming members of the Empire, and the princes were themselves limited by the Estates of their subjects. The republican towns of Germany and Italy were ruled by an entangled federation of unequal gilds, like their less autonomous congeners elsewhere. Even in the Church the "parliamentary" collective conception of government had its place and was gaining ground for a time in the Conciliar Movement. Rule under law and by consent was the reigning belief and the partial practice, founded on rights descended from the feudal, contractual, decentralised past.

In the fifteenth century this intricate, motley system of co-operative, diversely federated government was brought to moral bankruptcy by its failure to meet the needs or redress the evils of the times as well as by its inability to adapt itself to the changing conditions of the society which had given it birth. Feudal armies failed to defend France from the English invasions; barons, clergy, and towns equally failed to present a united front or to pursue a consistent policy; the mere maintenance of order and security was beyond their capacity and even alien to their desires. In England feud and faction, greed and misgovernment ran riot in the Wars of the Roses. The over-mighty subjects failed to give either victory or peace or justice. Like the French States General the English

[1] Cf. *supra*, Vol. IV, especially Chaps. XVIII, XIX, and XXI.

Parliament had proved unequal to its own aims. The same failure in a more veiled form was to be seen in the lands of the Empire. The feudal constitution of Germany meant in practice unremitting private war amid princes and cities, and this disorder was equally or more apparent within the princes' territories and the self-governing towns themselves. Feudal jurisdiction seemed to mean anarchy and brigandage; town autonomy a simmering class-war. In North Italy, again, with the exception of Venice, republican government had meant the exploitation of one class by another and the furious short-sighted rivalry of wealthy families. These defects were not new, but in the new conditions of larger units and problems wider and more complex they were far less tolerable and more obstructive. A curious inability to make any real sacrifice of personal and family immediate advantage to secure the working and profit of the State jeopardised the existence of that system of contract, co-operation, and consent in both lands of the Empire.

Common to all Europe, almost, save England, was the depression of the peasants. As the *élan* of increasing population, the cultivation of waste lands, and the need of a greater food-supply died down after the Plague became a regular visitation in Europe, the ruling classes became more apt to reimpose or increase old exactions on their rustic dependants. The more rapid intellectual progress of the upper classes gave them a fresh advantage over the more primitive lower. The North Italian town-dwelling landlord knew, indeed, that it was bad business to make his terms too hard for his tenants—the *mezzadria* worked for content and stability—but he kept them in firm subjection. The northern noble was both harsher and more extortionate in his narrower feudal outlook. Thus, in Germany the fifteenth century is an age of peasant discontent and revolt[1]. It is an age of disillusion and deadlock, when the old ways seem void of hope and profit.

In these circumstances the growth of untrammelled monarchy almost everywhere met a public need, and was to find its consummation in the early modern age. In France especially the kingship stood forth as the saviour of the country from foreign conquest, as the centre of unity and the expression of nationality, which was now become in the Hundred Years' War acutely self-conscious and a deciding factor in history. The continual inter-communication between European communities made the smaller differences between allied districts seem less and the great divergences between distant countries more severing and alien. Monarchy was the only force which could compel order and give security,

---

[1] Cf. *supra*, Vol. VII, Chap. XXII and for special cases the chapters on Bohemia, France, Spain, etc. in the present volume. In Germany the depression of the peasants was the more salient because the country had not suffered the special depopulation and misery of the Hundred Years' War. In France, there was more need to induce the peasant to recultivate, and perhaps too, his case was less noticeable in the general distress.

which stood above the strife of classes and personal ambitions, which could foster internal and external expansion. A public opinion rapidly formed which lifted the king, in spite of individual defects and particular oppressions, into unchallenged supremacy. In Spain, and in a more tempered shape in England, the same irresistible process was seen. Nobles and local powers, after the heyday of their uncurbed development, seemed smitten with paralysis before the advance of the central kingship directed with resolution and consistent purpose. Even in Germany and Italy the same phenomenon was clear. If the Emperor had too long been the chief of a loose federation to take effective advantage of it, the greater princes were able to master their nobles and towns in their own lands. Territorialism was but a fractional kind of monarchy. In Italy, with Venice as the only important exception, class disunion and city rivalry had produced the despot; and even in the splintered Papal States there were signs that despotism would be provincial as in Lombardy, and not a mere form of a city-autonomy, now out-of-date in a more interconnected world.

The general appearance of the despot, exalted above all competing authorities, was made possible by the decay of the nobles in independent military power and, again especially in France, in material wealth. The feudal noble as such had become an amateur in war; his inefficiency was shewn at Agincourt; he was outclassed by the professional soldier, who was very usually himself under new conditions of discipline and whole-time training. Now the maintenance of even a small regular army was beyond the resources of a feudal estate for any length of time. Only the kings, who could draw from every kind of wealth over a large territory, could achieve this. Only they could amass the artillery, which besides its growing importance in the field could shatter the once secure strong-hold of the feudal castle and the fortified autonomous town. Only they could levy for long periods the large numbers of foot, pikemen and archers, who were indispensable in a campaign, and who could repel the wildest charge of feudal knights. Forethought, co-ordination, system, and routine, which the Middle Ages had slowly brought forth, were all available to the new resolute monarchy, not to the disunited feudal survival with its purblind counsels. Ability gravitated to the king's service with its wide sphere, its wide outlook, and its manifold activities. In France, too, feudal independence had been sapped by the impoverish-ment of the nobles. Its origins lay far back. The nobles were un-productive; chivalry was a costly and wasteful mode of life; the strenuous noble stocks were prolific. From the time of the later Crusades all save the wealthy and the eldest sons found it steadily harder to live the life of their class in feudal society. The king's service became more and more their chief resource. As his officials, his troopers, and his pensioners, provided with posts and Church benefices misemployed, they could gain an honourable livelihood. The devotion of the lesser nobles as a whole to their sovereign, fortified by chivalry and loyalty, became a characteristic of the fifteenth century.

It was a kind of apotheosis. The nobles for honour and support, the townsmen for wealth and safety, the peasants for protection to live and labour, all looked to the national or territorial ruler by right divine, the embodiment of law, of order, of justice, and ancient right. The very advance in individual initiative and freedom which was taking place as the sequel of organised civilisation made the older forms of group and class life not only inefficient for men's growing needs but also fetters to their action and self-help. The single master who gave them security and opportunity was himself the representative individual in the State. Under him the individual could move more freely. Thus the political ideals of Western Europe were being transformed in correspondence with contemporary practice. The concerted action of Christendom under the leadership of the visionary Empire and the spiritual Papacy, always since the latter thirteenth century at least more a sentiment than a reality, lost its appeal with the defeat of the Council of Basle and the fall of Constantinople. So did the ideal of a graded government partitioned down among a feudal and ecclesiastical hierarchy co-operating with their chiefs in matters of general concern. This, too, had been diseased or moribund in practice, as Pope and kings centralised their dominion, long before feudalist and prelate by their own behaviour seemed to make its pretensions hollow. With comparatively few exceptions the most respectable bishops appeared, not as guides to holiness, but as shrewd men of affairs administering an extortionate and rigidly technical business and legal system. Chivalry appeared to have become in like manner a matter of parade and convention cloaking reckless greed and callous brutality. The discredit was not wholly just, for the solid achievements of churchman and knight in the past had created a more civilised world by which their successors were judged. Ancient faults became more glaring with a higher standard more diffused. None the less there had been a degeneracy in morale, as the first enthusiasms died down, and men discovered that the mere machinery for improvement did not necessarily imply a renovation in human nature. They grasped at the untried remedy of national or territorial monarchy.

Another facet of the same process was apparent in the obsolescence of the feudal tie of homage and fealty. Time had been when this contractual bond had constituted the suzerain's principal hold on his feudal inferiors; it was by means of it and the rights it conferred that he had fortified and given reality to the infant and shadowy conception of sovereignty and the State. In the fifteenth century, become complicated, inconsistent, and artificial, it exercised less and less moral compulsion on the vassal conscience. But it was replaced by the yet stronger charm of the allegiance of the subject to his natural lord, the sovereign of the State. Herein the continuous study of the Roman Civil

Law produced its full effect. From the legal theorists and the lawyers in the king's service the belief in absolute monarchic power spread to the theologians and infiltrated into the general thought. The community no longer appeared as an association of grades and diverse functions but as a mass of individuals bound together in the State, whose concentrated powers resided in its head—"amat enim unitatem suprema potestas[1]." The Roman Law had partly shaped the history of the later Middle Ages by its direct influence, but that influence grew more potent as the times became more apt for the reception of its maxims and conceptions. When despotism was men's refuge, its doctrine of the omnicompetent State and the absolute monarch took effect. Even if in Germany the Reception of Roman Law in 1495 did not benefit the Emperor, it strengthened the territorial princes. Yet the fifteenth century is still preparatory; the older notions still lived and struggled; the new were not fully accepted for many years, and were never the one temporal creed of Christendom.

Something of the same bankruptcy of older ideals, the same changing of conditions, and the same emergence of new impulses which blindly created the revolutionary future was to be seen in the economic aspects of fifteenth-century society. Roughly speaking, the two preceding centuries had seen the growth of capitalism in long-distance trading and in large-scale manufacture for export. But that capitalism had had its chief home in a certain number of great towns situated on the main routes of traffic, and in those towns it was regimented in wealthy gilds which controlled to some extent the individual capitalist. Not only that: the local retail trade was organised in its own gilds, all on the lines of strict regulation and of restraint of undercutting competition. Among the employees of the rich manufacturers, too, the revolutionary movements in the Low Countries, Italy, and Germany tended to introduce similar gilds, which in their turn worked for regulation and protection from native employers and outside rivals. In short, trade, even in its most capitalistic form, was subject to the local group system rooted in the older towns and by consequence was fettered by the narrow local spirit of monopoly which did not transcend its town of origin. Trade was being choked by the multitude of restrictions imposed by concerted action. But a change was coming in conditions. As the stretch of territory under a single monarchical authority widened, as for instance in the Low Countries under the house of Burgundy, it became impossible for the towns and the classes within them to play the dog-in-the-manger to the country round them. While the Flemish towns saw their carefully regulated cloth manufacture dwindle, a new race of capitalists employed the villagers without restrictions or traditions, pliant to changes of demand and supply, and captured the European market. In like manner

[1] Cf. Louis xi, "To us alone belongs and is due the general government and administration of the realm" (*supra*, p. 294).

the new free port of Antwerp drew to itself the international merchant and banker by the liberty he had there, unhindered by meddling, local greed, to manage business sensitive to far-off and uncontrollable events. How much this freedom meant can be seen later even in the older Flemish towns, where certain industries prospered because they were new and had no gild. To sum up, the tide of individualism, in the shape of the single person or private firm, whether in the Netherlands, France[1], South Germany, or Italy, was more and more eluding and undermining the joint control of the group. This, too, meant a decline at least in old ideals: the theory of the "just price", according to which a fair reward apportioned to his status and need could be dealt out by authority in due shares to each who was concerned in the production; the condemnation of interest on moral grounds; the duty of maintaining a joint control of quality, of product, of work, and of play. But the loss was less than it seems. Minute, vexatious regulations, incessantly and hypocritically evaded, were after all a nuisance and a clog; in spite of the very real decay of scruple, honesty and fairness could and did survive. Individual responsibility in the wider world that fostered it was a dynamic, creative force; it supplied a public need, and in the long run submitted to the sway of a public conscience.

These changes were being effected not only by the growth of wider areas under a single monarch who could bring peace and loosen restrictions, but also by changes in the trade-routes and in the commercial centres along those trade-routes. No little of the prosperity of Nuremberg and the Swabian and Rhine towns was due to the disorder of France in the Hundred Years' War. That England in the fifteenth century increasingly exported rough cloth instead of wool helped in the decay of Ghent and Bruges. Similar causes were beginning to destroy the cloth-trade of Florence. In the middle of the century the decay of the Scanian herring fisheries and the development of those of the North Sea were diminishing the prosperity of the Hansa towns of the Baltic and enhancing that of Holland and the English eastern coasts. Large-scale industry, in fact, was becoming diffused over Europe amid political changes which steadily weakened the predominance of the old autonomous towns with their unyielding traditions. The Hansa were worsted in their long contest with the Duke of Burgundy, against whose wide lands their commercial boycott was inefficient. The subjection of the Teutonic Order to Poland depressed their Prussian allies; that of Novgorod to the Great Prince of Muscovy left them helpless in the Russian trade. They could no longer insist on their methods and monopoly. In like manner the advance of the Ottoman Turks was depriving Venice and Genoa of their central position in European commerce and of their eastern outlets. The fall of Constantinople meant the loss of the Black Sea trade and most of that of the

---

[1] *E.g.* Jacques Cœur.

Aegean. Only the route to Alexandria, whither the spices came from India, remained to enrich Venice, and this was costly and precarious. The diminution of the papal income from beyond the Alps after the Great Schism prevented the return of the Papacy to Rome from being a sufficient makeweight, and Italy was becoming merely the source of a few expensive luxuries, spices, armour, glass, and silk, while the volume of European trade was moving north. Even in the Mediterranean, unified France and Spain were too powerful rivals for the city States. The country States, too, secure in their wide home market, could deliberately exclude foreign imports which competed with their own productions, whereas the retaliatory protection instituted by the autonomous Italian towns was useless as a weapon and a miserable compensation for a once European trade. A rapid decline in the cloth-making firms was visible. North Italy was beginning to live on stored-up wealth, and her unrivalled skill in banking. It is no wonder that investment in land was becoming the fashion in Florence and Venice, and that Venice turned to territorial ambitions both for their own sake and to secure her route to Germany. Over all the West the star of the city State was paling before the formation and cultural advance of the country State with its varied and abundant resources.

By a fatal coincidence the westerly countries, too, were enlarging both their products and their enterprise. As the shifting of the herring fisheries stimulated Dutch and English shipping, so had the multiplication of Spanish flocks, a new source of wool, and their share of the Bay salt of the Loire mouth profited both Spain and the Low Countries. The Portuguese, already active by sea as far as England and Flanders, were turning to the exploration of the African coast. The art of ship-building was advancing by slow experience among the westerly nations on their varied ocean coasts rather than in the limited, monotonous Mediterranean. It was the learned Prince Henry the Navigator of Portugal, himself no seaman, who planned and directed the enterprise in the spirit of a crusader: so might the Muslims of Morocco be evaded and the distant, legendary heathen be converted, and even the fabulous Prester John and his Christians be reached in the East. Continual expeditions crept slowly along the North African coast line. The difficult navigation round Cape Bojador was accomplished in 1434, and the immediate objective, the heathen negro population in fertile lands round the River Senegal, within twenty years. The progress was slow, but the profits in the trade in gold and ivory and the swarms of negro slaves were great. It was still in the Middle Ages when in 1486 Bartholomew Dias rounded the Cape of Good Hope and opened the route, soon to be traversed, to India. With that discovery the Italian transit trade to the East, cumbrous, scanty, and costly, rapidly became insignificant. It was a discovery made in the open sea away from routine by a nation State under a despotic king. So, too, was the expedition of Columbus which intended, like the Portuguese, to reach the

Spice Islands, and in fact unveiled the New World. The "oceanic" period of commerce, thus begun, when the main route and centre of wealth were in the countries of the Atlantic coast, belongs to modern times, but that revolution, which reduced the Mediterranean and Italy to a side artery, had taken its first steps earlier with the formation of national kingdoms in the West and the restriction of papal authority and revenue in the fifteenth century.

When we turn to the intellectual preoccupations of men, apart from their social or economic activity, we find even more the evidence of the sterility and decay of those leading ideas which had once been so fecund. The whole fabric of scholastic thought seemed to be smitten by a secret sense of failure. It had aspired to formulate a system of the philosophic explanation of the universe, where reason should be the loyal ally of faith and revelation, and "justify the ways of God to men." Its purpose had been religious and even devotional, yet it rested on a conviction not only of man's potential capacity to understand the reality of the spiritual and material world but also that man had discovered the infallible recipe to achieve that understanding. Shred by shred by the fourteenth-century thinkers that certitude was stripped away from scholasticism. The "sons of Ockham," the "moderni," denied the possibility of proving by reason any part of the Christian verity, or even of metaphysical verity. They were Christians by an act of theological faith alone. The "antiqui," the realist opponents of the new nominalists, could only reply by a lifeless adherence to Aquinas, a petrified repetition on all essentials. This agnosticism, which so severely limited the province of reason and was answered inadequately, produced its slow disintegrating effects on a study which thus renounced its own goal. When nothing great could be proved, men spent themselves on verbal subtleties. It was good to know how to reason, it was the avenue to promotion in the universities and the clerical career; so there flourished the compendium, the explanation of former explanations, the barren exploitation of method and teaching of dexterity, the alleviated path to a degree. The names of "antiqui" and "moderni" became badges of factions in the universities, indeed of universities themselves, changing sides at the order of their sovereign, and now numerous and no longer international as Paris had been. When Nicholas of Cusa attempted a system of compromise and contradiction, he bound it together by the tenet of intuition of the incomprehensible, indescribable infinite. But this intuition, vouchsafed to the individual mystic, was hardly of service to a common effort of mankind to grasp a coherent scheme of things. The same paralysis of will rather than of thought seemed to strike the consideration of those single sensible impressions, which to the Ockhamists appeared to give some secure foot-hold. In induction from them, as some fourteenth-century thinkers saw[1],

---

[1] Such as Jean Buridan, Albert of Saxony, and Nicole Oresme.

lay the hope of advance, but the true "modernus," Cardinal d'Ailly, was "palsied with a doubt" here too: God might give the illusion of a sensible impression without the external object to make it. A preference for the arbitrary aspect of omnipotence—not alien to earthly despotism—grew stronger: it was open to God to make evil good and good evil.

It was, perhaps, a natural concomitant of this disbelief in the validity of reason that led to the more pronounced belief in the crude, age-long superstitions handed down among the masses from a prehistoric past. They had always been there; they were, indeed, allied to the belief in stellar influences, in the mysterious properties of stones and times, in charms and spells, which had been part of the matrix of infant science; they were fostered by the ignorant panic roused to fever by the Black Death; now they became prominent and, so to say, official. The "witchcraft delusion," with its accompanying horrors, was a not unnatural vagary of educated men to whom anything was possible because nothing was disprovable. The extremes of scepticism and credulity met in that circle.

Yet the decadence of the great edifice of thought raised by the Middle Ages helped to clear the way for a fresh advance unhindered by its pre-possessions of doctrine, aim, and method. The stress laid upon sensible experience by the Ockhamists not only anticipated a distant future, it also expressed the less conscious mental orientation of men who were not schoolmen. The home of this new direction of thought and interest lay in Italy. It took its start from the solid acquisitions in knowledge and culture of earlier times, but it was fired by the appetite for more and wider-based knowledge, for which an unexhausted source lay open in the writings of classical antiquity. One constant feature of medieval development had been a slow approximation, however partial, towards the cultural standard of the ancients. As men became more literate and civilised, they became more capable of appreciating the higher civilisation of the past. They progressively absorbed what they became fit to realise. In Italy, with its classic temper, this particular evolution grew speedier in the fourteenth century. Dante still regarded Virgil as a sage of the undifferentiated former time, not essentially strange to his own; just as his contemporaries looked on Aristotle. With Petrarch and Boccaccio, and far more with their successors, the Latin classics seemed the relics of a nobler age, a greater race of men. True knowledge, true insight, and instructed modes of thought were there, to be learnt and imitated by their devotees. The humanist enthusiasm was afoot. It was clear from their Latin oracles that the yet unknown Greek literature was the fount and the main current of this dimly descried sea. Virgil pointed the way to Homer. The disasters of the time themselves were auspicious, for the Byzantine Empire in its struggle for existence against the Ottoman Turks was painfully for the first half of the fifteenth century courting the West and ready to give what the Italians had grown to wish; and the Byzantines in the long ebb of their culture and in the antiquarian passion for their greater past were at last in real mental contact with the West, which had grown literate as they grew "medieval." The coming of Chrysoloras and his foundation of Greek studies in Italy marks an epoch.

It is not here in question to narrate the bitter war between humanists and scholastic theologians, the strife and the compromise between the classical and the ascetic ideals of life, the long survival of medieval traditions, the contest between the outworn subtleties of the Schools and the pretentious rival imaginings of the Italian Neo-Platonists. But it is essential to remark that the humanists were engaged in a fresh and fervid study of facts, a method of experience. They were exploring Latin and Greek as concrete languages, learning the arts of expression and taste from ancient masters, finding out what they had thought and felt, seeing the world through their eyes, replacing the monotonous web of an *a priori* metaphysic by a variegated display of life and nature. Here lay their achievement; they were discoverers and cartographers of new lands of intellectual wealth and inspiration. That their own first efforts at rivalry might be vapid in style and shallow in thought was of little account: by the close of the fifteenth century their successors, steeped in the classics, were creating thought solid and profound, literature that with exquisite or reckless touch ran through the gamut of life itself.

The humanistic movement, in fact, did eminently in its sphere of learning with revolutionary consequences what others tended to do with reluctant or blindfold steps. The appreciation of the multitudinous direct facts of the visible, audible world, the joy in this life, the absorbing interest in man in his concrete variety, in his passions and capacities, replaced exhausted schemes of the unseen, supersensible universe, of refinements of the theory of knowledge, which were ending in questioning its possibility. In a time of failure and disillusion it brought triumphant hope, a boundless employment of man's faculties with a boundless reward. The earth renewed "its winter weeds outworn." If it seems strange that a tribe of pedantic grammarians should so exalt themselves, it is to be remembered that the ancient authors they idolised covered the whole field of knowledge and literature and gave the outlook, the freedom of spirit, and the new programme the age was seeking.

It was only slowly that the new humanism spread beyond the Alps, although the inclination towards scientific knowledge was early obvious, but the practical invention which was to have so great an influence in the diffusion of both was made in Germany on the Rhine. Printing by movable type, following, it seems, on some obscure preludes in Holland, was made into a workable method of reproducing books by John Gutenberg at Mayence round about the year 1450. In some ten years, by him and his allies Fust, the necromancer Faust of the legend, and Schoeffer, the new art had been proved capable of rivalling manuscripts in its beauty and accuracy, and far surpassing them in prolificness and accessibility. Journeymen and pupils carried it rapidly over Germany, Italy, and France; it entered England with Caxton; by 1500 tens of thousands of editions of books had been published in Western Europe. The humanists had sought far and wide for the rare manuscripts of long neglected classic works. Now those works were multiplied beyond the risk of destruction or of seclusion in a few libraries. New works shared the fortune of the old. The extension of literacy and education had been one of the achievements of the Middle Ages, and this invention at their close not only immensely widened the reading public but allowed the rapid participation and secure possession of learning, literature, and thought. It made indestructible the gains amassed by the effort of seven hundred years.

The same zeal to know and admiration for the visible, multifarious world and man, its denizen, which were vocal in the humanists, inspired also the plastic and pictorial art of the Italian Renaissance. The Italians from Giotto onwards shared in the general advance in artistic technique which was being made all through the West, and in the fifteenth century they were discoverers in perspective, in anatomy, in psychologic insight. Whatever ideal or religious forms it took, at the foundation of this art lay the instinct for reality: to represent men in their fashion as they lived, the earth as the eye might see it, heaven and hell as the abodes of verifiable human emotion and desire. But the passion for the beauty of what the natural existing world presented them was no less strong; Italian *quattrocento* art is filled with the delight in life, and the conscious mastery of the skill to express it. In nothing was the classic nature, akin to humanism, of this mastery displayed more than in the native Italian aptitude for form and composition. The picture becomes a harmonious whole, not a mere collection of observations however exact, skilled, and poignant. Not only in the formal arrangement of what they chose to shew but in grading the spiritual significance, in the choice of emphasis in their representations, the Italians excelled. In this lucidity in the world of fact, unhampered by metaphysical questioning, in the will to grasp and control it for human exploitation, they knew themselves like the ancients whose civilisation they emulated. There was an element of classical revival and imitation in their work which grew with the years and acted for long, though not permanently, as an inspiration and not a chilling fetter. For their art, like humanism, was home-grown and a true development from the later Middle Ages.

But if we can only speak of the fifteenth-century Renaissance in respect of Italian art, the essential realism, the sense of the individual, external fact, from which it grew, was rife in Europe, and so was the technical proficiency which was its condition. The portraiture, the scenes of devotion or homely life, the exquisiteness in minute, exact detail of the Flemings give the elements of the new mentality without their fusion in a new artistic creed. In architecture the builders seem to disguise the monotony of purpose they habitually revere, in the English perpendicular by the multitudinous, gorgeous incidents of the stained windows, in French flamboyant by the inexhaustible wealth of tracery and fretted stone. The decoration drew more interest than the design. Strong and full of vitality as the art remained, virtuosity in detail appealed most to its practitioners and accorded with the temper of the age. Romanesque and then Gothic art in its prime had revealed its structure, its details had a confessed architectural purpose; just as the design of its churches responded to doctrinal, ceremonial, or social needs—we see the uplifted presbytery of the Hildebrandine age, when the priesthood were the mediators between God and man, the processional, monastic church with its many altars for the unending *opus Dei*, the open-spaced church of the Friars built for preaching to the city throng. But flamboyant art conceals its essential functions with functionless decoration; the pillar can be twined with wreaths, the keystone apes a stalactite, even the vaulting which is visible may be merely a painted design; exquisite monuments and private chapels break up the unity of the whole. It was a fit emblem of a time when men led by personal or national instinct still subscribed mechanically to the formulae of Catholic Christendom.

There may be found an analogy to this phase of the plastic and pictorial arts in the vernacular literature of the fifteenth century, which, like them, appealed to the wider public. A tedious conventionality enwrapped the tale of chivalry and the moral allegory. In the lyrics, technique, ever more elaborated, replaces in general both genuine feeling and poetic inspiration. It was an age of the pedantic manufacture of literature on bygone themes under set rules. Yet here too men's real interests found expression and gave life. An unforced characterisation of his personages pervades the *Mort Darthur* of Malory. Historians, like Chastellain and Commynes, could draw portraits—realism is their true bent. Villon made the elaborate *ballade* vibrate with as poignant a personal truth as Dante's. Even the endless mysteries, allegoric and religious plays, awake to drama when they treat of persons, passions, and the absurdities of mankind. The living theme was what men felt and did. To this the new humanism arising in Italy brought a kind of consecration, and in its development it brought more tangible gains, form and plan and coherence, the rationality of the classics.

It is curious to see how the reforming, yet conservative endeavour to revivify asceticism and the monastic life[1], in its attempt to be both reactionary towards ancient prescriptions and appropriate to new needs, admitted the dangerous ally of humanism within the cloister. The Brethren of the Common Life were scribes, educators, and grammarians. The reformed Benedictines, renewing the long-forgotten manual labour of the Order, zealously copied and bound manuscripts. Both furthered, first

---

[1] See *supra*, Vol. v, Chap. xx, pp. 693–96, Vol. vii, Chap. xxvi, pp. 803–4, 810–12, Vol. viii, Chaps. xxiii, xxv.

unconsciously, then consciously, the new learning of humanism. In both, perhaps, the individual mystic was harboured. That the pen of the copyists might be snatched from their hands by Gutenberg's invention, that the scholar might stray from accepted solutions and ideals to new interpretations, that collective asceticism might prove an unequal rival to individual freedom and unalluring to the majority of fifteenth-century monks, however old-fashioned, may be claimed as signs that changes in men themselves and their surroundings were outrunning changes in their scheme of life.

The growing unreality of its professed aims was perhaps the source of the decadent aspect of the fifteenth century. The Church, feudalism, chivalry, the crusade, asceticism received a formal homage, less and less sincere. But beside them was the vivid desire of men to know, to dominate, and to possess, the intense interest in human capacity and human fate. Hence came that appetite for personal fame, for an immortality among future men, which was stimulated by the humanists. They could not really wish for a personality submerged in the undifferentiated blessedness of heaven. For the expression of personality, of all that a man embodied of talent and strength, the Italians used their untranslatable word, *virtù*; he should be assessed not by the group or institution to which he belonged, but by himself, on his naked merits. The century was full of the evils and the triumphs of this rampant individualism, the crumbling of a social system on its way to transformation. It is, perhaps, too easy to forget that these years also produced heroic patriotism, as in Joan of Arc, and unselfish devotion to secular and Christian learning. These, too, instances as they are of liberated personality, had their share in the coming of a new age.

In closing the survey of a wide historical period such as the Middle Ages, the student must inevitably be impressed by the relativity of history, and be conscious that he looks at the past through the medium of his own time, that contemporary perplexities and dominant factors will appear to him in higher relief among the bygone events he considers. And he will see that this, too, characterised history as seen by his predecessors. Democratic nationalism colours the spectacles of one generation, economic problems those of another, the cataclasm of war those of a third. Then, too, there is the influence of his personal temperament and prepossessions. The high lights of interest will fall on different aspects of the panorama. To one it will seem the jostling of an illimitable throng of men, a profusion of greater and lesser and indistinguishable stars; to another an almost impersonal conflict and consent of forces, material or spiritual, themselves diversely perceived and appraised by his kindred thinkers; to one a catalogue of single things, to another a vast, dim pattern working itself out with resistless impetus always unforeseen, whose unending variety is never staled. To different onlookers the same scene will be sombre or sunlit, the same sound may come plangent or muffled to the ear. For, had we the precise knowledge, history, which is mankind and all its fortunes, is too vast to be held in one view and subjected, as a medieval thinker would have done, to one simple interpretation. We take narrow views of a world of which each one of us is an infinitesimal part, secluded within a straitened limit. Perhaps only one general impression is universal—the turbulent movement, the infinite perspective and variety, in great things and in small, of that unfathomed sea.

LIST OF ABBREVIATIONS OF TITLES
OF PERIODICALS, SOCIETIES, ETC.

(1) The following abbreviations are used for titles of periodicals:

AB.   Analecta Bollandiana. Paris and Brussels. 1882 ff.

AHR.   American Historical Review. New York and London. 1895 ff.

AKKR.   Archiv für katholisches Kirchenrecht. Innsbruck. 1857-61. Mayence. 1862 ff.

AOG.   Archiv für Kunde österreichischer Geschichts-Quellen. Vienna. 1848-65; *continued as* Archiv für österreichische Geschichte. 1865 ff.

Arch. Ven. (*and* N. Arch. Ven. ; Arch. Ven.-Tri.). Archivio veneto. Venice. 40 vols. 1871–90; *continued as* Nuovo archivio veneto. 1st series. 20 vols. 1891–1900. New series. 42 vols. 1901–21. *And* Archivio veneto-tridentino. 10 vols. 1922–6. *And* Archivio veneto. 5th series. 1927 ff., in progress.

ASI.   Archivio storico italiano. Florence. Ser. i. 20 vols. and App. 9 vols. 1842–53. Index. 1857. Ser. nuova. 18 vols. 1855–63. Ser. iii. 26 vols. 1865–77. Indexes to ii and iii. 1874. Supplt. 1877. Ser. iv. 20 vols. 1878–87. Index. 1891. Ser. v. 50 vols. 1888–1912. Index. 1900. Ser. vi. Anni 71–81. 22 vols. 1913–23. Ser. vii. Anni 82 etc. 1924 ff., in progress. (Index up to 1927 in Catalogue of The London Library. Vol. i. 1913, and Supplts. 1920, 29.)

ASL.   Archivio storico lombardo. Milan. 1874 ff.

ASPN.   Archivio storico per le province napoletane. Naples. 1876 ff.

ASRSP.   Archivio della Società romana di storia patria. Rome. 1878 ff.

BEC.   Bibliothèque de l'École des chartes. Paris. 1839 ff.

BIHR.   Bulletin of the Institute of Historical Research. London. 1923 ff.

BISI.   Bullettino dell' Istituto storico italiano. Rome. 1886 ff.

BRAH.   Boletin de la R. Academia de la historia. Madrid. 1877 ff.

CQR.   Church Quarterly Review. London. 1875 ff.

DZG.   Deutsche Zeitschrift für Geschichtswissenschaft. Freiburg-im-Breisgau. 1889–98. *Continued as* HVJS. *See below.*

DZKR.   Deutsche Zeitschrift für Kirchenrecht. Freiburg-im-Breisgau. 1891 ff.

EHR.   English Historical Review. London. 1886 ff.

FDG.   Forschungen zur deutschen Geschichte. Göttingen. 1860 ff.

HJ.   Historisches Jahrbuch. Munich. 1880 ff.

HVJS.   Historische Vierteljahrsschrift. Leipsic. 1898 ff.

HZ.   Historische Zeitschrift (von Sybel). Munich and Berlin. 1859 ff.

JQR.   Jewish Quarterly Review. London. 1889–1908. New series. Philadelphia. 1910 ff.

MA.   Le moyen âge. Paris. 1888 ff.

MGWJ.   Monatsschrift für die Geschichte und Wissenschaft des Judenthums. Dresden, and later Breslau. 1851 ff.

MIOGF.   Mitt(h)eilungen des Instituts für österreichische Geschichtsforschung. Innsbruck. 1880 ff.

Neu. Arch. Neues Archiv der Gesellschaft für ältere deutsche Geschichtskunde. Hanover and Leipsic. 1876 ff.

NRDF (*and* RDF). Nouvelle Revue hist. de droit français et étranger. Paris. 1877–1921; *continued as* Revue hist. de droit français et étranger. Paris. 1922 ff.

QFIA.   Quellen und Forschungen aus italienischen Archiven und Bibliotheken. Rome. 1898 ff.

RABM.   Revista de Archivos, Bibliotecas, y Museos. Madrid. 1871 ff.

RBén.   Revue bénédictine. Maredsous. 1890 ff.

RDF.   *See above,* NRDF.

REJ.   Revue des études juives. Paris. 1880 ff.

RH.   Revue historique. Paris. 1876 ff.

RHE.   Revue d'histoire ecclésiastique. Louvain. 1900 ff.
RQ.   Römische Quartalschrift für christliche Alterthumskunde und für Kirchengeschichte. Rome. 1887 ff.
RQH.   Revue des questions historiques. Paris. 1866 ff.
SBAW.   Sitzungsberichte der (kön.) bayerischen Akademie der Wissenschaften. [Philos.-philol.-hist. Classe.] Munich. 1891 ff.
SKAW.   Sitzungsberichte der (kaiserlichen) Akademie der Wissenschaften. [Philos.-hist. Classe.] Vienna. 1848 ff.
SPAW.   Sitzungsberichte der (kön.) preussischen Akademie der Wissenschaften. Berlin. 1882 ff.
TRHS.   Transactions of the Royal Historical Society. London. 1871 ff.
ZDMG.   Zeitschrift der deutschen morgenländischen Gesellschaft. Leipsic. 1846 ff.
ZKG.   Zeitschrift für Kirchengeschichte. Gotha. 1877 ff.
ZR.   Zeitschrift für Rechtsgeschichte. Weimar. 1861–78. *Continued as*
ZSR.   Zeitschrift der Savigny-Stiftung für Rechtswissenschaft. Weimar. 1880 ff. [Each vol. contains a Romanistische, a Germanistische, and after 1911, a Kanonistische Abteilung.]
ZWT.   Zeitschrift für wissenschaftliche Theologie. Frankfort-on-Main. 1858 ff.

(2) Other abbreviations used are:

AcadIBL.   Académie des Inscriptions et Belles-Lettres.
AcadIP.   Académie Impériale de Pétersbourg. (*Now* Acad. des sciences de l'Union des républiques soviétiques socialistes. Leningrad.)
AllgDB.   Allgemeine deutsche Biographie. *See Gen. Bibl.* I.
ASBoll.   Acta Sanctorum Bollandiana. *See Gen. Bibl.* IV.
BAW.   (Königliche) bayerische Akademie der Wissenschaften. Munich.
BHE.   Bibliothèque de l'École des Hautes Études. *See Gen. Bibl.* V.
Bouquet.   *See* Rerum Gallicarum...scriptores *in Gen. Bibl.* IV.
Cal.SP.   Calendars of State Papers, Close Rolls, Patent Rolls, etc., issued by the State Paper Office, Public Record Office, and General Register House.
Class. hist.   Classiques de l'histoire de France au moyen âge. *See Gen. Bibl.* IV.
Coll. doc.   Collection de documents inédits sur l'histoire de France. *See Gen. Bibl.* IV.
Coll. textes.   Collection de textes pour servir à l'étude et à l'enseignement de l'histoire. *See Gen. Bibl.* IV.
CSEL.   Corpus scriptorum ecclesiasticorum latinorum. *See Gen. Bibl.* IV.
CSHB.   Corpus scriptorum historiae Byzantinae.
DNB.   Dictionary of National Biography. *See Gen. Bibl.* I.
EcfrAR.   Écoles françaises d'Athènes et de Rome. Paris.
EETS.   Early English Text Society. *See Gen. Bibl.* IV.
EncBr.   Encyclopaedia Britannica. *See Gen. Bibl.* I.
Fonti.   Fonti per la storia d' Italia. *See Gen. Bibl.* IV.
KAW.   (Kaiserliche) Akademie der Wissenschaften. Vienna.
Mansi.   *See Gen. Bibl.* IV *under* Councils, General.
MGH.   Monumenta Germaniae Historica. *See Gen. Bibl.* IV.
MHP.   Monumenta historiae patriae. Turin. *See Gen. Bibl.* IV.
MPG.   Migne's Patrologiae cursus completus. Ser. graeco-latina. [Greek texts with Latin translations in parallel columns.] *See Gen. Bibl.* IV.
MPL.   Migne's Patrologiae cursus completus. Ser. latina. *See Gen. Bibl.* IV.
PAW.   (Königliche) preussische Akademie der Wissenschaften. Berlin.
P.R.O.   Public Record Office.
RAH.   Real Academia de la Historia. Madrid.
RC.   Record Commissioners. *See Gen. Bibl.* IV.
Rolls.   Rerum Britannicarum medii aevi scriptores. *See Gen. Bibl.* IV.
RR.II.SS.   *See* Muratori *in Gen. Bibl.* IV.
SGUS.   Scriptores rerum Germanicarum in usum scholarum. *See* Monumenta Germaniae Historica *in Gen. Bibl.* IV.
SHF.   Société de l'histoire de France. *See Gen. Bibl.* IV.
SRD.   Scriptores rerum Danicarum medii aevi. *See Gen. Bibl.* IV.

Abh.	Abhandlungen.	mem.	memoir.
antiq.	antiquarian, antiquaire.	mém.	mémoire.
app.	appendix.	n.s.	new series.
coll.	collection.	progr.	programme.
disc.	discourse, discurso.	publ.	published, publié.
diss.	dissertation.	R. }	
docs.	documents.	r. }	real, reale.
ed., edn.	edited, edition.	repr.	reprinted.
enl.	enlarged.	rev.	revised.
Gesch.	Geschichte.	roy.	royal, royale.
gesch.	geschichtlich.	ser.	series.
hist.	history, histoire, historical, historique, historisch.	soc.	society, société, società.
		stor.	storico, storica.
Jahrb.	Jahrbuch.	Viert.	Vierteljahrsschrift.
k.	{ kaiserlich. königlich. koninklijk.		

GENERAL BIBLIOGRAPHY.

I. DICTIONARIES, BIBLIOGRAPHIES, AND GENERAL WORKS OF REFERENCE.

Allgemeine deutsche Biographie. Ed. Liliencron, R. von, and Wegele, F. X. (Hist. Commission BAW.) 56 vols. Leipsic. 1875–1912. (AllgDB.)

Ballester, R. Bibliografía de la historia de España. Gerona. 1921. [Select.]

Baxter, J. H. and Johnson, C. Medieval Latin word-list from British and Irish sources. London. 1934.

Below, G. von, and Meinecke, F. edd. Handbuch der mittelalt. und neu. Geschichte. Munich. 1903 ff., in progress. (Below-Meinecke.)

Bernheim, E. Lehrbuch der historischen Methode und der Geschichtsphilosophie. 5th and 6th enl. edn. Leipsic. 1908.

Biographie nationale de Belgique. Brussels. 1866 ff., in progress. (Acad. Roy. des sciences, des lettres, et des beaux arts.)

Biographie universelle, ancienne et moderne. Ed. Michaud, L. G. and others. 45 vols. (Publ. by Desplaces.) Paris. 1843–65. [Greatly improved edn. of earlier work, 1811–28, and supplt., 1832–62.]

Boüard, A. de. Manuel de diplomatique, française et pontificale. Vol. I. Paris. 1929, in progress.

Bresslau, H. Handbuch der Urkundenlehre für Deutschland und Italien. 2nd edn. enl. 2 vols. in 3 pts. Leipsic. 1912–31.

Cabrol, F. and Leclercq, H. Dictionnaire d'archéologie chrétienne et de liturgie. Vols. I–XII. i (in 23 pts.). Paris. 1907 ff., in progress.

Calvi, E. Bibliografia generale di Roma medioevale e moderna. Pt. I. Medio Evo. Rome. 1906. Supplt. 1908.

Capasso, B. Le fonti della storia delle provincie napolitane dal 568 al 1500. Ed. Mastrojanni, E. O. Naples. 1902.

Cappelli, A. Dizionario di abbreviature latine ed italiane. 3rd edn. Milan. 1929.

Ceillier, R. Histoire générale des auteurs sacrés et ecclésiastiques. 23 vols. Paris. 1729–63. New edn. 14 vols. in 15. Paris. 1858–69.

Chevalier, C. U. J. Répertoire des sources historiques du moyen âge. Bio-bibliographie. Paris. 1883–8. Rev. edn. 2 vols. 1905–7. Topo-bibliographie. Montbéliard. 1894–1903.

Dahlmann, F. C. and Waitz, G. Quellenkunde der deutschen Geschichte. 9th edn. Haering, H. Leipsic. 1931. Index. 1932.

Dictionary of National Biography. Ed. Stephen, L. and Lee, S. 63 vols. London. 1885–1900. 1st supplt. 3 vols. 1901. Errata vol. 1904. Re-issue. 22 vols. 1908–9. 2nd supplt. 3 vols. 1912. 3rd supplt. 1927. Corrigenda and addenda publ. in BIHR. 1923 ff., in progress. (DNB.)

Dictionnaire de biographie française. Ed. Balteau, J. and others. Vol. I. Paris. 1933 ff., in progress.

Du Cange, C. du Fresne. Glossarium ad scriptores mediae et infimae Latinitatis. Edns. of Henschel, 7 vols. Paris. 1840–50; and Favre, 10 vols. Niort. 1883–7.

—— Glossarium ad scriptores mediae et infimae Graecitatis. 2 vols. Lyons. 1688.

Egidi, P. La storia medioevale. (Guide bibliografiche, 8–9.) Rome. 1922. [Publications on Italy.]

Enciclopedia italiana di scienze, lettere, ed arti. Rome. 1929 ff., in progress.

Encyclopaedia Britannica. 11th and 13th edn. 32 vols. Cambridge. London and New York. 1910–26. 14th edn. 24 vols. London and New York. 1929. (EncBr.)

Encyclopaedia of Islam. A dictionary of the geography, ethnography, and biography of the Muhammadan peoples. Ed. Houtsma, M. T., Arnold, T. W., and Basset, R. Leiden and London. 1913 ff., in progress.

Ersch, J. S. and Gruber, J. G. Allgemeine Encyklopädie der Wissenschaften und Künste. Berlin. 1818–90. (Ersch-Gruber.) [Incomplete.]

Galbraith, V. H. An introduction to the use of the Public Records. Oxford. 1934.

824 *General Bibliography*

Giry, A. Manuel de diplomatique. 2nd edn. 2 vols. Paris. 1925.

Giuseppi, M. S. Guide to the Manuscripts preserved in the Public Record Office. 2 vols. London. 1923–4.

Grässe, J. G. T. Lehrbuch einer allgemeinen Litterärgeschichte aller bekannten Völker der Welt. 4 vols. Leipsic. 1837–59.

Gröber, G. *ed.* Grundriss der romanischen Philologie. 2 vols. Strasbourg. 1888–1902. 2nd edn. Vol. I. 1904–6. Neue Folge. I. iv. 1914.

Gross, C. Sources and Literature of English History from the earliest times to about 1485. 2nd edn. enl. London. 1915.

Hardy, T. D. Descriptive catalogue of materials relating to the history of Great Britain and Ireland to the end of the reign of Henry VII. 3 vols. in 4. (Rolls.) 1862–71.

Hastings, J. and Selbie, J. A. Encyclopaedia of Religion and Ethics. 13 vols. Edinburgh and New York. 1908–26.

Herre, P., Hofmeister, A., and Stübe, R. Quellenkunde zur Weltgeschichte. Leipsic. 1910.

Herzog, J. J. and Hauck, A. Real-Encyklopädie für protestantische Theologie und Kirche. 3rd edn. 24 vols. Leipsic. 1896–1913.

Holtzendorff, F. von. Encyklopädie der Rechtswissenschaft. 5th edn. Leipsic. 1890. 6th edn. Kohler, J. 2 vols. Leipsic. 1904. Vol. I. 7th edn. 1913. (Holtzendorff-Kohler.)

International bibliography of historical sciences. (Ed. for the International committee of historical sciences, Washington.) 1926 ff. Paris, London, etc. 1930 ff., in progress.

Jahresberichte für deutsche Geschichte. Ed. Brackmann, A. und Hartung, F. Jahrg. 1925 ff. Leipsic. 1927 ff., in progress.

Jansen, M. and Schmitz-Kallenberg, L. Historiographie und Quellen der deutschen Geschichte bis 1500. 2nd edn. (Meister's Grundriss, I. vii. *See below.*) 1914.

Lichtenberger, F. Encyclopédie des sciences religieuses. 13 vols. Paris. 1877–82.

Lorenz, O. Deutschlands Geschichtsquellen im Mittelalter seit der Mitte des 13 Jahrhts. 3rd edn. 2 vols. Berlin. 1886–7.

Maigne d'Arnis, W. H. Lexicon manuale ad scriptores mediae et infimae Latinitatis. (Publ. by Migne.) Paris. 1858. Repr. 1866 and 1890.

Meister, A. *ed.* Grundriss der Geschichtswissenschaft zur Einführung in das Studium der deutschen Geschichte des Mittelalters und der Neuzeit. Leipsic. 1906 ff. 2nd and 3rd edns. 1912 ff., in progress.

Molinier, A. Les sources de l'histoire de France des origines aux guerres d'Italie (1494). 6 vols. (Manuels de bibliographie historique, III. i.) Paris. 1901–6.

Monod, G. Bibliographie de l'histoire de France depuis les origines jusqu'en 1789. Paris. 1888.

Nouvelle Biographie générale,...avec les renseignements bibliographiques. Ed. Höfer, J. C. F. 46 vols. (Publ. by Didot frères.) Paris. 1854–66.

Oudin, Casimir. Commentarius de scriptoribus ecclesiae antiquae illorumque scriptis tam impressis quam manuscriptis adhuc extantibus. 3 vols. Frankfort-on-M. and Leipsic. 1722.

Paetow, L. J. Guide to the study of Medieval History. Rev. edn. (Mediaeval Acad. of America.) New York; and London. 1931.

Paul, H. *ed.* Grundriss der germanischen Philologie. 3rd edn. Strasbourg. 1911 ff.

Pirenne, H. Bibliographie de l'histoire de Belgique. 3rd edn., with the collaboration of Nowé, H. and Obreen, H. Brussels. 1931. [Till 1598 includes all the Netherlands.]

Potthast, A. Bibliotheca historica medii aevi. Wegweiser durch die Geschichtswerke des europäischen Mittelalters bis 1500. 2nd edn. 2 vols. Berlin. 1896.

Redlich, O. and Erben, W. Urkundenlehre. Pts. I and III. (Below-Meinecke. *See above.*) Munich. 1907, 11.

Rivista storica italiana. Turin. 1884 ff., in progress. [Up to 1921 contained quarterly classified bibliography of books and articles on Italian history.]

Sánchez Alonso, B. Fuentes de la historia española. 2nd edn. Vol. I. Madrid. 1927.

Solmi, A. La storia del diritto italiano. (Guide bibliografiche, 10.) Rome. 1922.

Thompson, E. M. Introduction to Greek and Latin Palaeography. London. 1912.

Vacant, A. and Mangenot, E. Dictionnaire de théologie catholique. Paris. 1909 ff.
Victoria History of the Counties of England. London. 1900 ff., in progress. (Vict. Co. Hist.)
Vildhaut, H. Handbuch der Quellenkunde zur deutschen Geschichte. 2nd edn. 2 vols. Werl. 1906, 9.
Villien, A. and Magnin, E. Dictionnaire de droit canonique. Paris. 1924 ff., in progress.
Wetzer, H. J. and Welte, B. Kirchenlexikon oder Encyklopädie der katholischen Theologie. 1847–60. 2nd edn. Kaulen, F. Freiburg-i.-B. 1882–1903. Index. 1903. (Wetzer-Kaulen.) French transl. Goschler, I. 26 vols. Paris. 1869–70.
Whitney, J. P. Bibliography of Church History. (Historical Assoc. Leaflet 55.) London. 1923.

II. ATLASES AND GEOGRAPHY.

Baudrillart-Vogt-Rouziès. Dictionnaire d'histoire et de géographie ecclésiastiques. Paris. 1911 ff., in progress.
Beekman, A. A. *ed.* Geschiedkundige Atlas van Nederland. The Hague. 1911 ff., in progress.
Droysen, G. Allgemeiner historischer Handatlas. Bielefeld. 1886.
Essen, L. van der, *ed.* Atlas de géographie historique de la Belgique. Brussels and Paris. 1919 ff., in progress.
Freeman, E. A. Historical Geography of Europe (with Atlas). London. 1881. 3rd edn. revised and ed. Bury, J. B. 1903.
Kretschmer, K. Historische Geographie von Mitteleuropa. (Below-Meinecke. *See above*, I.) Munich. 1904.
Longnon, A. Atlas historique de la France depuis César jusqu'à nos jours. (Text separate.) Paris. (1885–9.) 1912. [Incomplete.]
Poole, R. L. *ed.* Historical Atlas of Modern Europe. Oxford. 1902. [With valuable introductions.]
Putzger, F. W. Historischer Schul-Atlas. Ed. Baldamus, A. and others. 43rd edn. Bielefeld and Leipsic. 1922.
Schrader, F. *ed.* Atlas de géographie historique. New edn. Paris. 1907.
Shepherd, W. R. Historical atlas. 7th edn. New York and London. 1929.
Spruner-Menke. Hand-Atlas für die Geschichte des Mittelalters und der neueren Zeit. Gotha. 1880. (3rd edn. of Spruner's Hand-Atlas, etc. Ed. Menke, T.)

(FOR PLACE-NAMES:—)

Bischoff, H. T. and Möller, J. H. Vergleichendes Wörterbuch der alten, mittleren, und neuen Geographie. Gotha. 1892.
Deschamps, P. Dictionnaire de Géographie. (Supplt. to Brunet, J. C. Manuel du Libraire.) Paris. 1870. 2nd edn. 2 vols. 1878, 80.
Grässe, J. G. T. Orbis Latinus. Dresden. 1861. Ed. Benedict, F. Berlin. 1909. [Part I only.]
Martin, C. T. The Record Interpreter. London. 1892. 2nd edn. 1910. [For the British Isles.]
See also above, I. Chevalier, C. U. J. Répertoire etc., Topo-bibliographie.

III. CHRONOLOGY, NUMISMATICS, AND GENEALOGY.

(CHRONOLOGY:—)

L'Art de vérifier les dates et les faits historiques. 2e partie. Depuis la naissance de J.-C. 3rd edn. Paris. 3 vols. 1783 ff., and other edns. and reprints. Also 4th edn. by Saint-Allais. 18 vols. 1818–19.
Belviglieri, C. Tavole sincrone e genealogiche di storia italiana dal 306 a 1870. Florence. 1875. Repr. 1885.
Bond, J. J. Handybook of rules and tables for verifying dates. 4th edn. London. 1899.
Calvi, E. Tavole storiche dei comuni italiani. Rome. 1903–7. I. Liguria e Piemonte. II. Marche. III. Romagna. [Also useful bibliographies.] [All publ.]
Cappelli, A. Cronologia, cronografia, e calendario perpetuo dal principio dell' Era Cristiana ai giorni nostri. 2nd edn. Milan. 1930.

Eubel, C. Hierarchia catholica medii aevi. Vols. ɪ, ɪɪ. 2nd edn. Münster. 1913–14.
Gams, P. B. Series episcoporum ecclesiae catholicae. (With supplt.) Ratisbon. 1873, 86. Repr. 1931.
Grotefend, H. Taschenbuch der Zeitrechnung des deutschen Mittelalters und der Neuzeit. 3rd enl. edn. Hanover. 1910.
—— Zeitrechnung des deutschen Mittelalters und der Neuzeit. 2 vols. Hanover. 1891, 98.
Janus: ein Datumweiser für alle Jahrhunderte. By Doliarius, J. E. Leipsic. *n.d.*
Lane-Poole, S. The Mohammadan Dynasties. London. 1894. Repr. 1925.
Mas Latrie, J. M. J. L. de. Trésor de chronologie, d'histoire, et de géographie pour l'étude des documents du moyen âge. Paris. 1889.
Nicolas, Sir N. H. The chronology of history. Revised edn. London. 1838.
Poole, R. L. Medieval reckonings of time. (Helps for Students of History.) S.P.C.K. London. 1918.
Rühl, F. Chronologie des Mittelalters und der Neuzeit. Berlin. 1897.
Schram, R. Hilfstafeln für Chronologie. Vienna. 1883. New edn. Kalendariographische und chronologische Tafeln. Leipsic. 1908.
Stokvis, A. M. H. J. Manuel d'histoire, de généalogie, et de chronologie de tous les États du globe, etc. 3 vols. Leyden. 1888–93.
Stubbs, W. Registrum sacrum Anglicanum. 2nd edn. Oxford. 1897.
(*Note:*—Much information in such works as Gallia Christiana; Le Quien, Oriens Christianus; Ughelli, Italia sacra; for which see ɪv, *below.*)

(Numismatics:—)

Blanchet, A. and Dieudonné, A. Manuel de numismatique française. Vols. ɪ, ɪɪ. Paris. 1912, 16.
Brooke, G. C. English Coins. London. 1932.
Corpus nummorum italicorum. Vols. ɪ–xv. Rome. 1910 ff., in progress.
Dieudonné, A. Les Monnaies françaises. (Collection Payot, 34.) Paris. 1925.
Engel, A. and Serrure, R. Traité de numismatique du moyen âge. 3 vols. Paris. 1891–1905.
Grueber, H. A. Handbook of the Coins of Great Britain and Ireland in the British Museum. London. 1899.
Hill, G. F. Coins and Medals. (Helps for Students of History.) S.P.C.K. London. 1920. [Bibliographical guide.]
Luschin von Ebengreuth, A. Allgemeine Münzkunde und Geldgeschichte des Mittelalters und der neueren Zeit. (Below-Meinecke. *See above*, ɪ.) Munich. 1904. 2nd edn. 1926.
Martinori, E. La Moneta. Rome. 1915. [Dictionary of names of coins.]

(Genealogy:—)

Cokayne, G. E. Complete Peerage of England, Scotland, Ireland, Great Britain and the United Kingdom. 8 vols. Exeter. 1887–98. New enl. edn. Gibbs, V. and others. London. 1910 ff., in progress.
Fernández de Béthencourt, F. Historia genealógica y heráldica de la Monarquía Española, Casa Real, y Grandes de España. Madrid. 1897 ff., in progress.
Foras, E. A. de, and Mareschal de Luciane. Armorial et Nobiliaire de l'ancien duché de Savoie. Vols. ɪ–v. Grenoble. 1863 ff., in progress.
George, H. B. Genealogical Tables illustrative of Modern History. Oxford. 1873. 5th edn. rev. and enl. Weaver, J. R. H. 1916.
Grote, H. Stammtafeln mit Anhang calendarium medii aevi. (Münzstudien. Vol. ɪx.) Leipsic. 1877.
Guasco di Bisio, F. Dizionario feudale degli antichi stati sardi e della Lombardia dall' epoca carolingica ai nostri tempi (774–1909). 5 vols. (Biblioteca della soc. storica subalpina. Vols. 54–58.) Pinerolo. 1911.
Institut héraldique de France. Le Nobiliaire universel. 24 vols. Paris. 1854–1900.
Litta, P. (and continuators). Famiglie celebri italiane. 11 vols. Milan and Turin. 1819–99. 2nd series. Naples. 1902–23. [No more publ.]
Moreri, L. Le grand dictionnaire historique. Latest edn. 10 vols. Paris. 1759. English version, Collier, J. 2nd edn. with supplts. and app. 4 vols. London. 1701–16.

Voigtel, T. G. and Cohn, L. A. Stammtafeln zur Geschichte d. europäischen
Staaten. Vol. I. Die deutschen Staaten u. d. Niederlande. Brunswick. 1871.
See also L'Art de vérifier les dates (*above*), Lane-Poole, Mohammadan Dynasties
(*above*), and Stokvis (*above*).

IV. SOURCES AND COLLECTIONS OF SOURCES.

Achery, L. d'. Spicilegium sive collectio veterum aliquot scriptorum. 13 vols.
Paris. 1655(1665)–77. New edn. Barre, L. F. J. de la. 3 vols. Paris. 1723.
Acta Sanctorum Bollandiana. Jan.–Oct. VI. Antwerp, Brussels, and Tongerloo.
1643–1794. Oct. VII–XIII. Brussels, Paris and Rome, Paris. 1845–83. Nov.
Paris and Rome, Brussels. 1887 ff., in progress. [The reprint of Jan.–Oct. x
published by Palmé at Paris and Rome, 1863 ff., among other variations, has 3
instead of 2 vols. of Jan., and re-arranges the contents of the 7 vols. of June.]
(ASBoll.) [Supplemented by Analecta Bollandiana. 1882 ff. (AB.)]
Archivio storico italiano. (ASI.) *See List of Abbreviations* (1).
Biblioteca della società storica subalpina. Ed. Gabotto, F. and Tallone, A. Pinerolo,
etc. 1899 ff., in progress. [Contains charters and monographs.]
Böhmer, J. F. Regesta imperii. *See below*, Imperial Documents.
Bouquet. *See* Rerum Gallicarum...scriptores.
Camden Society. Publications. London. 1838 ff., in progress. (Now publ. by the
Roy. Hist. Soc.)
Classiques de l'histoire de France au moyen âge. General editor: Halphen, L.
Paris. 1924 ff., in progress. (Class. hist.) [Texts and French translations.]
Collection de chroniques Belges inédites. Brussels. 1836 ff., in progress.
Collection de documents inédits sur l'histoire de France. Paris. 1835 ff., in progress.
(Coll. doc.)
Collection de textes pour servir à l'étude et à l'enseignement de l'histoire. 49 vols.
Paris. 1886–1913. (Coll. textes.)
Corpus Iuris Canonici. Vol. I. Decretum Gratiani. Vol. II. Decretales Gregorii
Papae IX, etc. Ed. Friedberg, E. Leipsic. 1879, 81. [Critical edition.]
—— (Édition of Gregory XIII.) 3 vols. Lyons. 1584; and other 16th-century edns.
also. [Contains the medieval glosses.]
Corpus Iuris Civilis. 3 vols. Berlin. [Critical edn.]
Vol. I. Institutiones. Ed. Krueger, P. Digesta. Ed. Mommsen, T. 15th edn. 1928.
Vol. II. Codex Iustinianus. Ed. Krueger, P. 10th edn. 1929.
Vol. III. Novellae. Ed. Schoell, R. and Kroll, W. 5th edn. 1928.
—— Ed. Gothofredus, E. 3rd edn. 6 vols. Cologne. 1612; and other edns.
[Contains the medieval glosses and additions, such as the Libri Feudorum.]
Corpus scriptorum ecclesiasticorum latinorum. Vienna. 1866 ff., in progress. (CSEL.)
Corpus statutorum Italicorum. Ed. Sella, P. and others. Vols. I–XIV. Rome. 1912 ff.,
in progress.
Councils, General and other:
Mansi, J. D. Sacrorum conciliorum collectio. 31 vols. Florence and Venice.
1759–98. Repr. Martin, J. B. and Petit, L. (With continuation, vols. 32–50.)
Paris. 1901 ff., in progress. (Mansi.)
Finke, H. *ed.* Acta concilii Constanciensis. 4 vols. Münster. 1896–1928.
—— Forschungen und Quellen zur Geschichte des Konstanzer Konzils.
Paderborn. 1889.
Haller, J. and others, *edd.* Concilium Basiliense. Studien und Quellen zur
Geschichte des Konzils von Basel. 7 vols. Basel. 1896–1926.
Monumenta conciliorum generalium saeculi XV. Concilium Basiliense. Scriptores.
Vols. I, II, III. i–iv. (KAW.) Vienna. 1857–96.
Wilkins, D. Concilia Magnae Britanniae et Hiberniae. 4 vols. London. 1737.
Dugdale, W. Monasticon Anglicanum. 3 vols. London. 1655–73. New edn. by
Caley, J. and others. 6 vols. in 8. London. 1817–30. Repr. 1846.
Early English Text Society. Publications. London. 1864 ff., in progress. (EETS.)
España Sagrada. Ed. Florez, H. and others. 51 vols. Madrid. 1747–1879.
Fejér, G. Codex diplomaticus Hungariae ecclesiasticus et civilis. (Chronological
table by Knauz, F. Index by Czinár, M.) 45 vols. Buda-Pest. 1829–66.
Fontes rerum Austriacarum. Österreichische Geschichtsquellen. Abt. I. Scriptores.
Abt. II. Diplomataria et acta. (Hist. Commission KAW.) Vienna. 1849 ff.

Fontes rerum Bohemicarum. Ed. Emler, J. and others. Prague. 1873 ff.
Fonti per la storia d' Italia. Publ. by Istituto storico italiano. Rome. 1887 ff., in
 progress. (Chronicles, 39 vols. Letters, 8 vols. Diplomas, 8 vols. Statutes,
 7 vols. Laws, 1 vol. Antiquities, 3 vols. Poems, 1 vol.) (Fonti.)
Gallia Christiana (Vetus). Ed. Sainte-Marthe, S. de, and others. 4 vols. Paris. 1656.
—— (Nova). Vols. i–xiii. Ed. Sainte-Marthe, D. de, and others. Vols. xiv–xvi.
 Ed. Hauréau, B. Paris. 1715–1865. 2nd edn. Revised by Piolin, P. Vols. i–v,
 xi, xiii. Paris. 1870–8. Provincia Tolosana. New edn. Vol. i. Toulouse. 1892.
—— (Novissima). Ed. Albanès, J. H. and Chevalier, C. U. J. 7 vols. Montbéliard
 and Valence. 1895–1920.
Germania sacra. Publ. by Kaiser-Wilhelm-Institut für deutsche Geschichte. Berlin.
 1929, in progress.
Geschichtschreiber der deutschen Vorzeit etc. Ed. Pertz, Wattenbach, and others.
 New series. Leipsic. 1884, in progress. [German translations.]
Goldast, M. Monarchia S. Romani Imperii. Vol. i. Hanover. 1612. Vols. ii, iii.
 Frankfort. 1614, 13.
Graevius, J. G. and Burmannus, P. Thesaurus antiquitatum et historiarum Italiae
 etc. 30 vols. Leiden. 1704–23.
—— —— Thesaurus antiq. et histor. Siciliae, Sardiniae, Corsicae, etc. 15 vols.
 Leiden. 1723–5. [Forms a continuation of the preceding.]
Le Quien, M. Oriens Christianus. 3 vols. Paris. 1740.

Imperial Documents:—

Bachmann, A. *ed.* Urkunden und Actenstücke zur österreichischen Geschichte im
 Zeitalter Kaiser Friedrichs III und König Georgs von Böhmen (1440–71).
 (Fontes rerum Austriacarum. Abt. ii, Vol. xlii.) Vienna. 1879.
—— Briefe und Acten zur österreichisch-deutschen Geschichte im Zeitalter
 Kaiser Friedrichs III (1448–71.). (*Ibid.* Vol. xliv.). Vienna. 1885.
—— Urkundliche Nachträge zur österreichisch-deutschen Geschichte im
 Zeitalter Kaiser Friedrichs III (1458–82). (*Ibid.* Vol. xlvi.) Vienna. 1892.
Böhmer, J. F. Regesta imperii.
 Regesten d. Kaiserreichs...1314–1347. Frankfort. 1839. Additamenta i–iii.
 1841–65.
—— Regesta imperii. (New edn. in several parts by various editors.) Innsbruck.
 1877 ff. [*See also Gen. Bibl. of Vol.* v, p. 838.]
 v. Regesten d. Kaiserreichs...1198–1272. Ed. Ficker, J. and Winkelmann, E.
 3 vols. 1881–1901.
 vi. Regesten d. Kaiserreichs...1273–1313. Abtlg. 1 (1273–91). Ed. Redlich, O.
 Abtlg. 2 (1291–). Ed. Samanek, V. 1898 ff., in progress.
 viii. Regesten d. Kaiserreichs...1346–78. Ed. Huber, A. 1877. Additamentum i.
 1889.
 xi. Die Urkunden Kaiser Sigmunds, 1410–37. Ed. Altmann, W. 2 vols.
 Innsbruck. 1896–1900.
Chmel, J. *ed.* Regesta chronologico-diplomatica Ruperti regis Romanorum.
 Frankfort. 1834.
—— Urkunden und Actenstücke zur Geschichte K. Albrechts II (V als Herzog)
 aus den Jahren 1413–39. SKAW. iii (1849). 12–48.
—— Regesta chronologico-diplomatica Friderici III Romanorum Imperatoris
 (regis IV). 2 pts. Vienna. 1838, 40; repr. Vienna. 1859. [App. of docs.]
—— Materialien zur österreichischen Geschichte. (Beiträge zur Geschichte König
 Friedrich IV.) 2 vols. Vienna. 1837–40. (Pt. i also publ. at Linz. 1832.)
—— Urkunden, Briefe, und Actenstücke zur Geschichte Maximilians I und seiner
 Zeit. (Bibliothek des literar. Vereins in Stuttgart. x.) Stuttgart. 1845.
Deutsche Reichstagsakten. Vols. i–xiii, xv, xvi (1378–1442). Publ. by Hist.
 Commission. BAW. Munich. 1867 ff.
Lünig, J. C. *ed.* Codex Germaniae diplomaticus. 2 vols. Frankfort and Leipsic.
 1732–4.
—— Teutsches Reichsarchiv. 24 vols. Leipsic. 1710–22.
Müller, J. J. *ed.* Des h. Röm. Reiches...Reichstags-Theatrum...unter Kayser
 Friedrichs V (=III)...(1440–93). 3 pts. Jena. 1713. *Idem.* Reichstags-Thea-
 trum...unter Kayser Maximilians I...(1486–1500). 2 pts. Jena. 1718–19.

Winkelmann, E. *ed.* Acta imperii inedita seculi xiii et xiv. Urkunden und Briefe zur Geschichte des Kaiserreichs und des Königsreichs 'Sicilien (1198–1400). 2 vols. Innsbruck. 1880, 85.

Mabillon, J. Annales Ordinis S. Benedicti. 6 vols. Paris. 1703–39. 2nd edn. Lucca. 1739–45.

Marrier, M. and Quercetanus (Duchesne), A. Bibliotheca Cluniacensis. Paris. 1614.

Martène, E. and Durand, U. Thesaurus novus anecdotorum. 5 vols. Paris. 1717.

Mémoires et documents publiés par la Société de l'École des chartes. Paris. 1896 ff., in progress.

Migne, J. P. Patrologiae cursus completus. Series graeco-latina. Paris. 1857–66. 161 vols. in 166. (MPG.) Indices, Cavallerà, F. Paris. 1912; *also* Hopfner, T. Paris. 1928 ff., in progress. [This is the series containing Greek texts with Latin translations in parallel columns. The so-called Series graeca (81 vols. in 85. 1856–67) contains Latin translations only.]

—— —— Series latina. 221 vols. Paris. 1844–55. Index, 4 vols. 1862–4. (MPL.)

Mirbt, C. Quellen zur Geschichte des Papsttums und des römischen Katholizismus. 4th edn. Tübingen. 1924. (Mirbt. Quellen.)

Monumenta Germaniae Historica. Ed. Pertz, G. H., Mommsen, T., and others. Hanover and Berlin. 1826 ff. Index. 1890. [For full list of the different series *see Gen. Bibl. of Vol.* v, pp. 840–1.] (MGH.)

Deutsche Chroniken (Scriptores qui vernacula lingua usi sunt). i–vi. 1892 ff., in progress.

Epistolae selectae. i–iv. 1916 ff., in progress. 8°. (Epp. select.)

Fontes iuris Germanici antiqui. Nova Series. i. 8°. Hanover. 1933, in progress.

Legum sectiones quinque. 4°.

Sect. iv. Constitutiones etc. i–v, vi. i, viii. 1893 ff.

Scriptores. Vols. i–xxx. Fol. 1826–1934. And 4°. Vols. xxxi, xxxii. 1903, 1913. Now complete. (Script.)

Scriptores rerum Germanicarum in usum scholarum. Hanover. 1839 ff. Fresh series. 1890 ff., in progress. 8°. (SGUS.) [Contains revised editions of many of the Scriptores in Fol. edition.]

Scriptores rerum Germanicarum. Nova Series. i–iv. i, v–ix. Berlin. 1922 ff., in progress. (MGH. Script. N.S.)

Monumenta historiae patriae. 19 vols. Fol. 2 vols. 4°. Turin. 1836 ff. (MHP.)

Monumenta Hungariae historica. Ser. i. Diplomataria. Ser. ii. Scriptores. Ser. iii. Monumenta comitialia. Ser. iv. Acta extera. (Magyar Tudományos Akad.) Budapest. 1857 ff.

Muratori, L. A. Rerum Italicarum scriptores. 25 vols. Milan. 1723–51. Supplements: Tartini, J. M., 2 vols., Florence, 1748, 70; and Mittarelli, J. B., Venice, 1771; and Amari, M., Biblioteca arabo-sicula, versione italiana, and Appendix. Turin and Rome. 1880–1, 1889. Indices chronolog. Turin. 1885. New enl. edn. with chronicles printed as separate parts. Carducci, G., Fiorini, V., Fedele, P. Città di Castello and Bologna. 1900 ff., in progress. (RR.II.SS.)

—— Antiquitates italicae medii aevi. 6 vols. Milan. 1738–42. Indices chronolog. Turin. 1885.

Papal Documents (*for earlier Popes see Gen. Bibl. of Vol.* vi, p. 852; Vol. vii, pp. 822–3).

Analecta Vaticano-Belgica. Documents relatifs aux anciens diocèses de Cambrai, Liège, Thérouanne, et Tournai. (Institut historique belge de Rome.) Rome, Brussels, etc. 1906 ff., in progress.

Bossányi, A. *ed.* Regesta supplicationum, 1342–94. 2 vols. Budapest. 1916, 18.

Pastor, L. *ed.* Acta inedita historiam Pontificum Romanorum illustrantia. Ungedruckte Akten zur Geschichte der Päpste vornehmlich im 15, 16, und 17 Jahrht. Vol. i (1376–1464). Freiburg-i.-B. 1904.

Riezler, S. *ed.* Vatikanische Akten zur deutschen Geschichte in der Zeit Kaiser Ludwigs des Bayern. (Hist. Commission. BAW.) Innsbruck. 1891.

Repertorium Germanicum. [1378–1527.] Verzeichnis der in den päpstl. Registern und Kameralakten vorkommenen Personen, Kirchen, und Orte des Deutschen Reiches.... Vol. i (1378–94). Ed. Göller, E. Vol. ii (1378–1415). Ed. Tellenbach, G. Vol. iii (1409–17). Ed. Kühne, U. (K. Preuss. hist. Inst. in Rom.) Berlin. 1916 ff., in progress.

Repertorium Germanicum. Regesten aus den päpstl. Archiven zur Geschichte des Deutschen Reichs und seiner Territorien im 14 und 15 Jahrht. Pontificat Eugens IV (1431–47). Vol. i. Ed. Haller, J. and others. (K. Preuss. hist. Inst. in Rom.) Berlin. 1897.
Monumenta Vaticana res gestas Bohemicas illustrantia. Prague. 1903 ff.
   i. Acta Clementis VI. Ed. Klicman, L. 1903.
   ii. Acta Innocentii VI. Ed. Novák, J. F. 1907.
   v. Acta Urban: VI et Bonifatii IX. Ed. Krofta, K. 2 pts. 1903, 5.
Monumenta Poloniae Vaticana. Editiones collegii historici Acad. lit. Craco-viensis. Vol. i. Cracow. 1913.
Monumenta Vaticana historiam regni Hungarici illustrantia. Ser. i. Vols. i–vi. Ser. ii. Vols. i, ii. Budapest. 1884–91.
Calendar of entries in the Papal Registers relating to Great Britain and Ireland. Papal Letters. Vols. i–xii. Ed. Bliss, W. H. and others. (Cal.SP.) London. 1893–1933.
   Petitions to the Pope. Vol. i. Ed. Bliss, W. H. (Cal.SP.) London. 1896.
Calendar of Scottish supplications to Rome, 1418–22. Ed. Lindsay, Hon. E. R. and Cameron, A. J. (Scottish History Soc. 3rd ser. Vol. xxiii.) Edinburgh. 1934.
Theiner, A. *ed.* Vetera monumenta Hibernorum et Scotorum historiam illustrantia...ex Vaticani, Neapolis ac Florentiae tabulariis... (1216–1547). Rome. 1864.
—— Codex diplomaticus dominii temporalis S. Sedis. 3 vols. Rome. 1861–2.
Record Commissioners, Publications of the. London. 1802–69. (RC.)
Rerum Britannicarum medii aevi scriptores. (Chronicles and Memorials of Great Britain and Ireland during the Middle Ages.) Published under direction of the Master of the Rolls. London. 1858 ff. (Rolls.) [For convenient list see Gross (Section i, *above*), App. c.]
Rerum Gallicarum et Francicarum scriptores. (Recueil des hist. des Gaules et de la France.) Ed. Bouquet, M. and others. 24 vols. Paris. 1738–1904. Vols. i–xix re-ed. by Delisle, L. 1868–80. New series. 4°. AcadIBL. Paris. 1899 ff., in progress. (Bouquet.)
Rymer, T. Foedera. [1101–1654.] 20 vols. (xvi ff. by Sanderson, R.) London. 1704–35. 3rd edn. The Hague. 1739–45. New edn. [1069-1383] by Clarke, A., Holbrooke, F., and Caley, J. 4 vols. in 7 pts. (RC.) London. 1816–69. Syllabus by Hardy, T. D. 3 vols. London. 1869–85. Report (App. a–e only) by Cooper, C. P. (RC.) London. [1836?] Publ. 1869.
Scriptores rerum Danicarum medii aevi. Ed. Langebek, I. and others. 9 vols. Copenhagen. 1772–1878. (SRD.)
Selden Society. Publications. London. 1888 ff., in progress.
Société de l'histoire de France. Publications. Paris. 1834 ff., in progress. (SHF.)
Ughelli, F. Italia sacra. 2nd edn. Coleti, N. 10 vols. Venice. 1717–22.
Vic, C. de, and Vaissete, J. J. Histoire générale de Languedoc. New edn. Dulaurier, E. 16 vols. Toulouse. 1872–1904.

V. MODERN WORKS.

Altamira, R. Historia de España y de la civilización española. 3rd edn. 4 vols. Barcelona. 1913–14.
—— History of Spanish civilization. Transl. by Volkov, P. London. 1930.
Alzog, J. Universalgeschichte der Kirche. Mayence. 1841. Best edn. 10th by Kraus, F. X. 1882. Transl. (from 9th German edn.). Pabisch, F. J. and Byrne, T. S. Manual of Church History. 4 vols. Dublin. 1895–1900.
Baronius, C. Annales Ecclesiastici una cum critica historico-chronologica P. A. Pagii. [–1198.] Contin. by Raynaldus, O. [1198–1565.] Ed. Mansi, J. D. Lucca. 34 vols. 1738–46. Apparatus and Index, 4 vols. 1740, 1757–9. New edn. 37 vols. Bar-le-duc. 1864–83. [Not completed.]
Barraclough, G. Papal provisions. Oxford. 1935. [Bibliography.]
Bédier, J. and Hazard, P. *edd.* Histoire de la littérature française illustrée. 2 vols. Paris. 1923–4.
Bibliothèque de l'École des Hautes Études. Paris. 1869 ff., in progress. (BHE.)

Bréhier, L. L'Église et l'Orient au moyen âge. Les Croisades. 5th edn. Paris. 1928. [With bibliography.]

Brown, P. Hume. History of Scotland to the present time. (Library edn.) 3 vols. Cambridge. 1911.

Brunner, H. Deutsche Rechtsgeschichte. 2 vols. Leipsic. 1887, 92. Vol. i. 2nd edn. 1906. Vol. ii, ed. Schwerin, C. von. 1928.

—— Grundzüge der deutschen Rechtsgeschichte. 8th edn. Schwerin, C. von. Munich. 1930. [Bibliographies.]

Bryce, J. The Holy Roman Empire. New edn. London. 1906, and reprints.

Calmette, J. L'élaboration du monde moderne. ("Clio," 5.) Paris. 1934. [Valuable bibliographies.]

Cambridge History of English Literature. Ed. Ward, A. W. and Waller, A. R. 15 vols. Cambridge. 1907–27.

Cánovas del Castillo, A. *ed.* Historia general de la España. (By members of R. Acad. de la Hist.) Madrid. 1892 ff., in progress.

Carlyle, R. W. and A. J. A History of Mediaeval Political Theory in the West. Vols. i–v. Edinburgh and London. 1903 ff., in progress.

Coulton, G. G. Five Centuries of Religion. Vols. i–iii. Cambridge. 1923 ff., in progress.

Creighton, M. History of the Papacy during the period of the Reformation. 5 vols. London. 1882–94. New edn., with title, History of the Papacy from the Great Schism to the sack of Rome. 6 vols. London. 1897.

Cunningham, W. The growth of English Industry and Commerce. [Vol. i.] Early and Middle Ages. 5th edn. Cambridge. 1910.

Curtis, E. History of Mediaeval Ireland from 1110 to 1513. Dublin and London. 1923.

Eck, A. Le moyen âge russe. Paris. 1933.

England, A History of, in eight volumes. Ed. Oman, C. 8 vols. London. 1905–34.

—— The Oxford History of. Ed. Clark, G. N. [To be 14 vols.] Oxford. 1934 ff., in progress.

—— The Political History of. Ed. Hunt, W. and Poole, R. L. 12 vols. London. 1905–10.

Erben, W. Kriegsgeschichte des Mittelalters. (HZ. Beiheft 16.) Munich and Berlin. 1929. [Valuable bibliographies.]

Ficker, G. and Hermelink, H. Das Mittelalter. 2nd edn. (Handbuch d. Kirchengesch. für Studierende. Ed. Krüger, G. Vol. ii.) Tübingen. 1929.

Fleury, C. Histoire ecclésiastique. 20 vols. Paris. 1691–1720. Continued to end of 18th century under Vidal, O. Many editions. (Orig. edn. to 1414. 4 add. vols. by Fleury to 1517, publ. Paris. 1836–7.)

Gebhardt, B. Handbuch der deutschen Geschichte. 7th edn. by Holtzman, R. 2 vols. Stuttgart. 1930–1.

Gibbon, E. The History of the Decline and Fall of the Roman Empire. 1776–81. Ed. Bury, J. B. 7 vols. London. 1896–1900; best edn., rev. and illustrated. 7 vols. London. 1909–14. [Notes essential, especially for bibliography.]

Gierke, O. Das deutsche Genossenschaftsrecht. 4 vols. Berlin. 1868–1913.

—— Political Theories of the Middle Age. Transl. and ed. Maitland, F. W. Cambridge. 1900. [Translation of a section of the preceding.]

Gieseler, J. C. L. Lehrbuch der Kirchengeschichte. Vols. i–iii (in 8 pts.). 4th, 2nd, and 1st edns. Bonn. 1844–8; 35–53. Engl. transl. Davidson, S. and Hull, J. W. Vols. i–iii. Edinburgh. 1853 ff.

Gilson, E. La philosophie au moyen âge. 2 vols. Paris. 1922. [Bibliographies.]

Glotz, G. *ed.* Histoire générale. Section II. Histoire du moyen âge. [To be 10 vols.] Paris. 1928 ff., in progress.

Gregorovius, F. Geschichte der Stadt Rom im Mittelalter. 5th edn. 8 vols. Stuttgart. 1903–8. (Engl. transl. from 4th edn. by Mrs A. Hamilton. 8 vols. in 13. London. 1894–1902.)

Halphen, L. and Sagnac, P. *edd.* Peuples et civilisations. Histoire générale. Vol. vii. La fin du moyen âge. Pt. i (1285–1453); Pt. ii (1453–92). Paris. 1931.

Hanotaux, G. *ed.* Histoire de la nation française. 15 vols. Paris. 1920–9.

Harnack, C. G. A. Lehrbuch der Dogmengeschichte. 4th edn. 3 vols. (Sammlung theolog. Lehrbücher.) Tübingen. 1909–10. Engl. transl. of the 3rd edn. Buchanan, N. and others. 7 vols. London. 1894–9.

Hartmann, L. M. *ed.* Weltgeschichte in gemeinverständlicher Darstellung. Vol. v. Kaser, K. Das späte Mittelalter. Gotha. 1921.

Hauck, A. Kirchengeschichte Deutschlands. 5 vols. Leipsic. 1887–1920. Vols. i–iv. 4th edn. 1906–13. Vol. v. 2nd edn. 2 pts. 1911, 20.

Heeren, A. H. L. and others, *edd.* Geschichte der europäischen Staaten. Hamburg and Gotha. 1829 ff. Continued as section i of Allgemeine Staatengeschichte. Ed. Lamprecht, K. and Oncken, H. *Cited sub nom. auct.* (Heeren.)

Hefele, C. J. v., contin. Hergenröther, J. A. G. Conciliengeschichte. 9 vols. Freiburg-i.-B. 1855 ff. 2nd edn. 1873 ff. French transl. Delarc, O. 1869. New rev. Fr. transl. Leclercq, H. Vols. i–ix (in 18 pts.). Paris. 1907 ff., in progress. (Hefele-Leclercq.)

Heyd, W. Histoire du Commerce du Levant au moyen-âge. 2nd edn. (in French transl. by Raynaud, F.). 2 vols. Leipsic. 1885–6. Reprinted. 2 vols. Leipsic. 1923.

Hinschius, P. Das Kirchenrecht der Katholiken und Protestanten in Deutschland. Pt. i. System des kathol. Kirchenrechts, mit besonderer Rücksicht auf Deutschland. Vols. i–vi. i. Berlin. 1869–97.

Historische Studien. Ed. Ebering, E. Berlin. 1896 ff., in progress.

Holdsworth, W. S. History of English Law. 3rd edn. Vols. i–iii. London. 1922–3.

Kirchenrechtliche Abhandlungen. Ed. Stutz, U. Stuttgart, 1902 ff., in progress.

Köhler, G. Die Entwicklung des Kriegswesen und der Kriegsführung in der Ritterzeit von der Mitte des 11 Jahrhunderts bis zu den Hussitenkriegen. 3 vols. Breslau. 1886–90.

Kraus, F. X. Geschichte der christlichen Kunst. 2 vols. in 4. Freiburg-i.-B. 1896–1908.

Krumbacher, K. Geschichte der byzantinischen Literatur (527–1453). 2nd edn. (Handbuch d. klass. Altertums-Wissenschaft. Ed. Müller, I. von. Vol. ix. i.) Munich. 1897.

Lamprecht, K. Deutsche Geschichte. 12 vols. in 16. Berlin. 1891–1909. Vols. i–v. 3rd edn. 1902–6. Supplts. 2 vols. in 3. 1902–4.

Langen, J. Geschichte der römischen Kirche. 4 vols. Bonn. 1881.

Lavisse, E. *ed.* Histoire de France jusqu'à la Révolution. 9 vols. in 18. Paris. 1900–11. Illustrated edn. Paris. 1913. Vols. i–iv.

Lavisse, E. and Rambaud, A. *edd.* Histoire générale du iv⁰ siècle jusqu'à nos jours. Vols. i–iii. Paris. 1893–6.

Lea, H. C. History of the Inquisition of the Middle Ages. 3 vols. New York. 1887. French transl. Reinach, S., with introdn. by Frédéricq, P. 3 vols. Paris. 1900–2.

—— History of Sacerdotal Celibacy in the Christian Church. 3rd edn. 2 vols. London. 1907.

Loserth, J. Geschichte des späteren Mittelalters von 1197 bis 1492. (Below-Meinecke. *See above,* i.) Munich. 1903.

Manitius, M. Geschichte der lateinischen Literatur des Mittelalters. Vols. i–iii. (Handbuch d. klass. Altertums-Wissenschaft. Ed. Müller, I. von. Vol. ix. ii. 1–3.) Munich. 1911 ff., in progress.

Meister, A. Deutsche Verfassungsgeschichte von den Anfängen bis ins 15 Jahrht. 3rd edn. (Meister's Grundriss, ii. iii. *See above,* i.) Leipsic. 1922.

Merriman, R. B. The rise of the Spanish empire in the old world and in the new. Vols. i and ii. New York. 1918.

Milioukov, P. and others. Histoire de Russie. Vol. i. Paris. 1932.

Moeller, W. Hist. of the Christian Church (A.D. 1–1648). Transl. Rutherfurd and Freese. 3 vols. London. 1892–1900.

Mosheim, J. L. von. Institutionum historiae ecclesiasticae antiquae et recentioris libri iv. 4 vols. Helmstedt. 1755. Transl. Murdock, J., ed. Soames, H. 4 vols. London. 1841. 2nd rev. edn. 1850.

Müller, K. Kirchengeschichte. Vols. i, ii. Freiburg-i.-B. 1892.

Muratori, L. A. Annali d' Italia. 12 vols. Milan. 1744–9. Also other editions.

Norden, W. Das Papsttum und Byzanz. Berlin. 1903.

Oman, C. W. C. History of the Art of War in the Middle Ages. 2nd edn. enl. 2 vols. London. 1924.

Oncken, W. *ed.* Allgemeine Geschichte in Einzeldarstellungen. 45 vols. Berlin. 1879–93. *Cited sub nom. auct.* (Oncken.)

Pastor, L. Geschichte der Päpste seit dem Ausgang des Mittelalters. Vols. I–III. Freiburg-i.-B. 1886–96; and later edns. Engl. transl., ed. Antrobus, F. I. Vols. I–V. London. 1891–8.

Pertile, A. Storia del diritto italiano dalla caduta dell' impero Romano alla codificazione. 2nd edn. Del Giudice, P. 6 vols. Turin. 1892–1902. Index. Eusebio, L. Turin. 1893.

Petit de Julleville, L. *ed.* Histoire de la langue et de la littérature française. 8 vols. Paris. 1896–1900.

Pirenne, H. Histoire de Belgique. Vol. I. 5th edn. Brussels. 1929. Vol. II. 3rd edn. 1922.

Poole, R. L. Illustrations of the history of Medieval Thought and Learning. 2nd edn. London. 1920.

Propyläen-Weltgeschichte. Ed. Goetz, W. Vol. IV. Das Zeitalter der Gotik und Renaissance. Leipsic. 1932.

Rambaud, A. Histoire de la Russie depuis les origines jusqu'à nos jours. 6th edn. rev. by Haumant, E. Paris. 1914. Engl. transl. Lang, L. B. Rev. edn. 3 vols. Boston, Mass. 1886.

Ranke, L. von. Weltgeschichte. 9 vols. Leipsic. 1881–8. And later edns.

Rashdall, H. The Universities of Europe in the Middle Ages. 2 vols. in 3. Oxford. 1895. [A new edn. is in preparation.]

Salembier, L. Le Grand Schisme d'Occident. 5th edn. Paris. 1922.

Savigny, F. C. von. Geschichte des Römischen Rechts im Mittelalter. 2nd edn. 7 vols. Heidelberg. 1834–51. French transl. Guenoux, C. 4 vols. Paris. 1839.

Schröder, R. Lehrbuch der deutschen Rechtsgeschichte. 6th edn. Ed. Künnsberg, E. von. Berlin and Leipsic. 1922.

Schulte, J. F. v. Die Geschichte der Quellen und Literatur des Canonischen Rechts von Gratian bis auf die Gegenwart. 3 vols. Stuttgart. 1875–80.

Storia letteraria d' Italia scritta da una società di professori. Milan. 1900 ff.

Storia politica d' Italia scritta da una società d' amici. Ed. Villari, P. Vols. III (Lanzani, F.), IV (Cipolla, C.). Milan. 1882, 81.

Storia politica d' Italia scritta da una società di professori. Vol. V. Orsi, P. Signorie e principati (1300–1530). Milan. [1902].

Stubbs, W. Constitutional history of England. 3 vols. Oxford. 1873–8. (Frequently reprinted.) French transl. Lefebvre, G., with notes and studies by Petit-Dutaillis, C. 3 vols. Paris. 1907–27. English transl. of notes, etc. Ed. Tait, J. and Powicke, F. M. *as* Studies and notes supplementary to Stubbs' Constitutional history. Vol. I. Transl. Rhodes, W. E. Vol. II. Transl. Waugh, W. T. Vol. III. Transl. Robertson, M. I. E. and Treharne, R. F. Manchester. 1908–29.

Tiraboschi, G. Storia della letteratura italiana. New edn. 9 vols. in 16. Florence. 1805–13. Milan. 1822–6.

Ueberweg, F. Grundriss der Geschichte der Philosophie. 12th edn. Ed. Frischeisen-Köhler, M. and Praechter, K. 5 vols. Berlin. 1926–8. [Bibliography.]

Valois, N. La France et le Grand Schisme d'Occident. 4 vols. Paris. 1896–1902.

Viollet, P. Droit public. Histoire des institutions politiques et administratives de la France. 3 vols. Paris. 1890–1903.

—— Histoire du droit civil français. 3rd edn. Paris. 1905.

Weil, G. Geschichte der islamitischen Völker von Mohammed bis zur Zeit des Sultans Selim. Stuttgart. 1866.

Werminghoff, A. Geschichte der Kirchenverfassung Deutschlands im Mittelalter. Vol. I. Hanover and Leipsic. 1905.

Wulf, M. de. Histoire de la philosophie médiévale. 6th edn. Vol. I. Louvain. 1934. In progress. 3rd Engl. transl., based on 6th French edn., Messenger, E. C. Vol. I. London. 1935. In progress.

Zeller, J. Histoire d'Allemagne. Vols. I–IX. Paris. 1872–91. [No more publ.]

CHAPTER I.

THE COUNCILS OF CONSTANCE AND BASLE.

I. BIBLIOGRAPHIES.

Lists of sources and literature may be found in Dahlmann-Waitz, Quellenkunde; Molinier, Les sources de l'hist. de France, Vol. IV; Potthast, Bibliotheca historica; Paetow, Guide to the study of Medieval History (for all which *see Gen. Bibl.* I).

Reference should also be made to the Bibliography of Vol. VII, ch. x, pp. 867–8 for the Great Schism, and *infra* to those of Vol. VIII, chapters II and III, for the Hussite controversy.

II. SOURCES.

A. Collections.

Acta concilii Constanciensis. Ed. Finke, H. *See Gen. Bibl.* IV *under* Councils, General.

Concilia Germaniae. Ed. Schannat, J. F., Hartzheim, J. etc. Vol. v. Cologne. 1763.

Concilium Basiliense. Studien und Quellen zur Geschichte des Konzils von Basel. Ed. Haller, J. and others. *See Gen. Bibl.* IV *under* Councils, General.

Hardt, E. H. von der. Magnum oecumenicum Constantiense concilium. Vols. I–VI. Frankfort and Leipsic. 1696–1700. Vol. VII (Index). Berlin. 1742.

Mansi, J. D. Sacrorum conciliorum collectio. Vols. XXVII–XXXI, and XXXV. *See Gen. Bibl.* IV *under* Councils, General.

Martène, E. and Durand, U. Thesaurus novus anecdotorum. Vols. II and IV. *See Gen. Bibl.* IV.

——— Veterum scriptorum et monumentorum historicorum, dogmaticorum... amplissima collectio. Vols. VII, VIII. Paris. 1733.

Monumenta conciliorum generalium saeculi xv. Concilium Basiliense. *See Gen. Bibl.* IV *under* Councils, General. [Contains narratives of John of Ragusa, John of Segovia, Petrus Zatecensis, Gilles Carlier, Thomas Ebendorffer, John of Tours, etc.]

Raynaldus, O. Annales Ecclesiastici. Vols. XXVII, XXVIII. Ed. Mansi, J. D. *See Gen. Bibl.* v *under* Baronius.

Wilkins, D. Concilia Magnae Britanniae et Hiberniae. Vol. III. *See Gen. Bibl.* IV *under* Councils, General.

B. Documents and Controversial Writings.

Achery, L. d'. Spicilegium sive collectio veterum aliquot scriptorum. New edn. *See Gen. Bibl.* IV.

Acta Nicolai Gramis. Urkunden und Aktenstücke betreffend die Beziehungen Schlesiens zum Basler Konzil. Ed. Altmann, W. (Codex diplomaticus Silesiae. xv.) Breslau. 1890.

Acta varia ad Concilium Basileense pertinentia. *In* Martène and Durand. Veterum script. et monument. hist....collectio. Vol. VIII. *See above,* II A.

Baumgarten, P. M. Aus Kanzlei und Kammer Erörterungen zur kurialen Hof- und Verwaltungsgeschichte im 13, 14, und 15 Jahrht. Freiburg. 1907.

——— Von der apostolischen Kanzlei. Untersuchungen über die päpstlichen Tabellionen und die Vizekanzler der heil. röm. Kirche im 13, 14, und 15 Jahrht. Cologne. 1908.

Bourgeois du Chastenet, L. Nouvelle histoire du Concile de Constance. Paris. 1718. [Appendix of docs.]

Bresslau, H. Zur Geschichte Kaiser Sigmunds. FDG. XVIII. 1878.

Breviscoxa, Johannes. De fide et ecclesia, Romano pontifice, et concilio generali. *In* Gerson, J. Opera omnia. Vol. I. *See below.*

Caro, J. Aus der Kanzlei Kaiser Sigmunds. AOG. LIX. 1880.

Deutsche Reichstagsakten. Vols. x-xiii. *See Gen. Bibl.* iv *under* Imperial Documents.

Döllinger, J. J. Materialien zur Geschichte des 15 Jahrhts. *In* Beiträge zur polit., kirchl., und Cultur-Geschichte. Vol. ii. Ratisbon. 1863.

Ehrle, F. Aus den Acten des Afterconcils von Perpignan 1408. *In* Archiv für Lit.- und Kirchengeschichte des Mittelalters. v and vii. 1889, 91.

—— Der Cardinal Peter de Foix der Aeltere, die Acten seiner Legation in Aragonien und sein Testament. *Ibid.* vii. 1891.

—— Die kirchenrechtlichen Schriften Peters von Luna (Benedikts XIII). *Ibid.*

—— Neue Materialien zur Geschichte Peters von Luna. *Ibid.* vi, vii. 1890–1.

Finke, H. Forschungen und Quellen zur Geschichte des Konstanzer Konzils. *See Gen. Bibl.* iv *under* Councils, General.

Gerson, Johannes. Opera omnia. Ed. Ellies Du Pin, L. 5 vols. Antwerp. 1706.

Hippeau, C. Documents concernant les relations de la France avec la cour de Rome, depuis la fin du xive siècle jusqu'au commencement du xviie. *In* Archives des missions scient. et litt. Ser. ii. Vol. ii. Paris. 1865.

Jacobus Almainus. De auctoritate ecclesiae et conciliorum generalium adversus Thomam de Vio Caietanum. *In* Gerson, J., Opera omnia. Vol. ii. *See above.*

—— De dominio naturali, civili, et ecclesiastico. *Ibid.*

Lenz, M. Drei Tractate aus dem Schriftenencyklus des Constanzer Concilsuntersucht. Marburg. 1876.

Loserth, J. Beiträge zur Geschichte der husitischen Bewegung. iii. Der Tractatus de longevo schismate des Abtes Ludolf von Sagan. AÖG. lx. 1880.

Muralt, E. von. Urkunden der Kirchenversammlung zu Basel und Lausanne. *In* Anzeiger für schweizerische Gesch. Bern. 1881.

Nicolaus de Pelhřimov and Ulricus de Znojmo. Orationes...in Concilio Basiliensi anno 1443. Ed. Bartoš, F. M. (Archivum Taboriense. i.) Tábor. 1935.

Pinsson, F. Caroli VII...Pragmatica Sanctio. Paris. 1666.

Pulka, Petrus. Epistolae. Ed. Firnhaber, F. *in* AOG. xv. 1856.

Repertorium Germanicum. Regesten aus d. päpstl. Archiven zur Gesch. des Deutschen Reiches, etc. *See Gen. Bibl.* iv *under* Papal Documents.

Richerius, Edmundus. Libellus de ecclesiastica et politica potestate. Cologne. 1701.

—— Vindiciae doctrinae majorum scholae Parisiensis. Cologne. 1683.

Sanctiandree, Copiale prioratus. The letter-book of James Haldenstone, prior of St Andrews (1418–43). Ed. Baxter, J. H. (St Andrews Univ. publns. xxxi.) London. 1930.

Simonsfeld, H. Analekten zur Papst- und Conciliengeschichte im 14 und 15 Jahrht. *In* Abh. BAW. Hist.-Cl. xx. 1891–2.

Theodericus de Niem (Dietrich von Nieheim). De modis uniendi et reformandi ecclesiam in Concilio Universali. Ed. Heimpel, H. (*with title* Dialog über Union und Reform der Kirche, 1410.) Leipsic. 1933.

—— De scismate. Ed. Erler, G. Leipsic. 1890.

—— Nemus unionis. Ed. Schard, S. Basle. 1566.

Traitez des droits et libertez de l'Église Gallicane. (Preuves des libertez de l'Église Gallicane.) [Ed. Brunet, J. L.] Vol. iii. [Paris] 1731. [Contains proceedings at Bourges, etc.]

Traversari, Ambrogio. Latinae epistolae. Ed. Mehus, L. Florence. 1759.

Tudeschis, Nicolaus de. (Panormitanus.) De electione et electi potestate. *In* Prima super primo decretalium. Lyons. 1546. ff. 118–84.

—— De concilio Basiliensi. *In* Consilia, quaestiones, etc. Lyons. 1546. ff. 126–37.

—— Questiones subtilissime, Questio i. *Ibid.* ff. 138–43.

C. NARRATIVE.

Aeneas Silvius Piccolomini (Pius II). Briefwechsel. Ed. Wolkan, R. (Fontes rerum Austriacarum. Abt. ii. Vols. lxi, lxii, lxvii, lxviii.) Vienna. 1909–18.

—— Commentarii de gestis Basiliensis concilii. *In* Opera omnia. Basle. 1551. *Also in* Fasciculus rerum expetendarum.... Ed. Brown, E. Vol. i. London. 1690.

—— De rebus Basiliae gestis stante vel dissoluto concilio. Ed. Fea, C. *in* Pius II... a calumniis vindicatus. Rome. 1823.

Antoninus, St (Archbp. of Florence). Summa historialis. *In* Opera omnia. Vol. I. Florence. 1741.

Baluzius, S. Vitae paparum Avenionensium. New edn. by Mollat, G. 4 vols. Paris. 1914–27.

Basler Chroniken. Ed. Vischer, W. and others. 7 vols. (Hist. Gesellsch. in Basel.) Leipsic. 1872–1915.

Baye, Nicolas de. Journal. Ed. Tuetey, A. (SHF.) Paris. 1885.

Bruni, L. (Aretino). Rerum suo tempore gestarum commentarius. Ed. Santini, E. and Pierro, C. di. RR.II.SS. New edn. Vol. xix, pt. 3.

Cerretanis, Jacobus de. Diarium. Ed. Finke, H. *in* Forschungen...zur Gesch. d. Konst. Konzils. *See Gen. Bibl.* iv *under* Councils, General.

Dacher, Gebhard. Historia magnatum in Constantiensi concilio primis concilii annis xiv et xv. *In* Mansi. Vol. xxviii. *See Gen. Bibl.* iv *under* Councils, General.

Fillastre, Guillelmus. Diarium. Ed. Finke, H. *in* Forschungen...zur Gesch. d. Konst. Konzils. *See Gen. Bibl.* iv *under* Councils, General.

Gattaro of Padua, Andrea. Tagebuch der venezianischen Gesandten beim Conzil zu Basel, 1433–5. Ed. Wackernagel, R. *in* Basler Jahrb. 1885.

Knöpfler, A. Eine Tagebuch Fragment über das Konstanzer Konzil. HJ. xi. 1890.

Patricius, Augustinus. Summa concilii Basiliensis. *In* Concilia Germaniae. Vol. v. *See above,* ii A.

Ruppert, P. Die Chroniken der Stadt Konstanz. 2 vols. Constance. 1890–1.

Theodericus de Niem (Dietrich von Nieheim). Historia de vita Johannis XXIII. Ed. Hardt *in* Magnum oecumenicum Constant. concilium. Vol. ii. *See above,* ii A.

Ulrich von Richental. Chronik des Konstanzer Konzils. Ed. Buck, M. R. (Bibl. des lit. Vereins in Stuttgart, 158.) Tübingen. 1882.

Windecke, Eberhart. Denkwürdigkeiten zur Geschichte des Zeitalters Kaiser Sigmunds. Ed. Altmann, W. Berlin. 1893.

III. MODERN WORKS.

A. GENERAL.

Ballerini, J. De potestate ecclesiastica summorum pontificum et conciliorum generalium liber. Verona. 1768. *Also in* Migne. Theologiae cursus completus. Vol. iii.

Bess, B. Johannes Gerson und die kirchenpolitischen Parteien Frankreichs vor dem Konzil zu Pisa. Marburg. 1890. [diss.]

Blietmetzrieder, F. Das Generalkonzil im grossen abendländischen Schisma. Paderborn. 1904.

Bruce, H. The age of schism. (The Church Universal.) London. 1907.

Cameron, A. J. The Apostolic Camera and Scottish benefices, 1418–88. (St Andrews Univ. publns. xxxv.) London. 1934.

Capes, W. W. The English church in the fourteenth and fifteenth centuries. (Hist. of the English Church. Ed. Stephens and Hunt. iii.) London. 1900.

Connolly, J. L. John Gerson, reformer and mystic. Louvain. 1928.

Creighton, M. History of the Papacy. New edn. Vols. i–iii. *See Gen. Bibl.* v.

Delalonde. Étude historique et critique sur le Grand Schisme. Rouen. 1875.

Erler, G. Dietrich von Nieheim, sein Leben und seine Schriften. Leipsic. 1887.

Eubel, C. Aus den Ausgabebüchern der Schisma-Päpste Klemens VII und Benedikt XIII. RQ. xviii. 1904.

Fournier, P. Les officialités au moyen âge. Paris. 1880.

Gayet, L. Le Grand Schisme d'Occident. 2 vols. Rome. 1889.

Gottlob, A. Aus der Camera Apostolica des 15 Jahrhts. Beiträge des päpstl. Finanzwesens. Innsbruck. 1889.

Haller, J. Papsttum und Kirchenreform. Vier Kapitel zur Geschichte des ausgehenden Mittelalters. Vol. i. Berlin. 1903.

Hartwig, O. Zwei Untersuchungen über das Leben und die Schriften Heinrichs von Langenstein. Marburg. 1857–8.

Hasenohr, W. Der Patriarch Johannes Maurosii von Antiochien: ein Charakterbild aus der Zeit der Reformkonzilien. Berlin. 1909.

Hasghagen, J. Papsttum und Laiengewalten im Verhältnis zu Schisma und Konzilien. HVJS. xxiii. 1926.

Hauck, A. Kirchengeschichte Deutschlands. Vol. v. *See Gen. Bibl.* v.

—— Die Reception und Umbildung der allgemeinen Synode im Mittelalter. HVJS. x. 1907.

Hefele-Leclercq. Histoire des Conciles. Vol. vii. *See Gen. Bibl.* v.

Heimpel, H. Dietrich von Niem (c. 1340–1418). Münster-i.-W. 1932.

Hergenröther, J. von. Handbuch der allgemeinen Kirchengeschichte. Vol. ii, ed. Kirsch, J. P. Freiburg-i.-B. 1904.

Hofmann, W. von. Forschungen zur Geschichte der kurialen Behörden vom Schisma bis zur Reformation. 2 vols. (Bibl. des K. Preuss. hist. Inst. in Rom. xii, xiii.) Rome. 1914.

Jacob, E. F. Dietrich of Niem: his place in the Conciliar Movement. *In* Bulletin... John Rylands Library. xix (1935). 388–410.

—— Some English documents of the Conciliar Movement. *Ibid.* xv (1931). 358–94.

Kneer, A. Die Entstehung der conciliaren Theorie zur Geschichte des Schismas und der Kirchenpolitiken. (RQ. Supplt. i.) Rome. 1893.

—— Kardinal Zabarella. Münster. 1891. [diss.]

Kochendörffer, H. Päpstl. Kurialen während des grossen Schismas. Neu. Arch. xxx. 1905.

König, E. Kardinal Giordano Orsini: ein Lebensbild aus der Zeit der grossen Konzilien und des Humanismus. (Studien u. Darstellungen aus d. Gebiete d. Gesch. im Auftrage der Görres-Gesellsch. v.) Freiburg. 1906.

Lafontaine, A. Jehan Gerson (1363–1429). Paris. 1906.

Mandonnet, P. Beiträge zur Geschichte des Kardinals Giovanni Dominici, Zusammenberufung des Konzils zu Konstanz. HJ. xxi. 1900.

Masson, A. L. Jean Gerson, sa vie, son temps, ses œuvres. Lyons. 1894.

Merkle, S. Konzilsprotokolle oder Konzilstagebücher. HJ. xxv. 1904.

Pastor, L. von. Geschichte der Päpste. Vol. i. Engl. transl. Vols. i, ii. *See Gen. Bibl.* v.

Raumer, F. von. Die Kirchenversammlungen von Pisa, Kostnitz, und Basel. *In* Hist. Taschenbuch. n.s. Vol. x. Leipsic. 1849.

Rösler, A. Kardinal Johannes Dominici, 1357–1419: ein Reformatorenbild aus der Zeit des grossen Schismas. Freiburg. 1893.

Sauerland, H. V. Cardinal Johannes Dominici und sein Verhalten zu den kirchlichen Unionsbestrebungen während der Jahre 1406–15. ZKG. ix, x. 1888–9.

Scheuffgen, F. J. Beiträge zur Geschichte des grossen Schismas. Freiburg. 1889.

Schwab, J. B. Johannes Gerson, Professor der Theologie und Kanzler der Universität Paris. Würzburg. 1858.

Stewart, A. Scotland and the papacy during the Great Schism. *In* Scottish hist. review. iv. 1907.

Thomassy, R. Jean Gerson et le Grand Schisme d'Occident. 2nd edn. Paris. 1852.

Valois, N. La crise religieuse du xve siècle. Le pape et le concile (1418–50). 2 vols. Paris. 1909.

—— La France et le Grand Schisme d'Occident. Vol. iv. *See Gen. Bibl.* v.

Wenck, K. Konrad von Gelnhausen und die Quellen der konziliaren Theorie. HZ. lxxvii. 1896.

Werminghoff, A. Nationalkirchliche Bestrebungen im deutschen Mittelalter. (Kirchenrechtliche Abhandlungen. Ed. Stutz, U. lxi.) Stuttgart. 1910.

Wessenberg, J. H. von. Die grossen Kirchenversammlungen des 15 und 16 Jahrhts. 4 vols. Constance. 1840.

Workman, H. B. The dawn of the Reformation. Vol. ii. The age of Hus. London. 1902. [This gives a summary of Reichenthal's chronicle with its vivid details.]

Zimmermann, A. Die kirchlichen Verfassungskämpfe im 15 Jahrht. Breslau. 1882.

B. Constance and Pisa.

Bernhardt, W. Zur Geschichte des Konstanzer Konzils. Marburg. 1891.

Bess, B. Die Annatenverhandlungen der Natio Anglicana des Konstanzer Konzils. ZKG. xxii. 1901.

Bess, B. Johannes Falkenberg und der preussisch-polnische Streit. *In* Brieger Zeitschr. XVI. Gotha. 1896.
—— Studien zur Geschichte des Konstanzer Konzils. Marburg. 1891.
Blumenthal, H. Die Vorgeschichte des Konstanzer Konzils bis zur Berufung. Halle. 1897. [diss.]
Bofarull y Sans, F. Felipe de Malla y el Concil o de Constanza. Gerona. 1882.
Caro, J. Das Bündnis von Canterbury. Eine Episode a. d. Geschichte des Konstanzer Konzils. Gotha. 1880.
Chroust, A. Zu den Konstanzer Konkordaten. DZG. IV. 1890.
Coville, A. Jean Petit. La question du tyrannicide au commencement du XVe siècle. Paris. 1932.
Dax, L. Die Universitäten und die Konzilien von Pisa und Konstanz. Freiburg. 1910. [diss.]
Denifle, H. Les délégués des universités francaises au concile de Constance. *In* Revue des bibliothèques. 1892.
Dieterle, K. Die Stellung Neapels und der grossen italienischen Kommunen zum Konstanzer Konzil. RQ. XXIX. 1915.
Erler, G. Zur Geschichte des Pisanischen Concils. Leipsic. 1884. [progr.]
Fages, H. Histoire de Saint Vincent Ferrier. 2nd edn. 2 vols. Paris. 1901.
Figgis, J. N. Politics at the council of Constance. TRHS. n.s. Vol. XIII. 1899.
Finke, H. Bilder vom Konstanzer Konzil. Heidelberg. 1903.
—— Papst Gregor XII und König Sigismund im Jahre 1414. RQ. I. 1887.
—— Der Strassburger Elektenprozess vor dem Konstanzer Konzil. Strasbourg. 1884.
—— Zur Charakteristik des Hauptanklägers Johanns XXIII. *In* Miscellanea Francesco Ehrle. III. Rome. 1924.
Focke, W. Studien zur Geschichte der englischen Politik am Konstanzer Konzil. Freiburg. 1919. [diss.]
Fromme, L. Der erste Prioritätsstreit auf dem Konstanzer Konzil. RQ. X. 1896.
—— Die spanische Nation und das Konstanzer Konzil. Münster. 1896.
—— Die Wahl des Papstes Martin V. RQ. X. 1896.
Funk, F. X. Martin V und das Konzil zu Konstanz. *In* Kirchengeschichtliche Abhandlungen und Untersuchungen. Vol. I. Paderborn. 1897.
Göller, E. Die päpstliche Pönitentiarie von ihrem Ursprung bis zu ihrer Umgestaltung unter Pius V. Vol. I. Die päpstliche Pönitentiarie bis Eugen IV. Rome. 1907.
—— König Sigismunds Kirchenpolitik vom Tode Bonifaz IX bis zur Berufung des Konstanzer Konzils 1404–13. Freiburg. 1902. [diss.]
—— Zur Geschichte der apostolischen Kanzlei auf dem Konstanzer Konzil. RQ. XIX. 1906.
Haller, I. England und Rom unter Martin V. QFIA. VIII. 1905.
Höfler, C. Der Streit der Polen und der Deutschen vor dem Konstanzer Konzil. SBAW. 1879.
Hollerbach, J. Die gregorianische Partei, Sigmund und das Konstanzer Konzil. RQ. XXIII, XXIV. 1910.
Hollnsteiner, J. Kaiser Sigmund a. d. Konstanzer Konzil. MIOGF. XLI. 1926.
—— Studien zur Geschäftsordnung am Konstanzer Konzil. *In* Abh. aus dem Gebiete der mittleren und neueren Gesch.... Festgabe H. Finke gewidmet. Münster. 1925.
Hübler, B. Die Konstanzer Reformation und die Konkordate von 1418. Leipsic. 1867.
Katterbach, B. Der zweite literarische Kampf...im Jan. und Feb. 1415. Fulda. 1919.
Kehrmann, K. Die Capita agendorum. (Hist. Bibliothek, herausg. von der Redaktion der HZ.) Munich. 1903.
Keppler, J. Die Politik des Kardinalkollegiums in Konstanz, Jan.-Marz 1418. Münster. 1899. [diss.]
Kitts, E. J. In the days of the Councils. London. 1908.
—— Pope John XXIII and Master John Hus of Bohemia. London. 1910.
Kötzschke, K. R. Ruprecht von der Pfalz und das Konzil zu Pisa. Jena. 1889.

Lenfant, J. Histoire du concile de Constance. New edn. 2 vols. Amsterdam. 1727. Engl. transl. London. 1728, 30.

—— Histoire du concile de Pise. 2 vols. Amsterdam. 1724.

Lenné, A. Der erste literarische Kampf auf dem Konstanzer Konzil im Nov. und Dez. 1414. RQ. xxviii. 1914.

Lenz, M. König Sigismund und Heinrich der Fünfte von England. Ein Beitrag zur Geschichte der Zeit des Constanzer Concils. Berlin. 1874.

Marmor, J. Das Conzil zu Konstanz...1414–18. Nach Ulrich von Reichental's handschriftlicher Chronik. 2nd edn. Constance. 1874.

Miltenberger, F. Versuch einer Neuordnung der päpstlichen Kammer in den ersten Regierungsjahren Martins V. RQ. viii. 1894.

Müller, F. D. Der Kampf um die Auctorität auf dem Conzil zu Constanz. Berlin. 1860.

Müntz, A. Nicolas de Clémanges. Strasbourg. 1846.

Peter, H. G. Die Informationen Papst Johanns XXIII und dessen Flucht von Konstanz nach Schaffhausen. Freiburg. 1926.

Powers, G. C. Nationalism at the council of Constance. Washington. 1928. [diss.]

Reinke, G. Frankreich und Papst Johann XXIII. Münster. 1900. [diss.]

Rest, J. Kardinal Fillastre bis zur Absetzung Johanns XXIII auf dem Konstanzer Konzil. Freiburg. 1908. [diss.]

Riegel, J. Die Teilnehmerlisten des Konstanzer Konzils. Freiburg. 1916. [diss.]

Rossmann, W. De externo concilii Constantiensis apparatu. Jena. 1856. [diss.]

Salembier, L. Petrus de Alliaco. Lille. 1886.

Sauerland, H. B. Ergänzungen zu dem Itinerar Johannis XXIII. *In* Hist. Jahrb. der Görres-Gesellsch. xviii. Munich. 1897.

Sauerland, H. V. Das Leben des Dietrich von Nieheim nebst einer Uebersicht über dessen Schriften. Göttingen. 1875.

Schmid, G. Itinerarium Johannis XXIII zum Konzil von Constanz. *In* S. Ehses Festschrift zum 1100-jährigen Jubiläum des deutschen Campo Santo in Rom. Freiburg. 1897.

Schmitz, J. Die französische Politik und die Unionsverhandlungen des Konzils von Konstanz (1414–16). Bonn. 1879. [diss.]

Schmitz, L. Das Itinerar Johannis XXIII. *In* Hist. Jahrb. der Görres-Gesellsch. xvii. Munich. 1896.

—— Zur Geschichte des Konzils zu Pisa 1409. RQ. ix. 1895.

Siebeking, H. Die Organisation und Geschäftsordnung des Constanzer Konzils. Leipsic. 1872. [diss.]

Steinhausen, F. Analecta ad historiam concilii generalis Constantiensis. Berlin. 1862.

Stuhr, F. Die Organisation und Geschäftsordnung des Pisaner und Konstanzer Konzils. Schwerin. 1891. [diss.]

Telgmann. Das Konklave in Konstanz 1417. Strasbourg. 1900. [diss.]

Tosti, L. Storia del Concilio di Constanza. Naples. 1853.

Truttmann, A. Das Konklave auf dem Konzil zu Konstanz. Strasbourg. 1899. [diss.]

Tschackert, P. Peter von Ailli. Zur Geschichte des grossen abendländischen Schisma und der Reformconcilien von Pisa und Constanz. Gotha. 1877. [With appendix of extracts from MS. at Emmanuel College, Cambridge.]

Wylie, J. H. The council of Constance to the death of John Hus. London. 1900.

Zösmair, J. Herzog Friedrichs Flucht von Konstanz nach Tirol. Innsbruck. 1894. [progr.]

C. BASLE, FERRARA, AND FLORENCE.

Abert, F. P. Papst Eugen IV. Mayence. 1884.

Ady, C. M. Pius II (Aeneas Silvius Piccolomini), the humanist pope. London. 1913.

Altmann, W. Stellung der deutschen Nation des Basler Konzils zur Ausschreibung eines Zehnten. ZKG. xi. 1889.

—— Zur Geschichte der Erhebung des Peterspfennigs im Königreich Polen durch Beauftragte des Basler Konzils. *In* Zeitschr. der hist. Gesellsch. der Provinz Posen. Jahrg. v. 1890.

Ametller y Vinyas, J. Alfonso V de Aragón en Italia y la crisis religiosa del siglo xv. Ed. Collell, J. 2 vols. Gerona. 1903–4.

840   The Councils of Constance and Basle

Aschbach, J. Geschichte Kaiser Sigmunds. Vol. IV. Hamburg. 1845.

Bachmann, A. Die deutschen Könige und die kurfürstliche Neutralität, 1438-47. AOG. LXXV. 1889.

Bangen, J. H. Die römische Kurie, ihre gegenwärtige Zusammensetzung und ihr Geschäftsgang. Münster. 1854.

Bartoš, F. M. Husitika a bohemika několika knihoven jihoněmeckých a švýcarských. Prague. 1932.

Beer, R. Die Quellen für den "Liber diurnus concilii Basiliensis" des Petrus Bruneti. SKAW. cxxiv. 1891.

—— Urkundliche Beiträge zu Johannes de Segovias Geschichte des Basler Konzils. SKAW. cxxxv. 1896.

Bett, H. Nicholas of Cusa. London. 1932.

Birck, M. Enea Silvio de Piccolomini als Geschichtsschreiber des Basler Konzils. In Theol. Quartalsschr. Jahrg. LXXVI. 1894.

Bittner, L. Die "Protokolle" des Konzils zu Basel und ihre jüngste Ausgabe. In Zeitschr. für österreich. Gymnasien. XLIX. 1898.

Bressler, H. Die Stellung der deutschen Universitäten zum Basler Konzil, zum Schisma und zur Neutralität. Leipsic. 1885. [diss.]

Bretholz, B. Bischof Paul von Olmütz über den Abschluss der Basler Kompaktaten. MIOGF. XXI. 1900.

Brieger, T. Ein Leipziger Professor im Dienste des Basler Konzils. In Beiträge zur sächsischen Kirchengesch. XVI. 1902.

Brockhaus, C. Gregor von Heimburg. Ein Beitrag zur deutschen Geschichte des 15 Jahrhts. Leipsic. 1861.

Brockhaus, C. F. Nicolai Cusani de Concilii universalis potestate sententia explicatur. Leipsic. 1867. [diss.]

Bursche, E. Die Reformarbeiten des Basler Konzils. Lodz. 1921.

Cecconi, E. Studi storici sul concilio di Firenze. Florence. 1869.

Cohn, W. Die Basler Konzilflotte des Jahres 1437. In Basler Zeitschr. für Gesch. XII. 1913.

Dephoff, J. Zum Urkunden- und Kanzleiwesen des Konzils von Basel. Hildesheim. 1930.

Dombrowski, L. Die Beziehungen des deutschen Ordens zum Basler Konzil...bis 1438. Berlin. 1913. [diss.]

Düx, J. M. Der deutsche Cardinal Nikolaus von Cusa und die Kirche seiner Zeit. 2 vols. Ratisbon. 1847.

Eckstein, A. Zur Finanzlage Felix V und des Basler Konzils. Berlin. 1911.

Fechner, S. Giuliano Cesarini (1398-1444) bis zu seiner Ankunft in Basel am 9 Sept. 1431. Marburg. 1907. [diss.]

Figgis, J. N. The Conciliar movement and the Papalist reaction. In Studies of political thought from Gerson to Grotius. 2nd edn. Cambridge. 1916.

—— Lecture IV (Councils and unity), lecture V (National churches). In Our place in Christendom. London. 1916.

Gottschalk, A. Kaiser Sigmund als Vermittler zwischen Papst und Konzil, 1431-4. Erlangen. 1911. [diss.]

Haller, J. Die Belehnung Renés von Anjou mit dem Königreich Neapel. QFIA. IV. 1902.

—— Die Kirchenreform auf dem Konzil zu Basel. In Korrespondenzblatt des Gesamtvereins d. deutsch. Gesch.- und Altertumsvereine. Jahrg. XVIII. 1910.

—— Die Protokolle des Konzils in Basel. HZ. LXXIV. 1895.

—— Zur Geschichte des Konzils von Basel. In Zeitschr. f. Gesch. d. Oberrheins. n.s. Vol. XVI. 1901.

Hasse, K. P. Nikolaus von Kues. Berlin. 1913.

Hergenröther, J. von. Kardinal Julian Cäsarini. In Kathol. Wochenschr. Ed. Himmelstein, F. Würzburg. 1855.

Joachimsohn, P. Gregor Heimburg. Bamberg. 1891.

Lazarus, P. Das Basler Konzil. Seine Berufung und Leitung, seine Gliederung und seine Behördenorganisation. (Ebering's Hist. Studien, 100.) Berlin. 1912. [Bibliography.]

Lenfant, L. Histoire de la guerre des Hussites et du concile de Basle. Amsterdam. 1731. Supplt. by Beausobre, J. de. Lausanne. 1745.

Manger, H. Die Wahl Amadäus' von Savoyen zum Papste durch das Basler Konzil. Marburg. 1901. [diss.]

Meusel, A. Die Quellen des 'Libellus de ortu et autoritate Imperii Romani' des Enea Silvio de' Piccolomini (Pius II). Breslau. 1903.

Morpurgo-Castelnuovo, M. Il cardinal Domenico Capranica. ASRSP. LII. 1929.

Pérouse, G. Le cardinal Louis Aleman, président du concile de Bâle, et la fin du Grand Schisme. Paris. 1905.

Pleyel, K. Die Politik Nikolaus V. Stuttgart. 1927.

Preiswerk, E. Der Einfluss Aragons auf den Prozess des Basler Konzils gegen Papst Eugen IV. Basle. 1902. [diss.]

Pückert, W. Die kurfürstliche Neutralität während des Basler Konzils. Leipsic. 1858.

Redlich, V. Eine Universität an dem Konzil von Basel. *In* Hist. Jahrb. der Görres-Gesellsch. XLIX. Munich. 1929.

Reuter, H. Balduin von Wenden und Dahlum, Abt zu St Michaelis in Lüneburg und Erzbischof von Bremen. *In* Zeitschr. d. Gesellsch. f. niedersächs. Kirchengesch. XIV. 1909.

Richter, O. Die Organisation und Geschäftsordnung des Basler Konzils. Leipsic. 1877. [diss.]

Rotta, P. Il Cardinale Nicolò di Cusa. Milan. 1928.

Scharpff, F. A. Der Cardinal und Bischof Nicolaus von Cusa. Pt. I. Das kirchliche Wirken. Mayence. 1843. [no more publ.]

—— Der Cardinal und Bischof Nicolaus von Cusa als Reformator, etc. Tübingen. 1871.

Schmidlin, J. Die letzte Sessio des Basler Konzils. *In* Strassb. Diözes. Blatt. n.s. Vols. III, IV.

Schmidt, C. Kardinal Nikolaus Cusanus. Coblenz. 1907.

Schneider, F. Der europäische Friedenskongress von Arras (1435) und die Friedenspolitik Papst Eugens IV und des Basler Konzils. Greiz. 1919.

Schweizer, J. Le cardinal Louis de Lapalud et son procès pour la possession du siège épiscopal de Lausanne. Paris. 1929.

—— Nicolas de' Tudeschi....Seine Tätigkeit am Basler Konzil. Strasbourg. 1924. [diss.]

Stutt, H. Die nordwestdeutschen Diözesen und das Basler Konzil...1431–41. *In* Niedersächs. Jahrb. v. 1928.

Stutz, J. Felix V. *In* Zeitschr. für schweizerische Kirchengesch. XXIV. Stans. 1930.

Thommen, R. Basel und das Basler Konzil. *In* Basler Jahrb. 1895.

—— Zur Geschichte des Basler Konzils. *In* Anzeiger f. schweizerische Gesch. VII. 1894 ff.

Vacandard, E. An attempt at union between Greeks and Latins at the council of Ferrara-Florence. *In* Constructive Quarterly. June 1917.

Valois, N. Histoire de la Pragmatique Sanction de Bourges sous Charles VII. (Archives de l'hist. religieuse de la France, IV.) Paris. 1906.

Vansteenberghe, E. Le cardinal Nicolas de Cues (1401–66), l'action, la pensée. Lille and Paris. 1920.

Voigt, G. Enea Silvio de' Piccolomini als Papst Pius II und sein Zeitalter. 3 vols. Berlin. 1856–63.

Wackernagel, R. Geschichte der Stadt Basel. 3 vols. Basle. 1906–24.

Weber, G. Die selbständige Vermittlungspolitik der Kurfürsten...1437–8. (Ebering's Hist. Studien, 127.) Leipsic. 1915.

Wittram, R. Die französische Politik auf dem Basler Konzil während der Zeit seine Blüte. Riga. 1927.

Zeibig, H. J. Beiträge zur Geschichte d. Wirksamkeit des Basler Konzils in Oesterreich. SKAW. VIII. 1852.

Zellfelder, A. England und das Basler Konzil. (Ebering's Hist. Studien, 113.) Berlin. 1913. [Prints docs.]

Zlozisti, I. Die Gesandtschaft des Basler Konzils nach Avignon und Konstantinopel (1437–8). Halle. 1908. [diss.]

Zwölfer, R. Die Reform der Kirchenverfassung auf dem Konzil zu Basel. *In* Basler Zeitschr. für Gesch. XXVIII, XXIX. 1929–30.

CHAPTER II.

JOHN HUS.

I. BIBLIOGRAPHIES.

See Bibliography to ch. iii, *infra.*

II. SOURCES.

De Ecclesia. The Church. By John Hus. Transl. by Schaff, D. S. New York. 1915.
Documenta Mag. Joannis Hus vitam, doctrinam, causam in Constantiensi Concilio actam...illustrantia. Ed. Palacký, F. Prague. 1869.
Geschichtschreiber der husitischen Bewegung in Böhmen. Ed. Höfler, K. (Fontes rerum Austriacarum. Abt. i. Vols. ii, vi, vii.) Vienna. 1856–66. *Cf.* Palacký, F. Die Geschichte des Hussitenthums und Prof. C. Höfler. Kritische Studien. 2nd edn. Prague. 1868.
Historia et monumenta Joannis Hus et Hieronymi Pragensis, confessorum Christi. Ed. M. Flacius Illyricus. 2 vols. Nuremberg. 1558. 2nd edn. Frankfort. 1715.
Historické spisy Petra z Mladoňovic a jiné zprávy a paměti o M. J. Husovi a M. Jeronymovi z Prahy. (Historical writings of Peter of Mladoňovice and other accounts and memories of Master John Hus and Master Jerome of Prague.) Ed. Novotný, V. (Fontes rerum Bohemicarum. viii.) Prague. 1932.
Korrespondence a dokumenty M. Jana Husi. (Correspondence and documents of Master John Hus.) Ed. Novotný, V. Prague. 1920.
Letters of John Hus. Ed. Workman, H. B. and Pope, R. M. London. 1904.
Processus judiciarius contra Jeronimum de Praga habitus. Viennae aet. 1410–12. Ed. Klicman, L. Prague. 1898.
Sbírka pramenů českého hnutí náboženského ve xiv a xv stol. Vols. i–viii. Ed. Flajšhans, V. Prague. 1904 ff. [Collection of sources of the Bohemian Reformation Movement, containing the following works by Hus: Expositio decalogi, De corpore Christi, De sanguine Christi, Super iv sententiarum, Sermones de sanctis.]
Sebrané spisy české M. Jana Husi. (Complete works in Czech of Master John Hus.) Ed. Erben, K. J. 3 vols. Prague. 1865–8.

III. MODERN WORKS.

Berger, W. Johannes Hus und König Sigmund. Augsburg. 1871.
Bonnechose, É. de. Jean Hus, Gerson et le Concile de Constance. Paris. 1846. 3rd edn. 1860.
Creighton, M. History of the Papacy. Vol. i. *See Gen. Bibl.* v.
Denis, E. Huss et la guerre des Hussites. Paris. 1878. 2nd edn. 1931.
Flajšhans, V. Literární činnost Mistra Jan Husi. (The literary activities of Master John Hus.) Prague. 1900.
—— Mistr Jan řečený Hus z Husinec. (Master John, called Hus of Husinec.) Prague. 1904.
Gillet, E. The life and times of John Huss, or the Bohemian Reformation of the fifteenth century. Boston, Mass. 1863.
Herben, J. Huss and his followers. London. 1926.
Jakubec, J. Dějiny literatury české. (History of Czech literature.) 2nd edn. Prague. 1929.
Lechler, G. V. Johannes Hus. Halle. 1890.
—— Johann von Wiclif. 2 vols. Leipsic. 1873. Transl. and abridged by Lorimer, P. *as* John Wycliffe and his English precursors. London. [1884.]
Lenz, A. Učení Mistra Jana Husi. (The teachings of Master John Hus.) Prague 1875.

Loserth, J. Hus und Wiclif: zur Genesis der husitischen Lehre. 2nd edn. Munich and Berlin. 1925. Engl. transln. of 1st edn. by Evans, M. J. London. 1884.

Lützow, Francis, Count. The life and times of Master John Hus. London. 1909.

Mussolini, B. John Huss. Transl. by Parker, C. New York. 1929. [Italian original publ. in 1913.]

Nejedlý, Z. Počátky husitského zpěvu. (The origins of the Hussite songs.) Prague. 1907.

Novotný, V. and Kybal, V. M. Jan Hus. Život a učení. Vol. i. Život a dílo napsal V. Novotný. 2 částí. Praha. 1919–21. Vol. ii. Učení, napsal V. Kybal. část i–iii. Praha. 1923–31. (Master John Hus, his life and teaching. Vol. i. Life and work, by V. Novotný. 2 pts. Prague. 1919—21. Vol. ii. Teachings, by V. Kybal. Pts. i–iii. Prague. 1923–31.)

Palacký, F. Dějiny národa českého v Čechách a na Moravě. (History of the Czech nation in Bohemia and Moravia.) Vol. iii. 2nd edn. Prague. 1870–2.

—— Geschichte von Böhmen. Vol. iii. Prague. 1845.

Schaff, D. S. John Huss: his life, teachings, and death. New York. 1915.

Sedlák, J. Mistr Jan Hus. Prague. 1915.

Strunz, F. Johannes Hus. Munich. 1927.

Tomek, V. V. Děje university pražské. (History of Prague University.) Prague. 1849.

—— Dějepis města Prahy. (History of the city of Prague.) Vol. iii. 2nd edn. Prague. 189..

Vlček, J. Dějiny české literatury. (History of Czech literature.) Vol. i. 2nd edn. Prague. 1931.

Workman, H. B. The dawn of the Reformation. Vol. ii. The age of Hus. London. 1902.

Wratislaw, A. H. John Huss. London. 1882.

844

CHAPTER III.

BOHEMIA IN THE FIFTEENTH CENTURY.

I. BIBLIOGRAPHIES.

Zíbrt, Č. Bibliografie české historie. (Bibliography of Czech history.) Vol. II. Prague. 1902.

Kazimour, J. Bibliografie české historie. (Bibliography of Czech history.) [For the years 1904-14 published with the Český časopis historický (Czech Historical Review), for the years 1915-19, 1920-4, 1925-6, 1927-9 published independently. Prague. 1922-31.]

Krofta, K. Novější badání o Husovi a hnutí husitském. Kap. II : Hus, jeho přátelé a odpůrci. Kap. III : Husitství po Husovi. (The recent investigations about Hus and the Hussite movement. Ch. II. Hus, his friends and opponents. Ch. III. Hussitism after Hus.) [Critical review of literature from the middle of the nineteenth century. Contained in the Český časopis historický (Czech Historical Review). Prague. 1915.]

Goll, J. and Šusta, J. Posledních padesát let české práce dějepisné. Soubor kritických přehledů české literatury historické psaných pro francouzskou Revue historique. (The last fifty years of Czech historical research. A collection of critical surveys of Czech historical literature, written for the French Revue historique.) Prague. 1926.

Novotný, V. České dějepisectví v prvním desítiletí republiky. Bibliografický přehled prací vyšlých v let 1918-28 s kritickými poznámkami. (Czech historical writings in the first decade of the Republic. Bibliographical review of works issued in the years 1918-28, with critical notes.) Prague. 1928.

II. SOURCES.

Akty Jednoty bratrské. (Records of the Unity of Brethren.) 2 vols. Ed. Bídlo, J. Brno (Brünn). 1915, 23.

Archiv český čili staré písemné památky české i moravské. (The Bohemian archives, or old Bohemian and Moravian chronicles.) Ed. Palacký, F. 6 vols. Prague. 1840-72.

Geschichtschreiber der husitischen Bewegung in Böhmen. Ed. Höfler, K. (Fontes rerum Austriacarum. Abt. I. Vols. II, VI, VII.) Vienna. 1856-66.

Kronika Vavřince z Březové. (The Chronicle of Lawrence of Březová.) Ed. Goll, J. (Fontes rerum Bohemicarum. v.) Prague. 1893.

Listář a listinář Oldřicha z Rožmberka. (Records and documents of Oldřich of Rožmberk.) 2 vols. Prague. 1929, 31.

Manifesty města Prahy z doby husitské. (Manifestoes of the city of Prague during the Hussite period.) Ed. Bartoš, F. M. Prague. 1933.

Nicolaus de Pelhřimov and Ulricus de Znojmo. Orationes...in Concilio Basiliensi anno 1433. Ed. Bartoš, F. M. (Archivum Taboriense, I.) Tábor. 1935.

Postilla Petra Chelčického. (Postilla of Peter Chelčický.) Ed. Smetánka, E. 2 vols. Prague. 1900, 3.

Prameny k synodám strany pražské a táborské v let 1441-4. (Sources touching the synods of the Prague and Tábor parties in the years 1441-4.) Ed. Nejedlý, Z. Prague. 1900.

Rokycanova postila. (The postilla of Rokycana.) Ed. Šímek, F. Prague. 1928-30.

Sít víry Petra Chelčického. (The Net of Faith by Peter Chelčický.) Ed. Annenkov, J. S. and Jagič, V. St Petersburg. 1893. 2nd edn. ed. Smetánka, E. Prague. 1912. 3rd edn. 1929.

Peter Cheltschitski, Das Netz des Glaubens. Transl. by Vogl, C. Dachau. 1924.

Staří letopisové čeští. (Old Czech chronicles), 1378-1527. Ed. Palacký, F. Prague. 1829.

Táborské traktáty eucharistické. (Tabor eucharistic tractates.) Ed. Sedlák, J. Brno (Brünn). 1918.

Urkunden und Actenstücke zur österreichischen Geschichte im Zeitalter Kaiser Friedrichs III und König Georgs von Böhmen. Ed. Bachmann, A. 3 vols. (Fontes rerum Austriacarum. Abt. II. Vols. XLII, XLIV, XLVI.) Vienna. 1879–92. [*Cf. Gen. Bibl.* IV under Imperial Documents.]

Urkundliche Beiträge zur Geschichte Böhmens und seiner Nachbarländer im Zeitalter Georgs von Podiebrad, 1450–71. Ed. Palacký, F. (Fontes rerum Austriacarum. Abt. II. Vol. XX.) Vienna. 1860.

Urkundliche Beiträge zur Geschichte des Hussitenkrieges.... (1419–36). Ed. Palacký, F. 2 vols. Prague. 1873.

III. MODERN WORKS.

A. GENERAL.

Bachmann, A. Geschichte Böhmens. Vol. II (1400–1526). Gotha. 1905.

Baker, J. A forgotten great Englishman, or the life and work of Peter Payne the Wicliffite. London. 1894.

Bartoš, F. M. Do čtyř prazských artykulů. Otisk ze Sborníku příspěvků k dějinám m. Prahy, v. (The Four Articles of Prague. Reprinted from Collection of contributions to the history of the City of Prague, v.) Prague. 1925.

—— Husitika a bohemika několika knihoven jihoněmeckých a švýcarských. Prague. 1932.

—— Husitství a cizina. (Hussitism and the outside World.) Prague. 1931.

—— Literární činnost M. Jakoubka ze Stříbra. (The literary activities of Master Jakoubek of Stříbro.) Prague. 1925.

—— Literární činnost M. Jana Rokycany, M. Jana Příbrama, M. Petra Payna. (The literary activities of Masters John Rokycana, John Příbram, and Peter Payne.) Prague. 1928.

Bezold, F. König Sigmund und die Reichskriege gegen die Husiten. 3 vols. Munich. 1872–7.

—— Zur Geschichte des Husitenthums. Munich. 1874.

Birnbaum, V., Cibulka, J., Matějček, A., Pečírka, J., and Štech, V. V. Dějepis výtvarného umění v Čechách. (History of art in Bohemia.) Vol. I. Prague. 1923–31.

Denis, E. Fin de l'indépendance bohême. Paris. 1890. 2nd edn. 1930.

—— Huss et la guerre des Hussites. Paris. 1878.

Gindely, A. Böhmen und Mähren im Zeitalter der Reformation. Pt. I. Geschichte der böhmischen Brüder. Vol. I (1450–1564). Prague. 1857.

Goll, J. Čechy a Prusy ve středověku. (Bohemia and Prussia in the Middle Ages.) Prague. 1897.

—— Petr Chelčicky a Jednota bratrská v xv stol. (Peter Chelčický and the Unity of the Brethren in the 15th century.) Prague. 1916.

—— Quellen und Untersuchungen zur Geschichte der böhmischen Brüder. 2 vols. Prague. 1878, 82.

Grünhagen, C. Geschichte Schlesiens. Vol. I. Gotha. 1884.

—— Die Husitenkämpfe der Schlesier, 1420–35. Breslau. 1872.

Haupt, H. Hussitische Propaganda in Deutschland. *In* Raumers Historisches Taschenbuch. Leipsic. 1886.

Jakubec, J. Dějiny literatury české. (History of Czech literature.) Prague. 1929.

Jastrebov, N. Etjudy o Petrě Chelčickom i jego vremeni. I. (Study of Peter Chelčický and his times.) St Petersburg. 1908.

Jecht, R. Der Oberlausitzer Hussitenkrieg und das Land der Sechsstädte unter Kaiser Sigmund. 2 vols. Görlitz. 1911, 16.

Krummel, L. Geschichte der böhmischen Reformation. Gotha. 1866.

—— Utraquisten und Taboriten. Gotha. 1871.

Lützow, Francis, Count. Bohemia, an historical sketch. London. 1896. 2nd edn. (Everyman's Library.) London. 1910; repr. 1920.

—— The Hussite Wars. London. 1914.

Maurice, C. E. Bohemia from the earliest times to the fall of national independence in 1620. (Story of the Nations.) London. 1896.

Müller, J. T. Geschichte der böhmischen Brüder. Vol. i (1400–1526). Herrnhut. 1922.

Nejedlý, Z. Dějiny husitského zpevu za válek husitských. (History of Hussite songs during the Hussite Wars.) Prague. 1913.

—— Počátky husitského zpěvu. (The origins of the Hussite songs.) Prague. 1907.

Palacký, F. Dějiny národu českého v Čechách a na Moravě. (History of the Czech nation in Bohemia and Moravia.) Vols. iii–v. Prague. 1851–67. Vol. iii. 2nd edn. 1870–2.

—— Die Geschichte des Hussitenthums und Prof. C. Höfler. Kritische Studien. 2nd edn. Prague. 1868.

—— Geschichte von Böhmen. Vols. iii–v. Prague. 1845–67.

Palmov, J. Češskije bratja v svoich konfessiách. (The Bohemian Brethren and their Confessions.) Vol. i. Prague. 1904.

Pekař, J. Žižka a jeho doba. (Žižka and his times.) Vols. i–iii. Prague. 1927–30.

Preger, W. Ueber das Verhältnis der Taboriten zu den Waldesiern des 14 Jahrhts. *In* Abh. d. BAW. 1887.

Toman, H. Husitské válečnictví za doby Žižkovy a Prokopovy. (Hussite military tactics at the time of Žižka and Prokop.) Prague. 1898.

Tomek, V. V. Dějepis města Prahy. (History of the city of Prague.) Vols. iii–x. Prague. 1875–94.

—— Johann Žižka. 1882.

Urbánek, R. Věk poděbradský. (The Poděbrady era.) Vols. i–iii. Prague. 1915–32. [Forms Vol. iii of the Czech History ed. by V. Novotný.]

Vogl, C. Peter Cheltschizki. Zurich. 1926.

Winter, Z. Děje vysokých škol pražských. (History of Prague University and Colleges), 1409–1622. Prague. 1897.

—— Život církevní v Čechách. Kulturní historický obraz z xv a xvi stol. (Church life in Bohemia. Sketch of the history of culture in the 15th and 16th centuries.) Vols. i and ii. Prague. 1895–6.

B. Legal, Economic, and Social History.

Čelakovský, J. Povšechné české dějiny právní. (Outline of Czech legal history.) Prague. 1900.

Kapras, J. Právní dějiny zemí koruny české. (Legal history of the lands of the Bohemian crown.) 2 vols. Prague. 1913.

Krofta, K. Přehled dějin selského stavu v Čechách a na Moravě. (Outline of the history of the peasantry in Bohemia and Moravia.) Prague. 1919.

Peterka, O. Rechtsgeschichte der böhmischen Länder. 2 vols. Prague. 1923, 28.

Rieger, B. Zřízení krajské v Čechách. (Local government in Bohemia.) Vol. i. Prague. 1893.

Winter, Z. Dějiny řemesel a obchodu v Čechách v xiv a xv stol. (History of handicraft and commerce in Bohemia in the 14th and 15th centuries.) Prague. 1906.

CHAPTER IV.

THE EMPIRE IN THE FIFTEENTH CENTURY.

I. BIBLIOGRAPHIES.

A. General.

Standard bibliographies are: Dahlmann-Waitz, Quellenkunde; Potthast, A., Bibliotheca historica medii aevi; Lorenz, O., Deutschlands Geschichtsquellen; Vildhaut, H., Handbuch der Quellenkunde, Vol. II; Jansen, M. and Schmitz-Kallenberg, L., Historiographie und Quellen, for all which see *Gen. Bibl.* I. Detailed information on the archives and archive material is in Bresslau, H., Handbuch der Urkundenlehre für Deutschland und Italien. See *Gen. Bibl.* I. Useful bibliographies are also in Gebhardt, B., Handbuch der deutschen Geschichte, Vol. I. See *Gen. Bibl.* v. Annual reviews of historical literature are—Jahresberichte der deutschen Geschichte, ed. Loewe, V. and Stimming, M. Breslau. 1920–5; and Jahresberichte für deutsche Geschichte, ed. Brackmann, A., Hartung, F., and Loewe, V. Leipsic. 1927 ff. The historical literature of the years 1914–20 is reviewed in Hampe, K., Mittelalterliche Geschichte. Gotha. 1922.

B. Special.

Bemmann, R. Bibliographie der sächsischen Geschichte. Leipsic. 1918 ff.

Charmatz, R. Wegweiser durch die Literatur der österreichischen Geschichte. Stuttgart. 1913.

Erman, W. and Horn, E. Bibliographie der deutschen Universitäten. 3 vols. Leipsic. 1904–5.

Häberle, D. Pfälzische Bibliographie. Heidelberg, etc. 1908 ff.

Heyd, W. Bibliographie der württembergischen Geschichte. Stuttgart. 1895 ff.

Lautenschlager, F. Bibliographie der badischen Geschichte. Karlsruhe. 1929.

Loewe, V. Bibliographie der hannoverischen und braunschweigischen Geschichte. 2nd edn. Posen. 1908.

—— Bibliographie der schlesischen Geschichte. Breslau. 1927.

II. ORIGINAL DOCUMENTS.

A. General.

Albrecht Achilles, Die politische Korrespondenz des Kurfürsten. Ed. Priebatsch, F. 3 vols. Leipsic. 1894–8.

Altmann, W. Regesta Imperii. Die Urkunden Kaiser Sigmunds (1410–37). See *Gen. Bibl.* IV *under* Imperial Documents.

—— Urkundliche Beiträge zur Geschichte Kaiser Sigmunds. MIOGF. XVIII. 1897.

Bachmann, A. Briefe und Acten zur österreichisch-deutschen Geschichte im Zeitalter Kaiser Friedrichs III (1448-71). See *Gen. Bibl.* IV *under* Imperial Documents.

—— Urkundliche Nachträge zur österreichisch-deutschen Geschichte im Zeitalter Kaiser Friedrichs III (1458–82). *Ibid.*

Chmel, J. Regesta chronologico-diplomatica Rupertiregis Romanorum. *Ibid.*

—— Regesta chronologico-diplomatica Friderici III Romanorum Imp. *Ibid.*

—— Materialien zur österreichischen Geschichte. (Beiträge zur Geschichte König Friedrich IV.) *Ibid.*

Deutsche Reichstagsakten. *Ibid.*

Eneas Silvius Piccolomini (Pius II). Briefwechsel. Ed. Wolkan, R. 4 vols. (Fontes rerum Austriacarum. Abt. II. Vols. LXI, LXII, LXVII, LXVIII.) Vienna. 1909–18.

Heimburg, G. Various tracts printed in Goldast, M. Monarchia S. Romani Imperii. Vols. I, II. See *Gen. Bibl.* IV.

Janssen, J. Frankfurts Reichskorrespondenz. Vol. I (1376–1439). Vol. II (1440–86). Freiburg. 1863–6.

Müller, J. J. Reichstags-Theatrum...(1440–93). *See Gen. Bibl.* iv *under* Imperial Documents.
Repertorium Germanicum....Clemens VII von Avignon. *See Gen. Bibl.* iv *under* Papal Documents.
—— —— Pontificat Eugens IV. Vol. i. *Ibid.*
Werner, H. Die Reformation des Kaisers Sigmund. (Archiv für Kulturgesch. Ergänzungsbd. iii.) Berlin. 1908. (*Cf.* Doren, A. *in* HVJS. xxi. 1924; Beer, K. *in* MIOGF. xl. 1925, *and in* SKAW. ccvi. 1927.)
Winkelmann, E. Acta imperii inedita. Vol. ii. *See Gen. Bibl.* iv *under* Imperial Documents.

B. TERRITORIAL.

Bachmann, A. Urkunden und Actenstücke zur österreichischen Geschichte im Zeitalter Friedrichs III (1440–71). *See Gen. Bibl.* iv *under* Imperial Documents.
Krenner, F. von. Baierische Landtagshandlungen (1429–1513). 18 vols. Munich. 1803–5.
Kuske, B. Quellen zur Geschichte der kölner Handels und Verkehrs im Mittelalter. 3 vols. Bonn. 1918–23.
Oberndorff, L. Regesten der Pfalzgrafen am Rhein (1214–1508). Vol. ii, pts. 1–5. (Badische Hist. Commission.) Innsbruck. 1912–19.

III. NARRATIVE AUTHORITIES.

A. GENERAL.

Aeneas Sylvius Piccolomini (Pius II). Commentarii rerum memorabilium, libri xii. Frankfort. 1614.
—— De ritu, situ, moribus et condicione Theutonie descriptio. Basle. 1571.
—— Historia rerum Friderici III. Ed. Kollar A. F. *in* Analecta monument. omnis aevi Vindobonensia. Vol. ii. Vienna. 1762. German transl. Ilgen, T. (Geschichtschreiber der deutsch. Vorzeit. 2nd edn. 88, 89.) Leipsic. 1899.
Andreas presbyter Ratisbonensis. Werke. Ed. Leidinger, G. Munich. 1903.
Chroniken der deutschen Städte. Vols. i, ii, iii, x, xi, Nürnberg. Vols. iv, v, xxiii, xxxiv, Augsburg. Vols. vi, xvi, Braunschweig. Vol. vii, Magdeburg. Vol. ix, Strassburg. Vols. xii, xiii, xiv, Köln. Vol. xv, Landshut, Mühldorf, München. Vols. xvii, xviii, Mainz. Vol. xx, Dortmund. Vols. xxi, xxiv, Soest and Duisburg. (Hist. Commission BAW.) Vols. i–xxxii. Leipsic. 1862 ff. Vols. xxxiii ff. Stuttgart. 1928 ff.
Dietrich von Nieheim. De scismate libri tres. Ed. Erler, G. Leipsic. 1890.
—— Nemus unionis. Ed. Schard, S. Basle. 1560.
Ebendorfer, T., of Haselbach. Chronica regum Romanorum. Bks. vi and vii. Ed. Pribram, A. F. (MIOGF. Ergänzungsbd. iii.) Innsbruck. 1890.
Gobelinus Persona. Cosmidromius (–1418). Ed. Jansen, M. Münster. 1900.
Grünpeck, J. Historia Friderici III et Maximiliani I. Ed. Chmel, J. *in* Österreichischer Geschichtsforscher. Vol. i. Vienna. 1838. German transl. Ilgen, T. (Geschichtschreiber d. deutsch. Vorzeit. 2nd edn. 90.) Leipsic. 1899.
Justinger, C. Berner Chronik (–1421). Ed. Studer, G. Bern. 1870.
Korner, H. Chronica novella. Ed. Schwalm, J. Göttingen. 1895.
Limburger Chronik. Ed. Wyss, A. MGH. Deutsche Chroniken. iv. 1883.
Nauclerus, J. Memorabilium omnis aetatis et omnium gentium Chronici commentarii (–1500). 2 vols. Tübingen. 1516.
Rolewinck, W. Fasciculus temporum (–1474). Ed. Pistorius, J. Vol. ii. Ratisbon. 1726.
Schedel, H. Liber Chronicorum (–1492). Nuremberg. 1493.
Windecke, E. Denkwürdigkeiten zur Geschichte des Zeitalters Kaiser Sigmunds. Ed. Altmann, W. Berlin. 1893. German transl. Hagen, F. von. (Geschichtschreiber der deutsch. Vorzeit. 2nd edn. 87.) Leipsic. 1899.

B. Territorial.

Anonymi chronicon Austriacum. German transl. Rauch, A. *in* Rerum Austriacarum Script. Vol. iii. Vienna. 1794.

Arnpeck, V. Chronik Bayerns (–1495). Ed. Freyberg, M. von. Stuttgart. 1827.

Chronik der Bischöfe von Münster (–1424); *and* Münsterische Chronik (1424–96). Ed. Ficker, J. Münster. 1851.

Ebendorfer, T., of Haselbach. Chronicon Austriacum (–1463). Ed. Pez, H. *in* Script. rerum Austriacarum. Vol. ii. Ratisbon. 1745.

Engelhus, D. Chronica nova (–1433). Ed. Leibnitz, G. G. *in* Script. rerum Brunsvicensium. Vol. ii. Hanover. 1711.

Eyb, Ludwig von. Denkwürdigkeiten brandenburgischer Fürsten. Ed. Höfler, C. Baireuth. 1849.

Fütrer, U. Bayerische Chronik. Ed. Spiller, R. Munich. 1909.

Gerstenberg, W. Chroniken [of Thuringia and Hesse]. Ed. Diemar, H. Marburg. 1909.

Rolewinck, W. De laude veteris Saxoniae nunc Westphaliae dictae libellus. Ed. and transl. Tross, L. Cologne. 1865.

Schüren, G. van der. Chronik von Cleve und Mark. Ed. Scholten, R. Cleve. 1884.

Sefner, J. Chronica des Landes Österreich (–1398). Ed. Seemüller, J. MGH. Deutsche Chroniken. vi. 1909.

Unrest, J. Österreichische Chronik (1435–99). [Chronicon Austriacum.] Ed. Hahn, S. F. *in* Collectio monumentorum ineditorum. Vol. i. Brunswick. 1724.

Wevelinkhoven, F. von. Chronicle, with continuations to 1466. Ed. Ficker, J. Münster. 1851.

Wildenberg, H. E. von. Chronik von den Fürsten von Bayern. Ed. Roth, F. Munich. 1905.

IV. MODERN WORKS.

A. General.

Andreas, W. Deutschland vor der Reformation. Stuttgart. 1932.

Aschbach, J. Geschichte Kaiser Sigmunds. 4 vols. Hamburg. 1838–45.

Bachmann, A. Die deutsche Könige und die kurfürstliche Neutralität (1438–47). AOG. lxxv. 1889.

—— Deutsche Reichsgeschichte im Zeitalter Friedrichs III und Max. I (1461–86). 2 vols. Leipsic. 1884, 94.

Beckmann, G. Der Kampf Kaiser Sigmunds gegen die werdende Weltmacht der Osmanen (1392–1437). Gotha. 1902.

Bezold, F. von. König Sigmund und die Reichskriege gegen die Hussiten. 3 vols. Munich. 1872–7.

Bock, E. Der schwäbische Bund und seine Verfassung (1488–1534). Breslau. 1927.

Brandenburg, E. König Sigmund und Kurfürst Friedrich I von Brandenburg. Berlin. 1891.

Chmel, J. Geschichte Kaiser Friedrichs IV und seines Sohnes Maximilian I. 2 vols. Hamburg. 1840, 42.

Erben, W. Kriegsgeschichte des Mittelalters. *See Gen. Bibl.* v.

Finke, H. König Sigmunds reichstädtische Politik(1410–18). Tübingen. 1880. [diss.]

Franz, E. Nürnberg, Kaiser und Reich. Munich. 1930.

Goll, J. König Sigmund und Polen (1420–36). MIOGF. xv, xvi. 1894–5.

Heuer, O. Städtebundbestrebungen unter König Sigmund. Berlin. 1887. [diss.]

Hofmann, A. von. Politische Geschichte der Deutschen. Vol. iii. Stuttgart. 1923.

Janssen, J. Geschichte des deutschen Volkes seit dem Ausgange des Mittelalters. Vols. i, ii. Ed. Pastor, L. Freiburg. 1913–15. Engl. transl. Mitchell, M. A. and Christie, A. M. London. 1896.

Kaser, K. Deutsche Geschichte zur Zeit Maximilians I (1486–1519). Stuttgart. 1912.

Klopp, O. Deutschland und die Habsburger. Vienna. 1907.

Kraus, V. von. Deutsche Geschichte zur Zeit Albrechts II und Friedrichs III (1438–86). Stuttgart. 1905.

Lamprecht, K. Deutsche Geschichte. Vols. IV, V. *See Gen. Bibl.* v.
Leroux, A. Nouvelles recherches critiques sur les relations politiques de la France avec l'Allemagne de 1378 à 1461. Paris. 1892.
Lindner, T. Deutsche Geschichte unter den Habsburgern und Luxemburgern (1273–1437). 2 vols. Stuttgart. 1890–3.
Loserth, J. Geschichte des späteren Mittelalters von 1197 bis 1492. *See Gen. Bibl.* v.
Nahmer, E. von der. Die Wehrverfassung der deutschen Städte in der zweiten Hälfte des 14 Jahrhts. Marburg. 1888. [diss.]
Nitzsch, K. W. Geschichte des deutschen Volkes bis zum Augsburger Religionsfrieden. Vol. III. 2nd edn. Leipsic. 1892.
Pückert, W. Die kurfürstliche Neutralität während des Basler Konzils. Leipsic. 1858.
Quidde, L. Die Wahl Sigmunds zum römischen König. Göttingen. 1881. [diss.]
Schäfer, D. Deutsche Geschichte. 9th edn. 2 vols. Jena. 1922.
Schiff, O. König Sigmunds italienische Politik bis zur Romfahrt. Frankfort. 1909.
Schwerdfeger, J. Papst Johann XXIII und die Wahl Sigmunds zum römischen König. Vienna. 1898.
Weber, G. Die selbständige Vermittlungspolitik der Kurfürsten im Konflikt zwischen Papst und Konzil (1437–8). Berlin. 1915.
Wostry, W. König Albrecht II. 2 vols. Prague. 1906–7.

B. TERRITORIAL.

Bachmann, A. Geschichte Böhmens. Vol. II. Gotha. 1905.
Böttiger, C. W. Geschichte des Kurstaates und Königreichs Sachsen. Vol. I. 2nd edn. by Flathe, T. Gotha. 1867.
Bretholz, B. Geschichte Böhmens und Mährens. Vols. I, II. Reichenberg. 1921, 23.
Dändliker, K. Geschichte der Schweiz. Vol. II. 3rd edn. Zürich. 1902.
Derichsweiler, H. Geschichte Lothringens. Wiesbaden. 1901.
Dierauer, J. Geschichte der schweizerischen Eidgenossenschaft. Vol. I, 4th edn. Gotha. 1926. Vol. II, 3rd edn. Gotha. 1920.
Doeberl, M. Entwickelungsgeschichte Bayerns. Vol. I. 3rd edn. Munich. 1916.
Droysen, J. G. Geschichte der preussischen Politik. Vol. I. 2nd edn. Berlin. 1868.
Eichmann, J. Der Städtekrieg von 1449–50. Berlin. 1882.
Gäthgens, G. Die Beziehungen zwischen Brandenburg und Pommern unter Kurfürst Friedrich II. Giessen. 1890.
Grünhagen, C. Geschichte Schlesiens. Vol. I. Gotha. 1884.
Hansen, J. Westfalen und Rheinland im 15 Jahrht. Vol. I. Die Soester Fehde. Vol. II. Die Münsterische Stiftsfehde. Leipsic. 1888, 90.
—— Zur Vorgeschichte der Soester Fehde. Trèves. 1883.
Häusser, L. Geschichte der rheinischen Pfalz. 2 vols. Heidelberg. 1845.
Hausberg, H. Die Soester Fehde. Trèves. 1882.
Heidemann, J. Die Mark Brandenburg unter Jobst von Mähren. Berlin. 1881.
Heinemann, O. von. Geschichte von Hannover und Braunschweig. Vol. II. Gotha. 1886.
Hintze, O. Die Hohenzollern und ihr Werk. Berlin. 1915.
Huber, A. Geschichte Österreichs. Vols. II, III. Gotha. 1886, 88.
Jäger, J. Beiträge zur Geschichte des Erzstiftes Mainz unter Diether von Isenberg und Adolf II von Nassau. Osnabrück. 1894.
Kirchlechner, K. Aus den Tagen Herzog Sigmunds des Münzreichen und Kaiser Maximilians I. Linz. 1884.
Koser, R. Die Politik der Kurfürsten Friedrich II und Albrecht von Brandenburg. *In* Hohenzollern-Jahrb. XIII. Berlin.
Kretzschmar, H. Die Beziehungen zwischen Brandenburg und die wettinische Landen...(1464–86). *In* Forsch. zur brandenburg. und preussisch. Gesch. XXXV. Berlin. 1923.
Lorenz, O. and Scherer, W. Geschichte des Elsasses. 3rd edn. Berlin. 1886.
Nerlinger, H. Pierre de Hagenbach et la domination bourguignonne en Alsace (1469–74). Nancy. 1891.

Palacký, F. Geschichte von Böhmen. Vols. iii–v. Prague. 1845 ff.

Pflugk-Harttung, J. von. Die Erwerbung der Mark Brandenburg durch das Haus Hohenzollern. *In* Forsch. zur brandenburg. und preussisch. Gesch. xxix and xxxi.

Prutz, H. Preussische Geschichte. Vol. i. Stuttgart. 1899.

Rachfahl, F. Der Stettiner Erbfolgestreit (1464–72). Breslau. 1890.

Riezler, S. Geschichte Bayerns. Vols. ii, iii. 2nd edn. Gotha. 1927 ff.

Schalk, K. Aus der Zeit des österreichischen Faustrechts (1440–63). Vienna. 1919.

Schneider, E. Württembergische Geschichte. Stuttgart. 1896.

Stälin, P. F. Geschichte Württembergs. Vol. i. Gotha. 1882–7.

Stowasser, O. Ulrich von Eizing und das Testament König Albrechts II. (Mitteil. d. Vereins f. Gesch. d. Stadt Wien, iii.) Vienna. 1922.

Vancsa, M. Geschichte Nieder- und Oberösterreichs. Vol. ii. Stuttgart. 1927.

Waddington, A. Histoire de Prusse. Vol. i. Paris. 1911.

Weech, F. von. Badische Geschichte. 2nd edn. Karlsruhe. 1896.

Wehrmann, M. Geschichte von Pommern. Vol. i. 2nd edn. Gotha. 1919.

Witte, H. Die Armagnaken im Elsass. Strasbourg. 1889.

—— Zur Geschichte der Entstehung der Burgunderkriege. Hagenau. 1885.

Zeissberg, H. von. Die österreichische Erbfolgestreit (1457–8). AOG. lviii. 1879.

C. Biographical.

Allgemeine deutsche Biographie. *See Gen. Bibl.* i.

Birck, M. Der kölner Erzbischof Dietrich Graf von Mörs und Papst Eugen IV. Bonn. 1889.

Erler, G. Dietrich von Nieheim. Leipsic. 1887.

Fraknoi, W. Matthias Corvinus, König von Ungarn. Freiburg. 1891.

Hasse, K. P. Nikolaus von Kues. Berlin. 1913.

Höfler, K. A. K. Ruprecht von der Pfalz, römischer König. Freiburg. 1861.

Hufnagel, O. Kaspar Schlick als Kanzler Friedrichs III. (MIOGF. Ergänzungsbd. viii.) Innsbruck. 1911.

Jansen, M. Kaiser Maximilian I. Munich. 1905.

Joachimsohn, P. Gregor Heimburg. Bamberg. 1891.

Kanter, E. W. Markgraf Albrecht Achilles von Brandenburg. Berlin. 1911.

Kluckhohn, A. Ludwig der Reiche, Herzog von Bayern. Nördlingen. 1865.

Kremer, C. J. Geschichte des Kurfürsten Friedrichs I von der Pfalz. 2 vols. Leipsic. 1765.

Menzel, K. Diether von Isenburg, Erzbischof von Mainz (1459–63). Erlangen. 1868.

—— Kurfürst Friedrich der Siegreiche von der Pfalz (1454–63). Munich. 1861.

Rotta, P. Il Cardinale Nicolò di Cusa. Milan. 1928.

Vansteenberghe, E. Le cardinal Nicolas de Cues. Lille. 1920.

Voigt, G. Enea Silvio de' Piccolomini als Papst Pius II und sein Zeitalter. 3 vols. Berlin. 1856–63.

Werminghoff, A. Ludwig von Eyb der Ältere. Halle. 1919.

D. Legal and Constitutional.

Below, G. von. Der deutsche Staat des Mittelalters. 2nd edn. Leipsic. 1925.

—— Territorium und Stadt. Munich. 1923.

—— Die Ursachen der Rezeption des Römischen Rechts in Deutschland. Munich. 1905.

—— Vom Mittelalter zur Neuzeit. Leipsic. 1924.

Bemmann, R. Zur Geschichte des Reichstages im 15 Jahrht. Leipsic. 1907.

Brunner, H. Grundzüge der deutschen Rechtsgeschichte. *See Gen. Bibl.* v.

Eberbach, O. Die deutsche Reichsritterschaft in ihrer staatsrechtlich-politischen Entwickelung…(–1495). Leipsic. 1912.

Hartung, F. Deutsche Verfassungsgeschichte vom 15 Jahrht. bis zum Gegenwart. 2nd edn. Leipsic. 1928.

Lindner, T. Die Veme. Münster. 1888.

Meister, A. Deutsche Verfassungsgeschichte…bis ins 15 Jahrht. *See Gen. Bibl.* v.

Molitor, E. Die Reichsreformbestrebungen des 15 Jahrhts. Breslau. 1921.
Müller, J. Die Entstehung der Kreisverfassung Deutschlands (1383–1512). Gotha. 1914.
Schröder, R. Lehrbuch der deutschen Rechtsgeschichte. *See Gen. Bibl.* v.
Spangenberg, H. Vom Lehnstaat zum Ständestaat. Munich. 1912.
Thudichum, F. Femgericht und Inquisition. Giessen. 1889.
Vahlen, A. Der deutsche Reichstag unter König Wenzel. Leipsic. 1892.
Weizsäcker, J. Der Pfalzgraf als Richter über den König. Göttingen. 1886.
Wendt, H. Der deutsche Reichstag unter König Sigmund (1410–31). Breslau. 1889.
Zickel, E. Der deutsche Reichstag unter König Ruprecht von der Pfalz. Strasbourg. 1908. [diss.]

E. Ecclesiastical.

Bressler, H. Die Stellung der deutschen Universitäten zum Basler Konzil. Leipsic. 1885.
Denifle, H. Die Universitäten des Mittelalters bis 1400. Vol. i. Berlin. 1885.
Ficker, G. and Hermelink, H. Das Mittelalter. *See Gen. Bibl.* v.
Hashagen, J. Staat und Kirche vor der Reformation. Essen. 1931.
Hauck, A. Kirchengeschichte Deutschlands. Vol. v. 2nd edn. *See Gen. Bibl.* v.
Schairer, I. Das religiöse Volksleben am Ausgang des Mittelalters. Leipsic. 1914.
Schulte, A. Der Adel und die deutsche Kirche im Mittelalter. 2nd edn. 2 vols. (Kirchenrechtliche Abhandlungen. Ed. Stutz, U. 63, 64.) Stuttgart. 1922.
Valois, N. La France et le Grand Schisme d'Occident. *See Gen. Bibl.* v.
Werminghoff, A. Die deutschen Reichskriegsteuergesetze von 1422 und 1427 und die deutsche Kirche. Weimar. 1916.
—— Geschichte der Kirchenverfassung Deutschlands im Mittelalter. *See Gen. Bibl.* v.
—— Nationalkirchliche Bestrebungen im deutschen Mittelalter. Stuttgart. 1910.

F. Social and Economic.

Bechtel, H. Der Wirtschaftstil des deutschen Mittelalters. Munich. 1930.
Bens, G. Der deutsche Warenfernhandel im Mittelalter. Breslau. 1926.
Hasse, K. P. Die deutsche Renaissance. Vol. i. Meerane. 1920.
Hegel, K. Städte und Gilden der germanischen Völker im Mittelalter. 2 vols. Leipsic. 1891.
Joachimsen, P. Geschichtsauffassung und Geschichtsschreibung in Deutschland unter dem Einfluss des Humanismus. Vol. i. Leipsic. 1910.
Kiesskalt, E. Die Post—ein Werk Kaiser Friedrichs III, nicht der Taxis. Bamberg. 1926.
Lamprecht, K. Deutsches Wirtschaftsleben im Mittelalter. 4 vols. Leipsic. 1886.
Mayer, F. M. Geschichte Österreichs mit bes. Rücksicht auf das Kulturleben. 3rd edn. 2 vols. Vienna. 1909.
Parisot, R. Histoire de Lorraine. Vol. i. Paris. 1919.
Schulte, A. Geschichte des mittelalterlichen Handels und Verkehrs zwischen Westdeutschland und Italien. Leipsic. 1900.
Schultz, A. Deutsches Leben im 14 und 15 Jahrht. Leipsic. 1892.
Stadelmann, R. Vom Geist des ausgehenden Mittelalters. Halle. 1929.
Streider, J. Studien zur Geschichte kapitalischer Organisationsformen. 2nd edn. Munich. 1925.

CHAPTER V.

THE PAPACY AND NAPLES IN THE FIFTEENTH CENTURY.

[*See also* the Bibliography of ch. vi *below*.]

I. SPECIAL BIBLIOGRAPHIES.

Ady, C. M. Pius II. *See below*, iii c.
Calvi, E. Bibliografia generale di Roma medioevale e moderna. *See Gen. Bibl.* i.
Capasso, B. Le fonti della storia delle provincie napolitane dal 568 al 1500. *See Gen. Bibl.* i.
Creighton, M. History of the Papacy. New edn. Vols. i–v. *See Gen. Bibl.* v.
Pastor, L. Geschichte der Päpste. Vols. i–iii. *See Gen. Bibl.* v.

II. SOURCES.

A. COLLECTIONS.

Bonanni, F. Numismata Pontificum Romanorum. Vol. i. Rome. 1699.
Caruso, G. B. Bibliotheca historica regni Siciliae. 2 vols. Palermo. 1723.
Collezione di documenti storici antichi inediti ed editi rari delle città e terre Marchigiane. Ed. Ciavarini, C. 5 vols. Ancona. 1870–84.
Corpus nummorum italicorum. *See Gen. Bibl.* iii.
Del Re, G. Cronisti e scrittori sincroni Napoletani. 2 vols. Naples. 1845, 68.
Documenti per servire alla storia di Sicilia. (Soc. siciliana di stor. pat.) Palermo. 1876.
Fonti della storia delle Marche. (R. Dep. di stor. pat. per le Marche.) Ancona. 1896.
Fonti per la storia d' Italia. (Fonti.) *See Gen. Bibl.* iv.
Graevius, J. G. and Burmannus, P. Thesaurus antiquitatum et historiarum Italiae etc. *See Gen. Bibl.* iv.
—— Thesaurus antiquitatum et historiarum Siciliae, Sardiniae, Corsicae, etc. *See Gen. Bibl.* iv.
Gregorio, R. Bibliotheca scriptorum qui res in Sicilia gestas sub Aragonum imperio retulere. 2 vols. Palermo. 1791–2.
Monumenta historica ad provincias Parmensem et Placentinam pertinentia. 12 vols Parma. 1855–69.
Monumenti istorici pertinenti alle provincie di Romagna. Series iii. Cronache. (R. Dep. di stor. pat. per le provincie di Romagna.) Bologna. 1869.
Monumenti storici. Ed. Capasso, B. (Società Napoletana di storia patria.) 2 vols. in 3 pts. Naples. 1881–92.
Muratori, L. A. Rerum Italicarum scriptores. (RR.II.SS.) *See Gen. Bibl.* iv.
Pirri, R. Sicilia sacra. 3rd edn. by Mongitore, A. 2 vols. Palermo. 1733. Additions etc., by Mongitore, A. 2nd edn. Palermo. 1735.
Raccolta di tutti i più rinomati scrittori dell' istoria generale del regno di Napoli. [Ed. Gravier, G.] 25 vols. Naples. 1769–72.
Raccolta di varie croniche, diari, ed altri opuscoli, così Italiani come Latini, appartenenti alla storia del regno di Napoli. Ed. Pelliccia, A. A. 5 vols. Naples. 1780–2. [This contains, besides those listed separately, the chronicles of Antonio Afeltro, Antonello Coniger, and the Cronaca di Napoli d' incerto autore.]

B. DOCUMENTS.

Acta inedita historiam Pontificum Romanorum illustrantia. Ed. Pastor, L. Vol. i. (1376–1464.) *See Gen. Bibl.* iv *under* Papal Documents.
Bognetti, G. P. Per la storia dello stato visconteo. Un registro di decreti della cancelleria di Filippo Mario Visconti, e un trattato segreto con Alfonso d' Aragona. ASL. liv. 1927.

Caetani, G. Regesta chartarum. Regesto delle pergamena dell' archivio Caetani.
    Vol. I. Perugia. 1922. Vols. II–V. Sancasciano. 1926 ff.
Carusi, E. Alcuni documenti per la congiura dei baroni negli Abruzzi (1485–6). *In*
    Boll. della R. Dep. Abruzzese di stor. pat. III. 1910.
Codice Aragonese. Ed. Trinchera, F. 3 vols. Naples. 1866–74. *Also* ed. Messer, A. A.
    Paris. 1912. *See also below*, III B.
Codice diplomatico della città d' Orvieto. Ed. Fumi, L. (R. Dep....di stor. pat.
    Documenti di stor. Italiana. VIII.) Florence. 1884.
Commynes, Philippe de. Lettres et négociations. Ed. Kervyn de Lettenhove. 3 vols.
    (Acad. roy. de Belgique.) Brussels. 1867–74.
Dallari, U. Carteggio tra i Bentivoglio e gli Estensi dal 1401 al 1542 esistente nel-
    l' Archivio di Stato in Modena. *In* Atti e mem. della R. Dep. di stor. pat. per
    le provincie di Romagna. Ser. III. Vols. XVIII. and XIX. Bologna. 1902.
Durán y Sanpere, A. Un document catalá de la revolta de Génova de 1435. *In* Bol.
    R. Acad. de Buenas Letras de Barcelona. VIII. 1915–16.
Egidi, P. L' ultimo trattato internazionale del libero comune di Roma. ASRSP.
    XLVIII. 1925.
Epistolarium Honorati Caietani. Lettere familiari del cardinale Scarampo e corri-
    spondenza della guerra Angioina (1450–67). Ed. Caetani, G. Sancasciano. 1926.
Ferdinandi Primi instructionum liber (1486–8). Ed. Volpicella, L. (Soc. Napol. di
    stor. pat. Monumenti storici. Ser. II. Documenti.) Naples. 1916.
Filangieri, G. Nuovi documenti intorno la famiglia, le case e le vicende di Lucrezia
    d' Alagno. ASPN. XI. 1886.
Foucard, C. Otranto nel 1480 e nel 1481. (Dispacci degli oratori Estensi da Napoli,
    Roma, etc.) ASPN. VI. 1881.
Fumi, L. Nuove rivelazioni sulla congiura di Stefano Porcari. [from Milanese
    Archives.] Perugia. 1910.
Paladino, G. Per la storia della congiura dei baroni. Documenti inediti del-
    l' Archivio Estense, 1485–7. ASPN. XLIV–XLVIII. 1919–23.
Ribera, J. Tratado de paz o tregua entre Fernando I el Bastardo, rey de Nápoles, y
    Abuámer Otmán, rey de Túnez (1477). *In* Centenario della nascita di Michele
    Amari. Vol. II. Palermo. 1910.
Theiner, A. Codex diplomaticus dominii temporalis S. Sedis. *See Gen. Bibl.* IV *under*
    Papal Documents.
Varias noticias sobre la segunda expedición a Nápoles por el Rey D. Alonso V en 1432.
    In Col. de doc. inéd. para la hist. de España. XIII.

C. Narrative Sources.

Alberti, Leon Battista. De porciana conjuratione. Ed. Muratori. RR.II.SS. 1st
    edn. Vol. XXV.
Albinus, J. (Albino, G.). De gestis regum Neapolitanorum ab Aragonia. Naples.
    1589. *Also in* Raccolta di...scrittori. [Ed. Gravier, G.] Vol. V. *See above*, II A.
Angeluccio, Franceso d'. Cronaca delle cose dell' Aquila (1436–85). Ed. Muratori
    in Antiq. italicae. Vol. VI. *See Gen. Bibl.* IV.
Annales Forolivienses. Ed. Mazzatinti, G. RR.II.SS. New edn. Vol. XXII, pt. 2.
Antonio di Pietro dello Schiavo. Diario Romano (1404–17). Ed. Isoldi, F. RR.II.SS.
    New edn. Vol. XXIV, pt. 5.
Beccadelli, Antonio (Panormita). De dictis et factis Alphonsi regis Aragonum libri
    IV. Florence. 1491. Basle. 1538. [With the commentary of Aeneas Sylvius
    Piccolomini.]
Bernardini Azzurrini. Chronica breviora aliaque monumenta faventina. Ed. Messeri, A
    Vol. I. RR.II.SS. Vol. XXVIII, pt. 3.
Blondus, Flavius. Historiarum decades III. *In* Opera. Basle. 1559.
Bonincontri, L. Annales (1360–1458). Ed. Muratori. RR.II.SS. 1st edn. Vol. XXI.
Borbona, N. di. Cronaca delle cose dell' Aquila (1363–1424). Ed. Muratori *in* Antiq.
    italicae. Vol. VI. *See Gen. Bibl.* IV.
Borghi, Tobia. Continuatio Cronice dominorum de Malatestis (1353–1448). Ed
    Massèra, A. F. RR.II.SS. New edn. Vol. XVI, pt. 3 (appendix).

Borselli, G. Cronica gestorum ac factorum memorabilium civitatis Bononie ab urbe condita ad a. 1497. Ed. Sorbelli, A. RR.II.SS. New edn. Vol. xxiii, pt. 2.

Burckardi, J. Liber notarum. Vol. i (from 1483). Ed. Celani, E. RR.II.SS. New edn. Vol. xxxii.

Campano, G. A. De vita et gestis Braccii. Ed. Valentini, R. RR.II.SS. New edn. Vol. xix, pt. 4.

Cantari sulla guerra Aquilana di Braccio di anonimo contemporaneo. Ed. Valentini, R. (Fonti.) 1935. ["Ciminello."]

Capgrave, John. Ye solace of pilgrimes. A description of Rome *c.* A.D. 1450. Ed. Mills, C. A. London. 1911. (*Cf.* article by Balzani, U. ASRSP. xxxii. 1909.)

Caracciolus, Tristanus. Opuscula historica. Ed. Muratori. RR.II.SS. 1st edn. Vol. xxii. *Also in* Raccolta di...scrittori. [Ed. Gravier, G.] Vol. vi. *See above,* ii A.

Cardami, Lucio, da Gallipoli. Diario. Ed. Tafuri, G. B. *in* Istoria degli scrittori nati nel regno di Napoli. Vols. ii, iii. Naples. 1744–60.

Chaula, Thomas de. Gesta per Alphonsum Aragonum et Siciliae regem. Ed. Starrabba, R. Palermo. 1904.

Chronicon anonymi Neapolitani (1434–1506). *In* Pellegrino, C. Historia principum Langobardorum. New edn. Vol. iv. Naples. 1749.

Chronicon Estense. Ed. Bertoni, G. and Vicini, E. P. RR.II.SS. New edn. Vol. xv, pt. 3 in progress.

Cobelli, L. Cronache Forlivesi. Ed. Carducci, G. and Frati, E. (R. Dep. di stor. pat. per le provincie di Romagna. Monumenti istorici. Ser. iii.) Bologna. 1874.

Collenuccio, Pandolfo. Historia Neapolitana seu Compendio dell' istoria del regno di Napoli. Venice. 1613. *In* Raccolta di...scrittori. [Ed. Gravier, G.] Vols. xvii–xix. *See above,* ii A.

Commynes, Philippe de. Mémoires. Ed. Mandrot, B. de. 2 vols. Paris. 1901, 3. *Also* ed. Calmette, J. and Durville, G. 3 vols. (Class. hist.) Paris. 1924–5.

Conti, Sigismondo dei, da Foligno. Le storie de' suoi tempi, dal 1475 al 1510. Ed. Calabri, F. 2 vols. Rome. 1882–3.

Corpus chronicorum Bononiensium. Ed. Sorbelli, A. A. RR.II.SS. New edn. xviii, pt. 1, in progress.

Cronache della città di Fermo. Ed. Minicis, G. de. (R. Dep....di stor. pat. Documenti di storia Italiana. iv.) Florence. 1870.

Cronache della città di Perugia. Ed. Fabretti, A. Vols. i, ii. Turin. 1887–8.

Cronache e statuti della città di Viterbo. Ed. Ciampi, I. (R. Dep....di stor. pat. Documenti di storia Italiana. v.) Florence. 1872. [Contains the chronicles of Niccola della Tuccia and Giovanni di Juzzo.]

Cronache Malatestiane. Ed. Massèra, A. F. RR.II.SS. New edn. Vol. xv, pt. 2.

Cronache Siciliane dei secoli xiii, xiv, e xv. Ed. Giovanni, V. de'. Bologna. 1865.

Cronica gestorum in partibus Lombardie et reliquis Italie (1476–82). (Diarium Parmense.) Ed. Bonazzi, G. RR.II.SS. New edn. Vol. xxii, pt. 3.

Diario Ferrarese dall' anno 1409 fino al 1502. Ed. Pardi, G. RR.II.SS. New edn. Vol. xxiv, pt. 7.

Diurnali detti del duca di Monteleone. Ed. Faraglia, N. F. (Soc. Napol. di stor. pat. Monumenti storici. Ser. i. Cronache.) Naples. 1895. [Published imperfectly by Muratori *as* Diaria Neapolitana *in* RR.II.SS. 1st edn. Vol. xxi.]

Fazio, B. (Facius.) De rebus gestis ab Alphonso I Neapolitanorum rege. Lyons. 1560. *In* Raccolta di...scrittori. [Ed. Gravier, G.] Vol. iv. *See above,* ii A.

Ferrarese, G. Excerpta ex annalibus principum Estensium (1409–54). Ed. Muratori. 1st edn. Vol. xx.

Gaspare da Verona and Michele Canensi. Le vite di Paolo II. Ed. Zippel, G. RR.II.SS. New edn. Vol. iii, pt. 16.

Gherardi, Jacopo, da Volterra. Il diario Romano (1479–84). Ed. Carusi, E. RR.II. SS. New edn. Vol. xxiii, pt. 3.

Giacomo, Notaro. Cronaca di Napoli. Ed. Garzilli, P. Naples. 1845.

Godis, Petrus de. De coniuratione Porcaria dialogus (1453). Ed. Lehnerdt, M. (*with* Horatius Romanus, *below*). Leipsic. 1907.

Griffonibus, Matthaei de. Memoriale historicum de rebus Bononiensium. Ed. Frati, L. and Sorbelli, A. RR.II.SS. New edn. Vol. xviii, pt. 2.

Gubbio, Ser Guerriero da. Cronaca (1350–1472). Ed. Mazzatinti, G. RR.II.SS. New edn. Vol. xxi, pt. 4.
Hieronymus Foroliviensis. Chronicon (1397–1433). Ed. Pasini, A. RR.II.SS. New edn. Vol. xix, pt. 5.
Horatius Romanus. Porcaria. Ed. Lehnerdt, M. Leipsic. 1907.
Infessura, Stefano. Diario della città di Roma. Ed. Tommasini, O. (Fonti.) 1890.
Jacopino de' Bianchi detto de' Lancellotti. Cronaca Modenese (1469–1502). Ed. Borghi, C. (Mon. di stor. pat. delle provincie Modenesi. Cronache. Vol. i.) Parma. 1862.
Leostello, Joampiero, di Volterra. Effemeridi delle cose fatte per il duca di Calabria (1484–91). Ed. Filangieri, G. Naples. 1883.
Lignamine, J. P. de. Inclyti regis Ferdinandi vita. Extracts ed. Pontieri, E. ASPN. lviii. 1933.
Manetti, Jannotius. Chronicon Pistoriense seu historiae Pistoriensis libri iii (–1446). Ed. Muratori. RR.II.SS. 1st edn. Vol. xix.
—— Oratio gratulatoria in coronatione Friderici III imp. Romae sub Nicolao V pont. facta ad utrumque 1450. In Freher, M. Rerum german. script. Ed. Struve, B. G. Vol. iii. Strasbourg. 1717.
—— Vita Nicolai V papae libri iv. Ed. Muratori. RR.II.SS. 1st edn. Vol. iii.
Matteo di Cataluccio da Orvieto. Ricordi (1422–58). Ed. Fumi, L. RR.II.SS. New edn. Vol. xv, pt. 5 (Ephemerides Urbevetanae. Vol. i.)
Minuti, A. Vita di Muzio Attendolo Sforza. Ed. Lambertenghi, G. P. in Miscell. di storia italiana. Vol. vii. (R. Dep. di. stor. pat.) Turin. 1869.
Palmieri, M. Liber de temporibus. Ed. Scaramella, G. RR.II.SS. New edn. Vol. xxvi, pt. 1.
Paolo dello Mastro. Diario e memorie delle cose accadute in Roma (1422–82). Ed. Isoldi, F. RR.II.SS. New edn. Vol. xxiv, pt. 2.
Paolo di Lello Petrone. La Mesticanza (1434–1447). Ed. Isoldi, F. RR.II.SS. New edn. Vol. xxiv, pt. 2.
Passero, Giuliano. Giornali. Naples. 1785.
Peregrino Priscianus. Storia Ferrarese. Ed. Bertoni, G. and Vicini, E. P. RR.II.SS. New edn. Vol. xv, pt. 3.
Pius II. (Aeneas Sylvius Piccolomini.) Commentarii rerum memorabilium quae temporibus suis contigerunt. Frankfort. 1614. [Contains also the Commentarii of Jacobus Piccolomini.]
Platina. Liber de vita Christi ac omnium pontificum. Ed. Gaida, G. RR.II.SS. New edn. Vol. iii, pt. 1.
Pontani, Gaspare. Il diario Romano, già riferito Notaio del Nantiporto (1481–92). Ed. Toni, D. RR.II.SS. New edn. Vol. iii, pt. 2.
Pontanus, J. J. Opera omnia. 3 vols. Venice. 1518–19.
Raimo, Ludovico, etc. Annales. Ed. Muratori. RR.II.SS. 1st edn. Vol. xxiii. Also in Raccolta di varie croniche.... Ed. Pelliccia, A. A. Vol. i. See above, ii a.
Ritius, Michael. De regibus Neapolis et Siciliae libri iv. In De regibus Hispaniae, etc. Naples. 1645.
Sanudo, Marino. Commentarii della guerra di Ferrara. Ed. Manin, L. Venice. 1829.
Simonetta, J. De rebus gestis Francisci Sfortiae (1421–66). Ed. Muratori. RR.II. SS. 1st edn. Vol. xxi. Ed. Soranzo, G. Ibid. New edn. Vol. xxi, pt. 2, in progress.
Sozomen Pistoriensis. Chronicon universale (1411–55). Ed. Zaccagnini, G. RR.II.SS. New edn. Vol. xvi, pt. 1.
Stella, G. Annales Genuenses (1298–1435). Ed. Muratori. RR.II.SS. 1st edn. Vol. xx.
Tummulillis, Angelo de. Notabilia temporum (1343–1467). Ed. Corvisieri, C. (Fonti.) 1890.
Valla, Laurentius. Historiarum Ferdinandi regis Aragoniae libri iii. Rome. 1520. Also ed. Schott, A. in Hispaniae illustratae. Vol. i. Frankfort. 1603.
Vespasiano da Bisticci. Vite di uomini illustri. Ed. Frati, L. 3 vols. Bologna. 1892. Engl. transln. Waters, W. G. London. 1926.
Vita Martini V. Ed. Muratori. RR.II.SS. 1st edn. Vol. iii, pt. 2.

D. Sixteenth-Century Historians.

Ghirardacci, Fra C. Della historia di Bologna. Pt. 2 (1321–1425). Bologna. 1669.
Pt. 3 (1426–1509). Ed. Sorbelli, A. RR.II.SS. New edn. Vol. xxxiii, pt. 1.
Giovio (Jovius), P. Vitae illustrium virorum. 3 vols. Basle. 1576–8.
Porzio, Camillo. La congiura de' baroni del regno di Napoli contro il re Ferdinando
I. Rome. 1565. Ed. d'Aloe, S. Naples. 1859. Ed. Nolfi, M. Turin. 1895.
Ed. Vacoli, A. 1907.
Sansovino, F. Origini e fatti delle famiglie illustri d'Italia. Venice. 1582.
Summonte, G. A. Historia della città e regno di Napoli. 2nd edn. Almagiore, T.
4 vols. Naples. 1675.
Zurita, J. Anales de la Corona de Aragón. 6 vols. Saragossa. 1610.

III. MODERN WORKS.

A. General.

Ametller y Vinyas, J. Alfonso V de Aragón en Italia y la crisis religiosa del siglo
xv. Ed. Collell, J. and Roca Heras, J. M. 3 vols. Gerona and San Feliu de
Guixols. 1903–28.
Archivio della società romana di storia patria. Rome. 1878 ff. (ASRSP.)
Archivio storico per le province napoletane. Naples. 1876 ff. (ASPN.)
Armstrong, E. Italian studies. Ed. Ady, C. M. London. 1934.
Battistella, A. Il conte di Carmagnola; studio storico con documenti inediti.
Genoa. 1889.
Block, W. Die Condottieri. Studien über die sogenannten "unblutigen Schlachten."
(Ebering's Hist. Studien, 110.) Berlin. 1913.
Burckhardt, J. Die Kultur der Renaissance in Italien. 15th edn. rev. by Geiger, L.
and Goetz, W. Leipsic. 1926. Engl. transl. (illustrated). Middlemore, S. G. C.
London. 1929.
Calmette, J. La politique espagnole dans la guerre de Ferrare (1482–4). RH. xcii.
1906.
Carusi, E. La legazione del cardinale D. Capranica ad Alfonso di Aragona (Napoli,
29 luglio—7 agosto 1453). ASRSP. xxviii. 1905.
Cipolla, C. Storia delle signorie italiane del 1313 al 1530. 2 vols. (Storia politica
d'Italia scritta da una società d'amici. Ed. Villari, P. Vol. iv.) Milan. 1881.
Creighton, M. History of the Papacy. New edn. Vols. i–v. *See Gen. Bibl.* v.
Eubel, C. Hierarchia catholica medii aevi. *See Gen. Bibl.* iii.
Fedele, P. La pace del 1486 fra Ferdinando d'Aragona ed Innocenzo VIII. ASPN.
xxx. 1907.
Forgeot, H. Jean Balue, cardinal d'Angers (1421–91). (BHE. 106.) Paris. 1895.
Gabotto, F. Lo stato Sabaudo da Amedeo VIII ad Emanuele Filiberto. Turin. 3 vols.
1892–5.
Gams, B. Series episcoporum. *See Gen. Bibl.* iii.
Haller, J. Die Belehnung Renés von Anjou mit dem Königreich Neapel. QFIA.
iv. 1902.
Lea, H. C. History of the Inquisition of the Middle Ages. *See Gen. Bibl.* v.
Lengueglia, G. A. della. Guerre dei Ginovesi contro Alfonso [V] re d'Aragona.
Genoa. 1648.
Litta, P. Famiglie celebri italiane. *See Gen. Bibl.* iii.
Manfroni, C. Storia della marina italiana dal trattato di Ninfeo alla caduta di
Costantinopoli (1261–1453). Pt. i. Leghorn. 1902.
—— Storia della marina italiana dalla caduta di Costantinopoli alla battaglia di
Lepanto. Rome. 1897.
Orsi, P. Signorie e principati. (Storia politica d'Italia scritta da una società di
professori. Vol. v.) Milan. [1902.]
Pastor, L. von. Geschichte der Päpste. Vols. i–iii. *See Gen. Bibl.* v.
Picotti, G. B. La pubblicazione e i primi effetti della "Exsecrabilis" di Pio II.
ASRSP. xxxvii. 1924.
Piva, E. La guerra di Ferrara del 1482. Padua. 1893–4.
—— Origine e conclusione della pace e dell' alleanza fra i Veneziani e Sisto IV.
N. Arch. Ven. n.s. Vols. i–vii. 1901–4.

Pleyel, K. Die Politik Nikolaus V. Stuttgart. 1927.
Raynaldus, O. Annales ecclesiastici. Vols. xxvii–xxx. *See Gen. Bibl.* v *under*
     Baronius.
Ricotti, E. Storia delle compagnie di ventura in Italia. Turin. 1844–5. And later edns.
     4 vols.
Rossi, L. Niccolò V e le potenze d' Italia (1447–51). Pavia. 1906.
—— Venezia e il re di Napoli, Firenze, e Francesco Sforza (1450–1). N. Arch. Ven.
     n.s. Vol. x. 1905.
Semerau, A. Die Condottieri. Jena. 1909.
Soranzo, G. La lega italica (1454–5). Milan. 1924.
Valentini, R. Lo stato di Braccio e la guerra Aquilana nella politica di Martino V
     (1421–1424). ASRSP. lii. 1929.
Zanelli, A. Roberto Sanseverino e le trattative di pace tra Innocenzo VIII e il re di
     Napoli. ASRSP. xix. 1896.

B. Naples and Sicily.

Ametller y Vinyas, J. Don Alfonso V de Aragón y Lucrecia de Alagno. *In* Rev. de
     Gerona. xii. 1888.
Balaguer, V. Alonso V y su corte de literatos. *In* Rev. de España. xxxviii, xxxix.
     1874.
Bianchini, L. Storia delle finanze del regno di Napoli. 3rd edn. Naples. 1859.
—— Storia economico-civile della Sicilia. Naples. 1841.
Blasi, E. di. Storia civile del regno di Sicilia. New edn. 22 vols. Palermo. 1830.
—— Storia del regno di Sicilia. 3 vols. Palermo. 1844–7.
Bofarull, F. de. Alfonso V de Aragón en Napoles. *In* Homenaje a Menendez y
     Pelayo. i. Madrid. 1925.
Calisse, C. Storia del parlamento in Sicilia dalla fondazione alla caduta della
     monarchia. Turin. 1887. [Bibliography.]
Calmette, L. La politique espagnole dans l'affaire des barons napolitains (1485–92).
     RH. cx. 1912.
Candida-Gonzaga, B. Memorie delle famiglie nobili delle provincie meridionali
     d' Italia. 6 vols. Naples. 1876–83.
Carusi, E. Osservazioni sulla guerra per il ricupero d' Otranto e tre lettere inedite
     di re Ferrante a Sisto IV (1480–1). ASRSP. xxxii. 1909.
Caruso, G. B. Memorie istoriche di quanto è accaduto in Sicilia dal tempo de' suoi
     primieri abitatori sino alla coronazione del re Vittorio Amedeo. 2 vols.
     Palermo. 1742, 45.
Cerone, F. Alfonso il Magnanimo ed Abù Omer Othman [Tunis]…1432–57. *In*
     Archivio stor. per la Sicilia orientale. ix. Catania. 1912.
—— La politica orientale di Alfonso d' Aragona. Naples. 1903.
—— A proposito di alcuni documenti sulla seconda spedizione di Alfonsi V contra
     l'isola Gerba. *In* Anuari de l'Inst. d'Estudis Catalans. iii. Barcelona. 1909–10.
Cortese, N. Don Alfonso d' Aragona ed il conflitto fra Napoli e Venezia per la
     conquista di Cipro. Teramo. 1916.
Costanzo, A. di. Istoria del regno di Napoli. 3 vols. Milan. 1805.
Croce, B. La corte spagnuola di Alfonso d' Aragona a Napoli. Naples. 1894.
—— Lucrezia d' Alagno. *In* Nuova Antologia. l. Rome. 1915.
—— Storia del regno di Napoli. Bari. 1925.
Cruz Navarro, P. Alfonso V de Aragón en el Imperio de Oriente. Valencia. 1908.
Damians Manté, A. Desfeta de la armada d'Alfonso V d' Aragón en Gaeta. *In* Bull.
     de la Soc. arqueol. Luliana. Sept.–Dec. 1900.
Egidi, P. La politica del regno di Napoli negli ultimi mesi dell' anno 1480. ASPN.
     xxxv. 1910.
Faraglia, N. F. Storia della lotta tra Alfonso V d' Aragona e Renato d' Angiò.
     Lanciano. 1908.
—— Storia della regina Giovanna II d' Angiò. Lanciano. 1904.
Flandina, A. La spedizione di Alfonso nell' isola delle Gerbe e la presidenza del
     regno di Sicilia in quell' epoca. *In* Archivio stor. Siciliano. n.s. Vol. i. Palermo.
     1877.

Forcellini, F. Un episodio della congiura dei Baroni. ASPN. xxxvii. 1912.

Fossati, F. Alcuni dubbi sul contegno di Venezia durante la guerra per la ricuperazione di Otranto. N. Arch. Ven. n.s. Vol. xii. 1906.

Foucard, C. Descrizione della città di Napoli e statistica del regno nel 1444. ASPN. ii. 1877.

—— Proposta fatta dalla corte estense ad Alfonso I, re di Napoli (1445). ASPN. iv. 1879.

—— Otranto nel 1480 e nel 1481. ASPN. vi. 1881.

Gentile, P. Parlamenti del regno di Napoli, 1450–57. ASPN. xxxviii. 1913.

—— La politica interna di Alfonso V d' Aragona, 1443–50. Monte Cassino. 1909.

Giannone, P. Storia civile del regno di Napoli. New edn. 5 vols. Milan. 1844–7.

Gregorio, R. Considerazioni sopra la storia di Sicilia. 4 vols. Palermo. 1831–9.

Jiménez Soler, A. Itinerario del rey D. Alfonso de Aragón, el que ganó Nápoles. Saragossa. 1909.

La Lumia, I. Storie siciliane. 4 vols. Palermo. 1881–3.

—— Studi di storia siciliana. 2 vols. Palermo. 1870.

Lecoy de la Marche, A. Le roi René; sa vie, son administration, etc. 2 vols. Paris. 1875.

Mazio, P. La guerra di Fernando de Aragona e di Renato d' Anjou. *In* Il Saggiattore. i. 1844.

Meo, A. di. Annali critico-diplomatichi del regno di Napoli. 13 vols. Naples. 1785–1819.

Messer, A. A. Le Codice Aragonese. Étude générale. Publication du manuscrit de Paris. (Bibliothèque du xve siècle, xvii.) Paris. 1912.

Minieri Riccio, C. Alcuni fatti di Alfonso d' Aragona dal 15 Aprile, 1437 al 31 Maggio 1458. ASPN. vi. 1881.

Miret y Sans, J. La politica oriental de Alfonso V de Aragón. Barcelona. 1904.

Mongitore, A. Parlamenti generali del regno di Sicilia dell' anno 1446 sino al 1748. 2 vols. Palermo. 1749.

Montalto, L. La corte di Alfonso I d' Aragona. Vesti e gale. Naples. 1922.

N., M. Il pontefice Pio II e l' aragonese Ferdinando I, re di Napoli. *In* Bull. Senese di stor. pat. xx. Siena. 1913.

Nunziante, E. I primi anni di Ferdinando d' Aragona e l' invasione di Giovanni d' Angiò. ASPN. xvii–xxiii. 1892–8.

Paladino, G. La pace di Miglionico. ASPN. xliii. 1918.

Pasolini, P. D. Madama Lucrezia. *In* Rendiconti...R. Accad. dei Lincei. Ser. v. Vol. xxvi. 1917.

Pepe, L. Storia della successione degli Sforzeschi negli stati di Puglia e di Calabria. Trani. 1900.

Perito, E. Uno sguardo alla guerra d' Otranto e alle cedole della tesoreria aragonesa di quel tempo. ASPN. xl. 1915.

Pontieri, E. La Calabria del secolo xv e la rivolta di Antonio Centeglia. ASPN. xlix. 1924.

Scaduto, F. Stato e chiesa nelle Due Sicilie dai Normanni ai giorni nostri. Palermo. 1887.

Schipa, M. Contese sociali nel medio evo. ASPN. xxxi–xxxiii. 1906–8.

—— Nobili e popolani in Napoli nel medio evo. ASI. lxxx. 1925.

Tapia, C. de. Jus regni Neapolitani. 7 vols. Naples. 1605–43.

Toppi, N. De origine tribunalium. 2nd edn. 3 vols. Naples. 1666.

Vendrell Gallostra, F. La corte literaria de Alfonso V de Aragón y tres poetas de la misma. *In* Bol. R. Acad. Españ. xix. 1932.

Vita, O. Ricerche sulla storia di Sicilia sotto Ferdinando di Castiglia. Palermo. 1922.

C. Papal States.

Ady, C. M. Pius II (Aeneas Silvius Piccolomini), the Humanist Pope. London. 1913.

Armstrong, E. Aeneas Silvius Piccolomini, Pope Pius II. *In* Italian studies. *See above*, iii a.

Banchi, L. Il Piccinino nello stato di Siena e la lega italica, 1455–6. ASI. Ser. iv. Vol. iv. 1879.

Banchi, L. Ultime relazioni dei Senesi con papa Callisto III. ASI. Ser. iv. Vol. v. 1880.

Benadduci, G. Della signoria di Francesco Sforza nella Marca e peculiarmente in Tolentino (1433–47). Tolentino. 1892.

Bonazzi, L. Storia di Perugia dalle origini al 1860. Vol. i. Perugia. 1875.

Boüard, A. de. Le régime politique et les institutions de Rome au moyen âge. Paris. 1920.

Boulting, W. S. Aeneas Silvius. London. 1908.

Caetani, G. Domus Caietana. Storia documentata della famiglia Caetani. Vol. i, pt. 2. Sancasciano. 1927.

Calisse, C. I Prefetti di Vico. ASRSP. x, xi. 1887–8.

Cappelli, A. Niccolò di Leonello d' Este. *In* Atti e mem. della R. Dep. di stor. pat. per le provincie Modenesi e Parmensi. Vol. v. Modena. 1870.

Ciacconius, A. Vitae et res gestae Pontificum Romanorum et S.R.E. Cardinalium. Vols. ii, iii. Rome. 1677.

· Davies, G. S. Renascence: the sculptured tombs of the fifteenth century in Rome. London. 1910.

Dennistoun, J. Memoirs of the Dukes of Urbino. Ed. Hutton, E. 3 vols. London. 1908.

Fabretti, A. Biografie dei Capitani Venturieri dell' Umbria. 5 vols. Montepulciano. 1842–6.

Frantz, E. Sixtus IV und die Republik Florenz. Ratisbon. 1880.

Frizzi, A. Memorie per la storia di Ferrara. 2nd edn. 5 vols. Ferrara. 1847–50.

Gardner, E. G. Dukes and poets in Ferrara. London. 1904.

Gianandrea, A. Della signoria di Francesco Sforza nella Marca. ASL. viii, xii, and xxiii. 1881–96.

—— Della signoria di Francesco Sforza nella Marca secondo le mem. e i doc. dell' arch. Fabrianese. ASI. Ser. v. Vol. ii. 1888.

Gregorovius, F. Geschichte der Stadt Rom im Mittelalter. *See Gen. Bibl.* v.

Guiraud, J. L'État pontifical après le Grand Schisme. Étude de géographie politique. (EcfrAR.) Paris. 1896.

Heywood, W. History of Perugia. London. 1910.

Höfler, C. von. Don Rodrigo de Borja (Papst Alexander VI) und seine Söhne. Vienna. 1889.

Hofmann, W. von. Forschungen zur Geschichte der kurialen Behörden vom Schisma bis zur Reformation. 2 vols. Rome. 1914.

Hutton, E. Sigismondo Pandolfo Malatesta, lord of Rimini. London. 1906.

L'Épinois, H. de. Paul II et Pomponius Laetus. RQH. i. 1866.

Longhi, M. Niccolò Piccinino in Bologna (1438–43). *In* Atti e mem. della R. Dep. di stor. pat. per le provincie di Romagna. Ser. iii. Vols. xxiv, xxv. 1906–7.

Miller, W. Mediaeval Rome, 1073–1600. (Story of the Nations.) London. 1901.

Morpurgo-Castelnuovo, M. Il cardinale Domenico Capranica. ASRSP. lii. 1929.

Müntz, E. Les arts à la cour des papes pendant le xve et le xvie siècle. Recueil de documents inédits.... Vols. i–iii, pt. i (1417–84). (EcfrAR.) Paris. 1878–82.

—— Les arts à la cour des papes Innocent VIII, etc. (1484–1503.) (AcadIBL. Fondation E. Piot.) Paris. 1898.

Muratori, L. A. Delle antichità Estensi ed Italiane. 2 vols. Modena. 1717, 40.

Nasalli Rocca di Corneliano, E. Il cardinale Bessarione legato pontificio in Bologna. *In* Atti e mem. della R. Dep. di stor. pat. per le provincie di Romagna. Ser. iv. Vol. xx. 1930.

Paschini, P. Da medico a patriarca d'Aquileia, camerlengo e cardinale di S. Romana Chiesa. *In* Memorie storiche forogiuliesi. xxiii. 1927.

—— Lodovico cardinale camerlengo e i suoi maneggi sino alla morte di Eugenio IV (1447). *Ibid.* xxiv. 1928. xxvi. 1931.

—— La flotta di Callisto III (1455–8). ASRSP. liii–lv. 1930–2.

Peruzzi, A. Storia d'Ancona...all' anno 1532. 2 vols. Pesaro. 1835.

Pinzi, C. Storia della città di Viterbo lungo il medio evo. Vol. iv. Viterbo. 1913.

Prutz, H. Pius II Rüstungen zum Türkenkrieg. (Repr. from SBAW.) Munich. 1912.

Reumont, A. von. Geschichte der Stadt Rom. 3 vols. Berlin. 1867–70.

Rodocanachi, E. Les corporations ouvrières à Rome. 2 vols. Paris. 1894.

Rodocanachi, E. Histoire de Rome de 1354 à 1471. Paris. 1922.
—— Histoire de Rome. Une cour princière au Vatican...1471–1503. Paris. 1925.
Rosi, M. Della signoria di Francesco Sforza nella Marca, secondo le memorie dell' archivio Recanatense. Recanati. 1895.
Salimei, A. Serie cronologica dei senatori di Roma dal 1431 al 1447. ASRSP. LIII–LV. 1930–2.
Sanesi, G. Stefano Porcari e la sua congiura. Pistoia. 1887.
Schmarsow, A. Melozzo da Forlì. Ein Beitrag zur Kunst- und Kulturgeschichte Italiens im 15 Jahrht. Berlin. 1886. [Useful for Sixtus IV and nephews.]
Schürmeyer, W. Das Kardinalskollegium unter Pius II. (Ebering's Hist. Studien, 122.) Berlin. 1914.
Soranzo, G. Pio II e la politica italiana nella lotta contro i Malatesti (1457–63). Padua. 1911.
Tomassetti, G. La Campagna Romana antica, medioevale, e moderna. 3 vols. Rome. 1910–13.
Tommasini, O. Documenti relativi a Stefano Porcari. ASRSP. III. 1880.
Tonini, L. Storia civile e sacra Riminese. Vol. v. Rimini nella Signoria de' Malatesti. Pt. II. Rimini. 1881.
Torraca, F. Studi critici. Naples. 1907.
Ugolini, F. Storia dei conti e duchi d' Urbino. 2 vols. Florence. 1859.
Vast, H. Le cardinal Bessarion (1403–72). Paris. 1878.
Voigt, G. Enea Silvio de' Piccolomini als Papst Pius II und sein Zeitalter. 3 vols. Berlin. 1856–63.
Yriarte, C. Un Condottiere au xvᵉ siècle. Rimini. Paris. 1882.

CHAPTER VI.

FLORENCE AND NORTH ITALY, 1414–1492.

[*See also* the Bibliography of ch. v *above.*]

I. BIBLIOGRAPHIES.

General: Egidi, P. La storia medioevale. *See Gen. Bibl.* i.
Florence: Caggese, R. Firenze della decadenza di Roma al risorgimento d' Italia
    See below, iii b (i).
    Pieraccini, G. La stirpe de' Medici di Cafaggiolo. *Ibid.*
Milan: Ady, C. M. History of Milan under the Sforza. *See below,* iii b (ii).
    Verga, E. Storia della vita milanese. *Ibid.*
Venice: Brown, H. F. Venice. *See below,* iii b (iii).
    Foligno, C. Codice di materia veneta nelle biblioteche inglesi. N. Arch.
    Ven. n.s. Vols. x–xv. 1905–8.
    Kretschmayr, H. Geschichte von Venedig. Vol. ii. *See below,* iii b (iii).

II. SOURCES.

A. Documents.

Annali della Fabbrica del Duomo di Milano. Ed. Brigola. 9 vols. Milan. 1877–85.
Calendar of State Papers and Manuscripts existing in the archives and collections of
    Milan. Vol. i (1385–1618). Ed. Hinds, A. B. (Cal.SP.) London. 1912.
Calendar of State Papers and Manuscripts relating to English affairs preserved in
    the archives of Venice. Vol. i (1202–1509). Ed. Brown, R. *Ibid.* 1864.
Canestrini, G. Documenti per servire alla storia della milizia italiana. ASI. Vol. xv.
    1851.
—— La scienza e l' arte di Stato desunte dagli atti officiali della repubblica fiorentina
    e dei Medici. Pt. i. Vol. i. Florence. 1862.
Canestrini, G. and Desjardins, A. Négociations diplomatiques de la France avec la
    Toscane. Vol. i. Paris. 1859.
Cappelli, A. Lettere di Lorenzo dei Medici conservate nell' archivio di Modena con
    notizie tratte dai carteggi diplomatici degli oratori estensi a Firenze. *In* Atti e
    mem. della R. Dep. di stor. pat. per le provincie Modenesi e Parmensi. Vol. i.
    p. 231. Modena. 1864.
Commissioni di Rinaldo degli Albizzi. Ed. Guasti, C. 3 vols. Florence. 1867–73.
Dallari, U. Carteggio tra i Bentivoglio e gli Estensi dal 1401 al 1542 esistente nell'
    Archivio di Stato in Modena. *In* Atti e mem. della R. Dep. di stor. pat. per le
    provincie di Romagna. Ser. iii. Vols. xviii, pp. 1, 285; xix, p. 245. Bologna.
    1902.
Formentini, M. Il Ducato di Milano. Studii storici documentati. Milan. 1877.
Grunzweig, A. Correspondance de la filiale de Bruges des Medici. Pt. i. (Comm.
    roy. d'hist. de Belgique.) Brussels. 1931.
Inventari e Registri del R. Archivio di Stato in Milano.
    Vol. i. I registri viscontei. Ed. Manaresi, C. Milan. 1915.
    Vol. ii, pts. 1, 2. Gli atti cancellereschi viscontei. Ed. Vittani, G. Milan.
    1920–29.
    Vol. iii. I registri dell' ufficio degli statuti di Milano. Ed. Ferorelli, N. Milan.
    1920–26.
Karmin, D. La legge del catasto fiorentino del 1427. Testo, introduzione, e note.
    Florence. 1906.
Mandrot, B. de and Samaran, C. Dépêches des ambassadeurs milanais en France
    sous Louis XI et François Sforza. 4 vols. (SHF.) Paris. 1916–23.
Medici, Lorenzo de'. Lettere ad Innocenzo VIII. Ed. Moreni, D. Florence. 1830.
Medici Archives, Catalogue of the...Property of the Marquis Cosimo de' Medici and
    the Marquis Averardo de' Medici. London. [1917.]

Morbio, C. Codice Visconteo-Sforzesco, 1390–1497. Milan. 1846.
Müller, G. Documenti sulle relazioni delle città Toscane coll' oriente fino all' anno 1531. Florence. 1879.
Osio, L. and Cantù, C. Documenti diplomatici tratti degli Archivi Milanesi (1265–1447). 3 vols. Milan. 1864.
Predelli, R. I libri commemoriali della republica di Venezia. Regesti. 8 vols. (R. Dep. Ven. di stor. pat. Monumenti, Ser. I. Documenti. Vols. I, III, VII, VIII, X, XI, XIII, XVII.) Venice. 1876–1913. [Vols. VII–XI especially for 15th century.]
Provvisioni della repubblica fiorentina dei 10 e 19 Aprile 1480 per la formazione dell' Ordine dei Settanta. Ed. Capponi, G. ASI. Vol. I (1842). 315.
Statuta Populi et Communis Florentiae publica auctoritate collecta castigata et praeposita anno salutis MCCCCXV. 3 vols. Fribourg. 1778–83.
Suardis, P. de. Liber statutorum inclite civitatis Mediolani. Milan. 1480.

B. Chronicles, Biographies etc.

Allegretto, A. Diarii delle cose Sanesi del suo tempo (1450–96). Ed. Muratori. RR.II.SS. 1st edn. Vol. XXIII.
Anonimo Veronese. Cronaca 1446–88. Ed. Soranzo, G. (R. Dep. Ven. di storia patria. Monumenti. Ser. III. Vol. IV.) Venice. 1915.
Antoninus, St (Archbp. of Florence). Chronicon. 3 vols. Nuremberg. 1484. *Also* Fragments originaux (1378–1459). Ed. Moray, R. Paris. 1913.
Biglia, A. Rerum mediolanensium historiae (1402–31). Ed. Muratori. RR.II.SS. 1st edn. Vol. XIX.
Bonincontri, L. Annales (1360–1458). Ed. Muratori. RR.II.SS. 1st edn. Vol. XXI.
Borselli, G. Cronica gestorum ac factorum memorabilium civitatis Bononie ab urbe condita ad a. 1497. Ed. Sorbelli, A. RR.II.SS. New edn. Vol. XXIII, pt. 2.
Bracciolini, Poggio. Historiae Florentinae. Ed. Muratori. RR.II.SS. 1st edn. Vol. XX.
Bruni, L. (Aretino). Difesa contro i riprensori del popolo fiorentino nella impresa di Lucca. Ed. Guerra, P. Lucca. 1864.
—— Rerum suo tempore gestarum commentarius. Ed. Santini, E. and Pierro, C. di. RR.II.SS. New edn. Vol. XIX, pt. 3.
Buoninsegni, D. Storie della città di Firenze dall' anno 1410 al 1460. Florence. 1637.
Cagnola, G. P. Cronaca milanese (1023–1497). ASI. Vol. III (1842). 1.
Cambi, G. Istorie fiorentine. Ed. Luigi, S. *in* Delizie degli eruditi toscani. Vols. XX–XXIII. Florence. 1785.
Campano, G. A. De vita et gestis Braccii. Ed. Valentini, R. RR.II.SS. New edn. Vol. XIX, pt. 4.
Capponi, G. Ricordi. Ed. Muratori. RR.II.SS. 1st edn. Vol. XVIII.
Capponi, N. Commentarii di cose seguite in Italia dal 1419 al 1456. Ed. Muratori. RR.II.SS. 1st edn. Vol. XVIII.
Cavalcanti, G. Istorie fiorentine. 2 vols. Florence. 1838–9.
Cirneo, P. De bello ferrariensi (1482–4). Ed. Muratori. RR.II.SS. 1st edn. Vol. XXI.
Corio, B. Storia di Milano. Ed. Magri, E. 3 vols. Milan. 1855.
Cornazzano, A. De vita et gestis Bartholomei Colei. Ed. Graevius, J. G. *in* Thesaurus antiq. et hist. Italiae. Vol. IX, pt. 7. *See Gen. Bibl.* IV.
Corpus Chronicorum Bononiensium. Ed. Sorbelli, A. RR.II.SS. New edn. Vol. XVIII, pt. 1, in progress.
Crivelli, L. De vita rebusque gestis Sfortiae ac initiis filii ejus Francisci Sfortiae Vicecomitis (1369–1424). Ed. Muratori. RR.II.SS. 1st edn. Vol. XIX.
Cronica di Milano (948–1487). Ed. Lambertenghi, G. P. *in* Miscell. di storia italiana. Vol. VIII. (R. Dep. di stor. pat.) Turin. 1869.
Cronica gestorum in partibus Lombardie et reliquis Italie (1476–82). (Diarium Parmense.) Ed. Bonazzi, G. RR.II.SS. New edn. Vol. XXII, pt. 3.
Decembrio, P. C. Vita Philippi Mariae III Liguris Ducis. Ed. Butti, A., Fossati, F., and Petraglione, G. RR.II.SS. New edn. Vol. XX, pt. 1.
—— Vita Francisci Sfortiae. *Ibid.*, in progress.
—— Vita Nicolai Piccinini. Ed. Muratori. RR.II.SS. 1st edn. Vol. XX.

Dei, B. Cronica. Ed. Pagnini, G. F. *in* Della decima. Vol. II, p. 235. *See below*, III B (i).

Diario Ferrarese dall' anno 1409 fino al 1502. Ed. Pardi, G. RR.II.SS. New edn. Vol. XXIV, pt. 7, in progress. *Cf.* 1st edn. Vol. XXIV.

Ferrarese, Fra G. Excerpta ex annalibus principum estensium (1409–54). Ed. Muratori. RR.II.SS. 1st edn. Vol. XX.

Gallo, A. Commentarii de rebus Genuensium (1466–94). Ed. Pandiani, E. RR.II.SS. New edn. Vol. XXIII, pt. 1.

Gubbio, Ser Guerriero da. Cronaca (1350–1472). Ed. Mazzatinti, G. RR.II.SS. New edn. Vol. XXI, pt. 4. [Included in 1st edn. as Bernius, Chronicon Eugubinum.]

Ivani (Hyvanus), A. (da Sarzana). Historia de volaterrana calamitate. Ed. Mannucci, F. L. RR.II.SS. New edn. Vol. XXIII, pt. 4.

Landucci, L. Diario fiorentino (1450–1516). Florence. 1883. Engl. transl. Jervis, A. London. 1927.

Malipiero, D. Annali Veneti (1457–1500). Ed. Sagredo, A. ASI. Vol. VII, pts. 1, 2. 1843–4.

Medici, Cosimo de'. Ricordi. Ed. Lami, G. *in* Deliciae eruditorum. Vol. XII, p. 169. Florence. 1742.

—— Lorenzo de'. Ricordi. Ed. Santini, A. *in* La Toscana illustrata nella sua storia. Leghorn. 1755.

Minuti, A. Vita di Muzio Attendolo Sforza. Ed. Lambertenghi, G. P. *in* Miscell. di storia italiana. Vol. VII. (R. Dep. di stor. pat.) Turin. 1869.

Morelli, G. Ricordi. Ed. Luigi, S. *in* Delizie degli eruditi toscani. Vol. XIX. Florence. 1785.

Morelli, L. Cronaca (1347–1520). *Ibid.*

Morosini, P. Memoria storica intorno alla repubblica di Venezia. Venice. 1796. [A defence of Venetian policy in the 15th century dedicated to Cecco Simonetta.]

Palmieri, M. Annales (1429–74). Ed. Scaramella, G. RR.II.SS. New edn. Vol. XXVI, pt. 1.

Paullo, A. da. Cronaca Milanese, 1476–1515. *In* Miscell. di storia italiana. Vol. XIII. (R. Dep. di stor. pat.) Turin. 1862.

Pius II (Aeneas Silvius Piccolomini). Commentarii rerum memorabilium quae temporibus suis contigerunt. Rome. 1584. Frankfort. 1614.

—— De viris aetate sua claris. Ed. Mansi, J. D. *in* Pii II...Orationes. Vol. III. Lucca. 1759.

Platina, B. Historia urbis Mantuae ab ejus origine usque ad annum 1464. Ed. Muratori. RR.II.SS. 1st edn. Vol. XX.

Poliziano, A. Conjurationis Pactianae anni 1478 commentarius. *In* Opera. Basle. 1553.

Porcellio, P. Commentaria Comitis Jacobi Piccinino. Ed. Muratori. RR.II.SS. 1st edn. Vol. XX.

Pulci, L. La giostra di Lorenzo de' Medici messa in rima (1468). Florence. 1518.

Redusio, A. Chronicon Tarvisinum (1368–1428). Ed. Muratori. RR.II.SS. 1st edn. Vol. XIX.

Ricordi di Firenze dell' anno 1459 di autore anonimo. Ed. Volpi, G. RR.II.SS. New edn. Vol. XXVII, pt. 1.

Rinuccini, F. Ricordi storici (1282–1460) colla continuazione di Alamanno e Neri suoi figli sino al 1506. Florence. 1840.

Ripalta, A. Annales Placentini (1401–84). Ed. Muratori. RR.II.SS. 1st edn. Vol. XX.

Sabellico, M. A. Rerum venetarum ab urbe condita ad sua usque tempora. Venice. 1487.

Sanudo, Marino. Commentarii della guerra di Ferrara. Ed. Manin, L. Venice. 1829.

—— Le vite dei Duchi di Venezia. Ed. Muratori. RR.II.SS. 1st edn. Vol. XXII. Ed. Monticolo, G. *Ibid.* New edn. Vol. XXII, pt. 4, in progress.

Schivenoglio, A. Cronaca di Mantova (1445–84). Ed. D'Arco, C. *in* Raccolta di cronisti e documenti storici Lombardi inediti. Vol. II. Milan. 1857.

Senarega, B. De rebus genuensibus commentaria (1488–1514). Ed. Pandiani, E. RR.II.SS. New edn. Vol. XXIV, pt. 8.

Simonetta, J. De rebus gestis Francisci Sfortiae (1421–66). Ed. Muratori. RR.II. SS. 1st edn. Vol. XXI. Ed. Soranzo, G. *Ibid.* New edn. Vol. XXI, pt. 2, in progress

Soldo, C. da. Annales brixiani (1437–68). Ed. Muratori. RR.II.SS. 1st edn. Vol. xxi.

Sozomeni (Pistoriensis) Chronicon universale (1411–55). Ed. Zaccagnini, G. RR. II.SS. New edn. Vol. xvi, pt. 1.

Stella, G. Annales Genuenses (1298–1435). Ed. Muratori. RR.II.SS. 1st edn. Vol. xx.

Valori, N. Laurentii Medicei vita. Ed. Galletti, G. C. Florence. 1847. Ital. transl. Valori, F. Florence. 1568.

Vespasiano da Bisticci. Vite di uomini illustri. Ed. Frati, L. 3 vols. Bologna. 1892. Engl. transl. Waters, W. G. London. 1926.

C. Sixteenth-Century Historians.

[These, although not strictly contemporary, may be regarded as sources in view of the living tradition which they embody in varying degrees.]

Ammirato, S. Istorie fiorentine. 3 vols. Florence. 1641–7.

Barbuò, S. Sommario delle vite de' Duchi di Milano. Venice. 1584.

Bembo, P. Historiae Venetae (1487–1513). Venice. 1551.

Folieta, U. Historiae Genuensium. Genoa. 1585.

Ghirardacci, Fra C. Della historia di Bologna. Pt. 2 (1321–1425). Bologna. 1669. Pt. 3 (1426–1509). Ed. Sorbelli, A. RR.II.SS. New edn. Vol. xxxiii, pt. 1.

Giovio (Jovius), P. Illustrium virorum vitae. Florence. 1551.

Giustiniani, A. Castigatissimi annali della republica di Genoa. Genoa. 1537.

Guicciardini, F. Storia fiorentina. *In* Opere inedite. Vol. iii. Florence. 1859.

—— Storia d' Italia. Ed. Gherardi, A. Florence. 1919.

Machiavelli, N. Istorie fiorentine. Ed. Mazzoni, G. and Casella, M. *in* Tutte le opere. Florence. 1929. Engl. transl. Thomson, N. H. London. 1906.

Malavolti, O. Historia de' fatti e guerre de' Senesi. Venice. 1599.

Muzio, G. Historia de' fatti di Federico di Montefeltro, Duca d' Urbino. Venice. 1605.

Navagero, A. Storia della repubblica veneziana. Ed. Muratori. RR.II.SS. 1st edn. Vol. xxiii.

Nerli, F. Commentarii dei fatti civili occorsi dentro la città di Firenze dal 1215 al 1537. Augsburg. 1728.

Pitti, J. Istoria fiorentina al 1529. ASI. Vol. i (1842). 1.

Sansovino, F. Origine e fatti delle famiglie illustri d' Italia. Venice. 1582.

D. Treatises, Political and Social.

Alberti, L. B. Della famiglia. Ed. Bonucci, A. *in* Opere volgari. Vol. ii. Florence. 1843.

Carafa, D. De regentis et boni principis officiis. *In* Fabricius, J. A. Bibliotheca Latina. Vol. vi, app. 3. Padua. 1754.

Castiglione, B. Il Cortegiano. Venice. 1528. Ed. Cian, V. Florence. 1908. Engl. transl. Hoby, T. (Tudor Translations. xxiii.) London. 1900.

Ficino, M. Epistolae familiares. Venice. 1495. Ital. transl. Figliucci. Venice. 1546.

Garigiolli, G. L'Arte della Seta in Firenze, trattato del secolo xv. Florence. 1868.

Giannotti, D. Della repubblica fiorentina. *In* Opere politiche e letterarie. Vol. i. Florence. 1850.

—— Il libro della repubblica de' Vinitiani. Rome. 1540.

Guicciardini, F. Del Reggimento di Firenze. *In* Opere inedite. Vol. ii. Florence. 1858.

—— Ricordi politici e civili. *Ibid.* Vol. i. 1857.

Machiavelli, N. Discorsi sopra la prima deca di T. Livio. Engl. transl. Thomson, N. H. London. 1883.

—— Libro dell' arte della guerra. Engl. transl. Whitehorne, P. London. 1573.

—— Il Principe. Ed. Burd, L. A. Oxford. 1891. Engl. transl. Thomson, N. H. London. 1882.

[All three works ed. Mazzoni, G. and Casella, M. *in* Tutte le opere. Florence. 1929.]

Palmieri, M. Della vita civile. Milan. 1830.

Pazzi, A. de'. Discorso al Cardinale Giulio de' Medici, 1522. ASI. Vol. ɪ (1842). 420.
Sabadino degli Arienti, G. Gynevra delle clare donne. (Scelta di curiosità letterarie inedite o rare. ccxxɪɪɪ.) Bologna. 1888.
Salutati, C. Tractatus de tyranno. Ed. Ercole, F. (Quellen der Rechtsphilosophie. Vol. ɪ.) Berlin. 1914.
Sforza, F. I suggerimenti di buon vivere dettati da Francesco Sforza pel figliuolo Galeazzo Maria. Ed. Orano, D. Rome. 1901.
Uzzano, G. da. La pratica della mercatura. Ed. Pagnini, G. F. *in* Della decima. Vol. ɪv. *See below*, ɪɪɪ ʙ(i).
Valturius, G. De re militari. Verona. 1472.

III. MODERN WORKS.

A. General.

Antonini, F. La pace di Lodi ed i segreti maneggi che la prepararono. ASL. Anno ʟvɪɪ (1930). 233.
Banchi, L. Il Piccinino nello stato di Siena e la lega italica. ASI. Ser. ɪv. Vol. ɪv (1879). 44, 225.
Battistella, A. Il conte Carmagnola. Genoa. 1889.
Belotti, B. La vita di Bartolomeo Colleone. Bergamo. 1923. [Bibliography.]
Block, W. Die Condottieri. Studien über die sogenannten "unblutigen Schlachten." (Ebering's Hist. Studien. No. 110.) Berlin. 1913.
Burckhardt, J. Die Kultur der Renaissance in Italien. 15th edn. rev. by Geiger, L. and Goetz, W. Leipsic. 1926. Engl. transl. (illustrated). Middlemore, S. G. C. London. 1929.
Calmette, J. La politique espagnole dans la guerre de Ferrare (1482–4). RH. xcɪɪ (1906). 225.
Chabod, M. Di alcuni studi recenti sull' età comunale e signorile nell' Italia settentrionale. *In* Rivista stor. ital. Anno xʟɪɪ. Turin. 1925.
Cipolla, C. Storia delle signorie italiane dal 1313 al 1530. 2 vols. (Storia politica d' Italia scritta da una società d' amici. Ed. Villari, P. Vol. ɪv.) Milan. 1881.
Einstein, L. The Italian Renaissance in England. New York. 1902.
Ercole, F. Da Carlo VIII a Carlo V. La crisi della libertà italiana. Florence. 1932.
—— Impero e papato nella tradizione giuridica bolognese e nel diritto pubblico italiano del Rinascimento. *In* Atti e mem. della R. Dep. di stor. pat. per le provincie di Romagna. Ser. ɪv. Vol. ɪ, p. 1. Bologna. 1911. Repr. *in* Ercole, F. Dal comune al principato. Florence. 1929.
Fabretti, A. Biografie dei capitani venturieri dell' Umbria. 5 vols. Montepulciano. 1842–6.
Litta, P. Famiglie celebri italiane. *See Gen. Bibl.* ɪɪɪ.
Manfroni, C. Storia della marina italiana dalla caduta di Costantinopoli alla battaglia di Lepanto. Rome. 1897.
Miller, W. Essays on the Latin Orient. Cambridge. 1921.
—— The Latins in the Levant. London. 1908.
Muratori, L. A. Annali d' Italia. *See Gen. Bibl.* v.
—— Delle antichità estensi ed italiane. 2 vols. Modena. 1740.
Negri, P. Studi sulla crisi italiana alla fine del secolo xv. ASL. Anno ʟ (1923). 1; Anno ʟɪ (1924). 75.
Orsi, P. Signorie e principati. (Storia politica d' Italia scritta da una società di professori. Vol. v.) Milan. [1902.]
Picotti, G. B. Qualche osservazioni sui caratteri delle signorie italiane. *In* Rivista stor. ital. Anno xʟɪɪɪ. p. 7. Turin. 1926.
Piva, C. La guerra di Ferrara del 1482. Padova. 1893–4.
Ricotti, E. Storia delle compagnie di ventura in Italia. 4 vols. Turin. 1844–5. And later edns.
Semerau, A. Die Condottieri. Jena. 1909.

Sismondi, J. C. L. Histoire des républiques italiennes du moyen âge. 16 vols. Brussels. 1809.

Soranzo, G. La lega italica (1454–5). Milan. 1924.

—— Pio II e la politica italiana nella lotta contro i Malatesti (1457–63). Padua. 1911.

Symonds, J. A. The Renaissance in Italy. 7 vols. London. 1875–86. New edn. 1909.

Villari, P. Niccolò Machiavelli e i suoi tempi. 3 vols. Florence. 1878. Milan. 1913. Engl. transl. Villari, L. London. 1892.

Vita italiana nel rinascimento, La. Conferenze tenute a Firenze nel 1892. Milan. 1899.

B. LOCAL.

(i) *Florence.*

Armstrong, E. Lorenzo de' Medici. London. 1896.

Barbadoro, B. Le finanze della repubblica fiorentina. Florence. 1929.

Biagi, G. Men and manners of Old Florence. London. 1909.

Brinton, S. The Golden Age of the Medici. London. 1925.

Brosch, M. Albizzi und Medici. Leipsic. 1908.

Buser, B. Die Beziehungen der Mediceer zu Frankreich, 1434–94. Leipsic. 1879.

—— Lorenzo de' Medici als italienischer Staatsmann. Leipsic. 1879.

Caggese, R. Firenze dalla decadenza di Roma al risorgimento d' Italia. 3 vols. Florence. 1912–21. [Bibliography.]

Capponi, G. Storia della repubblica di Firenze. 2 vols. Florence. 1875.

Dami, B. Giovanni Bicci dei Medici. Florence. 1899.

Doren, A. Studien aus der florentiner Wirtschaftsgeschichte von 14 bis zum 16 Jahrht. 2 vols. Stuttgart. 1901, 8.

Ewart, D. K. Cosimo dei Medici. London. 1899.

Fabroni, A. Magni Cosmi Medicei vita. 2 vols. Pisa. 1788.

—— Laurentii Medicis Magnifici vita. 2 vols. Pisa. 1784.

Gelli, A. L' esilio di Cosimo de' Medici. ASI. Ser. IV. Vol. x (1882). 53, 149.

Horsburgh, E. L. S. Lorenzo the Magnificent and Florence in her golden age. London. 1908.

Hyett, F. A. Florence, her history and her art to the fall of the republic. London. 1903.

Levantini Pieroni, G. Lucrezia Tornabuoni. Florence. 1888.

Maguire, Y. The women of the Medici. London. 1927.

Marzi, D. La cancelleria della repubblica fiorentina. Rocca San Casciano. 1910.

Masi, E. Lorenzo il Magnifico. *In* La Vita italiana. *See above*, III A.

Morcay, R. Saint Antonin archevêque de Florence. Paris. 1914.

Pagnini, G. F. Della decima…della moneta e della mercatura de' Fiorentini fino al secolo XVI. 4 vols. Lisbon and Lucca. 1765–6.

Panella, A. Firenze. (Storie municipali d' Italia. Ed. Caggese, R. and Malatesta.) Rome. 1930.

Pellegrini, F. C. Sulla repubblica fiorentina a tempo di Cosimo il Vecchio. Pisa. 1889.

Perrens, F. Histoire de Florence depuis ses origines jusqu'à la domination des Médicis. Vol. VI. Paris. 1883.

—— Histoire de Florence depuis la domination des Médicis jusqu'à la chute de la république. 3 vols. Paris. 1888.

Picotti, G. B. La giovinezza di Leone X. Milan. 1928.

Pieraccini, G. La stirpe de' Medici di Cafaggiolo. 3 vols. Florence. 1924–5. [Bibliography.]

Reumont, A. von. Lorenzo de' Medici il Magnifico. 2 vols. Leipsic. 1874. Engl. transl. Harrison, R. London. 1876.

Rho, E. Lorenzo il Magnifico. Bari. 1926.

Ricchioni, A. La costituzione politica di Firenze ai tempi di Lorenzo il Magnifico. Siena. 1913.

Richards, G. R. B. Florentine merchants in the age of the Medici. Cambridge, Mass. 1932. [An account of the letters and documents in the Selfridge collection of Medici manuscripts, with translations of selections from them.]

Ridolfi, R. Studi Savonaroliani. Florence. 1935.
—— La visita del Savonarola al Magnifico morente e la leggenda della negata assoluzione. ASI. Ser. VII. Vol. x (1928). 204. [Evidence which appears conclusive against the Savonarolist version of Lorenzo's death-bed scene.]
Roscoe, W. Life of Lorenzo de' Medici. 10th edn. (Bohn's Standard Library.) London. 1851. Illustrations, historical and critical, of the Life, etc. London. 1822.
Ross, J. Lives of the early Medici as told in their correspondence. London. 1910. [An important collection of letters, translated for the most part from the originals in the Florentine Archives.]

(ii) *Milan.*

Ady, C. M. History of Milan under the Sforza. London. 1907. [Bibliography.]
Beltrami, L. Il Castello di Milano sotto il dominio degli Sforza (1450–1535). Milan. 1894.
—— La vita nel Castello di Milano al tempo degli Sforza. Milan. 1900.
Biscaro, G. Il banco Filippo Borromei e compagni di Londra (1436–9). ASL. Anno XL (1913). 37, 283.
Bognetti, G. P. Per la storia dello stato visconteo. Un registro di decreti della cancelleria di Filippo Maria Visconti. ASL. Anno LIV (1927). 237.
Cartwright, J. Beatrice d'Este, Duchess of Milan. London. 1899.
Casanova, E. L' uccisione di Galeazzo Maria Sforza. ASL. Anno XXVI (1899). 299.
Colombo, A. L' ingresso di Francesco Sforza in Milano e l' inizio di un nuovo principato. ASL. Anno XXXII (1905). 297.
Colombo, E. Il Re Renato alleato del Duca Francesco Sforza contra i Veneziani (1453–4). ASL. Anno XXI (1894). 79, 361.
Daverio, M. Memorie sulla storia del ex-ducato di Milano risguardanti il dominio dei Visconti. Milan. 1804.
Dina, A. Isabella d'Aragona, Duchessa di Milano e di Bari. ASL. Anno XLVIII (1921). 169.
Fumi, L. Chiesa e Stato nel dominio di Francesco Sforza. ASL. Anno LI (1924). 1.
Ghinzoni, P. Informazioni politiche sul Ducato di Milano 1461. ASL. Anno XIX (1892). 863.
Giudice, P. del. Il consiglio ducale e il senato di Milano. *In* Rendiconti Istituto Lombardo. Vol. XXXII. Milan. 1899.
Giulini, G. Memorie spettanti alla storia, al governo ed alla descrizione della città e della campagna di Milano ne' secoli bassi. Milan. 1771. 2nd edn. 7 vols. Milan. 1854–7.
Kagelmacher, E. Filippo Maria Visconti und König Sigismund. Berlin. 1885.
Latuada, S. Descrizione di Milano. 5 vols. Milan. 1737.
Magenta, C. I Visconti e gli Sforza nel Castello di Pavia. 2 vols. Milan. 1883.
Magnani, R. Relazioni private tra la corte Sforzesca di Milano e casa Medici, 1450–1500. Milan. 1910.
Malaguzzi-Valeri, F. La corte di Lodovico il Moro. 4 vols. Milan. 1913–23.
Muir, D. History of Milan under the Visconti. London. 1924.
Nulli, S. A. Lodovico il Moro. Milan. 1930.
Peluso, F. Storia della repubblica milanese, 1447–50. Milan. 1871.
Ratti, N. La famiglia Sforza. 2 vols. Rome. 1794–5.
Romano, G. Contributi alla storia della ricostituzione del ducato milanese sotto Filippo Maria Visconti (1412–21). ASL. Anno XXIII (1896). 231. Anno XXIV (1897). 67.
Rosmini, C. Storia di Milano. 4 vols. Milan. 1820–1.
Rossi, L. Lega tra il duca di Milano, i Fiorentini e Carlo VII. ASL. Anno XXXIII (1906). 246.
Solmi, E. Leonardo. Florence. 1900.
Sorbelli, A. Francesco Sforza a Genova (1458–66). Bologna. 1901.
Verga, E. Storia della vita milanese. Milan. 1909. New edn. 1931. [Bibliography.]
—— Un caso di conscienza di Filippo Maria Visconti. 1446. ASL. Anno XLV (1919). 427.

(iii) *Venice.*

Besta, E. Il Senato Veneziano, origine, costituzione, attribuzioni e riti. (Monumenti Storici di R. Dep. Ven. di storia patria. Miscellanea. Ser. II. Vol. v.) Venice. 1899.

Brown, H. F. Venice: a historical sketch of the republic. London. 1893.
—— Venetian studies. London. 1887.
—— Venice. *In* Cambridge Modern History. Vol. I, ch. VIII. Cambridge. 1902. [Bibliography.]

Cecchetti, B. La repubblica di Venezia e la corte di Roma nei rapporti della religione. Vol. I. Venice. 1874.

Daru, P. Histoire de la République de Venise. 2nd edn. 8 vols. Paris. 1821.

Harrington, J. The Commonwealth of Oceana. London. 1656.

Hazlitt, W. C. The Venetian Republic. 2 vols. London. 1858. 4th edn. 1915.

Kretschmayr, H. Geschichte von Venedig. Vol. II. Die Blüte. (Heeren. *See Gen. Bibl.* v.) Gotha. 1920. [Bibliography.]

Magnante, G. L' acquisto dell' isola di Cipro da parte della Repubblica di Venezia. Arch.Ven. Ser. v. Vol. v (1929). 78; Vol. VI (1929). 1.

Marin, C. A. Storia civile e politica del commercio de' Veneziani. Vol. VII. Venice. 1800.

Molmenti, P. La storia di Venezia nella vita privata. Turin. 1880. 6th edn. 3 vols. Bergamo. 1922–9. Engl. transl. Brown, H. F. London. 1906–8.

Musatti, E. Storia di Venezia. 2 vols. Milan. 1914–15.

Picotti, G. B. La dieta di Mantova e la politica de' Veneziani. (R. Dep. Ven. di storia patria. Miscellanea. Ser. IV. Vol. IV.) Venice. 1912.

Raulich, I. La prima guerra fra i Veneziani e Filippo Maria Visconti. *In* Rivista stor. ital. Anno v. pp. 441, 661. Turin. 1888.

Romanin, S. Storia documentata di Venezia. 10 vols. Venice. 1853–61. 2nd edn. 1913.

Rossi, L. Venezia e il re di Napoli, Firenze e Francesco Sforza (1450–1). N. Arch. Ven. n.s. Vol. x (1905). 5, 281.

Sagredo, A. Legge venete intorno agli ecclesiastici sino al secolo XVIII. ASI. Ser. III. Vol. II (1865). 92.

Sandi, V. Principi di storia civile della Repubblica di Venezia dalla sua fondazione sino all' anno 1700. Vols. III, IV. Venice. 1755–6.

Toderini, T. Francesco Sforza e Venezia. Documenti. 1436–70. Arch. Ven. Vol. IX, pt. 2 (1875). 116.

Verci, G. B. Storia della marca trivigiana. Vol. XIX. Venice. 1790.

(iv) *Other Cities.*

Ady, C. M. A charter of an Italian rural commune, 1488. EHR. XLVIII (1933). 269–76.

Ansidei, V. Appunti per la storia delle famiglie perugine Baglioni e degli Oddi. Perugia. 1901.

Baldi, B. Vita e fatti di Federico di Montefeltro, Duca d'Urbino. 3 vols. Rome. 1824.

Benadducci, G. Della Signoria di Francesco Sforza nella Marca. Tolentino. 1892.

Bent, T. Genoa: how the Republic rose and fell. London. 1881.

Brinton, S. The Gonzaga Lords of Mantua. London. 1927.

Cartwright, J. Isabella d'Este, Marchioness of Mantua. 2 vols. London. 1903.

Cognasso, F. Amedeo VIII. 2 vols. (Collana storica Sabauda.) Turin. 1930.

Dennistoun, J. Memoirs of the Dukes of Urbino. 3 vols. London. 1852. Ed. Hutton, E. 3 vols. London. 1908.

Douglas, R. L. History of Siena. London. 1902.

Frati, L. La vita privata di Bologna dal secolo XIII al XVII. Bologna. 1900.

Gabotto, F. Lo stato Sabaudo da Amadeo VIII a Emanuele Filiberto. 3 vols. Turin. 1892–5.

Gardner, E. G. Dukes and poets in Ferrara. London. 1904. [Bibliography.]

Gozzadini, G. Memorie per la vita di Giovanni II Bentivoglio. Bologna. 1839.

Heywood, W. History of Perugia. London. 1910.

Manfroni, C. Genova. (Storie municipali d' Italia. Ed. Caggese, к. and Malatesta.) Rome. 1929.

Marengo, E. Il Banco di San Giorgio. Genoa. 1911.

Mondolfo, U. G. Pandolfo Petrucci, Signore di Siena. Siena. 1899.

Oderici, F. Storie Bresciane. Vols. vii, viii. Brescia. 1857–8.

Palmieri, A. La montagna bolognese nel medio evo. Bologna. 1929.

Pardi, G. Borso d'Este, Duca di Ferrara, Modena e Reggio. (Studii Storici. Ed. Crivellucci, A. xv, xvi.) Pisa. 1906–7.

Pasolini, P. D. Caterina Sforza. 3 vols. Rome. 1893.

Pellini, P. Dell' historia di Perugia. Vols. i, ii. Venice. 1664.

Ricotti, E. Storia della monarchia piemontese. Vol. i. Florence. 1861.

Sizeranne, R. de la. Le vertueux condottière Federigo de Montefeltro duc d'Urbino. Paris. 1927.

Sorbelli, A. Il comune rurale dell' Appennino Emiliano nel sec. xiv e xv. Bologna. 1910.

Volta, L. C. Compendio cronologico critico della storia di Mantova. 5 vols. Mantua. 1807–38.

Zanelli, A. La signoria di Pandolfo Malatesta in Brescia. ASL. Anno lviii (1931). 126.

CHAPTER VII.

FRANCE, 1422–1461.

I. BIBLIOGRAPHIES.

Molinier, A. Les sources de l'histoire de France. Vol. IV. *See Gen. Bibl.* I.

Chevalier, C. U. J. Répertoire des sources historiques du moyen âge. Bio-bibliographie and Topo-bibliographie. *See Gen. Bibl.* I.

Petit-Dutaillis, C. Histoire politique de la France au XIVe et au XVe siècles. Revue de synthèse historique. 1902.

Pilot de Thorey, E. Catalogue des actes du Dauphin Louis II, devenu le roi de France Louis XI, relatifs à l'administration du Dauphiné. Vols. I, II. (Soc. de statistique...de l'Isère.) Grenoble. 1899. Vol. III, supplt., ed. Vellein, G. *Ibid.* 1911.

Lanéry d'Arc, P. Le livre d'or de Jeanne d'Arc. Bibliographie raisonnée et analytique des ouvrages relatifs à Jeanne d'Arc. Paris. 1894.

Terry, E. Jeanne d'Arc in periodical literature, 1894–1929. (Publn. of the Institute of French Studies.) New York. 1930.

Bradi, L. di. Jeanne d'Arc dans la littérature anglaise. (Nouvelle bibliothèque littéraire.) Paris. 1921.

Rudler, G. Michelet, historien de Jeanne d'Arc. 2 vols. Paris. 1925–6.

Mestre, J. B. Catalogue de la bibliothèque Alexandre Sorel consacré au souvenir de Jeanne d'Arc. [Bibliothèque de Compiègne.] *In* Procès-verbaux de la Soc. hist. de Compiègne. 1929.

II. SOURCES.

A. DOCUMENTS.

Thomas, A. Jean de Gerson et l'éducation des dauphins de France. Paris. 1930. [Publishes two educational opuscula of Gerson, and shews that they were addressed to an unknown master of Charles VII.]

Cosneau, E. Les grands traités de la guerre de Cent Ans. (Coll. textes.) Paris. 1889.

Denifle, H. La désolation des églises, monastères, hôpitaux en France vers le milieu du XVe siècle. Vol. I. Mâcon. 1897.

Longnon, A. Paris pendant la domination anglaise, 1420–36, documents extraits de la Chancellerie de France. (Mém. de la Soc. de l'hist. de Paris et de l'Île de France.) Paris. 1878.

Joubert, A. Documents inédits pour servir à l'histoire de la guerre de Cent Ans dans le Maine. Mamers. 1889.

Rowe, B. J. H. Discipline in the Norman garrisons under Bedford, 1422–35. EHR. XLVI. 1931.

Newhall, R. A. Bedford's ordinance on the watch of September 1428. EHR. L (1935). 36–60.

L'Averdy, C. C. F. de. Mémorial concernant la recherche à faire des minutes originales des différentes affaires qui ont eu lieu par rapport à Jeanne d'Arc. Paris. 1787.

Quicherat, J. Procès de condamnation et de réhabilitation de Jeanne d'Arc. 5 vols. (SHF.) Paris. 1841–9.

O'Reilly, E. Les deux procès de condamnation, les enquêtes et la sentence de réhabilitation de Jeanne d'Arc. 2 vols. Paris. 1868. [French transl. of the documents publ. by Quicherat, J.]

Champion, P. Procès de condamnation de Jeanne d'Arc. Texte et traduction. 2 vols. (Bibliothèque du XVe siècle. XXII, XXIII.) Paris. 1920–1. *Cf.* Reinach, S., Observations sur le texte du procès de condamnation de Jeanne d'Arc. RH. CXLVIII. 1925.

Champion, P. Notice des manuscrits du procès de réhabilitation de Jeanne d'Arc. (Bibliothèque du XVe siècle. XXXVII.) Paris. 1930.

Barrett, W. P. The trial of Jeanne d'Arc. London. 1931. [Complete English transl. of docs.]

Comptes de l'hôtel des rois de France au xive et au xve siècles. Ed. Douët d'Arcq, L. (SHF.) Paris. 1865.

Ordonnances des Rois de France de la troisième race. Vols. xiii and xiv. Paris. 1723 ff. [Preface by Bréquigny, L. G. O. F. de.]

Jacqueton, G. Documents relatifs à l'administration financière en France... 1443–1523. (Coll. textes.) Paris. 1891.

B. NARRATIVE SOURCES.

Chartier, Jean. Chronique de Charles VII (en français). Ed. Godefroy, D. *in* Histoire de Charles VII. Paris. 1661. *Also* ed. Vallet de Viriville, A. 3 vols. (Bibliothèque elzévirienne.) Paris. 1858.

—— Chronique latine. Ed. Vallet de Viriville, A. *in* Bulletin de la Soc. de l'hist. de France. Paris. 1858. *Cf.* Samaran, C., La chronique latine de Jean Chartier. *In* Annuaire-Bulletin de la Soc. de l'hist. de France, 1926, and BEC., 1926.

Berry, Gilles le Bouvier, dit le Héraut. Chronique du roy Charles VII. Ed. Godefroy, D. *op. cit.*

—— Le recouvrement de Normandie. Ed. with Engl. transl. Stevenson, J. *in* Narratives of the expulsion of the English from Normandy. (Rolls.) 1863. *Cf.* Bouvier, A. *in* Positions des thèses. École nat. des chartes. Paris. 1922.

Blondel, Robert. De reductione Normanniae. Ed. Stevenson, J. *op. cit.*

Bueil, Jean de. Le Jouvencel. Ed. Favre, C. and Lecestre, L. 2 vols. (SHF.) Paris. 1887, 89.

Basin, Thomas. Histoire des règnes de Charles VII, etc. Ed. Quicherat, J. 4 vols. (SHF.) Paris. 1855–9. Best edn., ed. Samaran, C. Vol. i. (Class. hist.) 1933. In progress.

Chronique Martiniane. Interpolation originale. Ed. Champion, P. (Bibl. du xve siècle. ii.) Paris. 1907.

Cousinot, Guillaume. Chronique [called sometimes Chronique de la Pucelle]. Ed. Vallet de Viriville, A. Paris. 1859. Republ. with addns. and corrections. Paris. 1892.

Cochon, Pierre. Chronique Normande. Ed. Beaurepaire, C. de *in* Bouquet. Vol. xxiii. *Also* ed. Vallet de Viriville, A. *in* Cousinot (*above*). [Cochon, apostolic notary, to be distinguished from the Bishop Pierre Cauchon.]

Morosini, Antonio. Chronique. Ed. Dorez, L. and Lefèvre-Pontalis, G. 4 vols. (SHF.) Paris. 1898–1902.

Maupoint, Jean. Journal Parisien. Ed. Fagniez, G. *in* Mém. de la Soc. de l'hist. de Paris et de l'Île-de-France. iv. Paris. 1878.

Journal d'un bourgeois de Paris, 1405–49. Ed. Tuetey, A. (Soc. de l'hist. de Paris et de l'Île-de-France.) Paris. 1881. Popular edn. Mary, A. Paris. 1929.

Gruel, Guillaume. Chronique d'Arthur de Richemont. Ed. Le Vavasseur, A. (SHF.) Paris. 1890.

Chronique du Mont-Saint-Michel, 1343–1468. Ed. Luce, S. 2 vols. (Soc. des anciens textes français.) Paris. 1879, 83.

Pastoralet, Le. Ed. Kervyn de Lettenhove *in* Chroniques rel. à l'hist. de la Belgique.... Vol. ii. Brussels. 1873.

Monstrelet, Enguerrand de. Chronique. Ed. Douët d'Arcq, L. 6 vols. (SHF.) Paris. 1857–62.

Escouchy, Mathieu d'. Chronique. Ed. Beaucourt, G. du Fresne de. (SHF.) Paris. 1863–4.

Fenin, Pierre de. Mémoires. Ed. Dupont, L. M. E. (SHF.) Paris. 1837.

Chastellain, Georges. Oeuvres. Ed. Kervyn de Lettenhove. 8 vols. (Acad. roy. de Belgique.) Brussels. 1863–6.

Wavrin, Jehan de. Anchiennes cronicques d'Engleterre. Ed. Dupont, L. M. E. 3 vols. (SHF.) Paris. 1858–63. *Also* ed. Hardy, W. and Hardy, E. L. C. P. 5 vols. (Rolls.) 1864–91.

Worcester, William of. Annales rerum Anglicarum. Ed. Stevenson, J. *in* Letters and papers illustrative of the wars of the English in France during the reign of Henry VI. Vol. ii. (Rolls.) 1864.

Planchenault, R. De l'utilité pour l'histoire de France de quelques chroniques anglaises de la première moitié du xve siècle. BEC. lxxxv. 1924.

La Marche, Olivier de. Mémoires. Ed. Beaune, H. and d'Arbaumont, J. 4 vols. (SHF.) Paris. 1883–8.

Leseur, Guillaume. Histoire de Gaston IV, comte de Foix. Ed. Courteault, H. 2 vols. (SHF.) Paris. 1893, 96.

Chartier, Alain. Oeuvres. Ed. Duchesne, A. Paris. 1617.

—— Le quadrilogue invectif. Ed. Droz, E. (Classiques français du moyen âge. xxxii.) Paris. 1923.

Cretton, A. La lettera di Alain Chartier su Giovanna d'Arco. ASI. Anno lxxxviii. 1930.

Chants historiques et populaires du temps de Charles VII, etc. Ed. Leroux de Lincy, A. J. V. Paris. 1857.

Lettres diverses du règne de Charles VII. Ed. Champollion-Figeac, J. J. *in* Lettres de rois, reines....des cours de France et d'Angleterre. Vol. ii. (Coll. doc.) Paris. 1847.

Lettres closes de Charles VI et de Charles VII adressées à l'Université de Toulouse. Ed. Thomas, A. *in* Annales du Midi. xxvii. 1915.

Lettres de Louis XI. Vol. i. (Louis dauphin.) Ed. Charavay, É. and Vaesen, J. (SHF.) Paris. 1883.

Epitaphes et poèmes sur Charles VII. Ed. Calmette, J. *in* Mélanges d'archéol. et d'hist. xxv. (École franc. de Rome.) 1905.

III. MODERN WORKS.

A. General.

Vallet de Viriville, A. Histoire de Charles VII, roi de France et de son époque. 3 vols. Paris. 1862–5. [Antiquated, but still useful.]

Beaucourt, G. du Fresne de. Histoire de Charles VII. 6 vols. Paris. 1881–91. [This general work always supplements and sometimes corrects Vallet de Viriville.]

Petit-Dutaillis, C. Charles VII, Louis XI, et les premières années de Charles VIII. *In* Lavisse, E. Histoire de France. Vol. iv, pt. 2. 1902. *See Gen. Bibl.* v.

Pirenne, H., Renaudet, A., Perroy, E., Handelsmann, M. and Halphen, L. La fin du moyen âge. 2 vols. (Peuples et civilisations. Histoire Générale. Ed. Halphen, L. and Sagnac, P. vii. i, ii.) Paris. 1931.

Brachet, A. Pathologie mentale des rois de France. Louis XI et ses ascendants. Paris. 1903.

Longnon, A. La formation de l'unité française. Paris. 1922.

Mirot, L. Manuel de géographie historique de la France. Paris. 1923.

Daumet, G. Étude sur l'alliance de la France et de la Castille au xive et au xve siècle. (BHE. 118.) Paris. 1898.

Mandrot, B. de. Les relations de Charles VII et de Louis XI avec les cantons suisses, 1444–83. *In* Jahrbuch für schweizerische Gesch. v–vi. Zurich. 1880–1.

Perret, P. M. Histoire des relations de la France avec Venise du xiiie siècle à l'avènement de Charles VIII. 2 vols. Paris. 1896.

Buser, B. Die Beziehungen der Mediceer zu Frankreich während der Jahre 1434–94 in ihrem Zusammenhang mit den allgemeinen Verhältnissen Italiens. Leipsic. 1879.

Barante, A. G. P. B. de. Histoire des ducs de Bourgogne. 12 vols. Paris. 1824–9.
Drouot, H. and Calmette, J. Histoire de Bourgogne. Paris. 1928.
Huizinga, J. L'état bourguignon, ses rapports avec la France et les origines d'une nationalité néerlandaise. MA. xl, xli. 1930–1.
La Borderie, A. de and Pocquet, B. Histoire de Bretagne. 6 vols. Rennes. 1896–1914.
Vic, C. de and Vaissete, J. J. Histoire générale de Languedoc. Vols. ix–xi. *See Gen. Bibl.* iv.

B. JOAN OF ARC.

[None of the histories of Joan of Arc can be called satisfactory and definitive: a selection is here given of the most striking and best known.]

Fabre, J. Jeanne d'Arc libératrice de la France. Paris. 1884; and later edns.
Wallon, H. Jeanne d'Arc. 2nd edn. 2 vols. Paris. 1867.
Sépet, M. Jeanne d'Arc. Paris. 1869; and reprints.
France, Anatole. Vie de Jeanne d'Arc. 2 vols. Paris. 1908.
Hanotaux, G. Jeanne d'Arc. Paris. 1911.
Dunand, P. H. Histoire complète de Jeanne d'Arc. New edn. 4 vols. Paris. 1910.
Goyau, G. Les étapes d'une gloire religieuse, sainte Jeanne d'Arc. Paris. 1920.
Lowell, F. C. Joan of Arc. Boston, Mass. 1896.
Lang, Andrew. The Maid of France. London. 1908. French transl. London. 1911. New edn., The story of Joan of Arc. London. 1925.
Paine, A. B. Joan of Arc, maid of France. London. 1925.
Quicherat, J. Aperçus nouveaux sur l'histoire de Jeanne d'Arc. Paris. 1850.
Luce, S. Jeanne d'Arc à Domrémy. Paris. 1886.
La nationalité de Jeanne d'Arc. *In* Intermédiaire. lxxxii. 1920.
Marin, P. Jeanne d'Arc tacticien et stratégiste. 4 vols. Paris. 1889–90.
Taylor, T. A. Joan of Arc, soldier and saint. London. 1920.

Pascal, E. Jeanne d'Arc au château de Chinon, l'audience du 8 mars 1428. Paris. 1924.
Thomas, A. Le siège d'Orléans, Jeanne d'Arc et les Capitouls de Toulouse. *In* Annales du Midi. i. 1889.
Prutz, H. Zur Geschichte der Jungfrau von Orléans. Der Krönungzug nach Reims. SBAW. 1923.

Brun, F. Jeanne d'Arc à Soissons. Meulan. 1920.

Couzet, H. Jeanne d'Arc devant Paris. Paris. 1925.
Lemier, E. Les dernières étapes de la vie de Jeanne d'Arc: Le Crotoy, Saint-Valery, Rouen. *In* Revue des études hist. 1929.
Thomas, A. Jeanne d'Arc au Crotoy. *In* Journal des Savants, December, 1930.
Sarrazin, A. Jeanne d'Arc et la Normandie au xve siècle. Rouen. 1896.
Queneday, R. La prison de Jeanne d'Arc à Rouen. *In* Bulletin archéol. Rouen. 1923. *Cf.* Mailly-Maître, *in* Bulletin de la Soc. des Antiquaires de France. 1928.
Champion, P. Les juges de Jeanne d'Arc. *In* Revue Universelle. i. 1920.
Sarrazin, A. Pierre Cauchon, juge de Jeanne d'Arc. Paris. 1901.
Wickevoort-Crommelin, H. S. M. Waarom werd Jeanne d'Arc verlaten? *In* Haagsch Maandblad. The Hague. 1929.
Chevalier, U. L'abjuration de Jeanne d'Arc au cimetière de St Ouen et l'authenticité de sa formule. Paris. 1902.
Boucher. La prétendue abjuration de Jeanne d'Arc au cimetière de St Ouen. *In* Bulletin de la Soc. d'émulation de la Seine-Inférieure. Rouen. 1922–3.
Sarrazin, A. Le bourreau de Jeanne d'Arc. Rouen. 1910.
Jordan, A. Les responsabilités dans les procès de Jeanne d'Arc. *In* Bulletin Joseph Lotte. March, 1932.
Billard, A. Jehanne d'Arc et ses juges. Paris. 1933. [docs.]

Grand-Carteret, J. Les images et le culte de Jeanne d'Arc à travers les siècles. *In* Revue de la Semaine. v. 1922.

Harmand, A. Jeanne d'Arc, ses costumes, ses armures. Paris. 1929. [Based on documents and customs of the time.]

Metman, É. Une épée de Jeanne d'Arc. *In* Revue de Bourgogne. 1911.

ffoulkes, C. J. The armour of Joan of Arc. *In* Burlington Magazine. December, 1909.

C. Other Personages.

Champion, P. Louis XI. Vol. i. Le Dauphin. Paris. 1927.

Thibault, M. La jeunesse de Louis XI, 1423–45. Paris. 1907.

Champion, P. La dauphine mélancolique [Marguerite d'Écosse]. Paris. 1921.

Lecoy de la Marche, A. Le roi René. 2 vols. Paris. 1875.

Perceval, C. S. On certain inaccuracies in the ordinary accounts of the early years of the reign of King Edward IV. *In* Archaeologia. xlvii. 1883. [Events relating to Margaret of Anjou.]

Hookham, M. A. The life and times of Margaret of Anjou. 2 vols. London. 1872.

Flourac, L. Jean 1ᵉʳ, comte de Foix. Repr. from Bulletin de la Soc. des sciences, lettres, et arts de Pau. xv–xvi. Paris. 1884.

Courteault, H. Gaston IV, comte de Foix, vicomte souverain de Béarn, prince de Navarre, 1423–72. (Bibliothèque méridionale. Ser. ii. Vol. iii.) Toulouse. 1895.

Pocquet du Haut-Jussé, B. A. François II, duc de Bretagne, et l'Angleterre. Paris. 1929. (Repr. from Mém. de la Soc. d'hist....de Bretagne. ix. Paris. 1928.)

Guibert, J. Jean II, duc d'Alençon. *In* Positions des thèses. École nat. des chartes. Paris. 1893.

Champion, P. Agnès Sorel, la dame de beauté. Paris. 1931.

D. Episodes and local events.

Tuetey, A. Les écorcheurs sous Charles VII. 2 vols. (Mém. de la Soc. de Montbéliard.) Montbéliard. 1874.

Rowe, B. J. H. John Duke of Bedford and the Norman 'Brigands.' EHR. xlvii. 1932.

Quicherat, J. Rodrigue de Villandrando, l'un des combattants pour l'indépendance française au xvᵉ siècle. Paris. 1879.

Thomas, A. Rodrigue de Villandrando en Rouergue. *In* Annales du Midi. ii. 1890.

—— Rodrigue de Villandrando en Auvergne. *Ibid.*

Clément-Simon, G. Un capitaine de routiers sous Charles VII, Jean de la Roche. RQH. lviii. 1895.

Pasquier, F. Louis, dauphin, et les routiers en Languedoc, 1439–44. Foix. 1895.

Newhall, R. A. The English conquest of Normandy. (Yale University publn.) New Haven. 1926.

Cheruel, A. Histoire de Rouen sous la domination anglaise au xvᵉ siècle. Rouen. 1840.

Flamare, H. de. Le Nivernais pendant la guerre de Cent Ans, le xvᵉ siècle. Vol. ii. Paris. 1925.

Villaret, A. Campagne des Anglais dans l'Orléanais, la Beauce Chartraine, le Gâtinais, 1421–8. Orléans. 1893.

Planchenault, R. La conquête du Maine par les Anglais; la campagne de 1424–5. *In* Revue hist. et archéol. du Maine. lxxxi. 1930.

Lefèvre-Pontalis, G. Épisodes de l'invasion anglaise; la guerre de partisans dans la Haute-Normandie. BEC. liv–lvii. 1893–5.

Dubois, F. Histoire du siège d'Orléans, 1428–9. Ed. Charpentier, P. and Cuissard, C. Orléans. 1894.

Champion, P. Guillaume de Flavy, capitaine de Compiègne. (Bibliothèque du xvᵉ siècle. i.) Paris. 1906.

Triger, R. Complots françaises à Argentan et à Séez. *In* Revue hist. et archéol. du Maine. lxxviii. 1922.

Planchenault, R. La délivrance du Mans en 1448. *Ibid.* lxxix. 1923.

Jullian, C. Histoire de Bordeaux. Bordeaux. 1895.

Labroue, E. La guerre de Cent Ans en Périgord. *In* Grande Revue. **xxx**, no. 8. 1906.

Brissaud, D. Les Anglais en Guyenne. Paris. 1875.

Ribadieu, H. Histoire de la conquête de la Guyenne. Paris. 1866.

Breuils. La campagne de Charles VII en Gascogne. RQH. **lvii**. 1895.

Mazon, A. Essai historique sur le Vivarais pendant la guerre de Cent Ans, 1337–1453. Tournon. 1890.

Samaran, C. La maison d'Armagnac au xve siècle. (Mém. et documents publ. par la Soc. de l'École des chartes. **vii**.) Paris. 1907.

Lodge, E. C. Gascony under English rule. London. 1926.

Le Cacheux, P. Rouen au temps de Jeanne d'Arc et pendant l'occupation anglaise (1419–49). (Soc. de l'hist. de Normandie.) Paris. 1931.

Witte, H. Die Armagnaken in Elsass, 1439–45. Strasbourg. 1889.

Cartellieri, O. Philippe le Bon et le roi de France en 1430–1. *In* Annales de Bourgogne. 1929.

E. Institutions and economic history.

Valois, N. Les Conseils du roi aux xive, xve, et xvie siècles. Paris. 1888.

Thomas, A. Les États Généraux sous Charles VII. *In* Cabinet historique. **xxiv**. 1878.

—— Le Midi et les États Généraux sous Charles VII. *In* Annales du Midi. **i**. 1889.

—— Les États provinciaux de la France centrale sous Charles VII. 2 vols. Paris. 1879–80.

—— Nouveaux documents sur les États provinciaux de la Haute-Marche. *In* Annales du Midi. **xxv**. 1913.

Billioud, J. Les États de Bourgogne aux xive et xve siècles. (Acad. des sciences... de Dijon.) Dijon. 1922.

Hirschauer, J. Les États d'Artois, de leurs origines à l'occupation française. 2 vols. Paris. 1923.

Dussert, A. Les États de Dauphiné, de la guerre de Cent Ans aux guerres de religion. Grenoble. 1923. (Repr. from Bulletin de l'Acad. Delphinale. 1922–3.)

Beaurepaire, C. de. Les États de Normandie sous la domination anglaise. Évreux. 1859.

Prentout, H. Les États provinciaux de Normandie. 3 vols. (Mém. de l'Acad. Nat....de Caen. n.s. Vols. **i–iii**.) Caen. 1925–7. *Also* publ. separately.

Rowe, B. J. H. The estates of Normandy under the Duke of Bedford, 1422–35. EHR. **xlvi**. 1931.

Le Sourd, A. Essai sur les États du Vivarais. Paris. 1926.

Aubert, F. Histoire du Parlement de Paris, de l'origine à François 1er. Vol. **i**. Paris. 1894.

Maugis, E. Histoire du Parlement de Paris de l'avènement des rois Valois à la mort d'Henri IV. 3 vols. Paris. 1913–16.

Neuville, D. Le Parlement royal à Poitiers, 1418–39. RH. **vi**. 1878.

Dubédat, J. B. Histoire du Parlement de Toulouse. 2 vols. Paris. 1885.

Thomas, A. Documents relatifs au Comté de la Marche et le Parlement de Poitiers. (BHE. 174.) Paris. 1910.

Vuitry, A. Études sur le régime financier de la France. 3 vols. Paris. 1878–83.

Borrelli de Serres, L. L. Recherches sur divers services publics. Vol. **iii**. Notices relatives aux xive–xve siècles. Paris. 1910.

Spont, A. La taille en Languedoc de 1450 à 1515. *In* Annales du Midi. **ii, iii**. 1890–1.

—— L'équivalent aux aides en Languedoc de 1450 à 1515. *Ibid.* **iii**. 1891.

Perroy, E. La fiscalité royale en Beaujolais. MA. **xxix**. 1930.

Doucet, R. Les finances anglaises en France à la fin de la guerre de Cent Ans, 1413–35. MA. xxvi. 1926.

Soudet, F. Ordonnances de l'Échiquier de Normandie aux xive et xve siècles. (Soc. de l'hist. de Normandie.) Paris. 1929.

Valois, N. Histoire de la Pragmatique Sanction de Bourges sous Charles VII. Paris. 1906.

Salvini, J. L'application de la Pragmatique Sanction sous Charles VII et Louis XI au chapitre cathédral de Paris. Paris. 1912.

Dupont-Ferrier, G. Les officiers royaux des bailliages et sénéchaussées et les institutions monarchiques locales en France à la fin du moyen âge. (BHE. 145.) Paris. 1902.

Dognon, P. Les institutions politiques et administratives du pays de Languedoc. (Bibliothèque méridionale. Ser. ii. Voï. iv.) Toulouse. 1896.

Dupont-Ferrier, G. Études sur les institutions financières de la France à la fin du moyen âge. 2 vols. Paris. 1930, 32.

—— Nouvelles études sur les institutions financières de la France à la fin du moyen âge. Les origines et le premier siècle de la Chambre ou Cour des Aides de Paris. Paris. 1933.

Lameere, E. Le grand conseil des ducs de Bourgogne de la maison de Valois. Brussels. 1906.

Cosneau, E. Le connétable de Richemont, Arthur de Bretagne. Paris. 1886. [Important for military decisions.]

Spont, A. La milice des francs-archers. RQH. lxi. 1897.

La Roncière, C. Bourel de. Histoire de la marine française. Vol. ii. Paris. 1900. 2nd edn. 1914.

Clément, P. Jacques Cœur et Charles VII, l'administration, les finances, l'industrie, le commerce et les arts au xve siècle. Paris. 1873.

Guiraud, L. Recherches et conclusions nouvelles sur le prétendu rôle de Jacques Cœur. *In* Mém. de la Soc. archéol. de Montpellier. Ser. ii. Vol. ii. 1900.

Thomas, A. L'évasion et la mort de Jacques Cœur. RH. xcviii. 1918.

Prutz, H. Jacques Cœur von Bourges. (Ebering's Hist. Studien. 93.) Berlin. 1911.

—— Jacques Cœur als Bauherr und Kunstfreund. SBAW. 1911.

—— Kritische Studien zur Geschichte Jacques Cœur, des Kaufmanns von Bourges. SBAW. 1909.

—— Jacques Cœur's Beziehungen zur römischen Kurie. SBAW. 1910.

Bouvier, R. Jacques Cœur, un financier colonial au xve siècle. Paris. 1928.

Kerr, A. B. Jacques Cœur, merchant prince of the Middle Ages. New York. 1927.

CHAPTER VIII.

FRANCE: LOUIS XI.

I. SPECIAL BIBLIOGRAPHIES.

A full account of the sources is given in Molinier, A. Les sources de l'histoire de France, Vol. v, pp. 1–146. *See Gen. Bibl.* i. Bibliographies will also be found in the following five works:

Petit-Dutaillis, C. Charles VII, Louis XI, etc. *See below,* iii a.
Champion, P. Louis XI. *See below,* iii a.
Calmette, J. and Périnelle, G. Louis XI et l'Angleterre. *See below,* iii c.
Samaran, C. La maison d'Armagnac au xvᵉ siècle. *See below,* iii c.
Lettres de Louis XI. Vol. xi. *See below,* ii a.

Chevalier, C. U. J. Répertoire des sources historiques au moyen âge. *See Gen. Bibl.* i.
    Bio-bibliographie. *Sub nom.* Louis XI, Commines, etc.
    Topo-bibliographie. *Sub nom.* Bien public, Cléry, etc.
Bibliographies in this volume to ch. v (Papacy), vi (Florence), ix (Burgundy), x (Low Countries), xv (Spain), xvi (Portugal); and in Vol. vii, ch. vii (Switzerland).
Cf. the critique of recent publications by Petit-Dutaillis, C. and by Samaran, C. *in* Revue historique. Bulletins historiques: Histoire de France, fin du moyen âge.

II. SOURCES.

A. Acts and Letters of the King.

Lettres de Louis XI, roi de France. Ed. Charavay, E., Vaesen, J. and Mandrot, B. de. 11 vols. (SHF.) Paris. 1883–1909.
Ordonnances des Rois de France de la troisième race. Vols. xv–xix. Paris. 1811–35.
Recueil des documents concernant le Poitou contenus dans les registres de la Chancellerie de France. Ed. Guérin, P. and Celier, L. Vols. x–xii. (Soc. des archives hist. du Poitou.) Poitiers. 1906–19. [394 acts of Louis XI.]
Pilot de Thorey, E. Catalogue des actes du Dauphin Louis II, devenu le roi de France Louis XI, relatifs à l'administration du Dauphiné. Vols. i, ii. (Soc. de statistique...de l'Isère.) Grenoble. 1899. Vol. iii, supplt., ed. Vellein, G. *Ibid.* 1911.

B. Various Letters and Despatches of Ambassadors.

Croy, Vicomte J. de. Une ambassade de Lucerne à Tours près de Louis XI en 1480. *In* Bulletin de la Soc. archéol. de Touraine. xviii. 1911–12.
Dépêches de Nicolas de Roberti, ambassadeur du duc de Ferrare auprès du roi Louis XI. 1478–80. Ed. Périnelle, G. *in* Mélanges d'archéol. et d'hist. xxiv. (École franç. de Rome.) 1904.
Dépêches des ambassadeurs milanais en France sous Louis XI et François Sforza. Ed. Mandrot, B. de and Samaran, C. 4 vols. (SHF.) Paris. 1916–23.
Dépêches des ambassadeurs milanais sur les campagnes de Charles le Hardi. Ed. Gingins la Sarraz, F. de. 2 vols. Geneva and Paris. 1858.
Lettres de M. de Pompadour à Alain d'Albret sur la mort de Louis XI. *In* Archives hist. de la Gironde. vi. 1864.
Lettres de Marie de Valois à Olivier de Coëtivy, 1458–72. Ed. Marchegay, P. *in* Annuaire départemental de la Soc. d'émulation de la Vendée. 1874.
Lettres et négociations de Philippe de Commines. Ed. Kervyn de Lettenhove. Vol. i. (Acad. roy. de Belgique.) Brussels. 1867.
Lettres missives originales du xvᵉ siècle. Ed. Marchegay, P. *in* Bulletin de la Soc. archéol. de Nantes. xi. 1872.

C. Other Official Documents.

Alliot, J. M. Visites archidiaconales de Josas. Paris. 1902.

Dognon, P. Arrêt rendu par le Grand Conseil en 1481 contre un seigneur de Rouergue. *In* Annales du Midi. 1898.

Bossebœuf, L. A. Comptes royaux inédits. *In* Bulletin de la Soc. archéol. de Touraine. XII. 1900.

Champollion-Figeac, J. J. Documents historiques inédits. Vols. II–IV. (Coll. doc.) Paris. 1843–8.

Cimber, M. L. [*i.e.* Lafaist, L.] and Danjou, A. Archives curieuses de l'histoire de France. Ser. I. Vol. I. Paris. 1834. [Extracts from the accounts and expenses of Louis XI, etc.]

Desjardins, A. Négociations diplomatiques de la France avec la Toscane. Vol. I. (Coll. doc.) Paris. 1859.

Douais, C. Un registre de la Monnaie de Toulouse, 1465–83. *In* Annales du Midi. 1899.

Douët d'Arcq, L. Comptes de l'hôtel des rois de France aux xive et xve siècles. (SHF.) Paris. 1865.

Fagniez, G. Documents relatifs à l'histoire de l'industrie et du commerce en France. Vol. II. xive et xve siècles. (Coll. textes. 31.) Paris. 1900.

Fawtier, R. Comptes du Trésor (......1477). (Recueil des historiens de la France. Documents financiers. II.) (Bouquet. n.s. *See Gen. Bibl.* IV.) AcadIBL. Paris. 1930.

Giraudet. Documents inédits sur les prisonniers du roi Louis XI à Tours. *In* Bulletin de la Soc. archéol. de Touraine. III. Tours. 1877.

Hamy, A. Cession du Boulonnais à Louis XI (Actes). *In* Mém. de la Soc. acad. de Boulogne. XIX. 1903.

Jacqueton, G. Documents relatifs à l'administration financière en France...1443–1523. (Coll. textes.) Paris. 1891.

La Trémoille, L. de. Archives d'un serviteur de Louis XI, documents et lettres. Nantes. 1888.

Lesort, A. Document inédit concernant la diplomatie de Louis XI. BEC. 1901.

Masselin, Jean. Journal des États Généraux en 1484. Ed. Bernier, A. (Coll. doc.) Paris. 1835.

Maulde, R. de. Procédures politiques du règne de Louis XII. (Coll. doc.) Paris. 1885.

Morice, P. H. Mémoires pour servir de preuves à l'histoire de Bretagne. 3 vols. Paris. 1742–6.

Palustre, L. Compte du roi Louis XI, 1462. *In* Bull. de la Soc. archéol. de Touraine. XI. Tours. 1873.

Parfouru, P. and Carsalade du Pont, J. de. Comptes consulaires de Riscle. 2 vols. (Arch. hist. de Gascogne.) Paris and Auch. 1892.

Pasquier, F. Un favori de Louis XI, Boffille de Juge. Documents inédits du Chartrier de Léran. (Archives hist. de l'Albigeois. x.) Albi. 1914.

Pelicier, P. Une enquête financière sous Louis XI. *In* Bulletin hist. et philol. du Comité des travaux hist. 1886.

Pelissier, L. G. Una relazione dell' entrata di Luigi XI a Parigi. ASI. Ser. v. Vol. XXI. 1898.

Pinsson, F. Pragmatica Sanctio. Paris. 1666.

Preuves des Mémoires de Philippe de Comines, Traités, instructions, etc., *in* Vols. II–IV of Mémoires de Comines. Nouv. édn. par MM. Godefroy, augmentée par N. Lenglet du Fresnoy. London and Paris. 1747.

Quicherat, J. Documents relatifs à la guerre du Bien Public. *In* Champollion-Figeac, J. J. Documents hist. inédits. Vol. II. *See above.*

Rapport au Grand Conseil de Louis XI sur les abus et les scandales de la Cour des Aides, 1468. BEC. Ser. II. Vol. v. 1848–9.

Reilhac, A. de. Jean de Reilhac, secrétaire des rois Charles VII, Louis XI, et Charles VIII. Documents pour servir à l'histoire de ces règnes. 3 vols. Paris. 1886–8.

Roolles des bans et arrières-bans de la province de Poictou, Xaintonge et Angoumois, 1467. Poitiers. 1667. Repr. Nantes. 1883.

Saige, G. Documents historiques relatifs à la Principauté de Monaco depuis le xv⁰ siècle. Vol. i. Monaco. 1888.

Vayssière, A. Louis XI et la Franche-Comté. Documents inédits. *In* Bulletin de la Soc. d'agriculture, sciences, et arts de Poligny. 18ᵉ année. 1877.

Vic, C. de and Vaissete, J. J. Histoire générale de Languedoc. Vol. xii. *See Gen. Bibl.* iv.

Webster, W. An unknown treaty between Edward IV and Louis XI. EHR. xii. 1897.

Würth-Paquet, F. X. Table chronologique des chartes relatives au Luxembourg. (Publns. de la sect. hist. de l'Institut de Luxembourg, xxxi ff.) Luxembourg. 1876 ff.

D. Chronicles, Memoirs, Reports.

Basin, Thomas. Histoire des règnes de Charles VII et de Louis XI. Apologie, etc. Ed. Quicherat, J. 4 vols. (SHF.) Paris. 1855–9. [New edn. by Samaran, C. *in* Class. hist. is forthcoming.]

—— Fragments inédits de l'histoire de Louis XI. Ed. Delisle, L. *in* Notices et extraits des manuscrits. xxiv, pt. 2. Paris. 1893.

—— Page inédite de l'histoire de Louis XI. Ed. Samaran, C. BEC. 1924.

Chastellain, Georges. Chronique. Ed. Kervyn de Lettenhove, *in* Oeuvres. Vols. i– v. (Acad. roy. de Belgique.) Brussels. 1863–4.

Chronique du Bec. Ed. Porée, A. A. (Soc. de l'hist. de Normandie.) Rouen and Paris. 1883.

Chronique du Mont St Michel. Ed. Luce, S. 2 vols. (Soc. des anciens textes français.) Paris. 1879, 83.

Chroniques de Yolande de France. Documents. Ed. Menabrea, L. (Acad. roy. de Savoie, i.) Chambéry. 1859.

Commynes, Philippe de. Mémoires. Ed. Dupont, L. M. E. 3 vols. (SHF.) Paris. 1840–7; *also* ed. Mandrot, B. de. 2 vols. (Textes pour l'enseignement de l'hist.) Paris. 1901, 3; *also* ed. Calmette, J. and Durville, G. 3 vols. (Class. hist.) Paris. 1924–5.

Cronique Martiniane. Interpolation originale. Ed. Champion, P. (Bibl. du xvᵉ siècle. ii.) Paris. 1907.

Deportemens des François et Allemands. (Mém. pour servir à l'hist. de la Franche-Comté. Publ. par l'Acad. de Besançon. vii.) Besançon. 1876.

Diesbach, Louis de, page de Louis XI. Chronique. French transl. Diesbach, M. de. Paris. 1901.

Du Clercq, Jacques. Mémoires. Ed. Reiffenberg, F. A. F. T. de. 4 vols. 2nd edn. Brussels. 1835–6.

Dupré. Journal de famille des Dupré, bourgeois de Mâcon, 1407–1520. Ed. Lex, L. and Bougenot, S. *in* Annales de l'Acad. de Mâcon. Ser. iii. Vol. ii. Mâcon. 1898.

Foulquart, Jehan. Mémoires. Pt. i. Ed. Barthélemy, E. de *in* Revue de Champagne. i. 1876.

Fragments d'une chronique du règne de Louis XI. Ed. Coulon, A. *in* Mélanges d'archéol. et d'hist. xv. (École franç. de Rome.) 1895.

Gaguin, Robert. Compendium de Francorum gestis. Paris. 1501.

Gros, Bernard. Livre de raison. Ed. Tholin, G. *in* Bull. hist. et philol. du Comité des travaux hist. 1889; and *in* Revue de l'Agenais. •xx. 1893.

Haynin, Jean de. Mémoires. [Ed. Chalon, R.] 2 vols. (Soc. des bibliophiles de Mons.) Mons. 1842.

La Marche, Olivier de. Mémoires. Ed. Beaune, H. and d'Arbaumont, J. 4 vols. (SHF.) Paris. 1883–8.

Ledoyen, Guillaume. Chronique rimée. Ed. Certain, E. de. BEC. Sér. iii. Vol. iii. 1852.

Le Prestre, Pierre. Chronique. Ed. Belleval, Marquis de, *in* Mém. de la Soc. d'émulation d'Abbeville. Ser. iii. Vol. ii. 1878.

Leseur, Guillaume. Histoire de Gaston IV, comte de Foix. Ed. Courteault, H. 2 vols. (SHF.) Paris. 1893, 96.

Livre des Trahisons de France envers la maison de Bourgogne. Ed. Kervyn de Lettenhove. (Chroniques relatives à l'hist. de Belgique sous la domination des ducs de Bourgogne. II.) Brussels. 1873.

Mailliard, Benoît. Chronique. Ed. Guigue, G. Lyons. 1883; supplt. 1901.

Maupoint, Jean. Journal parisien. Ed. Fagniez, G. *in* Mém. de la Soc. de l'hist. de Paris et de l'Île-de-France. IV. Paris. 1878.

Medici. Le Livre de Podio ou Chroniques d'Étienne de Médicis. Ed. Chassaing, A. 2 vols. Le Puy. 1869–74.

Molinet, Jean. Chronique. Ed. Buchon, J. A. Vols. I, II. (Coll. des chroniques nationales françaises. XLIII, XLIV.) Paris. 1827–8. Also publ. separately.

Robert, Gerard. Journal. (Pièces concernant l'hist. d'Artois. Publ. par l'Acad. d'Arras. I.) Arras. 1852.

Rogier, Jean. Mémoires. Ed. de Barthélemy. Rheims and Paris. 1875–6.

Rosmital, Léon de. De Leonis a Rosmital nobilis Bohemi itinere annis 1465–7 suscepto commentarius. (Bibliothek des literarischen Vereins. VII.) Stuttgart. 1844.

Roye, Jean de. Journal, connu sous le nom de Chronique scandaleuse. Ed. Mandrot, B. de. 2 vols. (SHF.) Paris. 1894, 96.

Vigneulles, Philippe de. Chronique. [From the Creation.] Ed. Bruneau, C. Vols. I, II. (Soc. d'hist. et d'archéol. de la Lorraine.) Metz. 1927 ff., in progress. Incomplete edn., under the title Gedenkbuch (1471–1522) by Michelant, D. H. Stuttgart. 1852.

Wavrin, Jehan de. Anchiennes cronicques d'Engleterre. Ed. Dupont, L. M. E. Vols. II, III. (SHF.) Paris. 1859, 63. Also ed. Hardy, W. and Hardy, E. L. C. P. Vol. V (Rolls). 1891.

E. LITERARY DOCUMENTS.

Baude. Les vers de maître Henri Baude. Ed. Quicherat, J. (Trésor des pièces rares ou inédites.) Paris. 1856.

Chastellain, Georges. Oeuvres diverses. Ed. Kervyn de Lettenhove *in* Oeuvres. Vols. VI, VII. (Acad. roy. de Belgique.) Brussels. 1864–5.

Déprez, E. La trahison du cardinal Balue. Chansons et ballades inédites. *In* Mélanges d'archéol. et d'hist. XIX. (École franç. de Rome.) 1899.

Leroux de Lincy, A. J. V. Chants historiques et populaires du temps de Charles VII et de Louis XI. Paris. 1857.

——— Recueil de chants historiques français. Ser. I. Paris. 1841.

Martial d'Auvergne. Vigiles de Charles VII. Ed. Coustelier, A. U. 2 vols. Paris. 1724.

Meschinot, Jean. Satires contre Louis XI. Ed. La Borderie, A. de *in* Jean Meschinot, sa vie et ses œuvres. BEC. 1895.

Rosier des Guerres. Ed. (with the completely incorrect title, Enseignements de Louis XI pour le dauphin), by Diamant-Berger, M. Paris. 1925. [Cf. Articles by Kaulek, J. and by Hellot *in* RH. XXI and XXIX; and by Samaran, C. *in* BEC. 1926.]

F. ICONOGRAPHIC DOCUMENTS.

Harcourt, L. d' and Maumené, C. Iconographie des rois de France, de Louis IX à Louis XIII. Paris. 1929.

[See the portraits reproduced in the above work; and *in* Champion, P. Louis XI (*see below*, III A), Delaborde, H. F. L'expédition de Charles VIII en Italie (*see below*, III C), Lavisse, E. Histoire de France, illustrated edn., Vol. IV, pt. 2 (*see Gen. Bibl.* V).

III. MODERN WORKS.

A. GENERAL.

The older histories of the reign are now valueless except that of J. Michelet, antiquated but still worth reading (Livres XIII–XVII of his Histoire de France). Michelet has utilised an immense work composed in the eighteenth century by Joachim Legrand (Bibl. Nat., Fonds français 6960–90) which contains 1. History of the reign (mediocre). 2. A very valuable collection of original documents. 3. Copies of documents, often faultily transcribed.

Petit-Dutaillis, C. Charles VII, Louis XI, etc. *In* Lavisse, E. Histoire de France. Vol. IV, pt. 2. 1902. *See Gen. Bibl.* v.

Champion, P. Louis XI. Vol. I. Le Dauphin. Vol. II. Le Roi. Paris. 1927. [Interesting, but disconnected.]

Brachet, A. Pathologie mentale des rois de France. Louis XI et ses ascendants. Paris. 1903.

Coville, A. La jeunesse et la vie privée de Louis XI. *In* Journal des Savants. May–June 1908.

Degert, A. Louis XI et ses ambassadeurs. RH. CLIV. 1927.

Dodu, G. Louis XI. RH. CLXVIII. 1931.

Doucet, R. Le gouvernement de Louis XI. *In* Revue des Cours et Conférences. Années 1922–3 and 1923–4.

Gandilhon, A. Contribution à l'histoire de la vie privée et de la cour de Louis XI. (Mém. de la Soc. hist. du Cher.) Bourges. 1906.

Mosher, O. W. Louis XI, king of France, as he appears in history and in literature. Toulouse. 1925. [diss.]

Thibault, M. La jeunesse de Louis XI. Paris. 1907.

B. BIOGRAPHIES OF THE MINISTERS OF LOUIS XI.

Anchier, C. Charles I de Melun, lieutenant général de Louis XI. MA. 1892.

Bardoux, A. Les grands baillis au XVe siècle. Jean de Doyat. RDF. IX. 1863.

—— Les légistes, leur influence sur la société française. Paris. 1877.

Bellet, C. Notice sur Jost de Silenen. Lyons. 1880.

Bernus, P. Louis XI et Pierre de Brézé. (Repr. from Revue de l'Anjou.) Angers. 1912.

Boislisle, A. de. Notice sur Étienne de Vesc, sénéchal de Beaucaire. *In* Annuaire Bulletin de la Soc. de l'hist. de France, 1878–83.

Bricard, G. Un serviteur et compère de Louis XI, Jean Bourré. Paris. 1893.

Carrière, V. Nicole Tilhart, secrétaire et général des finances de Louis XI. MA. 1905.

Chabannes, Comte H. de. Histoire de la maison de Chabannes. Vols. I, II. Dijon. 1892 ff.

Chartraire, Chanoine. Jean de Salazar, écuyer de Louis XI. *In* Bull. de la Soc. archéol. de Sens. XXXII. 1923.

Chéreau, A. Les Médecins de Louis XI. *In* Union médicale. n.s. Vol. XV. 1862.

—— Jacques Coitier, médecin de Louis XI. *In* Bulletin de la Soc. d'agriculture, sciences, et arts de Poligny. 1892 and 1893.

Douët d'Arcq, L. Procès criminel intenté contre Jacques de Brézé. BEC. Ser. II. Vol. V. 1848–9.

Feugère des Forts. Pierre d'Oriole, chancelier de France. *In* Positions des thèses. École nat. des chartes. Paris. 1891.

Fierville, C. Le cardinal Jean Jouffroy et son temps. Coutances. 1874.

Forgeot, H. Jean Balue, cardinal d'Angers. (BHE. 106.) Paris. 1895.

Lanier, A. Recherches sur Tristan Lermite. *In* Positions des mémoires pour le diplôme d'études supérieures. Faculté des lettres de Paris. Paris. 1897.

Mallat, J. Geoffroy de Pompadour. *In* Bulletin de la Soc. hist. et archéol. du Périgord. XXI. 1894.

Mandrot, B. de. Ymbert de Batarnay. Paris. 1886.

Marchegay, P. Louis XI, M. de Taillebourg et M. de Maigné. BEC. Ser. IV. Vol. I. 1855.

Péchenard, P. L. Jean Juvénal des Ursins. Paris. 1876.

Perret, P. M. Boffille de Juge. *In* Annales du Midi. 1891.

—— Jacques Galéot. BEC. 1891.

—— Le Maréchal d'Esquerdes. *In* Annuaire Bulletin de la Soc. de l'hist. de France. 1891.

—— Notice sur Louis Malet de Graville. Paris. 1889.

Picot, G. Le procès d'Olivier le Dain. *In* Comptes rendus des séances et travaux de l'Acad. des sciences morales et politiques. CVIII. 1877.

Renet, Abbé. Les Bissipat du Beauvaisis. *In* Mém. de la Soc. acad. de l'Oise. XIV. 1889.

Samaran, C. Jean de Bilhères-Lagraulas, diplomate français. Paris. 1921.

Vallet de Viriville, A. Notice historique sur Cousinot, introductory to his edn. of Chronique de la Pucelle ou Chronique de Cousinot. Paris. 1859.

C. The Nobility and Feudal Coalitions. Enlargement of the Domain. Foreign Policy. Army and Navy.

[Books referring to the contest between Louis XI and Charles the Bold are omitted.]

Aimond, C. Les relations de la France et du Verdunois de 1270 à 1552. Paris. 1910.

Arnaud d'Agnel, G. Politique des rois de France en Provence. Louis XI et Charles VIII. 2 vols. Paris and Marseilles. 1914.

Boissonnade, P. Histoire de la réunion de la Navarre à la Castille. Paris. 1893.

Buser, B. Die Beziehungen der Mediceer zu Frankreich. Leipsic. 1879.

Calmette, J. Louis XI, Jean II, et la révolution catalane. Toulouse and Paris. 1903.

—— La question du Roussillon sous Louis XI. *In* Annales du Midi. 1895–6.

—— and Périnelle, G. Louis XI et l'Angleterre. (Mém. et doc. publ. par la Soc. de l'École des chartes.) Paris. 1930.

—— and Vidal, P. Histoire du Roussillon. Paris. 1923.

Chaillan, M. Le roi René à son château de Gardanne. Paris. 1909.

Champion, P. Calendrier royal pour l'an 1471. Abbeville and Paris. 1928.

—— Vie de Charles d'Orléans. Paris. 1911.

Chazaud, A. M. Fiançailles, mariage et apanage du sire de Beaujeu. *In* Bulletin de la Soc. d'émulation de l'Allier. XI. 1870.

—— Une campagne de Louis XI. La ligue du Bien public en Bourbonnais. *Ibid.* XII. 1873.

Clerc, E. Various memoirs on Louis XI and Franche-Comté *in* Mém. de l'Acad. de Besançon, 1843, 1873, 1881.

Courteault, H. Gaston IV, comte de Foix. (Bibliothèque méridionale. Ser. II. Vol. III.) Toulouse. 1895.

Daumet, G. Étude sur l'alliance de la France et de la Castille au XIVe et au XVe siècle. (BHE. 118.) Paris. 1898.

Delaborde, H. F. L'expédition de Charles VIII en Italie. Paris. 1888.

Desdevises du Dézert, G. Don Carlos d'Aragon, prince de Viane. Paris. 1889.

Desjardins, A. Mémoire sur la politique extérieure de Louis XI et sur ses rapports avec l'Italie. Mém. AcadIBL. VIII, pt. 2. 1868.

Duhamel, L. Négociations de Charles VII et de Louis XI avec les évêques de Metz pour la châtellenie d'Épinal. *In* Annales de la Soc. d'émulation des Vosges. XII. 1867.

Dupuy, A. Histoire de la réunion de la Bretagne à la France. 2 vols. Paris. 1880.

Favre, C. [Jean de Bueil]. Biographical introdn. to his edn. of Jouvencel by Jean de Bueil. 2 vols. (SHF.) Paris. 1887, 89.

Fawtier, R. Organisation de l'artillerie royale au temps de Louis XI. *In* Essays in medieval history presented to T. F. Tout. Manchester. 1925.

Ghinzoni, P. Galeazzo Maria Sforza e Luigi XI. ASL. XII. 1885.

—— Spedizione Sforzesca in Francia, 1465–6. ASL. XVII. 1890.

Goechner, E. Les relations des ducs de Lorraine avec Louis XI. *In* Annales de l'Est. XII. 1898.

Huillard-Bréholles, J. L. A. Louis XI protecteur de la Confédération italienne. *In* Revue des Soc. Savantes. Ser. II. Vol. v. 1861.

Jaurgain, J. de. Deux comtes de Comminges: Jean de Lescun et Odet d'Aydie. (Repr. from Bull. de la Soc. archéol. du Gers.) Paris. 1919. [Cf. RH. cxxxviii. 1921. pp. 89 sqq.]

La Borderie, A. de and Pocquet, B. Histoire de Bretagne. Vol. IV (1364–1515). Rennes. 1906.

La Mure, J. M. de. Histoire des ducs de Bourbon. Ed. Chantelauze, R. Vol. II. Paris. 1868.

La Roncière, C. de. Histoire de la marine française. Vol. II. Paris. 1900.

Lecoy de la Marche, A. Le roi René. 2 vols. Paris. 1875.

—— Louis XI et la succession de Provence. RQH. XLIII. 1888.

Ledru, A. Louis XI et Colette de Chambes. (Repr. from Revue de l'Anjou.) Angers. 1882.

Luchaire, A. Alain le Grand, sire d'Albret. Paris. 1877.

Mandrot, B. de. Jacques d'Armagnac, duc de Nemours. RH. XLIII, XLIV. 1890.

—— Jean de Bourgogne, duc de Brabant, et le procès de sa succession. RH. XCIII. 1907.

—— Louis XI, Jean V d'Armagnac et le drame de Lectoure. RH. XXXVIII. 1888.

—— Les relations de Charles VII et de Louis XI avec les cantons suisses, 1444–83. *In* Jahrb. für schweizerische Geschichte. v–vi. Zürich. 1880–1.

Marchegay, P. La rançon d'Olivier de Coëtivy. BEC. XXXVIII. 1877.

Maulde la Clavière, R. de. Histoire de Louis XII. 3 vols. Paris. 1889–91.

—— Jeanne de France, duchesse d'Orléans et de Berry. Paris. 1883.

Neubauer, H. G. Die burgundische Frage, 1477–93. London. 1930. [diss.]

Perret, P. M. Histoire des relations de la France avec Venise du XIIIᵉ siècle à l'avènement de Charles VIII. 2 vols. Paris. 1896.

Pocquet du Haut-Jussé, B. A. François II, duc de Bretagne, et l'Angleterre. Paris. 1929. (Repr. from Mém. de la Soc. d'hist....de Bretagne. IX. Paris. 1928.)

—— Les papes et les ducs de Bretagne. 2 vols. (Bibl. des Écoles franç. d'Athènes et de Rome.) Paris. 1928.

Renet, M. Époque de Louis XI. Siège de Beauvais. Jeanne Hachette. *In* Beauvais et le Beauvaisis. Beauvais. 1898.

Rossignol, C. Histoire de la Bourgogne. Conquête de la Bourgogne après la mort de Charles le Téméraire. Dijon. 1853.

Salmon, A. Notice sur Simon de Quingey et sa captivité dans une cage de fer. BEC. Ser. III. Vol. IV. 1853.

Samaran, C. La maison d'Armagnac au XVᵉ siècle. (Mém. et doc. publ. par la Soc. de l'École des chartes. VII.) Paris. 1907.

Sorbelli, A. Francesco Sforza a Genova. (Saggio sulla politica italiana di Luigi XI.) Bologna. 1901.

Stein, H. Charles de France, frère de Louis XI. (Mém. et doc. publ. par la Soc. de l'École des chartes.) Paris. 1921.

Tauzin, L'abbé. Louis XI et la Gascogne. RQH. LIX. 1896.

Thomas, E. Étude sur les relations de Louis XI avec la Savoie. *In* Positions des thèses. École nat. des chartes. Paris. 1931.

Vaesen, J. Du droit d'occupation d'une terre sans seigneur selon Louis XI. *In* Revue d'hist. diplomatique. I. 1887.

D. RELIGIOUS AFFAIRS. LOUIS XI AND THE PAPACY.

Arnaud. Louis XI et les Vaudois du Dauphiné. *In* Bulletin hist. et philol. du Comité des travaux hist. 1895.

Baron, F. Le cardinal Pierre de Foix le Vieux et ses légations. Amiens. 1920–2.

Caillet, P. Jean de Bourbon, évêque du Puy (1413–85). (Publn. de la Soc. des études locales, sect. de la Haute-Loire.) Le Puy. 1929.

Chasseriaud, H. Étude sur la Pragmatique Sanction sous le règne de Louis XI. *In* Positions des thèses. École nat. des chartes. Paris. 1897.

Combet, J. Louis XI et le St Siège. Paris. 1903.

Labande, L. H. Avignon au xve siècle. (Mém. et doc. publ. par ordre du Prince de Monaco.) Paris. 1920.

Lesellier, J. Une curieuse correspondance inédite entre Louis XI et Sixte IV. *In* Mélanges d'archéol. et d'hist. xLV. (École franç. de Rome.) 1928.

Lucius, C. Pius II und Ludwig XI. (Heidelberger Abh. zur mittl. und neueren Gesch. 41.) Heidelberg. 1913.

Marx, J. L'Inquisition en Dauphiné. (BHE. 206.) Paris. 1914.

Petit-Dutaillis, C. Un nouveau document sur l'Église de France. Le registre des visites de Josas. RH. LXXXVIII. 1905.

Philippe, J. Guillaume Fichet. Annecy. 1892.

Rey, R. Louis XI et les États pontificaux de France au xve siècle. Grenoble. 1899.

Richard, P. Origines de la Nonciature de France. RQH. LXXVIII. 1905.

Salvini, J. L'application de la Pragmatique Sanction sous Charles VII et Louis XI au chapitre cathédral de Paris. Paris. 1912. (Repr. from Revue d'hist. de l'Église de France. III. 1912.)

Vast, H. Le cardinal Bessarion. Paris. 1878.

E. ADMINISTRATION. ASSEMBLIES OF ESTATES.

Aubert, F. Histoire du Parlement de Paris de l'origine à François I. 2 vols. Paris. 1894.

Billioud, J. Les États de Bourgogne aux xive et xve siècles. (Acad. des sciences… de Dijon.) Dijon. 1902.

Bonnault d'Houët, Baron de. Les Francs Archers de Compiègne. Paris. 1897.

Cadier, L. Les États de Béarn. Paris. 1888.

Clerc, E. Histoire des États Généraux en Franche-Comté. 2 vols. Lons-le-Saunier. 1881.

Cramer, O. Das innere Politik Ludwigs XI. Cologne. 1927. [With appendix: methodical classification of the letters of Louis XI.]

Dognon, P. Les institutions politiques et administratives du pays de Languedoc, du xiiie siècle aux guerres de religion. Toulouse and Paris. 1896.

—— La taille en Languedoc de Charles VII à François Ier. *In* Annales du Midi. 1891.

Dupont-Ferrier, G. Études sur les institutions financières de la France à la fin du moyen âge. 2 vols. Paris. 1930, 32.

—— Nouvelles études sur les institutions financières de la France à la fin du moyen âge. Les origines et le premier siècle de la Chambre ou Cour des Aides de Paris. Paris. 1933.

—— Les institutions bailliagères en Dauphiné, 1440–1515. Paris. 1902.

—— Les officiers royaux des bailliages et sénéchaussées…à la fin du moyen âge. (BHE. 145.) Paris. 1902.

Dussert, A. Les États du Dauphiné, de la guerre de Cent Ans aux guerres de religion. Grenoble. 1923. (Repr. from Bulletin de l'Acad. Delphinale. 1922–3.)

Hirschauer, C. Les États d'Artois, de leurs origines à l'occupation française. 2 vols. Paris and Brussels. 1923.

Le Sourd, A. Essai sur les États de Vivarais. Paris. 1926.

Maugis, E. Histoire du Parlement de Paris de l'avènement des rois Valois à la mort d'Henri IV. Vol. I. Paris. 1913.

Pasquier, F. La domination française en Cerdagne sous Louis XI. *In* Bulletin hist. et philol. du Comité des travaux hist. 1895.

Picot, G. Histoire des États Généraux. Vol. I. 2nd edn. Paris. 1888.

Prentout, H. Les États provinciaux de Normandie. 3 vols. (Mém. de l'Acad. Nat.… de Caen. n.s. Vols. I–III.) Caen. 1925–7. *Also* publ. separately.

Spont, H. L'équivalent aux aides en Languedoc de 1450 à 1515. *In* Annales du Midi. III. 1891.

—— La gabelle du sel en Languedoc au xve siècle. *Ibid.*

—— La milice des francs-archers. RQH. LXI. 1897.

—— La taille en Languedoc de 1450 à 1515. *In* Annales du Midi. II, III. 1890–1.

Valois, N. Inventaire des arrêts du Conseil d'État. Vol. I. Introduction, étude historique sur le Conseil du roi. (Coll. des inventaires et documents.) Paris. 1886.

Viollet, P. Élections des députés aux États Généraux de Tours en 1468 et en 1484. BÉC. Ser. VI. Vol. II. 1866.

F. THE COUNTRYSIDE AND THE TOWNS DURING THE REIGN OF LOUIS XI.
ECONOMIC AND SOCIAL CONDITIONS.

Beaurepaire, C. de. État des campagnes de la Haute Normandie dans les derniers temps du moyen âge. *In* Recueil des travaux de la Soc. libre d'agric.,...de l'Eure. Ser. III. Vol. VII. Évreux. 1865.

Bellecombe, A. de. Histoire des seigneurs de Montpezat et de l'abbaye de Pérignac. Auch and Paris. 1898.

Bezard, Y. La vie rurale dans le sud de la région parisienne, de 1450 à 1560. Paris. 1929.

Boissonnade, P. La renaissance de l'essor de la vie maritime en Poitou, Aunis, et Saintonge du xe au xve siècle. *In* Revue d'hist. économique. XII. 1924.

Borel, F. Les foires de Genève au xve siècle. Geneva. 1892.

Canel, A. Révolte de la Normandie sous Louis XI. *In* Recueil des travaux de la Soc. libre d'agric.,...de l'Eure. Ser. II. Vol. I. 1840. Évreux. 1841.

Dupont, G. Histoire du Cotentin et de ses îles. Vol. III. Caen. 1885.

Eberstadt, R. Das französische Gewerberecht in Frankreich vom 13 Jahrht. bis 1581. Leipsic. 1899.

Hauser, H. Ouvriers du temps passé, xve–xvie siècles. Paris. 1899.

La Roncière, C. de. Première guerre entre le protectionnisme et le libre échange. RQH. LVIII. 1895.

Maulde, H. de. Marchandises envoyées en Angleterre en 1471. BEC. 1896.

—— Note sur un projet d'exposition en 1470. *In* Comptes rendus...AcadIBL. 1889.

Tholin, G. Ville libre et barons. Paris and Agen. 1886.

On Louis XI and the Towns.

Sée, H. Louis XI et les villes. Paris. 1892.

Abbeville.

Ledieu, A. Budget d'Abbeville en 1464 et 1465. *In* Bulletin du Comité des travaux hist., section des sciences écon. et sociales. 1903.

Prarond, E. Abbeville aux temps de Charles VII, des ducs de Bourgogne et de Louis XI. Paris. 1899.

Agen.

Magen, A. Un essai d'organisation démocratique dans la ville d'Agen en 1481. *In* Travaux de la Soc. d'agriculture, sciences, et arts d'Agen. Ser. II. Vol. V. Agen. 1877.

Amiens.

Calonne, A. de. Histoire d'Amiens. Vol. I. Amiens. 1899.

Maugis, E. Essai sur le régime financier de la ville d'Amiens du milieu du xive à la fin du xvie siècle. Amiens. 1898.

—— Transformations du régime politique et social de la ville d'Amiens, des origines de la commune à la fin du xvie siècle. Paris. 1906.

Angers.

Marchegay, P. Sédition à Angers en 1461, dite la Tricoterie. *In* Revue de l'Anjou. II. 1853.

Varangot, J. Les institutions municipales d'Angers, de 1474 à 1584. *In* Positions des thèses. École nat. des chartes. Paris. 1932.

Arras.

Stein, H. Les habitants d'Évreux et le repeuplement d'Arras en 1479. BEC. 1923. [Special bibliography.]

—— La participation du pays de Languedoc au repeuplement d'Arras. BEC. 1931.

Avallon.

Quentin. Avallon au xve siècle. *In* Bull. de la Soc. archéol. de l'Yonne. VII. 1853.

Bordeaux.

Jullian, C. Histoire de Bordeaux. Bordeaux. 1895.

Malvezin, T. Histoire du commerce de Bordeaux. Vol. II. Bordeaux. 1892.

Caen.

Prentout, H. Louis XI et les foires de Caen. *In* Bulletin hist. et philol. du Comité des travaux hist. 1911.

Cambrai.

Dubrulle, H. Cambrai à la fin du moyen âge. Lille. 1903.
Lesort, A. La succession de Charles le Téméraire à Cambrai. *In* Mém. de la Soc. d'émulation de Cambrai. LV. 1903.

Compiègne.

Bazin, A. Compiègne sous Louis XI. Compiègne. 1907.

Cordes.

Portal, C. Histoire de Cordes. Cordes. 1902.

Grenoble.

Prudhomme, A. Histoire de Grenoble. Grenoble. 1888.

Lyon.

Brésard, M. Les foires de Lyon aux xve et xvie siècles. Paris. 1914.
Caillet, L. Relations de la commune de Lyon avec Charles VII et Louis XI. (Annales de l'Université de Lyon. xxi.) Lyons and Paris. 1909.
Vaesen, J. La juridiction commerciale à Lyon, 1463–1795. Lyons. 1879.
Valous, V. de. Étienne Turquet et les origines de la fabrique lyonnaise, 1466–1536. Lyons. 1868.

Montdidier.

Beauvillé, V. de. Histoire de la ville de Montdidier. Vol. i. 2nd edn. Paris. 1875.

Orléans.

Poullain, H. Orléans. Règne de Louis le Onzième. Orléans. 1888.

Paris.

Poëte, M. Une vie de cité. Paris de sa naissance à nos jours. Vol. ii. Paris. 1927.

Perpignan.

Vidal, P. Histoire de la ville de Perpignan. Paris. 1897.

Rouen.

Beaurepaire, C. de. Note sur six voyages de Louis XI à Rouen. *In* Travaux de l'Acad. de Rouen. LIX. 1856–7.
Giry, A. Les établissements de Rouen. 2 vols. (BHE. 55, 59.) Paris. 1883, 85.

Senlis.

Flammermont, J. Histoire des institutions municipales de Senlis. (BHE. 45.) Paris. 1881.

Toulouse.

Bonnafous, M. Toulouse et Louis XI. *In* Annales du Midi. 1927.

Tours.

Bossebœuf, L. A. [*sub nom.* Ariel Mouette]. Dix ans à Tours sous Louis XI. Tours. 1890.
—— Histoire de la fabrique de soieries de Tours. *In* Mém. de la Soc. archéol. de Touraine. xli. Tours. 1900.

Troyes.

Boutiot, T. Histoire de la ville de Troyes. Vol. iii. Troyes and Paris. 1873.

Tulle.

Fage, R. Louis XI et les fortifications de Tulle. *In* Bulletin de la Soc. des lettres, sciences, et arts de la Corrèze. xxii. 1910.

CHAPTER IX.

THE KINGDOM OF BURGUNDY OR ARLES FROM THE ELEVENTH TO THE FIFTEENTH CENTURY.

I. BIBLIOGRAPHIES.

Much information on the sources can be gathered from Molinier, A. Les sources de l'histoire de France. Vols. ii–vi. *See Gen. Bibl.* i. Some of the modern works listed below also contain bibliographies on their particular subjects.

II. DOCUMENTS.

Böhmer, J. F. Regesta imperii. Vols. v, vi, viii, xi. *See Gen. Bibl.* iv *under* Imperial Documents.
Boutaric, E. Notices et extraits de documents inédits relatifs à l'histoire de France sous Philippe-le-Bel. *In* Notices et extraits des manuscrits de la Bibl. Nat. xx. Paris. 1862.
Chevalier, C. U. J. Choix de documents historiques inédits sur le Dauphiné. *In* Bulletin de la Soc. de statistique de l'Isère. Ser. iii. Vol. vi. *Also* publ. separately. Lyons. 1874.
—— Regeste dauphinois ou répertoire...des documents imprimés et manuscrits relatifs à l'histoire du Dauphiné. Valence. 1912 ff.
Constitutiones et Acta publica imperatorum et regum. Vols. iii–vi. i, viii. MGH. Legum Sect. iv. 1904–26.
Diplomata regum et imperatorum Germaniae. Vol. v. Die Urkunden Heinrichs III. Vol. viii. Die Urkunden Lothars III. MGH. 1926–31.
Jaffé, P. Regesta Pontificum Romanorum. 2nd edn. by Loewenfeld, S. and others. 2 vols. Leipsic. 1885, 88.
Papal Registers and Letters. *See Gen. Bibl.* iv *supra, and also of* Vols. vi *and* vii, *under* Papal Documents.
Poupardin, R. Recueil des actes des rois de Provence (855–928). (Chartes et diplômes. AcadIBL.) Paris. 1920.
Riezler, S. Vatikanische Akten zur deutschen Geschichte in der Zeit Kaiser Ludwigs des Bayern. *See Gen. Bibl.* iv *under* Papal Documents.
Schwalm, J. Reise nach Italien im Herbst 1898. Neu. Arch. xxv, xxvi. 1899–1900.
Stumpf-Brentano, K. F. Die Reichskanzler vornehmlich des 10, 11, und 12 Jahrhts. 3 vols. Innsbruck. 1865–83.
Werunsky, E. Excerpta ex registris Clementis VI et Innocentii VI. *See Gen. Bibl.* iv *under* Papal Documents.
Winkelmann, E. Acta imperii inedita. *See Gen. Bibl.* iv *under* Imperial Documents.

III. MODERN WORKS.

A. The Kingdom and its Foreign Relations.

For the general history of the Arelat there may be consulted :

1. Lavisse, E. and Rambaud, A. Histoire générale. Vols. ii, iii. *See Gen. Bibl.* v
2. Lavisse, E. Histoire de France. Vols. ii, iii. MGH. *See Gen. Bibl.* v.
3. Jahrbücher der deutschen Geschichte. [Dealing with the reign of each emperor.] (Hist. Commission BAW.) Berlin and Leipsic. 1862 ff., in progress.
4. Kopp, J. E. Geschichte der eidgenössischen Bünde. Vol. v. Lucerne. 1851.

Bergengrün, A. Die politischen Beziehungen Deutschlands zu Frankreich während der Regierung Adolfs von Nassau. Strasbourg. 1884.
Bonnassieux, P. De la réunion de Lyon à la France. Lyons. 1875.

Faure, C. Histoire de la réunion de Vienne à la France. *In* Bulletin de l'Acad. Delphinale. xix, xx. 1906.

Fournier, P. Le royaume d'Arles et de Vienne. Étude sur la formation territoriale de la France dans l'est et le sud-est. Paris. 1891.

Funck-Brentano, F. Philippe le Bel et la noblesse Franc-Comtoise. BEC. xlix. 1888.

Gottlob, A. Kaiser Karls IV private und politische Beziehungen zu Frankreich. Innsbruck. 1883.

Grieser, R. Das Arelat in der europäischen Politik von der Mitte des 10 bis zum Ausgange des 14 Jahrhts. Jena. 1925.

Guiffrey, J. J. Histoire de la réunion du Dauphiné à la France. Paris. 1868.

Gutsche, F. Die Beziehungen zwischen Reich und Kurie vom Tode Bonifaz VIII bis zur Wahl Heinrichs VII, 1303-8. Marburg. 1913. [diss.]

Heller, J. Deutschland und Frankreich in ihren politischen Beziehungen vom Ende des Interregnums bis zum Tode Rudolfs von Habsburg. Göttingen. 1874.

Henneberg, H. Die politischen Beziehungen zwischen Deutschland und Frankreich unter König Albrecht I. Strasbourg. 1891. [diss.]

Hentze, C. England, Frankreich, und König Adolf von Nassau. Kiel. 1914.

Hofmeister, A. Deutschland und Burgund im früheren Mittelalter. Leipsic. 1914.

Hueffer, G. Die Stadt Lyon und die Westhälfte des Erzbistums in ihren politischen Beziehungen zum Deutschen Reich und zur französischen Krone (879-1312). Münster. 1878.

Jacob, L. Le royaume de Bourgogne sous les empereurs franconiens. Paris. 1906.

Kallmann, R. Die Beziehungen des Königreichs Burgund zu Kaiser und Reich. Berlin. 1888.

Kraussold, M. Die politischen Beziehungen zwischen Deutschland und Frankreich während der Regierung Heinrichs VII. Munich. 1900.

Leroux, A. Recherches critiques sur les relations politiques de la France avec l'Allemagne de 1292 à 1378. (BHE. 50.) Paris. 1882.

—— Nouvelles recherches...1378 à 1461. Paris. 1892.

——: La royauté française et le Saint-Empire Romain au moyen âge. RH. xlix. 1892.

Mendl, B. and Quicke, F. Les relations politiques entre l'empereur et le roi de France de 1355 à 1356. *In* Revue belge de philol. et d'hist. viii. 1929.

Poole, A. L. England and Burgundy in the last decade of the twelfth century. *In* Essays in history presented to Reginald Lane Poole. Oxford. 1927.

Poupardin, R. Le royaume de Bourgogne (888-1038). (BHE. 163.) Paris. 1907. [Bibliography.]

—— Le royaume de Provence sous les Carolingiens (855-933?). (BHE. 131.) Paris. 1901. [Bibliography.]

Previté-Orton, C. W. Italy and Provence, 900-950. EHR. xxxii (1917). 335-47.

Priesack, J. Die Reichspolitik des Erzbischofs Balduin von Trier in den Jahren 1314-28. Göttingen. 1894.

Reuter, E. Der Feldzug Rudolfs I von Habsburg gegen Burgund, 1289. Halle. 1901. [diss.]

Scheffer-Boichorst, P. Die Erhebung Wilhelms von Baux zum Könige des Arelats. SPAW. 1901.

Sievers, O. Die politischen Beziehungen Kaiser Ludwigs des Bayern zu Frankreich in den Jahren 1314-37. (Ebering's Hist. Studien, 2.) Berlin. 1896.

Sternfeld, R. Das Verhältniss des Arelats zu Kaiser und Reich vom Tode Friedrichs I bis zum Interregnum. Berlin. 1881.

Trog, E. Rudolf I und Rudolf II von Hochburgund. Basle. 1884.

Vogt, E. Reichspolitik des Erzbischofs Balduin von Trier, 1328-34. Gotha. 1901.

Welvert, E. Philippe le Bel et la maison de Luxembourg. BEC. xlv. 1884.

Wenck, K. Clemens V und Heinrich VII. Halle. 1882.

Werminghoff, A. Zur Geschichte der politischen Beziehungen zwischen Deutschland und Frankreich unter König Albrecht I. Neu.Arch. xxvi. 1901.

Werunsky, E. Geschichte Karls IV und seiner Zeit. 3 vols. Innsbruck. 1880-92.

Winckelmann, O. Die Beziehungen Kaiser Karls IV zum Königreich Arelat. Strasbourg. 1882.

B. Separate Provinces.

(i) *Dauphiné.*

Chevalier, Jules. Mémoires pour servir à l'histoire des comtés de Valentinois et de Diois. Paris. 1897–1906.

[Valbonnais, J. P. Moret de Bourchenu, Marquis de.] Histoire de Dauphiné. 2 vols. Geneva. 1721–2.

(ii) *Franche-Comté.*

Clerc, E. Essai sur l'histoire de la Franche-Comté. 2nd edn. 2 vols. Besançon. 1870.

Dunod de Charnage, F. I. Histoire du comté de Bourgogne, etc. (Histoire des Séquanois.) 3 vols. Dijon and Besançon. 1735–40.

(iii) *Lyonnais.*

Fabvier, E. Histoire de Lyon et des anciennes provinces du Lyonnais, du Forez, et du Beaujolais. 2 vols. Paris. 1845.

Steyert, A. Nouvelle histoire de Lyon et du Lyonnais. 3 vols. Lyons. 1895–9.

(iv) *County of Provence.*

Castrucci, F. Istoria della città d'Avignone et del Contado Venesino. Venice. 1678.

Kiener, F. Verfassungsgeschichte der Provence seit der Gothenherrschaft bis zur Errichtung der Konsulate, 510–1200. Leipsic. 1900.

Manteyer, G. de. La Provence du premier au douzième siècle. Études d'histoire et de géographie politique. (Mém. et documents publ. par la Soc. de l'École des chartes, VIII.) Paris. 1908.

Papon, J. P. Histoire générale de Provence. 4 vols. Paris. 1777–86.

Sternfeld, R. Karl von Anjou als Graf der Provence. Berlin. 1888.

(v) *Savoy.*

Cibrario, G. A. L. Storia della monarchia di Savoia. 3 vols. Turin. 1840–4.

Cognasso, F. Amedeo VIII. 2 vols. (Collana storica Sabauda.) Turin. 1930.

—— Il Conte Rosso. (*Ibid.*) Turin. 1931.

—— Il Conte Verde. (*Ibid.*) Turin. 1926.

—— Umberto Biancamano. (*Ibid.*) Turin. 1929.

Guichenon, S. Histoire de Bresse et de Bugey. 4 pts. Lyons. 1650.

—— Histoire généalogique de la royale maison de Savoye. 2 pts. Lyons. 1660.

Previté-Orton, C. W. The early history of the House of Savoy (1000–1233). Cambridge. 1912.

Wurstemberger, J. L. Peter der Zweite Graf von Savoyen, Markgraf in Italien sein Haus und seine Lande. 4 vols. Bern. 1856–8.

(vi) *Trans-Jurane Burgundy.*

See Bibliography to ch. VII in Vol. VII, pp. 850–2.

CHAPTER X.

THE LOW COUNTRIES.

I. BIBLIOGRAPHY.

Pirenne, H. Bibliographie de l'histoire de Belgique. 3rd edn. *See Gen. Bibl.* i. [Till 1598 includes all the Netherlands.]

II. SOURCES.

The publications of the Commission royale d'histoire de Belgique (Brussels. 1836 ff.), the Rijks geschiedkundige publicatiën (The Hague. 1904 ff.), and the Werken van het historisch genootschap (Utrecht. 1863 ff.) contain a number of documents and narrative sources, the latter especially towards the close of the Middle Ages. For the earlier period most of the narrative texts are in the MGH. For Belgian charters and diplomas, consult Wauters, A. Table chronologique des chartes et diplômes imprimés concernant l'histoire de la Belgique (–1350). 13 vols. (Comm. roy. d'hist. de Belgique.) Brussels. 1866 ff.

The most important narrative texts only are given, from the close of the 13th century.

Annales Gandenses (1296–1310). Ed. Funck-Brentano, F. (Coll. textes.) Paris. 1895.

Chastellain, G. Oeuvres. Ed. Kervyn de Lettenhove. 8 vols. (Acad. roy. de Belgique.) Brussels. 1863–6.

Chronicon comitum Flandrensium (–1428). Ed. Warnkoenig, L. *in* Corpus chronicorum Flandriae. Ed. Smet, J. J. de. Vol. i. (Comm. roy. d'hist. de Belgique.) Brussels. 1837.

Chroniques relatives à l'histoire de Belgique sous la domination des ducs de Bourgogne. Ed. Kervyn de Lettenhove. 3 vols. (*Ibid.*) Brussels. 1870–6.

Commynes, Philippe de. Mémoires (1464–98). Ed. Calmette, J. and Durville, G. 3 vols. (Class. hist.) Paris. 1924–5.

Documents relatifs aux troubles du pays de Liège sous les princes-évêques Louis de Bourbon et Jean de Horne (1455–1505). Ed. Ram, P. de. (Comm. roy. d'hist. de Belgique.) Brussels. 1844.

Dynter, E. de. Chronicon ducum Brabantiae (–1442). Ed. Ram, P. de. 3 vols. (*Ibid.*) Brussels. 1854-60.

Hemricourt, J. de. Guerres d'Awans et de Waroux. *In* Oeuvres; ed. Borman, C. de, Bayot, A., and Poncelet, E. 3 vols. (*Ibid.*) Brussels. 1910-31.

—— Miroir des nobles de Hesbaye. (*Ibid.*)

—— Patron de la temporalité des évêques de Liège. (*Ibid.*)

Hocsem, J. Gesta pontificum Leodiensium (1247–1348). Ed. Kurth, G. (*Ibid.*) Brussels. 1927.

Istore et croniques de Flandres (–1408). Ed. Kervyn de Lettenhove. 2 vols. (*Ibid.*) Brussels. 1879–80.

La Marche, Olivier de. Mémoires (1435–88). Ed. Beaune, H. and d'Arbaumont, J. 4 vols. (SHF.) Paris. 1884–8.

Mémoire du légat Onufrius sur les affaires de Liége. Ed. Bormans, S. (Comm. roy. d'hist. de Belgique.) Brussels. 1886.

Molinet, J. Chronique (1474–1506). Ed. Buchon, J. A. 5 vols. (Coll. des chroniques nationales françaises. xliii–xlvii.) Paris. 1827–8. Also publ. separately.

Monstrelet, E. de. Chronique (1400–44). Ed. Douët d'Arcq, L. 6 vols. (SHF.) Paris. 1857–62.

Muisit, G. le. Chronicon (1300–52). Ed. Lemaître, H. (SHF.) Paris. 1905.

III. MODERN WORKS.

A. GENERAL.

Blok, P. J. Geschiedenis van het Nederlandsche volk. 3rd edn. Vol. I. Leyden. 1923. [Standard history of the Northern Netherlands.]

Gosses, J. H. and Japikse, N. Handboek tot de staatkundige geschiedenis van Nederland. 2nd edn. The Hague. 1927.

Pirenne, H. Histoire de Belgique. *See Gen. Bibl.* v. [Standard history of Belgium.]

Poullet, E. Histoire politique nationale. Les institutions des anciens Pays-Bas. 2nd edn. 2 vols. Louvain. 1892.

B. BEFORE THE BURGUNDIAN PERIOD.

(a) *Political.*

Duvivier, C. La querelle des d'Avesnes et des Dampierre. 2 vols. Brussels. 1894.

Fris, V. De slag van Kortrik. Ghent. 1902.

Funck-Brentano, F. Philippe le Bel en Flandre. Paris. 1897.

Kern, F. Die Anfänge der französischen Ausdehnungspolitik bis zum Jahre 1308. Tübingen. 1910.

Lucas, H. S. The Low Countries and the Hundred Years War (1326–47). Ann Arbor. 1929.

Obreen, H. Floris V graaf van Holland en Zeeland. Ghent. 1907.

Pirenne, H. Le soulèvement de la Flandre maritime en 1323–8. Brussels. 1900.

Vanderkindere, L. La formation des principautés belges au moyen âge. 2 vols. Brussels. 1902.

Wrong, G. M. The crusade of 1383 known as that of the bishop of Norwich. London. 1892.

(b) *Economics and Institutions.*

Blok, P. J. Geschiedenis eener hollandsche Stad [Leyden]. 4 vols. The Hague. 1910–18.

Dillen, J. G. van. Het economisch Karakter der middeleeuwsche stad. Amsterdam. 1914.

Espinas, G. La draperie dans la Flandre française au moyen âge. Paris. 1923.

—— La vie urbaine de Douai au moyen âge. 4 vols. Paris. 1913.

Hirschauer, C. Les États provinciaux d'Artois de leurs origines à l'occupation française. 2 vols. Paris. 1923.

Kurth, G. La cité de Liège au moyen âge. 3 vols. Brussels. 1910.

Linden, H. van der. Histoire de la constitution de la ville de Louvain au moyen âge. Ghent. 1892.

Nowé, H. Les baillis comtaux en Flandre des origines à fin du XIVe siècle. Brussels. 1929.

Pirenne, H. Les anciennes démocraties des Pays-Bas. Paris. 1910. Transl. Saunders, J. V. *as* Belgian democracy; its early history. Manchester. 1915.

—— Histoire de la constitution de la ville de Dinant au moyen âge. Ghent. 1889.

Posthumus, N. W. De geschiedenis van de leidsche lakenindustrie. Vol. I. De Middeleeuwen. The Hague. 1908.

Warnkoenig, L. A. Flandrische Staats- und Rechtsgeschichte bis zum Jahre 1305. 3 vols. Tübingen. 1835–42. Rev. French transl. Gheldolf, A. Histoire de la Flandre et de ses institutions civiles et politiques. 5 vols. Brussels. 1835–64.

Wohlwill, A. Die Anfänge der landständischen Verfassung im Bistum Lüttich. Leipsic. 1867.

C. THE BURGUNDIAN PERIOD.

(a) *Political.*

Beaucourt, G. du Fresne de. Histoire de Charles VII. 6 vols. Paris. 1881–91.

Blok, P. J. De eerste jaren der bourgondische heerschappij in Holland. *In* Bijdragen voor vaderl. geschiedenis. Utrecht. 1885.

Cartellieri, O. Geschichte der Herzöge von Burgund. Vol. I. Philipp der Kühne. Leipsic. 1910.

—— Am Hofe der Herzöge von Burgund. Basle. 1926.

Dändliker, K. Ursachen und Vorspiel der Burgunderkriege. Zürich. 1876.
Delbrück, H. Die Perserkriege und die Burgunderkriege. Berlin. 1887.
Diemar, H. Die Entstehung des deutschen Reichskriegs gegen Herzog Karl den Kühnen. Marburg. 1896.
Hintzen, J. D. De Kruistochtplannen van Philips den Goede. Rotterdam. 1918.
Kallen, G. Die Belagerung von Neuss. Neuss. 1925.
Löher, F. von. Jakobäa von Bayern. 2 vols. Nördlingen. 1869.
Quicke, F. Les relations diplomatiques entre le roi des Romains Sigismond et la maison de Bourgogne. *In* Bulletin de la Commission roy. d'hist. de Belgique. Brussels. 1926.
Richter, F. Der Luxemburger Erbfolgestreit in den Jahren 1438–44. Trèves. 1889.
Schellhass, K. Zur Trierer Zusammenkunft im Jahre 1473. DZG. 1890.
Werveke, N. van. Definitive Erwerbung des Luxemburger Landes durch Philipp Herzog von Burgund. Luxemburg. 1886.

(*b*) *Economics and Institutions.*

Coornaert, E. La draperie-sayetterie d'Hondschoote. Paris. 1930.
Des Marez, G. L'organisation du travail à Bruxelles au xve siècle. Brussels. 1904.
Guillaume, G. Histoire des bandes d'ordonnance. Brussels. 1873.
Huizinga, J. L'état bourguignon, ses rapports avec la France et les origines d'une nationalité néerlandaise. MA. xl, xli. 1930-1.
—— Uit de voorgeschiedenis van ons nationaal besef. *In* Tien Studien. Haarlem. 1926.
—— The waning of the Middle Ages; a study of the forms of life, thought and art in France and the Netherlands in the xivth and xvth centuries. London. 1924. Dutch edn. Haarlem. 1919.
Lameere, E. Le Grand Conseil des ducs de Bourgogne. Brussels. 1900.
Pirenne, H. Les anciennes démocraties des Pays-Bas. *See above,* iii b (*b*).
Reiffenberg, F. A. F. T. de. Histoire de l'ordre de la Toison d'Or. Brussels. 1830.

D. HISTORICAL ATLASES.

Beekman, A. A. *ed.* Geschiedkundige Atlas van Nederland. The Hague. 1911 ff., in progress.
Essen, L. van der, *ed.* Atlas de géographie historique de la Belgique. Brussels and Paris. 1919 ff., in progress.

894

CHAPTER XI.

ENGLAND: THE LANCASTRIAN KINGS, 1399–1461.

I. BIBLIOGRAPHIES AND GUIDES TO THE SOURCES.

Bolland, W. C. Manual of Year Book Studies. Cambridge. 1925.
Flemming, J. H. England under the Lancastrians. *See below*, II B (i).
Fowler, R. C. Episcopal Registers of England and Wales. (Helps for Students of History, I.) S.P.C.K. London. 1918.
Giuseppi, M. S. Guide to the Manuscripts...in the P.R.O. *See Gen. Bibl.* I. [*See also* P.R.O. Lists and Indexes. *Cf.* Gross, Sources (*below*), p. 81, no. 473.]
Gross, C. Bibliography of British Municipal History. (Harvard Hist. Studies, v.) New York, 1897. [*See also* Interim Report of the Committee on House of Commons Personnel and Politics, 1264–1832. App. VIII, pp. 119–136. London. 1932.]
—— Sources and Literature of English History. *See Gen. Bibl.* I.
Hall, H. Repertory of British Archives. Pt. I, England. London. 1920.
—— Studies in English Official Historical Documents. Cambridge. 1908.
—— *ed.* Formula Book of English Official Historical Documents. 2 pts. Cambridge. 1908–9.
—— *ed.* Select Bibliography of English Mediaeval Economic History. London. 1914.
Holdsworth, W. S. Sources and Literature of English Law. Oxford. 1925.
Humphreys, A. L. Handbook to County Bibliography. London. 1917.
Kingsford, C. L. English Historical Literature in the fifteenth century. Oxford. 1913.
Morris, J. E. and Jordan, H. Introduction to the study of Local History and Antiquities. London. 1910.
Oman, C. W. C. History of England, 1377–1485. *See below*, III A.
Putnam, B. H. The Ancient Indictments in the Public Record Office. EHR. XXIX (1914). 479–505.
Richardson, H. G. Year Books and Plea Rolls as sources of historical information. TRHS. 4th ser. Vol. v (1922). 28–70.
Winfield, P. H. The chief Sources of English Legal History. Cambridge, Mass. 1925.

II. ORIGINAL AUTHORITIES.

A. CHRONICLES AND OTHER NARRATIVE SOURCES.

Account of the first battle of St Albans (1455). Ed. Bayley, J. *in* Archaeologia. (Soc. of Antiq. of London.) XX. (1824). 519–23.
Amundesham, J. Annales monasterii Sancti Albani, 1421–40, quibus praefigitur Chronicon rerum gestarum in monasterio Sancti Albani, 1422–31, a quodam ignoto compilatum. Ed. Riley, H. T. 2 vols. (Rolls.) 1870–1.
Annales monasterii de Bermundeseia (1042–1432). Ed. Luard, H. R. *in* Annales Monastici. Vol. III, pp. 421–87. (Rolls.) 1866.
Annales Ricardi et Henrici IV (1392–1406). Ed. Riley, H. T. *in* Johannis de Trokelowe et Henrici de Blaneforde Chronica et Annales. pp. 155–424. (Rolls.) 1866. [Now known to be by Thomas Walsingham. The continuation to 1420, discovered in MS. Bodley 462, is being edited by Mr V. H. Galbraith. See his Thomas Walsingham and the St Albans Chronicle. EHR. XLVII (1932). 12–30.]
Arnold, R. The Customs of London, otherwise called Arnold's Chronicle. Ed. Douce, F. London. 1811.
Berry, Hérault du Roy. Le recouvrement de Normandie. Ed. with Engl. transl. Stevenson, J. *in* Narratives of the Expulsion of the English from Normandy, 1449–50. pp. 239–376. (Rolls.) 1863.

Blacman, J. Collectarium mansuetudinum et bonorum morum Regis Henrici VI. Ed. with Engl. transl. James, M. R. Cambridge. 1919.

Blondel, R. De reductione Normanniae. Ed. Stevenson, J. *in* Narratives of the Expulsion of the English from Normandy, 1449–50. pp. 1–238. (Rolls.) 1863. *Also* ed. Héron, A. *in* Oeuvres de Robert Blondel. Vol. II. (Soc. de l'hist. de Normandie.) Rouen. 1893.

Brut, The, or the Chronicles of England. Ed. Brie, F. W. D. 2 pts. (EETS. Orig. ser. 131, 136.) London 1906, 8. [The critical introduction was never published. For a discussion of the various manuscripts, see the editor's Geschichte und Quellen der mittelenglischen Prosachronik, 'the Brute of England.' Marburg. 1905.]

Burton, Thomas of. Chronica monasterii de Melsa (continuatio 1396–1417). Ed. Bond, E. A. Vol. III, pp. 237–314. (Rolls.) 1868.

Capgrave, J. Chronicle of England (to 1417). Ed. Hingeston, F. C. (Rolls.) 1858.
—— Liber de illustribus Henricis. Ed. with Engl. transl. Hingeston, F. C. 2 vols. (Rolls.) 1858.

Chastellain, G. Oeuvres. Ed. Kervyn de Lettenhove. 8 vols. Brussels. 1863–6.

Chronica minor Sancti Benedicti de Hulmo (continuation to 1503). Ed. Ellis, H. *in* Chronica Johannis de Oxenedes. pp. 412–39. (Rolls.) 1859.

Chronicle of Dieulacres Abbey, 1381–1403. Ed. Clarke, M. V. and Galbraith, V. H. *in* The deposition of Richard II. *See below*, III C.

Chronicle of the Grey Friars of London. (1189–1556.) Ed. Nichols, J. G. (Camden Soc. LIII.) London. 1852. A better edn., ed. Howlett, R. *in* Monumenta Franciscana. Vol. II, pp. 141–260. (Rolls.) 1882.

Chronicle of John Strecche for the reign of Henry V (1414–1422). Ed. Taylor, F. *in* Bulletin...John Rylands Library. XVI. 1932.

Chronicle of London, 1089–1483. Ed. Tyrrell, E. and Nicolas, N. H. London. 1827.

Chronicles of London. Ed. Kingsford, C. L. Oxford. 1905.

Chronicon abbatiae de Evesham ad annum 1418. Ed. Macray, W. D. (Rolls.) 1863.

Chronicon abbatiae de Parco Ludae (1066–1413). Ed. Venables, E., with Engl. transl. by Maddison, A. R. (Lincolnshire Record Soc.) Horncastle. 1891.

Chronicon Angliae (incerti scriptoris) de regnis Henrici IV, Henrici V, et Henrici VI (to 1455). Ed. Giles, J. A. London. 1848. [That part which deals with the reign of Henry V (by Thomas Elmham to Nov. 1416) was edited more satisfactorily by Williams, B. *as* Henrici Quinti Angliae regis gesta. (English Hist. Soc.) London. 1850.]

Chronique de la traïson et mort de Richart Deux, Roy d'Engleterre (1397–1400). Ed. with Engl. transl. Williams, B. (English Hist. Soc.) London. 1846.

Chronique du religieux de Saint-Denys (1380–1422). Ed. with a French transl. of Latin text, Bellaguet, L. 6 vols. (Coll. doc.) Paris. 1839–52.

Cochon, P. Chronique Normande. Ed. de Beaurepaire, C. de R. (Soc. de l'hist. de Normandie.) Rouen. 1870.

Créton, J. Histoire du roy d'Angleterre Richard [II], traictant particulièrement la rebellion de ses subiectz. Ed. with Engl. transl. Webb, J. *in* Archaeologia, XX, pp. 1–423. London. 1824. A better text, ed. Buchon, J. A. C. (*as* Poème sur la déposition de Richard II) *in* Collection des chroniques nationales françaises XXIV, pp. 321–466. Paris. 1826.

Débat (Le) des Hérauts d'Armes de France et d'Angleterre. Ed. Meyer, P. (Soc. des Anciens Textes français.) Paris. 1877. Engl. transl. Pyne, H. London. 1870.

Elmham, T. Vita et Gesta Henrici Quinti. Ed. Hearne, T. Oxford. 1727. [Now known not to be by Elmham.]

English Chronicle of the reigns of Richard II, Henry IV, Henry V, and Henry VI. Ed. Davies, J. S. (Camden Soc. LXIV.) London. 1856.

Eulogium historiarum sive temporis. Continuatio (to 1413). Ed. Haydon, F. S. Vol. III, pp. 333–421. (Rolls.) 1863.

Fabyan, R. The new chronicles of England and France (to 1485). Ed. Ellis, H. London. 1811.

First English Life of Henry V. Ed. Kingsford, C. L. Oxford. 1911.

Froissart, J. Chroniques (1307–1400). Ed. Kervyn de Lettenhove. 25 vols in 26. Brussels. 1867–77. Engl. transl. Bourchier, J., Lord Berners. Chronicles of

England, France &c. Ed. Ker, W. P. 6 vols. (Tudor Transl. Library.) London. 1901–3.
Frulovisi, *see below* Livio.
Gruel, G. Chronique d'Arthur de Richemont. Ed. Le Vavasseur, A. (SHF.) Paris. 1890.
Hall, E. Chronicle of Lancaster and York (1399–1547). Ed. Ellis, H. London. 1809.
Hardyng, J. Chronicle (to 1461). Ed. Ellis, H. London. 1812.
—— Extracts from the first version of his Chronicle. Ed. Kingsford, C. L. EHR. xxvii (1912). 462–82; 740–53.
Higden, R. Polychronicon. Continuation. English translations of John Trevisa and of an unknown writer of the fifteenth century. Ed. Lumby, J. R. Vol. viii, pp. 429–587. (Rolls.) 1882.
Historia vitae et regni Ricardi II (1377–1402) a monacho quodam de Evesham consignata. Ed. Hearne, T. Oxford. 1729.
Historiae Croylandensis continuatio (1149–1486). Ed. Fulman, W. *in* Rerum Anglicarum Scriptores. Oxford. 1684. Engl. transl. by Riley, H. T. Ingulf's Chronicle of the Abbey of Croyland, with the continuations. (Bohn's Antiq. Library.) London. 1854.
Historians of the Church of York and its Archbishops. Ed. Raine, J. Vols. ii and iii. (Rolls.) 1886, 94.
An Historical Collection of the fifteenth century. Ed. Kingsford, C. L. EHR. xxix (1914). 505–15.
Historical Collections of a Citizen of London in the fifteenth century. Ed. Gairdner, J. (Camden Soc. n.s. Vol. xvii.) London. 1876. [containing: Page, J., Ballad of Siege of Rouen and Gregory's Chronicle (1189–1469).]
Journal d'un bourgeois de Paris, 1405–49. Ed. Tuetey, A. (Soc. de l'hist. de Paris et de l'Île-de-France.) Paris. 1881.
Juvénal des Ursins, J. Histoire de Charles VI, 1380–1422. Ed. Buchon, J.A.C. Paris. 1838.
Kirkstall Chronicle, 1355–1400. Ed. Clarke, M. V. and Denholm-Young, N. *in* Bulletin...John Rylands Library. xv (1931). 100–37.
Le Fèvre, J. Chronique (1408–35). Ed. Morand, F. 2 vols. (SHF.) Paris. 1876, 81.
Livio, T. (dei Frulovisi.) Vita Henrici Quinti regis Angliae (1413–22). Ed. Hearne, T. Oxford. 1716. [*See also* Wylie, J. H. Decembri's Version of the Vita Henrici Quinti by Tito Livio. EHR. xxiv (1909). 84–9; and Opera hactenus inedita T. L. de F., ed. Previté-Orton, C. W. pp. ix–xvi, xviii–xix.]
London Chronicle of 1460. Ed. Baskerville, G. EHR. xxviii (1913). 124–7.
Memorials of Henry V (Vita Henrici Quinti Roberto Redmanno auctore, versus rhythmici in laudem Henrici Quinti, Elmhami liber metricus de Henrico Quinto). Ed. Cole, C. A. (Rolls.) 1858.
Monstrelet, E. de. Chronique (1400–44). Ed. Douët d'Arcq, L. 6 vols. (SHF.) Paris. 1857–62. Engl. transl. by Johnes, T. 13 vols. London. 1810.
Otterbourne, T. Chronica regum Angliae (to 1420). Ed. Hearne, T. *in* Duo Rerum Anglicarum Scriptores Veteres. Vol. i, pp. 3–283. Oxford. 1732.
Pseudo-Elmham. *See above*, Elmham.
Registrum abbatiae Johannis Whethamstede Roberto Blakeney cappellano quondam adscriptum (1451–61). Ed. Riley, H. T. *in* Registra Quorundam Abbatum Monasterii Sancti Albani. 2 vols. (Rolls.) 1872.
Remarkable fragment of an old English Chronicle (1459–70). Ed. Hearne, T. *in* Thomae Sprotti Chronica, pp. 283–306. Oxford. 1719. Another edn. with modernised spelling *in* Chronicles of the White Rose of York, ed. Giles, J. pp. 1–30. London. 1845.
Ricart, R. The Maire of Bristowe is Kalendar. Ed. Smith, L. Toulmin. (Camden Soc. n.s. Vol. v.) London. 1872.
Rous, J. Historia regum Angliae (to 1485). Ed. Hearne, T. Oxford. 1745.
Six Town Chronicles. Ed. Flenley, R. Oxford. 1911. [*See also* Kingsford, C. L. Robert Bale, the London Chronicler. EHR. xxxi (1916). 126–8.]
Stone, J. Chronicle of Christ Church, Canterbury (1415–71). Ed. Searle W. G. (Cambridge Antiq. Soc. xxxiv.) Cambridge. 1902.

Stow, J. Annales or a General Chronicle of England. Ed. Howes, E. London. 1631.
—— A Summarie of the Chronicles of England. London. 1575.
Three Fifteenth-Century Chronicles. Ed. Gairdner, J. (Camden Soc. n.s. Vol. xxviii.) London. 1880.
Usk, Adam of. Chronicon, 1377–1421. Ed. with Engl. transl. Thompson, E. M. 2nd edn. (Roy. Soc. of Literature.) London. 1904.
Vergil, Polydore. Anglicae historiae libri xxvii. (to 1538). Leyden. 1651. An early English transl. of the three books dealing with the years 1422–85 was ed. Ellis, H. (Camden Soc. xxix.) London. 1844.
Walsingham, T. Gesta Abbatum Monasterii Sancti Albani. Ed. Riley, H. T. Vol. iii. (Rolls.) 1869.
—— Historia Anglicana (1272–1422). Ed. Riley, H. T. 2 vols. (Rolls.) 1863–4.
—— Ypodigma Neustriae (to 1419). Ed. Riley, H. T. (Rolls.) 1876.
Waurin, J. de. Recueil des croniques et anchiennes istories de la Grant Bretaigne (to 1471). Ed. Hardy, W. and Hardy, E. L. C. P. 5 vols. (Rolls.) 1864–91. Engl. transl. by same (to 1431). 3 vols. (Rolls.) 1864–91.
Worcester, William of. Annales rerum Anglicarum (1324–1468). Ed. Stevenson, J. *in* Letters and Papers illustrative of the wars of the English in France during the Reign of Henry VI. Vol. ii, pt. ii. pp. 743–93. (Rolls.) 1864.
—— Itinerarium. Ed. Nasmith, J. *in* Itineraria Symonis Simeonis et Willelmi de Worcestre. Cambridge. 1778.

B. Records.

(i) *General Collections.*

Coulton, G. G. Social Life in Britain from the Conquest to the Reformation. Cambridge. 1918.
English Constitutional Documents, 1307–1485. Ed. Lodge, E. C. and Thornton, G. A. Cambridge. 1935.
Flemming, J. H. England under the Lancastrians. (Univ. of Lond. Intermediate source-books of History. iii.) London. 1921.
Foedera, Conventions &c. Ed. Rymer, T. Edn. 1704–35. Vols. viii–xi. *See Gen. Bibl.* iv. [*See also* Hardy, T. D. Syllabus of Rymer's Foedera, and Report by Cooper, C. P. *Ibid.*]
Select Documents of English Constitutional History. Ed. Adams, G. B. and Stephens, H. M. New York. 1921.

(ii) *Chancery.*

Calendarium rotulorum chartarum (1199–1483) et inquisitionum ad quod damnum (1307–1461). (RC.) London. 1803.
Calendarium Inquisitionum post mortem sive escaetarum. 4 vols. (RC.) London. 1806–28.
Calendar of Charter Rolls. Vols. v, vi. (Cal.SP.) London. 1916, 27.
Calendar of Close Rolls. Henry IV (4 vols. wanting index volume). Henry V (2 vols). Henry VI (2 vols. 1422–35). In progress. (Cal.SP.) London. 1927 ff.
Calendar of Fine Rolls. Vols. xii–xv. (1399–1430.) In progress. (Cal.SP.) London. 1931–5.
Calendar of French Rolls (Henry V and Henry VI) *in* Deputy Keeper's 44th Report (1883), App. pp. 545–638 and 48th Report (1887), App. pp. 217–450.
Calendar of Norman Rolls (6–10 Henry V) *in* Deputy Keeper's Report xli (1880), App. pp. 671–810 and xlii (1881), App. pp. 313–472.
Calendar of Patent Rolls, Henry IV (4 vols.); Henry V (2 vols.); Henry VI (6 vols.). (Cal.SP.) London. 1901–11.
Catalogue of Ancient Deeds. 6 vols. (Cal.SP.) London. 1890–1915.
Rôles Normands et Français tirés des Archives de Londres. Ed. Brécquigny, L. G. O. F. de. (Soc. des Antiq. de Normandie, Mémoires. xxiii, pt. i.) Paris. 1858.
Rotuli Normanniae in Turre Londinensi asservati Johanne et Henrico Quinto Angliae Regibus. Ed. Hardy, T. D. (RC.) London. 1835.

(iii) *Exchequer.*

The Antient Kalendars and Inventories of the Treasury of His Majesty's Exchequer, together with other documents illustrating the history of that repository. Ed. Palgrave, F. 3 vols. (RC.) London. 1836.

Feudal Aids, Inquisitions, and Assessments relating to, 1284-1431. 6 vols. (Cal.SP.) London. 1899-1920.

Issues of the Exchequer (10 Henry III to 39 Henry VI). Ed. Devon, F. London. 1837. [Translated excerpts.]

Rotulorum originalium in curia scaccarii abbreviatio. 2 vols. (RC.) London. 1805, 10.

(iv) *Parliament and Council.*

Dugdale, W. A perfect copy of all summons of the nobility to the great councils and parliaments of the realm. London. 1685.

Official Return of Members of Parliament. Pt. i. London. 1878.

Proceedings and Ordinances of the Privy Council of England. Ed. Nicolas, N. H. Vols. i-vi. (RC.) London. 1834-7.

Prynne, W. A brief Register, Kalendar, and Survey of the several kinds of all parliamentary writs. 4 pts. London. 1659-64.

Reports from the Lords' Committees appointed to search the Journals of the House, Rolls of Parliament, and other records for all matters touching the Dignity of a Peer. 5 vols. London. 1820-9.

Rotuli Parliamentorum. [Ed. Strachey, J. and others.] Vols. iii-v [London. 1767]. Index. (RC.) London. 1832.

Statutes of the Realm. Vol. ii. (RC.) London. 1816.

(v) *Legal.*

Early Treatises on the Practice of the Justices of the Peace in the fifteenth and sixteenth centuries. Ed. Putnam, B. H. (Studies in Social and Legal History. vii.) Oxford. 1924.

Orders of the High Court of Chancery and Statutes of the Realm relating to Chancery. Ed. Sanders, G. W. 2 pts. London. 1845.

Public Works in Mediaeval Law. Ed. Flower, C. T. 2 vols. (Selden Soc. xxxii and xl.) London. 1915, 23. [*See also* Richardson, H. G. Early History of Commissions of Sewers. EHR. xxxiv (1919). 385-93.]

Select Cases before the King's Council, 1243-1482. Ed. Leadam, I. S. and Baldwin, J. F. (Selden Soc. xxxv.) Cambridge, Mass. 1918.

Select Cases concerning the Law Merchant, 1239-1779. Ed. Gross, C. and Hall, H. 3 vols. (*Ibid.* xxiii, xlvi, xlix.) London. 1908-32.

Select Cases from the Coroners' Rolls, 1265-1413. Ed. with Engl. transl. Gross, C. (*Ibid.* ix.) London. 1896.

Select Cases in Chancery, 1364-1471. Ed. Baildon, W. P. (*Ibid.* x.) London. 1896.

Select Cases in the Exchequer Chamber before all the Justices of England, 1377-1461. Ed. Hemmant, M. (*Ibid.* li.) London. 1933.

Select Pleas in the Court of Admiralty. Ed. Marsden, R. G. Vol. i, pt. 1. (1390-1404.) (*Ibid.* vi.) London. 1894.

Some Chancery Proceedings of the fifteenth century. Ed. Martin, C. T. *in* Archaeologia. lix (1904). 1-24.

Year Books of Henry VI: 1 Henry VI, A.D. 1422. Ed. Williams, C. H. (Selden Soc. l.) London. 1933.

[Year Books] Les Reports del Cases en ley, que furent argues en le temps de les Roys Henry le IV et Henry le V. London. 1679.

——— Henry VI. 2 vols. *Ibid.* 1679.

  [*See also* various editions published by R. Totell, 1550-87; Fitzherbert, A. La Graunde Abridgement. London. 1514. (and many later edns.); and Brooke, R. La Graunde Abridgement (a revision of Fitzherbert's edn.). London. 1568 (and later).]

(vi) *Letters and Papers.*

Aeneas Sylvius Piccolomini (Pope Pius II). Commentarii. Ed. Gobellinus, J. Rome. 1584.
—— Der Briefwechsel des Eneas Silvius Piccolomini. Ed. Wolkan, R. (Fontes rerum Austriacarum. Abt. ii. Vols. lxi–ii, lxvii–viii. Vienna. 1909–18.)
Caro, J. B. Aus der Kanzlei Sigmunds. AOG. lix. 1879.
Christ Church Letters relating to the affairs of the Priory of Christ Church, Canterbury. Ed. Sheppard, J. B. (Camden Soc. n.s. Vol. xix.) London. 1877.
Correspondence of Humphrey, Duke of Gloucester, and Pier Candido Decembrio. Ed. Borsa, M. EHR. xix (1904). 509–26. [*See also* Newman, W. L. Correspondence of Humphrey, Duke of Gloucester, and Pier Candido Decembrio. EHR. xx (1905). 484–98.]
Le Cotton MS. Galba B.I. Ed. Scott, E. and Gilliodts van Severen, L. (Acad. Roy....de Belgique.) Brussels. 1896.
Epistolae Academicae Oxon. (1421–1509.) Ed. Anstey, H. 2 vols. (Oxford Hist. Soc. xxxv, xxxvi.) Oxford. 1898.
Historical Papers and Letters from the Northern Registers. Ed. Raine, J. (Rolls.) 1873.
Letters of John Tiptoft, Earl of Worcester,...to the University of Oxford [1460.] Ed. Tait, J. EHR. xxxv (1920). 570–2.
Letters and Papers of John Shillingford, Mayor of Exeter, 1447–50. Ed. Moore, S. A. (Camden Soc. n.s. Vol. ii.) London. 1871.
Letters of the fifteenth and sixteenth centuries. Ed. Anderson, R. C. (Southampton Record Soc.) Southampton. 1921.
Letters of the Kings of England. Ed. Halliwell-Phillipps, J. O. 2 vols. London. 1846. [Translations only.]
Letters of Queen Margaret of Anjou and Bishop Beckington and others, written in the reigns of Henry V and Henry VI. Ed. Munro, C. (Camden Soc. lxxxvi.) London. 1863.
Lettres de rois, reines, et autres personnages des cours de France et d'Angleterre. Ed. Champollion-Figeac, A. Vol. ii. (Coll. doc.) Paris. 1847.
Literae Cantuarienses. Ed. Sheppard, J. B. Vol. iii. (Rolls.) 1889.
Mediaeval Post-Bag. Ed. Lyell, L. London. 1934. [Contains a few letters not before published.]
Memorials of St Edmund's Abbey. Ed. Arnold, T. Vol. iii. (Rolls.) 1896. [Letters from Register of Abbot Curteys, 1440–1444, pp. 241–79.]
Memorials of the reign of Henry VI. Official Correspondence of Thomas Bekynton, Secretary to Henry VI and Bishop of Bath and Wells. Ed. Williams, G. 2 vols. (Rolls.) 1872. [*See also* Journal by one of the Suite of Thomas Beckington, 1442. Ed. (in transl.) Nicolas, N. H. London. 1828.]
Original Letters illustrative of English History. Ed. Ellis, H. Three series. 11 vols. London. 1824–46.
Paston Letters, 1422–1509. Ed. Gairdner, J. (Library edn.) 6 vols. London. 1904.
Plumpton Correspondence. A series of letters, chiefly domestick, written in the reigns of Edward IV, Richard III, Henry VII, and Henry VIII. Ed. Stapleton, T. (Camden Soc. iv.) London. 1839.
Poggio Bracciolini, F. Epistolae. Ed. Tonelli, T. 3 vols. Florence. 1832–61.
Royal and historical letters during the reign of Henry IV. Ed. Hingeston, F. C. (Rolls.) 1860. [This covers the years 1399–1404. A second volume was suppressed but can be obtained in the larger libraries.]
Some Literary Correspondence of Humphrey, Duke of Gloucester. Ed. Creighton, M. EHR. x (1895). 99–104.
Stonor Letters and Papers, 1290–1483. Ed. Kingsford, C. L. 2 vols. (Camden Soc. 3rd ser. Vol. xxix, xxx.) London. 1919. The editor afterwards published a supplement in Camden Miscellany, xiii. (Camden Soc. 3rd ser. Vol. xxxiv.) 1924.
Trevelyan Papers. Ed. Collier, J. P. 3 vols. (Camden Soc. lxvii, lxxxiv, cv.) London. 1857–72.

(vii) *Ecclesiastical.*

(a) *General.*

Chapters of the Augustinian Canons. Ed. Salter, H. E. (Cant. and York Soc. LXX.) London. 1922.

Collectanea Anglo-Premonstratensia. Ed. Gasquet, F. A. 3 vols. (Camden Soc. 3rd ser. Vols. VI, X, XII.) London. 1904–6.

Documents illustrating the activities of the General and Provincial Chapters of the English Black Monks. Ed. Pantin, W. A. Vol. II. (Camden Soc. 3rd ser. Vol. XLVII.) London. 1933. [A third volume to come.]

Dugdale, W. Monasticon Anglicanum. *See Gen. Bibl.* IV.

Gascoigne, T. Loci e Libro Veritatum. Passages selected from Gascoigne's Theological Dictionary illustrating the condition of Church and State, 1403–1458. Ed. Rogers, J. E. Thorold. Oxford. 1881.

Godwin, F. De praesulibus Angliae commentarius. Ed. Richardson, G. 2 vols. Cambridge. 1743.

Grey Friars of London, their history with the Register of their convent. Ed. Kingsford, C. L. (British Soc. of Franciscan Studies.) Aberdeen. 1915.

Le Neve, J. Fasti Ecclesiae Anglicanae. Ed. Hardy, T. D. 3 vols. Oxford. 1854.

Lyndwood, W. Provinciale (seu constitutiones Angliae) continens constitutiones provinciales archiepiscoporum Cant' a Stephano Langtono ad Henricum Chichleium, cum annotationibus. 2 pts. Best edn. Oxford. 1679.

Snappe's Formulary and other Records. Ed. Salter, H. E. (Oxford Hist. Soc. LXXX.) Oxford. 1924. [For Archbishop Arundel's visitation of the University of Oxford.]

Some English documents of the Conciliar Movement. Ed. Jacob, E. F. *in* Bulletin ...John Rylands Library. xv (1931). 358–94.

Stubbs, W. Registrum sacrum Anglicanum. *See Gen. Bibl.* III.

A Visitation of Westminster in 1444. Ed. Galbraith, V. H. EHR. XXXVII (1922). 83–8.

Wilkins, D. Concilia Magnae Britanniae et Hiberniae. *See Gen. Bibl.* IV *under* Councils, General. [*See also* Jacob, E. F. Wilkins's *Concilia* and the fifteenth century. TRHS. 4th ser. Vol. xv (1932). 91–131.]

(b) *Episcopal Registers.*

[*See* Fowler, R. C. Episcopal Registers of England and Wales. (Helps for Students of History. I.) S.P.C.K. London. 1918.]

Bath and Wells.

Henry Bowet (1401–7). Ed. Holmes, T. S. (Somerset Record Soc. XIII.) London. 1899.

Nicholas Bubwith (1407–24). Ed. Holmes, T. S. 2 vols. (*Ibid.* XXIX, XXX.) 1914.

John Stafford (1425–43). Ed. Holmes, T. S. 2 vols. (*Ibid.* XXXI–II.) 1915–16.

Thomas Bekynton (1443–65). Ed. Maxwell-Lyte, H. C. and Dawes, M. C. B. 2 vols. (*Ibid.* XLIX, L.) 1934–5.

Chichester.

Medieval Registers of the Bishops of Chichester, 1396–1502. Ed. (abstracts) Walcott, M. E. C. *in* Trans. Roy. Soc. of Literature. 2nd ser. Vol. IX (1870). 215–44.

Robert Rede (1397–1415). Ed. (with Engl. transl.) Deedes, C. 2 pts. (Sussex Rec. Soc. VIII, IX.) London. 1908, 10.

Richard Praty (1438–45). Ed. (extracts) Deedes, C. (*Ibid.* IV.) Lewes. 1905.

Durham.

[Thomas Langley (1407–37). Ed. Whiting, C. E. To be published by the Surtees Soc.]

Ely.

Abstracts of Registers. Ed. Crosby, J. H. *in* Ely Diocesan Remembrancer (Cambridge):
John de Fordham (1388–1425). April—May, 1897 to May—June, 1902.
Thomas Bourchier (1444–54). June–July, 1902 to April–May, 1904.
William Gray (1454–78). May—June, 1904 to April 1908.
Ely Episcopal Records. A Calendar of the Episcopal Records in the Muniment Room of the Palace of Ely. Ed. Gibbons, A. Lincoln. 1891. [Includes extracts from registers 1375–1587.]

Exeter.

Edmund Stafford (1395–1419). Ed. Hingeston-Randolph, F. C. London. 1886.
Edmund Lacy (1420–55). Ed. Hingeston-Randolph, F. C. and Reichel, O. J. 2 pts. London. 1909, 15. [Calendars with copious extracts.]

Hereford.

(Published by Cantilupe Soc., Hereford, and Cant. and York Soc., London, jointly.)
John Trefnant (1389–1404). Ed. Capes, W. W. 1914–6.
Robert Mascall (1404–16). Ed. Parry, J. H. 1917.
Edmund Lacy (1417–20).
Thomas Poltone, or Poulton (1420–22). Ed. Parry, J. H. and Capes, W. W. 1918.
Thomas Spofford (1422–48). Ed. Bannister, A. T. 1917–9.
Richard Beauchamp (1449–50). Ed. Bannister, A. T. 1917–9.
Reginald Boulers (1451–3). Ed. Bannister, A. T. 1917–9.
John Stanbury (1453–74). Ed. Parry, J. H. and Bannister, A. T. 1919.

Lincoln.

Visitations of Religious Houses in the Diocese of Lincoln, 1420–1449. Ed. Thompson, A. Hamilton. 3 vols. (Lincoln Record Soc. and Cant. and York Soc. jointly.) London. 1915–27. [Richard Flemyng (1420–31), William Gray (1431–6), William Alnwick (1436–49).)]

St Davids.

The Episcopal Registers, 1397–1518. Ed. with transl. Isaacson, R. F. 2 vols. (Cymmrodorion Soc. Record Series. VI.) London. 1917.

Winchester.

William of Wykeham (1366–1404). Ed. Kirby, T. I. 2 vols. (Hampshire Record Soc.) London. 1896, 99.

York.

Documents relating to Diocesan and Provincial Visitations from the Registers of Henry Bowet, Archbishop of York (1407–23), and John Kempe, Archbishop of York (1425–52). Ed. Thompson, A. Hamilton. (Surtees Soc. CXXVII. Miscellanea. II, pp. 131–302.) Durham. 1916.

(viii) *Miscellaneous.*

Acta Concilii Constanciensis. Ed. Finke, H. *See Gen. Bibl.* IV *under* Councils, General.
A Book of London English, 1384–1425. Ed. Chambers, R. W. and Daunt, M. Oxford. 1931.
Borough Customs. Ed. Bateson, M. (Selden Soc. XVIII, XXI.) London. 1904, 6.
Calendar of entries in the Papal Registers relating to Great Britain and Ireland. Papal Letters. Vols. V–XII. *See Gen. Bibl.* IV *under* Papal Documents.
—— Petitions to the Pope. Vol. I (1342–1419). *Ibid.*
Calendar of Letter-Books preserved among the archives of the Corporation of the City of London. Ed. Sharpe, R. R. Books I and K. (1400–61.) London. 1909, 11.

Calendar of Select Pleas and Memoranda of the City of London, Preserved...at the Guildhall, A.D. 1381–1412. Ed. Thomas, A. H. Cambridge. 1932. [Introduction on the Law Merchant.]

Calendar of State Papers and Manuscripts existing in the Archives and Collections of Milan (1385–1618). Ed. Hinds, A. B. (Cal.SP.) London. 1912.

Calendar of State Papers and Manuscripts relating to English affairs in the Archives of Venice and Northern Italy. Ed. Brown, R. Vol. I (1202–1509). (Cal.SP.) London. 1864.

Cartulaire de l'ancienne Estaple de Bruges, 862–1492. Ed. Gilliodts van Severen, L. 4 vols. (Soc. d'Émulation de Bruges.) Bruges. 1904–6.

Collection générale des Documents français qui se trouvent en Angleterre. Ed. Delpit, J. (Coll. doc.) Paris. 1847.

Collection of all the Wills now known to be extant of the Kings and Queens of England. Ed. Nichols, J. London. 1780.

Concilium Basiliense. Studien und Quellen zur Geschichte des Konzils von Basel. Ed. Haller, J. and others. *See Gen. Bibl.* IV *under* Councils, General.

England from Chaucer to Caxton. Ed. Bennett, H. S. (English Life in English Literature; ed. Power, E. E. and Reed, A. W. I.) London. 1928.

Excerpta Historica. Ed. Bentley, S. 1831.

Expeditions to Prussia and the Holy Land made by Henry, Earl of Derby (afterwards King Henry IV) in the years 1390–1 and 1392–3, being the Accounts kept by his Treasurer during two years. Ed. Smith, L. Toulmin. (Camden Soc. n.s. Vol. LII.) 1894.

Fasciculi Zizaniorum, ascribed to Thomas Netter of Walden. Ed. Shirley, W. W. (Rolls.) London. 1858.

Fasciculus rerum expetendarum et fugiendarum...una cum appendice sive tomo II scriptorum veterum qui ecclesiae Romanae mores et abusus detegunt et damnant. Ed. Brown, E. 2 vols. London. 1690.

Fifty earliest English wills in the Court of Probate, London. Ed. Furnivall, F. J. (EETS. Orig. ser. 78.) London. 1882.

Hanseakten aus England, 1275–1412. Ed. Kunze, K. (Hansische Geschichtsquellen. VI.) Halle-a.-S. 1891.

Hanserecesse, 1431–76. Ed. Ropp, G. von der. 2te Abt. Vols. I–VII. (Verein für Hansische Geschichte.) Leipsic. 1876–92.

Hansisches Urkundenbuch. Ed. Höhlbaum, K., Kunze, K., Stein, W. 10 vols. Leipsic. 1876–1907.

Henrici VI Angliae Regis Miracula Postuma, ex codice Musei Britannici Regio 13 c. VIII. Ed. Grosjean, P. (Soc. des Bollandistes. Subsidia hagiographica, XXII.) Brussels. 1935. Another edition (extracts only with Engl. transl.). Miracles of King Henry VI. Ed. Knox, R. and Leslie, S. Cambridge. 1923.

Leland, J. Itinerary. Ed. Smith, L. Toulmin. 5 vols. London. 1906–10.

Letters and Papers illustrative of the wars of the English in France during the reign of Henry VI. Ed. Stevenson, J. 2 vols in 3. (Rolls.) 1861–4. [French documents translated.]

Memorials of London and London Life: a series of extracts from the archives of the City of London, 1276–1419. Transl. and ed. Riley, H. T. London. 1868.

Monumenta Juridica: the Black Book of the Admiralty. Ed. with Engl. transl Twiss, T. 4 vols. (Rolls.) 1871–6.

Munimenta Academica. Ed. Anstey, H. 2 vols. (Rolls.) 1868.

Stow, J. Survey of London. Ed. Kingsford, C. L. 2 vols. Oxford. 1908.

Testamenta Vetusta. Ed. Nicolas, N. H. 2 vols. London. 1826. [Translated selections.]

York Mercers and Merchant Adventurers 1356–1917. Ed. Sellers, M. (Surtees Soc. CXXIX.) Durham. 1918.

C. Contemporary Prose and Poetry.

An Alphabet of Tales. Ed. Banks, M. M. 2 vols. (EETS. Orig. ser. 126–7.) London. 1904–5.

Ancient English Christmas Carols, 1400–1700. Ed. Rickert, E. London. 1910.

Ashby, G. Poems. Ed. Bateson, M. (EETS. Extra ser. LXXVI.) London. 1899.

Audelay, J. Poems. Ed. Whiting, E. K. (EETS. Orig. ser. 184.) London. 1931.

Capgrave, J. Lives of St Augustine and St Gilbert of Sempringham. Ed. Munro, J. J. (EETS. Orig. ser. 140.) London. 1910.

—— Life of St Katharine of Alexandria. Ed. Horstmann, C. and Furnivall, F. J. (EETS. Orig. ser. 100.) London. 1893.

—— Ye Solace of Pilgrimes. Ed. Mills, C. A. (British and American Archaeol. Soc. of Rome.) London. 1911.

A Defence of the Proscription of the Yorkists in 1459. Ed. Gilson, J. P. EHR. XXVI (1911). 512–25.

Fortescue, Sir J. The Governance of England. Ed. Plummer, C. Oxford. 1885.

—— Works. Ed. Fortescue, T., Lord Clermont. London. 1869.

Frulovisi, Tito Livio dei. Opera hactenus inedita. Ed. Previté-Orton, C. W. Cambridge. 1932.

Glyn Cothi, Lewis. Poetical Works. Ed. Jones, J. and Davies, W. (Cymmrodorion Soc.) Oxford. 1837.

Gower, J. Works. Ed. Macaulay, G. C. 4 vols. Oxford. 1899–1902.

Guy of Warwick. The Second or Fifteenth-Century Version. Ed. Zupitza, J. 2 vols. (EETS. Extra ser. XXV–VI.) London. 1875–6.

Hoccleve, T. Minor Poems. Ed. Furnivall, F. J. and Gollancz, I. 2 vols. (EETS. Extra ser. LXI, LXXIII.) London. 1892, 1925.

—— Regement of Princes. Ed. Furnivall, F. J. (EETS. Extra ser. LXXII.) London. 1897.

Hymns to the Virgin and Christ, Parliament of Devils, and other Religious Poems. Ed. Furnivall, F. J. 2nd edn. (EETS. Orig. ser. 24.) London. 1895.

Jacob's Well. An English treatise on the Cleansing of Men's Conscience. Ed. Brandeis, A. (EETS. Orig. ser. 115.) London. 1900.

Laud Troy Book. Ed. Wülfing, J. E. 2 vols. (EETS. Orig. ser. 121–2.) London. 1902–3.

Libelle of Englyshe Polyce, a poem on the use of Sea-Power, 1436. Ed. Warner, Sir G. Oxford. 1926.

Life of Saint Cuthbert in English verse, c. 1450. Ed. Fowler, J. T. (Surtees Soc. LXXXVII.) Durham. 1891.

Lydgate, J. Assembly of Gods. Ed. Triggs, O. L. (EETS. Extra ser. LXIX.) London. 1896.

—— Fall of Princes. Ed. Bergen, H. 4 vols. (EETS. Extra ser. CXXI–IV.) London. 1924, 7.

—— Minor Poems, religious and secular. Ed. MacCracken, H. N. 2 vols. (EETS. Extra ser. CVII and Orig. ser. 192.) London. 1911, 34.

—— Pilgrimage of the Life of Man. Ed. Furnivall, F. J. and Locock, K. B. 3 vols. (EETS. Extra ser. LXXVII, LXXXIII, XCII.) London. 1899, 1901, 4.

—— Reson and Sensuallyte. Ed. Sieper, E. 2 vols. (EETS. Extra ser. LXXXIV, LXXXIX.) London. 1901, 3.

—— Serpent of Division. Ed. MacCracken, H. N. London. 1911.

—— Siege of Thebes. Ed. Erdmann, A. and Ekwall, E. 2 vols. (EETS. Extra ser. CVIII, CXXV.) London. 1911, 30.

—— Temple of Glas. Ed. Schick, J. (EETS. Extra ser. LX.) London. 1891.

—— Troy Book. Ed. Bergen, H. 4 vols. (EETS. Extra ser. XCVII, CIII, CVI, CXXVI.) London. 1906–35.

—— Two Nightingale Poems. Ed. Glauning, O. (EETS. Extra ser. LXXX.) London. 1900.

Lydgate, J. and Burgh, B. Secrees of old Philisoffres. Ed. Steele, R. (EETS. Extra ser. LXVI.) London. 1894.

Myrc or Mirk, J. Festial, a collection of Homilies. Ed. Erbe, T. (EETS. Extra ser. XCVI.) London. 1905. [Incomplete.]

—— Instructions for Parish Priests. Ed. Peacock, E. (EETS. Orig. ser. 31.) Revised edn. London. 1902.

Netter, T., of Walden. Doctrinale Fidei Ecclesiae. Ed. Blanciotti, B. 3 vols. Venice. 1757–9.

Oure Ladyes Myroure. Ed. Blunt, J. H. (EETS. Extra ser. XIX.) London. 1873.

Page, J. Siege of Rouen. Ed. Huscher, H. (Kölner Anglistische Arbeiten. i.) Leipsic. 1927.

Palladius on Husbondrie, englisht about 1420. Ed. Lodge, B. and Herrtage, S. J. 2 vols. (EETS. Orig. ser. 52, 72.) London. 1872, 79. Better edn.: Middle English translation of Palladius de re rustica. Ed. Liddell, M. Berlin. 1896.

Pecock, R. Book of Faith. Ed. Morrison, J. L. Glasgow. 1909.

—— Donet. Ed. Hitchcock, E. V. (EETS. Orig. ser. 156.) London. 1921.

—— Folewer to the Donet. Ed. Hitchcock, E. V. (EETS. Orig. ser. 164.) London. 1924.

—— The Repressor of Overmuch Blaming of the Clergy. Ed. Babington, C. 2 vols. (Rolls.) 1860.

—— Reule of Crysten Religioun. Ed. Greet, W. G. (EETS. Orig. ser. 171.) London. 1927.

Political Poems and Songs relating to English history, from the accession of Edward III to that of Richard III. Ed. Wright, T. 2 vols. (Rolls.) 1859, 61.

Political Poems of the Reigns of Henry VI and Edward IV. Ed. Madden, F. and Rokewode, J. G. *In* Archaeologia xxix (1842). 318–47.

Political, Religious, and Love Poems. Ed. Furnivall, F. J. 2nd edn. (EETS. Orig. ser. 15.) London. 1903.

Satirical Rhymes on the Defeat of the Flemings before Calais in 1436. Ed. Williams, B. *in* Archaeologia. xxxiii (1849). 129–32.

Songs, Carols, and other Miscellaneous Poems. (Richard Hill's Commonplace Book.) Ed. Dyboski, R. (EETS. Extra ser. ci.) London. 1908.

Three Prose Versions of the *Secreta Secretorum*. Ed. Steele, R. (EETS. Extra ser. lxxiv.) London. 1898.

Twenty-six Political and other Poems. Ed. Kail, J. (EETS. Orig. ser. 124.) London. 1904.

Two Fifteenth-Century Cookery Books. Ed. Austin, T. (EETS. Orig. ser. 91.) London. 1888.

Verses on the Exchequer in the fifteenth century. Ed. Haskins, C. H. and George, E. EHR. xxxvi (1921). 58–67.

III. MODERN WORKS.

A. General.

Belloc, H. History of England. Vol. iii. (1348–1525.) London. 1928.

Campbell, J. The lives of the Chief Justices of England. 3rd edn. 4 vols. London. 1874.

—— The lives of the Lord Chancellors of England. 4th edn. 10 vols. London. 1856–7.

Cokayne, G. E. Complete Peerage of England, Scotland, Ireland, etc. *See Gen. Bibl.* iii.

Dasent, A. I. The Speakers of the House of Commons. London. 1911.

Dugdale, W. The Baronage of England. 2 vols. London. 1675–6.

Foss, E. The Judges of England. 9 vols. London. 1848–64.

Hook, W. F. Lives of the Archbishops of Canterbury. 12 vols. London. 1860–76.

Jacob, E. F. The Fifteenth Century: some recent interpretations. *In* Bulletin... John Rylands Library. xiv (1930). 386–409.

Kingsford, C. L. Prejudice and promise in fifteenth-century England. Oxford. 1925.

Maitland, F. W. The Constitutional History of England. Cambridge. 1908.

Manning, J. A. The lives of the Speakers of the House of Commons. London. 1850.

Mediaeval England. Ed. Davis, H. W. C. (A new edition of Barnard's Companion to English History.) Oxford. 1924.

Oman, C. W. C. History of England, 1377–1485. (Political History of England. Ed. Hunt, W. and Poole, R. L. Vol. iv.) London. 1918.

Powicke, F. M. Medieval England, 1066–1485. London. 1931.

Ramsay, J. H. Lancaster and York, 1399–1485. 2 vols. Oxford. 1892.

Sharpe, R. R. London and the Kingdom. 3 vols. London. 1894.

Vickers, K. H. England in the Later Middle Ages. London. 1913.

B. Political and Biographical.

Alexander, J. J. Exeter Members of Parliament. Pt. II. 1377 to 1537. *In* Reports and Trans.... Devonshire Assn. for the Advancement of Science, Lit., and Art. LX (1928). 183–214.

Besant, Sir W. and Rice, J. Sir Richard Whittington, Lord Mayor of London. New edn. London. 1894. [*See also* Tait, J. *in* DNB. (1909 edn.) Vol. XXI. pp. 153—7.]

Blair, C. H. Hunter. Members of Parliament for Northumberland (6th October 1399—20th January 1558). *In* Archaeologia Aeliana. 4th ser. Vol. XII (1935). 82—132.

Brewer, T. Memoir of the life and times of John Carpenter (Town Clerk of London). 2nd edn. London. 1856.

Chandler, R. The life of William Waynflete, Bishop of Winchester. London. 1811.

Duck, A. Vita Henrici Chichele. Oxford. 1617. Engl. transl. London. 1699. [*See also* Jacob, E. F. Two lives of Archbishop Chichele, with an Appendix containing an early Book List of All Souls College. *In* Bulletin...John Rylands Library. XVI (1932). 428–81.]

Gasquet, F. A. The religious life of King Henry VI. London. 1923.

Harbin, S. W. Bates. Members of Parliament for the County of Somerset. *In* Proc.... Somerset Arch. and Nat. Hist. Soc. LXXX (1934). App. II. In progress.

Hornyold-Strickland, H. Biographical sketches of the Members of Parliament of Lancashire, 1290—1550. (Chetham Soc. New ser. Vol. 93.) Manchester. 1935.

Kingsford, C. L. Henry V. 2nd edn. London. 1923.

Lloyd, J. E. Owen Glendower. *Owen Glyn Dŵr*. Oxford. 1931.

Lodge, R. Cardinal Beaufort. Oxford. 1875.

Mirot, L. Isabelle de France, Reine d'Angleterre, Comtesse d'Angoulême, Duchesse d'Orléans (1389–1409). *In* Revue d'histoire diplomatique. XVIII–XIX. Paris. 1904–5.

Moberly, G. H. Life of William of Wykeham. 2nd edn. Winchester. 1893.

Oman, C. W. C. Warwick the Kingmaker. London. 1891.

Perry, G. G. Bishop Beckington and King Henry VI. EHR. IX (1894). 261–74.

Radford, L. B. Henry Beaufort. London. 1908.

Round, J. H. John Doreward, Speaker (1399, 1413). EHR. XXIX (1914). 717–9.

Scofield, C. L. The life and reign of Edward the Fourth. 2 vols. London. 1923.

Solloway, J. Archbishop Scrope. (York Minster Hist. Tracts. XV.) S.P.C.K. London. 1927.

Tyler, J. E. Henry of Monmouth, or memoirs of the life and character of Henry the Fifth as Prince of Wales and King of England. 2 vols. London. 1838.

Vernon Harcourt, L. W. The two Sir John Fastolfs. TRHS. 3rd ser. Vol. IV (1910). 47–62.

Vickers, K. H. Humphrey, Duke of Gloucester. London. 1907.

Waugh, W. T. Sir John Oldcastle. EHR. XX (1905). 434–56 and 637–58.

Weyman, H. T. Shropshire Members of Parliament (1325—1584) *In* Trans.... Shropshire Arch. and Nat. Hist. Soc. 4th ser. Vols. X (1925—6). 162—92 and XI (1927—8). 1—48.

Wylie, J. H. History of England under Henry the Fourth. 4 vols. London. 1884–98.

—— The reign of Henry the Fifth. 3 vols. (Vol. III completed by Waugh, W. T.) Cambridge. 1914–29.

C. Constitutional and Administrative.

Adams, G. B. Constitutional History of England. London. 1921.

Baldwin, J. F. The Chancery of the Duchy of Lancaster. *In* Bulletin...Institute of Hist. Research. IV (1926–7). 129–43.

—— The King's Council in England during the Middle Ages. Oxford. 1913.

Beard, C. A. The Office of Justice of the Peace in England. (Columbia Univ. Studies in Hist. XX.) New York. 1904.

Chrimes, S. B. 'House of Lords' and 'House of Commons' in the fifteenth century. EHR. XLIX (1934). 494–7.

—— The pretensions of the Duke of Gloucester in 1422. EHR. XLV (1930). 101–3.

Chrimes, S. B. Sir John Fortescue's Theory of Dominion. TRHS. 4th ser. Vol. xvii (1934). 117–47.

Clarke, M. V. and Galbraith, V. H. The deposition of Richard II. *In* Bulletin... John Rylands Library. xiv (1930). 125–81.

Crump, C. G. A note on the criticism of records. *Ibid.* viii (1924). 140—9.

Déprez, E. Études de Diplomatique Anglaise, 1272–1485. Le Sceau Privé, le Sceau secret, le Signet. Paris. 1908.

Evans, F. M. G. The Principal Secretary of State. Manchester. 1923.

Gray, H. L. The influence of the Commons on early legislation. (Harvard Hist. Studies. xxxiv.) Cambridge, Mass. 1932.

Holdsworth, W. S. History of English Law. *See Gen. Bibl.* v.

Jacob, E. F. Sir John Fortescue and the Law of Nature. *In* Bulletin...John Rylands Library. xviii (1934). 359–76.

Jenkinson, H. Exchequer Tallies. *In* Archaeologia lxii (1911). 367–80.

—— Medieval Tallies, public and private. *Ibid.* lxxiv (1925). 289–351.

Lapsley, G. T. The County Palatine of Durham. (Harvard Hist. Studies. viii.) New York. 1900.

—— The Parliamentary Title of Henry IV. EHR. xlix (1934). 423–49, 577–606.

Latham, L. C. Collection of the wages of the Knights of the Shire in the fourteenth and fifteenth centuries. EHR. xlviii (1933). 455–64.

Levett, A. E. Baronial Councils and their relation to Manorial Courts. In Mélanges d'hist. ...offerts à Ferdinand Lot. pp. 421–41. Paris. 1925.

McIlwain, C. H. The High Court of Parliament and its supremacy. New Haven. 1910.

McKisack, M. The parliamentary representation of King's Lynn before 1500. EHR. xlii (1927). 583–9.

—— The parliamentary representation of the English Boroughs during the Middle Ages. Oxford. 1932.

Maitland, F. W. Equity, also the forms of action at Common Law. Ed. Chaytor, A. H. and Whittaker, W. J. Cambridge. 1909.

Marsden, R. G. Early Prize Jurisdiction and Prize Law in England. EHR. xxiv (1909). 675-97.

Maxwell-Lyte, H. C. Historical notes on the use of the Great Seal of England. London. 1926.

Neale, J. E. The Commons' Privilege of Free-Speech in Parliament. *In* Tudor Studies. Ed. Seton-Watson, R. W. pp. 257–86. London. 1924.

Newhall, R. A. The war finances of Henry V and the Duke of Bedford. EHR. xxxvi (1921). 172–98.

Palgrave, F. An essay upon the original authority of the King's Council. (RC.) London. 1834.

Pike, L. O. Constitutional History of the House of Lords. London. 1894.

Plucknett, T. F. T. The Lancastrian Constitution. *In* Tudor Studies. Ed. Seton-Watson, R. W. pp. 161–81. London. 1924.

—— The place of the Council in the fifteenth century. TRHS. 4th ser. Vol. i (1918.) 157–89.

Pollard, A. F. The evolution of Parliament. 2nd edn. London. 1926.

Riess, L. Geschichte des Wahlrechts zum Englischen Parlament im Mittelalter. Leipsic. 1885.

Sillem, R. Commissions of the Peace, 1380–1485. *In* Bulletin...Institute of Hist. Research. x (1933). 81–103.

Skeel, C. A. J. The influence of the writings of Sir John Fortescue. TRHS. 3rd ser. Vol. x (1916.) 77–114.

Stubbs, W. Constitutional History of England. Vol. iii. *See also* Petit-Dutaillis, C. Studies and notes suppl. to Stubbs' Constitutional History. Vol. iii. *See Gen. Bibl.* v.

Thornley, I. D. Treason by words in the fifteenth century. EHR. xxxii (1917). 556–61.

Vernon Harcourt, L. W. His Grace the Steward and the Trial of Peers. London. 1907.

Williams, C. H. Fifteenth-Century Coram Rege Rolls. *In* Bulletin...Institute of Hist. Research. i (1924). 69–72.

Wittke, C. History of English parliamentary privilege. (Ohio State Univ. Studies, History and Polit. Science. vi.) Columbus, Ohio. 1921.

Wylie, J. H. The Council of Constance to the death of John Hus. London. 1900.

D. Economic and Social.

Abram, A. English life and manners in the Later Middle Ages. London. 1915.

—— Social life in the fifteenth century. London. 1909.

Bennett, H. S. The Pastons and their England: studies in an age of transition. Cambridge. 1922.

Carus-Wilson, E. M. The Merchant-Adventurers of Bristol in the fifteenth century. TRHS. 4th. ser. Vol. xi (1928). 61–82.

Cunningham, W. The growth of English Industry and Commerce. Vol. i. *See Gen. Bibl.* v.

Curtis, M. E. Some disputes between the City and the Cathedral authorities of Exeter. (Univ. College of the South-West of England. History of Exeter Research Group Monograph v.) Manchester. 1932.

Davenport, F. G. The decay of villeinage in East Anglia. TRHS. n.s. Vol. xiv (1900). 123–41.

Davis, E. J. and Peake, M. J. Loans from the City of London to Henry VI. *In* Bulletin...Institute of Hist. Research. iv (1927). 165–72.

Denton, W. England in the fifteenth century. London. 1888.

Engel, K. Die Organisation der deutsch-hansischen Kaufleute in England im 14 und 15 Jahrht. bis zum Utrechter Frieden von 1474. 2 pts. *In* Hansische Geschichtsblätter xix (1913). 445–517; xx (1914). 173–225.

Flenley, R. London and foreign merchants in the reign of Henry VI. EHR. xxv (1910). 644–55.

Giuseppi, M. S. Alien merchants in England in the fifteenth century. TRHS. n.s. Vol. ix (1895). 75–98.

Gras, N. S. B. The early English Customs System. (Harvard Econ. Studies. xviii.) Cambridge, Mass. 1918.

Gray, H. L. English Field Systems. (Harvard Hist. Studies. xxii.) Cambridge, Mass. 1915.

—— Incomes from land in England in 1436. EHR. xlix (1934). 607–39.

Green, A. S. (Mrs J. R.) Town life in the fifteenth century. 2 vols. London. 1894.

Gross, C. The Gild Merchant. A contribution to British municipal history. New edn. 2 vols. Oxford. 1927.

Hall, H. History of the Custom-Revenue in England. 2 vols. London. 1885. New edn. in one vol. 1892.

Haward, W. I. Economic aspects of the Wars of the Roses in East Anglia. EHR. xli (1926). 170–89.

—— Gilbert Debenham. A medieval rascal in real life. *In* History. xiii (1928–9). 300–14.

Kingsford, C. L. The beginnings of English maritime enterprise in the fifteenth century. *Ibid.* xiii (1928–9). 97–106, 193–203.

Kriehn, G. The English Rising of 1450. Strasbourg. 1892.

Lipson, E. An introduction to the Economic History of England. Vol. i. The Middle Ages. 5th edn. London. 1929.

Mace, F. A. Devonshire Ports in the fourteenth and fifteenth centuries. TRHS. 4th ser. Vol. viii (1925). 98–126.

McFarlane, K. B. Anglo-Flemish relations in 1415–16. *In* Bodleian Quarterly Record. vii (1932). 41–5.

Owen, L. V. D. England and the Low Countries, 1405–13. EHR. xxviii (1913). 13–33.

Page, T. W. The end of Villeinage in England. (Amer. Econ. Assocn. 3rd ser. Vol. i, no. 2.) New York. 1900.

Postan, M. M. Credit in Medieval Trade. *In* Econ. Hist. Review. i (1927–8). 234–61.

—— Private financial instruments in Medieval England. *In* Viert. für Sozial- und Wirtschaftsgeschichte. xxiii (1930). 26–75.

Redstone, V. The social condition of England during the Wars of the Roses. TRHS. n.s. Vol. xvi (1902). 159–200.

Rees, W. South Wales and the March, 1284–1415. A social and agrarian study. London. 1924.

Rogers, J. E. Thorold. History of agriculture and prices in England. Vols. i–iv. Oxford. 1866–82.

—— Six centuries of work and wages. 2 vols. London. 1884, 1886.

Salzman, L. F. English industries in the Middle Ages. New edn. Oxford. 1923.

—— English trade in the Middle Ages. Oxford. 1931.

Savine, A. Copyhold cases in the early Chancery proceedings. EHR. xvii (1902). 296–303.

Schanz, G. Englische Handelspolitik gegen Ende des Mittelalters, mit besonderer Berücksichtigung des Zeitalters der beiden ersten Tudors, Heinrich VII und Heinrich VIII. 2 vols. Leipsic. 1881.

Schulz, F. Die Hanse und England von Eduards III bis auf Heinrichs VIII Zeit. (Abhandlungen zur Verkehrs- und Seegeschichte. Vol. v. Hansische Geschichtsverein.) Berlin. 1911.

Steel, A. B. Receipt roll totals under Henry IV and Henry V. EHR. xlvii (1932). 204–15.

—— The present state of studies on the English Exchequer in the Middle Ages. AHR. xxxiv (1929). 485–512.

Stein, W. Die Hanse und England beim Ausgang des hundertjährigen Krieges. *In* Hansisches Geschichtsblätter. xxvi. Lübeck. 1921.

Studies in English Trade in the fifteenth century. Ed. Power, E. E. and Postan, M. M. London. 1933.

Tait, J. The Borough Community in England. EHR. xlv (1930). 529–51.

—— The Common Council of the Borough. EHR. xlvi (1931). 1–29.

Trenholme, N.M. The English Monastic Boroughs. A study in medieval history. (Univ. of Missouri Studies. ii, no. 3.) Columbia, Miss. 1927.

Unwin, G. The Gilds and Companies of London. London. 1908.

E. Ecclesiastical and Religious.

Blackie, E. M. Reginald Pecock. EHR. xxvi (1911). 448–68.

Capes, W. W. The English Church in the fourteenth and fifteenth centuries. (History of the English Church. Ed. Stephens, W. R. W. and Hunt, W. iii.) London. 1900.

Churchill, I. J. Canterbury Administration, illustrated from original records. 2 vols. (Church Hist. Soc.) S.P.C.K. London. 1933.

Coulton, G. G. A sidelight on the medieval visitation system. EHR. xlviii (1933). 89–91.

Deanesly, M. The Lollard Bible and other Medieval Biblical versions. Cambridge. 1920.

Gabel, L. C. Benefit of clergy in England in the later Middle Ages. (Smith College Studies in History. xiv. Nos 1–4.) Northampton, Mass. 1928–9.

Gairdner, J. Lollardy and the Reformation in England. Vol. i. London. 1908.

Graham, R. The English Province of the Order of Cluny in the fifteenth century. TRHS. 4th. ser. Vol. vii (1924). 98–130. Repr. *in* English Ecclesiastical Studies, pp. 62–90. London. 1929.

—— The Great Schism and the English Monasteries of the Cistercian Order. EHR. xliv (1929). 373–87.

—— The Papal Schism of 1378 and the English Province of the Order of Cluny. EHR. xxxviii (1923). 481–95. Repr. *in* English Ecclesiastical Studies. pp. 46–61. *op. cit.*

Haller, J. England und Rom unter Martin V. QFIA. viii. 1905.

Hodge, C. E. Cases from a fifteenth-century Archdeacon's Court. *In* Law Quarterly Rev. xlix (1933). 268–74.

Lapsley, G. T. The County Palatine of Durham. (Harvard Hist. Studies. viii.) New York. 1900.

Little, A. G. Introduction of the Observant Friars into England. *In* Proceedings of the British Academy. xi. London. 1924.

Maitland, F. W. Roman Canon Law in the Church of England. London. 1898.

Makower, F. The Constitutional History and Constitution of the Church of England. (Transl. from German.) London. 1895.

Ogle, A. The Canon Law in Mediaeval England. An examination of William Lyndwood's "Provinciale" in reply to the late Professor F. W. Maitland. London. 1912.

Owst, G. R. Literature and Pulpit in Medieval England. Cambridge. 1933.

—— Preaching in Medieval England: an introduction to Sermon Manuscripts of the period c. 1350-1450. Cambridge. 1926.

Pantin, W. A. The General and Provincial Chapters of the English Black Monks, 1215-1540. TRHS. 4th. ser. Vol. x (1927). 195-263.

Power, E. E. Medieval English Nunneries, c. 1275 to 1535. Cambridge. 1922.

Reid, E. J. B. Lollards at Colchester in 1414. EHR. xxix (1914). 101-4.

Snape, R. H. English monastic finances in the later Middle Ages. Cambridge. 1926.

Thompson, A. Hamilton. The Fifteenth Century. (York Minster Hist. Tracts. xvi.) S.P.C.K. London. 1927.

Valois, N. La crise religieuse du xvᵉ siècle. Le pape et le concile (1418-50). 2 vols. Paris. 1909.

Waugh, W. T. The Great Statute of Praemunire. EHR. xxxvii (1922). 173-205.

Zellfelder, A. England und das Basler Konzil. (Ebering's Hist. Studien. 113.) Berlin. 1913.

F. Learning, Literature, and the Arts.

Allen, F. J. The great Church Towers of England, chiefly of the Perpendicular Period. Cambridge. 1932.

Ayrton, M. and Silcock, A. Wrought Iron and its decorative use. London. 1929.

Bond, F. Fonts and Font Covers. London. 1908.

—— Gothic Architecture in England. London. 1912.

—— An introduction to English Church Architecture from the eleventh to the sixteenth century. 2 vols. London. 1913.

—— Screens and Galleries in English Churches. London. 1908.

—— Woodcarving in English Churches. 2 vols. London. 1910.

Borenius, T. English Primitives. In Proceedings of the British Acad. xi. London. 1925.

Borenius, T. and Tristram, E. W. English Medieval Painting. Florence and Paris. 1927.

Chambers, E. K. The Mediaeval Stage. 2 vols. Oxford. 1903.

Chambers, R. W. On the continuity of English prose from Alfred to More and his School. Repr. from Harpsfield, N. Life of Sir Thomas More. Ed. Hitchcock, E. V. and Chambers, R. W. London. 1932.

Coulton, G. G. Art and the Reformation. Oxford. 1928.

Cox, J. C. The Parish Churches of England. Ed. (with additional chapters) Ford, C. B. London. 1935.

Creighton, M. The Early Renaissance in England. Cambridge. 1895.

Crossley, F. H. English Church Monuments, A.D. 1150-1550. London. 1933.

Curzon of Kedleston, Marquis, and Tipping, H. Avray. Tattershall Castle, Lincolnshire. A historical and descriptive survey. London. 1929.

Emmerig, O. "The Bataile of Agyncourt" im Lichte geschichtlicher Quellenwerke. Nuremberg. 1906.

Gardner, A. A handbook of English Medieval Sculpture. Cambridge. 1935.

Gray, H. L. Greek Visitors to England in 1455-6. In Anniversary Essays in Medieval History by Students of C. H. Haskins. pp. 81-116. New York. 1929.

Harrison, F. The Medieval Stained Glass. (York Minster Hist. Tracts. xx.) York. 1927.

—— The Painted Glass of York Minster. York. 1928.

Hope, W. H. St John. The Funeral, Monument, and Chantry Chapel of King Henry V. In Archaeologia. lxv (1914). 129-186.

Hope, W. H. St John, and Prior, E. S. English Medieval Alabaster Work. (Society of Antiquaries.) London. 1913.

Howard, F. E. and Crossley, F. H. English Church Woodwork. A study in Crafts-manship during the Medieval Period, A.D. 1250–1550. 2nd edn. London. 1927.

Jacob, E. F. Changing views of the Renaissance. *In* History. XVI (1931–2). 214–29.

—— "Florida Verborum Venustas." Some early examples of euphuism in England. *In* Bulletin...John Rylands Library. XVII (1933). 264—90.

Knoop, D. and Jones, G. The Mediaeval Mason: an economic history of English Stone Building in the Later Middle Ages and Early Modern Times. Manchester. 1933.

Knowles, J. A. The York Glass-Painters. (York Minster Hist. Tracts. XXI.) S.P.C.K. London. 1927.

Leach, A. F. The Schools of Medieval England. London. 1915.

Mallet, C. E. History of the University of Oxford. Vol. I. London. 1924.

Maxwell-Lyte, H. C. History of the University of Oxford. London. 1886.

Millar, E. G. English illuminated manuscripts of the fourteenth and fifteenth centuries. Paris and Brussels. 1928.

Mullinger, J. B. The University of Cambridge from the earliest times to the Royal Injunctions of 1535. Cambridge. 1873.

Previté-Orton, C. W. The earlier career of Titus Livius de Frulovisiis. EHR. XXX (1915). 74–8.

Rashdall, H. The Universities of Europe in the Middle Ages. Vol. II, pt. II. Oxford. 1895.

Read, H. English Stained Glass. London and New York. 1926.

Rushforth, G. McN. Medieval Christian Imagery as illustrated by the painted windows of Great Malvern Priory Church. Oxford. 1935.

Sandys, J. E. History of Classical Scholarship. Vol. I. 3rd edn. Cambridge. 1921. Vol. II. *Ibid.* 1908.

Saunders, O. E. A history of English Art in the Middle Ages. Oxford. 1932. [Useful bibliographies.]

Savage, E. A. Old English Libraries. London. 1911.

Schirmer, W. F. Der Englische Frühhumanismus. Leipsic. 1931.

Thompson, A. Hamilton. Military Architecture in England during the Middle Ages. London. 1912.

Tout, T. F. The English Civil Service in the fourteenth century. *In* Bulletin... John Rylands Library. III (1916). 185—214. Repr. *in* Collected Papers. Vol. III. pp. 191–221. Manchester. 1934. [For Thomas Hoccleve.]

G. MILITARY AND NAVAL.

Anderson, R. C. The Grace de Dieu of 1446–86. EHR. XXXIV (1919). 584–6.

Bourel de la Roncière, C. Histoire de la marine française. Vol. II (La Guerre de Cent Ans.) pp. 211—97. Paris. 1900. [For English invasion and Battle of the Seine.]

Brooke, R. Visits to fields of battle in England of the fifteenth century. London. 1857.

Clowes, W. L. The Royal Navy: a history from the earliest times to the present. 2nd edn. Vols. I, II. London. 1911, 13.

Evans, H. T. Wales and the Wars of the Roses. Cambridge. 1915.

Newhall, R. A. The English Conquest of Normandy, 1416–1424. New Haven. 1924. [See also his War-Finances of Henry V and the Duke of Bedford. EHR. XXXVI (1921). 172–98.]

—— Henry V's policy of conciliation in Normandy, 1417–1422. *In* Anniversary Essays in Medieval History by Students of C. H. Haskins. New York. 1929.

Nicolas, N. H. History of the Battle of Agincourt. London. 1832.

—— History of the Royal Navy. 2 vols. London. 1847.

Oman, C. W. C. History of the Art of War in the Middle Ages. *See* Gen. Bibl. v.

Oppenheim, M. Administration of the Royal Navy. London. 1896.

Puiseux, L. L'émigration normande et la colonisation anglaise en Normandie au XVe siècle. Caen. 1866.

—— Siège et prise de Caen par les Anglais en 1417. Caen. 1858.

—— Siège et prise de Rouen par les Anglais (1418—1419). Caen. 1867.

Twemlow, F. R. The Battle of Bloreheath. Wolverhampton. 1912.
Wylie, J. H. Notes on the Agincourt Roll. TRHS. 3rd ser. Vol. v (1911). 105–40.

H. Miscellaneous.

Cartellieri, O. Beiträge zur Geschichte der Herzöge von Burgund. iv. König Heinrich V von England und Herzog Johann von Burgund im Jahre 1414. *In* Sitzungsberichte der Heidelberger Akad. der Wissensch. iv. Abh. ix. 1913. [Prints three important Anglo-Burgundian agreements.]
Champion, P. Vie de Charles d'Orléans. Paris. 1911.
Curtis, E. Richard, Duke of York, as Viceroy of Ireland, 1447–1460. *In* Journ. of the Roy. Soc. of Antiq. of Ireland. lxii, pt. ii (1932). 158–86.
D'Entrèves, A. P. San Tommaso d'Aquino e la Constituzione Inglese nell' Opera di Sir John Fortescue. *In* Atti della R. Accad. delle Scienze di Torino. lxii. 1927.
Fonblanque, E. B. de. Annals of the House of Percy. 2 vols. London. 1887.
Holtzmann, W. Die englische Heirat Pfalzgraf Ludwigs III. *In* Zeitschr. für die Gesch. des Oberrheins. xliii (1929). 1–38.
Johnston, C. E. Sir William Oldhall. EHR. xxv (1910). 715–22.
Kingsford, C. L. The Earl of Warwick at Calais in 1460. EHR. xxxvii (1922). 544–6.
—— The early biographies of Henry V. EHR. xxv (1910). 58–92.
—— A legend of Sigismund's visit to England. EHR. xxvi (1911). 750–1.
—— Two forfeitures in the year of Agincourt. *In* Archaeologia. lxx (1920). 71–100.
Lenz, M. König Sigismund und Heinrich V von England. Berlin. 1874.
Mirot, L. and Déprez, E. Les Ambassades anglaises pendant la Guerre de Cent Ans (1327–1450). BEC. lix–lxi. 1898–1900.
Pocquet du Haut-Jussé, B. A. François II, duc de Bretagne, et l'Angleterre (1458–1488). Paris. 1929. (Repr. from Mém....Soc. d'hist. de Bretagne. ix. 1928.)
Richardson, H. G. Illustrations of English history in the Mediaeval Registers of the Parlement of Paris. TRHS. 4th ser. Vol. x (1927). 55–85.
Scofield, C. L. The capture of Lord Rivers and Sir Anthony Woodville in 1460. EHR. xxxvii (1922). 253–5.
—— Sir John Fortescue in February 1461. EHR. xxvii (1912). 321–3.
Skeel, C. A. J. The pardon of Gilbert de Lannoy by Henry VI. *In* Cambridge Hist. Journ. i (1925). 322–3.
Thompson, G. Scott. Two centuries of family history. London. 1930.
Varenbergh, E. Histoire des relations diplomatiques entre le Comté de Flandre et l'Angleterre. Brussels. 1874.
Walser, E. Poggius Florentinus Leben und Werke. Leipsic and Berlin. 1914.
Waugh, W. T. Joan of Arc in English sources of the fifteenth century. *In* Hist. Essays in honour of James Tait, pp. 387–98. Manchester. 1933.
Wenck, K. Lucia Visconti. König Heinrich IV von England und Edmund von Kent. MIOGF. xviii. 1897.
Wylie, J. H. Dispensation by John XXIII for a son of Henry IV "propter defectum natalium," 15 Jan. 1412. EHR. xix (1904). 96–7.
—— Memorandum concerning a proposed marriage between Henry V and Catherine of France in 1414. EHR. xxix (1914). 322–3.

CHAPTER XII.

ENGLAND: THE YORKIST KINGS, 1461–1485.

I. SPECIAL BIBLIOGRAPHIES.

Gross, C. Sources and Literature of English History. *See Gen. Bibl.* i.
Oman, Sir C. History of England, 1377–1485. pp. 497–512. *See below*, iii a.
Scofield, C. L. The life and reign of Edward the Fourth. Vol. ii. pp. 485–94. *See below*, iii a.
Tucker, L. and Benham, A. R. Bibliography of fifteenth-century Literature. (Publications in Language and Literature, Univ. of Washington. 1928.)
Vickers, K. M. England in the Later Middle Ages. 3rd edn. London. 1921. pp. 509–17.

II. ORIGINAL AUTHORITIES.

A. Narrative Sources.

(i) *Guides.*

Chambers, R. W. More's "History of Richard III." *In* Modern Language Review. xxiii (1928). 405–23. Repr. in revised form *in* The English Works. *See below*, ii a (v).
Flenley, R. Six Town Chronicles. Oxford. 1911.
Kingsford, C. L. Chronicles of London. Oxford. 1905.
—— English Historical Literature in the fifteenth century. Oxford. 1913.
—— Prejudice and Promise in fifteenth-century England. Oxford. 1925.
Pollard, A. F. Sir Thomas More's "Richard III." *In* History. n.s. Vol. xvii (1933). 317–23.

(ii) *Monastic Chronicles.*

Bury St Edmunds. Memorials of St Edmund's Abbey. Ed. Arnold, T. Vol. iii. pp. 295–7. (Rolls.) 1896.
Canterbury. Chronicle of John Stone, Monk of Christ Church, 1415–1471. Ed. Searle, W. G. (Camb. Antiq. Soc., Octavo ser. xxxiv.) Cambridge. 1902.
Croyland. Historiae Croylandensis Continuatio. Ed. Fulman, W. *in* Rerum Anglicarum Scriptores. Oxford. 1684. Engl. transl. Riley, H. T. (Bohn's Antiq. Library.) London. 1854.
Ely. Brief notes. 1422–62 [Lambeth MS. 448]. Ed. Gairdner, J. *in* Three Fifteenth-Century Chronicles. pp. 148–63. (Camden Soc. n.s. Vol. xxviii.) London. 1880.
Gloucester. Gloucester Annals. Ed. Kingsford, C. L. *in* English Historical Literature. pp. 355–7. *See above*, ii a (i).
St Albans. Registrum Abbatiae Johannis Whethamstede. Ed. Riley, H. T. (Rolls.) 1872.

(iii) *Town Chronicles.*

Bristol. The Maire of Bristowe is Kalendar, by R. Ricart. Ed. Smith, L. Toulmin. (Camden Soc. n.s. Vol. v.) London. 1872.
Chester. B.M. Add. MS. 29777. Described by Flenley, R. *in* Six Town Chronicles. p. 31. Oxford. 1911.
Dublin. MS. 59 (Trin. Coll. Dublin). Described *Ibid.* p. 33, n.i.
Lynn. MS. Western 30745. Ed. by Flenley. *Ibid.* pp. 184–201.
London. [For a general discussion of the relation of manuscripts, *see* Kingsford, C. L. English Historical Literature, ch. iv (*above*, ii a (i)), Flenley, *op. cit.* Introduction, and Pollard, A. F. *in* The Times, 4 Dec. 1933.]
The Great Chronicle. Now in the Guildhall Library, London, and is being edited by A. H. Thomas. Not yet published.
B.M. MS. Cott. Vitellius A. xvi. Ed. Kingsford, C. L. *in* Chronicles of London pp. 153–263. Oxford. 1905.

Short English Chronicle [MS. Lambeth 306]. Ed. Gairdner, J. *in* Three Fifteenth-Century Chronicles. pp. 1–80.

Gregory's Chronicle [B.M. MS. Egerton 1995]. Ed. Gairdner, J. *in* Historical Collections of a Citizen of London. pp. 57–239. (Camden Soc. n.s. Vol. xvii.) London. 1876.

B.M. MS. Cott. Julius B. i. Ed. Nicolas, N. H. and Tyrrel, E. *in* A Chronicle of London, 1089–1483. London. 1827.

MS. Arundel xix. Ed. Nichols, J. G. *in* Chronicle of the Grey Friars of London. (Camden Soc. liii.) London. 1852.

MS. Balliol College 354. Ed. Dyboski, R. *in* Songs, Carols, etc. pp. 142–65. (EETS. Extra ser. ci.) London. 1907.

B.M. MS. Harl. Roll C. 8. *See* Kingsford, C. L. *in* Stow's Survey of London. Vol. i. pp. xxxiv, xcii. Oxford. 1908.

Bodleian MS. Gough. London 10. Ed. by Flenley, *op. cit.* pp. 153–66.

B.M. MS. Tanner 2. *Ibid.* pp. 168–84.

A London Chronicle of 1460. Ed. Baskerville, G. *in* EHR. xxviii (1913). 124–7.

(iv) Miscellaneous Narratives.

Account of the First Battle of St Albans, 1455. Ed. Bayley, J. *in* Archaeologia. xx (1824). 519–23.

Brief Latin Chronicle [MS. Arundel 5]. Ed. Gairdner, J. *in* Three Fifteenth-Century Chronicles. pp. 164–85.

Chronicle of the Rebellion in Lincolnshire, 1470. Ed. Nichols, J. G. *in* Camden Miscellany. Vol. i. (Camden Soc. xxxix.) London. 1847.

Chronicles of the White Rose of York. Ed. Giles, J. A. London. 1845. [Contains modernised versions of Warkworth, and other chronicles indifferently edited.]

Collections of a Yorkist Partisan, 1447–52. Ed. Kingsford, C. L. *in* English Historical Literature. pp. 358–68.

Hardyng, John. Chronicle. Ed. Ellis, H. London. 1812.

Historie of the Arrivall of Edward IV in England and the Finall Recoverye of his Kingdomes from Henry VI. Ed. Bruce, J. (Camden Soc.) London. 1838.

Narrative of the Tournament between Anthony Wydeville, Lord Scales, and the Bastard of Burgundy. Ed. Bentley, S. *in* Excerpta Historica. pp. 171–212. *See below*, ii b (ii).

Record of Bluemantle Pursuivant. 1471–2. Ed. Kingsford, C. L. *in* English Historical Literature. pp. 379–88.

Warkworth, J. A Chronicle of the first thirteen years of the Reign of King Edward the Fourth. Ed. Halliwell, J. O. (Camden Soc.) London. 1839. [For a French text, *see* Giles, J. A. La Révolte du Comte de Warwick. (Caxton Soc.) London. 1849; and Mlle Dupont, Mémoires de Commynes, *see below*, ii a (vi).]

Yorkist Notes. 1471. Ed. Kingsford, C. L. *in* English Historical Literature. pp. 374–5.

(v) Sixteenth-Century Narratives.

Fabyan, R. The New Chronicles of England and France. Ed. Ellis, H. London. 1811. (Earlier edns. 1516, etc.)

Hall, E. The Union of the Two Noble and Illustre Famelies of Lancastre and York....1548. Ed. Ellis, H. London. 1809.

Grafton, R. Continuation of Hardyng's Chronicle. Ed. Ellis, H. London. 1812.

Hearne's Fragment. A Remarkable Fragment of an Old English Chronicle. Ed. Hearne, T. Oxford. 1719. (Printed in Chronicles of the White Rose, pp. 5–30. *See above*, ii a (iv).)

More, Sir Thomas. History of King Richard III. Ed. Lumby, J. R. Cambridge. 1853. —— The English Works of Sir Thomas More. Ed. Campbell, W. E. and others. London. 1931. [Gives a facsimile of W. Rastell's edition, 1557.]

Rastell, J. The Pastime of People or the Chronicles of Divers Realms. London. 1529. Ed. Dibdin, T. F. London. 1811.

Rous, J. Historia Regum Angliae. Ed. Hearne, T. Oxford. 1716. —— The Rous Roll. Ed. Courthope, W. London. 1845.

Vergil, Polydore. Historiae Anglicae libri xxvi. Basle. 1534. Leyden. 1651.
—— Three books of Polydore Vergil's English History....from an early translation.
    Ed. Ellis, H. (Camden Soc. xxix.) London. 1844.

(vi) *Foreign.*

Basin, Thomas. Histoire des règnes de Charles VII et de Louis XI. Ed. Quicherat, J.
    4 vols. (SHF.) Paris. 1855-9. Histoire de Charles VII. Ed. Samaran, C. Vol. i.
    (Class. hist.) Paris. 1933, in progress.
Chastellain, Georges. Oeuvres. Ed. Kervyn de Lettenhove. 8 vols. (Acad. roy. de
    Belgique.) Brussels. 1863-6.
Chronique Scandaleuse. Journal de Jean de Roye connu sous le nom de Chronique
    Scandaleuse, 1460-83. Ed. Mandrot, B. de. 2 vols. (SHF.) Paris. 1894-6.
Commynes, P. de. Mémoires. Ed. Calmette, J. and Durville, G. 3 vols. (Class.
    hist.) Paris. 1924-5. *Also* ed. Mandrot, B. de. 2 vols. Paris. 1901, 3; Dupont,
    L. M. E. 3 vols. (SHF.) Paris. 1840-7.
Escouchy, Mathieu d'. Chronique. Ed. Beaucourt, G. du Fresne de. 3 vols. (SHF.)
    Paris. 1863-4.
La Marche, Olivier de. Mémoires. Ed. Beaune, H. and d'Arbaumont, J. 4 vols.
    (SHF.) Paris. 1883-8.
Molinet, Jean. Chronique (1474-1506). Ed. Buchon, J. A. 5 vols. (Coll. des chroni-
    ques nationales françaises. xliii-xlvii.) Paris. 1827-8. Also publ. separately.
Rozmital, Leo von. Ritter-, Hof-, und Pilger-Reise durch die Abendlände, 1465-7.
    Stuttgart. 1844.
Vespasiano da Bisticci. Vite di uomini illustri del secolo xv. Ed. Frati, L. 3 vols.
    Bologna. 1892-3. Engl. transl. by Waters, W. G. and E. The Vespasiano
    Memoirs. London. 1926.
Waurin, Jehan de. Recueil des croniques et anchiennes istories de la Grant
    Bretaigne. Ed. Hardy, W. and E. L. C. P. Vol. v. (Rolls.) 1891. *Also* ed.
    Dupont, L. M. E. 3 vols. (SHF.) 1858-63.

(vii) *Metrical.*

Political Poems and Songs relating to English History. Ed. Wright, T. (Rolls.) 1861.
Political Poems of the reigns of Henry VI and Edward IV. Ed. Madden, F. *in*
    Archaeologia. xxix (1842). 318-47.
Verses on the Battle of Towton. Ed. Gordon, M. G. *Ibid.* p. 343.
Kingsford, C. L. English History in Contemporary Poetry. Lancaster and York.
    London. 1913.

B. Records.

(i) *Guides.*

Giuseppi, M. S. Guide to the Manuscripts...in the P.R.O. Vol. i. *See Gen. Bibl.* i.
Hall, H. Repertory of British Archives. Pt. i, England. London. 1920.
—— Studies in English Official Historical Documents. Cambridge. 1908.
—— Formula Book of English Official Historical Documents. 2 pts. Cambridge.
    1908-9.
Holdsworth, W. S. Sources and Literature of English Law. Oxford. 1925.
Jenkinson, H. *ed.* Guide to archives and other collections of documents relating to
    Surrey. i. General introduction and scheme. Jenkinson, H.; ii. The Public
    Record Office. Giuseppi, M. S. (Surrey Record Soc. xxiii, xxiv.) London.
    1925-6.
Winfield, P. H. The Chief Sources of English Legal History. Cambridge, Mass.
    1925.

(ii) *General Collections.*

Bentley, S. Excerpta Historica or Illustrations of English History. London. 1831.
Champollion-Figeac, J. J. *ed.* Lettres de rois, reines, et autres personnages des
    cours de France et de l'Angleterre depuis Louis VII jusqu'à Henri IV. Paris.
    1839, 47.
Rymer, T. Foedera. Vols. xi, xii. *See Gen. Bibl.* iv.
Thornley, I. D. England under the Yorkists. London. 1920.

(iii) *State Papers.*

Calendar of State Papers, Milan. Vol. i. Ed. Hinds, A. B. (Cal.SP.) London. 1912.
Calendar of State Papers, Venice. Vol. i. Ed. Brown, R. (Cal.SP.) London. 1864.
Gairdner, J. Letters and Papers illustrative of the Reign of Richard III and Henry VII. (Rolls.) 1861–3.
Scott, E. and Gilliodts van Severen, L. Le Cotton Manuscrit Galba B. i. Brussels. 1896.
Vaesen, J. and Charavey, E. Lettres de Louis XI, roi de France. 11 vols. (SHF.) Paris. 1883–1909.

(iv) *Letters.*

(*a*) *Guides.*

Kingsford, C. L. Prejudice and Promise, ch. ii; *and* English Historical Literature, ch. viii [especially pp. 389–94 where there is a calendar of private letters of the fifteenth century which are contained in the Reports of the Historical Manuscripts Commission].
Bennett, H. S. The Pastons and their England. Cambridge. 1922. [*See* pp. 264–75 for a collation of the editions and original manuscripts of the Paston Letters.]

(*b*) *Collections.*

Ancient Correspondence. *See* P.R.O. Lists and Indexes. xv.
Ancient Petitions. *See* P.R.O. Lists and Indexes. i.
Anderson, R. C. Letters of the fifteenth and sixteenth centuries. (Southampton Record Soc.) 1921–2.
Anstey, H. Epistolae Academicae Oxon. (Oxford Hist. Soc. xxxv, xxxvi.) Oxford. 1898.
—— Munimenta Academica, or documents illustrative of academic life at Oxford. 2 vols. (Rolls.) 1869.
Collier, J. P. Trevelyan Papers. 3 vols. (Camden Soc. lxvii, lxxxiv, cv.) London. 1857–72.
Correspondence, Inventories, Account Rolls, and Law Proceedings of the Priory of Coldingham. Ed. Raine, J. (Surtees Soc.) London. 1841.
Ellis, Sir H. Original Letters. Ser. i–iii. London. 1825, 1827, 1846.
Gairdner, J. *ed.* The Paston Letters. 6 vols. London. 1904. Other edns.: by Gairdner. 3 vols. London. 1872–5; 3 vols. London. 1896; 4 vols. (with introdn. and supplt.) London. 1901.
—— Original Letters written during the reigns of Henry VI, Edward IV and Richard III.... Ed. Fenn, J. 5 vols. 1787–1823.
—— The Paston Letters. Ed. Ramsay, A. London. 1840–1.
Grunzweig, A. Correspondance de la filiale de Bruges des Medici. Pt. i. (Comm. roy. d'hist. de Belgique.) Brussels. 1931.
Kingsford, C. L. The Stonor Letters and Papers, 1290–1483. 2 vols. (Camden Soc. 3rd ser. Vols. xxix, xxx.) London. 1919.
—— Supplementary Stonor Letters and Papers, 1314–1482. *In* Camden Miscellany. Vol. xiii. (Camden Soc. 3rd ser. Vol. xxxiv.) London. 1924.
Malden, H. E. The Cely Papers, 1475–85. (*Ibid.* Vol. i.) London. 1900.
—— An unedited Cely Letter of 1482. TRHS. 3rd ser. Vol. x (1916). 159–65.
Sheppard, J. B. Literae Cantuarienses. (Rolls.) 1889.
—— Christ Church Letters. (Camden Soc. n.s. Vol. xix.) London. 1877.
Spingarn, J. E. Unpublished letters of an English Humanist [John Free]. *In* Journ. of Comparative Literature. i (1903). 47–65.
Stapleton, T. The Plumpton Correspondence. (Camden Soc.) London. 1839.
Tait, J. Letters of John Tiptoft, Earl of Worcester, and Archbishop Neville, to the University of Oxford. EHR. xxxv (1920). 570–4.

(v) *Chancery.*

(*a*) *Guides.*

List of Chancery Rolls. P.R.O. Lists and Indexes. xxvii. 1908.
Maxwell-Lyte, H. C. Historical notes on the use of the Great Seal of England. London. 1926.

(b) Enrolments.

Calendar of Charter Rolls. vi. 1427–1516. (Cal.SP.) London. 1927.
Calendar of Patent Rolls, 1452–1485. 4 vols. (Cal.SP.) London. 1897–1910.
[complete.]
Close Rolls [not yet calendared]. *See* Giuseppi, *op. cit.* and P.R.O. Lists and Indexes.
xxvii.
Fine Rolls [not yet calendared]. *See* Giuseppi, *op. cit.* and P.R.O. Lists and Indexes.
xxvii.

(c) Documents other than Enrolments.

For inquisitions *ad quod damnum*, inquisitions *post mortem*, and inquisitions miscel-
laneous. *See* P.R.O. Lists and Indexes.
Warrants for the Great Seal and Writs of Privy Seal. *See* Giuseppi, *op. cit.* pp. 68–9.
List of Sheriffs. P.R.O. Lists and Indexes. ix.

(vi) Documents in the Exchequer, Household, and Chamber.

[Not much material is as yet available in print. For unprinted sources *see* Giuseppi,
op. cit. and P.R.O. Lists and Indexes xvii, xxii, xxxviii.]
Issue Rolls. Issues of the Exchequer. Ed. Devon, F. London. 1837.
Customs Accounts. For description of these *see* Power and Postan. English Trade
in the fifteenth century. *See below*, iii b (vi).
The Aulnage Accounts, by Carus-Wilson, M. *In* Economic Hist. Review. ii (1929–
30). 114–23.
Wardrobe. Privy Purse Expenses of Elizabeth of York and Wardrobe Accounts of
Edward IV. Ed. Nicolas, N. H. London. 1830.
Household. Collection of Ordinances and Regulations for the government of the
royal household. (Soc. of Antiquaries.) London. 1790.

(vii) Records for the History of Parliament.

(a) Guides.

Gross. *op. cit.* pp. 635–40.
Interim Report of the Committee on House of Commons Personnel and Politics,
1264–1832. (Cmd. paper. 4130.) London. 1932.

(b) Records.

Parliament and Council Proceedings. Chancery and Exchequer. *See* Giuseppi, *op.
cit.*
Dugdale, W. A perfect copy of all summons of the nobility to the great councils
and parliaments of the realm. London. 1685.
Prynne, W. A brief register, kalendar, and survey of...parliamentary writs. 4 pts.
London. 1659–64.
Reports from the Lords' Committee appointed to search the Journals of the House,
Rolls of Parliament, and other records for all matters relating to the dignity of
a peer. 5 vols. London. 1820–9.
Rotuli Parliamentorum. [Ed. Strachey, J. and others.] Vols. v, vi. London. 1767.
Index. (RC.) London. 1832.
The Fane fragment of the 1461 Lords' Journal. Ed. by W. H. Dunham, jun. New
Haven. 1935.
Return of Members of Parliament. 3 vols. (Parl. Paper.) London. 1878.

(viii) Legal Records.

(a) Guides.

Beale, J. H. A Bibliography of Early English Law Books. (Ames Foundation.)
Harvard and London. 1926.
Bolland, W. C. Manual of Year Book Studies. Cambridge. 1925.
Harcourt, L. V. The Baga de Secretis. EHR. xxiii (1908). 508–29.
Holdsworth, W. S. History of English Law. *See Gen. Bibl.* v.
—— Sources and Literature of English Law. Oxford. 1925.
Maitland, F. W. Materials for English Legal History. *In* Collected Papers. Vol. ii.
pp. 1–60. Cambridge. 1911.

Putnam, B. H. The Ancient Indictments in the Public Record Office. EHR. xxix (1914). 479–505.

Richardson, H. G. Year Books and Plea Rolls as sources of historical information. TRHS. 4th ser. Vol. v (1922). 28–51.

Soule, C. C. Year-Book Bibliography. *In* Harvard Law Review. xiv (1901). 557–87.

Williams, C. H. Fifteenth-century Coram Rege Rolls. *In* Bulletin...Institute of Hist. Research. i (1924). 69–72.

Winfield, P. H. Chief Sources of English Legal History. Cambridge, Mass. 1925.

(*b*) *Statutes.*

Statutes of the Realm. Vol. ii. (RC.) London. 1810.

(*c*) *Records of Proceedings.*

(1) (*Conciliar Proceedings.*)

Early Chancery Proceedings. P.R.O. Lists and Indexes. xii.

Select Cases in Chancery, 1364–1471. Ed. Baildon, W. P. (Selden Soc. x.) London. 1896.

Select Cases before the King's Council. Ed. Leadam, I. S. and Baldwin, J. F. (Selden Soc. xxxv.) London. 1919.

Select Pleas of the Court of Star Chamber. Vol. i. 1477–1509. Ed. Leadam, I. S. (Selden Soc. xvi.) London. 1902.

Proceedings in the Court of Star Chamber. Ed. Bradford, G. (Somerset Record Soc.) 1911.

Yorkshire Star Chamber Proceedings. Ed. Brown, W. (Yorks. Archaeol. Soc.) 1909.

(2) (*Common Law Courts.*)

  i. King's Bench:

    (*a*) Indictments. For Ancient Indictments *see* Putnam *op. cit. above* (sect. *a*), and P.R.O. Lists and Indexes. For Baga de Secretis *see* Calendar in Deputy Keeper's Rep. iii. App. ii.

    (*b*) Plea Rolls. Coram Rege Rolls. *See* Lists and Indexes. iv.
Controlment Rolls. *See* Lists and Indexes. iv.

  ii. Justices Itinerant, Gaol Delivery, etc. *See* Lists and Indexes. iv.

  iii. Common Pleas.

    (*a*) Feet of Fines. Indexes and calendars have been printed by many local societies. *See* Index volumes of their transactions, and Gross, *op. cit.* pp. 457–63.

    (*b*) Plea Rolls. P.R.O. Lists and Indexes. iv. For specimen transcripts of extracts *see* Neilson, *op. cit. below* (sect. *d*).

(*d*) *Reports, Abridgments, etc.*

Year Book 10 Edward IV, 49 Henry VI (1470). Ed. Neilson, N. (Selden Soc. xlvii.) London. 1930.

[For other years, only the black letter editions are available. *See* Les Reports des cases.... London. 1679.]

Anthony Fitzherbert. La Graunde Abridgement. London. 1516 (and many later edns.).

Robert Brooke. La Graunde Abridgement. London. 1568 (and many later edns.).

Registrum omnium brevium tam originalium quam judicialium. 2 pts. London. 1531 (and other edns.).

Fitzherbert, A. La Novelle Natura Breuium. London. 1534 (and later edns.).

(*e*) *Treatises, legal and political.*

A Defence of the Proscription of the Yorkists in 1459. Ed. Gilson, J. P. EHR. xxvi (1911). 512–25.

Fortescue, Sir John. The Works of Sir John Fortescue collected by Thomas (Fortescue), Lord Clermont. 2 vols. London. 1869. [Contains the political tracts written in defence of the house of Lancaster, etc., as well as the major treatises. For other editions *see* Gross, *op. cit.* p. 402.]

Fortescue, Sir John. The Governance of England. Ed. Plummer, C. Oxford. 1885.
—— De Laudibus Legum Angliae. Printed in Clermont, and various other editions.
    See Gross, *op. cit.* p. 402.
Littleton, Sir Thomas. Tenures. Ed. Wambaugh, E. Washington. 1903. Consult
    pp. lxvii–lxxxiv for account of other editions.

(ix) *Ecclesiastical Records.*

(a) *General.*

Anglia Sacra. Ed. Wharton, H. London. 1691.
Calendar of entries in the Papal Registers relating to Great Britain and Ireland.
    Vols. xi, xii (1455–71). *See Gen. Bibl.* iv *under* Papal Documents.
Dugdale, W. Monasticon Anglicanum. *See Gen. Bibl.* iv.
Gibson, E. Codex Iuris Ecclesiastici Anglicani. 2 vols. Oxford. 1713.
Lyndwood, W. Provinciale seu Constitutiones Angliae. Oxford. 1679.
Neve, J. Fasti Ecclesiae Anglicanae. Ed. Hardy, T. D. Oxford. 1854.
Raine, J. Records of Northern Convocation. (Surtees Soc.) 1906.
Stubbs, W. Registrum sacrum Anglicanum. *See Gen. Bibl.* iii.
Wilkins, D. Concilia Magnae Britanniae et Hiberniae. *See Gen. Bibl.* iv *under*
    Councils, General.

(b) *Registers.*
(1) (*Guides.*)
    Fowler, R. C. Episcopal Registers of England and Wales. (Helps for Students
        of History.) S.P.C.K. London. 1918.
    Offer, C. J. The Bishop's Register. London. 1929. [Translated extracts from
        medieval episcopal registers.]

(2) (*Registers printed.*)
    Hereford. Richard Beauchamp, Reginald Boulers, and John Stanbury, 1449–74.
        Ed. Bannister, A. T. (Cant. and York Soc.) London. 1919.
    —— Thomas Myllyng, 1474–92. Ed. Bannister, A. T. *Ibid.* 1920.
    Lincoln. Lincoln Diocese Documents. Ed. Clark, A. (EETS. Orig. ser. 149.)
        London. 1914. [Contains extracts from Bishop Chedworth's register.]

(c) *Visitations.*

Collectanea Anglo-Premonstratensia. Ed. Gasquet, A. F. 3 vols. (Camden Soc.
    3rd ser. Vols. vi, x, xii.) London. 1904–6.
Extracts from Lincoln Episcopal Visitations in the fifteenth, sixteenth, and seventeenth
    centuries. *In* Archaeologia. xlviii (1885). 249–69.
Visitations and Memorials of Southwell Minster. Ed. Leach, A. F. (Camden Soc.
    n.s. Vol. xlviii.) London. 1891.

(d) *Miscellaneous.*

Lincoln Diocese Documents, 1450–1544. Ed. Clark, A. (EETS. Orig. ser. 149.)
    London. 1914.
Martin, C. T. Clerical Life in the fifteenth century as illustrated by proceedings of
    the Court of Chancery. *In* Archaeologia. lx (1906). 353–78.
Register of the Archdeacons of Richmond, 1442–77. Ed. Thompson, A. Hamilton,
    in Yorks. Archaeol. Journal. xxx.
The Medieval Records of a London City Church (St Mary at Hill). Ed. Littlehales, H.
    (EETS. Orig. ser. 125, 128.) London. 1904–5.

(e) *Wills.*

Skeel, C. A. J. Medieval Wills. *In* History. n.s. Vol. x (1926). 300–10. *See* for
    bibliographical note of chief collections.
Interim Report of the Committee on House of Commons Personnel (*see above*, sect.
    vii (*a*)). App. xi for a list of printed indexes of wills.

(x) *Town Records.*

(a) *Guides.*

Gross, C. Bibliography of British Municipal History including Gilds and Parliamentary Representation. (Harvard Hist. Studies. v.) New York. 1897.

Humphreys, A. L. Handbook to County Bibliography. London. 1917.

Thompson, A. H. Short Bibliography of Local History. (Hist. Assocn. Leaflet, 72.) London. 1928.

[*See* Interim Report of the Committee on House of Commons Personnel and Politics. App. VII. List of parliamentary cities and boroughs whose archives have been described in the reports of the Historical Manuscripts Commission; and App. VIII. Summary statement of information relative to the records of boroughs which returned burgesses to parliament before 1547.]

(b) *Select List of Town Records bearing on the Period.*

Barnstaple. Reprint of the Barnstaple Records. Ed. Chanter, J. R. and Wainwright, T. Barnstaple. 1900.

Bath. Municipal Records of Bath, 1189–1604. Ed. King, A. J. and Watts, B. H. Bath. 1885.

Beverley. Beverley Town Documents. Ed. Leach, A. F. (Selden Soc. XIV.) London. 1900.

Cambridge. Annals of Cambridge. By Cooper, C. H. Vol. I. Cambridge. 1842.

—— The Charters of the Borough of Cambridge. Ed. Maitland, F. W. and Bateson, M. Cambridge. 1901.

Colchester. Charters of the Borough of Colchester. Ed. Jeayes, I. H. Colchester. 1903.

Coventry. Coventry Leet Book; or Mayor's Register containing Records of City Court Leet. Ed. Harris, M. D. 4 pts. (EETS. Orig. ser.) London. 1907–13.

Leicester. Records of the Borough of Leicester. Ed. Bateson, M. 3 vols. Cambridge. 1899–1905.

London. Calendar of Letter Books...of the City of London. Letter Book L. Ed. Sharpe, R. R. London. 1912.

—— Aldermen of London. Ed. Beaven, A. B. 2 vols. London. 1908, 13.

Northampton, Records of the Borough of Northampton. Ed. Markham, C. A. and Cox, J. C. London. 1898.

Norwich. Records of the City of Norwich. Ed. Hudson, W. and Tingey, J. C. 2 vols. Norwich, etc. 1906–10.

Nottingham. Records of the Borough of Nottingham. Ed. Stevenson, W. H. 5 vols. Nottingham, etc. 1882–1900.

Reading. Reading Records. Ed. Guilding, J. M. 4 vols. London. 1892–6.

Rochester. Archives of Rochester. *In* Archaeologia Cantiana. VI.

Southampton. The Black Book of Southampton, 1385–1620. Ed. Wallis-Chapman, A. B. 3 vols. (Southampton Record Soc.) Southampton. 1912–15.

Winchester. Black Book of Winchester. Ed. Bird, W. H. B. Winchester. 1925.

York. Extracts from Municipal Records of York during the reign of Edward IV, Edward V, and Richard III. Ed. Davis, R. London. 1843.

(xi) *Wales, Scotland, Ireland.*

See Vol. VII, pp. 909–18.

(xii) *The Hansa.*

See Vol. VII, pp. 853–7.

III. MODERN WRITERS.

A. GENERAL NARRATIVES.

Gairdner, J. History of the life and reign of Richard III. New edn. Cambridge. 1898.

Kingsford, C. L. Prejudice and promise in fifteenth-century England. Oxford. 1925.

Oman, Sir C. History of England, 1377–1485. (Political History of England. Ed. Hunt, W. and Poole, R. L. Vol. IV.) London. 1918.
Ramsay, Sir J. H. Lancaster and York, 1399–1485. 2 vols. Oxford. 1892.
Scofield, C. L. The life and reign of Edward the Fourth. 2 vols. London. 1923.

B. STUDIES ON SPECIAL SUBJECTS.

(i) *Political and Military.*

Anderson, R. C. The Grace de Dieu of 1446–86. EHR. XXXIV (1919). 584–6.
Barnard, F. P. Edward IV's French Expedition of 1475. Oxford. 1925.
Calmette, J. and Périnelle, G. Louis XI et l'Angleterre. (Mém. et doc. publ. par la Société de l'École des chartes. XI.) Paris. 1930.
Champion, P. Louis XI. 2 vols. Paris. 1927. Engl. transl. Stephens, W. 1931.
—— Vie de Charles d'Orléans, 1394–1465. Paris. 1911.
Conway, A. E. The Maidstone sector of Buckingham's Rebellion, October 18, 1483. *In* Archaeologia Cantiana. XXXVII (1925). 97–119.
Gairdner, J. Battle of Bosworth. *In* Archaeologia. LV (1897). 159–78.
—— Did Henry VII murder the Princes? EHR. VI (1891). 444–64.
Kingsford, C. L. The beginnings of English maritime enterprise. *In* History. n.s. Vol. XIII (1928). 97–106; 193–203.
—— The Earl of Warwick at Calais. EHR. XXXVII (1922). 544–6.
Kirk, J. F. History of Charles the Bold. 3 vols. London. 1863–8.
Kriehn, G. The English Rising in 1450. Strasbourg. 1892.
Percival, C. S. Inaccuracies in the ordinary accounts of the early years of the reign of Edward IV. *In* Archaeologia. XLVII (1883). 265–94.
Pocquet du Haut-Jussé, B. A. François II, duc de Bretagne, et l'Angleterre. Paris. 1929. (Repr. from Mém. de la Soc. d'hist....de Bretagne. IX. Paris. 1928.)
Ransome, C. The Battle of Towton, 1461. EHR. IV (1889). 460–6.
Scofield, C. L. Henry Duke of Somerset and Edward IV. EHR. XXI (1906). 300–21.
—— The movements of the Earl of Warwick in the Summer of 1464. EHR. XXI (1906). 732–7.
—— Elizabeth Wydevile in the Sanctuary at Westminster. EHR. XXIV (1909). 90–1.
—— Jean Malet Seigneur de Graville and Edward IV. EHR. XXV (1910). 547–50.
—— Sir John Fortescue in February 1461. EHR. XXVII (1912). 321–3.
—— The early life of John de Vere, 13th Earl of Oxford. EHR. XXIX (1914). 228–45.
—— An Engagement of Service to Warwick the Kingmaker, 1462. EHR. XXIX (1914). 719–20.
—— Five indentures between Edward IV and Warwick the Kingmaker. EHR. XXXVI (1921). 67–70.
—— The capture of Lord Rivers and Sir Anthony Woodville, 19 January 1460. EHR. XXXVII (1922). 253–5.
Scott, J. R. Letters relating to Fauconberg's Kentish Rising, 1471. *In* Archaeologia Cantiana. II (1877). 359–64.
Webster, W. An unknown Treaty ¦between Edward IV and Louis XI. EHR. XII (1897). 521–3.

(ii) *Constitutional and Administrative.*

Adams, G. B. Constitutional History of England. London. 1921.
Baldwin, J. F. The King's Council in England during the Middle Ages. Oxford. 1913.
Beard, C. A. The office of Justice of the Peace in its Origin and Development. (Columbia Univ. Studies in Hist. XX.) New York. 1904.
Cave-Brown, J. Knights of the Shire for Kent, 1406–1500. *In* Archaeologia Cantiana. XXI (1895). 198–225.
Dicey, A. V. The Privy Council. Oxford. 1860.
Dowell, S. History of Taxation and Taxes in England. 2nd edn. 4 vols. London. 1888.

Ellis, Sir H. Enumeration and explanation of devices formerly borne as badges of cognizance by the House of York. *In* Archaeologia. xvii (1814). 226–7.

Gneist, R. Englische Verfassungsgeschichte. Berlin. 1882. Engl. transl. Ashworth, P. A. 2nd edn. 2 vols. London. 1889; one vol. edn. 1891.

Gray, H. L. The influence of the Commons on early legislation. (Harvard Hist. Studies. xxxiv.) Cambridge, Mass. 1932.

—— The First Benevolence. *In* Facts and factors in Economic History. Essays presented to E. F. Gay. pp. 90–113. Harvard. 1932.

Hall, H. History of the Custom-revenue in England. 2 vols. London. 1885. New edn. in 1 vol. 1892.

Harcourt, L. W. V. His Grace the Steward and Trial of Peers. London. 1907.

Hearnshaw, F. J. C. *ed.* The social and political ideas of some great thinkers of the Renaissance and the Reformation. London. 1925.

Holdsworth, W. S. History of English Law. *See Gen. Bibl.* v.

Lapsley, G. The County Palatine of Durham. (Harvard Hist. Studies. viii.) Cambridge, Mass. 1900.

McIlwain, C. H. The High Court of Parliament and its Supremacy. New Haven. 1910.

McKisack, M. The Parliamentary Representation of King's Lynn before 1500. EHR. xlii (1927). 583–9.

—— Representation of English Boroughs in the Middle Ages. London. 1932.

Maitland, F. W. The Constitutional History of England. Cambridge. 1908.

Maxwell-Lyte, H. C. Historical notes on the use of the Great Seal of England. London. 1926.

Milles, J. Observations on the Wardrobe Accounts for the year 1483 wherein are contained deliveries made for the coronation of King Richard III. *In* Archaeologia. i (1770). 361–83.

Percival, C. S. Remarks on an Admiralty Seal of Richard Duke of Gloucester. *In* Archaeologia. xlvi (1881). 366–70.

Pike, L. O. The Constitutional History of the House of Lords. London. 1894.

Plucknett, T. F. T. The place of the Council in the fifteenth century. TRHS. 4th ser. Vol. i (1918). 157–89.

—— The Lancastrian Constitution. *In* Tudor Studies: essays presented to A. F. Pollard. pp. 161–81. London. 1924.

Pollard, A. F. The evolution of Parliament. 2nd edn. London. 1926.

Putnam, B. H. Early treatises on the practice of the Justices of the Peace in the fifteenth and sixteenth centuries. (Oxford Studies in Social and Legal Hist. vii.) Oxford. 1924.

Reid, R. R. The King's Council in the North. London. 1921.

Scofield, C. L. A study of the Court of Star Chamber. Chicago. 1900.

—— A voluntary subsidy levied by Edward IV in the Province of Canterbury, 1462. EHR. xxiii (1908). 85–7.

Scott, J. R. Receipts and expenditure of Sir John Scott, 1463–6. *In* Archaeologia Cantiana. x (1876). 250–8.

Skeel, C. A. J. The Council in the Marches of Wales. London. 1903.

—— The influence of the writings of Sir John Fortescue. TRHS. 3rd ser. Vol. x (1916). 77–114.

—— The Council of the West. *Ibid.* 4th ser. Vol. iv. 1921.

Stubbs, W. The Constitutional History of England. Vol. iii. *See Gen. Bibl.* v.

Vinogradoff, P. Constitutional History and the Year Books. *In* Collected Papers. Vol. i. pp. 192–256. Oxford. 1928.

White, A. B. The making of the English Constitution. 2nd edn. New York. 1925.

Williams, C. H. A Norfolk Parliamentary Election, 1461. EHR. xl (1925). 79–86.

(iii) *Legal.*

Ames, J. B. Lectures on Legal History. Harvard. 1913.

Bailey, A. Some historical aspects of the English Law of Attainder and Forfeiture for High Treason. *In* Archaeologia. xlvii (1883). 409–28.

Barbour, W. T. The history of Contract in Early English Equity. (Oxford Studies in Social and Legal History. iv.) Oxford. 1914.

Bateson, M. The English and the Latin versions of a Peterborough Court Leet, 1461. EHR. xix (1904). 526–8.

—— Borough Customs. 2 vols. (Selden Soc. xviii, xxi.) London. 1904, 6.

Bolland, W. C. Manual of Year Book Studies. 1925.

—— The Year Books. Cambridge. 1921.

Foss, E. The Judges of England. Vol. iv (1377–1485). London. 1851.

Holdsworth, W. S. History of English Law. Vols. i–iii. *See Gen. Bibl.* v.

Jenks, E. A short history of English Law. London. 1913.

Kerly, D. M. An historical sketch of the Equitable Jurisdiction of the Court of Chancery. Cambridge. 1890.

Leadam, I. S. The security of Copyholders in the fifteenth and sixteenth centuries. EHR. viii (1893). 684–96.

Maitland, F. W. English Law and the Renaissance. Cambridge. 1901.

—— Equity, also the forms of action at Common Law. Cambridge. 1909.

Savine, A. Copyhold cases in the Early Chancery Proceedings. EHR. xviii (1902). 296–303.

Williams, C. H. A fifteenth-century Law Suit. *In* Law Quarterly Review. July 1924. 354–64.

—— Nicholas Statham's Will. *In* Bulletin...Institute of Hist. Research. iii (1925). 47–50.

Winfield, P. H. The History of Conspiracy and Abuse of Legal Procedure. Cambridge. 1921.

(iv) *Ecclesiastical.*

Capes, W. W. The English Church in the fourteenth and fifteenth centuries. (Hist. of the English Church. Ed. Stephens and Hunt. iii.) London. 1900.

Creighton, M. History of the Papacy. *See Gen. Bibl.* v.

Firth, C. B. The English Church in the reign of Edward IV. [Thesis accepted for D.Lit. (London), and deposited in the University Library.]

—— Benefit of Clergy in the time of Edward IV. EHR. xxxii (1917). 175–91.

Fueter, E. Religion und Kirche in England im 15 Jahrht. Tübingen. 1904.

Gabel, L. C. Benefit of Clergy in England in the later Middle Ages. (Smith College Studies in Hist. xiv.) Northampton, Mass. 1928–9.

Gairdner, J. Lollardy and the Reformation in England. 4 vols. London. 1908–13.

Gasquet, F. A. The eve of the Reformation. 3rd edn. London. 1905.

Graham, Rose. The English Province of the Order of Cluny in the fifteenth century. TRHS. 4th ser. Vol. vii (1924). 98–130.

Makower, F. The Constitutional History and Constitution of the Church of England. (Transl. from the German.) London. 1895.

Martin, C. T. Clerical life in the fifteenth century as illustrated by proceedings in the Court of Chancery. *In* Archaeologia. lix (1904). 1–24; lx (1906). 353–78.

Owst, G. R. Preaching in Medieval England. Cambridge. 1926.

—— Literature and Pulpit in Medieval England. Cambridge. 1933.

Power, E. Medieval English Nunneries. Cambridge. 1922.

Snape, R. H. English Monastic Finances in the later Middle Ages. Cambridge. 1926.

(v) *Biographical.*

Bensemann, W. Richard Nevil der Königmacher. Strasbourg. 1898.

Buck, G. Life and reign of Richard III. London. 1646.

Burrows, M. Memoir of William Grocyn. *In* Collectanea. Ser. ii. pp. 332–80. (Oxford Hist. Soc. xvi.) Oxford. 1890.

Chandler, R. The life of William Waynflete. London. 1811.

Churchill, G. B. Richard the Third up to Shakespeare. (Palaestra. x.) Berlin. 1900.

Cooper, C. H. Memoir of Margaret, Countess of Richmond and Derby. Cambridge. 1874.

Crotch, W. J. B. An Englishman of the fifteenth century [William Caxton]. *In* Economica. No. 28. London. 1930.

Gairdner, J. Life and Reign of Richard III. Cambridge. 1898.
Harris, M. D. Laurence Saunders, citizen of Coventry. EHR. IX (1894). 633–51.
Hookham, M. A. Life and times of Margaret of Anjou. 2 vols. London. 1872.
Jesse, J. H. Memoirs of Richard III. London. 1862. New edn. 2 vols. New York. 1894.
Johnston, C. E. Sir William Oldhall. EHR. xxv (1910). 715–22.
Kingsford, C. L. Robert Bale, the London chronicler. EHR. xxxi (1916). 126–8.
Kittridge, G. L. Who was Sir Thomas Malory? *In* Harvard Studies in Philol. v (1896). 85–106.
Legge, A. O. The unpopular King. [Life of Richard III]. 2 vols. London. 1885.
Markham, C. R. Richard III. London. 1906.
Martin, A. T. The identity of Sir Thomas Malory. *In* Archaeologia. LVI (1898–9). 165–82.
Oman, Sir C. Warwick the Kingmaker. London. 1899.
Ryan, G. H. and Redstone, L. J. Timperley of Hintlesham. London. 1931.
Schmidt, K. Margareta von Anjou vor und bei Shakespeare. (Palaestra. LIV.) Berlin. 1906.
Stratford, L. Edward the Fourth. London. 1910.
Walpole, H. Historic doubts on the life and reign of Richard III. London. 1768.

(vi) *Society and Economic Development.*

Abram, A. English life and manners in the Later Middle Ages. 1913.
—— Social England in the fifteenth century. London. 1909.
Adamson, J. W. The extent of literacy in England in the fifteenth and sixteenth centuries. *In* The Library. 4th ser. Vol. x. 1930.
Baldwin, F. E. Sumptuary Legislation and Personal Regulation in England. (John Hopkins Univ. Studies in Hist. and Political Science.) Baltimore. 1926.
Bennett, H. S. The Pastons and their England. Cambridge. 1922.
Brakel, S. van. Die Entwicklung und Organisation des Merchant Adventurers. *In* Viert. für Sozial- und Wirtschaftsgeschichte. v (1907). 401–32.
Carus-Wilson, E. M. The Merchant Adventurers of Bristol in the fifteenth century. TRHS. 4th ser. Vol. XI (1928). 61–82.
—— The Iceland Trade. *In* Power, E. E. and Postan, M. M. Studies in English Trade in the fifteenth century. pp. 155–82. London. 1933.
—— The Overseas Trade of Bristol. *Ibid.* pp. 183–246.
Cheney, E. P. Disappearance of English Serfdom. EHR. xv (1900). 20–37.
Cust, N. Gentlemen-Errant: being the journeys and adventures of four Noblemen in Europe during the fifteenth and sixteenth centuries. New York. 1909.
Daenell, E. Die Blütezeit der deutschen Hanse. 2 vols. Berlin. 1905–6.
Davenport, F. Decay of Villeinage in East Anglia. TRHS. n.s. Vol. XIV (1900). 123–41.
Denton, W. England in the fifteenth century. London. 1888.
Gray, H. L. English Foreign Trade from 1446–1482. *In* Power and Postan, *op. cit.* pp. 1–38.
Green, A. S. Town Life in the fifteenth century. London. 1894.
Haward, W. I. Gilbert Debenham. *In* History. n.s. Vol. XIII (1929). 300–14.
—— Economic aspects of the Wars of the Roses in East Anglia. EHR. XLI (1926). 170–89.
Huizinga, J. The Waning of the Middle Ages. London. 1924.
Kingsford, C. L. A London Merchant's house and its owners, 1360–1614. *In* Archaeologia. LXXIV (1925). 137–58.
—— On some London houses of the early Tudor period. *Ibid.* LXXI (1921). 17–54.
Knoop, D. and Jones, G. P. Masons and apprenticeship in Mediaeval England. *In* Economic Hist. Review. III (1931–2). 346–66.
Kramer, S. The English Craft Gilds. New York. 1927.
Latimer, J. History of the Society of Merchant Adventurers of the City of Bristol. Bristol. 1903.
Lingelbach, W. E. The Merchant Adventurers of England. Philadelphia. 1902.
McClenaghan, B. The Springs of Lavenham. Ipswich. 1924.

Mace, F. A. Devonshire ports in the fourteenth and fifteenth centuries. TRHS. 4th ser. Vol. VIII (1925). 98–126.

Michel, F. Histoire du commerce et de la navigation à Bordeaux. 2 vols. Bordeaux. 1867, 70.

Oliphant, T. L. K. Was the old English Aristocracy destroyed by the Wars of the Roses? TRHS. I (1869). 437–43.

Peake, M. London and the Wars of the Roses. *In* Bulletin...Institute of Hist. Research. IV (1926–7). 45–7. [Summary of thesis.]

Postan, M. M. Credit in Medieval Trade. *In* Economic Hist. Review. I (1927–8). 234–61.

—— The Financing of Trade in the later Middle Ages. *In* Bulletin...Institute of Hist. Research. V (1927–8). 176–8. [Summary of thesis.]

—— Private financial instruments in Medieval England. *In* Viert. für Sozial- und Wirtschaftsgeschichte. XXIII (1930). 26–75.

—— The economic and political relations of England and the Hanse, 1400–1475. *In* Power and Postan *below.* pp. 91–154.

Power, E. E. and Postan, M. M. *edd.* Studies in English Trade in the fifteenth century. London. 1933.

Power, E. The English Wool Trade in the Reign of Edward IV. *In* Cambridge Hist. Journ. II (1926). 17–35.

—— The Wool Trade in the fifteenth century. *In* Power and Postan, *op. cit.* pp. 39–90.

Pryce, G. Memorials of the Canynges Family and their times. Bristol. 1854.

Redstone, V. B. Social conditions of England during the Wars of the Roses. TRHS. n.s. Vol. XVI (1902). 159–200.

Rösler, M. Leben und Lernen in England im 15 und 16 Jahrht. *In* Englische Studien. Ed. Hoops, J. 61 (1926). 320–85; 62 (1928). 328–82.

Ryan, G. H. and Redstone, L. J. Timperley of Hintlesham. London. 1931.

Salter, F. R. The Hanse, Cologne, and the Crisis of 1468. *In* Economic Hist. Review. III (1931–2). 93–101.

Schanz, G. Englische Handelspolitik gegen Ende des Mittelalters. Leipsic. 1881.

Shillington, V. M. and Chapman, A. B. W. The commercial relations of England and Portugal. London. 1907.

Skeel, C. A. J. The Cattle Trade between Wales and England from the fifteenth to the nineteenth centuries. TRHS. 4th ser. Vol. IX (1926). 135–58.

Thompson, G. Scott. Two centuries of Family History. London. 1930.

Thrupp, S. The Grocers of London. A study of distributive trade. *In* Power and Postan, *op. cit.* pp. 247–92.

Unwin, G. Industrial organisation in the sixteenth and seventeenth centuries. Oxford. 1904.

Winston, J. E. English towns in the Wars of the Roses. Princeton. 1921.

(vii) *Cultural.*

(a) *Art.*

See below, Bibl. to ch. XXIV.

(b) *Education.*

Ady, C. M. Italian influences on English history during the period of the Renaissance. *In* History. IX (1925). 288–301.

Allen, P. S. Bishop Shirwood of Durham and his Library. EHR. XXV (1910). 445–56.

Chambers, E. K. The Medieval Stage. 2 vols. Oxford. 1903.

Creighton, M. The early Renaissance in England. Cambridge. 1895.

Deanesly, M. Vernacular books in England in the fourteenth and fifteenth centuries. *In* Modern Language Review. XV (1920). 349–58.

Einstein, L. D. The Italian Renaissance in England. New York. 1907.

Goetz, W. Mittelalter und Renaissance. HZ. XCVIII (1906–7). 30–54.

Gray, H. L. Greek visitors to England in 1455–6. *In* Anniversary essays in Medieval History by students of C. H. Haskins. pp. 81–116. New York. 1929.

Jacob, E. F. Changing views of the Renaissance. *In* History. xvi (1931). 214–29.
—— The Fifteenth Century. Some recent interpretations. *In* Bulletin...John Rylands Library. xiv. 1930.
Jenkinson, H. The teaching and practice of Handwriting in England. *In* History. xi (1926). 130–8 ; 211–18.
Lathrop, H. B. The Translations of John Tiptoft. *In* Modern Language Notes. Baltimore. 1926. pp. 496–501.
Leach, A. F. The Schools of Medieval England. London. 1915.
—— St Paul's School before Colet. *In* Archaeologia. lx (1910). 191–238.
Leland, J. Commentarii de Scriptoribus Britannicis. Oxford. 1709.
Mallet, C. E. History of the University of Oxford. Vol. i. London. 1924.
Maxwell-Lyte, H. C. History of Eton College. London. 1889.
—— History of the University of Oxford. London. 1885.
Moore, S. Patrons of Letters in Norfolk and Suffolk, c.1450. *In* Publns. Mod. Lang. Assocn. xxvii (1912). 188–207 ; xxviii (1913). 79–105.
Mullinger, J. B. The University of Cambridge...to...1535. Cambridge. 1873.
Parry, A. W. Education in England in the Middle Ages. London. 1920.
Rashdall, H. The Universities of Europe in the Middle Ages. *See Gen. Bibl.* v.
Sandys, J. E. History of Classical Scholarship. Vol. i. 3rd edn. Cambridge. 1921. Vol. ii. *Ibid.* 1908.
Schirmer, W. Der englische Frühhumanismus. Leipsic. 1931.
Voigt, G. Die Wiederbelebung des classischen Alterthums. 3rd edn. Berlin. 1893

(c) Books and Printing.

Aurner, N. S. Caxton: Mirrour of fifteenth-century letters. London. 1926.
Blades, R. H. Who was Caxton? *In* The Library. n.s. Vol. iv (1903). 113–43.
Blades, W. Life and typography of William Caxton. London. 1861–3.
—— Catalogue of Books printed by (or ascribed to the press of) William Caxton.... London. 1865.
Clark, J. W. Libraries in the Medieval and Renaissance period. Cambridge. 1894.
Crotch, W. J. B. Caxton Documents. *In* The Library. 4th ser. Vol. viii. 1928.
Duff, E. G. William Caxton. London. 1905.
—— The Printers, Stationers, and Bookbinders of London and Westminster in the fifteenth century. Aberdeen. 1899.
—— Early Printed Books. London. 1893.
—— Fifteenth-century English Books. (Oxford Bibliographical Soc.) 1917.
James, M. R. Another book written by the scribe of the Leicester Codex. *In* Journ. Theol. Studies. xii (1911). 465.
—— Descriptive catalogue of MSS. in the Library of Corpus Christi College, Cambridge. Cambridge. 1912.
—— Greek MSS. in England before the Renaissance. *In* The Library. n.s. Vol. vii. 1927.
Lathrop, H. B. The first English Printers and their Patrons. *Ibid.* 4th ser. Vol. iii. 1923.
Owst, G. R. Some books and book owners of fifteenth-century St Albans. *In* Trans. St Albans and Herts. Archaeol. Soc. 1928. pp. 176–95.
Plomer, H. R. The importation of Low Country and French Books into England 1480 and 1502–3. *Ibid.* Vol. ix. 1929.
—— The importation of Books into England in the fifteenth and sixteenth centuries. *Ibid.* Vol. iv. 1924.

CHAPTER XIII.

IRELAND, 1315—c. 1485.

See also the Bibliography to Vol. vii, ch. xviii (Ireland to 1315), to which the following is merely a supplement of additional works for this period.

I. ORIGINAL AUTHORITIES.

A. CALENDARS OF RECORDS AND COLLECTIONS OF DEEDS AND DOCUMENTS.

Irish Exchequer Rolls, Edward II to Richard III. MSS. in P.R.O., London. [Important for detailed history of the period.]
MS. Brit. Mus. Titus B. xi. Extracts *in* Gilbert, J. T., History of the Viceroys of Ireland. Dublin. 1865.
Statute Rolls of the Parliament of Ireland. Henry VI and 1–12 Edward IV. Ed. Berry, H. F. 2 vols. Dublin. 1910, 14.
Original documents containing the submissions of the Irish to Richard II in P.R.O., London. Printed in Curtis, E. Richard II in Ireland. *See below*, ii.
Calendar of the Carew MSS. (Miscellaneous). Ed. Brewer, J. S. and Bullen, W. (Rolls.) 1871. [Contains many extracts from documents not now to be found elsewhere.]
Calendar of Documents relating to Scotland. Ed. Bain, J. Vol. iii (1307–57). (Cal. SP.) Edinburgh. 1887.
Calendar of the Liber Ruber of Ossory (original compiled for the most part c. 1360). Ed. Lawlor, H. J. *in* Proc. Roy. Irish Acad. xxvii (c), pp. 159–208. Dublin. 1909.
Calendar of Ormond deeds, 1172–1350. Ed. Curtis, E. (Irish MSS. Commission.) Dublin. 1932.
Calendars of the Registers of Archbishops Sweteman (1362–80) and Fleming (1404–16). Ed. Lawlor, H. J. *in* Proc. Roy. Irish Acad. xxix, xxx. Dublin. The original Registers of these and other archbishops of Armagh from 1362–1550 (with short gaps) are in the Public Library, Armagh. Transcripts in Trin. Coll. Dublin.
Issues of the Exchequer (Hen. III to Hen. VI). Ed. Devon, F. (RC.) London. 1837.
Muniments of Edmund de Mortimer, third Earl of March, concerning his Liberty of Trim. Ed. Wood, H. *in* Proc. Roy. Irish Acad. xL (c), pp. 312–55. Dublin. 1932.
Plea Rolls relating to Bruce and De Lacy: transcribed by Gilbert, J. T., *in* Chartularies of St Mary's Abbey, Dublin. Vol. ii, App. 2. (Rolls.) 1884.
Proceedings and Ordinances of the Privy Council (1386–1542). Ed. Nicolas, N. H. 7 vols. (RC.) London. 1834–7.
Red Book of Ormond. Ed. White, N. B. (Irish MSS. Commission.) Dublin. 1932.
Roll of the Proceedings of the King's Council in Ireland..., 1392–3. Ed. Graves, J. (Rolls.) 1877.
Rotuli selecti ad res Anglicas et Hibernicas spectantes. Ed. Hunter, J. (RC.) London. 1834.

B. ANNALS AND NARRATIVE SOURCES.

Annales Hiberniae Fratris Johannis Clyn (contemporary from 1315 to 1349). Ed. Butler, R. (Irish Archaeol. Soc.) Dublin. 1849.
Annales Breves Hiberniae auctore Thaddaeo Dowling (to 1600). *Ibid.*
Annals of Ireland from 1443 to 1468, translated from the Irish by Dudley Firbisse (Dubhaltach MacFirbisigh) in 1666. Ed. O'Donovan, J. (Irish Archaeol. Soc. Miscellany, i, pp. 198–302.) Dublin. 1846.
The Bruce by John Barbour. Ed. Mackenzie, W. M. London. 1909. The text based mainly on Skeat's recension. EETS. 1870–89.

Cath Fhochairte Brighite. Ed. and transl. Morris, H. *in* Louth Archaeol. Journal. Vol. I, p. 87. [Preserves the Irish tradition of Edward Bruce's invasion.]

Chronicque de la traïson et mort de Richart deux. Ed. Williams, B. (English Hist. Soc.) London. 1846.

Créton, Jean. Histoire du roy d'Angleterre Richard, traictant particulièrement la rebellion de ses subiectz. Ed. with Engl. transl. Webb, J. *in* Archaeologia. xx. London. 1824.

Froissart, Jean. Chroniques. Ed. Kervyn de Lettenhove. 25 vols. in 26. Brussels. 1867-77. Engl. transl. Bourchier, J., Lord Berners. Chronicles of England, France, etc. Ed. Ker, W. P. 6 vols. (Tudor Transl. Library.) London. 1901-3. [Bks III and IV, ch. 198. Berners, Vol. VI, p. 147, gives Christede's account to Froissart of Richard II's first expedition to Ireland, 1394-5.]

Henry Marlebourgh's Chronicle of Ireland. MS. E . 3 . 20. Trin. Coll. Dublin. The part from 1285 to 1421 printed in Ware, J. Ancient Irish Histories. Vol. II. Dublin. 1809.

II. MODERN WORKS.

Armstrong, O. Edward Bruce's Invasion of Ireland. London. 1923.

Bryan, D. Gerald FitzGerald, the great Earl of Kildare (1456-1513). Dublin. 1933.

Clarke, M. V. The Irish Modus Tenendi Parliamentum. EHR. XLVIII (1933).

—— William of Windsor in Ireland, 1369-76. *In* Proc. Roy. Irish Acad. XLI (c), pp. 55-130. Dublin. 1932.

Conway, A. Henry VII's relations with Scotland and Ireland, 1485-98. With a chapter on the Acts of the Poynings Parliament 1494-5, by E. Curtis. Cambridge. 1932.

Curtis, E. Richard II in Ireland, 1394-5. Oxford. 1927. [Contains texts, translations, and annotations concerning the submissions of the Irish chiefs.]

—— Unpublished letters from Richard II in Ireland. *In* Proc. Roy. Irish Acad. XXXVII (c), pp. 276-303. Dublin. 1927.

—— Richard, Duke of York, as Viceroy of Ireland, 1447-60. *In* Journ. of the Roy. Soc. of Antiq. of Ireland, LXII, pt. II (1932), pp. 158-86.

Philips, W. Alison, *ed.* History of the Church of Ireland. Vol. I. London. 1933.

Quin, D. B. The Irish parliamentary subsidy in the fifteenth and sixteenth centuries. *In* Proc. Roy. Irish Acad. XLII (c), pp. 219-46. Dublin. 1935.

Richardson, H. G. and Sayles, G. O. The Irish Parliaments of Edward I. *In* Proc. Roy. Irish Acad. XXXVIII (c), pp. 128-47. Dublin. 1929.

Wood, H. The titles of the Chief Governors of Ireland. *In* Bulletin...Institute of Hist. Research. XIII (1935-6). 1—8.

CHAPTER XIV.

SCOTLAND, 1328-1488.

See the Bibliography to Vol. VII, ch. XIX, pp. 915-18.

ADDITIONS TO ORIGINAL AUTHORITIES.

Calendar of Scottish supplications to Rome, 1418-22. *See Gen. Bibl.* IV *under* Papal Documents.

Sanctiandree, Copiale prioratus. The letter-book of James Haldenstone, prior of St Andrews (1418-43.) Ed. Baxter, J. H. (St Andrews Univ. publns. XXXI.) London. 1930.

ADDITIONS TO MODERN WORKS.

Cameron, A. I. The Apostolic Camera and Scottish benefices, 1418-88. (St Andrews Univ. publns. XXXV.) London. 1934.

Hannay, R. K. The College of Justice: essays on the institution and development of the Court of Session. Edinburgh. 1933.

CHAPTER XV.

SPAIN, 1412–1516.

[For general histories of Spain, *see Gen. Bibl.* v. Some of the books and documents listed in the Bibliography of Vol. vi, ch. xx are also useful for this period.]

BIBLIOGRAPHIES.

The bibliography of the whole of Spanish history is to be found in Sánchez Alonso, B. Fuentes de la historia española e hispanoamericana. 2nd edn. 2 vols. Madrid. 1927.

Other bibliographies are listed in Vol. vi, ch. xii, pp. 912, 916, 917, 920.

For Neapolitan affairs, *see supra*, the Bibliography to ch. v, pp. 857-9.

For a select bibliography of works published before 1902 on the discovery of America, see the Bibliography to Vol. i, ch. i of the Cambridge Modern History. 1902. For works published 1900–1930, *see* the Bibliographie d'histoire coloniale. Paris. 1932, published by the Société de l'Histoire des Colonies Françaises. A very full bibliography up to 1926 may be found in Sánchez Alonso, B. (*see supra*), Vol. i, ch. v, *esp.* pp. 241-62.

I. KINGDOM OF CASTILE (1406–1474).

A. ORIGINAL DOCUMENTS.

(i) *Published*.

Altamira, R. Textos primitivos de legislación colonial española. Madrid. 1934.
Anonymous. Coplas de Ay panadera (1445). Ed. Gallardo, B. J. *in* Ensayo de una Bibl. española. i. Madrid. 1863.
Coplas del Provinzial. *In* Revue hispanique. iv.
Coplas de Mingo Revulgo. Ed. Gallardo, B. J. *op. cit.* i. *Also* ed. Menéndez y Pelayo, M. *in* Antología. iii.
Documentos relativos a Enrique IV de Castilla, siendo todavía príncipe de Asturias. *In* Col. de doc. inéd. para la hist. de España. xl.
Documentos relativos al reinado de Enrique IV. *In* Mem. Hist. Españ. (RAH.) v.
[Fernández de Córdoba, Gonzalo, el Gran Capitán.] Colección de cartas originales y autógrafas...que se guardan en la Biblioteca Nacional. RABM. 3rd ser. Vols. v and vii. 1901-2.
Foulché-Delbosc, R. Cancionero castellano del siglo xv. *In* Nueva Bibl. de autores españ. Ed. Menéndez y Pelayo, M. xix and xxii.
Guerra entre Castilla, Aragón y Navarra: Compromiso para terminarla (1431). *In* Col. de doc. inéd. del Arch. Gen....Aragón. xxxvii comp.
Honras por Enrique IV y proclamación de Isabel la Católica en la ciudad de Avila. Ed. Foronda y Aguilera, M. de. BRAH. lxiii. 1913.
[John II, King of Castile.] Carta...acerca de unos tesoros...en Soria. RABM. 1st ser. Vol. iv. 1874.
—— Carta...negando la obediencia al antipapa Luna (1416). Ed. Cagigas, I. de las. *In* Rev. del Centro de Estudios hist. de Granada. iv. 1914.
López de Ayala, Pedro. Rimado de Palacio. *In* Bibl. de autores españ. Ed. Rivadeneyra, M. xxxv. *Also* ed. Kuersteiner, A. F. (Bibliotheca hispanica. xxi, xxii.) New York. 1920.
Luna, Alvaro de. Lamentación. Spanish transl. from the Latin by Villafranca, J. de *in* Bibliotecario y el Trovador Español. Colec. de doc. Madrid. 1841.
Luna, Alvaro de, Testamento original de. Ed. Roca, P. RABM. 3rd ser. Vol. v. 1901.
Memorial que dieron los Grandes al Rey (John II?) para que no hiciese mercedes de las fincas de su patrimonio. *In* Col. de doc. inéd. para la hist. de España. xiv.

Noticias sobre el testamento de Enrique IV. Ed. Ferrer, P. RABM. 1st ser. Vol. IV. 1874.

Paz, J. Versión oficial de la batalla de Olmedo (1445). *In* Homenaje a M. Pidal. Vol. I. Madrid. 1925.

Peticiones originales hechas al señor Rey D. Enrique IV por diferentes Arzobispos, etc. *In* Col. de doc. inéd. para la hist. de España. XIV.

Testamento de la Reina D. Juana, mujer de Enrique IV...abril de 1475. *Ibid.* XIII.

Votos de dos consejeros de Enrique IV sobre la sucesión a esta corona de la Infanta D. Isabel. Ed. Fresca, F. G. RABM. 1st ser. Vol. III. 1873.

(ii) *Manuscripts.*

Concordia celebrada entre Enrique IV y el Reyno sobre varios puntos de Govierno y Legislación civil...1465. (18th cent. copy.) Nat. Lib., Madrid. 9546.

Documentos relativos a D. Alvaro de Luna. Nat. Lib., Madrid. 19701, 18696–7, 20056, 20260, 19710, 6185.

Documentos, Varios, pertenecientes al reinado de Juan II de Castilla. (18th cent. copy.) Nat. Lib., Madrid. 13105–8.

Documentos varios del reinado de Enrique IV. Nat. Lib., Madrid. 13106, 13124, 13110, 18736, 3668, 19703.

Documentos del Infante D. Alfonso, hermano de Enrique IV. Nat. Lib., Madrid. 13110, 13124, 13109.

Documentos sobre Juana la Beltraneja. Nat. Lib., Madrid. 2420, 6150.

Documentos [varios sobre las diferencias y pacificación...de Castilla en tiempo de Enrique IV y otros asuntos de su reinado]. (18th cent. copy.) Nat. Lib., Madrid. 13109–13110.

John II. Cartas y otros escritos. Nat. Lib., Madrid. 13104, 13119, 13107.

—— Cartas inéditas a D. Juana Pimentel, Muger de D. Albaro de Luna y a su Hijo D. Juan.... (18th cent.) Bibl. Municipal, Madrid. 4.

Juan II. Testamento de...1454, en Valladolid. (18th cent.) Nat. Lib., Madrid. 5578[54].

Luna, Alvaro de. Cartas y otros escritos. Nat. Lib., Madrid. 13109, 13105, 13107, 638, 13042.

Noticias sobre el reinado de Enrique IV. (18th cent.) Nat. Lib., Madrid. 18673[9].

B. Original Narrative Authorities.

(i) *Published.*

Bravo de Rojas, Lope. Notas manuscritas, por la mayor parte genealógicas, que puso a... la Crónica de D. Juan II de la edición de Logroño, año 1517... en 1555. Ed. D. R. F. *in* Col. de doc. inéd. para la hist. de España. XX.

[Crónica.] Comiença la Coronica de D. Alvaro de Luna.... Milan, 1546. *Also* ed. Flores, J. M. *in* Col. de Crónicas...de Castilla. Madrid. 1783.

[Enriquez del Castillo, Diego.] Comienza la historia del qvarto Rey D. Enrrique. *n.p., n.d.* Ed. Flores, J. M. de *in* Col. de crónicas...de Castilla. Madrid. 1787. *Also in* Bibl. de autores españ. LXX.

Escavias, P. de. Repertorio de Principes de España. [The section on Henry IV publ. by Sitges, J. B. *in* Enrique IV, etc.] *See below,* I c.

Fernández de Velasco, Pedro. Seguro de Tordesillas (1440). Sacóle a luz...Pedro Mantuano. Con la uida del Conde, etc. Milan. 1611. Madrid. 1784.

Luna, Alvaro de. El libro de las claras y virtuosas mugeres (1446). Ed. Menéndez y Pelayo, M. (Soc. de Bibliófilos Españ.) 1891.

[Martínez de la Puente, J.] Epítome de la Crónica del rey D. Jvan el segundo de Castilla. Madrid. 1678.

Memorias de D. Enrique IV de Castilla.... 2 vols. (RAH.) Madrid. 1913.

[Olid, Juan de?] Crónica del condestable Miguel Lucar Iranzo (1458–71). *In* Mem. Hist. Españ. (RAH.) VIII. 1855.

Palencia, Alfonso de. Gesta hispaniensia. [Madrid. 1834.]

—— (Incomplete transln. of the preceding by Paz y Melia, A.) 5 vols. Madrid. 1904–12.

Palencia, Alfonso de. Dos tratados. Ed. Fabié, A. M. (Libros de antaño. v.) Madrid. 1872.
[Paz y Melia, A. El cronista...Palencia. Su vida y...sus obras; sus Décadas y las Crónicas contempóraneas; ilustraciones de las Décadas. (Hispanic Soc. of America.) Madrid. 1914.]
Pérez de Guzman, Fernán. Crónica del Rey D. Juan II (1406–54). *In* Bibl. de autores españ. LXVIII. 1877. First publ. at Logroño 1517. Has also been attributed to Alvar Garcia de Santa Maria, under whose name it was publ. in Col. de doc. inéd. para la hist. de España. XCIX.
—— Mar de historias. Ed. Foulché-Delbosc, R. *in* Revue hisp. XXVIII. 1913.
—— Generaciones, semblanzas, y obras de...D. Enrique III y D. Juan II. Ed. Foulché-Delbosc, R. Maçon. 1907. Also repr. in the two works above.
Pulgar, Hernando del. Los Claros Varones de Espanna. Toledo. 1486. Ed. Domingues Bordona, J. (Clásicos castellanos, XLIX.) Madrid. 1923.
Quiriales, Alonso de. El Tumbo de Valdeiglesias y D. Alvaro de Luna. [2–3 June 1453.] Ed. Foronda, M. de. BRAH. XLI. 1902.
Rodriguez de Cuenca, Juan. Sumario de los Reyes de España. Madrid. 1781.
Santillana, Marqués de. Doctrinal de privados (1454). Ed. Ríos, J. Amador de los. 1852.
Valera, Diego de. Corónica de España (abreviada). Seville. 1482; and other edns.
—— Epistolas...(1441–86). Madrid. 1878.
—— Memorial de diversas hazañas. *In* Bibl. de autores españ. LXX. [Not a good edn.]

(ii) *Manuscripts.*

Cruz, Fray Jerónimo de la. Historia del...Rey D. Henrique Quarto.... (18th cent.) Nat. Lib., Madrid. 1350, 1776, 8220.
[Galindez de Carvajal, Lorenzo?] Crónica de Enrique IV. (17th cent.) Nat. Lib., Madrid. 13261.

C. Modern Works.

Amador de los Ríos, J. Memoria histórico-crítica de las treguas celebradas en 1349 entre los reyes de Castilla y de Granada. *In* Mem. RAH. IX.
—— El condestable D. Alvaro de Luna y sus doctrinas políticas y morales. *In* Rev. de España. XIX. 1871.
Azevedo, P. A. d'. O testamento de Excellente Senhora. *In* Archivo hist. portuguez. I. 1903.
[Caumont de la Force, C. R.] Histoire secrète de Henry IV Roy de Castille. Paris. 1695.
Cazabán, A. Quién fué y cómo fué D. Beltrán de la Cueva. *In* D. Lope de Sosa [review]. II. Jaén. 1914.
Cirot, G. Les Décades d'Alfonso de Palencia, la Chronique castillane de Henri IV attribuée à Palencia et le "Memorial de diversas hazañas" de Diego de Valera. *In* Bulletin hispanique. XI. 1909.
Corral, L. de. Don Alvaro de Luna. Valladolid. 1915.
Daumet, G. Étude sur l'alliance de la France et de la Castille au XIVe et au XVe siècle. (BHE. 118.) Paris. 1898.
Ebert, A. Historia Johannis II, Castellae regis, usque ad pugnam Olmedum commissam enarrata. Göttingen. 1844.
Espejo, C. El Contador mayor de Enrique IV, Juan Pérez de Vivero. *In* Bol. de la Soc. Cast. de Excursiones. III. 1907–8.
—— El leonés Fernand Alfón de Robres, contador mayor de Juan II. *Ibid.*
Fernández Duro, C. D. Francisco Fernández de la Cueva, Duque de Alburquerque. Madrid. 1884.
Floranes, R. de. Vida literaria del Canciller Mayor de Castilla D. Pedro López de Ayala. *In* Col. de doc. inéd. para la hist. de España. XIX, XX.
Foronda, M. de. El tumbo de Valdeiglesias y D. Alvaro de Luna. BRAH. XLI. 1902.

Foulché-Delbosc, R. Fernan Pérez de Guzman. Étude bibliographique. *In* Rev. hispanique. xvi. 1907.

Gil y Sanz, A. D. Alvaro de Luna y su obra. *In* Rev. de España. xcii. 1883.

Guzmán el Bueno y Padilla, J. Sitio de Gibraltar por el segundo Conde de Niebla [in 1433]. *In* La España moderna. xxxiv. 1891.

Histoire secrette du Connétable de Lune. Paris. 1720.

Jaén y Morente, A. Segovia y Enrique IV. Segovia. 1916.

Laurencin, M. de. Mosen Diego de Valera y el Arbol de Batallas. BRAH. lxxvi. 1920.

López Guijarro, S. Los españoles del reinado de Enrique IV. *In* Rev. de España. iv. 1868.

Maldonado, A. de. Hechos de D. Alonso de Monroy, Clavero y Maestro de la Orden de Alcántara. *In* Mem. Hist. Españ. (RAH.) vi.

Marañon, G. Ensayo biológico sobre Enrique IV de Castilla y su época. Madrid. 1930.

Martínez, M. Una crónica inédita de D. Juan II de Castilla. *In* La Ciudad de Dios (El Escorial). lxxxvi. 1911.

Medina, F. Vida del Cardenal D. Pedro Fernandez de Mendoza. *In* Mem. Hist. Españ. (RAH.) vi.

Menéndez y Pelayo, M. La sátira política en tiempo de Enrique IV. *In* La España moderna. lxxx. 1895. *See also* Antología de poetas liricos castellanos, introdn. to vol. iii.

Oliver, B. Las Hermandades de Castilla en tiempos de Enrique IV. BRAH. xiv. 1889. [A critique of Haebler, K. Die Kastilischen Hermandades zur Zeit Heinrich's IV. HZ. lvi. 1886.]

Palanco Romero, J. Estudios del reinado de Enrique IV. 1914.

—— La monarquía castellana en tiempo de Enrique IV. *In* Rev. del Centro de Estudios hist. de Granada. ii. 1912.

—— La nobleza en tiempo de Enrique IV. *Ibid.* iii. 1913.

Paz y Melia, A. La Biblia puesta en romance por Rabi Mosé Arragel de Guadalajara, 1423-33. *In* Homenaje a Menéndez y Pelayo. Vol. ii. Madrid. 1925.

Puymaigre, Comte de. La Cour littéraire de D. Juan II. Paris. 1873.

Puyol, J. Los cronistas de Enrique IV. BRAH. lxxviii, lxxix. 1921.

Rizzo y Ramírez, J. Juicio crítico y significación política de D. Alvaro de Luna. Madrid. 1865.

Rodríguez Villa, A. Bosquejo biográfico de D. Beltrán de la Cueva. Madrid. 1881.

Sáez, P. Liciniano. Demostración histórica del verdadero valor de todas las monedas que corrían en Castilla durante el reinado del S. d. Enrique IV. *In* Mem. RAH. 1805.

[Sitges, J. B.] Enrique IV y la excelente señora llamada vulgarmente la Beltraneja, 1425-1530. Madrid. 1912.

Sousa Viterbo, [F. de]. A Batalha de Touro. *In* Revista Militar. 31 March, etc. 1900.

II. KINGDOM OF ARAGON.

A. Original Documents.

(i) *Published.*

Alfonsello, Andreu. Los reys de Aragó y la seu de Girona desde l'any 1462 fins al 1482. Ed. Fita y Colomé, D. Fidel. 2nd edn. Barcelona. 1873.

Apéndice al Parlamento de Cataluña y Compromiso de Caspe. Barcelona. 1848.

Carreras y Candi, F. Dietari de la guerra de Cervera, 1462-5. Barcelona. 1907.

Carta de D. Fernando de Antequera sobre una derrota de los ingleses en Aragón en el año 1413. Ed. Alvarez de la Braña, R. RABM. 3rd ser. Vol. vii. 1902.

Cortes de los antiguos reinos de Aragón y de Valencia, y Principado de Cataluña. Vols. vii-x. (RAH.) Madrid.

González Hurtebise, E. Inventario de los bienes muebles de Alfonso V de Aragón como infante y como rey (1412-24). *In* Anuari de l'Inst. d'Estudis Catalans. i. 1907-8.

Levantamiento y guerra de Cataluña en tiempo de Juan II. *In* Col. de doc. inéd. del Archivo...de Aragón. xiv–xvi and xxvi.
[Louis XI, King of France.] Lettres...relatives à sa politique en Catalogne de 1461 à 1473. Ed. Pasquier, F. Foix. 1895.
—— Une lettre...à Sixte IV relative aux affaires d'Espagne. Ed. d'Herbomez, A. BEC. li. 1890.
Proceso contra el último Conde de Urgel y su familia. *In* Col. de doc. inéd. del Archivo...de Aragón. xxxv, xxxvi.
Varias noticias sobre la segunda expedición a Nápoles por el Rey D. Alonso V en 1432.... *In* Col. de doc. inéd. para la hist. de España. xiii.

(ii) *Manuscripts.*

Carta [de Juan II] a los nobles aragoneses establecidos en Castilla (1460). Nat. Lib., Madrid. 13236.
[Documentos varios del reinado de Alfonso V de Aragón.] Nat. Lib., Madrid. 840, 1358, 1334, 1299, 13106, 6176.
[Investidura del Reyno de Nápoles en favor de Alfonso V de Aragón.] Nat. Lib., Madrid. 6949.
Letters from Alfonso V and his widow Maria. Arch. Corona Aragón, Barcelona, R. 2939, 3276, 2410, 3108, 3162, 3168, etc.
Llibre de rebudes i dates de Guillen de Peralta, tresorer general de Joán II d'Aragó (julio-desembre de 1472). Bibl. Catalunya. 17.
Proceedings of the Town Council of Barcelona and the Diputación General, in the respective Archives.
Registro de la correspondencia de Fernando I de Nápoles (1458–60). (In Catalan, Italian, and Latin. 15th cent.) Bibl. Nat., Paris. 103 (no. 411 of the Catalogue of Morel-Fatio).
Varias noticias para la segunda expedición á Nápoles por...Alonso V en 1432.... [Enc. con la Relación y Comentario de los successos...por Vincart]. Nat. Lib., Madrid. 6357. From the "Libre ordinari de Dates fetes per En Bernat Sirvent..." [then royal treasurer].

B. Original Narrative Authorities.

Anonymous. La fi del Comte d'Urgel. Best text by an editor of the Veu de Catalunya. Barcelona. 1897. [*See* essay by Jiménez Soler, A. *in* Mem. de la R. Acad. de Buenas Letras de Barcelona. vii. 1901.]
Axarate, Blas de. Relación de la Batalla de Ponza. Ed. Paz y Melia, A. RABM. 3rd ser. Vol. i. 1897.
Beccadelli, Antonio (Panormita). De dictis et factis Alphonsi regis Aragonum libri iv. Florence. 1491. Basle. 1538. [With the commentary of Aeneas Sylvius Piccolomini.]
Boades, Mosen Bernardo. Libre dels feyts d'armes de Catalunya. Barcelona. 1873–1904.
Chaula, Thomas de. Gesta per Alphonsum Aragonum et Siciliae regem. Ed. Starrabba, R. Palermo. 1904.
Fazio, B. (Facius). De rebus gestis ab Alphonso I Neapolitanorum rege. Lyons. 1560. *Also in* Raccolta di...scrittori dell'istoria...di Napoli. [Ed. Gravier, G.] Vol. iv. Naples. 1769 ff.
García de Santa María, Gonzalo. Vida del serenísimo Rey D. Juan II de Aragón. *In* Col. de doc. inéd. para la hist. de España. lxxxviii. [Written in Latin and transl. into Spanish by the author.]
Tomich, Pere. Historias e conquestas d'Aragó e de Catalunya. Barcelona, 1886; and many early edns. [The anonymous addition to this chronicle reached Ferdinand II, the Catholic King.]

C. Modern Works.

Alós y de Dou, J. M. de. Mort y exequies del Rey D. Joan II d'Aragó. *In* Bol. de la R. Acad. de Buenas Letras de Barcelona. XI. 1924.

Ametller y Vinyas, J. Alfonso V de Aragón en Italia y la crisis religiosa del siglo XV. Ed. Collell, J. and Roca Heras, J. M. 3 vols. Gerona and San Feliu de Guixols. 1903–28.

Arco, R. del. El obispo de Huesca D. Domingo Ram y el Compromiso de Caspe. *In* Nuestro Tiempo. XIV. 1913.

Arezio, L. La Sardegna e Alfonso il Magnanimo (1435–44). *In* Archivio storico sardo. 1907.

Artigas y Coma, L. Relaciones de D. Fernando de Antequera con el principado de Cataluña. *In* Rev. de Aragón. IV. 1903.

Calmette, J. Louis XI, Jean II, et la révolution catalane (1461–73). Toulouse and Paris. 1903. (*See* Vidal, P. Louis XI, Jean II, et la révolution catalane du XVe siècle. Perpignan. 1903.)

—— La question du Roussillon sous Louis XI. *In* Annales du Midi. VII. 1895.

Carreras Candi, F. Pere Joan Ferrer, Militar y Senyor del Maresme, 1462–85. Barcelona. 1892.

Chaytor, H. J. A history of Aragon and Catalonia. London. 1933.

Coroleu e Inglada, J. El Condestable de Portugal, rey intruso de Cataluña [1464]. *In* Rev. de Gerona. II. 1878.

Dürr, E. Ludwig XI, die aragonesisch-kastilianischen Heirat und Karl der Kühne. MIOGF. XXXV. 1914.

Gaspar Remiro, M. Los cronistas hispano-judíos. Granada. 1919.

Grahit, E. El sitio de Gerona del año 1462. *In* Rev. de Gerona. III. 1879.

Janer, F. Examen de los sucesos y circunstancias que motivaron el Compromiso de Caspe, etc. Madrid. 1855.

Jiménez Soler, A. Causas de la estancia de Alfonso V en Italia. *In* Rev. crítica de hist. y lit. esp., port., e hisp.-amer. III. 1898.

—— D. Jaime de Aragón, último conde de Urgel. *In* Mem. R. Acad. de Buenas Letras de Barcelona. VII. 1901.

—— Retrato histórico de Alfonso V de Aragón. *In* Rev. Aragonesa. I. 1907.

—— Scriptura privada ó "La fi del Conde d' Urgell." Estudio crítico. *In* Rev. crítica de hist. y lit. esp., port., e hisp.-amer. IV. 1899.

Luna, M. Intervención de Benedicto XIII (D. Pedro de Luna) en el Compromiso de Caspe. RABM. 3rd ser. Vol. XXVIII. 1913.

Mery de la Canorque, Abbé. Le génie d'Alphonse V Roi d'Aragon et de Sicile. Brussels. 1765.

Preiswerk, E. Der Einfluss Aragons auf den Prozess des Basler Konzils gegen Papst Eugen IV. Basle. 1902. [diss.]

Pujol y Tubau, P. De la guerra contra Joan II. Conveni entre la vall de Ribes i el rei Lluis XI de França (any 1463). *In* Butl. del Centre Excurs. de Catalunya. XXIV. 1914.

Sancho Bonal, L. Historia del Compromiso de Caspe. Barcelona. 1912.

Soldevila, F. Història de Catalunya. Vol. I. Barcelona. 1934.

Soler, C. El fallo de Caspe. Barcelona. 1899.

III. THE CATHOLIC KINGS.

A. Original Documents.

(i) *Published.*

Asiento y promesa al caudillo de Baza y Almería Yahía Alnayar. *In* Col. de doc. inéd. para la hist. de España. VIII.

Avenencias de algunos sujetos comprendidos en las capitulaciones ajustadas entre los Reyes Católicos y el Rey Baudili para pasarse allende, sobre sus indemnizaciones. Año de 1493. *Ibid.*

Ayora, Gonzalo, Cartas de, cronista de los Reyes Católicos. Escribíalas al Rey D. Fernando en el año 1503 desde el Rosellón, sobre el estado de la guerra con los franceses. Dalas a luz D. G. V. Madrid. 1794. *Also in* Bibl. de autores españ. XIII.

Ayora, Gonzalo de. Carta...al rey Católico sobre la toma de Mazalquivir...1505. *In* Col. de doc. inéd. para la hist. de España. xlvii.
—— Carta...al rey D. Fernando. *In* Doc. escogidos del archivo de la Casa de Alba. Madrid. 1891.
Batalla de Toro. Carta del Rey Católico a...Bacza haciéndole saber la victoria.... *In* Col. de doc. inéd. para la hist. de España. xxiii.
[Boabdil.] Carta del Rey Mahomad (Baudili) a...Isabel I fecha en...Granada...año ochocientos noventa y dos (1487). *Ibid.* lxxxviii.
Cambronero, C. Acuerdos del Ayuntamiento de Madrid referentes a la guerra de Granada (1486–92). *In* Bol. de Archivos, Bibl., y Museos. Madrid. 1896.
Capitulación de la toma e entrega de Granada. Fecha en el Real de la Vega de Granada a 25...de noviembre de 1491.... *In* Col. de doc. inéd. para la hist. de España. viii.
Capitulación ajustada entre los Reyes Católicos y el último Rey de Granada Baudili. *Ibid.*
Capitulación de los Reyes Católicos con Muley Babdali, Rey de Granada, [15 de junio del] año 1493. *Ibid.*
Capitulación de Baudili para irse allende...firmada y sellada por el Rey Baudili en Andarax a 8 de julio de 1493. *Ibid.*
Capitulaciones de Granada. Ed. Garrido Atienza, M. Granada. 1910.
Carta de los judíos de España a los de Constantinopla y respuesta de estos últimos. RABM. 1st ser. Vol. ii. 1872.
Cartas, Dos, de los Reyes Católicos, hasta ahora inéditas. *In* Rev. de la Raza. 1922.
Cartas y documentos relativos al Gran Capitán. Ed. Torre, L. de and Rodríguez Pascual, R. RABM. 3rd ser. Vol. xxxiv. 1916. Vol. xxxv. 1916. Vol. xxxix. 1918. Vol. xliv. 1923.
Cédula y capitulación firmada de los Reyes Católicos sobre el rescate de los moros y moras, naturales de Málaga (4 Sept. 1487). *In* Col. de doc. inéd. para la hist. de España. viii.
Cedulario del Rey Católico (1508–90). Ed. Rodríguez Villa, A. BRAH. liv, lv. 1909.
Concordia entre...D. Fernando y D. Isabel ā cerca del regimiento de sus Reynos; y el poder que dió la Reyna al Rey, año de mccclxxv. *In* Dormer, D. J. Discursos varios de historia. Saragossa. 1683.
Copia de fragmento de carta de Sus Altezas...de marzo de 96...ampliando las instrucciones para la alianza y casamiento. *In* Col. de doc. inéd. para la hist. de España. lxxxviii. [Catherine of Aragon and the Prince of Wales.]
Correspondencia de D. Hugo de Moncada y otros personajes con el Rey Católico y el Emperador Carlos V. *Ibid.* xxiv.
Correspondencia de los Reyes Católicos con el Gran Capitán durante las campañas de Italia. Ed. Serrano y Pineda, I. RABM. 3rd ser. Vols. xx–xxix. 1909–13.
Corrispondenza dei Rei Cattolici col Gran Capitano durante la campagna d' Italia. Ed. Cerone, F. ASPN. xl. 1915.
Cortes de los antiguos Reinos de León y Castilla. Vol. iii (1407–73). Vol. iv (1474–1537). (RAH.) Madrid. 1861 ff.
Discurso político del Comendador mayor de Castilla...sobre si seria bien que el rey D. Fernando passara a Nápoles a assistir al aquisto de aquel Reyno. *n.p., n.d.*
Documentos de asunto económico corr. al rein. de los Reyes Católicos (1475–1516). Ed. Ibarra y Rodríguez, E. Madrid. 1917.
Documentos inéditos sobre la conquista del reino de Granada.... Ed. Fullana, F. de Paula, *in* Boletin hist. iii. Madrid. 1882.
Documentos referentes a la prisión de Boadil en 1483. Ed. Serrano, L. BRAH. lxxxiv. 1924.
Documentos relativos a los Reyes Católicos en la época de sus conquistas en Andalucía. *In* Col. de doc. inéd. para la hist. de España. xi and xix.
Documentos relativos al Rey Católico desde 1504–12. *Ibid.* xxxix.
Documentos relativos al gobierno de estos reinos, muerta...D. Isabel, entre Fernando V, su hija D. Juana y...Felipe I. *Ibid.* xiv.
Documentos sobre la ocupación de Melilla por el duque de Medinasidonia. [Cartas de 1497–1500.] *In* Col. de doc. inéd. para la hist. de España. xxxvi.

Documentos, Tres, inéditos referentes al matrimonio de los Reyes Católicos. 1468, 1469 y 1470. Ed. Danvila, M. BRAH. xxxix. 1901.
Documents inédits sur l'histoire de l'occupation espagnole en Afrique (1506–7ᴬ). Ed. La Primaudaie, F. É. de. Algiers. 1876.
Dote de D. Catalina, hija de los Reyes Católicos y tía del Emperador Carlos V, cuando casó en Inglaterra. [Docs. from Simancas. Ed. González, T.] *In* Col. de doc. inéd. para la hist. de España. i.
Edicto de los Reyes Católicos (31 marzo, 1492) desterrando de sus estados a todos los judíos. Ed. Fita, F. BRAH. xi. 1887.
Encinar, Diego de. Libro de provisiones...libradas por...los...Reyes .Católicos. *In* Bol. investig. hist. Buenos Aires. 1922.
Entrevista del Rey Católico con su yerno D. Felipe. RABM. 1st ser. Vol. v. 1875.
Expulsión de los judíos de España. *Ibid.* iv. 1874.
[Ferdinand V.] Cédula a los moros de Málaga. Ed. Rodríguez Villa, A. RABM. 1st ser. Vol. iii. 1873.
—— Carta...a Gonzalo Ruiz de Figueroa, su embajador en Venecia, dándole cuenta de todo lo que le había ocurrido con su yerno Felipe I. *In* Col. de doc. inéd. para la hist. de España. viii.
—— Copia de minuta de carta autógrafa...a la Reina su mujer. Ed. Pérez Gredilla, C. RABM. 3rd ser. Vol. i. 1897.
Gachard, L. P. Inventaire des papiers d'État concernant les négociations du gouvernement espagnol avec la cour de Rome, qui sônt conservés dans... Simancas: 1486–1612. *In* Compte-rendu des séances...Comm. Roy. d'Hist. (de Belgique), ou Recueil de ses Bulletins. 2nd ser. Vol. vi. 1854.
Gaspar Remiro, M. Documents relatifs à la Guerre de Grenade. *In* Revue hispan. xxx.
—— Últimos pactos y correspondencia íntima entre los Reyes Católicos y Boabdil sobre la entrega de Granada. Granada. 1910.
—— Documentos árabes de la corte nazari de Granada. RABM. 1912.
Gómez de Fuensalida, G. Correspondencia de...Embajador en Alemania, Flandes, e Inglaterra (1496–1509). Publ. by the Duke of Berwick and Alba. Madrid. 1907.
Gutierrez, M. Indice de documentos del reinado de Isabel I...que hay en el Archivo municipal de Cáceres. *In* Rev. de Extremadura. vi. 1904.
Hauser, H. Deux brefs inédits de Léon X à Ferdinand au lendemain de Marignan. RH. c. 1909.
Isabel I. Carta a los oficiales de la contratación de Sevilla.... *In* Col. de doc. inéd. para la hist. de España. xiii.
Laso de la Vega, G. Carta a los reyes D. Fernando y D. Isabel de su embajador en Roma en 1498, inédita.... San Sebastián. 1842.
Letters, despatches,...negotiations between England and Spain. Ed. Bergenroth, G. A. Supplt. to Vols. i and ii (Intended marriage of Henry VII with Queen Joanna, etc.). (Cal.SP.) London. 1868.
Linde, Baron de la. El testamento otorgado en Burgos por D. Fernando el Católico. 1512. *In* Rev. de hist. y geneal. españ. 1916–17.
López de Mendoza, Iñigo, conde de la Tendilla. Registro de la correspondencia... acerca del gobierno de las Alpujarras. RABM. 3rd ser. Vol. xvi. 1907.
Minuta de lo tocante al asiento que se dió a la ciudad de Granada por los Reyes Católicos acerca de su gobierno. *In* Col. de doc. inéd. para la hist. de España. viii.
Pactos, Últimos, y correspondencia íntima entre los Reyes Católicos y Boabdil sobre la entrega de Granada. Granada. 1910.
[Papers about the Inquisition in Catalonia.] *In* Col. de doc. inéd. para la hist. de España. xxviii.
Parra, Carta del doctor, médico, escrita desde Valladolid al Rey Católico, dándole noticia de la enfermedad y muerte de Felipe I. *In* Col. de doc. inéd. para la hist. de España. viii.
Paz, A. Colección de cartas originales y autógrafas del Gran Capitán que se guardan en la Biblioteca Nacional. RABM. v. 1901; vii. 1902.
Paz y Melia, A. Catálogo abreviado de papeles de la Inquisición. Madrid. 1914.

Paz y Espeso, J. Capitulaciones con la Casa de Austria y papeles de las negociaciones de Alemania, Sajonia, Polonia, Prusia, y Hamburgo, 1493–1796. Catálogo II, Secretaría del Estado, del Archivo general de Simancas. Vienna. 1913.

Philip I. Cartas...copiadas de las minutas existentes en el Archivo de Simancas. *In* Col. de doc. inéd. para la hist. de España. viii.

Pujol y Camps, C. Una carta del Gran Capitán. *In* Rev. de ciencias históricas. i. Barcelona. 1880.

Relación del caso de Granada...Principio de la rebelión de los moros después de la conquista (1499). *In* Col. de doc. inéd. para la hist. de España. xxxvi.

Relaciones de algunos sucesos de los últimos tiempos del reino de Granada, que publica la Sociedad de Bibliófilos españoles. Madrid. 1868.

[Riaño, J. F.] Una relación inédita de la toma de Granada. *In* La Alhambra. n.s. Vol. i. 1898.

Rodríguez Villa, A. Un cedulario del Rey Católico (1508–9). BRAH. liv, lv. 1909. [A register preserved in Acad. Hist. Madrid (Colec. Salazar K–4).]

—— Tratado entre las coronas de Castilla y Portugal sobre posesión de Guinea, costas, mares e islas de Africa. BRAH. xxxvi.

Roth von Schreckenstein, K. H. Briefe des Grafen Wolfgang zu Fürstenberg zur Geschichte der Meerfahrt des Königs Philipp von Castilien (1506). *In* Zeitschr. d. Gesellsch. für d. Gesch.-Alterth. i. Freiburg. 1867–9.

Sanz Arizmendi, C. Indice del Tumbo de los Reyes Católicos. *In* Revue hisp. lxii. 1924.

Testamento del...Rey D. Fernando el Cathólico, hecho en...Madrigalejo (22 Jan. 1516). *In* Dormer, D. J. Discursos varios de historia. Saragossa. 1683.

Testamento de la...Reyna Católica, D. Isabel hecho en...Medina del Campo (12 Oct. 1503). *In* Dormer, D. J. *Op. cit.*

Traslado de los capítulos del tratado de paces entre...Castilla y...Portugal...de 1480, relativos a la posesión y pertenencia de Guinea, costas, mares e islas de Africa. Ed. Fernández Duro, C. BRAH. xxxvi. 1900.

Traslado de una instrucción que dieron los Reyes Católicos al obispo de Túy...sus embajadores en Roma. *In* Col. de doc. inéd. para la hist. de España. vii.

Valera, Mosen Diego de. Epistolas [to the Catholic Kings]. (Soc. de Bibliófilos Españ. xvi.)

Zafra, Fernando de. Correspondencia sobre la empresa española en el Norte de Africa...1492–4. *In* Col. de doc. inéd. para la hist. de España. li.

(ii) *Manuscripts.*

Armada que D. Fernando de Castella mandou contra Gilves, e por capitão D. Garcia filho do Duque d'Alba, em 1510. Derrota dos christãos. Nat. Lib., Lisbon. 7638.

Batalha que foi entre...Luiz [XII]...e...Fernando de Castella, em Italia, anno de 1513 sobre o reino de Naples. Nat. Lib., Lisbon. 7638.

Cartas Reales de Fernando V, Isabel la Católica, D. Juana la Loca y Carlos I a varios personajes. (Copy of 1646.) Nat. Lib., Madrid. 18634[70].

[Cédulas varias de Dª Juana la Loca y de Carlos I.] Nat. Lib., Madrid. 19703, 13292[4], 18714[60].

[Cota, Sancho. Memorias, 1482–1538.] (16th cent.) Bibl. Nat., Paris. 355 (no. 171 of the Catalogue of Morel-Fatio. Incomplete MS.)

De lo que sucedió en España en cosas particulares desde la venida de Felippe I hasta su muerte. (18th-cent. copy.) Nat. Lib., Madrid. 13127.

[Documentos varios del reiuado de los Reyes Católicos.] Nat. Lib., Madrid. 638, 1763, 13127, 13110–12, 13031, 5790, 8512, 13089, 7456, 13123, 6150, 19703, 12976, 19365, 18700, 18620, 1490; Bibl. Nat., Paris. 318 (no. 172 of the Catalogue of Morel-Fatio).

[Documentos varios sobre el Gran Capitán.] Nat. Lib., Madrid. 1490, 4320, 1924, 1755, 2834, 7413, 6176.

Escritura de pacto entre D. Alfonso [V] de Portugal y varios nobles de Castilla, acerca del derecho que aquél tenía para penetrar en territorio castellano. (1469, 18th-cent. copy.) Nat. Lib., Madrid. 18759[11].

[Felipe I. Cartas y otros escritos.] Bibl. Nat., Paris. 143 (no. 442 of the catalogue of Morel-Fatio).

[Fernando V. Cartas y otros escritos.] Nat. Lib., Madrid. 11036, 11017, 11075, 11263, 10767, 10739, 10902, 10176, 13298, 11031, 10206, 19204, 5749, 1029, 9374, 1170, 11649, 18725, 9855, 18717, 9391, 18634, 5791, 6150, 2394, 95, 8512, 8755, 13069, 13040, 9408, 11592, 9175, 6916, 18700, 3202.

[Fernando V] Avisos políticos a sus Embajadores en Inglaterra, Alemania y Flandes, y cartas del mismo Rey. (17th cent.) Nat. Lib., Madrid. 1490.

Juana, Reina de Castilla: Dos cartas a D. Rampston de Viciana trasladando otras de Carlos I sobre la conversión de los moriscos de Valencia y sobre la victoria de Pavía. (Copy of 1779 by Pérez Bayer, ff. 48–54.) Nat. Lib., Madrid. 13208.

Noticia de lo que al...Consejo Real...pasó con...D. Juana en Burgos...un día después de la muerte de...D. Felipe. (18th cent.) Nat. Lib., Madrid. 18761[6].

Registro de cartas referentes al Gobierno de las Alpujarras. Años 1508 a 1520. (16th cent.) Nat. Lib., Madrid. 10230, 10231.

Relación de la prisión del Rey Boadil de Granada.... (1483, 19th-cent. copy.) Nat. Lib., Madrid. 20276[23].

Relación de los hechos de Pedro Navarro, 1510–12. (16th cent.) Escurial Lib. v. II. 4.

Tractatus matrimonii inter Arthurum Principem Waliae et Catherinam filiam Ferdinandi et Helisabet.... (17th-cent. copy.) Nat. Lib., Madrid. 18673[16].

B. Original Narrative Authorities.

(i) *Published.*

Abraham ben Solomon of Torrutiel. El libro de la tradición (–1500.) [An appendix to the Sefer ha-Ḳabbalah (Book of tradition) of Abraham ibn Daud ha-Levi.] Granada. 1922; and 1923.

d'Anghiera or Angleria, Pedro Martir. Opus epistolarum. Alcalá. 1530. Amsterdam. 1570.

—— De Orbe Novo Decades. Alcalá. 1516–30.

Ayora, Gonzalo de. Historia de la Reina Isabel *or* Crónica de los Reyes Católicos. (Fragments ed. by Cat, E. *in* Essai sur la vie et les ouvrages...G. de Ayora, suivi de fragments inédits de sa chronique. Paris. 1890.)

Baumstark, R. Isabelle von Castilien und Ferdinand von Aragonien. Freiburg. 1894.

Bernáldez, A. Historia de los Reyes Católicos D. Fernando y D. Isabel. 2 vols. Granada. 1856.

Cantalicio, G. B. Historie delle guerre fatte in Italia da...il Gran Capitano. Cozenza. 1595.

Coronica llamada Las dos Conquistas del Reyno de Nápoles.... Saragossa. 1559. [*See* Torre, L. de. De "re" bibliográfica. Algunas observaciones acerca de la llamada Crónica general del Gran Capitán. *In* Rev. de hist. y geneal. españ. I. 1912.]

Fernández de Oviedo, Gonzalo. Batallas y Quincuagenas, *or* Las Quincuagenas de la nobleza de España. Madrid. 1880. [Unfinished.]

Galíndez de Carvajal, Lorenzo. Anales breves (*or* Memorial y registro breve de los lugares donde el Rey y la Reyna Católicos...estuvieron cada año, desde el de 1468 hasta que Dios los llevò para si...). *In* Col. de doc. inéd. para la hist. de España. XVIII. *See also* Bibl. de autores españ. Crónicas. III. *Also* first edn., with variation in title, ed. by Floranes, R. in 1787.

García de Morales, A. La vida del Gran Capitán, según una Historia de Córdoba, inédita, del siglo XVII, del Padre Jesuíta. Ed. Ortí Belmonte, M. A. *in* Rev. del centro de estudios hist. de Granada. V–VII. 1915.

Gaspar Remiro, M. Entrada de los Reyes Católicos en Granada al tiempo de su rendición. *Ibid.* I. 1911.

Giovio (Jovius), P. La vita di...il Gran Capitano. Transl. by Domenichi, L. [from the Latin]. Florence. 1550.

Gómez de Castro, A. De rebus gestis Francisci Ximenii. Alcalá. 1569.

[González Simancas, M.] Notas históricas referentes al reinado de Doña Isabel la Católica. BRAH. XLIV. 1904.

Il grado di Gran Capitano nell' esercito di Ferdinand V. *In* Riv. del Coll. Araldico. Rome. 1908.

Guicciardini, F. Relazione di Spagna...(1512–13). *In* Opere inedite. Vol. VI. Ed. Canestrini, G. Florence. 1864.

—— La storia d' Italia. Ed. Gherardi, A. 4 vols. Florence. 1919.

Irving, Washington. Chronicle of the conquest of Granada. From the MSS. of Fray Antonio Agapida. 2 vols. London. 1829. Spanish transln. Montgomery, J. W. Madrid. 1831.

Langendries, A. Jeanne d'Aragon, mère de Charles-Quint, et ses derniers historiens. *In* Précis historiques. VII. Brussels. 1878.

Marineus, Lucius. Epistolarium libri XVII. Valladolid. 1513.

—— Sumario de...D. Fernando y D. Isabel. [Transl. from the Latin by Bravo, J.] Alcalá. 1530.

Medina y Mendoza, F. de. Vida del Cardenal D. Pedro González de Mendoza. *In* Mem. hist. español. (RAH.) VI.

Miranda, F. A. de. Los grandes hechos del Gran Capitán.... Seville. 1615.

Padilla, L. de. Crónica de Felipe I llamado el Hermoso. *In* Col. de doc. inéd. para la hist. de España. VIII. 1846. [Incomplete edn. MS. in the Escurial Library.]

[Palencia, Alfonso de.] Guerra de Granada. Transl. Paz y Melia, D. A. Madrid. 1909. [Latin original, in Nat. Lib., Madrid, not yet publd.]

Palma, A. de, el Bachiller. Divina retribución sobre la caída de España (1385–1476). (Soc. de Bibliófilos Españ. XVIII.) Madrid. 1879.

Perali, P. La guerra di Tripoli del 1511 in un diario orvietano dell' epoca. *In* La Bibliofilia. XIV. 1913.

Pérez de Hita, G. Historia de los bandos de los Zegries y Abencerrajes, *and* Segunda parte de las guerras civiles de Granada. Ed. Blanchard-Demonge, P. Madrid. 1913–15. [Valuable chiefly for its style and picturesqueness.]

Porreño, Baltasar. Vida y hechos del...Cardenal...D. Pedro González de Mendoça.... (17th cent.) Nat. Lib., Madrid. 9643.

Pulgar, Hernando del. Crónica de los...Reyes Católicos D. Fernando y D. Isabel (and anon. continuation). Valencia. 1780; *and in* Bibl. de autores españ. LXX. 1878. [First publ., in a Latin transln., by A. de Nebrija, to whom it was attributed.]

—— Letras or Cartas. *In* Bibl. de Autores Españ. XIII.

—— Libro de los claros varones de Castilla. (Clásicos castellanos, XLIX.) Madrid. 1923.

Quintanilla y Mendoza, P. Oranvm Ximenii virtvte catholicvm, sev de africano bello in Tremezinii Regno. Rome. 1658.

Rodríguez Villa, A. Crónicas del Gran Capitán. Nueva Bibl. de autores españ. X. Madrid. 1908. [Contains one chronicle hitherto unpublished, found in Arch. municipal de Montilla; those of Paolo Giovio and Pérez del Pulgar and one anonymous.]

Roesler, R. Johanna die Wahnsinnige, Königin von Castilien. Vienna. 1870. [Uses Bergenroth's discoveries at Simancas.]

Salazar y Mendoza, P. de: Crónica de el Gran Cardenal de España...D. Pedro Gonçalez de Mendoza.... Toledo. 1625.

Santisteban, Cristóbal. Tratado de las sucesiones de los reynos de Gerusalem, Nápoles, Sicilia y provincias de Pulla y Calabria, y del derecho que a ellos tienen los reyes catholicos don Fernando y donna Isabel. Saragossa. 1503.

Sucesos de las armadas, así españolas como turquescas. *In* Col. de doc. inéd. para la hist. de España. XIII.

Valera, Mosen Diego de. Crónica de los Reyes Católicos. Ed. Carriazo, J. M. de. Madrid. 1927. [Newly discovered text.]

Vallejo, J. de. Memorial de la vida de Fray Francisco Jiménez de Cisneros. Madrid. 1913.

Zakuth (Zacuto), Abraham. Sefer ha-Yuḥasin. (Book of Genealogies.) Ed. Shalom, S. Constantinople. 1566. Ed. Filipowski, H. and Emden, J. London. 1857.

Zurita y Castro, J. de. Anales de la Corona de Aragón. Saragossa. 1610–21. Vol. III (On Ferdinand the Catholic).

(ii) *Manuscripts.*

Barreda, Onofre Antonio de la. Vida de los señores reyes catholicos de Spaña, D. Fernando V⁰ i D. Isabel. (17th cent.) Bibl. Nat., Paris 360 (no. 162 of the Catalogue of Morel-Fatio).

[Crónica incompleta de los Reyes Católicos.] (16th cent.) Escurial Lib. L. I. 6.

[Florez, Alonso?] Crónica de los Reyes Católicos D. Fernando y D. Isabel. Acad. Hist. Madrid. Colec. Salazar. G. 20.

González Dávila, Gil. Historia original de los Reyes Católicos...hasta...1479. (Modern copy.) Nat. Lib., Madrid. 1763.

López de Palacios Rubios, J. Libellus de Insulis Occeanis quas vulgus Indias apellat. (16th-cent. copy.) Nat. Lib., Madrid. 17641. [Incomplete.]

Paz, F. Matías de. Circa dominium Catholici atque invictissimi regis Hyspaniae super Indios. (16th cent.) Acad. Hist. Madrid. Colec. Mateos Murillo.

Santa Cruz, Alonso de. Coronica de los Reyes Catholicos don Fern^do y d^a Isauel. (16th cent.) Nat. Lib., Madrid. 1620. [Gayangos discovered another MS. in the British Museum.]

Sumario de la Coronica de los Reyes Catholicos. (16th cent.) Escurial Lib. x. II. 23.

Tsaddic de Arévalo, R. Josef. Compendio del recuerdo justo (1467). Rabbinic MSS. in Bodleian Library, Oxford. [*See* Gaspar Remiro, M. Los cronistas hispanojudíos. Madrid. 1920.]

Zurita y Castro, Jerónimo de. Historia del Rey D. Fernando el Católico. De las empresas y ligas de Italia. Nat. Lib., Madrid. 1488-9, 6794 (fragment); Bibl. Nat., Paris. 96-7 (nos. 160-1 of the Catalogue of Morel-Fatio).

C. Modern Works.

(i) *General.*

Calmette, J. La France et l'Espagne à la fin du xve siècle. *In* Rev. des Pyrénées et de la France méridionale [et Espagne]. Toulouse. xvi. 1904.

Campillo, T. del. Aragón, Castilla y la unidad española. RABM. 1st ser. Vol. II. 1872.

Clemencín, D. Elogio de la Reina Católica D. Isabel. Madrid. 1820.

—— Ilustraciones sobre varios asuntos del reinado de D. Isabel la Católica. *In* Mem. RAH. vi. Madrid.

Costa, J. Tutela de pueblos en la Historia. Madrid. Fortanet. *n.d.*

Dieulafoy, J. Isabelle la Grande, reine de Castille, 1451-1504. Paris. 1920.

Estado de la cultura española y principalmente catalana en el siglo xv. Barcelona. 1893. [Composite.]

Flórez, E. Reinas católicas. Madrid. 1790.

Galindo de Vera, L. Historia, vicisitudes y política tradicional de España respecto de sus posesiones en las costas de Africa. *In* Mem. RAH. xi. 1884.

Hume, M. Isabel la Católica. *In* La España moderna. cccIII–cccv. 1914.

Kayserling, M. Geschichte der Juden in Spanien und Portugal. Berlin. 1861-7.

Lea, H. C. History of the Inquisition in Spain. 4 vols. New York. 1906-7.

López Ferreiro, A. Galicia en el último tercio del siglo xv. Santiago. 1883.

Mariégol, J. H. L'Espagne sous Ferdinand et Isabelle. Paris. 1892.

Nervo, Baron de. Isabelle la Catholique, 1451-1504. Paris. 1874.

Paz y Melia, A. Cuadros o narraciones de la sociedad española del siglo xv, según documentos coetáneos inéditos. Madrid. 1878.

Plunket, I. L. Isabel of Castile and the making of the Spanish nation, 1451-1504. New York. 1915.

Prescott, W. H. History of the reign of Ferdinand and Isabella, the Catholic, of Spain. 3 vols. London. 1838; and many later edns.

Sotto, R. de, conde de Clonard. Apuntes históricos sobre las expediciones de los españoles al Africa. *In* La Asamblea del Ejército [y de la Armada]. Vols. I–v; 2nd ser. Vols. I, II, IV, v, IX, x. Madrid. 1856 ff.

Vidal, J. Desorientación política y militar de la España de los Reyes Católicos. Estudio de las expediciones a Africa. *In* Memorial de Infantería. x. Toledo. 1916.

(ii) *Monographs*.

Albors y Albors, C. La Inquisición y el Cardenal de España. Valencia. 1896.

Altamira, R. Significación e importancia del reinado de los Reyes Católicos en relación con América. *In* Bol. de la Inst. libre de Enseñanza. Año lvi. Madrid. 1932.

Amezúa y Mayo, A. G. de. La batalla de Lucena y el verdadero retrato de Boabdil. Estudio histórico-artístico.... Madrid. 1915.

Barata, A. F. A batalha de Toro. Evora. 1896.

Barcia y Pavón, A. M. de. Retratos de Isabel la Católica procedentes de la Cartuja de Míraflores. Madrid. 1907.

Bernays, J. Petrus Martyr...und sein Opus epistolarum. Strasbourg. 1891.

Blum, N. La croisade de Ximenès en Afrique. Oràn. 1898.

Bullón, E. Un colaborador de los Reyes Católicos: Juan López de Vivero Palacios Rubios. Madrid. 1927.

Calmette, J. Une ambassade espagnole à la cour de Bourgogne en 1477. *In* Bulletin hisp. vii. 1905.

—— L'avènement de Ferdinand le Catholique et la " Leuda" de Collioure (1479). Perpignan. 1901.

—— Un incident franco-espagnol en 1484. *In* Rev. des Pyrénées et de la France méridionale [et Espagne]. Toulouse. xviii. 1906.

—— La politique espagnole dans la guerre de Ferrare (1482-4). *In* Rev. hispanique. xcii. 1906.

—— La politique espagnole dans l'affaire des barons napolitains (1485-92). RH. cx. 1912.

—— La politique espagnole dans la crise de l'indépendance bretonne (1488-92). RH. cxvii. 1914.

Carreres Zacarés, S. Por qué la conquista de Granada no se hizo un siglo, cuando menos, antes de lo que fué. Valencia. 1908.

Cotarelo y Valledor, A. Fray Diego de Deza. Madrid. 1905.

Creus, T. Un golpe de Estado hasta aquí desconocido en la historia de Cataluña. (Año 1488.) BRAH. xiii. 1888. (*See* Fita, F. El rey D. Fernando II de Aragón en la historia parlamentaria de Cataluña. BRAH. xii. 1888.)

Croce, B. Di un poema spagnuolo sincrono intorno alle imprese del Gran Capitano nel regno di Napoli. Naples. 1894.

Desdevises du Dezert, G. La politique de Ferdinand le Catholique. *In* Rev. hispanique. lvi. 1922.

Dubos, J. B. Histoire de la ligue faite en Cambray. 2 vols. Paris. 1709.

Duponcet, J. ?'. Histoire de Gonsalve de Cordoue, surnommé le Grand Capitaine. 2 vols. Paris. 1714.

Duran, J. La toma de Granada y los caballeros que concurrieron a ella. Madrid. 1893.

Eguilaz Yanguas, L. de. Reseña histórica de la conquista del reino de Granada... según los cronistas árabes. *In* Boletín del Centro Artístico. Granada. Jan. 1892. Another edition: Reseña histórica...seguida de un fotograbado de una carta autógrafa de Boabdil. Granada. 1894.

Feldherr. Der grosse Gonzalo Fernández de Córdova. *In* Oesterreichisches Archiv. 1831.

Filippi, G. Il convegno in Savona tra Luigi XII e Ferdinando il Cattolico. Savona. 1890.

Finke, H. Zur Charakteristik Philipps des Schönen. MIOGF. xxvi. 1905.

Fita, F. La inquisición anormal planteada en Sevilla. BRAH. xv. 1889.

Fiter Inglés, J. Expulsión de los judíos de Barcelona. Barcelona. 1876.

Florian, J. P. C. de. Gonsalve de Cordoue ou Grenade reconquise. 2nd edn. 3 vols. Paris. 1892.

Fuentes, J. Ceriñola, abril 1503. (Capítulo de un libro inédito.) Madrid. 1912.

—— El Gran Capitán. *In* Nuestro Tiempo. xxi. 1921.

Fuertes Arias, R. Estudio histórico acerca de Alfonso de Quintanilla, Contador mayor. 2 vols. Oviedo. 1909.

Gachard, L. P. Sur Jeanne la Folle. *In* Bulletins...Classe de Lettres...de l'Acad. Roy. de Belgique. 2nd ser. Vol. xxvii. 1869.
—— Jeanne la Folle et Charles-Quint.... *Ibid.* Vol. xxix. 1870; xxxiii. 1872.
—— Les derniers moments de Jeanne la Folle. *Ibid.* Vol. xxix. 1870.
Galindo de Vera, L. Conquistas de los españoles en Africa. Orán y Mazalquibir. *In* Rev. Hisp.-Amer. iv, vii, viii. 1882.
Garrido Atienza, M. Las capitulaciones para la entrega de Granada. Granada. 1910.
Gaspar Remiro, M. Granada en poder de los Reyes Católicos. Primeros años de su dominación. *In* Rev. del Centro de estudios hist. de Granada. i. 1911. Publ. separately. Granada. 1912.
Gerigk, J. Das Opus epistolarum des Petrus Martyr. Königsberg. 1881. [diss.]
Godard, L. Souvenirs de l'expédition de Ximenèz en Afrique. *In* Revue Africaine. v. 1861.
Gracián y Morales, B. El político D. Fernando el Catholico...que publica D. V. J. de Lastanosa. Huesca. 1646; and later edns.
Gray, A. Joanna of Castile and Aragon. *In* Tinsley's Magazine. xxxix. 1881.
Guillén Robles, F. Estudios sobre la dominación de los españoles en Berbería. Las Cabalgadas. *In* La España moderna. iii. 1889.
Haebler, K. Der Streit Ferdinand's des Katholischen und Philipp's I um die Regierung von Castilien, 1504–6. Dresden. 1882.
—— Tipografía ibérica del siglo xv. The Hague. 1908.
Hefele, C. J. El cardenal Jiménez de Cisneros y la Iglesia Española a fines del siglo xv. Barcelona. 1869.
Heidenheimer, H. Petrus Martyr Anglerius und sein Opus epistolarum. Berlin. 1881.
Heros, M. de los. Historia del conde Pedro Navarro. *In* Col. de doc. inéd. para la hist. de España. xxv compl.; xxvi. Publ. separately. Madrid. 1854.
Hillebrand, K. Une énigme de l'histoire. La captivité de Jeanne la Folle d'après des documents nouveaux. *In* Revue des Deux Mondes. 2nd ser. Vol. lxxxi. 1869.
Hoefler, C. R. von. Antoine de Lalaing, seigneur de Montigny, Vincenzo Quirino und D. Diego de Guevara als Berichterstatter über König Philipp I in den Jahren 1505–6. Vienna. 1884.
—— Donna Juana...Königin von Spanien. Vienna. 1885.
—— Kritische Untersuchungen über den Quellen der Geschichte Philipps des Schönen. SKAW. civ. 1883.
Huarte y Echenique, A. El Gran Cardenal de España D. Pedro González de Mendoza. Madrid. 1912.
Hume, M. Juana la Loca. *In* La España moderna. cccvi, cccvii. 1914.
Ibarra y Rodríguez, E. La conquista de Melilla en 1497. *Ibid.* lxi. 1894.
Iglesia, E. de la. Estudios históricos militares sobre las campañas del Gran Capitán.... Madrid. 1871.
Jiménez de la Espada, M. La guerra del moro a fines del siglo xv. BRAH. xxv. 1894.
Llorente, J. A. Cuál ha sido la opinión nacional de España acerca del establecimiento de la Inquisición. Madrid. 1812. [Inaug. disc. RAH.]
López de Ayala, I. Vida de Gonzalo Fernández de Aguilar y Córdoba, llamado el Gran Capitán. Madrid. 1793.
López Martínez, C. La santa Hermandad de los Reyes Católicos. Seville. 1921.
Martí y Monsó, J. Bustos de doña Isabel la Católica y doña Juana la Loca. *In* Bol. de la Soc. Cast. de Excursiones. ii. 1905–6.
Martín Arrúe, F. Guerra de Italia en 1515 y 1516. *In* Rev. téc. de Infantería y Caballería. i. Madrid. 1890.
Martínez de la Rosa, F. Hernán Pérez del Pulgar, el de las Hazañas. Madrid. 1834. [With a reprint of Breve parte de las hazañas del excelente nombrado Gran Capitán. A very rare book.]
Marx, A. The expulsion of the Jews from Spain. Two new accounts. JQR. xx. 1908.
Maulde-La Cravière, R. de. L'entrevue de Savone en 1507. *In* Rev. d'hist. diplomatique. iv. 1890.
Mazzei, P. Un MS. della Crónica de los Reyes Católicos di...Pulgar. *In* Rev. hispanique. lvi. 1922.

Merton, R. Cardinal Ximenes and the making of Spain. London. 1934.

Ocepin, Jáuregui, A. La conquista de Orán por el Cardenal Cisneros. *In* Estudios Franciscanos. xxvii. 1921.

Pasolini, P. D. La Battaglia di Ravenna (11 aprile 1512). *In* Nuova Antología. 5th ser. Vol. clvii. 1912.

Pella y Forgas, J. Consecuencias de la unión de las coronas de Aragón y Castilla. *In* Rev. España Regional. iv. 1888.

Pérez de Guzmán y Gallo, J. Dogmas de la política de Fernando V el Católico.... Madrid. 1906. [Inaug. disc. RAH.]

—— La posesión de las islas Chafarinas. BRAH. 1921.

Planella, J. Judíos y moriscos españoles. Rectificación de un juicio erróneo. *In* Razón y Fe. i. 1901.

Rodríguez Pascual, R. El testamento de Isabel la Católica y el problema de Marruecos. Madrid. 1922.

Rodríguez Villa, A. Las cuentas del Gran Capitán. BRAH. lvi. 1910.

—— D. Francisco de Rojas, Embajador de los Reyes Católicos. BRAH. xxviii; xxix. 1896.

—— Observaciones y documentos relativos a...Juana. RABM. 1st ser. Vol. iii. 1873.

—— La Reina D. Juana la Loca. Madrid. 1892.

Rosell, C. Expedición a Orán del Cardenal Cisneros. Madrid. 1857. [Inaug. disc. RAH.]

Saavedra Fajardo, D. de. Introducciones a la política y razón de Estado del Rey Católico D. Fernando. *In* Bibl. de autores españoles. xxv.

Schmidt, C. Peter Martyr Vermigli. Leben und ausgew. Schriften. Elberfeld. 1858.

Schumacher, H. A. Petrus Martyr, der Geschichtschreiber des Oceans. New York. 1879.

Serrano, L. Noticias inéditas del Gran Capitán. BRAH. lxxix. 1921.

Téllez-Girón y Fernández de Córdoba, L. Fernando el Católico como diplomático. Madrid. 1896. [disc.]

Torres Campos, R. Carácter de la conquista y colonización de las islas Canarias. Madrid. 1901.

Valladar, F. de P. Los Moriscos granadinos. *In* La Alhambra. n.s. Vol. xii. Granada. 1909.

Vera, F. de la. Sobre la política de los Reyes Católicos en Italia. *In* Rev. de España. 2nd ser. Vols. v, vi. 1846.

Vidart, L. Colón y la ingratitud de España. Madrid. 1892.

—— Colón y Robadilla. Madrid. 1892.

Vilanova, R. de. Noticias acerca de la institución del Cuerpo de Gentileshombres por Don Fernando el Católico en 1512. BRAH. lxxxii. 1923.

Villa-Real, F. Hernán Pérez del Pulgar. *In* Revista contemporánea. lxxviii–lxxxvi. 1890–2.

IV. NAVARRE.

A. Original Documents.

(i) *Published.*

Carrera, F. Dietari de la guerra de Cervera, 1462–5. Barcelona. 1897.

Documentos inéditos. Navarra, Castilla y Aragón en la segunda mitad del siglo xv. *In* Col. de doc. inéd. para la hist. de España. xl, xli.

Documents relatifs à don Carlos de Viane (1460–1). Ed. Calmette, J. *in* Mélanges d'archéol. et d'hist. École franç. de Rome. 1901.

Protesta de la Princesa D. Blanca, hermana del Príncipe de Viana, contra el pacto acordado por D. Juan II y Luis XI de Francia, sobre la sucesión al trono de Navarra. Ed. Sitges, J. B. *in* Bol. de la Com. de Monumentos...de Navarra. xiii. Pamplona. 1922.

(ii) *Manuscripts*.

Instrucción y memorial de las cosas que...Mosen Pierres de Peralta, condestable de Navarra, había de hacer en Castilla por pacto del Rey de Aragón y de Navarra (1467). Nat. Lib., Madrid. 19698[12 and 13].

Memorial sobre premios y recompensas a los hombres de armas en la conquista de Navarra. (1512.) Nat. Lib., Madrid. 18690[36].

[John, King of Navarre.] Testament de Jean, comte de Foix et d'Étampes, roi de Navarre (27 octobre 1500). Ed. Boucher de Molandon, M. *in* Bulletin du comité des travaux hist. Sect. d'hist. et de philol. 1885.

B. ORIGINAL NARRATIVE AUTHORITIES.

Correa, Luís. Historia de la conquista del reino de Navarra por el Duque de Alba...en ...1512. New edn. by Yanguas y Miranda, J. Pamplona. 1843.

[López de Palacios Rubios, J.] De iustitia et iure obtētionis ac retētionis regni Navarre. *n.p.*, *n.d.*

Viana, Carlos, Príncipe de. Crónica de los Reyes de Navarra [till 1425]. Ed. Yanguas y Miranda, J. Pamplona. 1843.

Historia de Navarra en los años 1512 y 1513. (18th cent.) Nat. Lib., Madrid. 9198.

C. MODERN WORKS.

Agapito y Revilla, J. Casamiento de Doña Juana de Navarra, hija natural de D. Carlos III el Noble, con Iñigo Ortíz, hijo de Diego López de Estuñiga, Justicia Mayor del rey de Castilla. BRAH. LXXXI. 1922.

Altadill, J. La biblioteca y monetario del Príncipe de Viana. *In* Bol. Com. Mon. Navarra. Pamplona. 1918.

B., J. Relaciones de la Santa Sede con los últimos reyes navarros y con sus legítimos herederos. *In* Bol. Com. Mon. Navarra. XII, XIII. Pamplona. 1921.

Balaguer y Merino, A. De la mort de l'infant En Carles...princep de Viana.... *In* La Renaixensa. III. Barcelona. 1873.

Baselga y Ramírez, M. Fragmentos inéditos para ilustrar la historia literaria del Príncipe D. Carlos de Viana. RABM. 3rd ser. Vol. I. 1897.

Beccaria, G. La regina Bianca di Navarra in Sicilia. Palermo. 1887.

Boissonnade, P. Histoire de la réunion de la Navarre à la Castille (1479–1521). Paris. 1893.

Calmette, J. Louis XI, Jean II, et la révolution catalane (1461–73). Toulouse and Paris. 1903.

—— La question du Roussillon sous Louis XI. *In* Annales du Midi. VII. 1895.

Campión, A. La excomunión de los últimos reyes legítimos de Navarra. *In* Bol. Com. Mon. Navarra. XII. Pamplona. 1921.

—— La visión de Don Carlos. Pamplona. 1907.

Codina, J. Guerras de Navarra y Cataluña desde...1451 hasta...1472. Barcelona. 1851.

Courteault, P. de. Gaston IV, comte de Foix, vicomte souverain de Béarn, prince de Navarre, 1423–72. Toulouse. 1895.

Desdevises du Dezert, G. D. Carlos d'Aragón, prince de Viane. Paris. 1889.

Queralt y Nuet, J. Relación histórica del...Príncipe D. Carlos de Viana...Escrita en...1706. *In* Col. de doc. inéd. para la hist. de España. LXXXVIII.

[Relación] sobre la muerte del Príncipe de Viana. *In* Bol. Com. Mon. Navarra. V. Pamplona. 1914.

Ruano Prieto, Fernando, barón de Velasco. Anexión del Reino de Navarra en tiempo del Rey Católico. Madrid. 1899.

—— Don Juan II de Aragón y el Príncipe de Viana. Bilbao. 1897.

CHAPTER XVI.

PORTUGAL IN THE MIDDLE AGES.

I. COLLECTIONS OF DOCUMENTS.

Alguns Documentos do Archivo nacional da Torre do Tombo acerca das navegações e conquistas Portuguesas. Lisbon. 1892.
Archivo historico Portugues. 10 vols. Lisbon. 1903–16.
Corpus codicum latinorum et portugallensium eorum qui in Archivo Municipali Portucalensi asservantur antiquissimorum. 2 vols. Oporto. 1899, 1917.
Narratio itineris navalis ad Terram Sanctam. Ed. Chroust, A. *in* MGH. Script. N.S. Vol. v. 1928. *Also* ed. Gazzera, C. *in* Mem. della R. Accad. delle Scienze di Torino. Ser. II. Vol. II. 1840. p. 177; repr. by Silva Lopes, J. B. de. Lisbon. 1844.
Elementos para a historia do Municipio de Lisboa. 17 vols. Lisbon. 1882–1911.
Ordinações do senhor Rei D. Affonso V. 5 vols. Coimbra. 1792.
Portugaliae Monumenta Historica. Ed. Herculano, A., *et al.* (Acad. das Sciencias de Lisboa). Lisbon. 1856 ff.
    Scriptores. 1856. Leges et consuetudines. 2 vols. 1856 ff.
    Diplomata et Chartae. 1868. Inquisitiones. 1878.
Vimaranis Monumenta Historica. Pt. I. 2nd edn. Guimarães. 1931. Pt. II. *Ibid.* 1929.

II. CHRONICLES.

Brandão, A. Monarchia Lusitana. Pt. III. Lisbon. 1632, 1690. Pt. IV. Lisbon. 1632, 1725.
Brandão, F. Monarchia Lusitana. Pt. V. Lisbon. 1650, 1752. Pt. VI. Lisbon. 1672, 1751.
Chronica do Condestabre de Portugal Nuno Alvares Pereira. Lisbon. 1526.
Eannes de Zurara, Gomes. Chronica do descobrimento e conquista de Guiné. Paris. 1841. Engl. transl. Beazley, C. R. and Prestage, E. 2 vols. (Hakluyt Society.) London. 1896, 99.
—— Chronica da tomada de Ceuta. Lisbon. 1644. Coimbra. 1915.
Goes, Damião de. Chronica do Principe D. João. Lisbon. 1567. Coimbra. 1905.
Lopes, Fernão. Chronica d'el Rei D. João I. Lisbon. 1644, 1915.
—— Chronica do senhor Rei D. Pedro I. *In* Livros ineditos da Historia Portuguesa. Vol. IV. Lisbon. 1816.
—— Chronica do senhor Rei D. Fernando. *Ibid.*
Pina, Ruy de. Chronica d'el Rei D. Affonso o IV. Lisbon. 1653.
—— Chronica do senhor Rei D. Duarte. *In* Livros ineditos. Vol. I. Lisbon. 1790.
—— Chronica do senhor Rei D. Affonso V. *Ibid.*
—— Chronica d'el Rei D. João II. *Ibid.* Vol. II. Lisbon. 1792.
Resende, Garcia de. Chronica de D. João II. Lisbon. 1545. Coimbra. 1798.

III. MODERN WORKS.

Almeida, Fortunato de. Historia da Igreja em Portugal. 6 vols. Coimbra. 1910–17.
Armitage-Smith, S. John of Gaunt. London. 1904.
Azevedo, J. Lucio de. Epocas de Portugal economico. Lisbon. 1929.
—— Historia dos Christãos novos Portugueses. Lisbon. 1921.
Azevedo, Luis G. de. Notas de historia medieval. *In* Revista de Historia. x. Lisbon. 1921.
—— Articles *in* Broteria. 1925, p. 319; 1926, p. 177; 1928, p. 73; 1929, pp. 22, 359; 1930, p. 303.
Beazley, C. R. Prince Henry the Navigator. London. 1895.
—— Prince Henry of Portugal. AHR. XVI, XVII. 1911–12.

Bensaude, Joaquim. L'Astronomie nautique au Portugal à l'époque des grandes découvertes. Berne. 1912.

Cá da Mosto, Alvise de. Le navigazioni Atlantiche. Ed. Caddeo, R. Milan. 1929.

—— Paesi nuovamente retrovati. Vicenza. 1507.

Coelho da Rocha, M. A. Ensaio sobre a historia do governo e legislação de Portugal. 7th edn. Coimbra. 1896.

Costa, Bernardo da. Historia da militar Ordem de Nosso Senhor Jesus Christo. Lisbon. 1771.

Costa Quintella, Ignacio de. Annaes da marinha portuguesa. 2 vols. Lisbon. 1839–40.

Erdmann, C. Der Kreuzzugsgedanke in Portugal. HZ. cxli. 1929.

—— Papsturkunden in Portugal. Berlin. 1927.

Ferreira, J. A. Fastos episcopaes da Igreja de Braga. Braga. 1928.

—— Memorias archeologico-historicas da cidade do Porto. Braga. 1923.

Ficalho, Conde de. Viagens de Pedro de Covilhan. Lisbon. 1891.

Gama Barros, H. de. Historia da Administração publica em Portugal nos seculos xii a xv. 4 vols. Lisbon. 1885–1922.

Herculano, A. Historia de Portugal. 4 vols. Lisbon. 1846–53. New edn. 8 vols. Lisbon. 1914–16.

Historia e Memorias da Academia Real das Sciencias de Lisboa. 12 vols. Lisbon. 1797–1839.

Lopes, D. Os Arabes nas obras de Alexandre Herculano. *In* Bol. da 2da classe da Acad. das Sciencias de Lisboa. Vols. iii, iv. 1910.

—— Historia de Arzila durante o dominio portugues. Coimbra. 1925.

Mayer, Ernesto. Historia de las instituciones sociales y politicas de España y Portugal durante los siglos v a xiv. 2 vols. Madrid. 1925–6.

Memorias de litteratura portuguesa. 8 vols. Lisbon. 1792–1814.

Merea, M. P. O poder real e as Cortes. Coimbra. 1923.

Oliveira Martins, J. P. de. Historia da Civilisação Iberica. Lisbon. 1883. Engl. transl. Bell, A. F. G. Oxford. 1930.

—— A vida de Nun' Alvares. Lisbon. 1893.

Portugalia. 2 vols. Oporto. 1899–1908.

Rebello da Silva, L. A. Memoria sobre a população e a agricultura de Portugal. Lisbon. 1868.

Reuter, A. E. Königtum und Episkopat in Portugal im 13 Jahrht. Berlin. 1928.

Ribeiro, J. P. Dissertações chronologicas e criticas sobre a historia e jurisprudencia de Portugal. 5 vols. Lisbon. 1810–36.

Saldanha Oliveira e Sousa, J. P. de. Coutos de Alcobaça. Lisbon. 1929.

Sanches-Albornoz Menduina, C. La Curia Regia Portuguesa, siglos xii a xiii. Madrid. 1920.

Sandoval, C. Ximenes de. Batalla de Aljubarrota. Madrid. 1872.

Santarem, Visconde de. Memorias para a historia e theoria das Cortes geraes. Lisbon. 1827–8.

—— Quadro Elementar das relações politicas e diplomaticas de Portugal com as diversas potencias do mundo. 18 vols. Paris and Lisbon. 1842–60.

Shillington, V. M. and Chapman, A. B. W. Commercial relations of England and Portugal. London. [1907.]

Sousa, A. C. de. Historia Genealogica da Casa Real Portuguesa. 12 vols. Lisbon. 1735–48. Provas. 6 vols. Lisbon. 1739–48.

Sousa Silva Costa Lobo, A. de. Historia da sociedade em Portugal no seculo xv. Lisbon. 1903.

Vieira Guimarães, J. A Ordem de Christo. Lisbon. 1901.

Vilhena, D. Thomas de. Historia da Ordem de Santa Cavallaria em Portugal. Coimbra. 1920.

Villa Franca, Conde de. D. João I e a alliança inglesa. Lisbon. 1884.

CHAPTER XVII.

THE SCANDINAVIAN KINGDOMS DURING THE FOURTEENTH AND FIFTEENTH CENTURIES.

[For bibliographies and other works covering the whole medieval period, *see* Vol. vi, pp. 909–11.]

I. AUTHORITIES.

A. DENMARK.

Regesta diplomatica historiae Danicae. Series ii. Vol. i (789–1536). Copenhagen. 1889.
Repertorium diplomaticum regni Danici mediaevalis. Ed. Erslev, K. Vols. i–iv. Copenhagen. 1895–1912.
Diplomatarium Christierni Primi. Ed. Wegener, C. F. Copenhagen. 1856.
Danske Kongers Haandfaestninger. *In* Aarsberetninger fra det Kongelige Geheimearchiv. Vol. ii, ed. Wegener, C. F. Copenhagen. 1856–9.
Acta pontificum Danica. Vols. i–vi (1316–1536). Copenhagen. 1904–15.

B. NORWAY AND HER DEPENDENCIES.

Norges gamle Love indtil 1387. Ed. Keyser, R. and others. Vols. iii–v. Christiania (Oslo). 1849–95. Anden raekke (1388–1604). Vols. i, ii. Christiania (Oslo). 1904–21. In progress.
Islandske Annaler indtil 1578. Ed. Storm, G. Christiania (Oslo). 1888.
Records of the Earldom of Orkney, 1299–1614. Ed. Clouston, J. Storer. Edinburgh. 1914.

C. SWEDEN.

Svenskt Diplomatarium. Vols. ii–v (1286–1347). Stockholm. 1837–65.
Svenskt Diplomatarium från och med år 1401. Vols. i–iv (1401–20). Stockholm. 1875–1904.
Sverges traktater med främmande magter. Ed. Rydberg, O. S. Vols. ii, iii. Stockholm. 1883, 95.
Privilegier, resolutioner och förordningar för Sveriges städer. Vol. i. Ed. Herlitz, N. Stockholm. 1927.
Bidrag till Skandinaviens historia ur utländska arkiver. Ed. Styffe, C. G. 5 vols. Stockholm. 1859–84.
Svenska Medeltidens Rim-Krönikor. Ed. Klemming, G. E. 3 vols. Stockholm. 1865–8. The text of Vol. i (Erikskrönikan) in new edn. by Pipping, R. Upsala. 1921.
Revelationes S. Birgittae. First printed in Rome 1475, often reprinted. English transl. (15th century) ed. Cumming, W. P. (EETS. Orig. ser. 178). London. 1929. Old Swedish transl. ed. Klemming, G. E. 4 vols. Stockholm. 1857–84.

II. MODERN WORKS.

A. SCANDINAVIA AS A WHOLE.

Allen, C. F. De tre nordiske Rigers Historie, 1497–1536. 5 vols. (to 1527). Copenhagen. 1864–72.
Christensen, W. Unionskongerne og Hansestaederne, 1439–66. Copenhagen. 1895.
Paludan-Müller, C. P. De första Konger af den Oldenborgske Slaegt. Copenhagen. 1874.

B. DENMARK.

Arup, E. Danmarks historie. Vol. II. Copenhagen. 1932.
Christensen, W. Dansk Statsforvaltning i det 15 århundrede. Copenhagen. 1903.
Erslev, K. Danmarks Historie under Dronning Margrethe og Erik af Pommern.
    2 vols. Copenhagen. 1882–1901.
—— Danmarks Riges Historie. Vol. II. Copenhagen. 1898–1905.
Jahn, F. H. Danmarks politisk-militaire Historie under Unionskongerne. Copen-
    hagen. 1835.
Lindbaek, J. Pavernes Forhold til Danmark under Kongerne Kristiern I og Hans.
    Copenhagen. 1907.
Olrik, J., and Christiansen, C. P. O. Det danske Folks Historie. Vols. II, III.
    Copenhagen. 1927–8.

C. NORWAY AND HER DEPENDENCIES.

Gjerset, K. History of the Norwegian people. Vol. II. New York. 1915.
Johnsen, O. A. Noregsveldets undergang. Christiania (Oslo). 1924.
Munch, P. A. Det norske Folks Historie. Anden Hovedafdeling. Unionsperioden.
    2 vols. Christiania (Oslo). 1862–3.
Nielsen, Y. Det norske rigsraad. Christiania (Oslo). 1880.
Sars, J. E. Udsigt over den norske Historie. Vol. III. Christiania (Oslo). 1887.
    Repr. *in* Samlede Vaerker. Vol. II. Christiania (Oslo). 1912.
Taranger, A. Norges historie fremstillet for det norske folk. Vol. III. Christiania
    (Oslo). 1915–17.
——
Clouston, J. Storer. History of Orkney. Kirkwall. 1932.

D. SWEDEN.

Andersson, I. Källstudier till Sveriges historia, 1230–1436. Lund. 1928.
Brilioth, Y. Svensk kyrka, kungadöme och påvemakt 1363–1414. Upsala. 1925.
Hallendorff, C., and Schück, A. History of Sweden. Stockholm. 1929.
Hildebrand, H. Sveriges historia intill tjugonda seklet. Vol. II. Medeltiden.
    Stockholm. 1905.
Odhner, C. T. Bidrag till svenska städernas historia före 1633. Upsala. 1860.
Schück, H. Minne af rikshöfvitsmannen Engelbrekt Engelbrektsson. Stockholm.
    1915.
—— Svenska folkets historia. Vol. I, pt. II. Lund. 1915.
——
Hornborg, E. Finlands hävder. Vol. I. Helsingfors. 1929.

CHAPTER XVIII.

POLAND AND LITHUANIA IN THE FOURTEENTH AND FIFTEENTH CENTURIES.

I. BIBLIOGRAPHIES.

Finkel, L. Bibliografia historyi polskiej. 3 vols. Cracow. 1891–1906; and supplt.
Potthast, A. Bibliotheca historica medii aevi. *See Gen. Bibl.* i.

II. DOCUMENTS.

Acta patriarchatus Constantinopolitani. i, ii. Ed. Miklosich, E. and Müller, J. Vienna. 1862.
Acta Tomiciana. i. Ed. Gorski, S. Poznań (Posen). 1852–76.
Ältesten grosspolnischen Grodbücher, Die. Ed. Lekszycki, J. von. Leipsic. 1887–9.
Aeneas Silvius Piccolomini (Pius II). Briefwechsel. Ed. Wolkan, R. (Fontes rerum Austriacarum. Abt. ii. Vols. lxi, lxii, lxvii, lxviii.) Vienna. 1909–18.
Akta kongresu Wyszegradzkiego. Ed. Ludewig, J. P. Leipsic. 1720–31.
Akty istoricheskie iz inostrannykh arkhivov. (Arkheograf. Kommissiya.) St Petersburg. 1841–2.
Akty izdavayenniye komissieyu dlya razbora drevnykh aktov v Vilnie. Vilna. 1865–88.
Akty otnosyashchiesya k istorii yuzhnoy i zapadnoy Rossii. i. (*Ibid.*) St Petersburg. 1863–89.
Akty otnosyashchiesya k istorii zapadnoy Rossii. (*Ibid.*) St Petersburg. 1846–53.
Akty sobrannye v bibliotekakh i arkhivakh...Akademii Nauk. (*Ibid.*) St Petersburg. 1836.
Akty unii horodelskiej. *In* Volumina legum. i. *See below.*
Archiv česky. ii. Ed. Palacký, F. Prague. 1840 ff.
Archiwum domowe. Towarzysz duch. kat. Tarnopol. 1864.
Arkhiv yugo-zapadnoy Rossii. Kiev. 1859–88.
Articuli Corczinenses. Ed. Bandtkie, J. W. *in* Jus Polonicum. *See below.*
Bachmann, A. Urkunden...zur österreichischen Geschichte...(1440–71). *See Gen. Bibl.* iv *under* Imperial Documents.
Bandtkie, J. W. Jus Culmense. Warsaw. 1814.
—— Jus Polonicum. Warsaw. 1831.
Beiträge zur Geschichte der Stadt Lemberg. AOG. lxiv. 1870.
Bershadsky, S. Dokumenty i regesty k istorii litovskikh Evreev. i. St Petersburg. 1882.
Bestätigungsdiplome Königs Kasimir d. Stadt Lemberg. SKAW. xlix.
Bischoff, F. Urkunden zur Geschichte der Armenier in Lemberg. AOG. xxxii. 1865.
Bobrzyński, M. Star. prawa polskiego pomniki. Cracow. 1882.
Böhmer, J. F. Regesta imperii. *See Gen. Bibl.* iv *under* Papal Documents.
Brock, J. De controversiis quae post pacem Thorunensem secundam inter Casimirum IV et terras Prussiae exortae sunt. Breslau. 1871.
Buja, M. Regesten d. Kriege. *In* Altpreuss. Monatsschr. 1869.
Callimachi Oratio coram Innocentio VIII. Cracow. 1524.
Caro, J. Liber cancellariae Stanislai Ciolek. Vienna. 1871–4.
Casimirus rex jus Culmense per totam Prussiam servari jubet. *In* Volumina legum. i. *See below.*
Chmel, J. Regesta...Ruperti regis Romanorum. *See Gen. Bibl.* iv *under* Imperial Documents.
—— Urkunden und Actenstücke zur Geschichte K. Albrechts II. *Ibid.*
—— Regesta...Friderici III. *Ibid.*
—— Materialien zur österreichischen Geschichte. *Ibid.*
—— Urkunden, Briefe, und Actenstücke zur Gesch. Maximilians I. *Ibid.*

Cieszkowski, A. Materyaly do historyi Jagiellonów z archiwów weneckich. *In* Rocznik Tow. Przyj. Nauk Poznańskiego. xv. Poznań (Posen). 1887.

Codex diplomaticus Lubecensis. Lübeck. 1843–84.

Codex diplomaticus Silesiae. Breslau. 1857–89.

Codex epistolaris Vitoldi. Ed. Prochaska, A. Cracow. 1888.

Concordia dominorum de Prussia cum rege Poloniae. SKAW. ii. 1850.

Confirmatio jurium majoris Poloniae. Ed. Bandtkie, J. W. *in* Jus Polonicum. *See above.*

Constitutiones et Acta publica imperatorum et regum. Vols. iv, i–vi.i, viii. MGH. Legum Sect. iv. 1906–26.

Danilowicz, J. Skarbiec diplomatów papieskich, cesarskich w bibliotece Muzeum Wileńskiego. Vilna. 1860–2.

Deutsche Reichstagsakten. *See Gen. Bibl.* iv *under* Imperial Documents.

Diplomata et documenta varia rebus Friderici III illustrandis. Publ. as appendix to Aeneas Silvius. Historia rer. Friderici III Imp. Ed. Kulpis, J. G. Strasbourg. 1685.

Dlugosz, J. Liber beneficiorum dioec. Cracoviensis. Cracow. 1863–4.

Dogiel, M. Codex diplomaticus regni Poloniae. Vilna. 1758.

Dokument do historyi Kopernika. *In* Wiek. No. 64. Warsaw. 1877.

Dokumenta dawnej ekonomii samborskiej. *In* Dodatek do Gazet. lwowskiej. i–iii. Lemberg. 1872.

Dokumenty i akty…Diplomataryusz Kalisza. Kalisz. 1869.

Dokumenty obyasnyayushchie istoryu zapadno-russkago. kraya. (Arkheograf. Kommissiya.) St Petersburg. 1865.

Dokumenty tyczące się biskupstwa Przemyskiego. *In* Przyj. chrześc. prawdy. i–ii. 1833, 40.

Dubiński, P. Zbiór praw i przywilejów Wilnowi nadanych. Vilna. 1788.

Dudik, B. Archive im Königreich Galizien. xxxix. Vienna. 1868.

Edictum Wielunense contra haeresiam Hussiticam sancitum. *In* Volumina legum. i. *See below.*

Ehmck, D. R. and Bippen, W. v. Bremisches Urkundenbuch. Bremen. 1873–80.

Ermisch, H. Schlesiens Verhältniss zu Polen und zu König Albrecht II. *In* Zeitschr. d. Vereins f. Gesch….Schlesiens. xii. 1875.

Fejér, G. Codex diplomaticus Hungariae ecclesiasticus et civilis. Buda. 1827–40.

Fiedler, J. Böhmens Herrschaft in Polen, urkundlicher Beitrag. AOG. xiv. 1855.

Finke, H. Acta concilii Constanciensis. *See Gen. Bibl.* iv *under* Councils.

Friderici III Epistolae. *In* Freher, M. Script. rerum Germanicarum. 3rd edn. by Struve, B. G. Vol. ii. Strasbourg. 1717.

Gercken, P. Codex diplomaticus Brandenburgensis. Salzwedel. 1769–85.

Geschichtsquellen der Provinz Sachsen. Ed. by Hist. Commission der Provinz Sachsen. Halle. 1870 ff.

Grabowski, M. and Przezdiecki, A. Źródla do dziejów polskich. Vilna. 1843–4.

Gramoty velikikh knyazey litovskikh s 1390. Ed. Antonovich and Kozlovsky. Kiev. 1868.

Grünhagen, C. Geschichtsquellen der Hussitenkriege. Breslau. 1871.

—— Urkunden der Stadt Brieg. (Codex diplomaticus Silesiae. ix.) Breslau. 1870.

—— and Markgraf, H. Lehns- und Besitzurkunden Schlesiens. Leipsic. 1881–3.

Halytskiy istoricheskiy Sbornyk. Lemberg. 1860.

Hasselbach, K. F. W. and Kosegarten, J. G. L. Codex Pomeraniae diplomaticus. Greifswald. 1842–62.

Helcel, A. Z. Pomniki z ksiąg…ziemi krakowskiej. Cracow. 1870.

Hennes, J. H. Codex diplomaticus ordinis sanctae Mariae Teutonicorum. Mayence. 1845.

Holovatskiy, J. F. Pamyatniki diplomaticheskoho i sudebnodilovoho yazyka ruskoho v drevnym halitskovolodimirskom knyazhestvi. Lemberg. 1867.

Hube, R. Statuta nieszawskie z roku 1454. Warsaw. 1875.

—— Wyrok lwowski z roku 1421. Warsaw. 1888.

Istoricheski Sbornik Mukhanova. Moscow. 1836.

Jablonowski, A. Sprawy woloskie za Jagiellonów, Akta i Listy. *In* Źródla dziejowe. x. Warsaw. 1878.

Jacobi, T. Codex epistolaris Joannis regis Bohemiae. Berlin. 1841.
Joannis Alberti Statutum Petricoviense. Ed. Bandtkie, J. W. *in* Jus Polonicum. *See above.*
Johannis Hus et Hieronymi Pragensis historia et monumenta. Frankfort. 1715.
Karbowiak, A. Ustawy bursy krakowskiej. Cracow. 1888.
Karpov, G. Istoriya borby moskovskago gosudarstva s polsko-litovskim. Moscow. 1867.
—— Spor mezhdu Litvoyu i Polsheyu o prava na Volynie i Podoliyu. Odessa. 1863.
Kazimierz Jagiellończyk potwierdza przywilej żydowski z roku 1264. Ed. Bandtkie, J. W. *in* Jus Polonicum. *See above.*
Kazimierz nadaje prawo magdeburg. m. Lwowa. Ed. Roepell, R. *in* Ueber d. Verbreitung d. Magdeburger Stadtrechts, u.s.w. *In* Abh. d. hist.-phil. Gesellsch. *in* Breslau. 1857.
Kestner, E. Beiträge zur Geschichte der Stadt Thorn. Thorn. 1883.
Kętrzyński, W. and Smolka, S. Codex diplomaticus monasterii Tynecensis. Lemberg. 1875.
Klose, S. B. Von Breslau. Dokumentirte Geschichte. Breslau. 1781–3.
Köhler, G. Codex diplomaticus Lusatiae superioris. Görlitz. 1851–6.
Konarski, S. Summarium privilegiorum concernentium fundationem Vilnensem. Vilna. 1739.
Korn, G. Breslauer Urkundenbuch. Breslau. 1870.
Krupowicz, M. Zbiór dyplomatów rządowych i aktów prywatnych do dziejów Litwy. Vilna. 1858.
Kulczyński, I. Specimen ecclesiae Ruthenicae. Rome. 1733, 1759.
Labęcki, H. Górnictwo w Polsce. Warsaw. 1841.
Lampe, E. Beiträge zur Gesch. Heinrich von Plauen. Danzig. 1889.
Lauda Cracoviensia. Ed. Bandtkie, J. W. *in* Jus Polonicum. *See above.*
Leges sumptuariae. Ed. Barącz, S. *in* Pamiętnik dziejów polskich. Lemberg. 1855.
Lengnich, G. Jus publicum regni Poloniae. 2 vols. Danzig. 1742–6, 1765.
Lewicki, A. Index actorum saeculi xv. Cracow. 1888.
—— Kazimierz potwierdza przywileje Polski. *In* Rozprawy...Wydz. hist-fil. Akad. Um. xx. Cracow.
Lichnowsky, E. M. von. Geschichte d. Hauses Habsburg. Vienna. 1836–44.
Liske, X. Akta grodzkie i ziemskie z archiwum t.z. Bernadyńskiego we Lwowie. Lemberg. 1868 ff.
List Andrzeja de Palatio o klęsce warneńskiej. Ed. Prochaska. Lemberg. 1882.
Listy Genueńczyków do Kazimierza Jagiellończyka z Kaffy. *In* Pamiętnik hist. lit. i.
Listy Jana Długosza do Zbig. Oleśnickiego. *In* Pamiętnik Warszawski. xiv. Warsaw. 1819.
Listy króla Kazimierza Jag. z roku 1455. *Ibid.*
Listy o Polsce Wincentego Dominica, pisane do Senatu genueńskiego. *In* Bibl. Ossol. pocz. nowy. ii. Lemberg.
Literae pacis perpetuae inter Poloniam et Ordinem Teutonicorum. *In* Volumina legum. i. *See below.*
Lites ac res gestae inter Polonos ordinemque Cruciferorum. Poznań (Posen). 1855.
Lubomirski, T. J. Judiciorum in Polonia libri antiquissimi. Warsaw. 1879.
—— Kodeks dyplomatyczny księstwa Mazowieckiego. Warsaw. 1862.
Lucas, D. Preussische Chronik. Königsberg. 1812.
Lünig, J. C. *See Gen. Bibl.* iv *under* Imperial Documents.
Malinowski, M. Dzieje Bernarda Wapowskiego. Vilna. 1847.
Markgraf, H. Annales Glogovienses mit Urkunden. *In* Script. rerum Silesiacarum. x. 1877. *See below,* iii A.
Martène, E. and Durand, U. Veterum scriptorum et monumentorum amplissima collectio. Paris. 1724–33.
Maurer, R. Urzędnicy kancelaryjni Wladyslawa Jagielly. *In* Biblioteka Warszawska. 1877. iii.
Monumenta Conciliorum generalium saeculi xv. Concilium Basiliense. *See Gen. Bibl.* iv *under* Councils.
Monumenta Hungariae historica. Ser. i. Diplomataria. (*Esp.* Codex dipl. Hungaricus Andegavensis. 7 vols.) Ser. ii. Scriptores. Ser. iv. Acta extera. (Magyar Tudományos Akad.) Budapest. 1857 ff.

Monumenta medii aevi historica res gestas Poloniae illustrantia. i–xi. (Academia Cracoviensis.) Cracow. 1874 ff.

Mosbach, A. Przyczynki do dziejów polskich. Poznań (Posen). 1860.
—— Wiadomości do dziejów polskich. Ostrów. 1860.

Muczkowski, J. Statuta necnon liber promotionum...in universitate...Jagellonica [Cracow]. Cracow. 1849.

Najdawniejsze księgi sądowe krakowskie. Ed. Ulanowski, B. Cracow. 1886.

Narbutt, M. T. Dzieje starożytne narodu litewskiego. Vilna. 1835–41.
—— Pomniki do dziejów litewskich. Vilna.

Niemcewicz, J. U. Zbiór pamiętników o dawnej Polsce. Lemberg. 1833.

Notaty historyczne do czasów Kazimierza Jagiell. *In* Biblioteka Warszawska. 1864. iii.

Obolensky, M. Stosunki diplomatyczne W. X. z Polską Litwą i Tartarami. iv. Moscow. 1842–7.
—— Yarlyk khana zolotoy Ordy Tokhtamisha. Kazan. 1850.

Ordinatio Sabinarum per Casimirum facta. Ed. Bandtkie, J. W. *in* Jus Polonicum. *See above.*

Palacký, F. Urkundliche Beiträge zur Geschichte Böhmens und seiner Nachbarländer im Zeitalter Georgs von Podiebrad. (Fontes rerum Austriacarum. Abt. ii. Vol. xx.) Vienna. 1860.
—— Urkundliche Beiträge zur Gesch. des Hussitenkrieges. 2 vols. Prague. 1872–3.

Pamyatniki diplomaticheskikh snoshenii drevney Rossii. (Sobstvennaya Ego Imp. Vel. Kantselyariya.) St Petersburg. 1851–71.

Panowie woloscy i polscy odbywają zjazd w Chocimiu. Ed. Papée, F. Cracow. 1878.

Papal Registers. *See Gen. Bibl.* iv *under* Papal Documents.

Paprocki, B. Herby rycerstwa polskiego. Cracow. 1584.

Pauli, Ż. Codex diplomaticus Universitatis studii generalis Cracoviensis. Cracow. 1870–84.

Pawlowski, F. Premislia sacra sive series et gesta episcoporum. Cracow. 1869.

Pelzel, F. M. Kaiser Carl IV. Prague. 1780–1.
—— Lebensgeschichte Venceslaus. Prague. 1788–96.

Perlbach, M. Königsberger Regesten. *In* Altpreuss. Monatsschr. xxvii. 1881.
—— Quellen-Beiträge zur Gesch. der Stadt Königsberg. Göttingen. 1878.

Perwolf, J. Prispevsky k českym dejinam xv–xvi stoleti. *In* Časopis Musea českého. Prague. 1880.

Petriceicu, H. Archiva istorica romanie. Bucharest. 1865–7.

Piekosiński, F. Akta sądu leńskiego wyższego w Grodku goleńskim. Cracow. 1889.
—— Codex diplomaticus civitatis Cracoviensis. *In* Monumenta...hist. res gestas Poloniae illustrantia. v and vii. 1879. *See above.*
—— Codex diplomaticus Minoris Poloniae. *Ibid.* iii. 1876 ff.
—— and Szujski, J. Libri antiquissimi civitatis Cracoviensis. *Ibid.* iv. 1878.

Pistorius, J. Polonicae Historiae Corpus. i. Basle. 1582.

Podobizny z rachunków miejskich lwowskich. Lemberg. 1889.

Potkański, K. Zapiski herbowe z dawnych ksiąg ziemskich. Cracow. 1886.

Prawa książąt mazowieckich. Poznań (Posen). 1877.

Privilegium juris Theutonici Cracoviae. Ed. Bandtkie, J. W. *in* Jus Polonicum. *See above.*
—— Ludovici Budae editum. *Ibid.*
—— Vladislai Jagiellonis. *Ibid.*
—— Varsaviae. Ed. Bandtkie, J. W. *in* Jus Culmense. *See above.*

Przezdziecki, A. Regesta wydatków królewskich w Krakowie. *In* Biblioteka Warszawska. 1852. iii.
—— Życie domowe Jadwigi i Jagielly z regestrów skarbowych. Warsaw. 1854.

Przywilej Przemyslawa ks. cieszyńskiego. *In* Pam. Sandom. i. Sandomierz. 1829.

Przywilej Wladyslawa Jagielly w Czerwińsku. *In* Volumina legum. i. *See below.*

Przywileje miasta Brześcia litewskiego. Vilna. 1842.

Pulaski, K. Stosunki z Mengli-Girejem, akta i listy. Warsaw. 1881.

Raczyński, E. Codex diplomaticus Lithuaniae. Breslau. 1845.
—— Codex diplomaticus Majoris Poloniae. Poznań (Posen). 1840.

Radzimiński, Ż. and Gorczak, B. Archiwum kziążąt Lubartowiczów Sanguszków w Slawucie. i. Lemberg. 1887.

Raumer, G. W. Codex diplomaticus Brandenburgensis continuatus. Berlin. 1831–3.
Riedel, A. F. Codex diplomaticus Brandenburgensis. Berlin. 1838–65.
Rogalski, L. Zbiór praw litewskich od r. 1389 do 1529. Poznań (Posen). 1841.
Rozgraniczenie królestwa od Marchii Brandenburg. i Pomorza. Ed. Raczyński, E. *in* Wspom. Wielkopolski. II. Poznań (Posen). 1843.
Rzyszczewski, L. and Muczkowski, A. Codex diplomaticus Poloniae. Warsaw. 1847–87.
Sbornik imperatorskago russkago istorich. obshchestva. xxxv. St Petersburg. 1867 ff.
Schirrmacher, F. W. Urkundenbuch d. Stadt Liegnitz. Liegnitz. 1868.
Schmidt, G. Beiträge zur Geschichte d. Hussitenkriege...1427–31. FDG. VI. 1866.
Schütz, C. Historia Prussiae. Danzig. 1769.
Scriptores rerum Prussicarum. Ed. Hirsch, T., Töppen, M., and Strehlke, E. 5 vols. Leipsic. 1861–74.
Siemieński, J. Diplomatie de l'ancienne Pologne. Poznań (Posen). 1929. [Docs.]
—— Les finances de l'ancienne Pologne. Poznań (Posen). 1929. [Docs.]
Smolka, S. Archiva w W. X. Poznańskiem. Cracow. 1875.
Sobranie gosudarstvennykh gramot i dogovorov v kol. inostrannykh diel. Moscow 1813–28.
Sokolowski, A. and Szujski, J. Codex epistolaris saeculi XV. Cracow. 1876.
Stadnicki, K. Synowie Gedymina. Lemberg. 1881.
Starodawne prawa polskiego pomniki. Ed. Helcel, A. Z. Cracow. 1857–89.
Statut Kazimierza Jagiellończyka. Vilna. 1826.
Statut Wiślicki. Ed. Piliński, A. Poznań (Posen). 1876.
Statut Ziemowita III. *In* Starodawne prawa polskiego pomniki. I.
Statuta Casimiri regis in conv. Petricoviensi. *In* Volumina legum. I. *See below.*
Statuta Casimiri III Visliciae et Petricoviae promulgata. *Ibid.*
Statuta Opatoviensia. Ed. Bandtkie, J. W. *in* Jus Polonicum. *See above.*
Statuta synodalia episc. Conradi, Petri et Rudolphi Vratislav. Breslau. 1475.
Statuta synodalia episcoporum Cracoviensium XIV et XV saeculi. Ed. Heyzmann. Cracow. 1875.
Stefan, wojewoda Moldawski, kupcom lwowskim przywilej ponawia. *In* Dodatek Gazety lwowskiej. No. 40. 1861.
Stenzel, G. A. Urkunden zur Geschichte des Bisthums Breslau im Mittelalter. Breslau. 1845.
—— and Tzschoppe, G. Urkundensammlung zur Gesch. d. Städte in Schlesien und Ober-Lausitz. Hamburg. 1832.
Strehlke, E. Tabulae Ordinis Teutonici. Berlin. 1869.
Stronczyński, K. Wzory pism dawnych. Warsaw. 1839.
Sudendorf, H. Registrum oder merkwürdige Urkunden für die deutsche Geschichte. Jena. 1849 ff.
Szaraniewicz, J. Starodawniye halytskiye horody. Lemberg. 1861–2.
Szujski, J. Uchwały zjazdu w Radomsku w roku 1384. *In* Rozprawy...Wydz. hist.-fil. Akad. Um. I. Cracow. 1874.
Testament Andrzeja, pierwszego biskupa Litwy. Ed. Narbutt. Vilna. 1856.
Theiner, A. Vetera monumenta historica Hungariam sacram illustrantia. 2 vols. Rome. 1859–60.
Thunert, F. Acten der Ständetage 1466–71. Leipsic. 1888.
Töppen, M. Acten der Ständetage Preussens unter dem Deutschen Orden. Leipsic. 1878–88.
Uchwały walnego zjazdu w Piotrkowie. Ed. Prochaska, A. *In* Ateneum. 1887. II.
Uchwały zjazdu piotrkowskiego 1406 i 1407 r. Zjazdy piotrkowskie z 1406 i 1471. *In* Rozprawy...Wydz. hist.-fil. Akad. Um. I and XXI. Cracow.
Ulanowski, B. Inscriptiones clenodiales. Cracow. 1885.
—— Laudum Vartense. *In* Rozprawy...Wydz. hist.-fil. Akad. Um. XXI. Cracow.
—— Libri formularum XV saec. Cracow. 1888.
—— Materyaly do historyi prawa i heraldyki. Cracow. 1886.
—— Roty przysiąg krakowskich z lat 1399–1418. Cracow. 1883.
—— Wybór zapisek kaliskich. *In* Archiwum Komisyi hist. III. Cracow. 1886.
—— Wyjątki z najdawniejszej księgi miejskiej lubelskiej. *Ibid.* IV.

Ulyanitsky, W. Materyaly dlya istorii otnoshenii Rossii, Polshy, Moldavii, Valakhii, i Turtsii v. xiv—xv v. Moscow. 1887.
Urkunden des Kloster Czarnowanz. Breslau. 1857.
Urkundl. Beiträge z. Geschichte d. Kriege d. Deutschen Ordens. *In* Allg. Archiv f. d. Geschichtskunde d. preuss. Staates. Ed. Ledebur, L. von. vii. Berlin, etc. 1832.
Voigt, J. Codex diplomaticus Prussicus. Königsberg. 1836–61.
—— Die Erwerbung d. Neumark. Berlin. 1863.
—— Geschichte Preussens. vi–ix. Königsberg. 1834–9.
—— and Schubert, J. Editio Lindenblatts Jahrbücher. Königsberg. 1823.
Volumina legum. Ed. Konarski, S. H. and others. Warsaw. 1732–68.
Wajda, K. Poselstwo czeskie (1465–66). *In* Dziennik Warszawski. No. 199. Warsaw. 1854.
Werunsky, E. Excerpta ex registris Clementis VI et Innocenti VI...historiam S. R. Imperii sub regimine Caroli IV illustrantia. Innsbruck. 1885.
Wiernicke, E. J. Geschichte Thorns. i, ii. Thorn. 1839, 42.
Wierzbowski, T. Hold Kazimierza Grzegorzowi w tajn. *In* Arch. watykańskim. Klosy. xxxiii. 1881.
—— Synopsis legatorum in Polonia. Rome. 1880.
Wiszniewski, M. Pomniki historyi i literatury polskiej. Cracow. 1835.
Woelky, C. P. Urkundenbuch d. Bisthums Culm. Danzig. 1884–7.
—— and Saage, M. Codex diplomaticus Warmiensis. Mayence. 1860–74.
Wojna Warneńska. Ed. Sękowski, J. J. S. *in* Collectanea. i. Warsaw. 1824.
Wolff, J. Senatorowie i dygnitarze W. X. Litewskiego. Cracow. 1885.
Wuttke, H. Städtebuch des Landes Posen. Leipsic. 1864.
Wypisy z aktów siewierskich. *In* Pam. Sandom. i. 1829.
Wyslocki, W. Liber diligentiarum. Cracow. 1886.
W. W. Przywilej Kazimierza W. dany Żydom. *In* Przewodnik nauk. lit. 1873.
Zakrzewski, J. Codex diplomaticus Majoris Poloniae. i. (Tow. Przyj. Nauk. Poznań.) Poznan (Posen). 1877–81.
Zeissberg, H. Analecten z. Gesch. d. xv Jahrh. *In* Zeitschr. f. d. österr. Gym. Vienna. 1871.
Zeitschrift des Vereins für Geschichte und Alterthum Schlesiens. Breslau. 1856 ff.
Zellmer, W. Zur polnischen Politik d. Kurfürsten Friedrich II von Brandenburg. Berlin. 1883.
Zieliński, F. Poszukiwanie historyczne nad finansami polskiemi w xiv i xv wiekach. *In* Biblioteka Warszawska. 1849. ii.
Zubrzycki, M. Kronika miasta Lwowa. Lemberg. 1844.

III. CHRONICLES, ETC.

A. Collections.

Monumenta Germaniae Historica. Scriptores. *See Gen. Bibl.* iv.
Monumenta historiae Warmiensis. (Hist. Verein für Ermland.) 8 vols. Mayence, etc. 1860–89.
Monumenta historica Boemiae. Ed. Dobner, G. 6 vols. Prague. 1764–86.
Monumenta Poloniae historica. Ed. Bielowski, A. and others. 6 vols. Lemberg, etc. 1864–93.
Polnoe Sobranie russkikh lêtopisey. (Arkheograf. Kommissiya.) St Petersburg. 1846 ff.
Scriptores rerum Bohemicarum. Vols. i, ii, ed. Pelzel, F. M. and Dobrovský, J. Prague. 1783–4. Vol. iii, ed. Palacký, F. 1829.
Scriptores rerum Hungaricarum. Ed. Schwandtner, J. G. 3 vols. Vienna. 1746–8.
Scriptores rerum Prussicarum. Ed. Hirsch, T., Töppen, M., and Strehlke, E. 5 vols. Leipsic. 1861–74.
Scriptores rerum Silesiacarum. Vols. i–v, ed. Stenzel, G. A. Breslau. 1835–51. Vols. vi–xvii, ed. by Verein für Gesch. und Alterthum Schlesiens. Breslau. 1871–1902.

B. SPECIAL.

Acta de interceptione castri Allenstein (1455–61). *In* Monumenta hist. Warmiensis. I. *See above*, III A.

Aeltere Hochmeister Chronik. Script. rerum Prussicarum. III. *See above*, III A.

Aeneas Sylvius (Pius II). De Polonia, Lithuania, et Prussia. Ed. Pistorius, J. *in* Polonicae Historiae Corpus. I. Basle. 1582.

—— De situ et origine Pruthenorum 1410–54. *In* Script. rerum Prussicarum. IV.

—— Historia Bohemica. *In* Opera geog. et hist. Frankfort and Leipsic. 1707.

Annales canonici Sambienses. *In* Monumenta Poloniae hist. *See above*, III A.

Annales Cujavienses. *Ibid.*

Annales Dunamundenses. *Ibid.*

Annales Glogovienses ad 1493. *In* Script. rerum Silesiacarum. x. *See above*, III A.

Annales Magdeburgenses (1453–60). MGH. Script. XVI.

Annales Magistratus Vratislaviensis. *In* Monumenta Poloniae hist. III.

Annales Miechovienses. *Ibid.*

Annales Poznanienses. *Ibid.*

Bitschen, A. Continuatio Chronicae Polonorum (1409–71). *In* Script. rerum Silesiacarum. II.

Blumenau, Laurentius. Historia de Ordine Theutonicorum (1226–1455). *In* Script. rerum Prussicarum. IV. *See above*, III A.

Boucicaut, Mémoires du maréchal. *In* Petitot, C. B. Collection...des mém. relatifs à l'hist. de France. VI, VII. Paris. 1819.

Calendarium Cartusiae Dantiscanae (1395–1564). (Necrologium Dantiscanum.) *In* Monumenta Poloniae hist. IV.

Callimachus Buonaccorsi, P. De Vita et moribus Gregorii Sanocensis. *In* Monumenta Poloniae hist. VI.

—— Historia de rege Vladislao IV. *Ibid.*

—— Vita et mores Sbignei Cardinalis. *Ibid.*

Chronica Hungariae. Ed. Florianus, M. *in* Historiae Hungaricae fontes domestici. Pt. I. Vol. III. Leipsic. 1884.

Chronica Hungarorum antiqua (Chronicon Budense). Buda. 1838.

Contarini, A. Itinerario nel anno 1472. Venice. 1574.

Dalimil Meseryczni Kronyka Boleslavská. Ed. Hanka. Prague. 1849, 51.

Danziger Chronik, Die. *In* Script. rerum Prussicarum. IV.

Dlugosz, J. Opera omnia. Ed. Przezdziecki, A. 14 vols. Cracow. 1863–87.

—— Historiae Polonicae libri XII (XIII). 2 vols. Leipsic. 1711–12. [*Also* ed. in the preceding.]

Eschenloer, P. Geschichte der Stadt Breslau. Ed. Kunisch, J. G. 2 vols. Breslau. 1827–8.

Expulsio Judaeorum 1453. *In* Monumenta Poloniae hist. III.

Fragment epopei lacinskiej z końca xv wieku. Ed. Kętrzyński. Lemberg. 1887.

Fragmentum expeditionis Ludovici regis Hungariae cum Casimiro 1351. Ed. Lewicki, A. *in* Kwartalnik hist. 1889. p. 205.

Geschichte von wegen eines Bundes (1422–62). *In* Script. rerum Prussicarum. IV.

Gesta abbatum monasterii s. Vincentii. *In* Script. rerum Silesiacarum. II.

Guilbert de Lannoy. Voyages et ambassades. Mons. 1830.

Henricus Sbignei de Gora. Tractatulus contra Cruciferos. *In* Monumenta Poloniae hist. IV.

Historia brevis magistri Theutonici. *In* Script. rerum Prussicarum. IV.

[Hus and Hussites.] Geschichtschreiber der husitischen Bewegung in Böhmen. Ed. Höfler, K. 3 vols. '(Fontes rerum Austriacarum. Abt. I. Vols. II, VI, VII.) Vienna. 1856–66.

Inventaria ecclesiae S. Mariae Vislicensis. *In* Monumenta Poloniae hist. V.

Joannes de Czarnkow. Chronicon Polonorum. Ed. Szlachtowski. *In* Monumenta Poloniae hist. II.

Joannis de Zredna, Epistolae. *In* Script. rerum Hungaricarum. II.

Johannes de Thurocz. Illustrissima Hungariae Chronica. *Ibid.*

Jonsdorff, B. Böhmische Chronik (1471–90). *In* Script. rerum Silesiacarum. XII.

Jüngere Hochmeisterchronik. *In* Script. rerum Prussicarum. V.

Jüngere livländische Reimchronik des Barthol-Hoeneke 1315-48. Ed. Höhlbaum, K. Leipsic. 1872.
Kalendarz czerwiński (1345-1425). *In* Monumenta Poloniae hist.
Kalendarz wladyslawski (1324-46). *Ibid.* II.
Korner, Hermann. Chronica novella. Ed. Eccardus, J. G. *in* Corpus hist. medii aevi. Leipsic. 1723.
Latopisiec Litwy. Ed. Danilowicz, J. Vilna. 1827.
Laurentius Corvinus. Cosmographia. Basle. 1496.
Libenwald, Memoriale Bartholomei. *In* Monumenta historiae Warmiensis. I.
Lindaus, J. Geschichte des 13-jährigen Krieges. *In* Script. rerum Prussicarum. IV.
Lubbe, Jacob. Familien Chronik (1400-1518). *In* Script. rerum Prussicarum. IV.
Narratio de interitu illustrissimi ducis Opoliensis Nicolai 1497 a. *In* Script. rerum Silesiacarum. XII.
Notae Caminenses (1495-96). MGH. XIX.
Notae Cracovienses (1331-1420). *In* Monumenta Poloniae hist. VI.
Notae de universitate studii Cracoviensis (1400-94). *Ibid.*
Notae Gnesnenses (1454-59). *Ibid.*
Notae Lublinenses (1456-97). *Ibid.* III.
Notatki kupca krakowskiego w podroży do Flandryi 1401-2. Ed. Pawiński, A. *in* Biblioteka Warszawska. 1872.
O Spustoszenie Sambora roku 1498. *In* Monumenta Poloniae hist. III.
Obwarowanie miasta Wilna murem obronnym. Ed. Narbutt *in* Ateneum. 1848. III.
Opis zabycia Tęczyńskiego i Proces. *In* Monumenta Poloniae hist. III.
Oratio contra Cruciferos 1464. *Ibid.* IV.
Ostroróg, J. Monumentum pro comitiis generalibus Regni sub rege Casimiro pro reipublicae ordinatione congestum. Ed. Bandtkie, J. W. Warsaw. 1831.
Pamię niki Janczara Polaka. Warsaw. 1828.
Podróż po Polsce z XV wieku. Ed. Przezdziecki, A. *in* Biblioteka Warszawska. 1844. IV.
Pole, Paul. Preussische Chronik (1422-1532). *In* Script. rerum Prussicarum. V.
Ratiborer Chronik (1300-1463). Ed. Weltzel *in* Zeitschr. d. Vereins f. Gesch.... Schlesiens. V.
Rocznik Jana z Targowiska (1386-1491). *In* Monumenta Poloniae hist. III.
Rocznik krośnieński (1427-98). *Ibid.*
Rocznik świętokrzyski (1484-90). *Ibid.*
Rosicz, S. Chronica et numerus episcoporum Vratislaviensium. *In* Script. rerum Silesiacarum. XII.
Schedel, H. De Sarmatia. Ed. Pistorius, J. *in* Polonicae Historiae Corpus. I. Basle. 1582.
Sermo de morte Vladislai. AOG. IX.
Spominki bochnieńskie (1423-47). *In* Monumenta Poloniae hist. III.
Spominki kazimierskie (1422-73). *Ibid.*
Spominki krakowskie (1410-61). *Ibid.*
Spominki lwowskie (1351-1454). *Ibid.*
Spominki mieszane (1072-1492). *Ibid.*
Spominki Minorytów samborskich (1455-1501). *Ibid.*
Spominki o haskach (1392-1515). *Ibid.*
Spominki plockie (1055-1357). *Ibid.*
Spominki przeworskie (1386 and 1482). *Ibid.*
Spominki sochaczewskie (1124-1462). *Ibid.*
Spominki wiślickie (1305-1479). *Ibid.*
Suffragia monasterii Mogilnensis (1179-1485). *In* Monumenta Poloniae hist. V.
Vita Caroli IV. Ed. Emler, J. *in* Fontes rerum Bohemicarum. III. Prague. 1882.
Vita fratris Nicolai de Magna Kosmin. *In* Monumenta Poloniae hist. V.
Vita Sbignei Cardinalis. Ed. Dlugosz, J. *in* Opera Omnia. I. *See above.*
Weinrich, C. Danziger Chronik (1461-95). *In* Script. rerum Pruss. IV.
Wigand von Marburg. Chronik. Ed. Voight, J. and Raczyński, E. Königsberg. 1840.
Wtargnięcie Turków w roku 1498. Ed. Sękowski, J. *in* Collectanea. I. Warsaw. 1824.
Zapiski. A. Przekory (1457-59). *In* Monumenta Poloniae hist. III.

IV. MODERN WORKS.

A. General.

Albertrandy, J. Dwadzieścia sześć lat panowania Wladyslawa Jagielly. Breslau. 1845.
—— Panowanie Kazimierza Jagiellończyka. Warsaw. 1826–7.
Altmann, W. Geschichte der Erhebung des Peterpfennigs in Polen. *In* Zeitschr. f. Gesch. v. Posen. 1889.
Balzer, O. O następstwie tronu w Polsce. i. Cracow. 1897.
Barbashev, A. Vitovt i yeǵo polityka do Grunwaldskoy bitvy. St Petersburg. 1885.
—— Vitovt, Posledniya dvadtsat lyet kniazheniya. St Petersburg. 1890.
Bobrzynski, M. Dzieje Polski w zarysie. Cracow. 1887.
—— O ustawodawstwie Nieszawskim. Cracow. 1874.
—— Sejmy za Olbrachta i Aleksandra. *In* Ateneum. 1876. ii.
—— and Smolka, S. Jan Dlugosz, jego życie i stanowisko. Cracow. 1893.
Bujak, C. Der Deutsche Orden und Herzog Witold von Litauen. Königsberg. 1869.
Caro, J. Geschichte Polens. Vols. ii–v. (Heeren. *See Gen. Bibl.* v.) Gotha. 1863-88.
Celichowski, Z. Spory i sprawy między Polakami i Zakonem krzyżackim. Poznań (Posen). 1890, 92.
Choiseul-Gouffier, S. Vladislav Jagellon et Hedvige. Paris. 1824.
Czermak, W. Jadwiga królowa polska. Lemberg. 1887.
—— Polska za času Kazimira Velikego. Prague. 1873.
Czermy, F. Panowanie Jana Olbrachta i Aleksandra Jagiellończyków. Cracow. 1871.
Dargun, L. O źródlach prawa miast polskich. Cracow. 1888.
Denis, E. Fin de l'indépendance de la Bohême. i. Paris. 1891.
Dzieduszycki, M. Zbigniew Oleśnicki. Cracow. 1854.
Fiedler, J. Böhmens Herrschaft in Polen. AOG. xiv. 1855.
Filevich, J. P. Bor'ba Polshy i Litvy-Rusy. Istor. ocherki. St Petersburg. 1890.
Finkel, L. Marcin Kromer. Cracow. 1883.
Foerster, R. Vladislaus Jagiello II rex Poloniae et Hungariae. Breslau. 1871.
Forsten. Bor'ba iz za gospodarstva na baltiyskom morie v xv i xvi stol. St Petersburg. 1884.
Golębiowski, L. Dzieje Polski. Warsaw. 1846–8.
Gorski, K. Bitwa pod Grunwaldem. *In* Biblioteka Warszawska. 1888. iii.
Gorzycki, K. J. Kwestya lennego zwierzchnictwa Polski do Pomorza. Lemberg. 1895.
—— Wplyw Stolicy apostolskiej na rokowania pokojowe Kazimierza W. z Czechami i Zakonem. Lemberg. 1893.
Grosse, L. Stosunki Polski z soborem Bazylejskim. Warsaw. 1885.
Halecki, O. La Pologne de 963 à 1914. Paris. 1933.
Hirschberg, A. Koalicya Francyi z Jagiellonami z roku 1500. Lemberg. 1882.
Hlebowicz, A. B. Krótki zarys życia Witolda. Vilna. 1821.
Hrushevsky, M. Pokhvala v. kn. Vitovta. *In* Zapiski Tov. Shevchenk. viii. Lemberg. 1895.
Hube, R. Prawo polskie w xiv wieku. Warsaw. 1881.
—— Statuta Nieszawskie z roku 1454. *In* Bibl. umiej. prawn. Warsaw. 1876.
Jounot, L. P. and Straszewicz, J. Hedvige reine de Pologne. Paris. 1838.
Karpov, G. Istoriya bor'by moskovskago gosudarstva s pol'sko-litovskim, 1462–1508. Moscow. 1867.
Karyeyev, M. Istor. ocherk polskago seyma. Moscow. 1888.
Klaczko, J. Une annexation d'autrefois. *In* Revue des deux mondes. 1869.
Kniazolucki, Z. Johann I Albrecht, König von Polen. Leipsic. 1875.
Kochanowski, J. K. Kazimierz Wielki. Warsaw. 1900.
Koneczny, F. Jagiello i Witold. Lemberg. 1893.
—— Polityka Zakonu 1389 i 1390. Cracow. 1889.
Konopczyński, L. Le Liberum Veto. Étude sur le développement du principe majoritaire. Paris. 1930.
Kotzebue, A. Switrigail. Leipsic. 1820.
Krasinski, W. O Czechachi Polsce w wiek. xiv–xvi. Warsaw. 1857.

Kutrzeba, S. Historya ustroju Polski w zarysie. Lemberg. 1908.
—— Sejm Walny dawnej Rzeczypospolitej Polskiej. *In* Biblioteka Skladnicy. Warsaw. 1923.
Kwiatkowski, S. Ostatnie lata Wladyslawa Warneńczyka. Lemberg. 1883.
Leniek, J. Kongres Wyszegradzki w roku 1335. Lemberg. 1884.
Lewicki, A. König Johann Albrechts Bericht über den Feldzug von 1497. Cracow. 1892.
—— Nieco o unii Litwy z Koroną. Cracow. 1893.
—— Powstanie Świdrygielly. Cracow. 1892.
—— Unia Florencka w Polsce. *In* Rozprawy...Wydz. hist.-fil. Akad. Um. xxxviii. Cracow. 1899.
—— Wstąpienie na tron Kazimierza Jagiellończyka. Cracow. 1886.
—— Zarys historyi Polskiej. Warsaw. 1913.
Lohmeyer, K. Witowd, Grossfürst von Littauen. Königsberg. 1885.
Lorenz, O. Deutsche Geschichte im xiii und xiv Jahrht. Vol. ii. Vienna. 1867.
Milewski, K. Historya Wladyslawa III. Warsaw. 1823.
Mniszech, M. Kazimierz Wielki. Warsaw. 1777.
Morawski, K. Poselstwo polskie na Koncylium Konstancyeńskiem 1414–18. Cracow. 1897.
Narbutt, T. Dzieje starożytne narodu litewskiego. 9 vols. Vilna. 1835–41.
Palacký, F. Dějiny naroda českého. Prague. 1848–67.
Papée, F. Polityka polska w czasach upadku Jerzego z Podiebradu. Cracow. 1878.
—— Przelom w stosunkach miejskich za Kazimierza Jagiellończyka. *In* Przewodnik nauk. lit. 1883.
Pawiński, A. Sejmiki ziemskie (1374–1505). Warsaw. 1895.
Piekosiński, F. Goście polscy na soborze konstancyjskim. Cracow. 1898.
—— Uwagi nad ustawodawstwem wiślicko-piotrkowskiem. *In* Rozprawy...Wydz. hist.-fil. Akad. Um. xxviii. Cracow. 1891.
—— Zdobycze szlachty polskiej w wieku xv. Cracow. 1900.
Pierling, P. La Prussie et le Saint-Siège. Paris. 1896.
Prochaska, A. Geneza i rojwój parlamentaryzmu za pierwszych Jagiellonów. Cracow. 1898.
—— Kwestya husycka 1425–29. *In* Ateneum. 1887. iii.
—— Na soborze w Konstancyi. Cracow. 1897.
—— O naprawie Rzeczypospolitej Ostroroga. *In* Kwartalnik hist. 1899.
—— Ostatnie lata Witolda. Warsaw. 1882.
—— Polska a Czechy w czasach husyckych. Cracow. 1878.
—— Polska i Husyci po odwolaniu Korybuta z Czech. *In* Przewodnik nauk. lit. 1883.
—— Przyczynki krytyczne do dziejów unii. Cracow. 1896.
—— Stosunki Krzyżakow z Gedyminem i Lokietkiem. *In* Kwartalnik hist. 1896.
—— Świdrygiello. *In* Przewodnik. nauk. lit. 1885.
—— Szkice historyczne w xv w. Cracow and Warsaw. 1885.
Przezdziecki, A. Życie domowe Jadwigi i Jagielly. *In* Biblioteka Warszawska. 1853. iii, iv. 1854. i, ii.
Przylęcki, S. Wspomnienia o Wladyslawie Warneńczyku. Lemberg. 1844.
Pulaski, K. Stosunki z Mendli-Girejem. Cracow. 1881.
—— Stosunki z Tatarszczyzną w polowie xv wieku. *In* Ateneum. 1882. ii.
R.G.K. Bitwa pod Grunwaldem. *In* Lwowianin. i. Lemberg. 1837.
Rakowski, K. Entstehung des Grossgrundbesitzes im xv und xvi Jahrht. in Polen. Poznań (Posen). 1899.
Rembowski, A. Reprezentacya stanowa w Polsce. *In* Biblioteka Warszawska. 1893.
Seredyński, W. Gregorz z Sanoka, arcyb. lwowski. Cracow. 1867.
Smolka, S. Kiejstut i Jagiello. Cracow. 1888.
—— Polska i Brandenburgia za czasów Jagielly. Warsaw. 1896.
—— Polska wobec wojen husyckich. *In* Ateneum. 1879. i.
—— Spór z Kościolem. Szkice Hist. ii. Warsaw. 1883.
Sokolowski, A. Ostatni obrońcy hussytyzmu w Polsce. Cracow. 1870.
—— Stosunki polsko-czeskie za czasów wojen husyckich. *In* Dziennik lit. 1868.

Stadnicki, K. Bracia Wladyslawa Jagielly. Lemberg. 1867.
—— Olgierd i Kiejstut. Lemberg. 1870.
—— Synowie Gedymina. Lemberg. 1881.
Sutowicz, J. Walka Kazimierza Jagiellończyka z Maciejem Korwinem. Cracow. 1877.
Szajnocha, K. Gedyminowicze. *In* Biblioteka Warszawska. 1853. IV.
—— Jadwiga i Jagiello. Lemberg. 1855–6.
—— Król Louis. *In* Biblioteka Warszawska. 1853. III.
—— Pierwsze odrodzenie się Polski. Lemberg. 1849.
—— Wiek Kazimierza W. Szkice hist. Lemberg. 1854.
Szujski, J. Charakterystyka Kazimierza W. *In* Przewodnik nauk. lit. 1876.
—— Odrodzenie i reformacya w Polsce. Cracow. 1881.
—— Opowiadania i roztrząsania historyczne. Cracow. 1876.
—— Warunki traktatu kaliskiego 1343 roku. Cracow. 1888.
Tatomir, L. Mieszczanin krakowski z xiv wieku. Lemberg. 1861.
—— O królu Kazimierzu Wielkim. Lemberg. 1868.
Thunert, F. Der grosse Krieg zwischen Polen und d. Deutschen Orden, 1410–11. *In* Zeitschr. d. Westpreuss. Geschichtsvereins. XVI. Danzig. 1886.
Toplicki. Abrégé de l'histoire de la maison de Jagiellon. Vilna. 1776.
Ulanowski, B. Przyczynki do hist. stosunków między kósciolem a państwem. 1446–7. Cracow. 1889.
—— Trzy zabitki do historyi parlamentaryzmu w Polsce w xv wieku. Cracow. 1893.
Ulyanitsky, V. Materialy dlya istorii otnosheniy Rosii, Polshy, Moldavii, Valakhii, i Turtsii v xiv–xv v. Moscow. 1887.
Vasilevsky, V. Obrashchenie Gedemina v katolichestvo. *In* Zhurnal Ministerstva narodnago prosveshchenia. CLXXIX. St Petersburg. 1872.
Wegner, L. Jan Ostroróg i jego pamiętnik. Poznań (Posen). 1858.
Werunsky, E. Geschichte Kaiser Karls IV. Innsbruck. 1880–92.
Zellmer, W. Zur polnischen Politik des Kurfürsten Friedrich II von Brandenburg. Pt. I. Berlin. 1883.

B. SPECIAL.

Abraham, W. Sprawa Muskaty. Cracow. 1893.
—— Statuta legata Gentilisa. Cracow. 1893.
—— Stanowisko komisyi papieskiej wobec koronacyi Lokietka. Lemberg. 1900.
Arndt, R. Die Beziehungen König Sigmunds zu Polen. Halle. 1897.
Badeni, S. H. Stanislaw Ciolek. Cracow. 1900.
Balzer, O. Laudum Cracoviense. Studya. Poznań (Posen). 1888.
Bitwa pod Plowcami. Przyj. dom v. Lemberg. 1855.
Bobrzyński, M. Bunt wojta krakowskiego Alberta z roku 1311. *In* Biblioteka Warszawska. 1877. III.
—— Wiadomość o uchwalach zjazdu Piotrkowskiego roku 1406. Cracow. 1873.
Brandowski, A. Baron Maciej Borkowicz. Poznań (Posen). 1879.
Breiter, E. Wladyslaw książe opolski. Lemberg. 1889.
Chyliński, M. Pamflet Falkenberga. *In* Ateneum. 1878. III.
Daenell, E. R. Polen und die Hanse um die Wende des 14 Jahrht. DZG. 1898.
Dubiecki, M. Kaffa…i jej stosunek do Polski w xv wieku. Obrazy i studya hist. II. Warsaw. 1899.
Gumplowicz, L. Prawodawstwo polskie względem Żydów. Cracow. 1867.
Hoszowski, K. Żywot Jana Muskaty. Cracow. 1866.
Hube, R. Przyczynki do objaśnień historyi Statuta wiślickiego. Warsaw. 1853.
—— Statut Wartski. *In* Biblioteka Warszawska. 1874. II.
—— Wyrok lwowski z roku 1421. Warsaw. 1888.
Jablonowski, A. Koleje dziejowe zreszenia się Slowian pólnocnych od polowy xv wieku. *In* Kwart. Klosów. I. Warsaw. 1877.
Jekel, F. J. Polens Handelsgeschichte. Vienna and Trieste. 1809.
Klöden, K. F. Die Mark Brandenburg unter K. Karl IV. Berlin. 1836–7.
Kubala, L. Jan Czarnkowski i jego kronika. Warsaw. 1871.
Kwiatkowski, S. Jan Giskra z Brandysu. Lemberg. 1886.

Lęgowski, J. Der Hochmeister des Deutschen Ordens Konrad von Wallenrod. Königsberg. 1879.

Lelewel, J. Krytyczny rozbiór wiślickiego statuta. *In* Rocznik Tow. Przyj. Nauk. xx, xxi. Warsaw. 1828–30.

Lewicki, A. Ein Blick in die Politik König Sigmunds gegen Polen. Vienna. 1886.

—— Król Zygmunt a Polska 1420–36. *In* Kwartalnik hist. 1896.

—— Powstanie Świdrygielly. Cracow. 1892.

—— Przymierze Zygmunta w. ks. litewskiego z Albrechtem II. Cracow. 1898.

Maurer, R. Stanislaus Ciolek. Brody. 1883.

Morawski, K. Historya Uniwersytetu Jagiellońskiego. Cracow. 1900.

Pfitzner, J. Grossfürst Witold von Litauen als Staatsmann. Brünn. 1930.

Potkański, K. Daty zjazdów koszyckich. Cracow. 1900.

—— Sprawa restitucyi roku 1374 i 1381. Cracow. 1900.

—— Zdrada Wincentego z Szamotul. Cracow. 1899.

Prochaska, A. Konfederacya Spytka z Melsztyna. Lemberg. 1887.

—— Konrad Wallenrod w poezyi i w dziejach. *In* Przewodnik nauk. lit. 1875.

—— Podole lennem Korony. Cracow. 1895.

—— Zawisza Czarny. Sykice hist. 1884.

—— Zjazd monarchów w Lucku. *In* Przewodnik nauk. lit. 1874.

Semkowicz, A. Żony Kazimierza Wielkiego. *In* Kwartalnik hist. 1898.

Smolka, S. Witold pod Grunwaldem. Szkice hist. i. Warsaw. 1882.

Sutowicz, J. Zjazd Lucki. Cracow. 1875.

Świeżowski, E. Sulimczyk, Esterka i inne kobiety Kazimierza Wielkiego. Warsaw. 1894.

—— Zjazd 1404 roku w Korczynie. *In* Ateneum. 1899. ii.

Szujski, J. Uchwaly zjazdu w Radomsku w roku 1384. *In* Rozprawy...Wydz. hist.-fil. Akad. Um. i. Cracow. 1874.

Taube, F. W. Ludwig d. Ältere als Markgraf von Brandenburg. Berlin. 1900.

Tosti, L. Storia di Bonifazio VIII e di suoi tempi. Monte Cassino. 1846.

Turkawski, D. M. Spytko z Melsztyna. Lemberg. 1876.

Ulanowski, B. Laudum Vartense. Cracow. 1887.

—— Zjazdy piotrkowskie 1406–7. Cracow. 1888.

Weinert, A. O starostwach w Polsce. Warsaw. 1877.

C. REGIONAL.

Abraham, W. Statuta synodu prow. w Kaliszu. Cracow. 1888.

Amanton, P. C. N. Vladislav duc de Cujavie. Dijon. 1842.

Andryashev, A. Ocherk istor. volynskoy zemli do kontsa xiv st. Kiev. 1887.

Boldt, F. Die Deutsche Orden und Littauen, 1370–86. Königsberg. 1870.

Czolowski, A. Początki Moldavii i wyprawa Kazimierza Wielkiego. *In* Kwartalnik hist. 1890.

Dovnar-Zapolsky, M. Gosudarstvennoye hozyaystvo litovskoy Rusi pri Yagellonakh. *In* Kiev-univ. Izvest. Kiev. 1900.

—— Iz istorii litovsko-polskoy bor'by za Volyn. Kiev. 1896.

Ermisch, H. Schlesiens Verhältniss zu Polen und zu Albrecht II. *In* Zeitschr. d. Vereins f. Gesch....Schlesiens. xii. 1875.

Fedorowicz, K. Dostojnicy i urzędnicy świeccy wojewodztwa krakowskiego 1374—1506. *In* Archiw. Kom. hist. Akad. Krak. Cracow. 1896.

Gorzycki, K. J. Kwestya lennego zwierzchnictwa Polski do Pomorza. Lemberg. 1895.

—— Połączenie Rusi Czerwonej z Polską. Lemberg. 1889.

Grünhagen, C. Schlesien unter Karl IV. *In* Zeitschr. d. Vereins f. Gesch.... Schlesiens. xvii.

Heinemann, O. Das Bündniss zwischen Polen und Pommern 1325, 1348, und 1466. *In* Zeitschr. d. hist. Gesellsch. f. d. Provinz Posen. xiii, xiv. 1898–9.

Heinl, K. Fürst Witold von Litauen in seinen Verhältnissen zum Deutschen Orden, 1382–1401. (Ebering's Hist. Studien, 165.) Berlin. 1925.

Jablonowski, A. Sprawy woloskie za Jagiellonów. Warsaw. 1878.

Kujot, S. Piotr Święca a Wladyslaw Lokietek. *In* Warta. iii. Poznań (Posen). 1876–7.
Kunasiewicz, S. Zajęcie Rusi. Lemberg. 1874.
Linnichenko, Y. A. Cherty iz istorii sosloviy v yugo-zapadnoy Rusi xiv–xv v. Moscow. 1894.
Lyubavsky, M. K. Oblastnoye dyelenie litovsko-russkago gosudarstva. Moscow. 1892.
—— Ocherk istorii litovsko-russkago gosudarstva. Moscow. 1910.
Milkovich, V. Studia krytychni nad istoryeyu russko-polskoyu. i. Lemberg. 1893.
Papée, F. La Lithuanie pendant les douze dernières années du règne de Casimir IV, 1480–92. Cracow. 1900.
Potkański, K. Walka o Poznań, 1306–12. Cracow. 1899.
Reifenkugel, K. Die Gründung der römisch-katholischen Bisthümer in den Territorien Halicz und Wladimir. Vienna. 1874.
Soloviev, S. Krestonostsy i Litva. *In* Otech. Zapiski. lxxxii. 1852.
Stadnicki, K. O początkach arcybiskupstwa i biskupstw katolickich na Rusi halickiej i Wolyniu. Lemberg. 1882.
—— Ziemia lwowska za rządow polskich w xiv i xv wieku. Lemberg. 1863.
Tatomir, L. Chrzest Litwy. Lemberg. 1886.
Wagner, A. Schlesisches aus dem vaticanischen Archive aus den Jahren 1316–71. *In* Zeitschr. d. Vereins f. Gesch....Schlesiens. xxv. 1891.
Wojcicki, K. Ksią e bialy Wladyslaw. Szkice hist. Cracow. 1869.

CHAPTER XIX.

HUNGARY, 1301–1490.

[*See also* the Bibliography of Vol. vi, ch. xiii (c), pp. 930–33.]

I. BIBLIOGRAPHIES.

Áldásy, A. A xv század nyugati elbeszélő forrásai. (Western narrative sources of history of the xvth century.) *In the Series:* A Magyar Történettudomány Kézikönyve. (Manual of historical sciences.) Ed. Hóman, B. i, vii (c). Budapest. 1928.

Bartoniek, E. Magyar történeti forráskiadványok. (Bibliography of Hungarian historical sources.) *Ibid.* i, iii (b). Budapest. 1929.

Bibliographia Hungariae. Verzeichnis der Ungarn betreffenden Schriften in nichtungarischer Sprache. Vol. i. Historica. (Ungarische Bibliothek. Ed. Gragger, R. iii, i.) Berlin. 1923.

Eckhart, F. Introduction à l'histoire hongroise. *See below,* iv a.

Flegler, A. Geschichte der ungarischen Geschichtsschreibung. 19..

Hóman, B. A forráskutatás és forráskritika története. (History of historical research and criticism in Hungary.) *In the series:* A Magyar Történettudomány Kézikönyve. Ed. Hóman, B. i, iii (a). Budapest. 1925.

Kont, I. Bibliographie française de la Hongrie (1521–1910). Paris. 1913.

Mangold, L. A magyarok oknyomozó története. (Pragmatic history of Hungary.) 4th edn. Budapest. 1903.

—— and Auner, M. Ungarn. *In* Jahresberichte der Geschichtswissenschaft. Jahrg. 1913. Berlin. 1916.

Szekfü, J. Der Staat Ungarn. *See below,* iv a.

Timon, Á. Ungarische Verfassungs- und Rechtsgeschichte. *See below,* iv a.

Ungarische Jahrbücher. Ed. Gragger, R. and others. Berlin. 1921 ff.

II. DOCUMENTARY SOURCES AND COLLECTIONS.

Altmann, W. Regesta Imperii. Die Urkunden Kaiser Sigmunds (1410–37). *See Gen. Bibl.* iv *under* Imperial Documents.

Berzeviczy, A., Gerevich, T., and Jakubovich, E. Beatrix magyar királyné életére vonatkozó okiratok. (Documents referring to the life of Queen Beatrice.) *In* Monumenta Hungariae historica. Ser. i. Vol. xxxix. Budapest. 1914.

Birk, E. Beiträge zur Geschichte der Königin Elisabeth und des Königs Ladislaus (1440–57). *In* Quellen und Forschungen zur vaterländ. Geschichte. 1849.

Bossányi, Á. Regesta supplicationum, 1342–94. *See Gen. Bibl.* iv *under* Papal Documents.

Chmel, J. Urkunden zur Geschichte Albrechts. Vienna. 1853.

Corpus Iuris Hungarici. Ed. Márkus, D. Budapest. 1896.

Diplomatarium Habsburgense seculi xv. Ed. Chmel, J. (Fontes rerum Austriacarum. Abt. ii. Vol. ii.) Vienna. 1850.

Fejér, G. Codex diplomaticus Hungariae ecclesiasticus et civilis. Vols. i–xi. Buda. 1829–44.

Fraknói, V. Oklevéltár a kegyuri jog történetéhez. (Monumenta historiam iuris patronatus illustrantia.) Budapest. 1899.

Kaprinai, S. Hungaria diplomatica temporibus Mathiae de Hunyad regis Hungariae. 2 pts. Vienna. 1767, 71.

Katona, S. Historia critica regum Hungariae. 42 vols. Buda, etc. 1778–1817.

Kovachich, J. N. Sylloge decretorum comitialium regni Hungariae. 2 vols. Pest. 1818.

Kronthal, B. and Wendt, H. Politische Correspondenz Breslaus im Zeitalter des Königs Mathias Corvinus. Abt. i, 1469–79. Abt. ii, 1479–90. Breslau. 1893–4.

Magyar Történelmi Tár. (Hungarian Historical Journal.) Vols. i–xxv. Pest. 1833–77. Vol. xxvi. Budapest. 1914.

Marczali, H. Enchiridion fontium historiae Hungaricae. Budapest. 1901.

Matthias Corvinus. Epistolae. Vols. i–iv. Kassa. 1744.
—— Mátyás király levelei. Külügyi osztály. (Epistolae regis Mathiae. Extera. 1458–90.) Ed. Fraknói, V. 2 vols. Budapest. 1893, 95.
Monumenta Vaticana historiam regni Hungariae illustrantia. Ser. i. Vols. i–vi. Ser. ii. Vols. i–iii. Budapest. 1881–1909.
Nagy, I. and Nagy, J. Codex diplomaticus Hungaricus Andegavensis. 7 vols. *In* Monumenta Hungariae historica. Ser. i. Vols. i–vii. Budapest. 1878 ff.
—— and Nyáry, A. Magyar diplomáciai emlékek Mátyás király korából. (Acta extera tempor. regis Mathiae.) 4 vols. *Ibid.* Ser. iv. Vols. iv–vii. 1875–8.
Schwandtner, J. G. Scriptores rerum Hungaricarum veteres ac genuini. 3 vols. Vienna. 1746–8.
Smičiklas, T. Codex diplomaticus regni Croatiae, Dalmatiae ac Slavoniae (–1373). Vols. ii–xiv. Agram (Zagreb). 1904–16.
Teleki, J. A Hunyadiak kora. (The age of the Hunyadis.) Vols. x–xii. Diplomatarium. Pest. 1853–7.
Teutsch, G. D. Beiträge zur Geschichte Siebenbürgens unter König Ludwig I (1342–82). AOG. iii. 1850.
Theiner, A. Vetera monumenta historica Hungariam sacram illustrantia. 2 vols. Rome. 1859–60.
—— Vetera monumenta Slavorum Meridionalium Historiam illustrantia. 2 vols. Rome and Agram (Zagreb). 1863–75.
Történelmi Tár. (Historical Journal.) Vols. i–xxiii. Budapest. 1878–99. Uj folyam. (New Series.) Vols. i–xii. Budapest. 1900–11.
Wenzel, G. Magyar diplomáciai emlékek az Anjoukorból. (Acta extera tempor. regum Andegavensium.) 3 vols. *In* Monumenta Hungariae historica. Ser. iv. Vols. i–iii. Budapest. 1874–6.
Zimmermann, F. and Werner, K. Urkundenbuch zur Geschichte der Deutschen in Siebenbürgen. Vols. i–iii. Hermannstadt. 1892–1902.

III. NARRATIVE SOURCES.

Aeneas Sylvius Piccolomini (Pius II). Asiae Europaeque descriptio. Paris. 1534.
—— Historia Bohemica. *In* Opera geog. et hist. Frankfort and Leipsic. 1707. *Also* ed. Prague. 1766.
—— Historia rerum Friderici III. Ed. Kollár, A. F. *in* Analecta monumentorum... Vindob. Vol. ii. Vienna. 1762.
Anonymi descriptio Europae Orientalis. Ed. Górka, O. Cracow. 1916.
Anonymus de obsidione Jaderensi. Ed. Schwandtner, J. G. *in* Script. rerum Hungar. Vol. iii. *See above*, ii.
Arnpeck, Veit. Chronicon Austriacum (–1488). Ed. Pez, H. *in* Script. rerum Austriacarum. Vol. i. Leipsic. 1721.
Bertrandon de la Brocquière. Le voyage d'outremer. Ed. d'Aussy, L. *in* Mém. de l'Institut National. Sciences morales et polit. Vol. v. 1804. *Also* ed. Schefer, C. (Recueil de voyages et de documents. Vol. xii.) Paris. 1893.
Bonfini, A. Rerum Hungaricarum decades. Ed. Bél, C. A. Leipsic. 1771.
Callimachus. Historia de rege Vladislavo IV. Ed. Schwandtner, J. G. *op. cit.* Vol. i. *Also in* Monumenta Poloniae Historica. Vol. vi. Cracow. 1893.
Chalcocondylas, Laonicus. Historiarum demonstrationes. Ed. Darkó, E. Budapest. 1921–7.
Chronicon Aulae Regiae. Ed. Loserth, J. (Fontes rerum Austriacarum. Abt. i. Vol. viii.) Vienna. 1875.
Chronicon Dubnicense. Ed. Florianus, M. *in* Historiae Hungaricae fontes domestici. Pt. i. Vol. iii. Leipsic. 1884.
Critobulus of Imbros. De rebus gestis Mechemetis II. Ed. Müller, C. *in* Fragmenta hist. Graecorum. Vol. v, i. Paris. 1870.
Cronica Hungarorum antiqua. Buda. 1473. [Facsimile reprint.] Budapest. 1900. *Also* ed. as Chronicon Budense. Buda. 1838.
Cureus, Joachim. Schlesische General Chronika. 2 vols. Wittenberg. 1835.
Dandolo, Andrea. Chronicon Venetum. Ed. Muratori, L. A. RR.II.SS. 1st edn. Vol. xii.

Daniero, T. Descrizione de l'Ungheria nei secoli xv e xvi. Budapest. 1881.
Dlugosz, J. Historiae Polonicae libri xii. (Opera omnia. Vols. x–xiv.) Cracow. 1873–8.
Ducas, Michael. Historia Byzantina (1341–1462). Ed. Bekker, I. (CSHB.) Bonn. 1834.
Endlicher, S. Aus den Denkwürdigkeiten der Helene Kottanerin. Leipsic. 1846.
Eschenloer, Peter. Geschichten der Stadt Breslau. Ed. Kunisch, J. 2 vols. Breslau. 1827–8.
—— Historia Wratislaviensis. Ed. Markgraf, H. *in* Scriptores rerum Silesiacarum. Vol. vii. Breslau. 1872.
Galeottus, Martius. Commentarius. Ed. Schwandtner, J. G. *op. cit.* Vol. i.
Gravina, Dominicus de. Chronicon de rebus in Apulia gestis (1330–50). Ed. Sorbelli, A. RR.II.SS. New edn. Vol. xii. pt. 3.
Hagen, Gregor. Chronica des Landes Österreich (–1398). MGH. Deutsche Chroniken. vi.
Madius de Barbazanis, Michael. Historia de gestis Romanorum imperatorum et summorum pontificum. Ed. Schwandtner, J. G. *op. cit.* Vol. iii.
Monaci, L. Chronicon de rebus Venetis. Venice. 1758.
Paulus de Paulo. Memoriale. Ed. Schwandtner, J. G. *op. cit.* Vol. iii.
Phrantzes, Georgius. Chronicon. Ed. Bekker, I. (CSHB.) Bonn. 1838.
Thuróczy, J. Chronica Hungarorum. Ed. Schwandtner, J. G. *op. cit.* Vol. i.
Unrest, Jacob. Chronicon Austriacum (1435–99). Ed. Hahn, S. F. *in* Collectio monumentorum ineditorum. Vol. i. Brunswick. 1724–6.
Windecke, Eberhard. Denkwürdigkeiten zur Geschichte des Zeitalters Kaiser Sigmunds (–1442). Ed. Altmann, W. Berlin. 1893. German transl. Hagen, F. von. (Geschichtschreiber der deutsch. Vorzeit. 2nd edn. 87.) Leipsic. 1899.

IV. MODERN WORKS.

A. GENERAL.

Domanovszky, S. Geschichte Ungarns. Munich. 1923.
Eckhart, F. Introduction à l'histoire hongroise. Paris. 1928. [Bibliographies.]
—— Short history of the Hungarian people. London. 1931.
Fraknói, V. Hunyadiak kora. (Age of the Hunyadis.) *In the series:* A magyar nemzet története. Ed. Szilágyi, S. Budapest. 1895.
Hóman, B. Magyar történet. (Hungarian History.) Vols. ii–iii. (13th–15th centuries.) Budapest. 1928, 32.
Horváth, J. A magyar irodalmi müveltség kezdetei. (Origins of literary erudition in Hungary.) Budapest. 1931.
Huber, A. Geschichte Österreichs. Vols. i–v. (Heeren. *See Gen. Bibl.* v.) Gotha. 1885–96.
Knatchbull-Hugessen, C. M. (Lord Brabourne). The political evolution of the Hungarian nation. 2 vols. London. 1908.
Miskolczy, I. Magyarország az Anjouk korában. (Hungary in the age of the Angevins.) Budapest. 1931.
Pór, A. and Schönherr. Az Anjouk kora. (The age of the Angevins.) *In the series:* A magyar nemzet története. (History of the Hungarian nation.) Ed. Szilágyi, S. Budapest.
Sayous, A. E. and Dolenecz, J. Histoire générale des Hongrois. Paris and Budapest. 1900.
Szalay, L. Geschichte Ungarns. 3 vols. Budapest. 1870–5.
Szekfü, J. Der Staat Ungarn. Stuttgart and Berlin. 1918.
Timon, Á. Ungarische Verfassungs- und Rechtsgeschichte. 2nd edn. Berlin. 1909.
Yolland, A. B. Hungary. (Nations' Histories.) London. 1917.

B. SPECIAL.

Berzeviczy, A. Béatrice d'Aragon. 2 vols. Paris. 1911–12.
Csánki, D. Magyarország történeti földrajza a Hunyadiak korában. (Historical geography of Hungary in the age of the Hunyadis.) Vols. i–iii. Budapest. 1890–1913.

Csánki, I. Mátyás udvara. (The court of King Matthias.) Budapest. 1884.

Deér, J. Ungarn in der Descriptio Europae Orientalis. MIOGF. XLII. 1931.

Domanovszky, S. Nagy Lajos hadjáratai Velence ellen. (Lewis the Great's campaigns against Venice.) *In* Századok.

Eckhart, F. Die Glaubwürdigen Orte Ungarns im Mittelalter. Innsbruck. 1914.

Fraknói, V. Magyarország összeköttetései a római Szentszékkel. (Hungary's relations with the Holy See.) 2 vols. Budapest. 1900, 03.

—— Mátyás király. (King Matthias.) Budapest. 1890.

Gábor, G. A megyei intézmény alakulása és müködése Nagy Lajos korában. (Development and functions of the counties in the age of Lewis I.) Budapest. 1908.

Hajnik, L. A magyar birósági szervezet és perjog az Árpád és vegyesházi királyok korában. (Hungarian judicatory organisation and procedure in the Middle Ages.) Budapest. 1899.

Hevesy, A. La bibliothèque du roi Mathias Corvin. Paris. 1923.

Hóman, B. La circolazione delle monete d' oro in Ungheria dal x al XIV secolo e la crisi europea dell' oro nel sec. XIV. *In* Rivista italiana di numismatica. 1922.

—— A magyar királyság pénzügyei és gazdaságpolitikája Károly Robert korában. (Public finances and economic policy in the age of King Charles Robert.) Budapest. 1921.

Illés, J. Anjoukori társadalom és adózás. (Society and taxation in the age of the Angevins.) Budapest. 1900.

Károlyi, Á. Adalékok Frigyes császár és Mátyás király viszályai történetéhez. (Notes on the feud between Emperor Frederick and King Matthias.) Budapest. 1892.

Misik, M. Husiti na Slovensku. 1928.

Nagy, B. A magyar jobbágy állapota 1514-ig. (Villein class in Hungary before 1514.) Budapest. 1896.

Ortvay, T. Magyarország egyházi földleirása a XIV sz. elején. (Ecclesiastical geography of Hungary in the 14th century.) 2 vols. Budapest.

Pór, A. Nagy Lajos. (Lewis the Great.) Budapest. 1892. [Also articles in the periodicals Századok, Erdélyi Museum, etc.]

Steinacker, H. Ueber Stand und Aufgaben der ungarischen Verfassungsgeschichte. MIOGF. XXVIII.

Szekfü, G. Serviensek és familiárisok. (*Servientes* and *familiares*.) Budapest. 1913.

Thallóczy, L. Tanulmányok a bosnyák bánság kezdeteiről. (Studies relating to the origins of the Bosnian Banate.) Budapest. 1905.

—— Bosnyák és szerb élet-és nemzedékrendi tanulmányok. (Studies relating to life and clan organisation in Bosnia and Serbia.) Budapest. 1908.

Tóth-Szabó, P. A cseh-huszita mozgalmak és uralom története. (History of Czech-Hussite movements and rule in Hungary.) Budapest. 1917.

CHAPTER XX.

POLITICAL THEORY IN THE LATER MIDDLE AGES.

I. ORIGINAL TEXTS.

A. Thirteenth Century.

Anon. [Ptolemy of Lucca?] Determinatio Compendiosa. Ed. Krammer, M. (MGH. Fontes iuris Germanici antiqui.) Hanover. 1909.
Aegidius Romanus Colonna. De Regimine Principum. Venice. 1498, etc.
—— De ecclesiastica potestate. Ed. Scholz, R. Weimar. 1929.
Aquinas, St Thomas. Opera omnia. Antwerp. 1612. Parma. 1852–72.
Boniface VIII, Pope. Decretals. *In* Corpus Iuris Canonici. Ed. Friedberg, E. Pt. II. *See Gen. Bibl.* IV.
—— Letters. *In* Raynaldus, O. Annales ecclesiastici. Vol. XIV. *See Gen. Bibl.* v *under* Baronius.
—— Registres. Ed. Digard, G. and others. Pts. I–XIV. EcfrAR. Paris. 1884 ff., in progress.
Dante Alighieri. Monarchia. Ed. Moore, E. and Toynbee, P. *in* Opere. 4th edn. Oxford. 1924. *Also* with introdn. by Reade, W. H. V. Oxford.. 1916.
Engelbert, abbot of Admont. De Regimine Principum. Ratisbon. [1725.]
—— De ortu, progressu et fine Romani Imperii liber. Basle. 1553. *Also in* Goldast, M. Politica Imperialia. Frankfort. 1614.
Jordanus of Osnabrück [and Alexander of Roes]. De praerogativa Romani Imperii (De translatione Imperii). Ed. Waitz, G. *in* Abh. d. k. Gesellsch. d. Wiss. zu Göttingen. XIV. 1868–9. *Also* ed. Grundmann, H. *in* Quellen zur Geistesgesch. d. Mittelalters.... Vol. II. (Veröff. d. Forschungs Inst. a. d. Univ. Leipzig.) Leipsic. 1930.
Vincentius Bellovacensis. Speculum Doctrinale, lib. VII–XI. Douai. 1624.

B. Fourteenth Century.

Alvarus Pelagius. De Planctu Ecclesiae. Lyons. 1517.
Anon. [Pierre Dubois?] Disputatio inter Militem et Clericum. *In* Goldast, M. Monarchia S. Romani Imperii. Vol. I. *See Gen. Bibl.* IV.
Anon. [Évrart de Trémaugon?] Somnium Viridarii (Songe du Vergier). *Ibid.*
Augustinus Triumphus. Summa de Potestate Ecclesiastica. Rome. 1583, etc.
Clement V, Pope. Decretals. *In* Corpus Iuris Canonici. Ed. Friedberg, E. Pt. II. *See Gen. Bibl.* IV.
—— Letters. *In* Raynaldus, O. Annales ecclesiastici. Vol. XV. *See Gen. Bibl.* v *under* Baronius.
Dubois, Pierre. De recuperatione Terre Sancte. Ed. Langlois, C. V. (Coll. textes, 9.) Paris. 1891.
Henricus de Langenstein. Consilium Pacis. *In* Gerson, J. Opera omnia. Vol. II. Antwerp. 1706.
Johannes Parisiensis. Tractatus de Potestate Regia et Papali. *In* Goldast, M. Monarchia. Vol. II.
John XXII, Pope. Decretals. *In* Corpus Iuris Canonici. *See Gen. Bibl.* IV.
—— Letters. *In* Raynaldus. *op. cit.* Vol. XV.
Landulfus de Colonna. De translatione Imperii. *In* Goldast, M. Monarchia. Vol. II.
Lupold of Bebenburg. De Iure Regni et Imperii. *In* Schard, S. De Jurisdictione. Basle. 1566.
Marsilius of Padua. Defensor Pacis. Ed. Previté-Orton, C. W. Cambridge. 1928. *Also* ed. Scholz, R. (MGH. Fontes iuris Germanici antiqui.) Hanover. 1932–3.
—— Defensor Minor. Ed. Brampton, C. K. Birmingham. 1922.
Michael de Cesena. Letters, etc. *In* Goldast, M. Monarchia. Vol. II.
Occam, William of. Opus nonaginta dierum. *In* Goldast, M. Monarchia. Vol. II.
—— Compendium errorum Papae Johannis XXII. *Ibid.*

Occam, William of. Octo quaestiones. Goldast, M. Monarchia. Vol. II.
—— Dialogus. *Ibid.*
—— De Imperatorum et Pontificum Potestate. Ed. Brampton, C. K. Oxford. 1927.
Peter Bertrand. De Jurisdictione ecclesiastica et politica. *In* Goldast, M. Monarchia. Vol. II.
Petrarca, Francesco. Epistolae de juribus imperii Romani. *Ibid.*
Wyclif, John. [*Cf.* the Bibliography to Vol. VII, ch. XVI.]
—— Tractatus de Civili Dominio. (Summa Theologiae. Books III–V.) Liber primus. Ed. Poole, R. L. 1885. Liber secundus. Ed. Loserth, J. 1900. Liber tertius. Ed. Loserth, J. 2 vols. 1903–4.
—— De Dominio Divino libri tres. Ed. Poole, R. L. 1890.
—— Tractatus de Ecclesia. (Summa Theologiae. Book VII.) Ed. Loserth, J. 1886.
—— Tractatus de Mandatis Divinis. (*Ibid.* Books I, II.) Ed. Loserth, J. and Matthew, F. D. 1922.
—— Tractatus de Officio Regis. (*Ibid.* Book VIII.) Ed. Pollard, A. W. and Sayle, C. 1887.
—— Tractatus de Potestate Pape. (*Ibid.* Book IX.) Ed. Loserth, J. 1907.
—— Opera minora. Ed. Loserth, J. 1913.
—— Polemical works. Ed. Buddensieg, R. 2 vols. 1883.
[The above were published at London by the Wyclif Society.]
—— Trialogus cum supplemento Trialogi. Ed. Lechler, G. V. Oxford. 1869.
—— Select English works. Ed. Arnold, J. 3 vols. Oxford. 1869–71.
—— English works... hitherto unprinted. Ed. Matthew, F. D. (EETS. Orig. ser. no. 74.) London. 1880.

C. Fifteenth Century.

Aeneas Sylvius Piccolomini (Pius II). De Ortu et Auctoritate Imperii Romani. *In* Schard, S. De Jurisdictione. Basle. 1566.
Alliaco, Petrus de. Treatises and speeches. *In* Gerson, J. Opera omnia. Vol. I. *See below.*
—— Tractatus de Ecclesiastica Potestate. *In* Hardt, E. H. von der. Constantiense Concilium. Vol. VI. Frankfort. 1699.
Almainus, Jacobus. Expositio de Suprema Potestate Ecclesiastica et Laica. *In* Goldast, M. Monarchia S. Romani Imperii. Vol. I. *See Gen. Bibl.* IV.
—— De Dominio Naturali, Civili, et Ecclesiastico. *In* Gerson, J. Opera omnia. Vol. II. *See below.*
Andlo, Petrus de. De Imperio Romano-Germanico. Nuremberg. 1657. Ed. Hürbin, J. *in* ZSR. German. Abt. XII, XIII, XVI. 1891 ff.
Antonio de Rosellio. De Potestate Imperatoris et Papae. *In* Goldast, M. Monarchia. Vol. I.
Cajetanus, Franciscus, pontifex. De Institutione Reipublicae libri IX. Strasbourg. 1594.
Gerson, Johannes. Opera omnia. Ed. Ellies Du Pin, L. 5 vols. Antwerp. 1706.
Heimburg, Gregory of. Admonitio de iniustis usurpationibus. *In* Goldast, M. Monarchia. Vol. I.
—— Controversial writings. *Ibid.* Vol. II.
Hus, Johannes. Determinatio de Ablatione Temporalium a Clericis. *Ibid.* Vol. I.
—— Documenta Mag. Joannis Hus vitam, doctrinam, causam in Constantiensi Concilio actam...illustrantia. Ed. Palacký, F. Prague. 1869.
Nicholas of Cusa. Opera omnia. Basle. 1565.
Theodoricus de Niem. De bono Romani pontificis regimine. Ed. Rattinger, D. HJ. v. 1884.
—— De modis uniendi et reformandi ecclesiam in Concilio Universali. Ed. Heimpel, H. (*with title* Dialog über Union und Reform der Kirche, 1410). Leipsic. 1933.
Turrecremata, Johannes a. Summa de Ecclesia. Venice. 1561.
—— De Potestate Papae. Ed. Friedrich, J. Innsbruck. 1871.
Zabarella, Franciscus de. Tractatus de Schismate. *In* Schard. *op. cit.*
—— Commentarius in v libros Decretalium. Venice. 1602.

D. LEGISTS.

Albericus de Rosate. Commentarii. Lyons. 1545.
Baldus de Ubaldis. Commentarii on the Corpus Iuris Civilis. Venice. 1572.
—— Commentarius in usus feudorum. Lyons. 1566.
—— Commentariolum super pace Constantine. Lyons. 1566.
—— Commentarii super tribus prioribus libris Decretalium. Lyons. 1585.
Bartolus de Sassoferrato. Opera. Basle. 1562.

E. DOCUMENTS OF IMPORTANCE INCLUDING MANY MINOR TREATISES.

Baillet, A. Histoire des démeslez du Pape Boniface VIII avec Philippe le Bel.
    2nd edn. Paris. 1718. [Supplements Dupuy, *below.*]
Boehmer, J. Fontes rerum Germanicarum. Vols. I, II. Stuttgart. 1843.
Corpus Iuris Canonici. Ed. Friedberg, E. *See Gen. Bibl.* IV.
Dupuy, P. Histoire du différend d'entre le Pape Boniface VIII et Philippes le Bel.
    Paris. 1655. [Very valuable collection of documents.]
Finke, H. Acta concilii Constanciensis. *See Gen. Bibl.* IV *under* Councils, General.
Goldast, M. Monarchia S. Romani Imperii. *See Gen. Bibl.* IV.
—— Politica Imperialia. Frankfort. 1614.
Haller, J. Concilium Basiliense. *See Gen. Bibl.* IV *under* Councils, General.
Mirbt, C. Quellen zur Geschichte des Papsttums. *See Gen. Bibl.* IV.
Scholz, R. Unbekannte kirchenpolitische Streitschriften aus der Zeit Ludwigs des
    Bayern. 2 vols. (Bibl. d. K. Preuss. Hist. Inst. in Rom, IX, X.) Rome. 1911, 14.

II. MODERN WORKS.

Battaglia, F. Marsilio da Padova. Florence. 1928.
Baumann, J. J. Die Staatslehre des heil. Thomas von Aquino. Leipsic. 1873.
Bellarmine, Cardl. R. De Scriptoribus Ecclesiasticis. Venice. 1728.
Berchtold, J. Die Bulle Unam Sanctam. Munich. 1887.
Bess, B. Johannes Gerson und die kirchenpolitischen Parteien Frankreichs.
    Marburg. 1890. [diss.]
Bryce, J. The Holy Roman Empire. *See Gen. Bibl.* V.
Carlyle, R. W. and A. J. History of Mediaeval Political Theory. *See Gen. Bibl.* V.
Connolly, J. L. John Gerson. Louvain. 1928.
Coville, A. Évrart de Trémaugon et le Songe du Verger. Paris. 1933.
—— Jean Petit. La question du tyrannicide au commencement du XVᵉ siècle.
    Paris. 1932.
Creighton, M. History of the Papacy. Vols. I, II. *See Gen. Bibl.* V.
Declareuil, J. Histoire générale du droit français. Paris. 1925.
Dunning, W. A. History of Political Theories, ancient and mediaeval. New York.
    1902.
Emerton, E. The Defensor Pacis of Marsiglio. Cambridge, Mass. 1920.
Ercole, F. Da Bartolo all' Althusio. Saggi sulla storia del pensiero pubblicistico del
    rinascimento italiano. Florence. 1932.
Féret, P. La Faculté de Théologie de Paris. Vols. I–V. Paris. 1894 ff.
Figgis, J. N. The Divine Right of Kings. 2nd edn. Cambridge. 1914.
—— From Gerson to Grotius. Cambridge. 1907.
Finke, H. Aus den Tagen Bonifaz VIII. Münster. 1902.
—— Zu Dietrich von Niem und Marsilius von Padua. RQ. VII.
Gierke, O. von. Das deutsche Genossenschaftsrecht. *See Gen. Bibl.* V.
—— Political Theories of the Middle Age. *See Gen. Bibl.* V.
—— Johannes Althusius. Breslau. 1880.
Gilson, E. The philosophy of St Thomas Aquinas. Cambridge. 1929.
Gosselin, J. E. A. Pouvoir du Pape au moyen âge. New edn. Paris. 1845. Engl.
    transl. Kelly, M. 2 vols. London. 1853.
Grabmann, M. Studien über den Einfluss der aristotelischen Philosophie auf die
    mittelalterlichen Theorien über das Verhältnis von Kirche und Staat. SBAW.
    1934. Heft 2.
Hauck, A. Der Gedanke der päpstlichen Weltherrschaft bis auf Bonifaz VIII.
    Leipsic. 1904.
Heimpel, H. Dietrich von Niem. Münster-i.-W. 1932.
Heitling, G. von. Zur Geschichte der aristotelischen Politik im Mittelalter. Munich.
    1914.

Jacob, E. F. Dietrich of Niem. *In* Bulletin...John Rylands Library. xix (1935). 388–410.

—— Nicholas of Cusa. *In* Social and political ideas of some great thinkers of the Renaissance and the Reformation. Ed. Hearnshaw, F. J. C. London. 1925.

Lagarde, G. de. Une adaptation de la politique d'Aristote au xive siècle. RDF. 4th ser. Vol. xi. 1932.

—— Marsile de Padoue et Guillaume de Nogaret. *Ibid.*

—— La naissance de l'esprit laïque au déclin du moyen âge. Vols. i, ii. Paris. 1934. In progress.

Lechler, J. John Wycliffe and his English precursors. London. [1884.]

Lemaire, A. Les lois fondamentales de la Monarchie Française. Paris. 1907.

Lottin, O. Le droit naturel chez S. Thomas. Bruges. 1926.

McIlwain, C. H. The growth of political thought in the West. London. 1932.

Maitland, F. W. Roman Canon Law in the Church of England. London. 1898.

Marca, P. de. De Concordia Sacerdotii et Imperii. Paris. 1704.

Meyer, E. H. Die staats- und völkerrechtlichen Ideen von Peter Dubois. Leipsic. 1908. [diss.]

—— Lupold von Bebenburg. Freiburg. 1909.

Müller, C. Der Kampf Ludwigs des Baiern mit der römischen Curie. 2 vols. Tübingen. 1879–80.

Negroni, C. Dante Alighieri e Bartolo da Sassoferrato. Lonigo. 1890.

Perouse, G. Le Cardinal Louis Aleman. Lyons. 1904.

Pollock, F. An introduction to the history of the science of politics. London. 1900.

Poole, R. L. Illustrations of the history of Medieval Thought. *See Gen. Bibl.* v.

—— Wycliffe and movements for reform. London. 1889.

Power, E. E. Pierre Dubois. *In* Social and political ideas of some great medieval thinkers. Ed. Hearnshaw, F. J. C. London. 1923.

Powicke, F. M. Pierre Dubois. *In* Historical essays by members of the Owens College, Manchester. Ed. Tout, T. F. and Tait, J. Manchester. 1907.

Rashdall, H. The Universities of Europe in the Middle Ages. *See Gen. Bibl.* v.

Réville, A. Le soulèvement des travailleurs d'Angleterre en 1381. Paris. 1898.

Riezler, S. Die literarischen Widersacher der Päpste zur Zeit Ludwigs des Baiers. Leipsic. 1874.

Rivière, J. Le problème de l'Église et de l'État au temps de Philippe le Bel. Louvain. 1926.

Rocquain, F. La Cour de Rome et l'esprit de Réforme avant Luther. 3 vols. Paris. 1897.

Salembier, L. Le Grand Schisme d'Occident. *See Gen. Bibl.* v.

Savigny, C. Geschichte des Römischen Rechts im Mittelalter. *See Gen. Bibl.* v.

Scholz, R. Marsilius von Padua und die Idee der Demokratie. *In* Zeitschr. für Politik. i (1908). 61.

—— Die Publizistik zur Zeit Philipps des Schönen. Stuttgart. 1903.

—— Studien über die politischen Streitschriften des 14 und 15 Jahrhts. QFIA. xiv. 1909.

Schraub, W. Jordan von Osnabrück und Alexander von Roes. Heidelberg. 1910.

Smith, A. L. Church and State in the Middle Ages. Oxford. 1913.

Sullivan, J. Marsiglio of Padua and William of Ockham. AHR. ii (1896–7). 409–26, 593–610.

Tooley, M. J. The authorship of the Defensor Pacis. TRHS. 4th ser. Vol. ix. 1926.

Valois, N. La crise religieuse du xve siècle. 2 vols. Paris. 1909.

—— La France et le Grand Schisme d'Occident. *See Gen. Bibl.* v.

—— Histoire de la Pragmatique Sanction de Bourges. Paris. 1906.

Vansteenberghe, E. Le cardinal Nicolas de Cues. Lille. 1920.

Vinogradoff, P. Roman Law in Medieval Europe. 2nd edn. Oxford. 1929.

Woolf, C. N. S. Bartolus of Sassoferrato. Cambridge. 1913.

Workman, H. B. John Wyclif. 2 vols. Oxford. 1926.

Wulf, M. de. Histoire de la philosophie médiévale. *See Gen. Bibl.* v.

Zeck, E. Der Publizist Pierre Dubois. Berlin. 1911.

CHAPTER XXI.

THE ART OF WAR IN THE FIFTEENTH CENTURY.

[Most of the books cited below are highly controversial, and none can be recommended without a caution that many of the views expressed in it have been disputed by other specialists of equal value.]

I. GENERAL HISTORIES.

Delbrück, H. Geschichte der Kriegskunst im Rahmen der politischen Geschichte. 6 vols. (Vols. i and ii, 3rd edn.) Berlin. 1920–9.

Delpech, H. La tactique au xiiie siècle. 2 vols. Paris. 1886.

Erben, W. Kriegsgeschichte des Mittelalters. [Bibliographies.] See Gen. Bibl. v.

Jähns, M. Handbuch einer Geschichte des Kriegswesens von der Urzeit bis zur Renaissance (with Atlas). Leipsic. 1878, 80.

Köhler, G. Die Entwickelung des Kriegswesens und der Kriegführung in der Ritterzeit...[1150–1450]. 3 vols., index, and supplt. Breslau. 1886–93.

Oman, Sir C. W. C. History of the art of War in the Middle Ages. See Gen. Bibl. v.

II. MONOGRAPHS ON PARTICULAR SECTIONS.

History of Swiss Warfare.

Elgger, C. von. Kriegswesen und Kriegskunst der schweizerischen Eidgenossen im 14, 15, und 16 Jahrht. Lucerne. 1873.

The Italian Condottieri.

Block, W. Die Condottieri. Studien über die sogenannten "unblutigen Schlachten." (Ebering's Hist. Studien, 110.) Berlin. 1913.

Ricotti, E. Storia delle compagnie di ventura in Italia. 4 vols. Turin. 1844–5. And later edns.

Late Renaissance Warfare in Italy.

Machiavelli, N. Libro dell' arte della guerra. Ed. Mazzoni, G. and Casella, M. in Tutte le opere. Florence. 1929. Engl. transl. Whitehorne, P. Lond. 1573. [Invaluable for criticism of his contemporaries, and an idealistic reconstruction of future tactics.]

Taylor, F. L. The art of War in Italy, 1494–1529. Cambridge. 1921.

Crusades.

Heermann, O. Die Gefechtsführung abendländischer Heere im Orient in der Epoche des ersten Kreuzzugs. Marburg. 1888.

Free Companies in France.

Luce, S. Histoire de Bertrand du Guesclin et de son époque. La jeunesse de Bertrand (1320–64). Paris. 1876.

Artillery.

Hime, H. W. L. The origin of Artillery. London. 1915.

Rathgen, B. Das Geschütz im Mittelalter. Berlin. 1928.

English Armies and Tactics.

Morris, J. E. The Welsh Wars of Edward I. Oxford. 1901.

—— The Archers at Crecy. EHR. xii (1897). 427–36.

Tout, T. F. The tactics of the battles of Boroughbridge and Morlaix. EHR. xix (1904). 711–15.

English Castles.

Thompson, A. Hamilton. English military architecture during the Middle Ages. London. 1912.

CHAPTER XXII.

MAGIC, WITCHCRAFT, ASTROLOGY, AND ALCHEMY.

I. ORIGINAL MATERIALS.

The source material for witchcraft and kindred topics is set forth with considerable fullness in Hansen's books. *See below*, II (*a*). That for the magic of the learned down to 1327 is indicated in Thorndike, Lynn. History of Magic and Experimental Science. *See below*, II (*a*). The following notices, therefore, chiefly deal with writings, especially astrological, of the fourteenth and fifteenth centuries, to which in many cases attention has not been hitherto called. Space will not permit full descriptions of manuscripts and incunabula. Printed editions are followed by the place and date of publication.

(*a*) CATALOGUES OF MANUSCRIPTS.

Catalogus codicum astrologorum Graecorum. Ed. Boll, F., Cumont, F., Kroll, W. *et al.* 10 vols. Brussels. 1898–1924. [Only a fraction of the material is medieval.]

Saxl, F. Verzeichnis astrologischer und mythologischer illustrierter Handschriften des lateinischen Mittelalters. 2 vols. Sitzungsb. der Heidelberger Akad. der Wissensch., Philos.-hist. Kl. Jahrg. 1915 and 1925–6 (publ. 1927).

Catalogue des manuscrits alchimiques grecs. Ed. Bidez, J., Cumont, F., Heiberg, J. L., and Lagercrantz, O. Vols. I–VIII. Brussels. 1924–32.

Catalogue of Latin and Vernacular Alchemical Manuscripts in Great Britain and Ireland dating from before the 16th century. By Singer, Dorothea Waley, and Anderson, Annie. 3 vols. Brussels. 1928–31.

Carbonelli, G. Sulle fonti storiche della Chimica e dell' Alchimia in Italia, tratte dallo spoglio dei ms. delle Biblioteche con speciale riguardo ai codici 74 di Pavia e 1166 Laurenziano. Rome. 1925.

Hauber, A. Planetenkinderbilder und Sternbilder. Strasbourg. 1916. [The old MS. described was written in 1404.]

(*b*) OLD ALCHEMICAL COLLECTIONS.

Verae alchemiae artisque metallicae citra aenigmata. (Gratarolus.) 2 vols. Basle. 1561.

Auriferae artis quam chemiam vocant antiquissimi auctores. 2 vols. Basle. 1572.

Philosophiae chimicae quatuor vetustissima scripta. Frankfort. 1605.

Zetzner, L. Theatrum chemicum. 4 vols. Ursel. 1602; 5 vols. Strasbourg. 1613–22; 6 vols. Strasbourg. 1659–61.

Ashmole, E. Theatrum chemicum Britannicum. London. 1652.

Manget, J. J. Bibliotheca chemica curiosa. 2 vols. Geneva. 1702.

(*c*) RECENT EDITIONS OF ALCHEMICAL TEXTS.

Liber claritatis totius alkimicae artis. Ed. Darmstaedter, E. *in* Archeion. VI (1925). 319–30; VII. 257–65; VIII. 95–103, 214–29; IX. 63–80, 191–208, 462–82.

Avicennae De congelatione et conglutinatione lapidum, being sections of the Kitab al-Ahifa, Latin and Arabic text with Engl. transln. Ed. Holmyard, E. J. and Mandeville, D. C. Paris. 1927.

Kitab al- 'Ilm al-Muktasab fi Zira 'at Adh-Dhahab, Arabic text with Engl. transln. Ed. Holmyard, E. J. Paris. 1923.

The 'Alchemy' ascribed to Michael Scot. Ed. Haskins, C. H. *in* Isis. x (1928). 350–9.

Michael Scot and Alchemy. Ed. Singer, D. W. *in* Isis. XIII (1929). 5–15.

Rasis de aluminibus et salibus. Latin transln. of Gerard of Cremona. Ed. Steele, R. *in* Isis. XII (1929). 10–46.

The Works of Geber, Englished by Richard Russell, 1678. Ed. Holmyard, E. J. London. 1928.

The Arabic Works of Jabir ibn Hayyan, with Engl. transln. Ed. Holmyard, E. J. Paris. 1928.

Marinelli, A. Libretto di alchimia inciso su lamine di piombo (secolo xiv). Florence. 1910.

Stapleton, H. E. and Azo, R. F. An alchemical compilation of the thirteenth century. *In* Memoirs of the Asiatic Soc. of Bengal. iii (1910). 86.

The Emerald Table. Latin transln. probably by Plato of Tivoli. Ed. Steele, R. and Singer, D. W. *in* Proc. Roy. Soc. of Medicine. London. xxi (1928). Sect. of the hist. of medicine, pp. 41–57.

(*d*) Works of Individual Authors Chiefly of the Fourteenth and Fifteenth Centuries on Astrology, Magic, and Witchcraft.

(*Arranged so far as possible in chronological order.*)

[For manuscripts of authors in the following list which exist in European libraries, the reader may consult Thorndike, Lynn. A History of Magic and Experimental Science. Vols. iii, iv. *See below*, ii (*a*).]

Gerardus de Silteo vel de Sileto, Dominican. Summa de astris in tres partes distributa.

Exafrenon pronosticorum temporis. Probably by Walter of Odington, author of an alchemical Icocedron, rather than by Richard of Wallingford.

Firminus de Bellavalle, De mutatione aeris (dictus Colliget astrologie). Ed. Ratdolt, Erhard. Venice. 1485; *also* Paris. 1539.

Perscrutator (Robert of York?). De impressionibus aeris, written at York in 1325.

Andalò di Negro. Introductorius ad iudicia astrologie.

—— Liber iudiciorum infirmitatum: de infusione spermatis, Ratio diversitatis partus.

Galfridus or Gaufredus de Meldis. Tracts on the comets of 1315 and 1337.

—— On the conjunction of Saturn and Jupiter in 1325.

—— On the causes of the Black Death; written after the event.

—— Astronomiae iudicialis compendium.

Gentilis Fulginatis. Determinatio ad preces cuiusdam de incubo.

Niccolo de Aquila *or* di Paganica. Compendium medicinalis astrologie, 1330.

John of Saxony. Commentary on Alcabitius, 1331. Venice. 1485, and later. Paris. 1520.

Augustine of Trent. Prediction for the year 1340. Edited in part by Thorndike, Lynn, *as* A pest tractate before the Black Death. *In* Sudhoffs Archiv für Gesch. der Medizin. Leipsic. xxiii (1930). 346–56.

Leo Hebreus. De coniunctione Saturni et Iovis anni Christi 1345.

Iohannes de Muris. Prediction from the conjunction of 1345.

—— Epistola ad Clementem VI, on conjunctions of 1365 and 1357.

—— A compilation on the art of geomancy.

John of Eschenden. Summa astrologiae iudicialis de accidentibus mundi quae anglicana vulgo nuncupatur, Venetiis, 1489.

—— Pronosticationes de eclipsi universali lune et de coniunctione trium planetarum superiorum...anno domini 1345.

—— Prognostication for an eclipse and conjunction in 1349.

—— On conjunctions of 1357 and 1365.

—— Weather prediction for the years 1368–1374.

John of Bassigniaco. Prognostications for 1352–1382.

Milo Toletanus. Prognosticon de coniunctione facta anno domini 1357.

John of Stendal. Scriptum super Alkabicium compilatum...anno domini 1359.

Reginald Lambourne. Letters concerning conjunctions of 1367 and lunar eclipses of 1363.

Pelerin de Prusse. Three books in French on astrological elections written in 1361 for the dauphin, later Charles V; later in the same MS. occur horoscopes of Charles V and his children.

John of Rupescissa. De quinta essentia.
Thomas of Bologna. Epistola ad Bernardum Trevirensem de lapide philosophico.
Nicolas Oresme. Against princes studying astrology.
—— De divinationibus, translated from the French into Latin.
—— Contra divinatores horoscopios, written in 1370.
—— Quotlibeta annexa questioni premissa.
—— De commensurabilitate motuum celi.
—— De configuratione qualitatum, *or* De uniformitate et difformitate intentionum.
—— Des divinations, in French.
—— De spera en francois que translata maistre Nicole Oresme.
—— De fascinatione, probably incorrectly attributed to Oresme and really by
    Engelbert, abbot of Admont, *c.* 1250–1331.
Henry of Hesse. De discretione spirituum.
—— Questio de cometa, 1368.
—— Contra coniunctionistas, composed in 1373.
—— De habitudine causarum et influxu nature communis respectu inferiorum.
—— De reductione effectuum in causas universales (*or*, in virtutes communes).
John of Legnano. Tracts on the conjunction of 1365 and the comet of 1368.
Coluccio Salutati. De fato et fortuna.
Matthaeus de Guarimbertis, archdeacon of Parma. Tractatus de directionibus et de
    aspectibus et de radiis. Nuremberg. 1535 (with Ptolemy's Quadripartitum);
    Rome. 1557 (with works of Luca Guarico).
A Miscellany of Astronomy, Astrology, and Geomancy made for the Emperor Wen-
    ceslas in 1392–1393, with illuminations.
Andreas de Sommaria. Quod astrologia non possit sciri, *or*, De stellis et motu earum,
    apparently composed between 1383 and 1407 A.D.
Nicolas Eymeric. Contra demonum invocatores.
—— Contra alchymistas ad abbatem de Rosis.
—— Contra astrologos imperitos atque necromanticos de occultis perperam iudi-
    cantes, ad Thomam Ulzinam.
Iacobus Engelhart, of Ulm, to Leopold III and the city council. Tractatus novus de
    cometis (including that of 1402).
James the Augustinian. Sopholegium, written between 1390 and 1409.
Blasius of Parma (Biagio Pelacani). Iudicium revolutionis anni 1405, 11 marcii cum
    horis et fractionibus.
Melletus de Russis (of Forlì). Iudicium…super anno 1405 post meridiem 11 marcii
    abbreviatum per conclusiones.
Petrus de Alliaco. De ymagine mundi,…De legibus et sectis contra superstitiosos
    astronomos,…Vigintiloquium de concordantia astronomice veritatis et narrationis
    cum theologia, De concordia astronomice veritatis et narrationis historice, Elu-
    cidarius astronomice concordie cum theologia et cum hystorica narratione,
    Apologetica defensio astronomice veritatis, Alia secunda apologetica defensio
    eiusdem, De concordantia discordantium astronomorum. [Louvain? 1480?]
Jehan Gerson. De probatione spirituum, De distinctione verarum visionum a falsis,
    Trilogium astrologie theologizate, An liceat christiano initia rerum observare ex
    celestium syderum respectu, De erroribus circa artem magicam: all to be found
    in his Opera. 4 vols. Strasbourg. 1494–1502.
Petrus de Monte Alcino. Iudicium for 1418.
—— Iudicia for 1419, 1421, 1430, 1448.
Iohannes de Rubeis. Iudicia for 1420 and 1421.
Leonard of Bertipaglia. Iudicium revolutionis anni 1427 incompleti.
Iohannes Paulus de Fundis. Iudicium for 1435.
—— Tractatus reprobationis eorum que scripsit Nicolaus Orrem in suo libello intitu-
    lato de proportionalitate motuum celestium contra astrologos et sacram astrorum
    scientiam compilatus per Iohannem Lauratium de Fundis.
—— Questio de fine seu durabilitate mundi.
—— A work of judicial astrology which follows his Commentary on the Sphere in
    one MS. may also be his.
Paris Controversy of 1437 as to days for bleeding.
Jean Ganivet. Amicus medicorum. Lyons. 1496, and later; Frankfort. 1614.

Jehan de Bruges. Le livre des grandes conjonctions, 1444 A.D.

Nicolaus de Dacia. Liber anaglypharum, *or*, Congeries anaglypharum astronomice facultatis (about A.D. 1456). Prologue *in* Quetif, J. and Echard, J. Scriptores ordinis praedicatorum. Vol. I. Paris. 1719. pp. 886-7.

Savonarola, Michael. Speculum physionomie.

—— Libellus de magnificis ornamentis regiae civitatis Paduae. Ed. Segarizzi, A. RR.II.SS. New edn. Vol. xxiv, Pt. II.

Alvearium ad corrigendam rem publicam Friderico Caesari castro Nurnbergico anno 1444 presentatum. Est liber astrologicus et mysticus.

Raphael de Pornasio, Inquisitor at Genoa 1430-1450. Liber de arte magica (not mentioned by Hansen).

Jacobus de Clusa Carthusiensis. De arte magica.

—— De apparitionibus animarum post exitum earum.... Esslingen. 1475.

Dionysius the Carthusian. Contra vitia superstitionum. *In* Opera. Venice. 1533. pp. 598-628.

Thomas Ebendorfer de Haselbach. Excerpts, De sortilegiis and De superstitionibus et benedictionibus, from his writings were published by Schönbach in the Zeitschr. des Vereins für Volkskunde. xii (1902). 1-14.

Iudicium super comete qui anno Domini 1456 per totum mensem Iunium apparuit, scriptum in alma universitate Viennensi.

Arnoldus de Palude. Astrologia, written about 1460.

Petrus Verruensis. Prenosticationes preiudicate super naturalibus.

Mandelkern, Laurentius. Chiromantia, anno 1464.

Antonius de Camera. Iudicium...super revolutionem anni 1464 in civitate Pisarum... ad honorem Petri de Medicis.

Antonius Francigena. Experimentum supra Saturnum probatum in Avenione...anno domini 1454, die 16 Oct.

Nicolaus de Comitibus, of Padua. Opus astronomicum ad Marmeriam (*or*, Naymerium) filium, composed about 1466.

Curatus de Ziessele iuxta Brugas. Compendium theologie naturalis ex astrologica veritate sumptum.

Guilielmus de Bechis, General of the Augustinians, 1460-70. De potestate spirituum.

Hartlieb, Johannes. Die Kunst Chiromantia. [Augsburg. 1475?] [A blockbook.]

Iudicium anni 1470.

Pietro Bono Avogaro. Astrological writings of 1456, 1475, and on the comet of 1472.

Leonardus Qualea. Astronomia medicinalis, composed 1470-5.

Conrad Hemgarter (Heingarter?) Thuricensis (*i.e.* of Zurich). Tractatus de cometis. Beromünster. 1474.

—— Nativity of John de la Gutte, with medical advice.

—— Iudicium anni 1476, addressed to Louis XI.

—— Commentary on Ptolemy's Quadripartitum.

—— Treatise of astrological medicine addressed to the Duke of Bourbon.

John of Glogau. Summa astrologiae.

—— Iudicium anni 1476.

Nicholas of Poland. Stellarum fata 1477.

Girolami Manfredi. Pronosticon ad annum 1479. Bologna. 1478. [It is impossible to list here all the other annual predictions by him and others which exist in print in great number.]

—— Centilogium de medicis et infirmis. Bologna. 1488; Venice. 1500; Nuremberg. 1530.

Ficino, Marsilio. De vita coelitus comparanda. Florence. 1489. Apologia in qua de medicina, astrologia, vita mundi, etiam de magis qui Christum statim natum salutaverunt agitur, composed 15 Sept. 1489. *In* Opera. Vol. I. p. 572. Basle. 1576.

Galeotto Marzio. De incognitis vulgo.

—— De doctrina promiscua. Florence. 1548.

—— De homine (composed about 1468). Oppenheim. 1610.

Iohannes Nannius of Viterbo. Glosa super apocalipsim de statu ecclesie...in consonantia ex iudiciis astrorum.

Ulric Molitor. De lamiis et phitonicis mulieribus. Facsimile reproduction of the 1486 edn. with French transln. *in* Bibliothèque magique des xve et xvie siècles. Vol. I. 1926.

Petrus Garsia. Determinationes magistrales contra conclusiones apologiales Ioannis Pici Mirandulani. Rome. 1489.

Georgius Medicus de Russia. Collecta super iudicium in eclipsibus faciendis, 1490 A.D.

Pico della Mirandola, Giovanni. Opera omnia. Venice. 1519; 1557. Basle. 1572.

Abiosus, Ioh. Bapt. Dialogus in defensionem astrologiae cum vaticinio a diluvio usque ad Christi annos 1702. Venice. 1494.

Publii Fausti Andrelini Foroliviensis...de influentia syderum...carmen. Paris. 1496.

Torrella, Hieronymus. De imaginibus astrologicis. Valencia. 1496.

Savonarola, Hieronymus. Contro l' astrologia divinatrice. [Florence. *c.* 1497]; Venice. 1536.

Symon de Phares. Recueil des plus celebres astrologues et quelques hommes doctes. Ed. from the unique MS. in the Bibl. Nat. by Wickersheimer, E. Paris. 1929.

Les Évangiles des Quenouilles. [By Fouquart de Cambray and others.] New edn. [by Jannet, P.] Paris. 1855.

Geiler von Kaisersberg (1445-1510). Zur Geschichte des Volksaberglaubens im Anfange des 16 Jahrhts. Ed. Stöber, A. Basle. 1856.

(e) Byzantine Magic.

Delatte, A. Anecdota atheniensia. Vol. I. Textes grecs inédits relatifs à l'histoire des religions. Liége. 1927.

(f) Incunabula of Calendars.

Hundert Kalender Inkunabeln. Ed. Heitz, P. and Häbler, K. Strasbourg. 1905.

II. MODERN WORKS.

(a) General Accounts.

Works on the philosophy and general history of magic and the like are omitted, since their treatment of the Middle Ages is certain to be duplicated and enlarged in works devoted entirely to the medieval period. Local histories of superstition may supply further detail, however, so that a few are included.

Hansen, J. Zauberwahn, Inquisition, und Hexenprozess im Mittelalter. Munich. 1900.

—— Quellen und Untersuchungen zur Geschichte des Hexenwahns und der Hexenverfolgung im Mittelalter. Bonn. 1901.

Thorndike, Lynn. History of Magic and Experimental Science. Vols. I, II. During the first thirteen centuries of our era. Vols. III, IV. Fourteenth and fifteenth centuries. New York. 1923, 34.

—— Science and Thought in the fifteenth century. New York. 1929.

Haskins, C. H. Studies in the history of Mediaeval Science. 2nd edn. Cambridge, Mass. 1927.

Maury, A. La magie et l'astrologie dans l'antiquité et au moyen âge. New edn. Paris. 1863.

Denis, F. Le monde enchanté, cosmographie et histoire naturelles fantastiques du moyen âge. Paris. 1843.

Garinet, J. Histoire de la magie en France depuis le commencement de la monarchie. Paris. 1818.

Meyer, K. Der Aberglaube des Mittelalters und der nächstfolgenden Jahrhte. Basle. 1856.

Schindler, H. B. Der Aberglaube des Mittelalters. Breslau. 1858.

Fehr, J. Der Aberglaube und die kathol. Kirche des Mittelalters. Stuttgart. 1857.

Carini, S. I. Sulle scienze occulte nel medio evo. Palermo. 1872.

Graf, A. Miti, leggende, e superstizioni del medio evo. 2 vols. Turin. 1892-3. 2nd edn. 1 vol. 1925.

Kittredge, G. L. Witchcraft in Old and New England. Cambridge, Mass. 1929. [Includes not a little on the period before 1500.]

Stoeber, A. Zur Geschichte des Volksaberglaubens im Anfange des 16 Jahrhts. 2nd edn. Basle. 1875.

Singer, C. From Magic to Science. New York. 1928.

Sigerist, H. E. Studien und Texte zu frühmittelalterlichen Rezeptliteratur. Leipsic. 1923.

(*b*) Local Studies.

Pradel, F. Griechische und süditalienische Gebete, Beschwörungen, und Rezepte des Mittelalters. Giessen. 1907.

Dobeneck, F. L. F. von. Des deutschen Mittelalters Volksglauben. 2 vols. Berlin. 1815.

Barthéty, H. La sorcellerie en Béarn et dans le pays Basque. Pau. 1879.

Blasio, A. de. Inciarmatori, maghi, e streghe di Benevento. Naples. 1900.

Canaan, T. Aberglaube und Volksmedizin im Lande der Bibel. Hamburg. 1914.

Courthion, L. Les veillées des Mayens, légendes et traditions Valaisannes. Geneva. 1896.

Grohmann, J. V. Aberglauben und Gebräuche aus Böhmen und Mähren. Leipsic. 1864.

Jeanneret, F. A. Les sorciers dans le pays de Neuchâtel au xve–xviie siècle. 1862.

Kaufmann, R. Pratiques et superstitions médicales en Poitou. Paris. 1906.

Lavanchy, J. M. Sabbats ou synagogues sur les bords du lac d'Annecy. Annecy. 1896.

Riezler, S. Geschichte der Hexenprocesse in Bayern. Stuttgart. 1896.

Rocal, G. Les vieilles coutumes dévotieuses et magiques du Périgord. Toulouse. 1922.

Stoll, O. Zur Kenntnis des Zauberglaubens, der Volksmagie und Volksmedizin in der Schweiz. *In* Jahresbericht d. geog.-ethnog. Gesellschaft in Zürich. 1909. pp. 37–208.

Stern, B. Medizin, Aberglaube, und Geschlechtsleben in der Türkei. Berlin. 1903.

Rapp, L. Die Hexenprocesse und ihre Gegner in Tirol. 2nd edn. Brixen. 1891.

Lespy, V. Les sorcières dans le Béarn 1393–1672. *In* Bulletin de la Soc. des sciences de Pau. iv. 1874.

Jove y Bravo, R. Mitos y supersticiones de Asturias. Oviedo. 1903.

Leber, C. Des magiciens, des sorciers, et des devins chez les français. *In* Collection des meilleurs dissertations, notices, et traités particuliers relatifs à l'hist. de France. Vol. xi. Paris. 1838. pp. 82–121.

(*c*) Biography and Studies of Individuals.

Naudé, G. Apologie pour tous les grands personnages qui ont esté faussement soupçonnez de magie. Paris. 1625.

Nitzsch, F. Augustinus' Lehre vom Wunder. Berlin. 1865.

Brown, J. W. An inquiry into the life and legend of Michael Scot. Edinburgh. 1897.

Pouchet, F. A. Histoire des sciences naturelles au moyen âge, ou Albert le Grand et son époque considérés comme point de départ de l'école expérimentale. Paris. 1853.

Mandonnet, P. Siger de Brabant et l'averroïsme latin au xiiie siècle. 2nd edn. 2 vols. Louvain. 1908, 11.

Boncompagni, B. Della vita e delle opere di Guido Bonatti astrologo ed astronomo del secolo decimoterzo. Repr. from Giornale Arcadico. cxxiii–iv. Rome. 1851.

Sante Ferrari. I tempi, la vita, le dottrine di Pietro d'Abano. *In* Atti dell' Università di Genova. xiv. 1900.

—— Per la biografia e per gli scritti di Pietro d'Abano. *In* Atti dell' Accad. dei Lincei. Mem. della classe di scienze morali. xv. Rome. 1918. pp. 629–727.

Ritter, H. Picatrix, ein arabisches Handbuch hellenisticher Magie. *In* Vorträge d. Bibliothek Warburg. Hamburg. 1923.

Birkenmajer, A. Henri Bate de Malines. Repr. from La Pologne au Congrès International de Bruxelles. Cracow. 1923.

Boffito, P. G. Perchè fu condannato al fuoco l' astrologo Cecco d' Ascoli? *In* Studi e documenti di storia e diritto. xx. Rome. 1899. pp. 357–82.

Wickersheimer, E. Henri de Saxe et le De secretis mulierum. Antwerp. 1923.

Gabory, É. La vie et la mort de Gilles de Raiz. Paris. 1926. [The most recent of numerous treatments of him.]

Franz, A. Der Magister Nicolaus Magni de Jawor. Freiburg-i.-B. 1898.

Villain, E. F. Histoire critique de Nicolas Flamel et de Pernelle, sa femme, recueillie d'actes anciens qui justifient l'origine et la médiocrité de leur fortune contre les imputations des alchimistes. Paris. 1761.

Hartwig, O. Henricus de Langestein dictus de Hassia. Marburg. 1857.

Simonini, R. Maino de Maineri ed il suo Libellus de preservatione ab epydemia. Modena. 1923.

Oreglia, G. Giovanni Pico della Mirandola e la Cabala. Cagarelli. 1894.

Massetani, G. La filosofia cabbalistica di Giovanni Pico della Mirandola. Empoli. 1897.

(d) Survival of Paganism.

Bouché-Leclercq, A. L'astrologie grecque. Paris. 1899.

Cumont, F. Oriental religions in Roman paganism. Chicago. 1911.

—— Astrology and religion among the Greeks and Romans. 2 vols. New York. 1912.

Grenier, Dom. Introduction à l'histoire générale de la province de Picardie. Amiens. 1856.

Hälsig, F. Der Zauberspruch bei den Germanen bis um die Mitte des 16 Jahrhts. Leipsic. 1910.

Hamilton, M. Incubation or the cure of disease in pagan temples and christian churches. London. 1906.

—— Greek Saints and their festivals. Edinburgh. 1910.

Indiculus superstitionum et paganarum rituum. Ed. Saupe, H. A. Leipsic. 1891.

Kampers, F. Die tiburtinische Sibylle des Mittelalters. Munich. 1894.

Mackenzie, W. Gaelic incantations, charms, and blessings from the Hebrides. Inverness. 1895.

Oberle, B. A. Ueberreste germanischen Heidentums in Christentum. Baden-Baden. 1883.

Patch, H. R. The Goddess Fortuna in medieval literature. Cambridge, Mass. 1927.

Rochholz, E. L. Deutscher Glaube und Brauch im Spiegel der heidnischen Vorzeit. Berlin. 1867.

Soltau, W. Das Fortleben des Heidentums in der altchristlichen Kirche. Berlin. 1906.

Steele, R. Dies Aegyptiaci. *In* Proc. Roy. Soc. of Medicine. London. xiii (1919). Sect. of the hist. of medicine, pp. 108–21.

Warburg, A. Heidnisch-antike Weissagung in Wort und Bild zu Luthers Zeiten. *In* Sitzungsb. der Heidelberger Akad. der Wissensch., Philos.-hist. Kl. 1919.

Vordemfelde, H. Die Germanische Religion in den deutschen Volksrechten. *In* Religionsgeschichtl. Versuche und Vorarbeiten. xviii. Giessen. 1923. [pp. 125–49 deal especially with witchcraft and sorcery.]

Boese, R. Superstitiones arelatenses e Caesario collectae. Marburg. 1908.

Maury, L. F. A. Les fées du moyen âge, recherches sur leur origine, leur histoire et leurs attributs, pour servir à la connaissance de la mythologie gauloise. Paris. 1843.

Schreiber, H. Die Feen in Europa. Freiburg-i.-B. 1842.

Wentz, W. Y. E. The fairy-faith in Celtic countries. Rennes. 1909.

(e) Anglo-Saxon.

Cockayne, O. Leechdoms, wortcunning, and starcraft of Early England. 3 vols. (Rolls.) London. 1864.

Singer, C. Early English magic and medicine. London. 1920.

(*f*) ARABIC AND HEBREW.

[*Further titles will be found below under sections* (*j*), (*n*), (*o*).]

Ahrens, W. Studien über die magischen Quadrate der Araber. *In* Der Islam. VII (1917). 186–250.

Lidzbarski, M. De propheticis quae dicuntur legendis arabicis. Leipsic. 1894.

Brecher, G. Das Transcendentale Magie und magische Heilarten im Talmud. Vienna. 1850.

Groff, W. N. Études sur la sorcellerie ou le rôle que la Bible a joué chez les sorciers. *In* Institut Égyptien. Cairo. 1897.

Vulliaud, P. La kabbale juive. Histoire et doctrines. 2 vols. Paris. 1923.

Wiedemann, E. and Hauser, F. Ueber Trinkgefässe und Tafelaufsätze nach al-Gazari und den Benu Musa. *In* Der Islam. VIII (1918). 55–93.

(*g*) DREAMS, VISIONS, AND PROPHECIES.

Achmet filius Sereimi. Oneirocriticon. Ed. Rigaltius, N. Paris. 1603. Greek text ed. Drexl, F. Leipsic. 1925.

Diepgen, P. Traum und Traumbedeutung als medizinisch-naturwissenschaftlichen Problem im Mittelalter. Berlin. 1912.

Rocquain, F. L'hypnotisme au moyen âge. *In* Notes et fragments d'histoire. Paris. 1906.

Voigt, M. Beiträge zur Geschichte der Visionenliteratur im Mittelalter. Leipsic. 1924.

Kampers, F. Kaiserprophetieen und Kaisersagen im Mittelalter. Munich. 1895.

—— Ueber die Prophezeiungen des Johannes de Rupescissa. HJ. XV (1894). 796–802.

Rohr, J. Die Prophetie im letzten Jahrht. vor der Reformation. HJ. XIX (1898). 447–86.

(*h*) BENEDICTIONS, CONJURATIONS, AND EXORCISMS.

Franz, A. Die kirchlichen Benedictionen im Mittelalter. 2 vols. Freiburg. 1909.

Probst, F. Kirchliche Benediktionen und ihre Verwaltung. Tübingen. 1857.

Carmichael, A. Carmina Gadelica: hymns and incantations. 2nd edn. London. 1928.

Klapper, J. Das Gebet im Zauberglauben des Mittelalters. *In* Mittheil. der schlesischen Gesellsch. für Volkskunde. IX. Breslau. 1907. pp. 5–41.

Dölger, F. J. Der Exorzismus im altchristlichen Taufritual. Paderborn. 1909.

(*i*) PSEUDO-LITERATURE AND SECRETS.

Lehmann, P. Pseudo-antike Literatur des Mittelalters. Leipsic. 1927.

Sackur, E. Sibyllinische Texte und Forschungen. Halle. 1898.

Steinschneider, M. Zur pseudepigraphischen Literatur insbesondere der geheimen Wissenschaften des Mittelalters; aus hebräischen und arabischen Quellen. Berlin. 1862.

Battelli, G. Segreti di magia e medicina medievale cavati da un codice del Tesoro. *In* Archivum Romanicum. V. Geneva. 1926.

Giannini, G. Una curiosa raccolta di segreti e di pratiche superstiziose fatta da un popolano Fiorentino del secolo XIV. Città di Castello. 1899.

(*j*) LAPIDARIES.

Pseudo-Aristotle. Lapidarius. Merseburg. 1473.

Lapidario del rey D. Alfonso X. Codice original [in coloured facsimile]. Madrid. 1879.

Camillus de Leonardis. Speculum lapidum. Venice. 1502.

Clément-Mullet, J. J. Essai sur la minéralogie arabe. *In* Journal Asiatique. Ser. VI. Vol. XI. Paris. 1868.

Evans, J. Magical jewels of the Middle Ages and the Renaissance particularly in England. Oxford. 1922.

Garrett, R. M.　Precious stones in Old English literature.　*In* Münchener Beiträge. xlvii. Erlangen. 1909.

Giordano, C.　Trattato delle virtù delle pietre preziose, scrittura inedita del secolo xv. Città di Castello. 1912.

Mély, F. de, and Ruelle, C. E.　Les lapidaires de l'antiquité et du moyen âge. Paris. 1896.

Pannier, L.　Les lapidaires français du moyen âge. Paris. 1882.

Rose, V.　Aristoteles De lapidibus und Arnoldus Saxo.　*In* Zeitschr. f. deutsches Alterthum. xviii (1875). 321–447.

Ruska, J.　Das Steinbuch des Aristoteles…nach der arabischen Handschrift. Heidelberg. 1912; to be supplemented by the article of C. F. Seybold *in* ZDMG. lxviii (1914). 606–26.

—— Griechische Planetendarstellungen in arabischen Steinbüchern.　*In* Sitzungsb. der Heidelberger Akad. der Wissensch., Philos.-hist. Kl. 1919.

Steinschneider, M.　Arabische Lapidarien. ZDMG. xlix. 1895.

Studer, P. and Evans, J.　Anglo-Norman Lapidaries. Paris. 1924.

(k) Herbs.

Arber, A.　Herbals: their origin and evolution. Cambridge. 1912.

Fischer, H.　Mittelalterliche Pflanzenkunde. Munich. 1929.

Gessmann, G. W.　Die Pflanze im Zauberglauben. Vienna. 1899.

Joret, C.　Les plantes dans l'antiquité et au moyen âge. 2 vols. Paris. 1897, 1904.

Unger, F.　Die Pflanze als Zaubermittel. Vienna. 1859.

(l) Magic in Literature.

Callcott, F.　The supernatural in early Spanish literature, studied in the works of the court of Alfonso X. New York. 1923.

Dickman, A. J.　Le rôle du surnaturel dans les Chansons de Geste. Iowa City. 1925.

Easter, D. B.　A study of the magic elements in the Romans d'Aventure and the Romans Bretons. Baltimore. 1906.

Hallauer, M.　Das wunderbare Element in den Chansons de Geste. Basle. 1918.

Curry, W. C.　Chaucer and the Medieval Sciences. London. 1926.

Kittredge, G. L.　A study of Gawain and the Green Knight. Cambridge, Mass. 1916.

Krappe, A. H.　Balor with the Evil Eye. New York. 1927.

Parry, J. J.　The Vita Merlini. (Univ. of Illinois Studies in Lang. and Lit. x, no. 3.) Urbana, Ill. 1925.

Paton, L. A.　Les prophecies de Merlin. Edited from MS. 593 in the Bibliothèque Municipale of Rennes. 2 vols. (Mod. Lang. Assocn. of America.) New York. 1926-7.

Robinson, F. N.　Satirists and enchanters in early Irish literature.　*In* Studies in the history of religion presented to C. H. Toy. New York. 1912. pp. 95–130.

Schiavo, G.　Fede e superstizione nell' antica poesia francese.　*In* Zeitschr. f. romanische Philol. xv. Halle. 1891.

Schröder, R.　Glaube und Aberglaube in den altfranzösischen Dichtungen. Erlangen. 1886.

Tatlock, J. S. P.　Astrology and magic in Chaucer's Franklin's Tale.　*In* Kittredge Anniversary Papers. Boston. 1913. pp. 339–50.

Tavenner, E.　Studies in magic from Latin literature. New York. 1916.

Waxman, S. M.　Chapters on magic in Spanish literature. New York. 1916.

(m) The Inquisition and other Trials for Magic.

Albe, E.　Autour de Jean XXII: Hugues Géraud, évêque de Cahors; l'affaire des poisons et des envoûtements en 1317. Cahors. 1904.

Champion, P.　Procès de condamnation de Jeanne d'Arc. 2 vols. Paris. 1920–1. [In the introduction her trial is briefly compared with other contemporary trials for sorcery.]

Cherveix, Jean de.　Deux cents viols par un maréchal de France. Relation du procès en hérésie, évocations, sodomie contre Gilles de Laval, sire de Rais, maréchal de France, conseiller du roi, d'après les MSS. de 1440. Paris. 1903.

Cognasso, F. Un processo per sortilegio alla corte di Amedeo VIII. *In* Bollettino storico-bibliog. subalpino. Anno xxvi. Turin. 1924. pp. 165–72.

Esquieu, L. Jean XXII et les sciences occultes. *In* Bulletin trimestrial de la Soc. des études litt., sciences, et arts du Lot. xxii-(1897). 186–96.

—— Une bulle du pape Jean XXII. *Ibid.* xxvii (1902). 38–46.

—— Le couteau magique de Jean XXII. Cahors. 1899.

Eubel, K. Vom Zaubereinwesen anfangs des 14 Jahrhts. HJ. xviii (1897). 608–31.

Français, J. L'Église et la sorcellerie. Paris. 1910.

Giraud, A. Étude sur les procès de sorcellerie en Normandie. Rouen. 1897.

Hauréau, B. Bernard Délicieux et l'inquisition albigeoise. Paris. 1887.

Hoensbroech, Graf von. Das Papstthum in seiner sozialkulturellen Wirksamkeit. Vol. i. Inquisition, Aberglaube, Teufelsspuk, und Hexenwahn. Leipsic. 1900. [Polemical.]

Lamothe-Langon, E. L. Histoire de l'inquisition en France. 3 vols. Paris. 1829. [Valuable for the publication of materials from the archives of Toulouse and Carcassonne no longer extant, but largely reprinted in Hansen, J. Quellen, etc. *See above*, ii (a).]

Langlois, C. V. Le fin d'Hugues Géraud. *In* La revue de Paris. 1906. pp. 531–52.

Lea, H. C. History of the Inquisition of the Middle Ages. *See Gen. Bibl.* v. [Chapter on magic and occult science in Vol. iii.]

Marx, J. L'inquisition en Dauphiné, étude sur le développement de la répression de l'hérésie et de la sorcellerie du xive siècle au temps de François I. Paris. 1914.

Menéndez y Pelayo, M. Historia de los heterodoxos españoles. 3 vols. Madrid. 1911–17.

Mollat, G. Guichard de Troyes et les révélations de la sorcellerie de Bourdenay. MA. xii. 1908.

Mouan. Documents inédits sur un procès de magie en Provence. *In* Mém. lus à la Sorbonne, Histoire. 1869. p. 173.

Pratt, Sister Antoinette Marie. The attitude of the Catholic Church towards witchcraft and the allied practices of sorcery and magic. Washington. 1915.

Reinach, S. La tête magique des Templiers. *In* Revue de l'hist. des religions. lxiii. Paris. 1910.

Rigault, A. Le procès de Guichard, évêque de Troyes, 1308–13. Paris. 1896.

Tanon, C. L. Histoire des tribunaux de l'inquisition en France. Paris. 1893.

Thorndike, Lynn. Relations of the Inquisition to Peter of Abano and Cecco d'Ascoli. *In* Speculum. i (1926). 338–43.

—— Franciscus Florentinus or Paduanus, an inquisitor of the fifteenth century, and his treatise on astrology and divination, magic and popular superstition. *In* Mélanges Mandonnet. Vol. ii. Paris. 1930. pp. 353–69.

Trummer, C. Vorträge über Tortur und Hexenverfolgungen. Hamburg. 1844.

Wright, T. Contemporary narrative of the proceedings against Dame Alice Kyteler... 1324. (Camden Soc. xxiv.) London. 1843.

(*n*) Astrology.

Baron, H. Willensfreiheit und Astrologie bei Marsilio Ficino und Pico della Mirandola. *In* Festschrift W. Goetz, 60 Geburtstage. Leipsic. 1927. pp. 145–70.

Bezold, F. von. Astrologische Geschichtskonstruction im Mittelalter. DZG. viii (1892). 29 sqq.

Bonnaud, R. Notes sur l'astrologie latine au vie siècle. *In* Revue belge de philol. et d'hist. x (1931). 557–77.

De la Ville de Mirmont (H.). L'astrologie chez les Gallo-Romains. Bordeaux. 1904. Repr. from Revue des études anciennes. 1902–6.

Duhem, P. L'astrologie au moyen âge. RQH. xxvi (1914). 349–91.

Gabotto, F. L'astrologia nel Quattrocento in rapporto colla civiltà. *In* Rivista di filosofia scientifica. viii (1889). 378 sqq.

—— Bartolomeo Manfredi e l'astrologia alla corte di Mantova. Turin. 1891.

—— Nuove ricerche e documenti sull'astrologia alla corte degli Estensi e degli Sforze. Turin. 1891.

Hauber, A. Zur Verbreitung des Astronomen Sûfi. *In* Der Islam. VIII (1918). 48–54.

Hauréau, B. Le Mathematicus de Bernard Silvestris. Paris. 1895.

Hellmann, G. Die Wettervorhersage im ausgehenden Mittelalter. *In* Beiträge z. Gesch. d. Meteorologie. Vol. II. pp. 169–229. (Veröff. d. preuss. meteorol. Inst., 296.) Berlin. 1917.

Hommel, F. Der Gestirndienst der alten Araber und die altisraelitische Ueberlieferung. Munich. 1901.

Jourdain, C. Nicolas Oresme et les astrologues de la cour de Charles V. *In* Excursions historiques et philosophiques à travers le moyen âge. Paris. 1888.

Lebeuf, J. De l'astrologie qui avait cours sous Charles V. *In* Dissertations sur l'hist. ecclés. et civile de Paris. Vol. III. Paris. 1743. pp. 445–56; repr. *in* Collection des meilleurs dissertations...relatifs à l'hist. de France. Ed. Leber, C. Vol. XV. Paris. 1838. pp. 397–408.

Levy, R. The Astrological Works of Abraham ibn Ezra. A literary and linguistic study with special reference to the old French translation of Hagin. Baltimore. 1927.

Loth, O. Al-Kindi als Astrolog. *In* Morgenländische Forschungen, Festschrift... H. L. Fleischer. Leipsic. 1875.

Marx, A. The correspondence between the Rabbis of Southern France and Maimonides about astrology. Repr. from the Hebrew Union College Annual. III. Cincinnati. 1926.

Mehren, A. F. Vues d'Avicenne sur l'astrologie et sur le rapport de la responsabilité humaine avec le destin. Louvain. 1885.

Nixon, J. A. A new Guy de Chauliac manuscript. *In* Seventeenth International Congress of Medicine. London. 1913. Sect. XXIII. pp. 419–24.

Pèrcopo, E. L'umanista Pomponio Gaurico e Luca Gaurico ultimo degli astrologi. Naples. 1895.

Rose, V. Ptolemaeus und die Schule von Toledo. *In* Hermes. VIII. Berlin. 1874. pp. 327–49.

Ruska, J. Zahl und Null bei Gabir ibn Hajjan mit ein Exkurs über Astrologie im Sasanidenreiche. *In* Archiv f. Gesch. d. Math. d. Naturwiss. u. d. Technik. XI (1929). 256–64.

Sánchez Pérez, J. A. El libro de las cruces. *In* Isis. XIV (1930). 77–132.

Soldati, B. La poesia astrologica nel quattrocento, ricerche e studi. Florence. 1906.

Soriano Viguera, J. La astronomia de Alfonso X el Sabio. Contribución al conocimiento de los trabajos astrónomicos desarrollados en la Escuela de Alfonso X el Sabio. Madrid. 1926.

Steinschneider, M. Maschallah. ZDMG. LVII (1899). 434–40.

Strauss, H. A. Der astrologische Gedanke in der deutschen Vergangenheit. Munich. 1926.

Sudhoff, K. Iatromathematiker vornehmlich im 15 und 16 Jahrht. Breslau. 1902.

Vera, F. El tratado de astrologia del Marqués de Villena. *In* Erudición Ibero-Ultramarina. I (1930). 18–67.

Wedel, T. C. The medieval attitude toward Astrology, particularly in England. New Haven. 1920.

Weigl, L. Studien zu dem unedierten astrologischen Lehrgedichte des Johannes Kamateros. Würzburg. 1902.

Wickersheimer, E. Figures médico-astrologiques des IXe, Xe, et XIe siècles. *In* Seventeenth International Congress of Medicine. London. 1913. Sect. XXIII. pp. 313–23.

(o) ALCHEMY.

Lenglet du Fresnoy, N. Hist. de la philosophie hermétique. 3 vols. Paris. 1742.

Wiegleb, J. C. Historisch-kritische Untersuchung der Alchemie. Weimar. 1777.

Berthelot, P. E. M. Les origines de l'alchimie. Paris. 1885.

—— La chimie au moyen âge. 3 vols. Paris. 1893.

Kopp, H. Die Alchemie in älterer und neuerer Zeit. Heidelberg. 1886.

Lippmann, E. O. von. Entstehung und Ausbreitung der Alchemie. Berlin. 1919.

Mieli, A. Pagine di storia della chimica. Rome. 1922.

Poisson, A. Histoire de l'alchimie, xive siècle. 1893.
—— Théories et symboles des alchimistes. Paris. 1891.
Luanco, J. R. de. La Alquimia en España. Barcelona. 1889.
Ray, P. C. History of Hindu Chemistry...to the middle of the sixteenth century. 2nd edn. 2 vols. London. 1903–25.
Reitzenstein, R. Alchemistische Lehrschriften und Märchen bei den Arabern. Giessen. 1923.
—— Zur Geschichte der Alchemie und des Mystizismus. *In* Göttingen Nachrichten. Jahrg. 1919, Phil.-hist. Kl. pp. 5 sqq.
Ruska, J. Arabische Alchemisten. 2 vols. Heidelberg. 1924, in progress.
—— Tabula Smaragdina: ein Beitrag zur Geschichte der hermetischen Literatur. 1926.
—— Turba philosophorum: ein Beitrag zur Geschichte der Alchemie. Berlin. 1931.
Hammer-Jensen, I. Die älteste Alchemie. Copenhagen. 1921.
Gessmann, G. W. Die Geheimsymbole der Alchymie, Arzneikunde, und Astrologie des Mittelalters. 2nd edn. Berlin. 1922.
Darmstaedter, E. Die Alchemie des Geber. Berlin. 1922.
Zachar, O. O alchymi a českych alchymistech. Prague. 1911.

Of the periodical literature on medieval alchemy only a few indications may be given.
Browne, C. A. The poem of the philosopher Theophrastos upon the Sacred Art. *In* The Scientific Monthly. 1920. pp. 193–214.
Plessner, M. Neue Materialen zur Geschichte der Tabula Smaragdina. *In* Der Islam. xvi (1927). 77–113.
Stapleton, H. E. Sal Ammoniac. *In* Memoirs of the Asiatic Soc. of Bengal. i (1906). 25–42.
Stapleton, H. E. and Azo, R. F. Alchemical equipment in the eleventh century. *Ibid.*, 47–70; and other articles.
Stapleton, H. E. Chemistry in Iraq and Persia in the tenth century A.D. *Ibid.* viii (1927).
Steinschneider, M. Zur alchemistischen Literatur der Araber. ZDMG. lviii (1904). 299–315.
Hammer-Jensen, I. Das sogenannte iv Buch der Meteorologie des Aristoteles. *In* Hermes. l. Berlin. 1915. pp. 113–36.
Wiedemann, E. Zur Alchemie bei den Arabern. (Abh. zur Gesch. d. Naturwiss. u. d. Medizin, vii.) Erlangen. 1922; and many similar articles.
Sudhoff, K. Eine alchemistische Schrift des 13 Jahrhts., betitelt 'Speculum alkimiae minus,' eines bisher unbekannten Mönches Simeon von Köln. *In* Archiv f. Gesch. d. Naturwiss. ix (1922). 53–67.
Diepgen, P. Studien zu Arnald von Villanova. iii, Arnald und die Alchemie. *In* Archiv f. Gesch. d. Medizin. iii (1910). 369–96.
Singer, D. W. The Alchemical Testament attributed to Raymund Lull. *In* Archeion. ix (1928). 43–52.
Ruska, J. Die siebzig Bücher des Gabir ibn Hajjan. *In* Studien z. Gesch. d. Chemie, Festgabe f. Edmund O. von Lippmann. Berlin. 1927. pp. 38–47.
Darmstaedter, E. Liber misericordiae Geber. *In* Archiv f. Gesch. d. Medizin. xviii (1925). 181–97.
Holmyard, E. J. Chemistry in Islâm. *In* Scientia. 1926. pp. 287–96.
[And various other articles by the last three authors named.]

(p) MAGIC BOOKS.

Jacoby, A. Die Zauberbücher von Mittelalter bis zur Neuzeit, ihre Sammlung und Bearbeitung. *In* Mitteil. d. schlesischen Gesellsch. f. Volkskunde. xxxi (1930). 208-28.
Thorndike, Lynn. Alfodhol und Almadel. *In* Speculum. ii (1927). 326-31; iv (1929). 90.

CHAPTER XXIII.

EDUCATION IN THE FOURTEENTH AND FIFTEENTH CENTURIES.

I. SPECIAL BIBLIOGRAPHIES.

[*See also* Bibliographies to Vol. v, ch. xxii, Vol. vi, ch. xvii, and Vol. vii, ch. xxv. Many of the books listed below contain important bibliographical material.]

Adamson, J. W. A guide to the history of education. (Helps for Students of History. No. 24.) S.P.C.K. London. 1920.

Monroe, W. S. Bibliography of education. New York. 1897.

Silvy, A. Essai d'une bibliographie historique de l'enseignement secondaire et supérieur en France avant la Révolution. Paris. 1894.

II. GENERAL WORKS.

Adamson, J. W. A short history of education. Cambridge. 1919.

Allen, P. S. The age of Erasmus. Oxford. 1914.

Allen, P. S. *ed.* Opus Epistolarum Des. Erasmi Roterodami. Oxford. 1906 ff., in progress.

Baumeister, A. Handbuch der Erziehungs- und Unterrichtslehre für höhere Schulen. 3rd edn. Munich. 1909.

Berlière, U. Les écoles abbatiales au moyen âge. RBén. vi (1889). 499–511.

—— Les collèges bénédictins aux universités du moyen âge. RBén. x (1893). 145–58.

Bernard, E. Les Dominicains dans l'université de Paris. Paris. 1883.

Bourbon, G. La licence d'enseigner et le rôle de l'écolâtre au moyen âge. RQH. xix (1876). 513–53.

Boyd, W. The history of western education. 3rd edn. London. 1932.

Büdinger, M. Von den Anfängen des Schulzwanges. (Festrede zur Feier des Stiftungstages der Hochschule Zürich am 29 April 1865 gehalten.) Zürich. 1865.

Chambers, E. K. The Mediaeval Stage. 2 vols. Oxford. 1903.

Clark, V. S. Studies in the Latin of the Middle Ages and the Renaissance. Lancaster, Pa. 1900.

Colson, F. H. *ed.* M. Fabii Quintiliani institutionis oratoriae liber i. Cambridge. 1924. [Valuable introdn.]

Comparetti, D. Virgilio nel medio evo. 2nd edn. Florence. 1896. Engl. transl. of 1st edn. Benecke, E. F. M. London. 1895.

Compayré, G. Histoire de la Pédagogie. Paris. 1883. Engl. transl., ed. Payne, W. H. 6th edn. Michigan. 1905.

Coulton, G. G. Monastic Schools in the Middle Ages. (Medieval Studies. No. 10.) London. 1913.

—— Religious education before the Reformation. *In* Ten Medieval Studies. Cambridge. 1930. pp. 108–22.

Creighton, M. Historical essays and reviews. London. 1902.

—— Historical lectures and addresses. London. 1903.

Cubberley, E. P. The history of education. Boston, Mass. 1920.

Deanesly, M. The Lollard Bible. Cambridge. 1920.

De Montmorency, J. E. G. State intervention in English education. Cambridge. 1902.

—— The progress of education in England. London. 1904.

ürr, F. A. De episcopo puerorum. Mayence. 1755; repr. *as* Commentatio de Episcopo puerorum *in* Schmidt, A. Thesaurus Juris Ecclesiastici. Vol. iii. pp. 58–83. Heidelberg. 1774.

Eckstein, F. A. Lateinischer und griechischer Unterricht. Ed. Heyden, H. Leipsic. 1887. [pp. 43–61. Lateinischer Unterricht im Mittelalter.]

Einstein, L. The Italian Renaissance in England. New York. 1902.

Falk, F. Die Schul- und Kinderfeste im Mittelalter. *In* Frankfürter zeitgemässe Broschüren. n.s. Vol. I. pp. 229–48. Frankfort-on-M. 1880.

Felder, H. Geschichte der wissenschaftlichen Studien im Franziskanerorden. Freiburg-i.-B. 1904.

Franz, A. Der Magister Nikolaus Magni de Jawor. Freiburg-i.-B. 1898.

Geiger, L. Renaissance und Humanismus in Italien und Deutschland. Berlin. 1882.

Glöckner, G. Das Ideal der Bildung und Erziehung bei Erasmus von Rotterdam. Dresden. 1889.

Graves, F. P. History of education during the Middle Ages and the transition to modern times. New York. 1912.

Grupp, G. Kulturgeschichte des Mittelalters. 3rd edn. Paderborn. 1921–4.

Haskins, C. H. Studies in mediaeval culture. Oxford. 1929.

—— Studies in the history of Mediaeval Science. 2nd edn. Cambridge, Mass. 1927.

Heppe, H. Geschichte des deutschen Volksschulwesens. 5 vols. Gotha. 1858–61.

—— Das Schulwesen des deutschen Mittelalters. Marburg. 1860.

Issaurat, C. La pédagogie, son évolution et son histoire. Paris. 1886.

Janssen, J. Geschichte des deutschen Volkes seit dem Ausgang des Mittelalters. Vol. I. Freiburg-i.-B. 1878. Engl. transl. Mitchell, M. A. and Christie, A. M. Vol. I. London. 1896.

Jourdain, C. Excursions historiques et philosophiques à travers le moyen âge. Paris. 1888.

Just, K. S. Zur Pädagogik des Mittelalters. (Pädagogische Studien. Ed. Rein, W. VI.) Leipsic. 1876.

Kämmel, H. J. Geschichte des deutschen Schulwesens im Übergange vom Mittelalter zur Neuzeit. Leipsic. 1882.

—— Mittelalterliches Schulwesen. *In* Schmid, K. A. Encykl. des gesammten Erziehungs- und Unterrichtswesens. Vol. IV. *See below.*

Kappes, M. Lehrbuch der Geschichte der Pädagogik. Münster-i.-W. 1898.

Kehr, C. Geschichte der Methodik des deutschen Volksschulunterrichts. 6 vols. 2nd edn. Gotha. 1889–90.

Langlois, C. V. Questions d'histoire et d'enseignement. Paris. 1902.

Little, A. G. Educational organisation of the mendicant friars in England. TRHS. VIII. 1894.

—— Studies in English Franciscan history. Manchester. 1917.

Lorenz, S. Volkserziehung und Volksunterricht im späteren Mittelalter. Paderborn. 1887.

Messer, A. Quintilian als Didaktiker. *In* Neue Jahrbücher für Philol. und Paedagogik. Leipsic. 1897.

Monroe, P. Cyclopedia of education. 5 vols. New York. 1911–13.

Müller, J. Quellenschriften und Geschichte des deutschsprachlichen Unterrichtes bis zur Mitte des 16 Jahrhts. (Anhang to Kehr, K. Geschichte der Methodik. Vol. IV. *See above.*)

—— Vor- und frühreformatorische Schulordnungen und Schulverträge in deutscher und niederländischer Sprache. (*esp.* Abt. 1.) *In* Müller I. and J. Sammlung selten gewordener pädagogischer Schriften früherer Zeiten. No. 12. Leipsic. 1885.

Power, E. E. Medieval English Nunneries. Cambridge. 1922.

Raumer, K. von. Geschichte der Pädagogik vom Wiederaufblühen klassischer Studien bis auf unsere Zeit. 7th edn. Stuttgart. 1897.

Rein, W. Encyclopädisches Handbuch der Pädagogik. 2nd edn. 10 vols. Langensalza. 1903–11.

Sandys, J. E. Harvard Lectures on the Revival of Learning. Cambridge. 1905.

—— History of Classical Scholarship. Vol. I. 3rd edn. Cambridge. 1921. Vol. II. *Ibid.* 1908.

Schiller, H. Lehrbuch der Geschichte der Pädagogik. 4th edn. Leipsic. 1904.

Schirmer, W. F. Der englische Frühhumanismus. Leipsic. 1931.

Schmid, K. A. Encyklopädie des gesammten Erziehungs- und Unterrichtswesens. 2nd edn. 10 vols. Leipsic. 1876–87.

—— Geschichte der Erziehung vom Anfang an bis auf unsere Zeit. 5 vols. Stuttgart. 1884–1902.

Schmidt, C. Histoire littéraire de l'Alsace à la fin du xvᵉ siècle. 2 vols. Paris. 1879.

Schmidt, K. Die Geschichte der Erziehung und des Unterrichts. Cöthen. 1863.

—— Geschichte der Pädagogik. 4th edn. 4 vols. Cöthen. 1890.

Schmitz, H. J. Das Volksschulwesen im Mittelalter. *In* Frankfürter zeitgemässe Broschüren. n.s. Vol. ii. pp. 303–31. Frankfort-on-M. 1881.

Stein, L. von. Die Verwaltungslehre. 2nd edn. Stuttgart. 1869. [*esp.* pt. v, Das Bildungswesen des Mittelalters.]

Tarsot, L. Les écoles et les écoliers à travers les âges. Paris. 1893.

Thurot, C. De l'organisation de l'enseignement dans l'université de Paris au moyen-âge. Paris. 1850.

Voigt, G. Die Wiederbelebung des classischen Alterthums. 3rd edn., ed. Lehnerdt, M. 2 vols. Berlin. 1893.

Watson, F. Encyclopedia and dictionary of education. 4 vols. London. 1921.

Willmann, O. Didaktik als Bildungslehre.... 5th edn. Brunswick. 1923.

Woodward, W. H. Desiderius Erasmus concerning the aim and method of Education. Cambridge. 1904. [Bibliography.]

—— Studies in education during the age of the Renaissance. Cambridge. 1906. [Bibliography.]

Ziegler, T. Geschichte der Pädagogik. (Vol. i, pt. i of Baumeister, A. Handbuch der Erziehungs- und Unterrichtslehre. *See above.*)

III. SUBJECTS OF STUDY.

Abelson, P. The seven liberal arts. New York. 1906.

Appuhn, G. W. A. F. Das Trivium und Quadrivium in Theorie und Praxis. Pt. i. Das Trivium. Erlangen. 1900. [no more publ.]

Baebler, J. J. Beiträge zu einer Geschichte der lateinischen Grammatik im Mittelalter. Halle. 1885.

Bursian, C. Geschichte der classischen Philologie in Deutschland. Leipsic. 1883.

Cantor, M. Vorlesungen über Geschichte der Mathematik. 3rd edn. Leipsic. 1899–1908. 4 vols. (Corrections *in* Acta Mathematica. Stockholm. 1880 ff.) 4th edn. of Vol. i. Leipsic. 1922.

Chase, W. J. The Distichs of Cato. Transl....with introdn. Madison, Wis. 1920.

—— The Ars Minor of Donatus. Transl....with introd. sketch. Madison, Wis. 1926.

Fierville, C. Une grammaire latine inédite du xiiiᵉ siècle. Paris. 1886.

Gunther, S. Geschichte des mathematischen Unterrichts im deutschen Mittelalter bis zum Jahre 1525. (Monumenta Germaniae Paedagogica. iii.) Berlin. 1887.

Haase, H. A. F. De medii aevi studiis philologicis disputatio. Breslau. 1856.

Keil, H. *ed.* Grammatici Latini. 8 vols. Leipsic. 1857–80.

Liliencron, F. R. von. Ueber den Inhalt der allgemeinen Bildung in der Zeit der Scholastik. Munich. 1876.

Meier, G. Die sieben freien Künste im Mittelalter. 2 pts. Einsiedeln. 1886-7.

Paetow, L. J. The arts course at medieval universities with special reference to grammar and rhetoric. Champaign, Illinois. 1910.

—— The Battle of the Seven Arts. Berkeley, California. 1914.

—— Morale Scolarium of John of Garland. Berkeley, California. 1927.

Reichling, D. *ed.* Das Doctrinale des Alexander de Villa-Dei. (Monumenta Germaniae Paedagogica. xii.) Berlin. 1893. [Bibliography.]

Thurot, C. Documents relatifs à l'histoire de la grammaire au moyen-âge. *In* Comptes rendus AcadIBL. n.s. Vol. vi. pp. 242 ff. Paris. 1870.

—— Notices et extraits de divers manuscrits latins pour servir à l'histoire des doctrines grammaticales au moyen-âge. *In* Notices et extraits des MSS. de la Bibliothèque Impériale. Vol. xxii. 1868.

Voigt, E. Das erste Lesebuch des Triviums in den Kloster- und Stiftsschulen des Mittelalters. *In* Mitteil. der Gesellschaft für deutsche Erziehungs- und Schulgesch. i. pp. 42–53. Berlin. 1891.

IV. PARTICULAR COUNTRIES AND SCHOOLS.

A. ENGLAND.

Cust, L. H. History of Eton College. London. 1899.

Furnivall, F. J. Education in early England. London. 1867.

Gardiner, D. English Girlhood at School. Oxford. 1929.

Heywood, J. and Wright, T. The ancient laws of the fifteenth century, for King's College, Cambridge, and for...Eton College. London. 1850.

Kirby, T. F. Annals of Winchester College from its foundation in the year 1382. London. 1892.

Knight, S. Life of Dr J. Colet,...founder of S. Paul's School. New edn. Oxford. 1823.

Leach, A. F. Articles on Schools in Vict. Co. Hist. (*See Gen. Bibl.* I.) Berkshire, Bedfordshire, Buckinghamshire, Derbyshire, Durham, Essex, Gloucestershire, Hampshire, Hertfordshire, Lancashire, Lincolnshire, Northamptonshire, Nottinghamshire, Somersetshire, Suffolk, Surrey, Sussex, Warwickshire, Yorkshire.

—— Documents illustrating early education in Worcester, 685–1700. London. 1913.

—— Early Yorkshire Schools. Vol. I. York, Beverley, Ripon. Vol. II. Pontefract, Howden, Northallerton, Acaster, Rotherham, Giggleswick, Sedbergh. (Yorkshire Archaeol. Soc. Record Series. Vol. XXVII. 1898. Vol. XXXIII. 1903.)

—— Educational charters and documents, 598 to 1909. Cambridge. 1911.

—— English Schools at the Reformation, 1546–8. London. 1896.

—— History of Warwick School.... London. 1906.

—— History of Winchester College. London. 1899.

—— Memorials of Beverley Minster. 2 vols. (Surtees Soc. 98, 108.) Durham. 1898, 1903.

—— The Schools of Medieval England. 2nd edn. London. 1916.

—— Some results of research in the history of Education in England; with suggestions for its continuance and extension. *In* Proc. British Acad. VI. London. 1915.

—— Visitations and memorials of Southwell Minster. (Camden Soc. N.S. XLVIII.) London. 1891.

Lloyd, A. H. The early history of Christ's College, Cambridge. Cambridge. 1934.

Lupton, J. H. Life of John Colet.... 2nd edn. London. 1909.

Lyte, H. C. Maxwell. History of Eton College, 1440–1910. 4th edn. London. 1911.

Parry, A. W. Education in England in the Middle Ages. London. 1920.

Seebohm, F. The Oxford Reformers of 1498. 3rd edn. London. 1887.

Todd, H. J. History of the College of Bonhommes, at Ashridge, in the county of Buckingham. London. 1823.

Vickers, K. H. Humphrey, Duke of Gloucester. London. 1907.

Watson, F. The English Grammar Schools to 1660: their curriculum and practice. Cambridge. 1908.

B. SCOTLAND.

Edgar, J. History of early Scottish education. Edinburgh. 1893.

Grant, J. History of the Burgh and Parish Schools of Scotland. Vol. I. pp. 1–75. London and Glasgow. 1876.

Kerr, J. Scottish education, school and university, from early times to 1908. Cambridge. 1910.

Strong, J. History of secondary education in Scotland. Oxford. 1909.

C. FRANCE.

Allain, E. L'instruction primaire en France avant la Révolution. Paris. 1881.

Beaurepaire, C. M. de R. de. Recherches sur l'instruction publique dans le diocèse de Rouen...avant 1789. 3 vols. Évreux. 1872.

Carré, G. L'enseignement secondaire à Troyes, du moyen-âge à la Révolution. Paris. 1888.

—— Histoire populaire de Troyes et du département de l'Aube. Troyes. 1889.

Clerval, A. Les écoles de Chartres au moyen-âge, du Ve au XVIe siècle. Paris. 1895.

Knepper, J. Das Schul- und Unterrichtswesen im Elsass von den Anfängen bis gegen das Jahr 1530. Strasbourg. 1905.

Maître, L. L'instruction publique dans les villes et les campagnes du Comté Nantais avant 1789. Nantes. 1882.

Muteau, C. Les écoles et collèges en province depuis les temps les plus reculés jusqu'en 1789. Paris. 1882.

Schmidt, C. G. A. La vie et les travaux de Jean Sturm. Strasbourg. 1855.

Thomas, A. Jean de Gerson et l'éducation des dauphins de France. Paris. 1930.

D. Germany.

Becker, D. J. Chronica eines fahrenden Schülers, oder Wanderbüchlein des Johannes Butzbach. Ratisbon. 1869; repr. Leipsic. [c. 1925.]

Beyschlag, D. E.   Versuch einer Schulgeschichte der Reichsstadt Nördlingen. Nördlingen. 1793.

Detten, G. von. Ueber die Stift- und Klosterschulen Sachsens im Mittelalter. *In* Frankfürter zeitgemässe Broschüren. n.s. Vol. xvii. Frankfort-on-M. 1896.

Eberhard, F. Das deutsche Volksschulwesen vor und nach der Reformation. *Ibid.*

Fechter, D. A. Geschichte des Schulwesens in Basel bis zum Jahr 1589. Basle. 1837-9.

—— Thomas Platter und Felix Platter, zwei Autobiographieen. Basle. 1840.

Heinemann, F. Geschichte des Schul- und Bildungslebens im alten Freiburg bis zum 17 Jahrht. Fribourg. 1895.

Kaemmel, O. Geschichte des Leipziger Schulwesens vom Anfänge des 13 bis gegen die Mitte des 19 Jahrhts. Leipsic. 1909.

Kehrbach, C.   Texte und Forschungen zur Geschichte der Erziehung und des Unterrichts in den Ländern deutscher Zunge. Berlin. 1897 ff. 5 pts. publ. Continued after 1903 as supplt. to Mitteilungen der Gesellschaft für deutsche Erziehungs- und Schulgeschichte.

Knabe, K. Geschichte des deutschen Schulwesens. Leipsic. 1905.

Monroe, P. Thomas Platter and the Educational Renaissance of the sixteenth century. New York. 1904.

Müller, J. Die Anfänge des sächsischen Schulwesens. *In* Neues Archiv für sächsische Gesch. und Alterthumskunde. viii. pp. 1-40, 243-71. Dresden. 1887.

Nohle, C. Deutsches Knabenschulwesen. *In* Rein, W. Encycl. Handbuch der Pädagogik. Vol. ii. pp. 32-96. *See above*, ii.

Paulsen, F. Das deutsche Bildungswesen in seiner geschichtlichen Entwickelung. Leipsic. 1906. Transl. by Lorenz, T. *as* German Education, past and present. London. 1908.

—— Geschichte des gelehrten Unterrichts auf den deutschen Schulen und Universitäten vom Ausgang des Mittelalters bis zur Gegenwart. 3rd edn., ed. Lehmann, R. 2 vols. Leipsic. 1919, 21.

Pernwerth von Bärnstein, A. Beiträge zur Geschichte und Literatur des deutschen Studententhums. Würzburg. 1882.

Schultz, A. Deutsches Leben im 14ten und 15ten Jahrht. Leipsic. 1892.

Schulze, F. and Szymank, P. Das deutsche Studententum von den ältesten Zeiten bis zur Gegenwart. 3rd edn. Leipsic. 1918.

Zingerle, J. V. Das deutsche Kinderspiel im Mittelalter. SKAW. lviii. 1868. 2nd edn. Innsbruck. 1873.

E. Netherlands.

Bonet-Maury, G. Gérard de Groote, un précurseur de la Réforme au xive siècle, d'après des documents inédits. Paris. 1878.

—— Les précurseurs de la Réforme et de la liberté de conscience dans les pays latins du xiie au xve siècle. Paris. 1904.

—— De opera scholastica Fratrum vitae communis. Paris. 1889.

Busch, J. Chronicon Windeshemense und Liber de reformatione monasteriorum. Ed. Grube, K. Halle. 1887.

Cramer, F. Geschichte der Erziehung und des Unterrichts in den Niederlanden während des Mittelalters. Stralsund. 1843.

Dillenburger, W. Geschichte des deutschen Humanismus; Alexander Hegius und Rudolf von Langen. *In* Zeitschr. für das Gymnasialwesen. xxiv (1870). 481–502.
Grube, K. Gerhard Groot und seine Stiftungen. (Zweite Vereinsschrift des Görres-Gesellschaft für 1883.) Cologne. 1883.
Hyma, A. The Christian Renaissance. A history of the "Devotio Moderna." New York and London. 1925.
Schoengen, M. Die Schule von Zwolle von ihren Anfängen bis zu dem Auftreten des Humanismus. Freiburg-i.-B. 1898.
Ullmann, C. Reformatoren vor der Reformation. 2 vols. Hamburg. 1841–2. 2nd edn. Gotha. 1866. Engl. transl. Menzies, R. 2 vols. Edinburgh. 1855, 60.

F. Italy.

Bisticci, Vespasiano da. Vite di uomini illustri. Ed. Aubel, E. Lanciano. 1911.
Dominici, G. Regola del governo di cura familiare. Ed. Salvi, D. Florence. 1860.
Giesebrecht, W. von. De litterarum studiis apud Italos primis medii aevi saeculis. Berlin. 1845.
Manacorda, G. Storia della scuola in Italia. Milan. 1914.
Rosmini, C. Idea dell' ottimo Precettore nella vita e disciplina di Vittorino da Feltre e de' suoi discepoli. Milan. 1845.
—— Vita e disciplina di Guarino Veronese, e de' suoi discepoli. 3 vols. Brescia. 1805–6.
Sabbadini, R. La scuola e gli studi di Guarino Guarini Veronese. Catania. 1896.
—— *ed.* Guarino da Verona. Epistolario. 3 vols. (R. Dep. Veneta di stor. pat. Miscellanea. Ser. iii. Vols. viii, xi, xiv.) Venice. 1915–19.
Vegio, Maffeo. De Educatione liberorum.... German transl. ed. Köhler, F. J. Gmünd. 1856.
Woodward, W. H. Vittorino da Feltre and other humanist educators. Cambridge. 1897. [Bibliography.]

CHAPTER XXIV.

PAINTING, SCULPTURE, AND THE ARTS.

I. GENERAL BIBLIOGRAPHIES.

Chevalier, C. U. J. Répertoire des sources historiques du moyen âge. Topo-bibliographie. *See Gen. Bibl.* I.

Schlosser, J. Die Kunstliteratur. Vienna. 1924. [Admirable especially for sources and early authorities.]

II. ORIGINAL AUTHORITIES.

[In many of the modern books given later, isolated documents and references in early authorities are quoted.]

A. TECHNICAL.

Alberti, Leone Battista. De pictura (1436). First publ. in Latin. Basle. 1540. Orig. Ital. text and parallel German transl. by Janitschek *in* Eitelberger's Quellenschriften. XI. Vienna. 1887. Ital. text (*with* Cinque ordini archi-tettonici) ed. Papini. Lanciano. 1911.

—— De statua (after 1464). Orig. Latin text with parallel German transl. first publ. by Janitschek, as above. Ital. transl. Bartoli. Florence. 1568.
[Masterly expositions of early Renaissance theory and practice.]

Cennini, Cennino. Il libro dell' arte o trattato della pittura. [*c.* 1390.] Three MS. versions, the best in the Riccardi Library, Florence. Ed. Thompson, D. V., jun. Yale. 1932. Engl. transl. Herringham, C. J. London. 1899; Thompson, D. V., jun. Yale. 1933. [Of outstanding importance for medieval practice in Italy.]

Merrifield, M. P. The ancient practice of painting. 2 vols. London. 1849. Contains Latin and Engl. versions of:
    Eraclius. (13th cent.) De coloribus et artibus Romanorum.
    La Bègue, Jehan. (15th cent.) Tabula de vocabulis synonymis et equivocis colorum.
    Anon. Bolognese MS. (15th cent.) Segreti per colori.

Theophilus. Schedula diversarum artium. (11th–12th cent.) MS. in Wolfenbüttel library first noticed by Lessing. 1774. Text and Engl. transl. Hendrie. London. 1847. Ed. with commentary and bibliog. Thompson, D. V., jun. Yale. 1932.

Villard de Honnecourt. Sketchbook. Original in Bibl. Nat., Paris. Facsimile, ed. Willis. London. 1859. Ed. Omont. Paris. 1906.

B. STATUTES, BIOGRAPHY, WORKS OF ART, ETC.

(i) *General.*

Schlosser, J. Quellenbuch zur Kunstgeschichte. (Eitelberger's Quellenschriften. Sonderausgabe.) Vienna. 1896.

(ii) *France.*

Boileau, Étienne. Livre des métiers de Paris (–1271). (Coll. doc.) Paris. 1837.

Champollin, F. Documents paléographiques relatifs à l'histoire des beaux-arts et des belles-lettres pendant le moyen âge. Paris. 1868.

Guiffrey, J. Inventaires des collections de Jean, duc de Berry. 2 vols. Paris. 1894, 96.

(iii) *Italy.*

Il codice anonimo Magliabecchiano *or* Gaddiano (active 1537–42). Ed. Frey. Berlin. 1892.

Il libro di Antonio Billi (1481–1538). Ed. Frey. Berlin. 1892.

Boccaccio. Decameron. Various editions and English translations.

Bocchi, Francesco. Bellezze della città di Fiorenze. Florence. 1591 and 1592. Ed. and expanded by Cinelli. Florence. 1677.

Campori, G. Raccolta di cataloghi ed inventari inediti sec. xv–xix. Modena. 1870.

Facius, Bartholomaeus. (*ob.* 1457.) De viris illustribus. Ed. Mehus. Florence. 1745. [Useful information also concerning 15th-century Flemish painters.]

Gaye, J. Carteggio inedito d' artisti dei secoli xiv, xv, xvi. 3 vols. Florence. 1839–40.

Ghiberti, Lorenzo. Commentarii. Ed. Schlosser. 2 vols. Berlin. 1912.

Malvasia, C. Felsina pittrice. Pt. i. Bologna. 1678.

Manetti, A. Vita del Brunellesco. Ed. Milanesi. Florence. 1887; *and* Frey *in* Ausgewählten Biographien Vasaris. Vol. iv. Berlin. 1887.

Michiel, Marc Antonio (L' Anonimo Morelliano). Notizie d' opere di disegno. Ed. Frizzoni. Bologna. 1884. Engl. transl. Williamson. London. 1903. [References to Netherlandish painters as well as Italian.]

Milanesi, G. Documenti per la storia dell' arte senese. Siena. 1854.

—— Lettere d' artisti italiani dei secoli xiv e xv. Rome. 1869.

Monticolo, G. I capitolari delle arti veneziane. Vols. i–iii (Fonti). Rome. 1896–1914, in progress.

Sacchetti, Novelle. Various editions and English translations.

Vasari. Le vite de più eccellenti architetti, pittori et scultori italiani, etc. Pts. i–ii. 1st edn. 2 vols. Florence. 1550; 2nd enl. edn. 3 vols. Florence. 1568; Ed. Milanesi. 9 vols. Florence. 1878–85; Ed. Frey. Berlin. 1884; Ghiberti. Berlin. 1886; Brunellesco. Berlin. 1887; Le Vite. 1911 (Vol. i, including the Pisani, alone issued); all with elaborate notes and critical apparatus. Engl. transl. from 2nd edn. by Vere, G. de. 10 vols. London. 1912.

Villani, Filippo. De origine civitatis Florentiae et ejusdem famosis civibus, *c.* 1400. Ital. transl. by Mazzuchelli. Florence. 1747; *and* Dragomanni. Florence. 1847; Latin text, by Galletti. Florence. 1847; sections relating to painting only in Frey. Il libro di Antonio Billi. Berlin. 1892.

(iv) *Netherlands.*

Becker, F. Schriftquellen zur Gesch. der altniederländischen Malerei. Pt. i. Leipsic. 1898. [diss.]

Butzbach, Johannes. Libellus de praeclaris picturae professoribus. 1505. Publ. by Schultz *in* Zahns Jahrb. für Kunstwissenschaft. ii. Leipsic. 1896.

Dehaisnes, C. Documents et extraits divers concernant l'histoire de l'art dans la Flandre, l'Artois, et le Hainaut avant le xve siècle. 2 vols. Lille. 1886.

Guicciardini, Lodovico. Descrittione di tutti i Paesi Bassi. Antwerp. 1567.

Lemaire, Jean. La couronne margaritique. 1510 (publ. Lyons. 1549). A poem, in which a list of artists appears, publ. by Crowe and Cavalcaselle *in* The early Flemish Painters. London. 1857.

Michelant. Inventaires des collections de Marguerite de l'Autriche (1480–1530). *In* Comptes rendus de la Comm. Roy. d'hist. Brussels. 1871.

Pinchart, A. Archives des arts, des sciences et des lettres. Documents inédits. 3 vols. Ghent. 1860–81.

Prost, B. and H. Inventaires, mobiliers, et extraits des comptes des ducs de Bourgogne. 2 vols. Paris. 1902, 13.

C. Iconography.

Dionysius, monk of Fourna d'Agrapha. Manuel d'iconographie chrétienne, grecque, et latine. Transl. from the Byzantine MS. by Durand, P. and ed. Didron, A. N. Paris. 1845.

Durandus, Gulielmus. Rationale divinorum officiorum. Written before 1286, latest edn. Naples. 1866. Bk. i transl. Neale and Webb. Leeds. 1843.

Jacobus de Voragine. Legenda Aurea. *c.* 1275. 1st edn. (in Latin). *c.* 1470. Engl. transl. from French (Caxton). 1483.

Vincent of Beauvais. (*ob. c.* 1264.) Speculum Historiale (third part of the Speculum Majus). 1st edn. Strasbourg. *c.* 1473–6; Douai. 4 vols. 1624.

Molanus, Joannes. De historia sanctorum imaginum et picturarum. 1st edn. 1580. Ed. Paquot. Louvain. 1771.

Honorius of Autun. (13th cent.) Speculum Ecclesiae. MPL. clxxii. Imperfect text corrected by Kelle. Untersuchungen über das Speculum Ecclesiae…. *In* SKAW. cxlv. 1902.

III. SECONDARY AUTHORITIES AND TEXT-BOOKS.

A. General.

Bréhier, L. L'art chrétien. 2nd edn. Paris. 1928.
Coulton, G. G. Art and the Reformation. Oxford. 1928.
Didron, A. N. Iconographie chrétienne. (Coll. doc.) Paris. 1843. Engl. transl. Millington and Stokes. London. 1886.
Dvořák, M. Idealismus und Naturalismus in der gotischen Skulptur und Malerei. HŽ. cxix.
Gonse, L. L'art gothique. Paris. 1890.
Karlinger, H. Die Kunst der Gotik. Berlin, 1927.
Kraus, F. X. Geschichte der christlichen Kunst. 2 vols. Freiburg-i.-B. 1895-1908. [Vol. ii, pt. i. Middle Ages.]
Laborde, L. E. S. J. de. Les ducs de Bourgogne. 3 vols. Paris. 1849. [Reproduces documents concerned with the arts.]
Lethaby, W. R. Mediaeval art. 2nd edn. London. 1912.
Lübke, W. Die Kunst des Mittelalters. Ed. Semrau, M. Stuttgart. 1901.
Mâle, É. L'art allemand et l'art français du moyen âge. Paris. 1917.
Marle, R. van. Iconographie de l'art profane au moyen âge et à la Renaissance. The Hague. 1931.
Michel, A. *ed.* Histoire de l'art. Paris. 1905-26. Vols. ii, iii. [With bibliographies.]
Swartwout, R. E. The monastic craftsman. Cambridge. 1932.
Thieme, U. and Becker, F. Allgemeines Lexikon der bildenden Künstler. Leipsic. 1907 ff., in progress. [Authoritative articles on artists.]
Van Mander, K. Schilderboek. 1st edn. Haarlem. 1604. French transl. Hymans. Paris. 1884. German transl. Munich. 1906.
Woermann, K. Geschichte der Kunst aller Zeiten und Völker. Vols. iii, iv. Leipsic. 1905.
Worringer, W. Form in Gothic. Engl. transl. Read. London. 1927.

(i) *England.*

Carter, J. Specimens of the ancient sculpture and painting now remaining in England from the earliest period to the reign of Henry VIII. London. 1838.
Lethaby, W. R. Westminster Abbey and the king's craftsmen. London. 1906.
—— Westminster Abbey re-examined. London. 1925.
Prior, E. S. English mediaeval art. Cambridge. 1922.
Royal Commission on Ancient and Historical Monuments: Great Britain and Ireland. Inventories of the historical monuments in various counties. London. 1910 ff., in progress. [Gives much information concerning sculpture, painting, and the applied arts.]
Saunders, O. E. History of English art in the Middle Ages. Oxford. 1932.
Vict. Co. Hist. *See Gen. Bibl.* i. [Chapters on the arts.]

(ii) *France.*

France: Ministère de l'Instruction Publique et des Beaux-Arts. Inventaire général des richesses d'art de la France. Paris. 1879 ff.
Mâle, É. L'art religieux du xiiie siècle en France. 3rd edn. Paris. 1910. Engl. transl. London. 1913.
—— L'art religieux de la fin du moyen âge en France. 2nd edn. Paris. 1922.
—— L'art religieux du xiie siècle en France. Paris. 1922.
[Three books of the first importance for the iconography of French medieval art.]
Viollet-le-Duc, M. Dictionnaire raisonné du mobilier français de l'époque carlovingienne à la Renaissance. 6 vols. Paris. 1872.

(iii) *Germany and Austria.*

Bau- und Kunstdenkmäler. [Various dates, editors, and places of publication. A series of illustrated surveys by provinces of works of art of all kinds in Germany.]

Baum, J. Die Malerei und Plastik des Mittelalters. (Handbuch der Kunstwissenschaft.) Potsdam. 1930.

Buchner, E. and Feuchtmayr, K. *edd.* Beiträge zur Geschichte der deutschen Kunst. I. Oberdeutsche Kunst der Spätgotik- und Reformationszeit. Augsburg. 1924. II. Augsburger Kunst der Spätgotik und Renaissance. Augsburg. 1928.

Dehio, G. Geschichte der deutschen Kunst. Vols. I, II. 2nd edn. Berlin. 1921.

—— L'influence de l'art français sur l'art allemand au XIIIᵉ siècle. *In* Revue archéol. Paris. 1900.

Ehrenberg, H. Deutsche Malerei und Plastik von 1350–1450. Neue Beiträge zu ihrer Kenntnis aus dem ehemaligen Deutschordensgebiet. Bonn. 1920.

Flechsig, E. Sächsische Bildnerei und Malerei von 14 Jahrht. bis zur Reformation. Leipsic. 1908 ff.

Habicht, V. C. Niedersächsische Kunst in England. Hanover. 1930.

London: Burlington Fine Arts Club. Catalogue of an exhibition of early German art. London. 1906.

Prague: Archeol. Commission bei der Böhmischen Kaiser-Franz-Josef-Academie. Topographie der historischen und Kunst-Denkmäler im Königreiche Böhmen. Prague. 1898 ff.

Vienna: K.K. Central-Commission zur Erforschung. (K.K. Zentral-Kommission für Denkmalpflege.) Oesterreichische Kunst-Topographie. Vienna. 1907 ff., in progress. [Vols. I–XXV.]

Vienna: Gotik in Oesterreich. Catalogue of exhibition of Gothic art at Vienna. 1926.

(iv) *Italy.*

Ancona, P. d'. L' uomo e le sue opere. Florence. 1923. [Valuable for iconography.]

Beltrami, L. L' arte negli arredi sacri della Lombardia. Milan. 1897. [Manuscripts, goldsmiths' work, and embroidery.]

Bertaux, É. L'art dans l'Italie méridionale. Paris. 1904.

Burckhardt, J. Der Cicerone. Leipsic. 1924.

Crowe, J. A. and Cavalcaselle, G. B. History of painting in Italy. Ed. Douglas, Strong, and Borenius. Vols. I–V. London. 1903 ff.

Dvořák, M. Geschichte der italienischen Kunst. Vol. I. Munich. 1927.

Gabelentz, H. von der. Die kirchliche Kunst im italienischen Mittelalter. Strasbourg. 1907. [For iconography.]

Molmenti, P. G. Venice. Transl. Brown, H. F. Pt. I. The Middle Ages. 2 vols. London. 1906.

Müntz, E. Les arts à la cour des papes pendant le XVᵉ et le XVIᵉ siècles. Vols. I–III, pt. I (1417–84). (EcfrAR.) Paris. 1878–82.

—— Les arts à la cour des papes...(1484–1503.) (AcadIBL. Fondation E. Piot.) Paris. 1898.

—— Les collections des Médicis au XVᵉ siècle. Paris. 1888. [The last two books quote original documents and inventories.]

—— Histoire de l'art pendant la Renaissance. Vol. I. Italy: The Primitives. Paris. 1889.

Ricci, C. L' arte in Italia. 2 vols. Bergamo. 1911.

Riegel, H. Beiträge zur Kunstgeschichte Italiens. Dresden. 1898.

Rumohr, C. F. von. Italienische Forschungen. Ed. Schlosser. Frankfort-on-M. 1920.

Schmarsow, A. Italienische Kunst im Zeitalter Dantes. Augsburg. 1928.

Thode, H. Franz von Assisi und die Anfänge der Kunst der Renaissance in Italien. 2nd edn. Berlin. 1904.

Toesca, P. Storia dell' arte italiana. Turin. 1927. In progress.

Venturi, A. Storia dell' arte italiana. Milan. 1901 ff. In progress. Vols. IV–VII.

(v) *Netherlands.*

Clemen, P. Belgische Kunstdenkmäler. 2 vols. Munich. 1923.
Dehaisnes, C. C. A. Histoire de l'art dans la Flandre, l'Artois, et la Hainaut avant le xvᵉ siècle. Lille. 1886.
Helbig, J. L'art mosan depuis l'introduction du Christianisme jusqu'à la fin du xviiiᵉ siècle. Vol. i. Brussels. 1906.
Pit, A. Les origines de l'art hollandais. Paris. 1894. [Principally painting, illumination, and engraving.]
Weale, W. H. J. Belgium, Aix-la-Chapelle, and Cologne. London. 1859. [A guidebook unique in its detailed archaeological information.]
—— Instrumenta ecclesiastica. Choix d'objets d'art religieux du moyen âge et de la Renaissance exposés à Malines en Septembre 1864. Brussels. 1866.
Wurzbach, A. von. Niederländisches Künstler-Lexikon. 3 vols. Vienna. 1906–11. [Authoritative articles on artists.]

B. Painting.

(i) *General.*

Hourticq, L. La peinture des origines au xviᵉ siècle. Paris. 1908.
Westlake, N. H. J. History of design in mural painting. London. 1901.
Woltmann, A. F. G. A. Geschichte der Malerei. Die Malerei des Mittelalters. Ed. Bernath, M. Leipsic. 1916.
—— and Woermann, K. History of painting. Ed. by Colvin, Sir S. 2 vols. London. 1880, 87.

(ii) *England.*

Bond, F. B. and Camm, Dom Bede. Rood screens and rood lofts. 2 vols. London. 1909.
Borenius, T. and Tristram, E. W. English medieval painting. Florence and Paris. 1927.
Constable, W. G. Devonshire rood screen paintings. *In* Connoisseur. lxxx, lxxxi.
—— East Anglian rood screen paintings. *Ibid.* lxxxiv.
James, M. R. The drawings of Matthew Paris. *In* Walpole Soc. Annual. xiv.
—— An English medieval sketchbook. *Ibid.* xiii.
—— The frescoes in the chapel at Eton College. Eton. 1907.
—— and Tristram, E. W. The wall paintings in Eton College chapel and in the Lady Chapel of Winchester Cathedral. *In* Walpole Soc. Annual. xvii.
Kendon, F. Mural paintings in English churches during the Middle Ages. London. 1923.
Keyser, C. E. List of buildings in Great Britain and Ireland having mural and other painted decorations of dates prior to the latter part of the sixteenth century. 3rd edn. London. 1883.
Lethaby, W. R. English primitives. *In* Burlington Magazine. vii, xx, xxix, xxx, xxxi, xxxiii.
—— London and Westminster painters in the Middle Ages. With notes on the plates by Tristram, E. W. *In* Walpole Soc. Annual. i.
—— Medieval paintings at Westminster. *In* Proc. British Academy. xiii. 1927.
Lindblom, A. La peinture gothique en Suède et en Norvège. Stockholm. 1916. [Studies its relation to English school.]
London: Burlington House. British primitive paintings from the twelfth to the early sixteenth century. [Introdn. by Constable, W. G.] London. 1923.
Page, W. The St Albans school of painting. *In* Archaeologia. lviii. 1902.
Tristram, E. W. Piers Plowman in English wall-painting. *In* Burlington Magazine. xxxi.

(iii) *France.*

Bouchot, H. L'exposition des primitifs français: la peinture en France sous les Valois. 2 vols. Paris. 1904–5.
—— Les primitifs français, 1292—1500: complément documentaire au catalogue officiel de l'exposition (1904). Paris. 1904.
Chamson, L. Nicolas Froment et l'école avignonaise. Paris. 1931.
Cox, T. Jehan Foucquet. London. 1931.

Dimier, L. Histoire de la peinture française. Moyen-âge et Renaissance. Paris. 1925.
—— Les primitifs français: biographie critique. Paris. 1911.
Durrieu, P. La peinture en France au début du xvᵉ siècle. *In* Revue de l'art anc. et mod. xix, xx. Paris. 1906.
Gélis-Didot, P. and Laffillée, H. La peinture décorative en France du xiᵉ au xviᵉ siècle. Paris. 1888–91.
Guiffrey, J. and Marcel, P. La peinture française: les primitifs. 2 series. Paris. 1910–12.
Labande, L. H. Les primitifs français. Marseilles. 1932.
Lafenestre, G. Jehan Fouquet. Paris. 1905.
Laffillée, H. La peinture murale en France avant la Renaissance. 1893.
Lemoisne, P. A. Gothic painting in France, 13th and 14th centuries. Florence and Paris. 1931.
Loo, G. H. de. L'exposition des "Primitifs Français" au point de vue de l'influence des frères Van Eyck sur la peinture française et provençale. Brussels. 1904.
Paris: Exposition des primitifs français, 1904. Catalogue. 2nd edn. Paris. 1904.
Weese, A. Skulptur und Malerei in Frankreich vom 15 bis zum 17 Jahrht. (Handbuch der Kunstwissenschaft.) Berlin. 1917.

(iv) *Germany.*

Aldenhoven, C. Geschichte der Kölner Malerschule. Lübeck. 1902. (Publn. of Köln. Gesellsch. für rheinische Geschichtskunde. xiii.)
Beyer, O. Norddeutsche gotische Malerei. Hamburg. 1924.
Borrmann, R. Aufnahmen mittelalterlicher Wand- und Deckenmalereien in Deutschland. Berlin. 1897–1902.
Brandt, H. Die Anfänge der deutschen Landschaftsmalerei im 14 und 15 Jahrht. Strasbourg. 1912.
Burger, F. and others. Die deutsche Malerei vom ausgehenden Mittelalter bis zum Ende der Renaissance. 3 vols. (Handbuch der Kunstwissenschaft.) Berlin. 1913–19.
Clemen, P. Die gotischen Monumentalmalereien der Rheinlande. 2 vols. Düsseldorf. 1930.
Ehl, H. Aelteste deutsche Malerei. Berlin. 1922.
Fischer, O. Die altdeutsche Malerei in Salzburg. Leipsic. 1908.
Forster, O. H. Die Kölnische Malerei von Meister Wilhelm bis Stephan Lochner. Cologne. 1923.
Ganz, P. Malerei der Frührenaissance in der Schweiz. Basle. 1924.
Gerstenberg, K. Hans Multscher. Leipsic. 1929.
Glaser, K. Die altdeutsche Malerei. Munich. 1924.
Habicht, V. C. Die mittelalterliche Malerei Niedersachsens. i. Von den Anfängen bis um 1450. Strasbourg. 1919.
Heise, C. G. Norddeutsche Malerei. Leipsic. 1918.
Janitschek, H. Der Malerei. (Geschichte der deutschen Kunst. Vol. iii.) Berlin. 1890.
Pächt, O. Oesterreichische Tafelmalerei der Gotik. Augsburg. 1929.
Reichmann, F. Gotische Wandmalerei in Niederösterreich. Vienna. 1925.
Reiners. Die Kölner Malerschule. Gladbach. 1925.
Schmitz, H. Die mittelalterliche Malerei in Soest. Münster. 1906.
Stange, A. Deutsche Malerei der Gotik. Berlin. 1934.
Thode, H. Die Malerschule von Nürnberg im 14 und 15 Jahrht. Frankfort-on-M. 1891.
Voss, H. Der Ursprung des Donaustiles. Leipsic. 1907.
Wendland, H. Konrad Witz. With Supplt. by Graber, H. Basle. 1924.
Worringer, W. Die Anfänge der Tafelmalerei. Leipsic. 1924.

(v) *Italy.*

Aubert, A. Die malerische Dekoration der San Francesco-Kirche in Assisi: ein Beitrag zur Lösung der Cimabue-Frage. Leipsic. 1907.
Baldinucci, F. Notizie de' professori del disegno da Cimabue, etc. Vols. i–iii. 1st edn. Florence. 1681–1728. Collected edn. Milan. 1811–12.

Berenson, B. The Italian painters of the Renaissance. Oxford. 1930.
—— Italian pictures of the Renaissance. Oxford. 1932.
—— A Sienese painter [Sassetta] of the Franciscan legend. London. 1909.
—— Studies in medieval painting. New Haven. 1930.
Borenius, T. The painters of Vicenza. London. 1919.
Brach, A. Giottos Schule in der Romagna. Strasbourg. 1902.
Crowe, J. A. and Cavalcaselle, G. B. History of painting in North Italy. Ed. Borenius, T. Vol. i. London. 1912.
De Wald, E. T. Pietro Lorenzetti. Harvard. 1930.
Douglas, L. Fra Angelico. London. 1900.
Escher, K. Malerei der Renaissance in Italien. (Handbuch der Kunstwissenschaft.) Berlin. 1922.
Manzoni, L. Statuti e matricole dell' arte dei pittori della città di Firenze, Perugia, Siena. Rome. 1904.
Gielly, L. Les primitifs siennois. Paris. 1926.
Gnoli, U. Pittori e miniatori nell' Umbria. Spoleto. 1923.
Gronau, G. Die Künstlerfamilie Bellini. Leipsic. 1909.
Jacobsen, E. Das Quattrocento in Siena. Strasbourg. 1908.
—— Sienesische Meister der Trecento in der Gemälde-Galerie zu Siena. Strasbourg. 1907.
—— Umbrische Malerei des 14, 15, und 16 Jahrhts. Strasbourg. 1914.
Kleinschmidt, B. Die Wandmalereien der Basilika San Francesco in Assisi. Berlin. 1930.
London: Burlington Fine Arts Club. School of Siena. London. 1904.
—— —— Pictures of the Early Venetian School. London. 1912.
—— —— Florentine painting before 1500. London. 1919.
Mesnil, J. Masaccio et les débuts de la Renaissance. Paris. 1927.
Muratoff, P. Fra Angelico. London. 1929.
Rintelen, F. Giotto und die Giotto-Apokryphen. Munich. 1912.
Sandberg-Vavala, E. La croce dipinta italiana e l' iconografia della passione. Verona. 1929.
—— La pittura veronese del Trecento e del primo Quattrocento. Verona. 1926.
Schmarsow, A. H. Masaccio, der Begründer des klassischen Stils der italienischen Malerei. Cassel. 1900.
Schottmüller, F. Fra Angelico da Fiesole. 2nd edn. Stuttgart. 1924.
Schubring, P. Altichiero und seine Schule. Leipsic. 1898.
—— Cassoni. 2 vols. Leipsic. 1915.
Sirén, O. Giottino und seine Stellung in der gleichzeitigen florentinischen Malerei. Leipsic. 1908.
—— Giotto and some of his followers. Cambridge, Mass. 1917.
—— Toskanische Maler im 13 Jahrht. Berlin. 1922.
Somare, E. Masaccio. Milan. 1925.
Suida, W. Florentinische Maler um die Mitte des 14 Jahrhts. Strasbourg. 1905.
Supino, I. B. Giotto. Florence. 1920.
Testi, L. La storia della pittura veneziana. Bergamo. 1900.
Toesca, P. Florentine painting of the Trecento. Florence. 1929.
—— Masolino da Panicale. Bergamo. 1908.
—— Pittura e miniatura nella Lombardia. Milan. 1912.
Van Marle, R. The development of the Italian schools of painting. The Hague. 1923 ff., in progress. [Vols. i-ix.]
—— La peinture romaine au moyen-âge, son développement du vie jusqu'à la fin du xiiie siècle. Strasbourg. 1921.
—— Simone Martini et les peintres de son école. Strasbourg. 1920.
Weigelt, C. H. Duccio di Buoninsegna. Leipsic. 1911.
—— Sienese painting of the Trecento. Florence and Paris. 1930.

(vi) *Netherlands.*

Bodenhausen, E. von. G. David und seine Schule. Munich. 1905.
Bruges: Ambacht van Beeldmakers. La corporation des peintres de Bruges: registres d'admission. Courtrai and Bruges. n.d.

Burger, W. Rogier van der Weyden. Leipsic. 1923.

Conway, Sir W. M. The Van Eycks and their followers. London. 1921.

Destrée, J. Hugo van der Goes. Brussels and Paris. 1914.

—— Rogier de la Pasture (Van der Weyden). 2 vols. Paris and Brussels. 1931.

Durrieu, P. Les débuts des Van Eyck. *In* Gazette des Beaux-Arts. xxix. 1903.

Fierens-Gevaert, H. Histoire de la peinture flamande des origines à la fin du xvᵉ siècle. 3 vols. Paris. 1927–30.

—— Les primitifs flamands. Vols. i–iii. Brussels. 1909 ff.

Friedlaender, M. J. Die altniederländische Malerei. (Illus.) Berlin. 1924 ff., in progress. i. Die Van Eyck; Petrus Christus. 1924. ii. Rogier van der Weyden und der Meister von Flémalle. 1924. iii. Dierick Bouts; Joos van Gent. 1925. iv. Hugo van der Goes. 1926. v. Geertgen van Haarlem à Hieronymus Bosch. 1927. vi. Memling; Gerard David. 1928.

—— Meisterwerke der niederländischen Malerei des 15 und 16 Jahrhts, auf der Ausstellung zu Brugge. Munich. 1903. [*Also*, Loo, G. H. de, *below.*]

—— Von Eyck bis Bruegel: Studien zur Geschichte der niederländischen Malerei. 2nd edn. Berlin. 1921.

Houtart, M. Jacques Daret. Tournai. 1908.

Jamot, P. Rogier van der Weyden et le prétendu Maître de Flémalle. *In* Gazette des Beaux-Arts. xlviii. 1928.

Loo, G. H. de. Bruges, 1902. Exposition de tableaux flamands des xivᵉ–xviᵉ siècles. Catalogue critique. Ghent. 1902.

—— Jacques Daret. *In* Burlington Magazine. xv. pp. 202–8; xix. pp. 218–25.

Maeterlinck, L. Une école primitive inconnue. Brussels. 1913.

—— L'énigme des primitifs français. Paris. 1923.

—— La pénétration française en Flandre, une école préeyckienne inconnue. Paris. 1925.

Réau, L. Les richesses d'art de la France. La Bourgogne. La peinture et les tapisseries. Paris. 1929.

Renders, E. La solution du problème Van der Weyden-Flémalle-Campin. Bruges. 1931.

Schmarsow, A. Hubert und Jan Van Eyck. Leipsic. 1924.

Tschudi, H. von. Der Meister von Flémalle. *In* Jahrb. der K. Preuss. Kunstsamml. Berlin. 1898.

Voll, K. Die altniederländische Malerei von Jan van Eyck bis Memling. Leipsic. 1906.

—— Entwicklungsgeschichte der Malerei in Einzeldarstellungen. i. Altniederländische und altdeutsche Meister. Munich. 1913.

Weale, W. H. J. Hubert and John van Eyck, their life and work. London and New York. 1908. 2nd edn. (with Brockwell, M. W.). London. 1912.

—— Peintres brugeois: les Christus, *c.* 1412–1530. Bruges. 1909.

Winkler, F. Die altniederländische Malerei. Berlin. 1924.

—— Der Meister von Flémalle und R. Van der Weyden. Strasbourg. 1913.

(vii) *Spain.*

Barcelona: Institut d'Estudis Catalans. Los pintures murals catalanes. Barcelona. 1908.

Figueiredo, J. de. O pintor Nuno Gonçalves. Lisbon. 1910.

Gudiol i Cunill, J. Els Primitius. (Vol. i in 2 pts. of: La pintura mig-eval catalana.) Barcelona. 1927.

Loga, V. von. Die Malerei in Spanien vom 14 bis 18 Jahrht. Berlin. 1923.

Mayer, A. L. Gotik in Spanien. Leipsic. 1928.

Post, C. R. History of Spanish painting. Cambridge, Mass. 1930. [Vols. i–iv (to *c.* 1450) publ.]

San Pere y Miquel, S. Los cuatrocentistas catalanes. 2 vols. Barcelona. 1906.

—— Els trescentistes. (Vol. ii in 2 pts. of: La pintura mig-eval catalana.) Barcelona. *n.d.*

Tormo y Monzò, E. Bartolomé Bermejo. Madrid. 1926.

—— Jacomart y el arte hispano-flamenco cuatrocentista. Madrid. 1913.

C. Manuscripts.

(i) *General.*

Bastard, A. de. Librairie de Jean de France, duc de Berry. Paris. 1834.

Berlin. Beschreibende Verzeichnisse der Miniaturen-Handschriften der preussischen Staatsbibliothek zu Berlin. 1. Kirchner, J. Philipps-Handschriften. Leipsic. 1926. 5. Wegener. Deutsche Handschriften bis 1500. Leipsic. 1928.

Bulletin de la Société Française de reproduction de manuscrits à peintures. 1911 ff., in progress. [Vols. i. ff.]

Byvanck, A. W. Les principaux manuscrits à peintures conservés dans les collections publiques du royaume des Pays-Bas. Paris. 1931.

Cambridge. Descriptive catalogues of the manuscripts in the libraries of Cambridge Colleges. By James, M. R. Cambridge. 1895–1913.

Delisle, L. Le cabinet des manuscrits de la Bibliothèque Impériale. 4 vols. Paris. 1868–81.

—— Mélanges de paléographie et de bibliographie. Paris. 1880.

Herbert, J. A. Illuminated manuscripts. London. 1911.

Kobell, L. von. Kunstvolle Miniaturen. Munich. 1890. [From mss. in Munich Collection.]

Kuhn, A. Die Illustration des Rosenromans. *In* Jahrb. der kunsthist. Samml. des allerh. Kaiserhauses. xxxi. 1912.

Leroquais, Abbé V. Les livres d'heures manuscrits de la Bibliothèque Nationale. Paris. 1927.

London: British Museum. Reproductions from illuminated manuscripts. 3 series. London. 1907–8.

—— Schools of illumination: Reproductions from manuscripts in the British Museum. 4 vols. London. 1914–22.

London: Burlington Fine Arts Club. Exhibition of illuminated manuscripts. (Catalogue by Cockerell, S. C.) London. 1908.

London: Palaeographical Society. Facsimiles of ancient manuscripts. London. 1873–94.

—— New Palaeographical Society. Facsimiles of ancient manuscripts. London. 1903 ff., in progress.

Martin, H. Les joyaux de l'enluminure à la Bibliothèque Nationale. Paris. 1928.

—— Les principaux manuscrits à peintures de la Bibliothèque de l'Arsenal à Paris. Paris. 1929.

Mély, F. de. Les primitifs et leurs signatures. i. Les miniaturistes. Paris. 1913.

Meurgey, J. Les principaux manuscrits à peintures du Musée Condé à Chantilly. Paris. 1930.

Middleton, J. H. Illuminated manuscripts in classical and mediaeval times. Cambridge. 1892.

Millar, E. G. The library of A. Chester Beatty. 2 vols. London. 1927, 30.

Morgan, J. P. Catalogue of manuscripts and early printed books. [iv.] Manuscripts. By M. R. James. London. 1906.

Schlosser, J. and Hermann, H. J. Beschreibendes Verzeichnis der illuminierten Handschriften in Oesterreich. Leipsic. 1923 ff., in progress. [Vols. i–vi.]

Shaw, H. and Madden, Sir F. Illuminated ornaments selected from the manuscripts and early printed books from the 6th to the 17th century. London. 1833.

Thompson, H. Yates. Catalogue of mss. in collection of H. Y. Thompson. By James, M. R. and others. Cambridge. 1898–1907.

—— Illustrations of 100 mss. 7 vols. London. 1907–8.

Warner, Sir G. F. Descriptive catalogue of illuminated manuscripts in the library of C. W. Dyson Perrins. 2 vols. Oxford. 1920.

—— Illuminated manuscripts in the British Museum. London. 1899–1903.

Wescher, P. Beschreibendes Verzeichnis der Miniaturen, Handschriften, und Einzelblätter des Kupferstichkabinetts der Staatlichen Museen Berlins. Leipsic. 1931.

Westwood, J. O. Illuminated illustrations of the Bible, copied from select manuscripts of the Middle Ages. London. 1846.

—— Palaeographia Sacra Pictoria: being a series of illustrations of the ancient versions of the Bible, copied from illuminated manuscripts. London. 1843–5.

Wickhoff, F. and Dvořák, M. Beschreibendes Verzeichnis der illuminierten Handschriften in Oesterreich. 7 vols. Leipsic. 1905–17. (Continued by Schlosser and Hermann, *see above.*)

(ii) *England.*

Cockerell, S. C. The Gorleston Psalter. London. 1907.
—— William de Brailes. (Roxburghe Club.) 1930.
—— and James, M. R. Two East Anglian psalters at the Bodleian Library. (Roxburghe Club.) 1926.
Goldschmidt, A. Der Albani-Psalter in Hildesheim und seine Beziehung zur symbolischen Kirchenskulptur des 13 Jahrhts. Berlin. 1895.
Herbert, J. A. The Sherborne missal. (Roxburghe Club.) 1920.
James, M. R. The Apocalypse in Latin and French. (Bodleian MS. Douce 180.) (Roxburghe Club.) 1922.
—— The Bestiary. (Roxburghe Club.) 1928.
—— An English Bible-picture book of the fourteenth century. (Holkham MS. 666.) *In* Walpole Society Annual. Vol. xi.
—— An English mediaeval sketch-book, no. 1916 in the Pepysian Library... Cambridge. *In* Walpole Society Annual. Vol. xiii. 1924–5.
—— The Trinity College Apocalypse. (Roxburghe Club.) 1909.
London: British Museum. Queen Mary's psalter: miniatures and drawings by an English artist of the 14th century. Introdn. by Warner, Sir G. F. London. 1912.
Millar, E. G. English illuminated manuscripts from the xth to the xiiith century. Paris and Brussels. 1925.
—— English illuminated manuscripts of the xivth and xvth centuries. Paris and Brussels. 1928.
—— The Luttrell Psalter. London. 1932. [Complete reprodn.]
Omont, H. Miniatures du psautier de St Louis...Université de Leyde. Leyden. 1902.
Paris: Bibliothèque Nationale. Psautier illustré. xiiie siècle. Paris. 1906.
Thompson, Sir E. Maunde. English illuminated manuscripts. London. 1895.
Thompson, H. Yates. Facsimiles...of six pages from a psalter, written and illuminated about 1325 for a member of the St. Omer family in Norfolk. London. 1900.
Saunders, O. E. English illumination. 2 vols. Florence and Paris. 1928.

(iii) *France.*

Blum, A. and Lauer, P. Miniature française aux xve et xvie siècles. Paris. 1930.
Cockerell, S. C. The book of hours of Yolande of Flanders. London. 1905.
—— A psalter and hours of Isabelle of France. London. 1905.
Delisle, L. Les grandes heures de la reine Anne de Bretagne et l'atelier de Jean Bourdichon. Paris. 1913.
—— Les heures dites de Jean Pucelle. Paris. 1910.
—— Notice de douze livres royaux. Paris. 1902.
—— Notice sur un psautier du xiiie siècle appartenant au Comte de Crawford. Paris. 1897.
—— and Meyer, P. L'Apocalypse en français au xiiie siècle. Paris. 1901.
Dewick, E. C. The Metz Pontifical. (Roxburghe Club.) 1902.
Durrieu, P. Les antiquités judaïques et le peintre J. Fouquet. Paris. 1908.
—— Le Maître des Heures du Maréchal de Boucicaut. (La peinture en France au début du xve siècle.) Paris. 1906.
Gruyer, F. A. Les Quarante Fouquet. Paris. 1897.
Haseloff, A. Les psautiers de Saint Louis. *In* Mém. de la Soc. nat. des Antiquaires de France. lix.
Lasteyrie, R. de. André Beauneveu et Jacquemart de Hesdin. Fondation Eugène Piot: Monuments et Mémoires. iii. pp. 71–119.
Martin, H. Le Boccace de Jean sans Peur. Brussels. 1911.
—— Légende de Saint Denis. (Soc. de l'hist. de Paris.) Paris. 1908.
—— La miniature française du xiiie au xve siècle. Paris. 1923.
—— Les miniaturistes français. Paris. 1906.

Martin, H. Psautier de St Louis et de Blanche de Castille. Paris. 1909.
Omont, H. Psautier de St Louis (Bibl. Nat.). Paris. 1902.
—— Vie et histoire de St Louis. Paris. 1906.
Paris: Soc. des Bibliophiles Français. Notice sur un manuscrit du xive siècle. Les Heures du Maréchal de Boucicaut. Paris. 1889.
Thompson, H. Yates. Hours of Joan II, Queen of Navarre. (Roxburghe Club.) 1899.
Vitzthum, G. Die Pariser Miniaturmalerei von der Zeit des hl. Ludwig bis zu Philipp von Valois, etc. Leipsic. 1907.
Vogelstein, J. Von französischer Buchmalerei. Munich. 1914.

(iv) *Germany, Austria, and Bohemia.*

Bruck, R. Die Malereien in der Handschriften des Königreichs Sachsen. Saxony: K. Sächsische Kommission, etc. Dresden. 1906.
Damrich, J. Die Regensburger Buchmalerei von der Mitte des 12 bis zum Ende des 13 Jahrhts. Munich. 1902.
Dvořák, M. Die Illuminatoren des Johann von Neumarkt. *In* Jahrb. d. kunsthist. Samml. des allerh. Kaiserhauses. xxii. 1901. p. 35.
Flechsig, E. *ed.* Sächsische Bildnerei und Malerei vom 14 Jahrht. bis zur Reformation. 2 vols. Leipsic. 1910, 12.
Freyhan, R. Der Willehalm-Codex der Landesbibliothek in Cassel. Marburg. 1927.
Haseloff, A. Eine thüringisch-sächsische Malerschule des 13 Jahrhts. Strasbourg. 1897.
Jacobi, F. Die deutsche Buchmalerei in ihren stilistischen Entwicklungsphasen. Munich. 1923.
—— Studien zur Geschichte der bayerischen Miniatur des 14 Jahrhts. Strasbourg. 1908.
Jerchel, H. Die ober und nieder-österreichische Buchmalerei der ersten Hälfte des 14 Jahrhts. *In* Jahrb. der kunsthist. Samml. in Wien. n.s. Vol. vi. 1932. p. 9.
Kletzel, O. Studien zur böhmischen Buchmalerei. i. Das Missale 111/205 von St. Florian, ein Werk böhmischer Buchmalerei des späteren 14 Jahrhts. ii. Das Missale Pragense in Zettau. *In* Marburger Jahrbuch. vii. 1933. pp. 1–76.
Leidinger, G. Miniaturen aus Handschriften der K. Hof. und Staatsbibliothek in München. Vols. i–viii. Munich. 1912–24.
Schlosser, J. Bilderhandschriften Königs Wenzel I. *In* Jahrb. der kunsthist. Samml. des allerh. Kaiserhauses. xiv. Vienna. 1893. pp. 214–17.
Vollmer, H. Materialien zur Bibelgeschichte und religiösen Volkskunde des Mittelalters. Berlin. 1912.
Winkler, E. Die Buchmalerei in Niederösterreich von 1150–1250. Vienna. 1923.

(v) *Italy.*

Ancona, P. d'. La miniatura fiorentina (secoli xi–xvi). 2 vols. Florence. 1914.
—— La miniature italienne du xe au xve siècle. French transl. Poirier. Paris. 1925.
Biagi, G. Biblioteca Mediceo-Laurenziana. Florence. 1914. [Reproductions from illuminated manuscripts...in the R. Medicean Laurentian Library.]
Gnoli, U. Pittori e miniatori nell' Umbria. Spoleto. 1923.
Hermann, H. J. Zur Geschichte der Miniaturmalerei am Hofe der Este in Ferrara. *In* Jahrb. d. kunsthist. Samml. des allerh. Kaiserhauses. xxi. 1900. p. 117.
James, M. R. and Berenson, B. Speculum humanae salvationis. Oxford. 1928. [Reprodn., with important commentary and introductions, of a MS. in the Riches collection.]
Malaguzzi Valeri, F. La miniatura in Bologna dal xiii al xviii secolo. ASI. xviii. 1896.
Schlosser, J. von. Ein veronesisches Bilderbuch und die höfische Kunst des 14 Jahrhts. *In* Jahrb. d. kunsthist. Samml. des allerh. Kaiserhauses. xvi. 1895. p. 144.

(vi) *Netherlands.*

Le Bréviaire Grimani de la Bibliothèque de S. Marco à Venise. Reprodn, ed. Vries, S. de, and others. 12 vols. Leyden. 1904–9.

Byvanck, A. W. and Hoogewerff, G. J. Noord-Nederlandsche miniaturen in handschriften der 14ᵉ, 15ᵉ, en 16ᵉ eeuwen. (Text and plates.) The Hague. 1921–5. French transl. The Hague. 1921–5.

Durrieu, P. Heures de Turin. Paris. 1902.

—— La miniature flamande au temps de la cour de Bourgogne (1415–1530). Brussels. 1921.

—— Quarante-cinq feuillets à peintures provenant des Très Belles Heures de Jean de France, duc de Berry. Paris. 1902.

—— Les Très Riches Heures de Jean, duc de Berry. Paris. 1904. [Complete reprodn., with elaborate introdn.]

Fierens-Gevaert, H. *ed.* Les Très Belles Heures de Jean de France, duc de Berry. Brussels. 1910. [Complete reprodn.]

Loo, G. H. de. Heures de Milan. Brussels. 1911.

Van den Gheyn, J. Le bréviaire de Philippe le Bon. Brussels. 1909.

Vogelsang, W. Holländische Miniaturen des späteren Mittelalters. Strasbourg. 1899.

Winkler, F. Die flämische Buchmalerei des 15 und 16 Jahrhts. Künstler und Werke von den Brüdern Van Eyck bis zu Simon Bening. Leipsic. 1925.

—— Studien zur Geschichte der niederländischen Miniaturmalerei des 15 und 16 Jahrhts. *In* Jahrb. d. kunsthist. Samml. des allerh. Kaiserhauses. xxxii. Vienna.

(vii) *Spain.*

Neuss, W. Die katalanische Bibelillustration um die Wende des ersten Jahrtausends und die altspanische Buchmalerei. Bonn. 1922.

D. Sculpture.

(i) *General.*

Berlin: Königl. Mus. Beschreibung der Bildwerke der christlichen Epoche. 2nd edn. Berlin. 1900–13. i. Die Elfenbeinbildwerke. (Text and atlas.) ii. Die italienischen Bronzen. iii. Altchristliche und mittelalter. Epochen, etc. 4 vols.

Brindley, W. and Weatherley, W. S. Ancient sepulchral monuments...of...various countries, and from the earliest periods down to the end of the eighteenth century. London. 1887.

Goldschmidt, A. Die Elfenbeinskulpturen. 3 vols. Berlin. 1914–23.

—— Die frühmittelalterliche Bronzetüren. Marburg. 1926.

London: Burlington Fine Arts Club. Catalogue of a collection of carvings in ivory. [Introdn. by Maclagan, E. R. D.] London. 1923.

Lübke, W. History of sculpture. Engl. transl. Bunnett, F. E. 2 vols. London. 1872.

Molinier, E. Histoire générale des arts appliqués à l'industrie. i. Les ivoires. Paris. 1896.

(ii) *England.*

Bond, F. Woodcarvings in English churches. 2 vols. London. 1910.

Gardner, S. English Gothic foliage sculpture. Cambridge. 1927.

Gough, R. Sepulchral monuments in Great Britain. 2 vols. London. 1786–96.

Hope, W. H. St J. The imagery and sculptures on the west front of Wells Cathedral Church. *In* Archaeologia. lix. 1904.

Howard, F. E. and Crossley, F. M. English church woodwork. London. 1927.

James, M. R. The sculptures in the Lady Chapel at Ely. London. 1895.

Longhurst, M. H. English ivories. London. 1926.

Prior, E. S. Catalogue of an exhibition of English medieval alabaster work. Soc. of Antiquaries. London. 1913.

—— and Gardner, A. An account of medieval figure-sculpture in England. Cambridge. 1912.

Seward, A. C. The foliage, flowers, and fruit of Southwell chapter house. *In* Camb. Antiq. Soc. Proceedings. xxxv. 1935.

Stothard, C. A. The monumental effigies of Great Britain. London. 1817–32.

(iii) *France.*

Aubert, M. French sculpture at the beginning of the Gothic period, 1140–1225. Florence and Paris. 1929.
—— Les richesses d'art de la France. La Bourgogne. La sculpture. 3 vols. Paris. 1930.
Baudot, A. de. La sculpture française au moyen âge et à la renaissance. Paris. 1884.
Boinet, A. Les sculptures de la cathédrale de Bourges. Paris. 1912.
Bréhier, L. La cathédrale de Reims. Paris. 1916.
Durand, G. Monographie de l'église de Notre-Dame, cathédrale d'Amiens. 3 vols. Amiens. 1901–3.
Gardner, A. French sculpture of the thirteenth century. London. 1915.
—— Medieval sculpture in France. Cambridge. 1931.
Houvet, E. Cathédrale de Chartres. 7 vols. Chelles. 1920–1.
Humbert, A. La sculpture sous les ducs de Bourgogne (1361–1483). Paris. 1913.
Kleinclausz, A. Claus Sluter et la sculpture bourguignonne au xvᵉ siècle. Paris. 1905.
Koechlin, R. Les ivoires gothiques français. 3 vols. Paris. 1924.
Lami, S. Dictionnaire des sculptures de l'école française du moyen âge au règne de Louis XIV. Paris. 1898.
Lasteyrie, R. de. Études de la sculpture francaise du moyen âge. Fondation Eugène Piot. viii. 1902.
Marignan, A. La décoration monumentale des églises de la France septentrionale du xiiᵉ au xiiiᵉ siècle. Paris. 1911.
Marriage, M. and E. The sculptures of Chartres cathedral. (Text in Engl. and French.) Cambridge. 1909.
Moreau-Nelaton, E. La cathédrale de Reims. Paris. 1915.
Pillion, L. Les sculpteurs français du xiiiᵉ siècle. Paris. 1912.
Sartor, M. La cathédrale de Reims. Études sur quelques statues du grand portail. Rheims. 1910. [Suggests an 18th-cent. origin for certain statues.]
Terret, V. La sculpture bourguignonne aux xiiᵉ et xiiiᵉ siècles. Paris. 1914.
Vitry, P. French sculpture during the reign of St Louis, 1226–1270. Florence and Paris. 1929.
—— and Brière, G. Documents de sculpture française du moyen âge. Paris. 1906.

(iv) *Germany.*

Baum, J. Altswäbische Kunst. Augsburg. 1923.
—— Gotische Bildwerke Schwabens. Stuttgart. 1921.
—— Die Malerei und Plastik des Mittelalters. (Handbuch der Kunstwissenschaft.) Potsdam. 1930.
Beenken, H. Bildhauer des 14 Jahrhts am Rhein und in Schwaben. (Deutsche Meister.) Leipsic. 1927.
Bode, W. Die Plastik. (Geschichte der deutschen Kunst. Vol. ii.) Berlin. 1887.
Goldschmidt, A. Die Skulpturen von Freiburg und Wechselburg. (Deutscher Verein für Kunstwissenschaft.) Berlin. 1924.
—— Studien zur Geschichte der sächsischen Skulptur in der Uebergangszeit vom romanischen zum gotischen Stil. Berlin. 1903.
Habicht, V. C. Die mittelalterliche Plastik Hildesheims. Strasbourg. 1917.
Hartmann, P. Die gotische Monumental-Plastik in Schwaben...bis zum...Beginn des 15 Jahrhts. Munich. 1910.
Hoehn, H. Nürnberger gotische Plastik. Nuremberg. 1922.
Jantzen, H. Deutsche Bildhauer des 13 Jahrhts. (Deutsche Meister.) Leipsic. 1925.
Karlinger, H. Die romanische Steinplastik in Altbayern und Salzburg, 1050–1260. (Deutscher Verein für Kunstwissenschaft.) Berlin. 1924.
Kautzsch, R. Der Mainz Dom und seine Denkmäler. 2 vols. Frankfort-on-M. 1925.
Kemmerich, M. Die frühmittelalterliche Porträtplastik in Deutschland bis zum Ende des 13 Jahrhts. Leipsic. 1909.

Kieslinger, F. Zur Geschichte der gotischen Plastik in Oesterreich. ɪ. Bis zum Eindringen des spätgotischen Faltenstiles. Vienna. 1923.

Künze, H. Die Plastik des 14 Jahrhts in Sachsen und Thüringen. (Deutscher Verein für Kunstwissenschaft.) Berlin. 1925.

Luebbecke, E. F. Die gotische Kölner Plastik. Strasbourg. 1910.

Lüthgen, E. Gotische Plastik in den Rheinlanden. Bonn. 1921.

—— Die niederrheinische Plastik von der Gotik bis zur Renaissance. Strasbourg. 1917.

Martin, K. Die Nürnberger Steinplastik im 14 Jahrht. Berlin. 1927.

Panofsky, E. Die deutsche Plastik des 11 bis 13 Jahrhts. 2 vols. Munich. 1924.

Pinder, W. Die deutsche Plastik des 14 Jahrhts. Munich. 1925.

—— Die deutsche Plastik des 15 Jahrhts. Munich. 1924.

—— Mittelalterliche Plastik Würzburgs. Würzburg. 1911.

—— and Hege, W. Der Bamberger Dom und seine Bildwerke. Berlin. 1933.

—— —— Der Naumburger Dom und seine Bildwerke. Berlin. 1931.

Schmitt, O. Gotische Skulpturen des Freiburger Münsters. 2 vols. Frankfort-on-M. 1926.

—— Gotische Skulpturen des Strassburger Münsters. 2 vols. Frankfort-on-M. 1924.

—— Oberrheinische Plastik im ausgehenden Mittelalter. Freiburg-i.-B. 1924.

Weese, A. Die Bamberger Domskulpturen. 2nd edn. 2 vols. Strasbourg. 1914.

Weigert, H. Die Stilstufen der deutschen Plastik von 1250 bis 1350. *In* Marburger Jahrbuch. Vol. ɪɪɪ. 1927.

Wiese, E. Schlesische Plastik vom Beginn des 14 bis zur Mitte des 15 Jahrhts. Leipsic. 1923.

(v) *Italy.*

Balcarres, Lord (Earl of Crawford). The evolution of Italian sculpture. London. 1909.

Bertaux, E. Donatello. Paris. 1910.

Bode, W. Denkmäler der Renaissance-Skulptur Toscanas. Munich. 1892–1905.

—— Florentiner Bildhauer der Renaissance. 3rd edn. Berlin. 1911. Engl. transl. London. 1908. [For Donatello.]

Brach, A. Nicola und Giovanni Pisano und die Plastik des 14 Jahrhts in Siena. Strasbourg. 1904.

Burger, F. Geschichte des florentinischen Grabmals...bis Michelangelo. Strasbourg. 1904.

Colasanti, A. Donatello. Rome. *n.d.*

Cruttwell, M. Donatello. London. 1911.

Fabriczy, C. von. Medaillen der italienischen Renaissance. Leipsic. 1903. Engl. transl. Hamilton. London. 1904.

Fechheimer, S. Donatello und die Reliefkunst. Strasbourg. 1904.

Filippini, L. La scultura del Trecento in Roma. Turin. 1908.

Graber, H. Beiträge zu Nicola Pisano. Strasbourg. 1911.

Hill, G. F. A corpus of Italian medals of the Renaissance before Cellini. (British Museum.) London. 1930.

—— Pisanello. London. 1905.

Mayer, A. L. Mittelalterliche Plastik in Italien. Munich. 1923.

Paniconi, E. Monumento al Cardinale G. de Braye, Orvieto. Rome. 1906.

Perkins, C. C. Tuscan sculptors. 2 vols. London. 1864.

Planiscig, L. Venezianische Bildhauer der Renaissance. Vienna. 1921.

Reymond, M. La sculpture florentine. 4 vols. Florence. 1897–1900.

Schottmueller, F. Donatello: ein Beitrag zum Verständnis seiner künstlerischen Tat. Munich. 1902.

Schubring, P. Donatello. Stuttgart. 1907.

—— Das italienische Grabmal der Frührenaissance. Berlin. 1904.

—— Die italienische Plastik des Quattrocento. Berlin. 1919.

—— Die Plastik Sienas im Quattrocento. Berlin. 1907.

Supino, J. B. La scultura delle porte di S. Petronio in Bologna. Florence. 1914.

—— La scultura in Bologna nel secolo xv. Bologna. 1910.

Venturi, A. Giovanni Pisano. Munich. 1927.
Wackernagel, M. Die Plastik des 11 und 12 Jahrhts in Apulien. (Rome: K. Preuss. Hist. Inst. Kunstgeschichtl. Forschungen, ii.) Leipsic. 1911.
Zimmermann, M. G. Öberitalienische Plastik im...Mittelalter. Leipsic. 1897.

(vi) *Netherlands.*

Bosschere, J. de. La sculpture anversoise aux xvᵉ et xviᵉ siècles. Brussels. 1909. [With bibliography.]
Devigne, M. La sculpture mosane du xiiᵉ au xviᵉ siècle. Paris and Brussels. 1932.
Dupierreux, R. La sculpture Wallonne. Les Amis de l'Art Wallon. Collection i. Brussels. 1914.
Vogelsang, W. Die Holzskulptur in den Niederlanden. Berlin. 1911.
Wauters, A. J. Sculpture en ivoire et les ivoiriers flamands. Brussels. 1885.

(vii) *Spain.*

Dieulafoy, M. La statuaire polychrome en Espagne. Paris. 1908.
Lafond, P. La sculpture espagnole. Paris. 1908.
Mayer, A. L. Mittelalterliche Plastik in Spanien. Munich. 1922.
Weise, G. Spanische Plastik. 2 vols. Reutlingen. 1925, 27.

E. STAINED GLASS.

(i) *General.*

Berlin: K. Akad. des Bauwesens. Vorbildliche Glasmalerei aus dem späten Mittelalter und der Renaissancezeit. 4 pts. Berlin. 1911–17.
Eden, F. S. Ancient stained and painted glass. Cambridge. 1913.
Heinersdorff, G. Die Glasmalerei. Berlin. 1914.
Knowles, J. A. The technique of glass painting in mediaeval and renaissance times. London. 1914.
Kolb, H. Glasmalereien des Mittelalters und der Renaissance. Stuttgart. 1884–9.
Oidtmann, H. Die Glasmalerei. i. Die Technik. ii. Die Geschichte. Cologne. 1892, 8.
Ottin, L. Le vitrail. Paris. *n.d.*
Roussel, J. Les vitraux. 2 vols. Paris. 1903, 11.
Schmarsow, A. Kompositionsgesetze frühgotischer Glasgemälde. Leipsic. 1919.
Warrington, W. History of stained glass from the earliest period of the art to the present time. London. 1848.
Westlake, N. H. J. History of design in painted glass. 4 vols. London. 1881–94.

(ii) *English.*

Drake, M. History of English glass painting, etc. London. 1912.
Heaton, C. Origin of the stained glass in Canterbury cathedral. *In* Burlington Magazine. xi. p. 172.
Knowles, J. A. Processes and methods of mediaeval glass painting. London. 1922.
—— The York school of glass painting. London. 1923.
Le Couteur, J. D. Ancient glass in Winchester. Winchester. 1920.
—— English medieval painted glass. London. 1926.
—— Notes on the great north window of Canterbury cathedral. *In* Archaeologia Cantiana. xxix. 1911. p. 323.
Nelson, P. Ancient painted glass in England, 1170–1500. London. 1913.
Read, H. English stained glass. London. 1926.

(iii) *French.*

Baudin, F. Le vitrail du xiiᵉ siècle au xviiiᵉ siècle en France. Paris. *n.d.*
Cahier, C. and Martin, A. Vitraux peints de Saint-Étienne de Bourges. Paris. 1842–4.
Delaporte, Y. (with illustrations by Houvet, E.). Les vitraux de la cathédrale de Chartres. Chartres. 1926.
Florival, A. de and Midoux, E. Les vitraux de la cathédrale de Laon. Paris. 1882–91.

Hucher, E. Vitraux peints de la cathédrale du Mans. Le Mans. 1868.
Lasteyrie, F. de. Histoire de la peinture sur verre d'après ses monuments en France. 2 vols. Paris. 1838, 57.
Magne, L. L'œuvre des peintres verriers français. 2 vols. Paris. 1885.
Meloizes, A. (Marquis des). Les vitraux de la cathédrale de Bourges postérieurs au xiiiᵉ siècle.
Rondot, N. Les peintres verriers de Troyes du xivᵉ et du xvᵉ siècle. Paris. 1867.

(iv) *Germany and Austria.*

Frankl, P. Die Glasmalerei des 15 Jahrhts in Bayern und Schwaben. Strasbourg. 1912.
Hertel, B. Die Glasgemälde des Kölner Domes. Berlin. 1925.
Kieslinger, F. Gotische Glasmalerei in Oesterreich bis 1450. Zurich. 1927.
Lind, K. Meisterwerke der kirchlichen Glasmalerei. Vienna. 1895-7.

(v) *Italy.*

Giusto, E. M. Le vetrate di S. Francesco in Assisi. Milan. 1911.
Monneret de Villard, U. Le vetrate del Duomo di Milano. 3 vols. Milan. 1918-20.

1004

CHAPTER XXV.

THE RENAISSANCE IN EUROPE.

[*See also* Bibliography of Vol. vii, ch. xxv.]

I. CONTEMPORARY SOURCES.

Barbari, F. Epistolae. Brescia. 1743.
Barzizza, G. Gasparino da. Opera. Ed. Furietti, J. A. 2 vols. Rome. 1723.
Beccatelli, Antonio. Epistolarum libri v. Venice. 1553.
Bekynton, Thomas. Correspondence. Ed. Williams, G. 2 vols. (Rolls.) 1872.
Burrows, M. *ed.* Collectanea. Series ii. (Oxford Hist. Soc. xvi.) Oxford. 1890.
Charles VIII. Lettres. Ed. Pélicier, P. 5 vols. Paris. 1898–1905.
Chaundler MSS, The. Ed. James, M. R. (Roxburghe Club.) London. 1916.
Christ Church letters. Ed. Sheppard, J. B. (Camden Soc. n.s. xix.) London. 1877.
Clamangiis, N. de. Opera. Leyden. 1613.
Cortesi, P. De hominibus doctis, dialogus. Florence. 1734.
Epistolae Academicae Oxon. Ed. Anstey, H. 2 vols. (Oxford Hist. Soc. xxxv, xxxvi.) Oxford. 1898.
Erasmus, D. Opus Epistolarum. Ed. Allen, P. S. Vol. i. Oxford. 1906.
Ficino, Marsilio. Opera. 2 vols. Venice. 1516.
—— Platonis opera. Florence. [*c.* 1494.]
—— Plotini opera. Florence. 1492.
Gaguin, R. Epistolae et orationes. Ed. Thuasne, L. 2 vols. Paris. 1904.
Gloria, A. I Monumenti dell' Università di Padova. 3 vols. Venice. 1884–8.
Martène, E. and Durand, U. Veterum Scriptorum et Monumentorum...amplissima Collectio. 9 vols. Paris. 1724–33. [Vol. ii (1311–1465). Selection from J. de Monstereul's letters.]
Montaiglon, A. de. Etat des gages des ouvriers italiens employés par Charles VIII. *In* Archives de l'art français. i, pp. 94 sqq. Paris. 1851.
Munimenta Academica Oxon. Ed. Anstey, H. 2 vols. (Rolls.) 1868.
Pico della Mirandola, G. Opera. Venice. 1478; Basle. 1557; Basle. 1601.
Pius II (Aeneas Sylvius Piccolomini). Opera. Basle. 1551.
Platina (Bartolommeo Sacchi). De vitis summorum pontificum opus. [Venice.] 1479. *Also* ed. Gaida, G. RR.II.SS. New edn. Vol. iii, pt. 1.
Poliziano, A. Opera. Venice. 1498.
—— Le Stanze, l' Orfeo e le Rime. Ed. Carducci, G. Florence. 1863. *Also* ed. Momigliano, A. Turin. [1921.]
Pontano, G. Opera. Venice. 1518.
Sannazaro, J. Opera. Venice. 1535.
Trithemius, J. De scriptoribus ecclesiasticis. Basle. 1494; Paris. 1512 (with a supplt.); Cologne. 1544 (with a second supplt.).
Vinci, Leonardo da. Frammenti letterari e filosofici. Ed. Solmi, E. Florence. 1904.
—— Leonardo da Vinci's Note-books. Arranged and rendered into English by McCurdy, E. London. 1906.
—— The literary works. Ed. with transl. Richter, J. P. 2 vols. London. 1883.
Wimpheling, J. Adolescentia. Strasbourg. 1500.

II. LATER WORKS.

Allen, P. S. The age of Erasmus. Oxford. 1914.
—— Bishop Shirwood of Durham and his library. EHR. xxv (1910). 445–56.
—— The letters of Rudolph Agricola. EHR. xxi (1906). 302–17.
Armstrong, E. Lorenzo de' Medici. (Heroes of the Nations.) New York and London. 1896.
Aschbach, T. R. von. Geschichte der Wiener Universität. Vols. i and ii. Vienna. 1865, 77.
Bauch, G. Die Anfänge des Humanismus in Ingoldstadt. Munich. 1901.
—— Die Universität Erfurt im Zeitalter des Frühhumanismus. Breslau. 1904.

Bett, H. Nicholas of Cusa. London. 1932.

Bezold, F. von. Konrad Celtis, der deutsche Erzhumanist. HZ. xLix (1883). 1 sqq., 193 sqq.

Bursian, C. Geschichte der classischen Philologie in Deutschland. Vol. i. pp. 91–118. Munich. 1883.

Campbell, M. F. A. G. Annales de la Typographie Néerlandaise au xvᵉ siècle. The Hague. 1874.

Claudin, A. Histoire de l'imprimerie en France au xvᵉ et au xviᵉ siècle. 4 vols. Paris. 1900–14.

Creighton, M. The Early Renaissance in England. Cambridge. 1895.. Repr. *in* Historical lectures and addresses. London. 1903.

—— History of the Papacy. Vol. v. (Ch. i, Humanism in Germany.) London. 1894.

Delaruelle, L. Guillaume Budé. Paris. 1907.

Delisle, L. Les livres d'heures du duc de Berry. *In* Gazette des Beaux-Arts. xxix (1884). 97 sqq. ; 281 sqq. ; 391 sqq.

—— Recherches sur la librairie de Charles V. 2 vols. Paris. 1907.

Della Torre, A. Storia dell' Accademia Platonica di Firenze. Florence. 1902.

Dimier, L. French Painting in the sixteenth century. London. 1904.

Dorez, L. and Thuasne, L. Pic de la Mirandole en France. Paris. 1897.

Dreydorff, G. Das System des Johannes Pico. Marburg. 1858.

Duhem, P. Études sur Léonard de Vinci. Series i–iii. Paris. 1906–13.

Einstein, L. The Italian Renaissance in England. New York. 1907.

Fierville, C. Le Cardinal Jean Jouffroy et son temps. Coutances. 1874.

Friedrich, J. Johann Wessel. Ratisbon. 1862.

Gallois, L. Les géographes allemands de la Renaissance. Paris. 1890.

Gasquet, F. A. The eve of the Reformation. pp. 14–50. London. 1900.

Geiger, L. Johann Reuchlin. Leipsic. 1871.

—— Renaissance und Humanismus in Italien und Deutschland. Berlin. 1882.

Geymüller, H. von. Die Baukunst der Renaissance in Frankreich. 2 vols. Stuttgart. 1898, 1901.

Gray, H. L. Greek visitors to England in 1455–6. *In* Anniversary essays in medieval history by students of C. H. Haskins. Boston and New York. 1929.

Haebler, C. Bibliografía ibérica del siglo xv. The Hague and Leipsic. 1903.

Hartfelder, K. Konrad Celtes und der Heidelberger Humanistenkreis. HZ. (1882). 15 sqq.

Hevesy, A. de. La Bibliothèque du roi Matthias Corvinus. Paris. 1923.

Imbart de la Tour, P. Les origines de la Réforme. Vol. ii. pp. 314–441. Paris. 1909.

James, M. R. Greek Manuscripts in England before the Renaissance. *In* The Library. 2nd ser. Vol. vii. pp. 337 sqq. Oxford. 1927.

—— The wanderings and homes of Manuscripts. (Helps for students of history.) S.P.C.K. London. 1919.

Janssen, J. History of the German People at the close of the Middle Ages. Transl. Mitchell, M. A. and Christie, A. M. Vol. i. Bk. i, ch. iv. London. 1896. [Untrustworthy.]

Kampschulte, F. W. Die Universität Erfurt in ihrem Verhältnisse zu dem Humanismus und der Reformation. Trèves. 1858.

Knepper, J. Jakob Wimpfeling. Freiburg. 1902.

Legrand, E. Bibliographie Hellénique. Vol. i. Paris. 1885.

Lupton, J. H. Life of John Colet. New edn. London. 1909.

Machly, J. Angelus Politianus. Leipsic. 1864.

McCurdy, E. Leonardo da Vinci. London. 1904, 1907.

—— The mind of Leonardo da Vinci. London. 1928.

McMurrich, J. F. Leonardo da Vinci the anatomist. London. 1930.

Mallet, C. E. History of the University of Oxford. Vol. i, ch. viii–x. London. 1924.

Mancini, G. Vita di Leon Battista Alberti. Florence. 1882.

Michel, A. Histoire de l'Art. Vol. iii, pt.2—vol. v, pt.1. Paris. 1908–12.

Müntz, E. La Renaissance en Italie et en France à l'époque de Charles VIII. Paris. 1883.

Omont, H. Georges Hermonyme de Sparte, maître de grec à Paris. Paris. 1885.
Osler, W. Thomas Linacre. Cambridge. 1908.
Palustre, L. L'Architecture de la Renaissance. Paris. 1892.
—— La Renaissance en France. Vols. I–III. Paris. 1879–89 [no more publ.].
Pater, W. Studies in the Renaissance. London. 1873.
Paulsen, F. Geschichte des gelehrten Unterrichts auf den deutschen Schulen und Universitäten. 2nd edn. Vol. I. pp. 49–170. Leipsic. 1896.
Pearson, K. The Ethic of Freethought. (Ch. VIII, Humanism in Germany.) London. 1888.
Philippe, J. Guillaume Fichet, sa vie, ses œuvres. Annecy. 1892.
Procter, R. An index to the Early Printed Books in the British Museum. Part I. 2 vols. London. 1898.
—— The printing of Greek in the fifteenth century. (Bibliog. Soc.) Oxford. 1900.
Pusino, I. Ficinos und Picos religiös-philosophische Anschauungen. ZKG. XLIV (1925). 504 sqq.
Reumont, A. von. Lorenzo de' Medici. 2 vols. Leipsic. 1874 ; 2nd edn. 1883. Engl. transl. Harrison, R. 2 vols. London. 1876.
Roscoe, W. Life of Lorenzo de' Medici. Liverpool. 1795.
Rotta, P. Il Cardinale Niccolò Cusano. Milan. 1928.
Saitta, G. La filosofia di Marsilio Ficino. Messina. 1923.
Savage, E. A. Old English libraries. London. 1911.
Schirmer, W. F. Der englische Frühhumanismus. Leipsic. 1931.
Schmid, K. A. and G. Geschichte der Erziehung. Vol. II. Pt. II, pp. 1–150 (by K. Hartfelder). Stuttgart. 1889.
Schmidt, C. Histoire littéraire de l'Alsace à la fin du XVe et au commencement du XVIe siècle. 2 vols. Paris. 1879.
Scholderer, V. Greek printing types. London. 1927.
Séailles, G. Léonard de Vinci. 2nd edn. Paris. 1906.
Seebohm, F. The Oxford Reformers of 1498. 3rd edn. London. 1887.
Seidlitz, W. von. Leonardo da Vinci. 2 vols. Berlin. 1909.
Semprini, G. Giovanni Pico della Mirandola. Todi. 1921.
Silbernagl, A. Johannes Trithemius. 2nd edn. Ratisbon. 1885.
Singer, C. ed. Studies in the history and method of Science. Oxford. 1917.
Solmi, E. Leonardo. 2nd edn. Florence. 1907.
Taylor, R. A. Leonardo the Florentine. London. 1927.
Thomas, A. De Joannis de Monsterolio vita et operibus. Paris. 1883.
Thorndike, L. Science and Thought in the fifteenth century. New York. 1929
Tilley, A. The Dawn of the French Renaissance. Cambridge. 1918.
Tomek, W. W. Geschichte der Prager Universität. Prague. 1849.
Vaissière, P. de. De R. Gaguini vita et operibus. Chartres. 1906.
Vansteenberghe, E. Le Cardinal Nicolas de Cues. Lille and Paris. 1920.
Vickers, K. H. Humphrey, Duke of Gloucester, London. 1907.
Vinci, Leonardo da. Conferenze Fiorentini. Milan. 1910.
Vitry, P. Michel Colombe et la sculpture française de son temps. Paris. 1901.
Ward, W. H. Architecture of the Renaissance in France. 2 vols. London. [1911.]
Wattenbach, W. Hartmann Schedel als Humanist. FDG. XI (1871). 349 sqq.
—— Peter Luder, der erste humanistische Lehrer in Heidelberg. In Zeitschr. für die Gesch. des Oberrheins. XXII (1869). 33 sqq.
Zeno, A. Dissertazioni Vossiane. 2 vols. Venice. 1752–3.
Ziegelbauer, M. Historia rei literariae ordinis S. Benedicti. Vol. III. pp. 217–333 (Vita Trithemii). Augsburg. 1754.
Ziegler, A. Regiomontanus. Dresden. 1874.

CHRONOLOGICAL TABLE

OF

LEADING EVENTS MENTIONED IN THIS VOLUME

1139 Afonso I Henriques becomes first King of Portugal.
1145–70 The (Gothic) west portal of Chartres Cathedral built.
1147 Afonso I captures Lisbon from the Moors.
1222 Andrew II of Hungary issues the Golden Bull.
1250–79 Afonso III, King of Portugal.
1254 Representatives of the towns sit in the Portuguese Cortes for the first
    time.
1260–78 Niccola Pisano *floruit*.
1266–1336 Giotto.
1267 Portugal completed by the final annexation of Algarve.
1279–1325 Dinis the Husbandman, King of Portugal.
1289 Strife between Church and State in Portugal ended by a Concordat.
1290 Expulsion of the Jews from England.
1300 Pierre Dubois writes *De Recuperatione Terrae Sanctae*.
1301 Death of Andrew III of Hungary and extinction of House of Árpád.
1302 (17–18 May) The Matins of Bruges.
    (11 July) Battle of Courtrai.
    (Nov.) Pope Boniface VIII issues *Unam Sanctam*.
1306 Expulsion of the Jews from France.
1308–42 Charles Robert of Anjou, King of Hungary.
1312 Philip the Fair annexes Lyons to France.
1315–41 Gedymin, Great Prince of Lithuania.
1315–18 Edward Bruce's rebellion in Ireland.
1319 Magnus, the infant king of Norway, elected King of Sweden. The
    nobles in control.
1320 Christopher, King of Denmark, submits to capitulations on his election.
1320–33 Vladyslav I the Short, King of Poland.
1320 (5 May) Peace of Paris between France and Flanders.
1321 Death of Dante Alighieri.
1324 Publication of the *Defensor Pacis* of Marsilio of Padua.
1328 (April) Independence of Scotland recognised by Treaty of Northampton.
    (23 Aug.) Battle of Mt. Cassel.
1329–71 David II, King of Scots.
1332 Battle of Dupplin Moor.
1332–9 Edward Balliol, intruded King of Scots.
1333–70 Casimir III the Great, King of Poland.
1337–45 James van Artevelde rules Ghent.
1340–75 Waldemar IV Atterdag, King of Denmark.
1340–84 Gerard Groote.
1342–82 Lewis I the Great, King of Hungary.
1345–77 Olgierd, Great Prince of Lithuania.
1345–1436 Bavarian dynasty in Holland and Hainault.
1346 Battle of Crécy.
1346–84 Louis de Maële, Count of Flanders.
1347 National code of law introduced in Sweden by King Magnus.
1347–50 Lewis the Great of Hungary occupies Naples.
1348–50 The Black Death.
1348–49 Massacre of Jews in Germany leads to their emigration to Poland.
1348 (?) Death of William of Ockham.
1349 Louis de Maële captures Ghent.
    The eldest grandson (subsequently eldest son) of the King of France
    becomes Dauphin of Viennois.

1351 The privileges of the nobility and the Golden Bull confirmed in Hungary.
1355 New frontier established between Dauphiné and Savoy.
1356 Duke Wenceslas of Brabant swears to the *Joyeuse Entrée*.
    Battle of Poitiers.
1358 Dalmatia ceded to Hungary by Venice.
1363–1404 Philip the Bold, Duke of Burgundy.
1363–1429 Jean Gerson.
1369 (Nov.)–1370 (May) Peace of Stralsund between Denmark and the Hansa.
1370–82 Lewis the Great of Hungary, King of Poland.
1371–90 Robert II (Stewart), King of Scots.
1374 The Pact of Koszice regulates the Polish succession and the rights of
    the *Szlachta*.
1375 Queen Margaret becomes regent of Denmark for her son King Olaf.
1376–1400 Wenceslas of Luxemburg, King of the Romans.
1377–1434 Jagiello, Great Prince of Lithuania.
1377 Pope Gregory XI condemns Wyclif's teaching in *De Civili Dominio*.
1378 Beginning of the Great Schism.
    (29 Nov.) Death of the Emperor Charles IV.
1378–1419 Wenceslas IV (King of the Romans), King of Bohemia.
1379 Victory of Alberico da Barbiano and the Compagnia di S. Giorgio
    establishes reputation of the Italian *condottieri* and Free Companies.
1380 Queen Margaret becomes regent of Norway for her son King Olaf.
1380–82 Philip van Artevelde rules Ghent.
1382 (27 Nov.) Battle of West-Roosebeke.
1384–1404 Philip the Bold, Count of Flanders and Franche Comté.
1384–98 Jadviga (Hedwig), Queen of Poland.
1385 John I elected King of Portugal.
    The Portuguese defeat the Castilians at Aljubarrota.
    Submission of Ghent to Philip the Bold.
1386 Conversion of Jagiello of Lithuania, and his marriage to Jadviga of
    Poland.
1386–1434 Vladyslav II (Jagiello), King of Poland.
1386 Battle of Sempach.
1387–1437 Sigismund of Luxemburg, King of Hungary.
1389 (Feb.) Queen Margaret of Denmark and Norway conquers Sweden.
    (15 May) Leagues of towns forbidden in the Public Peace of South
    Germany.
1390–1406 Robert III, King of Scots.
1394–95 Richard II's first expedition to Ireland.
1397 Union of the three Scandinavian kingdoms at Calmar.
1398–1430 Vitold, Grand Prince of Lithuania.
1399–1413 Henry IV, King of England.
1400–10 Rupert, Elector Palatine, King of the Romans.
1400–08 Revolt of Owen Glyn Dŵr in Wales.
1400–64 Nicholas of Cusa.
1401 Statute *De Haeretico comburendo* passed.
    King Rupert's failure against the Visconti.
1401–29 (?) Masaccio.
1402 John Hus begins preaching at the Bethlehem Chapel, Prague.
1402–12 Giovanni Maria Visconti, Duke of Milan.
1403 (20 July) Battle of Tewkesbury.
1404 John the Fearless becomes Duke of Burgundy, Count of Flanders etc.
1406–37 James I, King of Scots.
1407 (23 Nov.) Murder of the Duke of Orleans.
1408 Venice recovers Dalmatia.
1409 University of Prague becomes predominantly Czech.
1410 (15 July) Defeat of the Teutonic Knights by the Poles and Lithuanians
    at Tannenberg (Grunwald).
    (20 Sept.) Sigismund of Hungary elected King of the Romans.
    (1 Oct.) Jošt of Moravia elected King of the Romans.

1411 (Jan.) Death of Jošt.
    (July) Unanimous re-election of Sigismund as King of the Romans.
1412–47 Filippo Maria Visconti, Duke of Milan.
1412–16 Ferdinand I, King of Aragon.
1412 (Oct.) Death of Queen Margaret of Scandinavia.
1413–22 Henry V, King of England.
1414–35 Joanna II, Queen of Naples.
1414 (Nov.) Opening of the Council of Constance.
1415 (April) Frederick of Hohenzollern created Elector of Brandenburg.
    (29–31 May) Deposition of Pope John XXIII.
    (4 July) Abdication of Pope Gregory XII.
    (6 July) Execution of John Hus.
    (Aug.) Henry V invades Normandy.
    (Sept.) Czech nobility's protest against the execution of Hus.
    (24·Oct) Battle of Agincourt.
1416 (Feb.) Count Amadeus VIII created Duke of Savoy.
1416–58 Alfonso V the Magnanimous, King of Aragon.
1416 (30 May) Execution of Jerome of Prague.
    (15 Oct.) A Spanish nation formed at the Council of Constance.
1417 (26 July) Deposition of Pope Benedict XIII.
    (9 Oct.) The decree *Frequens* passed by the Council of Constance.
    (11 Nov.) Election of Pope Martin V.
1418 (22 April) Closing of the Council of Constance.
1419 (10 Sept.) Murder of John the Fearless, Duke of Burgundy.
1419–67 Philip the Good, Duke of Burgundy, Count of Flanders, etc.
1420 The "Four Articles of Prague" promulgated by the Hussites.
    Emergence of the Taborite party among the Hussites.
    (21 May) Treaty of Troyes between Henry V and Charles VI of France.
    Victories of the Hussites under Žižka over Sigismund.
1420–4 War between Alfonso V of Aragon and Louis III of Anjou for the succession to Naples.
1420 (19 Sept.) Pope Martin V re-enters Rome.
1421 Acquisition of Leghorn by Florence.
1422–61 Henry VI, King of England.
1422–61 Charles VII, King of France.
1423–4 Council of Siena.
1423 War breaks out between Florence and Visconti.
1424 (3 Jan.) Death of Sforza Attendolo.
    (3 June) Death of Braccio.
    (17 Aug.) Battle of Verneuil.
    (11 Oct.) Death of Žižka.
1425 Venice joins Florence in the war with Visconti.
1426–7 Venice wins Brescia and Bergamo.
1428 (3 July) Philip the Good acquires Holland and Hainault by Treaty of Delft.
1429 (8 May) St Joan of Arc raises siege of Orleans.
1429–33 War of Florence with Lucca.
1429 (19 June) Battle of Patay.
    (17 July) Charles VII crowned at Rheims.
1430 Philip the Good becomes Duke of Brabant.
1431 (20 Feb.) Death of Pope Martin V.
1431–47 Eugenius IV, Pope.
1431 (30 May) St Joan of Arc burnt at Rouen.
    (23 July) Opening of the Council of Basle.
    (14 Aug.) Victory of the Hussites at Taus (Domažlice).
    (14–18 Dec.) Eugenius IV attempts to dissolve Council of Basle.
1432 *The Adoration of the Lamb* by the Van Eycks completed.
1433 (31 May) Sigismund crowned Emperor at Rome.
    (Nov.) The *Compacts of Prague* accepted by the Bohemian Diet.

1434 (Feb.) Reconciliation of Eugenius IV and Council of Basle.
    (30 May) Prokop and the Taborites defeated at Lipany.
1434–44 Vladyslav III, King of Poland.
1434 (June) Eugenius IV flees from Rome to Florence.
    The Portuguese sailors round Cape Bojador.
    Revolt of Sweden from King Eric.
    (Oct.) Cosimo de' Medici returns from exile and becomes ruler of Florence.
    (Nov.) Death of Louis III of Anjou.
1435 (2 Feb.) Death of Joanna II of Naples.
1435–42 René of Anjou, King of Naples. Civil war with Alfonso V of Aragon.
1435 (5 Aug.) Alfonso V defeated and captured in sea-battle of Ponza.
    (Sept.) Agreement between the Emperor Sigismund and the Bohemian Diet.
    (15 Sept.) Death of Duke of Bedford.
    (21 Sept.) Treaty of Arras between France and Burgundy.
1436 (13 April) Charles VII recovers Paris.
    (5 July) The *Compacts of Prague* agreed to by the Council of Basle and the Hussites at Iglau (Jihlava).
1437–60 James II, King of Scots.
1437 (May–July) Breach between Eugenius IV and Council of Basle.
    End of the minority of Henry VI of England.
    (9 Dec.) Death of the Emperor Sigismund.
1438 (5 Jan.) Opening of the Council of Ferrara (Florence).
1438–9 Albert II of Austria, King of Hungary, and King of the Romans.
1438 (7 July) Charles VII issues the Pragmatic Sanction of Bourges.
    Revolt of Denmark from King Eric.
1439 (25 June) The Council of Basle deposes Eugenius IV.
    (5 July) Union of the Greek and Latin Churches decreed at the Council of Florence.
    (5 Nov.) The Council of Basle elects Amadeus VIII of Savoy as Pope Felix V.
1439–44 Vladyslav I (II of Poland), King of Hungary.
1440–93 Frederick III of Austria, King (Emperor) of the Romans.
1440–70 Frederick II, Elector of Brandenburg.
1440 The outbreak of the Praguerie in France.
1442 (2 June) Alfonso of Aragon captures Naples, and becomes sole king.
1443 (28 Sept.) Pope Eugenius re-enters Rome.
1444 George of Poděbrady leads the Hussites in Bohemia.
    (10 Nov.) Vladyslav of Hungary and Poland defeated and slain by the Turks at Varna.
1445 Charles VII issues the *Ordonnance* of Nancy on finance.
1445–6 Charles VII establishes the *Compagnies d'Ordonnance*.
1446–57 Ladislas V Posthumus, King of Hungary.
1446–52 John Hunyadi, regent of Hungary.
1447 Deaths of Humphrey, Duke of Gloucester, and Cardinal Beaufort.
1447–55 Nicholas V, Pope.
1447–92 Casimir IV, King of Poland.
1447–54 War of Milanese Succession.
1448–94 William Tilley of Selling *floruit*.
1448 (Feb.) Concordat of Vienna between Pope and Emperor.
    (April) Charles VII establishes the *Francs-Archers*.
    (July) The Council of Basle leaves Basle for Lausanne.
1448–81 Christian I (of Oldenburg), King of Denmark.
1449 (7 April) The Anti-Pope Felix V abdicates.
    (25 April) The Council of Basle-Lausanne dissolves. End of Conciliar Movement.
1449–53 War of Albert Achilles of Brandenburg-Anspach with Nuremberg.
1449 Charles VII recovers Normandy.
1450 (25 Feb.) Francesco Sforza becomes Duke of Milan.

1450 (15 April) Battle of Formigny.
     Fall and murder of the Duke of Suffolk.
     Rebellion of Jack Cade.
1451 Philip the Good becomes Duke of Luxemburg.
1452 (18 March) Frederick III crowned Emperor at Rome.
     (13 Oct.) Birth of Edward, Prince of Wales.
1452–1519 Leonardo da Vinci.
1453 (Jan.) Conspiracy of Porcaro at Rome.
     (6 Jan.) Frederick III creates Austria an arch-duchy.
     (29 May) Fall of Constantinople to the Turks. End of East Roman
        Empire.
     (17 July) Battle of Castillon.
1453–57 Ladislas Posthumus of Austria, King of Bohemia.
1453 (19 Oct.) Charles VII finally recovers Bordeaux. End of the Hundred
        Years' War.
1454 (9 April) Peace of Lodi.
     (22 May) First battle of St Albans. Beginning of Wars of the Roses.
     Statutes of Nieszawa in Poland, establishing the rights of the *Sejmiki*.
1454–66 War between Poland and the Teutonic Order.
1454–94 Angelo Poliziano (Politian).
1454 The Italian League formed.
1455–58 Calixtus III, Pope.
1456 John Hunyadi successfully defends Belgrade from the Turks.
     Charles VII annexes Dauphiné to the Crown of France.
     Gutenberg prints the "Mazarin Bible" at Mayence.
1458–90 Matthias Corvinus, King of Hungary.
1458–71 George of Poděbrady, King of Bohemia.
1458 (7 June) Death of Alfonso the Magnanimous, King of Aragon and Naples.
1458–79 John II, King of Aragon and Sicily.
1458–94 Ferdinand (Ferrante) I, King of Naples.
1458–64 Pius II, Pope.
1459–63 John "of Calabria's" war to recover Naples for René of Anjou.
1460 (18 Jan.) Pius II publishes the bull *Execrabilis* against appeals to a
        Council.
1460–88 James III, King of Scots.
1460 (Oct.) Richard, Duke of York, claims the crown of England,
     (30 Dec.) Richard of York defeated and slain at Wakefield.
1461–70 First reign of Edward IV, King of England.
1461 (29 March) Battle of Towton.
1461–83 Louis XI, King of France.
1463 Louis XI annexes Roussillon to France.
     Philip the Good summons the Estates General of the Netherlands.
     Death of Archduke Albert VI, and reunion of the eastern Habsburg
        dominions under the Emperor Frederick III.
1464 (Apr.) Francesco Sforza obtains Genoa as a French fief.
     (19 June) Louis XI establishes the French royal *Poste*.
     (1 Aug.) Death of Cosimo de' Medici.
1464–69 Piero de' Medici, ruler of Florence.
1464–71 Paul II, Pope.
1465 Revolt of the League of the Public Weal in France.
     Battle of Montlhéry (15 July). Peace of Conflans (Oct.).
     Printing introduced into Italy.
1466 (8 March) Death of Francesco Sforza, Duke of Milan.
1466–76 Galeazzo Sforza, Duke of Milan.
1466 (19 Oct.) Peace of Thorn between Poland and the Teutonic Order. The
        Order becomes vassal of Poland.
1467 The Unity of the Brotherhood institutes a separate Church in Bohemia.
1467–77 Charles the Bold, Duke of Burgundy, etc.
1467–94 Hans Memling *floruit*.
1468 (Oct.) Louis XI captured at Péronne. Treaty of Péronne.

1469–92 Lorenzo de' Medici, ruler of Florence.
1469 Matthias of Hungary obtains Moravia and Silesia.
1470–86 Albert Achilles, Elector of Brandenburg.
1470 Printing introduced into France.
    (Oct.) Henry VI of England restored to the throne.
1471–83 Second reign of Edward IV of England.
1471 (14 April, 4 May) Battles of Barnet and Tewkesbury.
    Sten Sture and the Swedes defeat Christian I of Denmark at Stockholm.
1471–1516 Vladislav II, King of Bohemia.
1471–84 Sixtus IV, Pope.
1472 Annexation of the Orkney and Shetland Islands to Scotland.
1473 *Dispositio Achillea* establishing absolute primogeniture for Brandenburg.
    Charles the Bold erects the Parlement of Malines for all the Netherlands.
1474–1504 Isabella the Catholic, Queen of Castile.
1475 (29 Aug.) Treaty of Picquigny between Louis XI and Edward IV.
    (Nov.) Charles the Bold annexes Lorraine.
1476 (2 March, 22 June) Charles the Bold defeated at Grandson and Morat by the Swiss.
1476–94 Gian Galeazzo Sforza, Duke of Milan.
1477 (5 Jan.) Defeat and death of Charles the Bold at Nancy
    Louis XI annexes the duchy of Burgundy and Franche Comté.
    (19 Aug.) Marriage of Archduke Maximilian of Austria with Mary, heiress of Charles the Bold.
    Printing introduced into England by Caxton.
1478 The Pazzi conspiracy against the Medici.
1478–80 War of Florence against the Papacy and Naples.
1478 Albert Achilles of Brandenburg defeats coalition headed by Matthias of Hungary.
    (7 Dec.) Moravia and Silesia ceded to Matthias of Hungary for life by the treaty of Olomouc.
1479–1516 Ferdinand II the Catholic, King of Aragon. He and Isabella of Castile become the "Catholic Kings of Spain".
1479 (7 Aug.) Battle of Guinegate between Maximilian and the French.
    Ludovico Sforza seizes the government of Milan.
1480–81 Otranto held by the Ottoman Turks.
1481–84 The Ferrarese War.
1481 Death of Charles of (Anjou-) Maine. Annexation of Provence to France.
1482 Berwick finally annexed to England.
    (23 Dec.) Peace of Arras between Maximilian and Louis XI.
1483 Edward V, King of England.
1483–85 Richard III, King of England,
1484–87 The Barons' Conspiracy in Naples.
1484–92 Innocent VIII, Pope.
1485 Treaty of Kutná Hora between Utraquists and Catholics in Bohemia.
    (22 Aug.) Battle of Bosworth, and accession of Henry VII, King of England.
1486 (16 Feb.) Archduke Maximilian elected King of the Romans.
1487 (July) Foundation of the Swabian League.
1488 Bartholomew Dias rounds the Cape of Good Hope.
1490 (6 March) Tyrol and the west Habsburg lands surrendered by Duke Sigismund to Maximilian.
    (11 July) Vladislav II of Bohemia elected King of Hungary.
    Moravia and Silesia reunited to Bohemia.
1492 (2 Jan.) Conquest of Granada by the Catholic Kings.
    (31 May) The Jews in Spain compelled to emigrate or become Christians.
    (12 Oct.) Columbus discovers America.
1495 Reception of Roman Law in Germany.
1498 Vasco da Gama reaches Calicut.
1502 (11 Feb.) The Muslims in Castile compelled to emigrate or become Christians.

INDEX

Aba, Amadé, 591

Abano, Peter of, 674, 678, 680, 685; his *Conciliator*, 677

Abbāsid dynasty, the, 664

Abbatia, Antonius de, alchemical writer, 682

'Abd-al-Mumin, emperor of Morocco, 510

Abenrakel, 669

Aberdeen, *studium generale* of, 470

Abingdon, 395

Abruzzi, the, governorship of, 164 sq.; Candola and, 177; Angevin predominance extirpated, *ib.*; 180, 198

Abū-'Abd-Allāhī Muhammad, "Az-Zaghal," uncle of Boabdil, in rivalry with Abū-l-Hasan and Boabdil, 488; dispossesses Abū-l-Hasan, 489; after Abū-l-Hasan's death, continues struggle with Boabdil, *ib.*; submits to Spain, *ib.*

Abū'l-Hākim, Muhammad Ibn 'Abd-al-Malik as-Sālihī al-Khwārazmī al-Kati, Arabian alchemist, 667

Academia Istropolitana, the, 615

Academy, the Roman, so-called, 188, 773 sq.

Acaster College School, 429

Achillini, Alessandro, 781

Achmet (Ahmed) ben Sirin, author of treatise on oneiromancy, 672

Acts of the Apostles, the, Greek MS. of, 799

Acuña Carillo, Alfonso de, archbishop of Toledo, 487

Adamitism, in Bohemia, 77

Adda, river, 178, 210 sq., 230

Aden, 524

Adige, river, 211

Adolf II, duke of Cleve, 141

Adolphus, 690

Adriatic, the, 160, 230

Adwert, abbey of, 789

Aegean, the, 812

Aeschines, 797

Aesop, the *Fables* of, 692

Afonso I (Henriques), count, then king of Portugal, and vassalage to Leon and Castile, 507; overthrows Teresa's rule, *ib.*; defeats her at St Mamede, 508; invades Galicia, *ib.*; defeats Alfonso at Cerneja, *ib.*; submits to emperor, *ib.*; overthrows Muslims at Ourique, *ib.*; and truce of Val de Vez, *ib.*; and peace at Zamora, 509; and Astorga, *ib.*; and Holy See, *ib.*; loses Astorga, *ib.*; takes Santarem and Lisbon, receives Sintra, gains Palmella, *ib.*; and Muslim states, 510; and his daughters' marriages, *ib.*; captured at Ciudad Rodrigo, *ib.*; besieged in Lisbon, 511; death of, *ib.*

Afonso II, king of Portugal, and canon law, 513; and civil war, *ib.*; and grant of tithes to episcopate, *ib.*; and dispute of the dean and bishop of Lisbon, *ib.*; and excommunication, 514; and confirmation of title-deeds, 513; and inquest into titles to landed property, 514; and invasion by Martin Sanches and king of Leon, *ib.*; and reconciliation with Church, *ib.*; death of, *ib.*; and Crown's appellate jurisdiction, 525

Afonso III, king of Portugal, invited to save Portugal, 515; accepts conditions, *ib.*; proceeds to Lisbon, *ib.*; and title of king, *ib.*; cedes Algarve, *ib.*; and marriage to Beatrice, illegitimate daughter of Alfonso X, *ib.*; and convention of Badajóz, 515 sq.; and policy in internal affairs, 516 sq.; his extravagance, 516; and clerical complaints, 517; his subterfuges, *ib.*; and Cortes of Leiria, 527; death of, 517

Afonso IV, king of Portugal, and conflict with Afonso Sanches, 518; and rebellion of Peter, *ib.*; and war with Castile, *ib.*; and Muslim invasion, 518 sq.; and abbey of Alcobaça, 526

Afonso V, king of Portugal, succeeds as minor, with successive regents queen Leonor and the Infant Peter, 522; takes over government, *ib.*; leases royal rights in Guinea trade to Fernão Gomes, *ib.*; captures Alcacer Ceguer in Morocco, and, ultimately, gains Tangier and Arzila, 523; after death of Henry IV of Castile, enters Castile and marries Joanna, *ib.*; fights drawn battle of Toro, *ib.*; makes peace with Ferdinand and Isabella at Alcaçovas, and concludes treaty of Toledo, *ib.*; promulgates *Ordenacões Afonsinas*, 522; handed over African forts and factories to Infant John, 524; effect of his liberalities and wars on treasury, 523; dominance of Braganza family, *ib.*; Afonso V and Cortes, 529; and agrarian legislation, 531

Afonso, infant of Portugal, 495, 524

Afonso Sanches, lord steward of Portugal, 518

Africa, North, 518; Spanish conquest of Peñon de la Gomera, Oran, Bougie, Tripoli, 521; Portuguese conquest of Ceuta, *ib.*; and expedition against Tangier, 521 sq.; and capture of Alcacer Ceguer, Tangier, and Arzila in Morocco, 522 sq.; 812

Africa, West, 506; stages in Portuguese exploration of, 521 sq.; exports of, 532

Agincourt, battle of, 383, 651 sq., 657; campaign of, 385 sq., 651; 808

Agnes of Aquitaine, marriage of, to the Emperor Henry III, 310 sq.

Agramontais, party of the, 485 sq.

Agricola, Rudolf, 712, 788 sqq.; his essay, *De formando studio*, 712

codification of law, 563; and provincial administration, 562 sq.; and *Szlachta*, 564; and urban development, 565; and learning, 566; and building, *ib.*; condition of Poland during his reign, as regards the peasantry, 564 sq.; and the towns, 565; death of, 566

Casimir IV, king of Poland, grand prince of Lithuania, and ecclesiastical magnates, 577; and policy as regards oligarchy, Turkish war, and the Order, 578; and statutes of Nieszawa, *ib.*; and territorial gains, *ib.*; and final settlement with Teutonic Order, *ib.*; and Tartar invasions, 579; and proposed Bohemian marriage for prince Vladislav, 101; and accession of Vladislav in Bohemia and Hungary, *ib.*, 579; death of, 579; *see also* genealogical table, 586; 95 sq., 100, 134, 155 sq., 267 *note* 2, 599, 612

Casimir, St, prince of Poland, 586, 616

Casimir V, duke of Stolpe or Stettin, 571

Cáslav, 70

"Caspe, Compromise of," 482

Cassel, castellany of, 342; battle of Mt, 342

Castagnaro, battle of, 648, 655

Castagno, Andrea del, 173

Castaldi, Pamfilo, 776

Castel d'Uovo, 164, 191

Castel Nuovo, 164 sq., 177 sq.

Castellis, Guido de, cardinal-priest of S. Marco, 509

Castiglione della Pescaja, 179

Castiglione d' Olona, Collegiata, Masolino's frescoes in, 766; and Baptistery, frescoes in, *ib.*

Castile and Leon, history of, chaps. XV, XVI *passim*, in fifteenth century, 479 sqq., 488, 498 sq.; administration of, 487; and America, 491 sq., 502 sq.; and north-west Africa, 493, 496; and Magrab and Canary Islands, 493; and Habsburg marriage, 495; and union of Spain, 498; and repression of lawlessness, *ib.*, 499; and municipal administration, 499; and peasant class, 499 sq.; and Muslims, 488, 490, 501; and Inquisition, 501 sq.; kings of, *see* Alfonso, Charles, Ferdinand, Henry, Isabella, Joanna, John, Peter, Philip, Sancho

Castillon, battle of, 253, 653

Castledermot, 451, 458

Castle-Island, castle of, 456

Castleknock, 451

Castro, Ignez de, 518

Catalans, the, in Rome, 175 sq.

Catalonia, election of Don Ferdinand to throne of, 479, 481; and count of Urgel, 482; Cortes of, and recognition of Ferdinand, *ib.*; section in, hostile to Ferdinand, *ib.*, 483; friction of Catalonians with Ferdinand in Cortes, and concerning Barcelona toll, 493; autonomy of Catalonia, *ib.*; succession of Alfonso V to throne of, *ib.*; and Charles of Viana, 269, 486;

army of *Generalitat* of, march against queen Joanna, 280, 486; peace offered to, by John II, 486; Louis XI and succession to, 279, 288; Ferdinand II succeeds to throne of, 487; effect on, of marriage of Infanta Joanna to archduke of Austria, 495; nomination of municipal councillors by Crown in, 499; effect of changed representation in Council of Hundred Jurats on, *ib.*; 748 sq.; counts of, *see* Aragon

Catharist teachings, and Hussitism, 76

Catherine of Valois, queen of England, 232 sq.

Catherine of Lancaster, queen of Castile, 521

Catherine of Foix, queen of Navarre, 496 sq.

Catholic Epistles, the, 799

Cato the Censor, 705; his *De agri cultura*, 783

Cato Uticensis, Marcus Porcius, 174

Cato, Walter, penitentiary of John XXII, 678

Caucasus, the, 587

Cauchon, Pierre, bishop of Beauvais, and custody of Joan of Arc, 249; presides over Inquisition that tried her, 250

"Causis," Michael "de," procurator of the Prague Chapter at the Papal Court, 58

Cavallini, Pietro, 751 sq., 757, 764

Cavriana, peace of, 170, 211

Caxton, William, 429, 431, 816

Cecco of Ascoli, execution of, 677 sqq.

Cele, John, 711

Celtes, Conrad, professor at Ingolstadt, 789 sq., 792 sqq., 795

Celys, the, 426

Cena, castle of, 484

Cennini, Bernardo, 776

Cerdagne, 279 sq., 494

Cerignola, battle of, 495

Cerneja, battle of, 508

Cerretanus, James, 4 *note* 2, 5 *note* 2

Cervia, saltpans of, 161

Cesarini, Giuliano, cardinal-bishop of Tusculum, legate, 23, 137, 182, 609

Cesena, Michael of, general of the Franciscans, 322 sq., 626 sq.

Ceuta, 521

Chabannes, Antoine de, count of Dammartin, grand master of France, 277, 282

Chalcondylas, 800

Champagne, ravaged by earl of Salisbury and John of Luxemburg, 241; fairs of, 335; 234, 244, 287

Champmol, abbey of, 734; portal of, 739; Puits de Moïse at, 739 sq.

Channel, the English, 384, 401

Chantilly, castle of, 734, 747

Chapelle, Bertrand de la, archbishop of Vienne, 324

Charenton, Enguerrand, painter, 748

Charlemagne, Western Emperor, 247 *note* 2, 309, 313, 564, 803

Charles IV, of Luxemburg, Western Emperor, king of Bohemia: and humanism,

Map 78

Germany

c. 1462

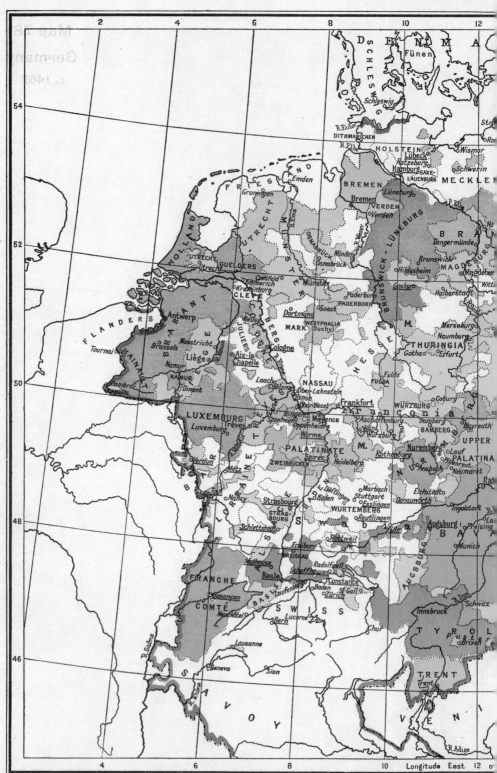

Map 78

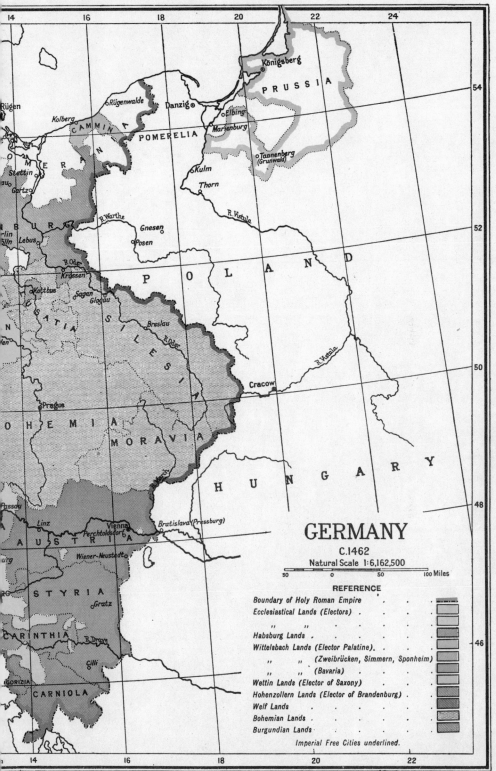

14 16 18 20 22 24

Rügen

Kolberg Rügenwalde Danzig Königsberg
CAMMINA PRUSSIA 54
POMER POMERELIA Elbing
Stettin Marienburg
Gartz Tannenberg (Grunwald)
BURG Kulm
Krossen Thorn
Kottbus R.Warthe R. Vistula
Sagan Gnesen
LUSATIA Glogau Posen 52
Lebus R.Oder
S I L E S I A P O L A N D
Breslau
R.Oder
Prague R. Vistula 50
B O H E M I A Cracow
M O R A V I A

H U N G A R Y 48
Passau
Linz Vienna
AUSTRIA Perchtoldsdorf Bratislava (Pressburg)
Wiener-Neustadt

GERMANY

C.1462

Natural Scale 1:6,162,500

50 0 50 100 Miles

STYRIA Gratz
CARINTHIA R.Drave
GORIZIA Cilli
CARNIOLA 46

REFERENCE

Boundary of Holy Roman Empire
Ecclesiastical Lands (Electors)
    "   "
Habsburg Lands
Wittelsbach Lands (Elector Palatine)
    "   "   (Zweibrücken, Simmern, Sponheim)
    "   "   (Bavaria)
Wettin Lands (Elector of Saxony)
Hohenzollern Lands (Elector of Brandenburg)
Welf Lands
Bohemian Lands
Burgundian Lands

Imperial Free Cities underlined.

14 16 18 20 22

W.& A.K.Johnston Ltd

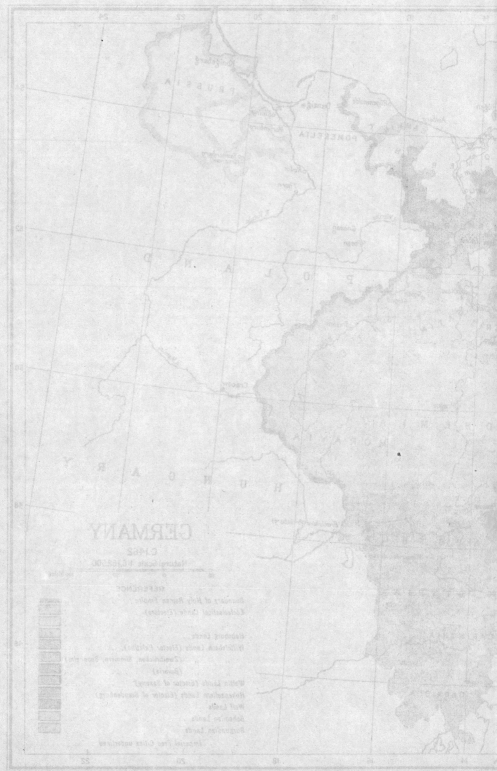

Map 79

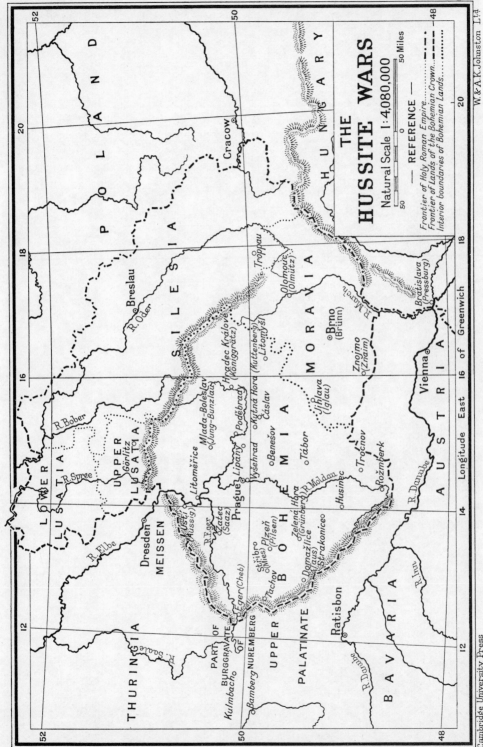

THE
HUSSITE WARS

Natural Scale 1:4,080,000

REFERENCE

Frontier of Holy Roman Empire........
Frontier of Lands of the Bohemian Crown.....
Interior boundaries of Bohemian Lands.......

50 Miles

W.& A.K.Johnston Ltð

Map 80

The Papal States
(15th century)

Savoy
under
Amadeus VIII

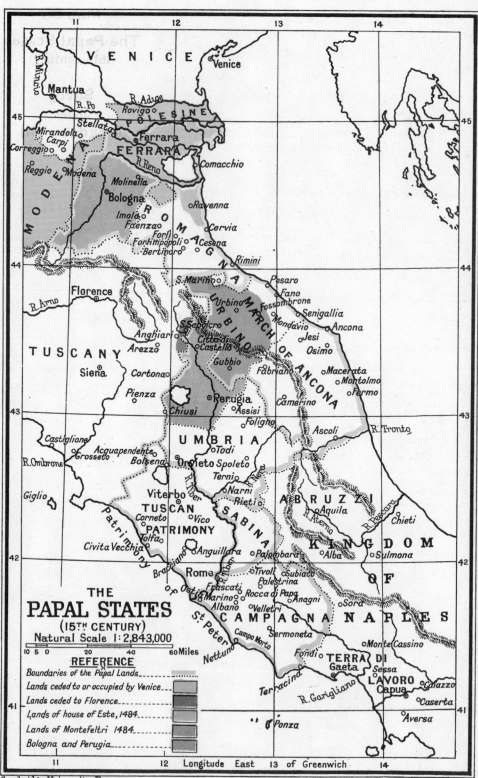

THE
PAPAL STATES
(15TH CENTURY)
Natural Scale 1:2,843,000

10 5 0   20   40   60 Miles

REFERENCE

Boundaries of the Papal Lands	-----------
Lands ceded to or occupied by Venice	-----------
Lands ceded to Florence	-----------
Lands of house of Este, 1484	-----------
Lands of Montefeltri 1484	-----------
Bologna and Perugia	-----------

Longitude East 13 of Greenwich

Cambridge University Press

Map 80

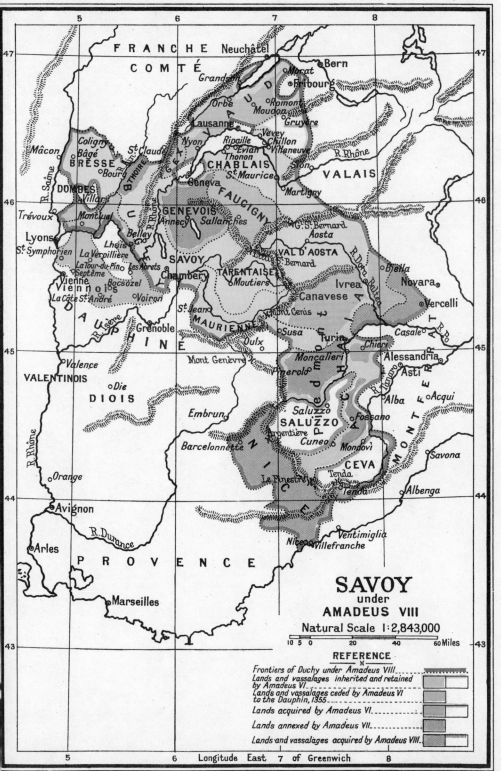

FRANCHE Neuchâtel
COMTÉ
Bern
Grandson
Morat
Fribourg
Orbe
Romont
Moudon
Gruyère
Lausanne
Nyon
Vevey
Ripaille
Chillon
Villeneuve
Evian
Thonon
Sion
CHABLAIS
R. Rhône
VALAIS
St. Maurice
Geneva
Martigny
FAUCIGNY
GENEVOIS
Annecy
Sallanches
G. St. Bernard
Aosta
Belley
SAVOY
Little
St. Bernard
R. Doire Baltée
Biella
VAL D'AOSTA
Ivrea
Novara
TARENTAISE
Chambéry
Moutiers
Canavese
Vercelli
St. Jean
Mont Cenis
MAURIENNE
Susa
Turin
Casale
Chieri
Alessandria
Moncalieri
Grenoble
Pinerolo
Asti
Mont Genèvre
Saluzzo
Alba
Acqui
Embrun
SALUZZO
Fossano
MONTFERRAT
Argentière
Cuneo
Barcelonnette
Mondovì
Savona
CEVA
Le Finestre
Tenda
Albenga
Ventimiglia
Nice
Villefranche

FR. Saône
Mâcon
Coligny
Bâgé
St. Claude
BRESSE
Bourg
Villars
DOMBES
Trévoux
Montluel
Lyons
St. Symphorien
Lhéis
La Verpillière
La Tour-du-Pin
Les Abrets
Septème
Vienne
Bocsözel
La Côte St. André
Voiron
Voreppe
R. Isère
Oulx
DAUPHINE

Valence
VALENTINOIS
Die
DIOIS

R. Rhône
Orange
Avignon
R. Durance
Arles

P R O V E N C E

Marseilles

SAVOY
under
AMADEUS VIII
Natural Scale 1:2,843,000

10 5 0   20   40   60 Miles

REFERENCE
Frontiers of Duchy under Amadeus VIII ....
Lands and vassalages inherited and retained
by Amadeus VI ....
Lands and vassalages ceded by Amadeus VI
to the Dauphin, 1355 ....
Lands acquired by Amadeus VI ....
Lands annexed by Amadeus VII ....
Lands and vassalages acquired by Amadeus VIII ......

Longitude East 7 of Greenwich

Map 80

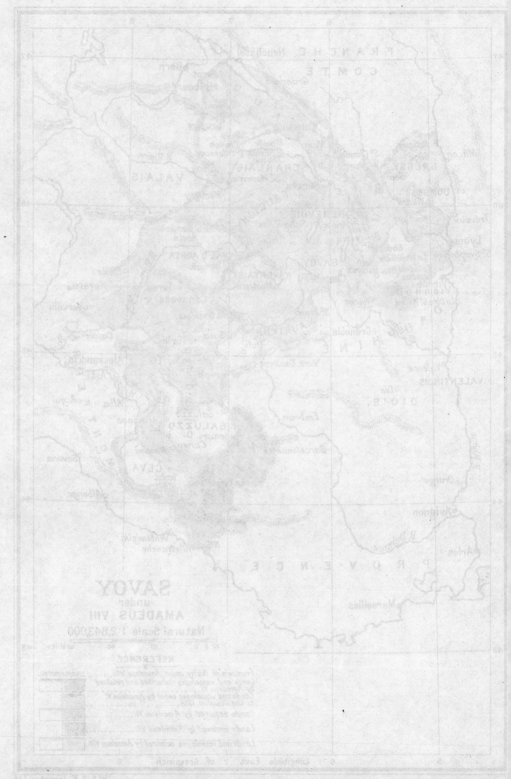

Map 81

The Growth
of the
Florentine Dominions

The Growth
of the
Venetian Dominions

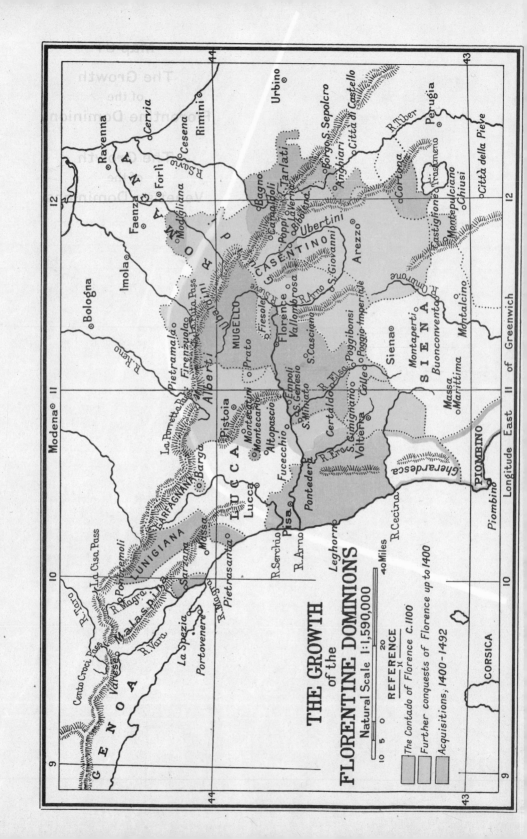

THE GROWTH
of the
FLORENTINE DOMINIONS

Natural Scale 1:1,590,000

REFERENCE

The Contado of Florence c.1100

Further conquests of Florence up to 1400

Acquisitions, 1400 - 1492

Map 81

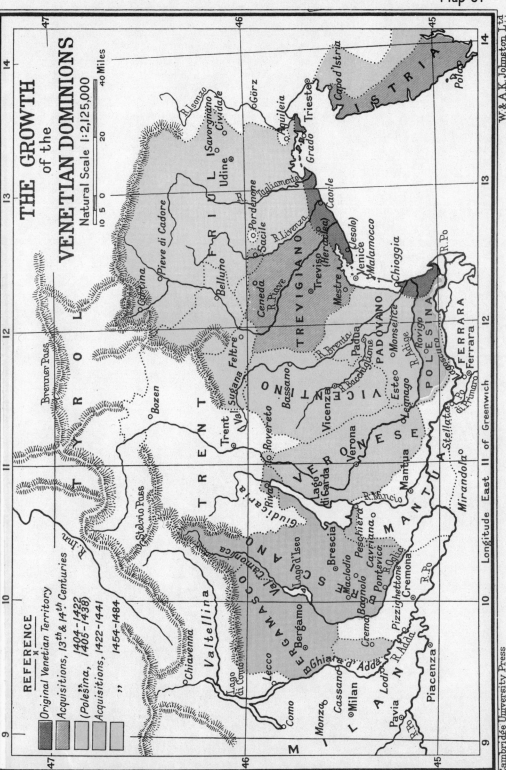

THE GROWTH
of the
VENETIAN DOMINIONS

Natural Scale 1:2,125,000

REFERENCE

Original Venetian Territory

Acquisitions, 13th & 14th Centuries

Acquisitions, 1404-1422
(Polesina, 1405-1438)

Acquisitions, 1422-1441

„ „ 1454-1484

Map 81

THE GROWTH
of the
VENETIAN DOMINIONS

Map 82

Dominions
of
Charles the Bold

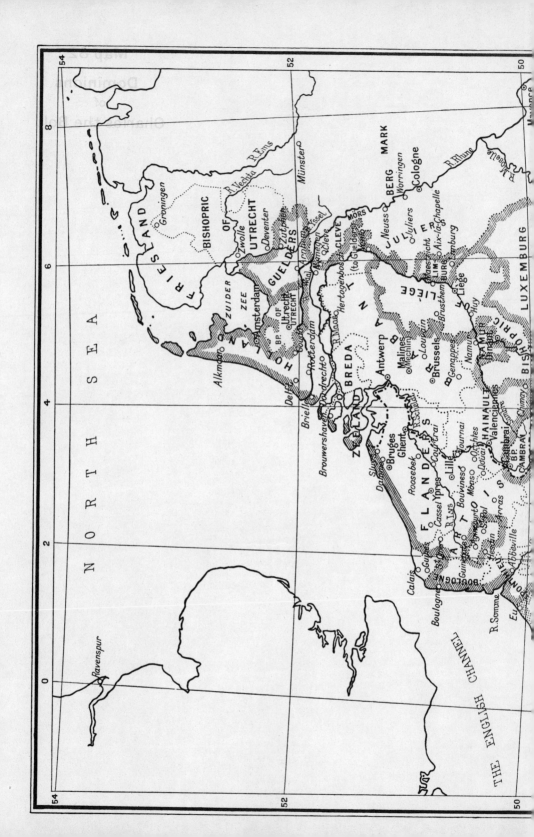

Map 82

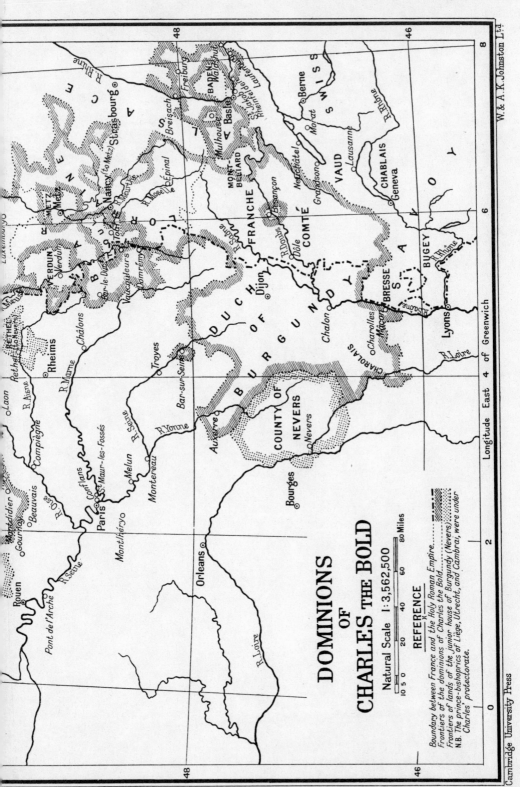

DOMINIONS
OF
CHARLES THE BOLD

Natural Scale 1:3,562,500

REFERENCE

Boundary between France and the Holy Roman Empire.
Frontiers of the dominions of Charles the Bold.
Frontiers of lands of the junior house of Burgundy (Nevers).
N.B. The prince-bishoprics of Liège, Utrecht, and Cambrai, were under Charles' protectorate.

10 5 0   20   40   60   80 Miles

Longitude East 4 of Greenwich

W. & A. K. Johnston Ltd.

Cambridge University Press

Map 82

DOMINIONS OF CHARLES THE BOLD

Natural Scale 1:3,825,500

REFERENCE

Map 83

France
in 1483

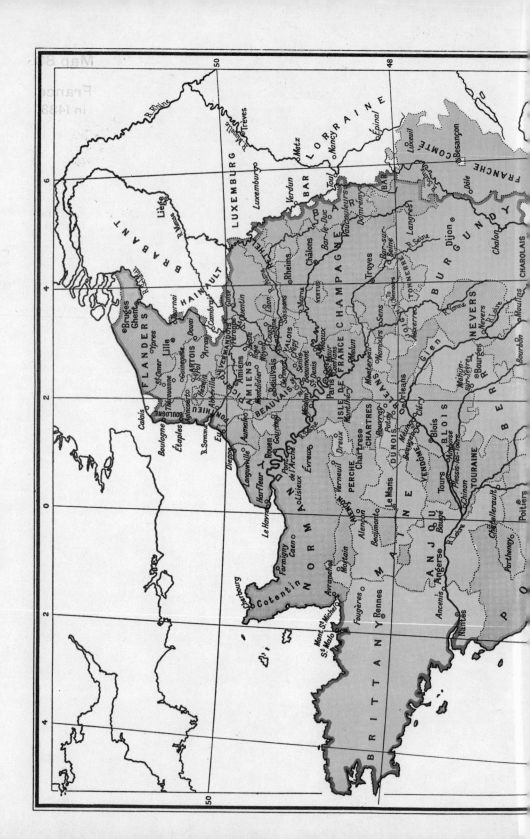

Map 8.

France
in 1483

R. Rhine

Treves

R. Moselle

LORRAINE

Metz

Nancy

Épinal

Luxeuil

Besançon

BAR

Toul

FRANCHE COMTE

LUXEMBURG

Luxemburg

Verdun

BAR

Voucouleurs

Domrémy

Dôle

Liège

R. Meuse

Bruges

Ghent

Ypres

Bar-le-Duc

Bar-sur-Seine

Langres

Dijon

BURGUNDY

Chalon

CHAROLAIS

BRABANT

HAINAULT

Tournai

Cambray

Rheims

Châlons

R. Marne

Troyes

TONNERRE

Sens

Nemours

Auxerre

R. Yonne

Gien

NEVERS

Nevers

R. Loire

Moulins

Douai

Lille

Guinegate

FLANDERS

St. Omer

Thérouanne

Arras

ARTOIS

Hesdin

Abbeville

Corbie

Péronne

VERMANDOIS

St. Quentin

Guise

Laon

Coucy

Soissons

VALOIS

Compiègne

Crépy

Meaux

Melun

ISLE DE FRANCE

Montlhéry

Étampes

Meun

ORLEANS

Orleans

Cléry

Beaugency

Blois

BLOIS

Amboise

Plessis-les-Tours

BERRY

Bourbon

Bourges

Melun-sur-Yèvre

Calais

BOULOGNE

Boulogne

Étaples

R. Somme

Eu

PONTHIEU

Aumale

Beauvais

BEAUVAIS

Montdidier

Amiens

Roye

Noyon

Senlis

St. Denis

Paris

Corbeil

Beaumont

CHARTRES

Chartres

VENDOME

Vendôme

Château-Renault

TOURAINE

Tours

Dieppe

Longueville

Rouen

Pont de l'Arche

Évreux

Dreux

Verneuil

PERCHE

DUNOIS

Châteaudun

Le Mans

MAINE

Harfleur

Le Havre

Lisieux

Caen

Formigny

Cherbourg

Cotentin

NORMANDY

Mortain

Avranches

Argentan

Séez

Alençon

Beaumont

ANJOU

Angers

Baugé

Chinon

R. Loire

Châtellerault

Poitiers

Parthenay

POITOU

Ancenis

Nantes

Mont St. Michel

St. Malo

Fougères

Rennes

BRITTANY

Map 84

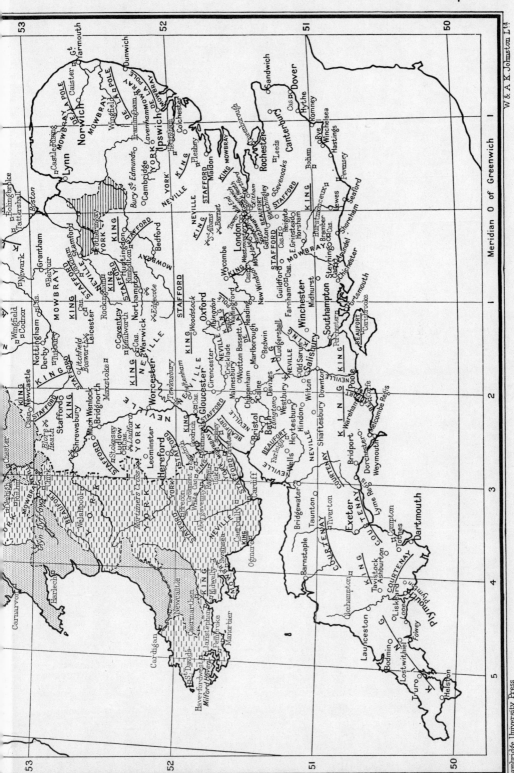

W & A K Johnston Ltᵈ

Meridian 0 of Greenwich

Map 85

Spain and Portugal
in 1474

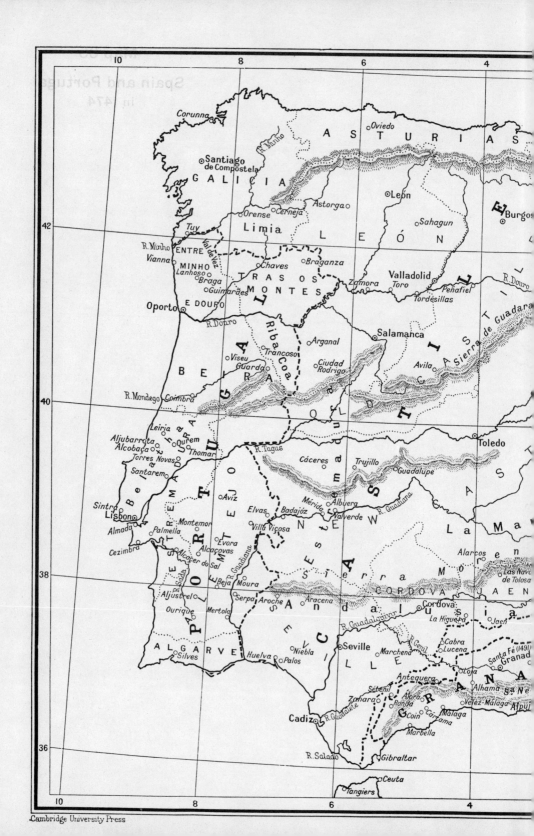

10   8   6   4

Corunna

ASTURIAS

Oviedo

Santiago
de Compostela

R.Minho

GALICIA

León

Astorga

Orense Cerneja

42

Tuy

Limia

LEÓN

Sahagun

Burgos

R.Minho ENTRE

Val de Vez

Chaves

Braganza

Vianna

MINHO

TRAS OS

Valladolid

Lanhoso

Braga

MONTES

Zamora

Toro

Penafiel

R.Douro

Guimarães

Tordesillas

Oporto

E DOURO

R.Douro

Ribacoa

Arganal

Salamanca

Sierra de Guadara

Viseu

Trancoso

Ciudad
Rodrigo

BEIRA

Guarda

Avila

40

R.Mondego Coimbra

CASTILE

Leiria

Toledo

Aljubarrota

Ourem

R.Tagus

Cáceres

Trujillo

Alcobaça

Thomar

Guadalupe

Torres Novas

ESTREMADURA

Aviz

Santarem

Mérida

Albuera

Elvas

Badajóz

R.Guadiana

Sintra

Valverde

La Ma

Lisbon

Montemor

Villa Viçosa

Almada

Palmella

Évora

Alarcos

Cezimbra

Alcaçovas

Las Navas
de Tolosa

Alcacer do Sal

Sierra M

38

Aljustrel

Beja

Moura

CORDOVA

JAEN

Ourique

Serpa

Aroche

Aracena

Andalu a

Cordova

Mertola

La Higuera

Jaen

R.Guadalquivir

R.Genl

Cabra

ALGARVE

Niebla

Seville

Marchena

Lucena

Loja

Santa Fé (491)

Silves

Huelva

Palos

Granada

Antequera

Setenil

Alhama

SaNe

Zahara

Abra

Ronda

Cartama

Velez-Malaga

Alpuj

Coin

Malaga

Cadiz

R.Guadalete

Marbella

36

R.Salado

Gibraltar

Ceuta

Tangiers

10   8   6   4

Cambridge University Press

Map 85

SPAIN AND PORTUGAL
IN 1474
Natural Scale 1: 4,800,000

20 10 0   20   40   60   80   100 Miles

— REFERENCE —

Frontiers of separate kingdoms .... – – – –
Frontiers of Granada in the 13th century .... – · – ·
Boundaries of the provinces of Spain and Portugal,
and of the three states of Aragon, Catalonia, and Valencia ....

Meridian 0 of Greenwich

W.& A.K. Johnston Ltd

Map 86

East Central Europe
in the 15th century

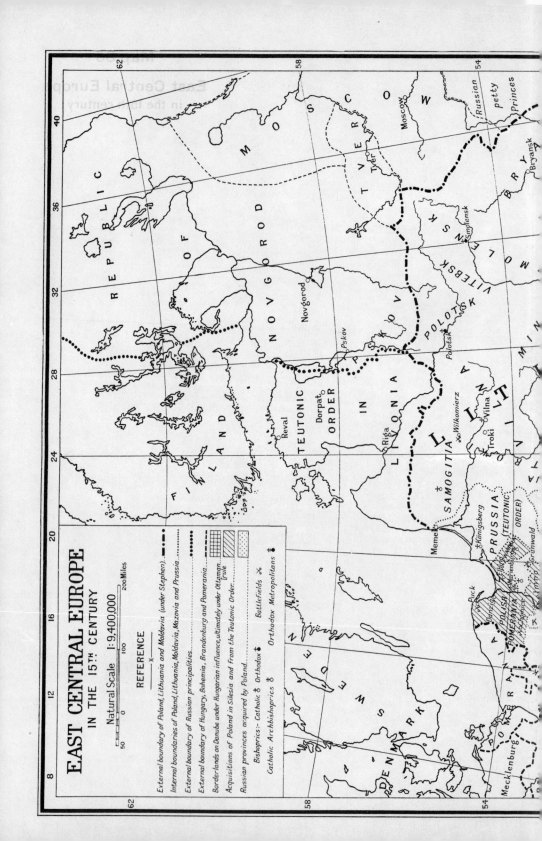

EAST CENTRAL EUROPE
IN THE 15ᵀᴴ CENTURY

Natural Scale 1: 9,400,000

50   0   100   200-Miles

REFERENCE

External boundary of Poland, Lithuania and Moldavia (under Stephen)
Internal boundaries of Poland, Lithuania, Moldavia, Mazovia and Prussia
External boundary of Russian principalities
External boundary of Hungary, Bohemia, Brandenburg and Pomerania
Borderlands on Danube under Hungarian influence, ultimately under Ottoman rule
Acquisitions of Poland in Silesia and from the Teutonic Order
Russian provinces acquired by Poland

Bishoprics:- Catholic ☩ & Orthodox ☩   Battlefields ✕
Catholic Archbishoprics ☩   Orthodox Metropolitans ☩

MOSCOW

REPUBLIC   OF

NOVGOROD

Novgorod

Moscow

TVER

Tver

VITEBSK

MOLENSK

Smolensk

Bryansk

Russian petty Princes

POLOTSK

Polotsk

PSKOV

Pskov

FINLAND

Reval

Dorpat

TEUTONIC ORDER

Riga

LIVONIA

IN

LITHUANIA

Wilkomierz

Vilna

Troki

SAMOGITIA

Memel

Königsberg

PRUSSIA (TEUTONIC ORDER)

Marienburg

Grunwald 1410

Puck

POLISH POMERANIA

Bydgoszcz

Marienwerder

MIN

MASOVIA

SWEDEN

DENMARK

Mecklenburg

POMER

Map 86

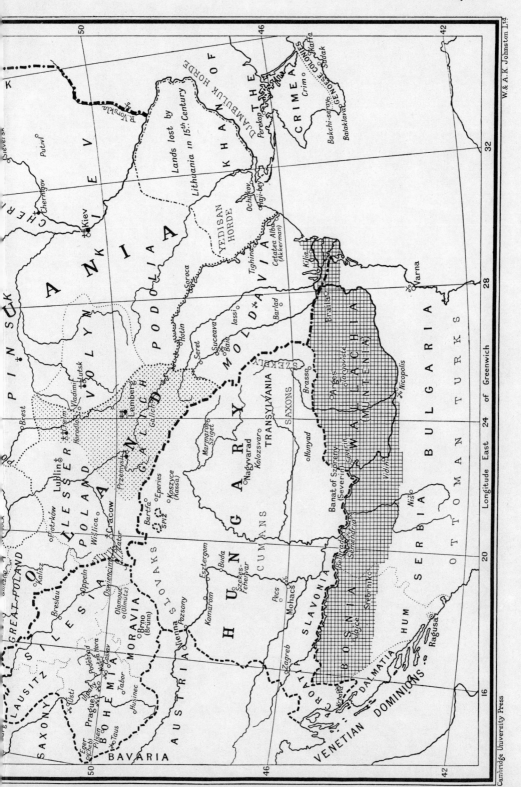

W. & A. K. Johnston Ltd

Cambridge University Press

Map 86